MACMILLAN
DICTIONARY
OF
INFORMATION
TECHNOLOGY

MACMILLAN
DICTIONARY
OF
INFORMATION
TECHNOLOGY

THIRD EDITION

Dennis Longley
Michael Shain

**MACMILLAN
REFERENCE
BOOKS**

First edition published 1982
Hardcover reprinted 1983
Paperback reprinted 1984

Second edition published 1985
Paperback reprinted 1985, 1986

Third edition first published 1989 by
THE MACMILLAN PRESS LTD.
London and Basingstoke

Associated companies in Auckland, Delhi, Dublin,
Gaborone, Hamburg, Harare, Hong Kong, Johannesburg,
Kuala Lumpur, Lagos, Manzini, Melbourne, Mexico City,
Nairobi, New York, Singapore, Tokyo.

British Library Cataloguing in Publication Data

Longley, Dennis
   Macmillan dictionary of information
   technology. — 3rd. ed.
   1. Information systems
   I. Title   II. Shain, Michael
   Dictionary of information technology
   001.5

   ISBN 0-333-44971-1
   ISBN 0-333-46050-2 Pbk

Printed in Great Britain

To Joanna, Gabrielle and Jonathan

Acknowledgements

In this dictionary material has been derived from a wide variety of sources. In some cases definitions are given within a particular context and the source body of the reference is given with the definition itself (eg. FIPS, AR). The references thus used are:

AFIPS	American Federation of Information Processing Societies
AFR	US Air Force Regulation
ANSI	American National Standards Institute
AR	US Army Regulation
DCID	US Director Central Intelligence Directive
DOD	US Department of Defence
DODD	US Department of Defence Directive
DOE	US Department of Energy
FIPS	US Federal Information Processing Standards
GAO	US General Accounting Office
MTR	Mitre Corporation
NSDD-145	US National Security Decision Directive 145

A number of definitions have been included from the *Philips New Media Systems Dictionary of Terms*, 2nd edition; and from the newsletter *Desktop Publisher*, with the kind permission of the publishers: Philips International BV and The Desktop Publishing Company Ltd. These terms are annotated Philips and Desktop in the text.

Many of the terms with reference AFR, AR, DCID, DOD, DODD, DOE, FIPS, GAO, MTR, NSDD-145, OMBC, and OPNAVINSI are contained in the Glossary of *Computer Security*, and are published with the kind permission of Douglas I Mansur and Major Mary C Curtis.

In addition the authors would like to express their further gratitude to the following: Mary Sandow-Quirk and Alan Tickle from the Faculty of Information Technology, QIT, Dr W Caelli from Eracom, and Maxwell James Longley; for their help and co-operation in compiling this third edition of the dictionary.

Introduction to the Third Edition

The early 1980's saw new products and services emerging as a consequence of the fusion of what had, until then, been largely considered as separate technologies: computing, communications and microelectronics. The IT industry was born out of this integration and almost overnight a new or unfamiliar terminology came into being.

The use of IT terms results from the integration of new disciplines and applications in industry. This in turn depends on both technological developments and market forces. The former are relatively predictable but the latter are not. Videotex, for example, was considered extremely important in the early 1980's, and no one forecast the expansion of facsimile, also a communications based technology, in the latter half of the 1980's.

The migration of terms used in IT from their original disciplines to new ones is well illustrated by developments in printing. Terms such as pica, points and ems were introduced on a speculative basis in the first edition of the Dictionary. These did not appear to have become of central importance in the second edition but now, with desk top publishing, they are in common use amongst computing and other professionals.

The language of IT is, as we have suggested, in a constant state of evolution due to ever varying developments within the discipline. For example, agreement has been reached on a range of international standards, particularly in communications: ISO-OSI, X.400, EDI etc., which should lead to a wider penetration of IT goods and services, with a consequent impact on IT terminology. Whilst agreement on standards will help to speed the integration of different computer based systems, there is a growing concern both amongst the public at large and corporate users of IT due to threats to data and computer security from such sources as viruses, hackers and wire tappers. The explosive growth in the power of personal computers and software remains unabated both for stand-alone applications, but also as workstations in office automation and to provide user-friendly access to corporate data.

Information technology is finding its place in the home through consumer electronics and increasingly low price, but powerful, personal computers. Both videotex and cable have not emerged as important forces here, but no doubt satellite television for domestic use will be an important factor.

Given the pace of these trends one can expect the emergence of new IT terms as the English language evolves to encompass these developments, both in the home and in the office. Meanwhile, the authors have attempted to capture, clarify and define these new terms as they come into focus.

How to use this dictionary

The design of the dictionary is based upon the principle that most readers never consult this section and so, to avoid confusion, sophisticated listing and cross reference techniques have not been employed.

The terms are retained in the normal order, ie **automatic widow adjust** is listed under automatic. They are sorted in alphabetical order of the complete term, ie **light pen** comes between **light emitting diode** and **light stability**. This order contrasts with some dictionaries in which the alphabetical order is based on a heavier weighting of the first word in a term, ie all terms commencing with **light** precede all terms commencing with **lighting**. In the alphabetical ordering digits are ranked before the letter 'A', ie **V.57** appears before **vacuum fluorescent display** and not at the end of the 'V' terms.

The area from which the head word is derived, is usually indicated in the definition, eg In computing, In printing … If more than one definition is related to a head word, then the entry is itemized to reflect this and the relevant field indicated in each sub-entry.

The terms normally appear in lower case characters, and proper nouns headed by an upper case, eg **Bildschirmtext**. Acronyms are presented in full upper case and the appropriate letters are amplified in the text, eg:

PERT — Program Evaluation and Review Technique.

The cross references are given under these headings: 'Compare', 'See' and 'Synonymous with'.

A significant feature of this dictionary is the use of extended entries dealing with important topics of the subject, ie artificial intelligence, banking networks, cable television, CD-Rom publishing, cellular radio, computer-based training, computer security, cryptography, data protection, desk-top publishing, expert systems, fiber optics, fifth generation computer, local area network, machine translation, outline information retrieval, open systems interconnection, proof of program correctness, smart card, video disk, visual display terminal and X.400.

A

AA. *See* AUDIO-ACTIVE.

AAs. *See* AUTHOR'S ALTERATIONS.

A, B and C series of paper sizes. In printing, a triple range of paper sizes adopted by International Standards Organization, of which the A Series is intended for all kinds of stationery and printed matter, the B Series as intermediate alternatives and the C Series for envelopes. The dimensions for the A series are given in millimetres:

A0 1189 x 841   A6 148 x 105
A1 841 x 594   A7 105 x 74
A2 594 x 420   A8 74 x 52
A3 420 x 297   A9 52 x 37
A4 297 x 210   A10 37 x 26
A5 210 x 148

All sizes are proportionate reductions of the basic A0 sheet, sides being in the ratio $1:\sqrt{2}$, with A0 being equal to 1 square metre, *Synonymous with* RA PAPER SIZES, SRA PAPER SIZES.

ABC. (1) American Broadcasting Corporation. (2) Australian Broadcasting Corporation.

ABCA. American Business Communications Association.

ABEND. In computing, an ABnormal END of a task prior to its completion on a mainframe because of an error. *See* ABORT.

aberration. (1) In optics, any systematic distortion of an image introduced by an optical element, such as a lens, prism or mirror. Aberrations common in early lenses were astigmatism, chromatic aberration, curvature of field, distortion and spherical aberration. *See* ASTIGMATISM, CHROMATIC ABERRATION, CURVATURE OF FIELD, DISTORTION, SPHERICAL ABERRATION. (2) In television, image distortion caused by signal interference or electron beam misalignment.

ABES. US Association for Broadcasting Engineering Standards.

ABI/Inform. In online information retrieval, Abstracted Business Information/Inform needs; a US database covering business management and administration.

ablative pit forming. In optical media, a technique for writing to optical discs in which the laser burns a small pit in the surface of the recording media. This technique has the disadvantage that the pits have comparatively ragged edges which may be a source of reading errors. *Compare* BUBBLE FORMING. *See* LASER, OPTICAL DIGITAL DISC.

ABN. In online information retrieval, Australian Bibliographic Network; a national online bibliographic facility based at the National Library of Australia that offers shared cataloguing, bibliographic verification and item location services.

abort. In computing, a routine undertaken when a situation arises during processing that makes it impossible or undesirable to continue; the activity is terminated in a controlled manner so as to minimize any damage to data. *See* ABEND.

above 890 decision. In communications, a decision of the Federal Communications Commission made in 1959 that allowed individual firms to build microwave systems for their own use utilizing frequencies above 890 MHz. This decision established a precedent in the USA for the provision of communication channels by entities other than the then established carriers, Western Union Telegraph Co. and AT&T. *See* MICROWAVE.

abscissa. In mathematics, the horizontal axis of a two-dimensional coordinate graph. *Compare* ORDINATE. *See* CARTESIAN COORDINATES, COORDINATE GRAPH. *Synonymous with* X-AXIS.

absolute address. (1) In programming, an address in a computer language that identifies a storage location or a device without the use of any intermediate reference. (2) In programming, an address that is permanently assigned by the machine designer to a storage location. (3) In programming, a pattern of characters that identifies a unique storage location or device without further modification. *Compare* RELATIVE ADDRESS. *See* ADDRESS, ADDRESSING MODE. *Synonymous with* MACHINE ADDRESS.

absolute assembler. In programming, a specific type of assembly language program designed to produce object code containing only absolute addresses and address references. *See* ABSOLUTE ADDRESS, ASSEMBLING, OBJECT CODE.

absolute code. In programming, a code that uses computer instructions with absolute addresses. *See* ABSOLUTE ADDRESS.

absolute disc address. In optical media, the address of an interactive compact disc sector in minutes, seconds and sector number. (Philips). *See* COMPACT DISC – INTERACTIVE, SECTOR ADDRESS, SECTOR STRUCTURE.

absolute loader. In programming, a routine that reads a computer program into main memory, beginning at the assembled origin. *See* ASSEMBLING, LOADER, MAIN MEMORY.

absolute rate. In information theory, the maximum number of bits of information that can be encoded in each character, assuming that all possible sequences are equally likely. If a language comprises C characters and each is equally likely to appear in any message sequence then the absolute rate of the language would be $\log_2 C$. In natural languages such as English the actual rate of the language is considerably less than the abso-

lute rate because such languages have a high degree of redundancy. *See* RATE.

absolute RGB coding. *Synonymous with* DIRECT RGB CODING.

absolute sector address. In optical media, the address part of an interactive compact disc sector header field. Its value corresponds to the absolute disc address. (Philips). *See* ABSOLUTE DISC ADDRESS, COMPACT DISC – INTERACTIVE.

absolute time. In optical media, the total time that a digital audio compact disc has been playing. It is included in the subcode and thus is available for display during playback. (Philips). *See* COMPACT DISC – DIGITAL AUDIO, SUBCODE CHANNEL.

absolute value. The value of a number regardless of a prefixed plus or minus sign (i.e. the absolute value of -5 is 5).

absorptance. The portion of the quantity of light incident on an object that is absorbed within the object, the energy ultimately being converted into heat. *Compare* REFLECTANCE, TRANSMITTANCE.

absorption. In communications, a loss of power of an electromagnetic wave during propagation through a medium. *See* ELECTROMAGNETIC RADIATION, TRANSMISSION LOSS.

absorption filter. In photography, a light filter that blocks certain wavelengths of light and transmits others.

ABSTI. Canadian Advisory Board on Scientific and Technical Information.

abstract. In library science, a summary containing the key points of a document. Indicative abstracts indicate the contents of a document. Informative abstracts convey the main findings methods and conclusions of a document.

abstract data type. In programming, a data type that is defined solely in terms of the operations that can be performed on objects of that type, and the range of values that it can take, without regard to the method of representation of the value. *See* TYPE.

AC. *See* ACCUMULATOR, ALTERNATING CURRENT.

Academy of Motion Picture Arts and Sciences. In filming, a US organization of film producers, directors, actors and technicians.

Academy of Television Arts and Sciences. In television, a US organization of television industry professionals.

ACARD. UK Advisory Council for Applied Research and Development.

ACC. *See* ACCUMULATOR.

ACCC. US Ad Hoc Committee for Competitive Communications.

acceleration potential. In electronics, the voltage between the cathode in a cathode ray tube and the face of the tube which attracts the beam of focused electrons, causing them to impinge on the phosphor dots. *See* CATHODE RAY TUBE, PHOSPHOR DOTS.

accent. In typesetting, a mark used to indicate a specific sound value, stress or pitch, or to indicate that an ordinarily mute vowel should be pronounced. *See* ACUTE, CEDILLA, CIRCUMFLEX, GRAVE, TILDE, UMLAUT.

acceptance angle. (1) In communications, the maximum angle, measured from the core centre line of a fiber optics cable, within which light may be coupled into a fiber for a uniformly illuminated optical waveguide. *See* FIBER OPTICS. (2) In photography, the angle in two dimensions covered by a lens or light meter.

acceptance testing. In computing, a series of tests designed to demonstrate the functional capabilities of a new computer system. It is usually conducted by the manufacturer to show the customer that the system is in working order. *See* ALPHA TESTING, BETA TESTING.

ACCESS. US Army Automated Catalog of Computer Equipment and Software Systems.

access. (1) In communications, the public availability of cable broadcasting time in the USA. (2) In programming, the manner in which files or data sets are referred to by the computer. *See* DIRECT ACCESS, RANDOM ACCESS, SEQUENTIAL ACCESS. (3) In computer security, a specific type of interaction between a subject and an object that results in the flow of information from one to the other. (DOD). *See* OBJECT, SUBJECT. (4) In optical media, the process of locating information in an interactive compact disc data store. (Philips). *See* COMPACT DISC – INTERACTIVE.

access arm. In memory systems, a mechanical device in a disk drive that positions the reading and writing mechanisms. *See* DISK DRIVE, HEAD.

access authorization. In computer security, the permission granted to a subject (e.g. person, terminal, program) to perform a set of operations in the system. Such authorizations are commonly expressed in an access privilege matrix giving details of the subjects, types of access (e.g. read, write) and time periods in which the accesses are allowed. *See* ACCESS MATRIX MODEL, SUBJECT.

access barred. In data communications, a situation in which a piece of data terminal equipment (DTE) cannot call the DTE specified in the selection signals. *See* DATA TERMINAL EQUIPMENT.

access charge. In communications, a charge made by a common carrier for the use of its local office facilities. *See* COMMON CARRIER, LOCAL OFFICE.

access control. (1) In computer security, procedures designed to limit entry to a physical area, or to limit use of a computer/communications system, or computer-stored data, to authorized personnel. The procedures may be based upon the knowledge, a possession, attribute or capability of the person seeking access. The procedure requires that the person performs a given test or responds to a challenge. If successful access is granted by opening a door, placing the computer in a certain mode of operation, establishing a communication channel or providing data with certain user privileges. *See* PASSWORD. (2) In data communications, the control of system usage, imposed by hardware, software and administrative controls. Such controls include system monitoring, user identification, ensuring data integrity, recording system access, and changes and methods for granting user access. *See* HARDWARE, SOFTWARE.

accession number. In library science, an arbitrary serial number given to each item as it enters a collection. *See* ASPECT CARD.

access line. In data communications, a telecommunications line that permanently connects a remote station to a data-switching exchange. *See* DATA-SWITCHING EXCHANGE.

access matrix model. In computer security, a model that relates subjects, objects and access types. A subject is an active entity capable of accessing objects (e.g. a program in execution, a user in a time-sharing system). An object is an entity to which access is controlled (e.g. a file, memory segment, program). An access type is just a kind of access to an object. An access type to a program may be execute, read source listing; to a file it may be read, write, append.

The access control matrix is a two-dimensional array with objects listed horizontally and subjects listed vertically, and each cell contains the access type that the given subject has for the corresponding object. *See* OBJECT, SUBJECT.

access mechanism. In computing, a mechanism for moving read and write heads to the requisite position on the storage device, or moving the storage medium to the heads, so that data may be accessed.

access protection. In optical media, the method of preventing unauthorized access to specific data of a confidential nature stored on an interactive compact disc. (Philips). *See* COMPACT DISC – INTERACTIVE.

access time. In memory systems, the time interval between the instant that data is requested from the storage device to the instant that it is delivered to the central processing unit, and vice versa. *See* CENTRAL PROCESSING UNIT. (2) In recording, the time interval between the moment that informa-

tion is requested in playback to the moment that it is delivered.

access type. In computer security, the form of access that is permitted to an object (e.g. read a file, write to a file, append information to a file, etc.). *See* ACCESS CONTROL, OBJECT.

accidental destruction. In data security, the unintentional overwriting or deletion of data (e.g. by faulty hardware or software). Backup is needed for recovery. *See* BACKUP COPY.

accidental threat. In computer security, the threat of unintentional damage to the system arising from incorrect use of the system or natural phenomena (e.g. flood, fire, etc.). *Compare* ACTIVE THREAT, DELIBERATE THREAT, LOGICAL THREAT, PASSIVE THREAT, PHYSICAL THREAT. *See* THREAT.

accordion fold. In printing, a method of folding paper in which each fold is in the opposite direction to the previous one. A printer can be fed with accordion-folded paper without continuous intervention of the operator. *Synonymous with* CONCERTINA FOLD, FANFOLD, ZIGZAG FOLDING.

accountability. In computer security, the quality or state that enables violations or attempted violations of automatic data-processing system security to be traced to individuals who may then be held responsible. (FIPS). *See* AUTOMATIC DATA-PROCESSING SYSTEM.

accreditation. In computer security, the authorization and approval granted to an automatic data-processing system or network to process sensitive data in an operational environment, and made on the basis of a certification by designated technical personnel of the extent to which design and implementation of the system meet prespecified technical requirements for achieving adequate data security. (FIPS). *See* APPROVAL/ACCREDITATION, AUTOMATIC DATA-PROCESSING SYSTEM, CERTIFICATION, DATA SECURITY.

accumulator. (ACC) In architecture, a device that functions as a holding register for arithmetic, logical and input/output operations. *See* INPUT/OUTPUT, REGISTER.

accuracy. In mathematics, the degree of exactness of an approximation or measurement. It denotes the absolute quality of the result with respect to its true value, as compared with precision which is concerned with the amount of detail used in specifying a result. Thus a two-digit result may be more accurate than an incorrect three-digit result, but it will be less precise. *Compare* PRECISION.

ACE. Association of Cinema Editors.

achromatic. In optics, pertaining to an optical device (e.g. a lens) that has been corrected in manufacture for chromatic aberration. *See* CHROMATIC ABERRATION.

achromatic colour. In computer graphics, an intermediate grey level in the monochromatic grey scale. *See* GREY SCALE.

ACIA. *See* ASYNCHRONOUS COMMUNICATIONS INTERFACE ADAPTOR.

ACICS. In online information retrieval, ACI Computer Services; a subdivision of the Australian company ACI which operates information retrieval services (including Ausinet) and information management services (including the ASCIS national school cataloguing project). *See* ASCIS, AUSINET.

Acimail. An electronic mail service that operates over the ACICS network. *See* ACICS.

ACK. *See* ACKNOWLEDGE CHARACTER.

acknowledge character. (ACK) In data communications, a character transmitted by a station as an affirmative response to the station with which the connection has been set up. *Compare* NEGATIVE ACKNOWLEDGEMENT. *See* ACKNOWLEDGEMENT, AFFIRMATIVE ACKNOWLEDGEMENT, STATION.

acknowledgement. In data communications, the transmission by a receiver of acknowledge characters as a response to a sender. *See* AFFIRMATIVE ACKNOWLEDGEMENT, NEGATIVE ACKNOWLEDGEMENT.

ACK0. *See* AFFIRMATIVE ACKNOWLEDGEMENT.

ACK1. *See* AFFIRMATIVE ACKNOWLEDGEMENT.

ACLS. American Council of Learned Societies.

ACM. *See* ASSOCIATION FOR COMPUTING MACHINERY.

acoustical feedback. In recording, the positive feedback between the microphone and loudspeaker in a sound system that usually results in an undesirable howling sound. *See* MICROPHONE, POSITIVE FEEDBACK.

acoustic coupler. In data communications, a device that interfaces an item of equipment, producing and receiving digital signals, to a telephone network. Sound transducers in the acoustic coupler produce sound tones corresponding to the digital signals; a telephone handset is placed in contact with the sound transducers so that these tones can be input into the telephone network. Similarly, tones from the network are converted back to digital signals. *See* TRANSDUCER.

acoustic eavesdropping. In communications security, the interception of sound waves created by the human voice or printing, punching or transmitting equipment. *Compare* ELECTRONIC EAVESDROPPING. *See* EAVESDROPPING.

acoustics. (1) The science concerned with the attributes of sound. (2) The characteristics of an enclosure (e.g. a room) as these affect the sound. *See* SOUND.

acquisition time. (1) In data communications, the amount of time required to attain synchronism. *See* SYNCHRONIZATION. (2) In communications, the time required to lock tracking equipment onto a signal from a communications satellite. *See* COMMUNICATIONS SATELLITE SYSTEM.

ACR. *See* AUDIO CASSETTE RECORDER.

ACRL. US Association of College and Research Libraries.

actinic light. In photography, light that is capable of causing photochemical changes in a photosensitive material.

action. In filming, the motion of a subject in camera range.

action cutting. In filming, a technique that is used to give an impression of uninterrupted action when there is a change of camera position. In editing it is achieved by overlapping the action of successive shots. *See* ACTION, EDIT.

action field. In photography, the portion of the area in front of the camera that is recorded.

action message. In computing, a message issued because of a condition that requires an operator response.

action paper. *Synonymous with* CARBON-LESS PAPER.

activating. (1) The process of getting a system (e.g. device or program) into a state ready for use. (2) In printing, the action of an activator on the exposed sensitized material in some photochemical process to cause development of the latent image. *See* ACTIVATOR, LATENT IMAGE.

activation. In data communications, the process by which a component of a node is made ready to perform the functions for which it was designed. *See* NODE.

activator. In printing, a liquid used for developing certain types of sensitized material. *See* ACTIVATING.

active attack. In communications security, an attack in which an opponent modifies transmitted information or injects information into the communications path. Active attacks can be subdivided into three categories: (a) message stream modification; (b) denial of message service; and (c) replay and masquerading.
Message stream modification can be aimed at changing the origination address, message contents, destination address or the order in which messages are transmitted. Denial of message service involves deleting, delaying messages or flooding the network with bogus messages. Replay attacks are based upon the recording and later playback of legitimate messages. Masquerading attempts to establish communication between a genuine and a fake user. *Compare* PASSIVE ATTACK. *See* ACTIVE WIRETAPPING, AUTHENTICATION, DELAY/DENIAL OF SERVICE, MASQUERADING, MESSAGE AUTHENTICATION, REPLAY.

active device. In electronics, a circuit which contains an amplifier providing gain. *Compare* PASSIVE DEVICE. *See* AMPLIFIER, GAIN.

active display. In optical media, the contents of a video memory currently being displayed as opposed to screen contents being held in memory for later display if needed. (Philips).

active file. In programming, a permanent or temporary file, having an expiration date that is later than the job date. *See* JOB, PERMANENT FILE.

active laser medium. In optoelectronics, the material within a laser (e.g. crystal, gas, glass, liquid or semiconductor) that emits coherent radiation as the result of stimulated electronic or molecular transitions to lower-energy states. *See* LASER, SEMICONDUCTOR.

active matrix. *See* LCD SCREENS.

active satellite. In communications, a satellite carrying a station that is intended to transmit or retransmit radio communication signals. *See* COMMUNICATIONS SATELLITE SYSTEM.

active state. In microelectronics, the digital state that causes a given action to occur. It may be either the high state or low state, depending on the circuit and pin in question.

active threat. In computer security, a potential breach of security, the nature of which, should it occur, would cause actual damage or alteration to the computer hardware, software or data. *Compare* ACCIDENTAL THREAT, DELIBERATE THREAT, LOGICAL THREAT, PASSIVE THREAT, PHYSICAL THREAT. *See* ACTIVE ATTACK, DENIAL OF SERVICE, MAS-

QUERADING, REPLAY, THREAT, TRAFFIC PADDING

active wire concentrator. (AWC) In data communications, cabinets with star connection to individual nodes. In some local area networks, they are connected in a ring, thus providing a combined ring/star configuration. See LOCAL AREA NETWORK, NODE, RING, STAR.

active wiretapping. In communications security, wiretapping for the purposes of obtaining access to data by the generation of false messages or control signals, alteration of communications of legitimate users or the denial of services to legitimate users. *Compare* PASSIVE WIRETAPPING. *See* DENIAL OF SERVICE, WIRETAPPING.

activity. In computing, the percentage of records in a file that are processed in a run. *See* VOLATILITY.

activity loading. In computing, a method of storing records on a file in which the most frequently processed records can be located most readily. *See* RECORD.

activity ratio. In computing, the ratio of the number of active records in a file to the total number of records in that file. *See* RECORD.

AC transfer. In recording, a videotape duplication by contact between a high-coercivity master and a low-coercivity slave in a high-frequency alternating current (AC) field. *See* COERCIVITY.

ACTSU. US Association of Computer Time Sharing Users.

ACTT. *See* ASSOCIATION OF CINEMATOGRAPH, TELEVISION AND ALLIED TECHNICIANS.

actual data transfer rate. In data communications, the average number of bits, characters or blocks per unit time transferred from a data source to a data sink. *See* SINK, SOURCE.

actuator. In hardware, a device that is capable of mechanical action under the control of a signal.

ACU. *See* AUTOMATIC CALLING UNIT.

acuity. (1) In physiology, the ability of the eye to perceive fine detail. (2) In physiology, the ability of the ear to detect very low sound levels or small changes in frequency.

acutance. In photography, the ability of a lens or film to reproduce edges sharply.

acute. In printing, an accent above the letter in the form of a diagonal stroke upwards from left to right. *Compare* GRAVE. *See* ACCENT.

Ada. A trademark; in programming, a language named after Augusta Ada, Countess of Lovelace, who assisted Babbage. Ada was developed for use in computer control and communication systems, where instruments or systems are monitored or governed by a program. Typical uses include factory production lines, data recording in laboratories, navigational systems, networking and interfacing of multiple processors. Ada is aimed at installations with a long lifespan where software modification and maintenance is a major concern. It originated in the US Department of Defense in the late 1970s. *See* HISTORY OF COMPUTING.

ADAPSO. US and Canadian Association of Data Processing Service Organizations.

adaptation. (1) In physiology, the ability to hear a particular sound in a high level of background noise. (2) In physiology, the ability of the eye to establish a range of luminance levels about a mean level, after a change in mean level. *See* LUMINANCE.

adaptive channel allocation. In communications, a method of multiplexing where channels are allocated according to demand rather than on a fixed predetermined plan. *See* MULTIPLEXING.

adaptive delta modulation. (ADM) In data communications, a form of delta modulation in which the value of delta is increased if successive error signals are of the same sign, and vice versa. *Compare* ADAPTIVE DELTA PULSE CODE MODULATION, ADAPTIVE PULSE CODE MODULATION, LINEAR DELTA MODULATION. *See* DELTA MODULATION.

adaptive delta pulse code modulation. (ADPCM) In codes, a modified form of delta pulse code modulation, used for compact disc recording, that can cope with large transient changes in an audio signal. Delta pulse code modulation assumes close correlation between successive samples; adaptive delta pulse code modulation is a variant of delta pulse code modulation in which the quantization steps are adapted to the dynamic amplitude variation. This adaptation can include a temporary switch to pulse code modulation. (Philips). *Compare* ADAPTIVE DELTA MODULATION, ADAPTIVE PULSE CODE MODULATION. *See* DELTA PULSE CODE MODULATION, PULSE CODE MODULATION, QUANTIZE.

adaptive prediction coding. In codes, an analog-to-digital conversion technique employing a one-level or multi-level sampling system in which the values of the signal at each sample time are adaptively predicted to be a linear function of the past values of the quantized signals. *See* ADAPTIVE DELTA PULSE CODE MODULATION, ANALOG-TO-DIGITAL CONVERTER.

adaptive pulse code modulation. In codes, a technique that effectively reduces occupied bandwidth per active speaker by reducing sampling rates during periods of overflow peak traffic. *Compare* ADAPTIVE DELTA MODULATION. *See* BANDWIDTH, PULSE CODE MODULATION.

adaptive routing. In data communications, a routing scheme for packets or messages in which the behaviour adapts to network changes such as line failures or variation of the traffic pattern. *Compare* DIRECTORY ROUTING, FIXED ROUTING. *See* CENTRALIZED ADAPTIVE ROUTING, DISTRIBUTED ADAPTIVE ROUTING, MESSAGE SWITCHING, PACKET SWITCHING, ROUTING.

adaptive systems. Systems that display the ability to learn to change, alter their state or otherwise react to a stimulus.

ADC. *See* ANALOG-TO-DIGITAL CONVERTER.

ADCCP. *See* ADVANCED DATA COMMUNICATIONS CONTROL PROCEDURE.

A/D converter. *See* ANALOG-TO-DIGITAL CONVERTER.

ADDA. In online information retrieval, Australian Database Development Association. The association comprises organizations that produce, develop or provide access to Australian databases or organizations or individuals with an interest in the area.

added entry. In library science, a secondary entry in a catalogue (i.e. any other than the main entry). *Compare* MAIN ENTRY.

addend. In mathematics, the operand of the addition operation; the number added to the augend to form a sum. *See* AUGEND, OPERAND.

addendum. In printing, supplementary material additional to the main body of a book and printed separately at the start or end of the text. (Desktop).

add-in. In hardware, an expansion card that slots into a microcomputer to provide additional facilities. This is a very simple method of enhancing a microcomputer. The boards available allow for additional random-access memory, enhanced graphics, modems, instrumentation, etc. *See* EXPANSION CARD, RANDOM-ACCESS MEMORY.

additive cipher. *Synonymous with* TRANSLATION CIPHER.

additive colour mixing. A means of reproducing colours by mixing lights. *Compare* SUBTRACTIVE COLOUR MIXING.

additive colour process. In filming, a technique of reproducing a colour image with black and white film. The image is photographed through three filters, each representing a primary colour, thus giving three black and white shots. The three black and white negatives are then converted into black and white positive transparencies. These three transparencies are projected simultaneously onto a screen through the appropriate primary colour filters thus providing a colour screen image. *See* PRIMARY COLOURS.

additive primary colours. In television, the red–orange, green and blue–violet colours.

In varying combinations, they produce all other colours and white. *Compare* SUBTRACTIVE PRIMARY COLOURS. *See* PRIMARY COLOURS, RGB, TRIAD.

add-on module. In hardware, a discrete module in either hardware or software to extend the specified performance of a system. (Philips). *See* EXPANSION CARD, INSERT MODULE.

address. (1) In programming, a character or group of characters that identifies a register, a particular part of storage or some other data source or destination. (2) In programming, to refer to a device or an item of data by its address. (3) In communications, the part of the selection signals that indicates the destination of a call. (4) In word processing, the location, identified by an address code of a specific section of the recording medium or storage.

addressability. In computer graphics, the number of addressable points within a specified display space or image space. *See* ALL-POINTS-ADDRESSABLE, DISPLAY SPACE, PIXEL.

addressable horizontal positions. (1) In micrographics, the number of positions within a specified film frame at which a full-length vertical line can be placed. (2) In computer graphics, a display line. *See* DISPLAY LINE.

addressable vertical positions. (1) In micrographics, the number of positions within a specified film frame at which a full-length horizontal line can be placed. (2) In computer graphics, a display column. *See* DISPLAY COLUMN.

address bus. In computing, a unidirectional bus over which digital information is transmitted to identify either a particular memory location or a particular input/output device. *Compare* CONTROL BUS, DATA BUS. *See* BUS, INPUT/OUTPUT UNIT, MICROCOMPUTER.

address data. In optical media, the part of the total data that is concerned with addressing. (Philips). *See* ADDRESSING.

address field. In programming, the specific portion of a computer word that contains either the address of the operand or the

information necessary to derive that address. *See* ADDRESS, OPERAND, WORD.

address format. In programming, the arrangement of the parts of a simple address, such as those required for identifying a channel, module or track on a magnetic disk. *See* ADDRESS, MAGNETIC DISK, TRACK.

addressing. (1) In programming, the assignment of addresses to the instructions of a program. *See* ADDRESS. (2) In communications, the means whereby the originator or control station selects the unit to which it is going to send a message. *See* STATION.

addressing mode. In programming, the method of specifying the location of data during the execution of a machine code instruction. At the simplest level, the operand may contain the actual address of the data or, in the immediate mode, the data itself. Locating the absolute address in the operand, however, is uneconomic, inflexible and inefficient for many operations, and facilities for address modification are required. *See* ABSOLUTE ADDRESS, ADDRESS, ADDRESS MODIFICATION, CENTRAL PROCESSING UNIT, MACHINE CODE INSTRUCTION, MEMORY MANAGEMENT.

address modification. In programming, an action that causes an address to be altered in a prescribed way by an arithmetic, syntactic or logic operation. *See* ADDRESSING MODE.

address register. In computing, a special register used by the central processing unit to store the address of data to be fetched from, or stored in, the computer memory. *See* ADDRESS, CENTRAL PROCESSING UNIT, REGISTER.

address space. In computing, the number of memory cells that can be accessed by the central processing unit. With 16-bit microprocessors the address bus normally has 20 lines giving an address space in excess of 1 megabyte. *See* BYTE, CENTRAL PROCESSING UNIT.

address track. In memory systems, a track on a magnetic disk containing the addresses of files, records, etc. stored on other tracks of the same device. *See* ADDRESS, MAGNETIC DISK, TRACK.

add time. In computing, the time required by a particular central processing unit to add two multidigit numbers, not including the time taken to read the numbers or store the result. Microcomputers are often rated by comparing add times as a criterion of their relative speed.

Adherography. In printing, the trade name for a duplicating process in which the image is formed by adherence of a powder to a sticky, latent image. *See* LATENT IMAGE.

ADI. American Documentation Institute.

ADIS. Automatic Data Interchange System.

adjacency. (1) In online information retrieval, a requirement that two or more terms immediately precede and follow each other, in the order specified, in order to be retrieved. (2) In character recognition, a condition in which the character-spacing reference lines of two consecutively printed characters on the same line are separated by less than a specified distance.

adjacent channel. In communications, the next channel or the one in close proximity, either physically or electrically, to the one in current use. *See* CHANNEL.

ADLC. *See* ADVANCED DATA LINK CONTROL.

ADM. *See* ADAPTIVE DELTA MODULATION.

administrative security. In data security, the management constraints, operational procedures, accountability procedures and supplemental controls established to provide an acceptable level of protection for sensitive data. (FIPS). *See* ACCOUNTABILITY. *Synonymous with* PROCEDURAL SECURITY.

Adonis. An experimental document delivery service system for biomedical literature that was operated by major European scientific publishers. It was followed by the Transdoc experimental system. *See* TRANSDOC.

ADP. *See* AUTOMATIC DATA-PROCESSING SYSTEM.

ADPCM. *See* ADAPTIVE DELTA PULSE CODE MODULATION.

ADRES. US Army Data Retrieval System.

ADSATIS. Australian Defence Science and Technology Information System.

ADSR. In man–machine interfaces, attack decay sustain release; the shape of the envelope that modulates the amplitude of a periodic waveform such as a sawtooth or sine wave. The sound generator chip of a microcomputer can be programmed to produce music by varying the ADSR and the modulating waveform. *Compare* TEMPO GENERATOR. *See* MODULATION, MUSIC SYNTHESIZER, SINE WAVE.

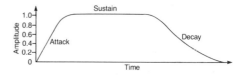

ADSR

advance. In filming, the number of frames between the picture and the synchronous sound on a composite film. *See* COMPOSITE.

advanced data communications control procedure. (ADCCP) In data communications, the operation of a data link using an advanced (i.e. synchronous data link control, high-level data link control) protocol. *See* HIGH-LEVEL DATA LINK CONTROL, PROTOCOL, SYNCHRONOUS DATA LINK CONTROL.

advanced data link control. (ADLC) In data communications, a link protocol used in high-level data link control and synchronous data link control systems. *See* HIGH-LEVEL DATA LINK CONTROL, SYNCHRONOUS DATA LINK CONTROL.

AECT. US Association for Educational Communication and Technology.

AEDS. US Association for Educational Data Systems.

aerial image. In optics, a real image formed at a plane in space in an optical system.

AEWIS. US Army Electronic Warfare Information System.

affiliate. In communications, a US broadcast station contracted to a network for more than 10 hours of programming a week.

affirmative acknowledgement. In data communications, the replies ACK0 and ACK1 in binary synchronous transmission indicate that the previous transmission block has been accepted by the receiver and that it is ready to accept the next block. ACK0 and ACK1 sent alternately provide sequential checking for a series of replies. ACK0 is also used as an affirmative reply to a station selection signal in a multidrop circuit, or to an initialization sequence in a point-to-point operation. *Compare* NEGATIVE ACKNOWLEDGEMENT. *See* BINARY SYNCHRONOUS COMMUNICATIONS, MULTIDROP CIRCUIT, POINT-TO-POINT.

AFI. *See* AMERICAN FILM INSTITUTE.

AFIPS. *See* AMERICAN FEDERATION OF INFORMATION PROCESSING SOCIETIES INC.

AFM. *See* AMERICAN FEDERATION OF MUSICIANS.

AFNOR. *See* ASSOCIATION FRANÇAISE DE NORMALISATION.

afterglow. *Synonymous with* PERSISTENCE.

after-image. In databases, a copy of a record after it has been modified by a user or program. If there is a system failure the after-images can be used to update the database from a previous dump. *Compare* BEFORE-IMAGE. *See* DUMP, TRANSACTION.

AFTRA. *See* AMERICAN FEDERATION OF TELEVISION AND RADIO ARTISTS.

agate. In printing, a type smaller than 6 point; 14 lines of agate make 1 inch of matter for newspaper advertising. *See* MATTER, POINT.

agate line. *See* AGATE.

AGC. *See* AUTOMATIC GAIN CONTROL.

agenda item. In communications, an Federal Communications Commission proceed-ing that has been placed on the Commission's formal agenda and a public notice given. *See* FEDERAL COMMUNICATIONS COMMISSION, SUNSHINE NOTICE.

aggregation. In mathematics, an abstraction whereby a relationship between objects is regarded as a higher-level object.

aging. In computing, identification of unprocessed or retained items in files according to their date, usually transaction date. Aging classifies items according to various ranges of dates.

Agricola. In online information retrieval, a database supplied by the US Department of Agriculture and dealing with agriculture, food and nutrition.

Agris. In online information retrieval, a database supplied by Food and Agriculture Organization of the United Nations (FAO), Agris Coordinating Center and dealing with agriculture.

AI. *See* ARTIFICIAL INTELLIGENCE.

A&I. Abstracting and indexing.

AIIA. Australian Information Industry Association.

AIM. US Associated Information Managers.

aiming symbol. In computer graphics, an indicator on a display screen (e.g. a circle) showing where a light pen may be detected at any given time. *Compare* TRACKING SYMBOL. *See* LIGHT PEN.

air. In printing, a US term for the amount of white space in a layout. (Desktop).

air gap. In memory systems, the very narrow gap between the two elements of a magnetic recording or playback head. *See* HARD DISK, HEAD.

air-quality. In communications, pertaining to program material developed in accordance with technical broadcasting standards.

AIS. Automated Information System.

AIT. *See* ARTIFICIAL INTELLIGENCE TECHNOLOGY.

ALA. American Library Association.

alarm. In computing, a visual or audio signal to signify that an error has arisen or an abnormal situation exists.

album descriptor. In optical media, the section of an interactive compact disc label identifying the album of which the disc is a part. (Philips). *See* COMPACT DISC – INTERACTIVE.

ALC. Automatic level control. *See* AUTOMATIC GAIN CONTROL.

ALE. *See* ANNUAL LOSS EXPECTANCY.

ALGOL. In programming, ALGOrithmic Language; an early block-structured language providing many elegant features that were lacking in other early high-level languages. It was largely superseded by Pascal. *See* HIGH-LEVEL LANGUAGE, PASCAL, PROGRAMMING.

algorithm. In programming, an unambiguous statement of the actions required to solve a problem in a finite number of steps (e.g. a precise description of the steps involved in determining the record with the highest value of a specified numerical attribute). *Compare* HEURISTIC. *See* ATTRIBUTE, PROGRAMMING, RECORD.

algorithmic language. A computer language (e.g. ALGOL) designed for expressing algorithms. *See* ALGOL.

aliasing. (1) An effect that occurs when a signal is sampled at a rate less than twice the highest frequency present in it. When a subsequent signal is recovered from the samples it will not contain the high-frequency component of the original signal, and instead it will display a false low-frequency signal. *See* NYQUIST SAMPLING THEOREM. (2) In computer graphics, an effect that occurs when a computer attempts to handle detail of a diagram that exceeds the basic resolving power of the system (e.g. the staircase effect produced when a low-resolution computer graphic system attempts to display a diagonal line). *Compare* ANTI-ALIASING.

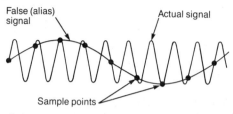

aliasing
A signal of 1kHz is sampled at 900 samples per second, instead of the required rate of more than 2 kilosamples per second, resulting in an alias at the difference frequency of 100 Hz.

align. In printing, to line up typeset or other graphic material as specified, using a base or vertical line as the reference point. (Desktop).

aligning edge. In character recognition, the edge of a form that, in conjunction with the leading edge, serves to position correctly the document that is to be optically scanned.

alignment. (1) In printing, the positioning of letters within a line that has an even appearance when looked at horizontally. (2) In communications, the simultaneous tuning of two or more circuits. (3) In recording, the positioning of microphones or loudspeakers for stereophonic effects.

alignment pin. In electronics, a pin or device that ensures the correct mating of two components designed to be connected.

ALIS. Automated Library Information System.

all in. In printing, all copy and proofs that are available. *Compare* ALL UP.

all in hand. In printing, the state of a job after all copy has been passed out to the typographers. *See* TYPOGRAPHY.

allocate. (1) In computing, to assign a resource, such as a disk file, to a specific task. *See* FILE, MAGNETIC DISK, TASK. (2) In computing, to assign memory allocations to main routines and subroutines. *See* SUBROUTINE.

allocation. *See* ASSIGNED FREQUENCY.

allophone. (1) In man–machine interfaces, a manifestation of a phoneme in a speech signal. A phoneme may be acoustically different depending upon word position, and an allophone is a positional variant of the same phoneme. *See* PHONEME, SPEECH SYNTHESIZER. (2) In acoustics, any of the variant forms of phoneme.

all-points-addressable. In computer graphics, pertaining to a system in which it is possible to address and display, or not display, each pixel on the display surface. *See* PIXEL.

all up. In printing, pertaining to the state of a print job after all copy has been set. *Compare* ALL IN.

Aloha. In computer networks, a packet-switched system initially developed at the University of Hawaii that uses radio broadcast techniques. *See* PACKET SWITCHING, SLOTTED ALOHA.

ALPAC. US National Academy of Sciences Automated Language Processing Advisory Committee. *See* MACHINE TRANSLATION.

alphabet. (1) An ordered set of all the letters and associated marks used in a language or work. (2) An ordered set of letters used in a code language (e.g. the 128 characters of the ASCII alphabet). *Compare* HIEROGLYPH. *See* AMERICAN STANDARD CODE FOR INFORMATION INTERCHANGE.

alpha beta technique. In artificial intelligence, a technique used in game-playing routines to determine the best set of moves for a given player. Players will pick the set of moves to maximize their score, whereas adversaries will always attempt to select moves that will minimize their losses. The successive set of moves can be represented by a tree structure, one player having the choice of branches from one level and the adversary the choice at the next level. The alpha beta technique eliminates the need for certain subtrees to be searched on the basis that both players using optimal strategies would never employ such subtrees, thus reducing the effort of searching for optimum moves. *See* MINIMAX, TREE STRUCTURE.

alphabetic character set. A character set that contains letters, but not digits. The set may contain control characters, special characters and the space character. *Compare* ALPHANUMERIC CHARACTER SET. *See* CHARACTER SET.

alphabetic shift. In peripherals, a control that selects the alphabetic character set on an alphanumeric keyboard. *See* ALPHABETIC CHARACTER SET.

alphabetic string. A character string comprising letters from the same alphabet. *See* STRING.

alphabet length. In printing, the measurement, in points, of the lower-case alphabet of a particular style and size. *See* POINT.

alphageometric. In computer graphics, a standard in which the codes can instruct the terminal to produce line drawings, fill areas with colour, etc. in addition to normal character display modes. *Compare* ALPHAMOSAIC. *See* NAPLPS, VIDEOTEX.

alphamosaic. In computer graphics, a standard in which the codes determine the alphanumeric character or mosaic pattern to be displayed in a character space. *Compare* ALPHAGEOMETRIC. *See* ALPHANUMERIC, CHARACTER SPACE, VIDEOTEX.

alphanumeric. (A/N) Pertaining to a set comprising letters, digits and normally associated characters (e.g. punctuation marks). *See* CHARACTER SET.

alphanumeric character set. A character set comprising both letters and digits. It may also contain control characters, special characters and the space character. *Compare* ALPHABETIC CHARACTER SET. *See* ALPHANUMERIC, CHARACTER SET.

alphanumeric data. Data that is represented by letters and digits and perhaps special characters and the space character. *See* ALPHANUMERIC.

alphanumerics mode. In videotex, the display mode in which the display characters are those of the alphanumerics set. *Compare* GRAPHICS MODE. *See* DISPLAY MODE.

alphanumerics set. In videotex, the set of 96 display characters comprising all the alphanumerics characters. *See* DISPLAY CHARACTER.

alphaphotographic. In videotex, a method of displaying alphanumeric characters and picture-quality graphics from individually transmitted and stored picture elements. *See* PICTURE PRESTEL.

alpha testing. In programming, the in-house testing of a package by a software house prior to beta testing. *Compare* BETA TESTING.

alpha wrap. In recording, a method of winding videotape around the drum of a helical scan device. The tape circumnavigates the drum producing a shape similar to the Greek letter alpha, leaving the drum at a higher level than that at which it entered. The video scans are diagonal on the tape and cover the width of it. The edge of the tape is also required for audio recording, and thus there is a compromise between good sound recording and drop out. *Compare* OMEGA WRAP. *See* DROP OUT, SOUND TRACK.

ALS. Automated Library Systems.

alternate mode. In computing, a method of using a virtual terminal by which each of two interacting systems or users has access to its data structure in turn. The associated protocols include facilities to allow the orderly transfer of control from one user to the other. *Compare* FREE-RUNNING MODE. *See* DATA STRUCTURE, VIRTUAL TERMINAL.

alternate route. In data communications, a secondary or backup route that is used if the normal routing path is not available.

alternate track. In memory systems, a track on a magnetic disk or other storage device that is automatically substituted for a damaged track. *See* MAGNETIC DISK, TRACK.

alternating current. (AC) In electronics, electric power supply in the form of a sine wave, normally a frequency of 60 Hz in the USA and 50 Hz in the UK. *Compare* DIRECT CURRENT.

ALU. *See* ARITHMETIC LOGIC UNIT.

Alvey. A research program, named after Mr John Alvey, of precompetitive research in advanced information technology costing some £300 million over five years. *Compare* ESPRIT.

AM. *See* AMPLITUDE MODULATION.

A-MAC. In television, a variant of C-MAC that requires a lower bandwidth per channel. *Compare* C-MAC. *See* MAC.

ambient noise level. In electronics, random, uncontrollable and irreducible noise level at a location or circuit. *See* NOISE.

ambisonics. In recording, the use of two or more sound channels to give the effect of more than one spatial dimension. *Compare* STEREO. *Synonymous with* SURROUND SOUND.

America: History & Life. (AHL) In online information retrieval, a database supplied by ABC–Clio Information Services and dealing with history, politics and political science.

American Federation of Information Processing Societies Inc. A federation founded in 1961 that includes the American Society for Information Science, American Statistical Association, Association for Computing Machinery, Association for Education Data Systems, Data Processing Management Association, IEEE Computer Society, Instrument Society of America, Society for Computer Simulation, Society for Industrial and Applied Mathematics, Society for Information Display. It is the US member of the International Federation of Information Processing. *See* INTERNATIONAL FEDERATION OF INFORMATION PROCESSING.

American Federation of Musicians. A US trade union representing musicians and vocalists.

American Federation of Television and Radio Artists. In broadcasting, a US trade union representing television and radio performers and sound effects specialists.

American Film Institute. (AFI) In filming, a US non-profit-making organization that offers educational opportunities within the industry.

American National Standards Institute. (ANSI) A body that organizes committees comprising computer users, manufacturers, etc. to develop and publish industry standards (e.g. ANSI FORTRAN, ANSI Standard Code for Periodical Identification).

American Research Bureau. (ARB) A US organization for television audience market research.

American Standard Code for Information Interchange. (ASCII) A standard, pronounced ASKEE, data transmission code that was introduced to achieve compatibility between data devices. It consists of seven information bits and one parity bit for error-checking purposes, thus allowing 128 code combinations. Of these, 32 are used for upper-case characters and a few punctuation marks, another group of 32 characters are used for numbers, spacing and additional punctuation symbols, the third group of 32 characters are assigned to lower-case characters and some rarely used punctuation symbols. The last set of 32 characters are allocated to machine and control commands (e.g. line feed, carriage return). *See* BIT, CARRIAGE CONTROL, INTERNATIONAL ALPHABET NUMBER 5, LOWER CASE, PARITY CHECKING, UPPER CASE.

American Standards Association. (ASA) A body with groups responsible for the establishment of data-processing standards. *See* NATIONAL BUREAU OF STANDARDS.

amorphous hydrogenated silicon. (a-Si-H) In optoelectronics, an improved form of amorphous silicon with high resistivity and low mobility. *Compare* AMORPHOUS SILICON. *See* RESISTANCE.

amorphous silicon. (a-Si) In optoelectronics, a high-yield photoconductor. *Compare* AMORPHOUS HYDROGENATED SILICON. *See* COPIER, PHOTOCONDUCTOR.

ampere. In electronics, the basic unit of electrical current. *See* CURRENT.

amplification. (1) In electronics, the strengthening of a weak signal. (2) In electronics, the ratio between some measure of the output signal and the input signal of a device. *Compare* ATTENUATION, GAIN.

amplified telephone. In communications, the general term for a hands-free telephone, using a loudspeaker and microphone unit rather than a telephone handset. *See* TELECONFERENCING.

amplifier. In electronics, a normally unidirectional device that increases the power or amplitude of an electrical signal. *See* AMPLITUDE.

amplitude. In electronics, the magnitude of the greatest deviation from the midpoint value of a periodic signal or phenomenon. *See* FREQUENCY, WAVELENGTH.

amplitude distortion. In electronics, a distortion caused by an undesired amplitude characteristic (e.g. in an amplifier the output signal would not be a faithful reproduction of the input signal).

amplitude frequency characteristic. In electronics, a graphical representation of the variation in output amplitude of a device with changes in input frequency at constant input amplitude.

amplitude modulation. (AM) In communications, a form of modulation in which the amplitude of the carrier signal is varied in accordance with the amplitude of the modulating signal. *Compare* FREQUENCY MODULATION, PHASE MODULATION, PULSE MODULATION. *See* CARRIER, MODULATION.

AMPS. In communications, advanced mobile phone service; a cellular radio system. *Compare* NMT, TACS. *See* CELLULAR RADIO.

ANA. *See* ARTICLE NUMBERING ASSOCIATION, ASSOCIATION OF NATIONAL ADVERTISERS.

analog. In computing and communications, pertaining to the form of conti-

CONTROL CHARACTERS

CHAR	OCTAL	BINARY
NUL	000	0000000
SOH	001	0000001
STX	002	0000010
ETX	003	0000011
EOT	004	0000100
ENQ	005	0000101
ACK	006	0000110
BEL	007	0000111
BS	010	0001000
HT	011	0001001
LF	012	0001010
VT	013	0001011
FF	014	0001100
CR	015	0001101
SO	016	0001110
SI	017	0001111
DLE	020	0010000
DC1	021	0010001
DC2	022	0010010
DC3	023	0010011
DC4	024	0010100
NAK	025	0010101
SYN	026	0010110
ETB	027	0010111
CAN	030	0011000
EM	031	0011001
SUB	032	0011010
ESC	033	0011011
FS	034	0011100
GS	035	0011101
RS	036	0011110
US	037	0011111
DEL	177	1111111

CONTROL CHARACTER KEY

NUL	=	All zeros
SOH	=	Start of heading
STX	=	Start of text
ETX	=	End of text
EOT	=	End of transmission
ENQ	=	Enquiry
ACK	=	Acknowledgement
BEL	=	Bell or attention signal
BS	=	Back space
HT	=	Horizontal tabulation
LF	=	Line feed
VT	=	Vertical tabulation
FF	=	Form Feed
CR	=	Carriage return
SO	=	Shift out
SI	=	Shift in
DLE	=	Data link escape
DC1	=	Device control 1
DC2	=	Device control 2
DC3	=	Device control 3
DC4	=	Device control 4
NAK	=	Negative acknowledgement
SYN	=	Synchronous/idle
ETB	=	End of transmitted block
CAN	=	Cancel (error in data)
EM	=	End of medium
SUB	=	Start of special sequence
ESC	=	Escape
FS	=	Information file separator
GS	=	Information group separator
RS	=	Information record separator
US	=	Information unit separator
DEL	=	Delete

PRINTABLE CHARACTERS

CHAR	OCTAL	BINARY
SP	040	0100000
!	041	0100001
"	042	0100010
#	043	0100011
$	044	0100100
%	045	0100101
&	046	0100110
'	047	0100111
(	050	0101000
)	051	0101001
*	052	0101010
+	053	0101011
,	054	0101100
-	055	0101101
.	056	0101110
/	057	0101111
0	060	0110000
1	061	0110001
2	062	0110010
3	063	0110011
4	064	0110100
5	065	0110101
6	066	0110110
7	067	0110111
8	070	0111000
9	071	0111001
:	072	0111010
;	073	0111011
<	074	0111100
=	075	0111101
>	076	0111110
?	077	0111111
@	100	1000000

PRINTABLE CHARACTERS

CHAR	OCTAL	BINARY
A	101	1000001
B	102	1000010
C	103	1000011
D	104	1000100
E	105	1000101
F	106	1000110
G	107	1000111
H	110	1001000
I	111	1001001
J	112	1001010
K	113	1001011
L	114	1001100
M	115	1001101
N	116	1001110
O	117	1001111
P	120	1010000
Q	121	1010001
R	122	1010010
S	123	1010011
T	124	1010100
U	125	1010101
V	126	1010110
W	127	1010111
X	130	1011000
Y	131	1011001
Z	132	1011010

PRINTABLE CHARACTERS

CHAR	OCTAL	BINARY
a	141	1100001
b	142	1100010
c	143	1100011
d	144	1100100
e	145	1100101
f	146	1100110
g	147	1100111
h	150	1101000
i	151	1101001
j	152	1101010
k	153	1101011
l	154	1101100
m	155	1101101
n	156	1101110
o	157	1101111
p	160	1110000
q	161	1110001
r	162	1110010
s	163	1110011
t	164	1110100
u	165	1110101
v	166	1110110
w	167	1110111
x	170	1111000
y	171	1111001
z	172	1111010

ASCII codes.

nuously variable physical quantities (e.g. a telephone conversation can be represented fully in analog form by a voltage derived from the telephone transmitters). *Compare* DIGITAL. *See* TRANSDUCER.

analog channel. In communications, a data channel such that the signal may take any form within the amplitude and frequency constraints imposed by the transmission technology. Voice-grade channels are analog channels. *See* ANALOG, VOICE-GRADE CHANNEL.

analog data. Data represented in a continuous form.

analog image synthesis. In filming, a computer graphics system used to produce special effects for films; images can be made to oscillate, shrink, spin, etc.

analog recording. A method of recording control information by a continuous, but varying signal. *Compare* DIGITAL RECORDING. *See* ANALOG SIGNAL.

analog signal. A signal that varies continuously according to the information in transmission (e.g. sound waves). *Compare* DIGITAL SIGNAL.

analog-to-digital converter. In peripherals, a device that accepts a continuous analog signal and produces a stream of digital signals corresponding to values of the analog signal at sampling instants. *Compare* DIGITAL-TO-ANALOG CONVERTER. *See* COMPUTERIZED INSTRUMENTATION, SAMPLE AND HOLD CIRCUIT.

analog transmission. In communications, the transmission of information by analog signal. *Compare* DIGITAL TRANSMISSION SYSTEM. *See* ANALOG SIGNAL.

analog video chip. *See* VIDEO CHIP.

analysis. The methodical investigation of a problem, and the separation of the problem into smaller related units for further detailed study. *Compare* SYNTHESIS. *See* SYSTEMS ANALYSIS.

analyst. A person who defines problems and develops algorithms and procedures for their solution. *See* SYSTEMS ANALYSIS.

analyst's workbench. In systems analysis, an integrated software package developed as an aid in the various tasks of a systems analyst (e.g. data collection, data analysis, data dictionary, production of high-level language specifications). *See* DATA ANALYSIS, DATA DICTIONARY.

anamorphic image. In optics, an image that has been squeezed in one direction, usually horizontal, by an anamorphic lens. *See* ANAMORPHIC LENS.

anamorphic lens. In photography, a lens that is designed to distort an image in a systematic way, usually by means of an element or elements having cylindrical rather than the usual spherical surfaces.

ANAPROP. In television, ANOmalous PROPagation; an effect caused by meteorological conditions that produces unwanted television reception from distant transmitters, resulting in poor reception from selected transmitters. *See* GHOST.

anastigmat lens. In optics, a lens optically corrected in manufacture for astigmatism. *See* ASTIGMATISM.

ancillary equipment. In communications, equipment located on a subscriber's premises (e.g. answering devices, automatic dialers) to provide a greater utility of a communications channel for individual subscribers.

AND. A logical operation, A AND B has the result true only if both of the logical variables A and B are true. The corresponding truth table is:

A	B	A AND B
0	0	0
1	0	0
0	1	0
1	1	1

Compare NAND, OR. *See* BOOLEAN ALGEBRA, TRUTH TABLE.

anechoic. In acoustics, pertaining to a enclosure neither having nor producing echoes. *See* ECHO.

angstrom. (Å). A unit of measurement equal to 10^{-10} metres (i.e. one ten-millionth of a millimetre). It is commonly used in the measurement of wavelengths of light.

angular misalignment loss. In communications, an optical power loss, in fiber optics, caused by the angular deviation from the optimum alignment of the source to optical waveguide, waveguide to waveguide, or waveguide to detector. *See* FIBER OPTICS.

ANI. (1) In data communications, advanced network integration; a data communications system that facilitates the interconnection of various nodes, transmission speeds, protocols, interfaces, formats and manufacturers' equipment into a single, cohesive network. (2) In communications. *See* AUTOMATIC NUMBER IDENTIFICATION.

Anik. In communications, a Canadian series of geostationary satellites. *See* GEOSTATIONARY SATELLITE, TELESAT.

animation. In video and computer graphics, the projection of a continuous sequence of related images, at a speed that matches the human eye's inherent persistence of vision, to create a flicker-free image. At the average cinematic screen illumination the human eye detects no flicker for frequencies of intermission above approximately 16 per second. US television generates images at 30 frames per second, whereas the European standard is 25 frames per second. Conflicts arise in the television and video recording of films employing 24 frames per second. US television uses three two pulldown. UK television transmits the film at 25 frames per second giving a speed increase of 4 per cent and a rise in the sound pitch. *See* COMPUTER ANIMATION, PERSISTENCE OF VISION, THREE TWO PULLDOWN.

anisochronous transmission. In data communications, a transmission process in which there is always an integral number of unit intervals between any two significant instants in the same group. Between two significant instants located in different groups there is not always an integral number of unit intervals. *Compare* ISOCHRONOUS TRANSMISSION. *See* ASYNCHRONOUS TRANSMISSION.

A/N. *See* ALPHANUMERIC.

annotation. A description or explanation usually in the form of a comment or note.

annual loss expectancy. (ALE) In risk management, a measure of the potential annual cost of a threat to system security. *See* RISK ANALYSIS, THREAT.

annunciator. A visual or audible device that provides information on the state of associated systems (e.g. a fire alarm device with a map of the location of sensors and an indication of which sensors, if any, have been actuated).

anode. In electronics, the positive terminal of a device. *Compare* CATHODE.

anomalistic period. In satellite communications, the time interval between two consecutive passages of a satellite through its apogee. *See* APOGEE.

ANSI. *See* AMERICAN NATIONAL STANDARDS INSTITUTE.

ANSI-SPARC. In databases, a schema developed as a general standard for the description of database management systems. The standard defines three schemata: (a) a conceptual schema which provides a logical description of the data; (b) one or more user schemata which represent the users' views of the data; and (c) a physical schema which describes the manner in which the data is stored in the computer. *See* SCHEMA.

answer back. In communications, a signal sent by a receiving unit to the sending station for identification or to indicate it is ready for transmission. *See* VOICE ANSWER BACK.

answering. In communications, the process of responding to a calling station to complete the establishment of a connection between data stations. *See* DATA STATION.

answering time. The elapse time between the appearance of a signal and the response made to it.

answerphone. In communications, a device that automatically answers a telephone call giving a prerecorded message and recording any received messages.

answer set. In online retrieval, a search statement or query and the computer's response. Each set is usually numbered.

antenna. In communications, a device that converts a high radio frequency signal into a corresponding electromagnetic wave, or vice versa. *See* RADIO FREQUENCY.

antenna array. An array of radiating and/or receiving elements arranged in a system. *See* ANTENNA.

antenna gain. In communications, the increase in power achieved by focusing an antenna, defined as the ratio of the power received from the antenna to the power that the receiver would receive if the transmission were isotropic. *See* ISOTROPIC ANTENNA.

antenna pattern. In communications, a diagram indicating the relative strength of the signal transmitted, or received, for every direction around an antenna. The diagram may indicate the amplitude, power or logarithmic amplitude of the signal. With directional antennae the pattern is in the form of a number of loops or lobes. The largest lobe is termed the main lobe. The antenna pattern should have the main lobe pointing towards the appropriate receiving or transmitting antennae. Receiving antennae patterns should also have a minimum in the direction of source of undesired signals. *See* ANTENNA GAIN, BACK LOBE, MAIN LOBE, SIDE LOBE.

anti-aliasing. In computer graphics, a method of disguising the aliasing errors introduced by low-resolution graphics displays. The jagged edges produced by boundary pixels may be softened by adjusting the shading intensities to create a smoother transition of colour changes. *Compare* ALIASING. *See* PIXEL.

anticipatory staging. In computing, a technique in which blocks of data are moved from one storage device to another, with a shorter access time, in anticipation that they will be required by the program and before

the program actually requests them. *Compare* DEMAND STAGING.

anti-coincidence circuit. In computing, a logic circuit that only provides an output if different signals are received on the input lines. *Compare* COINCIDENCE CIRCUIT.

anti-eavesdrop device. In communications security, a device that detects the presence of covert listening units by scanning radio frequency transmission frequencies. *See* ELECTRONIC COUNTERMEASURES SWEEPING.

Antiope. In videotex, French videotex system.

anti-passback. In computer security, pertaining to a system designed to prevent 'passing back' of an access card from an individual who has already gained entry. This measure ensures that a card used to enter an area must be used to exit the area before it can be reused for entry.

anti-surveillance. In computer security, pertaining to a system designed to prevent or detect the use of surveillance equipment. *See* ANTI-EAVESDROP DEVICE.

AO. Automated office. *See* OFFICE AUTOMATION.

AOCS. In communications, attitude and orbit control system; a system on a communications satellite that maintains it in the correct orbit and pointing in the correct direction. *See* COMMUNICATIONS SATELLITE SYSTEM.

AP. *See* ASSOCIATED PRESS

APD. *See* AVALANCHE PHOTODIODE.

aperture. (1) In computing, a part of a mask that permits retention of the corresponding portions of data. *See* MASK. (2) In optics. *See* LENS APERTURE. (3) In communications, the open end of a horn antenna. *See* HORN, MASK.

aperture antenna. In communications, a microwave antenna employing a horn, or a feed and reflector. *See* ANTENNA, APERTURE, HORN.

aperture card. In micrographics, an 80-column card which has a 35 x 48 millimetre microfilm frame inserted. Identifying information can be key-punched into the card, and their primary use is for graphic-type applications in which illustrations, such as engineering drawings, are stored.

aperture efficiency. In communications, the ratio of the effective aperture of an antenna to its physical area. *See* ANTENNA.

aperture illumination. In communications, the field pattern generated by an aperture antenna such as a horn. *See* APERTURE ANTENNA, HORN.

aperture mask. In television, a colour picture tube mask registering RGB beams. *See* BEAM, REGISTER, RGB.

apex. In printing, the point of a character where two lines meet at the top. An example of this is the point on the letter A. (Desktop).

Apilit. In online information retrieval, a database supplied by American Petroleum Institute (API), Central Abstracting and Indexing Service and dealing with energy.

Apipat. In online information retrieval, a database supplied by American Petroleum Institute (API), Central Abstracting and Indexing Service and dealing with energy patents.

APL. In programming, A Programming Language. APL is a language that began life as a functional notation to express mathematical algorithms and was subsequently adapted for use as a programming language. It is extremely concise and has found favour mainly in mathematical applications, although it has also been used for tasks such as data retrieval, teaching and simulation. As an interactive, and interpreted, language it is more suited to one-off jobs and experimental tasks than to large program construction.

apochromatic lens. In optics, a lens corrected for spherical and chromatic aberration.

See CHROMATIC ABERRATION, SPHERICAL ABERRATION.

apogee. In communications, the point at which the satellite is at its maximum distance from earth in its orbit. *Compare* PERIGEE.

Apollo. In data communications, Article Procurement with OnLine Local Ordering; a European project to provide high-speed digital information transfer. The project is aimed at long messages, in particular document facsimiles, transmitted from a small number (up to 10) information providers to a widely dispersed user population. It uses the EUTELSAT series of satellite communications. *See* ADONIS, DOCUMENT DELIVERY SERVICE, EUTELSAT.

append. (1) In programming, to attach a file to the end of another file. (2) In computer security, an access control privilege that enables a user to add information to a file, but not to modify any data already on the file.

application layer. In data communications, the topmost (i.e. seventh) layer in the ISO Open Systems Interconnections model. This layer provides a set of network services (e.g. file transfer, electronic mail) to the user application program. *Compare* DATA LINK LAYER, NETWORK LAYER, PHYSICAL LAYER, PRESENTATION LAYER, SESSION LAYER, TRANSPORT LAYER. *See* ELECTRONIC MAIL, OPEN SYSTEMS INTERCONNECTION, X.400.

application-oriented language. In programming, a language that has facilities or notations useful for solving problems in one or more specific classes of applications (e.g. numerical analysis, business data processing, simulation).

application program. In programming, a program, usually written in-house, for a specific user application (e.g. payroll). *See* IN-HOUSE.

application software. *See* APPLICATION PROGRAM.

application-specific design. *Synonymous with* CUSTOM DESIGN.

application-specific integrated circuit. In microelectronics, a semi-custom chip. *See* SEMI-CUSTOM DESIGN.

approach of end of medium indicator. On recording, a device that gives an audible or visual signal at a precise distance from the end of the recording medium.

approval/accreditation. In computer security, the official authorization that is granted to an automatic data-processing system to process sensitive information in its operational environment, based upon comprehensive security evaluation of the system's hardware, firmware and software security design, configuration and implementation, and of the other system's procedural, administrative, physical, tempest, personnel and communications security controls. (DOD). *See* ACCREDITATION, TEMPEST PROOFING.

approved circuit. *Synonymous with* PROTECTED WIRELINE DISTRIBUTION SYSTEM.

apron. In printing, a US term for additional white space allowed in the margins of text and illustrations when forming a foldout. (Desktop).

Aqualine. In online information retrieval, a database supplied by Water Research Centre and dealing with aquatic sciences and the environment.

Arabsat. In communications, an Arab League series of geostationary satellites. *See* GEOSTATIONARY SATELLITE, TELESAT.

ARB. *See* AMERICAN RESEARCH BUREAU.

arbitrated signature. In data security, a digital signature that involves a third party, the arbiter. The signed message is prepared by the sender and forwarded to the arbiter. The arbiter signs the message for the sender and subsequently validates it for the receiver. *See* DIGITAL SIGNATURE.

archetype. A work of communication (e.g. a book) that has the typical pattern, symbolism and forms for works of its kind, especially original classical works.

architecture. The specification of the relationships between parts of a computer system. All generations of computers prior to the fifth generation were based upon von Neumann architecture. This architecture was the turning point in computer design because it incorporated the concept of stored program control; thus decoupling the hardware design from the detailed consideration of algorithms relating to applications and providing the incredible flexibility of modern computers. The traditional von Neumann computer contains: (a) a single computing element incorporating a processor, communications and memory; (b) a linear organization of fixed-sized memory cells; (c) a one-level address space of memory cells; (d) a low-level machine language; (e) sequential centralized control of computation; and (f) a primitive input/output capability.

The von Neumann architecture was the keystone of computer development for over 40 years, but it was designed in an era when electronic devices were expensive, large, relatively unreliable and dissipated considerable thermal power. Moreover, the computer applications in the 1950s and 1960s were relatively straightforward and amenable to design by conventional high-level languages. The situation changed during the late 1970s; the software crisis can be, at least in part, attributed to the fact that relatively simple architectures can only be induced to perform complex processes by the design of sophisticated software. Moreover, the massive advances in microelectronics provide architecture designers with powerful, cheap, fast processors and memories. The wheel has thus undergone a complete revolution, and it is now more economical to design hardware modules for classes of problems. *See* DATAFLOW, FIFTH-GENERATION COMPUTER, HISTORY OF COMPUTING, LOW-LEVEL LANGUAGE, MAN–MACHINE INTERFACE, VON NEUMANN.

archival quality. In printing, the quality of the copy image expressed in terms of the specified number of years for which legibility is guaranteed when stored under stated conditions.

archiving. In computing, the storage of backup files and associated journals, usually for a given period of time. *See* FILE, JOURNAL.

ARDIS. US Army Research and Development Information System.

area. In databases, the CODASYL definition of an area is a named subdivision of the addressable storage space in the database which may contain occurrences of records and sets, or parts of sets of various types. *See* CODASYL, RECORD, SET.

area code. In communications, a three-digit number identifying a geographical area to permit direct distance dialing on the telephone system. *See* DIRECT DISTANCE DIALING. *Synonymous with* NUMBER PLAN AREA.

area composition. In printing, the operation of setting made up pages in varying formats for advertisements, tables, pages of periodicals, etc., following arrangement of these by use of the video layout system. *See* PHOTOTYPESETTING, VIDEO LAYOUT SYSTEM.

area exchange. In communications, an area organization established for administrative reasons for a telephone service covered on a single-rate basis, usually a city or large division, town or village. *See* RATE CENTRE.

area infill. In computer graphics, a technique used with pixel-based systems in which a defined area of the screen is filled with a specified colour or pattern. *See* PIXEL.

areal density. In recording, the number of bits that may be recorded per unit area on a recording medium. Areal densities vary from 0.1 megabits per square inch (open-reel tape recorders), 0.5 megabits per square inch (compact cassette), 100 megabits per square inch (8 mm VCR) and 1000 megabits per square inch (compact disc). *See* COMPACT CASSETTE, COMPACT DISC. (2) In memory systems, the number of bits per unit area that can be stored on a recording device. In magnetic and optical disc systems it is equal to the product of bits per inch (BPI) and tracks per inch (TPI). *See* BITS PER INCH, MAGNETIC DISK, OPTICAL DISC STORAGE, TRACKS PER INCH.

area search. In library science, the examination of a large group of documents to select those that belong to one group.

argument. (1) Any value of an independent variable. (2) In programming, a parameter passed between a calling program and a subprogram or statement function. *See* SUBROUTINE.

arithmetic. (1) The branch of mathematics concerned with the study of the positive real numbers and zero. (2) In programming, the operations of addition, subtraction, multiplication and division.

arithmetic capability. In word processing, the ability of a system to be used as a calculator or adding machine.

arithmetic instruction. In programming, an instruction in which the operation part specifies an operation that follows the rules of arithmetic. *See* INSTRUCTION.

arithmetic logic unit. (ALU) In computing, the unit in which arithmetic, logic and related operations are performed. *See* CENTRAL PROCESSING UNIT. *Synonymous with* MILL.

arithmetic mean. In mathematics, the average value of a number of values of a variable. It is calculated by summing all the component values and dividing the result by the number of values. *Synonymous with* AVERAGE.

arithmetic overflow. *See* OVERFLOW.

arithmetic shift. (1) In programming, a shift that does not affect the sign position. (2) In programming, a shift that is equivalent to the multiplication of a number by a positive or negative integral power of the radix. *Compare* LOGICAL SHIFT. *See* RADIX, SHIFT.

arithmetic unit. *See* ARITHMETIC LOGIC UNIT.

arm stealing. In backing storage, the rapid movement of read/write heads of a hard-disk drive, in a multiuser environment, when the system is responding to a succession of enquiries from different users. *See* HARD DISK, READ/WRITE HEAD.

ARPA. *See* DARPA.

ARQ. Automatic request for repetition. *Synonymous with* AUTOMATIC TRANSMISSION REQUEST.

array. In data structures, an ordered arrangement or pattern of items or numbers (e.g. a table of numbers). The use of arrays can substantially reduce programming effort in the processing of repetitive operations. *See* LOOP, VECTOR. (2) In communications, an assembly of spaced antenna elements designed to give an overall directional characteristic. *See* ANTENNA.

array processor. In computing, a computer system that is designed to perform identical operations on the elements of an array in parallel. It may be a self-contained unit or attached to a mainframe computer via an internal bus or input/output port. *See* ARRAY, INPUT/OUTPUT PORT, PARALLEL PROCESSING, SINGLE-INSTRUCTION STREAM MULTIPLE-DATA STREAM, *Synonymous with* VECTOR PROCESSOR.

art. In printing and filming, an abbreviation for artwork. *See* ARTWORK.

ARTbibliographies Modern. In online information retrieval, a database supplied by ABC–Clio Information Services and dealing with art.

ARTEMIS. Automatic Retrieval of Text through European Multipurpose Information Services; a document-delivery system proposed in a report published by the European Community in 1981.

Article Numbering Association. (ANA) A body concerned with the bar coding of retail goods. *See* BAR CODE, UNIVERSAL PRODUCT CODE.

articulator. In man–machine interfaces, a component of a music synthesizer that causes the sound to decay according to the characteristics of a particular instrument. The circuit effectively multiplies the analog signal of the sound by the approximate decay envelope. *See* ANALOG SIGNAL, MUSIC SYNTHESIZER.

artificial intelligence. (AI) The computational reproduction of intelligent action.
   (a) Introduction. In practice AI is a somewhat ill-defined discipline pertaining to many aspects of the simulation of human intellect and thought by logical systems embodied in computer programs. More precise definitions are elusive because the subject is still embryonic, with considerable disagreement as to its proper boundaries. The motivation for AI research is twofold. On the one hand, it is pursued in the hope that the application of rigorous computational methods and their attendant logic can throw light upon the operation of the human mind. More prosaically, the predominant drive behind AI research has been the desire to imbue machines with more flexible and informed patterns of behaviour, enabling some domains of human expertise to be cheaply replicated and possibly releasing workers from hazardous or monotonous tasks. The inception of AI cannot be as precisely dated as for, say, the advent of the digital computer, but investigations into most of its definitive branches were well under way by the mid 1960s. Much of the inspiration for AI can indeed be traced to Alan Turing and John von Neumann, the driving forces behind modern computer science.
   AI has often had a rough ride in terms of its research funding, but it is currently enjoying a resurgence with the advent of considerable government interest, following the Japanese decision to launch into the fifth-generation computer. Early successes, using very limited problems, sometimes generated over optimistic prophecies of superhuman machine intelligence and an new cybernetic age. However, it has been found that most situations become extremely complex once the problem has been expanded to a useful size. Moreover, it has emerged that the seemingly difficult logical/intellectual puzzles upon which artificial intelligence scored its initial successes are almost trivial, from the computational standpoint, in comparison with the 'mundane' human facilities of perception and day-to-day interactions in the real world. A more mature appreciation of the problems ahead has lead to some curtailment of the expectations of the technological advance that can be achieved in the immediate future.
   The central range of issues of AI is reasonably constant; a fact sometimes obscured by the large range of scenarios, programming languages and AI methods. Before any situation can be addressed by current computers, the pertinent details must be reduced to a precise, machine-

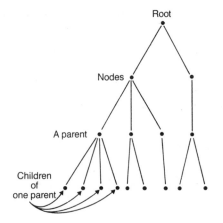

artificial intelligence
Fig. 1(a). A tree.

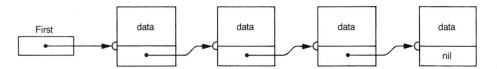

artificial intelligence
Fig. 1(b). A linked list.

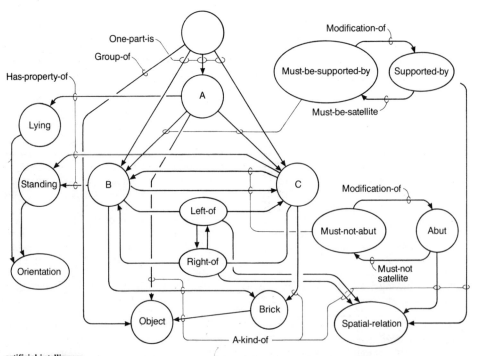

artificial intelligence
Fig. 1(c). Semantic network.

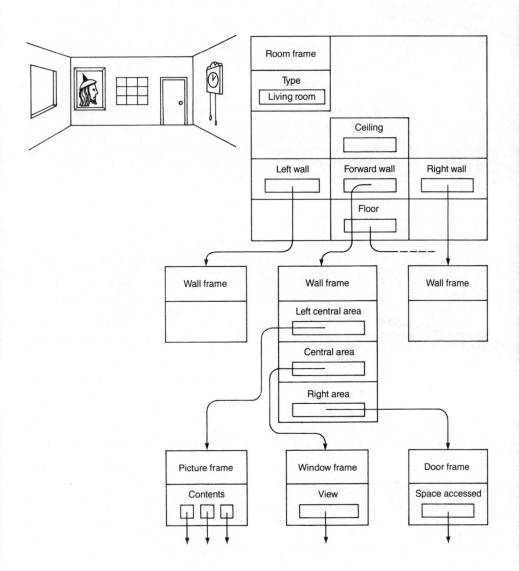

artificial intelligence
Fig. 1(d). A frame.

compatible formulation. In the development of a chess-playing program the board and pieces must obviously be codified to make them accessible to the program. There is rarely a unique solution to this problem, even for simple examples such as in chess it is necessary to ask 'what is the information required for, and how is it to be accessed, i.e. examined and modified?'. Various representations will tend to highlight some aspects of the data while obscuring others. For example, having decided upon some representation of the board, and the pieces, it will then be necessary to codify legal moves within such a representation. Whereas the board configurations will invariably be represented declaratively (i.e. as a set of explicitly detailed items which are read as data by the program) rules for the chess moves might be treated procedurally and embedded in the structure of the program code. Considerable importance is attached to this distinction between procedural and declarative representation because procedural knowledge, although more concise, is inflexible and often obscure. Knowledge representation is a crucial topic in AI, and can often determine the success or otherwise of a program. Inappropriate representations can render an operation extremely expensive in terms of processing power because vital data becomes difficult to access and modify.

A range of knowledge representations in current usage are illustrated in Fig. 1. Regular data, possessing well-defined properties for retrieval and modification, may be represented by trees (Fig. 1 (a)) or linked lists (Fig. 1 (b)). Semantic networks (Fig. 1 (c)) involve the decomposition of knowledge into irregular graphs, with objects at the nodes, and labelled arcs denoting the relationship between them. This provides greater versatility at the cost of more complexity in terms of traversing and updating the network; the notion of a legitimate insertion or deletion is related to the meanings associated with the affected arcs and nodes. Frames (Fig. 1 (d)) provide an alternative method of treating concepts with many irregular or divergent components, bearing some resemblance to the record construct of Pascal or COBOL; in these instances the meaning of the represented information is heavily conditioned by the procedural rules used to manipulate it.

Once the form of knowledge representation has been settled, the second characteristic feature of most AI programs is the search through the data for the answer in one guise or another. The chess-playing program can again illustrate this common theme. The program is expected to select a good move on the basis of the current board configuration. A straightforward, theoretically valid, approach simply tests every possible move up to the end game (i.e. for every move then every possible outcome is generated and tested until either White or Black checkmates or a stalemate occurs). This brute force technique is debarred by the combinational explosion in the number of moves that have to be inspected. In a typical game of chess there are 20 possible moves for a given board state, if the forward search is to be conducted over N stages then 20^N situations have to be inspected. Given that a typical game might occupy 40 sequential moves and that a supercomputer of the future could inspect a move in a microsecond, then the game would take an astronomical number of centuries to complete. It is clear that careful attention must be paid to pruning the search, and indeed some of the moves tested will represent ridiculous scenarios (e.g a player wantonly allowing an opponent to take a queen). Various strategies can be deployed to permit such pruning. If it is possible to evaluate a numerical value of a given board configuration (e.g. a high value indicates a significant probability that White will win from this board state) then a minimax search can be undertaken. At each juncture it is assumed that each player (i.e. the computer and its opponent) will select the moves giving the best board value (i.e. White selects the move giving the highest value and Black that giving the lowest). In this case only 20 calculations are required for each stage of the game. In practice it has proved impossible to develop a criterion for the evaluation of the 'value' of chess board states that is valid over all circumstances, but the illustration of the minimax approach remains valid.

(b) Landmark developments. The developments of AI may be described in terms of some landmark projects: (i) Shrdlu; (ii) Mycin; and (iii) Winston's computer learning by example.

(i) Shrdlu. AI workers have consistently been fascinated by the problem of developing programs capable of conducting a dialog with a human partner in conversational English. Famous attempts include Eliza and Parry. The former may be used to impersonate a non-directive psychoanalyst who responds to the user, who is assumed to be behaving as a clinically paranoid patient. Both Eliza and Parry achieved a surprising impression of an articulate, if somewhat idiosyncratic, person responding realistically, provided that the conversation remained within the carefully selected context. Neither program embodies any significant linguistic ability, relying instead upon the detection of a few trigger words, in the user's computer input, to unleash a standard response, manipulated with some grammatical constructs. The fundamental limitations of such systems, from the viewpoint of conducting an apparently intelligent conversation, can soon be revealed by the selection of appropriate user questions. Winograd's

Shrdlu represented a significant advance upon such programs because it required the computer to manipulate and answer queries about an imaginary world of toy blocks in response to the user's prompts. An excerpt from a typical exchange is given below.

User: Is there a large block behind the pyramid?

Shrdlu: Yes, three of them: a large red one, a large green cube and the blue one.

User: Put the small one onto the green cube which supports a pyramid.

Shrdlu: OK.

User: Put the little pyramid on top of it.

Shrdlu: OK.

User: Does the shortest thing the pyramid's support supports support anything green? (see Fig. 2).

Shrdlu: Yes, the green pyramid.

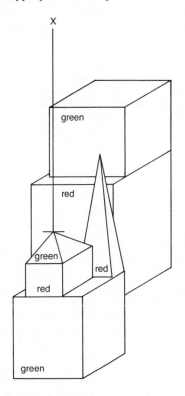

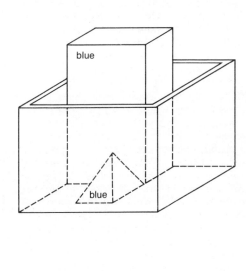

artificial intelligence
Fig. 2. 'Does the shortest thing the tallest pyramid's support supports support anything green?' Source: Adapted from T. Winograd, *Procedures as Representations for Data in a Computer Program for Understanding Natural Language*. (Ph.D. thesis), (Cambridge, Mass.: AI-TR-17, MIT AI Lab.), p. 49. Reprinted by permission.

In order to hold such a conversation, Shrdlu has to maintain a model of its world and represent its own capacity to act within that world. It can make sense of potentially ambiguous references to objects (e.g. 'it'), translate instructions into the necessary operations and request clarification for incomplete queries or commands. Although impressive, the program is nevertheless restricted to action in a very simple world and is less competent in language generation than comprehension.

(ii) Mycin. One of the most successful, and commercially viable, branches of AI application has been the creation of expert systems. In essence, these are the crystallization of rules and judgments, taken from human specialists, which attempt to convert a series of observations or measurements into the appropriate diagnosis within a restricted context. Practical examples have attempted medical diagnosis of certain conditions, mineral prospecting, classification of lunar samples and identification of naval movements from underwater sonar readings. Mycin is a highly regarded medical expert system, directed at the diagnosis and treatment of certain bacteriological infections, and it has fostered many derivatives. Mycin attempts to determine whether a patient has a serious infection, identify the bacteria involved, seek a generally suitable course of drug treatment and then tailor this to the patient's individual requirements.

To this end, Mycin comprises a suite of three sections: a consultation program; an explanation program; and a rule acquisition program. A physician interacts with the consultation program, entering observations and appending further data when so requested, and from this process a diagnosis and treatment are established. The explanation program provides the physician, on request, with the reasoning that led to a particular inference produced by the expert system, whereas the rule acquisition section is used by specialists during updating processes of the system's rule base.

The system rules are defined by a static database in production format (i.e. IF condition THEN action); the database also holds certain tables. Information on the patient is held in a dynamic database and updated during the operation of the system. Mycin attempts to 'back-chain' from the collected observations to elicit their likely causes. A typical rule of the system takes the form

IF: (i)   The stain of the organism is Gram-negative, AND
        (ii) the morphology of the organism is rod, AND
        (iii) the patient is a compromised host.
THEN: There is suggestive evidence (0.6) that the identity of the organism is *Pseudomonas*.

The figure 0.6 is an indication of probability in the range −1 (certainly not) to +1 (certainly is). Clinical tests on Mycin gave the same conclusion as a human physician in 75 per cent of cases, in a domain requiring considerable skill and expertise.

(iii) Winston learning by example. A fundamental issue in AI is that of learning skills through practical experience or of acquiring knowledge of conceptual categories through concise, but selective examples. Winston devised a program that could infer simple structural categories, in the 'blocks' world, by the provision of simple examples and near-misses. Positive instances allowed the program to construct descriptions of the features and relationships pertaining to this model; near-misses, through only just failing to qualify, delineated the critical aspects of the concept.

For example, the notions of an arch (Fig. 3) are first conveyed as a view of a typical prototype, and then a second view demonstrates that the top need not be flush with the sides. Counter-examples then inform that the arch must be sealed above and that it requires a passageway through the supports. Finally it is shown that non-rectangular blocks are legitimate components. Refinement of structural concepts proceeds by noting differences between the descriptions of examples and near-misses, elaborating and pruning the model appropriately. This program is again limited to a very basic domain of operation, but the rate at which sophisticated concepts can be acquired is quite impressive.

AI has spawned a multitude of new programming languages (e.g. Sail, Planner, Conniver, Smalltalk, Poplog), but the three that have entered popular usage are LISP, PROLOG and Logo. LISP is a list-oriented language which makes no distinction between the format of programs and data, and has widespread application in both AI and conventional programming. PROLOG is a declarative language, based upon first-order predicate calculus, that states the properties of an answer rather than the procedures necessary to attain it. Logo was developed as a teaching language, often used in conjunction with graphics or a robot turtle, that has found favour in educational circles and in particular in applications involving handicapped children. Many of the successful AI applications have still, however, been programmed in conventional high-level languages (e.g. Pascal and FORTRAN).

Current research in AI covers a wide range. The problems of perception, both for visual images and natural languages, evoke considerable interest. Computer vision has extended beyond the 'blocks world' of Shrdlu, etc. and is focusing attention upon the recovery of three-dimensional shape and object configurations from realistic images. Language perception now divides into the fields of speech technology, a hardware-oriented topic concerned with the transcription of the spoken word into stored text and natural language understanding which addresses the extraction of meaning from stored passages of text. Robotics research seeks an adequate theoretical underpinning for intricate problems of geometry, kinematics and control that arise in such systems. Automated task-planning remains a popular topic, particularly with reference to robotics, autonomous vehicles and computerized design/assembly schemes. Expert systems are naturally the focus of much attention, particularly with respect to problems in knowledge representation, derivation of probabilities, automatic explanation and the exercise of new logics. Mathematical reasoning, although more abstruse than the above-mentioned application areas, offers a neatly circumscribed and rigorous domain for testing of new approaches to theorem proving and some varieties of automatic programming. Finally, it should be noted that interest in novel computer architectures, particularly in the field of parallel processing and neural networks, continues to grow and the synthesis of AI with such hardware-driven disciplines remains an enticing possibility. *See* BACKWARD CHAINING, COBOL, DECLARATIVE LANGUAGE, EXPERT SYSTEMS,

fifth-generation computer, FORTRAN, LISP, Logo, machine vision, minimax, parallel processing, Pascal, PROLOG.

ARCH

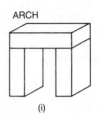

(i)

ARCH

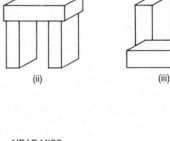

(ii)   (iii)

NEAR MISS

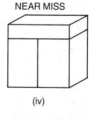

(iv)   (v)

artificial intelligence
Fig. 3. Description of an arch. Source: P.H. Winston (ed) *Psychology of Computer Vision*, 1975 (New York: McGraw-Hill). Reprinted by permission of the McGraw-Hill Book Company.

artificial intelligence technology. (AIT) In artificial intelligence, the commercial application of artificial intelligence. A particular area of development is in the use of expert system shells as an effective means of development for commercial applications packages. *See* EXPERT SYSTEMS.

art paper. In printing, a smooth-coated paper obtained by adding a coating of china clay compound on one or both sides of the paper. (Desktop). *Compare* MATT ART PAPER.

ARTS. In communications, advanced radio telephone service. *See* CELLULAR RADIO.

artwork. (1) In printing, matter prepared for photomechanical reproduction. (2) In filming, any kind of graphic work for a film (e.g. titles, diagrams, charts, scenery or animation drawings).

ARU. *See* AUDIO RESPONSE UNIT.

ASA. *See* AMERICAN STANDARDS ASSOCIATION.

ASA exposure index. In photography, letters used to refer to the numerical exposure index of a film under the system adopted by the American National Standards Institute.

ASC. American Society of Cinematographers.

ascender. In printing, the portion of a lower-case character, such as 'l', 'h', etc. that rises above the upper level of letters such as 'o', 'a', etc. *Compare* DESCENDER. *See* LOWER CASE.

ascertainment. In communications, the Federal Communication Commission licensing procedure that requires US broadcast stations to investigate local programming needs. *See* FEDERAL COMMUNICATIONS COMMISSION.

ASCII. *See* AMERICAN STANDARD CODE FOR INFORMATION INTERCHANGE.

ASCIS. Australian Schools Cataloguing Information Service.

ASET. Academy of Security Educators and Trainers.

a-Si. *See* AMORPHOUS SILICON.

ASIC. *See* APPLICATION-SPECIFIC INTEGRATED CIRCUIT.

a-Si:H. *See* AMORPHOUS HYDROGENATED SILICON.

ASIS. (1) American Society for Industrial Security. (2) American Society for Information Science.

ASLIB. *See* ASSOCIATION OF SPECIAL LIBRARIES AND INFORMATION BUREAUX.

aspect card. In library science, a card containing the accession numbers of documents in an information retrieval system. *See* ACCESSION NUMBER.

aspect ratio. In peripherals and television, the ratio of the horizontal to vertical dimensions of a display screen, normally 4:3.

aspect system. In library science, a method of indexing which assumes that a record represents a single subject and contains the necessary information on which documents have this subject in common. *See* ASPECT CARD.

ASSASSIN. In online information retrieval, Agricultural System for Storage and Subsequent Selection of Information; a software package for bibliographic information retrieval developed by ICI. *See* BIBLIOGRAPHIC DATABASE.

assemble. (1) In programming, to translate a source program using an assembler. *See* ASSEMBLING, SOURCE PROGRAM, TRANSLATOR. (2) In programming, to integrate subroutines into the main program. *See* SUBROUTINE. (3) In filming, the process of organizing and joining the film shots in the approximate sequence required for the completed version.

assembler. In programming, a program that translates a source program written in a low-level language to machine code. *Compare* COMPILER, INTERPRETER. *See* ASSEMBLING, LOW-LEVEL LANGUAGE, MACHINE CODE, SOURCE PROGRAM, TRANSLATOR.

assembling. In programming, the processes involved in translating a low-level program into an object code program. *Compare* COMPILER, INTERPRETER. *See* LOW-LEVEL LANGUAGE, OBJECT CODE.

assembly directive. In programming, an instruction in a low-level language that tells the assembler to perform certain actions (e.g. assign memory space to a variable or constant), but does not generate any machine code instructions. *See* ASSEMBLING, MACHINE CODE INSTRUCTION.

assembly language. In programming, a language that allows a programmer to develop a machine code program using symbols and mnemonics for storage locations and operations. This language greatly improves the comprehension of the program and enables modifications to be more readily incorporated. *Compare* HIGH-LEVEL LANGUAGE. *See* ASSEMBLING, LOW-LEVEL LANGUAGE, MACHINE CODE, TRANSLATOR.

assembly time. In programming, the time at which an assembler translates the source program into the corresponding object code. *See* ASSEMBLING, OBJECT CODE, SOURCE PROGRAM.

assertion. (1) In programming, a boolean expression that is stated to be true. In proof of program correctness, assertions are used to make statements about program states. *See* BOOLEAN ALGEBRA, PROOF OF PROGRAM CORRECTNESS. (2) In artificial intelligence, a hypothesis about the problem to be solved. The likelihood of an assertion is established by asking the user questions or rules may be used to deduce the likelihood from other assertions or stored data. *Compare* OBJECT. *See* EXPERT SYSTEMS, RULE.

assigned frequency. In communications, the Federal Communications Commission (FCC) licence of specific frequency and power to a broadcast station. The available radio frequencies for non-government use are reserved by the FCC for specific applications such as frequency-modulated broadcasting, television, aeronautical radio, amateur radio, etc. In the UK, the Home Office is responsible for such allocation and licensing. *See* FEDERAL COMMUNICATIONS COMMISSION.

assigned indexing. In library science, a method of indexing in which the indexer assigns the appropriate words to describe the document rather than relying on the author's choice. *Compare* DERIVED INDEXING. *See* INDEX.

assignment statement. In programming, a statement that results in the assignment of a value to a variable. The expression on the right-hand side of the statement is evaluated, and this value is assigned to the variable named on the left-hand side. *See* EXPRESSION, STATEMENT, VARIABLE.

Associated Press. (AP) A subscriber news service for broadcasting stations and newspapers. *See* BROADCASTING STATION, REUTERS.

associational editing. In filming, the juxtaposition of film or video shots in order to present contrast, comparisons, similarities or ideas.

Association for Computing Machinery. (ACM) A US professional computer science organization. Its objectives are to advance all aspects of information processing and to promote the interchange of such techniques between computer specialists and users.

Association Française de Normalisation. The French standards organization. *See* BRITISH STANDARDS INSTITUTION, DIN, NATIONAL BUREAU OF STANDARDS.

Association of Cinematograph, Television and Allied Technicians. In filming, a UK trade union representing members of the film and television technical trades.

Association of National Advertisers. A US organization concerned with the formulation of industry standards for advertising.

Association of Special Libraries and Information Bureaux. (ASLIB) In library science, an organization founded in 1926 and merged with British Society for International Bibliography in 1949. Its aims are to facilitate the coordination and systematic use of sources of knowledge and information in all public offices, in industry and commerce, and in all the arts and sciences.

associative law. In mathematics, a binary operation (i.e. one involving two variables) satisfies the associative law if

$$x * (y * z) = (x * y) * z$$

where x, y and z are the variables and $*$ represents the binary operation. *Compare* COMMUTATIVE LAW, DISTRIBUTIVE LAW.

associative processor. In computing, a device that uses associative storage methods (i.e. data is accessed by reading keys and comparing their values with those that identify the item sought). *See* ASSOCIATIVE STORAGE.

associative storage. In memory systems, a storage device in which the user identifies data by a part of its content rather than by its physical location. It provides a fast method of searching for data with certain keys. The computer system may also rearrange its storage of data without affecting the user's application programs. *See* APPLICATION PROGRAM, KEY, PHYSICAL DATA INDEPENDENCE. *Synonymous with* CONTENT-ADDRESSABLE MEMORY, SEARCH MEMORY.

astigmatism. In optics, a defect in the design of a lens that causes light rays passing through the lens to converge improperly.

astonisher. In printing, a term for an exclamation mark (!).

async. Asynchronous communication. *See* ASYNCHRONOUS TRANSMISSION.

asynchronous. Pertaining to actions and events that are not correlated with some reference time. *Compare* SYNCHRONOUS.

asynchronous attacks. (1) In computer security, a method of attempting two or more attacks at the same time in the hope that at least one will succeed while the other(s) are being dealt with. *See* COMPUTER FRAUD CONTROL. (2) In computer security, TOCTTOU attacks. *See* TOCTTOU PROBLEMS.

asynchronous communications interface adaptor. (ACIA) In computing, a device performing a similar function to a UART. *See* UART.

asynchronous computer. A computer in which each operation is initiated as a result of a signal generated by the completion of the previous operation or by the availability of the equipment required for the next operation. *Compare* SYNCHRONOUS COMPUTER.

asynchronous transmission. In data communications, a form of data transmission in which there can be variable time intervals between characters, but the bits within a character are sent with fixed time intervals. Start and stop elements are used to indicate the beginning and the end of characters. *Compare* SYNCHRONOUS TRANSMISSION.

ATA. American Translators Association.

ATM. *See* AUTOMATIC TELLER MACHINE.

atmospheric absorption. In communications, the loss of energy suffered by an electromagnetic wave due to dissipation in the atmosphere. *See* ELECTROMAGNETIC RADIATION.

atom. In programming, a value that cannot be decomposed further.

ATR. *See* AUDIO TAPE RECORDER.

ATS-6. In communications, Applications Technology Satellite-6; an US satellite leased to India for an experimental project to transmit educational television programs to remote villages. *See* COMMUNICATIONS SATELLITE SYSTEM.

attached processor. In computing, a processor with no input/output facilities. It is always linked to a processor with such facilities.

attaching device. In data communications, a device that is physically connected to a network and can communicate over the network. *See* NETWORK.

attack. In computer security, the realization of a threat. How often a threat is realized depends on such factors as the location, type and value of information being processed. *See* THREAT, VULNERABILITY.

attention interruption. In peripherals, an input/output interruption produced by an attention key on a terminal or some equivalent action. *See* ATTENTION KEY, INTERRUPT, INPUT/OUTPUT.

attention key. In peripherals, a key on a terminal that produces an input/output interruption in the processing unit. *See* INPUT/OUTPUT, INTERRUPT.

attenuation. In electronics and communications, the reduction in strength of an electrical signal as it passes through a circuit or an electromagnetic wave as it propagates through a transmission medium. *Compare* AMPLIFICATION. *See* ELECTROMAGNETIC RADIATION.

attribute. (1) In databases, a field that contains information about an entity (e.g. in a personnel database home address would be an attribute of entity employee). *See* DISPLAY ATTRIBUTE, ENTITY, FIELD. (2) In optical media, a word in a file descriptor indicating how the file is accessed, the file owner and the identification. *See* FILE DESCRIPTOR RECORD.

AT&T. American Telephone & Telegraph Co.

audience rating. In filming and broadcasting, a statement or scale of judgments made or used by an audience to evaluate a film or television programme.

audio-active. (AA) In an electronic learning laboratory, pertaining to a facility in which a student can hear a master tape, respond into a microphone and hear his or her response through headphones. *Compare* AUDIO-ACTIVE COMPARE, AUDIO-PASSIVE.

audio-active compare. In an electronic learning laboratory, pertaining to a facility in which a student can hear a master tape, respond into a microphone and have both sounds recorded on separate tape tracks for comparison. *Compare* AUDIO-ACTIVE, AUDIO-PASSIVE.

audio block. In optical media, a block of audio information in interactive compact disc format. (Philips). *See* COMPACT DISC – INTERACTIVE.

audio card. In audiovisual aids, a thin card with a strip of audiotape (usually 12 inches or less) across the bottom. Accompanying pictures or words are located above the tape. *Synonymous with* AUDIO PAGE.

audio cassette. *Synonymous with* COMPACT CASSETTE.

audio cassette recorder. (ACR) In memory systems, a recorder designed for using compact cassettes.

audio chip. In microelectronics, a dedicated circuit, either in analog or digital integrated circuit technology, designed to fulfil specific audio functions. (Philips). *Synonymous with* SOUND CHIP.

audio comparator. In recording, a monophonic, dual-track audio tape recorder that allows the user to record on one track and to play back on both. *See* AUDIO TAPE RECORDER, MONOPHONIC.

audio compressor. In audiovisual aids, an electronic device capable of the compression and expansion of an audio signal with respect to its speed without a corresponding increase or decrease in pitch.

audio conferencing. *Synonymous with* AUDIO TELECONFERENCING.

audio data. (1) In acoustics, audio data expressed in digital form. (2) In optical media, multiplexed and pulse code modulated stereo information, recorded on a digital audio compact disc with cross-interleaved Reed–Solomon code and subcode added. *See* COMPACT DISC – DIGITAL AUDIO, CROSS-INTERLEAVED REED–SOLOMON CODE, STEREO, SUBCODE CHANNEL. (3) In optical media, audio information, recorded on an interactive compact disc (CD-I), encoded with the CD-I specification. (Philips). *See* COMPACT DISC – INTERACTIVE.

audio frequency. The frequency of an audible sound wave. For normal hearing the range of frequencies lies between 20 and 20 000 Hz.

audio inquiry. *See* VOICE ANSWER BACK.

audio mix. In filming, the electronic combination of two or more sound elements into a single track, usually synchronized with a picture projection.

audio monitor. In recording, a studio-quality speaker for listening to the playback of a tape or record. It is also used for editing and quality checking.

audio mute. In acoustics, a facility for temporarily suppressing sound. (Philips).

audio page. *Synonymous with* AUDIO CARD.

audio-passive. In an electronic learning laboratory, a facility in which a student can listen to a master tape, usually through headphones. *Compare* AUDIO-ACTIVE, AUDIO-ACTIVE COMPARE.

audio quality level. In optical media, the reproduction quality of an audio signal. An interactive compact disc, for example, provides for five audio quality levels (i.e., in decreasing order of quality, digital audio compact disc, hi-fi, mid-fi, speech and synthesized speech). (Philips). *Compare* COMPACT DISC – DIGITAL AUDIO QUALITY, HI-FI QUALITY, MID-FI QUALITY, SPEECH QUALITY, SYNTHESIZED SPEECH QUALITY. *See* COMPACT DISC – INTERACTIVE.

audio response unit. In peripherals, an output device that provides a spoken response to digital enquiries transmitted to a computer, usually over a telephone link. *See* AUDIO TERMINAL.

audioslide. In audiovisual aids, a 2 x 2 inch slide with a brief audio recording on a magnetic coating on the slide mount. It requires a special projector for operation.

audio synthesis. *See* SPEECH SYNTHESIZER.

audio subcarrier. In television, a carrier modulated by the audio component of a television signal. *See* CARRIER.

audio tape. In recording, a tape having a coating on which sound can be recorded magnetically. *See* AUDIO TAPE RECORDER.

audio tape recorder. (ATR) In recording, a device for making a permanent or temporary record of a signal or program. It usually can play back as well as record. The tape may be on open reels or in a container called a cartridge or cassette. *See* AUDIO TAPE, CARTRIDGE, COMPACT CASSETTE.

audio teleconferencing. In communications, group voice communication relying on exchanges among more than two participants via voice. *Compare* VIDEO TELE-CONFERENCING. *See* TELECONFERENCING. *Synonymous with* AUDIO CONFERENCING.

audio terminal. In peripherals, a device associated with an audio response unit that enables keyed or dialed data to be entered for transmission to the computer. *See* AUDIO RESPONSE UNIT.

audio text. In acoustics, phonetically encoded speech. (Philips). *See* PHONETIC CODING.

audio track. In optical media, a digital audio compact disc (CD-DA) track as defined in the CD-DA specification; a separately addressable section of a CD-DA disc normally carrying a self-contained piece of music. It has a minimum duration of 4 seconds and a maximum duration of 72 minutes. One CD-DA disc can contain between one and 99 audio tracks, but the total disc playing time cannot exceed 72 minutes. (Philips). *Compare* DATA TRACK. *See* COMPACT DISC – DIGITAL AUDIO, TRACK. *Synonymous with* CD-DA TRACK.

audio tutorial instruction. In audiovisual aids, a teaching process in which audio tapes and audio equipment are the main educational tools.

audiovisual. A general term for non-book materials that can be viewed and/or listened to, such as films, filmstrips, tapes and overhead transparencies. *See* EDUCATIONAL TECHNOLOGY.

audiovisual aids. Any non-book material that can be used in educational technology. *See* EDUCATIONAL TECHNOLOGY.

audit. In computer security, to conduct the independent review and examination of system records and activities in order to test for adequacy of system controls, to ensure compliance with established policy and operational procedures, and to recommend any indicated changes in controls, policy or procedures. (FIPS). *See* AUDIT TRAIL.

audit data. In computer security, typical audit data produced in a time-sharing system includes information necessary to bill users, and security logs providing lists of attempts to use privileged commands.

audit trail. (1) A set of records that collectively provides documentary evidence of processing used to aid in tracing from original transactions forward to related records and reports and/or backwards from records and reports to their component source transactions. (DOD). (2) In computer security, a chronological record of system activities that is sufficient to enable the reconstruction, review and examination of the sequence of environments and activities surrounding or leading to each event in the path of a transaction from its inception to output of final results. (FIPS). (3) In programming, a clerical or automated method for tracing the transactions affecting the contents of a record. *See* RECORD.

augend. The number to which an addend is added to produce the sum in an arithmetic operation. *See* ADDEND.

aural transmitter. In broadcasting, equipment used to transmit the sound signal from a television broadcasting station.

Aurora. In communications, an US series of geostationary satellites. *See* GEOSTATIONARY SATELLITE, TELESAT.

Ausinet. In online retrieval, an Australian online information retrieval service operated by ACICS. *See* ACICS.

Aussat. In communications, an Australian geostationary satellite. *See* GEOSTATIONARY SATELLITE.

Austpac. In data communications, an public packet-switching service offered by Telecom Australia.

Australis. In online information retrieval, an online information retrieval service offered by the Australian Commonwealth Scientific (CSIRO) and Industrial Research Organization over its CSIRONET network.

authentication. (1) In computer security, the act of identifying or verifying the eligibility of a station, originator or individual to access specific categories of information. (FIPS). *See* ACCESS, PEER ENTITY AUTHEN-

TICATION. (2) In data security, processes that ensure everything about a teleprocessing transaction is genuine and that the message has not been altered or corrupted in transmission. The parties to the transaction must identify each other reliably, know that each message they receive comes from the other party and has not been modified or stored earlier and replayed by a third party. *See* DIGITAL SIGNATURE, MAC, MESSAGE AUTHENTICATION, REPLAY, WIRETAPPING.

authentication algorithm. In data security, the act of determining that a message comes from a source authorized to originate messages of that type and that the message is as authorized. (ANSI). *See* MESSAGE AUTHENTICATION.

authentication server. In data security, a trusted facility for arbitrated digital signatures. The authentication server signs a message, from a sender, by encrypting a data block, which comprises a concatenation of the message authenticator and the sender's identity, under the arbiter's secret key. The receiver also submits the signature to the authentication server; the server deciphers the signature and supplies the sender with the authenticator and the sender's identity. Communication between users and the authentication server are encrypted under pairs of keys shared only with the individual users. *See* ARBITRATED SIGNATURE, DIGITAL SIGNATURE, TRUSTED.

author. The writer of books, articles, computer software, computer-assisted learning packages, etc.

authoring. (1) In optical media, the work involved in producing the software for an interactive compact disc (CD-I) application, from the initial concept to the recording of the master tape required for the disc-mastering process. Authoring embraces the processes listed below.

(a) Encoding the required audio, video, text and binary data into CD-I data formats.
(b) Developing and producing the application software which operates on, uses or accesses the encoded CD-I data as required by the application.

(c) Structuring the encoded CD-I data and application software into the disc label, files and records corresponding to the access and playback requirements of the application.

(d) Verifying and validating the application so produced via, at least, a CD-I disc/ base case combination.

See BASE CASE SYSTEM, COMPACT DISC – INTER-ACTIVE. (2) In optical media, a structured approach to developing all elements of an interactive videodisc program with emphasis on preproduction. *See* PREPRODUCTION.

authoring process. In optical media, the process of developing and producing the complete software for an application. It involves the processes listed below.

(a) Designing the program content by creating the story board.

(b) Creating and capturing data, and preparing it for use.

(c) Developing the program that will appear on the disc.

(d) Simulating and testing the program in practice.

(e) Preparing the final master tape.

The first step in the process is the creation of an overall program design or story board. This is critical to the success of the project, as it defines not only the type of basic material or data required for the video, audio and text/graphics components, but also the interrelationships between them. The concept of interactivity, in which the response of the system depends upon the response of the user at each stage of the program, means that the whole project stands or falls upon the 'what happens then' response of the overall interactive compact disc (CD-I) system. This involves both the player and the disc, as well as the user. The key to this action and response relationship must be clearly defined in the story board design phase if the program is to be successful.

It is unlikely that the story board will get the design right at the first attempt. One of the essentials of CD-I program design is step-by-step evaluation of results, leading to redesign and re-evaluation in an on-going interactive process. With both the application data and the application software on the disc (all the information on a single medium), there is no opportunity to correct errors once the disc is released for replication and sale.

Thus, simulation, evaluation, validation, testing and, where needed, revision are essential steps in every phase of the CD-I authoring process. The controlling mechanism for this process is the story board.

Based on a first issue of the story board, design work proceeds along two parallel paths. The first involves content collection; the assembly and production, when needed, of the video, audio, text and graphics information required by the story board. This basic information may be in either digital or analog form, or may have to be generated from scratch.

Continuing along this first path, the collected data is tested and evaluated at each phase for correctness, and for the right balance of quality versus disc capacity. Although digital audio compact disc sound takes 100 per cent of the information channel from the disc to the player, monaural speech takes only 6 per cent of this capacity, leaving 94 per cent for other information (i.e. video, text/graphics, application software or indexing information). The choice of a balance between quality and data bandwidth is a key element in program design.

Once satisfactory, data is encoded and compressed to CD-I format and is prepared as data files onto a disc simulator. This is built around a large-capacity read/write store (typically hard discs are used with a capacity in excess of 1200 megabytes) and is part of the authoring studio equipment.

The second path involves the development and testing of the application software and user interfaces needed to interact with the data used in the program.

Each stage of this application software development is tested on its own and is slowly integrated and synchronized with the relevant data as it, in turn, is collected.

In this way, the integration and synchronization of each portion of the program is tested to prove that it works, as defined in the story board, before integration into the next level of the design.

Once completed, the program is then tested, revised and retested on the disc simulator until the overall design and balance have been proven.

Only at this stage can thought be given to

transferring the total program to the disc replication facility. (Philips). *See* COMPACT DISC – DIGITAL AUDIO, COMPACT DISC – INTERACTIVE, MONAURAL, STORY BOARD.

authoring system. (1) In optical media, a general term for the equipment, in hardware and software, needed for authoring interactive compact discs. (Philips). *See* AUTHORING, COMPACT DISC – INTERACTIVE. (2) In computer-aided learning, a computer system capable of executing an author language. *See* AUTHOR LANGUAGE.

authoring tool. In optical media, a computer programming aid used in authoring. (Philips). *See* AUTHORING.

authority file. In library science, a file of records relating to the decisions taken in the use of an indexing language. It identifies established forms of headings, index terms, preferred synonyms, etc. that may be used for information retrieval. *See* INDEXING LANGUAGE.

authorization. In computing, the right given to a user to communicate with or make use of a computer system or stored data.

authorization code. In computing, a code used to protect against unauthorized access to data and system facilities. The code normally consists of a user id and password. *See* PASSWORD, USER ID.

authorized file. In online information retrieval, a file for which the user's password is valid. *See* PASSWORD.

authorized power. In communications, the maximum power that may be used by a licensed radio station in the USA or a station that broadcasts any form of radio signal. The power limit is authorized and assigned by the Federal Communication Commission and is necessary to prevent interference with the many other users of the radio spectrum. It is set in accordance with the specific usage involved: television, frequency modulation, broadcast, citizen band, police radio, etc. *See* CITIZEN BAND, FREQUENCY MODULATION.

authorized user. In communications, a person or firm which, under the Communications Satellite Act of 1962, is permitted in the USA to deal directly with the Communications Satellite Corporation (COMSAT) to secure space segment and associated ground facilities.

author language. In applications, a programming language used for designing instructional programs for computer-aided instruction and computer-based training systems. *See* COMPUTER-AIDED INSTRUCTION, COMPUTER-BASED TRAINING.

author's alterations. (AAs) In printing, an indication in a proof that the cost of a correction is to be borne by the author or publisher and not by the printer. *Compare* PRINTER'S ERRORS.

auto abstract. In library science, an abstract produced by computer analyses. Sentences containing a high frequency of particular words are printed out in sequence.

auto answer. *Synonymous with* AUTOMATIC ANSWERING.

autodialer. In computing and videotex, a device that automatically dials a prerecorded telephone number for connection to a host computer.

autodial modem. In data communications, a modem that responds to call set up commands from a microcomputer. It listens for the answer tone and organizes itself to accept data. In comparison, with a manual modem, the user must dial using a telephone, listen for an answer, and then press the data button. *See* HAYES, MODEM.

autoidentifier. In computing and videotex, a device by which a terminal automatically identifies itself to a computer.

auto indexing. In computing, a system of indexing that superimposes additional information at any of several given addresses. *Compare* AUTOMATIC INDEXING.

auto kerning. In printing, the automatic reduction of unwanted white spaces between characters to produce a more aesthetic image. *See* KERNING.

automata theory. A mathematical study of the systems that receive discrete inputs, change their internal states according to the input, and their current states, and deliver outputs according to their internal states and inputs. *See* TURING MACHINE.

automatic. Pertaining to a process or device that, under specified conditions, functions without intervention by a human operator.

automatic abstracting. In library science, the production of an abstract by a computer. The abstract comprises complete sentences, derived from the original document, which are normally selected on the basis of the frequency of relevant terms within them. More refined methods introduce other criteria of significance (e.g. comparison with the expected frequency of occurrences; cue words in sentences — significantly, important — which indicate the author's emphasis; title and heading words and position of the sentence in the overall structure). *Compare* AUTOMATIC INDEXING. *See* ABSTRACT.

automatic answering. In data communications, a system in which the called station automatically responds to the calling signal; the call may be established whether or not the called station is attended. *See* CALL BACK. *Synonymous with* AUTO ANSWER.

automatic answering device. In communications, a machine feature that enables incoming phone calls to be answered and gives a prerecorded message. At the end of the message the unit usually switches from playback to record, thus permitting callers to leave messages.

automatic calling. In communications, a machine feature that allows a station to initiate a call automatically over a switched line. *See* STATION.

automatic calling unit. (ACU) In data communications, a device that enables a business machine to dial calls automatically over a network. *See* AUTODIALER.

automatic carriage return. In word processing, the automatic performance of a carriage return when the last word, which will fit onto a line of print, is typed. A system that has this facility will usually employ a buffer to hold the word currently being typed until it can decide whether to place the word on the current line, or to wrap it onto the next line. *See* BUFFER, CARRIAGE CONTROL, WRAPAROUND.

automatic centring. In word processing, the ability to centre automatically a word or portion of text.

automatic data-processing system. (ADP system) An assembly of computer hardware, firmware and software configured for the purpose of classifying, sorting, calculating, computing, summarizing, transmitting and receiving, storing and retrieving data with a minimum of human intervention. (DOD).

automatic decimal alignment. In word processing, the feature of a machine that enables numbers to be aligned automatically on either side of a decimal marker. *Synonymous with* AUTOMATIC DECIMAL TAB.

automatic decimal tab. *Synonymous with* AUTOMATIC DECIMAL ALIGNMENT.

automatic dialer. *See* AUTODIALER.

automatic dictionary. (1) In machine translation, a database that provides a word-for-word substitution from one language to another. *See* TERM BANK. (2) In online information retrieval, a system that substitutes codes for words or phrases in the encoding operation.

automatic document feeder. In printing, a device in which a quantity of original documents may be placed for automatic feeding.

automatic document handler. In printing, an automatic document feeder that incorporates additional facilities in order to recycle originals. *See* AUTOMATIC DOCUMENT FEEDER.

automatic exposure. In photography, the use in a camera of a device that opens up or closes down the lens iris, depending on subject brightness.

automatic file select. In word processing, a facility for making a selection from a data file based on the characters that appear in a specified data field (e.g. using a zip code field, the system can select all the addresses with a 1248 zip code for one letter, and print a different letter for all other codes, etc.).

automatic file sort. In word processing, a facility for performing sorts on files in alphabetical, or other order. This feature is useful for manipulating address lists so that changes need not be performed in alphabetical order.

automatic footers. *See* AUTOMATIC HEADERS/ FOOTERS.

automatic frequency control. In communications, a method of negative feedback in which a tuning error generates a control voltage, which is used to change the local oscillator frequency so as to minimize the error. *See* NEGATIVE FEEDBACK.

automatic gain control. (AGC) In electronics, circuitry that provides a consistent average output signal level for a wide range of input levels. For example, in a radio receiver this facility will automatically adjust the output volume to compensate for variations in signal strength. *See* GAIN. *Synonymous with* AUTOMATIC LEVEL CONTROL.

automatic headers/footers. In word processing, the ability to place header/footer text at the top or bottom of each page of a multipage document. The operator specifies the text once, and the header/footer (usually document title, company name or confidentiality requirements) is automatically added during printout.

automatic indexing. In library science, the selection of keywords from a document by a computer in order to develop index entries. Simple word counts techniques proved to be defective for several reasons and a more effective method is to count the number of occurrences of a word and compare it with an expected number derived from a predetermined frequency norm. *Compare* AUTO INDEXING, AUTOMATIC ABSTRACTING. *See* INDEX.

automatic letter writing. In word processing, the ability to produce a standard document as though it were typed specially for the recipient.

automatic level control. *Synonymous with* AUTOMATIC GAIN CONTROL.

automatic line/paragraph numbering. In word processing, a facility whereby the system automatically supplies an identifying number for each line or paragraph during input for use in defining locations during subsequent editing. The line/paragraph numbers are automatically deleted during final printout.

automatic line spacing. In word processing, the ability of a printer to perform different line spacings without the need for operator intervention.

automatic loader. In programming, a loader program implemented in a special read-only memory that allows loading of the first record or sector of a backing storage device. *See* BACKING STORAGE, LOADER, READ-ONLY MEMORY.

automatic lock. *Synonymous with* PIX LOCK.

automatic logging. In word processing, a facility in which a system automatically records titles and log numbers with all documents. *See* LOG.

automatic logon. In computing, a system by means of which a intelligent terminal can log onto a system directly without the user needing to key passwords or user numbers. This can represent a significant security hazard. *See* LOGON.

automatic margin adjust. In word processing, a facility to change margins with a single command. Line endings are adjusted without further intervention.

automatic message accounting. In communications, a process that records automatically all data concerning customer-dialed long-distance telephone calls for billing purposes.

automatic message-switching centre. In data communications, a centre where incoming messages are routed to outgoing destinations, according to their address information. *See* MESSAGE SWITCHING.

automatic noise suppression. In electronics, a means of suppressing unwanted signals (e.g. on a dictation machine, automatic noise suppression automatically reduces electrical noise during input to the recording medium or during playback, or both).

automatic number identification. (ANI) In communications, the automatic line identification of outward dialed telephone calls.

automatic pagination. In word processing, a facility that takes a multipage document and divides it into pages of a specified length in terms of line numbers. Often, this feature is joined with the capability to generate automatically page numbers.

automatic polling. In computing and data communications, a feature of a transmission control unit that enables it to handle negative responses to polling without interrupting the central processing unit. *See* CENTRAL PROCESSING UNIT, POLLING.

automatic program execution. In computing, a facility that automatically starts a specific program every time the operating system is loaded.

automatic programming. In programming, the process of using a computer to perform some stages of the work involved in preparing a computer program.

automatic program transfer. In an electronic learning laboratory, a facility that enables the transfer of program material to all students by the instructor.

automatic repeat key. *Synonymous with* TYPAMATIC KEY.

automatic request for repetition. *Synonymous with* AUTOMATIC RETRANSMISSION REQUEST.

automatic restart. In computing, a facility that performs automatically the initialization functions necessary to resume operation following an equipment or power failure. *See* INITIALIZATION.

automatic retransmission request. In data communications, a technique to ensure accurate transmission of data. Data to be transmitted is held in a buffer until the communication link is ready to deal with it.

The data is then despatched, and a copy is made at the same time. The copy is deposited in the buffer and erased when the sending device receives acknowledgement of correct receipt, as verified by an error-detecting code. If the receiving device detects an error in the data it informs the sending device, which then retransmits the buffered copy. *See* BUFFER, ERROR-DETECTING CODE. *Synonymous with* AUTOMATIC REQUEST FOR REPETITION.

automatic reverse. In recording, a facility in some recorders to reverse at the end of a tape without having to change reels.

automatic stop. In recording, a facility of a cassette recorder or dictation machine that enables it to stop the tape automatically when it reaches the end of its travel. The facility may also switch off the machine. *Synonymous with* AUTO STOP.

automatic tab memory. In word processing, a facility of a system which enables it to store a format of tab settings to be restored automatically to the typewriter at the time of printing. *See* TABULATION.

automatic teller machine. (ATM) In peripherals, a device that provides for cash withdrawals, payment of bills, account balance enquiries, deposits and transfers of funds between accounts. *See* BANKING NETWORKS, PIN MANAGEMENT AND SECURITY, SELF-BANKING.

automatic toning control. In printing, a built-in monitoring facility that regulates the supply of toner to the developing system of an electrostatic machine. *See* XEROGRAPHY.

automatic typewriter. The simplest form of word processor, used for repetitive output with little or no text editing. *See* TEXT EDITING.

automatic volume control. (AVC) In recording, a method of automatically maintaining a constant audio output volume over a range of input signals. *See* AUTOMATIC GAIN CONTROL.

automatic volume switching. In memory systems, access to a sequential data set that extends across two or more volumes, and to concatenated data sets stored on different volumes. *See* CONCATENATE, SEQUENTIAL DATA SET, VOLUME.

automatic widow adjust. In word processing, a facility which prevents the first line of a paragraph, title or heading from being the last line on a page. It may also prevent the last line from being the first line on a new page. *See* WIDOW.

automatic word recall. In office systems, an adjustable feature of an audio transcriber unit, whereby each time a foot pedal or hand control is depressed a measured portion of the previous dictation is replayed.

automatic word wraparound. (1) In word processing, the automatic placing of a word onto the next line if it does not fit onto the line being typed. It is frequently combined with with the automatic carriage return feature. (2) In word processing, systems that can wrap words during margin adjust procedures. *See* AUTOMATIC CARRIAGE RETURN.

automation. The technology concerned with the design and development of processes and systems that minimize the necessity for human intervention in their operation. *See* FEEDBACK.

autopositive. In photography, a material or process that provides a positive image of an original without the intervening negative stage.

auto stop. *Synonymous with* AUTOMATIC STOP.

autotrack. In communications, the automatic tracking of a satellite motion by a ground station antenna. *See* GROUND STATION ANTENNA.

auxiliary data field. In optical media, the last 288 bytes of a sector, on a read-only memory or interactive compact disc, either used for extra error detection and correction (mode 1 and form 1) or available as user data area (mode 2 and form 2). (Philips). *See* COMPACT DISC – INTERACTIVE, COMPACT DISC – READ-ONLY MEMORY, FORM I, FORM 2, MODE I, MODE 2.

auxiliary equipment. In computing, equipment not under the direct control of the central processing unit. *See* CENTRAL PROCESSING UNIT.

auxiliary storage. In computing, data storage other than the main storage, usually with slower access (e.g. magnetic tape or direct access devices). *See* DIRECT-ACCESS STORAGE DEVICE. *Synonymous with* BACKING STORAGE, SECONDARY STORAGE.

availability. In computing, a measure of the degree to which a system is ready for operation when required. *See* UPTIME.

available light. In photography, light that is in existence and not supplemented by additional photographic light.

available point. In computer graphics, an addressable point at which characteristics, such as colour, intensity or on/off condition, may be specified. *See* PIXEL.

available time. *Synonymous with* UPTIME.

avalanche photodiode. (APD) In electronics, a photodiode operated with a high reverse voltage. Hole electron pairs are produced by incident infrared or light energy, and these carriers are swept to the appropriate electrode. The electron carriers collide with other atoms releasing more electrons, hence increasing the sensitivity of the device. *Compare* PIN PHOTODIODE. *See* PHOTODIODE, SEMICONDUCTOR.

Avante-Garde. In printing, a grotesque typeface, rounder and lighter than Helvetica. *Compare* BOOKMAN, COURIER, HELVETICA, HELVETICA NARROW, NEW CENTURY SCHOOLBOOK, OLDSTYLE, PALATINO, SYMBOL, TIMES ROMAN, ZAPF CHANCERY, ZAPF DINGBATS. *See* GROTESQUE, TYPEFACE.

AVC. *See* AUTOMATIC VOLUME CONTROL.

average. *Synonymous with* ARITHMETIC MEAN.

average access time. In memory systems, the average time between the instant of a request for data and the delivery from a storage device.

average delay. In communications, the average time that a caller must wait for access to a communication facility.

AVIP.   *See* BAVIP.

AWC.   *See* ACTIVE WIRE CONCENTRATOR.

Az/El mount.   In communications, a form of mounting for a dish antenna that provides for both azimuth and elevation adjustments of the reflector. *Compare* POLAR MOUNT. *See* AZIMUTH, DISH ANTENNA.

azerty keyboard.   A keyboard arranged as on the standard typewriters of continental Europe, with the keys a, z, e, r, t, y on the upper left-hand side. *Compare* DVORAK KEYBOARD, MALTRON KEYBOARD, PRONTO KEYBOARD, QWERTY KEYBOARD. *See* KEYBOARD.

azimuth.   (1) In mathematics, a direction from a reference point measured in the horizontal plane. (2) In communications, the horizontal angle measured east from north, to the line from an observer to a satellite.

Compare ELEVATION. *See* COMMUNICATIONS SATELLITE SYSTEM.

azimuth alignment.   In recording, the precise alignment of recording/playback heads with the edge of tape or film. A very slight irregularity in alignment can cause a very considerable degradation in either or both recording and playback. *See* AZIMUTH LOSS.

azimuth loss.   In recording, the signal loss due to misalignment between the playback head and the signal recorded on tape. *See* AZIMUTH ALIGNMENT.

azimuth recording.   In recording, a technique in which the signal is recorded at different angles across the width of adjacent tracks on magnetic tape to reduce mutual interference between signals recorded on those tracks. *See* DIGITAL AUDIO TAPE.

B

B. *See* BYTE.

babble. In communications, the aggregate crosstalk from a number of interfering sources. *See* CROSSTALK.

backbone. In data communications, a high-speed link to which the rings of a multi-bridge ring local area network are connected by means of bridges. *See* BRIDGE.

backdoor. *See* TRAPDOOR.

back faces. In computer graphics, the facets of a three-dimensional object that cannot be seen from the current position of the observer. Deletion of current back faces can reduce the effort in computing the screen display of the object. *See* HIDDEN SURFACE.

backfile. In online information retrieval, those older sections of large databases which are held in separate files and are not available for online access.

Backbone

background.   *See* BACKGROUND PROGRAM.

background colour.   In videotex, the colour filling the parts of the character rectangle not occupied by the character itself. The background colour may be black or one of the seven display colours. It may be changed within a row by control characters. *Compare* FOREGROUND COLOUR. *See* CHARACTER RECTANGLE, CONTROL CHARACTER, DISPLAY COLOUR.

background image.   In computer graphics, the part of a display image that is not changed during a series of modifications. *Synonymous with* DISPLAY BACKGROUND.

background ink.   In character recognition, a type of ink that is not detected by the optical scan head because of its high reflective characteristics. It is used for print location guides, logotypes, instructions and any other desired preprinting that would otherwise interfere with the scan head reading.

background job.   In computing, a job of relatively low priority in a multitasking environment. Computer resources are only allocated to it when they are not required for higher-priority foreground tasks. *See* MULTITASKING.

background noise.   In communications, a noise signal received and demodulated with the required signal. *See* SIGNAL-TO-NOISE RATIO.

background noises.   In filming, small sounds that are either synchronous or non-synchronous and are often used to add realism to the sound track.

background plate.   In photography, an image on a glass slide used in a rear projection unit.

background printing.   *Synonymous with* OFFLINE PRINTING.

background processing.   (1) In computing, the execution of lower-priority computer programs when higher-priority programs do not require any system resource. *See* BACKGROUND PROGRAM. (2) In word processing, the execution of an operator's request such as printing a document while the operator is performing other tasks. *See* BACKGROUND, PRIORITY.

background program.   In computing, a program that does not involve interactions with a user and is run with a low priority in a multiprogramming environment. *Compare* FOREGROUND PROGRAM. *See* BATCH PROCESSING, MULTIPROGRAMMING.

background projection.   In filming, projection from the rear of still or moving images on a translucent screen in front of which titles or action are photographed. *Compare* FRONT PROJECTION.

background region.   In computing, a region in main memory to which a background job is assigned. *See* BACKGROUND JOB, MAIN MEMORY.

backing.   In filming, a coating on the back of a film stock (e.g. an anti-abrasion coating or an anti-halation coating). *See* HALATION.

backing copy.   In recording, the first video tape duplicate of a master, taken for protection purposes. *See* MASTER.

backing storage.   In peripherals, an intermediate storage medium (e.g. magnetic tape, magnetic disk, etc.) on to which data is entered for later processing by the central computer. Ideally computers would be provided with a single, non-volatile store which had random access, extremely low access times, of the order of nanoseconds, and massive capacity, of the order of gigabytes. However fast, random-access storage is expensive and economical high-capacity storage devices have slow access, of the order of milliseconds or even seconds, and provide only serial or direct access. In practice, therefore, computers are provided with hierarchies of memory: small, volatile cache memories for nanosecond access by the central processing unit, volatile random-access memories with capacities of the order of hundreds of kilobytes or more, with access times of the order of microseconds, and non-volatile backing stores of magnetic disk, magnetic tape, optical digital disc, magnetic bubble, etc. with storage capacities in the hundreds of kilobytes to gigabyte range. *See* BUBBLE MEMORY, CACHE MEMORY, CENTRAL PROCESSING UNIT, GIGABYTE, KILOBYTE, MAG-

NETIC DISK MAGNETIC TAPE MEGABYTE NANOSECOND OPTICAL DIGITAL DISC RANDOM-ACCESS MEMORY VOLATILE STORAGE *Synonymous with* AUXILIARY STORAGE.

backing up. In printing, to print the second side of printed sheet. (Desktop).

back lobe. In communications, a lobe opposite the main lobe in an antenna pattern. *Compare* MAIN LOBE, SIDE LOBE. *See* ANTENNA PATTERN. *Synonymous with* BACKWARD LOBE.

backlog. In computing, application programs that have been authorized, but not written. *See* APPLICATION PROGRAM.

back matter. In printing, the sections of a book that are placed at the end of main chapters or sections (e.g. index, glossary). *Compare* FRONT MATTER.

back number. In library science, any issue of a periodical that precedes the current issue.

backout. In programming, to return a file to an original state by deleting entries in the reverse chronological order to that in which they were inserted. *See* FILE, ROLLBACK.

backpack. In recording, a lightweight, portable television-recording or camera signal-transmitting equipment. *See* PORTA PAK.

backplane. In hardware, the connector blocks and wiring units that provide the means of interconnection between a computer and its peripherals. It normally comprises a series of multiway sockets connected to the internal bus of the computer. *See* BUS, MOTHERBOARD.

back porch. In television, a picture signal that lies between the trailing edge of the line sync pulse and the trailing edge of the corresponding blanking pulse. *Compare* FRONT PORCH. *See* BLANKING.

back referencing. In online information retrieval, referral to an earlier answer set. *See* ANSWER SET.

backscatter. In communications, a radio wave produced as a result of scattering of an incident wave, but travelling in the reverse direction. *See* FORWARD SCATTER.

backslant. In printing, letters that slant the opposite way from italic characters. (Desktop). *Compare* ITALIC.

backspace. In computing, to move the printing head on a printer back one character position or the cursor on a visual display unit back by the same amount. *See* VISUAL DISPLAY UNIT.

backspace character. In printing, a control character that causes the print or display position to move one position backward along the line without producing the printing or display of any graphic character. *See* CONTROL CHARACTER.

backspace mechanism. In printing, a typewriter device that performs an incremental movement between the paper carrier and the typing position contrary to the writing direction.

backtracking. In programming, a technique of searching for a goal that allows for the possibility that a given search path may prove to be a dead end. Algorithms using this method retreat from such dead ends and recommence the search along a different path which was not subjected to an earlier search. *See* PROLOG.

backup. In reliability, pertaining to a system, device, file or facility that can be brought into action in the event of a malfunction or loss of data. *See* BACKUP COPY, BACKUP DISKETTE, BACKUP/RESTORE.

backup copy. In computing, a copy of a file or data set that is kept for reference in case the original file or data set is destroyed. *See* BACKUP/RESTORE, DATA SET, FILE.

backup diskette. In memory systems, a diskette that contains information copied from another diskette. It is used in case the original information is unintentionally altered or destroyed. *See* BACKUP/RESTORE.

backup plan. *See* CONTINGENCY PLANNING.

backup/restore. In memory systems, the actions involved in transferring data from magnetic disk to tape, or disk, for backup, and the subsequent action of restoring the data to disk. *See* BACKUP.

backus naur form. (BNF) In computer programming, a metalanguage used to specify or describe the syntax of a language in which each symbol represents a set of strings of symbols. *See* METALANGUAGE, SYNTAX. *Synonymous with* BACKUS NORMAL FORM.

backus normal form. *Synonymous with* BACKUS NAUR FORM.

backward chaining. In artificial intelligence, a technique used in expert systems. A hypothesis is formulated, and rules that would lead to this hypothesis are selected from the knowledge base. Assertions are then sought from the database that match those rules, and if sufficient assertions are found the the hypothesis is considered to be validated. *Compare* FORWARD CHAINING. *See* ASSERTION, EXPERT SYSTEMS, RULE.

backward channel. In data communications, a channel, with a direction of transmission opposite to that in which user information is being transferred, which is used for error control or supervisory signals. *Compare* FORWARD CHANNEL.

backward lobe. *Synonymous with* BACK LOBE.

backward read. In memory systems, a technique used in a magnetic tape drive whereby data can be read when the tape is running backwards.

backwards learning. In data communications, a method of routing in which the switching nodes are able to deduce the behaviour of the network by observing the packets passing through, noting their source and the number of links through which they have travelled. *See* NODE, PACKET SWITCHING.

backward supervision. In data communications, pertaining to the use of supervisory sequences which are transmitted from the slave to a master station. *Compare* FOREWARD SUPERVISION. *See* MASTER, SLAVE, STATION, SUPERVISORY SIGNAL.

bad break. In printing, an incorrect end-of-line hyphenation or a page beginning with a widow, or the end of a hyphenated word. It may be produced by a manual operator or computer software. *See* HYPHENATION, SOFTWARE, WIDOW.

bad copy. In printing, a manuscript that is indistinct, illegible, improperly edited or otherwise unsatisfactory.

badge reader. In peripherals, a card, usually of plastic, containing a notched or magnetic stripe code for identifying an operator at a computer terminal. *See* MAGNETIC STRIPE.

bad letter. In printing, a letter that does not print or reproduce fully or clearly.

baffle. In recording, a non-resonant surface mounted on a loudspeaker to prevent air pressure cancellation effects between the front and rear of the speaker.

balance. (1) In printing, the appropriate placement of the various units of composition, illustration and ornamentation so that the appearance of the whole does not look disproportionate. (2) In recording, the arrangement of instruments and microphones to the best advantage.

balanced circuit. In communications, a line that is terminated with a matched load. *See* MATCHED LOAD.

balanced transmission. In data communications, a technique for high data rates that require two wires for each signal. *Compare* UNBALANCED TRANSMISSION. *See* DATA RATE.

balance stripe. In filming, the narrow band of magnetic coating on a magnetic film applied to the edge opposite the magnetic sound track to make the film lie flat when it passes over magnetic heads. The balance stripe is sometimes used to carry additional audio or magnetic cuing information. *See* MAGNETIC FILM, MAGNETIC HEAD.

balancing. In data processing, a test for equality between the values of two equivalent sets of items or one set of items and a control total. *See* HASH TOTAL.

ballistic technique. In printing, a method that is used in the printing head of a matrix printer. The needle is driven forward by a clapper which stops its own motion before the pin head meets the ribbon. The pin is thus in free flight at the point of contact. *Compare* NON-BALLISTIC TECHNIQUE. *See* MATRIX PRINTER.

balun. In communications, a passive device that is used to match an antenna to a cable having a different impedance. *See* IMPEDANCE MATCHING.

band. (1) In memory systems, a group of tracks on a magnetic drum or on one side of a magnetic disk. (2) In communications, a range of frequencies between two defined limits (e.g. the voice band in telephony is about 300–3000 Hz.

banding. In recording, an uneven variation in the rotational speed on a video tape playback head which causes variations in the picture hue. *See* HUE.

bandpass. In electronics, an amplifier or circuit having a frequency response characteristic that is uniform, within defined limits, across a given frequency range.

bandscrambler. *Synonymous with* BAND-SPLITTER.

bandsplitter. In communications security, a form of voice scrambler in which the frequency range of the voice message is split into bands, and the bands are then interchanged. The permutations of the bands may be changed, in a sequence known only to the transmitter and receiver, every few hundred milliseconds. Individual bands may also be inverted. *See* VOICE SCRAMBLING. *Synonymous with* BANDSCRAMBLER.

bandwidth. (1) In communications, a characteristic of a communication channel that is the amount of information that can be passed through it in a given amount of time, usually expressed in bits per second. (DOD). (2) In communications, the difference between the limiting frequencies in a band. (3) In electronics, the range of fre-

quencies within which a device can operate and meet a specified performance characteristic. *See* BIT.

bandwidth compression. In television, a method of reducing the bandwidth which is normally required for transmission by suppressing redundant information. *See* BAND-WIDTH, REDUNDANCY, VIDEO COMPRESSOR.

banking. In optical character recognition, a situation in which the first character of a line is misaligned with the the the left margin.

banking networks. An international bank may be divided into four main areas: lending, financial, operations and treasury functions. These separate activities are integrated into the bank's overall data-processing and communications network, and it is through this network that the bank conducts its day-to-day business.

(a) Introduction. A bank will have an internal network which is used to support the main business areas mentioned above (Fig. 1), and this network will interface with a number of external networks which serve specific sectors of the financial market place (Fig. 2). The internal applications include office automation and consolidation of banking transactions within a branch, or at a country level if the bank operates globally. Of particular concern to a bank is its overall financial exposure. For example, a bank could be lending to a multinational corporation through its branch offices in different countries. The bank in this instance can determine its total lending to the corporation by consolidating all its branch accounts with that company. This can be performed using the bank's own global network if it has one, or through the use of a value-added network provider such as Geisco.

Banks also use their networks to offer their corporate customers a wide range of services, particularly in the area of cash management. Corporate treasurers are required to manage their funds ever more efficiently and are placing increasing reliance upon timely information. The banks have risen to this challenge through the provision of funds transfer services over their networks. A corporate treasurer, via his bank, is able to evaluate his overall cash balance, obtain transaction summaries and initiate payment and funds transfers via a personal

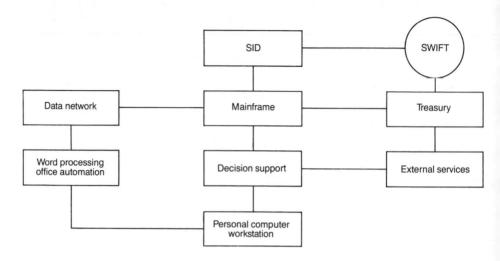

banking networks
Fig. 1. International bank system architecture.

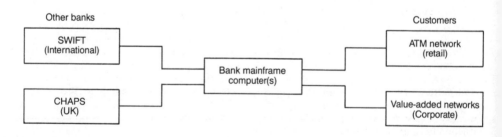

banking networks
Fig. 2. External network links.

computer linked into the bank's network. In this way the treasurer is able to set up a pre-authorized payment system with his suppliers.

In the last decade several electronic transfer systems have been developed to serve specific sectors of the banking community. Some of these are purely message-switching systems (e.g. SWIFT and BankWire); others are funds transfer and settlement systems (e.g. FedWire and CHIPS in the USA, CHAPS in the UK and SAGITTAIRE in France). The success of such systems has resulted, in some cases, in the danger of expansion beyond their capacity and the requirement for the system to be redesign based on improved technologies (SWIFT 11, FRCS '80 – the new FedWire). In addition, automated teller machines, point-of-sale devices and cash management services are rapidly being extended to serve individuals and companies. These systems all have the common objective of expediting business transactions and reducing costly paperwork.

Within an electronic payment system there are essentially three different elements which relate to payment:

(i) a message to convey the identity of the payer and receiver, and to indicate the accounts and responsibilities;
(ii) an account relationship encompassing the transfer and eventually the clearing and settlement;
(iii) a responsibility relationship to ensure delivery, determine value and authenticity and fulfil the obligation, and determine liability in the event of loss.

These three elements can be combined to form a complete national or international electronic system for payments featuring immediate or same-day transfers. A message-switching system, such as SWIFT, only processes the message and caters for some of the important aspects of responsibility relationships, such as delivery and authentication. The absence of account relationships within the scope of the message-switching system means that the exchange of value, the clearing and the settlement are delayed and performed separately. The distinction between a message-switching system and a payment system does not lie in the technology employed. However, for the same volume of transactions an electronic system for payments has to use more powerful and advanced equipment and software than a message-switching system because it has more complex operations to perform and must provide a higher level of security so that the parties involved may fulfil their obligations.

(b) Security in banking networks. Payment systems that are dependent upon the use of computers are exposed to a risk that has for some time caused grave concern to commerce and government. The particular concerns are the illegal use of technology to commit theft, fraud and sabotage, and to violate confidentiality.

Violations of confidentiality and privacy may well cause harm to the system that goes far beyond any direct financial loss involved. No system will be successful unless a sufficient number of individuals and companies are convinced that it is safe, reliable, flexible, convenient, economical and respects their privacy. Accordingly, measures to ensure security and reliability are essential if systems are to be accepted by users and thereby yield the anticipated increase in operational efficiency.

Although a totally secure computer system is unobtainable, it is possible to provide adequate levels of security consistent with the risks involved, within the constraints imposed by personnel, physical, technological and financial resources. The goals for a secure and reliable electronic payment system are listed below:

(i) Transaction message input to the system will never be unaccounted for, distorted, duplicated, accelerated or delayed without authorization.
(ii) The system will never be completely out of action, although the service it provides may on occasion be less than normal.
(iii) The failure of a single component or system path will not isolate any node.
(iv) Any error in the content format or processing of transaction messages input, transmitted or received will be detected and notified promptly to the operational personnel responsible for the system.

The risk of a security violation tends to be highest at the input and output stages in the transmission flow, and lowest during the electronic-processing phase, whereas the effects of security violations tend to be more serious during the latter phase, and less damaging at the input and output stages. This is due to several factors, including:

(i) the greater number of input and output stations vulnerable to violation;
(ii) the transfer of messages from human to electronic processing;

(iii) the greater complexity of the electronic transmission medium and associated procedures, with a corresponding increase in controls.

A breach or failure of the electronic-processing environment compromises the entire system; a breach of security in the input or output stages may only endanger individual transactions at a particular station, but could, on the other hand, jeopardize the integrity of the system as a whole. Adequate safeguards must be devised for both the electronic and the physical operating environments.

(c) SWIFT (Society for Worldwide Interbank Financial Telecommunication). SWIFT is a non-profit-making cooperative society. SWIFT's main purpose is to provide its member banks with their own fast, responsive and secure worldwide data transmission network for sending financial messages. It is used by some 1500 banks spread over 50 countries. In this context 'message' covers most international banking functions such as customer transfers, bank transfers, foreign exchange confirmations, credit/debit confirmations and statements. In the absence of any rivals its managing formats have evolved to become *de facto* standards for interbank worldwide communications.

The network functions are performed by three operating centres serving regional processors in the different countries. Each regional processor acts as the local concentrating point and operates on a store and forward basis. The operating centres validate the messages, acknowledge receipt of messages, store copies of them and control their delivery. Users are connected to the regional processors via public switched or private leased lines with their own choice of equipment which must comply with SWIFT's standards.

SWIFT ensures all members and users with overall security by following a set of underlying principles that have been, and still are, the major objectives of the SWIFT organization and the service it provides. Security in SWIFT is achieved by: (i) integrity and privacy of the data; and (ii) availability and reliability of the service. These objectives are attained by applying proven developments in the areas of computer security and control and computer audit.

Data privacy or data confidentiality on SWIFT is achieved primarily by encryption of all data that is not being processed. This entails the use of encryption devices on all links and circuits that are controlled by SWIFT, and the encryption of data in storage by means of proprietary encryption algorithms. Additionally, all functions that access data which is still being processed are protected by means of one-time passwords under the control of the security department. These controls also contribute to data integrity as they prevent access to data, which could result in inadvertent or fraudulent modifications, irrespective of the shortness of the time period in which data can be intercepted and/or manipulated.

Typical data integrity controls in the SWIFT system are unique sequencing of all messages, dual storage and real-time acknowledgement to the user, indicating the time of arrival. However, by far the most important data integrity control is the message authentication between sender and receiver. Authentication consists of a digital signature that is based on the contents of the message and the identity of the sender. Both the sender and receiver have exchanged a set of bilateral keys before transmission. The digital signature, known as the authenticator, will change if even a single bit is changed in the contents of the message. As such, when it is recalculated by the receiver and compared to the authenticator provided by the sender, the authenticity of the contents, as well as the authenticity of the sender, are guaranteed. The second most important control for data and functional integrity is the use of one-time passwords for gaining access to the system.

SWIFT availability is achieved by several measures, many of which are built into the organization in the form of contingency planning. Other typical availability controls are the duplication and, in some cases, triplication of equipment, extensive recovery schemes and automatic rerouting in case of the failure of some network nodes. Also, physical controls, such as access control and fire protection, and an uninterruptible power supply contribute extensively to the system's availability.

Many of the controls used on SWIFT for availability are not that common, nor is their purpose immediately obvious. For example the time-out control indirectly contributes to availability because it decreases the reaction time of the system when elements of the network fail. This function illustrates a general design principle for controls — known as 'hot mode' — which is applied wherever possible in the system. In hot mode all elements of the network are continuously monitored for proper functioning. Each element of the system is required to transmit continuously traffic or dummy traffic where necessary. Consequently, any absence of traffic immediately indicates a failure.

Error pattern recognition has been implemented on SWIFT to protect the system against the playful and untrained operator. Additionally, it contributes to integrity in case the 'playful operator' is really trying to penetrate the system. If a pattern of errors is recognized on any terminal and the threshold values are exceeded, the terminal will be disconnected automatically.

(Acknowledgement is made to *Security and Reliability in Electronic Systems for Payments*, published by the central banks of the Group of Ten countries and Switzerland under the aegis of the Bank for International Settlements. January, 1985.) *See* AUTHENTICATION, AUTOMATIC TELLER MACHINE, CHALLENGE/RESPONSE, CHAPS, CHIPS, CYCLIC REDUNDANCY CHECK, DIGITAL SIGNATURE, ELECTRONIC FUNDS TRANSFER, FRONT-END PROCESSOR, GATEWAY, PUBLIC DATA NETWORK, SAGITTAIRE, STORE AND FORWARD, SWIFT, VALUE-ADDED NETWORK SERVICE, WARM STANDBY, X.25.

bank paper. In office systems, uncoated paper produced for typewriting, similar to bond, but lighter. It is used for carbon copies. *Compare* BOND PAPER.

banner. In printing, a large headline or title extending across the full page width. (Desktop).

bar chart. A coordinate graph in which values are represented by vertical or horizontal bars, as distinct from a straight-line graph. *See* COORDINATE GRAPH. *Synonymous with* COLUMNAR GRAPH.

bar code. In peripherals, a code of parallel lines of discrete thickness printed on paper and used for fast error-free data entry into a computer. There is a wide variety of codes which may be numeric, limited alphabetic, alphanumeric or even encompass the full ASCII set. Often two bar widths are used, but some codes use four bar widths, although such codes have less tolerance in printing and present the scanning device with problems of resolving multiple bar widths. The code is read by moving a bar code pen across the code, or the code itself is moved past a fixed reader. Header and trailer codes are used before and behind the data bars so that the scanning device can synchronize to the speed of pen movement, the coding may also allow for correct reading even when the code is scanned in the reverse direction. Check codes may be employed either by appending a block check character or using parity check on bar combinations. The bar code is commonly used on product labels for retail outlets, on library books for check ins and check outs, and can be printed in computing books for entry of sample programs into microcomputers. *See* ALPHANUMERIC, AMERICAN STANDARD CODE FOR INFORMATION INTERCHANGE, EAN, OPTICAL BAR READER, PARITY CHECKING, UNIVERSAL PRODUCT CODE, WAND.

bar code camera. In peripherals, a bar code reading device that does not contain its own light source. The camera is focused to take a line image along the length of the coded label. It is a rugged device designed mainly for factory use, and it can read labels at a distance of 40 feet. *See* BAR CODE.

bar code scanner. *Synonymous with* OPTICAL BAR READER.

bar printer. In printing, an impact printer in which type characters are carried on a print bar. *See* IMPACT PRINTER.

barrel distortion. (1) In optics, a type of lens image distortion in which the sides of square objects are bent outwards. (2) In television, a form of distortion in the display, produced by the scanning system, which is identical in effect to the optical version. *Compare* PINCUSHION DISTORTION.

barrier box. *Synonymous with* DEMARCATION STRIP.

baryta paper. In printing, special matt-coated paper suitable for repro proofs. *See* REPRO PROOF.

base. (1) In mathematics, a reference value. (2) In mathematics, a number used in the floating point representation of numbers. *See* FLOATING POINT. (3) In mathematics, the value in which a number system is established. For example, binary arithmetic uses a base of 2. *See* RADIX. (4) In printing and filming, a supporting material for an emulsion or other sensitizing agent, usually cellulose triacetate. (5) In semiconductors, a region in a transistor into which minority carriers are injected. *Compare* COLLECTOR, EMITTER.

base address. In programming, an address that is used as a reference value. It is combined with a relative address to form an absolute address. *See* ABSOLUTE ADDRESS, ADDRESSING MODE, RELATIVE ADDRESS, RELOCATE.

base artwork. In printing, artwork requiring additional components such as halftones or line drawings to be added before the reproduction stage. (Desktop). *See* HALFTONE.

baseband. (1) In data communications, the frequency range of the information-bearing signals prior to combination with carrier wave by modulation. (2) In data communications, the transmission of signals at their original frequencies (i.e. unmodulated). *See* CARRIER, MODULATION.

baseband LAN. In data communications, a local area network (LAN) in which the data is encoded and transmitted without modulation of a carrier. *Compare* BROADBAND LAN. *See* BASEBAND, CARRIER, LOCAL AREA NETWORK.

baseband modem. *Synonymous with* LIMITED-DISTANCE MODEM.

baseband signalling. In communications, transmission of a signal at its original frequencies (i.e. unmodulated). *See* BASEBAND, MODULATION.

base case disc. In optical media, a hypothetical interactive compact disc that can exercise all the capabilities of a base case system. (Philips). *See* BASE CASE SYSTEM, COMPACT DISC − INTERACTIVE.

base case system. In optical media, the lowest-level system that can still carry the interactive compect disc (CD-I) logo. All CD-I systems must at least be able to operate in the way that a base case system does while playing a CD-I, no matter what their configuration or content. (Philips). *See* COMPACT DISC − INTERACTIVE.

baseline. (1) In printing, the line on which the bases of capital (upper-case) letters sit. (Desktop). (2) In printing, a horizontal reference line from which the location of characters and signs is derived. Normally characters without descenders are positioned on the base line. *See* DESCENDER.

BASIC. In programming, Beginners All-purpose Symbolic Instruction Code; the most commonly used language in microcomputers. It can be classed as a general-purpose teaching and hobbyist language. It is well suited to experimentation upon small to medium-sized programs both because it is interpretive and because it is easily learnt in the classroom. It has been increasingly shunned for professional applications due to its slow execution, paucity of program structure and poor readability. It originated Dartmouth College, USA in the 1960s. *See* INTERPRETER.

basic-mode link control. In data communications, control of data links by use of the control characters of the ISO/CCITT 7-bit character set for information-processing interchange. *See* PROTOCOL STANDARDS.

basic rate access. (BRA) In communications, a user network interface in an integrated services digital network system comparable to a single traditional telephone line. In some cases small offices will be served directly by external BRA lines, in other cases BRAs may connect to a small private branch exchange (PABX). BRA provides a user information transfer rate of 144 kilobits per second, simultaneously in both directions. It comprises two B channels, each with 64 kilobits per second capacity and one 16 kilobits per second D channel. The aggregate transmission rates, including framing and housekeeping overheads is 192 kilobits per second. Basic-rate access supports a passive bus wiring configuration. *Compare* PRIMARY RATE ACCESS. *See* B CHANNEL, D CHANNEL, INTEGRATED SERVICES DIGITAL NETWORK, PASSIVE BUS, PRIVATE AUTOMATIC BRANCH EXCHANGE.

basic service. In communications, a common carrier service limited to the provision of transmission capacity for the movement of information. In the USA basic services are regulated by the Federal Communications Commission. *See* COMPUTER INQUIRY 1980, ENHANCED SERVICES.

basic telecommunication access method. In computer networks, an access method that permits communication between terminals and computers. *See* TERMINAL.

basic weight. In printing, the weight in pounds of a ream (500 sheets) of paper to a given standard size. The basic weight of continuous forms for computer output is based on the size for bond paper (17 x 22 inches). *See* BOND PAPER.

bass. In recording, a standard audio frequency range of 0–60 Hz.

bass boost. In audio, the intensification of low frequencies in a sound by electronic means.

bastard size. In printing, any matter used in printing that is of non-standard size. *See* MATTER.

batch. (1) In computing, an accumulation of data to be processed. (2) In computing, a group of records or data-processing jobs brought together for processing or transmission. *See* JOB.

batched communication. In data communications, the transmission of a large body of data from one station to another in a network without intervening responses from the receiving unit. *Compare* INQUIRY/RESPONSE.

batch file. In computing, a file that contains one or more operating system commands. *See* OPERATING SYSTEM.

batch processing. (1) In computing, the processing of data where a number of similar input items are grouped for processing during the same machine run. (2) In computing, the technique of executing a set of computer programs such that each is completed before the next program is started. *Compare* MULTIACCESS PROCESSING, ONLINE SYSTEM, TRANSACTION PROCESSING.

batch region. In memory systems, one of several regions in main storage controlled by the operating system, where batch processing can be performed in a multiprogramming environment. *See* MULTIPROGRAMMING.

batch total. In computing, a total of some common component of a batch of data that enables control to be maintained over the validity of the data (e.g. the totalling of the cash value of daily receipts records so that at any time during the processing the cash total of the batch can be taken and related back to the original to ensure that no distortion of data has taken place).

battery-backed RAM. In memory systems, random-access memory (RAM) with a permanent power supply from batteries even when the power switch is turned off. It provides a non-volatile storage for portable microcomputers. *See* NON-VOLATILE STORAGE, RANDON-ACCESS MEMORY.

baud. In data communications, a measure of signalling speed in a digital communication circuit. The speed in bauds is equal to the number of discrete conditions or signal events per second (e.g., 1 baud equals 1 bit per second in a train of binary signals). Since the baud is a measure of all the signalling elements transmitted, including those used to coordinate transmission as well as the actual message transmitted, it is not necessarily equivalent to the data-signalling rate. *See* DATA-SIGNALLING RATE.

baudot code. In data communications, a code for the transmission of data in which five equal-length bits represent one character. This code is used in some teletypewriters where one start element and one stop element are added.

BAVIP. British Association of Viewdata Information Providers.

BBC. British Broadcasting Corporation.

BBS. Bulletin Board System. *See* BULLETIN BOARD.

BCC. *See* BLOCK CHARACTER CHECK.

BCD. *See* BINARY-CODED DECIMAL.

BCF. *See* BYTE CIPHER FEEDBACK.

B channel. In communications, a 64 kilobits per second integrated services digital network user interface carrying circuit mode or packet-switched mode user information (e.g. voice, data, facsimile and user-multiplexed information streams). *Compare* D CHANNEL, H CHANNEL. *See* CIRCUIT SWITCHING, FACSIMILE, INTEGRATED SERVICES DIGITAL NETWORK, MULTIPLEXING, PACKET SWITCHING.

BCPA. British Copyright Protection Association.

BCS. British Computer Society.

BDN. *See* BELL DATA NETWORK.

BDOS. In computing, basic disk operating system.

beam. (1) In electronics, the unidirectional, pinhead electron stream generated by the cathode gun in a cathode ray tube. *See* CATHODE RAY TUBE. (2) In communications, the radiation in a lobe of a directional antenna. *See* DIRECTIONAL ANTENNA.

beam deflection. In electronics, the process of changing the orientation of the electron beam in a cathode ray tube. *See* CATHODE RAY TUBE.

beam diversity. In satellite communications, a method of transmitting a band of frequencies twice (e.g. when a satellite is orbiting over the Atlantic Ocean one frequency can be used for different transmissions to both the USA and Europe simultaneously). *See* FREQUENCY REUSE.

beam penetration. In peripherals, a technique for colour cathode ray tube monitors in which the electron beam is voltage-controlled to penetrate a series of superimposed phosphor layers. If one phosphor layer emits red light when struck by elec-trons and the next layer is a green phosphor then the low-energy electron beams only penetrate the inner red layer, whereas high-energy beams reach the green phosphor layer. Intermediate-energy level beams will provide a combinational yellow colour. *Compare* SHADOWMASK. *See* CATHODE RAY TUBE, PHOSPHOR DOTS.

beam splitter. In optics, any prism or partial mirror that reflects part of a light beam and lets the rest pass through. It is used to separate colours or to produce two images in two different places.

beam width. In communications, the angular width of a beam within which the radiation exceeds some specified fraction of the maximum value. *See* BEAM.

beard. In printing, the space extending from the baseline of the typeface to a lower limit of body as it appears on the page. *See* BASELINE, BEVEL.

bearer. In data communications, a high-bandwidth channel. *See* CHANNEL.

bearer service. In communications, an integrated services digital network service that provides the means to convey information (i.e. speech, data, video, etc.), without any modification to the message. Alterations may, however, occur in the representation of the information (e.g. changes in the transcoding of speech). *Compare* TELESERVICES, UNRESTRICTED INFORMATION TRANSFER. *See* INTEGRATED SERVICES DIGITAL NETWORK.

before-image. In databases, a copy of a record, accessed by a user or program, before the record is modified. A record of all before-images may be used to restore a database to its original form if a set of processed transactions is to be aborted. *Compare* AFTER-IMAGE. *See* RECORD, ROLLBACK, TRANSACTION.

beginning of tape mark. In recording, an indicator on a magnetic tape used to indicate the beginning of the permissible recording area (e.g. a photoreflective string, a transparent section of tape, etc.). *See* MAGNETIC TAPE.

beginning of volume label. *See* LABEL.

bel. In electronics and communications, the basic unit of a logarithmic scale (to base 10) used for expressing ratios of powers. Two powers, A and B are related by N bels when $\log (A/B) = N$. *See* DECIBEL.

Bell Data Network. (BDN) In data communications, an AT&T system intended to provide subscribers with an extensive range of communication and database access facilities.

bells and whistles. In programming, pertaining to a software package with a large number of special features.

benchmarketing. In computing, an alleged practice of designing systems to perform well against a specific benchmark. *See* BENCHMARK TEST.

benchmark test. In computing, a procedure designed to evaluate the performance of a computer system under typical conditions of use. A program or group of programs can run in several computers for purposes of comparing speed, etc.

bend loss. *See* MACROBEND LOSS, MICROBEND LOSS.

BER. *See* BIT ERROR RATE.

bessel functions. In communications, a mathematical series that gives the relative amplitudes of the spectral components of a frequency-modulated carrier wave. *See* FREQUENCY MODULATION.

Beta. In recording, a video cassette format for half-inch tapes developed by Sony. *Compare* U-MATIC, VHS.

beta testing. In programming, the prerelease testing of software packages at selected customer sites. *Compare* ALPHA TESTING.

between-the-lines entry. (BTLE) In computer security, access, obtained through the use of active wiretapping by an unauthorized user, to a momentarily inactive terminal of a legitimate user assigned to a communications channel. (FIPS). *See* ACCESS, ACTIVE WIRETAPPING, PIGGYBACK ENTRY.

bevel. In typography, the sloping surface of a typeface extending from the top of the face to the shoulder. *See* SHOULDER.

Bezier. In computer graphics, a French mathematician who developed a mathematical method for the representation of smooth curves and surfaces. This technique was developed for the manufacture of car body panels using numerically controlled machine tools. *See* SPLINE.

bias. (1) In electronics, a reference electrical level. (2) In recording, a high-frequency AC carrier current (50–100 kHz) combined with an audio signal in a magnetic recording circuit to minimize non-linear distortion. (3) In statistics, a systematic deviation of a value from a reference value. (4) In communications, the uniform shifting of the beginning of all marking pulses on a teletypewriter from their proper positions in relation to the beginning of the start pulse.

biased. In mathematics, pertaining to a process used in the generation of random numbers that is more likely to produce some numbers than others. *See* RANDOM NUMBERS.

biased data. In data processing, a distribution of records that is non-random with respect to the sequencing or sorting criteria.

bibliographic coupling. In library science, a method of detecting documents dealing with the same subject by examining the articles cited in the bibliographies of the documents. If two documents contain many common references to other articles, then both documents are likely to deal with the same subject. *See* CITATION INDEX.

bibliographic database. In online information retrieval, a database whose records comprise bibliographic citations rather than the full text of documents or substantive information. *Compare* DIRECTORY DATABASE, FULL-TEXT DATABASE, NUMERIC DATABASE, REFERRAL DATABASE.

bibliographic utility. In online information retrieval, an organization that offers access to bibliographic databases which can be used to create catalogues for individual libraries. *See* BIBLIOGRAPHIC DATABASE.

bibliography. (1) An annotated catalogue of documents. (2) A list of documents relating to a specific subject or author. (3) An enumerative list of books. (4) The process of compiling catalogues or lists.

bicycling. In cable television, the showing of a program on several cable networks.

bid. In data communications, an attempt by a computer or station to gain control of a circuit so that it can transmit data.

bidirectional bus. In buses, a bus structure in which a single conductor is used to transmit data or signals in either direction, usually employed for data transmission between a peripheral unit and a central processing unit or memory. *See* BUS, CENTRAL PROCESSING UNIT, MEMORY, PERIPHERAL.

bidirectional microphone. In recording, a microphone that picks up sound primarily in two directions along a single axis. *Compare* UNIDIRECTIONAL MICROPHONE. *See* MICROPHONE.

bidirectional printing. In printing, a method of printing in which one line is printed from left to right and the next from right to left, thus saving time by avoiding unnecessary carriage movement. *Synonymous with* BUSTROPHEDON PRINTING.

bifurcation. A condition where two, and only two, outcomes are possible (e.g. on or off, 0 or 1).

Big Bang. In applications, a term that has been used to refer both to the deregulation of the UK stock market and to the development of an electronic market using modern information technology techniques, which became effective on 27 October 1987. The trading information system termed SEAQ (Stock Exchange Automatic Quotes) was developed on the TOPIC information distribution system. *See* DATA BROADCASTING, TOPIC.

Big Blue. A nickname for IBM. *See* IBM.

bigram. *Synonymous with* DIGRAM.

bijection. In mathematics, a function that maps a set of values $\{p\}$ onto a set of values $\{q\}$, such that each set has the same number of elements and there is a one-to-one relationship between the elements. Thus each value in $\{p\}$ is associated with just one value in $\{q\}$, and vice versa.

Bildschirmtext. (BTX) The Federal Republic of Germany public interactive videotex system.

bilinear interpolation. *Synonymous with* GOURAUD SHADING

binary. In mathematics and computing, a numbering system in which there are only two states, or conditions. The binary system is represented by the numbers 0 and 1. It is used in computing because bistable storage devices are reliable and cheap. *Compare* TERNARY. *See* BISTABLE.

binary arithmetic. In mathematics and computing, arithmetic performed with binary numbers. The arithmetic rules are extremely simple (e.g. $1 + 0 = 1$, $1 + 1 = 10$), and they can be implemented using simple logic circuits. *See* BINARY, LOGIC CIRCUIT.

binary code. In codes, a coding system employing groups of the binary digits 0 and 1 to represent a letter, digit or other character in a computer (e.g. the decimal number 6 is represented by binary 110, i.e. $(1 \times 4) + (1 \times 2) + (0 \times 1)$). *See* BINARY.

binary-coded decimal. (BCD) In data structures, a method of representing decimal numbers where each digit of the number is represented by one nibble. The four bits of the nibble can represent numbers in the range 0–15, but only the representations for 0–9 are employed. Moreover, one whole byte is sometimes used to represent the sign. This form of coding is less efficient in terms of storage space than the various binary forms, but it does allow very long decimal numbers to be represented precisely and is therefore often employed in applications involving financial transaction areas. *Compare* FLOATING POINT. *See* BIT, BYTE, NIBBLE.

binary counter. In hardware, a digital circuit, usually a series of cascaded flip flops, each storing one bit of a binary number. *See* BIT, FLIP FLOP.

binary digit. *Synonymous with* BIT.

binary number. In mathematics, a number expressed in binary notation. *See* BINARY ARITHMETIC, BINARY CODE.

binary phase shift keying. (BPSK) In data communications, a form of phase shift keying in which the carrier phase takes one of two possible values. *See* CARRIER, PHASE SHIFT KEYING.

binary search tree. In data structures, a tree structure that allows only two pointers at any node, except a leaf. Each node has only one key: one of the pointers is restricted to pointing to a key with a lower key value, if it exists; the other pointer is allowed to point to only a node with a higher key value, if it exists. *See* KEY, LEAF, NODE, TREE STRUCTURE.

binary synchronous communications. (BISYNC, BSC) In data communications, an IBM byte control protocol that sends data in frames marked by synchronization characters. After two synchronization characters, each frame has a start of header character, a header containing control and address information, a start of text character, the message text, an end of text character and a cyclic redundancy check character. The protocol supports both point-to-point and multipoint operation. *Compare* SYNCHRONOUS DATA LINK CONTROL. *See* CYCLIC REDUNDANCY CHECK, FRAME, HEADER, MULTIPOINT CONNECTION, POINT-TO-POINT.

binary thresholding. In computer graphics, a technique of allocating a black or white attribute to a pixel, depending upon the value of the grey scale. This technique produces a sharp black and white image. *See* GREY SCALE, MACHINE VISION, PIXEL.

binary-to-decimal conversion. In mathematics, the conversion of a binary number to the equivalent decimal number. For example, the binary-to-decimal conversion of the binary number 111 is the decimal number 7. *See* BINARY-CODED DECIMAL.

binaural. In recording, the use of two separate sound channels on headphones so that the left-hand sound channel is heard only in the left ear, and the right-hand channel is confined to the right ear. The spatial dimension in binaural sound is not confined to the location of the sound source. *Compare* MONAURAL.

bind. (1) In programming, to assign a value to a variable or parameter. (2) In programming, to assign an address to a variable. *See* BINDING TIME, PARAMETER, VARIABLE.

binding time. In programming, the stage at which the compiler replaces a symbolic name or address with its machine language form. *See* COMPILER.

biometrics. In computer security, an access control technology for positive personal identification. The techniques include recognition of eye blood vessel patterns, hand geometry, palm prints and signature analysis. *See* ACCESS CONTROL.

bionics. The technology that relates the functions, characteristics and phenomena of living systems to the development and exploitation of machine systems.

BIOS. In computing, basic input/output system; a section of the operating system that interfaces with the actual hardware environment of the microcomputer. It is a collection of subroutines for primitive input/output and disk accesses. *See* OPERATING SYSTEM.

biosensor. A biologically sensitive material immobilized in intimate contact with a suitable transducer system that converts the biochemical signal into a quantifiable and processible electrical signal. *See* BIONICS.

BIOSIS Previews. In online information retrieval, a database supplied by BioSciences Information Service (BIOSIS) and dealing with life sciences.

bipolar. (1) In data communications, pertaining to a signal that undertakes both positive and negative values. *Compare* UNIPOLAR. *See* NON-RETURN TO ZERO. (2) In electronics, pertaining to a type of semiconductor device. *Compare* UNIPOLAR. *See* TRANSISTOR.

bipolar transistor. *See* TRANSISTOR.

bird. In communications, a communications satellite. *See* COMMUNICATIONS SATELLITE SYSTEM.

birdies. In recording, extraneous whistles and chirps generated when two high-frequency tones intermodulate. It can occur in a tape recorder if the bias intermodulates with a high-frequency tone or its harmonics. *See* BIAS, INTERMODULATION DISTORTION.

birthday problem. In mathematics, pertaining to the calculation of the probability that if n people individually select a random number in the range 1, 2 , ..., n^2 then there is a significant probability that two people will select the same number. The name of the problem derives from the rather surprising fact that with a group of 23 randomly selected people there is an even chance that two of them will share a birthday.

bistable. Pertaining to a system or device that can only occupy one of two states. *See* FLIP FLOP.

BISYNC. *See* BINARY SYNCHRONOUS COMMUNICATIONS.

BIT. *See* BUILT-IN TEST.

bit. In mathematics, either of the characters 0 or 1; an abbreviated form of binary digit.

bit copier. In software protection, a program that reads the source disk at the bit level and writes at that level to the destination disk. If the source disk is copy-protected so will be the destination disk. *See* DEMON, WEAK BITS.

bit density. *See* DENSITY.

bit error. *Synonymous with* BIT INVERSION.

bit error rate. (BER) (1) In data communications, the ratio of incorrect to total number of bits in a message. *Compare* SYMBOL ERROR RATE. *See* BIT. (2) In data communications and storage, a measure of the capacity of a data medium to store, or transmit, bits without errors. It is expressed as the average number of bits the medium can handle with only one bit in error. Read-only memory and interactive compact discs, which employ three layers of error detection and correction (i.e. cross-interleaved Reed-Solomon code and error-detecting code/error-correcting code) have bit error rates of 10^{-18}. (Philips). *See* BIT, COMPACT DISC-INTERACTIVE, COMPACT DISC-READ-ONLY MEMORY, CROSS-INTERLEAVED REED-SOLOMON CODE, ERROR-CORRECTING CODE, ERROR-DETECTING CODE.

bit handling. In programming, a facility of some programming languages to manipulate the individual bits of a byte or word. *See* BIT, BYTE, INSTRUCTION SET, WORD.

bit interleaving. In data communications, a method of time division multiplexing in which the channel receives one bit in turn from each active terminal and delivers one bit in turn to each receiving terminal. *Compare* CHARACTER INTERLEAVING. *See* TIME DIVISION MULTIPLEXING.

bit inversion. In memory systems, a random error causing erroneous read out of a bit, a 1 becoming a 0, and vice versa. *See* BINARY ERROR. *Synonymous with* BIT ERROR.

bit map. (1) In data structures, a map in which each item is represented by a single bit of information. For example, a file directory may contain a bit map, the presence of a '1' bit denoting that the block is being used and a '0' that it is unused. (2) In computer graphics, the information displayed on a screen, corresponding to the contents of the memory-mapped part of main storage. *See* BIT-MAPPED GRAPHICS, MEMORY MAP.

bit-mapped display. *See* BIT-MAPPED GRAPHICS.

bit-mapped graphics. In computer graphics, a display technique in which the image is represented by an array of pixels, and the properties of the pixels are stored in the computer memory. With monochromatic displays the memory bits represent the grey scale of the image; a one-bit cell would provide for only a black/white image. With colour displays the number of colours varies with number of bits allocated per pixel. *See* BIT, FRAME STORE, GREY SCALE, PIXEL.

bit-oriented protocol. In data communications, a protocol that does not impose character assignments to the transmitted data bits. *Compare* CHARACTER-ORIENTED PROTOCOL. *See* BIT, CHARACTER, PROTOCOL.

bit packing. *See* PACKING.

bit parallel, byte serial. In data communications, transmission in which the individual bits of a byte are sent on individual lines, and the complete bytes are sent sequentially. *See* BIT, BYTE, PARALLEL TRANSMISSION, SERIAL TRANSMISSION.

bit pattern. In programming, the pattern of bits in a string, often a computer word. *See* BIT, STRING, WORD.

bit rate. In data communications, the speed at which bits are transmitted over a communications link, usually expressed in bits per second. *See* BAUD, DATA TRANSFER RATE.

bit sequence independence. In data communications, pertaining to a network that enables the transfer of digital data, as a sequence of bits, without placing any restriction upon the sequence of bits. *See* BIT, TRANSPARENT DATA COMMUNICATION CODE.

bit sequence transparent. *See* BIT SEQUENCE INDEPENDENCE.

bit slice microprocessor. In hardware, a microprocessor with an large-scale integrated arithmetic logic unit, which is made from bit slices, and associated control unit. *See* ARITHMETIC LOGIC UNIT, LARGE-SCALE INTEGRATION.

bits per inch. (BPI) In memory systems, the number of bits recorded per inch of track on a magnetizable recording surface.

bits per sample. In codes, the number of bits used to express the numerical value of a digitized sample. (Philips). *See* PULSE CODE MODULATION.

bits per second. *See* BIT RATE.

bit stream. In data communications, a binary signal without regard to grouping by character. *See* BIT.

bit string. In data communications, a string of binary digits in which each bit position is considered as an independent unit. *See* BIT, STRING.

bit stuffing. In data communications, a technique in which frames are delimited by the bit pattern 011 111 10. When five consecutive 1 bits appear in the message or control data an 0 bit is added to avoid confusion with the delimiter. *Compare* CHARACTER STUFFING, PULSE STUFFING. *See* SYNCHRONOUS DATA LINK CONTROL. *Synonymous with* ZERO BIT INSERTION.

black and white. In photography, the rendering of colour images into monochromatic values which are visually equivalent to, and acceptable as, substitutes for the colours of the images producing them.

black body. *See* COLOUR TEMPERATURE.

black box. In electronics, a device or system that has accessible inputs and outputs, but whose internal functions are unknown. All knowledge obtainable from a black box is derived solely from the output and input signals.

black clipping. In television and video, a control circuit in video cameras and recorders that is used to control the black level so that it does not affect or appear in the synchronization portion of the video signal. *See* BLACK LEVEL.

black crush. In television, an electronic effect that converts a live action image into a total black/white contrast without halftones.

black level. In television, a signal corresponding to zero luminance on the screen. *Compare* WHITE LEVEL. *See* LUMINANCE SIGNAL.

black shutter LCD. *See* LCD SCREENS.

black signal. In communications, the signal produced by facsimile scanning the darkest areas of a source document. *See* FACSIMILE.

BLAISE. In online information retrieval, British Library Automated Information Service; a commercial search service and bibliographic utility operated by the British Library. *See* BIBLIOGRAPHIC UTILITY.

blank. (1) In computing, a part of a data storage medium in which there are no characters. (2) In computer graphics, to suppress the display of all or part of a display image.

blank character. In computer graphics, the visual representation of the space character.

blanketing. In communications, the action of a powerful radio signal or interference signal in rendering a receiving set unable to detect the desired signals. *See* JAMMING.

blanking. In television, the suppression of the picture signal information during the return trace of the scanning line on the picture or camera tube. *See* BLANKING PULSE, SCANNING LINE.

blanking interval. In television, the time interval occupied by the blanking pulse. *See* BLANKING PULSE.

blanking level. In television, the level of a composite picture signal that separates the signals containing picture information from those containing synchronizing information. It usually corresponds to the black level. *See* BLACK LEVEL, COMPOSITE COLOUR VIDEO SIGNAL.

blanking pulse. In television, a pulse used in a television signal to effect blanking. *See* BLANKING.

blast through alphanumerics. In videotex, the set of letters and digits that may be displayed on a videotex terminal while it is being used in the graphics mode. *See* GRAPHICS MODE.

bleed. (1) In printing, the spreading of ink beyond the edges of a character. It causes problems in optical character recognition. *See* OPTICAL CHARACTER RECOGNITION. (2) In printing, to run a line or halftone image off the edge of a trimmed page or sheet. *See* HALFTONE.

blind. A device that is unreceptive to input data.

blind copy. In office systems, an electronic mail duplicate copy facility in which the distribution list of the message is not given to the individual recipients. *See* ELECTRONIC MAIL.

blind dialing. In data communications, a facility of some modems that allows the modem to dial when a dial tone is supposed to be present, but none is detected. This facility is important in some private branch exchange (PBX) systems that use non-standard lines which certain modems will interpret as a dead line. *See* MODEM.

blind TV. In television, a service for blind users in which a spoken commentary is added providing a description of the scene, particularly in periods when there is no dialogue.

blinking. In computer graphics, a flashing effect caused by an intentional change in the intensity of a character or group of characters on a visual display unit. *See* VISUAL DISPLAY UNIT.

BLLD. *See* BRITISH LIBRARY DOCUMENT SUPPLY CENTRE.

blob growing. In computer graphics, a feature analysis technique in which each pixel is examined until one is found that is of sufficient blackness to form part of the object. From that pixel, surrounding ones are then examined to determine if they too could form part of the object, *Synonymous with* REGION GROWING.

block. (1) In optical media, the user data portion of a sector of a read-only memory or interactive compact disc. (Philips). *See* BLOCK NUMBER, BLOCK ZERO, COMPACT DISC – INTERACTIVE, COMPACT DISC – READ-ONLY MEMORY, SECTOR. (2) In data structures, a group of words, documents or files treated as a unit. (3) In data structures, a collection of contiguous records stored as a unit. (4) In data communications, a group of bits transmitted as a unit and encoded for error control purposes. *See* BIT, ERROR-DETECTING CODE. (5) In word processing, the ability to define information so as to move it from one position to another within a text element or into another text element. *See* TEXT MOVE. (6) In computing, a unit storage area, normally 512 bytes. *See* BYTE. (7) In programming, a major program unit in a block-structured language. *See* BLOCK STRUCTURE, PASCAL.

blockage. In communications, the loss of energy in a reflector antenna due to the presence of obstacles (e.g. feed supports) in the aperture. *See* APERTURE ANTENNA.

block cancel character. In codes, a specific operational character designed to cause the portion of a block preceding it to be cancelled. *See* BLOCK.

block character check. (BCC) In data communications, an error control procedure that is used to detect errors on a block of data transmitted over a network. *See* BLOCK, ERROR-DETECTING CODE.

block cipher. In data security, a cipher in which the plaintext must be assembled into blocks with a block size determined by the cryptographic algorithm designer; the corresponding ciphertext block depends only upon the cryptographic key, the algorithm and the plaintext block. Thus for any given cryptographic key the cipher effectively provides a massive codebook with entries for every possible plaintext block and corresponding ciphertext block. *Compare* STREAM CIPHER. *See* BLOCK CIPHER CHAINING, CRYPTO-GRAPHIC KEY, DATA ENCRYPTION STANDARD, ELECTRONIC CODEBOOK.

block cipher chaining. In data security, a procedure using a block cipher in which the output ciphertext depends upon the key, the current and all previous plaintext blocks of the message. Chaining overcomes the cryptographic weakness of block ciphers which arises when the length of the message exceeds the block size and the messages are highly formatted or contain significant redundancy. *Compare* STREAM CIPHER CHAINING. *See* BLOCK SIZE, CIPHER BLOCK CHAINING.

block copy. In word processing, to copy a block of text from one area of a document and place the duplicate copy in another area of the document. *Compare* CUT AND PASTE.

block diagram. In electronics and systems analysis, a diagram of a system in which the principal parts are represented by suitably annotated geometrical figures to show both the function of components and their interrelations.

block error rate. In data communications, the ratio of the number of blocks incorrectly received to the total number of blocks sent. *See* BLOCK.

block gap. *See* INTERBLOCK GAP.

block in. In printing, to sketch in the main areas of an image prior to the design. (Desktop).

blocking. *See* BLOCKING FACTOR.

blocking factor. In memory systems, the number of logical records in each block. *See* BLOCK, LOGICAL RECORD.

block length. In memory systems, the number of bytes or words that form a block. *See* BLOCK.

block move. *Synonymous with* TEXT MOVE.

block multiplexer channel. In data communications, a multiplexer channel that interleaves blocks of data. *Compare* BYTE MULTIPLEXER CHANNEL. *See* BLOCK, CHANNEL, MULTIPLEXER.

block number. In optical media, the logical number of a read-only memory or interactive compact disc block after block zero. (Philips). *See* BLOCK, BLOCK ZERO.

block parity. In data communications, a method of parity checking in which an error in a block of data can be detected and corrected without the block being retransmitted. *See* ERROR-CORRECTING CODE, PARITY CHECKING.

block size. In data security, the number of bits in a block of a block cipher. The block size must be sufficiently large to thwart a message exhaustion attack. *See* BLOCK CIPHER, ELECTRONIC CODEBOOK, MESSAGE EXHAUSTION.

block structure. In programming, a technique by which a program is segmented into blocks or modules. This is an essential feature of top-down design and structured programming. Programs should be structured so that their overall function is clear and not obscured by the detail of constituent sets of operations. Communication between the individual blocks should not be affected by the detailed operation within blocks, and actions within modules should not have side effects upon other blocks. This form of program design is advantageous for all programs and is essential when a team of cooperating programmers is concerned with the design of the constituent modules. *See* BLOCK, INFORMATION HIDING, STRUCTURED PROGRAMMING, TOP-DOWN METHOD.

block sum check. *See* LONGITUDINAL PARITY CHECK.

block zero. In optical media, the first block on a read-only memory or interactive compact disc, with main channel or absolute disc address of 00 minutes, 02 seconds, 00 sector number. (Philips). *See* ABSOLUTE DISC ADDRESS, BLOCK, COMPACT DISC – INTERACTIVE, COMPACT DISC – READ-ONLY MEMORY, SECTOR.

bloom. (1) In photography and television, a dark area of a picture creating a halo around an unusually bright area. *Compare* FLARE. *See* HALATION. (2) In peripherals, excessive luminosity of the spot on a cathode ray tube display due to excessive beam intensity. *See* BEAM, SPOT.

bloop. In recording, the removal of unwanted sound from a magnetic sound track by erasing it by hand with a small magnet.

blooping tape. In recording, a tape used to cover unwanted portions of sound tracks. *See* BLOOP.

blow back. (1) In micrographics, a printed full-size copy of information stored on microform. *See* MICROFORM. (2) In peripherals, image enlargement on a cathode ray tube display. *See* CATHODE RAY TUBE.

blow up. In printing, an enlargement, particularly of pictorial information.

bluebird. In video, a type of charge-coupled device used in video cameras that is characterized by low inter-cell leakage. (Philips). *See* CHARGE-COUPLED DEVICE.

BNC connector. In communications, an industry standard coaxial cable connected to a bayonet style locking mechanism; frequently used in connecting closed circuit television equipment. *See* CLOSED CIRCUIT TELEVISION.

BNF. *See* BACKUS NAUR FORM.

board. (1) In electronics, a sheet of insulating material that houses electronic components on one or both sides. *See* BUBBLE BOARD, EXPANSION BOARD, MOTHERBOARD, PRINTED CIRCUIT BOARD. (2) In printing, paper of more than 200 gsm. (Desktop). *See* GSM. (3) In television, the control panel in a studio control room for the switching and mixing of video or audio program elements. *See* MIXING.

body. (1) In printing, a US term for the main text of the work, but not including headlines. (Desktop). (2) In word processing, the main text of a letter or other document.

body print. In computer security, a unique combination of physical attributes (e.g. pulse rate, respiration) which identifies a person.

body size. In printing, the height of type measured from the top of the tallest ascender to the bottom of the lowest descender. It is normally given in points, the standard unit of type size. (Desktop). *See* ASCENDER, DESCENDER, POINT.

boilerplate. In word processing, sections of standard text held as a library in memory for retrieval and use in documents. *Synonymous with* CANNED PARAGRAPHS, STANDARD PARAGRAPHS.

bold face. In printing, a heavier version of a particular typeface. *Compare* LIGHT FACE, VARIABLE TEXT.

bomb. In computing, a term used to denote a spectacular failure in a program that results in the disruption of the entire computer system. *See* TIME BOMB.

bond paper. In printing, a sized, finished writing paper of 50 gsm or more. It can be used for printing upon. (Desktop). *Compare* BANK PAPER. *See* GSM, SIZE.

Bookman. In printing, a typeface designed for ease of reading. *Compare* AVANTE-GARDE, COURIER, HELVETICA, HELVETICA NARROW, NEW CENTURY SCHOOLBOOK, OLDSTYLE, PALATINO, SYMBOL, TIMES ROMAN, ZAPF CHANCERY, ZAPF DINGBATS. *See* TYPEFACE.

boolean algebra. In mathematics, a branch of mathematics named after George Boole that is extremely important in the study of computers. The variables in this mathematical system can only take one of two values (i.e. TRUE or FALSE, 1 or 0). There are two binary operators (AND and OR) and a single unary operator (NOT). Its significance in computing is that the values of computer variables are stored as binary numbers, and the operations are performed on these numbers by logic circuits whose operations can be decomposed into the fundamental operations AND, OR and NOT. *See* AND, BINARY ARITHMETIC, COMPLEMENT, LOGICAL EXPRESSION, LOGICAL OPERATOR, LOGIC CIRCUIT, NOT, OR.

boolean logic. *See* BOOLEAN ALGEBRA.

boolean operator. *See* BOOLEAN ALGEBRA.

boom. In antennae, a metal backbone to which the array elements are attached.

boomy. In recording, a description of a sound which, when reproduced, lacks definition or contains an accentuation of low frequencies.

boot. *Synonymous with* BOOTSTRAP.

bootleg. To produce material illegally. *See* COPYRIGHT.

boot load. In computing, the action of loading the operating system, or monitor, into the computer after cold-start power-up. The boot load system is normally stored in programmable read-only memory. *See* BOOT RECORD, BOOTSTRAP, COLD START, MONITOR, PROGRAMMABLE READ-ONLY MEMORY.

boot record. (1) In optical media, an optional part of the interactive compact disc label bootstrap routine that is used to load the boot modules into memory. The boot program, be it in the system read-only memory or on disc, is used implicitly when starting up an interactive system. (Philips). *See* BOOTSTRAP, COMPACT DISC – INTERACTIVE, READ-ONLY MEMORY. (2) In computing, a record held on formatted disks that is loaded into computer memory and causes a check for the presence of operating system files in the directory when the system is started. If present the files are loaded into computer memory, otherwise an error message is displayed. *See* BOOT LOAD, DIRECTORY, RECORD.

bootstrap. A technique or device designed to bring itself into a desired state by means of its own action (e.g. a machine routine where the first few instructions are sufficient to initiate loading action into the computer from a peripheral device). *See* ROUTINE. *Synonymous with* BOOT.

border. In printing, a continuous decorative design or rule surrounding the matter on the page. (Desktop).

boresight. In communications, the centre of the antenna beam, usually measured in the direction of maximum gain. *See* ANTENNA, ANTENNA GAIN.

BORIS. In videotex, Canadian viewdata service. *See* VIEWDATA.

borrow. In mathematics, an arithmetically negative carry. It occurs in direct subtraction by raising the low-order digit of the minuend by one unit of the next higher-order digit. *Compare* CARRY. *See* MINUEND.

bottom-up method. In programming, a technique in which the lowest levels of instructions are combined to form a higher-level operation, which in turn may be used in the formulation of even higher-level routines. In this manner the programmer effectively forms a new instruction set which contains useful forms for a particular application area. *Compare* TOP-DOWN METHOD. *See* INSTRUCTION.

bounce. (1) In photography, diffused light having no direction. (2) In television, a short-duration variation in the luminance following a step change in the video signal. *See* LUMINANCE. (3) A fault on a keyboard in which a single key depression causes two or more characters to be transmitted. *See* DEBOUNCE.

bounds checking.   In computer security, the testing of computer program results for access to storage outside of its authorized limits. (FIPS). *See* ACCESS. *Synonymous with* MEMORY BOUNDS CHECKING.

bounds register.   In computer security, a hardware register that holds an address specifying a storage boundary. (FIPS). *See* BOUNDS CHECKING.

Bourne shell.   In computing, one of the widespread shells used with Unix. The Bourne shell is fast, compact and provides good constructs for writing programs. It is preferred to the C shell as a programming tool. *Compare* C SHELL. *See* SHELL, SHELL SCRIPT, UNIX.

box.   In printing, a section of text marked off by rules or white space and presented separately from the main text and illustrations. Longer boxed sections in magazines are sometimes referred to as sidebars. (Desktop).

boxed mode.   In videotex, a facility whereby an item of information from the teletext database is superimposed on the broadcast picture displayed on the television screen. It is usually displayed as white characters on a rectangular black background, giving a boxed effect, and is often used for news flashes or subtitles. *See* TELETEXT.

box in.   In printing, to enclose or encompass typed matter with a border of rules. *See* RULE.

BPCC.   British Printing and Publishing Communication Corporation.

BPI.   *See* BITS PER INCH.

BPMM.   In recording, bits per millimetre. *Compare* BITS PER INCH.

BPS.   Bits per second. *See* BIT RATE.

BPSK.   *See* BINARY PHASE SHIFT KEYING.

BRA.   *See* BASIC RATE ACCESS.

bracketed.   In printing, pertaining to a typeface having serifs that are joined to the stem of the type character by a continuous curve or bracket. *See* SERIF.

bracketing.   In photography, the practice of taking several camera shots with exposures around a mean value indicated by the light meter.

braille marks.   In audiovisual aids, special raised markings on equipment function controls that permit identification and operation by touch.

branch.   In programming, a jump instruction. *See* JUMP.

breach.   In computer security, the successful and repeatable defeat of security controls, with or without an arrest, which if carried to consummation, could result in a penetration of the system. *See* PENETRATION.

breadboard.   In electronics, a portable board on which experimental circuits can be laid out. *See* BOARD.

break.   (1) In data communications, to interrupt the transmitting end and seize control of the circuit at the receiving end. (2) In printing, a separation of continuous paper forms, usually at the perforation.

breakable.   In data security, pertaining to a cipher in which it is possible to determine the plaintext or key from the ciphertext or to determine the key from plaintext/ciphertext pairs. *See* CRYPTOGRAPHIC KEY, KNOWN PLAINTEXT.

break line.   In printing, a short line, particularly when at the end of a paragraph.

breakpoint.   (1) In programming, an instruction whose execution may be interrupted by an external intervention or by a monitor program. (2) In programming, a point in a program where control returns from the program to the user. The current state of the program can be examined for debugging purposes. *See* DEBUGGER.

breakup. In television, a momentary distortion in a picture.

breezeway. In television, a synchronizing waveform used in colour transmission and representing the time interval between the trailing edge of the horizontal synchronizing pulse and the start of the colour burst. *See* COLOUR BURST, COMPOSITE COLOUR VIDEO SIGNAL, HORIZONTAL SYNC PULSE, WAVEFORM.

brevity lists. In computer security, a code system that is used to reduce the length of time required to transmit information by the use of a few characters to represent long, stereotyped sentences. (FIPS). *See* CODE SYSTEM.

bridge. (1) In data communications, a device that provides connections between networks, particularly local area networks on a local basis. *Compare* GATEWAY. *See* LOCAL AREA NETWORK. (2) In communications, a connection provided at a telephone exchange to permit audio teleconferencing. *See* AUDIO TELECONFERENCING. (3) In communications, equipment and techniques used to match circuits to each other, ensuring minimum transmission impairment.

bridgeware. In programming, software, and possibly hardware, employed to enable a set of application programs, developed on one computer system, to run on another. It is often employed in the transition phase of changing computer systems. *See* EMULATOR.

bridging. In optical character recognition, a combination of peaks and smudges that may close or partially close a loop of a character thus making it unreadable.

briefcase-portable. In hardware, pertaining to a portable microcomputer that usually weighs between 0.5 to 5 kilograms and fits into an executive briefcase. *Compare* LAP-TOP COMPUTER, POCKET COMPUTER, SUITCASE-PORTABLE.

brightness. In optics, the visual and psychological sensation due to the perception of a luminous source.

brightness modulation. In computer graphics, a method of attenuating the brightness of an image as it recedes from the observer to give an impression of depth. *See* DEPTH CUE.

brightness range. In photography, the variations in intensity of light reflected from various objects or persons in the action field of a camera as measured by a light meter. *See* ACTION FIELD.

brightness ratio. In printing, the ratio between the darkest and brightest areas on a printed sheet. It is a term used in optical character recognition and facsimile. *See* FACSIMILE, OPTICAL CHARACTER RECOGNITION.

brilliance. In photography, the perceived brightness or darkness of a subject.

Bristol board. In printing, fine pasteboard with a smooth surface. It is ideal for drawing up artwork.

British Education Index. In online information retrieval, a database supplied by the British Library and dealing with education and educational institutions. *See* ONLINE INFORMATION RETRIEVAL.

British Library Document Supply Centre. A division of the British Library with responsibility for interlending. Formerly known as the British Library Lending Division (BLLD).

British Standards Institution. (BSI) The UK national body having a similar standards role to the American National Standards Institute and DIN.

British Telecom. The telecommunications part of the United Kingdom PTT. *See* PTT.

broadband. In communications, a frequency band that may be split into several narrower bands so that different kinds of transmission (e.g. voice, video and data) may occur simultaneously. *Synonymous with* WIDEBAND.

Broadband Exchange. In communications, a Western Union public switched telecommunications network. *See* PUBLIC SWITCHED NETWORK.

broadband LAN. In data communications, a local area network (LAN) in which the transmitted data is encoded, multiplexed and transmitted by carrier modulation. *Compare* BASEBAND LAN. *See* BROADBAND, CARRIER, LOCAL AREA NETWORK.

broadcast. (1) In data communications, a method of message routing in which the message is transmitted to all nodes in the network. *See* CARRIER SENSE MULTIPLE ACCESS — COLLISION DETECTION, ETHERNET, LOCAL AREA NETWORK. (2) In communications, the simultaneous transmission of data to a number of stations. *See* DATA BROADCASTING.

broadcast homes. In communications, a household owning one or more radio or television broadcast receivers.

broadcasting satellite service mode. In communications, a communications satellite mode of operation in which programmes or other material (e.g. data) are sent, by one-way transmission from a ground station via the satellite to many small receive-only ground stations. *See* COMMUNICATIONS SATELLITE SYSTEM, GROUND STATION.

broadcasting station. In communications, a centre consisting of one or more transmitters and associated antennae.

broadcast lines. In data communications, asynchronous serial lines that continuously carry broadcast information from a source computer via modems and leased lines, or dial-up telephone lines, to subscribers' host computers. *See* DATA BROADCASTING.

broadcast network. In data communications, a network in which messages are transmitted to all terminals; the receiving terminals check the address information in the message to determine whether or not to accept it. *See* CARRIER SENSE MULTIPLE ACCESS — COLLISION DETECTION, DATA BROADCASTING, PROMISCUOUS MODE.

broadcast satellite technique. In satellite communications, a method of maximizing channel bandwidth on a geostationary satellite. *See* GEOSTATIONARY SATELLITE.

broadcast videotex. *Synonymous with* TELETEXT.

broadsheet. In printing, a sheet of paper in its basic, uncut size; one which is printed on one side only. *Compare* TABLOID.

bromide print. (1) In photography, a normal photographic print made from a negative. (2) In printing, a preproduction plate in photolithography for proofing. *See* PHOTOLITHOGRAPHY.

browse. In peripherals, to scan a screen display rapidly by vertical scrolling. *Compare* BROWSING. *Synonymous with* HIGH-SPEED SCAN, HIGH-SPEED SCROLL.

browsing. In data security, the unauthorized searching of data held on a computer (e.g. confidential data or proprietary software). It is similar to passive wiretapping on communication channels, but is potentially more serious since data stored in a computer has a longer lifetime. Access controls are designed to prevent browsing. *Compare* BROWSE, SCAVENGING. *See* ACCESS CONTROL, PASSIVE WIRETAPPING.

BRS. In online information retrieval, an information retrieval service operated by Bibliographic Retrieval Services Inc. (USA).

brute-force technique. Any technique that depends mainly on computer power and time to arrive at a non-elegant solution to a problem.

BSC. *See* BINARY SYNCHRONOUS COMMUNICATIONS.

BSI. *See* BRITISH STANDARDS INSTITUTION.

B spline. In computer graphics, mathematical cubic equations for smooth two- and three-dimensional curves that touch specified points. *See* BEZIER, SPLINE.

BSS. Broadcast satellite service. *See* BROADCASTING SATELLITE SERVICE MODE.

BT. *See* BRITISH TELECOM.

BTLE. *See* BETWEEN-THE-LINES ENTRY.

BTX. *See* BILDSCHIRMTEXT.

bubble board. In electronics, an expansion board containing bubble memory which functions as if it were a floppy- or hard-disk drive. *See* BUBBLE MEMORY, EXPANSION BOARD, MAGNETIC DISK.

bubble chart. *Synonymous with* DATA FLOW DIAGRAM.

bubble forming. In optical media, a technique for writing to optical discs in which the laser raises the temperature of a spot in the media to about 2000°C. The lower layer of the recording media vaporizes and forces up the covering layer to a bubble. *Compare* ABLATIVE PIT FORMING. *See* LASER, OPTICAL DIGITAL DISC.

bubble jet. In printing, a technique for ink jet printers in which a bubble of ink is ejected from a nozzle by means of thermally generated bubbles. This technique provides for a much higher printing speed than conventional on-demand printers which rely on a piezoelectric element. *See* DROP ON DEMAND, INK JET PRINTER, PIEZOELECTRIC.

bubble memory. In memory systems, a solid-state storage device utilizing microscopic magnetic domains in an aluminum garnet substrate. The domains, or bubbles, are circulated within the substrate and are directed to the output by magnetic fields. This technology has the advantage over random-access memory in that it is non-volatile, and has the advantage over magnetic disk in that it has no mechanical moving parts. However, it is expensive compared with floppy disk, and there are no facilities to remove one set of data to a physical store (e.g. a cupboard) and replace it with another. *See* MAGNETIC DISK, NON-VOLATILE MEMORY, RANDOM-ACCESS MEMORY.

bucket. In memory systems, an area of storage that is referred to as a whole by some addressing system.

buckling. In audiovisual aids, the bending of film in a projector caused by a combination of tight winding and dryness.

buffer. (1) In memory systems, an area of storage that is temporarily reserved for use in performing an input/output operation into which data is read or from which data is written. (2) In data communications, a storage area used to compensate for differences in the rate of flow of data, or time of occurrence of events, when transferring data from one device to another. (3) In electronics, a device that allows one circuit to drive another when a direct interconnection would produce an excessive load on the driving circuit. *See* LOAD.

buffered device. In memory systems, a device that has input/output elements queued to a direct-access device before being written. *See* DIRECT ACCESS, INPUT/OUTPUT.

buffered input. In computing, the ability to enter new data or control instructions into the machine before current operations are completed. *See* BUFFER.

buffered network. In data communications, a system that employs buffers associated with each terminal to maximize the efficiency of the operation. *See* BUFFER.

buffer size. (1) In printing, the amount of memory in a printer used to hold data awaiting printing. The use of a printer buffer releases the central processing unit for other processing tasks. *See* CENTRAL PROCESSING UNIT. (2) In word processing, the number of characters of text and command codes that a system can manipulate at any one time.

bug. (1) In communications security. *Synonymous with* ELECTRONIC LISTENING DEVICE. (2) In programming and hardware, an error in a program or system. The term is reputed to have originated in the days of electromechanical computers using relays. An inexplicable error was traced to the wings of an insect lodged between the contacts of a relay of such a computer. *Compare* PROGRAM CRASH. *See* DEBUG, RELAY.

building block. In microelectronics, an electronic module suitable for building directly into a larger assembly. (Philips).

built-in test. (BIT) In reliability, a form of software redundancy using software-based test programs to check out a system. The programs are built into the system rather than being externally stored and loaded. Typically core elements of the system are tested at startup to ensure that a minimum system is available. If this initial test is satisfactory then the test is expanded to other units in order of priority. *See* SOFTWARE REDUNDANCY. *Synonymous with* SELF-TEST.

bulk eraser. In recording, a device that magnetically aligns all of the iron oxide molecules on a magnetic tape or film, thus eliminating any sound recording.

bulk storage. *Synonymous with* MASS STORAGE.

bulk update terminal. In videotex, a terminal used by an information provider for offline preparation, storage and fast transmission of pages to a videotex computer. *See* INFOMATION PROVIDER, OFFLINE, PAGE.

bulletin board. In applications, a remote public access system for personal computer users. A bulletin board is operated by a Sysop and provides a variety of services geared to the requirements of the user population. The bulletin boards run on different computers (e.g. Z80, 8086 systems, etc.). The user requires a communications software package and a modem to establish dial-up connection to the system. Access to system facilities is controlled by the Sysop, and users must initially be accepted by the Sysop and thereafter must identify themselves with a password upon login. The facilities provided by bulletin boards include: (a) posting messages for other users; (b) scanning and reading messages posted by other users; (c) uploading and downloading files.

Users are expected to assist each other by sharing ideas, posing technical questions and providing answers to posted questions based upon their knowledge and experience. The message facility can also be used for non-technical matters (e.g. for sale and wanted advertisements, as well as an electronic mail facility).

The file transfer facility enables users to provide, and access, public domain software. Copyrighted programs can also be provided on a shareware basis (i.e. the user downloads the program and makes a voluntary donation to the supplier if it proves to be useful). However, users should be aware that bulletin boards are ideal mechanisms for transmitting viruses. Bulletin boards may also be operated on a private basis (e.g. for the sales force of a company). *See* ELECTRONIC MAIL, MODEM, SHAREWARE, SYSOP, VIRUS.

bullets. (1) In printing, solid patches exposed onto phototypesetting film or paper to enable densitometer evaluation of the image density. *See* DENSITOMETER, PHOTOTYPESETTING. (2) In printing, large dots used to draw attention to paragraphs or to set them apart from the rest of the text.

Bundespost. The West German PTT. *See* PTT.

bundle. In optical fibers, a number of fibers grouped together in a single enclosure.

bundled software. In programming, software that is provided with a computer system . The cost of this software is part of the total price. *Compare* UNBUNDLING.

Bureau of Standards. The US government agency concerned with standards for measurement and performance.

burn in. (1) In photography, a prolonged exposure of image or part of an image to light. (2) In television, the after-image in a video tube when the camera has remained focused for too long on a bright or contrasting light source.

burning. In computing, the process of programming a read-only memory (i.e. a PROM). *See* PROM PROGRAMMER.

burn mark. In software protection, a fingerprint technique in which a laser is used to remove a small area of magnetic material on a floppy disk. A test program will write to, and then try to read data from, this area. If the read action is successful then the disk is a copy, and the protected program will be disabled. *See* EXECUTE PROTECTION.

burn resistance. In electronics, the ability of the cathode ray tube phosphor dots to withstand local overheating due to the conversion into heat of the residual energy of the electron beam (i.e. that part of the electron beam energy that is not converted into visible light). *See* PHOSPHOR DOTS.

burnt out. In electronics, pertaining to a device in which the essential working parts are inoperable due to abnormal use or excessive heat.

burst. (1) In data communications, a sequence of signals counted as a single entity in accordance with some defined criteria. (2) In printing, to separate continuous form paper into discrete sheets using a burster. *See* BURSTER.

burster. In printing and office systems, a form-handling device for detaching continuous stationery at the cross-perforations, usually using two sets of pressure rollers rotating at different speeds. *See* CONTINUOUS STATIONERY.

burst error. (1) In data communications, an error occurring in adjacent bits. *See* BIT.

(2) In codes, the corruption of a sequence of bits caused by, for example, a read error, a tracking error or electromagnetic interference. (Philips). *See* ELECTROMAGNETIC INTERFERENCE.

burst mode. In data communications, a mode in which data is transmitted at a specific data-signalling rate during controlled, intermittent intervals.

bus. (1) In data communications, a common group of hardware lines that are used to transmit information between digitally based devices or components. *See* ADDRESS BUS, CONTROL BUS, DATA BUS. *Synonymous with* HIGHWAY. (2) In data communications, a network topology in which workstations are connected by T junctions to one main cable. *Compare* RING, STAR. *See* LOCAL AREA NETWORK.

bus driver. In computing, an integrated circuit connected to the data bus to ensure that central processing unit signals are not affected by the capacitive loading arising from the connection of multiple units to the bus. *See* CENTRAL PROCESSING UNIT, DATA BUS.

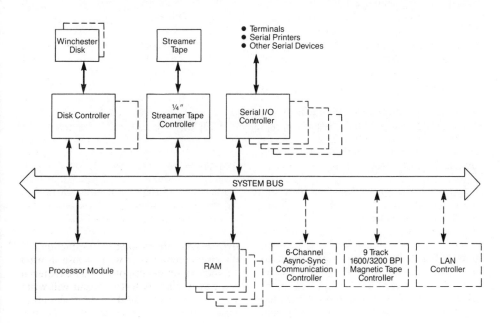

bus
An example of a microprocessor bus and interface options.

business graphics. In computer graphics, the use of graphic facilities to provide businessmen and managers with pictorial representation of information (e.g. pie graphs, histograms, maps, bar charts, etc.). *See* BAR CHART, HISTOGRAM, PIE GRAPH.

business quality. In printing, a quality of text image somewhat lower than that of near letter quality which is, nevertheless, adequate for internal memoranda, etc. *Compare* DRAFT QUALITY, LETTER QUALITY, NEAR LETTER QUALITY. *See* PRINTER.

bussback. In communications, the connection, by a common carrier or PTT, of the output portion of a circuit back to the input portion of a circuit. *See* LOOP CHECKING, PTT.

bustrophedon printing. *Synonymous with* BIDIRECTIONAL PRINTING.

bust this. In data communications, a phrase, used in place of a normal message ending, indicating that the complete message, including the heading, is to be disregarded. *See* CANTRAN.

busy. (1) In filming, pertaining to a background or setting that is distractingly over elaborate or detailed. (2) In communications, a telephone line or plant that is unavailable for more traffic. *See* BUSY HOUR.

busy byte. In architecture, a memory byte employed to prevent conflicts that can arise if processors, in multiprocessing systems, access common blocks of memory. *See* BYTE, DEADLOCK, MULTIPROCESSING.

busy hour. In communications, the period of a business day in which the communications traffic volume is at its maximum. *See* TRAFFIC.

butted slugs. In printing, type matter too wide to set in one line.

buzz. In television, an undesirable audible noise resulting from the interaction between sound and vision signals in a receiver.

buzz tester. In electronics, a device for testing electrical continuity in wiring; it emits a buzz only if there is an electrical short circuit between the two probes.

buzz word. A word used for the sake of its sound alone. *Compare* WEASEL WORD.

B-Y. In television, the blue primary colour difference signal.

bypass. In electronics, a parallel path, or shunt, around one or more elements of a circuit.

byte. (1) In data structures, a binary character operated upon as a unit and usually shorter than a computer word. A byte is the smallest addressable unit of storage and is usually eight bits long. (2) The representation of a character. *See* BIT, WORD. (3) In optical media, an eight-bit unit of compact disc data, representing one symbol before eight-to-fourteen modulation. (Philips). *See* COMPACT DISC, EIGHT-TO-FOURTEEN MODULATION, SYMBOL.

byte cipher feedback. In data security, cipher feedback in which the segments transmitted and fed back to the shift register are one byte in length. *See* BYTE, CIPHER FEEDBACK.

byte mode. *Synonymous with* MULTIPLEX MODE.

byte multiplexer channel. In data communications, a multiplexer channel that interleaves bytes of data from different sources. *Compare* BLOCK MULTIPLEXER CHANNEL. *See* MULTIPLEXER.

byte serial transmission. In data communications, the transmission of data in which successive bytes follow one another in sequence. The individual bits of each byte may be transmitted serially or simultaneously. *See* SERIAL TRANSMISSION.

C

C. (1) In programming, the successor to a language entitled B. It may be described as an intermediate-level programming language, in some respects similar to an assembly language, but with many features that support structured programming. This has made it very attractive in systems programming, and other applications where high-speed execution is important. C is significantly faster than many other compiled languages (e.g. Pascal) and also has the advantage of machine independence. It was originated by Ritchie at the Bell Laboratories in 1972. *See* ASSEMBLY LANGUAGE, BLOCK STRUCTURE, COMPILER, MACHINE INDEPENDENCE, PARAMETER PASSING, PASCAL. (2) In electronics. *See* COULOMB.

CAB Abstracts Database. In online information retrieval, a bibliographic database produced by the Australian Commonwealth Agricultural Bureaux. It covers agricultural and biological information.

cable. In electronics, a flexible electric wire sheathed in insulation.

Cable News Network. (CNN) In cable television, an all-news television cable network.

cable television. (CATV) A method of transmitting television programmes and information services into the home by twisted pair, coaxial or fiber optics cable. The topology of cable networks may take the form of tree and branch or switched star networks; the transmission medium choice between coaxial cable and fiber optics. The choice of network topology and transmission medium is significant if the network is to be used for a large number of channels and/or sophisticated information services. Many consumer receivers, however, can only be tuned to a limited number of frequencies and therefore require a frequency changer or set-top convertor to interface the television set to the cable system. Such a convertor can also contain decoding circuits which allow the viewer to receive premium services. Such services are subject to subscription charges, and the signals are encoded to prevent unauthorized (i.e. unpaid) viewing. The decoder itself may be addressable so that it can be programmed from a central point to receive different tiers of program and information. The set-top convertor may also be enhanced to enable user-originated information to transmit information upstream and thus provide interactive information services.

The tree and branch topology, as the name suggests, takes the form of a main trunk cable with periodic branches serving a cluster of subscribers; each individual subscriber is served by a further branch from this cable. Such a system provides a fixed amount of downstream bandwidth available throughout the system; all channels are simultaneously piped to a subscriber even though at any one time only one is used. A return (i.e. upstream) path can be provided for two-way communications, but suitable protocols must be employed to avoid the collision of such signals converging at the head end. In the alternative configuration, switched star, downstream video and data information is carried over trunk and subtrunk cables to local switching centres and thence is selected so that only the required signal is transmitted from the switching centre to the subscriber. Each subscriber is equipped with a keypad so that signals can be sent to the switching centre indicating the channel or service required. Alternatively, subscriber's data can be routed upstream, from the switching centre to the head end, usually via a data concentrator which serves a number of switching centres. The switching centre can also receive signals from the head end to predetermine the range of services made available to each subscriber. Thus this type of system is inherently interactive and two-way communication forms an integral part of the design. The switched star system requires no set-top encoding for premium services, since a subscriber can be allowed, or denied, access to particular services by programming the switching centre appropriately.

The transmission media may be coaxial cable or fiber optics. Although fiber optic cables are well suited to digital signals, there are technical problems in putting several analog television channel signals on a fiber system at a price low enough for the mass market. Fiber optic transmission is ideal for point-to-point connections, but it does not lend itself readily to successive tapping or subdividing since there is an unacceptable loss of energy at each tap. Thus fiber optics are fully compatible with the switched star system with its series of connections from set to switching centres, etc., and it is unlikely that fiber optics will be applicable in the final distribution network of tree and branch systems which require successive taps onto the final distribution lines. *See* COAXIAL CABLE, FIBER OPTICS, FREQUENCY DIVISION MULTIPLEXING, HEAD END, PREMIUM TELEVISION, SET-TOP CONVERTOR, SPACE DIVISION MULTIPLEXING, SWITCHED STAR, TREE AND BRANCH.

cable television relay pickup station. In cable television, a mobile broadcast station used to pick up programs from a location other than the studio and to transmit them to the head end by microwave transmission. *See* HEAD END, MICROWAVE TRANSMISSION.

cable television relay station. In cable television, formerly community antenna relay service, a fixed or mobile station that picks up signals and transmits them by a microwave link to a terminal point from which they are distributed to users by cable. *See* MICROWAVE TRANSMISSION.

cabletext. In videotex, a teletext system transmitted over a cable network. Unlike conventional broadcast teletext the system can employ the whole frame for codes instead of just a few lines not carrying video information. This enables a much larger database to be transmitted with acceptable user waiting times. *See* FRAME, TELETEXT.

caboose. *Synonymous with* STOP BIT.

cache memory. (1) In memory systems, a very high-speed buffer memory into which instructions from main storage are loaded and executed at a faster rate than if executed directly from main storage. (2) In computing, a buffer memory between a computer and a magnetic tape transport that provides a more constant flow of data to and from the read/write heads, thus reducing the number of stop and start operations. *See* MAGNETIC TAPE TRANSPORT.

CAD. *See* COMPUTER-AIDED DESIGN.

CAD/CAM. *See* COMPUTER-AIDED DESIGN, COMPUTER-AIDED MANUFACTURE.

cadmium sulphide meter. In photography, a light meter that uses cadmium sulphide as its light-sensitive component.

CAE. Computer-aided education. *See* COMPUTER-AIDED INSTRUCTION, COMPUTER-BASED TRAINING.

CAF. *See* CONTENT-ADDRESSABLE FILESTORE.

CAI. *See* COMPUTER-AIDED INSTRUCTION.

CAIRS. In online information retrieval, computer-assisted information retrieval systems.

CAL. *See* COMPUTER-ASSISTED LEARNING.

calendered finish. In printing, produced by passing paper through a series of metal rollers to give a very smooth surface. (Desktop).

caliper. In printing, thickness of a sheet of paper.

call. (1) In programming, the invocation of a program or subroutine. It usually involves setting up entry conditions and a jump to the appropriate entry point. *See* ENTRY POINT, JUMP. (2) In communications, a transmission for the purpose of identifying the transmitting station for which the transmission is intended. *See* CALL ACCEPTED SIGNAL, CALL CONTROL CHARACTER, CALL CONTROL PROCEDURE, CALL CONTROL SIGNAL, STATION. (3) In communications, an attempt to reach a user by telephone, whether or not successful.

call accepted signal. In data communications, a call control signal that is transmitted by the called data terminal equipment to indicate that it accepts the incoming call. *Compare* CALL NOT ACCEPTED SIGNAL. *See* CALL CONTROL SIGNAL, DATA TERMINAL EQUIPMENT.

call back. In computer security, a procedure established for positively identifying a terminal dialing into a computer system by disconnecting the calling terminal and re-establishing the connection by the computer system's dialing the telephone number of the calling terminal. (FIPS). *Compare* RING BACK. *See* DIAL-UP CONTROL, PORT PROTECTION DEVICE, TELEPHONE INTRUSION. *Synonymous with* DIAL BACK.

call control character. In data communications, a character that is used for call control. It may be used in association with defined signal conditions on other interchange circuits. *See* CALL CONTROL SIGNAL.

call control procedure. In data communications, the implementation of a set of protocols required to establish and release a call. *See* CALL.

call control signal. In data communications, one of the set of signals necessary to establish, maintain and release a call. *See* CALL, CALL ACCEPTED SIGNAL, CALL NOT ACCEPTED SIGNAL, CALL PROGRESS SIGNAL, CALL REQUEST.

call duration. *Synonymous with* HOLDING TIME.

called party. In communications, the location to which a connection is established on a switched line.

call forwarding. In communications, a diverter feature of certain central offices and private automatic branch exchanges, using a call device which causes an incoming telephone call to one station to be transferred automatically to another station. *Compare* CALL REDIRECTION. *See* CENTRAL OFFICE, STATION.

callier effect. In optics, the scattering of light as it passes through successive lenses.

calligraphy. The art of beautiful handwriting.

calling. In communications, the establishment of a connection between stations by the transmission of selection signals. *See* STATION.

calling sequence. In programming, the instruction that calls a subroutine or procedure and passes parameters to it. *See* CALL, PARAMETER PASSING, PROCEDURE, SUBROUTINE.

call letters. In communications, broadcast station identification, usually assigned by a licensing authority. In the USA the rule is generally 'W' — prefix, east of the Mississippi River; 'K' — prefix, west.

call not accepted signal. In data communications, a call control signal sent by the called data terminal equipment to indicate that the incoming call has not been accepted. *Compare* CALL ACCEPTED SIGNAL. *See* CALL CONTROL SIGNAL, DATA TERMINAL EQUIPMENT.

call progress signal. In data communications, a call control signal transmitted from the data circuit terminating equipment to the calling data terminal equipment to indicate the status of the call being established, the reason why connection could not be made or any other network condition. *See* CALL CONTROL SIGNAL, DATA CIRCUIT TERMINATING EQUIPMENT, DATA TERMINAL EQUIPMENT.

call redirection. In communications, a facility that allows calls to be passed automatically on to a nominated address when the recipient's user terminal is not operational or busy. *Compare* CALL FORWARDING. *See* CALL. *Synonymous with* CALL TRANSFER.

call request. In data communications, a call control signal sent by a data terminal equipment to the data circuit terminating equipment (or network) indicating that it wishes to make a call. *See* CALL CONTROL SIGNAL, DATA CIRCUIT TERMINATING EQUIPMENT, DATA TERMINAL EQUIPMENT.

call restriction.   In communications, a facility on a private automatic branch exchange system that prevents users from making toll calls without operator intervention. *See* PRIVATE AUTOMATIC BRANCH EXCHANGE, TOLL CALL.

call transfer.   *Synonymous with* CALL REDIRECTION.

CAM.   *See* COMPUTER-AIDED MANUFACTURE, CONTENT-ADDRESSABLE MEMORY.

Cambridge Ring.   In data communications, a local area network standard using a coaxial cable or twisted pair ring topology and a transmission rate of 1 megabit per second. It uses a message slot protocol. *Compare* ETHERNET. *See* COAXIAL CABLE, LOCAL AREA NETWORK, MESSAGE SLOT, RING, TWISTED PAIR.

camcorder.   In video, a combined video camera and portable video recorder. (Philips)

cameo.   (1) In printing, typefaces in which characters are reversed white out of solid or shaded ground. (2) In filming, the lighting of foreground objects, with a solid, dark tone background.

camera.   (1) In photography and filming, an optical or electronic device that consists essentially of a lens attached to a lightproof box containing a mechanism to advance the photographic film, a shutter for timed exposure of the film and a viewfinder. (2) In television, a device in which an image is converted into electrical signals for transmission. *See* PICKUP TUBE.

camera chain.   A television camera and its associated equipment, including power supply, cables and video controls.

camera light.   In television, a small spotlight mounted on a television camera and used for additional fill light on a performer, object or graphic card.

camera ready copy.   In printing, matter prepared for reproduction that is ready to go before a process camera. *See* PROCESS CAMERA.

camp on.   In communications, a method of holding a telephone call for a line that is in use and of signalling when it becomes free.

CAN.   *See* CANCEL CHARACTER.

cancel character.   (CAN) In codes, a character which indicates that the data with which it is associated has an error and should be discarded.

cancellation.   In data processing, the identification of transaction documents in order to prevent their further or repeated use after they have performed their function.

Cancerlit.   In online information retrieval, a database supplied by US National Institutes of Health, National Cancer Institute, International Cancer Research Data Bank Program and dealing with biomedicine.

candela.   In optics, the intensity of light given off by one-sixtieth of a square centimetre of platinum at a temperature of 2045 K. *See* INTENSITY.

candidate key.   In databases, a key in a relational database that has the properties of a primary key. It is a combination of attributes, in a relation, that uniquely distinguishes the tuple from any other in the relation. If any attribute is dropped from the candidate key then the uniqueness property is lost. For example a personnel database may contain employee's name and date of birth as fields within a relation; two employees may have the same name and two other employees may have the same date of birth, but the combination name and date of birth is likely to be a unique and hence a candidate key. *See* ATTRIBUTE, KEY, PRIMARY KEY, RELATIONAL DATABASE, TUPLE.

canned paragraphs.   *Synonymous with* BOILERPLATE.

CANOLE.   In online information retrieval, CAN OnLine Enquiry; an information service offered by the National Research Council of Canada.

canonical schema.   In databases, a model of a data system that represents the inherent structure of that system. It is independent of the software and hardware mechanisms used to store and manipulate the data. *See* SCHEMA.

CAN/SDI. In online information retrieval, an information dissemination service oofffered by the Canada Institute for Scientific and Technical Information.

Cansearch. In online information retrieval, an intermediary expert system intended to assist doctors in online searching of cancer therapy literature. *See* EXPERT SYSTEMS, INTERMEDIARY SYSTEM.

CANTRAN. In data communications, CANcel TRANSmission. *See* BUST THIS.

capability. In computing, pertaining to systems designed to provide protection against access to data or software by users or programs that do not have the requisite level of privilege. *See* CAPABILITY LIST, PRIVILEGE.

capability list. In computer security, list of the access rights of subjects to specified objects. *See* ACCESS CONTROL, CAPABILITY, OBJECT, SUBJECT.

capacitance. In electronics, the property of a system of conductors and dielectrics that permits the storage of electrically separated charges when a potential difference exists between the conductors. *Compare* INDUCTANCE, RESISTANCE. *See* CAPACITOR.

capacitance sensor. In computer security, a sensor with an action based upon the detection of changes in capacitance of a charged metallic object and ground. *See* CAPACITY-ACTIVATED TRANSDUCER.

capacitor. In electronics, a device that is designed to introduce capacitance into an electric circuit. *See* CAPACITANCE.

capacitor microphone. In recording, a microphone which uses a two-plate capacitor with one plate, the diaphragm, flexing under sound pressure. *Compare* CARBON MICROPHONE. *See* CAPACITOR, DIAPHRAGM, MICROPHONE.

capacity-activated transducer. (CAT) In electronics, a device operated by a change in capacitance (e.g. a switch operated when a

finger is placed close to it). *See* CAPACITANCE, TRANSDUCER.

cap line. In printing, an imaginary line across the top of capital letters. The distance from the cap line to the baseline is the cap size. (Desktop). *See* BASELINE.

caps. In printing, an abbreviation for capital letters. (Desktop).

capstan. In recording, a rotating device in a tape recorder used to drive the recording medium at a constant speed. *See* PINCH ROLLER.

CAPTAIN. In videotex, Character And Pattern Telephone Access Information Network; the Japanese videotex system.

caption. (1) In printing, the explanatory comment accompanying an illustration or diagram separated from the text. (2) In filming and television, text superimposed at the bottom of the frame for general information to viewers or to assist a class of viewers (e.g. explanatory information for the hard of hearing or those unable to follow a foreign language dialogue). *Synonymous with* SUBTITLE.

carbonless paper. In typing, paper especially treated to produce duplicate copies without the use of carbon interleaves or carbon coating. *Synonymous with* ACTION PAPER.

carbon microphone. In recording, a microphone in which the transducer is a container filled with carbon granules, the resistance of which varies as sound waves impinge on a diaphragm connected to the granules. *Compare* CAPACITOR MICROPHONE. *See* TRANSDUCER.

carbon ribbon. In office systems, a Mylar ribbon backed with a carbon film. It produces a cleaner print impression than that usually achieved with a fabric ribbon. *See* MYLAR.

carbon sets. In office systems, forms and paper manufactured with attached carbon paper.

card. In hardware, a unit bearing circuit components that can be plugged into a piece of equipment. *See* CARD CAGE, EXPANSION CARD, MODULE.

card cage. In hardware, a structure containing standard sockets for plug-in printed circuit boards and a motherboard for the interconnection of units used for microcomputers. It provides a basic system that can be configured with input/output boards, etc. to meet users' requirements. *See* INPUT/OUTPUT, MOTHERBOARD, PRINTED CIRCUIT BOARD.

cardinality. In databases, the number of tuples in a relation. *See* RELATION, TUPLE.

cardioid response. In communications and recording, a heart-shaped curve depicting the performance in a specified plane of a device such as a microphone or an antenna. *See* ANTENNA PATTERN, MICROPHONE.

caret mark. In printing, a proof-reading symbol in the form of an inverted V to indicate that something is to be inserted. *See* PROOF-READING.

CARIN. In optical media, Car Information and Navigation system developed by Philips for computerized on-the-road route planning and route following, using digital maps recorded on read-only memory compact discs, in association with navigation sensors. (Philips). *See* COMPACT DISC – READ-ONLY MEMORY.

carriage control. In printing, a means of controlling the movement of a printer carriage via a control character.

carriage return. (CR) In codes, a control character that causes a printer, or visual display unit, to locate the printing head or cursor at the beginning of the current line. *Compare* LINE FEED.

carrier. (1) In communications, a continuous-frequency voltage or electro magnetic wave capable of being modulated by a second signal which carries the informa-

tion to be transmitted. *See* MODULATION. (2) In printing, the substance in a xerography developer that conveys the toner, but does not itself become part of the viewable record. *See* TONER, XEROGRAPHY. (3) In micrographics, a device for holding a frame, or frames, of microfilm (e.g. an aperture card). *See* APERTURE CARD. (4) In memory systems, medium on which digital data or other information is stored or transmitted.

carrier beads. In printing, tiny iron spheres specially treated and used to move toner particles. *See* TONER.

carrier detect. *Synonymous with* RECEIVED LINE SIGNAL DETECTOR.

carrier sense multiple access — collision detection. (CSMA-CD) In data communications, a protocol in which a node with data to transmit listens to the network until it becomes quiet. Still listening it then transmits data. If it hears what has been transmitted then it knows that transmission is successful. Otherwise it is clear that two or more nodes have transmitted simultaneously, and the collision has caused a corruption in the data. The nodes then await a random interval before attempting to retransmit. *Compare* CONTROL TOKEN, MESSAGE SLOT. *See* ALOHA, LOCAL AREA NETWORK.

carrier signalling. In communications, signalling techniques used in multichannel carrier transmission. *See* COMMON-CHANNEL SIGNALLING, IN-BAND SIGNALLING, OUT-OF-BAND SIGNALLING, SEPARATE-CHANNEL SIGNALLING, SIGNALLING.

carrier system. In communications, a method of using a single path to obtain a number of channels. Signals are modulated with a different carrier frequency for each channel, and the received signals are demodulated at the receiving end. *See* CARRIER, FREQUENCY DIVISION MULTIPLEXING.

carrier-to-noise ratio. (C/N) In communications, the ratio of the power of the

Preamble	Start of frame delimiter	Destination node address on network	Source node address on network	Length	Logical link control frame	PAD	Cyclic redundancy check

carrier sense multiple access–collision detection frame format

carrier signal to that of the noise signal. *Compare* SIGNAL-TO-NOISE RATIO. *See* CARRIER, NOISE.

carrier wave. *See* CARRIER.

carry. In mathematics, a value, to be added to a digit in an addition process, that arises when the sum obtained by adding the digits in the preceding position exceeds the number base. *Compare* BORROW. *See* BASE.

carry forward. In printing, an instruction to transfer text to the next column or page.

CARS. In cable television, community antenna relay service; now known as cable television relay station. *See* CABLE TELEVISION RELAY STATION.

Carson's rule bandwidth. In communications, the theoretical bandwidth required to transmit a frequency-modulated signal without distortion. *See* FREQUENCY MODULATION.

Carterfone. In communications, a device for connecting a two-way mobile radio system with the telephone network. *See* CARTERFONE DECISION.

Carterfone Decision. In the USA the landmark interconnect decision of the Federal Communications Commission (FCC). In 1968, the FCC ruled that AT&T tariffs, which had forbidden the connection of any non-Bell company equipment to the Bell network, were unlawful. AT&T had banned the use of the Carterfone device on the grounds that its interconnection would cause harm to the network. The FCC decision resulted in tariff revisions, which permitted the interconnection of customer-provided equipment to the telephone network with appropriate terminating facilities to protect the network from harm. It subsequently evolved into the FCC's Registration Program for terminal equipment. *See* AT&T.

cartesian coordinates. In computer graphics, a method of specifying the location of a point in multidimensional space. The reference axes are at 90° to each other and the coordinates are given in terms of the perpendicular distance between the points

and the axes. *Compare* POLAR COORDINATES. *See* ABSCISSA, ORDINATE.

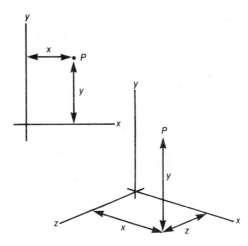

cartesian coordinates

cartridge. (1) In printing, pertaining to a thick, closely woven, general-purpose paper used for offset printing, drawing and wrapping. (Desktop). (2) In filming, recording and computing, a container holding film or magnetic tape, or disks, that permits quick insertion without threading.

cartridge disk. In computing, a hard-disk storage medium contained in a cartridge. *See* CARTRIDGE, HARD DISK.

cartridge paper. *See* CARTRIDGE.

cartridge tape drive. In computing, a storage system employing one-quarter-inch magnetic tape in a cartridge. It is sometimes used as a backup system for a Winchester disk drive. *See* BACKUP, CARTRIDGE, MAGNETIC TAPE, WINCHESTER DISK DRIVE.

CAS Databases. In online information retrieval, bibliographic databases produced by Chemical Abstracts Service(CAS) that provide comprehensive coverage of chemical literature.

CA Search. In online information retrieval, a database supplied by Chemical Abstracts Service (CAS) and dealing with chemistry.

case-bound. In printing, pertaining to a hardback book made with stiff outer covers.

Cases are usually covered with cloth, vinyl or leather. (Desktop).

case folding.   In software, a facility of some systems to accept input in either upper or lower case and then convert it into one case before subsequent processing. *See* LOWER CASE, UPPER CASE.

cassegrain.   In communications, a type of dish antenna in which a small reflector is mounted at the focal point. The received signals are first reflected by the antenna to this reflector and then reflected once more into the feedhorn mounted at the centre of the dish. *Compare* PRIME FOCUS. *See* DISH ANTENNA, FEEDHORN, FOCAL POINT.

cassette.   In recording, a case or container for audio and videotape motion picture film in reel-to-reel format. *See* CARTRIDGE, MAGNETIC TAPE CASSETTE.

cassette recorder.   In recording, a magnetic tape recorder using compact cassettes. *Compare* REEL-TO-REEL RECORDER. *See* COMPACT CASSETTE.

cast-coated.   In printing, pertaining to an art paper with exceptionally glossy-coated finish, usually on one side only. (Desktop).

casting off.   In printing, the process of calculating the amount of space required to print a defined amount of text in a specified font. *See* FONT.

CAT.   (1)   Computer-aided translation. *Synonymous with* MACHINE-AIDED TRANSLATION. (2) *See* CAPACITY-ACTIVATED TRANSDUCER.

catalogue.   In computing, a directory of all the files available to the computer.

catchline.   In printing, a temporary descriptive headline on galley proofs, etc.

catch word.   In printing, a word placed at the end of a block of text to indicate the first word of the next block or text following.

cathode.   In electronics, the negative terminal of a device. *Compare* ANODE.

cathode ray tube.   (CRT) In electronics, a device that converts electrical signals to a visual display. It comprises an evacuated glass envelope shaped as a television tube, an electron gun, which focuses deflection systems, and a screen coated with phosphors. The gun provides a stream of electrons that are focused into a thin beam and accelerated towards the tube face. When the beam strikes the phosphor screen a spot of light is produced. Electrical signals applied to the deflection system move the beam horizontally and vertically and trace a display. Alternatively, the deflection system causes the beam to trace out a regular raster pattern on the screen, and signal voltages applied to the gun vary the intensity of the beam and hence the brightness of the spot. Colour displays employ a screen with three types of phosphor which emit red, green and blue light when irradiated with electrons. The dots are arranged in tight groupings of three (triads) so that if all three are illuminated the effect of a white dot is produced. Three electron beams are used in this case, each controlling the intensity of one of the three colours, and each is focused upon the corresponding phosphor type.

The performance of high-quality monitors employing cathode ray tubes depends upon the bandwidth, dot pitch, resolution, line and frame frequencies, and the phosphors employed in the tube and its associated controlling circuits.

The bandwidth of the signal producing the raster display and the line frequency determine the maximum number of displayable dots per line. For example if the line frequency (i.e. the number of display lines drawn on the screen per second) is 24.75 kHz and the signal frequency is 22 MHz then a line is drawn in 1/24 750 seconds; during this time the signal will undergo 22 000 000/24 750 (= 889) cycles (i.e. 889 distinct pixels could be painted by the signal).

The dot pitch of the phosphor triads determines the degree to which the signal variations can be translated into distinct light dots on the screen. The resolution of a monitor is a function of the signal bandwidth, line frequency, dot pitch and display size. The width of a display line divided by the horizontal dot pitch gives the number of dots per line. For a display width of 213 millimetres and a horizontal dot pitch of 0.32 millimetres there are 662 dots per line. The line frequency divided by the frame frequency gives the number of vertical lines of the display. For example if the line frequency is 24.75 kHz and the frame frequency is 60 Hz then a complete frame is produced in 1/60 of a second and in that time 24 750/60 (= 412.5) vertical lines can be displayed. Increasing the line frequency enhances the number of vertical lines and hence the vertical resolution of the display. The vertical resolution can also be increased by interlacing the display lines in successive frames.

The display quality is also a function of the phosphors used on the screen. Long-persistence phosphors cause the emitted light to decay slowly after the electron excitation is removed. With colour displays the persistence of the three phosphors, representing green, red and blue, must be approximately equal, and such displays have a short persistence since the blue phosphors tend to have such a short persistence.

If interlacing is used it is necessary to use long-persistence phosphors to avoid flicker; the image of one set of lines must persist while the second interlaced set of lines is being painted. The disadvantage of long-persistence phosphors, however, is that an afterglow is visible for scrolled text or fast-moving graphics. *Compare* FLAT-SCREEN DISPLAY. *See* BANDWIDTH, DOT PITCH, FRAME, FRAME FREQUENCY, GUN, INTERLACE, LINE FREQUENCY, OSCILLOSCOPE, PERSISTENCE, PHOSPHOR DOTS, RASTER DISPLAY. *Synonymous with* DISPLAY TUBE.

CA television. *See* CABLE TELEVISION, COMMUNITY ANTENNA TELEVISION.

CATLINE. In online information retrieval, CATalog onLINE; a database supplied by National Library of Medicine (NLM) and dealing with biomedicine, books and periodicals — library holdings.

CAV. *See* CONSTANT ANGULAR VELOCITY.

CB. *See* CITIZEN BAND.

C band. In communications, the frequency range 4–8 GHz. *Compare* KU BAND, L BAND, S BAND.

CBC. (1) Canadian Broadcasting Corporation. (2) In data security. *See* CIPHER BLOCK CHAINING.

CBE. Computer-based education. *See* COMPUTER-ASSISTED LEARNING, COMPUTER-BASED TRAINING.

CBEMA. Canadian Business Equipment Manufacturers Association.

CBMS. Computer-based message system. *Synonymous with* ELECTRONIC MAIL.

CBT. *See* COMPUTER-BASED TRAINING.

CBX. *See* COMPUTERIZED BRANCH EXCHANGE.

c.c. In office systems, carbon copy; an instruction on a document that a duplicate copy is to be forwarded to the nominated person.

CCC. *See* COPYRIGHT CLEARANCE CENTER.

CCD. *See* CHARGE-COUPLED DEVICE.

CCEP. *See* COMMERCIAL COMSEC ENDORSEMENT PROGRAM.

CCETT. Centre Commune d'Etudes de Télévision et de Télécommunications.

CCIR. Comité Consultatif International Radio.

CCITT. Comité Consultatif International Télégraphique et Téléphonique. *See* PROTOCOL STANDARDS.

CCLN. US Council for Computerized Library Networks.

CCTA. UK Central Computer and Telecommunications Agency.

CC television. *See* CLOSED CIRCUIT TELEVISION.

CCU. *See* COMMUNICATION CONTROL UNIT.

CD. *See* COMPACT DISC.

CD-DA. *See* COMPACT DISC – DIGITAL AUDIO.

CD-DA quality. In optical media, the highest available sound quality on an interactive compact disc, identical with digital audio compact disc (CD-DA) sound. (Philips).

Compare HI-FI QUALITY, MID-FI QUALITY, SPEECH QUALITY, SYNTHESIZED-SPEECH QUALITY. *See* AUDIO QUALITY LEVEL, COMPACT DISC – DIGITAL AUDIO, COMPACT DISC – INTERACTIVE.

CD-DA track. *Synonymous with* AUDIO TRACK.

CD device driver. In optical media, the lowest software level to handle compact disc (CD) drives. The only software to communicate directly with the CD control unit, it resides in read-only memory on an interactive compact disc player. (Philips). *See* COMPACT DISC – INTERACTIVE, READ-ONLY MEMORY.

CD disc master. In optical media, a compact disc (CD) master disc produced by exposing a photosensitive coating on a glass substrate to a laser beam. The laser is modulated by the digital program information from the CD tape master, together with the subcode, which is generated during the disc mastering process from the subcode cue code, also on the CD tape master. The exposed coating is developed, covered with a silver coating and nickel-plated to form a 'metal father' recording mould. (Philips). *See* CD MASTERING, CUE CODE, LASER, METAL FATHER, SUBCODE CHANNEL.

CD graphics. In optical media, a technique for generating text, still pictures or animated graphics related to music from a digital audio compact disc not related to the graphics facilities of interactive compact discs. The graphic information is recorded in the subcode channels R–W. At present it is only used in Japan. *See* COMPACT DISC – DIGITAL AUDIO, COMPACT DISC – INTERACTIVE, SUBCODE CHANNEL.

CD-I. *See* COMPACT DISC – INTERACTIVE.

CD-I channel. In optical media, the main channel of an interactive compact disc (CD-I) track corresponding to the specifications of read-only compact disc, mode 2 and the CD-I logical and physical formats. *See* COMPACT DISC – INTERACTIVE, COMPACT DISC – READ-ONLY MEMORY, MODE 2, TRACK.

CD-I digital audio. In optical media, the quality levels of audio data on interactive compact discs (CD-I) are equivalent to LP record quality, frequency-modulated (FM) record quality, amplitude-modulated (AM) radio quality and telephone quality. Furthermore, digital audio compact disc (CD-DA) information can also be played on CD-I equipment.

In addition to CD-DA sound in 16-bit pulse code-modulated (PCM) format, CD-I audio data is also coded in 8- or 4-bit adaptive delta pulse code-modulated (ADPCM) formats. This technique is chosen as a way of coding sound more efficiently than for CD-DA, such that 50 per cent or less of the total data rate is occupied by audio information. At least 50 per cent of the data rate can therefore be used for other purposes, principally the transfer of visual information. The hi-fi music mode uses an 8-bit word size and a sampling rate of 37.8 kHz in order to take full advantage of the form 2 sector space of 2324 bytes, while remaining the highest integral fraction of 44.1 kHz (i.e. the 16-bit PCM sampling rate). Hi-fi music mode is equivalent in quality to a high-quality LP played for the first time. In order to use the same coding technique to span the requirement for various audio levels and still maintain optimal quality by proper post-filtering, the word size of the first level is reduced from 8 bits to 4 bits to give the mid-fi music mode. This is equivalent to FM broadcast-quality sound, as broadcast from the studio, and offers a maximum of four stereo or eight mono channels in parallel as opposed to the two stereo or four mono channels available in the hi-fi music mode. To achieve a further reduction in data rate, and thereby increase the number of audio channels to eight stereo or 16 mono, the sampling rate is reduced by half to 18.9 kHz. This results in the speech-mode-quality, which is equivalent to AM broadcast quality sound as broadcast from the studio.

It should be noted that a channel as described above is equivalent to some 70 minutes of uninterrupted playing time. Multiple channels can only be played with a one- to four-second gap between them. This gap is due to the fact that the laser read-out mechanism must be repositioned back to the beginning of the disc.

An alternative way of using the channels is as a sequence of up to 16 parallel channels of audio information. These channels could tell the same story, but in different languages, for example, so that the user could switch from one language to another at any time. This last case moves away from the question of what is on the disc alone to the question of how that information can be used in a CD-I system.

Audio information from the disc can reach the user in three different ways as described below.

(a) From the disc directly to the 16-bit PCM decoder, and out through the audio hi-fi system as CD-DA sound.
(b) From the disc directly through the ADPCM and PCM decoders and the hi-fi system as ADPCM sound.
(c) From disc into a microprocessor-controlled random-access memory, where it can either be held awaiting its singular or repeated use whenever a certain event occurs (e.g a ball bouncing on the screen which must be accompanied by the appropriate sound), or it can be slightly altered as a function of different events and then sent under microprocessor control through the ADPCM and PCM decoders and out to the hi-fi system. This approach allows for audio interactivity with a quality that has been unachievable in the past. (Philips).

See ADAPTIVE DELTA PULSE CODE MODULATION, COMPACT DISC – DIGITAL AUDIO, COMPACT DISC – INTERACTIVE, DELTA MODULATION, FORM I, FORM 2, HI-FI QUALITY, MID-FI QUALITY, LASER, PULSE CODE MODULATION, RANDOM-ACCESS MEMORY, SPEECH QUALITY.

CD-I digital video. In optical media, there are a range of video quality levels for interactive compact discs (CD-I) that offer a choice of resolution and colour depths to satisfy various pictorial functions in the applications. Three resolution levels are defined: (a) the best achievable resolution for pictures on present normal television receivers (normal resolution); (b) the best achievable resolution for characters displayed on present normal television receivers (double resolution); and (c) the best achievable resolution with the coming enhanced-quality television sets (high resolution). As for colour depth, the quality necessary depends on the type of image that is being handled. Natural stills use YUV (luminance and colour signals) coding for an

• Direct RGB configuration

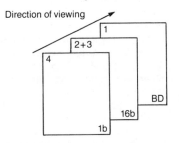

• Basic configuration

• Dual 4 bit configuration

BD = Backdrop (external video)

CD-I digital video
Visual effects: direct RGB configuration, basic configuration, and dual 4-bit configuration.

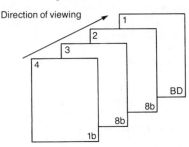

equivalent of 24 bit total colour depth per pixel; quality graphics employ colour look-up tables (CLUT), and user-manipulated graphics use direct RGB coding.

A key requirement is that the disc must be compatible regardless of where it is purchased and on which system it is used (i.e. playback should be independent of the particular television standard). Given these and other similarities and differences, CD-I video requirement are translated onto specifications related to three areas: (a) display resolution; (b) picture coding; and (c) visual effects.

CD-I systems will work with, and disc contents will be displayable on, normal television sets. The video coding adopted conforms, as far as possible, with prevailing industry conventions relating colour depth, visual effects and studio world consideration, while remaining independent of the television standard (525/625 lines).

The starting point for the specification of resolution, in addition to 525/625-line display systems compatibility, is to ensure the readability of text, the undistorted shape of graphics and the full-screen view of natural pictures on display. To do this, two sets of resolution areas are defined: one as a safety area for text and graphics; the other a full screen for natural and animated pictures. Moreover, three disc formats are defined: (a) a 525-line format for NTSC studios; (b) a 625-line format for PAL studios; and (c) a 525/625-line-compatible format that can be used in the international market to satisfy all compatibility requirements.

Each format is usable on each display system with, however, a quality penalty. The basic numbers for normal resolution (i.e. the best resolution visible on a non-interlaced television) are 384 x 280 pixels for the full-screen and 320 x 210 pixels for the safety area. For maximum readability of characters on a normal television display, the double-resolution mode is defined. This mode has twice the number of horizontal pixels as the normal-resolution mode. For future programs, but still keeping in line with the data rate limitations of compact discs, a high-resolution mode is defined as twice the horizontal and twice the vertical resolution of the normal-resolution mode, giving 768 x 560 pixels for full screen and 640 x 420 pixels for the safety area. This is also consistent with high-resolution or 525/625-line-compatible digital television.

The net distortion is at most 7 per cent for a 525- or 625-line disc on a 625- or 525-decoder, respectively, and 3.6 per cent for compatible discs on 525- or 625-line decoders. This is a considerable improvement on the 20 per cent distortion obtained when NTSC (525-line) material is transferred to PAL (625-line) systems for viewing. Also, it relates quite favourably to the fact that the eye can only resolve, at best, distortions of 5 per cent if the original and the distorted object are side by side on the same screen; if they are not side by side the eye can only resolve, at best, distortions of 10 per cent for objects of a familiar shape (e.g. circle, square, etc.). Even these low CD-I distortions will be reduced to zero when real-time pixel manipulation is added to CD-I equipment.

As far as picture coding is concerned, three target areas are defined by CD-I applications: (a) natural pictures; (b) graphics, complex graphics, minimum download-time complex graphics, locally created; and (c) animation.

In all cases it is necessary to use compression techniques to decrease the amount of data required for a given picture, and thus the loading time and the memory storage requirements. By using compression, the achievable update speed, the number of images that can be put on a disc and the number of video 'channels' available per unit are all increased. Clearly, video coding needs to be simple so that the decoding can be affordable, and it must also be capable of being performed in real time while still maintaining image quality.

The compression techniques chosen are given below.

(a) One-dimensional data YUV (delta YUV) for natural pictures.
(b) Direct RGB coding for high-quality end-user-manipulated grahics.
(c) Colour look-up table (CLUT) for graphics and fast update and manipulation.
(d) One-dimensional run length coding combined with CLUT for animation.

Each of the techniques gives optimal performance in the area of use for which they were chosen. In particular, with delta YUV coding there is no visible difference between the compressed and original pictures. If pictures coded in delta YUV or CLUT graphics are intermingled with audio data in speech mode quality, for example to explain their content or to enhance a story, then three full-screen pictures (normal-resolution-mode-compatible format) can be displayed every two seconds while the audio is playing. Moreover, for full-screen animations like cartoons, real motion is achievable with the run length coding specified.

The data rate of the CD-I data channel is

not high enough for visual effects such as cuts and wipes to be performed in the full motion video data stream (e.g. as is done in movies). Furthermore, for interactive use it is desirable to have not only more channel space (for more effective use of CD-I), but also the ability to vary the visual effects used on the same picture data as a function of end-user activity or computer software state. Visual effects are therefore approached at a higher level (e.g. via control functions in the data stream), rather than embedding them uniquely in a moving data stream.

As far as operations on a single visual plane are concerned, CD-I at the basic system level will be capable at least of: (a) cuts; (b) smooth X,Y-scrolling; (c) efficient updating of any part of a visual field independent of the contents of the rest of the visual field; (d) CLUT animation; and (e) trading off picture resolution against visual data throughput for constant visual field size.

The overlaying of images is based on the ability to have at least one hardware cursor plane available, one, two or three independent full-screen, full-picture visual planes available, and one backdrop plane available for use with external video at a pixel level. These plane combinations allow CD-I to be used for a variety of applications as encountered in games-like manipulation of objects over objects, or with a foreground over a background. In CD-I, the control of overlays is done by a transparency bit for the pixels of the cursor, and also the RGB plane. As for the use of the CLUT, a colour key is used to control the overlay of such planes, whereas for delta YUV the pixel-wise overlaying of regions under well-defined transparency/translucency conditions is used.

The final point concerning CD-I visuals is that of operations between two visual planes. There are two main categories of such operations: (a) wipes; and (b) dissolves or fades.

Wipes and dissolves are well known in the film and video industries, as well as in a simpler form, in professional slide shows. They are very important in maintaining an attractive presentation potential in CD-I for both stills and moving picture sequences. These effects, together with the other visual effects described, bring CD-I as close as possible to the present passive video world, while allowing for interactivity via either end user or software control of visual information. This multifaceted control of visual content and visual information flow as perceived and influenced by the end user makes CD-I potentially the richest artistic medium ever created. (Philips). *See* COLOUR LOOK-UP TABLE, COMPACT DISC – INTERACTIVE, CURSOR PLANE, DIRECT RGB CODING, DELTA YUV, HIGH RESOLUTION, NORMAL RESOLUTION, PIXEL, RUN LENGTH CODING, SAFETY AREA, TRANSPARENCY BIT, VIDEO STANDARDS, WIPE, YUV.

CD-I track. In optical media, a track on an interactive compact disc (CD-I) containing only mode 2 sectors conforming to the read-only memory mode 2 specification, as well as the CD-I specification. *See* COMPACT DISC – INTERACTIVE, COMPACT DISC – READ-ONLY MEMORY, MODE 2, SECTOR, TRACK.

CDMA. *See* CODE DIVISION MULTIPLE ACCESS.

CD mastering. In optical media, a compact disc (CD) master disc is produced from a master tape. In addition to the actual recorded program CDs also carry a control and display subcode, which is inserted during the encoding stage of the disc mastering, just prior to eight-to-fourteen modulation. The information for the subcode comes from the recording studio since it is related to the recorded program.

The recording studio therefore produces a digital master tape, assembled and edited into the required sequence, and in the correct CD pulse code-modulated format. It is required to be a U-matic tape, which carries the program on the video track, and SMPTE time code on audio channel 2. This is known as the CD master tape. The information concerning the subcode is then added, usually at the recording studio. This is in the form of a cue code, and it is inserted in audio channel 1 of the U-matic tape by means of a special subcode processor. The tape is now in the form required for disc mastering, and it is known as the CD tape master.

The CD tape master is played into the disc-mastering equipment. The recorded program is encoded into cross-interleaved Reed-Solomon Code (CIRC) for error protection, but the cue code is fed into another subcode processor which uses it to generate the actual subcode. This is then inserted into the CIRC-encoded program signal, which is then eight-to-fourteen modulated into the final CD signal. By using this signal to control the intensity of the recording laser, a pattern of pits is etched into the photographically sensitive recording surface on the glass substrate of the master disc. The master disc is developed and electroplated. The electroplating constitutes a 'metal father'. By two further stages of electroplating, copies of the metal father are produced. These are stampers supplied to the disc production plant for quantity disc production using compression or moulding techniques. (Philips). *See* COMPACT DISC, CROSS-INTERLEAVED REED-SOLOMON CODE, EIGHT-TO-FOURTEEN MODULATION, METAL FATHER, SMPTE, STAMPER, SUBCODE CHANNEL, U-MATIC.

CD master tape.   In optical media, a master tape for compact disc (CD); recorded on U-matic tape, with the digital program information on the video track and SMPTE time code on audio track 2. *See* AUDIO TRACK, COMPACT DISC, SMPTE, TRACK.

CD real-time operating system.   (CD RTOS) In optical media, the operating system used in interactive compact discs (CD-I) specified in such a manner that the real-time capabilities of CD-I are usable, as far as possible, in a device-independent way. The features of CD RTOS are:

(a) Mulitasking operating system with real-time response;
(b) Versatile modular design;
(c) Can be loaded from read-only memory;
(d) Supports a variety of arithmetic and input/output coprocessors;
(e) Device-independent and interrupt-driven;
(f) Can handle multilevel tree-structured disc directories;
(g) Supports both bit-addressable random-access files and real-time files;
(h) OS-9-compatible.

CD RTOS is composed of four major blocks as listed below.

(a) Libraries, which guarantee that the necessary specialized user library functions, such as high-level access and data

synchronization, as well as mathematical, input/output and other functions are available in CD-I systems. One of the most important of these is synchronization.
(b) CD RTOS kernel, which is a customized version of the OS-9 kernel.
(c) Managers, which define the virtual device level for graphics, visuals, text, audio, CD control, etc. The managers provide software support for graphics/visual devices, pointing devices and the CD-I audio-processing devices. Managers are also responsible for disc input/output, optimized disc access and reading.
(d) Drivers, which are interfaces between the virtual (i.e. hardware-independent) level and the actual hardware used by various manufacturers in their CD-I systems. (Philips).

See COMPACT DISC − INTERACTIVE, CO-PROCESSOR, DRIVER, INPUT/OUTPUT, KERNEL, MULTITASKING, OPERATING SYSTEM, OS-9, POINTING DEVICE, RANDOM ACCESS, REAL TIME, READ-ONLY MEMORY, TREE-STRUCTURED DIRECTORY, VIRTUAL.

CD-ROM.   *See* COMPACT DISC − READ-ONLY MEMORY.

CD-ROM channel.   In optical media, the main channel of a read-only compact disc (CD-ROM) track. *See* COMPACT DISC − READ-ONLY MEMORY, TRACK.

CD-ROM publishing.   In optical media, read-only memory compact discs (CD-ROM) can hold 550 megabytes of pre-recorded data, equivalent to 270 000 pages of text on A4 sheets. Moreover, the integrity of such data is assured against malicious modification or data loss from stray magnetic fields. The disc reader may be interfaced to a personal computer, thus providing fast access for viewing, and the retrieved data may also be subjected to local processing. For example, details of spare parts from a catalogue may be viewed and the prices input into a program to compute a total cost. In addition audio information and graphics can be included on the disc, providing for novel forms of encyclopaedias.
The application areas of CD-ROM publishing currently include census data,

medical and legal information, bibliographic databases, spare part catalogues, etc. The cost per storage byte and disc manufacturing costs are low compared to conventional storage techniques. Moreover, the small size of the discs considerably reduces media storage and transportation costs. If the data on the disc is subject to some limited degree of updating then such updated data may be supplied on magnetic discs which are loaded and run in conjunction with the CD-ROM discs.

The disc data must be structured into sections, chapters, paragraphs and indexes so that the constituent data can be accessed in a logical manner. From this data an inverted database is created, with a dictionary produced of all the words indexed. This information, together with search and retrieval software, is combined with the original data for transfer to the disc. The facilities that may be provided include those listed below.

(a) Comprehensive help screens enabling even first-time users to conduct effective searches.
(b) Boolean search options such as AND and OR.
(c) Proximity searching for words that are close to each other.
(d) Browsing of the dictionary of indexed words.
(e) Searching of words with a common prefix.
(f) Restriction of search to specific parts of a record.
(g) Windows for the simultaneous viewing of data from various sources or parts of the database.

The publishing process involves the preparation of data from machine-readable form and structuring of it into 2048-byte blocks. Each block is then processed to produce error-correcting codes and addresses which are appended to it. The disc data is then transferred to 19-mm video cassette recorder tape. This tape is used to prepare the master disc, which is in turn used for the mass manufacture of the CD-ROM discs. *Compare* VIEWBOOK. *See* CD MASTERING, COMPACT DISC – READ-ONLY MEMORY, INVERTED FILE.

CD RTOS. *See* CD REAL-TIME OPERATING SYSTEM.

CD tape master. In optical media, the tape used to produce the compact disc (CD) disc master; a CD master tape with subcode cue code on audio track 1. (Philips). *See* AUDIO TRACK, CD MASTERING, CUE CODE, SUBCODE CHANNEL.

CD track. In optical media, a separately addressable section of a compact disc (CD), normally carrying a self-contained piece of information. (Philips). *See* COMPACT DISC, TRACK.

CE. (1) Consumer electronics. (2) In computing. *See* CUSTOMER ENGINEERING.

cedilla. In printing, an accent positioned under the 'c' to indicate that it should be pronounced as an 's'. *See* ACCENT.

Ceefax. In videotex, the British Broadcasting Corporation's teletext system. *See* TELETEXT.

cel animation. In computer graphics, a method of producing animation films. A computer program produces the graphics for each frame of the film, and they are plotted onto individual cels with a graph plotter. *See* COMPUTER ANIMATION, FRAME, PLOTTER.

cell. (1) In programming, a position on a spreadsheet in which data or a formula may be entered. *See* SPREADSHEET. (2) In memory systems, the storage for one unit of information, usually one character or one word. *Compare* DATA CELL. (3) In communications, an area in a cellular radio system that is served by a transmitter. *See* CELLULAR RADIO.

cell library. In microelectronics, a technique of semi-custom design in which a fully documented range of commonly used predesigned macros is available and assembled to meet the requirements of an individual customer. A full mask has to be generated for the production of the cell library designed circuits.

The cells of the cell library correspond to gates or other functional entities, similar to small- or medium-scale integration packages. In this case, however, the cells are not interconnected on a printed circuit board assembly, but are connected together to form a monolithic integrated chip. The design processes involved are listed below.

(a) Decomposition of the customer requirements into the functional macros available in the cell library.
(b) Placement and routing (i.e. layout of the cells and design of interconnections and input/output pin connections).
(c) Simulation of the proposed overall circuit to check for logic errors, race hazards, etc.
(d) Customer acceptance of design.
(e) Generation of a complete set of masks and fabrication of the chip.

This technique is cheaper and faster than full-custom design of a chip, but the final result may have 30–50 per cent more silicon area and may not have the same operational efficiency as the full-custom design circuit. *Compare* HAND CRAFTING, MASTERCHIP. *See* CHIP, MACRO, MASK, MEDIUM-SCALE INTEGRATION, PRINTED CIRCUIT BOARD, RACE, SEMI-CUSTOM DESIGN, SMALL-SCALE INTEGRATION.

cellular radio. In communications, a method of providing a public mobile radio telephone service (e.g. for car telephones). The total area covered by the service is divided into cell clusters, typically 7, 12, 21 and 24 cells per cluster are used. The cells within a cluster share the total number of radio channels available for the service; low-powered transmitters are employed so that corresponding cells in adjacent clusters, which use the same radio frequencies, do not suffer mutual interference. The cell radius may be as high as 32 kilometres in a lightly populated rural area and as low as 1.1 kilometres in densely populated city areas.

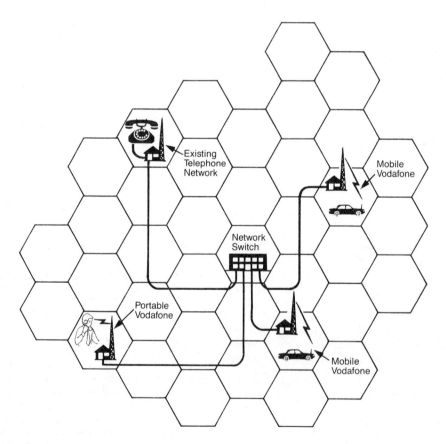

cellular radio
Structure of a cellular radio-telephone network.

To minimize co-channel interference, with small cell radii, sectored radio antenna, having a coverage angle of 120° may be employed.

The cellular technique enables different conversations to use the same frequencies in areas only several miles apart. As a mobile phone user moves from one cell to another the call is handed off (i.e. the switching centre compares signal strength as received at nearby cells). It searches the frequency set of the cell receiving the strongest signal for an open channel and commands the mobile unit to tune to that frequency. The system can now accept another call originating in the first cell on the previously occupied channel. To ensure that a minimum of calls is dropped cells typically overlap. When a call in progress moves into a busy cell, where there are no open channels, it can remain on its original cell until a channel opens or the user moves closer to a third cell with an open channel.

Cellular radio systems facilitate calling from a normal telephone to a mobile telephone even if the location of the called subscriber is not known and his equipment is not in use. The base station in each cell transmits regular identification signals which are constantly monitored by all mobile telephones in the area. If a mobile set detects a change of signal, indicating that it has travelled from one cell to another, it automatically transmits a brief identification to a new base station to inform the system that it has moved and to indicate the latest location. The specification for UK networks (TACS) calls for operation on a wide band of frequencies around 900 MHz. The specification allows for 600–1000 channels which should be adequate for the projected demand of 100 000 subscribers by the year 2000. *See* AMPS, DIRECTED RETRY, FREQUENCY RE-USE, HAND OFF, MTX, NMT, RBS, TACS, UPT.

cellular telephone. In communications, a portable telephone in a cellular radio system. *See* CELLULAR RADIO.

CENTO system. In communications, Central European Treaty Organization; a international microwave system. *See* MICROWAVE.

central computer. *Synonymous with* HOST COMPUTER.

centralized adaptive routing. In data communications, a method of routing in which the network routing centre controls routing based on address information supplied to it by each node. *Compare* DISTRIBUTED ADAPTIVE ROUTING. *See* ADAPTIVE ROUTING, NODE.

centralized computer network. In data communications, a computer network configuration in which a central node provides computing power, control or other services. *See* DATA COMMUNICATIONS.

central office. In communications, the place where common carriers locate their telephone switching equipment and terminate customer lines, etc. *See* EXCHANGE, LOCAL CENTRAL OFFICE. *Synonymous with* END OFFICE.

central processing unit. (CPU) In computing, the unit containing the circuits that control and perform the execution of instructions. It generally contains the arithmetic logic unit, a number of special registers and control circuits. The CPU handles the decoding and execution of instructions, performs arithmetic and logic functions, provides timing signals, etc. *See* ARITHMETIC LOGIC UNIT, MICROCOMPUTER, REGISTER.

centre of perspective. The eye position from which the image in a photograph would coincide dimensionally with the real subject.

centre operator. In videotex, an organization responsible for operating a service.

centrex. In communications, a telephone switching system enabling direct dialing without going through a switchboard. The system allows such services as direct inward dialing and direct distance dialing. *See* DIRECT DISTANCE DIALING, DIRECT INWARD DIALING.

centring. In word processing, the action of locating a text string so that its midpoint lines up with some reference position.

Centronics interface. In peripherals, a common interface between a microcomputer and a printer. The interface uses eight parallel wires to transmit the individual bits of a character, and status information is exchanged over a series of hardware status lines. *Compare* RS-232C. *See* PRINTER.

Century Schoolbook.   In printing, a popular serif typeface used in magazines and books for text setting. It has a large x height and an open appearance. (Desktop). *Compare* AVANTE-GARDE, BOOKMAN, COURIER, HELVETICA, HELVETICA NARROW, OLDSTYLE, PALATINO, SYMBOL, TIMES ROMAN, ZAPF CHANCERY, ZAPF DINGBATS. *See* SERIF, TYPEFACE, X HEIGHT.

CEPT.   Conference of European PTTs. *See* PTT.

CEPT videotex standard.   In videotex, a European standard for alphamosaic systems harmonizing the UK, French and West German standards. *Compare* NAPLPS. *See* CEPT.

certification.   In data security, a method of testing a proposed cryptosystem by subjecting it to attacks considered most favourable to the cryptanalyst. *See* CRYPTANALYSIS, WORST-CASE CONDITION.

CFB.   *See* CIPHER FEEDBACK.

CFD.   Compact floppy disk. *Synonymous with* MICROFLOPPY DISK.

chain.   (1) A set of operations that are to be performed sequentially. (2) In data structures, a set of data items linked in sequence by a series of pointers. *See* CHAIN LIST.

chained file.   In data structures, a file in which each entry contains the address of the next in sequential order. *See* CHAIN LIST.

chaining search.   In programming, a search in which each item contains the means for locating the next item to be considered in the search. *See* CHAIN.

chain list.   In data structures, a list in which each item contains a pointer to the next item in the list so that consecutive items do not have to be physically adjacent in storage. *Synonymous with* LINKED LIST.

chalking.   In printing, a powdering effect left on the surface of paper after the ink has failed to dry satisfactorily due to a fault in printing. (Desktop).

challenge/response.   In computer security, a technique in which the computer system generates a challenge in the form of a random number. The user performs a transformation on the challenge using a secret key unique to the user. The result of this mathematical transformation is entered into the system by the user as proof of identity. The system performs the same transformation using the stored secret key corresponding to the user id, compares the result with that entered by the user and thus authenticates the user. *See* ACCESS CONTROL, DYNAMIC PASSWORD, USER ID.

change dump.   In operations, a selective dump of those storage locations whose contents have changed. *See* SELECTIVE DUMP.

channel.   (1) In data communications, a path along which signals can be sent. (2) In computing, a special-purpose processor and associated circuitry which has the function of controlling input/output operations. The channel may be responsible for buffering of data, formatting and the control of data flows in accordance with the timing requirements of peripherals. (3) In broadcasting, a waveband approximately 6 Mhz wide assigned by the Federal Communications Commission.

Channel 2000.   *See* VIEWTEL.

channel-attached.   In computing, pertaining to devices that are directly connected to a computer by input/output channels. *Compare* LINK-ATTACHED. *See* CHANNEL.

channel bank.   In communications, equipment performing the operation of multiplexing; typically it is used for multiplexing voice-grade channels. *See* MULTIPLEXER.

channel capacity.   In data communications, the maximum rate at which information can be transmitted over a given channel. Channel capacity is normally measured in bauds, but may be stated in bits per second when specific terminating equipment is implied. *See* BAUD, CHANNEL.

channel group.   In communications, an assembly of 12 channels in a carrier system that occupy adjacent bands in the spectrum and are frequency division multiplexed. *See* CARRIER SYSTEM, CHANNEL, FREQUENCY DIVISION MULTIPLEXING, MASTER GROUP, SUPERGROUP.

channel isolation. In communications, a measure of the degree of crosstalk between two channels. It is measured in decibels. *See* CROSSTALK, DECIBEL.

channel overload. In computing, a situation in which the rate of transfer between a processor and input/output units is close to the maximum capacity of the channel. *See* CHANNEL, INPUT/OUTPUT UNIT.

CHAPS. In banking, Clearing House Automated Payment System; an electronic interbank system for sending guaranteed, unconditional sterling payments for same-day settlement from one settlement bank, on behalf of itself or its customers, to another settlement bank. (ANSI). *Compare* CHIPS. *See* BANKING NETWORKS, SWIFT.

chapter. In optical media, a consecutive sequence of frames. *See* FRAME.

chapter stop. In optical media, a code embedded in the vertical blanking interval of the videodisc. It enables the player to locate the beginning of chapters. *See* CHAPTER, VERTICAL BLANKING INTERVAL, VIDEODISC.

character. (1) In data structures, a representation of the letters of the alphabet (both upper and lower case), digits 0–9 and punctuation marks. The most common representation of characters in binary notation is the ASCII code, but the EBCDIC code is also employed. *Compare* STRING. *See* AMERICAN STANDARD CODE FOR INFORMATION INTERCHANGE, EBCDIC CODE, LOWER CASE, UPPER CASE. (2) In printing, a letter, number, punctuation mark or special graphic used for the production of text. (3) A letter, digit or other symbol that is used as part of the organization, control or representation of data. A character is often represented in the form of a spatial arrangement of adjacent or connected strokes or in the form of other physical conditions in data media.

character assembly. (1) In data communications, the process by which bits are put together to form characters as the bits arrive on a data link. *Compare* CHARACTER DISASSEMBLY. (2) In printing, a generic term covering all methods in which letters, figures, special characters and spaces are generated for reproduction.

character-based interface. In computing, the prompts and commands used by an operating system. With bit-mapped graphics, a more flexible and user-friendly interface is possible through the use of icons and pointing devices. *See* BIT-MAPPED GRAPHICS, ICON, POINTING DEVICE.

character byte. In videotex, the byte obtained by appending an odd parity bit to a character code. *See* PARITY.

character code. In codes, a method of representing characters by means of a unique set of binary digits. The two most common character codes are ASCII and EBCDIC. *See* AMERICAN STANDARD CODE FOR INFORMATION INTERCHANGE, EBCDIC CODE.

character disassembly. In data communications, the process by which characters are decomposed into bits for transmission over a data link. *Compare* CHARACTER ASSEMBLY.

character fill. In memory systems, the action of inserting a specified character into consecutive locations of a storage medium to overwrite existing data. *See* OVERWRITING.

character generator. (1) In computer graphics, a functional unit that converts the coded representation of a graphic character into the shape of the character for display. (2) In word processing, the means within the equipment for generating visual characters or symbols from coded data.

character interleaving. In data communications, a method of time division multiplexing in which the multiplexer stores a complete character before transmitting it down the line. *Compare* BIT INTERLEAVING. *See* TIME DIVISION MULTIPLEXING.

characteristic. In mathematics, the numeral that represents the exponent of a floating point number. *Compare* MANTISSA. *See* EXPONENT, FLOATING POINT.

characteristic curve. In photography, a graph displaying the relationship between the density in developed photographic emulsion and exposure.

character key. In word processing, a function key to process one character at a time. *See* FUNCTION KEY.

character mapping. *Synonymous with* CODE CONVERSION.

character-oriented protocol. In data communications, a protocol in which the sets of bits transmitted are recognized as specific characters. *Compare* BIT-ORIENTED PROTOCOL. *See* CHARACTER, PROTOCOL.

characterplexer. In data communications, a system in which data from a low-speed asynchronous channel is organized on a character basis, and each character is gated onto a high-speed synchronous trunk. *See* ASYNCHRONOUS TRANSMISSION, SYNCHRONOUS TRANSMISSION.

character printer. *Synonymous with* SERIAL PRINTER.

character recognition. In peripherals, the identification of graphic, phonic or other characters by automatic means, including magnetic, optical or mechanical. *See* MAGNETIC INK CHARACTER RECOGNITION, OPTICAL CHARACTER RECOGNITION.

character rectangle. In videotex, one of the 960 units in the regular matrix of 24 rows of 40 character positions in which characters are generated in the display of a page. *See* PAGE.

character rounding. In computer graphics, the technique of improving the shape of a displayed character within the constraints of the dot matrix. *See* DOT MATRIX.

character set. (1) In codes, a finite set of different characters that is considered complete for a particular application. (2) The set of characters available on a particular computer. *See* CHARACTER.

character size control. In word processing, a display option in which the operator can choose between a full page of text at normal character size or one-half page at double (vertical) size.

character skew. In character recognition, the angular shift of a character away from its intended position. *See* OPTICAL CHARACTER RECOGNITION, SKEW.

character space. In videotex, the space occupied by a character or graphic symbol on a videotex display. *See* CONTIGUOUS GRAPHICS, PAGE.

character spacing display. In word processing, a facility whereby the operator can view the character spacing for either 10 or 12 pitch, or for proportionally spaced characters. The screen display line may be identical to the line to be printed. *See* PITCH, PROPORTIONAL SPACING.

character-spacing reference line. In character recognition, a vertical line used for determining the horizontal spacing of characters.

characters per pica. In printing, the average number of characters in a given font that will fit within a given pica measure. *See* PICA.

characters per second. (CHPS) In data communications, a measure of transmission rate, usually between a terminal device and a computer. *Compare* BAUD.

character string. (1) In data structures, a string that consists solely of characters. (2) Connected sequence of characters.

character stroke. In character recognition, a line segment or mark used in optical character recognition (OCR). *See* OCR FONT.

character stuffing. In data communications, a method of delimiting frames with a special end-of-frame character. *Compare* BIT STUFFING.

character subset. In codes, a selection of characters from a character set comprising all characters that have a specified common feature. *See* CHARACTER SET.

character terminal. In data communications, a terminal that cannot form its own packets; it is connected to a packet assembler/disassembler for connection to a packet-switched network. *Compare* PACKET TERMINAL. *See* PACKET ASSEMBLER/DISASSEMBLER, PACKET SWITCHING.

charge. In electronics, a quantity of unbalanced electricity in a body (i.e. an excess or deficiency of electrons) giving the body a negative or positive potential, respectively.

charge-coupled device. (CCD) In microelectronics, a metal oxide semiconductor recirculating memory. Electrons are injected into the device and are moved along it as the result of voltages applied to a series of electrodes, thus providing an action similar to that of a shift register. *See* MEMORY, METAL OXIDE SEMICONDUCTOR, SHIFT REGISTER.

charging. In printing, the placing of an electrostatic charge onto the surface of a dielectric. *See* DIELECTRIC, ION DEPOSITION, LASER PRINTER.

chassis. In electronics, the metal base upon which the sockets, wiring and other electronic parts of an assembly are mounted.

check bit. In codes, a binary digit used in the process of determining the accuracy of processed or transmitted data. *See* PARITY CHECKING.

check digit. (1) In library science, a digit added to a sequence of digits to which it is arithmetically related. It allows the automatic detection of errors in the transcription of classification numbers. (2) In codes, one or more redundant digits used to check for the presence of errors in an associated set of digits. *See* CHECK KEY, CHECKSUM.

check key. In codes, a group of characters, derived from and appended to a data item, that can be used to detect errors in the data item during processing. *See* CHECK DIGIT, CHECKSUM.

checkpoint. In programming, a point at which information about the status of a program execution can be recorded so that the execution can be restarted later.

checksum. (1) In data security, a fixed-length block that is produced as a function of every bit in the message and used to check the integrity of the data. *See* MESSAGE AUTHENTICATION. (2) In codes, the summation of a set of data items for error detection purposes. The data items are either numerals, bits or other character strings regarded as numerals for the purpose of the calculation. *Compare* HASH TOTAL. *See* CHECK DIGIT, CHECK KEY, ERROR-DETECTING CODE.

Chemical Dictionary Databases. In online information retrieval, a dictionary non-bibliographic database that lists alterative names and unique identifiers (CA Registry Numbers) for chemical compounds.

Chemical Engineering Abstracts. In online information retrieval, a database supplied by the Royal Society of Chemistry and dealing with chemical engineering.

Chemical Industry Notes. In online information retrieval, a database supplied by Chemical Abstracts Service and dealing with the chemical industry.

chief programmer team. In programming, a team comprising a highly skilled programmer, termed the chief programmer, supported by other team members, typically a backup programmer, librarian, administrator and secretary. The chief programmer concept is based upon the premise that a single highly skilled programmer, suitably supported, is more productive than a team of programmers operating as equals.

Chill. In programming, a language, similar to Ada and adopted by CCITT as a standard, for programming computer-based telecommunication systems and computer-controlled exchanges. *See* ADA, CCITT.

chip. (1) In micrographics, a piece of microfilm smaller than a microfiche that contains coded information and microfiches. *See* MICROFICHE, MICROFILM. (2) In microelectronics, an integrated circuit device including its encapsulating package and circuit terminations. The phenomenal growth in the microelectronics industry is due to the technology that produces circuits of increasing complexity, high reliability, low power dissipation and cost on minute wafers of silicon. Silicon itself is a grey semiconductive material commonly found in the earth's crust.

The processes involved in the production of a chip are purification, ingot growth, wafer generation, imaging process, deposition and growth process, testing, chip separation, wiring and encapsulation. A silicon rod is initially purified by the zone-refining process; heating coils move along a cylinder containing the rod, and the impurities tend to collect in the localized molten region. As the heating coils move from one end of the rod to the other, the impurities are gradually separated from it. The polycrystalline silicon is then melted, and a single crystal seed is placed in contact with it. The seed crystal is then slowly rotated and drawn away from the molten silicon. forming a monocrystalline silicon cylinder. The ingots are then ground to produce a 'flat' that parallels the growth axis and sliced, into wafers of 500 micrometres thickness and 5 centimetres diameter, using diamond slicing saws. These wafers are then cleaned and chemically etched to produce a highly polished surface. The wafer forms the basis of a large number of individual chips, each with surface areas of the order of square millimetres. Each chip comprises a complicated pattern of embedded zones of various semiconductor materials.

The zones are produced by successive imaging and deposition or growth processes. An individual bipolar transistor, for example, is produced by forming minute zones of p- and n-type semiconductor material corresponding to the base, collector and emitter regions. The imaging process exposes certain areas of the chip surface, corresponding to circuit components, or parts thereof, to provide access windows for subsequent processes. In the photographic process a large mask is cut accurately by machine, and its image is then reduced photographically to wafer size. The wafer surface is coated with a photoresist material and, like all operations in chip manufacture, extreme precautions are taken to protect the surfaces from contamination.

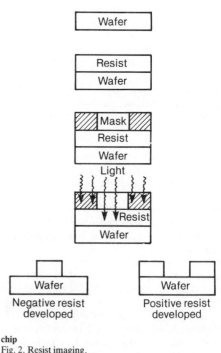

chip
Fig. 2. Resist imaging.

The mask is placed over the wafer surface, which is then exposed to ultraviolet light; the photoresist is developed with the consequent removal of the exposed (positive resist) or unexposed (negative resist) areas. An etching process then removes the exposed portions of the surface layer material, and finally the remainder of the photoresist is removed. The deposition and growth

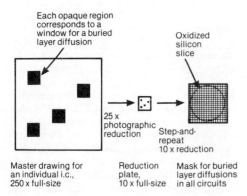

chip
Fig. 1. The production of one of a series of photographic masks required for the manufacture of an array of integrated circuits (not to scale).

processes add new layers to the wafer or introduce changes into the properties of chip material through windows produced by the imaging process. Silicon dioxide is a very stable material and is used to inhibit diffusion processes over certain parts of the surface or as an insulating layer (i.e. in metal oxide semiconductor components). The oxide layer is produced by heating the wafer in an oxygen or steam atmosphere.

Epitaxy is a deposition process wherein a single crystal layer is applied to a silicon wafer of the same crystal orientation. In this case the wafer surface is cleaned chemically, and the wafer is heated in a carefully controlled atmosphere of silicon tetrachloride and hydrogen which deposits silicon onto the wafer surface. The new layer is usually required to have a different level of p- or n-type concentration to that of the substrate, and the necessary dopant can be introduced into the vapour in the reactor.

Diffusion and ion implementation techniques enable atoms of impurities to be introduced into zones of the wafer, thus producing the individual circuit components or parts thereof. In the diffusion process windows, cut in the silicon dioxide layer by the imaging process, reveal the areas of surface that are to receive the impurity atoms. Dopants are introduced onto the surface of the heated wafer and are allowed to diffuse into the material. Ion implementation techniques are used to place impurity ions in semiconductor layers at variously controlled depths and with accurate control of the dopant ion concentrations. A beam of ions, produced by the collisions of electrons and neutral atoms, is accelerated and focused by electric fields onto the surface of the chip. The surface of the chip is masked by thick layers of silicon dioxide or photoresist material according to the required patterns of circuit components.

Aluminium metallization is used to provide an interconnection layer on the integrated circuits, making low-resistance contacts to the devices formed in the silicon, and connecting these to bonding pads on the chip's edge. Various techniques are employed to deposit a layer of aluminium about 2 micrometres thick on the chip. When the circuit components have been produced by the successive operations described above, the circuit operation is tested so that deficient chips can be elimi-

nated before the subsequent costly packaging operation. The wafer is separated into the individual chips by diamond scribing and cleaving. Each circuit chip is fixed to a suitable header and fine wires, of gold or aluminium, are bonded to circuit terminal pads to form connections between the chip components and the outside world. The chip is then encapsulated and circuits tested. *See* BASE, COLLECTOR, CUSTOM DESIGN, DOPANT, EMITTER, EPITAXIAL LAYER, ETCHING, INTEGRATED CIRCUIT, METAL OXIDE SEMICONDUCTOR, NEGATIVE RESIST, N-TYPE MATERIAL, PHOTORESIST, POSITIVE RESIST, P-TYPE MATERIAL, RESISTANCE, SEMICONDUCTOR, TRANSISTOR, WAFER.

chip architecture. In computing, the arrangement of chips forming a microprocessor chip (i.e. the arithmetic logic unit, general-purpose registers and the control bus structure). *See* ARITHMETIC LOGIC UNIT, CHIP, CONTROL BUS.

chip card. *Synonymous with* SMART CARD.

chip microprocessor. In microelectronics, a set of large-scale integration circuits on a single silicon chip capable of performing the essential functions of a central processing unit. *See* CENTRAL PROCESSING UNIT, CHIP, CHIP ARCHITECTURE, LARGE-SCALE INTEGRATION.

chip modem. In data communications, a modem contained in a single silicon chip. *See* CHIP, MODEM.

CHIPS. In banking, Clearing House Interbank Payments System; a private telecommunications payment service operated by the New York Clearing House Association for banks in the New York area that handles US dollar payments only. (ANSI). *Compare* CHAPS. *See* BANKING NETWORKS, SWIFT.

chip select line. In computing, a circuit which, when activated, enables or selects one and only one of several units. *See* CHIP.

chip set. In microelectronics, a single functional unit produced by the interconnection of a set of integrated circuits. *See* CHIP, MICROPROCESSOR.

chipspeech. In microelectronics, an integrated circuit that stores the sound of speech in digital form for playback. *See* SPEECH SYNTHESIZER.

chop. In mathematics, a method of rounding off numbers by truncating towards zero (i.e. 1.63 becomes 1.6 and −1.63 becomes −1.6). *See* ROUND-OFF ERRORS.

chord keying. In peripherals, a keyboard safeguard in which two or more keys must be depressed simultaneously in order to action critical commands from the keyboard.

CHPS. *See* CHARACTERS PER SECOND.

chroma. The measure of hue and saturation of a colour, undiluted with white, black or grey. *See* SATURATION.

chroma control. In television, the control regulating colour saturation in a receiver. *See* SATURATION.

chroma detector. In television, black and white circuitry eliminating colour burst by sensing absence of chrominance signal in a receiver. *See* COLOUR BURST, CHROMINANCE SIGNAL, COMPOSITE COLOUR VIDEO SIGNAL.

chroma key. *Synonymous with* COLOUR KEY.

chromatic aberration. In optics, a lens defect that causes colours to be focused at different points and so producing coloured fringe haloes.

chromatic dispersion. In optoelectronics, dispersion or distortion of a pulse in an optical waveguide due to differences in wave velocity caused by variation in the indices of refraction for different portions of the guide. *See* FIBER OPTICS, REFRACTIVE INDEX.

chromaticity. In optics, the colour quality of light definable by its dominant wavelength and its purity.

chrominance signal. In television, the transmitted signal providing information on hue and saturation. *See* COMPOSITE COLOUR VIDEO SIGNAL, HUE, LUMINANCE SIGNAL, SATURATION.

chromium dioxide. In audio recording, a magnetic tape coating that offers improved

signal-to-noise ratio. *See* SIGNAL-TO-NOISE RATIO.

C-MAC. In television, a standard to be used in direct-broadcast satellites to provide an enhanced picture quality. The synchronization, luminance, chrominance and sound signals are transmitted in time division multiplex. *Compare* A-MAC. *See* CHROMINANCE SIGNAL, LUMINANCE SIGNAL, MAC.

CMI. *See* COMPUTER-MANAGED INSTRUCTION.

CML. Computer-managed learning. *Synonymous with* COMPUTER-MANAGED INSTRUCTION.

CMOS. *See* COMPLEMENTARY METAL OXIDE SEMICONDUCTOR.

C/N. *See* CARRIER-TO-NOISE RATIO.

CNN. *See* CABLE NEWS NETWORK.

CNP. *See* COMMUNICATIONS NETWORK PROCESSOR.

COAM. In data communications, customer-owned and maintained communication equipment (e.g. terminals).

coated. In printing, printing papers that have had a surface covering of clay, etc. to give a smoother, more even finish with greater opacity. (Desktop).

coaxial cable. In electronics, a low-loss cable, used for high frequencies, that consists of a conductor within, and insulated from, a tube of braided copper. *See* SHIELDED CABLE.

COBOL. In programming, COmmon Business-Oriented Language. COBOL has found very extensive use in most areas of business computing, typically commercial, government and accounting systems. It is intended mainly for applications involving comparatively simple calculations and manipulations on large quantities of data and is therefore a compiled language. The language was designed for readability and thus is effectively self-documenting. It originated by the CODASYL committee in the early 1960s. *See* CODASYL, COMPILER.

CODASYL. In databases, Conference for Data System Languages; a group created by the US Department of Defense. It includes users and manufacturers and considers the development of COBOL and hardware-independent software for database management. *See* COBOL, DATABASE MANAGEMENT SYSTEM.

CODATA. Committee on Data for Science and Technology of the International Council of Scientific Unions.

code. (1) In programming, the instructions or statements of a program, or the act of generating them. (2) In data communications, a system of symbols used to convert alphanumeric information into a form suitable for communications transmission. *See* AMERICAN STANDARD CODE FOR INFORMATION INTERCHANGE, BAUDOT CODE, CHARACTER CODE. (3) A set of rules outlining the way in which data may be represented. (4) In data security, a method of sending secret messages. Each word or phrase is substituted by a corresponding group of symbols derived from a secret codebook. *Compare* CIPHER.

code area. In micrographics, a part of the film frame reserved for the retrieval code.

CODEC. In communications, coder/decoder; a device that converts analog signals (e.g. speech, television, music to digital form) for transmission over a digital network and to reconvert them back to analog form. *See* ANALOG SIGNAL, ANALOG-TO-DIGITAL CONVERTER, DIGITAL-TO-ANALOG CONVERTER.

code conversion. In data communications, a process for changing the bit grouping of one character in a code into the corresponding grouping for a character in a second code (e.g. from ASCII code to EBCDIC). *See* AMERICAN STANDARD CODE FOR INFORMATION INTERCHANGE, EBCDIC CODE. *Synonymous with* CHARACTER MAPPING.

coded image. In computer graphics, a display image that is represented in a form suitable for processing.

code division multiple access. (CDMA) In communications, a multiple-access technique whereby groups of users may transmit simultaneously using the same frequency bands. The signals are encoded so that information from a particular transmitter is only recovered by the appropriate receiving station. *Compare* FREQUENCY DIVISION MULTIPLE ACCESS, TIME DIVISION MULTIPLE ACCESS.

code extension character. In codes, a control character used to indicate that one or more of the succeeding code values are to be interpreted according to a special code. *See* ESCAPE CODE, LOCKING, SHIFT CODES.

code group. *See* CODE SYSTEM.

code-independent system. In data communications, a mode of transmission employing a character-oriented link protocol that is independent of the character set or code used by the data source. *See* LINK PROTOCOL.

code key. In word processing, a special typewriter key that, when depressed in conjunction with a designated key, initiates special modes of operation.

code level. In codes, the number of bits used to represent a character. *See* BIT, BYTE.

code line. In micrographics, a series of horizontal bars placed adjacent to each frame of a microfilm used to assist in the location of required frames. As the film passes rapidly in searching the bar is seen to rise (or fall), and the search is stopped when it attains a predetermined position. *See* MICROFILM.

coden. In library science, a five-character code with a unique mnemonic relationship to the title of a periodical or serial.

coder. In programming, a person who produces a program from a detailed specification of that program. *Compare* PROGRAMMER. *See* CODING.

code set. In codes, a finite and complete set of representations defined by a code. *See* CODE.

code system. (1) A means of converting information into a form suitable for communications or encryption (e.g. coded speech, Morse codes, teletypewriter codes). (FIPS). *See* BREVITY LISTS, ENCRYPTION. (2) In computer security, any system of communication in which groups of symbols are used to represent plaintext elements of varying length. (FIPS). *See* PLAINTEXT. (3) In data security, a cryptographic system in which cryptographic equivalents (usually called code groups) typically consisting of letters, digits or both in meaningless combinations are substituted for plaintext elements which may be words, phrases or sentences. (FIPS).

code value.   In codes, one element of a code set (e.g. the eight-bit code value for the delete character).

codeword.   In codes, a combination of message bits and parity bits formed into a word of fixed length. *See* ERROR SYNDROME, N,K CODE, PARITY CHECKING.

coding.   In programming, the process of producing a detailed program from a well-documented specification. The activity demands a knowledge of the detailed syntax of the language, but does not require design decisions associated with the overall development of the program. It may be performed automatically or by junior programming staff. *Compare* PROGRAMMING. *See* CODER.

coercivity.   In electronics, the reverse magnetic field necessary to reduce the magnetic flux to zero after the field has been increased to produce flux saturation and then reduced to zero. *See* DEGAUSS.

cognitive domain.   The category of instructional objectives relating to knowledge, information and other intellectual skills within human behaviour.

cogwheel effect.   In television, a staggered vertical image produced by the relative displacement of alternate scan lines. *See* SCANNING LINE.

coherence.   In optics, pertaining to electromagnetic radiation (e.g. light) where the individual waves are in phase. *See* IN PHASE, LASER.

coherent bundle.   In optoelectronics, a bundle of optical fibers in which the spatial coordinates are the same, or bear the same spatial relationship to each other, at the two ends of the bundle. *See* BUNDLE, FIBER OPTICS.

cohesion.   In systems analysis, a measure of the degree to which the elements within a given module relate to the accomplishment of a simple identifiable task. *See* STRUCTURED SYSTEMS ANALYSIS.

CoI.   Central Office of Information; the UK government agency dealing with information and publicity.

coincidence circuit.   (1) In electronics, a digital comparator circuit that detects the equality of two binary words. (2) In electronics, a circuit that detects the simultaneous occurrence of two digital events and produces an output. *Compare* ANTI-COINCIDENCE CIRCUIT.

coin denomination use.   In communications, a tone sent to a telephone operator to indicate the value of a coin inserted in a coinbox.

cold standby.   In reliability, the use of a backup computer in the event of a failure in the main system. Any data in the main memory of the computer at the time of failure, and not recorded in backing storage, will be lost. *Compare* WARM STANDBY, HOT STANDBY. *See* BACKING STORAGE.

cold start.   (1) In computing, the act of starting up a computer after power on. The computer has no programs in volatile storage, and they must be loaded from read-only memory or backing storage. *See* BOOT LOAD, VOLATILE STORAGE. (2) In computing, the restart process used when a serious failure has occurred in a system such that the contents of the memory become inaccessible and all information on the recent processing is lost. The computer must be reloaded and activity restarted as though at the beginning of the processing or from the last rescue dump. *See* RESCUE DUMP.

cold type.   In printing, type produced without the use of characters cast from molten metal, such as on a visual display unit. (Desktop). *See* VISUAL DISPLAY UNIT.

collate. (1) In data processing, to combine two or more similar sets of items to produce another similar set. (2) In printing, to check through the pagination or signatures of the sections of a book to ensure that they are complete and in the correct sequence for binding. *See* SIGNATURE.

collating marks. In printing, marks used to check for any displacement of printed material after gathering. They are black step marks printed on the back folds of sections and in progressively different positions. *See* GATHERING.

collect call. In communications, a telephone call in which the caller requests that the charge be paid by the called party.

collector. In electronics, a terminal on a transistor. *Compare* BASE, EMITTER. *See* TRANSISTOR.

collimator. In optics, a device for measuring the position of an image formed by a lens in relation to the film plane of a camera.

collision. In data communications, a transmission failure in a network caused by simultaneous transmission from two or more terminals. *See* CONTENTION CONTROL, CARRIER SENSE MULTIPLE ACCESS — COLLISION DETECTION.

collotype. In printing, a photomechanical, non-screen planographic process in which the printing is performed from a gelatine film. The process is used in art reproductions. *See* PHOTOMECHANICAL, PLANOGRAPHIC.

colophon. In printing, an inscription with information relating to the production of the book. It is usually placed at the end of a book.

colour. (1) The psychological sensation arising as a result of ocular perception of and discrimination between various wavelengths of light. (2) In printing, the degree of lightness or heaviness in appearance of a particular typeface.

colour balance. (1) In photography, the relative sensitivity of film to light of various wavelengths. (2) In television, adjustment of the colour controls to give a visually satisfying image, usually based on skin tones.

colour bars. In video, a bar-shaped test pattern on the leader of a video tape. It is used to match the playback to the original recording levels and phasing. *See* LEADER.

colour bar signals. In television, a video test signal for colour television equipment.

colour break-up. In peripherals, a separation of the primary colour components of a visual display unit image due to a rapid horizontal movement in the field of view. *See* VISUAL DISPLAY UNIT.

colour burst. In television, a signal of eight cycles of 3.58 MHz transmitted on the back porch of a composite colour signal. The phase of the following video signal is compared with that of the colour burst to determine the hue of the colour signal. *See* BACK PORCH, COMPOSITE COLOUR VIDEO SIGNAL, HUE.

colour cell. In peripherals, the smallest area of the phosphor screen of a display tube that can reproduce complete colour information. *See* CATHODE RAY TUBE, PHOSPHOR DOTS.

colour-compensating filter. In photography, a yellow, magenta or cyan filter which absorbs small amounts of either red, green or blue. It is used on cameras or in printers to make slight corrections in the colour of the light used. *See* FILTER.

colour contamination. In television, an error in the colour reproduction of an object due to defects in the optical, electronic or mechanical paths of the system.

colour decoder. In television, the apparatus for deriving the receiver primary signals from the colour picture signal and the colour burst. *See* COLOUR BURST, COMPOSITE COLOUR VIDEO SIGNAL.

colour encoder. In television, a device that produces an NTSC encoder colour signal from separate red, green and blue video inputs. It may also generate the colour burst. *See* COLOUR BURST, VIDEO STANDARDS.

colour key. In optical media, a system based upon matching to control overlay transparency. A technique in which parts of an image are determined to be transparent based upon their colour values. (Philips). *Synonymous with* CHROMA KEY.

colour look-up table. In computer graphics and optical media, a means of compressing the amount of information needed to store colour pictorial information by allowing only a specific number of colours (tints and brightnesses) and holding these values in a table. The colour of a given pixel is then defined as a value from this table. (Philips). *See* PIXEL.

colour raster printer. *See* ELECTROSTATIC PLOTTER.

colour saturation. *See* SATURATION.

colour separation. In printing, an electronic or photographic process to separate the various colours of an original, by the use of colour filters, so that separate printing plates can be produced. *See* FILTER.

colour shift. In television, an unwanted colour change in a transmitted picture.

colour temperature. In photography, a concept formulated for the purpose of reference to and standardization of colour of light sources. When a black body, such as a carbon filament, is heated until it glows, the colour of the radiant light is directly related to the temperature of the filament. It is measured in Kelvins (K). *See* BLACK BODY.

colour transparency. In photography, a usually positive colour picture on a transparent film.

colour work. In printing, the process of printing more than one colour on a sheet.

columnar graph. *Synonymous with* BAR CHART.

column balancing. In printing, a process in which text within columns is redistributed so that the amount of text is approximately equal in each column.

column inch. In printing, a measure of area used in newspapers and magazines to calcu-late the cost of display advertising. A column inch is one column wide and one inch deep. (Desktop).

column move and delete. In word processing, a facility permitting text to be manipulated by column, as compared with normal row manipulation. It is used in tabular work.

column rule. In printing, a light-faced vertical rule used to separate columns of type. (Desktop). *See* LIGHT FACE.

COM. *See* COMPUTER OUTPUT TO MICROFILM.

coma. In optics, a lens aberration resulting in a variation of magnification with aperture. Rays through the outer edges of a lens form a larger image than those through the centre.

comb. In memory systems, an assembly of seek arms in a multiple-disk, movable-head magnetic disk unit. The seek arms hold the read/write heads that are moved to the appropriate track of the disks. *See* HEAD, MAGNETIC DISK, MOVABLE-HEAD DISK, TRACK.

combination. In mathematics, a given number of different elements selected from a set without constraint on the order in which the selected elements are arranged. *Compare* PERMUTATION.

combinational circuit. *See* COMBINATIONAL LOGIC.

combinational logic. In electronics, a logic circuit in which the output depends only upon the instantaneous discrete states of the circuit inputs and is not a function of any previous inputs. *Compare* SEQUENTIAL LOGIC.

combinatorics. In mathematics, a branch of mathematics dealing with enumeration and counting problems.

combined station. In data communications, the station used in high-level data link control procedures. A combined station generates and interprets both commands and responses. *See* HIGH-LEVEL DATA LINK CONTROL.

combiner. (1) In cable television, a device enabling two or more input signals to be fed to a single output without interaction. (2) In communications, a device enabling two or more transmitters to use a single antenna simultaneously.

combi player. In optical media, a combined LaserVison and compact disc player. (Philips). *See* COMPACT DISC, LaserVision.

comet tail. In television, a smear on a television picture produced by a moving light source or hot spot. *See* HOT SPOT.

comic strip-oriented image. In micrographics, an image appearing on roll microfilm in such a way that the long edge of the film and the top edge of the image are parallel. *Compare* CINE-ORIENTED IMAGE.

COMINT. Communications intelligence.

command. In computing, a character string from a source external to a system that represents a request for system action.

command language. (1) In programming, a source language consisting principally of procedural operations, each capable of invoking a function to be executed. *See* PROCEDURE, SOURCE LANGUAGE. (2) In online information retrieval, a language comprising the instructions and terms used by the searcher to communicate with the host computer. Various online host computers use different command languages.

comma-separated value. *See* CSV.

comment. In programming, a phrase included in a computer program to assist the programmer in debugging operations by highlighting some aspect of the program. Comments are ignored by translators and have no effect upon the program execution. *See* DEBUG, TRANSLATOR.

commentary. In filming, the narration for a film spoken by an off-screen voice in voice-over situations. *See* VOICE OVER.

Commercial COMSEC Endorsement Program. In data security, a program established by NSA for the protection of government information. Following NSDD-145 this program will be adapted to make

NSA COMSEC modules available to the private sector. *See* NSA COMSEC MODULE.

commissioning. The process of running a system under normal working conditions during a trial period to ensure that it is operating according to specifications.

commit. In databases, a command to update the database according to the set of transactions input to the system. *Compare* ROLLBACK. *See* TRANSACTION.

common. In programming, a method of passing data between subroutines employed in FORTRAN and some versions of BASIC. A storage area is declared to be common and data placed in that area can be retrieved by a routine that has similarly declared a common area. *See* BASIC, FORTRAN, PARAMETER PASSING, SUBROUTINE.

common carrier. In communications, a company that supplies communication facilities to the public. The term is derived from the interstate commerce concept of carrying goods. In the USA a communication common carrier comes under the jurisdiction of relevant state organizations, and if it operates interstate facilities it will be subject to Federal Communications Commission regulations. Common carriers can carry telemetry, facsimile, television and data messages. *Compare* VALUE-ADDED NETWORK SERVICE. *See* TELEMETRY.

common-channel signalling. In communications, a signalling technique in which signalling information relating to a multiplicity of circuits and information for network management is conveyed over a single channel by addressed messages. *Compare* SEPARATE-CHANNEL SIGNALLING. *See* SIGNALLING.

communicating word processing. (CWP) In data communications, word processing equipment capable of transmitting and receiving text and data. With such systems internal mail or mail between connected external systems involves no paper-handling or postal system. *See* TELETEX.

communication. The process of transferring information in the various media from one point, person or device to another.

See DATA COMMUNICATIONS, TELECOMMU-
NICATIONS.

communication buffer. In communications, a terminal that has a buffer. *See*
BUFFER.

communication control unit. (CCU) In
data communications, a device employed to
control the transmission of data over telecommunication lines in a network. *See* COM-
MUNICATION SCANNER.

communication link. The physical means
of connecting one location to another for the
purpose of transmitting and receiving
information.

communication processor. *See* FRONT-END
PROCESSOR.

Communications Act, 1934. An Act of
Congress that established the Federal Com-
munications Commission. *See* FEDERAL
COMMUNICATIONS COMMISSION.

Communication Satellite Act, 1962. An
Act of Congress that established COMSAT.
See COMSAT.

communication scanner. In data communications, a device connected between communication lines and a communication
control unit. It is employed to monitor the
lines and data links for service requests. *See*
COMMUNICATION CONTROL UNIT.

communications computer. In data communications, a computer that manages the
control of lines and the routing of data in a
network. *See* ROUTING.

communication server. *See* SERVER. *Synonymous with* GATEWAY.

communications interface adaptor. In computing, an intelligent device on a bus-
organized computer system that provides
interface functions between the bus and a
modem. *See* BUS, MODEM, PERIPHERAL INTER-
FACE ADAPTOR, UART.

communications link controller. (CLC) In
data communications, an intelligent unit that
provides line-oriented interface functions
(e.g. error detection, synchronization,

acknowledgements) between a group of
modems and a computer or communications
network processor. *See* COMMUNICATIONS
NETWORK PROCESSOR, MODEM.

communications network processor. (CNP)
In data communications, an intelligent unit
that performs interface functions (e.g. buffering, code conversion, queue management) between a computer and one or more
communications link controllers. *See* COM-
MUNICATIONS LINK CONTROLLER.

communications satellite system. In communications, a system of earth-orbiting communications satellites and associated ground
stations for the purpose of transmitting telephone, television and data signals. *See* DISH
ANTENNA, EUTELSAT, GEOSTATIONARY SAT-
ELLITE, GROUND STATION, INTELSAT,
INTERSPUTNIK, TELEVISION RECEIVE-ONLY.

communications security. In data security,
the protection that ensures the authenticity
of telecommunications and that results from
the application of measures taken to deny
unauthorized persons information of value
which might be derived from the acquisition
of telecommunications. (FIPS). *See* COM-
PUTER SECURITY, DATA SECURITY.

communication theory. In mathematics,
the topic dealing with the transmission of
messages in the presence of noise. *See*
INFORMATION THEORY, NOISE, SHANNON'S LAW.

community antenna relay station. In television, a specific microwave frequency band
(12.75–12.95 MHz), provided by the Federal
Communications Commission for transmission of signals to cable television head
ends. *Compare* MASTER ANTENNA TELEVISION
SYSTEM. *See* CABLE TELEVISION RELAY PICKUP
STATION, HEAD END.

community antenna television. (CATV) In
cable television, a subscriber system in
which a single master antenna provides television reception for a whole geographical
area. *See* MASTER ANTENNA TELEVISION
SYSTEM.

commutative law. In mathematics, a binary
operation (i.e. one involving two variables)
satisfies the commutative law if

$$x * y = y * x$$

where x and y are the variables and $*$ represents the binary operation. *Compare* ASSOCIATIVE LAW, DISTRIBUTIVE LAW.

compact cassette. In recording, a 3.81-mm audio tape attached to two hubs inside a plastic container for self-threading, which may be used in fast forward and rewind modes. *See* CARTRIDGE.

compact disc. (CD) In optical media, a system for the reproduction of high-density digital data from an optical disc. Originally conceived as a medium for high-fidelity music reproduction, for which compact disc – digital audio is now an accepted world standard. Because of the very high disc data storage capacity compact discs are being applied as a text/data medium for electronic publishing (compact disc – read-only memory) and a multiple function (audio/video/text/data) medium for interactive programs (compact disc – interactive). (Philips). *See* COMPACT DISC – DIGITAL AUDIO, COMPACT DISC – INTERACTIVE, COMPACT DISC – READ-ONLY MEMORY.

compact disc – digital audio. (CD-DA) In optical media, a high-fidelity recording medium with pure sound reproduction, small size and immunity from surface scratching, developed jointly by Philips and Sony, and launched in October 1982.

The compact disc system records music, in the form of digital data, onto a light, but robust, 12-centimetre diameter disc, thereby virtually eliminating the problems of dynamic range, background noise, wow and flutter, and other sound disturbances common to earlier sound recording systems. 32-bit analog-to-digital conversion at a sampling rate of 44.1 kHz, in conjunction cross-interleaved Reed-Solomon code error correction and eight-to-fourteen modulation, gives a reproducible bandwidth of 10 Hz to 20 kHz within 0.2 dB, a signal-to-noise ratio of over 100 dB, a dynamic range of over 95 dB, and imperceptible wow and flutter.

The main distinguishing feature between compact disc and other audio recording systems, however, lies in its use of optical recording technology. With this technology a small laser is used to burn minute pits in an optically flat surface which is enclosed in a transparent sandwich disc construction. For playback the recorded surface is illuminated with a low-power laser. The light beam is concentrated onto the protected recording surface as the disc is rotated. Light is reflected from the recording surface and passed to a photosensor. The amount of light reflected from the disc surface changes depending on whether or not the beam is passing over a pit made during the recording process.

The pits, between 0.9 and 3.3 micrometres long and 0.6 micrometres wide are recorded on a spiral track at a pitch of 1.6 micrometres, 60 times the pitch of a LP record. The track is approximately 5 kilometres long. The music recorded in a normal recording studio is encoded into the CD-DA format and used to drive a recording laser to produce a master disc. Mechanical stamper discs are produced from the original master, and copy discs are then pressed in quantity from these stampers in a specially developed replication process.

The high recording density, achievable with optical recording techniques, results in over one hour of high-quality sound recorded on one side of the disc, the other side being used only for the disc label. CD-DA discs are designed for playback at constant linear velocity. This means that the speed, at which the track is scanned by the laser, pickup is a constant 1.25 metres per second. As a result, the speed of rotation of the disc changes as the disc is played. Play starts at the inside of the recording track and runs outwards. As the music is played, the rotational speed of the disc drops from some 500 rpm at the beginning of the disc to approximately 200 rpm at the end.

Apart from the main data channel, via which the hi-fi music is stored, an additional eight subchannels, with a much lower data capacity, are also available for control and display purposes. These subchannels, known as P, Q through to W are generally available to the recording studio. However, apart from the P and Q subchannels, little use is made of these subchannels in practice. Although the R to W channels have, in fact, been specified for a simple graphics application, no subchannel graphics decoders have as yet become generally available.

The disc surface is divided into three main portions: (a) the lead-in area at the centre or start of the disc; (b) the program area; and the lead-out area at the outside of the disc. In the lead-in area, the Q subchannel is used to store details of the contents of the disc. Up to 99 separate music tracks can be specified. A single track has a minimum duration of 4 seconds and a maximum duration of 72 minutes (the whole disc). The location of each track on a given disc, in terms of absolute time in minutes and seconds, relative to the start of the program area on the disc, as well as the running time of each track, is defined in the Q subchannel in the lead-in area. The P subchannel carries a music flag for the quick track finding using a simple decoder. (Philips). *See* CD MASTER-ING, CONSTANT LINEAR VELOCITY, CROSS-INTERLEAVING REED-SOLOMON CODE, EIGHT-TO-FOURTEEN MODULATION, FLUTTER, LASER, P CHANNEL, PHOTOSENSOR, Q CHANNEL, STAM-PER, TRACK, WOW.

compact disc drive. In optical media, a device that specifically reads digital data from read-only memory or interactive compact discs (CD-I). CD-I drives can also play digital audio compact discs. *See* COMPACT DISC − DIGITAL AUDIO, COMPACT DISC − INTER-ACTIVE, COMPACT DISC − READ-ONLY MEMORY.

compact disc − interactive. (CD-I) In optical media, a multi-application-based compact disc technology targeted at the consumer electronic and institutional markets.

The CD-I standard specifies a multi-media interactive information carrier that is mainly real-time audio- and video-driven, but also has text, binary data and computer program capabilities. It is both a media and a system specification, and defines what can be present on the disc, how it is coded and organized, and how disc/system compatibility can be maintained.

From a technical point of view, CD-I is based on the read-only memory compact disc (CD-ROM), but from a player/product view it is based on digital audio compact disc (CD-DA). Like CD-DA, it is dependent on processor hardware, but unlike CD-DA or CD-ROM, it is also system software-dependent. The hardware and system software dependence of CD-I is based on the real-time audio/video decoding and data-handling requirements that CD-I applications demand, as well as the requirements to maintain disc/system interchangeability. In

practice, this means that any CD-I disc can be played on any CD-I player. This degree of compatibility is achieved in the CD-I specification by defining a set of rules for a minimum-level system called the base case, which must be observed by all discs.

The CD-I specification also allows for mixing of CD-DA and CD-I tracks on CD-I discs and requires CD-DA decoding hardware in CD-I systems. The CD-I specification is a complete standard that:

(a) is applicable to the consumer market;
(b) can be realized as one disc, interactive, multimedia content carrier (i.e. a CD-I disc) by various content providers (e.g. publishers, the audiovisual industry, etc.);
(c) is capable of being produced by the existing CD manufacturing facilities;
(d) assures disc/system compatibility.

Present and potential future CD-I applications are categorized below.

(a) Education and training: do it yourself, home learning, reference books, albums, 'talking books'.
(b) Entertainment: 'music plus' (music with text, notes, pictures, etc.), action games, adventure games, activity simulation, edutainment.
(c) Creative leisure: drawing/painting, filming, composing.
(d) Work at home/while travelling: document processing, information retrieval and analysis.
(e) Travelling: maps, navigation, tourist information, real-time animation, diagnostics. (Philips).

See BASE CASE SYSTEM, CARIN, COMPACT DISC − DIGITAL AUDIO, COMPACT DISC − READ-ONLY MEMORY, EDUTAINMENT.

compact disc − read-only memory. (CD-ROM) In optical media, a derivative of digital audio compact (CD-DA) technology using the identical physical characteristics: disc size, rotational speed, read-out mechanism, disc mastering and replication processes. The distinction between CD-ROM and CD-DA lies in their application areas. CD-DA has a single application (i.e. hi-fi music), whereas the CD-ROM specification merely limits itself to the manner in which data is stored on the disc, leaving the question of application to the information providers making use of the medium.

The disc can be divided into tracks in the same manner as for CD-DA; in fact the specification allows for the possibility of combining CD-DA tracks with CD-ROM tracks on a single disc. CD-ROM also makes use of the cross-interleaved Reed-Solomon code error-correcting codes and eight-to-fourteen modulation as CD-DA. However the data recorded on the disc is organized into sectors of 2352 bytes. Each sector is subdivided: (a) 12 bytes of synchronization; (b) a four-byte header to identify the address and nature or mode, of the data in the block; (c) 2048 bytes for the main user data area; and (d) 288 bytes for the auxiliary data area.

The mode information for CD-ROM is listed below.

(a) Mode 0: used for CD-DA applications.
(b) Mode 1: the normal mode for CD-ROM, in which an additional level of error protection (EDC/ECC) is included in the auxiliary data area to reduce the chance of error to less than one bit per disc.
(c) Mode 2: allocates the auxiliary data area for additional user data; thus each sector contains 2336 bytes of user data.

The mode being used is fixed for the duration of a track. Details of the modes of all tracks are also held in the Q subchannel in the lead-in area of each disc.

The data rate from the disc is 175 kilobytes per second (i.e. 75 (175 000/2352) sectors per second). The minimum length of each track is 4 seconds, the minimum track thus containing 300 (4 x 75) sectors. The total disc has 72 minutes of playing time giving 663.5 (72 x 60 x 75 x 2048) megabytes of user data for mode 1 and 756.8 megabytes for mode 2. A CD-ROM can hold the equivalent of 165 000 pages of typed text, although some of the CD-ROM data space will be occupied by indexes necessary for data searching.

A number of CD-ROM drives are available together with standard hardware interfaces to connect CD-ROM drives to personal computers. CD-ROM is finding a well-defined place in the professional world for the distribution of bulk databases. Typical applications involve the replacement of text-based microfiche publishing or online databases. In order to locate data, on such a large-capacity disc as CD-ROM, personal computer versions of mainframe database retrieval software are normally used. Such software, adapted to the requirements of CD-ROM drives, used in conjunction with inverted files to identify the specific occurrence of each given word in the total database, can be used very effectively. Typical seek times of three to 10 seconds are now quite normal for text-based databases of several hundred megabytes.

A further feature of CD-ROM is that the data is stored in digital form, and as such data retrieved from the disc can be reproduced or re-edited by suitable word-processing software.

Although CD-ROM is best suited to text-based information, applications using drawings and pictures have also been demonstrated. However, no standard applications have yet been agreed between manufacturers, such applications in practice requiring specifically defined encoding and decoding hardware and software. Specific dedicated applications will nevertheless continue to grow for CD-ROM in selected market niches.

During 1985 and 1986 an ad hoc group of information providers and companies met in an attempt to extend the basic CD-ROM specification to cover such matters as file structure, file directory index and operating system. This group, known as the High Sierra group, after the the hotel at Lake Tahoe where the group first met, passed its recommendations to the standards committees. (Philips). See AUXILIARY DATA FIELD, CD MASTERING, CD-ROM PUBLISHING, COMPACT DISC – DIGITAL AUDIO, CROSS-INTERLEAVED REED-SOLOMON CODE, EDC/ECC, EIGHT-TO-FOURTEEN MODULATION, INFORMATION PROVIDER, INVERTED FILE, ONLINE INFORMATION RETRIEVAL, OPTICAL DIGITAL DISC, SECTOR, SUBCODE CHANNEL.

compact floppy disk. *Synonymous with* MICROFLOPPY DISK.

COMPANDOR. In communications, compressor expander; a device that compresses the range of signal amplitudes during telephone transmission to provide a more uniform response to strong and weak inputs. At the transmitting end, strong signals are attenuated, and weak signals are amplified; a reverse process occurs at the receiving end to restore signals to their original volume. *Compare* VOGAD.

comparator. (1) In electronics, a circuit that provides an output indicating whether two input signals are, or are not, equal. (2) In computing, a device for determining the similarity, or otherwise, of two words or patterns. *See* WORD.

compare instruction. In programming, a machine code instruction that checks for a zero difference between two specified words and returns the result true or false, which is then normally used by a conditional jump instruction. *See* CONDITIONAL JUMP.

compartmentalization. (1) In computer security, the isolation of the operating system, user programs and data files from one another in main storage in order to provide protection against unauthorized or concurrent access by other users or programs. (FIPS). *See* ACCESS. (2) In data security, the breaking down of sensitive data into small, isolated blocks for the purpose of reducing risk to the data. (FIPS). (3) In computer security, a principle of design that a failure or a harmful event in one part of a system should not be allowed to spread into another part of the system (e.g. smoke or harmful gases should not be allowed to spread outside a given area). *See* HARMFUL EVENT.

compatibility. (1) In optical media, the extent to which different types of compact discs can be interpreted by different types of players or drives. For example, all CD-DA discs are fully compatible with all digital audio compact disc players so that any player can reproduce music from any disc regardless of manufacturer. (Philips). *See* COMPACT DISC – DIGITAL AUDIO. (2) In data communications, pertaining to pairs of devices that have met the requirements for code, speed and signal level conversion to enable direct interconnections. (3) In computing, pertaining to machines on which programs may be interchanged without appreciable modification. *Compare* NON-COMPATIBILITY.

compatible data. In memory systems, data recorded on different storage media that can still be used in conjunction. (Philips).

COMPENDEX. In online information retrieval, Computerized Engineering Index; a database supplied by Engineering Information Inc. and dealing with engineering.

compiler. In programming, a program designed to translate a high-level language source program into a corresponding machine code program. The compiler checks for, and reports, any syntax errors in the source program. If the source program is syntax error-free then a complete object code program is produced. *Compare* ASSEMBLER, INTERPRETER. *See* HIGH-LEVEL LANGUAGE, MACHINE LANGUAGE, OBJECT CODE, SOURCE PROGRAM, SYNTAX.

complement. (1) In mathematics, to change a bit from 0 to 1, or vice versa, in binary arithmetic. *See* BIT, BOOLEAN ALGEBRA. (2) In mathematics, a number that is derived by subtracting the given number from another specified number. It is often used in the representation of negative numbers. *See* TWO'S COMPLEMENT.

complementary colours. In optics, those pairs of colours which give the effect of white when combined (e.g. red–cyan, green–magenta, blue–yellow).

complementary metal oxide semiconductor. (CMOS) In microelectronics, a semiconductor integrated circuit logic system using two complementary p- and n-channel transistors. Power consumption is very low because virtually no current flows except when the input changes from one logic value to the other. *See* METAL OXIDE SEMICONDUCTOR, N-CHANNEL MOS, P-CHANNEL MOS, TRANSISTOR.

complete mediation. In computer security, the principle of complete mediation, one of the principles of secure systems, which states that checks for access against access control information must be performed under all circumstances including normal operation, maintenance, recovery, etc. *See* PRINCIPLES OF SECURE SYSTEMS.

completeness check. In data processing, a test that data entries are made in fields that cannot be processed in a blank state. *See* FIELD.

complexity. In mathematics, pertaining to the difficulty of computational problems as measured by the resources required to complete the computation. It is an area of active research and has applications in the field of cryptography. *See* CRYPTOGRAPHY.

complex number. In mathematics, a number comprising a real and an imaginary part. Complex numbers are commonly used in engineering to describe periodic variables that have both a magnitude and a phase. *See* IMAGINARY NUMBER, PERIODIC, PHASE, REAL NUMBER.

component. An essential functional part of a subsystem or apparatus.

component television. In television, a domestic television that is assembled from a separate screen, tuner and loudspeakers to provide a high-performance system.

compose. *See* COMPOSITION.

composite. (1) In filming, a film that contains both audio and visual effects. (2) In number theory, an integer that is divisible, without remainder, by another integer. *Compare* PRIME NUMBER.

composite colour video signal. In television, the complete transmitted signal for colour television comprises the front porch, horizontal sync pulse, breezeway, colour burst and video signal. The phase of the video signal relative to the colour burst determines the hue, and the amplitude of the signal determines the saturation. *See* BREEZEWAY, COLOUR BURST, FRONT PORCH, HORIZONTAL SYNC PULSE, HUE, SATURATION.

composition. In printing, the process of preparing each line of text, arranging justification, hyphenation, etc. prior to printing. *Compare* PAGINATION. *See* JUSTIFICATION.

composition size. In printing, sizes of type up to, and sometimes including, 14 point. *See* POINT, TYPE SIZE.

compositor. A typographer. *See* COMPOSITION, TYPOGRAPHY.

compressed audio. In optical media, a method of digitally encoding and decoding several seconds of voice-quality audio per individual videodisc frame, thus producing a potential for several hours of audio per disc. *See* FRAME, VIDEODISC. *Synonymous with* STILL-FRAME AUDIO.

compression. (1) In optical media, a technique for reducing the amount of data needed to store audio or visual information on an interactive compact disc. The methods used are based upon the principle that, after the first picture or sound sample has been represented as data, the only further data required is that which represents relative changes. (Philips). *See* COMPACT DISC – INTERACTIVE, DIFFERENTIAL PULSE CODE MODULATION. (2) In communications, a process in which the effective gain applied to a signal is varied as a function of the signal magnitude, the effective gain being greater for small signals. *Compare* OVERMODULATION. *See* BANDWIDTH COMPRESSION, COMPANDOR, GAIN. (3) In codes. *See* DATA COMPRESSION.

compromise. In data security, an unauthorized disclosure or loss of sensitive information. (FIPS).

compromising emanations. In computer security, electromagnetic emanations that may convey data and that, if intercepted and analyzed, may compromise sensitive information being processed by any automatic data-processing system. (FIPS). *See* AUTOMATIC DATA-PROCESSING SYSTEM, COMPROMISE, ELECTROMAGNETIC EMANATIONS, TEMPEST PROOFING, VAN ECK PHENOMENON. *Synonymous with* RADIO FREQUENCY EMISSIONS.

computation. A process involving many calculations and often requiring high utilization of the central processing unit. *Compare* DATA PROCESSING. *See* CENTRAL PROCESSING UNIT.

computationally infeasible. In data security, pertaining to a computation that is theoretically achievable, but is infeasible in terms of the time taken to perform it with the current or predicted power of computers.

computationally secure. In data security, pertaining to a cipher that cannot be broken by systematic analysis with available resources. *See* CRYPTANALYSIS. *Synonymous with* COMPUTATIONALLY STRONG.

computationally strong. *Synonymous with* COMPUTATIONALLY SECURE.

computational stereo. In computer graphics, pertaining to the recovery of three-dimensional characteristics of a scene from information on multiple two-dimensional images taken from different viewpoints.

computer. A device that performs prespecified mathematical manipulations. Original attempts to develop computing devices, based upon mechanical or electromechanical technologies, were of limited success because it proved impossible to construct fast, sophisticated devices that were consistently reliable. The early electronic computers fell into two categories: analog and digital computers.

Analog computers were more successful than the early digital computers for a particular class of engineering problems and were successfully employed to simulate complex systems (e.g. aircraft systems, nuclear reactors). However, these computers had a limited range of application. With the concurrent development of digital computing, efforts were made to extend the range of analog computers by employing a combination of digital logic and analog computing devices, such computers being termed hybrid computers.

The rapid development of microelectronic techniques, however, had a major impact upon the cost and power of digital computers, and with their massive versatility they soon outdated the analog and digital computer. *See* ELECTRONIC DIGITAL COMPUTER, MICROCOMPUTER.

computer abuse. In computer security, the theft, fraud, embezzlement or damage in connection to computers, including: (a) unauthorized manipulation of computer input or output; (b) unauthorized access to the system through terminals; (c) unauthorized modification or use of application programs; (d) trespass on a data-processing installation and/or theft of equipment, files or output; (e) sabotage of a computer installation's equipment; and (f) unauthorized data interception. *Compare* INFORMATION SYSTEM ABUSE. *See* COMPUTER FRAUD CONTROL, COMPUTER SECURITY.

computer-aided design. (CAD) In applications, pertaining to systems that exploit computer technology in the design processes of engineering, manufacturing and construction. The system comprises computer hardware, software and appropriate peripherals (e.g. plotter and digitizing tablet). The system can be used to recall stored diagrams from memory, enhance them by adding lines and geometric patterns, modify them by changing shapes or moving subdiagrams, incorporate standard subdiagrams stored in a library, measure and annotate dimensions, display various levels of detail and perspective, and perform computations based upon information contained in the drawings.

CAD systems employ many of the techniques of computer graphics, but they also provide facilities for the accurate dimensioning of diagrams and the integration of graphics, file retrieval and computation geared to the requirements of the engineering designer. The first stage of the design process often involves a search of previous similar projects and the extraction of a drawing that can provide a starting point. One of the advantages of CAD systems is that such drawings can be stored, retrieved, modified and filed without damage to the original. The directory facility provides a list of stored files, and a tree-structured directory is particularly valuable if a large library of drawings and diagrams of subcomponents is to be accessed. Having selected the required file, its contents can be modified with an edit facility which accepts inputs from the keyboard, or a pointing device, and adds lines, geometric patterns, etc. to the drawing. Rubber-banding facilities permit the user to move sections of the drawing around the screen while retaining connecting lines to the fixed parts. Subcomponents can be extracted from the library files, scaled and positioned as required. Engineering diagrams often comprise layers of details superimposed one upon another (e.g. plumbing layouts, electrical wiring). CAD systems enable these layers to be stored separately so that various combinations can be viewed together, whereas the others are omitted to minimize diagram clutter. Pan and zoom allow the user to scan horizontally, or vertically, across a large diagram and display a selected portion in greater detail (e.g. to read the dimension of a line). Accurate dimensioning is an essential component of many engineering diagrams, and a flexible grid display can be used to check distances and areas, etc. It is also possible to command drawing lines to align themselves to the nearest grid lines. Additional dimensioning facilities can measure the distance between any two points, draw dimension lines and position associated text as required. Hard-copy versions of the diagrams can then be produced on an appropriate plotter.

The production of the final drawing is often, however, only an intermediate step in the design process. In many cases reports, based upon calculations performed on the contents of the diagrams, are required. Typically with building diagrams it will be necessary to produce a bill of materials and estimate the total cost of construction. Files with drawings of subcomponents can be supplemented with a database of other relevant information (e.g. supplier, cost, etc.). The user can then extract relevant information from a display diagram (e.g. using a light pen). This data is inputted to an appropriate program, combined with corresponding database information, calculations are performed, and the necessary reports generated. *Compare* COMPUTER-AIDED MANU- FACTURE. *See* COMPUTER GRAPHICS, DATABASE, DIGITIZING TABLET, DIRECTORY, LIGHT PEN, PLOTTER, POINTING DEVICE, RUBBER-BANDING, TREE-STRUCTURED DIRECTORY.

computer-aided instruction. (CAI) In applications, an application of computers in education and training, in which the computer is essentially regarded as an alternative to other conventional teaching aids such as tape/slide, videotape, text book or tutor. *Compare* COMPUTER-ASSISTED LEARNING, COMPUTER-MANAGED INSTRUCTION, INTELLI- GENT TUTORING SYSTEM. *See* COMPUTER-BASED TRAINING. *Synonymous with* COMPUTER- ASSISTED INSTRUCTION.

computer-aided manufacture. (CAM) In applications, the use of computers in all aspects of process control and manufac- turing. It involves the integration of all facets of manufacturing (e.g. automatic ordering of materials, prediction of material usage, factory scheduling, inventory control, prediction of machine changeovers, predic- tion of manpower requirements). *Compare* COMPUTER-AIDED DESIGN, *See* COMPUTER- AIDED TESTING.

computer-aided testing. In applications, the use of computers to control analog or digital test equipment. These techniques may be employed in the testing of subcom- ponents, components and complete systems.

computer-aided translation. *Synonymous with* MACHINE-AIDED TRANSLATION.

computer animation. In computer graphics, techniques that enable moving pic- tures to be produced by computer graphics. More sophisticated systems can generate the frames in real time (i.e. 30 frames per second in USA or 25 frames per second in UK). More commonly, however, the indi- vidual cels are produced and are later edited into a continuous sequence.

The facilities of an animation program normally include: (a) definition of objects and environments in two- and three- dimensional space; (b) conversion of the story board events into the computer code; (c) preview of animated sequences in wire- frame form; (d) allocation of colours to objects and environments; (e) specification of position of light sources; (f) use of inbet- weening techniques on key frames; (g) use of interpolation techniques with variable fairing when moving objects and the observer; (h) selective output of specific frames; (i) storage and retrieval images from a picture library; and (j) interactive modifi- cation of any element of any frame. *See* ANIMATION, CEL ANIMATION, CUSHIONING, FRAME, INBETWEENING, STORY BOARD, WIRE FRAME.

computer-assisted instruction. *Synony- mous with* COMPUTER-AIDED INSTRUCTION.

computer-assisted learning. (CAL) In applications, an application of computers in education and training in which the com- puter is used as a unique educational tool. It seeks to provide novel teaching strategies such as simulation/games and database/

enquiry. *Compare* COMPUTER-AIDED INSTRUC-
TION, COMPUTER-MANAGED INSTRUCTION,
INTELLIGENT TUTORING SYSTEM. *See*
COMPUTER-BASED TRAINING.

computer-assisted retrieval. In library
science, the use of computers in organizing,
identifying and retrieving documents stored
on microform. *See* MICROFORM.

computer-based message system. *Synonymous with* ELECTRONIC MAIL.

computer-based training. (CBT) In applications, the use of computers in training
schemes directed towards specific skills. It
covers all aspects of the use of computers in
education (i.e. computer-aided instruction
(CAI), computer-assisted learning (CAL),
computer-managed instruction (CMI) and
intelligent tutoring systems (ITS).

(a) Educational application of computers.
The potential of computers in education was
recognized in the 1950s, but the early
developments were hampered by the limited
processing and input/output facilities of
early mainframe computers, as well as their
very high capital cost. With the installation
of computers in college campuses in the
1960s there were more determined efforts to
revolutionize university teaching. The University of Illinois developed the PLATO
system, which was later marketed by the
Control Data Corp. and installed in a
number of sites throughout the world. In
spite of the early successes of such systems,
however, the concept of replacing conventional university and college teaching with
computers was not universally accepted. The
major factors were not only the comparatively high cost of hardware per student, the
high cost of courseware development, the
limitations of keyboard input and printer or
visual display unit text output and the inflex-
ibility of dumb terminals connected to a
large mainframe computer, but also the
academic debate on the objectives of the
educational process. It was commonly
argued that the computer systems were only
capable of injecting specific knowledge into
the student, and therefore did not satisfy the
wider perspectives of higher education.
There were, however, areas of training outside the higher-education sector where the
costs per student of conventional schemes
were already extremely high and the

requirement for high levels of trainee ultimate performance were paramount (e.g.
training airline pilots). It became clear that
developments in computer education would
succeed most readily in those areas where
there was a high training budget, a high cost
associated with inadequate training and
well-defined training objectives.

In the late 1970s there was a resurgence of
interest in the use of computers in
education, which arose from the power,
flexibility and low cost of microcomputers.
The proliferation of computers in schools
and colleges, the availability of high-quality
graphics, sound synthesizers, video tape and
videodisc systems, touch screens, light pens,
mice, etc., provided the essential interfaces
for exciting and productive student/
computer interactions. Moreover, many
teachers learnt to program computers, and
there was for the first time a large population
of potential courseware developers, who
were assisted by the availability of powerful
high-level programming languages and
authoring systems. Computing rapidly
expanded into all areas of schools, colleges
and universities, and there are now innu-
merable projects in computer-aided
education throughout the world. Nevertheless the most productive area of computing
education probably still lies outside the conventional educational sector (i.e. in those
training fields where the CBT system is not
competing directly with well-entrenched and
comparatively cost-effective traditional
methods).

(b) The role of computers in training. The
versatility of current computer systems enables them to play a variety of roles in the
training process. These are generally categorized as computer-managed instruction
(CMI), computer-aided instruction (CAI),
computer-assisted learning (CAL) and intelligent tutoring systems (ITS).

In many cases computers are primarily
deployed to assist in the management and
administration of large training schemes and
are not employed directly in the presentation of the training material itself. CMI
schemes are thus used to manage the
instructional process and to improve the
control and efficiency within the training
scheme. A typical system comprises CMI
software, a database and a reporting system
hosted by a powerful computer, which is
accessed by students, often located at

remote sites, and the training personnel.

When a student enters a CMI training scheme a registration program accepts and stores the student's personal information, associated training objectives and the instructor's recommendations and requirements into the student record database. The CMI scheme then generates a course of study for the student, based upon rules specified by the course designers. The course of study may include texts, videotapes, small classes or workshops, laboratory experiments, etc. The course may also specify tests to be taken at the completion of various stages of the course; these tests may be taken on- or offline. If the tests are offline they may be assessed by an instructor, and the marks entered manually into the computer. Alternatively, the trainee may complete a test by entering responses on a machine-readable card. With online tests the CMI can generate the requisite questions, and the student responds by keying in the answers. The CMI system analyzes the student's performance, makes the requisite test result entries into the student's record, produces reports for the instructor, on an individual or group basis, and provides a feedback information report for the student. The system then advises the student on the next phase of teaching activity to be undertaken. This phase may be remedial work, review activities or the succeeding unit of the course, depending upon the student results and rules of progression specified by the instructor. Such CMI schemes can massively reduce the routine administrative and assessment work of instructors. The scheduling routines within the system can avoid bottlenecks, provide instructors with resource schedules and give management detailed reports on student performance, overall performance of trainees in various activities, highlight areas where excessive amounts of remedial work are required, indicating weaknesses in certain modules or teaching activities, etc. The CDC PLATO system has a very sophisticated and proven learning management scheme termed PLM (PLATO Learning Management). Students can benefit from the facility to move through course material at their own pace. It is possible to interleave aspects of the training course with normal duties, thus reducing the training bill in terms of salary, travel and subsistence costs.

There are three techniques in which the computer is used directly in the teaching activity itself: CAI, CAL and ITS. CAI essentially regards the computer as an alternative to other conventional teaching aids such as tape/slide, videotape, text book or tutor. The three approaches of CAI are drill and practice, tutorial and Socratic.

Drill and practice is effectively an interactive testing system. The student is presented with a question and is required to enter an answer. Depending upon the correctness of the student's response the computer will select similar questions or move on to more advanced tests. Such drill and practice routines can be very effective in areas such as spelling, arithmetic, safety regulations, maintenance procedures, etc. With the comparatively low cost of microcomputers they can be cost-effective, reducing the number of trainers required for routine marking, providing students with early feedback on performance, reducing time spent on unnecessary testing, etc.

Unlike drill and practice, the tutorial and Socratic approaches involve the delivery of instructional material itself. Tutorial techniques are often dubbed as mere electronic page-turning; individual frames are presented as text, graphics, videodisc/videotape sequences, etc. and interspersed with questions. Depending upon the analysis of the student's response new or remedial frames are presented. Socratic techniques involve a more intelligent dialog between the student and the computer, with natural language responses entered by the student. In a restricted area of instruction it may be possible, with careful programming, to provide an apparently intelligent response from the computer by relying on the limited context of the dialogue. In general, however, Socratic methods make demands on the computer's processing power and software developer akin to that of natural language processing systems and artificial intelligence applications.

The advocates of CAL techniques regard the computer as a unique educational tool and seek to provide novel teaching strategies, such as simulation/games and database/enquiry. Simulation has proved to be a valuable tool in the training field. In this technique the interactions between a trainee and an expensive and/or hazardous system are modelled by a combination of computer and system hardware. Flight simulators have proved to be extremely valuable in the training of airline pilots. Flight simulators often comprised the complete flight cabin of a large aircraft suspended in a massive cradle so that it can move in conformity with the pilot's controls. A mainframe computer accepts the inputs from the aircraft controls and provides the requisite outputs to move the cabin, provides instrument displays and produces graphics corresponding to the views that pilots would have on entering or leaving the major airports. The cost of such simulators is of the order of several million dollars, but the systems are not only more economic than conventional training flights, but they also allow the instructor to test trainees' performance in hazardous situations. At the other end of the scale, it is possible to simulate a whole range of laboratory experiments on a microcomputer, possibly using a mouse or light pen to interact with a graphic display of equipment controls, thus providing a substitute for laboratories in remote locations, home teaching, etc.

Games, in the training context, are similar to simulations except that there is an element of competition between the users. In this case the simulation may be of a business enterprise, and the players, representing (say) executives of competing companies, are required to make management decisions, which are then entered into the computer. The calculated results of those decisions are then displayed, and further decisions are required.

Database/enquiry systems do not present information in an instructional sequence, but rather provide an effective reference library on a particular topic, and the trainee is required to decide which items are to be extracted and used in any given situation. This can provide an advanced form of training for maintenance engineers, managers, etc., who are placed in a problem-solving situation and required to determine the information that is pertinent and the manner in which it is to be used.

ITS use the concept of expert systems to provide an intelligent tutor which can interact with the trainee with near-natural language dialogues. The system contains a knowledge base corresponding to the material to be imparted with the rules of interaction, and interfaces which allow the tutoring system to respond to student questions, to analyze student responses and to guide the interaction to develop further the trainee's knowledge and skills. This is an area of active research; it has the capability of improving the training facilities that can be offered and of substantially reducing the cost of courseware development. Conventional CAI requires the instructor to provide a coded form of the requisite instructional material and to specify, in great detail, the various paths of student/computer interaction. If it is possible to reduce this effort to specifying the knowledge base and certain rules of trainee/computer interaction then courseware development becomes a less onerous task.

(c) CBT systems. The range of CBT systems used in industry extends from a simple, but highly effective, microcomputer package which has taught workers the calculation of mean values for a quality control system, to a flight simulator for a jumbo jet costing many million dollars. In general terms, however, CBT systems may be categorized as time-sharing, standalone and distributed.

The earliest powerful CBT systems comprised a large mainframe computer hosting local terminals on a time-sharing basis. Such systems were suitable for college campuses, and particularly for CMI where the central collection of data and the provision of central databases were essential. Attempts to extend the range of provision of CBT services to remote locations, however, have often proved to be too expensive for CAI and CAL applications where the students required continual terminal/host computer interaction; moreover, the limited communication channels inhibited applications involving more than the mere display of textual material.

Standalone CBT systems were initially restricted to powerful simulators, often comprising large mainframe computers and extensive engineering hardware. The advent of the microcomputer opened up the possibility of the cheap, versatile CBT workstation and provided the aforementioned resurgence of interest in CBT. Initially, the applications were restricted by the limited microcomputer random-access memory storage, processing power, graphics resolution and input/output facilities, but within a few years the microcomputer facilities expanded rapidly in all these regards. Current systems provide high-resolution graphics, pointing devices, voice recognizers and synthesizers, powerful processors and large main and backing storage memory. The videodisc systems open up an entirely new set of opportunities for CBT. A large collection of still video pictures can be accessed within a few seconds, short film sequences can be selected and displayed, and the use of dual sound tracks offers the possibility of bilingual disks for foreign language teaching. Interactive compact systems can provide a disc small enough to fit into a pocket and yet with a massive capacity for textual material (600 megabytes), audio tracks, still and animated images, and computer software. The reference material, including standard textbooks, software packages and spoken lectures with animated demonstrations, sufficient for an undergraduate course could be held on two or three such discs. It is also possible to link microcomputers to engineering and scientific equipment thus offering cheap, powerful system simulators which can extend the capabilities of small teaching laboratories.

Microcomputer standalone systems have the advantages of availability at remote sites, portability between sites and reliability; a fault in a time-sharing computer can close down the teaching activities of a whole class, whereas using standalone systems only one workstation is affected by a computer failure. In a large organization, however, it is often desirable to maintain control on the teaching activities, and in this case a distributed system may be employed. Such systems comprise one or more host computers, a communications network and workstations that can be operated as standalone devices or online terminals. The communications network may be used to distribute courseware to the workstations, and the host computers can provide CMI facilities. The distribution of courseware may be a significant feature in situations where it is subject to frequent amendment, and it is imperative that the training material be standardized throughout the organization.

(d) Comparative advantages of CBT. It is impossible to debate the comparative advantages of CBT in the abstract. Each class of application must be considered in terms of its instructional, logistic and economic objectives. CBT is effective when the training objectives are limited, clearly specified and unambiguous. This situation is common in industry, commerce, defence and government. If a new weapons system is to be introduced then the operators, maintenance engineers, etc. will be required to acquire mastery of specific skills if an organization introduces a new product line then the salesmen must be able to answer their customers' technical questions, if new legislation is introduced then government employees must be in a position to operate in conformity with the new regulations. It is argued that CBT is pedagogically unsound when the educational objectives extend beyond the mere transmission of skills or facts, since it provides no real practice in the process of seeking, distilling, analyzing and exercising judgement on information extracted from a variety of sources. Such criticism may be valid for electronic page-turning, or drill and practice methods, but managers, scientists and engineers need to extract information from electronic sources, process such information and interact with complex, real-time systems. Traditional teaching methods often fail to provide the corresponding educational environment. With the ever-increasing costs of college and university teaching laboratories there needs to be a reappraisal of the role of CAL simulation, gaming and database enquiry systems.

CBT systems have instructional advantages in the situations listed below.

(i)   Some of the information to be presented is in the form of still or moving images, or audio.

(ii) The trainee may react adversely or perform badly in conventional teaching situations.

(iii) The student is required to demonstrate dexterity skills or react to rapidly changing situations.

(iv) It is important to provide rapid feedback to the trainee.

(v)   There is a requirement to maintain close control of the training process (e.g. rapid feedback to management).

(vi) The quality and content of training is to be standardized over a large, scattered trainee population.

(e) Development and implementation of CBT systems. The total effort of developing and implementing a successful CBT system extends well beyond the mere production of the computer software. The essential phases for a successful project are given below.

(i)   Identification of the training application.
(ii) Identification of CBT system.
(iii) Feasibility study.
(iv) Selection of CBT system.
(v)   Design, development and implementation of courseware.
(vi) Management of system.

See COMPACT DISC – INTERACTIVE, COMPUTER-AIDED INSTRUCTION, COMPUTER-ASSISTED LEARNING, COMPUTER GRAPHICS, COMPUTER-MANAGED INSTRUCTION, INTELLIGENT TUTORING SYSTEM, LIGHT PEN, MOUSE, POINTING DEVICE, SPEECH RECOGNIZER, SPEECH SYNTHESIZER, TIME SHARING, TOUCHSCREEN, VIDEODISC.

computer bureau.   In legislation, as defined by the UK Data Protection Act 1984, a person carries on a computer bureau if he provides other persons with services in respect of data, and a person provides such services if:

(a)   as agent for other persons he causes them to be processed; or
(b)   he allows other persons to use equipment in his possession for the processing.

See DATA, DATA PROTECTION.

computer   conferencing.   In   communications, the use of a computer to handle group communication in simultaneous or asynchronous meetings. The latter allows participants to enter the conference at random. *See* TELECONFERENCING.

computer crime.   (1) In computer security, fraud, embezzlement unauthorized access and other 'white collar' crimes committed with the aid of or directly involving a computer system and/or network. (GAO). (2) In computer security, a misleading term because it is sometimes employed to cover unauthorized activities which do not meet the legal definition of a crime. The issue is further complicated by the absence of agreement on international criminal law. An indi-

vidual committing fraud at a terminal on a network by manipulating a computer in another country need not be breaking the law of either country. *See* COMPUTER ABUSE, COMPUTER FRAUD CONTROL, COMPUTER SECURITY.

computer   fraud   control.   In   computer security, the measures of effective control against computer fraud include: (a) prevention or reduction; (b) segregation of duties; (c) control of input and output; (d) control of amendments; (e) structured walk through; (f) good documentation; (g) job rotation; (h) split knowledge or dual control; (i) increasing the difficulty of concealment/realization; (j) good personnel procedures, (k) fidelity guarantee and computer crime insurance; (l) early detection; (m) monitoring of access violations; (n) reviewing unusual circumstances; (o) audit trails; (p) fraud detection models; (q) employer response; and (r) public prosecution. *See* AUDIT TRAIL, COMPUTER CRIME.

computer-generated information.   In applications, information produced by a computer without manual intervention, other than initiation or termination. (Philips).

computer graphics.   In applications, the use of computer equipment and techniques in inputting, manipulating, displaying and plotting graphic images. The graphics may be input in numerical form, by pointing devices or using a digital stream representing a camera image output. The manipulations may involve transformations, hidden-line and hidden-surface removal. Screen display may be in the form of vector or bit-mapped graphics, and the hard copy can be produced on graphic plotters. *See* BIT-MAPPED GRAPHICS, COMPUTER-AIDED DESIGN, COMPUTER ANIMATION, DIRECT-VIEW STORAGE TUBE, HIDDEN LINE, HIDDEN SURFACE, PLOTTER, RASTER DISPLAY, VECTOR REFRESH.

computer input from microfilm.   (CIM) In peripherals, the equipment and techniques employed to interpret microfilm images and convert them into a form suitable for input into a computer. *Compare* COMPUTER OUTPUT TO MICROFILM.

Computer Inquiry, 1980.   In the USA a Federal   Communications   Commission decision to restrict common-carrier regulation to the carrier's provision of basic services and to free enhanced services from regulation. This decision encouraged competition in the telecommunications market and increased the range of customer services and equipment. *See* BASIC SERVICE, COMMON CARRIER, ENHANCED SERVICES.

computer-integrated software engineering. (CISE) In programming, a formal systematic, computer-mediated and computer-enforced approach to systems development.

computer interpolation. In filming, a special effect produced by computer graphics in which one image is transformed into another by a mathematical process. *See* COMPUTER ANIMATION.

computerized branch exchange. (CBX) In communications, an intelligent private switchboard that may provide extra facilities (e.g. facsimile, database interrogation), in addition to routing incoming and outgoing telephone calls. *See* FACSIMILE, PRIVATE BRANCH EXCHANGE.

computerized composition. In printing, the use of a computer to make the computation decisions necessary to drive the typesetting machine. *See* COMPOSITION.

computerized instrumentation. In control and instrumentation, the use of computers, transducers, analog-to-digital converters and interface units to record, analyze and display data concerning a physical phenomenon. Computerized instrumentation can perform data acquisition, as well as data acquisition with alarming or online data analysis. With data acquisition the system simply accepts and stores the input data, possibly also providing some display of current data. The next level, data acquisition with alarming, provides the aforementioned data acquisition function plus an alarm facility. Typically some input level is monitored and compared with a set 'safety' level. When the input level moves outside its prespecified safety limits, alarms in the form of some combination of voice signals, screen display, data streams to disk or printer, etc. are actuated by the computer. Online data analysis performs some computational work on the input data as it is received and stores

the results, in addition to the simple data acquisition and possibly alarm functions. *See* ANALOG-TO-DIGITAL CONVERTER, TRANSDUCER.

computer language. *See* MACHINE LANGUAGE, PROGRAMMING LANGUAGE.

computer-managed instruction. (CMI) In applications, an application of computers to education and training in which the computer is used to manage the instructional process and to improve the control and efficiency within the training scheme. A typical system comprises CMI software, a database and a reporting system hosted by a powerful computer, which is accessed by students, often located at remote sites. *Compare* COMPUTER-AIDED INSTRUCTION, COMPUTER-ASSISTED LEARNING, INTELLIGENT TUTORING SYSTEM. *See* COMPUTER-BASED TRAINING. *Synonymous with* COMPUTER-MANAGED LEARNING.

computer-managed learning. (CML) *Synonymous with* COMPUTER-MANAGED INSTRUCTION.

computer micrographics. In computing, a technique in which a computer is used to convert data to or from film, or any other appropriate medium, in which the images are too small to be read by the naked eye. *See* COMPUTER INPUT FROM MICROFILM, COMPUTER OUTPUT TO MICROFILM, MICROGRAPHICS.

computer network. *See* DATA COMMUNICATIONS.

computer output to microfilm. In peripherals, the output of a computer may be printed directly onto microfilm (or microfiche). Four printing techniques are available: CRT recording; electron beam recording; laser beam recording; and fiber optics recording. These techniques can achieve very high throughput rates, of the order of 2 million lines per hour, and microform indexes can be automatically generated by the computer. *Compare* COMPUTER INPUT FROM MICROFILM. *See* CRT RECORDING, ELECTRON BEAM RECORDING, FIBER OPTICS RECORDING, LASER BEAM RECORDING.

computer power. In computing, a measure of the ability of a computer to perform a specified set of operations within a given time. *See* BENCHMARK TEST.

computer print out. *See* HARD COPY.

computer program bank. A centralized source of computer programs; usually protected against illegal copying and linked to automatic invoicing as, for example, in videotex. (Philips). *See* VIDEOTEX.

computer science. The study of computers, their underlying operations and applications. It includes the following topics: (a) data and information structures; (b) programming, programming languages, translators, formal language theory, proof of program correctness; (c) software engineering, operating systems; (d) architecture, logic circuits, automata theory; (e) theory of computation, design of algorithms; (f) systems analysis and design; (g) interfacing computers and peripherals, computer networks; (h) artificial intelligence; (i) information systems; (j) algorithms; and (k) computer applications, graphics, simulation, robotics, etc. *Compare* INFORMATION SCIENCE. *See* ARCHITECTURE, ARTIFICIAL INTELLIGENCE, AUTOMATA THEORY, COMPUTER GRAPHICS, DATABASE, DATA COMMUNICATIONS, DATA STRUCTURE, FORMAL LANGUAGE, PERIPHERAL, PROGRAMMING, PROOF OF PROGRAM CORRECTNESS, ROBOTICS, SOFTWARE ENGINEERING, TRANSLATOR.

computer security. The protection of the information and physical assets of a computer system. The protection of information aims to prevent the unauthorized disclosure, manipulation, destruction or alteration of data. The protection of physical assets implies security measures against theft, destruction or misuse of equipment (i.e. processors, peripherals, data storage media, communication lines and interfaces).

Unauthorized disclosure of information can be considered in relation to the disclosure of classified, protected or proprietary data. Military organizations, businesses, government offices, etc. have confidential data that is not to be revealed to unauthorized persons. Data protection and privacy legislation places a responsibility upon holders of personal data to maintain the confidentiality of that data; failure to do so can, under the terms of such legislation,

result in legal action against the data holder. Proprietary information (e.g. software, databases accessed by commercial online information retrieval systems, etc.) constitute the major assets of software houses and electronic publishers. Protection against illicit disclosure is vital for the financial well-being of such institutions.

Data manipulation refers to changing some attribute of data, such as security classification, file access privileges or data destination, which causes the data to be made available to illicit users or to be handled in an unauthorized manner.

Electronic and magnetic storage devices are designed to handle extremely volatile information. Whereas the destruction of paper-stored data can be a surprisingly difficult, time-consuming task, it is possible to destroy very rapidly computer-based information using a short section of code instructing an overwriting action, by removal of power from the volatile storage, by degaussing magnetic storage media or simply by stealing a box of floppy disks. The damage suffered by the erstwhile owner of the data may be out of all proportion to the benefit, if any, gained by the attacker or the effort required for the attack.

Unauthorized alteration of data can produce considerable personal or financial benefit to an attacker and/or corresponding disadvantage to the holder or subject of the data; Moreover, in the absence of special precautions such alterations may pass undetected. Bank account information, examination marks, credit ratings, criminal records, financial transactions and medical records represent information that people may wish to alter for their own benefit or to the detriment of another.

Physical assets security involves traditional security techniques which may be less esoteric, than those of the information security field, but are no less important. Theft of computing or associated equipment can often produce a loss to the owner that is out of all proportion to the benefit to the thief. A stolen floppy disk can represent the gain of a week's pocket money to a teenager, but the loss of irreplaceable financial data to a company. The malicious theft of a printed circuit board can close down a computer centre for some hours. Destruction of equipment can be accidental (e.g. natural disaster, fire, flood, etc.) or intentional (e.g. vandalism, terrorist action). The loss suffered by the organization can far exceed that of the cost of the equipment destroyed. Non-malicious misuse of computer or communication equipment can arise from employees conducting private businesses or simply playing computer games. Their deleterious effects depend upon the extent to which such activities impinge upon the normal operation of the organization (e.g. do these activities seriously affect the response time of the computer or occupy valuable disk storage space; or to the extent that they raise operating costs (e.g. public network communication charges). Malicious misuse of facilities can be aimed at deliberate over loading of the computer/communication system or attacking the reputation of the organization (e.g. hackers misusing a computer and publicising their exploits). *See* ACCESS CONTROL, COMPROMISE, COMPUTER CRIME, DATA, DATA PROTECTION, DATA SECURITY, DATA SUBJECT, DATA USER, DISCLOSING, HACKER, PERSONAL DATA, RISK ANALYSIS.

computer system. In computing, a configuration comprising one or more computers, associated peripherals and software that can share facilities for the performance of user tasks.

computer to plate. In printing, the production of plates for typesetting from computer-

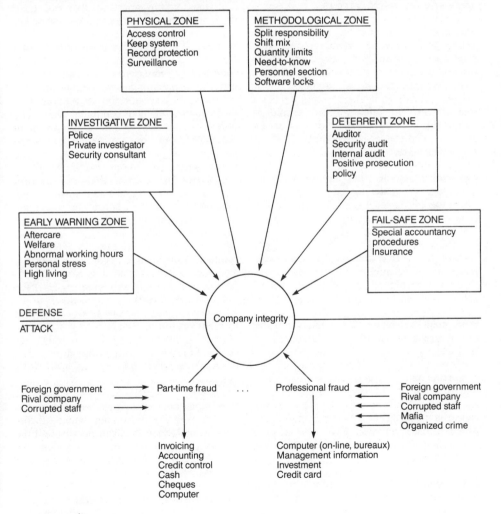

computer security
Copyright Kluwer Publishing Limited – source: *Handbook of Security*.

stored format without film or other intermediaries.

COMSAT. In communications, Communications Satellite organization; a private US company which competes in the domestic communications market. *Compare* INTELSAT, SBS. *See* COMMUNICATIONS SATELLITE SYSTEM.

COMSEC. Communications security. *See* COMMUNICATIONS SECURITY, NSA COMSEC MODULE.

concatenate. In programming, the joining of two or more strings into a single string. *See* CHARACTER STRING, STRING.

conceal. In videotex, a display mode during which certain characters are displayed as spaces until the viewer chooses to reveal them. This facility can be used in games, quizzes, etc. *Compare* REVEAL.

concealment. In codes, a technique in digital signal processing for the hiding of errors (e.g. by an interpolation scheme). (Philips). *See* INTERPOLATION.

concealment system. In computer security, a method of achieving confidentiality in which the existence of sensitive information is hidden by embedding it in irrelevant data. (FIPS). *See* CONFIDENTIALITY.

concentrator. In communications, a device that combines a number of individual message streams into a single message stream. *See* MULTIPLEXING.

conceptual schema. In databases, the overall logical structure of the database. *See* SCHEMA.

concertina fold. *Synonymous with* ACCORDION FOLD.

concordance program. In programming, a program that examines a body of text, providing a list of words giving each occurrence and its context.

concurrency. (1) In programming. *See* CONCURRENT PROGRAMMING, MULTIPROGRAMMING. (2) In databases, pertaining to situations when two or more users are attempting to access the same data record. *See* LOCKOUT, UPDATE INCONSISTENCY.

concurrent programming. In programming, the process of creating sections of a program, which are to be executed in parallel, and the subsequent execution. *See* PARALLEL PROCESSING.

condensed type. In printing, a style of typeface in which the characters have an elongated appearance. (Desktop). *Compare* EXPANDED TYPE. *See* TYPEFACE.

condenser lens. In audiovisual aids, one or more lenses between the projection lamp and slide, or film aperture, to concentrate the light in the aperture area. *See* APERTURE.

conditional branch. *See* CONDITIONAL JUMP.

conditional jump. In programming, an instruction to jump to another specified instruction if a specific condition exists (e.g. the equality of two computed variables) otherwise to select the next instruction in sequence. *Compare* UNCONDITIONAL JUMP.

conditioning. In data communications, procedures to ensure that transmission impairment on a circuit lies within limits specified in a tariff. It is used on telephone lines leased for data transmission to improve the transmission speed.

conductive shielding. In computer security, a special material placed around a component to prevent it from emitting EMI/RF radiation. *See* EMI/RF RADIATION, SHIELDING EFFECTIVENESS, TEMPEST PROOFING, VAN ECK PHENOMENON.

cone. In recording, a component of certain types of loudspeakers, used as a vibrator. *See* LOUDSPEAKER.

cone of vision. In computer graphics, the solid cone representing the three-dimensional space that can be viewed by a normal eye fixed upon a point in space. The angle of the cone is approximately 120°. *See* VIEWING PYRAMID.

conference call. In communications, a telephone call established among three or more stations so that each of the stations is able to communicate with the others. *See* DIAL-UP TELECONFERENCING, *Synonymous with* CONFERENCE CONNECTION.

conference connection. *Synonymous with* CONFERENCE CALL.

Conference Papers Index. (CPI) In online information retrieval, a database supplied by Cambridge Scientific Abstracts and dealing with science and technology.

confidentiality. In data security, a concept that applies to data that must be held in confidence and that describes the status and degree of protection that must be provided for such data about individuals as well as organizations. (FIPS).

configurably dumb terminal. In computer security, a terminal that may have extensive processing and storage facilities, but these facilities can be disabled to render the unit dumb (i.e. have no programmable memory) for computer security purposes. *See* DUMB TERMINAL.

configuration. (1) The composition of an electronic system, particularly in terms of its physical components. (Philips). (2) In computing, the set of hardware units, and their interconnections, for a particular period of operation.

configuration management. In computer security, the process of controlling modifications to the system's hardware, firmware, software and documentation that provides sufficient assurance that the system is protected against the introduction of improper modification before, during and after system implementation. (AFR).

confinement. In data security, the keeping of data within its proper security level. *Compare* SEEPAGE.

confinement channel. *See* COVERT CHANNEL.

confusion. (1) In data security, a technique in which the strength of a cipher system is increased by producing a complex relationship between the ciphertext and the cryptographic key. *Compare* DIFFUSION. *See* CIPHERTEXT, CRYPTOGRAPHIC KEY. (2) In data security, a characteristic of a cipher which

makes each letter of the cryptogram dependent on all the characters of the key. *See* CRYPTOGRAM, CRYPTOGRAPHIC KEY.

congestion. In communications, a state arising when the traffic demand exceeds the system capacity. *See* CHANNEL OVERLOAD.

Conit. In online information retrieval, a generic name for a number of experimental intermediary systems developed for online bibliographic retrieval. *See* BIBLIOGRAPHIC DATABASE, INTERMEDIARY SYSTEM.

conjunctive form. In mathematics, a logical expression of the form a AND b AND c. *Compare* DISJUNCTIVE FORM. *See* AND, BOOLEAN ALGEBRA.

connected word recognition. In man–machine interfaces, pertaining to systems that can recognize sets of human spoken words uttered without pauses. *Compare* ISOLATED WORD RECOGNITION. *See* CONTINUOUS SPEECH RECOGNITION.

connection trap. In databases, a false inference that can arise if attempts are made to join two individual statements (e.g. employee A works in department B, and department B is providing a service to project C, does not necessarily mean that employee A is working on project C). *See* JOIN.

connect time. In computing, the time in which a user of an interactive system is logged on. *See* LOGON.

CONSER. In library science, Cooperative Conversion of Serials; a US and Canadian project to develop a machine-readable database of serials held by libraries in the US and Canada. *See* MACHINE-READABLE.

console. In peripherals, the controlling terminal of a computer system.

constant. (1) In mathematics, a value that does not change. (2) In programming, a value, set in a program at compilation time, and not allowed to be altered during the execution of the program. *See* COMPILER, LITERAL.

constant angular velocity. (CAV) In optical media, a videodisc with one frame reproduced for each revolution giving freeze-frame facilities and individual frame addressability, a basic requirement for interactive videodisc application. *Compare* CONSTANT LINEAR VELOCITY. *See* FREEZE FRAME.

constant linear velocity. (CLV) In optical media, a disc rotation mode in which the disc rotation speed changes as the read radius changes so that the linear reading speed (i.e. the speed at which the readout device scans the track) is constant. This mode of recording maximizes the information storage capacity of digital data discs and the playing time of video or compact discs. It is therefore used in compact discs and non-interactive videodiscs. *Compare* CONSTANT ANGULAR VELOCITY. *See* COMPACT DISC, VIDEODISC.

constant-ratio code. *Synonymous with M OUT OF N CODE.*

contact. In electronics, a part of a switch designed to touch a similar contact to permit current to flow.

contact print. In photography, a print with direct emulsion-to-emulsion contact with the film being printed. *See* EMULSION.

contamination. (1) In television and filming, the faulty separation of colour signal paths. *See* COLOUR CONTAMINATION. (2) In data security, the introduction of data of one sensitivity and need-to-know with data of a lower sensitivity or different need-to-know. This can result in the contaminating data not receiving the required level of protection. (AFR). *See* DATA CONTAMINATION, NEED-TO-KNOW.

content-addressable filestore. (CAF) In memory systems, a disk-based associative processor used for storing and accessing large data files. The heads on the multidisk, magnetic disk system read data simultaneously as they scan each cylinder. Various fields of the accessed record can be used as a key, thus providing for very flexible search strategies. *See* ASSOCIATIVE PROCESSOR, CYLINDER, FIELD, HEAD, KEY, MAGNETIC DISK, RECORD.

content-addressable memory. (CAM) *Synonymous with* ASSOCIATIVE STORAGE.

contention. (1) In data communications, a situation in which two or more devices simultaneously attempt to access a common piece of equipment (e.g. two terminals attempting to access a processing unit). (2) In data networks, a method of line control on which terminals request or bid to transmit. If the channel is not available the terminals must wait until it is free. *See* CONTENTION CONTROL.

contention control. In data communications, a control strategy for a local area network in which any node that wishes to transmit does so. If two nodes transmit at the same time a collision occurs, and both messages are garbled. The transmitting nodes detect the collision and await a random interval before retransmitting the message. *See* ALOHA, CARRIER SENSE MULTIPLE ACCESS — COLLISION DETECTION, CONTENTION, ETHERNET, LOCAL AREA NETWORK.

contention delay. In data communications, the time spent waiting for a facility that is occupied by other using devices. *See* CONTENTION.

content provider. *Synonymous with* INFORMATION PROVIDER.

contextual operator. *Synonymous with* POSITIONAL OPERATOR.

contiguous. Adjoining. *See* CONTIGUOUS GRAPHICS.

contiguous graphics. In videotex, the set of graphic characters in which there are no gaps between adjacent cells in the character space. *Compare* SEPARATED GRAPHICS.

contingency planning. In computer security, the action of formulating plans by an organization to respond to the conceivable range of incidents, accidents and disasters that could occur (e.g. mistakes by operating staff, loss of personnel due to sickness, death or strikes, hacker activity, theft, fraud, vandalism, alteration or destruction of software or data, fire, flood, power failure, excessive weather conditions, electrical disturbances, failure of environmental protection (air conditioning, fumes, dust), terrorist attack, aircraft, vehicle, meteorite or satellite impact, chemical spillage, building construction failure, nuclear reactor incidents or other radiation effects, earthquakes, volcanos, avalanches, etc.). *See* RISK ANALYSIS.

continuation page.   In videotex, a page that cannot be addressed directly by its page number. If a continuation page exists, it is displayed by first retrieving the main page either via menu selection or its page number. The user must then view in sequence the associated continuation pages. *See* PAGE.

continuity check.   In data communications, a check made to verify that an information path exists in a channel or channels. *See* CHANNEL.

continuous-flow.   In printing, pertaining to ink jet printers in which electrostatic charges deflect ink drops from a continuous stream of ink onto the printing medium. *Compare* DROP ON DEMAND. *See* INK JET PRINTER, *Synonymous with* DEFLECTED PRINTER.

continuous loop.   In audiovisual aids, a loop of film or tape made by splicing the ends together for continuous projection or operation.

continuous speech recognition.   (CSR) In man–machine interfaces, the recognition of words spoken in a continuous stream is complicated by such factors as: (a) age, sex and identity of human speaker; (b) environmental conditions; (c) syntax and lexicon of phrases; and (d) number of lexical identities.
It is difficult to determine where one word ends and the other begins, and such problems rise sharply with the size of the vocabulary because simple methods of matching become too expensive. *Compare* CONTINUOUS SPEECH UNDERSTANDING. *See* SPEECH RECOGNIZER.

continuous speech understanding.   (CSU) In man–machine interfaces, the interpretation of data received from a human spoken voice in the light of stored knowledge concerning syllables, words, sentences, conversation rules and the subject under discussion. The requirements compared with continuous speech recognition are somewhat relaxed because the sense of the total phrase is required rather than the recognition of each word. *Compare* CONTINUOUS SPEECH RECOGNITION. *See* SPEECH RECOGNIZER.

continuous stationery.   In printing, paper forming one continuous piece, perforated at page intervals and with sprocket holes along the edges. *See* ACCORDION FOLD, SPROCKET FEED.

continuous tone.   In printing, an image in which the subject has continuous shades of colour or grey without being broken up by dots. Continuous tones cannot be reproduced in that form for printing, but must be screened to translate the image into dots. (Desktop). *Compare* HALFTONE.

contrast.   (1) In printing, the degree of tones in a photograph ranging from highlight to shadow. (Desktop). *See* HIGHLIGHT. (2) In optics, the ratio between the maximum and minimum intensities of incident light on a subject. (3) In photography, the ratio between the optically most dense and least dense areas of a positive or negative film. (4) In television, the subjective assessment of the difference in appearance of two parts of a field of view seen simultaneously or successively. *See* CRUSHING. (5) In computer graphics, the difference in brightness or colour between a display image and the area in which it is displayed.

contrast stretching.   In computer graphics, a technique of image processing in which the difference between grey levels is enhanced to improve the visual effects of a bland image. *See* GREY SCALE, IMAGE PROCESSING.

control block.   In programming, a block of memory holding control information concerning the program.

control bus.   In computing, a bus used to select an area of main storage and to transmit signals required for regulating the computer operation. *Compare* ADDRESS BUS, DATA BUS. *See* BUS, MAIN MEMORY.

control character.   In codes, a character whose occurrence in a particular context initiates a control action (e.g. carriage return on a printer).

control computer.   In applications, a special-purpose computer that controls a device or process. It receives input signals from a device or process transducers, or commands from operators, processes them according to a prestored program and produces signals to device or process activators (e.g. to move a robot arm, provide information for the operator, etc.). *See* TRANSDUCER.

control-driven. In computing, pertaining to an architecture in which instructions are executed as soon as they are selected by the control sequence. *Compare* DATAFLOW. *See* ARCHITECTURE, VON NEUMANN.

controlled reading device. In audiovisual aids, a device for progressively disclosing or exposing visual information.

controlled vocabulary. In library science, a list of standardized terms used to index items for storage and retrieval. These standardized terms are also known as descriptors and are contained in a thesaurus. *See* INDEXING LANGUAGE, THESAURUS.

controller. (1) In data communications, a device, which may contain a stored program, that directs the transmission of data over a network. (2) In computing, a peripheral controller. *See* PERIPHERAL CONTROL UNIT.

control mode. In data communications, a necessary state for all terminals on a line to allow line control actions or terminal selection to occur.

control read-only memory. In memory systems, a microprogrammed control block within a microprocessor that decodes control logic. *See* MICROPROCESSOR, MICROPROGRAM.

control token. In data communications, a bit pattern passed around a local area network for control purposes. Any node, upon receiving the control token, may remove it from the network, send a message and then pass on the control token. *Compare* CARRIER SENSE MULTIPLE ACCESS — COLLISION DETECT, DAISY CHAIN, MESSAGE SLOT, REGISTER INSERTION. *See* LOCAL AREA NETWORK, TOKEN BUS, TOKEN RING.

control track. In recording, a video tape track that contains timing pulses to facilitate synchronization of reading head on playback. *See* TACH PULSE.

control unit. In computing, a part of the central processing unit that holds the instruction code of the computer and that perfoms such functions as fetching instructions and operands, decoding instructions, allocating instructions to arithmetic logic units, storing results of ALU operations, etc. *See* ARITHMETIC LOGIC UNIT, CENTRAL PROCESSING UNIT, INSTRUCTION.

conversational mode. *Synonymous with* INTERACTIVE MODE.

converter. *See* CODE CONVERSION.

cooperative processing. In distributed processing, an environment that enables the services and data of either a microcomputer or a host computer to be transparent to an application program running in the microcomputer.

The objective of cooperative processing is to obtain the best features of both personal computers and mainframes. The desirable characteristics of personal computers are listed below.

(a) They are designed for the non-computing professional.
(b) They assume no knowledge of computers and are easy to operate.
(c) They are single-user systems guaranteeing privacy of programs and data.
(d) They are autonomous, giving service of constant response time, independent of mainframe downtime and loading.

Large corporations cannot, however, divide their information processing over a multitude of personal computers for the following reasons.

(a) Cost of individual workstations is too high.
(b) Corporate data cannot be divided between a large number of independent, non-communicating storage devices.

Cooperative processing, linking microcomputers to a mainframe, provides an optimum combination of microcomputer and main-frame systems. Thus:

(a) The loss of a single microcomputer does not affect any other microcomputer connected to the same mainframe.
(b) The human interface to the total system is simple inasmuch as the personal computer is designed for a single user. Moreover, the single user's requirements can be customized on the personal computer without negotiation with central computer staff.
(c) The mainframe can offload trivial user transactions to the personal computer and devote its capacity, with high efficiency, to heavy computation tasks and intensive input/output operations.

The cooperative-processing interface provides a set of virtual services and data in such a manner that their local and remote locations are transparent to the user. *See* MAINFRAME, TRANSPARENT, VIRTUAL.

coordinate graph. In mathematics, a visual representation of a relationship between two variables produced by plotting a series of points relative to axes at right angles to each other. *See* CARTESIAN COORDINATES.

copagination. In printing, a specific form of pagination where a numbered page of one document corresponds precisely to the subject matter on the same page number of another document. *See* PAGINATION.

copier. In office systems, the conventional office copier employs xerography in which an image of the original hard copy is projected onto a drum, causing changes in the electric potential according to the light intensity of the image. A variation in electric potential affects the amount of toner on the plate and hence the image transferred onto the duplicate hard copy. With conventional xerography the image was handled in analog form giving limited capability for any form of image processing apart from that which can be achieved with optical effects (e.g. reducing the size of the image).

Copiers incorporating digital scanners and laser printers can overcome the inherent limitations of conventional xerographic devices, and may be integrated with other office information-processing systems. If the hard-copy image is converted into digital form, then the printing system of the copier may also be able to process signals received over data communication lines. Similarly the digital image produced by the scanner could be transmitted to a remote location for printing. Thus the functions of facsimile may be integrated within the copier.

A digital signal may, moreover, be processed locally providing sophisticated local editing facilities (e.g. cutting and pasting, blanking out parts of the image, image black to white reversal, independent enlargement/reduction of horizontal/vertical dimensions, mask/trim functions, image overlay, frame erase function, book copying).

The image overlay feature enables two original images to be merged; unwanted borders can be eliminated with the frame erase function. Book copying enables facing pages of a book to be copied sequentially without the need for the operator to repositioning the book.

The development of copiers has been aided by the advent of the amorphous silicon (a-Si) high-yield photoconductor drum used in the printing system. Amorphous silicon is non-toxic, facilitating the disposal of used drums, is sensitive to all colours and is highly durable.

Most copiers are still restricted to black/white reproduction. Colour copying is possible either as single-colour imaging and full-colour reproduction. In the former case interchangeable colour toner/developers provide the facility to replace the black image with a selected colour. Full-colour reproduction produces high-quality, multi-coloured copies in one pass, but such devices are expensive and slow in comparison with current black/white copiers.

Two-sided copying is termed duplexing. In general both the original and duplicate copy must be flipped over and re-inserted for the second side. Some devices automatically flip over and re-feed the duplicate copy, but only relatively sophisticated units will automatically turn over the original. *See* AMORPHOUS SILICON, FACSIMILE, INTELLIGENT COPIER/PRINTER, LASER PRINTER, OPTICAL SCANNER, SINGLE-COLOUR IMAGING, TONER, XEROGRAPHY.

copperplate printing. In printing, an intaglio process in which the printing is performed direct from an engraved copper plate. *See* INTAGLIO.

coprime. In number theory, pertaining to a pair of integers with a greatest common divisor of one (e.g. 8 and 15). *See* PRIME NUMBER. *Synonymous with* MUTUALLY PRIME.

coprocessor. In computing, a form of multiprocessing in which two or more processors share the same instruction stream. This technique enables processors to be designed for a specific range of tasks, and therefore perform their allotted function with high efficiency. *See* MULTIPROCESSING, PROCESSOR.

copy. (1) In printing, matter that is to be set in type or reproduced. *Synonymous with* MANUSCRIPT. (2) In computing, the reproduction of source data in an identical form, but not necessarily on the same storage medium (e.g. from magnetic disk to magnetic tape). (3) In office equipment, a product of a document-copying process. *See* COPIER.

copy-protected. In software protection, pertaining to software distributed on floppy disks rendered 'uncopyable' by physical means. *See* COPY PROTECTION.

copy protection. In software protection, techniques used to prevent the unauthorized duplication of software. The term is a misnomer since any program can be copied, but with certain protection measures it may not be executable after it has been copied. *Compare* EXECUTE PROTECTION.

copy reader. In printing, one who assists an editor in preparing copy for printing.

copyright. (1) A legal document that establishes the ownership of an artistic creation (e.g. motion picture, literary work, musical composition). (2) In software and publishing, the right to prevent copying. The copyright owner has the right to prevent copying of the form in which an idea is expressed, but not the idea itself. Computer programs are protected under the same laws which cover literary works in those countries that have copyright legislation. However, the use of an idea or an algorithm obtained by studying the source code of a copyrighted program is not, in itself, an infringement of copyright.

Copyright Clearance Center. (CCC) A US non-profit-making organization offering licensing arrangements for the photocopying of documents.

Copyright Licensing Agency. A UK organization comprising the Publisher's Association, Association of Learned and Professional Society Publishers, Periodical Publishers Association, Society of Authors and the Writers Guild.

Coral. In programming, a programming language similar to ALGOL developed for military applications. *See* ALGOL.

cordless telephone. (CT) In communications, a portable telephone with a low-powered radio receiver/transmitter permitting communication with a local base unit. The power of the signals must not exceed 10 milliwatts, thus restricting the maximum distance between the portable and base unit to less than 200 metres. *See* UPT.

Core. In computer graphics, a graphics standard similar to graphical kernel system, developed by SIGGRAPH. It provides for two- and three-dimensional graphics. *See* GRAPHIC KERNEL SYSTEM, SIGGRAPH.

core. In optoelectronics, the central primary light-conducting region of an optical fiber. *See* FIBER OPTICS.

coring out. In recording, the use of digital filtering techniques to remove noise from a signal. *See* NOISE.

corner marks. In printing, marks printed on a sheet to indicate the trim or register marks. (Desktop).

coroutine. In programming, a procedure that can pass control to any other routine, suspend itself and continue later. *Compare* SUBROUTINE. *See* PROCEDURE.

corporate electronic publishing. In printing, use of desk-top publishing by organizations to produce in-house publications (e.g. manuals, reports, advertising material, etc.). *See* DESK-TOP PUBLISHING.

corporate identity. *See* HOUSE STYLE.

corrective maintenance. In computing, the activity of detecting, isolating and correcting failures after occurrence. *Compare* PREVEN-TIVE MAINTENANCE.

correctness. *See* PROOF OF PROGRAM COR-RECTNESS.

corrupt data. In data security, data that is accidentally or maliciously modified (e.g. by active wiretapping). *See* ACTIVE WIRETAPPING.

corruption. In memory systems and data communications, data that has been changed in an undesired manner either during transmission or in storage (e.g. a corrupt floppy disk). *See* FLOPPY DISK.

COSATI. US Committee on Scientific and Technical Information of the Federal Council for Science and Technology. COSATI is composed of federal agency officials with responsibility for operating scientific and technical information systems.

COSMOS. *See* COMPLEMENTARY METAL OXIDE SEMICONDUCTOR.

cost–risk analysis. In risk management, the assessment of the costs of potential risk or loss or compromise of data in an automatic data-processing system without data protection versus the cost of providing data protection. (FIPS). *See* AUTOMATIC DATA-PROCESSING SYSTEM, COMPROMISE, RISK ANALYSIS.

coulomb. In electronics, a unit of electric charge. It represents the quantity of charge passing in a conductor when a current of one ampere flows for one second. *See* AMPERE.

countdown. In video, a cuing signal on the leader of videotape and films. *See* LEADER.

counter. In computing, a register for storing a number, which is increased or decreased by a fixed amount each time an event occurs. *See* REGISTER.

countermeasure. In computer security, any method (e.g. physical, hardware, software,

personnel, procedural, etc.) used to counteract a threat to the system. *See* THREAT.

coupled. *See* LOOSELY COUPLED, TIGHTLY COUPLED.

coupler. (1) In optoelectronics, a component used to interconnect three or more optical conductors. (2) In printing, a chemical compound that reacts with another compound to form a dye in a document-copying machine.

coupling loss. In optoelectronics, the loss of power in a light pulse at the interface of two devices (e.g. a laser and an optical fiber). *Compare* MACROBEND LOSS, MICRO-BEND LOSS. *See* FIBER OPTICS, LASER.

Courier. In printing, a typeface commonly used for business typewriters. *Compare* AVANTE-GARDE, BOOKMAN, HELVETICA, HELVETICA NARROW, NEW CENTURY SCHOOL-BOOK, OLDSTYLE, PALATINO, SYMBOL, TIMES ROMAN, ZAPF CHANCERY, ZAPF DINGBATS. *See* TYPEFACE.

coverage. In broadcasting, the population within the service area of a transmitter capable of receiving the programmes.

covert. Disguised. *See* COVERT CHANNEL.

covert channel. In computer security, a communication channel that allows a process to transfer information in a manner that violates the system's security policy. (DOD). *Compare* OVERT CHANNEL. *See* COVERT STORAGE CHANNEL, COVERT TIMING CHANNEL, SECURITY POLICY.

cover time. In data security, the length of time that it is believed a cipher will resist a particular attack. *See* MINIMAL COVER TIME.

covert storage channel. In computer security, a covert channel that involves the direct or indirect writing of a storage location by one process and the direct or indirect reading of the storage location by another process. Covert storage channels typically involve a finite resource (e.g. sectors on a disk) that is shared by two subjects at different security levels. (DOD). *Compare* COVERT TIMING CHANNEL. *See* COVERT CHANNEL.

covert timing channel. In computer security, a covert channel in which one process signals information to another by modulating its own use of system resources (e.g. central processing unit time) in such a way that this manipulation affects the real response time observed by the second process. (DOD). *Compare* COVERT STORAGE CHANNEL. *See* COVERT CHANNEL.

CPM. *See* CRITICAL PATH METHOD.

cps. Cycles per second. *See* HERTZ.

CPU. *See* CENTRAL PROCESSING UNIT.

CPU-bound. In computing, pertaining to a process that makes extensive use of the central processing unit (CPU) and spends a low proportion of time on input/output operations. In concurrent programming systems it is necessary to ensure that CPU-bound processes do not affect overall system performance by locking out other processes. *Compare* INPUT/OUTPUT-BOUND. *See* CENTRAL PROCESSING UNIT, CONCURRENT PROGRAMMING, SCHEDULER.

CR. *See* CARRIAGE RETURN.

cracker. In software protection, a hacker who specializes in overcoming software protection systems. *Compare* CRASHER. *See* HACKER.

cracking. In software protection, a small routine that bypasses a protection scheme. *Compare* DEMON.

crash. In computing, a failure in a component or system during operations that renders it unavailable for use.

crasher. In computer security, a hacker who deliberately attempts to cause serious interference to the operation of a computer system. *Compare* CRACKER. *See* HACKER.

crawl. In filming, a device upon which television or film credits are mounted and

which makes them appear to crawl up the screen.

Cray-1. In computing, a well-known supercomputer. *See* PARALLEL PROCESSING, SUPERCOMPUTER.

CRC. *See* CYCLIC REDUNDANCY CHECK.

credit card. In banking, a card that enables the subscriber to purchase goods or services from a variety of outlets and then refund the appropriate financial institution, on a periodic basis. *See* SMART CARD.

creep. In video, a slippage between video tape and the recorder capstan that affects playback synchronization. *See* CAPSTAN.

crispening. In recording, the use of digital storage and processing techniques to improve the quality of an image. *See* IMAGE PROCESSING.

critical fusion frequency. In computer graphics, the frequency of a flickering stimulus at which the flicker appears to stop and the individual sensations are fused into a continuous, uniform sensation. *See* COMPUTER ANIMATION, FLICKER, PERSISTENCE OF VISION.

critical path method. (CPM) A management technique for control of large-scale projects involving analysis and determination of each critical step necessary for project completion. *See* PERT.

critical processing. In computer security, applications defined as being of such importance in the operation of an organization that little or no loss of availability is acceptable. *Compare* DISCRETIONARY PROCESSING.

critical region. In programming, a section of code that may only be executed by one process at any one time. *See* PROCESS.

CRN. In communications, cellular radio network. *See* CELLULAR RADIO.

CROM. *See* CONTROL READ-ONLY MEMORY.

cropping. In printing, the elimination of parts of a photograph or other original that are not required to be printed. Cropping allows the remaining parts of the image to be enlarged to fill the space. (Desktop).

cross-assembler. In programming, an assembler that runs on one type of computer and produces machine code for another. *Compare* CROSS-COMPILER. *See* ASSEMBLING.

cross-check. In mathematics, a method of validating the results of a calculation by repeating it using an alternative method.

cross-compiler. In programming, a compiler that generates object code for execution on a different computer than that on which it is running. *Compare* CROSS-ASSEMBLER. *See* COMPILER.

cross-fade. In recording, a transition in sound or image, with the element fading out as a second element fades in.

crossfire. *Synonymous with* CROSSTALK.

cross head. In printing, a heading set in the body of the text used to break it into easily readable sections. (Desktop).

cross-interleaved Reed-Solomon code. (CIRC) In codes, an error protection code, specially developed for the compact disc (CD), comprising two Reed-Solomon codes interleaved crosswise.

CIRC makes it possible for a CD player decoder to detect and correct, or conceal, large burst errors. Errors of up to 4000 data bits (2.5 millimetres of track) can be corrected. Errors up to 12 304 data bits can be concealed.

The CIRC encoder uses two stages of encoding and three stages of interleaving.

The 12 pulse code-modulated audio samples (24 symbols) of one compact disc audio frame are fed in parallel to the first encoder. The second symbol of each audio sample is delayed by two symbols, so that the symbols of two successive frames are interleaved. The first encoder then adds four parity symbols, making 24 in all.

These 28 symbols are fed to the second encoder through delay lines of different lengths. The second encoder adds four more parity symbols, making 32 in all. Finally, alternative audio signals are delayed by one symbol. The total effect is to spread the symbols of one frame over eight frames.

The two stages of CIRC encoding make it possible for the CIRC decoder in a CD player to correct two symbols in each received frame directly, or to correct four symbols in each received frame by erasure and calculation. Furthermore, it allows detection of up to 32 successive incorrect symbols so that interpolated values can be substituted. Because of the dispersion of symbols over eight frames, up to 4000 wrong data bits can be corrected and up to 12 304 wrong data bits can be concealed. The final (one symbol) delay provides protection against random errors. (Philips). *See* BIT, COMPACT DISC, CONCEALMENT, DELAY LINE, FRAME, PULSE CODE MODULATION, SYMBOL.

cross-modulation. In communications, an interference between two or more modulated signals, with different carrier frequencies, produced by non-linearities in the transmission path. *See* INTERFERENCE, MODULATION, NON-LINEAR.

cross-own. In broadcasting, the ownership of both a television station and newspaper in a single market area.

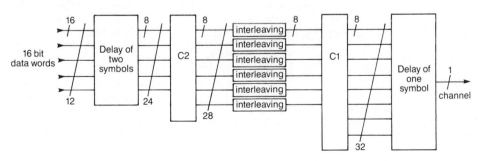

cross-interleaved Reed-Solomon code
CIRC – encoder principle.

cross-programs. In software, programs written for one computer that can generate machine code to run on another type of computer. *See* CROSS-ASSEMBLER, CROSS-COMPILER.

cross-referenced page. In videotex, a page that can be selected from a page which is not its parent. *See* PARENT.

cross-section. In communications, the signal transmission capacity of a transmission system normally measured in terms of the number of two-way voice channels.

crosstalk. In communications, an unwanted transfer of energy from one communications channel to another channel. (FIPS). *Synonymous with* CROSSFIRE.

CRT. *See* CATHODE RAY TUBE.

CRTC. Canadian Radio Television and Telecommunications Commission.

CRT controller. In peripherals, a device used to interface a microcomputer to a cathode ray tube (CRT) display. The controller generates four sets of signals: (a) the address of the character in screen memory to be displayed; (b) the row of the dot matrix pattern to be displayed next; (c) raster scan synchronization signals; and (d) a display enable signal. In addition, the controller normally provides the cursor display and accepts light pen input signals. *See* CATHODE RAY TUBE, CURSOR, DOT MATRIX, LIGHT PEN, RASTER SCAN.

CRT recording. In applications, a technique used in the production of computer output microfilm. The image on the face of a cathode ray tube (CRT) is focused onto microfilm. *Compare* ELECTRON BEAM RECORDING, FIBER OPTICS RECORDING. *See* CATHODE RAY TUBE, COMPUTER OUTPUT TO MICROFILM.

crushing. In television, an unwanted change in the contrast gradient of a picture. *See* CONTRAST.

cryogenics. The application of temperatures close to the absolute zero. *See* SUPERCONDUCTIVITY.

cryptanalysis. In data security, the steps and operations performed in converting encrypted messages into plaintext without initial knowledge of the key employed in the encryption algorithm. (FIPS). *See* ENCRYPT, KEY, PLAINTEXT.

cryptogram. *Synonymous with* CIPHERTEXT.

cryptographic algorithm. In data security, a set of rules specifying the procedure required to encipher and decipher data. *See* CIPHER.

cryptographic authentication. In authentication, the use of encryption-related techniques to provide authentication. *See* MESSAGE AUTHENTICATION.

cryptographic bit stream. In data security, the stream of bits which is combined with the plaintext to form the ciphertext in stream cipher. *See* STREAM CIPHER. *Synonymous with* KEY STREAM, RUNNING KEY.

cryptographic checksum. In data security, a checksum computed using a secret key. *See* CHECKSUM, MAC.

cryptographic control. In data security, the use of cryptographic techniques to protect information when transmitted over a link or when stored in a computer. *See* WIRETAPPING.

cryptographic key. In data security, a code used in association with a cryptographic algorithm, for enciphering and deciphering data.

cryptography. The science and study of secret writing. A cipher is a secret method of writing, whereby plaintext is transformed into ciphertext. The process of transforming plaintext into ciphertext is called encipherment or encryption; the reverse process of

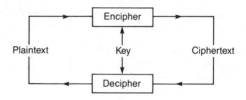

cryptography
Fig. 1. Cryptographic key.

transforming ciphertext into plaintext is called decipherment or decryption. Both encipherment and decipherment are controlled by one or more cryptographic keys.

Classical cryptography provide secrecy for information sent over channels where eavesdropping and message interception are possible. The sender selects a cipher and encryption key, and either gives it directly to the receiver or else sends it indirectly over a slow, but secure channel, typically a trusted courier. Messages and replies were transmitted over the insecure channel in ciphertext.

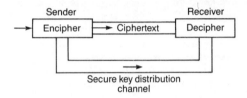

cryptography
Fig. 2. Classical information channel.

A cryptographic system is analogous to a resettable combination lock used to secure a safe. The combination is kept secret and can be changed whenever it is suspected of having fallen into the wrong hands. Although unauthorized persons know the set of all possible keys or combinations, they may be unable to discover the exact combination with a reasonable expenditure of time and money. The effort to try all possible combinations is a measure of the security of the lock, or cipher.

Modern cryptography protects data transmitted over high-speed links or information stored in computer systems. There are two principal objectives: (a) secrecy (or privacy) to prevent the unauthorized disclosure of data; and (b) authenticity (or integrity) to prevent the unauthorized modification of data. Modern ciphers, such as the data encryption standard, offer a high degree of security and can only be broken by an attacker with knowledge of the key being used. In general, the algorithm used for encryption/decryption with modern cryptosystems is published, but the key is kept secret. *See* CRYPTANALYSIS, CRYPTOGRAPHIC KEY, DATA ENCRYPTION STANDARD, DIGITAL SIGNATURE, PUBLIC KEY CRYPTOGRAPHY.

cryptology. In data security, the art of devising ciphers and breaking them. *See* CRYPTANALYSIS, CRYPTOGRAPHY.

cryptomanagement. In data security, the procedures that must be implemented and operated to ensure that cryptographic systems provide the required degree of security.

crystal microphone. In recording, a microphone in which the transducer is a piezoelectric crystal. When the crystal is deformed by a sound wave, the small voltage generated is used as an audio signal. *See* PIEZOELECTRIC.

C shell. In programming, a widely used Unix shell, preferred for interactive computing. *Compare* BOURNE SHELL. *See* INTERACTIVE, SHELL, UNIX.

CSIRONET. In data communications, a computer network operated by the Australian Commonwealth Scientific and Industrial Research Organization.

CSMA-CD. *See* CARRIER SENSE MULTIPLE ACCESS — COLLISION DETECTION.

CSR. *See* CONTINUOUS SPEECH RECOGNITION.

CSU. *See* CONTINUOUS SPEECH UNDERSTANDING.

CSV. In data structures, comma separated value; a free-format file standard in which a comma is used to delimit fields and quotation marks surround text. *See* DATA FORMAT.

CT. *See* CORDLESS TELEPHONE.

CTRL. In peripherals, a key on a computer terminal which, when pressed in conjunction with another key, is used to perform a control or manipulation function (e.g. to terminate an editing operation).

CTS. *See* CLEAR TO SEND.

cue code. In optical media, a code used in compact disc (CD) tape mastering. It is recorded on audio track 1 of the CD tape master and contains the information necessary to generate subcode during disc mastering. (Philips). *See* CD MASTERING, CD TAPE MASTER, SUBCODE CHANNEL.

CUG.   *See* CLOSED USER GROUP.

culling.   In computer graphics, the removal of back faces. *See* BACK FACES.

cumulative index.   In library science, an index that comprises the combination of a number of separate indexes. *See* INDEX.

curie point.   In recording, the temperature at which the residual recorded signal on magnetic tape or disc is lost or severely reduced.

current.   In electronics, an electric current flows through a conductor when there is an overall movement of electrons or other charge-carrying elements through it. *See* ELECTRON.

current awareness service.   In library science, a service that provides information and/or documents to users, based upon their known fields of interest or activity. *See* SELECTIVE DISSEMINATION OF INFORMATION.

current loop interface.   In data communications, an unofficial interface standard popular with low-cost home computers. It has two versions — 20 and 60 milliamps — and usually works over distances of 1500 feet with data rates up to 9600 bits per second. *Compare* RS-232C.

cursive.   In printing, describing typefaces that resemble written script. (Desktop). *See* TYPEFACE, ZAPF CHANCERY.

cursor.   (1) In peripherals, a symbol or character on a screen display that indicates a position, or a path to be followed. It is moved by the application program to guide the user and by the user to define a requirement. (Philips). (2) In peripherals, a short line or character on a visual display unit indicating where the next character is to be typed.

cursor control.   In peripherals, a facility in some visual display units enabling the cursor

to be moved around the screen under keyboard control. *See* CURSOR, KEYBOARD.

cursor home.   In peripherals, the operation of moving the cursor to the top left-hand corner of the screen.

cursor plane.   In optical media, the plane in which the cursor is presented in multiplane video representations. *See* MULTIPLANE.

curvature of field.   In optics, an aberration in which the focal point of a lens image falls on a curved rather than a flat plane. *See* ABERRATION.

cushioning.   In computer graphics, a technique that is used in computer animation to smooth the movement of an object to give a realistic impression of inertia. *Synonymous with* FAIRING.

custodian of data.   In data security, the individual or group that has been entrusted with the possession of, and responsibility for, the security of specified data.

custom design.   In microelectronics, the design of a microelectronic circuit to meet the specifications of an individual customer. *See* FULL-CUSTOM DESIGN, SEMI-CUSTOM DESIGN. *Synonymous with* APPLICATION-SPECIFIC DESIGN, CUSTOM-SPECIFIC DESIGN.

customer engineering.   (CE) In computing, pertaining to the department of a manufacturer that is responsible for field maintenance and repair of installed equipment.

custom-specific design.   *Synonymous with* CUSTOM DESIGN.

cut.   In filming, to remove unwanted portions of film during editing.

cut and paste.   (1) In peripherals, an electronic technique for the manipulation, of textual or pictorial information on a display screen, in a manner similar to the cut and paste technique used in editing such information on paper. (2) In word processing, the facility to delete a section of text and relocate it elsewhere, in one or more places, of the stored document. *Compare* BLOCK COPY.

cut in. In filming and video, a direct change from one image to another. (Philips).

cut-in notes. In printing, notes set into the text at the outer edge of a paragraph with white space forming three sides of a square around them.

cutoff. In communications, the point of degradation at which a signal becomes unusable because of attenuation or distortion. *See* ATTENUATION, DISTORTION.

cutoff frequency. In electronics, the upper or lower frequency limits of the useful frequency band of a filter. *See* FILTER.

cutout. In printing, a halftone where the background has been removed to produce a silhouette. (Desktop). *See* HALFTONE.

CVBS. In television, composite video broadcast signal; the standard form of colour television broadcast signal in which the intensity and relation of the red, green and blue components are represented by a luminance signal and a chrominance signal. (Philips). *See* CHROMINANCE SIGNAL, COMPOSITE COLOUR VIDEO SIGNAL, LUMINANCE SIGNAL.

CWP. *See* COMMUNICATING WORD PROCESSING.

cyan. In optics, the colour that is the complement of red (i.e. blue-green). *See* COMPLEMENTARY COLOURS.

cybernetics. The technology concerned with the study of control and information flows in artificial and natural systems.

cycle. In computing, the basic time unit of a central processing unit. *See* CENTRAL PROCESSING UNIT.

cycles per second. *See* HERTZ.

cycle stealing. In computing, a technique in which a peripheral uses one or more processor cycles to access main storage, locking out the processor from main storage for that period. *Compare* DIRECT MEMORY ACCESS.

cycle time. *See* CYCLE.

cyclic code. *See* GREY CODE.

cyclic redundancy check. (CRC) In codes, a method for detecting errors in the transmission or transfer of data using a polynomial code and a cyclic check field. *See* POLYNOMIAL CODE.

cylinder. In memory systems, the set of tracks of magnetic disks, on a unit with multiple read/write heads that can be read without mechanical movements of the heads. *See* MAGNETIC DISK.

cylinder machine. In printing, a machine bed from which impressions are made by a cylinder. *Compare* PLATEN PRESS. *See* CYLINDER.

cyrillic alphabet. The Russian alphabet, derived from Greek and incorporating characters expressing Slavic sounds.

D

DAA. *See* DATA ACCESS ARRANGEMENT.

DAC. (1) Data authentication code. *Synonymous with* MAC. (2) In computer security. *See* DISCRETIONARY ACCESS CONTROL. (3) In electronics. *See* DIGITAL-TO-ANALOG CONVERTER.

D/A converter. *See* DIGITAL-TO-ANALOG CONVERTER.

DAD. Digital audio disc. *Synonymous with* COMPACT DISC.

dagger. In printing, a type character used as a second order of reference marks in footnotes. It is sometimes called an obelisk or long cross. *See* REFERENCE MARK.

dailies. In filming, visual and audio workprints representing the results of a day's shooting. *Compare* INSTANTLIES.

daisy chain. (1) In computing, a method by which signals are propagated along a bus, allowing the central processing unit (CPU) interrupt control signal to pass along the chain. The first device in the chain, next to the CPU, has the highest priority. *See* BUS, INTERRUPT. (2) In data communications, a technique in a local area network to pass permission for a node to transmit; dedicated wires are used to pass control information from one node to the next. *Compare* CONTROL TOKEN, MESSAGE SLOT. *See* LOCAL AREA NETWORK.

daisy wheel. In printing, a print element used in conjunction with a daisy wheel character printer. It is a removable flat disc with spokes radiating out on stalks from a central hub, the entire print 'wheel' resembling a daisy. The daisy wheel is available in a variety of type styles and may be 10, 12 or 15 pitch or proportionally spaced. *Compare* LASER PRINTER, MATRIX PRINTER. *See* PITCH, PRINTER, PROPORTIONAL SPACING. *Synonymous with* PRINT WHEEL.

DAMA. *See* DEMAND-ASSIGNED MULTIPLE ACCESS.

dark current. In optoelectronics, the current that flows in a photodetector when there is no radiant energy or light flux incident upon its sensitive surface. *See* PHOTOCELL.

dark trace tube. In computer graphics, a cathode ray tube (CRT) in which the electron beam causes the phosphor surface of the tube to darken rather than to brighten. *See* CATHODE RAY TUBE.

DARPA. Defense Advanced Research Projects Agency; originally ARPA.

DASD. *See* DIRECT-ACCESS STORAGE DEVICE.

DAT. *See* DIGITAL AUDIO TAPE.

data. (1) Programs, files or other information stored in, or processed by, a computer system. (FIPS). (2) In legislation, as defined by the UK Data Protection Act, 1984, information recorded in a form in which it can be processed by equipment operating automatically in response to instructions given for that purpose. *See* DATA PROTECTION. (3) Information that is to be input, processed in some way and output by the computer. There is usually no restriction on the meaning associated with the data when it is processed by a computer, but it must be in a format that the computer can interpret. This is usually the responsibility of the programmer who has to define whether the data is numeric or alphanumeric, and its method of coding (e.g. binary, octal, etc.). (4) A

130

representation of facts, concepts or instructions in a formalized manner in order that it may be communicated, interpreted or processed by human or automatic means. *Compare* INFORMATION.

data above voice. (DAV) In data communications, a system for carrying digital data on a portion of the radio spectrum above the frequency used for voice transmission. *Compare* DATA IN VOICE, DATA UNDER VOICE.

data abstraction. *See* ABSTRACT DATA TYPE.

data access arrangement. (DAA) In communications, a unit containing an isolation transformer, for interconnecting user equipment to a telephone network. It is designed to prevent harmful voltages or signals entering the network.

data acquisition. (1) In computing, the process of identifying, isolating and gathering source data to be processed centrally. *See* COMPUTERIZED INSTRUMENTATION, DATA CAPTURE.

data aggregate. In databases, a CODASYL term for a named collection of data items within a record. *See* CODASYL.

data analysis. In databases, the development of the appropriate data structures to represent the data of a given application area. *See* DATA MODELLING, DATA STRUCTURE, NORMAL FORMS.

databank. A term that is often considered to be synonymous with database, but may be used to distinguish numeric databases from bibliographic or textual data. *See* BIBLIOGRAPHIC DATABASE, DATABASE, DIRECTORY DATABASE, FULL-TEXT DATABASE, NUMERIC DATABASE, REFERRAL DATABASE.

database. (1) An extensive and comprehensive set of records collected and organized in a meaningful manner to serve a particular purpose. (DODD). (2) In software, a collection of stored operational data used by the applications system of an enterprise. The precursor of database systems was sets of individual files maintained by departments of the enterprise for prespecified purposes and processed by individual application programs. This arrangement was inefficient in terms of the programming effort required to operate the system, failed to provide the management with the whole range of information available from the stored data and was too inflexible for evolving enterprises.

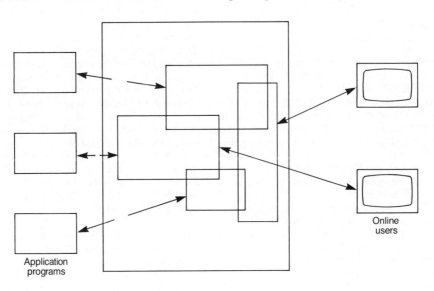

Application programs

Online users

database
Fig. 1. Unintegrated system of files.

Database systems integrate stored data, and special software termed database management systems (DBMS) provide a buffer between the stored data and application programs.

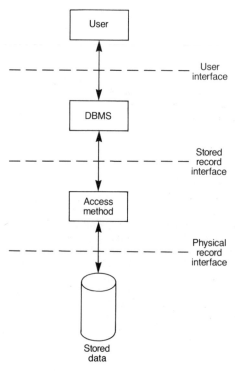

Fig. 2. Integrated data.

The advantages gained from this approach are: (a) the physical storage systems are decoupled from the application program; (b) the redundancy of stored data can be reduced; (c) problems of inconsistency in the stored data are reduced; (d) stored data can be shared amongst users; (e) data control standards can be enforced; (f) security restrictions can be applied; (g) data integrity can be maintained; and (h) ad hoc enquiries are facilitated.

The presence of the DBMS implies that individual programs can communicate data to the DBMS which has responsibility for accessing or updating the corresponding item in physical storage. This physical data independence allows the physical storage arrangements to be changed (e.g. to accommodate larger masses of data or to optimize data access) without modification to the application programs. The integration of stored data ensures that data items are not unnecessarily duplicated across files (e.g. employee information stored on personnel and payroll files). This reduction in data redundancy also minimizes the danger of data inconsistency (e.g. if the personnel department updated its file when a employee resigned then there would be an inconsistency with the corresponding item on the payroll file until the accounts department took the same action). Sharing of data between departments is obviously facilitated by the database approach, and this provides more relevant information for managers (e.g. it is possible to correlate details of employee qualifications with salary).

The major advantage of database systems became apparent as the volume of stored data increased, and the systems moved from batch to interactive modes. The dangers of incorrect, invalid or insecure data becomes acute in these circumstances, but with an integrated store of data it is possible to assign responsibility for overall control of the database to a database administrator (DBA). The DBA is given the authority and responsibility to ensure that the installation standards are enforced. This overcomes the problems arising from idiosyncratic data formats produced by individual programmers and facilitates both maintenance and data interchange between installations. The value and confidential nature of corporate data have compelled organizations to adopt stricter attitudes to data access. The existence of a central electronic store has enhanced the dangers of unauthorized access. The function of the DBA to enforce central control is thus vital to organizations. It is important to protect the data from accidental as well as malicious damage, and the DBA must initiate and enforce operating procedures and validity controls which minimize the danger of incorrect insertions or modifications (e.g. input data is rejected if it is in an incorrect format or does not conform to prespecified criteria).

The initial developments of databases concentrated upon the design of the inter-relationships between data items and the optimization of access strategies. The two major approaches were hierarchical and network databases. The former have a tree structure, with individual items being accessed by searches along branches from parent to child nodes. Alternatively, network databases allow pointers between data items that contravene the tree requirements of only one parent per node. Indexes and inverted files greatly facilitate access to individual items and reduce time-consuming multiple disk accesses. Inverted files permit fast searches on attributes other than the primary key. For example, if an employee file is sorted alphabetically by employee name then a search for all the employees in a particular department involves a comprehensive search of all the employees in the organization. An inverted file containing department and employee name, sorted by department name, would provide the necessary information in a fraction of the time.

The aforementioned approaches to database design, however, imposed a rigid structure on the database and led to very complex indexing arrangements. The relational database concept introduced by E.F. Codd revolutionized database concepts and removed the demand for complex indexes. The relational database is based upon the simplest possible data structure (i.e. tables or flat files). These tables, termed relations, can be manipulated to provide a view of the data appropriate to the particular application. This development provides yet a further degree of data independence (i.e. logical data independence). The users can be effectively provided with an individual database, which is a subset of the total database, geared to their particular requirements. This individual database does not involve any physical partitioning or rearrangement of the stored data. It does not therefore reintroduce the dangers of duplication or inconsistency inherent in the production of multiple 'private' databases. The provision of local views also simplifies security procedures since individual users are only provided with a subschema consistent with their security grading.

The modern trend is to employ relational databases accessed interactively with simple query languages or processed by fourth-generation languages. Whereas earlier databases were primarily processed by application programs in batch mode, current systems are designed to support both this mode and online access for ad hoc queries and updates by a large and diffuse user population.

The online access in a multiuser environment demands both a simple user interface and a sophisticated DBMS which guarantees security and integrity under all operating conditions. The database must be protected against aborted transactions which could leave it in an inconsistent state (e.g. a partial bank transaction which credits one account, but does not debit another). It must also be possible to reconstruct the database in the case of system failure. Concurrent users must be protected against mutual interference particularly if both are updating the same record.

The total population of database users is expanding rapidly. At one end of the spectrum there are massive databases designed for corporate bodies and public databases serving national and international users. At the other, there are a multiplicity of microcomputer DBMS designed for small businesses and professional users (e.g. dBase). *See* APPLICATION PROGRAM, DATABASE ADMINISTRATOR, DATABASE SECURITY, DATA INDEPENDENCE, dBASE, FLAT FILE, FOURTH-GENERATION LANGUAGE, HIERARCHICAL DATABASE, INVERTED FILE, LOCKOUT, LOGICAL DATA INDEPENDENCE, NETWORK DATABASE, PRIMARY KEY, QUERY LANGUAGE, RELATIONAL DATABASE, ROLLBACK, SCHEMA, SUBSCHEMA, TREE STRUCTURE.

database administrator. (DBA) In databases, a person who is responsible for a database system, particularly for defining the rules by which data is accessed, modified and stored. *See* DATABASE.

database language. *See* DATABASE MANAGEMENT SYSTEM, DATA DESCRIPTION LANGUAGE, DATA MANIPULATION LANGUAGE, QUERY LANGUAGE.

database machine. In computing, a combination of hardware and software specifically designed to speed up database operations. Most current developments are concerned with either enhancing the technology of magnetic disk storage mechanisms or finding suitable roles for other memory technologies (e.g. bubble memory). *See* BUBBLE MEMORY, MAGNETIC DISK.

database management system. (DBMS) In databases, a set of programs that facilitates the creation and maintenance of a database and the execution of programs using the database. *See* DATA INDEPENDENCE.

database producer. In online information retrieval, the person or organization that compiles a database. The producer may be a commercial enterprise, professional organization or government agency. It is not necessarily the producer who makes the database available to the database vendor. *Compare* DATABASE VENDOR.

database publishing. *See* ELECTRONIC PUBLISHING.

database security. The application of databases has increased rapidly in recent years; there has been a proliferation of individual databases on micro- and minicomputers and an expansion in the capacity of large systems serving organizational, national and international user populations. The integration of an organization's files into a single database increases the risk of unauthorized access and malicious modification of the organization's data. Moreover, the advent of data protection legislation places a legal responsibility on holders of personal data to protect that information against malicious modification and unauthorized access. Thus the problems of database security are increasing both in terms of the magnitude of the problem and the penalties associated with lax security.

Ideally the security arrangements for a database should meet the requirements listed below.

(a) No person or groups of persons should be able to access, modify, add or delete illegally the data.
(b) No unauthorized person, or unauthorized group of persons, should be able to infer the value of a confidential item by manipulating queries or performing computations on released data.
(c) The security arrangements should be flexible and users provided with privileges appropriate to their function and needs.
(d) The security mechanisms should not significantly degrade the performance of the database management system.
(e) The accessibility of the system should not be reduced for legitimate users.

(f) There should be no significant expansion of stored data.
(g) The cost of the security arrangements should not be incompatible with the function of the database.

The security problems for all databases fall into two broad categories — integrity preservation and security — but the nature of the problem is related to the function, size and user population of the database.

Integrity preservation concerns the preservation of the database contents against non-malicious errors. Security is concerned with access control (i.e. the database is only viewed and/or modified by authorized users). *See* ACCESS CONTROL, DATABASE MANAGEMENT SYSTEM, DATA SECURITY, INFERENCE CONTROL.

Data Base Task Group. (DBTG) In databases, the CODASYL committee responsible for producing their database facilities and associated data description language and data manipulation language. *See* CODASYL, DATA DESCRIPTION LANGUAGE, DATA MANIPULATION LANGUAGE.

database vendor. In online information retrieval, an organization that makes available access to a number of databases provided by a variety of database producers. *Compare* DATABASE PRODUCER. *Synonymous with* HOST.

data bits. In data communications, the number of bits transmitted per character, not including checking and timing bits. *See* BIT.

data broadcasting. In data communications, a technique in which information is updated continuously, and the updates are transmitted to subscribers over broadcast lines. There is no interaction with the end user. Moreover, unlike broadcast techniques such as teletext, the updated information is not transmitted cyclically, and therefore any failure to capture a particular transmission can lead to a subscriber's data loss. With conventional data transmission techniques the subscriber's computer could fail to receive the data if it is undertaking other processing or if it is temporarily offline. Moreover, the data is non-specific so that the subscriber will often discard a substantial

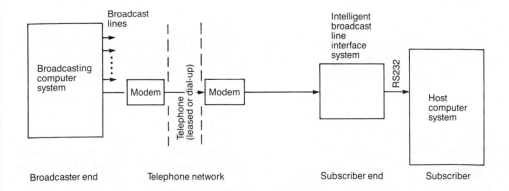

Broadcast lines

Broadcasting computer system

Modem

Telephone (leased or dial-up)

Modem

Intelligent broadcast line interface system

RS232

Host computer system

Broadcaster end   Telephone network   Subscriber end   Subscriber

data broadcasting

proportion of the updates. With data-broadcasting systems an intelligent broadcast line interface unit performs the data handling and only transfers the data relevant to the host.

The Stock Exchange system is an application area for data broadcasting since a large volume of trading information is transmitted to a wide stockbroker user population. *See* BIG BANG, BROADCAST LINES.

data bus. (1) In computing, a bus system that interconnects the central processing unit, memory and all the peripheral input/output devices of a computer system for the purpose of exchanging data. *Compare* ADDRESS BUS, CONTROL BUS. *See* BUS, MICRO-COMPUTER. (2) In optoelectronics, an optical waveguide used as a common trunk line to which a number of terminals can be interconnected using optical couplers. *See* COUPLER.

data bus coupler. In optoelectronics, a component that interconnects a number of optical waveguides and provides an inherently bidirectional system by mixing and splitting all signals in it. *See* DATA BUS.

data capture. In computing, the act of obtaining data by means of peripheral devices (e.g. a point-of-sale terminal). *See* POINT-OF-SALE TERMINAL.

data carrier. In memory systems, any medium such as magnetic tape or disk used to carry data. *See* MAGNETIC DISK, MAGNETIC TAPE, OPTICAL DIGITAL DISC.

data carrier detect. (DCD) In data communications, an interface signal from a modem to data terminal equipment indicating that a carrier signal of adequate quality is being received. *See* CARRIER, DATA TERMINAL EQUIPMENT.

data cassette. In memory systems, a compact cassette manufactured specifically for data recording, often with a short recording time of 10 or 15 minutes. (Philips). *See* COMPACT CASSETTE.

data cell. In data structures, the smallest unit of data which cannot be further subdivided (e.g. a bit). *Compare* CELL. *See* BIT.

Datacentralen. In online information retrieval, a Danish online service connected with Euronet DIANE. *See* DIANE.

data chain. In data structures, blocks of data linked together by pointers. *See* CHAINED FILE.

data channel. (1) In optical media, a channel of a compact disc carrying data, as opposed to audio information. (Philips). *See* COMPACT DISC. (2) In optical media, a channel carrying mode 1 data on a read-only memory compact disc. (Philips). *See* COMPACT DISC – READ-ONLY MEMORY, MODE 1. (3) In data communications. *See* CHANNEL.

data circuit. In data communications, a circuit that enables two-way communication to be carried out between any two data-terminating devices such as computers, visual display units, etc.

data circuit terminating equipment. (DCE) In data communications, a piece of equipment located at either end of a data circuit that provides all the functions needed to establish, maintain and terminate a connection. It also carries out the signal conversion and coding between the data terminal equipment and the telephone line. *Compare* DATA TERMINAL EQUIPMENT. *See* MODEM.

data collection. In computing, an activity in which data from several locations is accumulated at one place prior to processing.

data collection platform. In communications, a small, unattended ground station used to transmit automatically data to a central point via a satellite. *See* GROUND STATION.

data communications. The transmission of data between a person and a program, or between one program and another, when the sender and receiver are remote from each other. Data communications may take place between workstations and computers within a limited geographical region such as an office building or college campus, in which case the network is classified as a local area network. If the various installations are located at different cities connected by public telephone networks, high-speed data communication lines or satellites, then the network is classified as wide area. Local area networks are normally owned and operated by a single organization whereas wide area networks comprise hosts, belonging to one or more organizations, and a communication system operated by a common carrier. A typical wide area network is illustrated in the diagram.

Data circuit terminating equipment (DCE) provides an interface between the host computers and the network. A communications network node allows for store and forward facilities so that messages may be routed from one node to another, temporarily stored and then rerouted towards their destinations.

At the lowest level of operation the network may be considered as simply passing signals, representing bits, from one location to another. In wide area networks the communication can be organized on a circuit- or packet-switching basis. In circuit switching a connection is established between sender and receiver which is only released when one party terminates the call (e.g. as in a telephone connection). In packet switching, on the other hand, the users establish a connection between their terminal or host and the nearest communications network node.

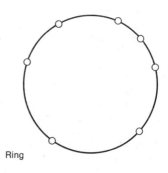

Ring

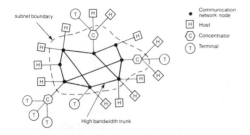

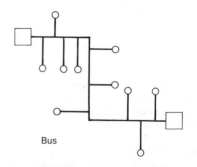

Bus

data communications
Fig. 1. A typical point to point wide area network .

data communications
Fig. 2. Ring and bus networks.

Whenever data is to be transmitted it is sent as a series of packets, typically 10–1000 bytes long. Packets are routed from communications network node to communications network node within the communication network until they reach the communications network node that services the destination host.

In local networks the DCE is provided by an interface cards in the constituent workstations or microcomputers. The networks are organized either on a bus or ring basis as shown in the diagram.

The Ethernet network, properly a trademark of the Xerox Corp., is now commonly used as a generic term for a linear or tree-shaped network using CSMA-CD (carrier sense multiple access — collision detection) mode. Ring networks operate on a different principle, and the whole ring is regarded as a massive circular shift register. After each shift the workstation interface can read or write the bit just shifted into it.

The consideration of the physical transfer of bits around the network does not allow for the problems that can arise from transmission errors (i.e. error control) or the possibility that a receiver is unable to accept data as fast as the sender can transmit (i.e. flow control). This aspect of data communications is handled by agreed protocols governing the exchange of signals, between transmitters and receivers, concerning the states of data transmission. A typical protocol is HDLC (high-level data link control). The raw data must first be organized into groups, or frames, so that each individual frame can be checked and acknowledged. The frames must, of course, be delimited, and if additional bits are used as delimiters then these bits must be so recognized so that they are not confused with data. Three common techniques are character count, character stuffing and bit stuffing. Using character count a fixed-format frame header indicates the number of characters in a frame. In theory the receiver simply counts the incoming characters and hence detects the end of the frame. However, this technique is extremely sensitive to transmission errors in the count field and lost characters can wreck frame synchronization. Character stuffing uses a special 'end of frame' character to terminate frames, but this forces a specific character code into the protocol. Bit stuffing is used by modern protocols for wide

area networks; in this case frames are delimited by the bit pattern 0 111 111 0, if five consecutive 1s appear in the data stream a 0 is stuffed into the bit stream and subsequently removed by the receiver.

Local area networks can use any of the above methods, but can also simply detect the end of a frame by the absence of a signal on the cable. Frame headers will also contain some form of checksum to provide for the detection, but not correction, of transmission errors. With the increased use of satellite communication, with their long propagation times, the use of error-correcting codes (e.g. Hamming codes), which do not necessarily require retransmission of data, becomes increasingly economic, but conventional local and wide area networks simply call for the retransmission of corrupted frames.

When two people communicate over a telephone they automatically employ a number of informal conventions to ensure that meaningful conversation takes place; the speaker will listen for comments of affirmation and if the listener is silent for an extended period then the speaker will enquire 'Are you still there?'. Similar protocols are required between the sender and receiver in a communication network, and the design of standardized effective protocols is an essential element of a successful system. At the simplest level there is the stop-and-wait protocol. In this case host A sends a frame to B and awaits specific permission from B to send the next one. If host A puts a sequence number on the frame header, together with some error-detecting code, then on receipt of a positive acknowledgement from B it forwards the next frame; on receipt of a negative acknowledgement, indicating errors detected by B, the frame is retransmitted by A. Unfortunately, such simple protocols can easily fail and when additional features are built into the protocol to overcome detected problems, they provide additional complexity and sources of new error conditions. Thus the design of effective protocols is a task of some complexity. For example, in the case where host A awaits receipt of positive, or negative, acknowledgement from B before forwarding another frame, a complete deadlock arises if either the message, or acknowledgement, frame is lost in transmission. To overcome this problem host A can be required to retransmit a frame if no acknowledgement is received after a specified period. However, if a satellite transmission is employed, then the minimum propagation delay for message and acknowledgement frame is 540 milliseconds. In this case host A must await at least this period of time before it can assume that a frame is lost. Thus a 1000-bit frame sent over a 1 megabit per second channel takes only 1 millisecond, but frames can only be sent every 540 milliseconds if the simple stop-and-wait protocol is employed. The transmission rate can be improved by the use of sliding window protocols. In this case the sender is allowed to have multiple unacknowledged frames outstanding simultaneously. If each frame is given a unique sequence number then host A could send out frames at high speed and retransmit individual frames if either negative acknowledgements are received or if no acknowledgement for a particular sequence number arrives in a given time interval. However, this technique produces a problem because the sequence numbers will become very large, thus necessitating an excessive overhead in the size of the frame header. The frame sequence numbers can simply be limited to a fixed size, and thereafter repeat themselves. The protocols then need to be designed with care to ensure that losses in message or acknowledgement frames do not lead to confusion between frames with identical sequence numbers.

The high-level data link control (HDLC) protocol uses a designated flag field to delimit frames with bit stuffing and a checksum field for error detection. There are three types of frame: information, supervisory and unnumbered. The information frames from A to B contain data, but also indicate the sequence number of the current frame and the frames correctly received from B to A. Attaching an acknowledgement field to an outgoing data frame is known as piggybacking. Supervisory frames are used to send acknowledgements when no information frames are transmitted and for other control purposes (e.g. negative acknowledgement, receiver temporarily not ready). Unnumbered frames are employed for a variety of control purposes.

The protocols described so far relate to point-to-point transmissions. Radio or satellite data communication networks, and some local area networks, operate in a broadcast mode (i.e. every host receives every message transmitted). The broadcast mode can lead to collisions when two hosts are transmitting simultaneously and protocols are required to enable recovery and successful retransmission following such collisions. In the Cambridge Ring local area network the 1 megabit per second ring contains several small slots around it, each slot consisting of 16 bits of data, an eight-bit source address, an eight-bit destination address, a bit indicating whether the slot is empty or full, and a number of control bits. A host transmits by awaiting a free slot and filling it up; the corresponding destination accepts the data and inserts acknowledgement information in the control bits which are subsequently read by the transmitting host.

A wide area network provides for a variety of paths from a transmitting to a receiving host, and inevitably some of these paths will be subject to congestion whereas others may be relatively idle. Routing decisions must be taken to pass messages onto the appropriate output lines of an intermediate processor and such routing decisions should also aim to minimize link congestion.

The network can either provide a datagram or a virtual circuit service. In the former case each packet carries a full destination address and is treated in a manner unrelated to any other packet, thus there is no guarantee that packets will be delivered in the same sequence that they were transmitted. In the case of a virtual circuit service a setup packet chooses a route for subsequent traffic and initializes all nodes along the route accordingly. The simplest routing technique is static or directory routing in which each node has a table, indexed by destination, stating which outgoing line is to be used. This static technique makes no attempt to respond to network conditions and can therefore lead to unnecessary congestion. Attempts to provide a more flexible approach, with monitoring of traffic and centralized routing decisions, are, however, fraught with problems. Unlike congestion problems of rail or road traffic the information about traffic conditions flows at the same speed as the packets themselves, and difficulties arise because the information about congestion is often out of date when it is received. Dynamic routing requires no feedback from the network; it simply assigns a packet to the output line with the shortest transmission queue, provided that the packet did not arrive on that line.

The X.25 protocol is a CCITT recommendation which relates to the interface between a host computer and a packet-switching network. The interface is defined in three layers: the first deals with the circuit interface between DTE and DCE, the second with the frames in which packets are sent, whereas layer 3 is concerned with the packet-level interface. To set up a virtual circuit a cell request packet is sent into the network. This packet contains the addresses of the source and destination host, a number selected by the host to designate the virtual circuit details of facilities requested by the host, and optional user data. The called host accepts or rejects the set-up request by sending back a control packet with appropriate bits in one of the specified fields. When the virtual circuit has been established full-duplex operation between the hosts is permitted, and data packets are transmitted with facilities, similar to HDLC, for the acknowledgement of error-free packages. The call is terminated by a clear request packet sent by either host and the return of the corresponding clear confirmation packet.

The rapid expansion in national and international data communication traffic has necessitated the development of standards governing all aspects of system hardware, software and protocols and of particular relevance are the ISO Open Systems Interconnection reference model and the IBM's SNA. *See* BIT STUFFING, CAMBRIDGE RING, CARRIER SENSE MULTIPLE ACCESS — MULTIPLE DETECTION, CHECKSUM, CIRCUIT SWITCHING, COMMON CARRIER, DATAGRAM, DATA CIRCUIT TERMINATING EQUIPMENT, DATA TERMINAL EQUIPMENT, ETHERNET, FRAME, FULL-DUPLEX, HAMMING CODE, HIGH-LEVEL DATA LINK CONTROL, HOST COMPUTER, INTEGRATED SERVICES DIGITAL NETWORK, LOCAL AREA NETWORK, OPEN SYSTEMS INTERCONNECTION, PACKET SWITCHING, PIGGYBACKING, POINT-TO-POINT, PROTOCOL, PROTOCOL STANDARDS, RING, SLIDING WINDOW PROTOCOL, STOP-AND-WAIT PROTOCOL, STORE AND FORWARD, SYSTEM NETWORK ARCHITECTURE, VIRTUAL CIRCUIT, WIDE AREA NETWORK, X-SERIES RECOMMENDATIONS OF CCITT.

data compaction. In codes, any method for encoding data to reduce the amount of time or memory required for transmission or storage, respectively. *Compare* DATA COMPRESSION, DATA REDUCTION. *Synonymous with* DATA TRANSMISSION.

data compression. (1) In codes, the reduction of the size of data by coding techniques which exploit redundancies in the data. *Compare* DATA COMPRESSION, DATA REDUCTION. *See* REDUNDANCY. (2) In memory systems, a technique that saves storage space by eliminating gaps, empty fields, redundancies or unnecessary data to shorten the length of records or blocks. *See* NULL SUPPRESSION.

data concentrator. *See* CONCENTRATOR.

data confidentiality. In data security the state that exists when the data is held in confidence and protected from unauthorized disclosure. *See* DATA INTEGRITY.

data connection. In data communications, the interconnection of a number of circuits designed to carry data signals. Special switching equipment is required so that data may be transmitted between data terminal equipment. *See* DATA TERMINAL EQUIPMENT, SWITCHING.

data contamination. In computer security, a deliberate or accidental process or act that results in a change in the integrity of the original data. (FIPS). *Compare* DATA INTEGRITY. *See* DATA DIDDLING. *Synonymous with* DATA CORRUPTION.

data-controlled oscillator. (DCO) In man–machine interfaces, an oscillator whose frequency can be determined by a digital input signal. It is used in music synthesizer systems. *See* MUSIC SYNTHESIZER, OSCILLATOR.

data corruption. *Synonymous with* DATA CONTAMINATION.

data coupler. In data communications, a device that enables the connection of customer-provided modems to the telephone network. It limits the power applied to the line and provides network control and signalling functions. *See* MODEM.

data-dependent protection. In data security, protection of data at a level commensurate with the sensitivity level of the individual data elements, rather than with the sensitivity of the entire file which includes the data elements. (FIPS).

data description language. (DDL) In databases, the language for describing the data. Such languages provide very detailed definitions of the structures and relationship of the data. In some cases the language is only concerned with the logical structure of the database, in others it is also concerned with descriptions relating to the manner in which the data is organized on physical storage devices. *Compare* DATA MANIPULATION LANGUAGE.

data dictionary. In databases, a centralized repository of information about the stored data, providing details of the meaning, relationship to other data, origin, usage and format. It is a vital part of the database management system providing information on the nature and usage of stored data, thus giving the database administrator overall control of an evolving database. *See* DATABASE ADMINISTRATOR, DATABASE MANAGEMENT SYSTEM.

data diddling. In data security, the changing of stored data values for illegal purposes. *See* DATA CONTAMINATION.

data-driven. In computing, pertaining to dataflow architecture in which the processor performs a computation as soon as all the necessary input data is available. *Compare* CONTROL-DRIVEN, DEMAND-DRIVEN, VON NEUMANN. *See* DATAFLOW, PARALLEL PROCESSING.

data-driven action tagging. In optical media, the technique for identifying or tagging events on the different data streams (audio, video, text/data), in interactive compact discs, so that they can be synchronized according to the requirements of the application program. (Philips). *See* COMPACT DISC – INTERACTIVE.

data element. *Synonymous with* DATA ITEM.

data-encrypting key. In data security, a cryptographic key used for encrypting (and decrypting) data. (FIPS). *Compare* KEY-ENCRYPTING KEY. *Synonymous with* DATA KEY, PRIMARY KEY.

data encryption algorithm. (DEA) In data security, an ANSI encryption standard, ANSI X3.92 — 1981, identical to the cryptographic function that forms part of the data encryption standard, FIPS Publication 46. *See* AMERICAN NATIONAL STANDARDS INSTITUTE, DATA ENCRYPTION STANDARD.

data encryption standard. (DES) In data security, an algorithm to be implemented in electronic hardware devices and used for the cryptographic protection of stored or transmitted data. The standard was published by the National Bureau of Standards in January 1977 as FIPS Publication 46. DES uses 64-bit data blocks and a 64-bit key; the cryptographic key, however, employs eight parity bits, and thus from a cryptographic viewpoint it is only a 56-bit key. *See* CRYPTOGRAPHIC KEY, PARITY BIT.

data entry. In peripherals, the entering data into a computer system for processing. The equipment used can include a card reader, badge reader or keyboard. *See* BADGE READER.

data exchange. In computing, the use of data by more than one system or program.

dataflow. In computing, a conceptual parallel-processing architecture in which the processor performs the computation as soon as all the necessary input data is available, or waits until the results of the computation are demanded by other processors. *Compare* CONTROL-DRIVEN. *See* DATA-DRIVEN, DEMAND-DRIVEN, PARALLEL PROCESSING.

data flow control. *See* INFORMATION FLOW CONTROL.

data flow diagram. (DFD) In systems analysis, a graphical representation of the logical flow of data through a program or system. The diagram comprises circles, connected by arrowed lines, with appropriate labels and annotations. The circle represents functions that transform the data, and the connecting lines indicate the flow of data from one processing unit to another. Additional symbols may be employed to indicate that the data on multiple inputs or outputs, of a processing unit, must be present simultaneously, mutually exclusively, etc. *Compare* STRUCTURE CHART. *See* STRUCTURED SYSTEMS ANALYSIS. *Synonymous with* BUBBLE CHART.

data format. In memory systems, the arrangement of data on a data medium (e.g. a floppy disk). *See* CSV, DIF, FILE TRANSFER.

datagram. In data communications, a self-contained packet in a packet-switching system that contains sufficient routing information to enable it to reach its required destination. *See* DATAGRAM SERVICE, PACKET.

datagram service. In data communications, a packet-switching service in which packets from a source, each of which contains the destination address, are entered into the network and are delivered to the destination in an order that may be independent of their order of entry. *Compare* VIRTUAL CALL SERVICE. *See* DATAGRAM.

data haven. In data security, a country that does not have data protection legislation. Data exported to such a country may therefore escape restrictions on processing and storage applied in Europe and the North America. *See* DATA PROTECTION.

data independence. In databases, pertaining to the structure of data that removes the close coupling with user programs, so that the logical or physical structure of the database may be changed without affecting the application programmer's view of the data. *See* LOGICAL DATA INDEPENDENCE, PHYSICAL DATA INDEPENDENCE.

data input voice answer back. (DIVA) In data communications, a system in which a user sends input to a computer using a terminal (e.g. a touchtone telephone) and receives a voice answer back from the computer, which may be either actual recorded or synthesized human voice. *See* AUDIO RESPONSE UNIT, SPEECH SYNTHESIZER.

data integrity. In data security, the state that exists when computerized data is the same as that in the source documents and has not been exposed to accidental or malicious alteration or destruction. (FIPS). *Compare* DATA CONTAMINATION. *Synonymous with* INFORMATION INTEGRITY.

data interchange format. *See* DIF.

data in voice. In data communications, the type of transmission in which digital data displaces voice circuits in a radio communications channel. *Compare* DATA UNDER VOICE, DATA ABOVE VOICE.

data item. In databases, the smallest unit of data that has independent meaning (e.g. an employee's name in a personnel record). *See* FIELD, RECORD. *Synonymous with* DATA ELEMENT.

data key. *Synonymous with* DATA-ENCRYPTING KEY.

data leakage. *Synonymous with* SEEPAGE.

dataline. In videotex, one of the lines of the television field blanking interval used to

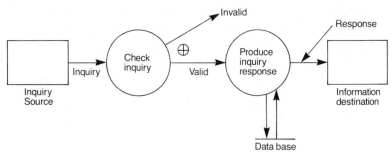

data flow diagram

carry information for the teletext character row. A dataline is identified by the clock run in sequence followed by a framing code at the appropriate time on a line in the field interval. *See* CLOCK RUN-IN, FIELD BLANKING, FRAMING CODE, TELETEXT.

data link. (1) In data communications, a physical means of connecting two locations (e.g. a telephone wire). (2) In data communications, the physical medium of transmission, the protocol and the associated devices and programs that together enable data to be transferred from a data source to a data sink. *See* DATA LINK LAYER, DATA SINK, DATA SOURCE, PROTOCOL.

data link control standard. In data communications, a set of conventions for sending and receiving data to and from a data network.

data link encryption. In data security, encryption of data over the physical circuit. With this form of encryption the data enters the intermediate and final nodes in plaintext. *Compare* END-TO-END ENCRYPTION, NODE ENCRYPTION. *See* NETWORK ENCRYPTION, PLAINTEXT. *Synonymous with* LINK ENCRYPTION, LINK-TO-LINK ENCRYPTION.

data link layer. In data communications, a layer in the ISO Open Systems Interconnection model. The function of this layer is to convert an unreliable transmission channel into a reliable one for use by the layer above it (i.e. the network layer). The raw data bit stream is organized into frames each containing a checksum for detecting errors. *Compare* APPLICATION LAYER, NETWORK LAYER, PHYSICAL LAYER, PRESENTATION LAYER, SESSION LAYER, TRANSPORT LAYER. *See* BIT STREAM, CHECKSUM, FRAME, OPEN SYSTEMS INTERCONNECTION.

data logging. In computing, the process of recording events in time sequence. *See* LOGGING.

data management. In databases, the organization and performance of functions that provide for the creation of stored data, access to it, regulation of input/output devices and the enforcement of data storage conventions.

data manipulation language. (DML) In databases, a language used by a programmer to manipulate the transfer of data between the database and the application program. It is normally hosted by another language to provide a framework for it and the necessary routines to handle the data. *Compare* DATA DESCRIPTION LANGUAGE.

data medium. (1) In memory systems, a physical quantity (e.g. a magnetic field, light) that can be varied to represent data. (2) In memory systems, the material that is affected by the physical quantity representing the data (e.g. magnetic materials, photographic emulsion). (3) In memory systems, a particular type of storage (e.g. semiconductor). *See* COMPACT DISC – READ-ONLY MEMORY, MAGNETIC DISK, MAGNETIC TAPE, PHOTODIGITAL MEMORY, SEMICONDUCTOR.

data modelling. In databases, the identification of the fundamental groups of data and their interrelationships. *See* DATA ANALYSIS.

data name. In programming, a character or group of characters used to identify an item of data. For example, the constant π can be used to refer to the number 3.14159.

data origination. In computing, the translation of information from its original form into machine-readable form or directly into electrical signals.

data origin authentication. In data security, the positive identification of the source or sender of data received.

data owner. In data security, the statutory authority responsible for a particular type or category of information; the individual or organization responsible for the actual data contained therein. (DODD). *See* OWNERSHIP.

Datapac network. In data communications, a commercial network which links the US network Telenet with the Trans-Canada network.

Dataphone Digital Service. (DDS) In data communications, an American Telephone and Telegraph Co. digital data transmission system. *See* TELENET.

dataplex. In data communications, a generic term used in the UK for services that involve multiplexing. *See* MULTIPLEXING.

dataplug. In communications, a proprietary name for a device that enables both telephone conversations and data to be multiplexed on a twisted pair cable connected to a private automated branch exchange (PABX). *See* MULTIPLEXING, PRIVATE AUTOMATED BRANCH EXCHANGE.

data preparation. In computing, the operation of transferring information in written form into a machine-readable form.

data processing. (dp) In applications, the activities that are concerned with the manipulation of a substantial mass of data to meet specified objectives (e.g. handling, sorting, merging, computing). *Compare* COMPUTATION, WORD PROCESSING. *Synonymous with* DATA TRANSACTIONS.

Data Processing Management Association. (DPMA) A UK professional data-processing organization whose main objective is the development and promotion of business methods and education in data processing and data-processing management.

data protection. In data security, the problems arising from the use of computers to store and correlate personal information on private citizens has been the subject of a number of UK and European committees. This matter was considered by the Younger Committee (1972), two White Papers (1975), Lindop Committee (1976), Council of Europe Convention, OECD guidelines and a White Paper (1982). The UK Data Protection Act, 1984, is based on eight data protection principles broadly in line with the recommendations of the Council of Europe Convention for the Protection of Individuals with regard to the automatic processing of personal data. The eight principles are:

(a) The information to be contained in personal data shall be obtained, and personal data shall be processed, fairly and lawfully.

(b) Personal data shall be held only for one or more specified and lawful purposes.

(c) Personal data held for any purpose or purposes shall not be used or disclosed in any manner incompatible with that purpose or those purposes.

(d) Personal data held for any purpose or purposes shall be adequate, relevant and not excessive in relation to that purpose or those purposes.

(e) Personal data shall be accurate and, where necessary, kept up to date.

(f) Personal data held for any purpose or purposes shall not be kept for longer than is necessary for that purpose or those purposes.

(g) A data subject shall be entitled: (i) to have access at reasonable intervals and without undue delay or expense to personal data of which he or she is the subject; and (ii) where appropriate, to have such data corrected or erased.

(h) Appropriate security measures shall be taken against unauthorized access to, or alteration, disclosure or destruction of personal data and against accidental loss or destruction of personal data.

In addition, the Act established a new office of Data Registrar, a national position, and a Data Protection Tribunal. It is the responsibility of the Registrar to set up and maintain a register of data users and persons carrying on computer bureaux. The Tribunal will hear appeals on behalf of users against decisions of or actions by the Registrar. The Act requires that all users of automated personal data must register their systems with the Registrar and comply with the principles except in specified exempted categories, which will include, for example, national security. It will be an offence to process or exchange automated personal data:

(a) while not being registered as a user,
(b) while being prevented by order of the Registrar from so doing,
(c) for purposes or exchanges which have not been registered.

The person who is the subject of information contained in a computer file is given the right to check that information, to receive a copy of the record and to take actions against loss where data is inaccurate or has been misused. *See* PRIVACY.

Data Protection Authority. The office of the UK Data Protection Registrar. *See* DATA PROTECTION.

Data Protection Convention. A convention, developed by the Council of Europe, describing the principles for the regulation of computer data to protect the privacy of the individual. *See* DATA PROTECTION.

Data Protection Registrar. *See* DATA PROTECTION.

data quality. (DQ) The correctness, relevance and accessibility of data appropriate for their use.

data rate. (1) In data communications, the amount of data transferred per unit time on a data link, usually expressed in bits per second. (2) In peripherals, the rate, usually expressed in terms of bytes or word per second, at which data is transferred between the units of a computer system. *See* BIT, BYTE, WORD.

data reduction. In computing, the process of transforming raw data into a useful simplified form. This often involves such operations as adjusting, scaling, smoothing, compacting and editing of data. *Compare* DATA COMPRESSION.

data retrieval. *See* INFORMATION RETRIEVAL.

data security. (1) The protection of data from accidental or malicious modification, destruction, or disclosure. (FIPS). (2) The protection against the unauthorized disclosure, manipulation, destruction or alteration of information. Disclosure refers to the disclosure of protected information such as classified or proprietary information, or information subject to data protection legislation. Manipulation is concerned with changing some attribute of the information such as file ownership, security classification, data destination, etc. Data can be destroyed quickly and efficiently, without leaving a trace, in electronic or magnetic storage devices; degaussing, removing the power from volatile storage and overwriting are effective methods of destroying data. Data alteration involves making changes in the stored data itself (e.g. financial amounts, measured values or system control parameters). *See* ACCESS CONTROL, COMPUTER SECURITY, CRYPTOGRAPHIC CONTROL, INFERENCE CONTROL, INFORMATION FLOW CONTROL. *Synonymous with* INFORMATION SECURITY.

data set. (DS) (1) In data communications, a circuit termination device used to provide an interface between a data communication circuit and a data terminal. Typically modulation/demodulation functions are performed in a data set. *See* MODEM. (2) In databases, a named collection of data items, bearing a logical relation to each other and ordered in a prescribed manner, it may also contain data for accessing the data (e.g. indices).

data set ready. (DSR) In data communications, a signal used in modems to indicate that the power is on and that the modem is ready to receive data for transmission. *See* DATA SET, MODEM, RS-232C.

data sheet. In electronics, a manufacturer's specification of an integrated circuit or device, parameters, functions and pin connections. *See* INTEGRATED CIRCUIT.

data-signalling rate. In data communications, the aggregate rate at which binary digits are transmitted over a circuit, expressed in bits per second. *Compare* DATA TRANSFER RATE. *See* BIT.

data-signalling rate selector. In data communications, a signal employed when a modem allows switching between two transmission speeds. If the modem at the calling end sets the speed for the connection then the calling computer uses the data-signalling rate selector (data terminal equipment source) to determine the line speed. The calling modem signals the speed to the answering modem, which informs the called computer by setting the data-signalling rate selector (data circuit terminating equipment) source to the appropriate value. *See* DATA CIRCUIT TERMINATING EQUIPMENT, DATA TERMINAL EQUIPMENT, MODEM, RS-232C.

data sink. In data communications, that part of a data terminal device that receives data. *Compare* DATA SOURCE.

Datasolve. In online information retrieval, a database vendor specializing in full-text databases. *See* DATABASE VENDOR, FULL-TEXT DATABASE.

data source.   In data communications, the part of a data terminal device that inputs data into a link. *Compare* DATA SINK.

Data-Star.   In online information retrieval, a Swiss online information retrieval service.

data station.   In data communications, the assembly of equipment which includes the data terminal equipment and data circuit terminating equipment. *See* DATA CIRCUIT TERMINATING EQUIPMENT, DATA TERMINAL EQUIPMENT.

data stream.   (1) In data security, the plaintext or the ciphertext considered as a sequence of cryptographic characters in a stream cipher. *See* CIPHERTEXT, PLAINTEXT. (2) In data communications, a continuous stream of serial data being transmitted in character or binary digit form through a channel. The data stream may contain control and format information.

data structure.   A system of relationships between items of data. Well-designed high-level languages permit the programmer to define and manipulate appropriate data structures which greatly reduce the complexity of programs. *See* ARRAY, HIGH-LEVEL LANGUAGE, LIST, QUEUE, STACK.

data subject.   In legislation, as defined by the UK Data Protection Act, 1984, an individual who is the subject of personal data. *See* DATA PROTECTION, PERSONAL DATA.

data-switching exchange.   In data communications, equipment installed at a single location used to switch data traffic. *See* CIRCUIT SWITCHING, MESSAGE SWITCHING, PACKET SWITCHING.

data tablet.   *See* DIGITIZING TABLET.

data terminal equipment.   (DTE) In data communications, any piece of equipment at which a communication path begins or ends (e.g. a visual display unit). *Compare* DATA CIRCUIT TERMINATING EQUIPMENT.

data terminal ready.   In data communications, a signal used in conjunction with an auto-answer modem to indicate that it is ready to receive a call. *See* AUTOMATIC ANSWERING, RS-232C.

data track.   In optical media, a read-only memory or interactive compact disc track containing data, as opposed to digital audio compact disc information; one of the two track types identified in the table of contents. (Philips). *Compare* AUDIO TRACK. *See* COMPACT DISC − DIGITAL AUDIO, COMPACT DISC -INTERACTIVE, COMPACT DISC − READ-ONLY MEMORY, TRACK.

data transactions.   *Synonymous with* DATA PROCESSING.

data transfer rate.   In data communications, the average number of bits or bytes that pass between devices per unit time. The average disk transfer rate from a device, (e.g. magnetic disk drive) will depend upon the electrical and mechanical properties of that device, but the upper limit of the instantaneous rate may be a function of the interface or transmission path. *Compare* DATA-SIGNALLING RATE. *See* MAGNETIC DISK.

data transmission.   *See* DATA COMMUNICATIONS.

data transparency.   In data communications, a technique whereby any pattern of bits, including those normally reserved for control purposes, may be transmitted as a block. *See* BLOCK, TRANSPARENT.

data transport system.   *See* WIDE AREA NETWORK.

data type.   *See* ABSTRACT DATA TYPE, TYPE.

data under voice.   (DUV) In data communications, a transmission system that carries digital data on a portion of the radio spectrum below the frequency used for voice transmission. *Compare* DATA ABOVE VOICE, DATA IN VOICE.

data user.   In legislation, as defined by the UK Data Protection Act, 1984, a person who holds data. A person holds data if:

(a) the data forms part of a collection of data processed or intended to be processed by, or on behalf of, that person;

(b) that person (either alone or jointly, or in common with other persons) controls the contents and use of the data comprised in the collection; and

(c) the data is in the form in which it have been, or is intended to be, processed as mentioned above or (though not for the time being in that form) in a form into which it has been converted after being so processed and with a view to being further so processed on a subsequent occasion.

See DATA PROTECTION, PERSONAL DATA.

data validation.   In computing, the act of checking that data fits certain defined criteria.

data word.   In programming, an item of data stored as a single word. *See* WORD.

data word size.   In data structures, the length of a data word, in bits, that a particular central processing unit is designed to handle. *See* CENTRAL PROCESSING UNIT, DATA WORD.

Datel.   In data communications, a generic name for British Telecom data transmission services other than dedicated data networks. *See* PSS.

daughter board.   In computing, a printed circuit board that plugs into a motherboard. *See* MOTHERBOARD, PRINTED CIRCUIT BOARD.

DAV.   *See* DATA ABOVE VOICE.

DB.   *See* DELAYED BROADCAST.

db.   *See* DECIBEL.

DBA.   *See* DATABASE ADMINISTRATOR.

dBASE.   In databases, a popular set of database management system packages for microcomputers. It employs a relational database structure; the database can be created, modified and interrogated by user commands. Reports may also be generated as tables with specified headings with totals, subtotals, etc. Complex sets of operations may be achieved by the development of command files similar to batch files in operating systems. *See* BATCH FILE, DATABASE

MANAGEMENT SYSTEM, FILE, RELATIONAL DATABASE.

DBMS.   *See* DATABASE MANAGEMENT SYSTEM.

DBS.   *See* DIRECT BROADCAST SATELLITE.

DBTG.   *See* DATA BASE TASK GROUP.

DC.   *See* DIRECT CURRENT.

DCD.   *See* DATA CARRIER DETECT.

DCE.   *See* DATA CIRCUIT TERMINATING EQUIPMENT.

D channel.   In communications, a 16 or 64 kilobits per second integrated services digital network user interface carrying packet-signalling information to control the establishment, modification and disestablishment of call and service. The D channel also provides additional functions such as identifying the incoming call, automatically transferring an incoming call to another station and allowing users to move back and forth among multiple calls without the need for multiple lines. The D channels can be used in parallel with other channels for user data (e.g. telemetry) and for the true integration of voice, data and image transmission. *Compare* B CHANNEL, H CHANNEL. *See* INTEGRATED SERVICES DIGITAL NETWORK, PACKET SWITCHING, SIGNALLING, TELEMETRY.

DCID.   US Director Central Intelligence Directive.

DCO.   *See* DATA-CONTROLLED OSCILLATOR.

DDC.   *See* DEWEY DECIMAL CLASSIFICATION.

DDD.   *See* DIRECT DISTANCE DIALING.

DDL.   (1) in databases. *See* DATA DESCRIPTION LANGUAGE. (2) In printing, document description language. *See* DESK-TOP PUBLISHING.

DDS.   (1) In data communications. *See* DATAPHONE DIGITAL SERVICE. (2) In data communications, direct digital service. *See* INTEGRATED SERVICES DIGITAL NETWORK.

DEA.   *See* DATA ENCRYPTION ALGORITHM.

DEA 1. In data security, International Standards Organization terminology for data encryption standard. *Compare* DEA 2. *See* DATA ENCRYPTION ALGORITHM, DATA ENCRYPTION STANDARD.

DEA 2. In data security, International Standards Organization terminology for RSA. *Compare* DEA 1. *See* RSA.

dead. In acoustics, describing an enclosed space in which reverberation is reduced to a very low level.

deadlock. In computing, an error condition in which processing cannot continue because each of two elements of the process is waiting for an action from the other. *Synonymous with* DEADLY EMBRACE.

deadly embrace. *Synonymous with* DEADLOCK.

dead matter. In printing, set type no longer intended for use.

dead spot. In recording, a point in space where sound waves originating from a common source cancel one another because of a 180° phase difference. *See* OUT OF PHASE.

de-archive. In word processing, the retrieval of stored text held on a disk or diskette and placing the text on the system disk or diskette.

deblocking. In data structures, the removal of each logical record from a block. *Compare* BLOCKING. *See* BLOCK, LOGICAL RECORD.

debounce. In electronic circuits, the prevention of spurious signals arising from mechanical bounce of electrical contacts (e.g. on keyboards). *See* BOUNCE.

debug. In computing, to detect, isolate and correct a mistake in a computer program or the computer system itself. *See* BUG, DEBUGGER.

debugger. In programming, a program to assist in testing and tracing errors in an application program. The debugger allows the user to step through a low-level language program, one instruction at a time, providing details of register contents, etc. after each execution. *See* INSTRUCTION, LOW-LEVEL LANGUAGE.

decade. A group, set or series of ten objects or events.

decentralized computer network. In data communications, a computer network in which some of the functions that control the network are distributed over several network nodes. *See* NODE.

decibel. (db) In electronics and communications, one-tenth of a bel, a measure of signal strength relative to a given reference level. A decibel is ten times the common logarithm (base 10) of that ratio. *See* BEL, LOGARITHM.

decibel meter. An instrument for measuring electric power level in decibels above or below an arbitrary reference level. One application is for the measurement of sound intensity. *See* DECIBEL.

decimal tab. *See* AUTOMATIC DECIMAL ALIGNMENT.

decipher. In data security, to convert ciphertext to plaintext. *Compare* DECRYPT, ENCIPHER. *See* CIPHERTEXT, PLAINTEXT.

decision support system. (DSS) In applications, an information-processing system used to aid decision-making, usually within a given organization. It differs from other information systems both in its emphasis on the synergism between the computer and the expert user, and in its application to underspecified or semistructured decision-making tasks. The system should be embedded in an organization's decision-making system and provide interactive ad hoc analytical capabilities including modelling. A DSS may include a database, a knowledge base, modelling tools and a language system that allows the user to build and test decision-making models in an interactive manner. *See* DATABASE, KNOWLEDGE BASE.

decision table. In systems analysis, a table that identifies the conditions of a system and the actions associated with each unique set of conditions. *Compare* DECISION TREE. *See* STRUCTURED SYSTEMS ANALYSIS.

Grade T,O,S,	T	T	O	O	S	S
Years of service	≤ 1	> 1	≤ 1	> 1	≤ 1	> 1
Bonus				√	√	√
Holiday Entitlement		√			√	√

T – Trainee   O – Operator   S – Supervisor

decision table

decision tree. In computing, a set of rules in the form of a tree. At each node the rule is examined, and a decision is correspondingly made to take a particular branch which leads either to the next rule to be examined or a leaf denoting the end result. *Compare* DECISION TABLE. *See* EXPERT SYSTEMS, LEAF, TREE STRUCTURE.

deckle edge. In printing, the ragged edge of handmade paper, sometimes simulated on machine-made paper.

declaration. In programming, a instruction in source code that identifies a resource or value that the program will use during execution. *See* SOURCE CODE.

declarative language. *Synonymous with* NON-PROCEDURAL LANGUAGE.

decode. To translate or determine the meaning of coded information. *Compare* DECIPHER, ENCODE. *See* DECODER.

decoder. (1) In computing, a logic device designed to convert data from one number system to another (e.g. from binary to decimal). (2) In videotex, a device used to decode videotex signals and to display them on a television screen. (3) In television, the receiver circuitry, between the signal detector and the screen, that decodes the broadcast signals.

decoding hardware. In optical media, the equipment required to interpret the encoded data recorded on a compact disc. (Philips). *See* COMPACT DISC.

decollator. In computing, a forms-handling device for separating out the folds of a continuous form into singles.

deconcentrator. *Compare* CONCENTRATOR.

decrement. The numerical quantity by which a variable is decreased (e.g. the numerical contents of a counter or store in a computer program). *Compare* INCREMENT.

decrypt. In data security, to convert, by use of the appropriate key, encrypted (encoded or enciphered) text into its equivalent plaintext. (FIPS). *Compare* DECIPHER, ENCRYPT. *See* DECIPHER, ENCODE, KEY, PLAINTEXT.

dedicated. Indicating equipment reserved for one user or type of application. *See* DEDICATED ACCESS, DEDICATED CHANNEL.

dedicated access. In data communications, a permanent connection between a terminal and a service network or computer.

dedicated channel. In data communications, a circuit or channel that has been reserved or committed for a specific use or application (e.g. for emergency purposes).

DEE. Data encryption equipment.

de-emphasis. In recording and communications, the attenuation of some high-frequency signals from a demodulated frequency-modulated signal, to remove noise and to compensate for the pre-emphasis stage. *Compare* PRE-EMPHASIS.

deep dish. *See* DISH ANTENNA.

default. In programming, pertaining to the choice made in the absence of specific instructions by the user.

default format statement. In word processing, a facility that is automatically invoked whenever the operator fails to specify some or all of the details relating to the layout and design of the printed work. *See* DEFAULT, FORMAT.

defect skipping. In memory systems, a technique in which magnetic material defects on a disk are identified during the manufacturing stage, and their size and location are written on a defect map track on the disk. *See* MAGNETIC DISK, TRACK.

defensive depth. In computer security, a principle of design that an attacker should be compelled to overcome a series of safeguards to achieve his objective, (e.g. access to a highly sensitive area should require passage through the maximum number of controlled areas, and violation of one control point should initiate an alert and reinforce all adjacent control points).

definition. In visual reproduction, a measure of perceivable detail.

deflected printer. *Synonymous with* CONTINUOUS FLOW.

deflection yoke. In peripherals, an assembly of one or more coils, whose magnetic field deflects the electron beam of a cathode ray tube and hence moves the spot to another point on the screen. *See* CATHODE RAY TUBE.

defocus. In filming, to cause the action to become out of focus during a shot by focusing the lens to a close point and reducing the depth of field. *See* DEPTH OF FIELD.

degauss. (1) In computer security, to apply a variable alternating current (AC) field for the purpose of demagnetizing magnetic recording media, usually tapes. The process involves increasing the AC field gradually from zero to a maximum value and back to zero, which leaves a very low residue of magnetic induction on the media. (FIPS). (2) Loosely, to erase. (FIPS)

degaussing pencil. In recording, an electromagnetic device for delicate sound track editing. *See* DEGAUS.

degradation. In data communications, a deterioration in the characteristics of a signal for whatever reason.

DEL. *See* DELETE CHARACTER.

delay characteristics. In data communications, the average time required for the operations such as call setup, data transfer

and call clearing in a packet-switching network. *See* PACKET SWITCHING.

delay/denial of service. In communications security, attacks undertaken to prevent messages from reaching their destinations within an acceptable time. This effect can be achieved by active wiretapping, a Trojan horse, message transmission or misrouting of messages. Active wiretapping can be used to remove or delay messages in the network. A Trojan horse can receive coded signals from an attacker to initiate a system disruption. Unauthorized message transmissions can be used to flood the network so as to diminish the network performance, whereas misrouting of messages can prevent them from attaining their intended destinations either at all or within acceptable time periods. *See* ACTIVE WIRETAPPING, BANKING NETWORKS, DENIAL OF SERVICE, TROJAN HORSE.

delay distortion. In data communications, a distortion caused by different propagation speeds of signals in a transmission medium arising from differences in their frequencies. This type of distortion does not affect voice, but can have a serious effect on some data transmission.

delayed broadcast. (DB) In television, a videotape or film, previously broadcast by a network, shown by a local station.

delay equalizer. In communications, a corrective network used to render the phase delay, or the rate of change of phase shift with frequency, of a system, substantially constant over the desired frequency range. *See* PHASE DELAY. *Synonymous with* PHASE EQUALIZER.

delay line. In electronics, a device that causes a time delay in the transmission of a pulse.

delay vector. In data communications, a list of the estimated transit times for a packet from one node to every other node in a packet-switching network. It is used in adaptive routing systems. *See* ADAPTIVE ROUTING, PACKET SWITCHING.

delete. (1) In memory systems, to remove a file from tape or disk. *See* MAGNETIC DISK,

MAGNETIC TAPE. (2) In word processing, a function that enables portions of text held in storage to be deleted.

delete character. (DEL) In codes, a control character used to delete an erroneous or unwanted character (e.g. a character transmitted down a communications circuit).

deliberate threat. In computer security, a threat of a person or persons to damage consciously and willingly the computer system. *Compare* ACCIDENTAL THREAT, ACTIVE THREAT, LOGICAL THREAT, PASSIVE THREAT, PHYSICAL THREAT. *See* THREAT.

delimiter. In data structures, a specified character used to denote the end of a field. *See* FIELD. *Synonymous with* SEPARATOR.

delivery assurance. In data security, pertaining to the level of damage associated with the delay or denial of messages. Delivery assurance is concerned, not only with the loss of messages, but also with preventing the addition or replay of messages. *See* DELAY/DENIAL OF SERVICE, END-TO-END ASSURANCE, REPLAY.

delta modulation. (DM) In data communications, a technique for the representation of waveforms by pulse trains. The signal to be represented is compared with an estimated value for the signal, and an error signal, given by the difference of the true and estimated signal, is generated. This signal is fed into a sign quantifier which has one of two output signals; if the input signal is equal to or greater than zero a fixed positive output is produced, otherwise the output is set at a fixed negative value. The output of the sign quantifier is sampled at a prespecified rate; a positive pulse is produced for a positive output of the sign quantifier, and vice versa.

The pulse train provides for the representation of the original waveform (e.g. for transmission), and it is also used in the estimation of the input signal. The output pulse train is integrated, and the output of the integrator multiplied by a constant, delta. This signal is then used as the estimate of the incoming waveform, to generate the error signal. A similar system at the receiving end enables an estimate of the original waveform to be produced.

If the incoming waveform is a unit step function, then the first estimate will be zero, and after the first pulse it will be raised to a value delta. If this fedback signal is still less than the input further positive pulses will be transmitted and fed back, increasing the fedback signal each time, until eventually the error signal becomes negative. The estimated signal will then vary between two values, one above and one below that of the input signal. If the value of delta is low then the estimated signal will be a good approximation of the input signal. On the other hand a low value of delta can prevent the estimated signal from ever catching up with a input signal increasing, or decreasing, at a rapid rate.

If the value of delta is fixed then the system is termed linear delta modulation. A variation of this technique (i.e. adaptive delta modulation) allows the value of delta to be varied during the modulation phase, thus overcoming the problem of changing the estimated signal at a sufficiently high rate. *Compare* PULSE CODE MODULATION. *See* ADAPTIVE DELTA MODULATION, DELTA PULSE CODE MODULATION, DIFFERENTIAL PULSE CODE MODULATION, LINEAR DELTA MODULATION.

delta pulse code modulation. (DPCM) In data communications, a form of differential pulse code modulation in which only one bit is transmitted, indicating a positive or negative change to the signal. *See* DELTA MODULATION, DIFFERENTIAL PULSE CODE MODULATION.

delta routing. In data communications, a method of routing, in a packet-switching network, in which a central routing controller receives information from nodes and issues routing instructions, but leaves a degree of discretion to individual nodes. *See* NODE, PACKET SWITCHING, ROUTING.

delta YUV. (DYUV) In codes, a high-efficiency image-coding scheme for natural pictures used in interactive compact discs. Delta coding takes advantage of the fact that there is a high correlation between adjacent pixel values, making it possible to encode only the differences between the absolute YU or YV pixel values. This coding scheme is applied per line (i.e. in one dimension). (Philips). *See* COMPACT DISC – INTERACTIVE, PIXEL, YUV ENCODING.

demand-assigned multiple access. (DAMA) In communications, the capability to allocate circuits to users only at those times when they are actually required for traffic. *See* FREQUENCY DIVISION MULTIPLE ACCESS, TIME DIVISION MULTIPLE ACCESS.

demand-driven. In computing, pertaining to a dataflow architecture in which the processor does not perform a computation until the results of the computation are required elsewhere. *Compare* CONTROL-DRIVEN, DATA-DRIVEN, VON NEUMANN. *See* DATAFLOW, PARALLEL PROCESSING.

demand multiplexing. In data communications, a form of time division multiplexing in which time slots are allocated according to demand. *See* TIME DIVISION MULTIPLEXING. *Synonymous with* DYNAMIC MULTIPLEXING.

demand paging. In memory systems, a form of paging in which no attempt is made to forecast the pages in backing store that will be required by the process; pages are therefore brought into main memory as demanded. *See* BACKING STORAGE, PAGING.

demand staging. In databases, a technique in which blocks of data are moved from a storage device to one with a shorter access time when they are requested by a program. *Compare* ANTICIPATORY STAGING.

demarcation strip. In data communications, a terminal board which acts as a physical interface between a business machine and the common carrier. *See* COMMON CARRIER. *Synonymous with* BARRIER BOX.

demodulation. In communications, the process by which an original modulating signal is recovered from a modulated wave. Demodulation techniques are used in both radio and television receivers and in data communications equipment. *Compare* MODULATION.

demodulator. (1) In communications, a device that performs the function of demodulation in a radio or television receiver. *See* DEMODULATION. (2) In data communications, a device that performs the function of demodulation on a data transmission circuit. It is usually found in conjunction with the device performing the modulation, together forming a modem. *See* MODEM.

demon. (1) In programming, a suspended process that waits for a certain kind of event to occur. It is then automatically actuated, performs its job and either terminates or suspends itself in wait for the next event. It is used in artificial intelligence applications. *See* ARTIFICIAL INTELLIGENCE, COROUTINE. (2) In software protection, a program used to break some software protection schemes. The demon is used initially to intercept and monitor all disk requests made by the protected program. If a copy of the protected program is made with, for example, a bit copier the demon will emulate the fingerprint used by the source program, and so be able to bypass the software protection scheme. The demon is not effective against programs that address the disk control directly, rather than via the operating system or BIOS. *See* BIOS, BIT COPIER, EXECUTE PROTECTION, FINGERPRINT, OPERATING SYSTEM.

demultiplexing. In data communications, the dividing of one or more information streams into a larger number of streams. *Compare* MULTIPLEXING.

denial. In communications, a condition that occurs in a telephone network when no circuits are available and a busy tone is returned to the calling party.

denial of service. *See* DELAY/DENIAL OF SERVICE.

dense index. In databases, an index that contains an entry for every record to be searched. *Compare* NON-DENSE INDEX. *See* INDEX, RECORD.

densitometer. In photography, a device used for measuring the density of photographic images. *See* DENSITY.

density. (1) In photography, a quantitative measure of the light-stopping characteristics of developed film. The density of a transparent surface is the logarithm of the ratio between the amount of incident light and the amount of light transmitted. (2) In printing, the blackness or darkness of a typed, printed or carbon image. *See* OPACITY. (3) In memory systems. *See* PACKING DENSITY.

depth cue. In computer graphics, a cue employed to avoid visual ambiguities when three-dimensional objects are displayed on a flat screen. These cues include hidden line removal, shading and brightness modulation. *See* BRIGHTNESS MODULATION, HIDDEN LINE, SHADING.

depth indexing. In library science, indexing as fully as possible by making specific entries for all relevant concepts mentioned in the text. *See* EXHAUSTIVITY.

depth of field. (D/F) In photography, the distance range before a camera in which objects are considered to be in sharp focus. The depth of field increases with smaller lens apertures. *Compare* DEPTH OF FOCUS.

depth of focus. In photography, the range of positions of a film in relation to the camera lens in which an acceptably sharp focus can be obtained. *Compare* DEPTH OF FIELD.

deque. In data structures, a double-ended queue; a queue in which insertions and deletions can be made from either end. *See* QUEUE.

deregulation. In legislation, a change in the operation of state-owned companies to allow for a wider range of suppliers for equipment and services.

derived indexing. In library science, a method of indexing in which the indexing information is derived solely from the document. A method well suited to the derivation of indexes by computer processing. *Compare* ASSIGNED INDEXING. *See* INDEX.

derived PIN. In banking, a personal identification number (PIN) that is generated from some information related to the customer's account number or identity. The PIN is derived by an algorithm involving a secret key. Such PINs may be verified at any location, with access to the secret key used in the algorithm, without requiring storage of the PIN on the customer's card. *See* PIN, PIN MANAGEMENT AND SECURITY.

derived sound. In recording, sound taken from the left- and right-hand stereo tracks and played on a third, middle speaker.

DES. *See* DATA ENCRYPTION STANDARD.

descender. In printing, the lower portion of the letters g, j, p, q, y, with the addition of f in italic. *Compare* ASCENDER. *See* ITALIC, TRUE DESCENDER.

descrambler. (1) In communications, a device attached to a user's television receiver to enable the reception of scrambled signals emanating from subscription television services. In some scrambling systems the video signal is enciphered digitally, and the descrambler can be individually addressed by the transmitter. Thus it is possible for the transmitter to send a coded signal to deactivate the scrambler of an individual subscriber who has not paid the regular fee. *Compare* SET-TOP CONVERTER. *See* SUBSCRIPTION TELEVISION. (2) In communications security. *See* VOICE SCRAMBLING.

descriptor. (1) In library science, a standardized word or phrase applied to a document in order to convey all or some of its content. *Synonymous with* KEYWORD. (2) In programming, stored information that contains details on how other information is stored. A program can thus refer to the descriptor of, for example, a file and then correctly interpret the data referred to. *See* FILE DESCRIPTOR.

design standard. Specific design criteria defining both result and method of performance per a standard. (ANSI). *Compare* PERFORMANCE STANDARD.

desk checking. In programming, the manual process in which representative data is traced through program logic to determine that the logical processing is as intended.

desk-top manager. In computing, an operating environment which provides desktop functions (e.g. diary, address book, calculator) and from which other applications may be called (e.g. spreadsheet, word processing). *See* SPREADSHEET, WORD PROCESSING.

desk-top organizers. In computing, software and expansion boards for personal computers that provide useful functions for executives (e.g. diary, telephone listing, calculators, etc.).

desk-top publishing. (DTP) In printing, a low-cost production system in which text and graphics are composed on a high-resolution display via special user friendly software, and the resulting screen image is exactly reproduced on a laser printer. DTP systems may be centred on microcomputers or more powerful intelligent workstations, and the former category of systems is discussed below.

(a) Origin. DTP systems exploit two key technological developments: (i) low-cost laser printer engines which offer high-quality resolution at 300 or more dots per inch; and (ii) sophisticated printer controllers which enable type to be scaled to any size. The result is that a laser printer can imitate the quality of a phototypesetter at one-tenth of the cost.

The market for personal computer DTP originated with Apple's introduction in 1985 of the LaserWriter, the low-cost laser printer, coupled with appropriate software both on the Macintosh microcomputer and Laser-Writer. Aldus Corp. developed PageMaker, a page composition system for the Macintosh, and Adobe Systems Inc. developed PostScript, a page description command language for driving the Laser-Writer. The result was the Apple DTP system, which capitalized on the Macintosh's ability to handle icons using its high-resolution, bit-mapped display. This, together with the low-cost Apple laser printer enabled the user to reproduce the screen image on the printer (i.e. what you see is what you get, or WYSIWYG).

WYSIWYG (pronounced Wiseywig) systems are best used in conjunction with a simple means to operate user interface based on windows, icons, mouse and pulldown menus (WIMPS). At the very least, this must be combined with a word processor program capable of integrating text and graphics. Ideally, it will also provide a choice of typographical fonts, in a selection of sizes and styles, and with an excellent standard of output.

(b) Benefits of DTP. Effective use of DTP has several important benefits: (i) cost saving; (ii) control; and (iii) quality. In manufacturing industries it has been estimated that the cost of producing technical product documentation lies anywhere between $350 and $1900 a page. In the aircraft industry, the typical commercial jet aircraft has over 8000 technical manuals, representing 15 per cent or more of the cost of manufacture. In other business environments, publishing may take between 6 and 10 per cent of an organization's total costs. The true cost of corporate publishing has rarely been appreciated because the activity is widely dispersed and not accounted for under a single budget.

Most organizations subcontract their typesetting and paste-up work, and it is this origination work which accounts for at least one-half to two-thirds of the final bill. Surprisingly, the cost is greater than the actual platemaking, paper and printing. DTP is targeted at precisely these areas of origination charges, since typesetting is eliminated, and the paste-up and design phase is dramatically shortened by on-screen manipulation. A six-fold saving using DTP in the cost of producing an in-house newsletter is not atypical, and firms that have switched to producing a DTP version of a weekly client newsletter can expect a payback in under two years.

With DTP a firm can anticipate a rapid contraction in the production cycle. It collapses the multiple stages of typesetting, proofing, paste-up and revision into a single operation, often performed by one person. Changes can be made to publication up to the very last minute. DTP therefore puts production control into the hands of the user. Because a company no longer needs to rely on outside suppliers, it now controls its schedules and budgets. It also offers design flexibility. For example, the Aldus PageMaker software for either the IBM PC or Macintosh accommodates up to 10 columns of varying width per page. In addition illustrations can be scaled and cropped to fit a given space, screen graphics or text can be displayed in varying shades of grey, and print type can vary from 4 points to 127 points. The ability to store boilerplate text and graphics for re-use is a particular advantage.

Although the resolution of the DTP laser printer is inferior to phototypeset copy for many applications, laser printing can improve the overall quality of a firm's printed output. The majority of business documents (i.e. sales letters, price lists, reports, etc.) have until now been either typewritten or computer-printed. However, laser printing provides professional quality of typesetting, but at a far-lower cost. Given these advantages, it is not surprising that DTP has enjoyed a rapid expansion, particularly in companies with a microcomputing background. It is for this reason that a number of stockbroking and investment firms have adopted DTP systems to produce their client reports, culling several days off the print cycle and enabling them to include late breaking price information.

(c) DTP software and hardware. It was mentioned earlier that a DTP system requires two programs, or groups of programs: one to help make up the page on the screen; the other to print the page on a laser printer as it appears on the screen. For page make-up the following facilities are important:

(i) Page layout. It should be easy to set up headlines, columns of text, graphics, running headers and footers. It should also be possible to rearrange design elements and to experiment until the page is right. Text threading, where editing changes made to text placed over several columns must be carried through the entire document, is necessary.

(ii) Text composition functions. This involves a choice of several typefaces and sizes and the ability to vary inter-line spacing. The software should offer automatic hyphenation (e.g. Aldus uses a 90 000 word dictionary). In addition, font-based, kerning, tracking, adjustable character set width and the flagging of too many hyphenated lines in a row ('ladders' of hyphens) are required.

(iii) Style sheets. Most documents employ a standard formatting pattern. The user should not have to re-specify typeface, point size, leading, line length and indents. This information should be stored as a style sheet, which can be invoked when needed.

(iv) Graphics. Aldus PageMaker established the industry standard by including a relatively complete set of graphic capabilities: the ability to draw rules, boxes, circles and other shapes, to fill areas with patterns and to layer graphics and text. These tools should be powerful enough to support basic drawing functions and to be used for creation of pages that combine text and graphics.

Other graphics requirements include the ability to accept pixel images from other sources, including computer-aided design files in industry standard formats. One should be able to scale, rotate and crop images, and to magnify an image in order to edit individual pixels. In this context, paint program tools such as airbrushes and area flood fill are useful. The user should be able to annotate margins with text and run text around them, as well as superimposing text over a graphic field.

The other important software component in DTP is the page description language (PDL). This is a command language used for driving the laser printer, and it is designed to be device-independent. The PDL interfaces with the page make-up program running in the host microcomputer, and the micro-processor in the laser printer. DTP users need never concern themselves with the PDL, unless non-standard manipulations are required. One of the most popular PDLs is PostScript from Adobe. This is an interpretive language and is therefore relatively slow, with some complex pages taking minutes to set and print.

A laser printer essentially consists of three hardware elements: a laser engine; a controller for the engine; and a raster image processor (RIP). The RIP is a hardware-dependent device, and it is used to build up an image of a complete page on the photo-sensitive drum of a laser engine. The RIP interprets the PDL instructions, which will include page layout details, font, point size, tint and other details. The PDL therefore acts as a common layout language offering portability between applications and printers.

An A4 page consists of about 100 square inches, and at a resolution of 300 dots per inch 90 000 dots need to be delivered to the printer for each square inch (i.e. 9 million for the whole page). Assuming a white dot is represented by a binary 0 and a black dot by a binary 1, every eight dots require one byte, which means that a full page takes over 1 megabyte of storage; hence the RIP requires a large amount of random-access memory. At standard serial (RS-232C) connection speeds this would take 18 minutes to transmit, but fortunately most pages contain a high proportion of spaces handled by the RIP data compression facilities.

The RIP can either be built onto the printer along with a selection of read-only memory (ROM) fonts, or it can be supplied as a separate unit.

(d) Fonts and digital scanning. Until quite recently, character fonts were formed from a pixel-based matrix both for screen display and printing, and were dependent upon the resolution of these devices. Fonts used in DTP are independent of the resolution of the output device since they are based upon splines, which describe the outline of each character geometrically. This approach enables PageMaker to stretch, compress or distort any character placed as an object. Only the font need be specified for the laser printer to print smoothly to the resolution available.

Fonts may either be permanently stored in ROM in the printer's RIP or downloaded from the host microcomputer. Downloaded fonts are not as fast as the inbuilt variety and take up valuable RAM space, up to 40 kilobytes per family. Moreover, software-based fonts are more expensive when they are not bundled in with the printer. Because the graphics screen monitor only has a resolution of about 72 pixels per inch, and the laser printer starts at 300 dots per inch, the operator will only see an approximation of the page layout on the screen.

Most users will want to incorporate pictures from a wide variety of sources and, in order to capture these images, many have to be digitally scanned. Until quite recently, scanners were expensive, but now the cost of a 300 dot per inch scanner may typically be only half that of a laser printer. However, although the scanner gives new freedom in illustration, scanners capture a vast amount of information, all of it necessarily without form. This is in contrast with the underlying notation of the PDL's vector graphics or the spline-based character's font. Scanners therefore create a dot volume problem, and it is exacerbated if halftones are used. Also, because of the lack of form of scanned images, they are less amenable to transformations and processing.

(e) Future trends. Word processing quickly became the driving force behind the purchase of many home, small business and office microcomputers. The performance and versatility of these systems were, however, initially restricted by the cost and performance of conventional printers. The advent of the laser printer and the development sophisticated software to enable ready manipulation of text and graphics provide a logical extension of the word processor to the sophisticated DTP system for a wide variety of businesses, colleges, public service institutions, etc. The DTP system may then be connected to organizational databases so that attractive reports, brochures, handbooks, etc. can be produced incorporating the current relevant data for the organization. Networking of DTP devices will enable expensive peripheral devices to be shared while providing managers, administrators, marketing executives, public relation officers, etc. with facilities to develop high-quality printed material at their desks. *See* AREA INFILL, AUTOMATIC HEADERS/FOOTERS, BIT-MAPPED GRAPHICS, BOILERPLATE, COMPUTER-AIDED DESIGN, DATA COMPRESSION, ICON, INTERPRETIVE LANGUAGE, KERNING, LASER PRINTER, MOUSE, OPTICAL SCANNER, PAGE DESCRIPTION LANGUAGE, PIXEL, RS-232C, SPLINE, STYLE SHEETS, WIMPS, WINDOW, WORD PROCESSING.

despun antenna. In communications, a satellite antenna whose main beam points to a fixed area on the surface of the earth even though the satellite rotates. *See* COMMUNICATIONS SATELLITE SYSTEM.

destructive cursor. In peripherals, a cursor on a visual display unit that erases any character through which it passes as it moves. *Compare* NON-DESTRUCTIVE CURSOR. *See* CURSOR, VISUAL DISPLAY UNIT.

destructive readout. (DRO) In memory systems, a reading action of stored data that necessarily erases the data held. *Compare* NON-DESTRUCTIVE READOUT.

detail paper. In printing, thin, hard, semi-transparent paper used for sketches and layouts.

determinism. In computing, the degree to which the movements of data and addresses during program execution can be predetermined and followed as they are operated upon by the processor subsystems.

deterrent. In computer security, a device that inhibits unauthorized action. Locked doors are an example of physical deterrents, whereas a surveillance camera can effect a psychological deterrent.

developing. In photography, the chemical process of bringing forth permanent image in film. Developing represents the first stage of this process, the later stages being fixation and drying. *See* FIXATION.

development centre. In computing, a department that commits the necessary hardware and software to application development. *See* INFORMATION CENTRE.

development tool. In programming, a software package designed as an aid to program development. (Philips). *Synonymous with* SOFTWARE TOOL.

device assignment. In computing, pertaining to a facility of logical to physical assignments that allows peripheral devices to be operated as required, by an application program, without the requirement for physical disconnection and connection. *See* LOGICAL.

device control character. In data communications, a character in a data transmission code available for controlling a device (e.g. turning it on or off).

device controller. *Synonymous with* PERIPHERAL CONTROL UNIT.

device driver. In peripherals, a hardware or software unit that interfaces between a peripheral and a central processing unit. It performs functions such as interrupts, passing addresses, error detection and data buffering. *See* CENTRAL PROCESSING UNIT, ERROR-DETECTING CODE, INTERRUPT.

device independence. In programming, the technique of writing application programs so that they are independent of the physical characteristics of peripheral devices. *See* PERIPHERAL.

Dewey decimal classification. (DDC) In library science, a system devised by Melvil Dewey to classify areas of knowledge, and still in use in a modified form (i.e. Universal Decimal Classification). In this system, there are ten main numbered classes (e.g. philosophy = 100) and each area is subdivided progressively into ten subclasses, and so on. *See* CLASSIFICATION.

D/F. *See* DEPTH OF FIELD.

DFD. *See* DATA FLOW DIAGRAM.

DFET. In microelectronics, depletion mode field effect transistor, a normally on device. *Compare* EFET. *See* FIELD EFFECT TRANSISTOR.

DFT. *See* DIAGNOSTIC FUNCTION TEST.

DG XIII. Directorate General Section XIII of the Commission of European Communities, which deals with the information market and innovation.

DGT. Director Generale des Télécommunications.

diacritic. In printing, an accent placed above or below certain letters. *See* ACCENT.

diagnostic function test. (DFT) In electronics, a program that tests the overall system reliability.

diagnostics. In computing, programs and techniques used to detect and isolate faults in a system, component or program. A diagnostic program will usually produce a print out containing an analysis of the operation being checked in order to assist with fault finding and correction. *Compare* DEBUGGER. *Synonymous with* SERVICE SOFTWARE.

diagonal cut. In photography and recording, a joint at an oblique angle to the edges of the film or tape. The diagonal cut is commonly used with magnetic tape to minimize the noise of the splice.

dial access. In data communications, the connection through the public switched telephone network, from a terminal to a service, network or computer.

dial back. *Synonymous with* CALL BACK.

Dialcom. In data communications, a US electronic mail service. *See* ELECTRONIC MAIL, TELECOM GOLD.

dial conference. In communications, a private automatic branch exchange (PABX) facility enabling an extension user to call several parties, all of whom are able to communicate with one another.

Dialog. In online information retrieval, the computer programs which allow online searching of the Lockheed Corp.'s databases.

dialog. In computing, a series of inquiries and related responses in an interactive session that is similar to a corresponding conversation between two people. *See* INTERACTIVE.

Dialog Information Retrieval Services. In online information retrieval, a major US database vendor. *See* DATABASE VENDOR.

Dialorder. In online information retrieval, a document delivery service offered by Dialog Information Retrieval Services. *See* DOCUMENT DELIVERY SERVICE.

dial tone. In communications, a single-frequency signal that indicates to the telephone caller that the receiving unit is ready to receive dial pulses. *See* DIAL PULSE.

dial-up. Pertaining to systems that can be accessed over a telephone network.

dial-up control. In computer security, a security system that is used to deal with misuse of computer systems by hackers. Such misuse can cause problems from illegal access and corruption of files, as well as simply tying up the telephone line. Some dial-up systems require user identification, and verification, before the modem tone is transmitted; this process thwarts the hacker who dials telephone numbers in a sequence until a modem tone is received. *See* CALL BACK, MODEM, TELEPHONE INTRUSION.

dial-up teleconferencing. In communications, a teleconferencing network that is established over dial-up circuits with or without operator assistance. *See* TELECONFERENCING.

DIANE. Direct Information Access Network for Europe; information services offered over the Euronet system. *See* EURONET.

diaphragm. (1) In photography, an iris in a lens used to control the amount of light passing through the lens; the diaphragm setting will affect the depth of field. *See* DEPTH OF FIELD. (2) In audio recording, a sound wave sensing element in a microphone.

diapositive. In photography, a positive transparency.

dibit. In data communications, a group of two bits. The four possible states of a dibit are 00, 01, 10, 11. *Compare* DIGRAM, TRIBIT.

dichroic. In optics, a thin, layered coating used on filters and mirrors to control the spectral qualities of light. Dichroic filters are used to alter the colour temperature of lights, and in colour printers to absorb certain wavelengths and pass others. *See* COLOUR TEMPERATURE, WAVELENGTH.

dictionary. (1) In word processing, a set of words contained in a spelling check program. *See* SPELLING CHECK PROGRAM. (2) In programming, a list of names generated by a compiler. *Compare* DATA DICTIONARY. *See* COMPILER. (3) In databases, a database of specifications of data and information-processing resources.

DID. *See* DIRECT INWARD DIALING.

Didot point. In printing, a measurement system established by Francois Didot, now used in most European countries as an alternative to the Anglo-American point system. The Didot point is now accepted as 0.375 millimetres (0.0148 inches). *Compare* POINT.

dielectric. In electronics, a material that resists the passage of electricity (i.e. an insulating material).

DIF. In programming, data interchange format; a *de facto* standard, developed by Software Arts Inc., to standardize ASCII data exchange between application programs running on different computers. It is used by many spreadsheet and database management systems. *See* AMERICAN STANDARD CODE FOR INFORMATION INTERCHANGE, DATABASE MANAGEMENT SYSTEM, DATA FORMAT, SPREADSHEET.

differential modulation. In data communications, a form of modulation in which the amplitude or phase of the carrier signal is determined by a change in the amplitude of the modulating signal from one symbol to the next. *Compare* DIRECT MODULATION. *See* DELTA MODULATION, DELTA PULSE CODE MODULATION, SYMBOL.

differential pulse code modulation. (1) In data communications, a version of pulse code modulation (PCM) in which the difference in value between a sample and the previous sample is encoded. Because fewer bits are required for transmission than under PCM, this technique is used in satellite communications. *See* PULSE CODE MODULATION, SAMPLING. (2) In optical media, a technique used to encode video and audio data in interactive compact discs. (Philips). *See* ADAPTIVE DELTA PULSE CODE MODULATION, COMPACT DISC – INTERACTIVE, DELTA YUV.

diffusion. (1) In microelectronics, a process in which controlled amounts of an impurity dopant material are inserted into a silicon crystal. *See* CHIP. (2) In data security, a characteristic of ciphering algorithms which conceal the statistical properties of the plaintext by diluting them in the ciphertext. *Compare* CONFUSION. *See* CIPHERTEXT, PLAINTEXT.

digiography. The processes concerned with the digital storage of images.

digipad. *Synonymous with* DIGITIZING TABLET.

digipulse telephone. In communications, a pushbutton telephone containing equipment that converts calling signals from the keypad into pulses similar to those generated by a rotary dial. *See* TOUCHTONE.

digit. A graphic character that represents a whole number (e.g. one of the characters 0–9).

digital. Pertaining to digits or the representation of data or physical quantities by digits. *Compare* ANALOG.

digital audio chip. *See* AUDIO CHIP.

digital audio compact disc. *See* COMPACT DISC – DIGITAL AUDIO.

digital audio tape. (DAT) In recording, a system in which digitally encoded sound is recorded on magnetic tape. In this system sound signals are sampled, quantized and the quantized signals represented as binary pulse trains are recorded on magnetic tape. This technique has the advantages of the high-quality reproduction associated with compact discs coupled with the user record facilities of magnetic tape systems. The problems, from a technological viewpoint, lie in the data transfer rate, approximately 2 magabits per second, coupled with the requirement to employ convenient cassette sizes. A further consideration is that the user should not be able to record compact disc or other prerecorded DAT information on such tapes, since unrestricted illegal copying would cause serious problems for the music-recording industry.

The recording density for compact cassettes is of the order of 20 kilobits per inch, and thus a data transfer rate of 2 megabits per second would consume some 100 inches of compact cassette tape per second. To overcome this problem two formats for DAT have been proposed, R-DAT and S-DAT; each is designed to provide the necessary data transfer rate while ensuring that the consumer equipment and cassettes are suitable for the domestic market. The R-DAT format employs the helical scan technique developed for video tape recorders, whereas S-DAT retains the conventional linear recording of audio tape systems, but uses 22 parallel tracks to provide the necessary data rate.

In the R-DAT system the audio input signal is digitized by a analog-to-digital converter; redundancy is added to the signal for error detection and correction purposes. The signal is then interleaved and an eight-to-ten modulation is performed. The output from this digital signal processing is then amplified and recorded on tape via the helical scanning head. In the playback mode the above-mentioned sequence of operations is reversed, the error detection and correction

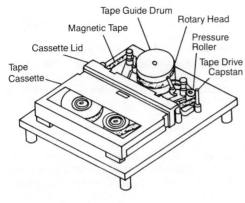

digital audio tape
Fig. 1. R-DAT

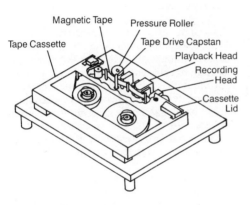

digital audio tape
Fig. 2. S-DAT

system removing most of the errors introduced in the recording/playback processing; time base fluctuations, caused by the variation in mechanical speeds of the tape drive system, are absorbed within the digital memory. The adjacent tracks on the tape are very close, the tape pitch is of the order of 20 micrometres, but interference between tracks is minimized by azimuth recording, with an azimuth angle of plus or minus 20°. This technique provides a high areal density for the tape.

The coding system for R-DAT is similar to compact disc with 48-, 44.1- and 32-kHz sampling rates and 16-bit linear quantization. Eight-to-ten modulation suppresses the DC component of the signal, which cannot be recorded on magnetic tape; a double Reed-

Solomon code is used for error correction and detection, and interleaving provides for error bursts. A subcode channel with a transmission capacity of some 300 kilobits per second is provided for data such as time codes, table of content codes, etc.

The S-DAT system is quite incompatible with the R-DAT, and it employs 22 tracks across the width of the tape and a multitrack stationary read/write head; two of the tracks are used for cue and auxiliary purposes. The linear density of the track is 64 kilobits per second and the tape speed is 47.6 millimetres per second. The S-DAT format is not, however, likely to be accepted as the standard for digital audio tape recording. *Compare* COMPACT DISC. *See* ANALOG-TO-DIGITAL CONVERTER, AREAL DENSITY, AZIMUTH RECORDING, COMPACT DISC DIGITAL AUDIO, CROSS-INTERLEAVED REED-SOLOMON CODE, HELICAL SCAN, PULSE CODE MODULATION, QUANTIZE, R-DAT, S-DAT, SUBCODE CHANNEL.

digital camera. In photography, a camera that produces images in digital form; they may be used as a graphical input device. *See* MAVICA.

digital computer. *See* ELECTRONIC DIGITAL COMPUTER.

digital filter. In electronics, a filter in which the input signal is in digital form and subjected to mathematical manipulation. The advantage of this technique, over conventional, analog, filters lies in the wide range of filtering operations and the precision of the computations. *See* FILTER.

digital magnetic tape. In recording, magnetic tape with a thin base layer for precision tape head contact and a high linear density (approximately 20 times that of analog tape) to accommodate the bit-packing requirements of 20 kilobits per inch. (Philips). *See* DIGITAL AUDIO TAPE.

digital multiplex interface. *See* DMT.

digital multiplex switching system. (DMS) In data communications, the use of pulse code modulation and time division multiplexing systems over circuit switched lines. *See* CIRCUIT SWITCHING, PULSE CODE MODULATION, TIME DIVISION MULTIPLEXING.

digital optical recording. *See* OPTICAL DIGITAL DISC.

digital optical technology. In optical media, the combination of digital and optical techniques. (Philips). *See* COMPACT DISC, FIBER OPTICS, VIDEODISC.

digital plotter. In peripherals, a plotter in which an automatically controlled pen is moved in incremental steps. *See* PLOTTER.

digital production master. In optical media, a digitally recorded audio tape used in editing to produce a master tape. It may be a studio mix, an equalized copy from a mastering suite or a transfer from a previous master. (Philips). *See* CD MASTERING.

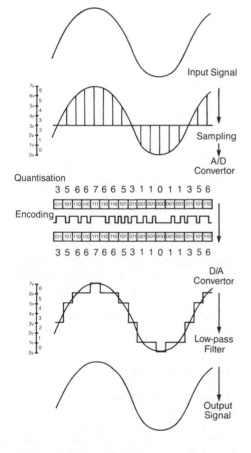

digital recording

digital recording. In recording, a recording of audio or video signals in digital form. The analog signal to be recorded is sampled at a rate at least double that of the highest frequency in the signal to be reproduced; the instantaneous amplitude of the signal is quantized and stored in digital form. (Philips). *See* ANALOG SIGNAL, COMPACT DISC, DIGITAL AUDIO TAPE, DIGITAL SIGNAL, NYQUIST SAMPLING THEOREM, QUANTIZE.

digital signal. A discrete or discontinuous electric signal, one whose various states are at discrete intervals apart. *Compare* ANALOG SIGNAL.

digital signalling. In data communications, the use of a digital transmission channel for the setting up, control and release of calls. *See* SIGNALLING.

digital signature. In data security, a data block appended to a message, or a complete encrypted message, such that the recipient can authenticate the message contents and/or prove that it could only have originated with the purported sender. The digital signature is a function of: (a) the message, transaction or document to be signed; (b) secret information known only to the sender; and (c) public information employed in the validation process.

Message authentication enables the receiver of a message to ensure that the contents cannot be changed accidentally or deliberately by a third party. However, since both the sender and the receiver share the same secret information there is no method of resolving disputes. The receiver can compute the authenticator and could therefore change a message, or forge a new message, develop the authenticator and claim that it was transmitted by the sender sharing the same secret key for authentication. Conversely the sender could disown an authenticated message and claim that the receiver produced a forged message using the common secret key.

The essence of a digital signature is that the receiver must be able to prove that a message originated with a given sender, but must not be able to construct the signed message. Thus the sender requires secret information to construct the signed message and the receiver must be able to access public information for use in the validation of the message. In the

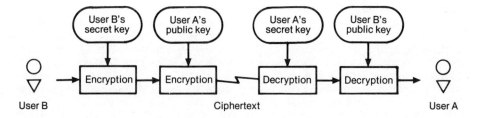

digital signature
A can prove that the message was enciphered by B. B can prove that the clear text was deciphered by A. In each case secret keys available only to B and A were used.

case of a dispute the receiver must be in a position to supply non-secret information to a judge (i.e. the signed message and the publicly available information) in order to prove the authentication and origin of the message. *Compare* DYNAMIC PASSWORD. *See* MESSAGE AUTHENTICATION, PUBLIC KEY CRYPTOGRAPHY, RSA. *Synonymous with* ELECTRONIC SIGNATURE.

digital speech interpolation. (DSI) In communications, a technique that is used to enhance the effective capacity of telephone networks in which speech is conveyed by pulse code modulation. The channel does not transmit bits during pauses in speech. *Compare* TIME ASSIGNMENT SPEECH INTERPOLATION. *See* PULSE CODE MODULATION.

digital switching. In communications, a process in which connections are established by operations on digital signals without their first being converted to analog signals. *See* DIGITAL SIGNAL.

digital technology. Technology based on the processing of numerical (usually binary) values. The approach is inherently more flexible and consistent, potentially faster and more accurate than analog technology. (Philips).

digital telephone. In communications, a telephone that performs pulse code modulation and may therefore be connected directly to a digital network. In addition to the high-quality voice transmission such telephones may provide extra facilities such as:

(a) alphanumeric display for: indication of called numbers, internal calling numbers and names, external calling number, time and date, reminder messages, call processing information, mailbox messages, call failure indication, call-alerting information and user prompts;

(b) user programmable keys, and single function keys for call transfer, automatic call back, call forwarding and last-number redial,

(c) hand-free operation,

(d) security feature (e.g. card reader for access control).

See ALPHANUMERIC, INTEGRATED SERVICES DIGITAL NETWORK, PULSE CODE MODULATION.

digital television. In television, the use of television receivers employing digital amplifier circuitry. This technique produces enhanced picture and sound quality and reduced deterioration resulting from ageing. (Philips).

digital-to-analog converter. (DAC) In peripherals, a device that converts a digital value to a corresponding analog signal. In general the analog signal is a total output current at a node. The input currents are controlled by internal switches operated by the digital input. *Compare* ANALOG-TO-DIGITAL CONVERTER.

digital transmission system. In data communications, a network in which analog information is digitized via a modulation technique and transmitted in a discrete form as a series of pulses. At the receiving station, the analog data is reconstituted from the digitized signals. Digital transmission systems support high data rates and error detection, and minimize effects due to noise. *See* PULSE CODE MODULATION.

digital typography. In applications, the production of type from data stored in digital form. Individual letter forms are represented by digital code stored in a computer. Algorithms convert this code into the appropriate graphic form, which is then displayed on a cathode ray tube and projected onto film, or written directly onto film by a laser. The number of bits required to represent a particular letter form may be reduced by the use of splines to represent its constituent curves. The algorithms can provide a high degree of flexibility in the production of the individual letterforms, thus enabling the designer to produce visually pleasing images for a wide range of type sizes. *See* ALGORITHM, LASER, SPLINE.

digital video. In video, the use of digital technology in television and video recording systems. The digital technology may be used to replace analog circuitry in video equipment. This development not only allows the video market to exploit the downward spiral of digital technology costs, but also provides enhanced facilities for video equipment. For example, home television could provide digital features such as PIP (picture-in-picture) and MPIP (multi-picture-in-picture) allowing several programs to be monitored simultaneously, freeze frame and zoom. Moreover, digital processing of signals can provide noise reduction, elimination of ghosts, caused by signal reflections, and higher-quality images. Switching between different television broadcast standards could be achieved with the minimum of replicated hardware.

It is unlikely that video signals will be broadcast digitally because the bandwidth requirements are extremely high. The digital technology therefore involves the capture of an analog-transmitted signal, analog-to-digital conversion and storage of the image in a frame store, for processing, and subsequent digital-to-analog conversion for signals to drive the audio and picture output devices. *See* ANALOG-TO-DIGITAL CONVERTER, BANDWIDTH, DIGITAL-TO-ANALOG CONVERTER, FRAME STORE, FREEZE FRAME, GHOST, MPIP, PIP, ZOOM.

digital video chip. *See* VIDEO CHIP.

digitize. The process of converting analog signals to digital form. Once the signal is in a digital form, it can be processed using digital techniques and then reconverted to analog form. *See* PULSE CODE MODULATION.

digitizing pad. *Synonymous with* DIGITIZING TABLET.

digitizing tablet. In peripherals, a pointing device capable of very high resolution that facilitates the accurate input of drawings, diagrams, etc. A drawing can be placed directly on the tablet, and the user traces out lines or inputs significant coordinate positions with a stylus, or cursor with cross hairs. The tablets often include areas mapped out as custom keyboards so that the user may input commands or data/text by pointing to the appropriate rectangle.

The digitizing tablet consists of a flat pad about one inch in thickness and a grid is embedded on the underside of the tablet, the resolution of the system is dictated by grid spacing and can be as high as one-thousandth of an inch. The stylus or cursor normally acts as a receiving antenna which receives phased signals injected into the grid, although in some systems the roles are reversed. In either case the phase and timing of the received signal is decoded by the tablet's electronic circuitry to provide the X,Y-coordinate of the stylus position.

Some digitizing tablets use flexible membranes operating in a similar manner to a pressure-sensitive touchscreen, and in this case data can be input with a finger or stylus. *See* POINTING DEVICE, TOUCHSCREEN. *Synonymous with* DIGIPAD, DIGITIZING PAD, ELECTRONIC PEN, GRAPHICS TABLET, TOUCH PAD.

digram. A two letter combination (e.g. 'th'). *Compare* DIBIT, TRIGRAM. *Synonymous with* BIGRAM.

DIMDI. Deutsches Institute für Medizinische Dokumentation und Information.

dimension. In programming, the number of subscripts required to access an element of an array. *See* ARRAY.

DIN. Deutsche Industrie Norm; the West German standards organization. *See* ASSOCIATION FRANÇAISE DE NORMALISATION, BRITISH STANDARDS INSTITUTION.

din. (1) In photography, a European unit of measurement used to indicate film exposure indexes. (2) In electronics, a multi-pin connector based on West German standards. *See* DIN.

diode. In electronics, a device that has a low electrical resistance in one direction and a very high resistance in the other, thus enabling current signals to pass in only one direction. *See* SEMICONDUCTOR DEVICES.

dioptre. In optics, a unit expressing the power of a lens.

dioptre lens. In photography, a lens attachment for close-up work.

diphone. In acoustics, two phonemes which together produce a characteristic sound. The sounds that constitute speech are largely the result of the association of diphones. This fact provides the basis for speech synthesis. (Philips). *See* SPEECH SYNTHESIZER.

diplex. In communications, a facility that permits two signals to be transmitted simultaneously, and in the same direction, over a channel. *Compare* FULL DUPLEX.

diplex operation. In communications, the use of a single circuit, carrier or antenna for the simultaneous transmission or reception of two signals. *Compare* FULL DUPLEX. *See* CARRIER.

dipole. In communications, a symmetrical antenna which is centre-fed. In its simplest form it consists of a single straight wire a half-wavelength long which radiates uniformly in all directions. *See* ANTENNA, WAVELENGTH.

direct access. In memory systems, pertaining to the ability to obtain data from, or to enter data into, a storage device in such a way that the process depends only on the location of that data and not on a reference to data previously accessed. Strictly speaking direct access and random access are synonymous, but in common parlance random access is used for main memory, whereas direct access is applied to magnetic disk systems, although in this case the access time depends upon the relative location of the read/write heads and the data. *Compare*

SEQUENTIAL ACCESS. *See* DIRECT-ACCESS STORAGE DEVICE, RANDOM ACCESS.

direct-access storage device. (DASD) In memory systems, a storage device that provides direct access to data in such a way that the access time is independent of the location of the data. Magnetic disks are considered to be DASDs because the access time is effectively independent of the location of the data, whereas magnetic tape access involves reading all previous records. *Compare* MAGNETIC TAPE. *See* DIRECT ACCESS, MAGNETIC DISK.

direct address. *Synonymous with* ABSOLUTE ADDRESS.

direct broadcast satellite. (DBS) In communications, a geostationary satellite used for broadcasting television and radio services. The satellite receives signals from a ground station and it then retransmits over a wide geographical area. Consumers may receive such services via a domestic disc antenna or a cable network employing a master antenna. *See* CABLE TELEVISION, C-MAC, DISH ANTENNA, GEOSTATIONARY SATELLITE, GROUND STATION, TELEVISION RECEIVE-ONLY.

direct-call facility. In data communications, a method which facilitates fast set-up of calls; the network interprets the call request signal and establishes connection to one or more data stations. Thus the user is not required to supply address selection signals.

direct colour print. In photography, a colour print made in one step from the original colour film.

direct current. (DC) In electronics, current produced by a constant voltage source (e.g. a battery). *Compare* ALTERNATING CURRENT. *See* CURRENT.

direct data access arrangement. In data communications, a unit containing an isolation transformer, for interconnecting user equipment to a telephone network. It is designed to prevent harmful voltages or signals entering the network.

direct digital service. *See* INTEGRATED SERVICES DIGITAL NETWORK.

direct distance dialing.   (DDD) In communications, a service that enables the subscriber to call other subscribers outside the local area without operator assistance. *Synonymous with* SUBSCRIBER TRUNK DIALING.

directed retry.   In communications, a facility in a cellular radio system allowing the subscriber's equipment to make a second attempt at gaining access if the first fails due to congestion. The second attempt will be made on the second strongest signal from a neighbouring cell. *See* CELLULAR RADIO.

direct-image film.   In photography, a film that will retain the same polarity as the previous generation or the original material (i.e. black for black).

direct impression.   In printing, a method of type composition using a typewriter.

direct inward dialing.   (DID) In communications, a feature of some private branch exchanges where incoming calls are routed to extensions without operator assistance. *Compare* DIRECT OUTWARD DIALING. *See* PRIVATE BRANCH EXCHANGE.

directional antenna.   In communications, an antenna that radiates, or receives, radio waves more effectively in some directions than others. *Compare* ISOTROPIC ANTENNA.

directional microphone.   A microphone that has greater sound sensitivity in one direction than in others. Directional microphones are often used in film and television production in order to avoid recording unwanted sounds. *Compare* OMNIDIRECTIONAL MICROPHONE. *See* BIDIRECTIONAL MICROPHONE, UNIDIRECTIONAL MICROPHONE.

directional pattern.   In audio recording, the directional sensitivity of a microphone. The basic patterns are omnidirectional (non-directional), bidirectional and unidirectional. *See* UNIDIRECTIONAL MICROPHONE, OMNIDIRECTIONAL MICROPHONE, BIDIRECTIONAL MICROPHONE.

directivity.   In communications, the ratio in decibels of the radiation intensity produced by an antenna in a given direction to the average value of the radiation intensities in all directions in space. *See* ANTENNA, DECIBEL.

direct-line attachment.   (DLA) In data communications, a device connected between a deta terminal equipment cable and a telecommunication line for protective purposes. *See* DATA TERMINAL EQUIPMENT.

direct memory access.   (DMA) In memory systems, a technique that allows a peripherals device to gain direct access to the main memory of the computer. When the peripheral initiates direct memory access the processor is compelled to stop all bus activity while the peripheral occupies the bus. This method allows extremely high data transfer rates. *Compare* CYCLE STEALING. *See* BUS, MAIN MEMORY, PROCESSOR.

direct modulation.   In data communications, a form of modulation in which the amplitude or phase of the carrier signal is determined by the amplitude of the modulating signal. *Compare* DIFFERENTIAL MODULATION. *See* PULSE CODE MODULATION.

directory.   (1) In programming, a record, containing details of the location of a file held in backing storage, which is accessed by the operating system. *See* FILE, OPERATING SYSTEM, RECORD. (2) In databases, a file that stores relationships between records in other files. The directory contains an overview of the data held, and since it occupies less storage space than the data files searches and operations performed on the directory are more efficient than those performed on the data files themselves. *Compare* DATA DICTIONARY. (3) In data communications, a table containing routing information. *See* DIRECTORY ROUTING.

directory database.   In online information retrieval, a non-bibliographic database offering directory-type information about companies, research grants, organizations, etc. *Compare* BIBLIOGRAPHIC DATABASE, FULL-TEXT DATABASE, NUMERIC DATABASE, REFERRAL DATABASE.

directory routing.   In data communications, a routing method that uses a directory at each node. The directory contains details of the preferred, and possibly second preference, outgoing link for each destination. *Compare* ADAPTIVE ROUTING. *See* PRIVATE BRANCH EXCHANGE.

direct outward dialing. In communications, a feature of private branch exchanges that allows a user to gain access to the exchange network without the assistance of the operator. *Compare* DIRECT INWARD DIALING.

direct ray. In communications, the shortest possible path for a wave between the transmitting and receiving antennae. *See* ANTENNA.

direct read after write. (DRAW) In optical media, an error protection technique used on WORM discs. A data block is read after writing to check for the presence of errors. It slows down the effective writing rate since the disc must complete a rotation, after writing, for the read action. *Compare* DIRECT READ DURING WRITE. *See* OPTICAL DIGITAL DISC, WORM.

direct read during write. (DRDW) In optical media, an error protection technique used on WORM discs. A data block is read as it is written to check for the presence of errors. It has a higher effective writing rate than direct read after write (DRAW) at the expense of more complex technology. *Compare* DIRECT READ AFTER WRITE. *See* OPTICAL DIGITAL DISC, WORM.

direct RGB coding. In codes, a picture coding scheme used in interactive compact discs for high-quality (e.g. modelled) graphics that can easily be changed by the user. Images are encoded on disc as red, green and blue (RGB) components using five bits for each colour plus one overlay or control bit. (Philips). *Compare* RGB ENCODING. *See* COMPACT DISC − INTERACTIVE, OVERLAY CONTROL. *Synonymous with* ABSOLUTE RGB CODING.

direct video input. In peripherals, a method of connecting a microcomputer output to a television set. The signal is fed as if it came from the output of the video detector. The display is better than that provided by the RF modulation method, which involves signal degradation due to a modulation/demodulation stage and interference from external sources, but it requires a television set with a connector for video input. *Compare* RF MODULATION METHOD. *Synonymous with* RGB INPUT.

direct-view storage tube. (dvst) In computer graphics, a device for displaying computer-generated images. It has the form of a cathode ray tube in which the electron beam is designed not to write to the phosphor directly, but to a fine wire mesh grid coated with dielectric and mounted just behind the screen. The movement of the beam causes a relative positive charge to be deposited on the grid. This charge will be retained for up to an hour. A flood gun produces a continuous flood of electrons towards the screen; electrons from the flood are attracted by the positive charges on the grid, accelerated through it and impact upon the screen phosphor. In those areas where no positive charge is deposited the electrons from the flood gun are repelled. Thus the computer output causes an image to be printed on the storage grid, where it remains for up to one hour, and this image is transferred to the screen by the combined action of the flood gun and grid. *Compare* RASTER DISPLAY, VECTOR REFRESH. *See* CATHODE RAY TUBE, DIELECTRIC, GUN.

direct voice input. In computing, pertaining to a computer input device capable of accepting spoken commands. *See* SPEECH RECOGNIZER.

DIRS. In online information retrieval, DIMDI Information Retrieval Service. *See* DIMDI.

DIS. International Standards Organization Draft International Standard. *See* ISO.

disable. To prevent a function from being recognized or acted upon.

disambiguation. In machine translation, the process of making a meaning transparent to the computer; one of the processes performed in pre-editing. *See* PRE-EDITING.

disassembler. (1) In programming, a program that accepts a machine code program as input and produces a corresponding assembly language program (e.g. with all operation codes replaced with their mnemonics). This provides the user with an equivalent listing of the machine code program that is much easier to read and diagnose. *See* ASSEMBLY LANGUAGE, MACHINE CODE, MNEMONIC, OPERATION CODE. (2) In data communications, a device that extracts the message content from packets. *See* PACKET ASSEMBLER/DISASSEMBLER, PACKET SWITCHING.

disaster dump. In computing, a dump undertaken for analysis after an unrecoverable program error has occurred. *Compare* RESCUE DUMP, SELECTIVE DUMP. *See* DUMP, POST MORTEM DUMP.

disaster plan. *See* CONTINGENCY PLANNING.

disc. *See* COMPACT DISC, VIDEODISC.

disc bootstrap routine. In optical media, an optional routine on an interactive compact disc to add or replace operating system capabilities in a base case system. (Philips). *See* BASE CASE SYSTEM, BOOTSTRAP, CD REAL-TIME OPERATING SYSTEM, COMPACT DISC – INTERACTIVE, OPERATING SYSTEM.

disc interchangeability. In optical media, the ability to exchange discs between players of different manufacture. This is an essential feature of both digital audio and interactive compact discs. (Philips). *See* COMPACT DISC – DIGITAL AUDIO, COMPACT DISC – INTERACTIVE, COMPATIBILITY, INTERCHANGEABILITY.

disc label. In optical media, the identity in terms of its volume and album description of an interactive compact disc. It is recorded on the first track of the disc. (Philips). *See* COMPACT DISC – INTERACTIVE, SUPER TABLE OF CONTENTS.

disclosing. In legislation, as defined by the UK Data Protection Act, 1984, pertaining to disclosing in relation to data and including the disclosure of information extracted from that data; and, where the identification of the individual who is the subject of personal data depends partly on the information constituting the data and partly on other information in the possession of the data user, the data shall not be regarded as disclosed or transferred unless the other information is also disclosed or transferred. *See* DATA, DATA PROTECTION, PERSONAL DATA.

disc mastering. *See* CD MASTERING.

disc memory. *Synonymous with* DISC STORAGE.

disconnect signal. In communications, a signal transmitted over the telephone line to indicate that the established connection should be broken.

discrepancy reports. In data processing, a listing of items that have violated some detective control and require further investigation.

disc replication. In optical media, the production of copy video or compact discs from a master disc, usually for commercial distribution. (Philips). *See* COMPACT DISC, VIDEODISC.

discrete. Describing data that is in the form of distinct elements such as characters. *Compare* ANALOG SIGNAL.

discretionary access control. (DAC) In access control, a means of restricting access to objects based on the identity of subjects and/or groups to which they belong. The controls are discretionary in the sense that a subject with a certain access permission is capable of passing that permission (perhaps indirectly) on to any other subject. (DOD). *Compare* MANDATORY ACCESS CONTROL. *See* OBJECT, SUBJECT.

discretionary hyphen. In printing, a specially coded hyphen which is only displayed when formatting of the hyphenated word puts it at the end of a line. (Desktop). *Compare* REQUIRED HYPHEN. *Synonymous with* SOFT HYPHEN.

discretionary processing. In computer security, the activities that may be interrupted for some period of time. A loss of ability to process such applications for some period of time will not seriously affect the well-being of the organization. *Compare* CRITICAL PROCESSING.

discretionary protection. Access control that identifies individual users and their need-to-know and that limits users to the information that they are allowed to see. It is used on systems that process information with the same level of sensitivity. (AFR). *See* DISCRETIONARY ACCESS CONTROL, NEED-TO-KNOW.

discretionary security. (1) In computer security, security measures initiated by the entities themselves. (2) In computer security, those aspects of a security policy which involve the provision of security services as a result of a request by an entity requiring an instance of communication. *Compare* MANDATORY SECURITY.

discriminator. In electronics, a circuit that extracts the audio and video signals from the intermediate-frequency signal in a satellite receiver. *See* TELEVISION RECEIVE-ONLY.

disc storage. In memory systems, data storage on optical or magnetic disc, characterized by low cost and relatively fast access as compared with tape storage. (Philips). *Compare* MAGNETIC TAPE. *See* MAGNETIC DISK, OPTICAL DIGITAL DISC. *Synonymous with* DISC MEMORY.

dish. In communications, describing an antenna having a concave reflecting surface. *See* DISH ANTENNA.

dish antenna. In communications, an antenna with a large reflecting dish commonly used in to receive the very low-power signals from communication satellites. The primary function of the reflector is to capture and reflect the incident electromagnetic radiation, received from the satellite, to the focal point of the antenna where the feedhorn is located. A secondary function of the dish is to shield the feedhorn from terrestrial noise signals. The antennae are classified as parabolic and spherical depending upon the shape of the reflector. The focal point of the dish is some distance in front of the centre of the reflector, and the feedhorn is fixed in this position, usually by a tripod mounted on the dish. The reflector may be manufactured from aluminium, fiber glass or wire screen; the fiber glass variety has an embedded wire screen. The dishes are categorized as deep or shallow, the latter having comparatively long focal lengths and hence the feedhorns are located some distance from the dish. The longer focal length of the shallow dish provides a high antenna gain, but the deep dishes give more shielding against terrestrial noise.

The diameter of the dish is a function of the satellite signal frequency, C band antennae are 8–12 feet in diameter, whereas the higher-frequency Ku band dishes need only be 2–6 feet in diameter. As mentioned above the feedhorn is normally held at the focal point by a tripod mounted on the dish; this method is termed prime focus. An alternative feedhorn mounting — cassegrain — employs a small reflector at the focal point which causes the doubly reflected radiation to be directed into the feedhorn mounted in the centre of the dish.

The performance of the antenna is measured in terms of gain measured in decibels. The gain is a relative measure against a reference standard isotropic antenna (i.e. one that receives signals equally in all directions). *See* ANTENNA GAIN, CASSEGRAIN, C BAND, DECIBEL, F/D RATIO, FEEDHORN, KU BAND, NOISE, PARABOLIC ANTENNA, PRIME FOCUS, SPHERICAL ANTENNA.

disjoint. Having no common areas.

disjunctive form. In mathematics, a logical expression of the form a OR b OR c. *Compare* CONJUNCTIVE FORM. *See* BOOLEAN ALGEBRA, OR.

disk. *See* FLOPPY DISK, MAGNETIC DISK.

disk cartridge. In memory systems, a hard disk permanently housed in a protective plastic cover which can be loaded onto a disk drive. *See* DISK DRIVE, HARD DISK.

disk crash. (1) In memory systems, a read/write head making destructive contact with a hard disk surface. (2) In memory systems, any hardware or software malfunction producing inaccessibility of disk data. *See* HARD DISK, MAGNETIC DISK.

disk drive. In memory systems, a mechanism for rotating a disk pack or a magnetic disk and controlling its movements. *See* DISK PACK, HARD DISK, WINCHESTER DISK DRIVE.

diskette. *Synonymous with* FLOPPY DISK.

disk interface. In memory systems, an interface that specifies the electrical connections between a controller and the disk drive. *See* DISK DRIVE.

disk magazine. In applications, a computer magazine supplied on a floppy disk. Such magazines can contain the usual features of a computer magazine, including advertisements. However, the user can select the various features from a menu, and programs featured in the magazine can be directly loaded into the computer and run. This form of magazine can also provide a more varied form of input — animated graphics, tunes, etc. Animated program demonstrations showing both intermediate results and highlighting the program lines executed can provide a very user friendly explanation of program operation. *Compare* VIEWBOOK. *See* ELECTRONIC PUBLISHING.

disk operating system. (DOS) In computing, an operating system for computers with disk drives in which the relevant routines are loaded from disk as required. *See* OPERATING SYSTEM.

disk pack. In memory systems, a set of disks on a common spindle, handled as a single unit.

disk server. In memory systems, a hard disk system providing backing storage to a number of networked microcomputer users. *See* FILE SERVER, INTELLIGENT DISK SERVER, SERVER.

dispatching algorithm. *Synonymous with* SCHEDULER.

displacement. *Synonymous with* RELATIVE ADDRESS.

display. (1) In peripherals, a device that is used for the presentation of visual information which varies with time. (Philips). *See* VISUAL DISPLAY UNIT. (2) In peripherals, the visual image on the screen of a display unit or monitor. (Philips). (3) In peripherals, a device for visual presentation of information on any temporary character-imaging device.

display attribute. In computer graphics, a particular property that is assigned to all or part of a display (e.g. character colour, size, blinking status, intensity, etc.). *See* PIXEL.

display background. *Synonymous with* BACKGROUND IMAGE.

display character. In videotex, one of many different shapes that can be generated in a character rectangle as part of a page. The display characters consist of alphanumeric, separated graphics and contiguous graphic sets. *See* CONTIGUOUS GRAPHICS, SEPARATED GRAPHICS.

display character generator. In peripherals, a device on a visual dislay unit that converts the digital code for a character into signals that cause the electron beam to create the character on the screen. *See* CHARACTER GENERATOR, VISUAL DISPLAY UNIT.

display color. In videotex, one of the seven colors (white, yellow, cyan, green, magenta, red and blue) used to depict a display character. *See* DISPLAY CHARACTER.

display column. In computer graphics, the display positions that form a vertical line on the display screen.

display device. *See* VISUAL DISPLAY UNIT.

display file. In computer graphics, a file of coordinates that is continually scanned to drive the display beam of a vector display device. If the file is too long the system is unable to refresh the graphics at an acceptable rate and flicker results. *See* FLICKER, VECTOR REFRESH.

display highlights. *See* HIGHLIGHT.

display line. In peripherals, the length of the horizontal scan line, of the raster scan of a visual display unit or television set, during which information is displayed. This is less than the screen width. *Compare* SCREEN OVERSCAN. *See* RASTER SCAN, VISUAL DISPLAY UNIT.

display mode. In videotex, pertaining to the three character sets used in creating and displaying a videotex page (i.e. alphanumerics set, separated graphics set and contiguous graphics set). *See* ALPHANUMERICS SET, CONTIGUOUS GRAPHICS, SEPARATED GRAPHICS.

display processor. In computing, a specialized input/output processor that accesses a file containing information to be displayed, reformats the information and passes it to the display device at a rate according to its timing requirements. *See* FILE.

display resolution. In peripherals and television, the measure of the number of pixels, and thus the amount of detail, that a screen can display. Horizontal resolution is a function of the bandwidth; vertical resolution is a function of the number of scan lines. Present-day colour television sets, with a bandwidth of 4–5 MHz, can display 40 alphanumeric characters per line. High-resolution monitors, with a bandwidth of 20 MHz or more, can usually display 80 and sometimes 132 characters per line. (Philips). *See* BANDWIDTH, PIXEL, SCANNING LINE.

display size. In printing, any size of type above 14 point, as distinct from text size or composition size. *See* COMPOSITION SIZE, POINT, TEXT SIZE.

display space. In computer graphics, the portion of a display surface that is available for the display of the image.

display tube. *Synonymous with* CATHODE RAY TUBE.

display type. In printing, larger type used for headings, etc.; normally 18 point or larger. (Desktop). *See* COMPOSITION SIZE, POINT.

display unit. In peripherals, a terminal device capable of producing a visible record or display of information; normally used in reference to cathode ray tube displays. *See* CATHODE RAY TUBE, VISUAL DISPLAY UNIT.

Dissertation Abstracts Online. In online information retrieval, a database supplied by University Microfilms International Inc. and dealing with dissertations.

dissolve. *See* GLOBAL DISSOLVE, LOCAL DISSOLVE, MATCH DISSOLVE.

distortion. (1) In data communications, any undesired change in waveform. The principal sources of distortion of waveforms are: (a) non-linear relationship between input and output; (b) non-uniform transmission at different frequencies; and (c) a phase shift not proportional to frequency. *See* INTERMODULATION DISTORTION. (2) In optics, any systematic malformation of an image caused by the optical system involved. Common optical distortions include positive (barrel) distortion and negative (pincushion) distortion. (3) In audio, any discrepancy in signal waveform or phase between the input and output signal of an amplifier or transmitting system.

distortion optics. In photography, optical devices used on a camera to achieve special image effects.

distributed adaptive routing. In data communications, a method of routing in which the decisions are made on the basis of exchange of information between the nodes of a network. *Compare* CENTRALIZED ADAPTIVE ROUTING. *See* ADAPTIVE ROUTING.

distributed database. In databases, a database that is located on a number of different computers which are often in different geographic locations. The database may have been designed as a single entity (e.g. to serve branches of a large organization) or it may have arisen as the result of a merger of a number of originally isolated systems.

distributed data processing. (1) In data communications, the distribution of processing functions and data throughout an organization to the locations where they are needed. *See* COOPERATIVE PROCESSING, END-USER COMPUTING. *Synonymous with* DISTRIBUTED PROCESSING. (2) In computing, a collection of processes interconnected so as to decentralize resources and provide an environment for execution of application programs. *See* APPLICATION PROGRAM, DISTRIBUTED NETWORK, PROCESSOR.

distributed function. In data communications, the use of programmable terminals and other devices to carry out operations that were previously performed by the central processing unit (e.g. network management and data formatting). *See* DATA FORMAT, NETWORK MANAGEMENT.

distributed logic. In computing, a system employing linked devices with local processing power (e.g. local word-processing termi-

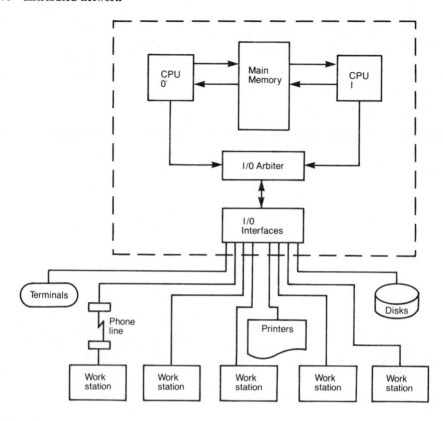

distributed network

nals sharing some common storage and printers). *See* SHARED LOGIC.

distributed network. In computing, any combination of loosely and tightly coupled systems. A typical configuration is illustrated in the diagram. The master comprises a tightly coupled multiprocessor with a large memory shared by two central processing units (CPUs). The input/output arbiter allows both processors to access all input/output devices. If one CPU develops hardware problems the remaining processor can continue to run all programs albeit at a slower rate. The workstations can be complete processors with memory, disk and input/output devices. Each can run in a standalone mode; when a user requests services not available locally the workstation can request assistance from the master.

Distributed networks can have very flexible architectures (e.g. star networks with all the workstations directly connected to the master or ring networks with cables daisy chaining from one office to the next). *See* CENTRAL PROCESSING UNIT, DAISY CHAIN, LOOSELY COUPLED, MULTIPROCESSOR, RING, STAR, TIGHTLY COUPLED, WORKSTATION.

distributed processing. *Synonymous with* DISTRIBUTED DATA PROCESSING.

distribution point. (1) In cable television, a point from which signals are taken from the trunk network, or head end, to feed branch or spur cables serving subscribers. *See* SPUR. (2) In communications, the final point on a local line network from which twisted pairs of wires are run to a subscriber's premises. *See* HEAD END.

distributive law. In mathematics, two binary operations satisfy the distributive law if

$$x + (y * z) = (x + y) * (x + z)$$
$$x * (y + z) = (x * y) + (x * z)$$

where x, y and z are the variables, and $*$ and $+$ represent the binary operations. *Compare* ASSOCIATIVE LAW, COMMUTATIVE LAW.

dittogram. In printing, a repeated letter caused by a typesetting error (e.g. a worrd).

DIV. *See* DATA IN VOICE.

DIVA. *See* DATA INPUT VOICE ANSWER BACK.

divergence. In peripherals, the failure of the beams in a colour display tube to land at the same colour cell on the screen.

dividend. In mathematics, the number that is to be divided in a division operation. *Compare* DIVISOR.

division. In databases, an operation in relational databases. If a relation A has two attributes X, Y and relation B has one attribute Z; with Y and Z defined over the same domain then the operation 'Divide A by B over Y and Z' produces a quotient defined on the same domain as X. The quotient contains tuples X; the dividend (A) contains tuples (X, Y) and the divisor (B) contains tuples Z. The value X appears only if A contains pairs (X, Y) for all values of Y in B. *Compare* JOIN, PROJECTION, SELECTION. *See* ATTRIBUTE, DOMAIN, RELATIONAL DATABASE, TUPLE.

divisor. In mathematics, the number by which the dividend is divided. *Compare* DIVIDEND.

DLA. *See* DIRECT-LINE ATTACHMENT.

DM. *See* DELTA MODULATION.

DMA. *See* DIRECT MEMORY ACCESS.

DMI. In data communications, digital multiplexed interface; a derivative of the integrated services digital network primary access rate developed by AT&T for direct connection between a host computer and a private automated branch exchange. *See* INTEGRATED SERVICES DIGITAL NETWORK, MULTIPLEXING, PRIMARY RATE ACCESS.

DML. *See* DATA MANIPULATION LANGUAGE.

DMS. *See* DIGITAL MULTIPLEX SWITCHING SYSTEM.

DOC. Canadian Department of Communications.

DOCDEL. In online information retrieval, document delivery; a European program comprising a number individual document delivery projects within the DIANE service. *See* DIANE, DOCUMENT DELIVERY SERVICE, EURODOCDEL, TRANSDOC.

docket. In communications, the record of an FCC or US state regulatory proceeding. *See* SUNSHINE NOTICE.

document. (1) Information and the medium on which it is recorded. The medium has some degree of permanence, and it may be in machine-readable or printed form. *See* MACHINE-READABLE. (2) In word processing, a portion of text treated as a single unit, whether it be a few short lines or a multipage report. *See* STANDARD DOCUMENT.

document assembly. *See* DOCUMENT MERGE.

documentation. In systems analysis, the preparation and production of documents for systems analysis, programming and system operation. Good documentation is an essential element in maintaining a computer system, particularly when changes or modifications have to be made subsequently to the computer software or hardware. *See* HARDWARE, SOFTWARE.

document delivery service. In online information retrieval, a service in which the user searches a database for information on relevant publications and then orders a copy of a selected publication via the terminal. The appropriate print copy is then delivered by post. The electronic storage, retrieval and delivery of full-text documents are increasingly viable with developments in telecommunications. *See* DOCDEL.

document description language. *See* DESKTOP PUBLISHING.

document fulfilment agency. In online information retrieval, an organization that provides copies of documents requested by users. The document details may be obtained by online search and the request forwarded to the agency over a telecommunications network. *See* DOCUMENT DELIVERY SERVICE.

document management. In office systems, a process that is concerned with: (a) text and image handling; (b) integration into corporate information system; (c) control of quality of content, access and security; (d) enforcement of corporate graphics policy; (e) continuous updating; (f) streamlined generation of text and image; and (g) shortening production cycle.

document mark. In micrographics, an optical mark, usually rectangular, within the recording area, and usually below the image on a roll of microfilm, that is used for counting images or frames automatically.

document merge. In word processing, the ability of the system to create a new document from previously recorded text. This facility is very useful in applications such as contracts' preparation, where a company's standard clauses can be selected, assembled and then merged on a word processor. *See* BOILERPLATE.

document processing. In applications, the machine processing of documents that can be read both by people and machines (e.g. bank cheques). The documents may contain information in optical character recognition or MICR fonts, but current document readers are capable of reading a variety of conventional printing fonts. *See* DOCUMENT READER, FONT, MICR, OPTICAL CHARACTER RECOGNITION.

document reader. In peripherals, a device capable of reading documents into a computer. Original document readers could deal with only special machine-readable parts of the document (i.e. those in optical character recognition) or MICR fonts. Current devices can read conventional printed pages in a variety of fonts. *See* DOCUMENT PROCESSING, FONT, OPTICAL SCANNER.

document retrieval system. In online information retrieval, a system that provides a complete copy of the document instead of just a citation or reference. *See* DOCUMENT DELIVERY SERVICE.

document stop. In micrographics, a device incorporated in most rotary cameras that prevents the entry of more than one document at a time. *See* ROTARY CAMERA.

DOD. US Department of Defense.

DODCSC. Department of Defense Computer Security Center. *See* NATIONAL COMPUTER SECURITY CENTER.

DODD. US Department of Defense Directive.

DOD security criteria. *See* ORANGE BOOK.

Dolby. In recording, a proprietary noise reduction system used on audio tape and cassettes.

domain. (1) In computer security, the set of objects that a subject has the ability to access. (DOD). *See* ACCESS, OBJECT, SUBJECT. (2) In computing, the resources under the control of one or more associated host processors on a network. (3) In programming, the set of values assigned to the independent variables of a function.

Domesday project. In optical media, a British Broadcasting Corporation project to produce interactive videodiscs with maps, demographic data and data collected by government and research agencies, providing a comprehensive picture of Great Britain in the 1980s. *See* VIDEODISC.

dominate. In computer security, a security level S_1 is said to dominate security level S_2 if the hierarchical classification of S_1 is greater than or equal to that of S_2 and the non-hierarchical categories of S_1 include all those of S_2 as a subset. (DOD). *See* SECURITY LEVEL.

DOMSAT decision. In communications, an Federal Communications Commission decision allowing open entry into the provision of domestic satellite communication services. *See* COMMUNICATIONS SATELLITE SYSTEM. *Synonymous with* OPEN SKIES POLICY.

dongle. In software protection, a small hardware device, supplied by a software producer and inserted in the serial port of a microcomputer. The package will not run unless the device is present. Dongles are not popular, partly because they tie up a microcomputer port, and in any case there are more effective software techniques for protection purposes. *Compare* FINGERPRINT. *See* EXECUTE PROTECTION.

don't care. In computing, pertaining to outputs corresponding to a subset of input signals that will not arise (e.g. in a device that is designed to accept a four-bit binary number and produce a corresponding decimal digit there are five inputs corresponding to numbers 10–15 that should not arise). The circuit designer is not constrained to produce particular outputs for such inputs, and this provides for flexibility and optimization in the circuit design.

dopant. In microelectronics, an element that is diffused into semiconductor material to give it n- or p-type properties. *See* DIFFUSION, N-TYPE MATERIAL, P-TYPE MATERIAL, SEMICONDUCTOR.

dope vector. In data structures, an array used to assist the accessing of a multidimensional array. *See* ARRAY.

Doppler shift. In communications, a change in frequency of a received signal due to relative motion between the transmitter and receiver.

DOR. In memory systems, digital optical recording. *See* OPTICAL DIGITAL DISC.

DOS. *See* DISK OPERATING SYSTEM.

dot matrix. (1) In computer graphics, a two-dimensional pattern of dots used for constructing a display image. This type of matrix is used to represent characters by dots. (2) In printing, a pattern of dots used as the basis for character formation in a matrix printer. *Compare* FULLY FORMED CHARACTER. *See* MATRIX PRINTER.

A 5 × 7 dot matrix

dot matrix

dot pitch. In peripherals, the distance between two corresponding dots in two adjacent triads. *Compare* SLIT PITCH. *See* TRIAD.

dot printer. *Synonymous with* MATRIX PRINTER, NEEDLE PRINTER.

double dagger. In printing, a character used as a third order of reference marks; also known as double obelisk. *See* REFERENCE MARK.

double density. In memory systems, a technique to increase the storage capacity of a floppy disk. The packing density is increased by the modified frequency modulation or modified modified frequency-modulated recording techniques. *Compare* DOUBLE-SIDED. *See* FLOPPY DISK, MODIFIED FREQUENCY MODULATION, PACKING DENSITY.

double document. In micrographics, a defect in a microfilm in which two documents have been photographed simultaneously on a rotary camera. *See* ROTARY CAMERA.

double-ended queue. *See* DEQUE.

double exposure. In photography, the recording of two or more images on a single strip of film. *Synonymous with* MULTI-EXPOSURE.

double-frequency scanning. In television, a method of scanning at twice the normal frequency so that double the number of lines can be shown within one frame without the loss of quality or the line flicker of normal interlaced scanning. This technique improves the vertical resolution of the display. (Philips). *See* DISPLAY RESOLUTION, INTERLACE, SCANNING LINE.

double obelisk. *See* DOUBLE DAGGER.

double-page spread. (DPS) In printing, two facing pages of newspaper or magazine where the textual material on the left-hand side continues across to the right-hand side. (Desktop).

double-precision arithmetic. In data structures, pertaining to arithmetic performed on a number comprising two words. It is used when the limited number of bits in one word does not provide sufficient precision. *See* PRECISION.

double resolution. In optical media, an interactive compact display resolution mode between the normal-and high-resolution modes, with 768 horizontal pixels and 280 vertical pixels. (Philips). *See* COMPACT DISC-INTERACTIVE, DISPLAY RESOLUTION, PIXEL.

double sideband. In communications, the frequency bands occupied by a modulated carrier wave, above and below the carrier frequency. *See* CARRIER, MODULATION.

double-sided. In memory systems, pertaining to a technique to increase the total storage capacity of a floppy disk. Data is recorded on both sides of the disk, and read/write heads of the disk drive are placed on both sides of the disk positioned 180° apart. *Compare* DOUBLE-DENSITY. *See* FLOPPY DISK.

double-sided copying. In printing, the production of printed sheets, with printing on both sides, without manual intervention. *See* INTELLIGENT COPIER/PRINTER.

double word. In data structures, a numeric entity comprising twice the number of bits contained in a normal computer word. For a 16-bit processor the double word is 32 bits wide; for a 32-bit processor it is 64 bits wide. It occupies two successive memory locations. (Philips). *See* BIT, WORD.

double-written. In optical media, data written twice on an interactive compact disc with a four-byte separation. This achieves a data integrity level equivalent to mode 1. (Philips). *See* BYTE, COMPACT DISC – INTERACTIVE, MODE 1.

down. In computing, pertaining to a device or system that is inoperative. *Compare* UP. *See* DOWNTIME.

downconverter. In communications, a circuit used in satellite receiver systems to change the signal frequency to an intermediate frequency by a channel converter; it is inserted between the local area network and the satellite receiver. *See* INTERMEDIATE FRE-

QUENCY, LOCAL AREA NETWORK, TELEVISION RECEIVE-ONLY.

downlink. In communications, a transmission path from a communications satellite to a ground station. *Compare* UPLINK. *See* GROUND STATION.

download. In computing, the transfer of programs or data between computers; usually from a mainframe to a microcomputer. *Compare* UPLOAD. *See* MAINFRAME.

downstream. In communications, the direction of message flow (i.e. towards the destination of the message). *Compare* UPSTREAM.

downstroke. In printing, the heavy stroke in type character derived from the broad line created by the downward movement of a pen in calligraphy.

downtime. In computing, the time during which a device is inoperable due to a fault. *Compare* IDLE TIME. *See* DOWN, MTBF.

dp. *See* DATA PROCESSING.

DPCM. *See* DELTA PULSE CODE MODULATION.

DPM. In data processing, data-processing manager.

DPMA. *See* DATA PROCESSING MANAGEMENT ASSOCIATION.

DPS. *See* DOUBLE-PAGE SPREAD.

DQ. *See* DATA QUALITY.

draft quality. In printing, one of the two or more printing modes available on some printers, normally of the dot matrix type. When operating in draft-quality mode, the printer operates at its maximum printing rate, producing a limited printing quality suitable for draft copies of documents. (Philips). *Compare* BUSINESS QUALITY, LETTER QUALITY, NEAR LETTER QUALITY. *See* DOT MATRIX, PRINTER.

dragging. In computer graphics, a facility to position a shape precisely on a screen (i.e. the object is dragged to the new position).

The image must be refreshed at a sufficient rate to permit continual visual feedback of the movement.

drain. (1) In electronics, the current supplied by a battery or power supply to a circuit. (2) In electronics, a terminal on an field effect transistor. *See* FIELD EFFECT TRANSISTOR, GATE, SOURCE, TERMINAL.

DRAM. In memory systems, dynamic random-access memory. *See* DYNAMIC MEMORY, RANDOM-ACCESS MEMORY.

DRAW. *See* DIRECT READ AFTER WRITE.

DRCS. *See* DYNAMICALLY REDEFINABLE CHARACTER SET.

DRDW. *See* DIRECT READ DURING WRITE.

D region. In communications, that part of the ionosphere, between 50 and 90 kilometres, responsible for most of the attenuation of radio waves in the frequency range 1–100 MHz. *See* ATTENUATION, IONOSPHERE.

drift. In electronics, the tendency of a circuit to alter its characteristics with time and temperature changes.

driver. (1) In hardware, a circuit used to boost the power of signals on a bus. *See* BUS, RECEIVER, TRANSMITTER. (2) In software, a routine that performs low-level input/output functions for an input/output device. *See* INPUT/OUTPUT UNIT.

DRO. *See* DESTRUCTIVE READOUT.

drop. In communications, that portion of outside telephone plant which extends from the telephone distribution cable to the subscriber's premises.

drop cap. In printing, the letter at the beginning of a line of text set in a larger size type and extending into lines of type below.

drop in. In memory systems, a error in reading from, or writing to, a magnetic storage device which reveals itself as the reading of a binary digit when no such bit was recorded. *Compare* DROP OUT. *See* BIT, MAGNETIC DISK, MAGNETIC TAPE.

drop line. In cable television, a cable that branches off from a feeder cable to provide signals to the subscriber's home. *See* FEEDER CABLE.

drop on demand. In printing, pertaining to ink jet printers in which the ink is only dropped onto the medium on demand. *Compare* CONTINUOUS FLOW. *See* INK JET PRINTER. *Synonymous with* NON-DEFLECTED PRINTER.

drop out. (1) In memory systems, a error in reading from, or writing to, a magnetic storage device that reveals itself as the failure to read a binary digit when such a bit was previously written. *Compare* DROP IN. *See* BIT, MAGNETIC DISK, MAGNETIC TAPE. (2) In data communications, the loss of discrete data signals due to noise or attenuation. (3) In video recording, loss of video information caused by irregularities in the oxide surface of the tape. Drop out results in a horizontal streak in the television picture during playback.

drum. (1) In filming, a flywheel that is used in a film projector to ensure smooth film movement over the sound head. (2) In recording, a slotted helical scan record/playback head assembly on a video recorder. *See* HELICAL SCAN.

drum plotter. In peripherals, a plotter in which the pen usually moves only in a horizontal direction and the paper itself moves on a cylindrical drum to add the vertical dimension. *Compare* FLATBED PLOTTER, PINCH PLOTTER. *See* PLOTTER.

drum printer. In printing, a line printer in which the type is mounted on a rotating drum that contains a full character set for each printing position.

dry circuit. In communications, a circuit for the transmission of voice signals that carries no direct current.

dry transfer. In printing, characters, drawings, etc. applied to the artwork from a transfer sheet by rubbing.

DS. *See* DATA SET.

DSE. *See* DATA-SWITCHING EXCHANGE.

DSI. *See* DIGITAL SPEECH INTERPOLATION.

DSR. *See* DATA SET READY.

DSS. *See* DECISION SUPPORT SYSTEM.

DTE. *See* DATA TERMINAL EQUIPMENT.

DTMF. In communications, dual-tone multifrequency signalling; a signalling method in which two frequencies, each selected from a group of four, are used to transmit numerical address information. *See* MULTIFREQUENCY SIGNAL.

DTP. *See* DESK-TOP PUBLISHING.

dual channel. In recording, a device with two separate paths that do not interact unless deliberately mixed (e.g. stereo equipment).

dual column. In word processing, a facility for printing in two columns on a page when the text was entered in a single-column format.

dual control. In data security, a process of utilizing two or more separate entities (usually persons), operating in concert, to protect sensitive functions or information. Both entities are equally responsible for the physical protection of materials involved in vulnerable transactions. No single person shall be able to access or to utilize the materials (e.g. cryptographic key). *See* CRYPTOGRAPHIC KEY, SPLIT KNOWLEDGE.

dual drive. In memory systems, a floppy disk drive for two disks using only one spindle motor and one positioner. *See* FLOPPY DISK.

dual processor. In computing, a system with two central processing units; one is normally dedicated to information processing whereas the other is primarily concerned with system operations. *See* CENTRAL PROCESSING UNIT, MULTIPROCESSING.

dual redundancy. In reliability, a form of modular redundancy using two replicated units. One unit may be a standby spare which replaces the active unit when a fault is detected. Alternatively the two units are operated synchronously and their outputs compared. When a mismatch occurs an interrupt is raised, and a fault recognition program is employed to identify and isolate the faulty module. *Compare* NMR, TRIPLE MODULAR REDUNDANCY. *See* MODULAR REDUNDANCY.

dual-tone multifrequency signalling. *See* DTMF.

dubbed sound. In recording, the transfer of a sound recording from one medium to another.

dubbing. *See* DUBBED SOUND. *Synonymous with* LOOPING.

duct. In communications, an underground pipe in which cables may be installed.

ductal. In calligraphy, handwritten characters whose basic form is the result of a smooth series of movements of the writing tool in the plane of the writing surface. *Compare* GLYPTAL.

dumb device. In peripherals, a device, usually a terminal, that can only transmit or receive data to or from a servicing computer. *Compare* INTELLIGENT DEVICE.

dumb terminal. In peripherals, a terminal (or computer using dumb terminal software) which allows communications with other computers, but does not enhance the data exchanged, or provide additional features such as upload/download. *Compare* EDITING TERMINAL, INTELLIGENT TERMINAL. *See* CONFIGURABLY DUMB TERMINAL, DUMB DEVICE.

dummy. A device which has the appearance of a specified unit, but does not have the capability to function as such.

dump. (1) In computing, a bulk transfer of data from one medium to another (e.g. the transfer of the contents of a part of main memory to a line printer). *See* CHANGE DUMP, FORMATTED DUMP, LINE PRINTER, MAIN MEMORY, POST MORTEM DUMP, RESCUE DUMP, SELECTIVE DUMP, STATIC DUMP. (2) In databases, pertaining to the regular backup of a database for security purposes. *See* BACKUP.

dumpster diving. In computer security, a method of obtaining confidential information by examining the contents of legitimate users' wastepaper baskets, dustbins, etc.

Dunn camera. In computer graphics, a photographic peripheral for computers that facilitates the high-quality capture of colour graphics. The red, green and blue images are displayed in sequence upon a flat accurate monochrome screen masked from extraneous light. A polaroid camera is exposed to these images through red, green and blue filters, respectively, without advancing the film, thus producing an accurate colour image.

duodecimal. In mathematics, a system of twelve choices or states. *Compare* HEXADECIMAL.

duplex. *Synonymous with* FULL-DUPLEX.

duplex circuit. In communications, a circuit used for transmission of signals in both directions at the same time. *See* FULL-DUPLEX, HALF-DUPLEX.

duplexing. In office systems, two-sided copying. *See* COPIER.

Dural. In programming, a language that is an extension of PROLOG. *See* PROLOG.

DUV. *See* DATA UNDER VOICE.

Dvorak keyboard. In peripherals, a keyboard layout that locates the most frequently used keys in the centre of the keyboard. *Compare* AZERTY KEYBOARD, MALTRON KEYBOARD, PRONTO KEYBOARD, QWERTY KEYBOARD. *See* KEYBOARD.

dvst. *See* DIRECT-VIEW STORAGE TUBE.

dyadic. In mathematics, an operation that has two and only two operands. *Compare* UNARY OPERATION.

dye transfer. In printing, a photographic colour print with a full-colour image produced using special coated papers.

dynamic allocation. In computing, the assignment of system resources to a program at the time of execution rather than when it is loaded into main storage. *See* MAIN STORAGE.

dynamically redefinable character set. (DRCS) In videotex, the ability to load a new character set in a videotex terminal by transmitting the set over the telephone network from a videotex computer. *See* CHARACTER GENERATOR.

dynamic loading. In computer graphics and optical media, the updating of the contents of the colour look-up table during the horizontal retrace period (up to four colours) or during the vertical retrace period (up to 256 colours). (Philips). *See* COLOUR LOOK-UP TABLE.

dynamic memory. In memory systems, a form of volatile semiconductor memory in which the stored information degrades with time. *Compare* STATIC RANDOM-ACCESS MEMORY. *See* VOLATILE STORAGE.

dynamic microphone. In acoustics, a microphone that generates a voltage in proportion to the sound pressure changes on a diaphragm. This is achieved by attaching a voice coil to the diaphragm. *See* DIAPHRAGM, MICROPHONE.

dynamic multiplexing. *Synonymous with* DEMAND MULTIPLEXING.

dynamic password. In computer security, an access control method based on the use of random numbers and effective against replay attacks. A user is given a device, rather like a pocket calculator, but having a protected data encryption standard key. This key is also stored in protected form in a computer system. After log on at a terminal the user is challenged by a random number. This number is entered into the device to produce a response number which in turn is keyed into the terminal by the user. The response is the DES output of the challenge, encrypted under the secret key. The computer checks the response by performing the same calculation on the random number using the secret key corresponding to the user id. Since the key is unique to the user, the user's identity can be confirmed; the security is further enhanced through the use of a PIN in conjunction with the cryptographic device. *Compare* DIGITAL SIGNATURE. *See* CHALLENGE/RESPONSE, DATA ENCRYPTION STANDARD, PIN, REPLAY.

dynamic programming. In mathematics, an operations research technique for optimizing a multi-stage system when one of a number of choices may be taken at each stage. *Compare* LINEAR PROGRAMMING.

dynamic range. In audio recording, the difference in amplitude between the softest and loudest sounds. *See* DISTORTION.

dynamic track following. In video recording, a technique adopted by Philips in which the read head is dynamically aligned with the correct track position through the use of guidance signals.

DYUV. *See* DELTA YUV.

E

E13B. In character recognition, a magnetic ink character recognition font consisting of 10 numerals and four symbols. It is widely used in automatic cheque sorting and banking. *See* FONT, MAGNETIC INK CHARACTER RECOGNITION.

EAN. In codes, European article number; a four-bar width bar code said to be the European counterpart of universal product code. *See* BAR CODE, UNIVERSAL PRODUCT CODE.

EAPROM. In memory systems, electrically alterable programmable read-only memory. *Synonymous with* ELECTRICALLY PROGRAMMABLE READ-ONLY MEMORY.

EAROM. *See* ELECTRICALLY ALTERABLE READ-ONLY MEMORY.

earth. *Synonymous with* GROUND.

earth coverage. *See* GLOBAL BEAM.

earth station. *Synonymous with* GROUND STATION.

eavesdropping. In computer security, the unauthorized interception of information-bearing emanations through the use of methods other than wiretapping. (FIPS). *Compare* WIRETAPPING. *See* COMPROMISING EMANATIONS, ELECTRONIC COUNTERMEASURES SWEEPING, PASSIVE ATTACK.

eavesdropping node. *Synonymous with* PROMISCUOUS MODE.

EBCDIC code. In codes, Extended Binary-Coded Decimal Interchange Code (pronounced ip-sa-dik), one of two international data codes used in IBM equipment. An eight-bit code that gives 256 combinations to represent a selection of graphic (printing) and non-graphic (control) codes. It is used by IBM for representing characters and control values on large computers. *Compare* AMERICAN STANDARD CODE FOR INFORMATION INTERCHANGE, ISO-7.

EBNF. *See* EXTENDED BACKUS NAUR FORM.

EBR. *See* ELECTRON BEAM RECORDING.

EBU. European Broadcasting Union.

ECB. *See* ELECTRONIC CODEBOOK.

ECC. *See* ERROR-CORRECTING CODE.

ECCM. In data security, electronic ecounter-countermeasures. *Compare* ECM. *See* ELECTRONIC COUNTERMEASURES SWEEPING.

ECHO. In online information retrieval, European Commission Host Organization; a database vendor based in Luxembourg and offering access to EEC databases. *See* DATABASE VENDOR.

echo. (1) In broadcasting, a sound generated in an echo chamber to simulate reverberation. *See* ECHO CHAMBER. (2) In audio recording, an electronic technique for creating a time-delayed signal to be added to the original source. (3) In high-frequency radio communications, a signal received after travelling around the world. (4) In television, the second image on a display due to a signal received via a reflecting path. This image is displaced to the right of the original. (5) In communications, an interference due to reflection of the transmitted signal from the receiving end. *See* ECHO SUPPRESSOR.

		Bit Positions 0, 1, 2, 3															
Bit Positions 4, 5, 6, 7		0000	0001	0010	0011	0100	0101	0110	0111	1000	1001	1010	1011	1100	1101	1110	1111
	Hex	0	1	2	3	4	5	6	7	8	9	A	B	C	D	E	F
0000	0	NUL	DLE			SP	&	R̄H̄Ȳ						2	3	½	0
0001	1	SOH	DC1			RSP	/			a	j	°		A	J	NSP	1
0010	2	STX	DC2		SYN					b	k	s		B	K	S	2
0011	3	ETX	DC3	WUS	IRT					c	l	t		C	L	T	3
0100	4									d	m	u		D	M	U	4
0101	5	HT	NL	LF						e	n	v		E	N	V	5
0110	6	RCR	BS	ETB	NBS					f	o	w		F	O	W	6
0111	7	DEL		ESC	EOT					g	p	x		G	P	X	7
1000	8				SBS					h	q	y		H	Q	Y	8
1001	9	SPS			IT	|	±			i	r	z		I	R	Z	9
1010	A	RPT	UBS	SW	EOP	¼ $	¾]	# ¾	:					S̄H̄Ȳ			
1011	B			CU2		.	$ £	,	£ #								
1100	C	FF				<	*	%	@								
1101	D		IGS	ENQ	NAK	(	)	—	'								
1110	E		IRS			+	;	>									
1111	F		ITB	BEL	! ¼	μ	?	"									

Options

BS	Backspace
CRE	Carrier return
DEL	Delete
CU2	MCII Format control
HT	Horizontal tab
INX	Index
IRT	Index return
IT	Indent tab
NBS	Numeric backspace
NSP	Numeric space
PE	Page end
RCR	Required carrier return
RHY	Required hyphen
RPT	Repeat
RSP	Required space
SBS	Subscript
SHY	Syllable hyphen
SP	Space
SPS	Superscript
STP	Stop
SW	Switch
UBS	Unit backspace
WUS	Word underscore
PRE	Prefix

EBCDIC code

echo chamber. An acoustic or electronic device that can prolong the decay of a reverberating sound wave by up to two seconds. *See* ECHO.

echocheck. *Synonymous with* ECHOPLEX.

echoplex. In data communications, a method employing an echo of received data for error checking. A computer, receiving data from a communication link operating in a full-duplex mode, returns the received data to the transmitter thus allowing it to verify that data was correctly received. *Compare* LOCAL ECHO. *See* FULL-DUPLEX. *Synonymous with* ECHOCHECK.

echo suppressor. In data communications, conventional telephone networks have echo suppressors to inhibit annoying echoes during telephone conversations. These devices detect the presence of a voice signal in one direction and inhibit signal flow in the opposite direction. These devices prevent full-duplex data communications and must therefore be suppressed for data transfer. *See* FULL DUPLEX.

ECL.   *See* EMITTER COUPLED LOGIC.

eclipse.   In communications, a situation in which a satellite is in the shadow of the earth. *See* COMMUNICATIONS SATELLITE SYSTEM.

ECM.   In data security, electronic countermeasures. *Compare* ECCM. *See* ELECTRONIC COUNTERMEASURES SWEEPING.

ECMA.   European Computer Manufacturers Association. *See* ECMA-101.

ECMA-101.   In standards, a specification for the transmission of documents so that they can be worked on by the receiver without the need for subsequent, extensive formatting.

A document needs to be described in terms of its graphical contents, such as textual characters, including attributes such as super- and subscripts, underlining, italics, pictorial symbols used in diagrams and format attributes such as indentations, paragraphing, pagination, etc. Without some standard method of specifying these characteristics the document can only be transmitted as a text string. ECMA-101 caters for the transmission of character text and photographic (i.e. facsimile) images. The recipient can then (say) merge a received document with an existing one; the document will be automatically restructured (e.g. footnotes going to the appropriate place) without reformatting by the recipient. *See* ELECTRONIC DOCUMENT INTERCHANGE.

Ecom.   In data communications, an electronic mail service operated by US Postal Service. *See* ELECTRONIC MAIL.

ECOMA.   European Computer Measurement Association.

economy of mechanism.   In computer security, the principle of keeping the security design as small and simple as possible. The greater the complexity of the system the greater the potential of errors.

ECSA.   European Computer Services Association.

ED.   *See* ENERGY DISPERSAL.

EDAC.   In data communications, error detection and correction. *See* FORWARD ERROR CORRECTION.

EDC.   *See* ERROR-DETECTING CODE.

EDC/ECC.   In codes, error-detecting code/error-correcting code. *See* ERROR-CORRECTING CODE, ERROR-DETECTING CODE.

edge board.   In computing, a device similar to an edge card, but the term usually implies a somewhat larger circuit board. *See* EDGE CARD.

edge card.   In computing, a circuit board with contact strips along one edge. It is designed to mate with an edge connector. *See* EDGE BOARD, EDGE CONNECTOR.

edge connector.   In computing, an electrical slot-shaped socket enabling an edge card to be connected to the motherboard. *See* EDGE CARD, MOTHERBOARD.

edge emitting LED.   In optoelectronics, an light-emitting diode (LED) with a spectral output that emanates from an edge, having a higher output intensity and greater coupling efficiency to an optical fiber, or integrated optical circuit, than a surface emitting LED. *See* FIBER OPTICS, LIGHT-EMITTING DIODE.

EDI.   Electronic data interchange. *See* ELECTRONIC DOCUMENT INTERCHANGE.

edit.   (1) In computing, a procedure used to change or modify the form of data input to the system. This may involve testing input for correct format and adding or deleting characters. *See* EDITOR. (2) In filming, the creative alteration of a recorded original, whether by assembling, shortening, transposing or synchronizing the original film or tape material.

editing run.   In computing, a program run that checks new data for validity against a series of predefined rules and identifies any errors for correction and resubmission. Typical tests include checking that dates and numbers fall within expected ranges, verification of check digits, etc.

editing symbols. In micrographics, alpha-numerical and geometric symbols on micro-film readable with the unaided eye and used to provide cutting, loading and other preparation instructions.

editing terminal. (1) In peripherals, a visual display terminal with an internal memory to allow for the insertion, modification and deletion of data without necessitating immediate interaction with the host computer. *Compare* DUMB TERMINAL, INTELLIGENT TERMINAL. *See* VISUAL DISPLAY TERMINAL. (2) In printing, a visual display unit on which the result of keyboarding held on tape or disk is displayed for editing purposes, using an attached keyboard, prior to processing the copy on a typesetting machine. (3) In videotex, a terminal used for building up a page display consisting of alphamosaic characters. *Compare* GRAPHIC DISPLAY TERMINAL. *See* ALPHAMOSAIC.

edition. In publishing, the complete output of a publication from one set of printing forms. An edition may be of one or more impressions, but a new edition implies some change in content and/or style of production. *See* FORM.

editor. (1) In computing, a software tool that is used as an aid in producing and modifying and source programs under development. *See* LINE EDITOR, SCREEN EDITOR, SOURCE PROGRAM, TEXT EDITOR. (2) In filming, one who edits film.

editorial processing centre. (EPC) In publishing, a centre enabling a number of small publishing operations to be combined into one that is sufficiently large to render the application of computer techniques economically sound. The centre permits functions such as writing, refereeing, editing and proofing to be performed online. It also facilitates computer typesetting and the automation of certain business management functions. *See* ONLINE.

EDP. (1) Educational data processing. (2) *See* ELECTRONIC DATA PROCESSING.

EDP capability. In word processing, the ability of a machine to either perform some associated data processing, or else for it to be used independently for electronic data-processing (EDP) tasks. *See* ELECTRONIC DATA PROCESSING.

EDS. *See* EXCHANGEABLE DISK STORAGE.

educational technology. In applications, a systematic approach to the design and evaluation of teaching and learning methods and methodologies and to the application and exploitation of media and of the current knowledge of communication techniques in education, both formal and informal. *See* COMPUTER-BASED TRAINING, EDUCATIONAL TELEVISION, INTERACTIVE VIDEODISC SYSTEMS.

educational television. (ETV) A generic term applied to any television program, or equipment, related to some form of education or instruction.

edutainment. In domestic applications, a portmanteau word signifying educational entertainment (i.e. learning in an easy, enjoyable way). (Philips). *Compare* INFOTAINMENT.

EEMAC. Electrical and Electronic Manufacturers' Association of Canada.

EEROM. Electrically erasable read-only memory. *Synonymous with* ELECTRICALLY ALTERABLE READ-ONLY MEMORY.

EFET. In microelectronics, enhancement mode field effect transistor; a normally off device. *Compare* DFET. *See* FIELD EFFECT TRANSISTOR.

effective address. In computing, an address that is derived by performing an address modification. *See* ADDRESSING MODE.

effective aperture. (1) In optics, the ratio between the focal length and the diameter of the iris diaphragm. Thus although the geometry of the lens may indicate an f-number of 2.8, due to shortcomings of the camera system the lens may only have an effective value of 4.0. *See* F-NUMBER. (2) In communications, a measure of the power available at the terminals of antennae. *See* ANTENNA.

effective bandwidth. In communications, the frequency range over which the performance of the system is within the specified operational limits. *See* BANDWIDTH.

effective isotropic radiated power. (EIRP) In communications, the product of the power supplied to an antenna and its gain. *See* ANTENNA GAIN, DISH ANTENNA, ISOTROPIC ANTENNA.

effective search speed. In memory systems, the rate at which a storage medium (e.g. a floppy disk) can be searched to reach the beginning of a particular text passage. *See* FLOPPY DISK.

EFM. *See* EIGHT-TO-FOURTEEN MODULATION.

EFT. *See* ELECTRONIC FUNDS TRANSFER.

EFTPOS. *See* ELECTRONIC FUNDS TRANSFER POINT OF SALE.

EFTS. Electronic funds transfer system. *See* ELECTRONIC FUNDS TRANSFER.

Egyptian. In printing, a term for a style of typefaces having square serifs and almost uniform thickness of strokes. (Desktop). *Compare* AVANTE-GARDE, BOOKMAN, COURIER, HELVETICA, HELVETICA NARROW, NEW CENTURY SCHOOLBOOK, OLDSTYLE, PALATINO, SYMBOL, TIMES ROMAN, ZAPF CHANCERY, ZAPF DINGBATS. *See* SERIF, TYPEFACE.

EHF. *See* EXTREMELY HIGH-FREQUENCY.

EIA. *See* ELECTRONIC INDUSTRIES ASSOCIATION.

EIAJ standards. In recording, the tape standards promoted by the Electronic Industry Association of Japan which allows for the compatibility of the equipment of several manufacturers.

EIES. In data communications, Electronic Information Exchange Service; an experimental computer network supported by the US National Science Foundation.

eight sheet. In printing, a poster measuring 60 x 80 inches (153 x 203 cm) and traditionally made up of eight individual sheets.

(Desktop). *Compare* SIXTEEN SHEET, THIRTY-TWO SHEET.

eight-to-fourteen modulation. (EFM) In codes, a code used in compact discs to improve disc storage capacity. In compact discs, the pulse code-modulated signal produced by analog-to-digital conversion is a simple non-return to zero bit stream; it is not self-clocking and there is no restriction on run length.

EFM is applied to produce a signal format suitable for recording. EFM imposes a minimum run length of three 0 bits and a maximum run length of eleven 0 bits. It also changes the signal into a non-return to zero inverted bit stream, in which a 1 is represented by a transition and a 0 by no transition. Finally EFM introduces a unique synchronization pattern to each frame of audio information.

	data bits	channel bits
0	00000000	01001000100000
1	00000001	10000100000000
2	00000010	10010000100000
3	00000011	10001000100000
4	00000100	01000100000000
5	00000101	00000100010000
6	00000110	00010000100000
7	00000111	00100100000000
8	00001000	01001001000000
9	00001001	10000001000000
10	00001010	10010001000000

eight-to-fourteen modulation
Fig. 1. Part of the eight-to-fourteen code conversion table.

EFM greatly reduces the number of transitions for the same amount of data. This means that the data can be read more reliably, with much less risk of interference between symbols. It also means that 25 per cent more data can be recorded on the same data area. At the same time EFM ensures that there are always enough transitions to allow bit clock regeneration in the compact disc player. The data is thus made self-clocking.

EFM also minimizes the difference between the number of 1s and 0s in the bit stream. This suppresses low-frequency components which could otherwise interfere with the player's focusing, tracking and motor control servos. Finally the synchronization pattern allows each frame to be recognized. This is essential, particularly for error correction and subcode separation.

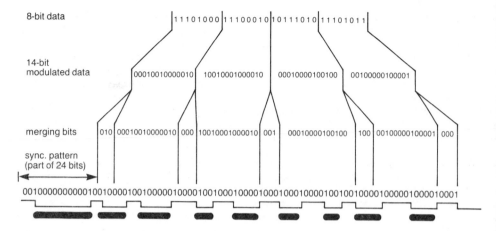

eight-to-fourteen modulation
Fig. 2. A '1' is represented by the transition from a land to a pit, or from a pit to a land. 'O's are represented by the run length between transitions, i.e. the length of a pit, or a land.

EFM changes each eight-bit symbol in the signal into a 14-bit symbol. The 14-bit symbols all have a minimum of three and a maximum of 11 successive 0s. 256 such symbols are needed to match all the possible eight-bit combinations. (In fact 267 14-bit symbols meet this requirement; 11 are not used.) The 256 14-bit symbols form a look-up table held in a read-only memory.

The run length conditions must be maintained between symbols, as well as within them. This is achieved by inserting two merging bits. A third merging bit maintains the balance between the number of 0s and 1s in the bit stream. Thus, each eight-bit symbol becomes a 17-bit symbol (14 + 3). The synchronization pattern consists of 24 bits, and is uniquely identifiable; it, too, has three merging bits.

An EFM audio frame is composed of 33 17-bit symbols (24 audio, 8 parity and 1 subcode) plus a 27-bit synchronization pattern, giving a total of 588 channel bits. This is the signal written to disc, where each 1 is represented by the beginning or end of a pit. (Philips). *See* ANALOG-TO-DIGITAL CONVERTER, BIT STREAM, COMPACT DISC, LOOK-UP TABLE, NON-RETURN TO ZERO, NON-RETURN TO ZERO INVERTED, PULSE CODE MODULATION, RUN LENGTH, SERVO, SUBCODE CHANNEL.

EIRP. *See* EFFECTIVE ISOTROPIC RADIATED POWER.

EL. *See* ELECTROLUMINESCENT DISPLAY.

electret. In electronics, a dielectric solid which retains a charge at its opposite sides after a voltage application in the assembly process.

electret microphone. *See* ELECTRET, MICROPHONE.

electrically alterable programmable read-only memopry. *Synonymous with* ELECTRICALLY PROGRAMMABLE READ-ONLY MEMORY.

electrically alterable read-only memory. (EAROM) In memory systems, a read-only memory that can be programmed by applying a voltage to selected pins and erased either by exposure to ultraviolet light or by reversing the polarity used in writing. *Compare* ELECTRICALLY PROGRAMMABLE READ-ONLY MEMORY. *See* READ-ONLY MEMORY. *Synonymous with* ELECTRICALLY ERASABLE READ-ONLY MEMORY, EROM.

electrically erasable read-only memory. *Synonymous with* ELECTRICALLY ALTERABLE READ-ONLY MEMORY.

electrically programmable read-only memory. (EPROM) In memory systems, a read-only memory that can be programmed by applying a voltage to selected pins. The term is applied both to devices that may, and may not, be reprogrammed. *See* ELECTRICALLY ALTERABLE READ-ONLY MEMORY, PROGRAMMABLE READ-ONLY MEMORY.

electrical metallic tubing. (EMT) In communications security, a form of conduit providing some physical and electrical protection for cables.

electroacoustic tablet. In peripherals, a digitizing tablet in which the position of the stylus is determined by the time of travel of sound waves to the stylus contact point. *See* DIGITIZING TABLET.

electrode. In electronics, that part of a circuit that acts as a source of electrical charges or controls or collects them.

electroerosion printer. In printing, a non-impact printer in which the current from a tiny needle removes the thin aluminium coating from a black sheet of paper. *See* NON-IMPACT PRINTER, PRINTER.

electroluminescence. (EL) In optoelectronics, the emission of light by a phosphorescent substance under the influence of an electromagnetic field. (Philips). *See* PHOSPHOR DOTS.

electroluminescent display. In peripherals, a form of flat-screen display employing electroluminescence. The displays have a viewing angle of 120° and their yellow display colour is easy to read. *See* ELECTROLUMINESCENCE, FLAT-SCREEN DISPLAY.

electromagnet. A device consisting of a ferromagnetic core and an electric coil that produces an appreciable magnetic effect while a current flows in the coil.

electromagnetic emanations. In computer security, signals transmitted as radiation through the air and through conductors, particularly through power supply leads and printer cables. *See* COMPROMISING EMANATIONS, VAN ECK PHENOMENON. *Synonymous with* ELECTROMAGNETIC EMISSIONS, RADIO FREQUENCY EMISSIONS.

electromagnetic emissions. *Synonymous with* ELECTROMAGNETIC EMANATIONS.

electromagnetic interference. (EMI) In computer security, a source of error conditions in computers caused by the pickup of stray electromagnetic radiation. *Compare* ELECTROMAGNETIC EMANATIONS. *Synonymous with* RADIO FREQUENCY INTERFERENCE.

electromagnetic radiation. In communications and optics, a radio or light energy wave associated with electric and magnetic fields. Electromagnetic radiation requires no supporting medium and is propagated through space at a velocity of approximately 3×10^8 metres per second. The nature of electromagnetic radiations depends upon their frequency and includes light waves and microwaves. In radiocommunications, the carrier signal is an electromagnetic wave which is transmitted and received by an antenna. *See* ANTENNA, CARRIER WAVE, LIGHT, MICROWAVE.

electromagnetic interference/radio fraquency radiation. *See* EMI/RF RADIATION.

electromagnetic spectrum. The range of frequencies over which electromagnetic radiations are propagated. The lowest frequencies are radio waves; increases of frequency produce infrared radiation, light, ultraviolet radiation, X-rays, gamma-rays and finally cosmic rays. *See* ELECTROMAGNETIC RADIATION, INFRARED, LIGHT, ULTRAVIOLET.

electromotive force. *Synonymous with* VOLTAGE.

electron. In electronics, an elementary particle containing the smallest electrical charge. The mass of the electron is approximately 1/1837 of the mass of the hydrogen atom. *Compare* PROTON.

electron beam recording. (EBR) (1) In television and filming, a technique of producing film from high-quality videotape. (2) In applications, a technique used in the production of computer output microfilm. A beam of electrons is directed onto energy-sensitive microfilm. *Compare* CRT RECORDING, FIBER OPTICS RECORDING. *See* COMPUTER OUTPUT TO MICROFILM, MICROFILM.

electron gun. *See* GUN.

electronic blackboard. In data communications, a system for sending handwriting and hand-drawn graphics over a telephone line. The sender may use either a light pen or digitizing tablet, and the appropriate image appears on a television monitor at the remote location. *See* DIGITIZING TABLET, LIGHT PEN, Sketchphone, TELEWRITING.

electronic card file. In programming, a program used on personal computers to simulate a card filing system. (Philips).

electronic cheque book. *See* SMART CARD.

electronic codebook. (ECB) In data security, a straightforward method of data encryption standard (DES) operation. Each 64-bit data block of the message is encrypted, transmitted and decrypted by the receiver. DES effectively acts as a codebook with 2^{64} entries. This method is vulnerable to a degree of attack when messages are likely to contain common phrases (e.g. message headings) since the ciphertext of consecutive messages will have some identical blocks. *Compare* CIPHER BLOCK CHAINING, CIPHER FEEDBACK, OUTPUT FEEDBACK. *See* DATA ENCRYPTION STANDARD. *Synonymous with* NATIVE MODE.

electronic composition. In printing, the use of a computer for text manipulation prior to typesetting.

electronic countermeasures sweeping. In communications security, the process of identifying and removing electronic listening devices from an area or piece of communication equipment. *See* ELECTRONIC LISTENING DEVICE.

electronic data processing. (EDP) In computing, data processing performed largely by electronic, as compared with manual or mechanical, techniques, usually involving company-wide transactions. *Compare* PERSONAL COMPUTING.

electronic digital computer. In computing, in its simplest form a device, with a central processing unit (CPU), that accepts a set of instructions and data, performs computations or manipulations upon that data according to the instructions and delivers the results. The basic computer comprises an input device, a memory, a control and arithmetic unit and an output device. The input device translates sets of signals from some external form (e.g. a keyboard on a com-

puter terminal) into a set of voltages that represent binary codes of the input data. These voltages are directed to the memory where they cause an electronic device to assume one of two states (i.e. they store the bits of the input data). The control unit of CPU takes each instruction from the program, held in memory, in a sequence determined by the program and previous results of program computations. The instruction is decoded and the corresponding actions are performed in the arithmetic unit. For example, a sequence of three instructions might require that a number be extracted from a memory location and stored in an arithmetic unit register. The second instruction then extracts another number from a second memory location and adds it to the first number in the register, and the third instruction moves the sum held in the register to a third memory location. At another part of the program an instruction will require that the certain memory locations be sent to an output device such as a printer. This operation involves the reverse of the input operation (i.e. the states of the memory location are converted to a pulse train and sent to an output device). *See* ARCHITECTURE, ARITHMETIC UNIT, BYTE, BINARY CODE, COMPUTER, CENTRAL PROCESSING UNIT, INFORMATION PROCESSOR, MEMORY, MICROCOMPUTER.

electronic document interchange. In computing and communications, the transmission of documents from one computer to another over a network. Consider the case of a vehicle manufacturer with many different component suppliers. If all parties have computer systems in which a standard has been agreed for electronic data interchange, such as X.400, then everyone benefits. Much paper work is eliminated, suppliers can respond more rapidly to production requirements and the manufacturer does not have to rekey supplier invoice details. This eliminates transcription errors and reduces handling costs, particularly if the participants are multinational organizations using a global network. *See* ECMA-101, ODETTE, X.400.

electronic eavesdropping. In data security, the interception of wireless transmissions (e.g. radio or microwave transmissions) or information-bearing electromagnetic energy emanating from electronic devices. *Compare* ACOUSTIC EAVESDROPPING, ELECTRONIC LISTENING DEVICE. *See* COMPROMISING EMANATIONS, EAVESDROPPING.

electronic editing. In recording, the insertion or assembling of program elements on video tape without physically cutting the tape. *See* EDITOR.

electronic encyclopaedia. In applications, a database providing a comprehensive information service in text and/or audiovisual form. Electronic textual encyclopaedias provide the user with online access to large databases either directly or via a videotex gateway service. The access protocol may be menu-driven or by keyword search. Audiovisual information may be packed onto sets of videodiscs or interactive compact discs and accessed by appropriate software indexes loaded into microcomputers controlling the disc player. The two forms of database have complementary characteristics; the online textual database may be updated by the information provider to reflect changes in the state of knowledge, or extensions and contractions in the perceived user requirements. The disc set of information is static and located at the user's premises, but provides information in the form of high-quality freeze-frame images or short film sequences with accompanying sound. The two forms of database may be combined with the online database providing both updated textual information and frame addresses to select appropriate still images (interactive compact disc or videodisc) or film sequences (videodisc) on the disc. *See* COMPACT DISC – INTERACTIVE, FREEZE FRAME, GATEWAY, INTERACTIVE VIDEODISC SYSTEMS, MENU SELECTION, ONLINE INFORMATION RETRIEVAL.

electronic filing. In applications, an aspect of office automation which is concerned with the filing of typical office records (e.g. memoranda, reports, diagrams) on magnetic tape or disk. In some cases microfilm techniques is used for the storage of bulky objects and the system normally allows for the recording of a catalogue of paper objects which cannot conveniently be read into the computer system. *See* MAGNETIC DISK, MAGNETIC TAPE.

electronic funds transfer. (EFT) In data communications, an automated system for transferring funds from one bank account to another using electronic equipment and data communications rather than paper media (e.g. cheques) and the postal system. *Compare* ELECTRON FUNDS TRANSFER POINT OF SALE. *See* BANKING NETWORKS, KEY MANAGEMENT, MESSAGE AUTHENTICATION, PIN MANAGEMENT AND SECURITY.

electronic funds transfer point of sale. (EFTPOS) In peripherals, a point of sale terminal that is connected by communication line to a financial institution's computer. The terminal normally reads and transmits the information recorded on the magnetic stripe of a credit card and provides for the input of transaction details via a keyboard. *Compare* ELECTRONIC FUNDS TRANSFER. *See* POINT OF SALE.

electronic glass. In peripherals, a transparent solid electrical conductor. It is used in a variety of devices (e.g. touchscreen units). *See* TOUCHSCREEN.

Electronic Industries Association. (EIA) A standards organization specializing in the electrical and functional characteristics of interface equipment.

electronic journal. In applications, an electronic publishing system which can bypass traditional scientific journal publishing. All the stages in the preparation of the electronic journal, i.e. writing, refereeing, editing, proofing and publishing, are performed within a distributed computing system. *Compare* VIDEO CASSETTE JOURNAL. *See* ELECTRONIC PUBLISHING.

electronic keyboard. In peripherals, a keyboard in which characters are generated or encoded by electronic means as opposed to mechanical methods. Electronic keyboards have a different feel, and in order to simulate their mechanical equivalent some have an artificial bottoming feel and/or audible click to assure the operator a key has actually been depressed. *See* KEYBOARD.

electronic learning laboratory. In educational technology, a system consisting of instructors, control equipment and a number of student positions or stations. The control equipment is capable of producing, copying, monitoring and distributing educational material to one or more students for study or response. The communications network may be either wired, or broadcast, and student positions are usually equipped with headphones, microphones, signalling devices, and recording and viewing facilities.

electronic listening device. In communications security, a device used to collect and transmit information to an eavesdropper. Such devices may be secreted in a room or connected to telephone equipment. The bug is used to listen into a conversation in a room and comprises a miniature microphone, amplifier, transmitter and power source. It can transmit the conversation in the form of a radio frequency signal which can be received as far as 10 kilometres away, depending upon the radio frequency used, the power of the transmitter and the density of the buildings in the transmission path.

Telephone taps are similar to bugs except that they do not contain a microphone, or power source, and are connected in series or parallel with a telephone line. Since they require no power source they can remain in operation indefinitely and need not be inserted into a secure area such as an office. The telephone tap can be connected to the appropriate telephone line at various points (e.g. at distribution frames located on the same floor, in the basement or outside the office building). Such taps may be used to eavesdrop on conversations, facsimile, telex or computer data. *Compare* ELECTRONIC EAVESDROPPING. *See* ELECTRONIC COUNTERMEASURES SWEEPING, FACSIMILE, TELEX. *Synonymous with* BUG.

electronic lock. In television, a device, used in cable television systems, that enables the authorized user to deny other users of the receiver access to certain channels (e.g. to prevent children from viewing unsuitable material).

electronic mail. (EM) In data communications, a facility that enables users to exchange information addressed to a particular individual, or a group, using computer communication facilities. The options available in various systems can be classified as Send, Receive, File options and Addressing options.

The Send options include Carbon Copy, Blind Copy, Reply Requested, Express,

Registered and Delayed Delivery. The Carbon Copy option sends a copy of messages to all designated users, whereas Blind Copy performs a similar function without indicating the distribution list to individual recipients. Reply Requested indicates that the correspondence should be responded to. Express will receive some type of special handling on receipt (e.g. alerting the workstation). Registered option will give an indication of delivery to the intended recipient and Delayed Delivery arranges for the mail to be delivered at a specified time/date.

The Receive options include Forward, Reply, Save, Delete and Scan. The Forward option sends the message to another user, with comments as appropriate, not on the original address list. Reply allows an immediate reply to the message whether requested or not. The Save option retains the message in an existing or new file for later editing, merging, review, etc. Delete disposes of a message after reading, and Scan allows a browse through pending mail, looking only at originators, subject headings, etc.

The File options available are Editing and Merging. The former allows reading of messages selected by date interval, search by keyword, originator, etc. Editing provides an off- or online edit capability, and Merging allows the insertion of preformatted information into a message during preparation.

The Addressing options comprise Group Addressing, Standard Distribution, Hidden Distribution and Account Number/Name Association. Group Addressing provides for the use of multiple user account numbers in the address list. Standard Distribution provides for prestored distribution lists whilst Hidden Distribution is similar to Blind Copy (i.e. no addressee sees the distribution list). The Account Number/Name Association permits address by name rather than by user number.

Electronic mailbox facilities may be provided within an organization or over a national or international network (e.g. Telecom Gold, or Dialcom). *See* DIALCOM, TELECOM GOLD. *Synonymous with* COMPUTER-BASED MESSAGE SYSTEM.

electronic mailbox. *See* ELECTRONIC MAIL.

electronic mark-up. In printing, the insertion of codes, within the text of a stored document, which are interpreted by a computer to control the format when the document is printed. *See* GENERIC CODING, STANDARD GENERALIZED MARK-UP LANGUAGE.

electronic message system. In communications, the transmission of information over networks. Examples include communicating word processors, teleconferencing, videotex and electronic mail. *See* ELECTRONIC MAIL, TELECONFERENCING, TELETEX, VIDEOTEX,

electronic messaging. *See* BULLETIN BOARD.

electronic news gathering. (ENG) The production of television news using hand-held cameras and video cassette recorders.

electronic office. *Synonymous with* OFFICE OF THE FUTURE.

electronic pen. *Synonymous with* DIGITIZING TABLET.

Electronic Post. In data communications, a UK Post Office service in which the text of bulk mail is transmitted over data communication networks, printed at receiving terminals and then distributed locally by normal postal delivery.

electronic publishing. (1) In applications, the writing, editing, transfer and publishing of information in electronic form. *See* BULLETIN BOARD, CD-ROM PUBLISHING, DESK-TOP PUBLISHING, ELECTRONIC ENCYCLOPAEDIA, ELECTRONIC JOURNAL, ONLINE INFORMATION RETRIEVAL, VIDEOTEX, VIEWBOOK. *Synonymous with* TELEPUBLISHING. (2) In printing. *Synonymous with* DESK-TOP PUBLISHING.

Electronic Publishing Abstracts. (EPA) In online information retrieval, a database supplied by the Paper, Printing and Packaging Industries Association.

electronic pulse. *See* PULSE.

electronic purse. *See* SMART CARD.

electronics. A branch of technology dealing with the motion and behaviour of electrons, especially those in semiconductor circuits. Although the term derives from vacuum tube technology, it is now concerned with the solid-state circuits and devices used in computing and communications. *See* CHIP, MICROELECTRONICS, SOLID-STATE DEVICE.

electronic signature. *Synonymous with* DIGITAL SIGNATURE.

electronic switching system. (ESS) In communications, a switching system using a special-purpose computer to direct and control the switching of telephone circuits.

electronic telephone. A telephone set that contains extra circuitry to provide additional features and improved performance.

electronic token. *See* INTELLIGENT TOKEN, SMART CARD.

electronic typewriter. In word processing, a typewriter with limited word-processing facilities. It normally has a one-line display which allows text to be corrected before it is printed.

electronic viewfinder. In television, a small cathode ray tube built into a camera to enable the operator to view the camera image.

electronic wallet. *See* SMART CARD.

Electronic Yellow Pages. In online information retrieval, directory databases that provide online access to the yellow page sections of US telephone directories. *See* DIRECTORY DATABASE.

electro-optic effect. In optoelectronics, the change in refractive index of a material when subjected to an electric field. The effect can be used to modulate a light beam in a material. *See* MODULATION, REFRACTIVE INDEX.

electrophotoadhesive process. In printing, an electrophotographic imaging process in which a toner image is formed xerographically on a photoconductive layer which is only weakly bonded to a base material. An adhesive-coated transfer sheet is pressed onto the unfixed toner image and is then removed with the toner image adhering. *See*

ELECTROPHOTOGRAPHIC PROCESS, PHOTOCON-
DUCTIVITY, XEROGRAPHY.

electrophotographic process. In printing, a
printing process that involves the stages: (a)
uniformly electrostatically charging a photoconductor surface; (b) creating a latent electrostatic image on the photoconductor; (c)
attracting negatively charged toner to the
discharged areas of the photoconductor; (d)
transferring the toner to paper; and (e)
fusing the toner. *See* ION DEPOSITION, LASER
PRINTER, LATENT IMAGE, PHOTOCONDUCTOR,
TONER, XEROGRAPHY.

electrosensitive paper. Printer paper with a
thin coating of aluminium or other conductive material. The print becomes visible after
a matrix print head causes an electric current
to flow onto the conductive surface, producing a darkening effect.

electrostatic loudspeaker. A speaker consisting of two large conducting electrodes,
one or both of which are flexible. The electrodes are maintained at a high voltage and
are separated by an insulating material.
Voltages at audio frequency are applied to
the electrodes, the resulting movement
creates a sound wave. *See* ELECTRODE.

electrostatic plotter. In peripherals, a plotter that produces a raster image by charging
the medium with static electricity; the latent
image attracts a toner which is then fused to
the medium by heat. The image head consists of an array of closely spaced electrical
contacts, termed nibs, which extend across
the width of the paper. A 1 or 0 signal is
passed to the head by the plotter controller,
and for a 1 signal an electrical charge is
passed to the paper. The paper is continuously moved past the writing array;
toner is applied and fused to the paper at the
toner/fusing station. With colour plotters the
paper may be rewound, passed over the
writing head and a different colour toner
applied at a second toner/fusing station. The
process is then repeated for the next colour
in the process. Some colour plotters have a
separate image head and toner/fusing station
for each colour thus requiring only one pass
of the paper.
   The dot density for printers can range
from 100 to 500 dots per inch, for large

diagrams the total storage capacity for the
complete raster image may be as high as
several hundred megabytes. Thus, for paper
speeds of 1 inch per second, the data rate to
the image head may be hundreds of
kilobytes per second. Any delay in the transfer of data to the image head would cause
the paper speed to be reduced, and this in
turn may cause colour bars to appear across
the image due to an extended period spent at
the fusing station.
   The problems of storage and data transfer
are such that the host computer may dele-
gate the image rasterization process to a
plotter controller and pass the diagram to be
plotted in the form of vectors; the vector/
rasterization computations being undertaken in the controller. The rasterization
process may be undertaken one row at a
time to reduce the storage requirements of
the controller. The vectors are sorted on the
basis of the minimum value of the X-
coordinates. Thus the first vectors to be
printed by the image head are processed,
and the first rows of the raster image are
formed and passed to the image head. As
the paper moves past the image head other
vectors are processed and included in the
raster image. *Compare* ELECTROSTATIC PRIN-
TER. *See* NIB, RASTER IMAGING, TONER.

electrostatic printer. In printing, a form of
printer in which the image is applied to the
paper as an electrostatic charge. Particles of
pigment are then attracted to the paper and
bonded to it. The term is sometimes used to
embrace   electrophotographic   printers.
Compare ELECTROSTATIC PLOTTER, IMPACT
PRINTER. *See* ELECTROPHOTOGRAPHIC PROCESS,
LASER PRINTER.

electrostatic storage. In memory systems,
the storage of data on a dielectric in the form
of charges that can persist for a short time
after the electrostatic charging mechanism is
removed (e.g. the screen of a cathode ray
tube can be used for this purpose). *See*
DIELECTRIC.

electrotype. In printing, a duplicate letterpress plate made from an original by electroplating. *See* LETTERPRESS.

electrowriter. *See* DIGITIZING PAD.

element. (1) In a set, an object, entity or
concept having the properties that define the

set. *See* SET. (2) In a printer, the removable type element. *See* DAISY WHEEL.

elementary cable section. In communications, the physical means of transmission between the output terminals of one device (e.g. a repeater) and the input terminals of the next device in the system. *See* REPEATER.

elevation. In communications, the angle measured from the local horizontal line up to the line from an observer to a satellite. *Compare* AZIMUTH. *See* COMMUNICATIONS SATELLITE SYSTEM.

ELF. *See* EXTREMELY LOW-FREQUENCY.

Elhill. In online information retrieval, software originally created for the online searching of the US National Library of Medicine databases. It is now also used to search BLAISE and other databases. *See* BLAISE.

elite. In printing, typewriter spaces of 12 characters to the inch. *Compare* PICA. *See* TYPEWRITER FACES. *Synonymous with* TWELVE PITCH.

ellipsis. In printing, a sign (...) used to indicate that something has been left out of a phrase or sentence.

elliptical orbit. In communications, an orbit in which the trajectory of a communications satellite around the earth maps out an ellipse. *Compare* CIRCULAR ORBIT. *See* COMMUNICATIONS SATELLITE SYSTEM, GEOSTATIONARY ORBIT, GEOSYNCHRONOUS ORBIT.

ELV. In communications, expendable launch vehicle. *See* COMMUNICATIONS SATELLITE SYSTEM.

EM. *See* ELECTRONIC MAIL, END OF MEDIUM.

em. In printing, a square unit with edges equal in size to the chosen point size. It gets its name from the letter M which originally was as wide as type the type size. (Desktop). *Compare* EN, POINT. *See* EM DASH, EM RULE.

emanations. *See* COMPROMISING EMANATIONS, ELECTROMAGNETIC EMANATIONS, EMANATION SECURITY.

emanation security. In computer security, the protection that results from all measures designed to deny unauthorized persons information of value that might be derived from intercept and analysis of compromising emanations. (FIPS). *See* COMPROMISING EMANATIONS, TEMPEST PROOFING.

embedded code. In programming, sections of assembler or machine language embedded into a high-level language program. It is used to reduce storage requirements, increase execution speed or to provide some function not available in the high-level language. *See* ASSEMBLER, HIGH-LEVEL LANGUAGE, MACHINE LANGUAGE.

embedded computer. In applications, a computer serving as an intelligent active component in an electronic or electromechanical system (e.g. a camera or a washing machine).

embedded pointers. In databases, pointers that are embedded within the data records rather than stored in the directory. *See* DIRECTORY, POINTER.

embossment. In character recognition, the distance between a specified part of a printed character and the undistorted surface of the document.

em dash. In printing, a dash used for punctuation the length of one em. (Desktop). *See* EM.

emergency plan. *See* CONTINGENCY PLANNING.

EMF. Electromotive force. *Synonymous with* VOLTAGE.

EMI. *See* ELECTROMAGNETIC INTERFERENCE.

EMI/RF radiation. In communications security, electromagnetic interference/radio frequency radiation; unwanted signals produced from sources such as motors, generators, car ignitions and radio broadcasts. *See* CONDUCTIVE SHIELDING, ELECTROMAGNETIC INTERFERENCE.

emitter. In electronics, a terminal of a bipolar transistor. *Compare* BASE, COLLECTOR. *See* TRANSISTOR.

emitter-coupled logic. In microelectronics, a transistor logic circuit, characterized by fast action and high power dissipation used in high-speed mainframe computers. *See* EMITTER, LOGIC CIRCUIT, MAINFRAME, TRANSISTOR.

emphasis. *See* PRE-EMPHASIS.

empty slot. In data communications, a packet which continually circulates around a ring network. Whenever a node on the circuit wants to send information it waits for an empty slot and then fills it with data and address information. *See* CAMBRIDGE RING, PACKET SWITCHING.

em quad. In printing, a type having no face and used for creating white space in letterpress printing. The width of the space is equal to an em. *Compare* EN QUAD. *See* EM.

em rule. In printing, a sign used to indicate the omission of a word.

EMS. Electronic mail service. *See* ELECTRONIC MAIL.

ems per hour. In printing, a unit of measurement used to evaluate the speed of text production by an operator or machine. An average of two characters is assumed to equal one em. *See* EM.

EMT. *See* ELECTRICAL METALLIC TUBING.

emulator. In computing, special-purpose hardware or software that enables one system to act as if it were another. It is used, for example, to minimize reprogramming effort when a new computer replaces an existing one.

emulsion. (1) In photography, the essential light-sensitive coating on photographic film comprising gelatine and silver salts. (2) In recording, iron oxide on magnetic tape.

emulsion laser storage. In memory systems, a digital storage medium in which a controlled laser beam is used to expose very small areas on a photosensitive surface.

en. In printing, a measure equal to half the width of an em. *See* EM.

enable. In electronics, a pulse signal used for control purposes (e.g. to open a gate) thus permitting other operations. *See* GATE.

encipher. In data security, to convert plaintext to ciphertext by the use of a cipher. *Compare* DECIPHER, ENCODE, ENCRYPT. *See* CIPHERTEXT, CRYPTOGRAPHY, PLAINTEXT.

encode. (1) In data security, to convert plaintext into unintelligible form by means of a code system. (FIPS). *Compare* ENCIPHER. *See* CODE SYSTEM. (2) In data communications, to convert data, by means of a code, in such a way that it may be subsequently reconverted to its original form. (3) In data communications, to convert from one system of communication to another. *Compare* DECODE. *See* CODE.

encrypt. In data security, to convert plaintext into unintelligible form by means of a cryptographic system or to convert data by a code system. *Compare* ENCIPHER, DECRYPT. *See* CODE, CRYPTOGRAPHY.

encryption. In data security, the process of transforming data to an unintelligible form in such a way that the original data either cannot be obtained (one-way encryption) or cannot be obtained without using the inverse decryption process (two-way encryption). (FIPS). *See* ENCRYPT, END-TO-END ENCRYPTION, IRREVERSIBLE ENCRYPTION, LINK ENCRYPTION, REVERSIBLE ENCRYPTION.

endless loop. In programming, an error state in which there is no exit from a loop of instructions. *See* LOOP. (2) In recording, a sealed continuous loop of magnetic cassette tape.

end of address. (EOA) In data communications, a control character indicating to the receiver that the last character of the address has been transmitted and successive characters relate to the message. *See* CONTROL CHARACTER.

end of block. (EOB) In data communications, a control character indicating to the receiver that the last character of a block has been transmitted. *See* BLOCK, CONTROL CHARACTER.

end of copy signal. In document transmission, a signal indicating the end of transmission.

end of document. (EOD) In character recognition, a mark on a document, recognizable by a detector, indicating that the last position where data can be entered has been passed.

end office. *Synonymous with* CENTRAL OFFICE.

end of file. (EOF) In data structures, a character indicating that the last record of a file has been read. *See* FILE, RECORD.

end of medium. (EM) In data communications, a control character indicating the physical end, end of used portion or end of the required portion of the data recorded on the medium. *See* CONTROL CHARACTER.

end of message. (EOM) In data communications, a control character indicating an end of message; used to separate messages in a multi-message stream. *See* CONTROL CHARACTER, END OF TEXT.

end of page indicator. On a typewriter, a device giving a warning of the approach of the end of page during the typing operation.

end of text. (ETX) In data communications, a control character indicating to the receiver that the previous character was the last in a message text. *Compare* END OF TRANSMISSION BLOCK, START OF TEXT. *See* CONTROL CHARACTER.

end of transmission. (EOT) In data communications, a control character indicating to the receiver that transmission has been completed. *See* CONTROL CHARACTER.

end of transmission block. (ETB) In data communications, a control character, used when the transmitted data is divided into blocks, to indicate to the receiver the end of a transmission block. *Compare* END OF TEXT. *See* CONTROL CHARACTER.

endorsement. In data processing, the marking of a form or document so as to direct or to restrict its further use in processing.

end pages. In videotex, the pages, at the leaves of a tree-structured database, containing the information. *See* INDEX PAGE, LEAF, TREE STRUCTURE.

end papers. In printing, the four-page leaves at the front and end of a book that are pasted to the insides of the front and back covers. (Desktop).

end-to-end assurance. In data security, the provision of assurance to the sender of a message that it was, or will be, correctly received. *See* DELIVERY ASSURANCE.

end-to-end control. In data communications, a technique for ensuring that information transferred between two data terminals is not lost or corrupted. *See* DATA TERMINAL EQUIPMENT, HANDSHAKING.

end-to-end encryption. In communications security, encryption of information at the origin within a communications network and postponing decryption to the final destination point. (FIPS). *Compare* DATALINK ENCRYPTION, NODE ENCRYPTION. *See* ENCRYPT, NETWORK ENCRYPTION.

end-to-end signalling. In communications, a method of signalling in which signals are sent from one end of a multilink connection to the other without intermediate storage.

end user. In applications, the source or destination of information flowing through a system.

end-user computing. In applications, personal computing performed by an end user, including program development, via a personal computer or terminal linked to a mainframe. *See* FOURTH-GENERATION LANGUAGE, INFORMATION CENTRE, PERSONAL COMPUTING.

end-user device. In peripherals, a device (e.g. a visual display unit) that provides the final output of an operation without need for further processing. *See* DUMB TERMINAL, VISUAL DISPLAY UNIT.

energy. The capacity for doing work.

energy dispersal. (ED) In communications, a technique of inserting a constantly changing waveform in a transmitted satellite signal to reduce interference with terrestrial services using the same frequency. *See* COMMUNICATIONS SATELLITE SYSTEM.

Energyline. In online information retrieval, a database supplied by EIC/Intelligence and dealing with energy.

ENG. *See* ELECTRONIC NEWS GATHERING.

enhanced-quality television. In television, a generation of high-definition television receivers, with a double-scan frequency resulting in twice the number of lines, increased bandwidth and improved, or enhanced, features. (Philips). *Synonymous with* HIGH-RESOLUTION TELEVISION.

enhanced services. In communications, a service that uses the basic facilities supplied by a common carrier to provide additional, different or restructured benefits. In the USA enhanced services are not regulated by the Federal Communications Commission. *See* BASIC SERVICE, COMPUTER INQUIRY 1980, VALUE-ADDED NETWORK SERVICE.

ENQ. *See* ENQUIRY CHARACTER.

en quad. In printing, a spacing bar of half the width of an em quad. *Compare* EM QUAD. *Synonymous with* NUT.

enquiry character. (ENQ) In data communications, a control character used to request a response from a remote station. The response may include station identification and the type of equipment in service.

entity. In databases, an object or event about which information is stored in a database. *Compare* ATTRIBUTE, RELATIONSHIP.

entity identifier. In databases, a key that uniquely identifies an entity or data relevant to that entity. *See* ENTITY, KEY.

entity relationship. In data structures, a model of data dealing with attributes of entities and the relationships between them.

See ATTRIBUTE, ENTITY, RELATIONAL DATABASE.

entrapment. In computer security, a technique in which certain vulnerabilities are made attractive to a potential attacker. These vulnerabilities are then heavily instrumented to detect and record any attacks. This technique has the disadvantage that intentional efforts to attract a user to attempt an attack may be of doubtful legality. *See* PSEUDO-FLAW, VULNERABILITY.

entropy. In mathematics, the mean value of the measure of information conveyed by the occurrence of any one of a finite number of mutually exclusive events. The entropy $H(x)$ for event x with a probability of occurrence of $p(x)$ is given by

$$H(x) = -p(x) \log p(x).$$

See INFORMATION THEORY.

entry. (1) In library science, the record of a book, publication or other item in a catalogue or other library record. (2) In word processing, the typing and introduction of text into the system. (3) In databases, information stored about an object or event.

entry assist. In peripherals, a function that allows a display terminal to operate like a typewriter, providing such facilities as margins, tabbing, a bell to signal end of line and word deletion.

entry point. In programming, the starting address of a subroutine to which control is passed from the main program. *See* SUBROUTINE.

envelope. (1) In electronics, the gas-tight enclosure of a cathode ray tube or vacuum tube. *See* CATHODE RAY TUBE. (2) In communications, the amplitude variations of an amplitude-modulated carrier wave. *See* AMPLITUDE MODULATION, ENVELOPE PATTERN. (3) In data communications, a byte to which a number of additional bits have been added for control and checking purposes.

envelope delay. *See* DELAY DISTORTION.

envelope pattern. In communications, the pattern formed by the amplitude variations of a modulated waveform. (Philips). *See* AMPLITUDE MODULATION, ENVELOPE.

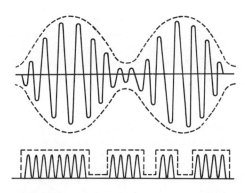

envelope pattern

Enviroline. In online information retrieval, a database supplied by EIC/Intelligence and dealing with the environment.

environment. In computing, the state of all registers, memory locations and other operative conditions.

EOA. *See* END OF ADDRESS.

EOB. *See* END OF BLOCK.

EOD. *See* END OF DOCUMENT.

EOF. *See* END OF FILE.

EOM. *See* END OF MESSAGE.

EOT. *See* END OF TRANSMISSION.

EPA. *See* ELECTRONIC PUBLISHING ABSTRACTS.

EPC. *See* EDITORIAL PROCESSING CENTRE.

EPIC. In applications, Exchange Price Information Computer; the UK Stock Exchange information system providing data to information services including TOPIC. *See* BIG BANG, SEAQ, TOPIC.

episcope. In audiovisual aids, a projector for displaying opaque subject matter on a screen (e.g. the pages of a book).

epitaxial layer. In microelectronics, a thin layer, of the order of 10 micrometres, of

doped semiconductor material that is grown onto a substrate. *See* CHIP.

EPO. European Patent Office.

EPOS. Electronic point of sale. *See* POINT OF SALE.

EPROM. (1) In memory systems. *See* ELECTRICALLY PROGRAMMABLE READ-ONLY MEMORY. (2) In memory systems, erasable programmed read-only memory. *See* PROGRAMMABLE READ-ONLY MEMORY.

Epub. In data communications, an electronic publishing service offered by Telecom Gold. *See* ELECTRONIC PUBLISHING, TELECOM GOLD.

equalization. In communications, a general term for a system designed to compensate for some form of deficiency in frequency response. *See* LOADING.

equatorial orbit. In communications, the path of a satellite when its orbital plane includes the earth's equator. *Compare* INCLINED ORBIT, POLAR ORBIT. *See* COMMUNICATIONS SATELLITE SYSTEM, GEOSTATIONARY ORBIT.

EQUIVALENCE. A logical operation, A EQUIVALENCE B has the result true if A EXCLUSIVE OR B is false. The corresponding truth table is:

A	B	A EQUIVALENCE B
0	0	1
1	0	0
0	1	0
1	1	1

Compare EXCLUSIVE OR. *See* TRUTH TABLE.

erasable medium. In memory systems, a medium from which information can be erased to allow the writing of new information. (Philips). *Compare* READ-ONLY MEMORY. *See* READ/WRITE MEDIUM.

erasable optical disc. In optical media, an optical disc using magneto-optical recording thus allowing stored information to be erased and overwritten. Writing and reading depend upon the physical effects of small reverse-polarized magnetic domains in a thin polarized magnetic layer. Writing is performed by reversing the polarization of the domain, while under the influence of an external magnetic field, by heating it above the compensation point temperature with a short laser pulse. Reading is performed by measuring the Kerr effect, which rotates polarized light when it is reflected under the influence of a magnetic field. (Philips). *See* KERR EFFECT, LASER, OPTICAL DIGITAL DISC.

erasable programmed read-only memory. *See* PROM.

erasable read-only memory. *Synonymous with* ELECTRICALLY ALTERABLE READ-ONLY MEMORY.

erasable storage. (1) In memory systems, a storage device whose data may be altered during the course of computation. (2) In memory systems, an area of storage used for temporary purposes. (3) In memory systems, a storage medium that can be erased and reused repeatedly (e.g. magnetic disk storage). *See* ERASABLE OPTICAL DISC, MAGNETIC DISK.

erase. In computing, to replace all the binary digits in a storage device by binary 0s.

erase head. In recording, a small degaussing device in the path of the tape that removes previously recorded signals. *See* DEGAUSS.

erecting system. In optics, a system that produces a top-side-up image (e.g. a camera viewfinder).

E region. In communications, a layer in the ionosphere occupying a region between 90 and 150 kilometres above the earth. *Compare* D REGION, F REGION. *See* IONOSPHERE.

ergonomics. The study of people in relation to their working environment. It is concerned with the design of man–machine interfaces to improve factors affecting health, efficiency, comfort and safety. *See* RSI.

ERIC. In online information retrieval, Educational Resources Information Center; a database supplied by US Department of Education, National Institute of Education, and dealing with education and educational institutions.

erlang. In communications, a unit of telecommunication traffic intensity determined by the product of the number of calls carried by the circuit in one hour and the average duration of the call in hours. *See* ERLANG HOUR, TRAFFIC.

erlang B model. In communications, the preferred method for the calculation of the number of channels required to carry a given amount of traffic. *See* ERLANG.

erlang hour. In communications, a unit of traffic volume, equal to the mean traffic intensity of one erlang maintained for one hour. *See* ERLANG, TRAFFIC.

EROM. In memory systems, erasable read-only memory. *Synonymous with* ELECTRICALLY ALTERABLE READ-ONLY MEMORY.

erratum. In publishing, an item omitted from a book and acknowledged by the subsequent inclusion of an erratum slip.

error. In mathematics, a discrepancy between a computed, or measured, value and some objective standard. *Compare* FAULT. *See* ERROR CONDITION.

error burst. In data communications, a series of consecutive errors. It is not unusual for errors to occur in groups or clusters.

error condition. In computing, a state that results from an attempt to execute invalid instructions or operate on invalid data. *See* ERROR ROUTINE, INSTRUCTION.

error-correcting code. (ECC) In codes, a code designed to detect an error, in a word or character, identify the incorrect bit or bits and replace them with the correct ones. The number of incorrect bits that can be corrected depends upon the number of redundant bits used in the code. *Compare* ERROR-DETECTING CODE. *See* HAMMING CODE, REDUNDANCY. *Synonymous with* SELF-CORRECTING CODE.

error-detecting code. (EDC) In codes, a code designed to detect, but not correct, an error in a word or character. The number of incorrect bits that can be detected depends upon the number of redundant bits in the code. *Compare* ERROR-CORRECTING CODE. *See* PARITY CHECKING. *Synonymous with* SELF-CHECKING CODE.

error message. In computing, a statement indicating that the computer has detected an error in the translation or execution phase of a program.

error rate. In data communications, the frequency of occurrence of errors, defined as the ratio of the number of bits incorrectly received to the total number of bits received.

error routine. In programming, a routine that is entered when an error condition arises during execution. The error routine may simply produce an error message, or it may attempt to recover from the error condition so that processing can continue. *See* ERROR CONDITION, ERROR MESSAGE.

error syndrome. In codes, a word indicating that a codeword is correct or incorrect. *See* CODEWORD.

error-trapping. In computing, pertaining to a program that takes over control when an error occurs in the system (e.g. disk read or write error). *See* MAGNETIC DISK.

ES. *See* EXPERT SYSTEMS.

ESA. European Space Agency.

ESA-IRS. In online information retrieval, a service operated by the European Space Agency (Italy).

ESC. *See* ESCAPE CODE.

escape character. *See* ESCAPE CODE.

escape code. (ESC) In codes, a code combination that causes a device to recognize all subsequent code combinations as having an alternate meaning to their normal representation. Escape codes are used for indicating a sequence of control messages in American Standard Code for Information Interchange (ASCII). *See* AMERICAN STANDARD CODE FOR INFORMATION INTERCHANGE. *Synonymous with* FLAG CODE.

escrow agent. In software protection, an honest broker who is used to solve disagreements between a software supplier and a licensee. A supplier deposits the source code with the agent for safekeeping, and a licensee will have rights to use it in the event of liquidation of the supplier or failure to give adequate support. *See* SOURCE CODE.

espionage. In legislation, the illegal gathering of proprietary or secret information by any means.

ESPRIT. European Strategic Programme for Research in Information Technology; launched in 1984, it aims at concentrating on long-term research for information technology product leadership. *Compare* ALVEY.

ESS. *See* ELECTRONIC SWITCHING SYSTEM.

ETB. *See* END OF TRANSMISSION BLOCK.

etching. In microelectronics, the process of removing material, on a chip, left exposed by the exposure and development of the photoresist. *See* CHIP.

etch type. In printing, type that is produced by direct etching of a printing surface (e.g. by a laser, electron beam, etc.). *Compare* COLD TYPE, STRIKE ON.

Ethernet. A trademark, in data communications, a local area network standard using baseband mode of transmission at 10 megabits per second, coaxial cable, bus topology and carrier sense multiple access — collision detection protocol. It was originally developed by Xerox. *Compare* CAMBRIDGE RING. *See* BASEBAND, BUS, CARRIER SENSE MULTIPLE ACCESS — COLLISION DETECTION, COAXIAL CABLE, LOCAL AREA NETWORK, MEGABIT.

ETS. Japanese satellite programme.

ETV. *See* EDUCATIONAL TELEVISION.

ETX. *See* END OF TEXT.

Euler circle. *See* VENN DIAGRAM.

EURIPA. European Information Providers Association.

Euroconnector. In electronics, a connector the transmission of RGB or CVBS video signals, audio signals and RC-5 control signals. It is used to interconnect video and audio equipment, and has been adopted as an industry standard. (Philips). *See* CVBS, RGB.

EURODICAUTOM. In machine translation, European Dictionaire Automatique; a term bank operated by the EEC to provide assistance in translation of scientific and technical documents. It can give corresponding phrases or sentences in several languages, terms or expressions accompanied by illustrative contexts and/or definitions as well as term-by-term definitions. *See* MACHINE-AIDED TRANSLATION, TERM BANK.

EURODOCDEL. In information retrieval, European Document Delivery; a project in the DOCDEL program to demonstrate the degree to which the physical components of a document delivery system can be spread over several countries. *See* DOCDEL, DOCUMENT DELIVERY SERVICE, Transdoc.

Euronet. In data communications, the data transmission network provided for the EEC by the telecommunication authorities of member countries. Users of Euronet are able to access specialized scientific, technical and economic information via a packet switched network, which in turn is connected to the public telephone system of member countries. *See* DIANE, PACKET SWITCHING.

European article number. *See* EAN.

Eurotra. In machine translation, proposed state of the art system. The proposal was initiated by the EEC in 1977 and is mainly intended for the translation of committee minutes, technical memoranda, etc. *See* MACHINE TRANSLATION.

EUTELSAT. In communications, European Telecommunications Satellite organization; a 21-nation satellite cooperative established in 1977 by members of CEPT and located in Paris. *Compare* INTELSAT,

INTERSPUTNIK. *See* CEPT, GEOSTATIONARY SATELLITE.

evaluative database. In online information retrieval, a full-text database that also offers evaluations of document contents. *See* FULL-TEXT DATABASE.

EVE. European Videoconferencing Experimentation project. *See* VIDEOCONFERENCING.

even parity. *See* PARITY.

even word spacing. *Synonymous with* FIXED WORD SPACING.

even working. In printing, a piece of print that is contained in sections of 16, 32, 48 or 64 pages.

EX. *See* EXCHANGE.

exception dictionary. In word processing, a store of word breaks that do not conform to the usual rules. *See* HYPHENATION.

Excerpta Medica. In online information retrieval, a database supplied by Excerpta Medica and dealing with biomedicine.

exchange. (EX) In communications, the generic term for an assembly of telephone equipment providing for the interconnection of incoming and outgoing lines, with the necessary signalling and supervision facilities, housed in one building. *See* CENTRAL OFFICE, TOLL CENTRE.

exchangeable disk. *See* DISK PACK.

exchangeable disk storage. (EDS) In backing storage, one or more disk units with disk packs that can be replaced by an operator. *Compare* FIXED-DISK STORAGE. *See* DISK PACK.

exchange line. *Synonymous with* LOCAL LOOP.

Exchange Price Information Computer. *See* EPIC.

exchange text string. In word processing, a function that enables a text string to be changed for another text string at one, or a number, of points throughout the text. *See* SEARCH AND REPLACE, STRING.

exclusion.   A logical operation, A EXCLU-SION B is true if A is true and B is false. The corresponding truth table is:

A	B	A EXCLUSION B
0	0	0
1	0	1
0	1	0
1	1	0

See TRUTH TABLE. (2) In some telephone systems, a feature permitting a user to exclude or prevent other users from access to a line or channel.

exclusion word dictionary.   In computing, a dictionary of syntactical words, articles and propositions that are ignored when a computer scans titles in the making of a keyword in context (KWIC) index. *See* KEYWORD IN CONTEXT.

exclusiveness.   In library science, a classification principle that it should not be possible to class a specific subject in more than one term of an array. *See* ARRAY.

EXCLUSIVE OR.   A logical operation, A EXCLUSIVE OR B is true if either, but not both, A or B is true. The corresponding truth table is:

A	B	A EXCLUSIVE OR B
0	0	0
1	0	1
0	1	1
1	1	0

Compare EQUIVALENCE. *See* OR, TRUTH TABLE.

executable code.   In programming, a set of instructions, or a computer program, in the machine language for a specific computer or microprocessor, and which can thus be executed directly. (Philips). *See* MACHINE LANGUAGE.

executable object code.   In programming, the output from a compiler's or assembler's linkage editor or linker, which is in the machine code for a particular processor, with each loadable program being one

named file. In interactive compact discs such an object file does not contain audio or video data. (Philips). *See* ASSEMBLER, COMPACT DISC – INTERACTIVE, COMPILER, EXECUTABLE CODE, MACHINE LANGUAGE.

execute.   In computing, to run a program or to carry out an instruction. *See* RUN.

execute protection.   In software protection, the use of protection measures to prevent a program from being executed after it has been copied. Most protection schemes depend upon the source diskette being uniquely defined by a fingerprint which cannot be copied across to another floppy disk. When the protected program starts execution, it checks for the presence of the fingerprint, such as burn mark or weak bits. If it is present the execution will proceed, if not it will terminate. The fingerprint must have three attributes: it must be unique, uncopyable and detectable.

The disadvantage of such protection schemes is that they prevent the legitimate taking of backup copies of software and the protected program usually cannot work on a hard disk. In general, because most copy protection schemes require a test for the presence of a fingerprint, they can be bypassed by a patch. Given the current generation of debugging tools, the task is not too difficult for an expert. A sufficiently smart copy program can copy almost any characteristic. What cannot be copied with a copy program can usually be made to work with other tools. *Compare* COPY PROTECTION. *See* BIT COPIER, BURN MARK, DEBUGGER, DEMON, DONGLE, FINGERPRINT, FLOPPY DISK, INSTALL/DEINSTALL, PATCH, WEAK BITS.

execution time.   In computing, the time taken for a central processing unit to perform a a specified instruction. *See* CENTRAL PROCESSING UNIT, RUN TIME. *Synonymous with* INSTRUCTION TIME.

exerciser.   In computing, a test system or program designed to detect faults in a program or circuit under development.

exhaustive attack.   In data security, attack aimed at discovering secret data by trying all possibilities and checking for correctness. *See* KEY EXHAUSTION.

exhaustivity. In library science, the extent to which a document is analyzed to establish the subject content that has to be specified for search and indexing purposes. The greater the proportion of concepts covered the greater the exhaustivity. *Compare* SPECI-FICITY.

existential quantifier. In mathematics, a symbol employed in predicate calculus, and relational calculus, which is read as 'there exists'. *Compare* UNIVERSAL QUANTIFIER. *See* PREDICATE, RELATIONAL CALCULUS.

exit. In programming, an instruction which, upon execution, relinquishes all further control by that program.

expanded type. In printing, a typeface with a slightly wider body giving a flatter appearance. (Desktop). *Compare* CONDENSED TYPE. *See* TYPEFACE.

expander board. *Synonymous with* EXPANSION CARD.

expandor. In communications, a device that expands the range of amplitudes of speech signals. *Compare* COMPANDOR.

expansion board. *Synonymous with* EXPANSION CARD.

expansion card. In computing, a card added to the system in order to mount additional chips or circuits so as to extend the system capability (e.g. modem, additional read-only memory). In a micro-computer an expansion card normally con- nects directly to the system bus. *See* ADD-IN, BUS, MICROCOMPUTER, MODEM, RANDOM-ACCESS MEMORY. *Synonymous with* EXPANDER CARD, EXPANSION BOARD.

Expert. In online information retrieval, a rule-based system for the automation of search strategy formulation and searching of online databases. *See* EXPERT SYSTEMS.

expert systems. (ES) In applications, com- puter systems that reflect the decision- making processes of a human specialist. They embody organized knowledge con- cerning a defined area of expertise and are intended to operate as skilful, cost-effective consultants. An expert system comprises a knowledge base, inference engine, expla- nation program, knowledge-refining pro- gram and natural language processor.

The knowledge base contains the distilled and codified knowledge of the human expert, or experts. It is much more than a simple database of facts; the expert must formulate rules, often based upon years of experience rather than deterministic laws, and in many cases such rules are probabilis- tic. Much research is being conducted into the methods of structuring knowledge bases; one of the most common is the production system in which rules are formulated on an IF... THEN... basis. The knowledge base may be constructed directly by the expert or by a knowledge engineer who assists the expert to express the knowledge in the required format.

The inference engine is a program that drives the system; attempting to match known facts, elicited from the user, with the

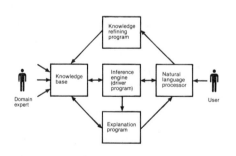

expert systems
Fig. 1.

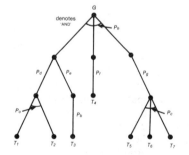

expert systems
Fig. 2. AND/OR tree representing rules.

rules in the knowledge base. The ultimate goal (e.g. decision on the presence of minerals in a given region or identification of a disease) is not attained in one step. The inference engine must set up subgoals; those successful subgoals are then used in higher-level rules. The facts elicited from the user, and inferred from application of the productions, may often be expressed only in terms of probabilities. Sometimes the requirement for more information from the user is recognized by the inference engine, and the user may be asked to input that information or even to perform (say) laboratory tests to obtain it. If the user does not supply the requested information, then the system will attempt to infer it. The inference engine may establish subgoals from an AND/OR tree.

The initial facts (T) are entered at the bottom of the tree causing rules to be fired, thus establishing goals or subgoals. An essential part of the design of the inference engine lies in the strategy for exploring the trees to determine the most efficient method of goal achievement. The explanation program is essential to establish user confidence in the system. It is human nature to query the conclusions of an expert, and the explanation program will enable the system to state the rule and input information leading to a particular conclusion. This facility can also expand upon the requirement for further information giving explanations of the terms used or a statement on why the additional information is required. A 'what if' facility in the explanation program can also enable the user to explore certain paths in the knowledge base.

The knowledge refining program enables the expert to update the knowledge base in the light of experience of the system or the acquisition of new knowledge in this field. The natural language processor facilitates the man–machine dialogue and enables the user to communicate with the system in a natural manner.

Expert systems software is available on current computer systems and can also be implemented on microcomputers. Expert systems have been employed by chemists to determine chemical structures (Congen), in geology to provide a consultant system for mineral exploration (Prospector), in medicine to provide advice on diagnosis and therapy for infectious diseases (Mycin). The range and versatility of existing systems is, however, limited both by the substantial effort involved in the development of the knowledge base and by the power of the inference engine necessary for determining goals in a massive knowledge base. *Compare* DATABASE. *See* ARTIFICIAL INTELLIGENCE, KEY MANAGEMENT, KNOWLEDGE ENGINEERING, RISK ANALYSIS, TEXT ANIMATION, WHAT IF.

expiration date. In computing, the date at which a file is no longer protected from deletion by the system.

expired password. In computer security, a password that must be changed by the user before log in may be completed. (DOD). *See* LOGON, PASSWORD.

explosion. In online information retrieval, a technique employed in online searching whereby a search may be expanded from a particular term to include all those below it in the hierarchy.

exponent. In mathematics, a number indicating how many times another number, the base, is to be repeated as a factor. Positive exponents denote multiplication, negative exponents denote division and fractional exponents denote a root. *See* BASE.

exponentiation. In mathematics, the operation of raising a number to a power. *See* EXPONENT.

exponentiation cipher. In data security, a cipher in which the encryption/decryption processes involve raising plaintext/ciphertext messages to specified powers (i.e. exponentiation) in modulo arithmetic. *See* EXPONENTIATION, RSA.

export. *See* IMPORT/EXPORT.

exposing. In photography, the action of submitting any sensitized material to radiation, light or heat, which will act upon it to form an image or latent image. *See* PHOTOGRAPHY.

exposure end point. In photography, the energy required to expose light-sensitive material to a stated density value. *See* DENSITY.

expression. (1) A mathematical identity or relationship. (2) In programming, a source language combination of one or more operations. (3) In programming, a notation, within a program, that represents a value.

extended area service.   In communications, a telephone exchange service without toll charges that extends over an area, where there is a community of interest, in return for higher exchange rates. *See* TOLL CHARGE.

extended backus naur form.   (EBNR) In programming, a metalanguage described by the rules: (a) a name on the left-hand side of an equals sign is defined on the right-hand side as a sequence of symbols; (b) a name on the right-hand side of an equals sign is defined elsewhere; (c) a period terminates a definition of a rule; (d) characters enclosed in double quotes stand for themselves; (e) alternatives are separated by vertical bars; (f) optional features are enclosed in square brackets; (g) features enclosed in curly brackets may appear zero, one or any number of times. *See* BACKUS NAUR FORM, METALANGUAGE.

extended character set.   In printing, a character set including characters not included in the conventional English alphabet.

extended disc.   In optical media, a hypothetical interactive compact disc that can exercise all the capabilities of an 'extended' system as defined by the compact disc 'extended' system specification. The base case specification is a subset of the 'extended' system specification. (Philips). *See* BASE CASE SYSTEM, COMPACT DISC – INTERACTIVE, EXTENDED SYSTEM.

extended system.   In optical media, a system conforming to base case specification, plus any extensions that conform to the 'extended' interactive compact disc system specification. (Philips). *See* BASE CASE SYSTEM, COMPACT DISC – INTERACTIVE, EXTENDED DISC.

extender.   In photography, a device used to hold a lens away from the camera for close-up work. *See* DIOPTRE LENS. *Synonymous with* EXTENSION TUBE.

extensible language.   In programming, a language that permits a user to define new elements (e.g. data structures, operators,

types of statements, control structures) in terms of existing elements in the language.

extension.   (1) In optical media, an upward compatible module to replace an existing interactive compact disc (CD) player module in read-only memory. During initialization, all modules in CD real-time operating system (except the protection modules) may be replaced by extended modules which have revision numbers higher than those they replace. (2) In optical media, an interactive compact disc (CD-I) player hardware module supporting a functional extension conforming to the CD-I 'extended' system specification. During initialization, CD real-time operating system identifies the extension and includes the software modules from it. (Philips). *See* CD REAL-TIME OPERATING SYSTEM, COMPACT DISC – INTERACTIVE, EXTENDED SYSTEM. (3) In data structures, a part of a file description. Commonly a file description takes the form — diskdrive: filename: extension — and the extension is employed to indicate the class of file: text, BASIC source program, command file, etc.

extension group hunting.   In communications, a private automatic branch exchange facility whereby a number of extensions can be associated in a group so that an incoming call automatically hunts for, and is connected to, the first free extension.

extension tube.   *Synonymous with* EXTENDER.

external data file.   In data structures, a file containing data that is stored separately from the program that processes it.

external interrupt.   In computing, an interrupt not caused by an event in the instruction sequence that is interrupted; one caused by a device external to the processor (e.g. a peripheral). *See* INTERRUPT, PERIPHERAL.

external label.   In memory systems, an identification label attached to the outside of a file medium holder (e.g. a sticky label attached to the case of a magnetic disk). *Compare* INTERNAL LABEL.

external schema.   *Synonymous with* SUBSCHEMA.

external storage. *See* AUXILIARY STORAGE.

extract. (1) The process of selecting, and removing, a group of items, according to some specified criteria, from a larger set of the items. (2) In distributed processing, to pull out specific items from mainframe file for downloading into a microcomputer. *See* DOWNLOAD. (3) In computing, the process of removing specific information from a computer word by the logical action of a mask. *See* MASK.

extra terrestrial noise. In communications, random noise originating in outer space and detected on the earth. The sun produces extra terrestrial noise. *See* GALACTIC NOISE, HELIOS NOISE, NOISE.

extremely high-frequency. (EHF) In communications, the range of frequencies from 30–300 GHz.

extremely low-frequency. In communications, frequencies of less than 100 Hz.

eye coordinates. In computer graphics, a set of coordinates based on a line from the observer's eye along the direction of sight and two axes at right angles to this line. *Compare* SCREEN COORDINATES, WORLD COORDINATES. *See* CARTESIAN COORDINATES.

eye-legible copy. In micrographics, a microform record that contains title, or other lettering, legible to the naked eye. *See* MICROFORM.

eyepiece. In photography, the lens of a camera viewfinder at which the operator's eye is placed.

F

F2F. *See* FREQUENCY DOUBLE FREQUENCY.

f. In photography, a symbol denoting the relationship between the camera lens opening and its focal length. *See* FOCAL LENGTH.

face. (1) In printing, the printing surface of type. (2) In printing, the design of a particular type, hence typeface. *See* TYPEFACE.

facilities management. (FM) In computing, the use of an independent service organization to manage and operate a computing installation.

facility. In data communications, a transmission path between two or more locations without terminating or signalling equipment.

facsimile. In communications, pertaining to the transmission of images over communication links which have a lower bandwidth than that necessary for video signals. The image is scanned by a light beam and a signal, representing the brightness of the section of the image under the scanning beam, is transmitted over the link in the form of a modulated analog or digital signal. At the receiving station the signal drives an energy source to reproduce the image by photographic, thermal or xerographic techniques.

There are seven stages in the transmission of a document by digital facsimile methods.

(a) The document is scanned, by an image scanner, in a raster pattern, and a bit map of the black/white image is formed; typically with a resolution of 200 pixels per inch.
(b) The data representing the bit mapped is compressed. A typical document will represent some 3.7 million bits of data, some 85 per cent of which will represent white spaces. If the boundaries of the black dots are specified the data may be compressed. Moreover, successive scan lines are often identical or similar. Thus it is more economical to represent successive lines by their differences.
(c) The compressed bit pattern representing the image is then packaged for transmission over communication lines. If it is to be transmitted over a public switched telephone network (PSTN) then the digital pulse train must be converted to an analog signal by a modem; with digital transmission networks, such as integrated services digital network (ISTN) no such conversion is required.
(d) The compressed data signal is transmitted over the communication link.
(e) The receiving end, if necessary, uses a modem to produce to the original digital pulse train.
(f) The data is expanded to its original bit map pattern by a decompressor which reverses the action of the data compression algorithms.
(g) The bit map data is used to drive a printer to reproduce the image document.

CCITT has described four groups of facsimile service:

Group	Signal	Compression	Page Speed	Network
1	Analog	None	6 min	PSTN
2	Analog	Limited	3 min	PSTN
3	Digital	Complex	< 1 min	PSTN
4	Digital	Complex	< 10 sec	ISDN, DDS

See CCITT, DATA COMPRESSION, DDS, GROUP 1 FACSIMILE, GROUP 2 FACSIMILE, GROUP 3 FACSIMILE, GROUP 4 FACSIMILE, INTEGRATED SERVICES DIGITAL NETWORK,

MODEM PUBLIC SWITCHED DIGITAL NETWORK, RASTER SCAN, TWO-DIMENSIONAL CODING

facsimile character generation. In computer graphics, the technique of writing characters on a display screen by copying those already written and stored in a master set. *See* CHARACTER GENERATOR.

facsimile laser platemaker. In printing, a technique by which a complete page may be transmitted, and the received image is employed to make a printing plate. *See* FACSIMILE.

facsimile mail. In communications, an extension of a facsimile service providing features such as: (a) timed delivery of documents; (b) broadcast facility; (c) message wait indication; (d) confidential mail; (e) text-to-facsimile conversion; and (f) teletex-to-facsimile conversion. *See* FACSIMILE, INTEGRATED SERVICES DIGITAL NETWORK, TELETEX.

factoring. In data security, the security of the RSA cryptography system depends on the computational infeasibility of factoring a large number of, say, 200 digits, made up of two prime numbers each of about 100 digits. Unless the prime numbers are known, the fastest computer would take several billion years to factor it using current technology and mathematical techniques. *See* PRIME NUMBER, PUBLIC KEY CRYPTOGRAPHY, RSA.

fade. *See* FADE IN, FADE OUT.

fade in. In recording, the gradual increase of a video or audio signal from zero to normal level. *Compare* FADE OUT.

fade out. In recording, the gradual reduction of a video or audio signal to zero. *Compare* FADE IN.

fading. (1) In communications, pertaining to variations in the received signal strength due to varying ionization conditions over the propagation path. Fading can affect television reception of a broadcast signal. (2) In recording. *See* FADE IN, FADE OUT.

fail safe. In computer security, automatic termination and protection of programs and/or processing systems when a hardware or software failure is detected in an auto-

mated information system. (FIPS). *Compare* FAIL SOFT.

fail soft. (1) In computer security, the selective termination of affected nonessential processing when a hardware or software failure is detected in an automated system. (FIPS). *Compare* FAIL SAFE. (2) In reliability, pertaining to a system that continues to operate, albeit in a degraded manner, even when a part of the system has failed.

fairing. *Synonymous with* CUSHIONING.

fall back. In computing, backup procedures to be used in the event of a services or machine failure. These procedures may be manual or involve the use of other computers and databases. *See* BACKUP.

false drop. In online information retrieval, irrelevant items, retrieved during an online search, that arise from the use of inappropriate search terms. *See* SEARCH STATEMENT. *Synonymous with* FALSE RETRIEVE, NOISE.

false retrieve. *Synonymous with* FALSE DROP.

FAM. *See* FAST-ACCESS MEMORY.

family. (1) In computing, a manufacturer's range of processors marketed to enable a customer to upgrade an installation with a more powerful unit without having to change the rest of the installation or programs. (2) In printing, a complete range of design variants of a particular typeface.

FAMOS. *See* FLOATING GATE AVALANCHE INJECTION MOS.

FAMT. Fully automatic machine translation. *See* MACHINE TRANSLATION.

fan antenna. In communications, an antenna in which the elements are spread in relative positions similar to the ribs of a fan. *See* ANTENNA.

fanfold. *Synonymous with* ACCORDION FOLD.

fanin. In electronics, the maximum number of inputs that can be connected to a processing unit, without affecting operation of the unit. *Compare* FANOUT.

fanning strip. In electronics, a strip of insulating material with holes through which individual pairs of a cable may be passed for support and identification.

fanout. (1) In communications, a single output that becomes an input to multiple branches. (2) In electronics, the maximum number of outputs that can be serviced by a processing unit, without affecting operation of the unit. *Compare* FANIN.

farad. In electronics, the unit of capacitance. A capacitor has a capacitance of one farad when a charge of one coulomb produces one volt of potential difference between its terminals. In practice electronic devices have capacitances of the order of picofarads. *See* CAPACITANCE, COULOMB, PICO.

far-end crosstalk. In communications, crosstalk that travels along the disturbed circuit in the same direction as signals in that circuit. *See* CROSSTALK.

fast. In photography, pertaining to lenses which have an f-value near one, and to films having a relatively high sensitivity to light. *See* FAST LENS, F-NUMBER.

fast-access memory. (FAM) In memory systems, a memory with a speed intermediate between that of main memory and fixed-head disk. *See* FIXED-HEAD DISK, MAIN MEMORY.

fast lens. In photography, a lens that has a large light-collecting capacity (i.e. an f-number of 2.8 or less). *See* F-NUMBER.

FAT. *See* FILE ALLOCATION TABLE.

fatal error. In programming, an error that causes all subsequent processing to be meaningless.

father file. In data structures, a method used in the updating of disk or magnetic tape files so that in the event of a serious corruption or loss of data the master file can be reconstituted. When a new file is created, as a result of updates to a current file, the old master file is termed the 'father file'. The new, updated file is called the 'son file', whereas the file originally used to create the father file becomes the 'grandfather file'. *See* FILE.

fault. In reliability, a condition that causes a device, component or element to fail to perform in a required manner. The fault may be either physical or logical. *Compare* ERROR. *See* BUG. *Synonymous with* LOOPHOLE.

fault diagnosis. In reliability, an activity that strives to locate a fault and to confine its damage. *See* FAULT.

fault tolerance. In reliability, the capability of a system to function correctly according to its design specifications despite the presence of transient or permanent faults. *See* FAULT.

FAW. *See* FRAME ALIGNMENT WORD.

fax. (1) In filming, a term for facilities (i.e. equipment used by technicians in the production of a film). (2) In communications, a term for facsimile. *See* FACSIMILE.

FC. *See* FONT CHANGE.

FCC. *See* FEDERAL COMMUNICATIONS COMMISSION.

FD. *See* FULL-DUPLEX.

FDM. *See* FREQUENCY DIVISION MULTIPLEXING.

FDMA. *See* FREQUENCY DIVISION MULTIPLE ACCESS.

F/D ratio. In communications, the ratio of focal length to diameter of a dish antenna. *See* DISH ANTENNA, FOCAL LENGTH.

FDS. *See* FIXED-DISK STORAGE.

FDX. *See* FULL-DUPLEX.

FE. *See* FORMAT EFFECTOR.

feasibility study. The first stage in the implementation of a system where the proposed system is evaluated for both technical and financial considerations. It is used as the basis for deciding to proceed with an outline system design, which is the next stage. This is followed by the detailed design and implementation, with each stage representing a more substantial financial commitment. *See* SYSTEMS ANALYSIS.

feature analysis. In computer graphics, a technique to obtain information on a stored image by comparing features of the image (e.g. dimensions, dimension ratios, perimeters, brightness levels, contrast, numbers of corners and edges, orientation, etc.), with corresponding features of known objects. Blob growing and a technique of examining the parts of the image where the contrast is changing rapidly to determine the edges are included in feature analysis. *Compare* FONT-INDEPENDENT, TEMPLATE MATCHING. *See* BLOB GROWING, MACHINE VISION.

FEC. *See* FORWARD ERROR CORRECTION.

Federal Communications Commission. (FCC) The independent regulatory agency, established by Congress in the Communications Act, 1934, and empowered by that Act to regulate interstate and foreign radio and wire communications services originating in the USA.

Federal Register Abstracts. In online information retrieval, a database supplied by Capitol Services Inc. (CSI) and dealing with US federal government.

Federal State Joint Board. In communications, a board established by the Federal Communications Commission and composed of commissioners representing state and federal jurisdictions. *See* FEDERAL COMMUNICATIONS COMMISSION.

FEDS. *See* FIXED AND EXCHANGEABLE DISK STORAGE.

feedback. (1) A process in which part of the output of a system is returned to it as input. Feedback may be positive, tending to increase the overall output, or negative, which will have the opposite effect. *See* NEGATIVE FEEDBACK, POSITIVE FEEDBACK. (2) Information concerning the result of a function or activity, particularly when used for control or modification. For example, system feedback optimizes the performance of a system, user feedback adapts the func-

tion of a product to suit the requirement of the user, and market feedback helps to tune marketing policies to actual market conditions. (Philips).

feeder cable. (1) In communications, the principal cable from a central office. (2) In communications, a transmission line that supports one or more signals over a number of receiving points. *See* CENTRAL OFFICE.

feedhorn. In communications, a metal device that feeds signals to a transmitting antenna, and from a receiving antenna. Originally feedhorns were rectangular in shape, but satellite antenna feedhorns often comprise concentric rings which maximize the signal from the centre of the dish and attenuate that received from the outer rim, thus reducing the effect of terrestrial noise. *See* DISH ANTENNA, NOISE.

feed reel. In recording and filming, a reel from which film or tape is passed through a mechanism and onto a take-up reel.

femtosecond. A thousandth of a picosecond (i.e. 10^{-15} seconds); approximately the time required for light to traverse one-third of the width of a human hair. *Compare* PICOSECOND.

FEP. *See* FRONT-END PROCESSOR.

ferric oxide. In memory systems and recording, the magnetizable constituent deposited on a tape or disk in the form of a dispersion of fine particles within the coating.

ferrite. In electronics, a non-metallic solid used in radio frequency operations. Ferrite materials have high permeability, high resistance and low eddy current loss. *See* PERMEABILITY, RESISTANCE.

ferroelectric display. In peripherals, a liquid crystal screen display employing polarized glass. *See* LCD SCREENS.

ferromagnetic. In electronics, pertaining to a material such as iron or nickel that has a very high magnetic permeability. *See* PERMEABILITY.

FET. *See* FIELD EFFECT TRANSISTOR.

fetch. In computing, the process of getting the next instruction from memory. *See* INSTRUCTION, MEMORY.

fetch protection. In computer security, a system-provided restriction to prevent a program from accessing data in another user's segment of storage. (FIPS). *See* ACCESS, BOUNDS CHECKING.

FF. *See* FORM FEED CHARACTER.

FHDS. In memory systems, fixed-head disk storage. *See* DISK DRIVE.

Fiat Shamir algorithm. In data security, an algorithm, with a similarity to RSA, that facilitates authentication between two parties. It is particularly suitable for smart card applications since it makes less demands upon the computational power at the user end. *See* RSA, SMART CARD, ZERO KNOWLEDGE PROOF.

fiber crosstalk. In optoelectronics, exchange of light wave energy between a core and the cladding of a fiber optic cable, the cladding and the ambient surrounding or between differently indexed layers. The crosstalk is deliberately reduced by making the cladding lossy. *See* CLADDING, CORE, FIBER OPTICS.

fiber optics. In communications, a technique that deals with the communication of signals by the transmission of light through extremely pure fibers of glass or plastic. A fiber optic cable comprises a plastic or glass core surrounded by a layer of plastic or glass

cladding, which in turn is surrounded by a plastic jacket to protect the core from moisture and abrasion. The diameter of the core varies with the type of fiber from 2 to 200 micrometres. Light signals are inserted from light-emitting diodes (LEDs) or injection lasers, propagated by refraction or internal reflection, and are collected by light detectors at the receiving end.

The propagation along the cable is either reflective or refractive depending upon the type of cable — stepped index monomode, stepped index multimode or graded index multimode. Here the term index refers to refractive index, and as the names suggest the refractive index of stepped index fibers is constant throughout the core and changes sharply at the core-cladding interface, whereas in the case of multimode-graded index fibers, the index falls off gradually from the centre of the core to its outer edges. In monomode cables the core diameter is very low (2–10 micrometres) and there is only one path — along the centre of the core — for the light signals. With stepped index multimode fibers the light rays travel at varying angles to the axis and are internally reflected at the core-cladding interface. In this case rays will travel along paths of different lengths, and thus signal pulses are spread out and distorted. In the graded index fiber light rays travel faster near the outer edge of the core, than along the axis, because the refractive index is lower. This effect tends to reduce the dispersion because rays travelling along the longer paths tend to travel faster.

The light signals are produced either by LEDs or injection lasers. The comparative advantages of the injection laser over the LED are higher power output and a narrow beam, but they tend to be more expensive and have shorter working lives. The transmitted light is normally in the infrared bandwidth, the signal attenuation is very sensitive to wavelength, tending to decrease with increased wavelength. The advantages of fiber optic cables over conventional coaxial are immunity from electromagnetic interference, high data-carrying capacity, low signal attenuation, security, raw material cost, chemical stability and freedom from cochannel interference. From a data security viewpoint fiber optic cables have the advantage that they do not emit radiating signals and are relatively difficult to tap, although

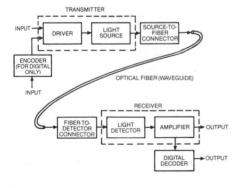

fiber optics
Fig. 1. Basic elements of a fiber optic transmission system.

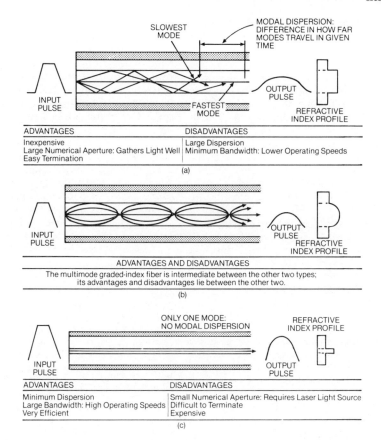

ADVANTAGES	DISADVANTAGES
Inexpensive Large Numerical Aperture: Gathers Light Well Easy Termination	Large Dispersion Minimum Bandwidth: Lower Operating Speeds

(a)

ADVANTAGES AND DISADVANTAGES

The multimode graded-index fiber is intermediate between the other two types; its advantages and disadvantages lie between the other two.

(b)

ADVANTAGES	DISADVANTAGES
Minimum Dispersion Large Bandwidth: High Operating Speeds Very Efficient	Small Numerical Aperture: Requires Laser Light Source Difficult to Terminate Expensive

(c)

fiber optics
Fig. 2. (a) multimode step index fiber; (b) multimode graded index fiber; (c) single mode step index fiber.

they can be subject to an active wiretap with a rogue fiber. *See* COMPROMISING EMANATIONS, FIBER OPTICS RECORDING, INFRARED, REFRACTIVE INDEX, ROGUE FIBER, SOLITON, TEMPEST PROOFING, TOTAL INTERNAL REFLECTION, WIRETAPPING.

fiber optics recording. In micrographics, a technique used in the production of computer output microfilm. A matrix of luminous fibers is selectively illuminated to form a single line of characters. The film is exposed to this line of characters and then incremented, permitting the next line of characters to be generated. *Compare* CRT RECORDING, ELECTRON BEAM RECORDING. *See* FIBER OPTICS.

fibonacci sequence. (1) In mathematics, a series of numbers in which each number is equal to the sum of the two preceding numbers in series: 0, 1, 1, 2, 3, 5, 8, 13, 21, etc. (2) In programming, a search in which at each step a division is made in accordance with the fibonacci sequence.

fiche. *See* MICROFICHE.

FID. International Federation of Documentation.

fidelity. In recording, the ability of a reproducing unit to recreate at its output a faithful reproduction of the input signal. *See* HI-FI.

field. (1) In mathematics, a set of integers for which addition, subtraction, multiplication, division (except by zero) are defined and the commutative, associative and distributive laws apply. A complete residue system, which is modulo a prime, forms a field. *See* ASSOCIATIVE LAW, COMMUTATIVE LAW, DISTRIBUTIVE LAW. (2) In computing, a physical space on a data-recording medium that is reserved for one or more related data elements. (3) In data structures, an element of a record. *See* RECORD. (4) In communications, the energy associated with magnetic and electric sources. Electromagnetic fields are types of composite fields radiated from a source into the surrounding space (e.g. light waves). *See* ELECTROMAGNETIC RADIATION. (5) In television, a scan of a picture by a series of evenly spaced lines from top to bottom. *Compare* FRAME. (6) In photography, the portion of the object in front of the camera represented within the limits of the camera aperture at the focal plane. Area of field thus varies with the focal length of lens and camera to subject distance.

field blanking. In television, the time interval between two successive fields within which picture information is suppressed and field sync pulses are transmitted. *See* FIELD SYNC PULSE, TELETEXT.

field correlator. In optical media, a device used to overcome field dominance problems during recording on a videodisc. The correlator accepts two successive fields and compares them line by line. If any difference is detected then one field is selected to be dominant, and the device replaces the second field with a copy of the dominant field. *See* FIELD, FIELD DOMINANCE.

field data code. In codes, a standardized military data transmission code consisting of seven data bits plus one parity bit. *See* DATA BITS, PARITY BIT.

field dominance. In optical media, a phenomenon in freeze frame recording on a constant angular velocity videodisc. The two fields selected for recording on one rotation should relate to the same instantaneous scene. If video material is mixed then the field dominance may change so that the fields selected for freeze frame viewing relate to successive video scenes giving a flicker effect. *See* CONSTANT ANGULAR VELOCITY, FIELD, FREEZE FRAME.

field effect transistor. (FET) In electronics, a semiconductor device that combines the small size and low power consumption of a bipolar transistor with a high input impedance. It is named field effect because the control action is effected by a field produced by an input voltage as compared with the control effect of the base current in a bipolar transistor. *See* IMPEDANCE, TRANSISTOR.

field frequency. In television, the number of fields scanned per second. Field frequency is usually the same as that of the power supply (e.g. for a power supply of 60 Hz the field frequency will be 60 fields per second, interlaced to produce 30 pictures per second). *See* FIELD, INTERLACE.

field-programmable. In microelectronics, pertaining to a technique in which the final stage of fabrication of a chip involves destroying certain connections already made on the chip. *Compare* MASK-PROGRAMMABLE. *See* PROGRAMMABLE READ-ONLY MEMORY, SEMI-CUSTOM DESIGN.

field-programmable device. *See* FIELD-PROGRAMMABLE, FIELD-PROGRAMMABLE LOGIC ARRAY.

field-programmable logic array. (FPLA) In memory systems, a programmable logic array that may be programmed by the user as compared with devices that are programmed by the manufacturer. *See* FIELD-PROGRAMMABLE, PROGRAMMABLE LOGIC ARRAY.

field separator. (FS) In codes, a character that may be used to delimit fields or other items of data in the storage, transfer or transmission of data. *See* FIELD.

field strength. In communications, the value of either the electric or magnetic field for a specified direction of the field.

field sweep. In peripherals, a general term for the movement of the electron beam spot in the vertical direction on the screen of a raster display visual display unit. *See* FIELD SYNC PULSE, RASTER SCAN, VISUAL DISPLAY UNIT.

field sync pulse. In television, a pulse used for initiating the field sweep and generated during the field-blanking interval. *See* FIELD BLANKING, FIELD SWEEP.

FIFO. *See* FIRST IN FIRST OUT.

fifth-generation computer. In computing, a knowledge–information-processing system based on innovative theories and technologies, that can offer the advanced functions expected to be required in the 1990s, overcoming the technical limitations inherent in conventional computers. The previous four generations of computers have exploited successive developments of new hardware techniques but all were based upon the same von Neumann architecture. The fifth-generation machine breaks with this tradition and represents a unification of four current, separate areas of research: knowledge-based expert systems, very high-level programming languages, decentralized computing and very large-scale integration (VLSI) technology.

Knowledge-based systems embody modules of organized knowledge, which support sophisticated problem-solving and inference functions to provide users with intelligent advice on specialized topics. This development will involve the production of large database machines employing relational database organization and linked to storage systems with 10 gigabytes' capacity. The processing involved will be performed initially by powerful serial inference engines. These knowledge-based systems will communicate in an extremely user friendly manner using voice, images and graphics; the dialog will be conducted in genuine natural languages.

The very high-level programming languages allow the programmer to specify 'what is to be performed' rather than the traditional 'how to perform it' approach of procedural languages such as COBOL or Pascal. PROLOG is an example of such a language and is regarded as a stepping stone for the new machine. The demands on computer processors produced by the above-mentioned developments force a radical rethink of the conventional von Neumann architecture. The fifth-generation computer systems will involve multiple processors comprising, in some cases, geographically separated computers, linked by communications networks, and in other cases miniature microcomputers residing on the same board or even on a single chip. The control mechanisms must ensure highly efficient non-sequential operations and employ dataflow or reduction architectures. Dataflow devices operate with individual actions performed when the input data becomes available. In reduction program organization the requirement for a result triggers the execution of the instruction that generates the value, and the control mechanism is recursive rather than sequential or parallel. VLSI technology can yield high-performance general- and special-purpose computers at a modest cost.

The fifth-generation computer systems may be viewed as forming a new computer family in which members provide powerful facilities for problem solving and inference, database management and intelligent input/output. Interfaces will be developed allowing both software modules and hardware units to be configured for applications or sets of applications. The resultant configuration can then be considered as building blocks for even larger systems. High-speed local area networks will interconnect hardware units of a single system whereas global networks will link together computer systems for social organizations. *Compare* SUPERCOMPUTER. *See* COBOL, DATABASE MACHINE, DATAFLOW, EXPERT SYSTEMS, GIGA, HARDWARE, INFERENCE ENGINE, LOCAL AREA NETWORK, PARALLEL COMPUTER, PASCAL, PROLOG, RECURSIVE ROUTINE, RELATIONAL DATABASE, SOFTWARE, VERY LARGE-SCALE INTEGRATION.

FIGS. *See* FIGURES SHIFT.

figure. In printing, a traditional term for a line illustration incorporated within the body of type in the pages of a book, as distinct from a photographic plate. *See* PLATE.

figure space. In printing, a unit of measure equal to the width of the en space in a given font. *See* EN, FONT.

figures shift. (FIGS) In codes, a code combination in the five-level baudot code that causes all subsequent code combinations to be recognized as upper-case characters (i.e. numerics, special symbols or control codes). *See* ESCAPE CODE, SHIFT CODES.

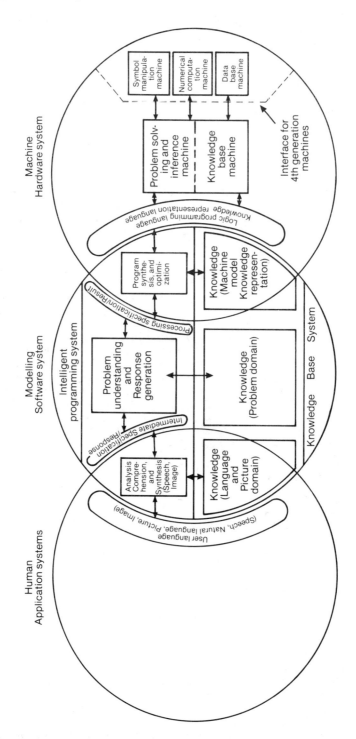

fifth generation computer
A conceptual diagram of a fifth generation system.

file. In data structures, a collection of records that are logically related to each other and handled as a unit, for example, by giving them a single name. A file may exist on magnetic tape, disk, etc. *See* MAGNETIC DISK, MAGNETIC TAPE, RECORD.

file access. In data security, access control procedures that determine the files that may be accessed by an authorized computer user and the operations that may be performed using those files.

file allocation table. (FAT) In computing, a table used by the operating system to allocate space on a magnetic disk for a file. The sectors allocated may be randomly scattered over the disk, and the table locates and chains together the sectors for each file. *See* FILE, MAGNETIC DISK, OPERATING SYSTEM, SECTOR.

file cleanup. In computing, the removal of superfluous data from a file. *Synonymous with* FILE TIDYING.

file conversion. In computing, the process of changing the file medium or structure, often because of the requirements of a new program or a change of hardware. *See* FILE, HARDWARE.

file descriptor. In computing, information normally stored as a header record on magnetic disk, or magnetic tape, giving details of the file name, generation number, expiry date, date of last access and structure of records. *See* FILE, GENERATOR, MAGNETIC DISK, MAGNETIC TAPE.

file descriptor record. In optical media, a sector on an interactive compact disc file that contains a list of the data segments, their starting logical sector number (block number), size and file attributes. (Philips). *See* COMPACT DISC – INTERACTIVE, FILE, RECORD, SECTOR.

file gap. In memory systems, an area on a tape or disk used to signify the end of a file, and possibly the start of the next file. *See* INTERBLOCK GAP.

file layout. In computing, the arrangement and structure of data in a file, including the order and field size of each element. *See* FIELD, FILE. *Synonymous with* FILE ORGANIZATION.

file lock. In computing, a facility to deny access to a file. It is used in multiuser systems to prevent two users from simultaneously writing to the same file. *Compare* RECORD LOCK. *See* FILE ACCESS, MULTIUSER.

file maintenance. In computing, the activity of keeping a file up to date by adding, changing, or deleting data (e.g. the addition of new programs to a program library on magnetic disks). *See* FILE LAYOUT, FILE MANAGEMENT.

file management. In computing, a procedure or set of processes for creating and maintaining files. *See* FILE, FILE LAYOUT, FILE MAINTENANCE.

file manager. In optical media, an interactive compact disc system software module that handles input/output requests for a class of similar devices. (Philips). *See* COMPACT DISC – INTERACTIVE, INPUT/OUTPUT.

filename. In computing, a character string that uniquely identifies a file. Files can be identified by two names, external and internal. The external filename is that used by the operating system and comprises all the higher-level owners of a file in a tree-structured directory plus the extension. An internal filename can be allocated to a file within a program, the open file instruction will relate the internal and external filenames and in subsequent read or write instructions the internal filename is used. *See* EXTENSION, FILE, OPEN, OPERATING SYSTEM, PATH, TREE-STRUCTURED DIRECTORY.

file organization. *Synonymous with* FILE LAYOUT.

file processing. In computing, the periodic updating of master files to reflect the effects of current data (e.g. a monthly stock run updating the master stock file). *See* RUN.

file protection. In data security, a method of protecting files against unauthorized access by another user. If a common directory is employed the directory entries will contain a tag indicating the owner and type of protection required. Several levels of protection may be provided (e.g. allow write, allow read, allow execute and allow append). The latter level of protection permits users to write records at the end of the file but not read or modify existing records, a useful facility for gathering statistics from a variety of users. *Compare* MEMORY PROTECTION. *See* DIRECTORY, FILE, FILE ACCESS, RECORD.

file protect ring. In memory systems, a ring which when removed from a magnetic tape reel will prevent data from being written to the tape. *See* FILE PROTECTION.

file protect tab. In memory systems, a sticky tag that is used to cover a hole on an 8-inch floppy disk, or removed from a 5.25-inch disk, to enable writing to the disk. *See* FLOPPY DISK.

filer. In programming, a computer program to handle the filing function of transferring certain data or information from the machine memory to an external storage medium. (Philips).

file security. In data security, the arrangements for ensuring the privacy or inaccessibility of files from unauthorized users. *See* FILE ACCESS, FILE PROTECTION.

file server. In memory systems, a sophisticated form of disk server that maintains a complete logical file system. Networked microcomputer users can access information in the same directory areas, and the file server mechanisms will deal with the problems of unauthorized access, concurrent accesses, etc. A heterogeneous mix of microcomputers can also be accommodated by software, which resides in the microcomputers and converts operating systems requests into equivalent file server requests. *See* DISK SERVER, FILE, SERVER.

file storage. In memory systems, peripherals that can store a mass of data. These include magnetic disk units, magnetic tape units and magnetic card units. *See* MAGNETIC CARD, MAGNETIC DISK, MAGNETIC TAPE.

file tidying. *Synonymous with* FILE CLEANUP.

file transfer. In computing, the downloading of a file from a host to a microcomputer, or the uploading from a microcomputer to a host, where the microcomputer is able to emulate a visual display unit either with a special card or by software alone. *See* DOWNLOAD, TERMINAL EMULATION, UPLOAD, VISUAL DISPLAY UNIT.

file updating. In computing, one of the most common operations in data and transaction processing. The contents of a file are changed without altering the fundamental structure. In batch-processing systems the changes to be made to the file were sorted in a sequence, corresponding to the sequence of records stored on the file, and the file records are inserted, modified or deleted, according to the input data, in one program run. The advent of direct-access storage devices has enabled efficient random access of file records so that individual transactions can be handled interactively. *See* BATCH PROCESSING, DATA PROCESSING, FILE, INTERACTIVE, RECORD, TRANSACTION PROCESSING.

fill character. In data structures, a character, usually a space, added to a set of characters to make the set a given length.

filled cable. In communications, a cable in which the gaps between the pairs are filled with a jelly-like compound to prevent the ingress of moisture.

filler. In publishing, extra material used to complete a column or page, usually of little importance. (Desktop).

film. In filming, a roll of cellulose triacetate, coated with light-sensitive emulsions and iron oxide, and with sprocket holes along each edge. *See* EMULSION.

film advance. In printing, the distance in points by which the film in the photounit of a phototypesetting machine is advanced between lines. *See* PHOTOTYPESETTING, POINT.

film assembly. In printing, the arrangement of film negatives or positives in position for making photolithographic printing plates. *See* PHOTOLITHOGRAPHY.

film base. In filming and recording, the flexible, usually transparent, support on which photographic emulsions and magnetic coatings are deposited.

film chain. In television, equipment necessary to present film or slide images via television. It ordinarily includes a pickup television camera, motion picture projector adapted for television frame rate, slide projector and a multiplexer all mounted on a rigid frame. *Compare* MULTIPLEXER. *See* FILM PICKUP.

film pickup. In television, the electronic scanning of motion picture film and transmission of the images by television. *See* FILM CHAIN.

filmsetter. *Synonymous with* PHOTOCOMPOSITION.

film strip. In audiovisual aids, a series of still pictures on a strip of film, usually single-frame 35-mm, but sometimes 110-, Super 8- or 16-mm formats. The film strip may be silent or provided with an accompanying sound program (tape or record). Film strips may be advanced manually as desired or in response to an audible beep in the audio source. Some film strip equipment can be automatically advanced through inaudible pulses on the tape or record.

filter. (1) In computing and communications, a hardware or software system that separates signals, material or data in some prespecified manner. (2) In electronics, a circuit that is frequency selective and so capable of attenuating some components of a signal while allowing other components to pass through uniformly. For example, a low-pass filter attenuates all frequencies in a signal that are above a specified frequency. (3) In optics, an element commonly used in conjunction with a lens system and designed to absorb selectively specific components of the visible spectra.

filter factor. In photography, a number designating the extent to which light is absorbed through the introduction of a filter. *See* FILTER.

final route chain. In communications, the final part of a network over which telephone calls are routed when all other direct, or high-usage, paths are busy.

find text string. In word processing, a command that enables a series of characters or words to be found within the text.

fine mode. In communications, a mode of operation on facsimile systems in which the scanning rate is decreased to provide more dots per inch and hence higher-quality reproduction. *See* FACSIMILE.

fingerprint. In software protection, a method of giving a unique mark, or signature, to a floppy disk, that cannot be duplicated. A special test routine detects if a signature is present, and if it is not found the protected program will be disabled. *Compare* DONGLE. *See* BURN MARK, EXECUTE PROTECTION, WEAK BITS. *Synonymous with* SIGNATURE, UNIQUE IDENTIFICATION.

Fintel. In online information retrieval, a UK database containing business, industrial and financial information. It is based on extensive indexing of the *Financial Times*.

FIPS. Federal Information Processing Standard.

FIPS pub. Federal Information Processing Standard Publication.

firmware. In memory systems, a program or data that has been permanently stored in a computer memory (i.e. a ROM, PROM, EROM or EPROM). This method of implementing software contrasts with programs held on magnetic media and which must first be loaded into the RAM memory of the computer before they can be used. *Compare* HARDWARE, SOFTWARE. *See* ELECTRICALLY PROGRAMMABLE READ-ONLY MEMORY, MICROCODE, PROGRAMMABLE READ-ONLY MEMORY, RANDOM-ACCESS MEMORY, READ-ONLY MEMORY.

First Computer Inquiry. *See* COMPUTER INQUIRY, 1980.

first-generation computer. In computing, vacuum tube-based electronic computers, of which the Univac 1 in 1951 was one of the earliest. *Compare* FIFTH-GENERATION COMPUTER, FOURTH-GENERATION COMPUTER,

SECOND-GENERATION COMPUTER, THIRD-GENERATION COMPUTER

first-generation image. In printing, the copy of a document, generally used as a master, produced directly by a camera.

first-generation language. In programming, a machine code or assembly language. *Compare* FIRST-GENERATION COMPUTER, FOURTH GENERATION LANGUAGE, SECOND GENERATION LANGUAGE, THIRD GENERATION LANGUAGE. *See* ASSEMBLY LANGUAGE, MACHINE CODE.

first in first out. (FIFO) In data structures, a method of storing and retrieving items from a structure such that the first element stored is the first one retrieved. *Compare* LAST IN FIRST OUT. *See* QUEUE.

first line form advance. In word processing, a forms-feeding device that automatically advances the stationery to the first line on a new page once the current page is completed. This avoids the need to record keystrokes for multiple line advances.

first normal form. (FNF) In databases, a property of a relation, in a relational database. A relation is in first normal form if it does not have any repeating groups (i.e. the data can be expressed in the form of a flat file). *Compare* SECOND NORMAL FORM, THIRD NORMAL FORM. *See* FLAT FILE, NORMAL FORMS, RELATIONAL DATABASE, REPEATING GROUP.

first-party release. In communications, a method of operation in which the release of a connection begins as soon as either party restores his telephone, modem, etc. to its quiescent state.

first point of Aries. In communications, a reference point in space used in satellite communications.

first silicon. In microelectronics, chips developed from the first masks and used for testing and debugging. *Compare* FIRST WORKING SILICON. *See* CHIP.

first working silicon. In microelectronics, chips produced as a result of testing and debugging the first silicon. *Compare* FIRST SILICON. *See* CHIP, DEBUG.

fisheye lens. In photography, an extremely wide-angle lens, about 150°–180°, producing a very distorted circular image.

FIT. Fédération Internationale des Traducteurs.

FIU. US Federation of Information Users.

five-two-five line. In television, the standard number of horizontal sweeps per frame used in America and Japan. *Compare* SIX-TWO-FIVE LINE. *See* FRAME, VIDEO STANDARDS.

fix. *See* FIXATION.

fixation. In photography, that part in the chemical development of films and prints where the images are made permanent. *See* DEVELOPING.

fixed and exchangeable disk storage. (FEDS) In memory systems, a magnetic disk unit in which some disks are fixed and others may be exchanged by an operator. *See* EXCHANGEABLE DISK STORAGE, FIXED DISK STORAGE.

fixed data. (1) In word processing, data, text or format instructions entered initially and available for subsequent reuse in documents. *Compare* VARIABLE TEXT. *See* BOILERPLATE. (2) In peripherals, data that is written on the display screen of a visual display unit, but which cannot be altered by the operator. *See* VISUAL DISPLAY UNIT. *Synonymous with* PROTECTED FIELD.

fixed-disk storage. (FDS) In memory systems, storage on non-exchangeable magnetic disks. *Compare* EXCHANGEABLE DISK STORAGE.

fixed-head disk. In memory systems, a disk system with a dedicated magnetic head fixed over each track. In the more common type of disk unit, the head is located on an arm, and so there is a delay while the head is positioned to seek the data. By eliminating the head-positioning delay, this method provides very high-speed access. *Compare*

MOVABLE-HEAD DISK. *See* HARD DISK, HEAD, MAGNETIC DISK.

fixed-head disk storage. *See* DISK DRIVE.

fixed-length record. In data structures, a record that always has the same length as all other records with which it is logically or physically associated. *Compare* VARIABLE-LENGTH RECORD. *See* RECORD.

fixed point. In mathematics, a number system in which each number is represented by a set of digits, and the position of the radix point is implied by the manner in which the numbers are used. *Compare* FLOATING POINT. *See* FIXED-POINT ARITHMETIC, RADIX.

fixed-point arithmetic. In computing, arithmetic using fixed-point numbers. *See* FIXED POINT.

fixed routing. In data communications, a method of routing messages in which the behaviour of the network is predetermined, taking no account of changes in traffic or network components. *Compare* ADAPTIVE ROUTING, FREE ROUTING.

fixed-satellite service. (FSS) In communications, a Federal Communications Commission term for a satellite service using non-mobile earth stations. *See* COMMUNICATIONS SATELLITE SYSTEM, EARTH STATION.

fixed-spaced font. In printing, a font in which the characters are contained in cells of fixed size. *See* MONOSPACE. *Synonymous with* UNIFORMLY SPACED FONT.

fixed word spacing. In printing, pertaining to printers in which the word spaces are standard, any extra spaces being left to the end of the line. *Synonymous with* EVEN WORD SPACING.

FL. *See* FOCAL LENGTH.

flag. (1) In publishing, the designed title of a newspaper as it appears at the top of page one. (Desktop). (2) In data communications, a character, typically consisting of eight bits, used to mark the start of a frame in a packet. *See* FRAME, PACKET SWITCHING. (3) In computing, a signal set up to indicate

that a specific condition has occurred. For example, when a buffer is full.

flag bit. *See* FLAG.

flag code. *Synonymous with* ESCAPE CODE.

flagging. In recording, television picture distortion caused by incorrect video tape playback head-timing coordination. *See* TIME BASE CORRECTOR.

flag sequence. In data communications, a sequence of bits used to identify the beginning and end of a frame. *See* FLAG, FRAME, PACKET SWITCHING.

flare. (1) In television, an unwanted component in the picture signal output from a camera, caused by the scattering of light in the optical system. Flare is often described in terms of its position in the picture (e.g. edge flare, bottom flare). (2) In photography, an area of film emulsion exposed in some way other than directly through the lens, such as internal reflections between the various surfaces of the lens component. *Compare* FOG. *See* HALATION.

flash. (1) In filming, a bright spot in a film frame caused by overexposure or unwanted reflection. *Compare* BLOOM. (2) In peripherals and videotex, a display mode in which the characters are blanked out at regular intervals under the control of a timing device in the receiver. In videotex it is used to highlight a part of the page. *See* CHARACTER.

flash card. In micrographics, a document introduced during the recording of a microfilm to facilitate its indexing. *See* INDEX.

flashing. In filming, the process of exposing film to a weak light before or after camera exposure, but before processing, to reduce contrast.

flat. (1) In printing, an assemblage of various film negatives or positives attached, in register, to a piece of film or suitable masking material ready to be exposed to a plate. (2) In printing, a lack of contrast and definition of material in printed matter.

flatbed camera. *Synonymous with* PLANETARY CAMERA.

flatbed plotter.   In peripherals, a plotter in which the paper is fixed in position on a flat surface and the pens move in X–Y-axes to draw an image. *Compare* DRUM PLOTTER, PINCH PLOTTER. *See* PLOTTER.

flatbed transmitter.   In communications, facsimile apparatus that holds the source document flat for scanning line by line. *See* FACSIMILE.

flat file.   In databases, a file comprising a collection of records of the same type which do not contain repeating groups. A flat file can be represented by a two-dimensional array of data items. A relational database comprises a set of well-structured flat files. *See* RECORD, RELATIONAL DATABASE, REPEATING GROUP.

flat pack.   In computing, a package where the leads extending from it are in the same plane, so that they can be spot welded to terminals on a substrate or soldered to a printed circuit board. *See* PACKAGE, SUBSTRATE.

flat rate.   In communications, a method of pricing for a service (e.g. a telephone subscriber may pay a fixed monthly charge and be allowed to make an unlimited number of local calls).

flat-screen display.   In peripherals, a form of display that uses a comparatively thin display tube, as compared with the conventional cathode ray tube. The four major types of flat-screen display used as visual display units are liquid crystal displays, vacuum fluorescent, electroluminescent and plasma discharge. *Compare* CATHODE RAY TUBE. *See* ELECTROLUMINESCENT DISPLAY, LCD SCREENS, PLASMA PANEL, VACUUM FLUORESCENT DISPLAY, VISUAL DISPLAY UNIT.

flat shading.   In computer graphics, a method of displaying the brightness of patches of an object represented by a graphics display. The brightness at the corners of the patch are evaluated, and the average value is used for the whole patch. *Compare* GOURAUD SHADING.

flexography.   In printing, a relief or surface process that uses curved rubber plates. It is particularly convenient for printing on paper bags and packaging material.

flicker.   (1) In optical media, a phenomenon that occurs in a freeze frame display from a videodisc when the two fields are not identically matched, creating two different alternating pictures. *See* FIELD, FIELD DOMINANCE, FREEZE FRAME. (2) In peripherals, a visual awareness that the luminance of a cathode ray tube is being interrupted at a constant rate. *See* CATHODE RAY TUBE. (3) In peripherals, an effect caused by a low refresh rate in a display device. *See* REFRESH RATE, VECTOR REFRESH.

flip flop.   In electronics, a circuit that can be used as a one-bit storage device for digital data. It can assume either one of two stable states at a given time.

flipover.   In filming and television, an optical effect in which the picture appears to turn from left to right, or vice versa, to reveal a picture on the reverse side.

flippy floppy.   In memory systems, a floppy disk that can be flipped over so that a single-sided drive can read either side. *See* FLOPPY DISK, SINGLE-SIDED DRIVE.

floating gate avalanche injection MOS. (FAMOS) In memory systems, a type of programmable read-only memory using storage cells similar to field effect transistors. An applied voltage produces a static charge, which allows the storage cell to conduct during the read action, for a 1 bit. Exposure to ultraviolet light enables the charge to leak away thus permitting reprogramming. *See* BIT, FIELD EFFECT TRANSISTOR, METAL OXIDE SEMICONDUCTOR, PROGRAMMABLE READ-ONLY MEMORY.

floating point.   In data structures, an approximate method of representing a large range of real numbers with a limited number of bits. The floating point representation provides a signed magnitude and a signed exponent (e.g. -1.173 e^{-5} corresponds to -1.173 x 10^{-5} or $-0.000\ 011\ 73$. *Compare* BINARY-CODED DECIMAL, FIXED POINT. *See* EXPONENT, MAGNITUDE, PRECISION, TWO'S COMPLEMENT.

floating voltage. In electronics, a network or component having no terminal at ground potential. *See* GROUND.

flooding. In data communications, a routing method in which each node replicates incoming packets and sends copies to its neighbours, thus ensuring that the actual destination is reached quickly and with certainty, although with considerable use of transmission capacity. *See* NODE, PACKET SWITCHING, ROUTING.

flood testing. In data communications, a method of testing the overall throughput of a system when all the terminals in a network are in use. *Compare* SATURATION TESTING.

floppy. In memory systems, an abbreviation for floppy disk or a floppy-disk drive. *See* FLOPPY DISK.

floppy disk. In memory systems, a thin flexible magnetic-coated disk contained in a rigid or semi-rigid protective jacket. The floppy disk provides microcomputer users with a cheap, high-capacity, direct-access backing store. The floppy disk is contained within an envelope which is coated in its exterior to provide a cleaning action. The envelope has a number of apertures for the drive spindle, index hole to signal the start of a sector and a write-inhibit notch. *Compare* HARD DISK. *See* BYTE, DIRECT-ACCESS STORAGE DEVICE. *Synonymous with* DISKETTE.

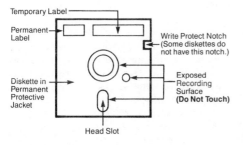

floppy disk

FLOPS. In computing, floating point operations per second; a measure of computer performance. *Compare* KIPS, LIPS, MIPS. *See* FLOATING POINT.

flow analysis. *See* INFORMATION FLOW ANALYSIS.

flowchart. A graphical representation of an algorithm in which annotated blocks represent the operations performed, and the links correspond to the flow of data.

flow control. In data communications, the control of data flow to prevent overspill of queues or buffers or loss of data because the intended receiver is unable to accept it. *See* BUFFER.

flush left. In printing, pertaining to text that lines up vertically on the left with a ragged right margin. *Compare* FLUSH RIGHT. *See* RAGGED SETTING.

flush right. In printing, pertaining to text that lines up vertically on the right with a ragged left margin. *Compare* FLUSH LEFT. *See* RAGGED SETTING.

flutter. In recording, a form of audio frequency distortion arising in reproduction from disc, film or tape that is caused by variations of speed in the transport system. *See* WOW.

flux. (1) In recording, a measure of the magnetic effect produced by a magnetic recording head, or a tape as it passes a head. (2) In optics, the amount of light energy incident or reflected from a body, measured in lumens. *See* LUMEN, MAGNETIC HEAD.

fly back. In peripherals, the rapid return of a scanning beam from the end of a line or field scan to the start of the next in a raster scan. *See* RASTER SCAN.

fly fold. In printing, a method of folding paper.

flying-spot scanner. (1) In character recognition, a technique for reading a document. The surface of the document is scanned with a moving spot of light, and the reflected ray is directed to a photocell. *See* OPTICAL CHARACTER RECOGNITION, PHOTOCELL. (2) In television, a method of scanning used for film transmission in which a moving, horizontal spot of light from a cathode ray tube is passed through the film and detected on a photocell. *See* PHOTOCELL, SCAN.

FM. *See* FACILITIES MANAGEMENT, FREQUENCY MODULATION.

FNF. *See* FIRST NORMAL FORM.

FNP. *See* FRONT-END NETWORK PROCESSOR.

f-number. In optics, a measure of the amount of light passed by a lens; the smaller the f-number the 'faster' the lens. It is the ratio of the focal length to the maximum diameter of the lens opening and is usually inscribed on the lens. *See* FOCAL LENGTH, F-STOP.

focal length. (FL) (1) In communications, the distance between the focal point and the centre of a dish antenna. *See* DISH ANTENNA, FOCAL POINT. (2) In optics, the distance from the optical centre of a lens to the film plane when the lens is focused at infinity.

focal plane. In photography, a plane that is perpendicular to the optical axis of a lens and is the location of an image for an object at infinity. *See* FOCAL LENGTH, INFINITY, OPTICAL AXIS.

focal point. (1) In optics, the point through which all parallel rays, incident to a lens, pass or appear to pass. *See* FOCAL PLANE. (2) In communications, a point in front of a dish antenna through which all parallel electromagnetic rays, incident upon the reflector, pass. *See* FOCAL LENGTH.

Focus Committee. A UK Department of Industry committee formed to coordinate British national and international information technology standards activities.

focusing. (1) In peripherals, a process for ensuring that the electron beam in a cathode ray tube is contained in a small spot area on the phosphor screen. *See* CATHODE RAY TUBE. (2) In photography, the maximum definition of an image attainable with a lens on a screen or film.

fog. In photography, a region of a film emulsion that has developed as a result of exposure to unwanted light, such as that arising from leaks in the camera. *Compare* FLARE.

FOI. In legislation, freedom of information; information or activities related to the US Freedom of Information Act. *See* DATA PROTECTION.

folding. In peripherals, a facility that maps a large character set onto a smaller one (e.g. all lower-case characters may be represented by upper case for a printer that does not have a full set of output characters).

follow me diversion. In communications, a private automatic branch exchange (PABX) facility that enables a user to have incoming calls automatically diverted to another extension. *See* PRIVATE AUTOMATIC BRANCH EXCHANGE.

font. In printing, a character set of given size, style and face in printers and terminals. The set may contain lower case, capitals, small capitals, numerals, ligatures, punctuation marks, reference marks, signs and spaces. *See* FACE, LIGATURES, LOWER CASE, REFERENCE MARK, SMALL CAPITALS, UPPER CASE.

font change. (FC) In printing, a control character to change the font of a printing or display device. *See* FONT.

font disk. (1) In printing, a plastic or glass disk containing the master character images that are used to form typeset characters. (2) In printing, the master characters stored in digital form on a magnetic disk. *See* MAGNETIC DISK, PHOTOTYPESETTING.

font-independent. In office systems, describing a technique used in optical scanners in which the topological features of alphanumeric characters are recognized, independent of their font, thus allowing the scanner to accept proportional fonts. *Compare* FEATURE ANALYSIS, FONT-SPECIFIC, TEMPLATE MATCHING. *See* ALPHANUMERIC, FONT, INTELLIGENT PAGE READER, OPTICAL SCANNER, PROPORTIONAL SPACING.

font-specific. In office systems, pertaining to a technique used in optical scanners in which the topological features of alphanumeric characters, in a given font, are recognized from the binary matrix representing the page image. *Compare* FONT-INDEPENDENT, TEMPLATE MATCHING. *See* ALPHANUMERIC, FONT, OPTICAL SCANNER.

foot candle. In optics, a measure of light illumination, defined as that illumination falling on a surface of one square foot when the uniform flux is one lumen. *See* LUMEN.

footcandle meter. In optics, a light meter calibrated in foot candles.

footer. In printing, information placed at the bottom of a page, usually for the purposes of identification. *Compare* HEADER.

footprint. (1) In communications, the geographical area throughout which signals may be transmitted to, or received from, a particular communications satellite. Within this area, the field strength of the beam from the satellite must exceed a specific value. *See* COMMUNICATIONS SATELLITE SYSTEM.

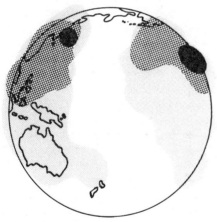

footprint
Intelsat V footprint over the Pacific Ocean showing regions of different signal strengths.

(2) In computing, the area of a desk occupied by a microcomputer. *See* FIELD STRENGTH.

forbidden combination. In data structures, a combination of bits that is not valid according to the criteria set by the programmer or system designer. *Compare* ILLEGAL CHARACTER.

foreground. (1) In filming, the action area in a shot that nearest to the camera. (2) In programming. *See* FOREGROUND PROGRAM.

foreground colour. In videotex, the colours in which characters are presented on an alphamosaic display. *Compare* BACKGROUND COLOUR. *See* ALPHAMOSAIC, VIDEOTEX.

foreground program. In computing, a program that has a high priority and so takes precedence over other programs that are running concurrently in a multiprogramming environment. *Compare* BACKGROUND PROGRAM. *See* MULTIPROGRAMMING.

foreign exchange service. In communications, a facility that connects a telephone subscriber to a central office that does not normally serve that customer's location.

foreshortening. In photography, an illusion of depth reduction produced by a telephoto lens. *See* TELEPHOTO LENS.

forgery. In legislation, the fabrication of information by one party and the claim that such information was received in a communication from another party. *See* DIGITAL SIGNATURE.

forgiving system. In programming, a software package designed so that mistakes made by inexperienced users can be easily corrected. *See* USER FRIENDLY.

form. In office systems, a document in which certain items have been precoded and against which variable information is entered.

form 1. In optical media, the interactive compact disc sector format with error-detecting code/error-correcting code; it is equivalent to read-only memory compact disc mode 1, but with the form identity included in a subheader to permit interleaving of form 1 and form 2 sectors to meet the requirements of real-time operation. (Philips). *Compare* FORM 2. *See* COMPACT DISC – INTERACTIVE, COMPACT DISC – READ-ONLY MEMORY, ERROR-CORRECTING CODE, ERROR-DETECTING CODE, MODE 1.

Form 1

sync. 12 B	header 4 B	subheader 8 B	user data 2048 B	EDC 4 B	ECC P-parity 172 B	ECC Q-parity 104 B

Form 2

sync. 12 B	header 4 B	subheader 8 B	user data 2324 B	reserved 4 B

form 1 and form 2
CD-I forms.

form 2. In optical media, an interactive compact disc sector format with an auxiliary data field instead of error-detecting code/error-correcting code error correction and detection. It is equivalent to read-only memory compact disc mode 2, but with the form identity included in a subheader to permit interleaving of form 1 and form 2 sectors to meet the requirements of real-time operation. (Philips). *Compare* FORM 1. *See* COMPACT DISC – INTERACTIVE, COMPACT DISC – READ-ONLY MEMORY, ERROR-CORRECTING CODE, ERROR-DETECTING CODE, INTERLEAVING, MODE 2.

formal language. In programming, a formal language defines a set of symbols — the alphabet — and a set of strings of those symbols. The significance of formal languages in programming is that a given program may be considered as a string of a formal language (i.e. the programming language). The program is produced by writing expressions according to the syntax of the language; this is equivalent to using productions of a corresponding grammar. The translator checks if the program is one of the strings of the language and reports syntax errors if it is not. *See* GRAMMAR, SYNTAX, TRANSLATOR.

formant. In man–machine interfaces, pertaining to a resonant frequency of the vocal tract. *See* SPEECH SYNTHESIZER.

formant synthesizer. In man–machine interfaces, a vocal tract synthesizer in which the coefficients of the digital filter are determined from the frequency transform of the original utterance. *Compare* LPC CODER. *See* SPEECH SYNTHESIZER, VOCAL TRACT SYNTHESIZER.

format. (1) In data structures, the predetermined mandatory order, organization or position of symbols in a computer instruction, data or word, data transmission message, etc. The order is mandatory so that the computer can understand and interpret the information. *See* INSTRUCTION, WORD. (2) In computing, a command to format a disk. *See* FORMATTING. (3) In filming, the dimensions of a film stock and its perforations, and size and shape of the image frame. (4) In a book, the dimensions of the printed page.

format effector. (FE) In codes, a control character used to position printed, displayed or recorded data. *See* CONTROL CHARACTER.

formatted dump. In computing, a dump in which certain data areas are isolated and identified. *Compare* POST MORTEM DUMP, RESCUE DUMP, SELECTIVE DUMP. *See* DUMP.

formatting. In computing, an operation that initializes blank disks; initiating data is written so that the tracks are divided into sectors. No files can be written to the disk until this operation has been performed. *See* FLOPPY DISK, FORMAT, MAGNETIC DISK, SECTOR, TRACK.

forme. In printing, type or blocks assembled in pages and imposed in a metal chase ready for printing. (Desktop). *See* IMPOSITION, WORK AND TUMBLE, WORK AND TURN.

form feed. In printing, the mechanical device that positions and advances paper through a printer. *See* FORM FEED CHARACTER, PRINTER.

form feed character. (FF) In printing, a control character that causes a printer to move a form to the next predetermined position. *See* FORM FEED. *Synonymous with* PAGE END CHARACTER.

form letter. In word processing, a standard letter in which the name and address are either individually or automatically typed. *See* BOILERPLATE, MAIL MERGE. *Synonymous with* REPETITIVE LETTER.

form mode. In computing, pertaining to sophisticated microprocessor-based terminals intended for data entry. Typically the computer displays a form for the operator to fill out using cursor control and local editing facilities. *Compare* PAGE MODE, SCROLL MODE.

forms flash. In micrographics, the method by which document formats are superimposed on a frame of computer output microfilm containing other data. *See* MICROFILM.

forms mode. In word processing, the storing of a format for a particular form. The format can provide automatic carriage position and other operator aids. *See* FORMAT.

formula. In mathematics, a rule expressed as an equation, e.g. $F = MA$ is a formula derived from Newton's laws of motion.

FORTH. In programming, a FOuRTH-generation language; FORTH can be considered as a 'high-level assembly language', whose operation is strongly machine-oriented and is therefore fast, but it provides most of the notational convenience associated with a high-level language. It is also easy to learn, and thus is popular with microcomputer users who often find that BASIC is excessively slow in execution. Forth has found many uses in real time and automation due to its speed and flexibility. In spite of its name it is not a fourth-generation language in the common usage of that term. It was originated by Charles Moore in the early 1970s. *See* ASSEMBLY LANGUAGE, BASIC.

fortnightly decision. In television, the 1968 Supreme Court decision which allows cable television operators to record and retransmit broadcast television programs without regard to any copyright restrictions.

FORTRAN. In programming, FORmula TRANslation; a compiled general-purpose language providing very efficient execution, especially for number-crunching operations. It has therefore gained considerable popularity among the scientific and technical communities, where speed of execution is of primary importance. It was originated in IBM in the late 1950s. *See* NUMBER CRUNCHING.

forward chaining. In artificial intelligence, a technique employed in expert systems in which the rules that match the question are fired. This firing then produces conditions in which further rules can be matched, and so on, until sufficient rules corresponding to a conclusion are fired. *Compare* BACKWARD CHAINING. *See* EXPERT SYSTEMS.

forward channel. In data communications, a transmission channel in which the direction of transmission coincides with that in which the user information is being transferred. *Compare* BACKWARD CHANNEL.

forward echo. In communications, an echo, in a transmission line, travelling in the same direction as the original wave, and formed by energy reflected back from one irregularity and then onwards again by a second. If forward echoes add in a systematic way they can impair the overall performance of the transmission line. *See* ECHO.

forward error correction. (FEC) In codes, a method using a redundant code that enables both error detection and some error correction without retransmission. *See* ERROR-CORRECTING CODE, ERROR-DETECTING CODE, Hamming CODE.

forward scatter. In communications, a radio wave produced as a result of scattering and propagating in the same general direction as the incident wave. *Compare* BACK SCATTER.

forward supervision. In data communications, use of supervisory sequences sent from the primary to a secondary station or node. *Compare* BACKWARD SUPERVISION. *See* NODE, PRIMARY STATION, SUPERVISORY SEQUENCE.

FOSDIC. In micrographics, film optical-scanning device for input into computers; a storage and retrieval system using direct input into a computer from 16-mm microfilm. *See* COMPUTER INPUT FROM MICROFILM.

FOTS. Fiber optics transmission system. *See* FIBER OPTICS.

four-colour process. In printing, a method of producing full-colour pictures by superimposing impressions from plates with cyan, magenta, yellow and black inks. *See* SUBTRACTIVE COLOUR MIXING.

four eyes. In data security, pertaining to security measures that require transactions to be endorsed by a second employee.

Fourier series. In communications, a mathematical series that can be applied to the analysis of periodic waveforms. Any periodic waveform may be expressed as the weighted sum of the fundamental frequency and its harmonics. *See* FUNDAMENTAL FREQUENCY, HARMONIC, PERIODIC.

four-one-four. *See* MILWAUKEE 414.

fourth-generation computer. In computing, pertaining to the generation of computers developed in the mid-1970s using large-scale integration technology. *Compare* FIFTH-GENERATION COMPUTER, FIRST-GENERATION COMPUTER, SECOND-GENERATION COMPUTER, THIRD-GENERATION COMPUTER.

fourth-generation language. In programming, a user friendly language that enables one to obtain the desired information with less effort than that associated with conventional procedural languages. The term fourth-generation language is widely used and has been applied to such a diverse range of products that no one succinct definition could adequately cover the host of current interpretations. The desirable attributes of a fourth-generation language include: (a) support of non-procedural programming; (b) support of procedural programming; (c) an active data dictionary; (d) provision of powerful, convenient and flexible database management; (e) human-oriented language; and (f) provision of a shield between the user and the machine. *Compare* FOURTH-GENERATION COMPUTER. *See* DATABASE MANAGEMENT SYSTEM, DATA DICTIONARY, NON-PROCEDURAL LANGUAGE, PROCEDURAL LANGUAGE.

four-track recorder. In recording, the ability to store four different sound or data channels on an audio tape. Conventionally, tracks 1 and 3 are recorded in the 'forward' direction, with track 2 and 4 recorded in the 'reverse' direction.

four-wire circuit. In communications, a two-way circuit where the signals simultaneously follow separate and distinct paths in opposite directions in the transmission medium. A telephone circuit carries voice signals both ways, and in the local loop this is achieved over two wires because the waveforms travelling each way can be distinguished. In the trunk network where amplifiers and multiplexers are used, the two directions of transmission have to be physically separated. It is called a four-wire circuit because, in its primitive form, it uses a pair of wires for each direction. *Compare* SINGLE-WIRE CIRCUIT, TWO-WIRE CIRCUIT. *See* TRUNK.

FPLA. *See* FIELD-PROGRAMMABLE LOGIC ARRAY.

fpm. Frames per minute.

fps. *See* FRAMES PER SECOND.

FRA. Federal Radio Act.

frame. (1) In computing, the array of bits across the width of magnetic tape. *See* BIT. (2) In data communications, a complete sequence of bits identified by an opening synchronization character, and usually including a field containing the user's data. (3) In television, a single television tube picture scan combining interleaved information. *Compare* FIELD. (4) In videotex, a page of data displayed on a terminal. *Compare* PAGE. (5) In artificial intelligence, a data structure for representing a stereotype situation. This concept may be useful in dealing with linguistic ambiguities which arise in machine translation. *See* DATA STRUCTURE. (6) In filming, an individual picture on a film, filmstrip or videotape. The size of the frame is determined by the limits of the camera aperture. (7) In optical media, one complete pattern of digital audio information on a digital audio compact disc, comprising six pulse code-modulated stereo samples, with cross-interleaved Reed-Solomon code and one subcode symbol, eight-to-fourteen-modulated, with a synchronization pattern. (Philips). *See* COMPACT DISC – DIGITAL AUDIO, CROSS-INTERLEAVED REED-SOLOMON CODE, EIGHT-TO-FOURTEEN MODULATION, PULSE CODE MODULATION, SUBCODE CHANNEL.

frame alignment word. (FAW) In data communications, a pattern of bits that identifies the start of a frame. *See* FRAME.

frame frequency. In television, the number of frames transmitted per second; it is 30 in the USA and 25 in the UK. *See* FRAME. *Synonymous with* VERTICAL SCAN FREQUENCY.

frame grabber. (1) In recording, an electronic technique for storing and regenerating a video frame from a helical video tape signal. This method avoids the need for the continuous head to tape contact which would otherwise be required in freeze frame operation. *Compare* FREEZE FRAME. (2) In recording, an electronic device for extracting a complete frame from a video signal and storing it in memory for further processing. (Philips). *See* FRAME.

framesnatch. In television, a home control unit for receiving and storing a particular cable television frame, transmitted as one of many.

frames per second. (fps) (1) In filming, film speed through a camera or projector gate. (2) In television, a transmission standard related to the power supply frequency. *See* FRAME FREQUENCY, GATE.

frame store. (1) In memory systems, a section of computer memory that stores the attributes of pixels for a given screen display. The value stored for a pixel may be the brightness for a monochrome display or the colour for a colour display. If one byte is employed, for the colour attribute then 256 colours may be displayed simultaneously. The actual range of colours may be extended by using the value, stored for a pixel, to refer to a table. If each entry in the table contains (say) three bytes then 256 x 256 x 256 colours

may be displayed; although only 256 will be available at any one time. The range of colours may be altered by changing the values in the look-up table. *See* COLOUR LOOK-UP TABLE, FRAME, PIXEL. (2) In television and recording, a store that holds a single television frame. *See* FRAME, FRAME GRABBER.

framing. (1) In data communications, the process by which groupings, representing one or more characters, are selected within a continuous bit stream. *See* FRAMING BITS. (2) In data communications, the method by which individual frames, in a time division multiplexing system, are recognized so that the time slots can be identified correctly. *See* TIME DIVISION MULTIPLEXING. (3) In filming, the positioning and movement of a camera by a cameraman so as to eliminate unwanted action and to achieve good composition.

framing bits. In data communications, bits used to make possible the separation of characters in a bit stream, but otherwise carrying no information. *See* BIT STREAM.

framing code. In videotex, a technique for enabling a receiver to achieve byte synchronization with the broadcast teletext signal. *See* SYNCHRONIZATION, TELETEXT.

framing pattern. In data communications, a unique pattern of framing bits. *See* FRAMING BITS.

FRC. Federal Radio Commission.

free indexing. In library science, a method of coordinate indexing in which words or phrases assigned as index terms for a given document are considered by the indexer to be appropriate even though they may not appear in the document. *See* INDEX.

free line. In communications, the state of a line when it is available for traffic.

free routing. In data communications, a method of routing in which messages are sent over any available channel towards the destination, without dependence upon any prespecified routing plan. *Compare* FIXED ROUTING.

free-running mode. In computing, a method of allowing two or more users of a database to have access simultaneously. The possibility that conflict between them may cause difficulties must be taken into account in the system design. This problem is avoided in the alternate mode. *Compare* ALTERNATE MODE.

free-space loss. In communications, a measure of the radiation dilution with distance of an antenna transmitting uniformly in all directions. It is defined as the ratio of the power received by an isotropic antenna to the power transmitted by an isotropic antenna, in decibels. *See* ANTENNA GAIN, ISOTROPIC ANTENNA.

free-text searching. In online information retrieval, a means of directly searching all the fields with subject content in a document for relevant terms. It is required when a controlled vocabulary has not been used to index the documents in a database. *See* CONTROLLED VOCABULARY.

freeware. *Synonymous with* SHAREWARE.

free wheeling. In data communications, a technique in which the simplest protocol is used by teletype compatible terminals. The computer transmitting the data does not know whether it is received or not, or whether it is received correctly. *Compare* STOP-AND-WAIT PROTOCOL. *See* PROTOCOL, TELETYPEWRITER.

freeze frame. (1) In filming, a frame of motion picture film that has been repeatedly printed to give the appearance of frozen motion. (2) In recording, a disc player or video tape recorder in which an identical effect is created by continually re-reading the frame. *Compare* FRAME GRABBER. *Synonymous with* STILL FRAME.

F region. In communications, that part of the ionosphere lying more than 150 kilometres from the surface of the earth. *Compare* D REGION, E REGION. *See* IONOSPHERE.

french fold. In printing, a sheet that has been printed on one side only and then folded with two right angle folds to form a four-page uncut section. (Desktop).

frequency. In communications, the frequency of a periodic wave is the number of

times the cycle of the waveform is repeated in a second, measured in hertz (Hz). *Compare* PERIOD. *See* HERTZ.

frequency agility. In communications security, a technique to counteract jamming in which the transmitted frequency is varied according to some sequence, known only to the transmitter and legitimate receiver, during transmission. *See* JAMMING.

frequency band. *See* BAND.

frequency coordination. In communications, an internationally agreed consultative procedure designed to prevent interference between terrestrial and satellite services sharing the same frequency bands. *See* BAND, COMMUNICATIONS SATELLITE SYSTEM.

frequency divider. In electronics, one or more flip flops used to divide down a square-wave input frequency. Each flip flop output changes at half its input frequency. *See* FLIP FLOP.

frequency division multiple access. (FDMA) In communications, a technique whereby groups of users (e.g. several ground stations in a satellite communication system) are allocated frequencies to use a common channel employing frequency division multiplexing techniques. The allocation of frequencies may be made on a fixed or on demand basis. *Compare* CODE DIVISION MULTIPLE ACCESS, TIME DIVISION MULTIPLE ACCESS. *See* COMMUNICATIONS SATELLITE SYSTEM, FREQUENCY DIVISION MULTIPLEXING, GROUND STATION.

frequency division multiplexing. (FDM) In communications, a process whereby two or more signals may be transmitted over a common wideband path, by using different parts of the frequency band for each signal. At the other end of the line the signals are separated and identified by selective filters which demultiplex them. *Compare* TIME DIVISION MULTIPLEXING. *See* FILTER.

frequency domain. In electronics, pertaining to the computation of the effect of a linear circuit on a periodic waveform by an analysis of the effects upon individual sinusoidal components of the waveform. *Compare* TIME DOMAIN.

frequency double frequency. (F2F) In memory systems, a method of recording binary data on magnetic media where each 1 bit is encoded as two flux transitions in a bit cell and each 0 bit as one flux transition. *See* BIT, FLUX.

frequency modulation. (1) (FM) In communications, a form of modulation in which the instantaneous frequency of a carrier wave is caused to depart from the normal carrier frequency by an amount proportional to the instantaneous amplitude of the modulating envelope. *Compare* AMPLITUDE MODULATION, PHASE MODULATION, PULSE MODULATION. *See* MODULATION. (2) In memory systems, a method of recording data on a magnetizable surface. The direction of current in the recording coil is reversed at intervals determined by a clock sequence. If a 1 bit is to be recorded then the current is also reversed at the midpoint between clock pulses. These current changes produce corresponding changes in the orientation of the magnetic particles on the disk surface. *See* FREQUENCY DOUBLE FREQUENCY, MAGNETIC DISK, MODIFIED FREQUENCY MODULATION.

frequency multiplexing. *See* FREQUENCY DIVISION MULTIPLEXING.

frequency response. In electronics, the variation of the gain of a device as a function of the frequency of the input signal. *See* FREQUENCY, GAIN.

frequency reuse. (1) In communications, a technique of satellite communications to increase the total capacity of the system. *See* POLARIZATION FREQUENCY REUSE, SPATIAL FREQUENCY REUSE. (2) In communications, pertaining to the reuse of identical sets of frequency channels over a total area covered by a cellular radio network. The area is divided into cell clusters; each cluster may use the total number of channels allocated for the service, and disjoint subsets of these channels are allocated to individual cells in the cluster. The geometric arrangement of the cells is such that the distance between cells, sharing the same channels, is sufficient to minimize cochannel interference. *See* CELLULAR RADIO.

frequency shift keying. (FSK) In data communications, a method of signalling in which a carrier is frequency-modulated by a signal that has a fixed number of discrete values. *See* FREQUENCY MODULATION.

friction feeder. In printing, a device that feeds single sheets of paper into a machine from the paper stack.

frilling. In photography, the puckering and peeling of a photographic emulsion from its support during processing.

front-end network processor. (FNP) In computing, a front-end processor that handles the interface functions between a computer and a data network. *See* FRONT-END PROCESSOR.

front-end processor. (FEP) In computing, a small computer used to handle communication interfacing (e.g. polling, multiplexing, error detection) for another computer. *Compare* INTEGRAL CONTROLLER. *See* MULTIPLEXING, POLLING.

front-end system. *Synonymous with* INTERMEDIARY SYSTEM.

front matter. In printing, the sections of a book that are placed before the main chapters or sections (e.g. preface, table of contents). *Compare* BACK MATTER.

front porch. In television, that part of the video signal waveform between the start of the line-blanking pulse and the leading edge of the line sync pulse. *Compare* BACK PORCH. *See* VIDEO SIGNAL.

front projection. In filming, television and still photography, a method of projecting a background image along the axis of a camera lens on a particular subject and a screen behind the subject; usually, a two-way mirror is interposed between the camera and main subject. *Compare* BACKGROUND PROJECTION.

frying. In acoustics, noise in a carbon microphone produced by small irregularities in the current in the absence of any input.

FS. *See* FIELD SEPARATOR.

FSK. *See* FREQUENCY SHIFT KEYING.

FSS. *See* FIXED-SATELLITE SERVICE.

f-stop. In optics, a lens calibration equal to the ratio of focal length to aperture opening. The lowest f-stop of a given lens is the setting that passes the most light and is equal to the f-number of the lens. *See* F-NUMBER. *Synonymous with* LENS STOP.

FTS. In communications, Federal Telecommunications System; a network employed US federal agencies.

full-coat magnetic film. In recording, magnetic film, as distinguished from magnetic audio tape, which is completely covered on one side with an iron oxide coating. Magnetic film is used in conjunction with a magnetic film recorder. *See* MAGNETIC FILM, MAGNETIC FILM RECORDER.

full-custom design. In microelectronics, the custom design to meet a specific customer's requirements using hand-crafting or computer-aided design techniques at the device level to produce a chip with minimum silicon area and optimum design performance. *Compare* SEMI-CUSTOM DESIGN. *See* CHIP, COMPUTER-AIDED DESIGN, CUSTOM DESIGN, HAND CRAFTING.

full-duplex. (FD, FDX) In data communications, a mode of information transmission in which data is transferred in both directions simultaneously. *Compare* HALF-DUPLEX, SIMPLEX.

full-frame time code. In recording, a standardized SMPTE method of address coding a video tape. It gives an accurate frame count rather than an accurate check time. *See* SMPTE.

full measure. In printing, a line set to the entire line width. (Desktop).

full point. In printing, a full stop. (Desktop).

full-text database. In online information retrieval, a database, comprising the full text of documents which can be retrieved *in toto*, as compared with bibliographic citations to documents. *Compare* BIBLIOGRAPHIC DATABASE, DIRECTORY DATABASE, NUMERIC DATABASE, REFERRAL DATABASE.

full-text retrieval. In information retrieval, a method of locating a document in an information retrieval system. Occurrences of a specified string of text is used to locate the document, as compared with a technique of matching preselected keywords stored with the document.

fully connected network. In data communications, a network in which each node is directly connected with every other node. *See* NODE.

fully distributed costs. In communications, a system for determining the costs of different services provided by a common carrier. In the USA the total allowable operating expenses and rate base are apportioned among the various services in accordance with fixed procedures established by the FCC.

fully formed character. In printing, pertaining to printers in which the character is produced by a single action, as in a typewriter. *Compare* DOT MATRIX.

fully functional-dependent. In databases, a collection of attributes A of a relation R is fully functionally dependent on another collection of attributes, B, of relation R if A is functionally dependent on the whole of B, but not on any subset of B. Suppose a relation contains employee name, employee number and department, and every employee in a particular department has a unique number. Then the employee name is fully functionally dependent upon the employee number and department, because two employees in different departments may have the same number. *See* ATTRIBUTE, FUNCTIONAL DEPENDENCE, NORMAL FORMS, RELATION.

function. (1) In mathematics, an entity whose value depends in a specified manner on the values of one or more independent variables. (2) In programming, a form of subroutine that enables programmers to define higher-level operations (e.g.

CUBEROOT would be defined and used in instructions in the form

a:= CUBEROOT(b),

where CUBEROOT returns the cube root of 'b'). *See* SUBROUTINE.

functional dependence. In databases, an indication of the interrelationships of attributes in a relation. Attribute A of a relation R is functionally dependent on attribute B of relation R if, at every instant of time, each value of B has no more than one value of A associated with it. Suppose a relation contains employee name, employee number and department, if every employee has a unique number then the employee name is functionally dependent upon the employee number. Note that the employee number is not functionally dependent upon the employee name since two employees may have identical names. *See* ATTRIBUTE, FULLY FUNCTIONAL DEPENDENT, NORMAL FORMS, RELATION.

functional diagram. A diagram that represents the working relationships between the parts of a system.

functional partitioning. In programming and systems analysis, a method of program or system design in which the elements of each module should only be concerned with the achievement of a single goal. *See* MODULE.

functional unit. In a computer system, a piece of hardware and/or software capable of accomplishing a specified objective. *See* HARDWARE, SOFTWARE.

function codes. In printing, codes that control the operation of the typesetter as distinct from those that produce the characters.

function key. In peripherals, a key (e.g. ENTER or SEND) that causes the transmission of a signal not associated with a printable or displayable character. Detection of the signal usually causes the system to perform some predefined function for the operator. *Compare* PROGRAM FUNCTION KEY.

fundamental frequency. In a complex, repetitive waveform, the repetition frequency of one cycle of this waveform. *See* FOURIER SERIES.

fuzzy logic. In mathematics, a form of logic in which the variables may assume a continuum of values between 1 and 0. It is used in expert systems when logical rules relate the input data and assertions to goals and subgoals, but the data is often expressed in terms of likelihood rather than certainty. *See* ASSERTION, EXPERT SYSTEMS, FUZZY SET, RULE.

fuzzy-sector technique. *Synonymous with* WEAK BITS.

fuzzy set. In mathematics, a set in which membership can be expressed as a continuum of values between 0 and 1. A value of 1 corresponds to definite membership, a value of 0 corresponds to definite non-membership. The concept of fuzzy sets has applications in information retrieval where it may not be possible to give a definite yes/no answer on the relevance of a document to a given area of search. *See* FUZZY LOGIC, SET.

G

G. *See* GIGA.

GaAs. *See* GALLIUM ARSENIDE.

gain. (1) In electronics, the degree to which the amplitude of a signal is increased when it passes through an amplifier, repeater or antenna. (2) In electronics, the ratio of output power from an amplifier system to the input power. Gain is normally measured in decibels. *See* AMPLIFICATION, DECIBEL.

galactic. In databases, pertaining to data that is extensive and accessible from many places and by many applications.

galactic noise. In communications, noise originating in outer space. *Compare* HELIOS NOISE. *See* NOISE SKY NOISE.

Galaxy. In communications, a US series of geostationary communications satellites. *See* GEOSTATIONARY SATELLITE.

galley proof. In printing, a rough proof of composed text, normally in a column produced before the text is made up into a page. *Compare* PAGE PROOF. *See* PROOF. *Synonymous with* GALLEY SLIP.

galley slip. *Synonymous with* GALLEY PROOF.

gallium arsenide. (GaAs) In microelectronics, a material used for microchips that can provide high-speed performance and low-power consumption, as well as an improved radiation tolerance and operating temperature range. *See* CHIP.

game theory. In mathematics, a method of analyzing situations in which competitive participants are each seeking to make decisions to maximize their own gains at the expense of the other participants. *See* ALPHA BETA TECHNIQUE, MINIMAX.

gamma. (1) In photography, a measure of the extent of development, and hence the contrast characteristics of a film. (2) In television, the relationship between the logarithm of the reproduced signal luminance on the screen to the logarithm of the original scene luminance. For the reproduction of a visual scene, it is important that variations in light and shade are reproduced with similar variations in luminance. *See* CONTRAST, LUMINANCE.

gamut. In computer graphics, the range of colours that can be displayed on a given monitor. *See* MONITOR.

gap. (1) In memory systems, the space between two records or blocks on a tape or disk. A gap is usually set to a predetermined value, such as all zeros. It allows blocks to be rewritten in a slightly expanded or reduced format due to speed variations of the driving mechanism. *See* INTERBLOCK GAP, MAGNETIC DISK, MAGNETIC TAPE. (2) In memory systems, the space between the read or write head and the recording media (i.e. tape or disk). *See* AIR GAP, GAP LOSS.

gap loss. In memory systems, the loss of signal from a magnetic disk reading head when it is not directly in line with the information that has been recorded. *See* GAP.

garbage. (1) In television and video, interference of audio and/or video signals on adjacent frequency bands. (2) In computing, data and programs in store that are no longer required. *See* GARBAGE COLLECTION. (3) In communications, radio frequency spillover interference onto adjacent frequency bands.

garbage collection. (1) In computing, an expression for cleaning dead records from a file. (2) In computing, the removal of items marked deleted from main memory to provide space for new programs or data. *See* FILE, MAIN MEMORY.

garbage in garbage out. (GIGO) In computing, an adage reflecting the fact that the quality of the output of a computer is dependent on the quality of the input.

gas plasma displays. *See* PLASMA PANEL.

gate. (1) In photography, the aperture in a camera or projector in which the frame is exposed or projected. (2) In electronics, the input terminal of a field effect transistor. *See* FIELD EFFECT TRANSISTOR. (3) In electronics, a generic term for a circuit element that can be turned on or off in response to one or more control signals.

gate array. *See* UNCOMMITTED GATE ARRAY.

gate fold. In printing, an oversize page where both sides fold into the gutter in overlapping layers. It is used to accommodate maps in books. (Desktop). *See* GUTTER.

gateway. In data communications, equipment used to interface networks so that a terminal can communicate with a terminal or computer on another network. *Compare* BRIDGE. *Synonymous with* COMMUNICATION SERVER.

gateway software. In online information retrieval, dedicated communications software that acts as an interface between end users and online databases. The software typically offers automatic dialing and logon, offline search formulation, downloading and may also allow text or data processing. *Compare* INTERMEDIARY SYSTEM. *See* AUTOMATIC LOGON, DOWNLOAD, TEXT PROCESSING.

gathering. In printing, the operation of inserting the printed pages, sections or signatures of a book in the correct order for binding. *See* SECTION, SIGNATURE.

gaussian distribution. In mathematics, a probability distribution derived by Gauss for the distribution of errors in experimental measurement. It is used in communications

to determine the probability that a signal carrying information will exceed a random noise voltage on the channel. *Compare* POISSON DISTRIBUTION, UNIFORM DISTRIBUTION.

GEAC. In library science, a Canadian company offering automated systems to libraries.

general-purpose. Pertaining to a system that can be applied to a wide variety of tasks without essential modification. *Compare* SPECIAL-PURPOSE. *See* GENERAL-PURPOSE INTERFACE BUS, GENERAL-PURPOSE TERMINAL.

general-purpose interface bus. (GPIB) In computing, a bus widely used to facilitate the connection between a computer and a wide range of peripheral devices or instruments. *See* BUS.

general-purpose terminal. (GPT) In peripherals, a terminal that may be employed for a variety of functions (e.g. database interrogation, online program development, data entry). *See* DATABASE, TERMINAL.

generation. (1) In computing, a measure of the remoteness of a file from the original file. *See* FATHER FILE. (2) In computing, pertaining to the technology used for the fabrication the components of a computer. *See* FIFTH-GENERATION COMPUTER, FIRST-GENERATION COMPUTER, FOURTH-GENERATION COMPUTER, SECOND-GENERATION COMPUTER, THIRD-GENERATION COMPUTER. (3) In programming, pertaining to the class of facilities offered in programming languages. *See* FIRST-GENERATION LANGUAGE, FOURTH-GENERATION LANGUAGE, SECOND-GENERATION LANGUAGE, THIRD-GENERATION LANGUAGE. (4) In printing and micrographics, a measure of the remoteness of the copy from the original matter, the first copy being the first generation.

generator. In programming, a program that creates other programs that carry out specific tasks (e.g. a report program generator). *See* REPORT PROGRAM GENERATOR.

generic coding. In printing, codes incorporated within the text of a machine-readable document so that the text may be suitably handled in a variety of situations (e.g. printed in a required format, input to a database, etc.). Standardization of such codes is required when the documents are to be handled by a variety of users. *See* STANDARD GENERALIZED MARK-UP LANGUAGE.

generic mark-up. *See* GENERIC CODING.

genlock. In television, a device for synchronizing video signals generated from different sources.

Geoarchive. In online information retrieval, a database supplied by Geosystems and dealing with earth sciences.

geometric distortion. (1) In television, a defect in the displayed picture in which the two-dimensional linearity is distorted. (2) In recording, video tape velocity and time base changes which produce a distorted image on playback. *See* TIME BASE CORRECTOR.

Georef. In online information retrieval, a database supplied by American Geological Institute and dealing with earth sciences.

geostationary orbit. In communications, a circular orbit of 42 242-kilometre radius that lies in the plane of the equator. A satellite in this orbit appear to remain stationary to an observer on the ground. *Compare* GEOSYNCHRONOUS ORBIT. *See* GEOSTATIONARY SATELLITE.

geostationary satellite. In communications, a satellite that appears stationary to observers on the earth's surface. These satellites have to be located at a height of about 35 870 kilometres (22 291 miles) above the equator, the radius of their orbit is 42 242 kilometres. At this height the combined effect of the satellite's momentum and the earth's gravitational pull keep the craft in the desired circular orbit with respect to the earth's centre. A satellite in such an orbit offers the following advantages:

(a)   It remains almost stationary to the earth antennae, so the cost of computer controlled tracking of the satellite is avoided. A fixed antenna is sufficient.
(b)   There is no necessity to switch from one satellite to another as one disappears over the horizon.

(c)   There are no breaks in transmission.
(d)   Because of its considerable distance from the earth, the satellite is in line of sight from 42.4 per cent of the earth's surface. A large number of ground stations may thus intercommunicate.
(e)   There is almost no Doppler shift. This is the case of satellites in ordinary elliptical orbits, and more complicated receiving equipment is required, especially when a large number of ground stations intercommunicate.

The disadvantages of geostationary satellites are:

(f)   The polar regions are not covered.
(g)   Because of the distance of the satellite from the earth, the received signal power is weak and the signal propagation delay is 270 milliseconds from ground station to satellite.

See COMMUNICATIONS SATELLITE SYSTEM, DISH ANTENNA, DOPPLER SHIFT, EUTELSAT, GEOSTATIONARY ORBIT, GEOSYNCHRONOUS ORBIT, GROUND STATION, INTELSAT, INTERSPUTNIK, TELEVISION RECEIVE-ONLY.

geosynchronous orbit. In communications, a circular orbit of 42 242 kilometres radius that does not lie in the equatorial plane. A satellite in this orbit will have the same period of rotation as the earth, but the inclination of the orbit, to the equatorial plane, means that to an observer on earth the position of the satellite changes with time. *Compare* GEOSTATIONARY ORBIT. *See* GEOSTATIONARY SATELLITE.

ghost. (1) In filming, an unanticipated disturbance of an image arising from the original illumination of the subject; image transfer in duplication or in projection. (2) In television, a secondary picture tube image, displaced to the right of the main image and generally caused by a reflected signal arriving at the antenna. Sometimes ghosting can be caused in cable systems where there is a long mismatched feeder cable between the antenna and the television receiver. *See* ANAPROP, IMPEDANCE MATCHING.

GHz. *See* GIGAHERTZ.

GIDEP. US Government Industry Data Exchange Program.

giga. One thousand million (i.e. 10^9).

gigabyte. In memory systems, 2^{30} bytes (i.e. 1 073 741 824 bytes). *See* MEGABYTE.

gigahertz. In communications, a frequency of one thousand megahertz. *See* MEGAHERTZ.

GIGO. *See* GARBAGE IN GARBAGE OUT.

GKS. *See* GRAPHICAL KERNEL SYSTEM.

glare. In optics, a visual condition caused by excessive luminance variations within the field of vision (e.g. when bright sources of light such as windows or lamps or their reflected images fall in the line of sight). *See* LUMINANCE.

glass master. In optical media, an optical master disc produced by exposing a photosensitive coating on a glass substrate to a laser beam, then developing the exposed coating and covering it with a silver coating. (Philips). *See* CD DISC MASTER, CD MASTERING, LASER.

glitch. (1) In television, random picture noise appearing as an ascending horizontal bar. (2) In electronics, a short-duration disturbance that can affect a timing or pulse waveform. (3) A fault or a failure.

global. In programming, pertaining to information that is available to more than one subroutine or program. *Compare* LOCAL.

global beam. In communications, a satellite beam pattern with a footprint that can cover that part of the earth's surface as seen from the satellite (i.e. up to 40 per cent of the earth's surface). These beams are extensively used to transmit television from one hemisphere to another. With such a large beam the received signal strength is low, and thus very large dish antennae are required. *Compare* HEMISPHERIC BEAM, SPOT BEAM, ZONE BEAM. *See* COMMUNICATIONS SATELLITE SYSTEM, DISH ANTENNA, FOOTPRINT, TELEVISION RECEIVE-ONLY.

global dissolve. In video and filming, a slow change from one picture to another. (Philips). *Compare* LOCAL DISSOLVE.

global fade. In video and filming, a fade affecting the whole of a video picture. (Philips). *Compare* LOCAL FADE. *See* FADE IN, FADE OUT.

global search and replace. *See* SEARCH AND REPLACE.

glossary function. In word processing, a facility in which commonly used phrases can be selected by invoking the glossary command and inserted into the appropriate place in the document.

glyph. In printing, a graphical symbol conveying information (e.g. horizontal arrows on a keyboard key). *See* ICON, PICTOGRAPH.

glyptal. In printing, pertaining to characters engraved onto a steel punch. *Compare* DUCTAL.

GMT. In peripherals, graphics mouse technology. *See* MOUSE.

goal. In artificial intelligence, a state attained as a result of the application of rules in an expert system. The ultimate goal, or goals, of the system is to provide the user with the desired results of the consultation (e.g. the probability that the site contains specified minerals). In general the goal will only be attained after investigation of a hierarchy of subgoals. *See* EXPERT SYSTEMS, RULE.

golden ratio. In printing, the rule devised to give proportions of height to width when laying out text and illustrations to produce the most optically pleasing result. (Desktop).

Gorizont. In communications, a series of Russian C band geostationary satellites within the Statsionar system; gorizont is Russian for horizon. *See* C BAND, GEOSTATIONARY SATELLITE, INTERSPUTNIK, MOLNIYA, RADUGA, STATSIONAR.

gothic. In printing, typefaces with no serifs and broad, even strokes. (Desktop). *See* SERIF, TYPEFACE.

Gouraud shading. In computer graphics, a method of displaying the brightness of patches of an object represented by a graphics display. The brightness at the corners of the patch is evaluated, the brightness is then interpolated along the edges of the patch, and then interpolated from edge to edge across a scan line. *Compare* FLAT SHADING. *See* INTERPOLATION. *Synonymous with* BILINEAR INTERPOLATION.

GPIB. *See* GENERAL-PURPOSE INTERFACE BUS.

GPT. *See* GENERAL-PURPOSE TERMINAL.

graceful degradation. (1) In optical media, the degradation of an interactive compact disc audio or video quality due to increasing error content. (Philips). *See* COMPACT DISC – INTERACTIVE. (2) In reliability. *See* FAIL SOFT.

graded index multimode. *See* FIBER OPTICS.

grade of service. In communications, a measure of the quality of the service in terms of the availability of circuits when calls are to be made. Grade of service is measured during the busiest hour of the day and is usually expressed as the fraction of calls likely to fail at the first attempt owing to equipment limitations. *See* CONGESTION.

grain. (1) In peripherals, the particle size of the phosphor coating in the interior surface of a cathode ray tube face. *See* CATHODE RAY TUBE, PHOSPHOR DOTS. (2) In printing, direction of the fibers in a sheet of paper.

graininess. In photography, the characteristic of a photographic image which under normal viewing conditions appears to be made up of small particles or grains. This effect is due to the grouping together, or clumping, of the individual silver grains in the film emulsion.

grammar. In programming, a method of specifying a formal language. A grammar comprises a set of rules, or productions, a set of terminal symbols, a set of non-terminal symbols and a starting symbol. The rules provide for the production of one string of symbols from another; non-terminal symbols may be converted into strings containing terminal and/or non-terminal symbols. The starting string must be the specified starting symbol for the grammar, and applicable productions may be applied successively until the resultant string contains only terminal symbols. This final string will then be a legal string in the corresponding language. *See* FORMAL LANGUAGE, STRING.

grammar-checking program. In word processing, a software package that aids operators to check for common grammatical errors in a document (e.g. 'we is' instead of 'we are'). *Compare* SPELLING CHECK PROGRAM.

grandfather file. *See* FATHER FILE.

granularity. In computer security, the extent of isolation with which a particular instance of a security service or mechanism is invoked. *See* ISOLATION.

graph. In mathematics, a diagram representing some form of relationship between two or more variables. *See* COORDINATE GRAPH.

graphic. A symbol produced by a process such as handwriting, drawing or printing.

graphical kernel system. (GKS) In computer graphics, a standard developed by the German standards organization, DIN, that defines an interface between an application program and a graphics mode. It shields the application programmer from the differences among various computers and graphics devices, thus providing the applications programmer with a single graphics language that manages the detail of the image input and output. *Compare* CORE. *See* DIN.

graphic arts-quality. In printing, pertaining to a photocomposition machine that can offer the facilities of traditional composition methods of change of type face and font, variable spacing, right-hand justification, proportional spacing for characters and variable leading between lines. *See* FACE, FONT, PHOTOTYPESETTING.

graphic display terminal. (1) In peripherals, a VDU which is capable of displaying graphical information. The screen is divided into discrete addressable elements which form the display picture. (2) In printing, a visual display that enables the phototypeset matter to be viewed as it appears on the font disk. *See* COMPUTER GRAPHICS,

PHOTOTYPESETTING, PIXEL *Synonymous with* PAGE VIEW TERMINAL.

graphic primitive. In computer graphics, one of a collection of elements (e.g. point, line, polygon, circle, polyhedron). Images of more complex objects can be developed by suitable juxtaposition and scaling of primitives; boolean operators can effectively add, or subtract, one primitive from another (e.g. removing a small cube from the corner of a large one). *See* BOOLEAN OPERATOR, NAPLPS.

graphics. (1) In filming, printed or hand-painted titles, charts, graphs, etc. (2) In computing, the ability to present data in the form of drawings, pictures, diagrams, etc.

graphics character. In videotex, one of 127 different shapes that can be generated in a character rectangle as part of a page. There are alphanumerics characters to provide text and graphics characters to provide an elementary, mosaic type of pictorial representation. There are three sets — alphanumerics, contiguous graphics and separated graphics — each of 96 display characters, some of which are common. *See* ALPHANUMERICS SET, CHARACTER RECTANGLE, CONTIGUOUS GRAPHICS, SEPARATED GRAPHICS.

graphics language. In programming, a programming language used for the processing and display of graphic data. *See* PROGRAMMING LANGUAGE.

graphics mode. In videotex, the display mode in which the display characters are those of one or other of the graphics sets, depending on whether contiguous or separated graphics are used. *Compare* ALPHANUMERIC MODE. *See* CONTIGUOUS GRAPHICS, DISPLAY CHARACTER, DISPLAY MODE, SEPARATED GRAPHICS.

graphics mouse technology. *See* MOUSE.

graphics package. In computer graphics, software packages designed for graphics applications. They require the user to interact in real time or to produce a command file, or program, which is processed by the package to produce the graphic display.

graphics set. *See* CONTIGUOUS GRAPHICS, SEPARATED GRAPHICS.

Graphics Standards Planning Committee. (GSPC) A committee formed by SIGGRAPH to generate a working document that could be used as groundwork for a computer graphics application standard. *See* SIGGRAPH.

graphics tablet. *Synonymous with* DIGITIZING TABLET.

graphic terminal. *See* GRAPHIC DISPLAY TERMINAL.

graph plotter. *See* PLOTTER.

grave. In printing, an accent above the letter in the form of a diagonal stroke downwards left to right. *Compare* ACUTE. *See* ACCENT.

gravure. *See* PHOTOGRAVURE.

Green Book. In optical media, the informal name for the interactive compact disc specification. (Philips). *Compare* RED BOOK, YELLOW BOOK. *See* COMPACT DISC – INTERACTIVE.

green disc. In optical media, an interactive compact disc. (Philips). *Compare* RED DISC, YELLOW DISC. *See* COMPACT DISC – INTERACTIVE.

grey code. In codes, a binary code in which sequential numbers are represented by binary expressions, each of which differs from the preceding expression in only one place:

DECIMAL	BINARY	GREY
0	000	000
1	001	001
2	010	011
3	011	010
4	100	110
5	101	111

grey literature. In library science, literature that is generally available (e.g. institutional reports), but which is not formally listed and priced. *See* SIGLE.

grey scale. (1) In filming and television, a range of ten discrete luminance values (1 = pure white, 10 = pure black) for evaluating the shading in a black and white television or for exposure tests. A television picture tube cannot adequately reproduce the extremes of the scale. In colour television, the grey scale test is important since at no place on the scale should colour be visible. *See* LUMINANCE. (2) In computer graphics, a range of values that may be assigned to a pixel to indicate a shade of grey between black and white. *See* PIXEL.

grid. (1) In printing, a systematic division of a page into areas to enable designers to ensure consistency. The grid acts as measuring guide and shows text, illustrations and trim sizes. (Desktop). *See* TRIM MARKS. (2) In optical character recognition, two sets of parallel lines crossing at right angles used for specifying or measuring character images.

grid gauge. In micrographics an inspection tool that is used to check the position of images on microfiche. *See* MICROFICHE.

Grosch's law. In computing, a law formulated by H. Grosch in the early 1950s, which stated that the performance of a computer rises as the square of the price. This law was approximately true at the time when large computers provided an economy of scale. Developments in large-scale integration and very large-scale integration have invalidated this law. *See* LARGE-SCALE INTEGRATION, VERY LARGE-SCALE INTEGRATION.

grotesque. *Synonymous with* SANS SERIF.

ground. In electronics, a conducting connection, whether by design or accident, by which an electric circuit or piece of equipment is connected to the earth. *Synonymous with* EARTH.

ground absorption. In communications, absorption of energy from a wave at or near the surface of the ground.

ground station. In communications, a location containing receiving and/or transmitting units and an antenna for communication with a satellite. *See* COMMUNICATIONS SATELLITE SYSTEM, DOWNLINK, UPLINK. *Synonymous with* EARTH STATION.

ground station antenna. In communications, an antenna used to receive and transmit signals to and from a commu-nications satellite. *See* COMMUNICATIONS SATELLITE SYSTEM, DISH ANTENNA, GROUND STATION.

group. (1) In communications, an assembly of 12 telephone channels forming a 48-kHz frequency band of a carrier transmission system. *See* CHANNEL. (2) In data structures, a set of related records that have the same value for a particular field in all of the records. *See* FIELD, RECORD.

Group 1 facsimile. In communications, a CCITT-defined facsimile service. It has analog transmission, no data compression and is transmitted over a public switched telephone network with a page speed of 10 minutes. *Compare* GROUP 2 FACSIMILE, GROUP 3 FACSIMILE, GROUP 4 FACSIMILE. *See* ANALOG, CCITT, DATA COMPRESSION, FACSIMILE, PUBLIC SWITCHED TELEPHONE NETWORK.

Group 2 facsimile. In communications, a CCITT-defined facsimile service. It has analog transmission, limited data compression and is transmitted over a public switched telephone network with a page speed of 3 minutes. *Compare* GROUP 1 FACSIMILE, GROUP 3 FACSIMILE, GROUP 4 FACSIMILE. *See* ANALOG, CCITT, DATA COMPRESSION, FACSIMILE, PUBLIC SWITCHED TELEPHONE NETWORK.

Group 3 facsimile. In communications, a CCITT-defined facsimile service. It has digital transmission, complex data compression and is transmitted over a public switched telephone network with a page speed of less than 1 minute. *Compare* GROUP 1 FACSIMILE, GROUP 2 FACSIMILE, GROUP 4 FACSIMILE. *See* CCITT, DATA COMPRESSION, FACSIMILE, PUBLIC SWITCHED TELEPHONE NETWORK.

Group 4 facsimile. In communications, a CCITT-defined facsimile service. It has digital transmission, complex data compression and is transmitted over a digital network (e.g. integrated services digital network) with a page speed of less than 10 seconds. This standard is subdivided into three classes with mandatory resolutions of 200 bits per inch (Classes 1 and 2) and 300 bits per inch (Class 3); optional bits per inch resolutions are 300/400 (Class 1) and 200/240/400 (Classes 2 and 3). *Compare* GROUP 1 FACSIMILE, GROUP 2 FACSIMILE, GROUP 3 FACSI-

MILE *See* CCITT, DATA COMPRESSION, FACSI-MILE, INTEGRATED SERVICES DIGITAL NETWORK.

group delay. In communications, a modulated radio frequency signal consists of a group of waves, within an overall wave envelope which may travel at slightly different speeds. The group delay is the time of propagation of the modulated wave envelope transmitted between two points. *See* MODULATION.

GSIS. US Group for the Standardization of Information Services.

gsm. In printing, grams per square metre; the unit of measurement for the weight of paper. (Desktop).

GSPC. *See* GRAPHICS STANDARDS PLANNING COMMITTEE.

G/T. In communications, the ratio of antenna gain to noise temperature; it is used to characterize ground stations. *See* ANTENNA GAIN, GROUND STATION, NOISE TEMPERATURE.

guard band. (1) In backing storage, the blank portion of a magnetic tape that separates two tracks of information, thus preventing signal interference. (2) In communications, a narrow band of unused frequencies between allocated channels which intended to minimize the possibility of mutual interference. For example, most television channels have a guard band of 0.5 MHz on each side of the channel. *Compare* GUARD TIME. *See* FREQUENCY DIVISION MULTIPLEXING, INTERFERENCE.

guarding. (1) The function of preventing the false operation of a device. (2) In prin-ting, a method of attaching a single leaf to a section of a book or periodical.

guard time. In data communications, an empty time interval used to separate time division multiple access bursts. *Compare* GUARD BAND. *See* TIME DIVISION MULTIPLE ACCESS.

guide. In recording, a device that delineates the path for tape in a tape recorder. *See* TAPE RECORDER.

guide bars. In codes, lines on a bar code that indicate the beginning and end of the bar code pattern and also separate items in the coding pattern. In universal product codes the guide bars comprise two thin black lines that are slightly longer than the code lines. *See* BAR CODE, UNIVERSAL PRODUCT CODE.

guided wave. In communications, an electromagnetic wave travelling along a waveguide. *See* ELECTROMAGNETIC RADIATION, WAVEGUIDE.

gulp. In data structures, a small group of bytes. *See* BYTE.

gun. In peripherals, that part of the cathode ray tube which provides a continuous source of electrons for the beam. In a colour tube, there are three guns, one for each of the additive primaries: red–orange, green and blue–violet. *See* CATHODE RAY TUBE.

gutter. (1) In printing, the central blank area between left and right pages. (Desktop). (2) In printing, the space between columns in a multi-column format.

H

hacker. (1) In programming, a computing enthusiast. The term is normally applied to people who take delight in experimenting with system hardware, software and communication systems. *See* CRACKER. (2) In data security, an unauthorized user who tries to gain entry to a computer network by defeating the system's access controls. *See* ACCESS CONTROL, CRASHER, PHRACKER, TELEPHONE INTRUSION. *Synonymous with* TERMINAL THIEF.

hack hack. *Synonymous with* SCANNING.

hairlines. In printing, the thinnest of the strokes in a typeface. (Desktop). *See* TYPEFACE.

halation. (1) In photography, a flare or halo effect caused by excessive light bouncing back through the emulsion of a film base. *See* EMULSION. (2) In television, a dark area on a picture tube surrounding an overloaded bright area.

half-duplex. (HD, HDX) In data communications, transmission that takes place one way at a time on a two-way circuit. *Compare* FULL-DUPLEX. *See* DUPLEX.

half-height. In memory systems, describing hard- and floppy-disk drives that are half the height of conventional microcomputer drives. *See* FLOPPY DISK, HARD DISK.

half-space. In word processing, the vertical distance advanced by a sheet of paper when moved through a distance of half a character space parallel to the typing line.

half-title. In printing, a right-hand page containing only the title, preceding the title page of the book.

halftone. (ht) (1) In printing, an illustration reproduced by breaking down the original tone into a pattern of dots of varying size. Light areas have small dots and darker areas or shadows have larger dots. (Desktop). *Compare* CONTINUOUS TONE. (2) In communications, a facsimile picture having a range of tones lying between picture black and picture white.

halftone screen. In printing, a glass plate or film placed between the original photograph and the film to be exposed. The screen carries a network of parallel lines. The number of lines to the inch controls the coarseness of the final dot formation. The screen used depends on the printing process and the paper to be used, the higher the quality the more lines can be used. (Desktop). *See* HALFTONE.

half up. In printing, artwork one and a half times the size that it will be reproduced. (Desktop). *See* ARTWORK.

halfword. In data structures, a contiguous sequence of bits, bytes or characters that occupy the space of half of a computer word and is capable of being addressed as a unit. *See* WORD.

halide. In photography, a chemical compound of halogen and silver that renders the silver light-sensitive.

halo. *See* HALATION.

Hamming code. In codes, a forward error-detecting code capable of detecting and correcting single-bit errors and detecting, but not correcting most multiple-bit errors. *See* FORWARD ERROR CORRECTION.

Hamming distance. *Synonymous with* SIGNALLING DISTANCE.

HAMT. *See* HUMAN-AIDED MACHINE TRANS-LATION.

hand control. In peripherals, a hand-operated device for manipulating a screen display. (Philips). *See* POINTING DEVICE.

hand crafting. In microelectronics, the detailed design of a chip at the transistor, rather than cell, level to achieve optimum performance. This technique is employed for high-volume production of chips. *Compare* CELL LIBRARY. *See* FULL-CUSTOM DESIGN.

handler. In computing, a program under the control of the operating system that controls a specific peripheral, such as a disk or printer, and also handles interrupts. *See* INTERRUPT.

hand off. In communications, a procedure employed in cellular radio when a subscriber moves from one cell to another. During voice communication the signal strength of the subscriber is constantly monitored; as the signal strength falls to some specified lower limit the stations in adjacent cells are commanded to monitor the call. The call is then handed off to the station receiving the highest acceptable signal. Signalling information is sent to the subscriber's equipment, causing it to change to a frequency selected by the station taking over the call. *See* CELLULAR RADIO.

handshaking. (1) In data communications, the exchange of predetermined signals when a connection is first made across an interface, in order to confirm it is working satisfactorily and to prevent data loss. *See* INTERFACE, PROTOCOL. (2) In data security, a procedure to ensure that communication has been established between two genuine nodes in a communications network. Handshaking procedures are designed to ensure that an attacker cannot elicit information from one node by operating a fake node (i.e. masquerading). *See* MASQUERADING.

hand viewer. In micrographics, a small portable magnetizing device used for viewing microfilm with magnification ranges from 5x to 15x. *See* MICROFILM.

hanging indent. In printing, an indentation of all lines, in a block of text, beyond that of the first line.

hanging punctuation. In printing, punctuation that is allowed to fall outside the margins instead of staying within the measure of the text. (Desktop).

hangover. (1) In television, an effect due to the camera tube in which a field image persists after a scan thus contaminating the following field scan. *See* FIELD. (2) In communications, a defect in a facsimile image whereby an abrupt tonal change on the original copy is reproduced as a gradual transition at the receiving terminal. *See* SCAN.

hang up. In computing, an unwanted or unforeseen halt in a program run, due to faulty coding or hardware errors. *See* RUN.

hard. (1) In photography, pertaining to any paper that produces a high-contrast image. (2) In electronics, pertaining to materials that retain their magnetism where the magnetic field is removed. *Compare* SOFT.

hardback. In printing, a case-bound book with a separate stiff board cover. (Desktop). *Compare* SOFTBACK. *See* CASE-BOUND.

hard copy. In peripherals, output in a permanent form, usually by printing on paper, but it can include computer output to microfilm. *Compare* SOFT COPY. *See* COMPUTER OUTPUT TO MICROFILM.

hard disk. In memory systems, a direct-access storage device with a rigid magnetic disk. High packing densities and data rates demand that the disk rotates at high speed with the read/write heads of the order of 1 micrometre above the disk surface. These requirements demand exacting engineering and an ultra-clean operating environment. *Compare* FLOPPY DISK. *See* DIRECT-ACCESS STORAGE DEVICE, HEAD CRASH, PACKING DENSITY, WINCHESTER DISK DRIVE.

hard error. (1) In data communications, a error in a network such that the source of the error must be removed, or the network reconfigured, before reliable operation can be resumed. *Compare* SOFT ERROR. (2) In memory systems, an error in reading data from a magnetic disk that cannot be corrected. The loss of data is considered to be irrecoverable. *Compare* SOFT ERROR. *See* MAGNETIC DISK.

hardware. In computing, physical equipment such as a disk drive, processor or printer, as opposed to programs, procedures, rules and associated documentation (i.e. software). *Compare* FIRMWARE, SOFTWARE.

hardware compatibility. In computing, compatibility between discrete pieces of hardware which may differ in function, type or manufacture (e.g plug-in modules or peripheral devices exchangeable from one computer to another). (Philips). *See* PERIPHERAL, PLUG-COMPATIBLE MANUFACTURER.

hardware-dependent. In computing, pertaining to a system that is dependent on a specific hardware configuration for its operation. (Philips). *Compare* SOFTWARE-DEPENDENT.

hardware handshaking. In data communications, the passing of control characters (e.g. ACK, NAK, XON, XOFF) between two devices, such as for the purpose of controlling the flow of information between the devices. (AFR). *See* ACK, HANDSHAKING, XON/XOFF PROTOCOL.

hardware interrupt. In computing, an interrupt activated by a peripheral or some other external device. *Compare* SOFTWARE INTERRUPT. *See* INTERRUPT.

hardware redundancy. In reliability, the use of extra circuitry or equipment to provide a degree of fault tolerance. *See* DUAL REDUNDANCY, HYBRID REDUNDANCY, MODULAR REDUNDANCY, NMR, SELF-CHECKING CIRCUIT, STRUCTURAL REDUNDANCY, TRIPLE MODULAR REDUNDANCY.

hardware security. In computer security, computer equipment features or devices used in a data-processing system to preclude unauthorized access to data or system resources.

hardwired. In computing, the implementation of a facility using logic circuits (hardware) rather than by using software. *See* HARDWARE, LOGIC CIRCUIT.

harmful event. In computer security, an instance of a threat acting upon a system vulnerability, in which the system is adversely affected. This may include physical damage to elements of the system or may be manifested in: (a) denial of service; (b) unauthorized use of data or system resources; (c) unauthorized manipulation of data or programs for fraudulent purposes; or (d) unauthorized disclosure of information. *See* THREAT, VULNERABILITY.

harmonic. In mathematics, pertaining to an oscillation with a frequency that is a multiple of a fundamental frequency. *See* FOURIER SERIES.

harmonic distortion. In electronics, a distortion caused by the non-linear processing of an input signal. For example, in an overloaded amplifier, additional sinusoidal components in the output signal are produced, these being integral multiples of the sinusoidal components of the input. *See* DISTORTION, OVERLOAD.

harmonic generator. In man–machine interfaces, a component of a music synthesizer that adds harmonics to the fundamental frequency in order to reproduce the timbre of a musical instrument. A square wave of the fundamental frequency is passed through a series of flip flops which produce square wave outputs double the frequency of the input. These outputs are added together to produce the desired sound. *See* FLIP FLOP, FOURIER SERIES, HARMONIC.

hartley. In mathematics, a unit of information based on a scale of ten (i.e. the amount of information that can be derived from the knowledge of the occurrence of one random event out of 10 equiprobable events). *See* INFORMATION CONTENT.

Hart's rules. In printing, rules contained in a book first published in 1903 by Horace Hart for compositors and print readers in connection with abbreviation, hyphenation, punctuation and spelling.

hash total. In computing, a figure obtained by some operations upon all the items in a collection of data and used for control purposes. A recalculation of the hash total, and comparison with a previous computed value, provides a check on the loss or corruption of the data. *Compare* CHECKSUM.

hat box. *Synonymous with* SHRINK-WRAPPED LICENCE.

Hayes. In data communications, a US industry modem standard for call setup and flow control procedures. The Hayes modem commands can be initiated by a program in a personal computer (e.g. for auto dial or auto answer). Most asynchronous personal computer communication software conform to the Hayes protocols. *See* ASYNCHRONOUS, AUTOMATIC ANSWERING, AUTODIALER.

hazard. In electronics, an undesirable transient output that may occur when a circuit changes its state (e.g. a flip flop condition in which both outputs are at zero for an instant during a change in state). *Compare* RACE. *See* FLIP FLOP.

H channel. In communications, an integrated services digital network user interface with a capacity of either 384 (H0), 1536 (H11) or 1920 (H12) kilobits per second. The channel carries circuit mode or packet mode user information such as voice, data, video/image and user multiplexed information. *Compare* B CHANNEL, D CHANNEL. *See* CIRCUIT SWITCHING, INTEGRATED SERVICES DIGITAL NETWORK, MULTIPLEXING, PACKET SWITCHING.

HD. *See* HALF-DUPLEX.

HDLC. *See* HIGH-LEVEL DATA LINK CONTROL.

HDTV. In television, high-definition television. *See* ENHANCED-QUALITY TELEVISION.

HDVS. In television, high-definition video system; a proposed new television standard with 1125 lines and a wide television screen. It requires a higher bandwidth signal, equivalent to about four current channels, and it may therefore be limited to satellite or cable systems. *See* BANDWIDTH, MAC.

HDX. *See* HALF-DUPLEX.

head. (1) In printing, the margin at the top of the page. (Desktop). (2) In peripherals, a specially designed electromagnetic trans-

ducer which can read, record or erase data on a magnetic disk, tape, cartridge or cassette. *See* CASSETTE, MAGNETIC DISK, MAGNETIC TAPE, MAGNETIC HEAD, TRANSDUCER. (3) In data structures, a special data item that points to the beginning of a list. *See* LIST. (4) In filming, the beginning of a reel of tape or film.

head alignment. In peripherals, the electrical adjustment of a magnetic tape head for optimum performance characteristics. *See* MAGNETIC HEAD.

head crash. In peripherals, a failure in a disk drive in which the head touches the rapidly rotating surface of a hard disk resulting in physical damage and data corruption. *See* HARD DISK, HEAD.

head demagnetizer. In video recording, a device that provides an alternating magnetic field used during routine maintenance to remove any residual magnetism from recording or playback heads. *See* RESIDUAL MAGNETISM.

head drum. In recording, the component of a video recorder holding the rotating heads. *See* HEAD, HEAD ROTOR, VIDEO TAPE RECORDING.

head end. In television, equipment that interfaces the antenna output with the cable network. It performs the function of pre-amplification, a combination of channels and change of frequency levels. *See* CABLE TELEVISION.

header. (1) In data communications, the first part of a message or packet that contains information essential for handling the packet or message, but which is not part of the text of the message (e.g. routing, destination information). *See* PACKET SWITCHING. (2) In data structures, coded information that gives details of a collection of data (e.g. length), but which is not part of the data itself. *See* HEADER LABEL. (3) In printing, information placed at the top of a page, usually for the purposes of identification. *Compare* FOOTER.

header field. In optical media, that part of an interactive or read-only memory compact disc data sector. It contains the absolute sector address and mode byte. (Philips). *See* COMPACT DISC – INTERACTIVE, COMPACT DISC – READ-ONLY MEMORY, MODE 1, MODE 2, SECTOR.

header label. In data structures, a label that precedes data records of a file and contains descriptive information about the file (e.g. file name, reel number, retention period, etc.). *See* FILE, HEADER.

heading. In library science, the word, name or phrase at the beginning of an entry to indicate some special aspect of the document (e.g. authorship, subject content, title). *See* ENTRY.

head level. In printing, the character size and typeface employed for words at the start of a chapter or section in a chapter.

headlife. In video, the average life of a recording head between adjustment overhauls.

head of form. (HOF) In printing, the first line where data can be entered on a form. In continuous stationery it is the first printing line, typically the fourth line below the fold. *See* CONTINUOUS STATIONERY, FORM.

head rotor. In recording, a rotating drum holding one or more recording heads of a video recorder. *See* HEAD, HEAD DRUM, VIDEO TAPE RECORDING.

head slot. In memory systems, an opening in the protective envelope of a floppy disk to allow the read/write head to make contact with the disk. *See* HEAD. *Synonymous with* READ/WRITE SLOT.

head wheel. In recording, the rotating wheel holding the read/write heads of a tape record/playback assembly.

heap. In memory systems, an area of storage used for the allocation of data structures; unlike the stack there are no restrictions on modes of access to the stored data. *Compare* STACK.

heat fixing. In printing, the use of heat to retain an image on the copy material.

Heaviside layer. In communications, the original name for the E region in the

ionosphere; named after the British physicist who discovered it in 1902. *See* E REGION, IONOSPHERE.

helical scan. (1) In recording, a format in which the video heads and and tape meet at an angle to produce a long, diagonal series of tracks, each diagonal stripe containing the full information for one field of video picture. It is so called because of the helical path the tape describes between supply and take-up reels. It offers a still picture, but is more susceptible than quadruplex to tape stretch and slippage. *Compare* QUADRUPLEX, TRANSVERSE SCAN. *See* FIELD, FREEZE FRAME. (2) In recording, a technique used in digital audio tape recorders to produce a high data transfer rate with acceptable linear tape speeds and tape usage. It is similar in operation to that used on video tape recorders. *See* DIGITAL AUDIO TAPE, VIDEO TAPE RECORDING.

helios noise. In communications, interference to satellite communications caused by the sun when an orbiting satellite passes between it and a tracking ground station. *Compare* GALACTIC NOISE. *See* COMMUNICATIONS SATELLITE SYSTEM, GROUND STATION, SUN OUTAGE.

hello screen. In computing, the first screen display produced when an application package is executed. *See* APPLICATION PROGRAM, LOGO SCREEN.

help. In programming, a facility provided by some software packages that enables a user to obtain information on certain aspects of the package during operation. In some packages the help facility is invoked by a program function key, and its contents depend upon the stage of the package from which it is called. *See* SOFTWARE PACKAGE.

Helvetica. In printing, a traditional sans serif typeface, commonly used for children's books for its clarity and readability. *Compare* AVANTE-GARDE, BOOKMAN, COURIER, HELVETICA NARROW, NEW CENTURY SCHOOLBOOK, OLDSTYLE, PALATINO, SYMBOL, TIMES ROMAN, ZAPF CHANCERY, ZAPF DINGBATS. *See* SANS SERIF, TYPEFACE.

Helvetica Narrow. In printing, a typeface that is a condensed version of Helvetica.

Compare Avante-Garde, Bookman, Courier, Helvetica, New Century Schoolbook, Oldstyle, Palatino, Symbol, Times Roman, Zapf Chancery, Zapf Dingbats. *See* typeface.

hemispheric beam. In communications, a satellite beam pattern with a footprint that can cover up to 20 per cent of the earth's surface. It is commonly used to provide television coverage to rural areas. *Compare* global beam, spot beam, zone beam. *See* communications satellite system, footprint.

Hershey symbols. In computer graphics, a complete set of fonts available for most computer systems. *See* font.

hertz. (Hz) The unit of frequency; one cycle per second.

heterogeneous computer network. In data communications, a network of dissimilar host computers, such as those produced by different manufacturers. *Compare* homogeneous computer network. *See* host computer.

heterogeneous multiplex. In data communications, a multiplex structure in which the information-bearing channels are not transmitting at the same data-signalling rate. *Compare* homogeneous multiplex. *See* data-signalling rate.

heuristic. In mathematics, a trial and error approach involving successive evaluations at each step made in the process of reaching the final result. In contrast, an algorithm represents a consistent approach in arriving at an optimal result. *Compare* algorithm.

heuristic searching. In library science, a search for information, or a document, by the user in which the search may be modified as each bit of information or document retrieved influences the user's view of it.

hex. *See* hexadecimal.

hexadecimal. In mathematics, a numbering system with a radix of 16. This system is used because a byte, comprising eight bits, can be conveniently expressed as two hexadecimal digits. Digits between decimal 10 and 15 are represented by the letters A to F, respectively (e.g. the decimal number 26 can be represented as hexadecimal 1A). *Compare* duodecimal, octal. *See* byte, radix.

Hex-Intel format. In data structures, a standard format for storing binary information on magnetic tape or disk. *See* binary, magnetic disk, magnetic tape.

hex pad. In peripherals, a keypad designed for hexadecimal inputs (i.e. it has sixteen keys labelled 0–9 and A–F). *See* hexadecimal, keypad.

HF. *See* high frequency.

hidden line. In computer graphics, data describing objects is stored in the form of coordinates or as a set of equations describing curves or surfaces. When this data is used to compute the object display each point is seen irrespective of its position in space. Hidden line algorithms are thus required to remove those lines that are normally masked by intervening faces and are thus invisible to the viewer. *Compare* hidden surface.

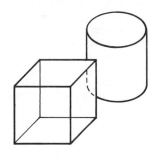

hidden line

hidden object. *See* persistent object.

hidden sections. In computer security, menu options or entire sub-menus not visible or accessible to a user due to lack of adequate authorization. *See* menu.

hidden surface. In computer graphics, the removal of hidden surfaces is similar to that of the removal of hidden lines, but is normally associated with frame stores capable of holding details of coloured surfaces. *Compare* FRAME STORE, HIDDEN LINE.

hierarchical classification. In library science, a classification that splits items into initial sets and then successively splits those sets into even finer ones. *See* CLASSIFICATION, DEWEY DECIMAL CLASSIFICATION.

hierarchical computer network. In computer networks, a network in which operations relating to control and processing are performed at several levels by computers specially suited for the tasks they have to execute.

hierarchical database. A database that allows records to be related to one another on a one to n mapping (e.g. an employee's record may point to a number of dependent's records). The records are thus interrelated by a tree structure. *Compare* NETWORK DATABASE, RELATIONAL DATABASE. *See* TREE DATABASE, TREE STRUCTURE.

hierarchical directory. *Synonymous with* TREE-STRUCTURED DIRECTORY.

hierarchical document design. A procedure for producing complex documentation (e.g. for a new technological product) in which the document is distributed among a team of contributors, each viewing it simultaneously as a complete document with all the section numbering, referencing and other structures appropriate to each level. The referencing of the document allows for modifications to be automatically fed to all appropriate sections, for example, if a diagram is changed in the design database then its inclusion by reference allows each document using it to be automatically updated. *See* TEAM DOCUMENTATION.

hierarchy. In databases, a method of organizing data into ranks, each rank having a higher precedence than those below it. *See* HIERARCHICAL DATABASE.

hieroglyph. In printing, a picture standing for a word or concept or sound. Derived from the Greek for sacred writing, it is used to describe the mode of writing used by the ancient Egyptians. *Compare* ALPHABET. *See* HIRAGANA.

hi-fi. In recording, pertaining to high-quality audio reproduction from radio, disc, tape or microphone.

hi-fi quality. In optical media, a second level sound quality of the interactive compact disc. The bandwidth of 17 000 Hz is obtained using eight-bit adaptive delta pulse code modulation at a sampling frequency of 37.8 kHz, and the sound quality is comparable to LP record sound quality. (Philips). *Compare* COMPACT DISC – DIGITAL AUDIO, QUALITY, MID-FI QUALITY, SPEECH QUALITY, SYNTHESIZED SPEECH QUALITY. *See* AUDIO QUALITY LEVEL, BANDWIDTH, COMPACT DISC – INTERACTIVE, SAMPLING.

high-definition television. *See* ENHANCED-QUALITY TELEVISION.

high-definition video system. *See* HDVS.

high frequency. In communications, the range of frequencies from 3 to 30 MHz. *See* MHz.

high-level data link control. (HDLC) In data communications, a standard data communications interface defined by the International Standards Organization. It has a data format that is virtually identical with synchronous data link control. *See* PROTOCOL, SYNCHRONOUS DATA LINK CONTROL.

high-level data link control station. In data communications, a process located at one end of a communications link that sends and receives high-level data link control (HDLC) frames in accordance with the HDLC procedures. *See* FRAME, HIGH-LEVEL DATA LINK CONTROL.

high-level language. In programming, a language that enables programmers to specify a set of instructions in a form geared to the nature of the problem rather than the detailed operation of the computer. As a comparison, consider the instruction 'take the next flight to New York' with the mass of detailed instructions implied by this action: 'stand up, turn left, walk three paces, open door, …'. High-level languages can be designed for specific application areas and provide facilities geared to the requirements of that area.

High-level languages may be classified

into two broad groups: procedural and non-procedural. In the case of procedural languages the programmer is still concerned with the manner in which the task is to be performed, but is relieved from the problem of specifying the very detailed computer steps. With non-procedural languages the programmer need, effectively, only specify the nature of the desired result (e.g. 'who is the grandfather of Jack?').

Fourth-generation languages provide a simple user friendly syntax and reduce the effort of specifying detailed, often repetitive information, common in languages such as COBOL, and hence in providing end users with more intimate contact with organizations' computer systems.

The programs must adhere to well-defined rules of syntax. There are three programs involved when a high-level language is used: the source program, the translator and the object program. The programmer writes a source program. A specially designed computer program, the translator, converts and checks the syntax of the source program and either reports errors or, if error-free, produces the corresponding set of machine code instructions, or instructions in some lower-level language (i.e. the object program) which is then executed. In the case of a class of translators known as interpreters the process of compilation and execution is effectively combined. *Compare* ASSEMBLY LANGUAGE, LOW-LEVEL LANGUAGE. *See* COBOL, COMPILER, FOURTH-GENERATION LANGUAGE, INTERPRETER, NON-PROCEDURAL LANGUAGE, OBJECT PROGRAM, PROCEDURAL LANGUAGE, PROGRAMMING, SOURCE PROGRAM, SYNTAX, TRANSLATOR.

high-level protocol. In data communications, a protocol that enables users to carry out functions at a higher level than merely transporting streams or blocks of data. *Compare* LOW-LEVEL PROTOCOL. *See* PROTOCOL.

highlight. (1) In printing, the lightest area in a photograph or illustration. (Desktop). (2) In word processing, a facility that intensifies the characters on the display screen. It is usually used in such text operations as deleting, copying and moving words or characters to make the operator fully aware of which portions of the text will be affected when the command is executed. *See* COMMAND, DISPLAY, REVERSE VIDEO.

high-pass filter. In electronics, a filter passing signals having frequencies above a predetermined cutoff frequency. *Compare* LOW-PASS FILTER. *See* CUTOFF FREQUENCY.

high reduction. In micrographics, a reduction in the range 31x to 60x. *Compare* LOW REDUCTION, MEDIUM REDUCTION, VERY HIGH REDUCTION, ULTRA HIGH REDUCTION. *See* REDUCTION.

high resolution. (hi res) In peripherals, the degree of detailed visual definition (800 x 600 pixels) that gives readable 80-column text display. The monitors used with professional computers normally have high resolution, as will the new generation enhanced-quality television. (Philips). *See* ENHANCED-QUALITY TELEVISION, PIXEL. (2) In optical media, an interactive compact disc display resolution mode of 768 pixels (horizontal) by 560 pixels (vertical). (Philips). *Compare* LOW RESOLUTION, NORMAL RESOLUTION. *See* COMPACT DISC – DIGITAL AUDIO, DIGITAL VIDEO, PIXEL. (3) In computer graphics, pertaining to graphics displays capable of presenting high-quality graphics. Current high-quality systems can have resolutions in excess of several thousand lines. *Compare* LOW RESOLUTION.

high-resolution   television. *Synonymous with* ENHANCED-QUALITY TELEVISION.

High Sierra group. In optical media, an ad hoc standards group set up to recommend compatible standards for read-only memory compact discs. The group includes representatives from the hardware, software and publishing industries, and was named after the hotel at Lake Tahoe where it first met in the summer in 1985. (Philips). *See* COMPACT DISC – READ-ONLY MEMORY.

high-speed. In data communications, describing transmission speeds in excess of those normally attainable over voice-grade channels (i.e. in excess of 9600 bits per second). *See* MEDIUM SPEED, NARROWBAND.

high-speed duplication. In recording, the production of one or more tape copies from a master tape at a speed many times faster than the original recording.

high-speed multiplex link. In data communications, a high-speed link over which many signals are combined and subsequently separated at the far end of the circuit. *See* MULTIPLEXING.

high-speed scan. *Synonymous with* BROWSE.

high-speed scroll. *Synonymous with* BROWSE.

high-speed skip. In word processing, a rapid vertical advance of a form on a printer to the areas where information is to be printed. *See* FORM FEED, VERTICAL TAB. *Synonymous with* SLEW.

high-usage trunk. In communications, a voice circuit directly connecting switching centres generating high volumes of traffic to each other. Since these trunks are specially designed for such traffic, they will always be selected first in routing calls between the locations they connect. *See* SWITCHING CENTRE.

highway. *Synonymous with* BUS.

hill climbing. In mathematics, a search technique for finding an optimum value. Starting from an arbitrary point the value of the appropriate function is measured at a number of test points in the vicinity. A move is then made in the 'best' direction as indicated by the test values. The process is repeated until all the neighbouring test points indicate 'lower' function values than that of the search point.

Hiragana. In printing, a character set of symbols used in one of the two common Japanese phonetic alphabets. *See* KANJI, KATAKANA.

hi res. *See* HIGH RESOLUTION.

HIS. *See* HOME INTERACTIVE SYSTEMS.

hiss. In recording, audio frequency noise having a continuous spectrum, often audible during tape playback.

histogram. In mathematics, a representation of some type of distribution in which the frequency percentage is plotted on the

ordinate and the varying quantity on the abscissa. *See* ABSCISSA, ORDINATE.

Historical Abstracts. In online information retrieval, a database supplied by ABC–Clio Information Services and dealing with history, social sciences and humanities.

history of computing.
1647   Pascal produced a mechanical calculator working on principle of a notched wheel.
1694   Leibnitz developed mechanical calculator for multiplication and division. He considered the use of binary arithmetic in calculations.
1801   Jacquard used punched cards to control automatic looms.
1821   Babbage presented mechanical calculating machine (difference engine) to the Royal Astronomical Society.
1833–71 Babbage, assisted by Ada Lovelace, worked on design of a general-purpose computing machine (analytical engine).
1854   Boole developed an algebra for logic.
1890   Hollerith won competition for analyzing census data using punched card systems.
1930   Bush developed a differential analyzer with thermionic valves.
1935   Zuse introduced the use of binary operations in a mechanical calculator.
1936   Turing produced theoretical model for computation — the Turing machine.
1943   Colossus 1 electronic calculator using thermionic valves developed for cryptanalytic applications.
1943   Harvard MK 1 computer based upon electromagnetic relays.
1946   ENIAC, thermionic valve computer used to produce ballistic tables for guns and missiles.
1947   EDVAC — stored program control computer designed by von Neumann.
1948   Manchester University Mark 1 computer.
1948   Bell Laboratories develop the transistor.
1949   EDSAC, Cambridge — significant software developments including first operating system.

1951   Leo — early commercial computers.
1954–57 NCR 304 — first transistorized
computer.
1970   DEC PDP8 — first minicomputer.
1971   Intel — first microprocessor 8008.
1972   Unimation — first industrial robots.
1979   Japan outlined plans for fifth-
generation computer.
1983   Very large-scale integration, Alvey
Committee.

See ALVEY, BOOLEAN ALGEBRA, FIFTH-
GENERATION COMPUTER, MICROCOMPUTER,
MICROPROCESSOR, OPERATING SYSTEM, TRAN-
SISTOR, TURING MACHINE, VON NEUMANN.

hit.   (1) In recording, a momentary interference in an audio signal. (2) In databases,
a comparison of two items of data in which
specified conditions are satisfied. (3) In data
communications, a momentary line disturbance that could result in the corruption of
characters being transmitted.

hit on the fly printer.   *Synonymous with* ON
THE FLY PRINTER.

hit on the line.   In communications, a general term used to describe short-term disturbances caused by external interferences
such as impulse noise produced by lightning
or man-made interference. *See* NOISE.

HLL.   *See* HIGH-LEVEL LANGUAGE.

HMOS.   In microelectronics, high-speed
metal oxide semiconductor; a metal oxide
semiconductor technology with a short channel between source and drain. *See* DRAIN,
METAL OXIDE SEMICONDUCTOR, SOURCE.

HOF.   *See* HEAD OF FORM.

hold.   In television, the synchronization of
a sweep time base with a pulse signal. In
some receivers, preset controls are marked
vertical hold and horizontal hold. *See* TIME
BASE.

hold graphics.   In videotex, a display mode
that removes a gap in a graphic display when
the colour is changed. The new colour code
occupies a character space, but in this mode
the screen space is occupied by a repeat of

the previous graphic character. *See*
ALPHAMOSAIC.

holding line.   In printing, an outline for
indicating the boundary of a solid or halftone image. *See* HALFTONE.

holding time.   In communications, the total
time that a circuit or device is occupied in
connection with a particular call. *Synonymous with* CALL DURATION.

hold time.   In computing, the interval of
time during which a signal on a computer
bus must be kept constant in order to transfer its value from one device to another. *See*
BUS.

hole.   In electronics, a vacancy for an electron in the atomic structure of a semiconductor. An electron in a neighbouring atom
may move into this vacancy, thus creating a
similar vacancy in its own atom. This
movement of electrons produces the effect
of a positive carrier moving in the opposite
direction of electron flow; p-type impurities
have such holes in their atomic structure and
therefore introduce carriers when they are
added to pure semiconductors. *See* ELEC-
TRON, P-TYPE MATERIAL, SEMICONDUCTOR.

hologram.   In optics, a three-dimensional
image produced through a combination of
photography and laser beams. Diffracted
laser light from a subject is used to capture a
two-dimensional interference pattern in
photographic film. These interference patterns, when illuminated by light from a
similar laser, produce a three-dimensional
image of the original subject. *See* INTERFER-
ENCE PATTERN, LASER.

holograph.   In publishing, a manuscript
written entirely in the author's own hand.

holographic memory.   In memory systems,
a system in which an image (a hologram) of a
page of binary data is stored as a two-
dimensional interference pattern. This
memory is illuminated by a laser beam, and
the image is formed on the surface of an
array of photocells. The system is experimental, but it is claimed that extremely high
bit-packing densities can be achieved. *See*

INTERFERENCE PATTERN, LASER, PACKING DENSITY, PHOTOCELL.

holography. *See* HOLOGRAM.

home banking. In applications, the use of a domestic communications terminal, usually viewdata, to conduct transactions on the user's bank account. *Compare* SELF-BANKING.

homebus. In communications, a small area network for use in domestic environments for transmission of video, audio data and control information around the house. The transmission medium may be coaxial or optical cable, or a combination of cables and wiring, depending on the particular transmission requirement. (Philips).

home computer. *Synonymous with* MICRO-COMPUTER.

home interactive systems. (HIS) In applications, domestic systems involving interactivity (e.g. a video game), as opposed to passive devices such as television sets which do not require continuing action on the part of the viewer. (Philips).

home monitoring. In applications, a system or equipment to monitor the status of various areas within the home and report it to some central location. Applications include intruder alarm systems, fire or smoke detection, garage door control and room temperature control. (Philips).

homogeneous computer network. In data communications, a network of similar host computers, such as those of one model of one manufacturer. *Compare* HETEROGENEOUS COMPUTER NETWORK.

homogeneous multiplex. In data communications, a multiplex structure in which the information-bearing channels are transmitting at the same data-signalling rate. *Compare* HETEROGENEOUS MULTIPLEX. *See* DATA-SIGNALLING RATE.

homograph. One of several words having the same spelling, but different meaning. *Compare* SYNONYM. *Synonymous with* HOMONYM.

homonym. *Synonymous with* HOMOGRAPH.

hooking. In recording, distortion of a television picture caused by errors in the head-timing coordination of a video tape recorder. *See* VIDEO TAPE RECORDING.

hop. In communications, a transmission path from one point on the earth to another via the ionosphere without any intermediate reflections from the earth's surface. *See* IONOSPHERE.

horizontal. In television, a signal that produces a scanning line of 0.4 nanosecond's duration across a television tube. *See* SCANNING LINE.

horizontal blanking. In peripherals, the blanking out of the retrace path area on the screen during the horizontal retrace of a raster scan on a cathode ray tube. *See* CATHODE RAY TUBE, RASTER SCAN.

horizontal justification. In printing, a technique employed to ensure that printed text just fills a line. Any spaces at the end of the line of the unjustified text are distributed as extra spaces between words. *Compare* VERTICAL JUSTIFICATION. *See* JUSTIFICATION.

horizontal line update. In peripherals and television, the modification of all, or part, of a single line in a video image. (Philips).

horizontal motion index. In peripherals, a number on a screen display indicating the horizontal position of the cursor in terms of character spaces.

horizontal parity. *See* LONGITUDINAL PARITY CHECK.

horizontal recording. *Synonymous with* LONGITUDINAL RECORDING.

horizontal resolution. In television, the ability of a camera to reproduce changes in intensity along a scan line. *Compare* VERTICAL RESOLUTION. *See* SCANNING LINE.

horizontal retrace period. In television, the time during which the horizontal line scan on a television screen returns to the beginning of the next line. (Philips). *Compare* VERTICAL RETRACE PERIOD. *See* SCANNING LINE.

horizontal scan frequency. *Synonymous with* LINE FREQUENCY.

horizontal sync pulse. In television, the pulse that follows the front porch in the composite colour video signal. It is used to synchronize the sweep circuits of the receiver with those of the camera. *See* COMPOSITE COLOUR VIDEO SIGNAL, FRONT PORCH.

horizontal wraparound. In peripherals, the continuation of cursor movement, on a visual display unit, from the last character position in a row to the first character in the next row, or vice versa. *Compare* VERTICAL WRAPAROUND.

horn. In communications, a form of directional radiator or antenna, in which a feed waveguide is flared at its end in one or more dimensions to provide a radiating aperture. *See* ANTENNA, WAVEGUIDE.

host. (1) In computing. *See* HOST COMPUTER. (2) In online information retrieval. *Synonymous with* DATABASE VENDOR.

host computer. (1) In computing, a computer that primarily provides services such as computation, database access or special programming languages over a network. *Synonymous with* CENTRAL COMPUTER, HOST. (2) A computer used to prepare programs to be run on other systems (e.g. a computer used to test programs to be run on a microcomputer). *See* CROSS-COMPILER.

host processor. In computing, a processor that controls all or part of a user application network. *See* HOST COMPUTER.

host system. In computing, a system used to prepare programs, etc. for use on another computer. *See* HOST COMPUTER.

hot frame. In filming, a deliberately overexposed frame used to provide a cue during editing.

hot key. In computing, a feature of a distributed processing emulation package that enables a user to switch automatically from a session, with the local microcomputer's operating system to a session with the host by pressing a single key. *See* COOPERATIVE PROCESSING, SESSION. *Synonymous with* SESSION HOLD.

hot mode. In communications security, a technique in which each terminal is required to generate continuously messages or dummy messages, if necessary; any lack of communication from a terminal then indicates a system failure. *See* BANKING NETWORKS, DELAY/DENIAL OF SERVICE.

hot-potato routing. In data communications, a method of routing in which a packet of data is transmitted from a node as soon as possible, even though the line chosen may not be optimal from a routing viewpoint. *See* PACKET SWITCHING.

hot spot. In filming and television, an area of too much brightness.

hot standby. In reliability, a method of hardware backup that is automatically switched into operation when a system failure is detected. *Compare* COLD STANDBY, WARM STANDBY.

hot zone. In word processing, an area of adjustable width immediately to the left of the right-hand margin. The system detects any word starting in the hot zone that will exceed its width. It may then pause to allow an operator to decide whether to hyphenate and start a new line, or to overrun the margin. Some word-processing systems are programmed to make such decisions automatically. *See* HYPHENATION. *Synonymous with* LINE END ZONE.

house corrections. In printing, errors made during composition and corrected at printer's cost.

housekeeping. In computing, supporting operations that are secondary to the main processing objectives (e.g. initialization, file creation and maintenance activities). *See* FILE, INITIALIZATION.

housekeeping information. In data communications, signals that are added to information signals, but are intended only for the receiving equipment so that it may function properly.

house style. In printing, the style of preferred spelling, punctuation, hyphenation and indentation used by a publishing house or in a particular publication to ensure consistent typesetting. (Desktop).

HR. *See* HIGH REDUCTION.

HRTV. High-resolution television. *See* ENHANCED-QUALITY TELEVISION.

Hseline. In online information retrieval, a database supplied by Health and Safety Executive, Library and Information Services (England) and dealing with safety.

ht. *See* HALFTONE.

hub polling. In data communications, a method of polling on multidrop lines that reduces the time lost in line turnaround. The controller first polls the terminal furthest from it. The addressed terminal turns the line around (i.e. arranges for the signal to be sent in the opposite direction); the line turnaround may take hundreds of milliseconds on a telephone network with echo suppressors. If the terminal has data to transmit it sends it to the controller; however, if it has no data it forwards a polling message to its nearest neighbour. If this terminal has no data it, in turn, forwards a polling message to the nearest neighbour on the controller side. In conventional polling the controller addresses each terminal directly, and each terminal must turn the line around to send a 'no data' message. *See* ECHO SUPPRESSOR, MULTIDROP CIRCUIT, POLLING.

hue. In optics, the name of a colour (e.g. red, yellow) or the quality of a colour as determined by its frequency in the spectrum. *Compare* SATURATION. *See* COLOUR.

hue control. In television, an essential control with NTSC receivers used for adjusting the hue of the picture. *See* HUE, VIDEO STANDARDS.

Huffman code. In codes, a code in which frequently occurring characters are assigned

fewer symbols than less frequently occurring characters.

hum. In electronics, undesirable low-frequency currents interfering with a desired signal and usually caused by a poorly screened alternating mains supply. *See* EMI/RF RADIATION.

human-aided machine translation. (HAMT) In applications, a machine translation system in which the computer retains the initiative, but works with a human consultant, who need not be a translator. The computer recognizes when a certain problem has arisen in the translation process and communicates the nature of the difficulty to the consultant. *Compare* MACHINE-AIDED TRANSLATION.

humanist. In printing, an example of typeface.

human-oriented language. In programming, a language that has more affinity with a human language than a machine language. *See* HIGH-LEVEL LANGUAGE, MACHINE LANGUAGE.

human window. In artificial intelligence, an explanation facility within an expert system. *See* EXPERT SYSTEMS.

hum bars. In television, broad moving or stationary horizontal picture bars on the receiver screen due to a variation in the direct-current power supply at the alternating-current power supply frequency. *See* FIELD FREQUENCY, PICTURE.

hunting. In control systems, an undesired oscillation generally of low frequency that persists after external stimuli disappear. *See* FEEDBACK.

hybrid computer. A computer system that combines the elements of both digital and analog techniques. *See* COMPUTER.

hybrid integrated circuit. In microelectronics, a type of integrated circuit in which active chips are attached to the surface of a passive (e.g. ceramic) substrate. *See* CHIP.

hybrid redundancy. In reliability, a form of modular redundancy combining the concepts of NMR and standby spare. When the voting system detects a faulty unit that unit is switched out and replaced by a standby spare. If three active and two standby spares are employed then the system will continue to function after three modules have failed. An NMR system with five modules can only tolerate a failure in two units. *See* MODULAR REDUNDANCY, NMR.

hypercube. In computing, a form of parallel-processing architecture in which processors are connected as nodes in multiple dimensions with direct-channel connections between neighbouring nodes. *See* PARALLEL PROCESSING.

hyphenation. In word processing, the practice of dividing a word into two parts if it cannot fit on the current line. Word-processing systems are designed to handle hyphenation in various ways, one of which may call for the use of an exception dictionary. *See* EXCEPTION DICTIONARY.

hyphen drop. In word processing, a software facility which ensures that a hyphenated word at the end of a line loses its hyphen if it subsequently appears elsewhere in the text and no longer requires hyphenation. *See* HYPHENATION.

hysteresis. In electronics, a closed circuit that demonstrates the relationship between magnetizing force and magnetic flux, in a magnetic substance, when the magnetizing force is taken through a complete cycle. *See* SATURATION.

Hz. *See* HERTZ.

I

I.100. In communications, a series of CCITT recommendations providing general introduction about the concepts of integrated digital services networks. *See* INTEGRATED DIGITAL SERVICES NETWORK.

I.200. In communications, a series of CCITT recommendations dealing with integrated digital services network services. The services have been broadly categorized as bearer services and teleservices. Bearer services provide the means of conveying information (i.e. speech, video, data, etc.) between users in real time and without modification to the message. Teleservices use bearer services to transfer information, but also employ higher-level functions. Such services include electronic mail, videotex, facsimile and stereo program sound. *See* ELECTRONIC MAIL, FACSIMILE, VIDEOTEX.

IA5. *See* INTERNATIONAL ALPHABET NUMBER 5.

I&A. Indexing and abstracting.

IACBDT. UNESCO International Advisory Committee on Bibliography, Documentation and Terminology.

IACDT. UNESCO International Advisory Committee for Documentation and Technology.

IADIS. Irish Association for Documentation and Information Services.

IAM. Intermediate-access memory. *Synonymous with* FAST-ACCESS MEMORY.

IARD. Information Analysis and Retrieval Division of the American Institute of Physics.

IBA. UK Independent Broadcasting Authority.

IBG. *See* INTERBLOCK GAP.

IBI. *See* INTERGOVERNMENTAL BUREAU FOR INFORMATICS.

IBM. International Business Machines.

IBM-compatible. In computing, pertaining to a personal computer, produced by a manufacturer other than IBM, that is claimed to have facilities similar to and can run software developed for the IBM PC. *See* PERSONAL COMPUTER, SOFTWARE.

IC. *See* INTEGRATED CIRCUIT.

ICAI. *See* INTELLIGENT COMPUTER-ASSISTED INSTRUCTION.

ICIC. UNESCO International Copyright Information Center.

ICIREPAT. International Cooperation in Information Retrieval among Examining Patent Offices.

ICOGRADA. *See* INTERNATIONAL COUNCIL OF GRAPHIC DESIGN ASSOCIATIONS.

icon. In computer graphics, a pictorial representation of an object in a computer graphic display. It is used in display systems for executive workstations to represent the functional component of an executive desk (e.g. documents, folders, in trays). *Compare* SPRITES. *See* MOUSE, WIMPS.

ICOT. *See* INSTITUTE FOR NEW GENERATION COMPUTER TECHNOLOGY.

IC/P. *See* INTELLIGENT COPIER/PRINTER.

ICR. (1) In peripherals. *See* INTELLIGENT CHARACTER RECOGNITION. (2) International Council for Reprography.

ICSSD. International Committee for Social Sciences Documentation and Information.

ID. *See* IDENTIFICATION CHARACTER.

IDD. In communications, international direct distance dialing. *See* DIRECT DISTANCE DIALING.

IDDS. In data communications, International Digital Data Service.

ideal format. In photography, a popular negative format (60 x 70 mm), an alternative to 35-mm format (24 x 36 mm), which is smaller and more elongated.

IDEM. In data communications, Inter-Departmental Electronic Mail; a UK governmental electronic mail service. *See* ELECTRONIC MAIL, X.400.

identification. (1) In computer security, the process that enables, generally by the use of unique machine-readable names, recognition of users or resources as identical to those previously described to an automatic data-processing system. (FIPS). *See* ACCESS. (2) In data communications, the procedure carried out by a host computer in verifying the identity of an individual line, device, subscriber, etc. requiring access. *See* HOST COMPUTER.

identification character. (ID) In data communications, a character that identifies a remote data station to the central station. *See* IDENTIFICATION.

identifier. (1) In data structures, a character or group of characters used to identify, indicate or name a body of data. (2) In programming, a name or string of characters employed to identify a variable, procedure, data structure or some other element of a program. *See* DATA STRUCTURE, PROCEDURE. (3) In online information retrieval, a word or phrase assigned to a document in addition to, or instead of, standard descriptors. *See* DESCRIPTOR.

identity authentication. In computer security, a set of manual or automated procedures which verify that users requesting access are who they claim to be.

identity operation. In mathematics, a boolean operation that results in a boolean value of 1 only if all the operands have the same boolean value. *See* BOOLEAN ALGEBRA, OPERAND.

identity token. In computer security, a smart card, a metal key or some other physical token carried by a system's user that allows user identity validation. *See* INTELLIGENT TOKEN, SMART CARD.

identity validation. In computer security, the performance of tests, such as the checking of a password, that enables an information system to recognize users or resources as identical to those previously described to the system. *See* AUTHENTICATION.

ideogram. In printing, a symbol or character conveying the idea, expression or part thereof (e.g. a Kanji character). (Philips). *See* KANJI.

idle. In communications, the state of a line or switching equipment on the line when it is not in use.

idle character. In data communications, a control character transmitted on a telecommunication line when there is no information to be transmitted. The character will not be displayed or printed by the accepting terminal.

idle time. In computing, operable time during which some or all of a computer system is not being used. *Compare* DOWN TIME.

IDMS. *See* INTEGRATED DATA MANAGEMENT SYSTEM.

IDP. UK Institute of Data Processing.

IEC. *See* INTERNATIONAL ELECTROTECHNICAL COMMISSION.

IEE. UK Institution of Electrical Engineers.

IEEE. US Institute of Electrical and Electronics Engineering.

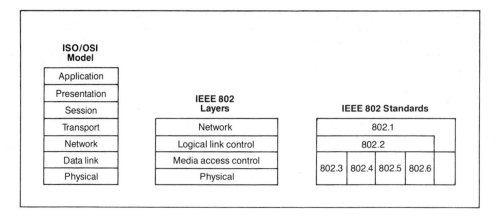

IEEE 802
Relationship between the ISO/OSI model to the IEEE 802 standards. See Open System Interconnection.

IEEE-488. In peripherals, a standard microcomputer interface for computers. *Compare* RS-232C.

IEEE-802. In data communications, a standard for local area networks dealing with the physical and data link layers. *See* DATA LINK LAYER, PHYSICAL LAYER.

IERE. UK Institution of Electronic and Radio Engineers.

IF. *See* INTERMEDIATE FREQUENCY.

IFIP. *See* INTERNATIONAL FEDERATION FOR INFORMATION PROCESSING.

IFRB. *See* INTERNATIONAL FREQUENCY REGISTRATION BOARD.

IIA. US Information Industry Association.

IIC. International Institute of Communications.

IIL. In microelectronics. *See* INTEGRATED INJECTION LOGIC.

IInfSc. (IIS) UK Institute of Information Scientists.

IIS. *See* IINFSC.

IKBS. Intelligent knowledge-based system. *See* EXPERT SYSTEMS.

ILD. In optoelectronics, injection laser diode; a semiconductor laser. *See* LASER, SEMICONDUCTOR LASER.

ILL. *See* INTERLIBRARY LOAN.

illegal character. In data structures, a character or combination of bits that does not meet some predetermined criteria (e.g. the character is not a member of some specified alphabet). *Compare* FORBIDDEN COMBINATION.

illegal operation. In computing, an action that a computer is unable to perform.

illuminance. In optics, that part of the luminous flux which is incident on a unit area of a surface (i.e. a measure of the quantity of light with which a surface is illuminated). It is measured in units of lux. *See* LUX.

image. In memory systems, an exact logical duplicate stored in a different medium.

image area. (1) In micrographics, the part of a microfilm display reserved for an image. *See* MICROFILM. (2) In word processing, the area of a display device in which characters can be displayed.

image carrier. In printing, a disk, grid, filmstrip, or magnetic tape that holds details of typefaces used by a phototypesetter. It has the same function as a set of type matrices in machine composition. *See* MACHINE COMPOSITION, MATRIX, PHOTOTYPESETTING.

image communications. *See* FACSIMILE.

image converter. In television, a camera tube that produces a visible image of an object illuminated by infrared or ultraviolet light.

image degradation. In photography, a loss of picture detail and good contrast as a result of successive duplication.

image distortion. In optics, a fault in a lens that produces an unwanted modification in the appearance of an object. *See* ABERRATION.

image duplication. In filming and video, a technique in which identical images are displayed on separate parts of the screen.

image enhancer. In filming and video, a signal-processing device that produces a sharper image by increasing luminance detail. *Compare* IMAGE INTENSIFIER. *See* CRISPENING, LUMINANCE.

image following. In computer graphics, a data compression technique for images in which the coordinates of non-white pixels are stored. *Compare* RUN LENGTH CODING, VECTOR GENERATION. *See* PIXEL.

image intensifier. In photography, an electronic device attached between a lens and the camera to increase the intensity of low light signals. *Compare* IMAGE ENHANCER.

image lag. In filming and video, an image that momentarily remains on the screen after the camera has been moved.

image master. In printing, the matrix holding the type fonts in a phototypesetter (i.e. disk, filmstrip, etc.). *See* MATRIX, PHOTOTYPESETTING.

image plane. (1) In video, pertaining to a method of creating complex images by combining individual images in real time. In digital video interactive compact disc there are a maximum of five image planes, including the cursor and backdrop planes. (Phi-

lips). *See* COMPACT DISC – INTERACTIVE, DIGITAL VIDEO. (2) In photography, the plane, perpendicular to the optical axis of a lens, at which an image is formed by the lens. This plane is normally coincident with the plane occupied by the emulsion surface of the film.

image printer. In printing, a printer that composes an image of a complete page before printing. *See* PRINTER.

image processing. In computer graphics, the use of computers to analyze, enhance or interpret images. The original image may be a drawing, photograph, television frame, output from a body scanner, etc. which is represented as a two-dimensional array of data in the computer. Each element of the array contains the attribute and grey level or colour of a pixel. Typical processing operations include contrast enhancement by computations involving comparisons of the brightness of individual pixels relative to the average brightness of their surrounding area, bright outlining of objects, correction of over- or underexposure of sections of the image, recognition and counting of predefined objects and comparisons of pictures. Application areas of image processing include satellite photographs, medical physics, robotic vision, undersea exploration, etc. *See* GREY SCALE, MACHINE VISION, PATTERN RECOGNITION, PIXEL. *Synonymous with* PICTURE PROCESSING.

image replacement. In filming, a special-effects technique in which parts of an image in a shot are removed and replaced with another image. *See* SPECIAL EFFECTS.

image retention. *See* LAG.

image sensors. In television, devices that produce an electrical signal corresponding to the intensity of incident light. An optical image is focused on a matrix of sensors which are then scanned to produce a television picture signal. *See* PICKUP TUBE.

image spread. In photography, the slight extension of the developed silver grains beyond the edges of images formed by the action of light striking the film emulsion.

image stability. In peripherals, the perceived freedom from flicker and movement of character images on the display screen of a visual display unit. The main causes of image instability are fluctuations of the voltage supply. *See* FLICKER, JITTER, VISUAL DISPLAY UNIT.

image storage space. In memory systems, the storage locations occupied by a digitized or coded image. *See* CODED IMAGE.

imaginary number. In mathematics, a real number multiplied by the square root of −1. *Compare* REAL NUMBER. *See* COMPLEX NUMBER.

imaging. In printing, the techniques used for creating and displaying a phototypesetting image (e.g. on a cathode ray tube). *See* CATHODE RAY TUBE, PHOTOTYPESETTING.

Imax. In filming, type of special-purpose cinema using a 70 foot high, 135 foot wide screen which surrounds an audience. The system uses six separate sound tracks and nine speakers.

immediate-access store. In memory systems, main storage having a very fast access. *See* MAIN MEMORY.

immediate data. In programming, data contained in a low-level language instruction rather than in a separate storage location. It is used for data that is predefined by the program and does not change in the course of the program execution. *See* LOW-LEVEL LANGUAGE.

IM&M. In applications, information movement and management; a specific market segment concerned with the effective management and movement of business information. Products that can be included in this area include:

(a) Single number routing. Allows customers to call a general number and for it to be routed directly to the right person.
(b) User friendly database access. Access to databases with minimum keystrokes and user training.
(c) Universal data networking. Permitting the information exchange between dissimilar office systems so that the format required by the user's workstation is recognized and the information is translated into that format irrespective of its source.
(d) Information manager. A facility that would screen, sort and organize information before it is presented to the user.
(e) Librarian. Performing extensive information searches over a wide range of sources and presenting the user only with usable information.
(f) Multimedia and interactive imaging. Presentation of information in the medium and format that would maximize its impact on the user.
(g) Remote access. Providing the user with remote access to the network from any suitable terminal and guaranteeing security procedures.

impact. In computer security, the damage to an organization resulting from a harmful event. It is usually measured in monetary terms per occurrence. In more complex cases it may be measured qualitatively (e.g low to high) or by comparison. *See* HARMFUL EVENT, LOSS.

impact paper. In printing, a coated paper used for multipart forms in which pressure on the top sheet causes the character to appear on the front of all sheets, thus eliminating the need for ribbon and carbon paper.

impact printer. In printing, a printer in which printing is the result of mechanical impacts. A key or ball with the desired symbol strikes a carbon or nylon ribbon which is then impacted onto the paper. *Compare* INK JET PRINTER, NON-IMPACT PRINTER. *See* DAISY WHEEL, PRINTER, THIMBLE.

impairment scale. In television, a subjective scale used in the classification of degradations caused to the screen image by imperfections in transmission links or equipment. Usually the scale has five levels ranging from imperceptible to very annoying.

impedance. In electronics, the property of a circuit that determines the magnitude and phase of the current flowing for a given applied voltage. The three basic elements of impedance are resistance, capacitance and inductance. *See* CAPACITANCE, INDUCTANCE, PHASE, RESISTANCE.

impedance matching. In electronics, the process of matching the impedance of a load or terminating device to that of the driving unit or network. Impedance matching is performed to maximize power transfer or to avoid reflection of signals back into the network. *Compare* IMPEDANCE MISMATCH. *See* IMPEDANCE.

impedance matching transformer. In recording, a small transformer used to match a low-impedance microphone output with the high-impedance input of an amplifier. *See* IMPEDANCE MATCHING.

impedance mismatch. In communications, a terminating device whose impedance does not match that of the network. *Compare* IMPEDANCE MATCHING.

imperative language. *Synonymous with* NON-PROCEDURAL LANGUAGE.

impersonation. In computer security, an attempt to gain access to a system by posing as an authorized user. (FIPS). *See* ACCESS. *Synonymous with* MASQUERADING, MIMIC-KING.

imported signal. In television, a program that is taken off the air outside the system's normal reception area and forwarded for local distribution over a cable television service. *See* CABLE TELEVISION.

import/export. Pertaining to the acquisition of information by one system and the acceptance of that information by another system.

imposition. In printing, the arrangement of pages on a printed sheet such that when the sheet is finally printed on both sides, folded and trimmed the pages will appear in the correct order. (Desktop).

impression. In printing, all copies of a book or other work printed at one time.

imprint. (1) In publishing, the publisher's name printed on the title page of a book. (2) In printing, the printer's name, usually placed at the back of the title page.

imprint position. In printing, the position where a character is to be typed on a sheet of paper.

impulse. *Synonymous with* PULSE.

impulsive noise. In communications, interference characterized by short-duration disturbances separated by quiescent intervals (e.g. the interference with radio reception caused by the ignition system on a car).

in-band signalling. In communications, a system in which control signals are transmitted inside the band normally used for voice transmission. *Compare* OUT-OF-BAND SIGNALLING. *See* BAND.

inbetweening. In computer graphics, a term derived from conventional animation to describe the actions of a human animator in producing the intermediate stages between two separate images representing two significant stages in a movement. Computer programs have been devised to perform this task; the programs are supplied with the desired starting and end coordinates plus the required percentage transformation at each stage. *See* COMPUTER ANIMATION.

in camera matte shot. In filming, a special-effects technique in which a film is exposed twice, with different masks partially covering the camera lens each time. *See* MATTE.

in camera process. In photography, a camera in which the development of the image takes place within the device itself, as in Polaroid and Kodak instant picture cameras.

incandescent. A light produced by a current passing through a filament at high temperature in a gas-filled tube or bulb.

inclined orbit. In communications, a communications satellite orbit that is neither equatorial nor polar. *Compare* EQUATORIAL ORBIT, POLAR ORBIT. *See* COMMUNICATIONS SATELLITE SYSTEM.

incoming message. In data communications, a message transmitted from a station to the computer. *See* STATION.

incoming traffic. In data communications, traffic passing through a network and having its origin in another network. *See* TRAFFIC.

incoming trunk. In communications, a trunk coming into a central office. *See* CENTRAL OFFICE, TRUNK.

incompatibility. *Compare* COMPATIBILITY.

increment. (1) In programming, a value used to increase the value in a counter or register. *Compare* DECREMENT. (2) In peripherals, to move a document, in a document reader, forward from one timing mark to the next so that a new line of characters is visible to the scan head. *See* DOCUMENT READER.

incremental plotter. In peripherals, a plotter that is able to draw straight lines and curves produced as a sequence of short straight lines. *See* PLOTTER.

indefeasible right of use. (IRU) In communications, a guarantee given to a subscriber for access to facilities on the cable network either until ownership of the network changes or they are conveyed to another subscriber.

indent. In word processing, to begin a line or lines with a blank space. In word-processing systems a margin indent is usually handled automatically.

independent telephone company. In communications, any telephone company in the USA that is not part of the Bell System. *See* RBOC, UNITED STATES INDEPENDENT TELEPHONE ASSOCIATION.

independent verification and validation. (IV&V) In computer security, the process of determining whether or not the products of a given phase of the software development cycle fulfil the requirements established during the previous phase, and the process of evaluating software at the end of the software development process to ensure compliance with software requirements.

index. (1) In data structures, a subscript of integer value that identifies the location of an item of data with respect to some other data item. (2) In databases, a list of the contents of a file, or document, with keys or references for locating the contents. (3) In library science, an organized or systematic list that specifies, indicates or designates the information, contents or topics in a document or groups of documents. Indexes can be organized under a variety of ways (e.g. authors, titles, dates, countries, institutions). *See* INDEXING LANGUAGE. (4) In printing, an alphabetical list of subjects contained within a book together with page numbers. (5) In data structures, a list of the contents of a file or of a document with keys or references for locating the contents. (6) In micrographics, a guide for locating information on microform. *See* CODE LINE.

index build. In databases, the automatic process of creating an alternate index based on results obtained from using the current access methods.

indexed file. In data structures, a file with an associated index that contains pointers to records, or groups of records, in the file. *See* FILE, INDEX, POINTER.

indexed sequential storage. In databases, a method in which records are stored in ascending order of primary keys and one index points to the highest key on a physical sector (e.g. track, cylinder, etc.). *See* CYLINDER, NON-DENSE INDEX, PRIMARY KEY, TRACK.

indexing language. In library science, a language used for naming subjects in an index. Its vocabulary introduces a measure of control of the terms used in indexing and its syntax is formalized to permit only certain constructions (e.g. aluminium heat treatment instead of heat treatment of aluminium). *See* SYNTAX.

index page. In videotex, a page that classifies a particular subject into divisions along with routing numbers to branch the user to the appropriate pages. *See* END PAGES. *Synonymous with* ROUTING PAGE.

indicative abstract. *See* ABSTRACT.

indirect electrostatic process. In printing, a process in which an image is formed on a sheet by an electrostatic technique and subsequently transferred to an unsensitized copying medium. *See* XEROGRAPHY.

indirect letterpress. *Synonymous with* LETTERSET.

indirect ray. In communications, a wave travelling along a path between transmitter and receiver that is not the shortest (e.g. at very high or ultra high frequencies reflection from an aircraft). *See* GHOST, ULTRA HIGH FREQUENCY, VERY HIGH FREQUENCY.

individual accountability. In computer security, pertaining to measures to associate positively the identity of users with their access to machines, material, data, etc. and the time, method and degree of access.

induced interference. In communications, noise induced in a circuit as a result of electromagnetic coupling with an external source. *See* NOISE.

inductance. In electronics, an electromagnetic phenomena in which a change in current induces a change in voltage in the same or adjoining circuit. Due to the very rapid current changes in digital computing circuits, even a straight connecting wire has significant inductance, and computer circuits must be designed to avoid undesired inductive coupling. *Compare* CAPACITANCE, RESISTANCE.

inductive coordination. In communications, consultation agreements between the electricity supply authorities and the communications authorities designed to prevent induced interference. *See* INDUCED INTERFERENCE.

inductrial player. *See* INTERACTIVE VIDEO DISC SYSTEMS.

inexact reasoning. In artificial intelligence, a technique for using imprecise rules in expert systems and manipulating combinations of such rules. *See* EXPERT SYSTEMS, FUZZY LOGIC. *Synonymous with* PLAUSIBLE REASONING.

inference. In data security, the deduction of confidential information relating to an individual by correlation of statistical evidence relating to a group of individuals. *See* INFERENCE CONTROL.

inference control. In database security, a control employed to prevent an enquirer from using data in a statistical database to obtain information concerning an individual. For example, if an individual were the only member of a particular ethnic group in a community, and the database contained the sums of welfare payments to all ethnic groups in the community, then an enquiry on the total payments for the whole community, coupled with a second enquiry on the payments to all ethnic groups except that of the individual in question, would reveal details of payments to that individual. *See* DATABASE SECURITY, STATISTICAL DATABASE.

inference engine. In programming, the part of an expert system which drives the system. It attempts to match the known facts about a particular problem with the rules. When one or more successful matches are found the inference engine uses an internal strategy to determine which rule should fire; the selected rule fires and the action part of the rule is used to update the known facts database, interact with the user, etc. *See* EXPERT SYSTEMS.

inferior figure. In printing, a small character, either a figure or a lower-case letter, set at the bottom of a larger character (e.g. in chemical formulae) and projecting slightly below the line. *Synonymous with* SUBSCRIPT.

infinity. (1) In optics, the position of a subject with respect to a camera lens that produces parallel light beams; in practice, a distance exceeding 30 feet. (2) In mathematics, a quantity greater than any assignable number.

infix notation. In programming, the conventional notation for mathematical expressions in which the operators are placed between the corresponding operands (e.g. $(a - b)/c$). *Compare* POSTFIX NOTATION, PREFIX NOTATION. *See* OPERAND, OPERATOR.

Infobank. In online information retrieval, a computerized information retrieval service offered by Computer Science of Australia on its network Infonet. It provides access to statistical databases containing social, economic and demographic data.

Infonet. *See* INFOBANK.

informatics. (1) The science concerned with the collection, transmission, storage, processing and display of information. (2) Translation of the French term *informatique*, which is normally considered to be equivalent to data processing.

information. (1) Knowledge that was unknown to the receiver prior to its receipt. Information can only be derived from data that is accurate, timely, relevant and unexpected. (2) The meanings assigned to data by the agreed conventions used in its representation. If the content of a message is known prior to its receipt then no new information is conveyed. The information $I(x)$ for event x of probability $p(x)$ is given by $I(x) = -\log p(x)$ (i.e. the information is highest for the least probable event). *See* INFORMATION CONTENT, INFORMATION THEORY.

information-bearer channel. In data communications, a channel capable of carrying both control and message information. It may therefore operate at a greater signalling rate than that required solely for user's data. *See* BEARER.

information broker. An individual or organization that offers information on request for a fee. *Compare* INFORMATION PROVIDER.

information carrier. In memory systems and communications, any medium (e.g. magnetic tape, compact disc, transmission line, broadcast channel, etc.) by which information is carried from its point of origin to its point of use. (Philips). *See* CARRIER, COMPACT DISC, MAGNETIC TAPE.

information centre. In computing, a service strategy as well as an organization within a data-processing department that provides a direct interface to, and supports services for, end user computing. *Compare* REFERRAL CENTRE. *See* END-USER COMPUTING, FOURTH-GENERATION LANGUAGE.

information channel. In data communications, the hardware forming the link between terminals in a data transmission system.

information content. A measure of the information conveyed by the occurrence of a symbol emitted by a source, measured in hartleys or shannons. It is defined as the negative of the logarithm of the probability that this particular symbol will be emitted. If logarithms to the base 2 are used, the unit is the shannon, if base 10 is chosen, the unit is the hartley. In practice, the probability of a particular symbol being emitted may be conditional on the symbols that preceded it. Each successive result of tossing a coin would have an information content of 1 shannon. *See* HARTLEY, INFORMATION THEORY, SHANNON.

information feedback system. *See* ECHOPLEX.

information flow analysis. In data security, the tracing of the flow of specific information types through an information system to determine whether the controls applied to the information are appropriate.

information flow control. (1) In data security, control on the flow of information within a computer system and as it leaves the computer system. (2) In data security, controls concerned with the right of dissemination of information, irrespective of what object holds the information. Whilst access controls regulate the accessing of objects, information flow control addresses what subjects might do with the information contained in them. *See* ACCESS CONTROL, LEAKAGE, OBJECT, SUBJECT.

information hiding. In programming, a principle in the design of program modules. Only the information essential to the user of the module (i.e. the interface) should be made available; details of how the module is implemented are hidden. This principle facilitates the development of large programs by independent programmers. The designer of a module is free to change its implementation details provided that the interface is not affected and the user can opt to use a different module with the same function and interface. *See* MODULA 2, MODULE.

information integrity. *Synonymous with* DATA INTEGRITY.

information interchange. In data communications, the sending and receiving of data in such a manner that the information content or meaning assigned to the data is not altered during transmission. *See* MESSAGE AUTHENTICATION.

information management. The use of information technology in the decision-making process. Managers have increasingly to take decisions in decreasing periods of time on increasing amounts of information. This pressure is in part due to the pervasive nature of today's communications and computing; the remedy lies in the more efficient use of information technology itself. *Compare* INFORMATION RESOURCES MANAGEMENT. *See* INFORMATION TECHNOLOGY.

information management system. In applications, a system designed to organize, catalogue, locate, store, retrieve and maintain information. Such systems are usually operated in real time and are accessed via visual display units. *See* CATALOGUE, REAL TIME, VISUAL DISPLAY UNIT.

information networks. In databases, the interconnection of a physically dispersed group of databases linked via telecommunications so that the total information resource may be shared by a larger population of users.

information processor. In computing, a device that stores information and instructions, receives input data or signals, processes its input and stores information according to its stored program and delivers output information or signals. The term computer is really a misnomer because the vast majority of the world's computers are not concerned with arithmetic or mathematical operations, but with the processing of textual information or communication and control signals. *See* COMMUNICATIONS COMPUTER, CONTROL COMPUTER, WORD PROCESSING.

information provider. (IP) In videotex, a name given to an organization providing information. Unlike other forms of publishing, an information provider is required to create an integrated system of cross-references to aid user access. *Compare* INFORMATION BROKER. *See* CROSS-REFERENCED PAGE. *Synonymous with* CONTENT PROVIDER.

information rate. In data communications, the number of symbols emitted by a source per second multiplied by the average information content per symbol. *See* INFORMATION CONTENT.

information redundancy. In reliability, the use of additional bits in a digital signal to enable the validity of the representation to be checked. *See* ERROR-CORRECTING CODE, ERROR-DETECTING CODE, REDUNDANCY.

information resources management. The planning, budgeting, organizing, directing, training and control associated with an organization's information. The term encompasses both information itself and the related resources, such as personnel, equipment, funds and technology. *Compare* INFORMATION MANAGEMENT.

information retrieval. (IR) In applications, the techniques for storing and searching large quantities of data and making selected data available. These techniques can include online storage, keyword in context (KWIC) indexes and database methods. *See* DATABASE, KEYWORD IN CONTEXT, ONLINE INFORMATION RETRIEVAL.

information retrieval centre. (IRC) In applications, a system designed to recover specific information for a user from a mass of data. *See* ONLINE INFORMATION RETRIEVAL.

information science. The study of the generation, communication and organization of information. *Compare* COMPUTER SCIENCE.

information security. *Synonymous with* DATA SECURITY.

information system. The organized collection, processing, transmission and dissemination of information in accordance with defined procedures, whether automated or manual. (DODD).

information system abuse. In data security, willful or negligent activity that affects the availability, confidentiality or integrity of information systems resources. It includes fraud, embezzlement, theft, malicious damage, unauthorized use, denial of service and misappropriation. (AFR). *Compare* COMPUTER ABUSE. *See* INFORMATION SECURITY.

information systems director. In applications, the expanded role of the data-processing manager to reflect the strategic importance of information systems in the corporate environment. *See* INFORMATION CENTRE.

information technology. (IT) The acquisition, processing, storage and dissemination of vocal, pictorial, textual and numerical information by a microelectronics-based combination of computing, telecommunications and video. Information technology has arisen as a separate technology by the convergence of computing, telecommunications and video techniques, computing providing the capability for processing and storing information, telecommunications providing the vehicle for communicating it and video providing high-quality display of images. This convergence has been catalyzed by the availability of complex, reliable and cost-effective microelectronic components and equipment. Global developments in electronics have also stimulated the search for common international standards, particularly in computing and telecommunications, which are paving the way for wide-scale applications of information technology.

information theory. In mathematics, the theory concerned with the information rate, channel capacity, noise and other factors affecting information transmission. Initially developed for electrical communications, it is now applied to business systems and other areas concerned with information units and the flow of information in networks. *See* INFORMATION CONTENT, SHANNON'S LAW.

information transfer channel. In data communications, the functional connection between the source and sink data terminal equipments, including the circuit and associated line plant. *See* DATA TERMINAL EQUIPMENT, SINK, SOURCE.

information vendor. *See* HOST.

informative abstract. *See* ABSTRACT.

infotainment. In applications, a combination of information and entertainment services. Videotex, employing the domestic television set as a display device, created the first consumer link between information and entertainment services, and its database may contain both information pages and interactive games or quizzes. Cable television provides the major example of this form of service, particularly with its potential for educational programs, cabletext, telebanking, teleshopping, etc. *Compare* EDUTAINMENT. *See* CABLE TELEVISION, CABLETEXT, TELEBANKING, TELESHOPPING.

infrared. In optics and communications, electromagnetic radiation wavelengths extending from visible red light to the shortest microwaves (780–100 000 nanometres).

infrared cinematography. In filming, the use of film that is sensitive to infrared light and that may either be black and white or colour.

infrared matte. In filming, a process in which a matte is produced by filming a subject before a background that reflects infrared light. The infrared light is then filtered out. *See* INFRARED, MATTE.

infrasonic frequency. In recording, a frequency below that of sound waves audible to the human ear. It is usually taken as a frequency below 15 Hz. *Compare* ULTRASONIC. *Synonymous with* SUBAUDIO FREQUENCY.

inhibit. In electronics, to prevent a process from taking place (i.e. an inhibit input prevents a logic element from carrying out its defined function).

in-house. (1) In filming, pertaining to a unit that is a part of the company for which it makes films. (2) In computing, pertaining to a system whose parts, including terminals, are situated at one location. (3) In printing, pertaining to work carried out by an organization whose main business is not printing, but which has its own printing plant. *See* IN-HOUSE SYSTEM.

in-house system. In communications, a communications system that does not use the facilities of a common carrier and is often contained within a building or complex of buildings. *See* COMMON CARRIER, LOCAL AREA NETWORK. *Synonymous with* IN-PLANT SYSTEM.

INIS. *See* INTERNATIONAL NUCLEAR INFORMATION SYSTEM.

initialization. In programming, the process of setting the values of a variable to a specified value at the start of program execution.

injection laser. In optoelectronics, a semiconductor laser used as a light source for optical fiber communication systems. *See* FIBER OPTICS, SEMICONDUCTOR LASER.

inking. (1) In computer graphics, creating a line by moving the pointer as in a line drawing on paper. (2) In filming, drawing lines for artwork for animation. (3) In printing, the process by which ink is transferred from the master to copy paper.

ink jet printer. In printing, a non-impact printer in which ink jets shoot coloured dots onto a substrate, and these dots are blended by the coating of the surface. High-quality colour images can be obtained because the ink jets do not merely overprint to produce the effect of hues they can blend the colours to achieve an effect of depth and perspective. There are basically two kinds of colour ink jet printer: deflected and non-deflected. In the formar case electrostatic charges are employed to deflect ink drops from a continuous stream onto the medium. In non-deflected printers the ink drops are produced on demand. The major difficulty in the design of ink jet printers arises from misfiring, which occurs when the jet becomes clogged, contaminated or blocked by air bubbles. *Compare* IMPACT PRINTER, LASER PRINTER. *See* BUBBLE JET, CONTINUOUS FLOW, DROP ON DEMAND, NON-IMPACT PRINTER, PRINTER.

ink squeakout. In character recognition, the displacement of ink from the centre of a printed optical recognition character (OCR). *See* OCR FONT.

ink uniformity. In character recognition, the variation in light intensity over the surface of optical character recognition (OCR) characters. *See* OCR FONT.

inlay. In television, a method of combining video signals from two sources into the one picture.

inline. In computing, a method of processing data without their previously having been edited or sorted.

inline recovery. In computing, a recovery in which the affected process is resumed from a safe point preceding the occurrence of the error. *See* RECOVERABLE ERROR.

INMARSAT. In communications, International Maritime Satellite organization; a service designed to provide telephone, telex, data, facsimile, distress and safety communications for the shipping and offshore industries. The organization operates a system of satellites and has it headquarters in London. It is a 44-member country cooperative financed by each of its signatories. *See* COMMUNICATIONS SATELLITE SYSTEM.

INPADOC. In online information retrieval, a database supplied by International Patent Documentation Center and dealing with patents.

in phase. (1) In filming, the precise coordination of the film movement through a gate with the rotation of the camera shutter. *See* GATE, PHASE. (2) In electronics and communications, pertaining to signals that have a zero phase shift relative to each other (e.g. two sinusoidal waves of the same frequency whose maximum and minimum values coincide). *Compare* OUT OF PHASE. *See* SINUSOIDAL.

in-plant system. *Synonymous with* IN-HOUSE SYSTEM.

in pro. In printing, an abbreviation for 'in proportion': used when giving instructions for reducing or enlarging originals.

input. (1) In computing, a signal transmitted from a peripheral device to the central processing unit. *Compare* OUTPUT. *See* CENTRAL PROCESSING UNIT. (2) In electronics, a signal transmitted into a circuit or unit, usually to achieve some desired output

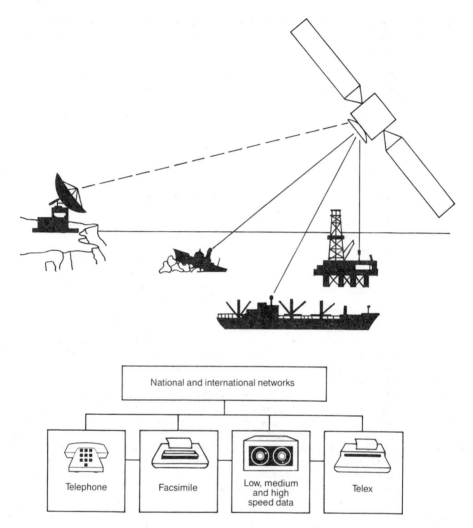

INMARSAT

or else to induce a change in the state of the circuit.

input-bound. Pertaining to a system in which the speed of performance is restricted by the rate at which input may be entered into it. *Compare* OUTPUT-BOUND. *See* INPUT UNIT.

input data validation. In programming, a control technique used to detect inaccurate or incomplete input data. This may include format checks, completeness checks, reasonableness checks and limit checks.

input device. *Synonymous with* INPUT UNIT.

input field. In peripherals, an unprotected field on the display surface of a visual display in which data can be entered, modified or erased. For example, in a transaction processing system for a retail store an operator might order stock replacements. A form would be displayed on the screen and the operator would only be permitted to input or modify data in certain parts of that form. *Compare* PROTECTED FIELD.

input/output. In computing and programming, pertaining to devices, systems, data and techniques concerned with the communication between the processor and an end user or a network.

input/output-bound. In computing, pertaining to computer applications in which there is relatively little processing compared to the amount of reading or writing to external devices. This is often the case in commercial processing, (e.g. for payroll, stock control processing). *Compare* CPU-BOUND. *See* INPUT-BOUND, OUTPUT-BOUND.

input/output channel. *See* CHANNEL.

input/output controller. In peripherals, a device that controls one or more units of peripheral equipment. Such controllers can relieve the central processor of routine peripheral control actions (e.g. raising/lowering pens on a plotter). *See* PLOTTER.

input/output device. *Synonymous with* INPUT/OUTPUT UNIT.

input/output functions. In optical media, the transfer functions read and play in an interactive compact disc system. These functions can perform the physical transfer of data from the disc. (Philips). *See* COMPACT DISC – INTERACTIVE.

input/output interface. In peripherals, an interface that can transmit an interrupt signal from a peripheral device to the central processing unit. *See* CENTRAL PROCESSING UNIT, INTERFACE, INTERRUPT.

input/output port. In peripherals, a special chip in a microcomputer that sits on the central processing unit data bus, enabling an external device to be connected to the computer for input/output operations. (Philips).

input/output statement. In programming, any instruction that results in a transfer of data between main storage and input/output units. *See* INPUT/OUTPUT UNITS, STATEMENT.

input/output unit. In peripherals, a device designed to communicate with a computer either inputting or receiving data, or both. The role of input/output units is to convert the signals of the processor to, and from, data flows which can be interpreted by people, other devices or networks. *See* COM-

PUTERIZED INSTRUMENTATION, INPUT UNIT, KEYBOARD, MODEM, OUTPUT UNIT, POINTING DEVICE, PLOTTER, PRINTER, SPEECH RECOGNIZER, SPEECH SYNTHESIZER, TERMINAL, VISUAL DISPLAY UNIT. *Synonymous with* INPUT/OUTPUT DEVICE.

input port. In data communications, an interface used for transferring information into a computer. (Philips). *See* INPUT/OPUTPUT PORT, PORT.

input primitive. In computer graphics, a basic data item from an input device. *See* DATA ITEM.

input unit. In peripherals, a device by which data can be entered into a computer system. *Compare* INPUT/OUTPUT UNIT, OUTPUT UNIT. *See* BAR CODE SCANNER, DOCUMENT READER, KEYBOARD, POINTING DEVICE, SPEECH RECOGNIZER. *Synonymous with* INPUT DEVICE.

inquiry. In computing, a request for information from storage that may be initiated at a local or remote point by use of a keyboard terminal or similar device.

inquiry/response. In applications, a method of transaction handling in which a user interrogates the computer via a terminal and obtains a response almost immediately. *Compare* BATCHED COMMUNICATION. *See* CONVERSATIONAL MODE.

In-Search. *See* PRO-SEARCH.

insert. (1) In word processing, adding characters, words, sentences or paragraphs into copy. (2) In printing, adding a separately printed piece into a book or periodical after binding.

insertion loss. In communications, the power that is absorbed by the insertion of a passive element into a channel or electronic device. This usually occurs when a filter or equalizer is added to a communications channel. *See* CHANNEL, EQUALIZATION, FILTER.

insert module. In computing, a module which, when inserted into equipment of a system, enables it to perform additional functions (e.g. additional memory capacity for a microcomputer, external interface connections, software programs stored in read-only memory, videotex decoders for television receivers. (Philips). *See* ADD-ON MODULE, EXPANSION BOARD, VIDEOTEX. *Synonymous with* PLUG-IN MODULE.

Inspec. In library science, a series of abstracts comprising:

(a) Computer and Control Abstracts, an abstracting publication covering computer and control engineering;
(b) Electrical and Electronics Abstracts, an abstracting publication covering electrical and electronics engineering;
(c) IT Focus, an abstracting publication covering information technology;
(d) Physics Abstracts, an abstracting publication covering physics. *See* ABSTRACT.

installation. In computing, a general term for a particular computing system in the context of the work it does and the staff who manage, operate and service the system.

install/deinstall. In software protection, an execute protection method on a floppy disk that can be carried across to a hard disk. When installed on a hard disk, the protected software marks the hard disk in some manner, and at the same time the floppy disk is deactivated so it cannot be copied to another hard disk. If the user wishes to change machines, the program must be deinstalled, thereby reactivating the floppy-disk copy and deactivating the hard-disk copy. *See* EXECUTE PROTECTION, FLOPPY DISK, HARD DISK.

instantiation. In programming, a more defined version of some partially defined object. *See* PROLOG.

instantlies. In television, the television equivalent of dailies. *Compare* DAILIES.

instant replay. In television, a technique used in live broadcasting in which a scene is played back, sometimes in slow motion or freeze frame, immediately after it occurred. *See* FREEZE FRAME.

Institute for New Generation Computer Technology. The Japanese fifth-generation computer research laboratory. *See* FIFTH-GENERATION COMPUTER.

Institute for Scientific Information. A Major US database producer best known for Scisearch and Social Scisearch databases. *See* DATABASE PRODUCER, SCISEARCH, SOCIAL SCISEARCH.

instruction. (1) In programming, a basic directive made by a programmer in a form that the computer can accept and execute. (2) In programming, a statement that specifies what operation is to be performed and the value or location of the operands. *See* LOCATION, OPERAND.

instruction cycle. In computing, the sequence of fetching an instruction stored in computer memory and then executing it. *See* INSTRUCTION.

instruction cycle time. In computing, the time taken to complete one instruction cycle. It represents a measure of computer speed. *See* INSTRUCTION CYCLE.

instruction execution time. *See* EXECUTION TIME.

instruction format. In programming, the allocation of the bits of a machine code instruction to the operation code, operands, etc. *See* BIT, INSTRUCTION SET, MACHINE CODE INSTRUCTION, OPERAND, OPERATION CODE.

instruction repertoire. *Synonymous with* INSTRUCTION SET.

instruction set. In programming, the complete list of machine code instruction types that can be decoded and executed by a given type of central processing unit. The instructions comprise an operation code and one or more operands which employ one of the addressing modes available to the set. *See* ADDRESSING MODE, CENTRAL PROCESSING UNIT, MACHINE CODE INSTRUCTION, OPERAND, OPERATION CODE. *Synonymous with* INSTRUCTION REPERTOIRE.

instruction time. *Synonymous with* EXECUTION TIME.

in sync. In recording, the exact alignment of sound and picture. *See* SYNCHRONIZATION.

intaglio. In printing, a general term for graphic printing carried out under pressure, usually in a cylinder or rolling press. The printing plate holds ink in etched lines and paper is forced into these recesses under the action of the cylinder. *Compare* LETTER-PRESS, LITHOGRAPHY.

INTAMIC. *See* INTERNATIONAL ASSOCIATION FOR MICROCIRCUIT CARDS.

integer. In data structures, a signed whole number. In binary notation special conventions are required to represent negative integers, and the most common form is the two's complement. In this notation the first bit is a sign bit (1 for negative, 0 for positive). The two's complement of a negative number is obtained by reversing the 0 and 1 digits and then adding one to the least significant position. One byte can thus represent numbers in the range -128 to $+127$ and 16 bits can represent $-32\,768$ to $32\,767$. *Compare* ORDINAL. *See* BIT, BYTE, TWO'S COMPLEMENT.

integral controller. In data communications, a communication unit built into a mini- or mainframe computer. *Compare* CLUSTER CONTROL UNIT, FRONT-END PROCESSOR.

integrated circuit. (IC) In electronics, a combination of interconnected circuit elements inseparably associated on or within a continuous substrate. An integrated circuit may contain a few to many thousands of transistors, resistors, diodes and capacitors. *See* LARGE-SCALE INTEGRATION, VERY LARGE-SCALE INTEGRATION.

integrated computing. In programming, the concurrent use of data by two or more software packages (e.g. a graphics package which displays spreadsheet data). *See* SPREADSHEET.

integrated database. A database that has been consolidated to eliminate redundant data. *See* DATABASE.

Integrated Data Management System. (IDMS) In databases, a proprietary system, specified by CODASYL, that provides facilities for structuring and using large databases. *See* CODASYL.

integrated data processing. In applications, a systematic approach to all aspects of data capture and data processing in order to maximize overall efficiency. *See* DATA PROCESSING.

integrated digital network. In data communications, a network in which digital transmission and digital switching are used. *See* DIGITAL SWITCHING, DIGITAL TRANSMISSION SYSTEM, INTEGRATED SERVICES DIGITAL NETWORK.

integrated home system. In applications, a number of related home systems integrated into a larger system (e.g. combination units for television and radio, modular audio video systems). (Philips).

integrated injection logic. (IIL) In microelectronics, a logic circuit of very low power consumption in which the switching speed is proportional to the amount of current injected. *See* LOGIC CIRCUIT.

integrated modem. In data communications, a modem that is an integral part of the device with which it operates. *See* MODEM.

integrated optical circuit. In optoelectronics, the optical equivalent of a microelectronic circuit. It acts on the light in a lightwave system to carry out communications functions: generating, detecting, switching and transmitting light.

integrated product. In computing, a product with more than one normally separate functions integrated together (e.g. a computer with a built-in disk drive, display and printer, or an interactive compact disc player). (Philips). *See* COMPACT DISC – INTERACTIVE, DISK DRIVE.

integrated publishing. In office systems, systems that encompass various desk-top devices and shared departmental and company-wide services linked together with a system-wide office network. The network allows the free flow of information among users and gives desk-top devices access to shared services such as images scanners, high-speed laser printers and mass storage units. *See* DESK-TOP PUBLISHING, LASER PRINTER, OPTICAL SCANNER.

integrated services digital network. (ISDN) In communications, an integrated digital network in which the same digital switches and digital paths are used to establish different services (e.g. telephony and data).

The ISDN concept represents a logical development in the provision of public communication services, recognizing the economies made possible by the advent of digital technologies, the increasing demands for a wide range of communication services and the need to provide the customer with a single interface to which can be connected a wide variety of user communication devices (i.e. voice, facsimile, data, videotex, alarm sensors, etc.). The public telephone networks throughout the world have expanded rapidly in terms of volume and user facilities in the last three decades. The analog technology of the voice network, however, has been ill-suited to demands of computer data communications which first arose in the 1960s and exploded in the following two decades. The necessary conversion of digital data to a form compatible with voice signals demanded expensive modems at each end of the communication link and severely limited data rates: low-cost devices operated at a few hundred bits per second and the expensive end of the modem range could only provide data rates of a few thousand bits per second. Data communications requirements for organizations concerned with large-scale data transfers were thus met with separate, dedicated high-speed data communication channels. However, a wide range of users looked to the telephone system to provide a variety of services (e.g. electronic mail, facsimile, videotex, telemetry, bulletin board connections, etc.) and to enhance the provision of voice communications in terms of quality and services. If these services were to be conducted within a voice service then it was logical that voice signals should be made to conform with data signals rather than vice versa. Use of pulse code modulation, which converts voice signals to binary pulse trains, allows the communication link to concern itself with only one type of signal for all transmissions. The signalling aspects of telephony (i.e. the control signals which set up and close down calls) had already been converted from analog to digital form in most advanced countries to benefit from the

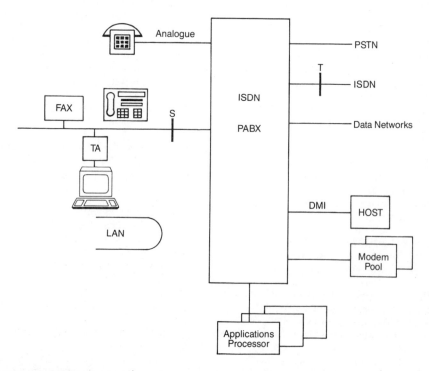

integrated services digital network
Fig. 1. ISDN PABX interfaces.

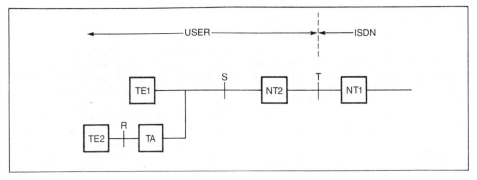

Definitions:

NT1 — Network Terminator 1, which includes transmission functions.

NT2 — Network Terminator 2, which includes switching and multiplexing functions

R — ISDN R reference point.

S — ISDN S reference point.

T — ISDN T reference point.

TA — Terminal Adapter.

TE1 — Terminal Equipment Type 1, a type of terminal equipment which conforms to the standard interface at the S reference point.

TE2 — Terminal Equipment Type 2, a type of terminal equipment which does not conform to the standard interface at the S reference point.

integrated services digital network
Fig. 2. CCITT ISDN reference configuration (user part).

advances in microelectronics and digital technology. Thus the concept of a communications system that concerned itself only with the transmission of digital data and used digital signals for signalling purposes, originally proposed in the 1960s, has excited the communications world for nearly two decades. The success of such a venture is, however, inextricably linked with the economic realities of communication traffic, the development of international standards, the national and international politics of communications, the marketing policies of manufacturers and readiness of consumers to adapt to new ideas, and to pay for them.

An organization that installs an ISDN private automatic branch exchange (PABX) will provide its users with interfaces illustrated in Fig. 1. At the users' side of the PABX the interfaces will support analog telephones, digital telephones, facsimile, computer terminals, personal computers, multifunctional workstations and gateways to local area networks. Clearly such interfaces will also support alarm systems, videotex, electronic mail and even slow-scan video systems for monitoring or alarm purposes. The actual interface types are analog

telephone, terminal equipment designed to interwork with public ISDN, and terminal adaptors, which are employed to connect equipment not conforming to ISDN standard interfaces (Fig. 2).

ISDN defines three reference points R, S and T. The R interface is for those existing devices (TE2 equipment) not designed to interface with ISDN networks, and which therefore require a terminal adaptor. The S interface allows a wide variety of devices (TE1 equipment), which have been designed with ISDN interfaces, to be directly connected to the ISDN system, thus providing the user with a guaranteed common connection facility for a wide range of office or home equipment. The T reference point is the interface between the network terminator 2 (NT2), which includes switching and multiplexing functions, and network terminator 1 (NT1), which provides ISDN line termination functions at the user end.

The facilities that can be connected directly to the PABX include digital telephone, facsimile, multifunctional workstations and local area networks. Digital telephones may have a range of features including those listed below.

(a) Alphanumeric display for indication of called numbers, internal calling numbers and names, external calling number, time and date, reminder messages, call-processing information, mailbox messages, call failure indication, call-alerting information and user prompts.
(b) User-programmable keys, and single function keys for call transfer, automatic call back, call forwarding and last number redial.
(c) Hand-free operation.
(d) Security feature (e.g. card reader for access control).

The facsimile devices that can be connected to the system include existing analog and Group 4 facsimile connected directly to an S interface. A particular feature of the ISDN environment is likely to be the multifunctional workstation capable of integrating voice, text, image and data with a wide variety of features including:

(a) Access to mailboxes.
(b) Enhanced voice features similar to those of the digital telephone.
(c) Terminal emulation for dialogues with a remote host computer.
(d) Teletex functions.
(e) Access to private and public databases (e.g. videotex).
(f) Exchange and display of documents between two or more terminals.
(g) Personal computing functions, word processing, spreadsheets, etc.
(h) Telephone directories.
(i) Pointing device facilities (e.g. light pen, mouse).

Local area networks (LANs) may have gateways to the ISDN network allowing LANs to be interconnected, and thus providing users with the combined advantages of LANs (i.e. communication or bursts of high-speed data transfers between local users) and PABX systems, which are mainly switch-oriented and related to voice communication traffic. LANs operated in different sites of an organization, linked via ISDN, therefore provide the appearance of a large integrated network.

The PABX in an ISDN system will not be restricted to merely switching and information transport functions. Facilities for the storage and processing of information, as performed in the application processors (Fig. 1) will provide functions such as facsimile mail, text mail and voice mail.

Current facsimile facilities have proved a boon to organizational communications, but they suffer from the same disadvantages as the conventional telephone system: communication has to be established with the receiving party, communication must take place at the time the user establishes the connection; and with multiple addresses a new connection has to be established for each receiving party. Facsimile mail may provide features such as: (a) timed delivery of documents; (b) broadcast facility; (c) message wait indication; (d) confidential mail; (e) text-to-facsimile conversion; and (f) teletex-to-facsimile conversion.

Text mail facilities are similar to the electronic mail provided by computer networks, but with the added advantages that the mail may be delivered via digital telephones or multifunction workstations. Future developments could well include conversion services providing 'text to voice' and 'text to facsimile' delivery services.

Voice mail employs store-and-forward techniques for voice communications, allowing messages to be delivered on demand to the recipient. Individual users may be assigned a mailbox and access to it will normally be controlled by password. Messages may be transmitted for timed delivery, broadcast to selected groups and 'text to mail' facilities will allow recipients to receive text-originated messages from telephone extensions.

The interface between the ISDN PABX and the network will be at the T interface (Fig. 1 and Fig. 2); the user's NT2 connecting to the networks NT1, at one end of the communication line and the line terminator (LT) interfaces with the ISDN exchange at the other end of the link. The interfaces to the ISDN network may be provided at the basic rate and primary access rate. There are two classes of channel in ISDN. The B channel is used for messages at 64 kilobits per second and the D channel (16 kilobits per second or 64 kilobits per second) provides both out of band common channel signalling and auxiliary message services (e.g. alarm systems monitoring). Basic rate access (2B + D) comprises two B channels and one D (16 Kbits per sec) channel giving a total capacity of 144 kilobits per second. If connection to the ISDN network is via a PABX the terminals will be connected to the PABX using basic rate access either individually or as clusters of terminals sharing the channel. The primary rate access comprises 32 x 64 kilobits per second channels in Europe and Australia; in North America and Japan it comprises 24 x 64 kilobits per second channels. The European primary access rate comprises 30 B channels for user information, one 64 kilobits per second D channel for signalling and one channel for system synchronization and alarms. Signalling between ISDN customer equipment and the ISDN exchange is conducted over D channels. Signalling between ISDN exchanges employs CCITT No 7 signalling, and X.25 or X.75 protocols are used for connections between ISDN exchanges and public data switched networks.

International standards are of paramount importance in integrated, and international communication systems. A CCITT set up a special study group as early as 1968 to consider all questions related to pulse code modulation; in 1984 the I series of recommendations was adopted. In this series of recommendation I.100 serves as a general introduction to the concepts of ISDN, I.200 is concerned with services, I.300 with network aspects and I.400 with user network interfaces.

The user advantages of ISDN are summarized below.

(a) Flexibility in the allocation of bandwidth to applications and specific routes.
(b) Control over the allocation of network resources.
(c) Reconfiguration of routes in a virtual private network and of the bandwidth allocations.
(d) Diversity in terms of alternate network routes.
(e) Cost control from the network management information, which facilitates reconfiguration and network development processes.
(f) Integrated network interfaces for a range of telecommunication types of service, thus reducing the proliferation of modems, etc.
(g) User-signalling capability, which facilitates in-house applications development to provide for integrated services (e.g. encryption, telemetering, surveillance, etc.).
(h) Opportunities of value-added services, voice prompts, database access, electronic mail, etc.

See BASIC RATE ACCESS, BAUD, B CHANNEL, BULLETIN BOARD, CCITT, D CHANNEL, DIGITAL TELEPHONE, DMI, ELECTRONIC MAIL, FACSIMILE, FACSIMILE MAIL, GROUP 4 FACSIMILE, H CHANNEL, I-SERIES RECOMMENDATIONS OF CCITT, LIGHT PEN, LOCAL AREA NETWORK, MODEM, MOUSE, NO 7 SIGNALLING, NT1, NT2, OUT-OF-BAND SIGNALLING, POINTING DEVICE, PRIMARY RATE ACCESS, PRIVATE AUTOMATIC BRANCH EXCHANGE, PULSE CODE MODULATION, R INTERFACE, S INTERFACE, STORE AND FORWARD, TE1, TE2, TELEMETERING, TELETEX, TERMINAL ADAPTOR, TEXT-TO-SPEECH SYNTHESIS, T INTERFACE, VIDEOTEX, VOICE MAIL, X.25, X.75.

integrated software. In programming, the integration of application packages may be achieved by: (a) easy transfer of program control and data between applications; (b) the extension of the aforementioned approach to a consistent operating environment; (c) the development of families of generic products, from manufacturers, having common command structures; and (d) the ability to integrate standard software packages into an operating shell. See INTEGRATED COMPUTING, SHELL.

integrated system. In applications, a system in which several elements are integrated and used for more than one function (e.g. an audio installation with record player, tuner tape deck, amplifier and loudspeakers). (Philips).

integrated word-processing equipment. In word processing, equipment that has its associated control unit contained within the body of the machine, as opposed to a general-purpose microcomputer system that runs a word-processing software package. See WORD-PROCESSING PACKAGE.

integrity. (1) In data security, the process of preventing undetected alteration of data. This term is preferred to authentication because the latter is commonly used in data communications to refer to peer entity verification. *Compare* AUTHENTICATION. *See* DATA INTEGRITY, SYSTEM INTEGRITY. (2) In computing, the preservation of files for their intended purpose. *See* DATA INTEGRITY.

Intel Hex.   In data structures, a format for storing binary information. The major features of the format are: (a) ASCII code is used to encode all information: (b) load addresses are included; and (c) checksum bytes are included for error detection and recovery.

An Intel Hex file is divided into records. Each record commences with a colon, a two-digit (ASCII) hexadecimal number specifying the number of bytes in the record, a four-digit hexadecimal number giving the load address for the record, a two-digit file type, the data bytes each encoded as a two-digit hexadecimal number and a two-digit checksum. *See* AMERICAN STANDARD CODE FOR INFORMATION INTERCHANGE, BINARY CODE, BYTE, CHECKSUM, HEXADECIMAL.

intelligence.   (1) The product resulting from the collection, evaluation, analysis, integration and interpretation of all information concerning one or more aspects of foreign countries or areas, which is immediately or potentially significant to the development and execution of plans, policies, and operations. (DODD). (2) In computing, a property of a device containing local processing power. *See* INTELLIGENT DEVICE. (3) The definition of natural intelligence is of increasing importance in the discussion of the performance of artificial intelligence systems. Suggested definitions include; (a) a concept related to comprehensive invention, direction and criticism or judgement; (b) the aggregate or global capacity of individuals to act purposefully, to think rationally and to deal effectively with their environments; and (c) the general capacity of individuals consciously to adjust their thinking to new requirements and a general adaptability to new problems and conditions. *See* ARTIFICIAL INTELLIGENCE.

intelligent cathode ray tube.   *See* INTELLIGENT TERMINAL.

intelligent character recognition.   (ICR) In peripherals, a form of optical character recognition that is not restricted to a particular font. *See* FONT, FONT-INDEPENDENT, OPTICAL CHARACTER RECOGNITION, OPTICAL SCANNER.

intelligent computer-assisted instruction.   (ICAI) In applications, a development of computer-assisted instruction in which course material is represented independently of teaching procedures so that exercises and remedial comments can be generated according to student performance. Such systems carry on a dialogue with the student and use the student's responses to diagnose comprehension. *See* COMPUTER-ASSISTED INSTRUCTION, COMPUTER-BASED TRAINING, INTELLIGENT TUTORING SYSTEM.

intelligent copier/printer.   (IC/P) In office systems, a non-impact, normally laser printer, output device that accepts electronic and hard-copy input and produces hard-copy output of at least letter-quality print. Such systems may have document-scanning capabilities thus distinguishing them from ordinary page printers. They may have user selectable fonts and document-formatting capabilities and are normally employed in printing standard letter-sized documents on plain bond paper.

The devices may have document scanners and hence perform the function of traditional photocopiers. On the other hand they may receive their inputs from local or remote computers/word processors, as electronic mail from networks or as images transmitted by facsimile.

The IC/Ps may be employed in centralized, satellite, office cluster and workstation environments. Centralized systems are often categorized by high-price, high-volume outputs with speeds in excess of 80 pages per minute. Satellite systems are normally employed at remote site printing departments controlled by a centralized processing system. The volume, ranging from about 20 000 to 40 000 pages per month is less than that associated with centralized sites, and speeds range from 35 to 80 pages per minute. The office cluster represents a further stage in decentralization and provides a local departmental facility with speeds from 10 to 35 pages per minute. The personal workstation provides a low-speed, below 10 ppm, service for a individual worker.

The current application areas for IC/Ps are data processing, word processing, office automation and electronic printing/publishing. *See* COPIER, FACSIMILE, ELECTRONIC MAIL, ELECTRONIC PUBLISHING, LASER PRINTER, LETTER QUALITY.

intelligent device. In peripherals, any device or peripheral which can be programmed. *Compare* DUMB DEVICE. *See* INTELLIGENT TERMINAL.

intelligent disk server. In memory systems, a disk server that provides a simple mechanism for networked microcomputers to request and gain access to centralized peripherals and disk volumes. The system can manage the efficient sharing of printers, tape drives, plotters, etc. and also can provide a degree of security by controlling individual user access to facilities. *See* DISK SERVER, FILE SERVER.

intelligent intermediary system. *Synonymous with* INTERMEDIARY SYSTEM.

intelligent knowledge-based system. *See* EXPERT SYSTEMS.

intelligent page reader. In office systems, an optical scanner employing font-independent pattern recognition. *See* FONT-INDEPENDENT, OPTICAL SCANNER.

intelligent player. In optical media, a videodisc or compact disc player with additional computing facilities built in, enabling the player to interact with the user, or to operate under program control; interactive compact disc players are intelligent players. (Philips). *See* COMPACT DISC – INTERACTIVE, INTERACTIVE VIDEODISC SYSTEMS.

intelligent terminal. In peripherals, a device with a visual display unit, keyboard, processor memory and local software connected to a host computer. The terminal has sufficient processing capability to provide user prompts, editing capabilities, etc. and can continue to operate in a limited mode for a certain time without communication with the host computer. Intelligent terminals are commonly employed in retail stores, banks, industrial data collection, etc. *See* HOST COMPUTER, INTELLIGENCE, TERMINAL.

intelligent token. In banking, a form of smart card, with facilities to sign messages, that can be used for access control, prepayment systems, electronic funds transfer, message authentication and negotiable documents. The card contains both a display and keyboard. It employs public key cryptography techniques and stores the corresponding private key. *See* DIGITAL SIGNATURE, MESSAGE AUTHENTICATION, PRIVATE KEY, PUBLIC KEY CRYPTOGRAPHY, SUPERSMART CARD.

intelligent tutoring system. (ITS) In applications, an application of computers in education and training that uses the concept of expert systems to provide an intelligent tutor that can interact with the trainee with near-natural language dialogues. *Compare* COMPUTER-AIDED INSTRUCTION, COMPUTER-ASSISTED LEARNING, COMPUTER-BASED TRAINING, COMPUTER-MANAGED INSTRUCTION, INTELLIGENT COMPUTER-ASSISTED INSTRUCTION.

Intelmatique. The international marketing agency of the French PTT.

Intelpost. A UK, US and Australian facsimile service offered by INTELSAT. *See* INTELSAT.

INTELSAT. In communications, International Telecommunications Satellite organization; an international organization with 109 member countries that initiated the world's first global satellite communications system. INTELSAT I, known as Early Bird, provided the first relay telephone and television service between Europe and North America in 1965. The early INTELSAT I, II and III series satellites are no longer operational. The INTELSAT IV, V and VA series satellites provide international communications across the Atlantic, Pacific and Indian Oceans. Satellites are leased to member counties, and a number of in-orbit spare satellites can be moved to required geostationary locations as required. *Compare* COMSAT, EUTELSAT, INTERSPUTNIK. *See* GEOSTATIONARY SATELLITE.

intensity. (1) In wave propagation, the intensity of a beam is proportional to the square of the amplitude of oscillation. It is a measure of the strength of the radiation. With light waves, intensity is an indication of brightness, and in sound it is a measure of loudness. (2) In computer graphics, the amount of light emitted from a point in the display. *See* DECIBEL.

intensity depth cue. In computer graphics, a depth cue in which the light brightness decreases with the distance from the observer. *See* DEPTH CUE, THREE-DIMENSIONAL GRAPHICS.

interactive. In computing, a conversational type system in which a continuous dialogue can take place between a user and the computer. *See* INQUIRY/RESPONSE.

interactive cable television. In television, a cable television system with facilities for the user to send signals upstream (e.g. for telebanking, teleshopping, voting on referenda). *See* CABLE TELEVISION, TELEBANKING, TELESHOPPING.

interactive compact disc. *See* COMPACT DISC – INTERACTIVE.

interactive computing. In computing, use of a computer such that the user is in control and may enter data or make other demands on the system, which responds by the immediate processing of user requests and returning appropriate replies to these requests. (FIPS).

interactive graphics. In computer graphics, pertaining to systems designed to enable the user to explore a multitude of conditions, imposed on a design model in real time. The user can employ a variety of pointing devices (e.g. joystick, keyboard, lightpen, mouse, touchscreen, trackerball, voice recognizer, etc.). *See* JOYSTICK, LIGHT PEN, MOUSE, POINTING DEVICE, SPEECH RECOGNIZER, TOUCHSCREEN, TRACKER BALL.

interactive media. In communications, teleconference systems that allow direct exchanges among people via one or more communication channels (e.g. voice, writing or vision), thus supporting a high degree of interpersonal communication. *See* TELECONFERENCING.

interactive mode. (1) In information presentation, a mode in which information is presented in a sequence determined by a dialogue between the information medium and the recipient (e.g. interactive compact disc, interactive videodisc). (Philips). *Com-*

pare LINEAR MODE. *See* COMPACT DISC – INTERACTIVE, INTERACTIVE VIDEODISC SYSTEMS. (2) In computing, a system which supports a continuous dialogue with a user. *See* INQUIRY/RESPONSE.

interactive system. A system capable of using an interactive medium to supply information to the user. (Philips). *See* INTERACTIVE MODE. *Synonymous with* CONVERSATIONAL MODE.

interactive television. *See* INTERACTIVE CABLE TELEVISION.

interactive videodisc systems. In optical media, some videodisc systems provide facilities for freeze frame, fast/slow motion and random access to individual frames. These facilities can be exploited for a variety of applications (e.g. education, training, sales promotions, information storage/retrieval). The four forms of interactive systems are classified as level one, level two, level three and level four.

Level one systems include consumer videodisc players and are characterized by individual frame addressability, worst-frame access (1–54 000) less than 20 seconds, limited memory and no processing power. At the simplest level, the user controls the playback with a keypad (e.g. search for a particular frame, playing from that point in normal mode, stopping at a point of interest, moving forward or reversing frame by frame, fast or slow motion, etc.). The disc can also contain coded control information so that, for example, the player automatically switches from normal play to freeze frame when a control code is read from the disc. Some discs also contain teletext-coded information so that the user may view teletext menus which display details of starting frame numbers for various sequences or select teletext-style subtitles providing additional information relating to sequences.

Level two systems, sometimes called industrial players, have the capabilities of level one systems plus improved worst-case access times, two-way computer/communications capabilities and a built-in microprocessor. Such systems provide capabilities for automatic programming of control sequences. These systems relieve the viewer of the requirement for manual control during playback, but require control sequences to be keyed in manually prior to play-back. A possible development is to encode the control program onto the beginning of the disc and to download it from the disc to the built-in microprocessor.

Level three systems comprise a level one or level two player interfaced to a micro-computer. This provides the most versatile form of interaction since the control program can employ the processing and memory power of the microcomputer and is independent of the information contained on the disc. The facilities depend upon the player; some systems provide for two-way communication so that the computer awaits acknowledgement signals, or even frame numbers, from the player.

Level four systems are sophisticated players with extensive memory, control and processing facilities.

Some players have teletext encoders so that computer-generated text or alphamo-saic graphics can be superimposed upon the videodisc pictures. More advanced user friendly facilities (e.g. touchscreen, voice recognition, etc.) can also be incorporated into most microcomputer configurations. *Compare* COMPACT DISC – INTERACTIVE. *See* FRAME, FREEZE FRAME, TELETEXT, TOUCH-SCREEN, VIDEODISC, VOICE RECOGNITION.

interactive videotex. *See* VIDEOTEX. *Synonymous with* VIEWDATA.

interblock gap. (IGB) In memory systems, the space on a magnetic tape between the end of one block of data and the beginning of the next. Such spacing facilitates tape stop/start operations. *Synonymous with* INTERRECORD GAP.

intercarrier buzz. In television receivers, an occasional noise heard on the reproduced sound that may have several causes, includ-ing intermodulation between the sound and vision carrier signals. *See* CARRIER, INTERMO-DULATION DISTORTION.

intercepting. In communications, the rerouting of a call or message that is initially directed to a disconnected, or non-existent, telephone number; a specified operator location or terminal can be designated to receive such calls or messages.

Intercept Strategy. A strategy of the UK Department of Trade and Industry to pro-vide guidelines on the likely content of Open Systems Interconnection standards so as to assist organizations in their implementation plans. *See* OPEN SYSTEMS INTERCONNECTION.

interchangeability. The characteristics that makes it possible to change components of a system for other components from a differ-ent source, and still obtain performance within the system specification. For example, all compact cassettes and compact discs are interchangeable, as are digital audio and interactive compact discs and players. (Philips). *See* COMPACT CASSETTE, COMPACT DISC, COMPACT DISC – DIGITAL AUDIO, COMPACT DISC – INTERACTIVE, DISC INTER-CHANGEABILITY.

intercharacter spacing. In word process-ing, the creation of variable spaces between the characters of individual words in order to create a justified column of text. Some soph-isticated systems offer spacing assigned according to character width, giving a print like quality. *Compare* INTERWORD SPACING. *See* JUSTIFY.

intercom. In communications, a service that supports voice intercommunications between two or more stations located in the same building or localized area.

interconnectability. In computing, the ability of two or more devices to be con-nected together. (Philips).

interconnection. (1) In communications, the connection of a piece of telephone equipment to the telephone network. (2) In communications, the interconnection of common carrier networks. *See* CARTERFONE DECISION, INTERFACE.

interdiction. In computer security, the act of impeding or denying the use of system resources to user. (FIPS). *See* DELAY/DENIAL OF SERVICE, DENIAL OF SERVICE.

interexchange. (IX) In communications, services and channels supported by one or more exchanges or rate centres. *See* EXCHANGE, RATE CENTRE.

interface. (1) The common boundary between independent systems or modules, where communications takes place. (2) In data communications, a shared boundary between two related devices or components defined for the purpose of specifying the type and form of signals passing between them (e.g. the EIA RS-232C interface represents a standard set of signal characteristics — time, duration, voltage and current — specified by the Electronic Industries Association (EIA) for use in communications terminals). It also includes a standard plug/socket connector arrangement. *See* RS-232C. (3) In programming, a specification of the communication between modules of a program. *See* INFORMATION HIDING.

interface box. In computing, a self-contained unit or box containing circuitry that allows two or more units to work together as a system. (Philips).

interface processor. In data communications, a processor that acts as the interface between a terminal or a computer, and a network or a computer that is used to control the flow of data into the network. *See* INTERFACE.

interference. (1) In communications, any unwanted signals appearing in a channel at a level sufficient to impair the performance of the channel to a significant extent. Interference may be a result of natural or man-made noises and signals. (2) In optics and communications, the addition or combination of waves. If a crest of one wave meets the trough of another of equal amplitude and frequency, the wave is destroyed at that point; conversely, the superimposition of one crest upon another leads to an increased effect. *See* HOLOGRAM.

interference fading. In communications, fading caused by the interaction of two or more radio waves of similar amplitude, but differing in phase. *See* FADING.

interference immunity. (1) In communications, the degree to which a receiving system can reject interfering signals. (2) In communications, the effectiveness of a directional antenna system designed to reject interfering signals. *See* ANTENNA.

interference pattern. In optics, the resulting distribution of energy when waves of the

same frequency and kind are superimposed. *See* HOLOGRAM.

Intergovernmental Bureau for Informatics. (IBI) An organization developed by UNESCO with the remit 'to permanently assist people in the field of informatics to help them live in the context created by this discipline, to understand better its impact on society and to derive the maximum benefit from its possibilities'. *See* INFORMATICS.

interlace. In television and peripherals, a system of scanning a picture using two fields. The first line-by-line scan sweeps alternate line positions on the picture, the second sweeps the gaps between the first, completing the total structure of the picture. Interlace scanning reveals a higher level of character detail in a visual display unit or videotex terminal and helps to reduce flicker. *See* FIELD, FLICKER, POSITIVE INTERLACE, RANDOM INTERLACE, SCANNING LINE.

interleaving. (1) In memory systems, the act of accessing two or more bytes or streams of data from separate storage units simultaneously. *See* BYTE. (2) In peripherals, the alternating of two or more operations or functions at the same time from the one computer. (3) In optical media, the interspacing of interactive compact disc sectors at intervals that correspond to the nature of the data. For audio, a regular interspaced pattern is used which depends on the sound quality level required. The subheader indicates the interleaving pattern at file, channel and data type levels. (Philips). *See* AUDIO QUALITY LEVEL, COMPACT DISC – INTERACTIVE, SUBHEADER. (4) In printing, the placing of extra sheets, usually blank, placed between printed sheets as they come off a press to avoid ink being transferred from one printed sheet to another. *See* SET OFF.

interlibrary loan. (ILL) In library science, a book or microform lent between libraries for a particular reader. *See* MICROFORM.

interlinear spacing. In printing, the electronic equivalent of the mechanical insertion of spaces between print lines in a photo-typesetting system. *See* PHOTOTYPESETTING.

interlingua. In machine translation, a language-independent representation of meaning. If source languages can be analyzed to an interlingua and target languages synthesized from this representation of meaning then multiple source language/target language pairs can be handled. *See* SOURCE LANGUAGE, TARGET LANGUAGE.

interlock. (1) To prevent a machine or device from commencing further operations until the current one is completed. (2) In recording, an arrangement that can synchronize separate sound and picture tracks. The simplest method is by the use of a synchronous drive motor connecting both picture viewer and sound reproducer. *See* INTERLOCK PROJECTOR.

interlock projector. In audiovisual aids, a projector used to produce the picture while synchronized sound is played back on an accompanying machine. *See* INTERLOCK.

intermediary. In online information retrieval, an information retrieval specialist who acts as the interface between an online database and the end user of the information to be retrieved. *See* END USER.

intermediary system. In online information retrieval, a kind of expert system used to assist end users searching online databases. Such systems offer assistance with query definition, database selection, search strategy formulation and search revision. *Compare* GATEWAY SOFTWARE. *See* EXPERT SYSTEMS, SEARCH STRATEGY. *Synonymous with* FRONT-END SYSTEM, INTELLIGENT INTERMEDIARY SYSTEM.

intermediate-access memory. *Synonymous with* FAST-ACCESS MEMORY.

intermediate frequency. (IF) In communications, the frequency to which the received signal is changed by the frequency changer in a superheterodyne receiver.

intermediate materials. In optical media, all the media (i.e. 16-mm film, video tape, 35-mm slides, etc.) selected for assembly onto the videodisc premaster.

intermediate reversal negative. In filming, a negative made directly from another negative without the creation of a positive. It is used to eliminate one generation of printing. *See* GENERATION.

intermediate text block. (ITB) In data communications, a control character used to end an intermediate block of characters. *See* END OF TEXT.

intermittent error. An error that occurs intermittently in a random way. It is extremely difficult to reproduce and therefore to correct.

intermodulation distortion. In electronics, a distortion resulting from the interaction of two or more frequencies when there is a non-linear relationship between input and output signals (e.g. an overloaded audio amplifier may cause such distortion). In wideband frequency division multiplexing transmission systems, the result of intermodulation is usually called intermodulation noise. *See* FREQUENCY DIVISION MULTIPLEXING, NOISE.

intermodulation noise. *See* INTERMODULATION DISTORTION.

internal label. In memory systems, a machine-readable label recorded on a data medium such as magnetic tape or disk that provides information about a set of data recorded on the medium. *Compare* EXTERNAL LABEL.

internally stored program. In memory systems, a program stored in read-only memory, as compared to one loaded into the machine from disk or tape. *See* READ-ONLY MEMORY.

internal security controls. In computer security, hardware, firmware, and software features within an automated system that restrict access to resources (hardware, software, and data) to only authorized subjects (persons, programs, or devices). Controls can also provide limit checks, reasonability checks, etc. (AFR). *See* FIRMWARE, REASONABLENESS CHECK, SUBJECT.

internal storage. *Synonymous with* MAIN MEMORY.

International Alphabet Number 5. In codes, a subset of IS0-7 in which characters for national use are either specified or not used. *See* ISO-7.

International Association for Microcircuit Cards. (INTAMIC) An organization of financial institutions created to study the microcircuit card and to investigate its application in financial fields. *See* MICROCIRCUIT CARD.

International Council of Graphic Design Associations. A body set up to provide a central focus for all aspects of graphic design.

International Electrotechnical Commission. (IEC) A body responsible for electrical standardization, including standards for materials, components and methods of measurement. Some of the IEC's work relates to telecommunications applications in the fields of wires, cables, waveguides and community antenna television systems. *See* COMMUNITY ANTENNA TELEVISION.

International Federation for Information Processing. (IFIP) A federation of professional and technical societies concerned with information processing. One society is admitted from each participating country.

International Frequency Registration Board. (IFRB) A body responsible for maintaining a master list of radio frequencies used throughout the world. It tries to prevent a country from introducing a new frequency if it would interfere with existing radio services. *See* INTERNATIONAL TELECOMMUNICATIONS UNION.

International Network Working Group. (INWG) A forum for discussing network standards and protocols. It is a working group within the International Federation for Information Processing with the title 'International Packet Switching for Computer Sharing'. *See* INTERNATIONAL FEDERATION FOR INFORMATION PROCESSING.

International Nuclear Information System. (INIS) In online information retrieval, a database supplied by International Atomic Energy Agency (IAEA), INIS Section, in cooperation with partici-

pating member states and dealing with nuclear science.

international number. In communications, all the digits that have to be dialed after the international prefix to obtain access to a telephone subscriber in another country. *See* INTERNATIONAL PREFIX.

International Packet Switching Service. (IPSS) In data communications, a packet switching system operated between Europe and the USA. *See* PACKET SWITCHING.

international paper sizes. *See* A, B AND C SERIES OF PAPER SIZES.

international phonetic alphabet. In communications, an internationally agreed code for spelling out letters of words over a voice circuit. A Alpha, B Bravo, C Charlie, D Delta, E Echo, F Foxtrot, G Golf, H Hotel, I India, J Julia, K Kilo, L Lima, M Mike, N November, O Oscar, P Papa, Q Quebec, R Romeo, S Sierra, T Tango, U Uniform, V Victor, W Whisky, X Xray, Y Yankee, Z Zulu.

international prefix. In communications, the dialing code for access to a telephone exchange controlling international calls. *See* EXCHANGE.

International Radio and Television Organization. (IRTO) A group that sets radio and television transmission standards.

International Record Carrier. In communications, a common carrier engaged in providing a service between the USA and foreign destinations, and between the continental USA and other areas such as Puerto Rico, Hawaii and Guam. These services include telex, private line service and alternate voice data service. *See* COMMON CARRIER.

international standard book number. (ISBN) In book publishing, a unique 10-digit number allocated to each published book, with a separate number for each edition. The first part of the number consists of a group identifier (country or group of countries), the second part is the publisher identifier, the third part is the title identifier, and the last part is a single check digit. *See* CHECK DIGIT.

international standard recording code. (ISRC) In recording, a code used by record manufacturers, giving information about country of origin, owner, year of issue and serial number of individual music tracks. It may optionally appear in digital audio compact disc subcode. (Philips). *See* COMPACT DISC – DIGITAL AUDIO, SUBCODE CHANNEL.

international standard serial number. (ISSN) In library science, a unique number for the identification of serial publications. It consists of eight digits, seven of which uniquely identify the serial, and the eighth is a check digit. *Compare* INTERNATIONAL STANDARD BOOK NUMBER.

International Standards Organization. (ISO) An agency of the United Nations concerned with international standardization across a broad field of industrial products. *See* PROTOCOL STANDARDS.

International Telecommunications Union. (ITU) A body that promotes international collaboration in telecommunications with a view to improving the efficiency of world services. It is a specialized agency of the United Nations and has three permanent committees: the IFRB (International Frequency Registration Board), the CCIR and the CCITT. Its regulations have the status of formal treaties between the participating countries and are binding on signatories who have acceded to them. *See* PROTOCOL STANDARDS.

internegative. In film processing, a colour negative duplicate made from a colour positive. Internegatives are used for release printing in order to protect the source film from damage. *See* PRINT.

internetworking. In data communications, the process of connecting together separate heterogeneous computer networks, which may have different protocols. The junctions between the networks are termed gateways, and these junctions are responsible for ensuring that messages passing into another network conform to the necessary protocols of that network. *See* GATEWAY, HETEROGENEOUS COMPUTER NETWORK, PROTOCOL.

interpolation. In mathematics, the process of filling in intermediate values, or terms, of a series between known values of the terms.

interpolation scheme. In codes, a method of substituting estimated values for missing or erroneous data. (Philips). *See* CONCEALMENT.

interpositive. In filming, any positive duplicate of a film. It is used for further printing.

interpreter. In programming, a translator that accepts one line of a source program at a time, and performs the corresponding actions. Interpreters differ from compilers in two important respects: (a) they do not check the syntax of the whole program before execution; (b) they repeat the process of translation every time a particular source program is executed. Debugging is easier and less frustrating than with compilers, but interpreted programs are much slower than compiled programs in execution. Moreover, a syntax error can lurk undetected, for many program test runs in a program instruction that is only accessed in exceptional circumstances. *Compare* ASSEMBLER, COMPILER. *See* BASIC, EXECUTE, MACHINE LANGUAGE, SOURCE PROGRAM, TRANSLATOR.

interpretive language. In programming, a language that is designed to be translated by an interpreter. Some interpretive languages may also be compiled (e.g. BASIC). *See* INTERPRETER, TRANSLATOR.

interrecord gap. *Synonymous with* INTERBLOCK GAP.

interrogation. In peripherals, the process of sending a signal to a peripheral (e.g. a terminal) to determine its status. Polling is a form of interrogation applied to a number of terminals in sequence. *See* PERIPHERAL, POLLING, TERMINAL.

interrupt. (1) In computing, a facility that enables a central processing unit to handle concurrently a number of input/output devices on a priority basis. An interrupt is sent from an input/output device to the central processing unit (CPU) requesting action (e.g. to receive data). The CPU suspends execution of the current task, transfers control to a specified location in memory which then calls a routine to deal with the interrupt. On completion, control is returned to the interrupted task. *See* CENTRAL PROCESSING UNIT, INPUT/OUTPUT UNIT. (2) In data communications, to take action at a receiving station that causes the transmitting station to terminate a transmission.

intersatellite link. In communications, a link to enable the direct transmission of messages between satellites (i.e. without the use of intermediate ground stations). *See* COMMUNICATIONS SATELLITE SYSTEM, GROUND STATION.

Intersputnik. In communications, an international satellite cooperative of 14 communist member countries using Statsionarsatellites. *Compare* EUTELSAT, INTELSAT. *See* COMMUNICATIONS SATELLITE SYSTEM, Statsionar.

interstate communicator. In communications, any service that crosses the boundary of two or more states of the USA and that may therefore be subject to Federal Communications Commission regulation.

interstation muting. In communications, the suppression of the audio output of a radio receiver during a tuning change from one broadcast station to another. With frequency-modulated receivers this is particularly useful since in the absence of an input signal the receiver is a noise generator. *See* FREQUENCY MODULATION, NOISE.

Interstream One. In communications, a service to link packet switch service and UK telex networks provided by British Telecom. *See* PACKET SWITCHING, TELEX.

intersymbol dependence. In data security, a property of a cipher in which every bit of a ciphertext block is a sufficiently complex function of every preceding bit in the input plaintext.

intertitles. In filming and video, additional textual information displayed on the screen. *See* CAPTION, SUBTITLES.

intertoll trunk. In communications, a trunk between toll-switching offices in different exchanges used for routing long distance calls. *See* TOLL-SWITCHING OFFICE, TRUNK.

intervention signal. In data communications, a control signal designed for the equipment at either end of a channel rather than for the channel itself.

interword spacing. In word processing, the creation of spaces between words to create justified columns of text. *Compare* INTERCHARACTER SPACING. *See* JUSTIFY.

intonation contour. In acoustics, the frequency contour for a group of intonation, or pitch, variations arranged to cover a complete utterance in speech synthesis. (Philips). *See* SPEECH SYNTHESIZER.

intruder. In data security, a person who seeks to make illegal use of a data communication system. The intruder may listen in and attempt to decipher a ciphertext message or seek to interfere actively with the messages. *See* ATTACKER, CIPHERTEXT, TROJAN HORSE, WIRETAPPING.

intrusion. In legislation, trespassing by any means upon private property or controlled public property.

intrusion tone. In communications, an indication, that a third party is taking part in a call, in the form of an audible signal superimposed upon the conversation.

invariant. In mathematics, a property that remains true after a given transformation.

inverse square law. In optics and communications, the intensity of the radiation falling on a given surface varies inversely as the square of its distance from the source. In the case of light, the intensity of illumination on an object thus varies as the square of the distance from the object to the light source. *See* INTENSITY.

inverse video. *Synonymous with* REVERSE VIDEO.

inversion. In mathematics, a complementation process in binary arithmetic where all the 1s in a binary number are changed to 0s, and vice versa. *See* COMPLEMENT.

inverted file. In databases, a file structure that facilitates searches for attributes by the provision of special lists or indices (e.g. a personnel file uses an employee number as the primary key, but an inverted file might provide a list in departmental order, with associated employee numbers). Thus all the employees in a given department could be accessed without an exhaustive search of the total personnel file.

inverter. In electronics, a logic circuit to perform a NOT operation. *See* NOT.

invitation. In data communications, the process in which a processor contacts a station in order to allow the station to transmit an available message. *See* POLLING.

INWG. *See* INTERNATIONAL NETWORK WORKING GROUP.

I/O. *See* INPUT/OUTPUT.

IOB. A United Nations Inter-Organization Board for Information Systems and Related Activities.

IoL. UK Institute of Linguists.

ion. In electronics, a charged particle. An atom is normally electrically neutral, the total charge of the electrons being equal and opposite to the positive nucleus. If an atom gains an extra electron, it becomes a negative ion; if it loses an electron, it becomes a positive ion.

ion deposition. In printing, a non-impact printing technique that does not require special papers, heat fusing or complex developers. There are four phases to the operation of the printer. A signal, representing the image to be printed, causes an array of charged particles to be directed, from an ion cartridge towards a rotating printing cylinder. This cylinder then holds a latent image, and as this image rotates past a toner station a toner is attracted towards it. This toner is then transferred to paper, held on another cylinder and in high pressure contact with printing cylinder. The toner is transferred to the paper by cold fusion; the printing cylinder is extremely hard and the high pressure enables more than 98 per cent of the toner to be transferred to the paper. The printing cylinder then rotates the remaining toner past a scraping head to remove any residue, and any remaining electrical charge is neutralized by a solid-state erase head. *Compare* LASER PRINTER. *See* TONER.

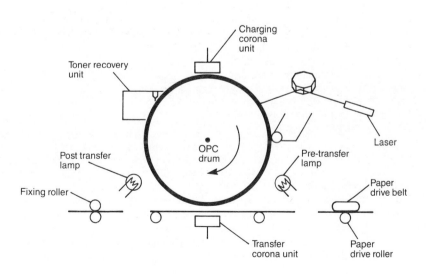

ion deposition
Ionographic printers have four stages to the printing process.

ionic. In printing, a range of typefaces commonly used in newspaper work.

ionosphere. In communications, a layer in the earth's atmosphere consisting of charged particles which cause a radio wave to be reflected back to earth. For reference purposes the ionosphere is divided into three regions: the D region occupying the spherical shell from 50 to 90 kilometres above the earth, the E region from 90 to 150 kilometres and the F region. *See* D REGION, E REGION, F REGION.

IP. *See* INFORMATION PROVIDER.

IPA. In online information retrieval, International Pharmaceutical Abstracts; a database supplied by American Society of Hospital Pharmacists and dealing with pharmaceuticals and the pharmaceutical industry. (2) International Phonetic Association.

IPG. Information Policy Group of the Organization for Economic Cooperation and Development.

ips. Inches per second

IPSS. *See* INTERNATIONAL PACKET SWITCHING SERVICE.

IP terminal. In videotex, an editing terminal used for creating or updating videotex pages. The terminal is designed to facilitate the use of colour, alphanumeric and graphics characters. Page creation can be carried out either online, or else in an offline mode where pages are held on disk for subsequent online connection to the videotex database. *See* BULK UPDATE TERMINAL, PAGE.

IR. *See* INFORMATION RETRIEVAL.

IRC. (1) In information retrieval. *See* INFORMATION RETRIEVAL CENTRE. (2) In memory system, interrecord gap. *See* INTERBLOCK GAP.

IRE. US Institute of Radio Engineers.

irradiation. In filming, the scattering of light by the silver grains in the emulsion, producing a noticeable reduction of image definition in thick emulsions. *See* EMULSION.

irreversible encryption. *Synonymous with* ONE-WAY CIPHER.

IRT. UK Institute of Reprographic Technology.

IRU. *See* INDEFEASIBLE RIGHT OF USE.

ISAM. Indexed sequential access method.

isarithmic control. In data communications, the control of flow in a packet-switched network so as to maintain the total number of packets in transit below a certain limit. *See* FLOW CONTROL, PACKET SWITCHING.

ISBN. *See* INTERNATIONAL STANDARD BOOK NUMBER.

ISDN. *See* INTEGRATED SERVICES DIGITAL NETWORK.

I-series recommendations of CCITT. In communications, detailed recommendations for integrated services digital networks. *Compare* V-SERIES RECOMMENDATIONS OF CCITT, X-SERIES RECOMMENDATIONS OF CCITT. *See* INTEGRATED SERVICES DIGITAL NETWORK.

ISI. *See* INSTITUTE FOR SCIENTIFIC INFORMATION.

ISO. *See* INTERNATIONAL STANDARDS ORGANIZATION.

ISO-7. In codes, a seven-bit code with 128 characters that is identical with ASCII, which is the US version of this code, with the exception that certain bit patterns can be optionally allocated to national characters. *See* AMERICAN STANDARD CODE FOR INFORMATION INTERCHANGE, INTERNATIONAL ALPHABET NUMBER 5.

isochronous transmission. In data communications, a data transmission process in which any two significant events are always separated by an integral number of unit intervals. *Compare* ANISOCHRONOUS TRANS-

MISSION. *See* ASYNCHRONOUS TRANSMISSION, SYNCHRONOUS TRANSMISSION.

isolated adaptive routing. In data communications, a method of signal switching in which the routing decisions are made solely on the basis of information available in each node. *See* ADAPTIVE ROUTING.

isolated word recognition. In man–machine interfaces, pertaining to systems that can recognize individual human spoken words separated by pauses. Typically the system can recognize words from a 50–300 word vocabulary. *Compare* CONNECTED WORD RECOGNITION. *See* SPEECH RECOGNIZER.

isolation. (1) In computer security, the containment of users and resources in an automatic data-processing system in such a way that users and processes are separate from one another, as well as from the protection controls of the operating system. (FIPS). *See* COMPARTMENTALIZATION, ISOLATION ENFORCEMENT, OPERATING SYSTEM. (2) In communications, methods employed to prevent high voltages being applied to common carrier networks. *See* COMMON CARRIER.

isolation enforcement. In data security, a technique to ensure that secure information is partitioned into disjoint sets so that it cannot be transmitted from one secure application to another, which does not have the necessary access privilege. The isolation can be achieved by physical, temporal, logical or cryptographic separation. *See* CRYPTOGRAPHY, TEMPEST PROOFING.

isometric projection. In computer graphics, a method of representing three-dimensional shapes in two-dimensional space; naturally vertical lines remain so, but horizontal lines are drawn at 30° to the horizontal. The regularity of such projections facilitates computer representation and hidden-line algorithms. *Compare* OBLIQUE PROJECTION, ORTHOGRAPHIC PROJECTION, PERSPECTIVE PROJECTION. *See* HIDDEN LINE.

ISO OSI. *See* OPEN SYSTEMS INTERCONNECTION.

isotropic. Pertaining to systems or substances that demonstrate the same properties in all directions. *See* ISOTROPIC ANTENNA.

isotropic antenna. In communications, a theoretical antenna radiating uniformly in all directions. *Compare* DIRECTIONAL ANTENNA. *See* ANTENNA GAIN, DISH ANTENNA, EFFECTIVE ISOTROPIC RADIATED POWER.

isotropic recording. In memory systems, a method of magnetizing a magnetic disk that has advantages over both longitudinal and vertical recording techniques. *Compare* LONGITUDINAL RECORDING, VERTICAL RECORDING. *See* FLUX, MAGNETIC DISK, READ/WRITE HEAD.

ISRC. *See* INTERNATIONAL STANDARD RECORDING CODE.

ISRD. Information System Requirements Document.

ISSN. *See* INTERNATIONAL STANDARD SERIAL NUMBER.

ISSO. Information system security officer.

IT. *See* INFORMATION TECHNOLOGY.

italic. In printing, a 15th century typeface with characters that have a noticeable inclination to the right. *Compare* BACKSLANT.

ITB. *See* INTERMEDIATE TEXT BLOCK.

item. In data structures, a group of related characters treated as a unit (e.g. a record may consist of a number of items, which in turn may consist of other items). *See* RECORD.

iteration. In programming, a process that repeats the same series of processing steps until a predetermined state or branch condition is reached. *Compare* RECURSIVE ROUTINE. *See* LOOP.

ITS. (1) Invitation to send. (2) In applications. *See* INVITATION TO SEND.

ITU. *See* INTERNATIONAL TELECOMMUNICATIONS UNION.

IV&V. *See* INDEPENDENT VERIFICATION AND VALIDATION.

IVIPA. International Videotex Information Providers Association.

ivory board. In printing, a smooth, high-white board used for business cards, etc. (Desktop).

IWP. International Word Processing Organizations.

IWR. *See* ISOLATED WORD RECOGNITION.

IX. *See* INTEREXCHANGE.

J

jabber control. In data communications, a facility in a local area network to interrupt automatically transmission of an abnormally long-output data stream. *See* LOCAL AREA NETWORK.

Jackson structured programming. In programming, a proprietary brand of structured programming, developed by Michael Jackson, widely favoured in data-processing environments. The technique employs hierarchical structures in which the major task of the program is successively decomposed into subtasks, until the eventual subtasks are reduced in complexity to the point that the corresponding subprogram can be written directly. *See* STRUCTURED PROGRAMMING.

jam. (1) In photography, a fault in a camera due either to mechanical failure or a pile up of film. (2) In computer peripherals, a pile up of card in a card reader.

jamming. In communications security, a deliberate form of radiation interference aimed at radio, microwave or satellite transmissions. The use of high-energy transmitters forces the jammer to use more powerful, and hence more expensive, transmission systems. Spread spectrum bandwidth transmission is distributed over a band of frequencies, thus also increasing the problem of the jammer, whereas the frequency agility technique changes the transmitted frequency randomly over the spectrum during transmission. *See* EMI/RF RADIATION, FREQUENCY AGILITY.

JAPATIC. Japanese Patent Information Centre.

JCL. *See* JOB CONTROL LANGUAGE.

JEIDA. Japan Electronic Industry Development Association.

jitter. (1) In television and computer graphics, a signal instability resulting in sudden, small, irregular variations due mainly to synchronizing defects in the associated equipment. (2) In facsimile, raggedness in the received copy caused by erroneous displacement of recorded spots in the direction of scanning.

job. In computing, a full description of a unit of work for a computer. A job normally includes all the necessary application programs, files and instructions to the operating system. *See* BACKGROUND JOB.

job control language. (JCL) In computing, a problem-oriented language used for specifying the environment for running a particular batch of work.

job-oriented terminal. In peripherals, a terminal designed for a particular application.

job priority. In computing, a value assigned to a job that determines the priority used in scheduling the job and allocating resources to it in a multiprogramming environment. *See* BATCH PROCESSING, MULTIPROGRAMMING.

job queue. In computing, the set of programs and data being processed by a computer, the order of processing being determined by the job priorities. *See* JOB PRIORITY.

job step. In computing, a unit of work associated with an application program. *See* APPLICATION PROGRAM.

jog. In recording, a frame-by-frame movement of a video tape during editing. This is possible on helical scan systems because of their freeze frame capability. *See* FREEZE FRAME, HELICAL SCAN.

joggle. In stationery, to align the edges of a stack of sheets by using vibration.

join. In databases, an operator in relational algebra. A join operation on two relations that share a common data item type produces a combined relation with attributes specified in the join operation. *Compare* DIVISION, PROJECTION, SELECTION. *See* RELATIONAL ALGEBRA, RELATIONAL DATABASE.

Josephson junction. In electronics, a superconducting device that can act as an extremely fast, low-power dissipating switch. It is the junction between two metals held at extremely low temperatures. *See* SUPERCONDUCTIVITY.

journal. (1) In communications, a list of all messages sent and received by a terminal. (2) In computing, a chronological record of changes made to a set of data, often used for reconstructing a previous version of the set in the event of corruption. *See* CORRUPTION.

JOVIAL. In programming, Jule's Own Version of International Algorithmic Language; a multipurpose programming language developed for military applications. *See* PROGRAMMING LANGUAGE.

joystick. (1) In peripherals, a rotary lever employed as a pointing device that enables an operator to alter or move images on the display. *See* POINTING DEVICE. (2) In filming, a device connected to a cable for remote lens control.

JSP. *See* JACKSON STRUCTURED PROGRAMMING.

j-type defects. In micrographics, defects in microfilm appearing as tiny spots 10–150 micrometres in diameter.

judder. In facsimile, an irregular movement of the moving parts in a transmitter or receiver causing straight lines in the source document to be reproduced in a wavy manner.

jukebox. In memory systems, a device that automatically retrieves a item containing stored information (e.g. videodisc, microfiche, etc.) from a central store.

Julian date. In programming, a date format in which the year is represented by numerals in positions 1 and 2, the day is represented as a number, in the range 1-366, in positions 3 to 5, with zeros in unused high-order positions.

jumbo chip. *See.* WAFER SILICON INTEGRATION.

jump. (1) In programming, a departure from the consecutive sequence in which instructions are executed. A jump instruction may be conditional or unconditional. In the former case the decision to continue with the current sequence, or to move control to a given instruction elsewhere in the program depends upon the current value of specified variables. *See* CONDITIONAL JUMP, UNCONDITIONAL JUMP. (2) In printing, to carry over a portion of a newspaper or periodical feature from one page to another.

jumper. In electronics, a short wire used for the temporary connection of two points in an electric circuit.

junction. In electronics, the boundary region between two semiconductors having different electrical properties, or between a metal and a semiconductor. This boundary region is used to control the current flow through a semiconductor. *See* SEMICONDUCTOR.

junk. In satellite communications, satellites that are still in orbit, but are no longer operating.

justification. *See* JUSTIFY.

justify. (1) In printing, to set lines of type to their full measure. (2) In word processing, to print a document with even right- and left-hand margins. *Compare* RAGGED SETTING. (3) In programming, to shift the contents of a register to a specified position. *See* REGISTER.

justify inhibit. In word processing, to inhibit the justification routine so that text is processed without being justified. *See* JUSTIFY.

K

K. *See* KILO.

Kanji. A set of ideograms used in Chinese and Japanese writing. *Compare* HIRAGANA, KATAKANA.

Karnaugh map. In mathematics, a method of representing a logical expression that facilitates the simplification of that expression.

Katakana. A character set of symbols used in one of the two common Japanese phonetic alphabets. It is often employed to write foreign words phonetically. *Compare* HIRAGANA, KANJI.

Kb. *See* KILOBYTE.

KDD. The Japanese international PTT. *See* PTT.

keep. In printing, a line of text intended to be printed in the same column. If necessary the column is continued in the next column or on the following page.

keep in. In printing, instruction to a compositor to use narrow wordspaces. *Compare* KEEP OUT.

keep it simple stupid. (KISS) In computing, an adage warning against the dangers of unnecessary sophistication.

keep out. In printing, instruction to a compositor to set type matter widely spaced so that it makes as many lines as possible. *Compare* KEEP IN.

kern. In printing, that part of a piece of type that overhangs the body and so overlaps onto an adjacent piece. *See* KERNING.

kernel. (1) In computer security. *See* SECURITY KERNEL. (2) In operating systems, the lowest level of an operating system, comprising rigorously tested routines responsible for the allocation of hardware resources to the operating system processes and the programs running under the operating system.

kernelized. In data security, pertaining to an operating system designed to partition classes of users so that they can only access those facilities for which they have authorization. Such systems give the impression that different computers are available to users of different kernels.

kerning. In printing, a backspacing technique whereby one character is tucked into another (e.g. an A and a V) in order to avoid the optical impression of excessive spacing that can arise from the varying shapes of characters and combinations of characters. *Compare* SIDE BEARINGS. *See* KERN.

Kerr effect. In optical media, the rotation of plane of polarization when a beam of polarized light passes through a magnetic field. *See* ERASABLE OPTICAL DISC, OPTICAL DIGITAL DISC, POLARIZED.

key. (1) In data security, a symbol or sequence of symbols (or electrical or mechanical correlates of symbols) that control the operations of encryption and decryption. (FIPS). *See* CRYPTOGRAPHIC KEY, DECRYPT, ENCRYPT. (2) In databases, one or more characters used for identifying a set of data. *See* PRIMARY KEY, SECONDARY KEY. (3) In peripherals, a lever on a keyboard. *See* KEYBOARD.

keyboard. In peripherals, the standard data input and operator control device for a microcomputer. The depression of a key causes a coded electrical signal to be input to the computer. The ergonomic design of keyboards is of increasing importance as microcomputers become standard office components for word processing, information retrieval, etc., and reports on RSI impact upon employer/employee relationships. Draft DIN standards have now been formulated following an ergonomic study of keyboards in West Germany. These standards relate to the keyboard height, measured from the work surface to the middle row of keys, the angle of tilt, the intercentre key spacing, key travel, key-operating force and the minimum legend size. The key layouts may be azerty, qwerty, Dvorak, Pronto and Maltron; the last is said to provide greater operator comfort, but requires retraining of typists.

Microcomputer keyboards normally provide more keys than conventional typewriters. A common layout includes conventional alphanumeric characters, function keys, a numeric keypad and specific control keys. The alphanumeric keys are used for text and numeric data entry. The role of function keys varies with application packages (e.g. save file, display graphs, etc.). The numeric keypad facilitates entry of tables of numerals, and control keys provide for cursor movements, rebooting the operating system, etc.

Keyboards may have varying degrees of intelligence, and microprocessor-controlled keyboards with electrically programmable read-only memories enable the code sequence generated by key depressions to be changed. The immediate effect of a key depression depends upon the current state of the interface with the central processing unit (CPU); if the processor is engaged on other tasks then the keyboard may appear to be dead, but a few keystrokes are stored in buffer and processed when the CPU becomes available. A bleep is commonly emitted to indicate that the keyboard buffer is full.

The operating functions of the key may be N-key rollover or lockout. In the former case N keys can be depressed virtually simultaneously and the keyboard will remember the sequence of depressions. Lockout systems, on the other hand, register only the first depression.

The main keyswitch technologies are capacitive, mechanical contact, membrane and reed. The life of a keyswitch ranges from 100- to 200-million depressions for capacitive devices, which involve no physical contact, to about 20-million depressions for mechanical keyswitches. *See* AZERTY KEYBOARD, CAPACITY-ACTIVATED TRANSDUCER, DVORAK KEYBOARD, ELECTRICALLY PROGRAMMABLE READ-ONLY MEMORY, LOCKOUT, MALTRON KEYBOARD, MEMBRANE SWITCH, N-KEY ROLLOVER, PROGRAM FUNCTION KEY, PRONTO KEYBOARD, QWERTY KEYBOARD, RSI.

keyboard control logic. In peripherals, the logic circuitry built into a keyboard, to interpret the individual keystrokes and convert them into the electronic signals needed to control the computer to which the keyboard is connected. (Philips). *See* KEYBOARD.

keyboarding. In peripherals, the operation of entering text via keyboards.

keyboard input functions. In peripherals, operating system subroutines that obtain the status of, or retrieve data from, a keyboard or keypad. (Philips). *See* KEYBOARD, KEYPAD.

keyboard overlay. In peripherals, a template placed over a keyboard to indicate the key functions for a particular operation or software package.

keyboard remapping. In distributed processing, a feature of a terminal emulator package that redefines the keys on a microcomputer keyboard to imitate the keyboard on a mainframe terminal. Since some terminals have more keys than the microcomputer some keys will be represented by a sequence of key depressions on the microcomputer keyboard. *See* TERMINAL EMULATION.

keyboard scan. In peripherals, the periodic sampling of the switches activated by the keys of a keyboard to determine whether a key has been depressed and, if so, its identity.

key controller. In peripherals and television, a control unit with a keypad. (Philips). *See* KEYPAD.

key distribution and control. In data security, the processes involved in the distribution and control of cryptographic keys include: (a) appointment of cryptographic personnel (b) responsibilities of cryptographic personnel; (c) shipment and receipt of keying material; (d) storage of keying material and encryption/authentication device physical keys; (e) use of keying material, (f) destruction of keying material; and (g) archiving of keys. *See* CRYPTOGRAPHIC KEY, DUAL CONTROL, SECURITY LIFE.

key-encrypting key. In data security, a key used in the encryption of another cryptographic key, so that it may be transmitted over an insecure channel or stored in insecure storage. *Compare* DATA-ENCRYPTING KEY. *See* CRYPTOGRAPHIC KEY, KEY MANAGEMENT. *Synonymous with* SECONDARY KEY.

key exhaustion. In data security, an exhaustive cryptanalytic attack technique in which the attacker possesses a fragment of the plaintext, the corresponding ciphertext and has knowledge of the cryptographic algorithm. A trial key is selected, the plaintext is encrypted with this key, and the result compared with the known ciphertext. Alternatively, if only ciphertext is available then it is decrypted with the trial key, and the resulting plaintext is inspected to see if it corresponds to a meaningful message. *Compare* MESSAGE EXHAUSTION. *See* CRYPTOGRAPHIC KEY, EXHAUSTIVE ATTACK, KNOWN PLAINTEXT.

keyforce. In peripherals, the force required to depress a key to ensure positive contact and the actioning of the keystroke.

key generator. In data security, a device, including associated alarms and self-tests, for generating cryptographic keys. Key generation must be undertaken in such a manner so as to ensure that: (a) the result of the generation process is unpredictable; (b) the range of keys that can be produced is equal to the full range of valid keys; (c) there is no substantial skew in the probability distribution of the keys produced; (d) an attacker cannot influence the generation process; (e) an attacker cannot change the output from the generator; and (f) an attacker cannot monitor the generator output. *See* CRYPTOGRAPHIC KEY, KEY MANAGEMENT.

key gun. In key management, a device for transporting electronically stored cryptographic keys. A typical key gun is the size of a pocket calculator, and it has connectors to receive keys from a source and to deliver them to the destination device (e.g. a terminal). Electrical or optical coupling may be employed for the device connection.

key letter in context. (KLIC) In library science, a method similar to keyword in context (KWIC), but based on letters instead of terms. Permuted term lists are sorted on each letter in every term with the balance of term displayed. *See* KEYWORD IN CONTEXT.

keyline. In printing, an outline drawn or set on artwork showing the size and position of an illustration or halftone. (Desktop). *See* HALFTONE.

key management. In data security, the processes concerned with the generation, distribution, storage and destruction of cryptographic keys. Encipherment effectively transfers the problem of ensuring the secrecy of a mass of data to that of protecting the secrecy of a cryptographic key. The problems associated with the various aspects of key management depend upon the range of the cryptographic techniques, the environment and applications in which the cryptographic keys are employed. *See* CRYPTOGRAPHIC KEY, DATA ENCRYPTION STANDARD, KEY GENERATOR.

key notarization. In data security, a method of applying additional security to a cryptographic key utilizing the identities of the originator and the ultimate recipient. *See* CRYPTOGRAPHIC KEY, KEY MANAGEMENT.

keypad. In peripherals, a simplified keyboard consisting of a small set of pushbuttons as on certain telephones or on the control unit of a videotex terminal. *See* KEYBOARD, VIDEOTEX.

key phrase in context. (KPIC) In library science, a method similar to keyword in context (KWIC), but based on phrases instead of words. *Compare* KEY LETTER IN CONTEXT, KEYWORD IN CONTEXT.

keyplate. In printing, the first plate used in the production of a coloured print. Subsequent plates overprint the first image, which provides the key for registering other colours. *See* REGISTER.

key space. In data security, the range of all possible values that a cryptographic key may assume. In a cipher system the key space must be large enough to thwart key exhaustion cryptanalytic attacks. *Compare* MESSAGE SPACE. *See* KEY EXHAUSTION.

keystone waveform. In television, a correction waveform sometimes used in scanning to correct for certain types of geometric distortion. *See* GEOMETRIC DISTORTION, KEYSTONING.

keystoning. (1) In optics, a geometrical image distortion arising when a plane surface is photographed at an angle other than perpendicular to the lens axis. (2) In audiovisual aids, distortion of a projected image, usually of a wide-top, narrow-bottom effect. To avoid keystoning the screen must be placed at right angles to the projection axis.

key stream. *Synonymous with* CRYPTOGRAPHIC BIT STREAM.

keystroke. The act of depressing one of the keys on a keyboard or a typewriter.

keystroke verification. In computing, the re-entry of data by a keyboard operator to check the accuracy of the prior entry of the same data by a different operator.

key telephone set. In communications, a telephone set with special buttons to provide such capabilities as switching between lines, call holding or alerting of other telephone users.

key travel. In peripherals, the displacement of a key from rest to fully depressed position.

key variant. In data security, a master cryptographic key derived from another master key by a simple mathematical operation (e.g. inverting selected bits). This technique permits the use of a hierarchy of master keys while only demanding secure storage for one of them.

keyword. (1) In computer security. *Synonymous with* PASSWORD. (2) In library science, one of the significant and informative words in a title or document that describes the content of that document. *See* KEY, KEYWORD AND CONTEXT, KEYWORD IN CONTEXT, KEYWORD OUT OF CONTEXT. *Synonymous with* DESCRIPTOR.

keyword and context. (KWAC) In library science, an index of titles of documents permuted to bring each significant word to the beginning, in alphabetical order, followed by the remaining words that follow it in the title, and then followed by that part of the original title that came before the significant word. *See* KEYWORD IN CONTEXT.

keyword in context. (KWIC) In library science, a form of automatic indexing of documents. Keywords are extracted from the title, abstract or some portion of the text and stored with the associated title or surrounding portion of text. A search for the keyword can produce the context of that keyword in the document plus a document number. *Compare* KEYWORD OUT OF CONTEXT. *See* KEYWORD, ONLINE INFORMATION RETRIEVAL.

keyword out of context. (KWOC) In library science, a method of indexing in which the titles are printed in full under as many keywords as the indexer considers useful. *Compare* KEYWORD IN CONTEXT. *See* INDEX, KEYWORD.

kHz. *See* KILOHERTZ.

kilo. A prefix denoting 1000, but in some computer applications it refers to 1024 because it corresponds to the binary number 10 000 000 000.

kilobit. (Kb) One-thousand and twenty-four bits. *See* BIT, KILO.

kilobyte. One-thousand and twenty-four bytes. *See* BYTE, KILO.

kilohertz. One-thousand hertz. *See* HERTZ.

Kilostream. In data communications, a fully digital service provided by British Telecom that operates over a specially provided digital network that links main telephone exchanges. *Compare* MEGASTREAM, SAT-STREAM, SWITCHSTREAM. *See* X-STREAM.

kinesthetic feedback. In physiology, an indication that an action has been effected (e.g. the actioning of a keystroke) by the sensation of touch, position or movement.

KIPS. (1) Knowledge information-processing system. *Synonymous with* FIFTH-GENERATION COMPUTER. (2) In architecture, kiloinstructions per second; a measure of computing power. *Compare* LIPS, MIPS. *See* INSTRUCTION.

KISS. *See* KEEP IT SIMPLE STUPID.

KLIC. *See* KEY LETTER IN CONTEXT.

kludge. In computing, a clever solution to a problem using unconventional methods; the major problem of kludges is that they may lead to unforeseen side effects or later maintenance problems.

knapsack cipher. In public key cryptography, an early form of public key crypto-system proposed by Merkle and Hellman in 1978. Its name relates to the mathematical problem of selecting a subset of a set of cylindrical rods of different lengths such that they will exactly fit in a cylindrical knapsack. Successful cryptanalytic attacks have been reported in relation to some knapsack ciphers. *Compare* RSA. *See* CRYPTANALYSIS, PUBLIC KEY CRYPTOGRAPHY.

know-how. Includes both the know-how of design and manufacturing, and the know-how and related technical information that is needed to achieve a significant development, production or use. The term know-how includes services, processes, procedures, specifications, design data and criteria, and testing techniques. (DODD).

knowledge base. In programming, a database containing the codified knowledge of a human expert or experts. *See* EXPERT SYSTEMS.

knowledge engineering. In programming, the process of building expert systems. *See* EXPERT SYSTEMS.

known plaintext. In data security, techniques employed in cryptanalysis when the cryptanalyst has matched plaintext and ciphertext available. *Compare* CIPHERTEXT ONLY. *See* CIPHERTEXT, CRYPTANALYSIS, PLAINTEXT.

KPIC. Key phrase in context. *See* KEY LETTER IN CONTEXT, KEYWORD IN CONTEXT.

Ku band. In communications, the frequency range 12–18 GHz. *Compare* C BAND, L BAND, S BAND.

KWAC. *See* KEYWORD AND CONTEXT.

KWIC. *See* KEYWORD IN CONTEXT.

KWOC. *See* KEYWORD OUT OF CONTEXT.

L

LA. UK Library Association.

LAA. Library Association of Australia.

label. (1) In computer security, a piece of information that represents the security level of an object and that describes the sensitivity of the information in the object. (DOD). *See* OBJECT. (2) In programming, one or more characters or a symbol used to identify a program statement or the entry point of a subroutine. The use of labels, as compared with consecutive statement numbers, provides for more meaningful program statements and avoids the necessity of extensive renumbering when substantial modifications are made. *See* STATEMENT, SUBROUTINE. (3) In filming, words superimposed on a film to indicate names, or functions, of objects shown in the film.

laboratory effects. In recording, special audio and optical effects that can be produced in the processing of film or video tape (e.g. a night effect or the sound of an explosion).

lag. (1) In electronics, the delay in change of an output with respect to changes in the input voltage, current or power. (2) In television, a persistence of the electrical charge image on the phosphor screen for a small number of frames. (3) In visual perception, the retention of an image by the eye after removal of the stimulus. When a succession of still pictures is presented to the eye, as in films or television, the visual sensation retained by the retina decays relatively slowly, thus providing an illusion of continuous movement. *See* PERSISTENCE OF VISION.

laid. In printing, paper with a watermark pattern showing the wire marks used in the paper-making process. It is usually applied to high-quality stationery. (Desktop). *See* WATERMARK.

laminate. In printing, a thin, transparent plastic coating applied to paper or board to provide protection and give it a glossy finish. (Desktop). *See* BOARD.

LAN. *See* LOCAL AREA NETWORK.

landscape. (1) In printing, work in which the width used is greater than the height. (2) In printing, indicating the orientation of tables or illustrations that are printed sideways. (Desktop). *Compare* PORTRAIT.

language. In programming and communications, a set of characters, conventions and rules used to convey information. A language may be formally considered to consist of pragmatics, semantics and syntax. *See* FORMAL LANGUAGE, GRAMMAR, PRAGMATICS, SEMANTICS, SYNTAX.

language processor. (1) In programming, a computer or other functional unit for processing programs written in a specified programming language. (2) In programming. *See* TRANSLATOR.

language support environment. In programming, hardware and software facilities supplied by a manufacturer to assist in the development of programs written in a particular language.

language translator. *See* TRANSLATOR.

LAP. In data communications, link access protocol; a data link layer protocol that is a subset of high-level data link control and is used in X.25-based networks. *See* DATA LINK

LAYER, HIGH-LEVEL DATA LINK CONTROL, PROTOCOL, X.25.

lap. In printing, a small overlap where two colours meet to safeguard against a gap that might otherwise occur due to a lack of register. *See* REGISTER.

lapel microphone. In recording and audiovisual aids, a microphone clipped to a speaker's clothing. *Compare* LAVALIER MICROPHONE.

lap-top computer. In computing, a battery-powered portable personal computer, often with a LCD screen; intended for use by travelling executives. *Compare* BRIEFCASE-PORTABLE, SUITCASE-PORTABLE. *See* LCD SCREENS.

large face. In typesetting, the larger of two sizes available on the same body of typeface. *See* TYPE SIZE.

large-scale integration. (LSI) In microelectronics, pertaining to a fabrication technology that produces between 10 000 and 100 000 transistors per chip. *Compare* MEDIUM-SCALE INTEGRATION, SMALL-SCALE INTEGRATION, SUPER-LARGE-SCALE INTEGRATION, ULTRA-LARGE-SCALE INTEGRATION, VERY LARGE-SCALE INTEGRATION. *See* CHIP, TRANSISTOR.

laser. In optoelectronics, Light Amplification by Stimulated Emission of Radiation; a device that emits light rays that are in phase, travelling in the same direction and essentially of the same wavelength (i.e. colour). A laser beam does not diverge by a significant amount and maintains a high energy density.

Conventional light sources accept energy, in some form, and use it to raise the energy level of electrons bound to nuclei. When these electrons return to their original state photons are produced. The light wavelength corresponding to these emitted photons depends upon the energy level changes of the electrons. In lasers a large number of electrons are raised to a specific energy level. An incident photon of the correct frequency causes an excited electron to fall to its lower-energy level and to emit a photon. These two photons can now stimu-

late two more excited electrons to undergo similar energy jumps. This multiplier effect produces the virtual simultaneous emission of photons of identical frequencies, thus providing a high-energy pulse of coherent, monochromatic light. Lasers are used in optical signalling devices, high-speed printers, fiber optics and holography. *See* COHERENCE, ELECTRON, FIBER OPTICS, HOLOGRAM, LASER PRINTER, PHOTON.

laser beam recording. (LBR) In applications, a technique employed in a microfilm recorder whereby the output characters from a computer are written directly to microfilm by laser. Typically the beam is divided into a number of separate rays which produce a dot matrix pattern. *See* COMPUTER OUTPUT TO MICROFILM, DOT MATRIX, LASER.

laser COM. In micrographics, the use of a laser to write directly on a microfilm (i.e. COM) to produce instantaneous storage without any need for chemical processing. *See* COMPUTER OUTPUT TO MICROFILM.

laser disc. In optical media, any disc recorded and read by a laser. (Philips). *See* COMPACT DISC, LASER, LaserVision, VIDEODISC.

laser graphics. In computer graphics, a method of producing spectacular large-scale graphic displays using lasers and computer-controlled scanners. The scanners are high-speed precision motor-driven mirrors, which deflect single or multiple laser beams to trace out an image several times a second. The mirrors deflect each point of the image at high speed creating the illusion of a solid line. The images can be projected onto a screen or non-solid objects such as smoke or mist. The movements of the scanners can be determined by a computer program. *See* LASER.

laser kinescope. In television, an experimental television projector in which the image is first produced by focusing an electron beam on a tiny screen which emits laser light; the laser light is then focused onto a large screen. *See* LASER, PROJECTION TELEVISION.

laser line follower. In peripherals, a graphic information input device in which a laser beam follows and traces continuous lines. *See* LASER.

laser printer. In printers, a fast, high-quality, non-impact printer. The six stages involved in the laser printer are cleaning, conditioning, writing, developing, transferring and fusing. The printing centres around a belt consisting of a polyester film covered with a photosensitive material.

The cleaning station comprises an erase lamp and magnetic brush assembly. The photosensitive material exhibits a reduction in its electrical resistance with incident light intensity. The erase lamp illuminates the photosensitive belt allowing any residual electronic charge to leak away, and the magnetic brush assembly removes any debris. The conditioning station applies a uniform electrostatic charge to the photosensitive surface. An electrical discharge is produced by a high voltage applied to a thin wire, ionizing the air and allowing passage of electrical charge from the wire to the belt.

A laser beam, modulated according to the raster pattern to be printed, applies the latent image to the belt at the writing station. The beam scans along the horizontal axis of the belt and creates a raster image of 'dots' or 'no dots' line by line. The electric charge on the belt is dissipated at any point illuminated by the laser beam due to the action of the photosensitive material.

The electrostatic image on the belt next rotates past the developing station where a cloud of toner is created by a rotating magnetic brush. The toner is composed of a black plastic resin mixed with iron and coated with carbon. It has an electrical charge and only settles on the uncharged 'dots' on the belt that were illuminated by the laser beam. At the transfer stage the toner image is placed on paper as a result of a second conditioning process which places a uniform electrostatic charge on the paper. This charge is opposite to that of the toner, and thus the toner image is attracted to the paper. The belt then returns to the cleaning station, and the paper proceeds to the fusing station where a high-intensity lamp provides the necessary heat to melt the toner in the paper. *Compare* INK JET PRINTER, ION DEPOSITION, LED PRINTER, MAGNETOGRAPHY. *See* CHARGE, ELECTROPHOTOGRAPHIC PROCESS, ELECTROSTATIC PRINTER, LASER, RASTER, XEROGRAPHY.

LaserVision. In optical media, an optical videodisc produced by Philips.

laser xerography. *See* LASER PRINTER.

last in first out. (LIFO) In data structures, a system in which the next item to be selected is the one most recently added to the list. *Compare* FIRST IN FIRST OUT. *See* STACK.

latch. In hardware, a circuit that accepts signals and holds the corresponding data until it is required. It is commonly used in microprocessor interfacing systems. *See* INTERFACE.

latency. In backing storage, the delay between the instant a request is made for a an item of data and the instant the transfer starts. *See* ROTATIONAL LATENCY, SEEK LATENCY.

latent image. In photography and printing, the invisible image formed in the sensitized material after exposure, but before development.

lateral reversal. To reverse an image from right to left so that it will appear as a mirror image.

launch amplifier. In cable television, the final amplifier at the head end of a system. *See* HEAD END.

launch vehicle. In communications, a rocket or space shuttle used to lift a communications satellite into orbit. *See* COMMUNICATIONS SATELLITE SYSTEM.

lavalier microphone. In recording and audiovisual aids, a small microphone suspended from a cord around a speaker's neck. *Compare* LAPEL MICROPHONE.

layer. (1) In radio communications, one of the three regions that form the ionosphere. *See* D REGION, E REGION, F REGION. (2) In data communications. *See* APPLICATION LAYER, DATA LINK LAYER, NETWORK LAYER, PHYSICAL LAYER, PRESENTATION LAYER, SESSION LAYER, TRANSPORT LAYER.

lay in. In recording, the synchronization of sound tracks to a picture.

layout. (1) In programming, the specification of the format for input/output data. *See* FORMAT. (2) In printing, a plan designed to show how the printed result is to be produced and to give an indication of how it will look.

L band. In communications, the frequency range 1–2 GHz. *Compare* C BAND, KU BAND, S BAND.

LBR. *See* LASER BEAM RECORDING.

LC. US Library of Congress.

LCA. Lower-case alphabet. *See* LOWER CASE.

LCD. *See* LIQUID CRYSTAL DISPLAY.

LCD screens. In peripherals, a form of flat-screen visual display unit employing liquid crystal displays (LCD). This type of display has no flicker and requires only 50–100 milliwatts. It is lighter, flatter and requires less power that a conventional cathode ray tube (CRT) display and is therefore favoured in portable microcomputers. Early LCD screens had a poor contrast and a limited viewing angle, and were therefore less attractive to the user than CRTs. The contrast and viewing angles of LCDs are improved by the use of super-twisted nematic crystal displays. The readability can also be improved by the use of back lighting using either an electroluminescent panel or fluorescent tube. A high-contrast display can be achieved by a black shutter LCD in which the active segments become transparent which, when backlit, produces a contrast of 16:1, compared with 4.5:1 for super-twisted nematic displays, and a wide viewing angle. *See* CATHODE RAY TUBE, ELECTROLUMINESCENCE, FLAT-SCREEN DISPLAY, LIQUID CRYSTAL DISPLAY, SUPER-TWISTED NEMATIC.

LCG. Linear congruential generator. *See* RANDOM NUMBERS.

LCMARC. In library science, US Library of Congress Machine-Readable Cataloging; a database of bibliographic records of US publications which is compiled at the Library of Congress. *See* MARC.

LCP. Link control procedure. *See* LINK PROTOCOL.

LD4. In data communications, a high-speed, coaxial cable, digital transmission system operating at 274 megabits per second.

LDDS. Limited-distance data set. *See* LIMITED-DISTANCE MODEM.

LDM. *See* LINEAR DELTA MODULATION.

LDS. *See* LOCAL DISTRIBUTION SERVICE.

LDX. *See* LONG-DISTANCE XEROGRAPHY.

lead. *See* LEADING.

leader. (1) In photography and filming, any kind of non-image film used for editing, threading or identification purposes. (2) In printing, a line of dots used to direct the eye along a printed line. (3) In computing, the blank section of magnetic or paper tape preceding the start of the recorded information, used for threading purposes. *See* MAGNETIC TAPE.

leading. In printing, space added between lines of type to space out text and provide visual separation of the lines. It is measured in points or fractions thereof. The name is derived from strips of lead which used to be inserted between lines of metal type. (Desktop). *See* POINT.

leading zero. In programming, a zero, used as a fill character, that precedes the most significant digit of a number. *See* FILL CHARACTER.

lead-in pages. In videotex, routing pages which direct a user to required areas of the database. *See* END PAGES.

lead-in track. In optical media, a track on a compact disc, before the program tracks, containing the table of contents. (Philips). *See* COMPACT DISC, TABLE OF CONTENTS, TRACK.

leaf. In data structures, the node at the end of a path in a tree structure. *Compare* ROOT. *See* TREE STRUCTURE.

leakage. In data security, the unauthorized flow of information from a user, with access privileges, to a user lacking such privileges. *See* INFORMATION FLOW CONTROL.

leased circuit. In data communications, a circuit hired by subscribers for their exclusive and permanent use. It may be a point-to-point or multidrop connection. *See* MULTIDROP CIRCUIT, POINT-TO-POINT. *Synonymous with* LEASED CIRCUIT, NON-SWITCHED LINE.

leased line. *Synonymous with* LEASED CIRCUIT.

least common mechanism. In computer security, one of the principles of secure systems. *See* PRINCIPLES OF SECURE SYSTEMS.

least cost network design. In data communications, a network of optimum design which meets the design specification at the least possible cost.

least privilege. *See* PRINCIPLE OF LEAST PRIVILEGE.

least significant bit. (LSB) In data structures, the bit that occupies the rightmost position in a binary number. *Compare* MOST SIGNIFICANT BIT.

least significant digit. (LSD) In data structures, the digit that occupies the rightmost position in a number and therefore has least weight. *Compare* MOST SIGNIFICANT DIGIT.

LED. *See* LIGHT-EMITTING DIODE.

LED printer. In printing, a device similar in operation to a laser printer except that the moving laser beam is replaced with light from an array of light-emitting diodes (LEDs). The light is conducted from the LEDs to the photosensitive surface by a matching set of rod lenses. This device has the advantage that it has fewer moving parts than the laser printer. *Compare* LASER PRINTER. *See* LIGHT-EMITTING DIODE.

left-hand margin indent. In word processing, a feature that enables blocks of recorded text to be identified with different left-hand margins, irrespective of any amendments made to the text and while still retaining the original, fixed, left-hand margin settings.

left-justified. (1) In printing, pertaining to text that has been moved so that the left margin is straight. (2) In program execution, the shifting of a number to the left-hand end of a register. *Compare* RIGHT-JUSTIFIED. *See* JUSTIFY, REGISTER.

legend. (1) In printing, the descriptive matter printed below an illustration, mostly referred to as caption. (2) In printing, an explanation of signs or symbols used in timetables or maps. (Desktop). *See* CAPTION.

lens. (1) In photography, a transparent optical system through which light is refracted to produce an image. (2) In electronics, a system of magnets or electromagnets used to focus a beam of electrons in a cathode ray tube. *See* CATHODE RAY TUBE, FOCUSING.

lens aperture. An orifice, usually an adjustable iris, that limits the amount of light passing through a lens.

lens coating. In photography, a coating used to reduce reflections from a lens surface.

lens speed. In photography, the f-number of a lens. *See* F-NUMBER, F-STOP.

lens stop. *Synonymous with* F-STOP.

lettering safety. In television, the area within a television frame in which text can be clearly read. *Compare* SAFETY AREA.

letterpress. In printing, a process in which an impression is taken from the inked surfaces of type or blocks. *Compare* INTAGLIO, LITHOGRAPHY. *Synonymous with* RELIEF PRINTING.

letter quality. In printing, a quality of text image, produced by top of the range fully formed character printers. It equates to that of high-quality office typewriters. *Compare* BUSINESS QUALITY, DRAFT QUALITY, NEAR LETTER QUALITY. *See* FULLY FORMED CHARACTER, PRINTER.

letterset. In printing, a contraction of letterpress offset; a process in which a rotary letterpress transfers an inked image from an offset cylinder, as with offset lithography. *See* LETTERPRESS, OFFSET PRINTING, LITHOGRAPHY. *Synonymous with* INDIRECT LETTERPRESS.

letterspacing. In printing, the insertion of spaces between the letters of a word or words to lengthen the measure, to improve the appearance of the line or for emphasis. *See* MEASURE.

level. (1) In electronics and communications, a general term for the magnitude of a signal. It is used for voltage, current and power. (2) In data communications, the number of bits in each character of an information-coding system. (3) In data communications, the number of discrete signal elements that can be transmitted in a given modulation scheme. *See* MODULATION.

level four. In optical media, pertaining to a sophisticated videodisc player with extensive memory, control and processing facilities. *Compare* LEVEL ONE, LEVEL THREE, LEVEL TWO. *See* INTERACTIVE VIDEODISC SYSTEMS.

level one. In optical media, pertaining to a videodisc player with freeze frame, picture stop, chapter stop, frame addressability and dual channel audio, but with limited memory and virtually no processing power. *Compare* LEVEL FOUR, LEVEL THREE, LEVEL TWO. *See* CHAPTER STOP, FREEZE FRAME, INTERACTIVE VIDEODISC SYSTEMS, PICTURE STOP.

level three. In optical media, pertaining to a level one or level two videodisc player interfaced with an external computer. *Compare* LEVEL FOUR, LEVEL ONE, LEVEL TWO. *See* INTERACTIVE VIDEODISC SYSTEMS.

level two. In optical media, pertaining to a videodisc player with level one facilities plus on-board, programmable memory and improved access times. *Compare* LEVEL FOUR, LEVEL ONE, LEVEL THREE. *See* INTERACTIVE VIDEODISC SYSTEMS.

lexical scan. In programming, a stage in the compilation process in which the source code statements are decomposed into essential components (e.g. constants, reserved words, names, operators). *See* COMPILER, OPERATOR, RESERVED WORD.

Lexis. In online information retrieval, a database supplied by Mead Data Central and others, and dealing with communications, energy, industry, US federal government, labour and employment, financal law, international law, UK law, US federal law, US state law, patents, US securities, taxes and US trade. *Compare* CLIRS DATABASES.

LF. *See* LINE FEED.

library. (1) In programming, a collection of subroutines and programs written for a particular computer and available to a programmer for insertion into his own coding. (2) In computing, a repository for demountable recorded media, such as magnetic disk packs and magnetic tapes. (3) In computing, any collection of related files. *See* FILE.

library picture. In printing, a picture taken from an existing library and not specially commissioned. (Desktop).

library science. The knowledge and skill concerned with the administration of libraries and their contents.

library subroutine. In programming, a set of standard routines kept on backing storage for use by application programmers. *See* SUBROUTINE.

license. In broadcasting, the permission granted by the Federal Commnications Commission to operate a broadcast facility in the USA. *See* FEDERAL COMMUNICATIONS COMMISSION.

LIFO. *See* LAST IN FIRST OUT.

lifter. In recording, a device that removes the magnetic tape from contact with the head on fast wind or rewind.

ligatures. In printing, two or more letters joined together, forming one type character, or a stroke connecting two letters. *Synonymous with* TIED LETTERS.

light. In physiology, that part of the electromagnetic spectrum, from 400 to 750 nanometres, of which the human observer is aware through the stimulation of the retina. It is not synonymous with radiant energy, nor is it merely a sensation. *See* ELECTROMAGNETIC RADIATION.

light button. *Synonymous with* VIRTUAL PUSH BUTTON.

light conduit. In optoelectronics, an assembly of fibers in a fiber optics cable that is used for the transmission of light sources rather than encoded optical signals. *See* FIBER OPTICS.

light control. (1) Control based on the use of light. (Philips). (2) In filming and video, the control of lighting levels.

light-emitting diode. (LED) In electronics, a semiconductor diode that glows when supplied with a specified voltage. LEDs are commonly used as alphanumeric display devices. They can also be used as light sources in optical fiber transmission systems, although their low power output and relatively wide bandwidth make them less attractive than lasers. *Compare* LIQUID CRYSTAL DISPLAY. *See* FIBER OPTICS, LASER.

light face. In printing, type having finer strokes than the medium typeface. *Compare* BOLD FACE.

light guide. *See* FIBER OPTICS.

light pen. (1) In peripherals, a light-sensitive device that is shaped like a pen and connected to a visual display unit. The tip of the light pen contains a light-sensitive element which, when placed against the screen, reacts to the presence of the scanning spot of the raster display. A pulse is thus generated, and the timing of this pulse, relative to the start of the raster scan, enables the computer to identify the location of the pen on the screen. *See* POINTING DEVICE, RASTER, SCANNING SPOT, VISUAL DISPLAY UNIT. (2) In optical media, the laser unit for an optical disc player complete with optics and photodiodes. (Philips). *See* COMPACT DISC, LASER, OPTICAL VIDEODISC.

light stability. In character recognition, the degree of resistance to a change in colour when the image is subject to varying intensities of light. *See* OPTICAL CHARACTER RECOGNITION.

light-struck. In photography, pertaining to film that has been accidentally exposed to light.

limit check. In programming, a test on a number to see if it is within a stipulated range. *See* VALIDATION.

limited animation. In filming, animation in which only a part of the image moves. *See* ANIMATION.

limited-distance modem. In data communications, a modem that does not apply a complex modulation scheme to the data before transmission, but applies the digital input (or a simple transformation of it) to the transmission channel. It is used only for short distances of transmission. *Synonymous with* BASEBAND MODEM.

limited syntax. In machine translation, a restricted range of sentence constructions. Documents may be formed using this syntax to facilitate machine translation. *See* SYNTAX.

limiter. In electronics, a device that restricts the amplitude of a signal to a predetermined threshold level. Limiters may act on positive or negative values of a signal, or both.

limiting resolution. In television, a measure of overall system resolution, usually expressed in terms of the maximum number of lines per picture height discriminated on a test chart. For a number of lines N (alternate black and white lines) the width of each line is $1/N$ times the picture height. *See* RESOLUTION.

Lindop Committee. In data security, a UK committee that considered the problems of data protection. Its recommendations formed the basis for the Data Protection Act. *See* DATA PROTECTION, PRIVACY.

line. (1) In communications, a metallic conductor used for transmission purposes. (2) In data communications, a string of characters accepted by a central computer as a single block of input (e.g. all the characters entered prior to a carriage return command). (3) In television and facsimile, the path traced by a scanning spot. *See* SCANNING SPOT. (4) In printing, a unit of measurement used to describe the body size of large faces. *See* BODY SIZE.

linear. In electronics, a circuit that produces an output which varies in direct proportion to the input. No actual device is ever linear because there will always be an upper limit on the output. However, the term is usually applied to devices that provide a linear response over the normal range of input signals.

linear array. In radio communications, an antenna array in which the centres of the radiating elements lie in a straight line. *See* RADIATING ELEMENT.

linear congruential generator. *See* RANDOM NUMBERS.

linear delta modulation. (LDM) In data communications, a form of delta modulation in which the value of delta is kept constant. *Compare* ADAPTIVE DELTA MODULATION. *See* DELTA MODULATION.

linear function. In mathematics, a function that comprises the sum of terms, each of which is a constant multiplied by one, and only one, of the variables which are of first order only. For example $P = 5X + 10Y$.

linear mode. In information presentation, presentation of information (e.g films, television programmes) in a fixed sequence, uninfluenced by the recipient. (Philips). *Compare* INTERACTIVE MODE.

linear predictive coding. (LPC) In man–machine interfaces, a technique of encoding sampled speech sounds in which redundant information is ignored. *See* SPEECH SYNTHESIZER.

linear programming. In mathematics, a technique for finding the maximum or minimum value of a linear function when certain constraints are placed upon linear functions of the variables. It is a widely used optimizing technique in business and industry. *Compare* DYNAMIC PROGRAMMING. *See* LINEAR FUNCTION.

line blanking interval. In television, the time interval represented by the line blanking pulse width. *See* BLANKING INTERVAL.

line busy tone. In communications, an audible signal sent to a telephone calling party to indicate that the called party is busy. *See* BUSY.

linecaster. In typesetting, a machine that can cast an entire line of type as compared with one casting a character at a time.

line communications. In communications, the transmission and reception of electric signals over a cable. *See* CABLE.

line concentrator. In communications, a switching stage in a telephone local office that concentrates the traffic from a number of incoming lines to a smaller number of outlets to subsequent switching stages. *Compare* MULTIPLEXER.

line control. In data communications, the sequence of signals used to control a channel. *See* CHANNEL.

line counter. In word processing, a facility for counting and possibly controlling the number of lines printed on each page.

line driver. In data communications, a hardware component that interfaces a device to a line, providing functions such as adding control characters to output data, interpreting control characters on incoming data, buffering incoming data, converting parallel to serial transmission, etc. *See* BUS DRIVER, PARALLEL TRANSMISSION, SERIAL TRANSMISSION.

line drive signal. In television, the signal applied to the camera control unit to initiate scanning. *See* SCANNING LINE.

line editor. In programming, a text editor where the user must select individual lines to modify the text. *Compare* SCREEN EDITOR. *See* TEXT EDITOR.

line end zone. In word processing, a length of line, corresponding to a specified number of character positions prior to the right-hand margin, which automatically terminates the line. *Synonymous with* HOT ZONE.

line engraving.   In printing, a letterpress printing block consisting of solid areas and lines, reproduced direct from a black and white original without any intermediate tones. *See* LETTERPRESS.

line extender.   In cable television, an amplifier that compensates for signal loss in a spur feeder, enabling the network to cover a greater area. *See* ATTENUATION, SPUR.

line feed.   (LF) In printing, advancement of paper or a form on a printer one line at a time so that the printing mechanism is positioned for printing the next line. *Compare* CARRIAGE RETURN.

line folding.   In communications, when a teletypewriter or similar equipment receives a text message longer than the maximum allowed by the printer, the excess characters will be printed on the next line due to the generation of a local new line signal. Although the appearance of the message may be marred, the meaning is preserved. *See* TELETYPEWRITER.

line frequency.   In television, the number of scanning lines swept in one second. In a 525-line, 30-pictures per second system, the line frequency is 525 x 30 = 15 750 Hz. *See* SCANNING LINE. *Synonymous with* HORIZONTAL SCAN FREQUENCY.

line group.   In communications, one or more lines of the same type that can be activated and deactivated as a unit.

line impedance.   In communications, the impedance of a telecommunication line. *See* IMPEDANCE.

line increment.   In printing, the smallest separation possible between two lines of type for a particular machine.

line level.   (1) In data communications, the signal strength on a communications channel. *See* DECIBEL. (2) In data communications, a set of protocols concerned with the transmission and control of a transparent

stream of bits along a communications channel. *See* PROTOCOL, TRANSPARENT.

line load.   In communications, the amount of traffic on a line, expressed as a percentage of its utilization to its total capacity. *See* TRAFFIC.

line multiplication.   In optical media, a technique used in interactive compact discs to make a high-resolution line information compatible with a lower-resolution system. (Philips). *See* COMPACT DISC – INTERACTIVE, HIGH RESOLUTION, LOW RESOLUTION.

line noise.   In communications, noise originating in a telecommunications line. *Compare* HELIOS NOISE. *See* NOISE.

line of sight.   In communications, a situation in which there is an unobstructed straight-line path from the transmitting to the receiving antenna. A necessary condition for microwave relay systems. *See* ANTENNA, MICROWAVE RELAY.

line printer.   In printing, a device that prints an entire line of characters as one unit. *Compare* PAGE PRINTER, SERIAL PRINTER. *See* PRINTER.

line protocol.   *Synonymous with* LINK PROTOCOL.

line spacing.   *See* AUTOMATIC LINE SPACING.

line speed.   In data communications, the rate, measured in bauds, at which signals may be transmitted over a given channel. Effective speed varies with the capabilities of the equipment used and the amount of noise on the line. *See* BAUD, SHANNON'S LAW.

lines per minute.   (LPM) In peripherals, a measure of the speed of a line printer. *See* LINE PRINTER.

line sweep.   In television, the horizontal movement of the scanning spot at line frequency. *See* LINE FREQUENCY, SCANNING SPOT.

line switching.   *Synonymous with* CIRCUIT SWITCHING.

line sync pulse.   In television, a synchronizing pulse transmitted during the line blanking interval. *See* LINE BLANKING INTERVAL, VIDEO SIGNAL.

line termination equipment. (LTE) In data communications, data circuit terminating equipment, usually for a non-telephone circuit. *See* DATA CIRCUIT TERMINATING EQUIPMENT.

line testing. In computer graphics, a term derived from conventional animation in which an animation test is conducted on raw line information before the image is coloured. Similarly with computer animation, wire frame images are tested before hidden line algorithm and shading operations are performed. In some cases the computer may be able to produce the animation test in real time, but normally the individual frames are photographed and the developed film is played back. *See* COMPUTER ANIMATION, HIDDEN LINE, WIRE FRAME.

line transient. In electronics, an unwanted voltage pulse of very short duration, which can often produce errors in digital circuits not designed to minimize the effects of such interference. *See* PULSE.

line update. In computer graphics, the modification of a single line, or part of a line, of graphics stored on a file. (Philips). *Compare* RECTANGULAR UPDATE. *See* FILE.

lining figures. In printing, numerals that align horizontally at the top and bottom (e.g. 1234567890) as opposed to old-style numerals. *See* OLD-STYLE FIGURES. *Synonymous with* RANGING FIGURES.

link. (1) In communications, a transmission path of specified characteristics between two points (e.g. a telephone wire or a microwave beam). As well as the physical aspect of transmission, a link includes the protocol, associated devices and software (i.e. it can also be logical). *See* PROTOCOL, LOGICAL CHANNEL. (2) In programming, a routine that interfaces two separate programs and through which control information is passed. *See* LINKING.

link access protocol. *See* LAP.

linkage. In data security, the purposeful combination of data or information from

one information system with that from another system in the hope of deriving additional information; in particular, the combination of computer files from two or more sources. (FIPS).

linkage editor. In programming, a program that combines separately compiled routines into a single application program. This utility enables a programmer to provide a series of commonly used routines and incorporate them into application programs as required. *See* APPLICATION PROGRAM, LINKING, ROUTINE.

link-attached. In data communications, pertaining to devices that are connected by data link to a controlling unit. *Compare* CHANNEL-ATTACHED.

link control procedure. *Synonymous with* LINK PROTOCOL.

linked list. *Synonymous with* CHAIN LIST.

link encryption. In data security, end-to-end encryption within each link in a communications network. (FIPS). *Compare* END-TO-END ENCRYPTION, NODE ENCRYPTION. *See* NETWORK ENCRYPTION. *Synonymous with* DATALINK ENCRYPTION, LINK-TO-LINK ENCRYPTION.

linking. In programming, the processes involved in joining together the subprograms in object code form to produce an executable code file. *See* LINKAGE EDITOR, OBJECT CODE.

link loss. In communications, the microwave transmission loss, in decibels, of signals between the transmitting and receiving ground stations of a communications satellite system. *See* COMMUNICATIONS SATELLITE SYSTEM, DECIBEL, FOOTPRINT, MICROWAVE TRANSMISSION.

link protocol. In data communications, a protocol controlling the transfer of data over a communication line so that a meaningful exchange of information may take place. Link protocols deal with message formats, error recovery procedures, control characters, block lengths, etc. *See* ADVANCED DATA CONTROL COMMUNICATIONS PROCEDURE, BINARY SYNCHRONOUS COMMUNICATIONS, HIGH-LEVEL DATA LINK CONTROL, PROTOCOL,

SYNCHRONOUS DATA LINK CONTROL *Synonymous with* LINE PROTOCOL, LINK CONTROL PROCEDURE.

link-to-link encryption. *Synonymous with* DATA LINK ENCRYPTION, LINK ENCRYPTION.

LIPS. In architecture, logical inferences per second; a measure of the power of an inference engine and denoting the number of syllogistic inferences per second that can be performed. One syllogistic inference is equivalent to 100–1000 conventional computer instructions. *Compare* KIPS, MIPS. *See* INFERENCE ENGINE, SYLLOGISM.

liquid crystal display. (LCD) In information presentation, a visual display used in pocket calculators, watches and many other portable products, because of its low power consumption. It is manufactured from two glass plates sandwiched together with a special fluid. When a voltage is applied, the light polarization in the liquid changes and, the image becomes visible through a polarizing filter. (Philips). *Compare* LIGHT-EMITTING DIODE. *See* LCD SCREENS, OPTOELECTRONICS.

LISP. In programming, LISt-Processing language: a symbol manipulation language with a simple format that makes no explicit distinction between programs and data. The predominant applications lie in the artificial intelligence field (e.g. expert systems, theorem proving and natural language parsing), but it has also been used for text editors and even system programming. There is a LISP machine which has been programmed throughout in LISP and offers fast performance. It originated at MIT in 1965. *See* ARTIFICIAL INTELLIGENCE, EXPERT SYSTEMS, PROLOG.

list. (1) In data structures, an ordered set of items of data. *See* CHAIN LIST, LIST PROCESSING. (2) In programming, to print or display items of data that meet specific criteria.

listening centre. In audiovisual aids, an audio distribution device that allows several individuals to listen to audio materials at the same time.

listening mode. In data communications, a mode in which a station can monitor messages on a line, but can neither transmit nor receive them.

listing. In programming, a printout with details of source program statements and the data produced by executing that program. *See* HARD COPY.

list processing. (1) In programming, the manipulation of lists. Items may be added to or deleted from lists by modification of pointers on the affected and adjacent items. It is not necessary to move physically the adjacent records in storage. *See* LISP, LIST. (2) In word processing, a facility to maintain and manipulate files in the form of lists (e.g. customer/address list).

literal. (1) In printing, an error by the compositor in substituting one character for another. (2) In computer programming, an item in a source program that contains a value rather than the address of that value.

literature search. In library science, a systematic and exhaustive search for published material on a specific subject, together with the preparation of annotated bibliographies or abstracts. Such searches are now commonly performed using online databases. *See* DATABASE, ONLINE INFORMATION RETRIEVAL.

lith film. In printing, a photographic film having a high definition and contrast that is used for lithographic printing. *See* PHOTOLITHOGRAPHY.

lithography. In printing, a method in which a very thin metal plate, usually made of zinc or aluminium, is bent to fit around a

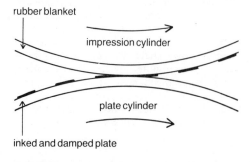

lithography
The printing surface lies in the same plane as the non-printing areas on the plate cylinder.

printing cylinder. A greasy substance is applied to the area to be printed, and the non-printing areas, which have a fine, grained surface, are dampened with water. A very fine film of water is retained by the fine surface. A greasy printing ink is used which adheres to the greasy image, but is rejected by the water on the non-image area. *Compare* INTAGLIO. *See* OFFSET PRINTING.

LLL. *See* LOW-LEVEL LANGUAGE.

LNA. *See* LOW-NOISE AMPLIFIER.

load. (1) In programming, to enter data or a program into a computer memory from an auxiliary storage device. *Compare* SAVE. (2) In electronics, a device that receives power. (3) In memory systems, to prepare a peripheral device so that data can be accessed.

loader. In operating systems, a program designed to load other programs into main memory from external bulk storage devices. *See* MAIN MEMORY.

loading. In communications, a method of improving the transmission characteristics of a telephone line by inserting a series of inductances along the line at regular intervals. Such a line behaves in a similar way to a low-pass filter. *See* INDUCTANCE, LOW-PASS FILTER.

load life. In electronics, the number of hours a device may dissipate power under specified operating conditions while remaining within its specified operational performance. *Compare* SHELF LIFE.

load point. In computing, the point on a reel of magnetic tape at which the recording area begins. *See* MAGNETIC TAPE.

load sharing. In computing, a technique whereby computers on a network share work loads to attain a reasonably uniform distribution. This is achieved by the off-loading of jobs from a heavily loaded computer to one that is more lightly loaded. *See* JOB.

load time. In video, the time taken to present a complete picture on the screen. (Philips).

lobe. *See* ANTENNA PATTERN.

lobe-attaching unit. In data communications, a unit that allows data stations to be connected to, and disconnected from, a ring network without disrupting the operation of the network. *See* DATA STATION, RING.

LOC. In programming, lines of codes; a measure of the cost of developing a software package.

local. (1) In distributed processing, the mode of operation of a microcomputer or terminal when a processing or an output operation is carried out locally rather than at the host. *See* HOST COMPUTER. (2) In programming, a variable that is defined and used only in one part of a program. *Compare* GLOBAL. (3) In communications, pertaining to a device that is accessed directly (i.e. not via a telecommunications link).

local area network. (LAN) In data communications, a high-bandwidth, bidirectional communications network that operates over a limited geographical area, typically an office building or a college campus. The incentive for the development of LANs arose from the proliferation of micro- and minicomputers in large organizations and the perceived trend to supply office workers with more communication devices (e.g. videotex, facsimile, communicating word processors, video and speech systems, etc.). It is clearly desirable that a unified approach be adopted to the intercommunication of such varied devices. LANs provide the computer user with the opportunity to communicate with other workers, to supply and access data, and to share expensive peripherals, hard-disk storage devices, sophisticated printers, etc. The LAN comprises a cable network linking the constituent nodes. Each node corresponds to a user workstation equipped with a physical network interface device. The topology of the network may be ring, star or bus.

The star network is the logical successor to the traditional mainframe computer — multiterminal configuration — but although it provides for a simple access protocol it has three disadvantages: network failure with central controller breakdown; low speed with controller bottlenecks; and extensive wiring.

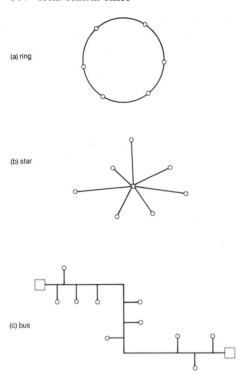

(a) ring

(b) star

(c) bus

local area network
Fig. 1. (a) ring; (b) star; (c) bus.

An important consideration to the LAN user is the interface card that connects the workstation to the network. The internal high-speed bus structures of computers facilitate the interconnection to the LAN, and the interface card can be simply plugged into the backplane. The interface must also contain the software to handle data transfers. The ISO-OSI seven-layer structure is significant in the design of LAN standards, particularly where the LANs require gateways to other LANs and wide area networks; the lower two layers of the ISO-OSI reference model are applied to the LAN concept.

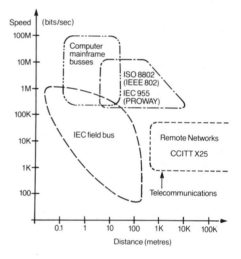

local area network
Fig. 2. Distance and speed relationships for LAN standards.

The mode of transmission may be either baseband or broadband; the transmission medium may be twisted pair copper wire, coaxial cable or fiber optics.

The access protocols available for bus and ring networks are carrier sense multiple access — collision detection (CSMA-CD) control token or message slot. The success of LANs will depend upon the confidence of users in the establishment of standards which will guarantee trouble-free interconnection and operation of a wide range of user devices. Two of the most widely discussed standards are Ethernet and Cambridge Ring. Other systems using CSMA-CD protocols often describe themselves as Ethernet-type. Both these systems transmit data in the baseband mode at 10 and 1 megabits per second, respectively. IBM has also developed a LAN standard using a baseband ring and token-passing protocol. The various protocol standards for LANs are defined in IEEE-802. IEEE-802.3 deals with CSMA-CD bus, IEEE-802.4 deals with token bus, and IEEE-802.5 covers token ring.

Compare WIDE AREA NETWORK. *See* BACK-PLANE, BANDWIDTH, BASEBAND, CARRIER SENSE MULTIPLE ACCESS – COLLISION DETECTION, CAMBRIDGE RING, COAXIAL CABLE, CONTROL TOKEN, ECMA, ETHERNET, FACSIMILE, FIBER OPTICS, GATEWAY, ISO-OSI, MESSAGE SLOT, NODE, PROTOCOL, TOPOLOGY, TWISTED PAIR, VIDEOTEX.

local central office. In communications, a central office which provides facilities for the terminating telephone subscriber lines and is connected by trunks to other central offices. *See* CENTRAL OFFICE, TRUNK.

local dissolve. In video and filming, a slow change from one part of a picture to another. *Compare* GLOBAL DISSOLVE, LOCAL FADE. *See* COMPACT DISC – INTERACTIVE, DIGITAL VIDEO, DISPLAY RESOLUTION, PIXEL.

local distribution service. (LDS) In cable television, a community antenna relay station located within a system and used for the transmission of signals, by microwave link, to one or more locations from which they are distributed to users by cable. *See* CARS, MICROWAVE TRANSMISSION.

local echo. In data communications, a technique in which the communications software in a transmitting computer displays the data transmitted into the communication link on the local terminal. *Compare* ECHO-PLEX. *See* TERMINAL. *Synonymous with* LOCAL SOFTWARE ECHO.

local exchange. *Synonymous with* LOCAL OFFICE.

local fade. In filming and video, a fade affecting a portion of an image. (Philips). *Compare* GLOBAL FADE, LOCAL DISSOLVE. *See* FADE, TRANSITION.

local loop. In communications, a link connecting a telephone subscriber to the local central office. *See* LOCAL CENTRAL OFFICE. *Synonymous with* EXCHANGE LINE.

local mode. In data communications, an internal operating state of a data terminal. In this condition a terminal is not able to accept incoming calls.

local office. In communications, a telephone exchange in which subscriber's lines are terminated. *Synonymous with* LOCAL EXCHANGE.

local origination. In cable television, pertaining to television programs produced within the local community.

local service area. In communications, the geographical area containing the telephone stations that a flat-rate customer may call without incurring toll charges. *See* TOLL CHARGE.

local software echo. *Synonymous with* LOCAL ECHO.

local switching office. *See* TOLL OFFICE.

local variable. *See* LOCAL.

location. In memory systems, a storage position that can hold a computer word. *See* WORD.

locator device. In peripherals, an input device that provides coordinate data (e.g. digitizing tablet). *See* DIGITIZING TABLET.

loc cit. In printing, an abbreviation for *loco citato*, Latin for 'in the place cited'; used particularly in footnotes.

lock. *See* FILE LOCK, RECORD LOCK.

Lockheed. *See* DIALOG INFORMATION RETRIEVAL SERVICES.

locking. (1) In codes, a characteristic of code extension characters that enforces a change in interpretation to all coded representations, or all those of a given class, until the next code extension character appears. *See* CODE EXTENSION CHARACTER. (2) In electronics, a term used for the synchronization of a repetitive signal source with timing signals. *See* CLOCKING.

lockout. (1) In peripherals, a keyboard action that only registers the first key depression when a number of keys are depressed virtually simultaneously. *Compare* ROLLOVER. *See* KEYBOARD, TWO-KEY LOCKOUT. (2) In databases, a technique in database systems to avoid update inconsistency. Only one user is allowed to access an item for update or modification at any one time. A disadvantage of this technique is that it can lead to a deadly embrace. If users A and B both wish to update a pair of records (X and Y) then lockout can produce the following sequence: (a) user A acquires X; (b) user B acquires Y; (c) user A requests Y, but it is locked by user B; (d) user B requests X, but it is locked by user A. *See* RECORD, UPDATE INCONSISTENCY. (3) In communications, the inability of a subscriber on a circuit controlled by an echo suppressor to get through to a called party because of either excessive local noise or continuous speech from one party. *See* ECHO SUPPRESSOR. (4) In programming, a technique used to prevent access to critical data by two separate programs in a multiprogramming environment. *Compare* LOCK UP. *See* FILE LOCK, RECORD LOCK.

lock up. In programming, an unwanted state of a system from which it cannot escape (e.g. a deadly embrace in the claiming of common resources). *Compare* LOCKOUT.

lockword. In data security, a password associated with a file or a data set. A file creator may specify a lockword for a file, or data set within a file, and thereafter users must input the lockword to gain access to the file or data set. *See* DATABASE SECURITY, DATA SET, FILE ACCESS, PASSWORD.

log. In computing, a record or journal of a sequence of events or the jobs run through a computer.

logarithm. In mathematics, the logarithm of a number is the power to which the base must be raised to give that number. Thus in decimal arithmetic the logarithm of 100 (to base 10) is 2, since 10 x 10 = 100. *See* BASE.

log file. *See* LOG.

logging. In computer security, a record kept either manually or by the computer system to keep track of events that take place with respect to the system.

logic. (1) In philosophy, the discipline concerned with reasoning and thought. (2) In electronics, the physical circuits that implement logical operations and functions. (3) In computing, the electronic components of the system. *See* LOGICAL OPERATOR.

logical. (1) Conceptual or virtual, as compared with physical or actual (e.g. a program may use a logical filename 'Pay', but during a particular program run the actual file accessed may be stored on a disk under the name 'Accounts'). (2) In data structures, a two-state quantity that can be stored as a single bit; often used for such purposes as status flags. *See* FLAG.

logical access control. In computer security, the use of procedures related to information and knowledge (e.g. passwords) rather than physical security. *See* ACCESS CONTROL.

logical channel. In data communications, a circuit that is used for packet-switching operations between a terminal and a network node. The circuit may be a permanent virtual connection or one set up for the duration of the call. *See* PACKET SWITCHING, PERMANENT VIRTUAL CIRCUIT, VIRTUAL CIRCUIT.

logical comparison. In programming, a logic operation to determine whether two character strings are equal. *See* LOGICAL OPERATOR, STRING.

logical completeness measure. In computer security, a means for assessing the effectiveness and degree to which a set of security and access control mechanisms meet the requirements of a set of security specifications. (FIPS). *See* ACCESS CONTROL.

logical database. In databases, a database as viewed by its users. This structure of the data need not be the same as that of the physical database. *Compare* PHYSICAL DATABASE.

logical data independence. In databases, pertaining to the structure of the data that permits the schema to be changed without affecting the application programmer's view of the data. *Compare* PHYSICAL DATA INDEPENDENCE. *See* DATA INDEPENDENCE, SCHEMA.

logical expression. In mathematics, a statement that contains logical operators and operands and can be reduced to a value that is only either true or false (e.g. the boolean formulae for an EXCLUSIVE OR function Z = (A AND NOT B) OR (NOT A AND B) is a logical expression). *See* AND, BOOLEAN ALGEBRA, EXCLUSIVE OR, LOGICAL OPERATOR, NOT, OR.

logical inferences per second. *See* LIPS.

logical operator. In programming, an operator that can be used in a logical expression to indicate the action to be performed on the terms in the expression. The logical operators are AND, OR, and NOT. All logic expressions can be written in terms of these three basic operations. *See* AND, LOGIC OPERATION, NOT, OR.

logical record. In programming, a record which is defined in terms of its functions rather than the physical manner in which it is stored. *Compare* PHYSICAL RECORD. *See* RECORD.

logical security. In data security, security provided by the operating system and basic software. *See* OPERATING SYSTEM.

logical shift. In programming, a shift operation which can take one of two forms: left or right. The bits in a specified storage register are shifted a given number of places, in the appropriate direction, and zeros are shifted in at the other end. *Compare* ARITHMETIC SHIFT. *See* REGISTER, SHIFT.

logical threat. In computer security, a threat of the possibility of destruction or alteration of software or data. It is realized by logical manipulation within the system rather than by a physical attack. For example, the threat could arise from an unauthorized user with dishonest motives or from an unauthorized user who managed to access the system either on-site or from a remote location through a network. *Compare* ACCIDENTAL THREAT, ACTIVE THREAT, DELIBERATE THREAT, PASSIVE THREAT, PHYSICAL THREAT. *See* THREAT.

logical unit. In data communications, a port through which a user gains access to the services of a network. *See* PORT.

logical variable. In mathematics, a variable in a logical expression. It may only assume one of two values: true or false. *See* BOOLEAN ALGEBRA.

logic bomb. In data security, a part of a program that is triggered by a combination of events in the system and activates a fraud or sabotages the system. *See* SABOTAGE, TIME BOMB, TROJAN HORSE.

logic card. In hardware, a circuit board that contains components and wiring which performs one or more complex logic functions or operations. The board is designed for easy removal from the motherboard of a computer. *See* MOTHERBOARD.

logic circuit. In electronics, a circuit comprising one or more gates or flip flops that performs a particular logic function. *See* FLIP FLOP, GATE.

logic device. *See* LOGIC CIRCUIT.

logic level. In electronics, the value of a physical quantity (e.g. a current or voltage) used to represent the logic state of a signal in a circuit. In binary logic there are two logic levels corresponding to the two logic states of 1 and 0. In a circuit, for example, a signal of +5 volts may correspond to a logical 1 (the high or true state) and −2 volts may correspond to a logical 0 (the low or false state). *See* LOGIC STATE.

logic map. *See* KARNAUGH MAP.

logic operation. In mathematics, an operation performed upon variables which can only take one of two values (e.g. TRUE or FALSE, 0 or 1). The operations may relate to a single variable or to a pair of variables. The basic operations are AND, OR and NOT, and these may be combined giving NAND, NOR, XOR and EQUIVALENCE. These operations may be performed on electrical signals with logic circuits termed gates. *See* AND, BOOLEAN ALGEBRA, EQUIVALENCE, GATE, LOGIC CIRCUIT, NOR, NOT, XOR.

logic probe. In electronics, a probe using a light-emitting diode or light bulb to indicate whether a signal is 0, 1 or undetermined. *See* LIGHT-EMITTING DIODE.

logic state. In mathematics, one of the two possible states of a binary variable, usually designated the 1 state and the 0 state.

logic state analyzer. In electronics, a digital test and diagnostic system equipped with an oscilloscope and capable of displaying bus and other digital states as 0s and 1s. *See* OSCILLOSCOPE.

logic symbol. In electronics, a symbol used to represent a logic element graphically.

login. *Synonymous with* LOGON.

Logo. In programming, an interactive programming language; specifically designed for teaching the concepts of programming and computer applications which has thus found application in schools. The simple format makes it suitable even for quite young children who are attracted by its picture-drawing capabilities. It can also be used for computer-assisted learning in such areas as mathematics and has fulfilled a therapeutic role for disabled children. It originated in Bolt Beranek and Newman Inc., Massachusetts, in the late 1960s. *See* COMPUTER-ASSISTED LEARNING, TURTLEGRAPHICS.

logo. *See* LOGOTYPE.

logoff. In computing, an instruction to a computer system by a user that a session is to be terminated. *Compare* LOGON. *Synonymous with* LOGOUT, SIGN OFF, SIGN OUT.

logogram. A sign or character that represents a word.

logon. (1) In computer security, procedure used to establish the identity of the user and the levels of authorization and access permitted. *Synonymous with* LOGIN, SIGN IN, SIGN ON. (2) In computing, a request by a user for access to a computer, usually a time-sharing system. In initiating a connection, the user may have to supply identification such as an account number and password. *Compare* LOGOFF. *See* PASSWORD, TIME SHARING. *Synonymous with* LOGIN.

logo screen. In programming, a initial screen that is displayed giving details of the owner or developer when an application program is run. *See* APPLICATION PROGRAM.

logotype. In printing, several letters, or a word cast on one body of type, often used for a trade name. *See* HOUSE STYLE.

logout. *Synonymous with* LOGOFF.

long cross. *Synonymous with* DAGGER.

long-distance xerography. In communications, a communications system combining facsimile and xerography. *See* FACSIMILE, XEROGRAPHY.

long-haul network. *Synonymous with* WIDE AREA NETWORK.

longitudinal parity check. (1) In computing, a parity check performed on a group of binary digits in a longitudinal direction for each track on a magnetic tape. (2) In data communications, a system of error checking performed at the receiving station after a block check character has been accumulated. *See* BLOCK CHARACTER CHECK, PARITY CHECKING. *Synonymous with* LONGITUDINAL REDUNDANCY CHECK.

longitudinal recording. In computing, the conventional method of magnetizing a magnetic disk. The air gap of the read/write head is comparatively wide, producing a horizontal magnetic field in the recording layer of the disk. The gamma oxide particles in the recording layer are needle-shaped and line up horizontally with the applied field. A comparatively wide dead zone exists between adjacent recorded bits because the identical north or south poles of two adjacent bits repel each other. The information density in most longitudinal systems has been limited to approximately 9000 flux changes per inch. *Compare* ISOTROPIC RECORDING, VERTICAL RECORDING. *See* FLUX, MAGNETIC DISK, READ/WRITE HEAD. *Synonymous with* HORIZONTAL RECORDING.

longitudinal redundancy check. *Synonymous with* LONGITUDINAL PARITY CHECK.

long letters. In printing, letter designs that occupy the maximum area of the typeface and include an ascender or descender. *See* ASCENDER, DESCENDER.

long-persistence phosphors. *See* LONG-PERSISTENCE SCREEN.

long-persistence screen. In peripherals, a screen with a coating of phosphors designed to retain an image for a relatively long period after the original signal has been removed. *See* CATHODE RAY TUBE, DIRECT-VIEW STORAGE TUBE, LAG, PHOSPHOR DOTS.

look angles. In communications, the elevation and azimuth angles for a communications antenna pointed at a communications satellite. *See* SUBSATELLITE POINT.

look-up table. In programming, a method of storing the values of an arbitrary function $F(n)$ where $n = 1, 2, 3, \ldots$. The function values are stored in sequential memory positions; given the value of n the corresponding storage location is calculated and the required function value retrieved.

loop. (1) In programming, a sequence of instructions that is repeated until some specific condition occurs. (2) In communications, a link or channel. (3) In filming, a purposely slack section of film in a camera or projector so that a frame can remain motionless at the aperture for the correct period while the feed and take-up spools are in motion.

loop antenna. In communications, an antenna comprising a closed circuit consisting of one or more turns of wire.

loopback test. *Synonymous with* LOOP CHECKING.

loop checking. In data communications, a method of detecting transmission errors in which received data is returned to the sending station for comparison with the original data. *Synonymous with* LOOPBACK TEST.

looped outlet. In cable television, a junction box in a subscriber's premises through which a spur cable passes. The box usually contains isolation and attenuation circuits. *See* ATTENUATION, ISOLATION, SPUR.

loop film. In recording, a length of film or tape spliced head to tail for continuous playing.

loophole. In computer security, an error, omission or oversight in software or hardware that permits circumventing the access control process. (FIPS). *See* ACCESS CONTROL. *Synonymous with* FAULT.

looping. *Synonymous with* DUBBING.

loop invariant. In programming, a predicate developed to prove the correctness of a program loop. The properties of the predicate are: (a) the predicate is true before the first evaluation of the condition for continuing or terminating the loop; (b) it is true before the first loop statement is evaluated; (c) if it is true before the execution of the loop statements, when the condition for loop continuation is true, then it is true after the execution of the loop statements; and (d) when the condition for loop termination is true then the loop invariant reduces to the postcondition. *See* LOOP, POSTCONDITION, PRECONDITION, PREDICATE, PROOF OF PROGRAM CORRECTNESS.

loop network. In communications, a network configuration in which there is a single path between all nodes and the path is a closed circuit. *Compare* STAR. *See* NODE, RING.

loop plant. In communications, all the cables, ducts, joint boxes, cabinets, poles and ancillary equipment used to connect subscribers to their local office or exchange.

loosely coupled. In computing, pertaining to a multiprocessing system in which the group of constituent processors is connected together with serial or parallel data links, allowing data and files to be transferred from one system to another. *Compare* TIGHTLY COUPLED. *See* MULTIPROCESSING.

loss. (1) In computer security, the quantitative measure of expected deprivation due to a threat acting upon a vulnerable system resource. *See* ANNUAL LOSS EXPECTANCY, THREAT, VULNERABILITY. (2) In communications, a general term for the loss of signal energy during transmission along a circuit, expressed as the ratio of the signal power at the start of the circuit to the signal power at the receiver, usually expressed in decibels. *See* ATTENUATION, DECIBEL, SIGNAL.

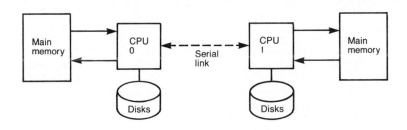

loosely coupled
A loosely coupled system.

lost call. In communications, a request for a telephone connection that is abandoned owing to congestion.

lost time. In communications, that fraction of the scanning line period which is not available for facsimile transmissions.

loudness. In audio, a subjective experience of the intensity of a sound wave. The loudness of a noise is determined by the amplitude of the wave, its frequency and the sensitivity of the listener to sound waves at a particular frequency. *See* FREQUENCY, INTENSITY.

loudspeaker. In acoustics, a transducer that converts electrical energy into sound energy. Most loudspeakers are of the moving-coil variety in which signals are supplied to a coil, attached to a large diaphragm, which is relatively free to move in a strong, transverse magnetic field. *See* ELECTROSTATIC LOUDSPEAKER. *Synonymous with* SPEAKER.

lower case. In printing, the small letters in typefaces (e.g. a, b, c, etc.). *Compare* UPPER CASE.

lowest useful frequency. In communications, the lowest frequency in the high-frequency band that can be used for transmission over a given path at a specified time.

low frequency. In communications, the frequency range from 30 to 300 kHz.

low-level language. (LLL) In programming, a language that is closely related to the machine code language of a computer (i.e. one that is translated by an assembler). LLL may be more efficient in operation (i.e. faster, require less memory, etc.). However, such languages are difficult to write, and their application is restricted to specific hardware configurations. *Compare* HIGH-LEVEL LANGUAGE. *See* ASSEMBLER, MACHINE LANGUAGE, PORTABILITY, TRANSLATOR.

low-level protocol. In data communications, a protocol that is concerned with the mechanics of communication within a network. *Compare* HIGH-LEVEL PROTOCOL. *See* PROTOCOL.

low-noise amplifier. (LNA) In electronics, an amplifier designed to minimize the noise introduced in the early stages of amplification. It is used as the first stage of amplification in satellite receiver systems. *See* AMPLIFIER, TELEVISION RECEIVE-ONLY.

low-pass filter. In electronics, a frequency-selective network that attenuates signals with frequencies above a predefined value, but passes signals with lower frequencies. *Compare* HIGH-PASS FILTER. *See* ATTENUATION, CUTOFF FREQUENCY.

low reduction. (LR) In micrographics, a reduction of less than 15x. *Compare* HIGH REDUCTION, MEDIUM REDUCTION, ULTRA HIGH REDUCTION, VERY HIGH REDUCTION. *See* REDUCTION.

low resolution. (1) In television, a degree of detailed visual definition below the 400 x 300 pixels presented by normal domestic colour television sets. (Philips). *Compare* HIGH RESOLUTION, NORMAL RESOLUTION. *See* PIXEL. (2) In computer graphics, a term used by some manufacturers to refer to a mode of operation providing a comparatively low number of horizontal and vertical pixels. *Compare* HIGH RESOLUTION. *See* PIXEL.

low-speed. In data communications, pertaining to systems that operate at less than 2400 bits per second.

low water mark. In data security, pertaining to two or more security levels, the least of the hierarchical classifications, and the set intersection of the non-hierarchical categories. (DCID).

LPC. *See* LINEAR PREDICTIVE CODING.

LPC coder. In man–machine interfaces, linear predictive coder; a vocal tract synthesizer in which the coefficients of the digital filter are determined by a technique which seeks to minimize the difference between the output of the filter and the original utterance. *Compare* FORMANT SYNTHESIZER. *See* SPEECH SYNTHESIZER, VOCAL TRACT SYNTHESIZER.

LPM. *See* LINES PER MINUTE.

LR. *See* LOW REDUCTION.

LRC. Longitudinal redundancy check. *See* LONGITUDINAL PARITY CHECK.

LSB. *See* LEAST SIGNIFICANT BIT.

LSD. *See* LEAST SIGNIFICANT DIGIT.

LSI. *See* LARGE-SCALE INTEGRATION.

LTE. *See* LINE TERMINATION EQUIPMENT.

luggable. *Synonymous with* SUITCASE-PORTABLE.

lumen. In optics, a unit of illumination, defined as the luminous flux emitted by a standard candle into a solid angle of one steradian. *See* CANDELA, FLUX, STERADIAN.

luminaire. In filming, all the components of a lighting system (i.e. support, housing, lens, bulb and cable).

luminance. In optics, the measured radiance of a light source using a photometer, as distinguished from brightness, the subjective visual sensation of luminance. *See* BRIGHTNESS.

luminance signal. In television, the part of the composite colour video signal that is responsible for the luminance information. Because the eye is less sensitive to colour changes than changes in contrast, more bandwidth is required for the luminance signal than the chrominance signal. *Compare* CHROMINANCE SIGNAL. *See* COMPOSITE COLOUR VIDEO SIGNAL.

lux. In optics, one lumen per square millimetre. *See* LUMEN.

LV. *See* LASERVISION.

M

M. Mega; a prefix for one million.

m. Milli; a prefix for one-thousandth.

MAC. (1) In television, multiplexed analog components; the technique adopted as a standard for direct-broadcast satellite in which the transmission format is a multiplex of time-compressed video components and a digital burst which carries synchronization, sound and data services. *See* DIRECT-BROADCAST SATELLITE. (2) In data security, message authentication code. *See* MESSAGE AUTHENTICATION. *Synonymous with* DAC.

machine. In computing, an adjective which is commonly associated with computer (e.g. machine address).

machine address. *Synonymous with* ABSOLUTE ADDRESS.

machine-aided translation. (MAT) In machine translation, the use of a computer to assist a human translator. At one end of the spectrum the human translator may only be required to undertake some pre- and/or post-editing, the remainder of the task being performed by machine translation. At the other extreme, the translator is provided with a range of information, text-processing and communication facilities. The electronic facilities provided to the translator may include sophisticated term banks combined with multilingual word processor systems so that terms extracted from the term bank may be automatically incorporated into the translated text, with all the necessary character sets, accents, etc. of the appropriate target language. *See* ACCENT, LIMITED SYNTAX, POST-EDITING, PRE-EDITING, TARGET LANGUAGE. *Synonymous with* COMPUTER-AIDED TRANSLATION.

machine check. In computing, an error condition arising as a result of an equipment malfunction.

machine code. *Synonymous with* MACHINE LANGUAGE.

machine code instruction. In programming, an instruction expressed in the machine language for the particular processor. High- and low-level language instructions are eventually translated into corresponding machine code instructions before they are executed by the processor. *See* HIGH-LEVEL LANGUAGE, LOW-LEVEL LANGUAGE, MACHINE LANGUAGE, PROCESSOR, TRANSLATOR.

machine cognition. *See* ARTIFICIAL INTELLIGENCE.

machine composition. In printing, any process that results in the production of type matter by means of composing machines and keyboards.

machine cycle. In computing, the minimum length of time taken by a computer to perform a given series of tasks. *Compare* MEMORY CYCLE.

machine-glazed. (MG) In printing, pertaining to paper with a high-gloss finish on one side only. (Desktop). *See* CAST-COATED.

machine independence. In programming, a software design philosophy that allows programs written for one type of computer to be run without change on another type of computer. *See* PORTABILITY.

machine instruction. *See* MACHINE CODE INSTRUCTION.

machine language. In programming, a language for programs that can be expressed directly in a binary format acceptable to the central processing unit. All other programming languages (e.g. low- or high-level languages) have to be translated into binary machine code before being executed in the central processing unit. *Compare* HIGH-LEVEL LANGUAGE, LOW-LEVEL LANGUAGE. *See* MACHINE CODE INSTRUCTION, TRANSLATOR. *Synonymous with* MACHINE CODE.

machine learning. In artificial intelligence, a process by which a device improves its performance based on the results of past actions. *See* ADAPTIVE SYSTEMS, ARTIFICIAL INTELLIGENCE.

machine proof. In printing, the first copies taken off a printing machine for checking purposes before full production starts.

machine-readable. In memory systems, pertaining to data which is in a form that can be input directly into the machine (e.g. on magnetic tape). *Compare* MANUAL INPUT. *See* BAR CODE, MAGNETIC INK CHARACTER RECOGNITION, MAGNETIC TAPE, OPTICAL CHARACTER RECOGNITION.

machine sheet. In printing, a printed sheet from off the press during a run.

machine translation. (MT) In applications, the use of a computer to translate natural language text into the corresponding text of another language. A significant proportion of conventional computing activity is spent in compilation, or interpretation; processes used when a program, expressed in a high-level language, is translated into another lower-level language. The processes involved in accepting several pages of a high-level language program with paragraphs written in English-like phrases such as

WHILE ONGOING DO CALC-TAX;

into a stream of binary numbers representing machine instructions may appear to have considerable similarity with that of translating from English to French. The program text is subjected to parsing, and the syntactical rules of the words and phrases are identified, and then the subcomponents are looked up in a dictionary and substitutions of the target language terms are

made. Computer scientists have devoted considerable effort to the design of highly efficient compilers, and it was natural that the parallels with the tasks of foreign language translation were spotted in the 1950s and 1960s when attempts were made to produce natural language translation. These early attempts did not, however, produce the expected rates of success, in spite of the money and expertise expended on research projects.

The human translators have three important functions not required of the compiler: (a) they must resolve ambiguities which arise from the very free syntax of natural language, often without the opportunity to refer back to the original author; (b) they must deal with a very large and dynamic vocabulary; and (c) they must produce a final text that has a 'style' acceptable to the ultimate user.

The resolution of ambiguities demands a knowledge of the conceptual framework surrounding the text, and it is unlikely that computer systems will be able to emulate completely the skill and versatility of human translators in the foreseeable future. Consider the following sentences. The boy went into a supermarket. He put a bag of flour into the basket and some chocolate into his pocket. At the checkout counter his face reddened, and he said 'I didn't mean to take it'. In the translation into German it is necessary to give a gender to 'it' contained in the phrase 'mean to take it'. To do so requires that 'it' is assigned to chocolate and not to bag of flour, but how do the human translators know this? They must use the concepts of supermarket shopping, shoplifting, sense of guilt and blushing to perform this task. The vocabulary can also present problems particularly with homographs that again require a knowledge of context for correct translation. Finally the process of learning to produce prose that is acceptable to a well-educated reader is not amenable to codification in a computer program.

The initial attempts to emulate human translators and their subsequent failures caused a reaction against machine translation research, particularly in the USA in the 1970s. The demand for translation services in the commercial, political and military fields has, however, grown in magnitude to the extent that it has become imperative to reconsider the nature of the translation workload and to re-examine the capabilities of machine translation against that workload.

In at least two areas of application (i.e. information acquisition and information dissemination) the user either may be prepared to accept a much lower standard of translation output or the sheer volume of translation material may render it imperative that cheaper, faster translation facilities be provided.

In many professions it is important to gain a timely overview of information of developments occurring in foreign countries. The only source of such information may be in articles, research papers, etc. written in a foreign language. An imperfect translation may well be sufficient for this task. The reader may merely need to scan a large number of papers to select those containing material of interest. The selected papers may then be handed over to human translators, or the reader may be able to glean the relevant facts from the imperfect translation.

The information dissemination problem has exploded as manufacturers and service providers seek to expand their overseas markets. Tender documents and maintenance and training manuals must be provided in the purchaser's language and be included in the total cost of the product. Human translation at an average rate of four to six pages per day can be totally incompatible with the problem of producing cratefuls of technical manual translations.

The demand for some form of machine translation was recognized by the EEC in the late 1970s. The Commission initiated the Eurotra project to produce high-quality translations of written texts for the languages Danish, Dutch, English, French, German, Greek and Italian, with possible extension to Spanish and Portuguese. This project has a budget of $25 million and involves 100 part- or full-time scientific staff in 16 locations throughout Europe.

The act of translation may be considered to comprise two or more of the phases: (a) analysis of the source language; (b) transfer and synthesis of the target language. The three approaches to machine translation can be categorized as direct translation, deep analysis and analysis combined with transfer.

With direct translation the analysis phase is only taken to the level required for the production of a specific target language. The source language dictionary thus contains details of the behaviour of the target language. This technique requires that an implementation be geared completely to the source language/target language pair. If an additional language is to be included then the total design effort must be duplicated to accommodate the additional target language. This approach is quite uneconomic for organizations such as the EEC; with nine languages and requirements for translation from any one to another would require 72 such systems.

The deep analysis approach uses an interlingua (i.e. a language-independent representation of meaning). In this case the source language is analyzed to an interlingua representation, and the target language is then synthesized from this representation. In this case nine languages would only require nine source language analyzers and nine target language synthesizers; a translation of a document from one language to the remaining eight would only require one analysis and eight syntheses. Unfortunately it has not yet proved possible to specify an interlingua. Even if one were specified it would probably be incomplete and unable to handle every sentence produced by authors, who have been known to break grammatical rules.

The analysis and transfer technique, adopted by Eurotra, involves an analysis deeper than that of direct translation, but not to the level of an interlingua. This analysis is followed by a transfer from a structure, peculiar to the source language, to a structure peculiar to the target language, and then a synthesis to the final output in the target language. This technique, for nine languages, requires nine analyzers, 72 transfer modules and nine synthesizers. On the face of it this appears to be even less attractive than the 72 systems required for direct translation. However, current research suggests that the transfer modules and bilingual dictionaries can be kept sufficiently small to render this a feasible approach.

An alternative approach to machine translation is simply to reduce the demands made upon the machine translation process. If the subject area of the source text is well defined then the syntax and vocabulary can become a manageable subset of natural language. Thus there are systems that successfully translate weather forecasts from one language to another. If the requirement for a style of target text, similar to that produced by a good human translator, is relaxed, then a crude form of translation with mechanical translation of words and phrases can be achieved by computers. In military intelligence work it is necessary to scan vast quantities of foreign documents, but the reader is often only interested initially in the appearance of a combination of key phrases or words. Thus a very crude translation process is often adequate for the task of selecting those documents that prove to be of sufficient interest to warrant full human translation.

The most important relaxation, however, is that the process be fully automated. There is a continuum of translator/computer systems that promise to reduce the cost and improve the turnaround of the translation task (i.e. from the fully automated machine translation, through the human-assisted machine translation to the machine-assisted translation down to the provision of comprehensive text-processing facilities for translators).

The human-assisted machine translation systems interact with a consultant, and the computer reports detected problems in the text which prevent it from continuing with the analysis, or finding a term in the internal dictionary. Machine-aided translations can range from translation systems which demand pre- and post-editing by human translators through automatic dictionaries to merely word-processing systems of greater or lesser complexity. Pre-editing enables the translator to remove ambiguities and simplify the syntax of the source text, whereas post-editing involves the redrafting of output text to produce a style more acceptable to the user. Translators argue that the effort of post-editing can exceed that of a complete translation from scratch. However, in human translation organizations it is not uncommon for high-level translators to post-edit the work of junior translators.

A form of machine-aided translation for business correspondence can be even be provided on microcomputers. The Tick-Tack software system effectively provides building blocks from which sentences, paragraphs and even entire business letters in a foreign language can be constructed. The user selects a stock phrase (e.g 'referring to your letter of the ...') supplying appropriate

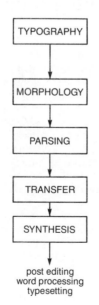

He saw the personal computer manual on the table.

com — puter computer	TYPOGRAPHY	divides text into words, phrases, sentences and paragraphs
		determines typographic attributes
saw = verb, past saw = noun	MORPHOLOGY	consults lexicon to determine morphological attributes of words and phrase
He saw (the ((personal computer) manual)) on (the table). **OR** He saw (the (personal (computer manual))) on (the table).	PARSING	analyzes sentences to determine roles of words and phrases in each sentence
Il voir (le ((individuel ordinateur) manuel)) sur (le table).	TRANSFER	substitutes target language words and phrases for source language words and phrases
Il a vu le manuel de l'ordinateur individuel sur la table.	SYNTHESIS	constructs meaningful and grammatically correct sentences in the target language

post editing
word processing
typesetting

machine translation
Stages in machine translation. Courtesy *TOVNA*.

parameters (e.g. a date) and the foreign language version is then presented.

Alternatively the computer may be used to assist the translator's productivity. A translator's workstation would combine the facilities of a multilingual character set word processor, with grammar, style and spelling checkers, access to term banks and electronic mail for the rapid transmission of source, draft and final documents, queries with document authors, etc. *See* HUMAN-AIDED MACHINE TRANSLATION, MACHINE-AIDED TRANSLATION, SOURCE LANGUAGE, TARGET LANGUAGE, TERM BANK.

machine vision. In peripherals, the techniques employed to determine information on a physical object by illuminating the object, detecting the reflected light with a photoelectric device and analyzing the subsequent electrical signals. The term machine vision is usually restricted to applications involving two- or three-dimensional objects (i.e it would not include bar code scanners).

The major application areas of machine vision are inspection, recognition, gauging and robot guidance. Inspection systems are often linked to automatic manufacture (e.g. checking the existence of components on a printed circuit board, caps on bottles containing pharmaceuticals, etc.). Recognition symbols identify objects or images. This area includes optical character recognition, and such devices could be used to read labels on boxes for automatic routing of units. Gauging systems measure distances such as the depth of a hole or the width of a door frame. Robot guidance systems identify parts and determine their location and orientation. This information is passed to the robot which will grasp, handle or process (e.g. spray paint) the part.

There are two phases of the machine vision process: image acquisition and computing. Image acquisition is performed by a camera which captures the image of the illuminated object and produces corresponding electrical signals. Front lighting is used for reading surfaces of flat objects; side lighting reveals an object's contours. If a silhouette is adequate for the application then back lighting may be employed. In some cases (e.g. if the objects are moving past the camera on an assembly line) it may be necessary to freeze the images by the use of strobe lighting.

Vidicons may be employed for image acquisition. They are comparatively cheap, rugged and have a high resolution. They suffer, however, from blooming and produce image distortion near the screen edges. In addition they can be damaged by exceptionally bright light. Solid-state cameras are more rugged than Vidicons; they cannot be damaged by bright light. They also do not suffer from blooming and are accurate over the whole image. Moreover, their arrays of discrete sensing elements render them better suited to image digitization than the continuous photoconductive surface of the Vidicon. The disadvantages of solid-state cameras are their price and comparatively low resolution.

If a camera is moved close to an object then the resolution, related to the number of pixels covering a given area of the image, will be increased, but only a limited area of the object's surface will be viewed. The resolution is also a function of the pixel grid of the camera. Commonly pixel grids vary from 126 x 126 to 1000 x 1000.

The image must be converted to a digital form and stored in random-access memory. Data compression techniques, such as image following, run length coding and vector generation, may be employed to reduce the storage demands of the image.

The second phase — computing — involves processing, analysis and interpretation. The processing of the image aims to enhance it by filtering, integration and contrast enhancement techniques. In inspection applications, the use of integration to remove small defects in the image may have the effect of hiding actual defects in the object that were the *raison d'être* of the inspection systems. Binary thresholding can produce sharp black/white images for some simple tasks, but the current trend is to operate with grey scales thus maintaining accuracy and consistency.

The image analysis phase provides measurements of the image by template matching or feature analysis. Template-matching and feature analysis techniques can provide information on the object by checking against standard patterns or comparing features such as dimension ratios with known objects.

The final stage — image interpretation — makes decisions on the basis of the information provided by the previous stages. With inspection systems a decision is made that a test object is, or is not, of acceptable quality. A recognition system decides that the test object belongs to a given class, or not. A gauging system determines the dimension in question, and the robot guidance system determines the actions to be performed by the robot.

Machine vision systems are often computationally demanding, and the speed of response of such systems may be significantly improved by the advent of parallel processing. *See* BINARY THRESHOLDING, BLOOM, DATA COMPRESSION, FEATURE ANALYSIS, IMAGE FOLLOWING, IMAGE PROCESSING, OPTICAL SCANNER, PARALLEL PROCESSING, PHOTOCONDUCTIVITY, PIXEL, RANDOM-ACCESS MEMORY, RESOLUTION, RUN LENGTH CODING, SOLID-STATE CAMERA, STROBOSCOPIC EFFECT, TEMPLATE MATCHING, VECTOR GENERATION, VIDICON.

Macintosh. In computing, a microcomputer manufactured by Apple using the WIMPS system. *See* WIMPS.

mackle. In printing, a spot or blemish on a printed sheet caused by a double impression, wrinkling, etc.

MAC residue. In computer security, the 32 bits, of the 64-bit output checksum generated to form the MAC, that are not transmitted as part of the authentication block. *See* CHECKSUM, MAC.

macro. (1) In microelectronics, a logic assembly that meets functional requirements at the medium-scale integration level (e.g. counters, adders, etc.). *See* CELL LIBRARY, COUNTER, MEDIUM-SCALE INTEGRATION. (2) In programming. *Synonymous with* MACROINSTRUCTION. (3) In programming, a sequence of user keyboard actions in a spreadsheet program. The user specifies the macro, which may include loops and conditional jumps, and thereafter the sequence can be invoked by the single depression of a specified pair of keys. *See* CONDITIONAL JUMP, LOOP, SPREADSHEET.

macroassembler. In programming, an assembler equipped with a facility for defining and expanding macroinstructions. *See* ASSEMBLER, MACROINSTRUCTION.

macrobend loss. In fiber optics, the leakage of light when the optical cable is bent. *Compare* MICROBEND LOSS.

macro chip. *See* WAFER SILICON INTEGRATION.

macrocode. *Synonymous with* MACROINSTRUCTION.

macroinstruction. In programming, an instruction that for a predefined sequence of other instructions. When a macroinstruction is encountered within a program it is called by the controlling system and is expanded into a series of machine language instructions. This technique can be used as a form of bottom-up programming. *See* ASSEMBLING, BOTTOM-UP METHOD. *Synonymous with* MACRO, MACROCODE.

macrolanguage. In programming, the representations and rules for writing macroinstructions. *See* MACROINSTRUCTION.

macroprogramming. In programming, the use of macroinstructions. *See* MACROINSTRUCTION.

magazine. (1) In teletext, a group of up to 100 pages, each carrying a common magazine number in the range of 1–8. Up to eight magazines may be transmitted in sequence, or independently, on a television program channel. (2) In filming, a container for film that is used for supply, shooting or storage purposes.

MAGB. Microfilm Association of Great Britain.

mag film. *Synonymous with* MAGNETIC FILM.

magnetically encoded card. In computer security and banking, a card that can be used for access control or for authority to initiate a transaction. The plastic card contains magnetically coded information on the surface, or embedded within it. The card may be of the magnetic spot or magnetic stripe type. *Compare* SMART CARD, SUPERSMART CARD. *See* MAGNETIC SPOT CARD, MAGNETIC STRIPE CARD.

magnetic bubble memory. *See* BUBBLE MEMORY.

magnetic card. (1) In audiovisual aids, a card with a magnetizable stripe on which sound can be stored by magnetic recording. (2) In word processing, a recording medium in the form of a paper or plastic card on which recordings can be made on one side only. (3) In computer security and banking. *See* MAGNETICALLY ENCODED CARD.

magnetic cartridge. *See* MAGNETIC TAPE CARTRIDGE.

magnetic character. In character recognition, a character printed with magnetic ink. *See* MAGNETIC INK.

magnetic disk. In memory systems, a flat disk with a magnetizable surface layer on which data can be stored by magnetic recording. There are two main types of disk — hard and floppy — the former being rigid using a metal or glass base, the latter having a flexible plastic base. The hard disk rotates at high speed (2400 rpm) so that data may be accessed without undue delay. A disk is logically formatted into tracks, with each track having a number of sectors. *Compare* MAGNETIC TAPE. *See* FLOPPY DISK, MAGNETIC DISK UNIT, SECTOR, TRACK, WINCHESTER DISK DRIVE.

magnetic disk unit. In memory systems, a device containing a disk drive, magnetic heads and associated controls. *See* MAGNETIC DISK.

magnetic field intensity. In electronics, the magnetic force required to produce a desired magnetic flux. *See* MAGNETIC FLUX.

magnetic film. In recording, standard-width film that is coated with an iron oxide compound. It is used for recording and reproducing sound. *Synonymous with* MAG FILM.

magnetic film recorder. In recording, a sound recorder that uses perforated magnetic film, as distinguished from a magnetic tape recorder. *Synonymous with* MAGNETIC FILM.

magnetic flux. In electronics, lines of force representing a magnetic field. (DOD).

magnetic focusing. In electronics, the focusing of an electron beam in a cathode ray tube by a magnetic field. *See* CATHODE RAY TUBE.

magnetic hand scanner. In peripherals, a hand-held device that reads information from a magnetic stripe. *See* MAGNETIC STRIPE.

magnetic head. In memory systems, a transducer for converting electrical variations into magnetic variations for storage on magnetic media, or for reconverting information stored in this way into corresponding electrical signals. *See* MAGNETIC DISK, MAGNETIC TAPE, TRANSDUCER.

magnetic ink. In peripherals, an ink containing magnetic particles which can be detected by a suitable magnetic sensor. *See* MAGNETIC INK CHARACTER RECOGNITION.

magnetic ink character recognition. (MICR) In character recognition, the identification of characters printed with ink that contains particles of a magnetic material. MICR is used in the banking industry to record transmitted codes and account numbers on cheques for data processing. *Compare* OPTICAL CHARACTER RECOGNITION.

magnetic keyboard. A word processor. *See* WORD PROCESSING.

magnetic master. In recording, the soundtrack from which the release print soundtrack is made.

magnetic medium. In memory systems, a magnetically sensitive carrier for the storage and distribution of information (e.g. hard disk, floppy disk, compact cassette, video cassette). (Philips). *See* COMPACT CASSETTE, FLOPPY DISK, HARD DISK, MAGNETIC TAPE, VIDEO CASSETTE.

magnetic original. In recording, a magnetic tape or film soundtrack containing the original live sound.

magnetic printing. In printing, a process in which a magnetic image is formed on a ferromagnetic layer. The image is developed by applying fine ferromagnetic particles, then transferring and fixing the image to paper. *Compare* ELECTROPHOTOGRAPHIC PROCESS. *See* FERROMAGNETIC, MAGNETOGRAPHY.

magnetic recording. In recording, a method of impressing signals onto a moving magnetic material by means of a magnetic field produced by a magnetic head. *See* MAGNETIC HEAD.

magnetic saturation. In electronics, the condition in which an increase in magnetizing force produces or results in little or no increase in magnetic flux. *See* HYSTERESIS, MAGNETIC FLUX.

magnetic screen. In electronics, a sheet of metal used to confine a magnetic field within a prescribed volume.

magnetic sheet. *See* MAGNETIC CARD.

magnetic sound. In recording, sound recorded on a magnetic medium. *Compare* OPTICAL SOUND TRACK. *See* MAGNETIC RECORDING.

magnetic spot card. In computer security, a card with magnetic spots embedded in the laminated material to provide coding of a unique identifier and used for access control. *Compare* MAGNETIC STRIPE CARD. *See* ACCESS CONTROL, MAGNETICALLY ENCODED CARD.

magnetic storm. In communications, a disturbance in the earth's magnetic field associated with abnormal solar activity and capable of seriously affecting both radio and wire transmission.

magnetic stripe. (1) In filming, a stripe of iron oxide placed on a clear film for recording and reproduction. (2) In computer security and banking. *See* MAGNETIC STRIPE CARD.

magnetic stripe card. In computer security and banking, a plastic card with a narrow magnetic stripe that may be employed for access control or authority to initiate a transaction. The data is normally encoded in three horizontal tracks along the stripe. The magnetic fields may be of low- or high-level intensity. The former are employed for credit cards, whereas some high-security access control systems employ high-intensity field materials because they provide greater stability. Magnetic stripe cards can be encoded or re-encoded with relatively inexpensive equipment. Special magnetic stripes are therefore sometimes employed to inhibit the production of counterfeit cards. *Compare* MAGNETIC SPOT CARD. *See* MAGNETICALLY ENCODED CARD, SANDWICH TAPE, WATERMARK TAPE. *Synonymous with* MAG STRIPE CARD.

magnetic tape. (1) In memory systems and recording, a recording medium consisting of a thin tape with a coating of a fine magnetic material, used for recording analog or digital data in the form of variations in the magnetic levels in the tape coating. (Philips). *Compare* MAGNETIC DISK. *See* DIGITAL AUDIO TAPE. (2) In memory systems, a common storage medium for computer software and data. In personal computer applications the tape is 1/2- or 1/4-inch wide and comprises a magnetic coating of fine particles of ferric oxide suspended in an inert binder on a polyester backing. It is stored on reels, cassettes or cartridges. The tape is mounted on a magnetic tape transport, which is connected to the computer by means of a tape controller. Magnetic tapes are commonly employed to convey software, or data, from one computer installation to another, and therefore the format of data recorded on the tape must conform to specific standards. *Compare* MAGNETIC DISK. *See* MAGNETIC TAPE CASSETTE, MAGNETIC TAPE CONTROLLER, MAGNETIC TAPE FORMAT, MAGNETIC TAPE TRANSPORT.

magnetic tape cartridge. In memory systems, a container with one or two reels holding magnetic tape that can be loaded onto a magnetic tape transport, without handling of the tape by the operator. There are a number of cartridge types for 1/2-inch, 1/4-inch and 0.15-inch tapes, the last are normally classified as magnetic tape cassettes. The 1/4-inch tape cartridges (QIC) are popular for tape streamers, and a typical 450-foot tape with 6400 bits per inch recording density has a storage capacity of 14 megabytes. QIC standards for 1/4-inch cartridge systems have been formulated in recent years. *See* BIT, BYTE, MAGNETIC TAPE CASSETTE, MAGNETIC TAPE TRANSPORT.

magnetic tape cassette. (MTC) In memory systems, a container with two reels holding 0.15-inch magnetic tape that can be played or recorded on a domestic audio cassette player. The tape has two tracks; the second track is selected by removing and turning over the cassette. *Compare* MINICASSETTE. *See* MAGNETIC TAPE CASSETTE, MAGNETIC TAPE TRANSPORT.

magnetic tape controller. In memory systems, a device that interfaces a magnetic tape transport to a computer. The device is responsible for data formatting and maintaining communication with the computer. *See* MAGNETIC TAPE FORMAT, MAGNETIC TAPE TRANSPORT.

magnetic tape drive. *Synonymous with* MAGNETIC TAPE TRANSPORT.

magnetic tape format. In memory systems, the format of data recorded on magnetic tape allowing the system to recognize, control and verify the data. Tape formats are concerned with the logical level of data presented to the computer and the physical level of the patterns of magnetization on the tape. The logical level normally deals with the name, characteristics of the entire tape or the next file, signals to delimit individual files and the data blocks. The physical format contains additional data to aid synchronization, identify individual data blocks, check bits, interblock gaps, etc. The formats commonly employed in magnetic tape recording are phase encoding, non-return to zero inverted (NRZI) and group-coded recording. QIC standards now define formats for 1/4-inch cartridge tape systems. *See* CHECK BIT, INTERBLOCK GAP, MAGNETIC TAPE, NON-RETURN TO ZERO INVERTED.

magnetic tape label. In memory systems, one or more records at the beginning of a magnetic tape that identify and describe the data recorded on the tape. It also contains other information, such as the serial number of the reel holding the tape. *See* MAGNETIC TAPE FORMAT, RECORD.

magnetic tape recorder. *Synonymous with* TAPE RECORDER.

magnetic tape transport. In memory systems, a peripheral unit for magnetic tape storage. The transport moves magnetic tape from a feed reel, past one or more heads for read, write or erase actions, to a take-up reel. An electrical signal applied to the write head induces flux changes in the magnetic coating on the tape, and movement of the magnetic coating past a read head induces corresponding electrical signals for output to the computer. The tape normally passes over an erase head prior to the writing action. The read/write heads may be separate units, allowing for the reading and checking of written data, or they may be a single head used either for read or write actions.

The magnetic tape transport has a long and continuing association with computers, but it has appeared in some radically different physical manifestations. The early mainframe computers used large, sophisticated and expensive magnetic tape transports as their prime method of backing storage. The applications were largely concerned with commercial batch data processing in which master files were updated by transaction files, sorted to correspond to the sequential records, on the master file. This mode of operation was compatible with the serial access of magnetic tape. The tape had to move over the read/write heads at a constant speed, and the data to and from the computer was intermittent. A major design feature of the tape transport was thus concerned with mechanisms, such as vacuum column or tension arm, which protect the tape against damage during rapid acceleration of the driving mechanism. The magnetic tapes were commonly used to distribute software and to pass computer data from one installation to another. Tape formats were therefore standardized.

The move to transaction processing and database systems produced a demand for direct-access storage devices, and magnetic disk drives replaced magnetic tape transports for online access. Magnetic tape drives were retained, however, for backup and archiving. In the mid-1970s the home computer market demanded a cheap mass storage system for distribution and offline storage of software. The audio cassette player was widely used for this purpose. Its low price made it attractive for this purpose, but the data rate of these units was kept low by the performance of domestic audio cassette recorders; it could take tens of minutes to save a program and perform a second verify run to ensure that the data was correctly recorded. There were a number of common cassette standards developed to cope with the vagaries of the domestic audio cassette recorder (e.g. Kansas City standard).

Business microcomputer applications demanded the performance of magnetic disks for backing storage, but the advent of the Winchester disk drives, with their fixed disks, revived the demand for magnetic tape systems as backup devices. Conventional mainframe tape transports were too expensive for this market, and smaller units, using 1/2- or 1/4-inch tapes, in reel-to-reel or cartridge form were produced for this purpose. These devices appear as start/stop drives or tape streamers. Start/stop units are based upon the traditional magnetic tape transport systems and allow individual records to be written and read. The drive can read a record, bring the tape to a halt within a specified interblock gap, and then accelerate the tape to running speed so that it can write the next record immediately after the interblock gap. The devices make heavy demands upon the drive systems which must use tension arms to maintain correct tensions and limit the torque requirements on the reel servo mechanisms. The tape streamer is a mechanically simpler and cheaper drive designed for continuous backup data flows. The new data is added to the end of a written tape, or the tape is erased and then rewritten. The tape streamer read/write head must be repositioned if there is an interruption in the data flow from the computer or accepted by the computer. Each reposition cycle can take as long a one second, and in some systems cache memories are employed as buffers to maintain a continuous data flow and hence reduce the time lost in repositioning.

A further development was the introduction of the mini-cassette drive. These mini-cassettes resemble those used in pocket dictation machines, but they are manufactured to higher specifications, ensuring that they provide reliable digital storage media. The storage capacity is of the order of 200 kilobytes, comparable with the lower end of the floppy disk range, and they can transfer data at 9600 baud with necessary error checking and correction. The cost of the mini-cassette recorders is low compared with floppy disk drives, and they have applications both in the home computer market and scientific/industrial fields, where they can be employed to download software or for data logging and acquisition. *See* BATCH PROCESSING, BAUD, BYTE, DATABASE, DATA ACQUISITION, DIRECT-ACCESS STORAGE DEVICE, INTERBLOCK GAP, MINI-CASSETTE, READ/WRITE HEAD, RECORD, TAPE STREAMER, TRANSACTION PROCESSING, WINCHESTER DISK DRIVE. *Syno-*

nymous with MAGNETIC TAPE DRIVE, MAGNETIC TAPE UNIT, TAPE DECK, TAPE DRIVE, TAPE TRANSPORT.

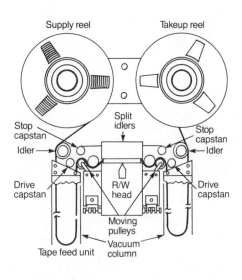

magnetic tape transport

magnetic tape unit. *Synonymous with* MAGNETIC TAPE TRANSPORT.

magnetic thin-film storage. *See* THIN-FILM MEMORY.

magnetic transfer. In recording, a transfer from one magnetic medium to another (e.g. magnetic tape to perforated magnetic film for editing).

magnetic workprint. In recording, a re-recorded sound track used for editing purposes, usually on a perforated magnetic film with coded edge numbers.

magnetography. In printing, a technique in which magnetic dots are created on paper to form a latent image. Toner is attracted to the dots and fixed to the paper by pressure rollers and heat fusing. *Compare* LASER PRINTER. *See* LATENT IMAGE, MAGNETIC PRINTING, TONER.

magnitude. In mathematics, the absolute value of a number, irrespective of sign.

magoptical. In recording, a sound track that has both an optical and a magnetic stripe track. *See* MAGNATIC SOUND, OPTICAL SOUND TRACK.

mag stripe card. *Synonymous with* MAGNETIC STRIPE CARD.

MAHT. Machine-aided human translation. *See* MACHINE-AIDED TRANSLATION.

mail box. *See* ELECTRONIC MAIL.

mail merge. In word processing, a program for producing form letters in which a name and address file is merged with the text file containing the letter. *See* FORM LETTER, MERGE.

main beam. In communications, the electromagnetic waves contained within the main lobe of an antenna array. *See* ANTENNA, ELECTROMAGNETIC RADIATION, MAIN LOBE.

main cable. In communications, a cable that links to a cross-connection point in a local line network to which other main cables are connected.

main channel. (1) In optical media, the only accessible, absolutely addressable, information channel recorded on a read-only memory or interactive compact disc. (Philips). *Compare* SUBCODE CHANNEL. *See* COMPACT DISC − INTERACTIVE, COMPACT DISC − READ-ONLY MEMORY. (2) In optical media, the main channel carries the digital audio (music) information on a digital audio compact disc. (Philips). *Compare* SUBCODE CHANNEL. *See* COMPACT DISC − DIGITAL AUDIO.

main distributing frame. (MDF) In communications, the cable racking on which all distribution and trunk cables into a central office are terminated. The bulky processing units of the early computers resembled the MDF, hence the origin of the term mainframe for a large computer.

main entry. In library science, the basic catalogue entry with the fullest particulars for the complete identification of the work. *Compare* ADDED ENTRY.

mainframe. In computing, a term normally applied to a large general-purpose computer installation serving a major section of an organization or institution. *Compare* MICROCOMPUTER, MINICOMPUTER.

mainframe on a chip. *Synonymous with* MICROMAINFRAME.

main index. In videotex, the topmost index in the database that directs a user to other indexes or services. *See* ROUTING PAGE, TREE STRUCTURE.

main lobe. In communications, the predominant lobe in an antenna pattern. *Compare* BACK LOBE, SIDE LOBE. *See* ANTENNA PATTERN.

main memory. In memory systems, a program-addressable random-access store that transfers instructions/data to, and from, the central processing unit registers for processing. The main memory also transfers data to, and from, backing storage and peripherals. *See* ADDRESS, BACKING STORAGE, PERIPHERAL, RANDOM-ACCESS MEMORY. *Synonymous with* INTERNAL STORAGE, MAIN STORAGE.

main program. In programming, the part of the program which is effectively a statement of the actions of the whole program expressed in terms of the constituent procedures. *See* PROCEDURE.

main station. In communications, a telephone, telex or teletypewriter exchange terminal connected to the local central office via a local loop and having a unique dial number. *See* LOCAL LOOP.

main storage. *Synonymous with* MAIN MEMORY.

maintenance. (1) In reliability, any activity intended to keep a machine in a specified, operational condition, including preventive maintenance and corrective maintenance. *See* CORRECTIVE MAINTENANCE, PREVENTIVE MAINTENANCE. (2) In programming. *See* SOFTWARE MAINTENANCE.

majuscule. In printing, a capital letter. *Compare* MINUSCULE.

make-up. In printing, the arrangement of type matter into pages. *Synonymous with* PAGE MAKE-UP.

make v buy. In computing and data communications, the choice senior management faces in either developing in-house software or purchasing products/services from external suppliers.

malicious logic. In computer security, hardware, software or firmware that is intentionally included in a system for the purpose of causing loss or harm (e.g. Trojan horse). (DOD). *See* TROJAN HORSE.

Maltron keyboard. In peripherals, a keyboard layout radically different from conventional keyboards. The keyboard is divided into two distinct groups with a centrally located numeric keypad. A set of thumb keys for each hand are used for cursor control and other frequently used functions. This keyboard design is said to offer greater operator comfort. *Compare* AZERTY KEYBOARD, DVORAK KEYBOARD, PRONTO KEYBOARD, QWERTY KEYBOARD. *See* KEYBOARD.

managed data network. (MDN) In operations, the use of one independent service organization to manage or operate a corporation's data communications. *Compare* VALUE-ADDED NETWORK SERVICE.

Management Contents. In online information retrieval, database supplied by Management Contents and dealing with business, industry and business management.

management information system. (MIS) (1) In applications, a system designed to provide management and supervisory staff with required data that is accurate, relevant and timely, possibly on a real-time basis. *See* DATABASE, REAL-TIME. (2) In applications, a system in which data is recorded and processed for operational purposes. The problems are detected for higher management decision-making, and information on the progress, or lack of it, in achieving management objectives is fed back to higher levels.

mandatory access control. In computer security, a means of restricting access to objects based on the sensitivity (as represented by a label) of the information contained in the objects and the formal authorization (i.e. clearance) of subjects to access information of such sensitivity.

(DOD). *Compare* DISCRETIONARY ACCESS CONTROL. *See* MANDATORY SECURITY, OBJECT, SUBJECT.

mandatory security. In computer security, the aspect of the security policy insisted upon by system administrators. It requires the provision of security services for one or more instances of communication. *Compare* DISCRETIONARY SECURITY. *See* MANDATORY ACCESS CONTROL.

manipulation detection. In computer security, a mechanism that is used to detect whether data has been modified, either accidentally or intentionally.

man–machine interface. (MMI) In peripherals, pertaining to technologies designed to improve the communication between the user and the computer. In hardware terms this includes voice analysis and synthesis, pointing devices, graphics displays, etc. In software terms it relates to methods that render packages more user friendly (e.g. natural language dialogues, windows, icons, WIMPS, etc.). *See* COMPUTER GRAPHICS, ICON, POINTING DEVICE, SPEECH RECOGNIZER, VOICE SYNTHESIS, WIMPS, WINDOWS.

man-made noise. In communications, interference caused by electrical machines, car ignition systems, etc. *See* INTERFERENCE.

man month. The amount of useful work that an individual can contribute when tackling a given task within one month; often used to assess the cost of writing a program or designing a system.

mantissa. In mathematics, the positive fractional part of the representation of a logarithm. In the expression log 643 = 2.808, the mantissa is 0.808 and the characteristic is 2. *Compare* CHARACTERISTIC. *See* LOGARITHM.

manual input. In operations, the entry of data by hand into a computer, usually involving a keyboard. *Compare* MACHINE-READABLE.

manuscript. In printing, any handwritten matter intended for typesetting. *Synonymous with* COPY.

MAP. In data communications, manufacturing automation protocol; a specification based upon the Open System Interconnection model to provide for communication within a factory environment. Efficient data communications in this field assist in the integration of activities, such as order processing, inventory management, work in progress, etc., within the overall business strategy. *Compare* TOP. *See* OPEN SYSTEMS INTERCONNECTION.

mapping. (1) In mathematics, a relationship between two or more quantities. (2) In databases, the relationship between a given logical structure and its physical representation. *See* LOGICAL DATABASE, PHYSICAL DATABASE.

MARC. In library science, machine-readable catalog; a system initially developed in the US Library of Congress with the purpose of organizing and disseminating bibliographic data in machine-readable form for incorporation into national and local records for the purpose of documentation. *See* MACHINE-READABLE.

margin. In printing, the space surrounding the type area, comprising head, tail, back and foredge. *See* HEAD, TAIL.

mark. In communications, an impulse on a data circuit that corresponds to the active condition of the receiving apparatus. *Compare* SPACE.

market feedback. *See* FEEDBACK.

Markov process. In mathematics, a random process in which the probability of a transition to a new state depends only upon the current state. *See* PROBABILITY THEORY, RANDOM PROCESS.

mark scanning. In character recognition, the automatic optical sensing of marks usually recorded manually on paper or another data carrier.

mark sense. In character recognition, to mark a position on a form with an electrically conductive pencil for machine reading. *See* MACHINE-READABLE.

markup. *Synonymous with* TYPE MARKUP.

mask. (1) In microelectronics, a photographically produced stencil used in semiconductor manufacture to control areas of metal deposited on a silicon substrate or to limit the regions of doping during the diffusion process. *See* CHIP, DOPANT, MASKED ROM. (2) In computing, a pattern of characters used to control the retention and elimination of portions of another pattern of characters. (3) In photography, a device used to restrict the light from one area, while admitting whole or reduced illumination to another area.

masked ROM. In memory systems, a read-only memory (ROM) whose contents are produced during its manufacture by a masking technique, in contrast to a programmable ROM (PROM) whose contents are programmed after manufacture by means of a PROM programming device. ROM masking is a high-volume method of production used when 1000 or more identical ROMs are to be made. *See* MASK, PROGRAMMABLE READ-ONLY MEMORY, READ-ONLY MEMORY.

masking. (1) In audio, an effect in which a sound may apparently be suppressed by another which might be louder or at a different frequency, or both. (2) In television, the minimizing of colour errors that may appear in the process of synthesizing colour information to three primary signals. *See* RGB.

mask-programmable. In microelectronics, pertaining to a technique in which the final stage of fabrication of a chip involves making certain final connections. *Compare* FIELD-PROGRAMMABLE. *See* SEMI-CUSTOM DESIGN.

masquerading. In data security, an attempt to gain access to a system by posing as an authorized user. (AR). *Compare* SPOOFING. *Synonymous with* IMPERSONATION, MIMICKING.

massaging. In printing, the manipulation of input copy, particularly on a visual display unit, in order to produce a desired layout.

mass media. In communications, newspapers, television and radio. *See* MEDIA.

mass storage. In memory systems, a device having a large storage capacity (e.g. magnetic disk, optical disc). *See* COMPACT DISC – READ-ONLY MEMORY, MAGNETIC DISK, OPTICAL DIGITAL DISC. *Synonymous with* BULK STORAGE.

mass storage system. (MSS) In memory systems, a storage system with more than a terabit capacity. Such systems normally hold the data cells in a rack, or honeycomb, of storage units. A mechanical system moves the appropriate cell to and from the read/write head. The data cells may be magnetic tape cartridge or cassette, magnetic card or photodigital systems. Access times range from three to about 20 seconds. *See* MAGNETIC CARD, MAGNETIC TAPE, PHOTODIGITAL MEMORY.

master. (1) In recording, a sound track on which other tracks have been combined. (2) In printing, a sheet of material that carries an image of the text or other material to be copied. *See* MASTER PROOF.

master antenna television system. (MATV) In cable television, an antenna arrangement that serves a localized cluster of television receivers. *Compare* COMMUNITY ANTENNA TELEVISION.

masterchip. In microelectronics, a technique of semi-custom design using a large-scale integration circuit, containing an uncommitted array of identical cells, which may be fabricated up to, but excluding, the final metallization interconnect process. The customization thus consists of the design and implementation of the interconnection of cells on the chip to meet customer requirements. The uncommitted masterchip wafers can be manufactured in quantity and held pending final design specifications from customers.

There are a variety of cells that may be used in masterchip processes, ranging from individual transistors to fully functional entities such as NAND or NOR gates. This technique has the advantage that all the stages and fabrication of chip design, up to the final interconnections, are standard, thus providing a fast and inexpensive route to the design of the final semi-custom chip. However, the final chip produced will be less efficient, in terms of chip size and performance than that provided by the cell library method. The relative inefficiency of the masterchip approach arises because the chip will normally contain many unused cells. *Compare* CELL LIBRARY. *See* LARGE-SCALE INTEGRATION, SEMI-CUSTOM DESIGN, UNCOMMITTED COMPONENTS ARRAY, UNCOMMITTED GATE ARRAY, UNCOMMITTED LOGIC ARRAY. *Synonymous with* MASTERSLICE.

master clock. In computing, the primary source of timing signals used to control the sequencing of pulses. *See* CLOCK.

master disc. In recording, an original disc from which copies can be made by a replication process. (Philips). *See* CD MASTERING, MASTERING, METAL FATHER, STAMPER.

master file. In data structures, a file containing relatively permanent information that is used as a source of reference and is updated periodically. *See* FILE.

master group. In communications, an assembly of ten supergroups in a 2520-kHz band, the basic master group extending from 564 to 3084 kHz. In the UK, a master group contains only five supergroups separated by 8 kHz in a 1232-kHz band. *See* SUPERGROUP.

mastering. (1) In optical media, the production of the master disc. (Philips). *See* CD MASTERING, MASTER DISC. (2) In optical media, a real-time process in which a premaster video tape is used to modulate a laser beam onto a photosensitive glass master videodisc. *See* VIDEO DISC.

master key. In data security, a long-life key to a cryptographic function. It is used to encrypt long-term data or other cryptographic keys. *See* CRYPTOGRAPHIC KEY, KEY-ENCRYPTING KEY.

master proof. In printing, the final version of a galley proof or page proof used for a print run. *See* GALLEY PROOF, PAGE PROOF.

masterslice. *Synonymous with* MASTERCHIP.

master station. In data communications, a station that has accepted an invitation to pass data to one or more slave stations. At any one time, there can only be one master station on a link. *See* SLAVE, STATION.

masthead. In publishing, details of publisher and editorial staff usually printed on the contents page. (Desktop).

MAT. *See* MACHINE-AIDED TRANSLATION.

match dissolve. In video and filming, a dissolve that links images having similar form or content. *Compare* GLOBAL DISSOLVE, LOCAL DISSOLVE.

matched load. In electronics, a load connected to the output of a device, or a node on a transmission system, that absorbs all the transmitted signal without reflection. *See* IMPEDANCE MATCHING.

match image cut. In filming, a cut from one shot to another that is of the same shape (e.g. from a golfball to a globe of the world).

matching. In programming, the process of comparing two files to determine whether there is a corresponding item, or group of items, in each file. *See* FILE, ITEM.

matching transformer. In electronics, a transformer used for coupling two systems having different impedances. *See* IMPEDANCE MATCHING.

mathematical model. A formal statement of the mathematical relationship between the elements of a system that are of particular interest. Mathematical models usually represent a simplified form of reality and are often used for prediction.

mathematics. The study of the relationships between quantities or objects, organized so that certain facts can be proved or derived from others by the use of logic. *See* LOGIC.

matrix. (1) In mathematics, a multidimensional array of quantities, manipulated in accordance with the rules of matrix algebra. (2) In computing, a logic network whose configuration is an array of intersections of its input/output leads, with logic circuits connected at some of these intersections. The network usually functions as an encoder or decoder. *See* LOGIC CIRCUIT. (3) In television, the means by which colour data is transformed from one reference system to another. (4) In printing, the set of type faces

used by a photocomposition machine. *See* PHOTOTYPESETTING. (5) In photography, a dyed emulsion image strip which together with two other strips, is combined on a film base to produce colour film.

matrix printer. In printing, a printer in which each character is represented by a pattern of dots. It is commonly used as a microcomputer peripheral; it has the advantage of relatively low cost and high flexibility. The font is determined by an internal read-only memory holding the matrix patterns for each code. The quality of the printed output can range from the functional (e.g. for program listings) to that approaching letter quality. *Compare* DAISY WHEEL, LASER PRINTER. *See* FONT, LETTER QUALITY, PAPER, PRINTER. *Synonymous with* DOT PRINTER, NEEDLE PRINTER.

matt art. In printing, pertaining to a coated printing paper with a dull surface. *Compare* ART PAPER.

matte. (1) In filming, a mask used to blank off one part of a negative during exposure to allow superimposition of another shot. *See* MATTER SCAN, MATTING. (2) In television, the electronic insertion of an image into a selected background. *See* COLOUR KEY.

matter. In printing, the body of a printed work as distinct from headings.

matte scan. In filming, a technique in which a computer is used to precisely direct and time a camera in matte photography. *See* MATTE.

matting. In filming, the insertion of an image into a background using optical or electronic techniques. *See* MATTE.

MATV. *See* MASTER ANTENNA TELEVISION SYSTEM.

Mavica. In photography, a camera system developed by Sony. The images are stored on a magnetic disk and can be replayed on a television set; up to 50 individual pictures can be stored on one disk.

maximum-usable frequency. In communications, the highest radio frequency that can be used for transmission purposes via the ionosphere. *See* IONOSPHERE.

Mb. *See* MEGABYTE.

MCC. *See* MISCELLANEOUS COMMON CARRIER.

MDF. *See* MAIN DISTRIBUTING FRAME.

MDN. *See* MANAGED DATA NETWORK.

Mead Data General Company. In online information retrieval, a database producer and vendor best known for the Lexis and Nexis databases. *See* DATABASE PRODUCER, DATABASE VENDOR, LEXIS, NEXIS.

mean busy hour. In communications, an uninterrupted period of one hour, starting at the same time on each of a number of weekdays, during which the highest average telephone traffic is measured. *See* BUSY HOUR, TRAFFIC.

mean grade. In audio and television, the average of a subjective assessment by a number of observers of the quality of a reproduction. *See* IMPAIRMENT SCALE.

mean life. In reliability, the average or expected life of a given item of equipment, normally a function of design parameters and usage. *Compare* MEAN TIME BETWEEN FAILURE.

mean time between failure. (MTBF) In reliability, for a given period in the life of a piece of equipment, the average of the periods of time between consecutive failures under stated conditions. *Compare* MEAN LIFE, MEAN TIME TO RECOVER, MEAN TIME TO REPAIR.

mean time to recover. In reliability, the average time required to bring a system into operation after repair. This may include reprocessing from the last checkpoint. *Compare* MEAN TIME BETWEEN FAILURE, MEAN TIME TO REPAIR. *See* CHECKPOINT.

mean time to repair. (MTTR) In reliability, the average time needed to repair, or to maintain correctively, a piece of equip-

ment. *Compare* MEAN TIME BETWEEN FAILURE, MEAN TIME TO RECOVER.

measure. In printing, the width to which type is set (i.e. the maximum length of the lines).

measured service. In communications, service that is provided on the basis of the number of message units accrued during the charging period, rather than on a flat-rate basis. *See* FLAT RATE.

media. (1) In memory systems, the material on which data and instructions are recorded (e.g. magnetic disk, floppy disk, magnetic tape, etc.). (2) In communications, the means whereby information is conveyed within the communications industry (i.e. books, cinema, newspapers, radio, television).

media centre. In audiovisual aids, a place where a full range of media-related information sources and associated equipment is available.

media drive. In word processing, the device used for recording on or reading from a recording medium. *See* DISK DRIVE, MAGNETIC TAPE TRANSPORT.

media technology. The range of activities and techniques that lie on the intersection of computing, publishing and film making (e.g. the production of an interactive videodisc or interactive compact disc encyclopaedia). *See* COMPACT DISC − INTERACTIVE, VIDEODISC.

mediated instruction. In audiovisual aids, a package that is designed for use without the need for a teacher or instructor.

medium. (1) In memory systems, a physical means of representing information for storage or transfer (e.g. tape, disk, paper). (2) A means of communicating information (e.g. video, audio, printed publications). (Philips). *See* MASS MEDIA.

medium frequency. (MF) In communications, the range of frequencies from 300 to 3000 kHz.

medium lens. In photography, a lens whose focal length is near the normal focal length for the film dimensions being used. *See* FOCAL LENGTH.

medium reduction. (MR) In micrographics, a reduction in the range 16x to 30x. *Compare* HIGH REDUCTION, LOW REDUCTION, ULTRA HIGH REDUCTION, VERY HIGH REDUCTION. *See* REDUCTION.

medium-scale integration. (MSI) In microelectronics, pertaining to a fabrication technology that produces between 100 and 10 000 transistors per chip. *Compare* LARGE-SCALE INTEGRATION, SMALL-SCALE INTEGRATION, SUPER LARGE-SCALE INTEGRATION, ULTRA LARGE-SCALE INTEGRATION, VERY LARGE-SCALE INTEGRATION. *See* CHIP, TRANSISTOR.

medium-speed. In data communications, pertaining to transmission rates between 2400 baud and the limit of a voice-grade circuit (i.e. 9600 baud). *See* BAUD, VOICE-GRADE CHANNEL.

Medlars. In online information retrieval, Medical Literature Analysis and Retrieval; the whole US National Library of Medicine database system including medline. *See* MEDLINE.

Medline. In online information retrieval, a database supplied by National Library of Medicine and dealing with biomedicine.

meet me conference. In communications, a switchboard facility enabling a conference call to be established by each participating extension user dialing a designated conference code. *See* CONFERENCE CALL, TELECONFERENCING.

megabit. (Mbit) One million bits. *See* BIT.

megabyte. (Mbyte) In computing, a unit of storage equal to 1 048 576 bytes. *See* BYTE.

megahertz. (MHz) One million hertz. *See* HERTZ.

Megastream. In data communications, a very high-speed digital communications service on a point-to-point basis offered by British Telecom. *Compare* KILOSTREAM, SATSTREAM, SWITCHSTREAM. *See* X-STREAM.

membrane switch. In electronics, a layer construction comprising a tough membrane with a conductive rear surface that effects a contact closure with a very small movement. *See* KEYBOARD.

memomotion. In filming, a time lapse photographic technique that is used mostly in connection with time and motion study analysis. *See* TIME LAPSE CINEMATOGRAPHY.

memory. Any facility for holding data. It is often used to describe main or internal memory, in which case a distinction must be made from external memory. (Philips). *See* BACKING STORAGE, DISC MEMORY, MAIN MEMORY, RANDOM-ACCESS MEMORY, READ-ONLY MEMORY, WORM.

memory access time. *See* ACCESS TIME.

memory allocation. In computing, the setting aside of contiguous memory locations for programming or device-handling purposes. *See* MEMORY MAP.

memory bank. In memory systems, a block of memory locations corresponding to contiguous addresses. *See* ADDRESS.

memory bounds. In computer security, the limits in the range of storage addresses for a protected region in memory. (FIPS).

memory bounds checking. *Synonymous with* BOUNDS CHECKING.

memory control logic. In memory systems, logic circuitry to control the movement of information to, from or within a memory. (Philips). *See* MEMORY.

memory cycle. In memory systems, the time required to send an address to memory as well as the reading or writing into that memory location. *Compare* MACHINE CYCLE. *See* ADDRESS.

memory dump. *Synonymous with* DUMP.

memory hierarchy. *See* BACKING STORAGE.

memory management. In memory systems, a combination of hardware and software elements that allocates main memory to programs and data in a multiprogramming system. *See* MAIN MEMORY.

memory map. In memory systems, a tabulation of all the memory locations that a processor can address and the facilities present at these locations. *See* INPUT/OUTPUT UNIT, MAIN MEMORY.

memory protection. In computing, a hardware or software method of ensuring that a application program does not access data, or write, in a memory location allocated to another user or a system utility. When a task accesses a given block of memory a check is made to determine whether it has the right to do so and an interrupt is generated if unauthorized access is attempted. *Compare* FILE PROTECTION. *See* APPLICATION PROGRAM, BOUNDS CHECKING.

memory workspace. In programming, the amount of memory required by a program in addition to that required for its own storage. Workspace is generally used for input/output device buffer areas and for holding temporary results. *See* INPUT/OUTPUT UNIT. *Synonymous with* WORK SPACE.

mental poker. In cryptography, a form of communication in which information can be concealed from individual parties exchanging data, but which also ensures that the concealed information can be checked subsequently by all parties. In its simplest form it involves two poker players communicating over a telephone. The cryptographic system employed must meet the specifications listed below.

(a) Both players must receive poker hands that are (i) disjoint, (ii) concealed from the other player and (iii) are equally likely for each player.
(b) Any additional cards drawn during play must conform to the above requirements, and a player must be able to reveal a card without compromising the security of other cards in the hand.
(c) At the end of the game the players must be able to confirm that the game was played fairly and no player cheated.

menu. (1) In information presentation, a display of a list of available functions for selection by an operator. (Philips). (2) In videotex, a list of up to nine choices on a page for selection by a user for routing to various parts of the database. *See* MAIN INDEX, MENU SELECTION, PAGE.

menu-driven. In programming, pertaining to the course of events in an application program, interactively controlled by means of menu selection. (Philips). *See* MENU.

menu selection. In programming, a technique in which a user is provided with a list of options and details of the keys to be depressed for the selection of each option. Thus the user needs no specific training or reference manuals to use the system. *See* MENU.

Mercury. In communications, a private consortium of Cable and Wireless, British Petroleum and Barclays Bank, acting as a carrier for voice and data traffic. They offer all digital services in the UK based upon a combination of high-speed fiber optics and microwave techniques. *See* FIBER OPTICS, MICROWAVE TRANSMISSION.

merge. In programming, the combining of two ordered files of information items in such a way as to maintain the ordering of the original files in the resulting file. *See* FILE.

meridional ray. In fiber optics, a ray of light that passes through the axis of the fiber as a result of an internal reflection and is confined to a single plane. *See* TOTAL INTERNAL REFLECTION.

mesh. In data communications, a configuration in which there are two or more paths between any two nodes. *Compare* RING, STAR. *See* NODE.

Mesh. In online information retrieval, a thesaurus of medical subject terms used to search Medline and some other Medlars databases. *See* MEDLARS, MEDLINE, THESAURUS.

meshbeat. *See* MOIRE.

message. (1) In data communications, an arbitrary amount of information whose beginning and end are defined or implied. *See* MESSAGE FORMAT. (2) A communication containing one or more transactions or one or more items of related information. (ANSI).

message analysis.   In communications and computing, the study of the structure, length and online time of a typical message. This information may be used to plan enhancement to an existing network.

message authentication.   In data security, the processes undertaken to ensure that: (a) the message originated with the purported sender; (b) the message contents have not been accidentally or intentionally altered or rearranged; (c) the message has been received in the sequence that it was sent by the originator; and (d) the message was received by the intended recipient. *See* AUTHENTICATION.

message certification.   In data security, a procedure in which a receiver provides proof to a sender that a particular message has been received. The acknowledgement from the receiver should be signed to ensure that it has not originated from an attacker. *See* DIGITAL SIGNATURE.

message circuit.   In communications, a circuit used to provide long-distance telephone or toll services to the general public, as opposed to private line services. *See* TOLL CALL.

message exhaustion.   In data security, a form of attack in which all possible plaintext combinations are encrypted and the corresponding ciphertext stored for future reference. In public key cryptography, the encrypting key is known by the cryptanalyst and thus the received ciphertext can be checked against the stored plaintext/ciphertext pairs. If the encryption key is not known then the process is conducted for all possible keys; if subsequently a fragment of plaintext and corresponding ciphertext is available then the stored plaintext/ciphertext pairs can be searched and the corresponding key determined. *Compare* KEY EXHAUSTION. *See* BLOCK CIPHER, BLOCK SIZE, CRYPTOGRAPHIC KEY, PUBLIC KEY CRYPTOGRAPHY.

message format.   In data communications, rules for the placement of such portions of a message as the heading, address, text and

end of the message. *See* ADDRESS, MESSAGE HEADING, MESSAGE TEXT.

message heading.   In data communications, the leading part of a message that contains such information as the source or destination code of the message, the message priority and the type of message. *Compare* MESSAGE TEXT.

message identifier.   In data security, a field of up to eight acceptable characters that may be used to identify a financial message or transaction. Typically, this field is a sequence number. (ANSI)

message numbering.   In data communications, a unique number given to each message in a system for identification purposes.

message routing.   In data communications, the process of selecting a route in a message-switching system. *See* MESSAGE SWITCHING, ROUTING.

message slot.   In data communications, sequences of bits, sufficient to hold a full message, that are continually circulated around a ring local area network. A slot may be empty or full, and any node, on detecting an empty slot, may mark the slot as full and place a message in it. *Compare* CONTROL TOKEN, DAISY CHAIN. *See* CAMBRIDGE RING, LOCAL AREA NETWORK.

message space.   In data security, the set of all possible messages that can be encrypted with a given cipher. *Compare* KEY SPACE.

message stream modification.   *See* ACTIVATION.

message switching.   In data communications, a technique for increasing the throughput of a network by the sequential switching of prestored messages. Unlike packet switching, messages are transmitted in their entirety and once in a network the system takes over responsibility for their delivery. *Compare* CIRCUIT SWITCHING, PACKET SWITCHING. *See* STORE AND FORWARD.

message-switching centre.   In data communications, a centre in which messages are routed according to information contained

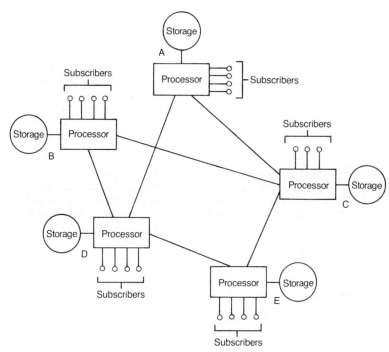

message switching

within the messages themselves. *Synonymous with* RELAY CENTRE.

message text. In data communications, the part of a message that is relevant to the party receiving the message. The message text excludes the header and control information. *Compare* MESSAGE HEADING.

Metadex. In online information retrieval, databases, supplied by the American Society for Metals and the UK Metals Society, that deal with metallurgy.

metalanguage. In computer programming, a language that is used to describe a class of languages. *See* BACKUS NAUR FORM.

metal father. In recording, a recording mould formed by nickel plating on a master disc. It can be used directly for replication, or as the basis for the production, by two further stages of plating of stampers, for large-quantity production. (Philips). *See* MASTER DISC, MASTERING, MOTHER, STAMPER.

metallic ink. In printing, printing inks that produce an effect of gold, silver, bronze or metallic colours. (Desktop).

metal oxide semiconductor. (MOS) In semiconductors, a technology for fabricating high-density integrated circuits. Most large-scale integration devices, such as microprocessors, are based on MOS technology. *See* CHIP, LARGE-SCALE INTEGRATION.

metal powder. (MP) In recording, a form of magnetic tape providing a high areal density. *See* AREAL DENSITY.

MF. *See* MEDIUM FREQUENCY, MICROFICHE, MICROFILM.

MF keypad. In communications, a keypad producing multifrequency signals that can be used with suitable types of telephone exchanges both for call set-up purposes and subsequently to transmit low-speed data (i.e. less than 600 baud). *See* KEYPAD, MULTI-FREQUENCY SIGNAL.

MFLOPS. In computing, mega floating point instructions per second. *See* FLOPS.

MF signal. *See* MULTIFREQUENCY SIGNAL.

MG. *See* MACHINE-GLAZED.

MHD. *See* MOVABLE-HEAD DISK.

MHz. *See* MEGAHERTZ.

MICR. *See* MAGNETIC INK CHARACTER RECOGNITION.

micro. (1) A Greek word meaning small. (2) A prefix representing one-millionth. (3) *See* MICROCOMPUTER.

microbend loss. In fiber optics, the leakage of light caused by minute sharp curves in the optical cable that may result from imperfections when the glass fiber meets the sheathing that covers it. *Compare* MACROBEND LOSS.

microcard. In micrographics, an opaque card with images reproduced photographically in rows and columns. *Compare* MICROFICHE.

microcassette. In recording, an audio cassette much smaller than the compact cassette, used mainly for office work. *Compare* COMPACT CASSETTE.

microcircuit card. *Synonymous with* SMART CARD.

microcode. In computing, a level of computer instruction below a machine code instruction. *Compare* NANOCODE. *See* MACHINE CODE INSTRUCTION.

microcomputer. A term applied to desktop computers designed for hobbyists, small businesses or educational applications, as compared with a microprocessor which is the central processing chip of the microcomputer. The power of some current business microcomputers rivals that of early minicomputers and exceeds that of small mainframe computers produced in the 1960s. The term microcomputer is used to describe a stored program desk-top digital computer built from microelectronic components (i.e. chips). The components making up the computer are assembled on printed circuit boards, which are then mounted in cases with power supplies and peripherals to produce the complete system. Many microcomputers are now supplied as three separate units. The main unit contains circuit boards, power supplies and disk drives; the keyboard unit and monitor (visual display) unit are connected to it by cables.

(a) The processor. At the simplest level the processor is the central processing unit (CPU) which communicates with the other components by means of logic signals carried on a group of electrical conductors (copper tracks on the circuit board), known as the bus. The memory holds lists of binary numbers which represent numerically coded program instructions or other numerical information (i.e. data). Memory capacity is usually quoted in units of bytes or kilobytes. A peripheral controller provides the means for connecting peripheral equipment such as keyboards, printers, disks and displays.

The actions of the microcomputer are controlled by the processor, which in turn is controlled by program instructions in the memory. When the system is switched on the processor starts fetch/execute instructions from the memory. A fetch/execute cycle, which is performed for each instruction, consists of the following steps: (i) obtain the next instruction from the memory; (ii) interpret the code; (iii) execute the actions specified. This cycle is repeated indefinitely until the processor is switched off or is instructed to stop. It is, of course, necessary for a suitable program to be present in the memory when the computer is switched on. This program is sometimes called the firmware and may provide the means for a user to operate the system (e.g. BASIC systems for home computers) or may read a copy of an operating system program from a disk unit and put it in the memory (e.g. PC.DOS for the IBM PC).

The power of a computer system is partly dependent on the amount of information, measured in bits, which the processor can handle in a single operation. Here it is necessary to consider both the operations inside the processor chip, using the internal bus, and outside, using the external bus.

(b) The buses. The collection of conductors connecting the processor to the other components in the computer is referred to as the processor bus. The detailed structure of each bus is dependent on the particular processor design being studied. There is, however, a general similarity in structure for all processors. Communication on the bus uses electronic signals which assume either a low-voltage or high-voltage state in order to

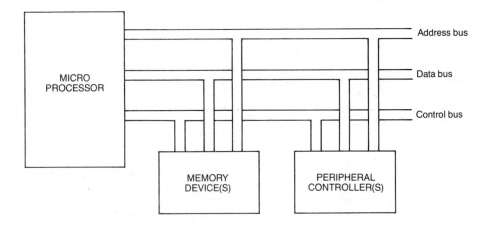

microcomputer
bus structure of a microcomputer.

represent: (i) binary 0 or 1 digit; (ii) true or false logic states; (iii) active or inactive control signal states.

The processor bus consists of the following three parts: (i) the address bus; (ii) the data bus; (iii) the control bus.

The address bus is used by the processor to present a binary number which identifies a place in memory, or a particular peripheral controller, for a data transfer operation. The number of bits in the address bus determine the maximum limit for directly addressable memory which can be connected. 16-bit addresses allow a maximum of 64 kilobytes of memory to be directly addressed.

The data bus is the external bus referred to in the overall view above. It carries binary numbers between the processor and memory or peripheral controllers selected by the address on the address bus.

The control bus conveys control signals to the various parts of the system. The details here are most heavily dependent on the processor being considered. Examples of necessary control functions are synchronization of use of the data bus, or specification of the direction of data transfer.

The processor uses the bus in order to transfer binary data between itself and other components in the system. The term read transaction refers to a transfer into the processor, and write transaction refers to a transfer out of the processor. Transactions are synchronized by a master clock signal and take one or more clock cycles depending on processor design. A bus transaction starts with the address being provided by the processor. Logic circuits connected to the address bus use this address to select the appropriate place in memory, or particular peripheral controller (referred to as address decoding). Finally data is transferred using the data bus. A fetch/execute cycle in the processor, in general, requires one or more read transactions to obtain the instruction from memory followed by other read or write transactions during instruction execution.

The foregoing description has explained the nature and operation of the main components in the microcomputer. The need for logic circuits for address decoding has been mentioned. There is also a need for transmitter, receiver and buffer circuits for the bus signals and for other control logic. Reducing the numbers of the separate components used in a design reduces costs and increases reliability.

(c) Memory. The memory of the computer holds lists of binary numbers representing program instructions and data. These numbers are stored in a line of separate memory locations identified by a unique integer address ranging from zero upwards. The memory locations are all of the same capacity, usually eight bits.

Two main types of memory component are used: read-only memory (ROM) and random-access memory (RAM). ROM is used for holding fixed program (firmware) or data and, as its name implies, can only be read by the processor, not written to. The contents of ROM are non-volatile, which is to say that the contents are not lost when power is switched off. Some ROM components are manufactured containing the required program and data values, and these cannot be altered. This is economic where a large number (i.e. more than 1000) of components are required all with the same contents.

For lower-volume requirements, where perhaps program and data are subject to change during development and testing, so-called programmable memories (PROMs) are available. Program or data values can be written to these after manufacture by a special process called, confusingly, 'programming'. Most PROMs can also be erased and reprogrammed.

The term RAM is applied to components that can be read from, or written to, by the processor. (A better name would be random-access read/write memory.) There are two types of circuit used: static and dynamic. The circuits in a static RAM are flip flops (bistables), which retain the stored bit value as long as power is maintained. The other type uses a capacitor to store a charge representing the bit value, and this requires refreshing, by being read and rewritten, every two milliseconds. Both types of RAM are volatile in that the contents are lost when power is switched off. In some equipment this limitation is overcome by the use of battery backup techniques.

(d) Peripheral controllers. A microcomputer requires peripheral equipment in order to perform a useful function. Input peripherals (e.g. a keyboard) provide data for the processor to read, whereas output peripherals (e.g. a printer) accept data written by the processor. There are also peripherals used for file storage (e.g. magnetic disks) which the processor can both read from and write to. In order to connect peripherals to a microcomputer an interface is necessary. Externally this takes the form of a socket which brings the electronic signals, at the appropriate voltage levels, to the specified pin positions. Internally a peripheral controller is necessary to provide the means for the processor to operate the signals via the processor bus. Peripheral con-

troller circuitry may be dedicated to a specific peripheral type (e.g. a display or a disk) or may be a general-purpose type, which can handle a number of different applications by program control. Two main types of general-purpose interface are used: parallel and serial.

With the parallel interface, a number of ports are provided to permit the transfer of a collection of bits (e.g. eight) simultaneously. Each bit requires its own wire to carry the signal. Generally there are also control and status signals on separate wires for control of the data flow in a similar manner to that of control signals on the processor bus. This type of parallel interface is commonly used for keyboard and printer interfaces. Provided that a suitable program can be produced the interface can also be adapted for many other purposes (e.g. control of a robot arm, motors, valves or lamp displays).

The serial interface uses a single wire for transmitting data one bit at a time to a receiver. This technique originated for telecommunications purposes and is widely used for remote communication over the telephone network. There is an internationally agreed standard (RS-232C), which, among other things, specifies connector size, allocation of pins, voltage levels and rates of transmitting bits. The standard was originally specified for connections to modems, but has found much wider usage for interconnection of assorted microcomputers and (suitable) peripherals. RS-232C interfaces in microcomputers provide both a transmitter circuit and a receiver circuit which are capable of independent and simultaneous operation. Over short distances it is possible to interconnect two systems with only three wires, transmitter data out, receiver data in and a ground return. *Compare* MAINFRAME, MICROPROCESSOR, MINICOMPUTER. *See* BUS, BYTE, CHIP, CENTRAL PROCESSING UNIT, FIRMWARE, FLIP FLOP, INSTRUCTION, MAGNETIC DISK, MEMORY, MICROPROCESSOR, PC.DOS, PERIPHERAL, PROGRAM, PROGRAMMABLE READ-ONLY MEMORY, RANDOM-ACCESS MEMORY, READ-ONLY MEMORY, RS-232C, SERIAL TRANSMISSION, SOFTWARE. *Synonymous with* HOST COMPUTER.

microcomputer on a chip. In computing, a microprocessor plus clock, read-only memory and random-access memory on a single chip. *Compare* MAINFRAME ON A CHIP.

See CHIP, CLOCK, MICROPROCESSOR, RANDOM-ACCESS MEMORY, READ-ONLY MEMORY.

microdata file. In data security, a file containing information on individuals, private households, enterprises, etc. *See* INFERENCE CONTROL.

microelectronics. The branch of electronics concerned with the design and manufacture of chips and integrated circuits. Advances in this field over the past decade fundamentally changed the economics and power of computing, communication and information technology devices. *See* CHIP, MICROCOMPUTER.

microfiche. (MF) In micrographics, a microform storage medium in which many microimages are arranged in a grid pattern on a sheet of film, usually containing a title that can be read without magnification. The most common microfiche has dimensions 148.75 x 105 millimetres and reductions range from 20x to 48x. *Compare* MICROCARD, ULTRAFICHE. *See* MICROFORM, MICROIMAGE, REDUCTION.

microfiche book. In micrographics, a set of microfiches bound in hard or soft cover so that they can be easily removed. It is used to reduce the size of lengthy reports for ease of postage and storage. *See* MICROFICHE.

microfiche reader. In micrographics, an optical device for producing an enlarged image, usually on a screen, from a microfiche. *See* MICROFICHE,.

microfilm. (MF) In micrographics, a film in the form of a roll that contains microimages arranged sequentially. It is used in data processing and for documentation and record compilation. *See* MICROIMAGE.

microfloppy disk. In backing storage, a floppy disk of less than 5.25 inches nominal diameter. There is a range of sizes from 3 to 4 inches, but the 3.5-inch disk tends to predominate. These disks benefit from low size inasmuch as the disk drive requires less power, higher track densities (typically 135 tracks per inch) can be achieved, and the disk fits conveniently into the user's pocket. The term floppy is somewhat misleading because the disks normally have rigid jackets

with an automatic shutter which protects against contamination by dust, fingerprints, etc. The capacity of such disks is of the order of 500 kilobytes. These devices do not use an index hole to locate the start of sectors. *Compare* MINIFLOPPY DISK. *See* BYTE, FLOPPY DISK, TRACK. *Synonymous with* COMPACT FLOPPY DISK.

microfont. In micrographics, an uppercase font designed by the National Microfilm Association specifically for microfilm applications. *See* FONT, MICROFILM, NATIONAL MICROFILM ASSOCIATION.

microform. In micrographics, a medium that contains microimages, such as microfiche and microfilm. *See* MICROFICHE, MICROFILM, MICROIMAGE.

microformat. In micrographics, any audiovisual format containing images too small to be seen without magnification.

microform reader. In micrographics, a display device with a built-in screen and magnification arranged so that a microform may be read comfortably at normal reading distances. *See* MICROFORM.

microform reader/printer. In micrographics, a microform reader with a printer attachment for producing hard copy printout at the original size. *See* MICROFORM READER.

micrographics. The condensing, storing and retrieving of graphic information. Micrographics involves the use of all types of microforms and microimages. *See* MICROFORM, MICROIMAGE, MICROPHOTOGRAPHY.

microimage. In photography, an image too small to be read without some form of magnification. *See* MICROPRINT.

microinstruction. In computing, a bit pattern that is stored in a microprogram memory word and specifies the action on individual computing elements and associated subunits (e.g. main memory, input/output interfaces). *See* MICROCODE, MICROPROGRAM.

micromainframe. In microelectronics, a term used to describe the capabilities of the

32-bit microprocessor. *Synonymous with* MAINFRAME ON A CHIP.

micromainframe link. *See* COOPERATIVE PROCESSING.

micrometre. *Synonymous with* MICRON.

micron. One-millionth of a metre. *Synonymous with* MICROMETRE.

micro-opaque. In micrographics, a sheet of opaque material bearing one or more microimages. *See* MICROIMAGE.

microperforated paper. In printing, continuous stationary with extremely fine perforations so that the separated sheets have the appearance of cut sheets. *See* continuous stationery.

microphone. In recording, a transducer that generates electrical voltages from air pressure waves. Microphones vary in their pickup patterns (i.e. directionality) and the method used to generate the electric signal. The pickup pattern may be omnidirectional, cardiod, bidirectional and unidirectional. There are several methods of generating signals from sound waves, and they vary in sound quality, impedance and cost. Generating methods include: ceramic, where a piezoelectric transducer is used; condenser, where a change in capacitance of a diaphragm is detected; dynamic, where a diaphragm induces vibrations in a moving coil; electret, which is similar to the condenser microphone except that the diaphragm is permanently charged. *See* BIDIRECTIONAL MICROPHONE, CARDIOID RESPONSE, ELECTRET, IMPEDANCE, MOVING-COIL MICROPHONE, OMNIDIRECTIONAL MICROPHONE, TRANSDUCER, UNIDIRECTIONAL MICROPHONE.

microphone pickup pattern. In recording, the locus of maximum sensitivity of a microphone.

microphonics. In electronics, a noise caused by mechanical vibration of one or more components of a system.

microphotography. In micrographics, the application of photography to produce copy in sizes too small to be read without magnification. *Compare* PHOTOMICROGRAPHY.

microprint. In micrographics, microimages on opaque stock produced by printing as distinct from microimages produced on photosensitive materials. *See* MICROIMAGE.

microprocessor. In computing, a large-scale integration implementation on a single chip of a complete central processing unit consisting of an arithmetic logic unit and a control unit. Various microprocessors are capable of accepting coded instructions for execution in 8-, 16- or 32-bit word format and acts as the central processor unit, or a coprocessor, in a microcomputer. *See* ARITHMETIC LOGIC UNIT, CENTRAL PROCESSING UNIT, CONTROL UNIT, COPROCESSOR, MICROCOMPUTER, WORD.

microprogram. In computing, a sequence of microinstructions maintained in a special storage. These instructions are initiated by the introduction of a computer instruction into an instruction register of the computer. *See* HARDWIRED, MICROCODE, MICROINSTRUCTION.

microprogrammable computer. In computing, a computer in which the instruction set is not fixed, but can be tailored to individual needs by the programming of read-only memories or other memory devices. *See* MICROPROGRAM, READ-ONLY MEMORY.

microprojector. In audiovisual aids, a device for enlarging and projecting microscope slides.

micropublishing. In micrographics, the issue of new or reformatted information in multiple-copy microform for sale or distribution to the public. *See* MICROFILM.

microrecording. In micrographics, a copying technique producing reduced-size copy such that an optical device is required in order to read it.

microsecond. One-millionth of a second.

microwave. In communications, a range of frequencies from about 1 GHz to the lower end of the infrared spectrum (3000 GHz) (i.e. a wavelength range from 30 centimetres to 0.1 millimetre). *See* INFRARED.

microwave interference. In communications, the interference between satellite ground station communications and terrestrial receivers. *See* COMMUNICATIONS SATELLITE SYSTEM, GROUND STATION, MAIN BEAM, MICROWAVE TRANSMISSION.

microwave relay. In communications, a station used for the reception and retransmission of microwave signals. *See* MICROWAVE.

microwave transmission. In communications, the transmission of microwaves which due to their high frequency may be modulated for very high information throughput. Many individual telephone and telex circuits may be multiplexed for transmission over trunk routes by microwaves. They are transmitted via highly directional dish-shaped antennae in line of sight in both terrestrial and satellite communication. *See* DISH ANTENNA, GEOSTATIONARY SATELLITE, LINE OF SIGHT, MICROWAVE.

mid-fi quality. In optical media, the third audio quality level in an interactive compact disc system. A bandwidth of 12 000 Hz is obtained by using four-bit adaptive delta pulse code modulation at a sampling rate of 37.7 kHz. It is comparable with frequency-modulated broadcast sound quality. (Philips). *Compare* CD-DA QUALITY, HI-FI QUALITY, SPEECH QUALITY, SYNTHESIZED SPEECH QUALITY. *See* ADAPTIVE DELTA PULSE CODE MODULATION, AUDIO QUALITY LEVEL, COMPACT DISC – INTERACTIVE, FREQUENCY MODULATION, SAMPLING.

migration. In databases, a technique in which the use of fast-access store is optimized by moving the less frequently accessed items to a slower, low-cost storage device. *See* FAST-ACCESS MEMORY.

mill. *Synonymous with* ARITHMETIC LOGIC UNIT.

milli. A prefix representing one-thousandth.

milliampere. In electronics, a current flow of one-thousandth of an ampere. *See* AMPERE.

millisecond. (ms) A unit of time equal to one-thousandth of a second.

Milwaukee 414. In computer security, a group of seven youths in the Milwaukee, Wisconsin area who gained illegitimate access to computers spread across the US and Canada in 1983. The group was named after the Milwaukee's area telephone code. *See* HACKER, TELEPHONE INTRUSION.

MIMD. *See* MULTIPLE-INSTRUCTION STREAM MULTIPLE-DATA STREAM.

mimicking. *Synonymous with* IMPERSONATION, MASQUERADING.

minicassette. In backing storage, a cassette similar to those used in pocket dictation units and designed for backing storage. *Compare* MAGNETIC TAPE CASSETTE. *See* MAGNETIC TAPE TRANSPORT.

minicomputer. In computing, a term first used to distinguish smaller computers from mainframes. There is no universally accepted definition of minicomputers, but they are usually faster and more expensive than a microcomputer, the cost being largely a function of memory size and input/output ports. *Compare* MAINFRAME, MICROCOMPUTER. *See* INPUT/OUT PORT, WORD.

minifloppy disk. In backing storage, a 5.25-inch floppy disk. Such disks are also commonly termed floppy, but were named minifloppy following the introduction of the microfloppy disk. *Compare* MICROFLOPPY DISK. *See* FLOPPY DISK.

minimal cover time. In cryptography, the shortest cover time for any conceivable attack. *See* COVER TIME.

minimax. In artificial intelligence, a state that is a minimum when considered from one viewpoint and a maximum when viewed from another. In game playing it represents a local optimum move from the viewpoint of both players. *See* ALPHA BETA TECHNIQUE, GAME THEORY.

minimax test. In computer graphics, a test employed to determine if two objects are likely to intersect. Rectangular boundaries are drawn around the objects. The minimum and maximum coordinates of the boundaries are then checked for overlap. This technique can speed up hidden line algorithms. *See* HIDDEN LINE.

minimum-weight routing. In data communications, a method of optimizing the transmission of a message by associating a weighting factor with each link in the network. The chosen route is the one which minimizes the sum of the weights of the lines it uses. If the weights chosen are the transit delays associated with lines, a minimum delay routing is obtained. *See* ADAPTIVE ROUTING, DIRECTORY ROUTING.

Minitel. In videotex, a low-cost videotex terminal used in France in conjunction with the central videotex computer system. It was introduced to provide an electronic telephone directory service, but now also provides a variety of information services. (Philips).

minuend. In mathematics, the number from which another number, the subtrahend, is subtracted. *Compare* SUBTRAHEND.

minuscule. In printing, a lower-case character. *Compare* MAJUSCULE. *See* LOWER CASE.

MIPS. In computing, million instructions per second; a measure of computing power. *Compare* KIPS, LIPS. *See* INSTRUCTION.

mirroring. In computer graphics, the rotation of all, or part of, a display image through 180° about an axis in the plane of the display.

MIS. *See* MANAGEMENT INFORMATION SYSTEM.

miscellaneous common carrier. (MCC) In communications, common carriers not engaged in providing telephone or telegraph services. Usually these carriers are responsible for radio and TV transmission services using terrestrial microwave links. *See* COMMON CARRIER.

MISD. *See* MULTIPLE-INSTRUCTION STREAM SINGLE-DATA STREAM.

mismatch. *Synonymous with* IMPEDANCE MISMATCH.

MITI. Japanese Ministry of Trade and Industry.

mix. In video and filming, the combination of two or more images into a single image. (Philips). *Compare* OVERLAY.

mixed highs. In television, the high-frequency components of the picture signal that are intended to be reproduced in monochrome in a colour picture. Systems such as NTSC and PAL use this principle, which is based on the fact that the eye cannot observe colour in fine detail, but is aware of variations in luminance. *See* COMPOSITE COLOUR VIDEO SIGNAL, LUMINANCE SIGNAL.

mixer. (1) In electronics, a circuit that accepts two signal inputs at different frequencies and generates an output consisting of combinations of sum and difference frequencies. (2) In broadcasting, equipment for combining signal inputs prior to being modulated for transmission. *See* MODULATION.

mixing. (1) In printing, the use of more than one typeface in a word or line of text. (2) In recording, the process of combining sound tracks to produce a master.

mixing studio. In recording, a facility equipped with electronic mixers capable of combining two or more audio signals into a single final sound track, usually synchronized with a picture. *See* MIXER.

MKS system. A system of units based on the metre, kilogram, second.

MLA Bibliography. In online information retrieval, a database supplied by Modern Language Association of America and dealing with language and linguistics.

MLS. (1) In online retrieval, machine literature searching. (2) In computer security, multilevel security. *See* MULTILEVEL SECURE.

MMI. *See* MAN–MACHINE INTERFACE.

MMU. In memory systems, memory management unit. *See* MEMORY MANAGEMENT.

mnemonic. An abbreviation or set of symbols chosen to help the reader to remember by association.

mnemonic code. *See* SYMBOLIC LANGUAGE.

mobile earth terminal. In communications, a mobile radio station used for space communication. *See* COMMUNICATIONS SATELLITE SYSTEM.

mobile unit. In filming and television, a production equipment system for use away from a studio.

mockingbird. In computer security, a computer program or process that mimicks the legitimate behaviour of a normal system feature (or other apparently useful function), but performs malicious activities once invoked by the user. *Compare* TROJAN HORSE, VIRUS.

mock up. In printing, the rough visual of a publication or design. (Desktop).

mode. (1) In data security, pertaining to the manner in which a block cipher may be operated (e.g. electronic codebook, cipher block chaining, etc.). *See* BLOCK CIPHER, CIPHER BLOCK CHAINING, ELECTRONIC CODE-BOOK. (2) In computing, an option in a method of operation (e.g. binary mode, alphanumeric mode, etc.). (3) In mathematics, the most frequently occurring value in a statistical sample. (4) In fiber optics, the manner in which light rays travel along the fiber. *See* MODE DISPERSION, MONOMODE FIBER, MULTIMODE FIBER.

mode 1. In optical media, one of the two sector formats defined for read-only memory compact discs. It incorporates error-detecting code/error-correcting code error detection and correction. (Philips). *Compare* FORM 1, MODE 2. *See* COMPACT DISC – READ-ONLY MEMORY, ERROR-CORRECTING CODE, ERROR-DETECTING CODE, SECTOR.

Mode 1 (153.6 K Bytes per sec.)

S	H	User data		ED	8x0	EC
(12)	(8)	(	2048 bytes user data	)(	288	)

Mode 2 (175.6 bytes per sec.)

S	H	User data	
(12)	(8)	(	2336 bytes user data	)

— 1 Mode per track
— 1 to 99 tracks per disc

mode 1, mode 2
CD-ROM modes.

mode 2. In optical media, one of the two physical sector formats defined for read-only memory compact discs. It incorporates an auxiliary data field instead of error-detecting code/error-correcting code error detection and correction. (Philips). *Compare* FORM 2, MODE 1. *See* COMPACT DISC – READ-ONLY MEMORY, ERROR-CORRECTING CODE, ERROR-DETECTING CODE, SECTOR.

mode byte. In optical media, the byte in the header field of a sector that defines whether a sector is in mode 1 OR MODE 2. (Philips). *See* BYTE, COMPACT DISC – READ-ONLY MEMORY, MODE 1, MODE 2, SECTOR.

mode dispersion. In fiber optics, the dispersion that arises from the different paths traversed by the light rays in an optical fiber. This dispersion causes a distortion of the received pulse. *See* MODE, MONOMODE FIBER, MULTIMODE FIBER,

model. The representation of a particular system in a logical form (e.g. through software) to predict some future occurrence.

modem. In data communications, modulator/demodulator; a device that modulates the transmitted signal and demodulates the received signal at a data station (e.g. a modem is used to convert a digital signal from a computer into an analog signal for transmission over a network and is commonly employed for the intercommunication of microcomputers over the telephone network). A modem may work in half-duplex or full-duplex mode over a two- or four-wire circuit. *See* FOUR-WIRE CIRCUIT, FULL-DUPLEX, HALF-DUPLEX, LIMITED-DISTANCE MODEM, MODULATION.

modern face. In printing, a class of typeface having considerable differences between thick and thin strokes, serifs at right angles to their strokes and central thickening of curves. *See* SERIF, TYPEFACE.

modified frequency modulation. In memory systems, a method of recording data onto a magnetic disk similar to frequency modulation except that fewer flux reversals are required to encode a given quantity of data. Like frequency modulation the flux is reversed between clock pulses to write a 1 bit; however the flux is only changed at a clock pulse if the previous bit was a 0 bit and the bit to be written is also a 0 bit. *Compare* FREQUENCY MODULATION.

Modula 2. In programming, a language that is a development of Pascal and provides facilities for concurrent programming. It includes methods of describing parallel computation together with the necessary means of interaction and synchronization. The significant feature of this language, from which its name is derived, is the development of modules which can be imported into programs, with specified access to abstract data types. *See* ABSTRACT DATA TYPE, CONCURRENT PROGRAMMING, MODULE, PARALLEL PROCESSING, PASCAL.

modular. In computing, a building block approach to hardware and software design in which a system is first analyzed in terms of functional subassemblies (modules) and then synthesized using these modules. Electronic fabrication consists largely in assembling circuits out of standard hardware components. *See* HARDWARE, SOFTWARE.

modular redundancy. In reliability, a method of hardware redundancy in which a module is replicated and the multiple copies run in parallel. The outputs of the modules are compared, and differences between them indicate the presence of a fault. *Compare* STRUCTURAL REDUNDANCY. *See* DUAL REDUNDANCY, HARDWARE REDUNDANCY, HYBRID REDUNDANCY, NMR, TRIPLE MODULAR REDUNDANCY.

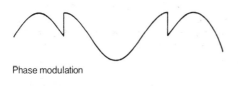

Phase modulation

Unmodulated carrier

Frequency modulation

Amplitude modulation

modulation

modulating signal. In communications, a signal that is impressed upon a carrier wave to vary it in some specified manner. *See* CARRIER, MODULATION.

modulation. In communications, a process by which information is impressed upon a carrier wave for transmission purposes. The term covers both processes where some characteristic of a continuous wave, such as its frequency or amplitude, is varied in accordance with a modulating signal such as a speech, television or facsimile waveform, and pulse modulation techniques in which the modulating signal operates on a pulse train. *Compare* DEMODULATION. *See* AMPLITUDE MODULATION, FREQUENCY MODULATION, MODULATING SIGNAL, PHASE MODULATION, PULSE MODULATION.

modulation rate. In communications, the reciprocal of the shortest time interval between successive significant instances of the modulated signal. If this measure is expressed in seconds, the modulation rate is in bauds. *See* BAUD, MODULATION.

modulator. In communications, the equipment or apparatus that modifies some characteristic of a signal. *See* MODULATION.

module. In computing, a hardware or software subassembly used in a modular system. *See* MODULA 2, MODULAR.

modulo N check. In programming, a means of checking the values of data whereby an operand is divided by a number N and the remainder is used as a check digit. Often N is taken to be 11, thus 81 modulo 11 is 4. *See* OPERAND.

moire. (1) In optics, an undesirable effect caused by one set of closely spaced lines moving in relation to another. (2) In television, the spurious pattern in the reproduced picture caused by interference beats between two sets of periodic structures in the image. The most common cause of moire is the interference between scanning lines and some other periodic structure such as a line pattern or dot pattern in the original scene, a mesh or dot pattern in the camera sensor, or the phosphor dots or other structure in a shadowmask picture tube. *See* INTERFERENCE, SCANNING LINE, SHADOWMASK.

Molniya. In communications, a series of Russian communications satellites; molniya is Russian for lightning. *See* COMMUNICATIONS SATELLITE SYSTEM, GORIZONT, INTERSPUTNIK, RADUGA, STATSIONAR.

monaural. In recording, the use of a single sound channel applied to one ear. *Compare* BINAURAL.

monitor. (1) In electronics, a supervisory system that can detect a circuit failure (e.g. a voltage monitor, which signals a failure condition when a power supply goes outside given limits). (2) A visual display unit used to display the status of a system. *See* VISUAL DISPLAY UNIT. (3) In television, a high-quality viewing unit, often used in closed circuit systems. (4) In filming, a rear projection unit used in editing. *See* BACKGROUND PROJECTION.

monitor speaker. In recording, a loudspeaker used for listening during recording and mixing.

monoalphabetic cipher. In data security, a substitution cipher in which each letter of the alphabet maps onto another letter with each individual pairing arbitrarily fixed by the cryptographer. *Compare* POLYALPHABETIC CIPHER. *See* CIPHER, CRYPTOGRAPHY, SUBSTITUTION CIPHER.

monochrome. (1) In photography, pictures that have no colour, only black, white or grey tones. (2) In television, the signal used for controlling the luminance values in the picture. *See* LUMINANCE.

monograph. A publication dealing with a single subject or person.

monoline. In printing, a typeface in which all the letter strokes are of equal thickness.

monolithic. In microelectronics, an integrated circuit fabricated on a single monocrystalline silicon chip. *See* INTEGRATED CIRCUIT.

monomode fiber. In fiber optics, a fiber with a very narrow core (2–10 micrometres); the only path for transmission is along the axis, thus producing low dispersion. *Compare* MULTIMODE FIBER. *See* MODE, MODE DISPERSION.

monophonic. In recording, sound reproduction using a single output signal or made with a single channel audio tape recorder. *Compare* QUADRUPHONIC, STEREOPHONIC.

monospace. In printing, a font in which all characters occupy the same amount of horizontal width regardless of the character. (Desktop). *Compare* PROPORTIONAL SPACING. *See* FONT.

monostable. In electronics, pertaining to a circuit used for delaying or lengthening a pulse. It remains in its stable state until it receives an input pulse when it then moves into a second state for a specified period.

montage. In printing, a single image formed from assembling of several images. (Desktop).

MOS. *See* METAL OXIDE SEMICONDUCTOR.

mosaic. (1) In television, the area of a television camera that is scanned by the electronic beam and that stores the image. *See* PICKUP TUBE. (2) In videotex, a display character that can have one of 128 different shapes. *See* ALPHAMOSAIC, DISPLAY CHARACTER.

mosaic graphics. In optical media, a low-resolution graphics, in interactive compact disc systems, achieved by repeating pixels or lines by a certain factor. (Philips). *Compare* HIGH RESOLUTION. *See* COMPACT DISC – INTERACTIVE, DIGITAL VIDEO, PIXEL.

MOSFET. In semiconductors, metal oxide semiconductor field effect transistor; a device that has an extremely high input impedance, low switching speed and low power consumption. *See* FIELD EFFECT TRANSISTOR.

most significant bit. (MSB) In mathematics, the leftmost bit in a binary number, having the greatest impact on the value of the number. *Compare* LEAST SIGNIFICANT BIT. *See* BINARY NUMBER.

most significant digit. (MSD) In mathematics, the leftmost digit in a number. *Compare* LEAST SIGNIFICANT DIGIT.

mother. In recording and optical media, a negative mould that is used in disc replication, intermediate between the metal father and stamper. It is formed by nickel plating on a metal father. (Philips). *See* CD MASTERING, METAL FATHER, STAMPER.

motherboard. In computing, a printed circuit board holding the major units of a computer (e.g. central processing unit, memory chips). The motherboard may also contain connectors into which daughter boards may be plugged in order to enhance the capabilities of the system. *See* BACK-PLANE, DAUGHTER BOARD, EXPANSION CARD.

motion picture. In filming, a succession of still images that gives the subjective impression of motion when used in a device that maintains persistence of vision. *See* PERSISTENCE OF VISION.

Motion Picture Association of America. (MPAA) An association of American motion picture producers and distributors.

motor boating. In audio, a very low-frequency oscillation often resulting from a positive feedback path in an amplifier system. *See* POSITIVE FEEDBACK.

mouse. In peripherals, a popular pointing device comprising a palm-sized device, with one or more control buttons, that is moved over a flat surface, producing a corresponding movement of a cursor on a cathode ray tube screen. The user can draw diagrams or make selections by moving the mouse until the cursor attains a designated area, or particular icon, and pressing a control button.

The mouse is connected to the computer by a flexible lead, and it senses the direction and distance of motion. There are three basic forms of mouse: mechanical, optical and acoustic mechanical. In the mechanical device a rubber-coated ball on the underside of the unit rotates as the mouse is moved over the desk top; the motion is measured by digital output shaft encoders. The shaft encoders may rely on electrical contacts for their action, or interrupted light optical encoders may be employed; the latter are less susceptible to mechanical wear and tear. The mechanical device requires no tablet; the user can move it over a desk top, lift it up, shift it to another position and continue moving it. The user can thus concentrate on the movement of the screen cursor and does not therefore need to switch attention between the screen and tablet, as is the case with the digitizing tablet.

The optical mouse requires no moving parts, but it must be operated on a tablet with a grid of optical marks, either lines or dots. Light from a light-emitting diode on the mouse is reflected back from the pad, and optical sensors detect the movement of the mouse over the grid.

The acoustic mechanical mouse also has no moving parts; strain gauges are used to determine direction, and a piezoelectric transducer determines speed. It requires no tablet and works on most surfaces.

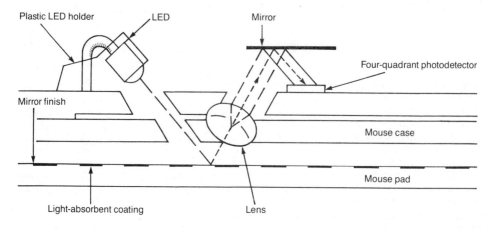

mouse
Optical mouse.

A resolution of 4 points per millimetre is possible with mouse units; text manipulation can be achieved with resolutions of only 0.08 points per millimetre. The mouse may be provided with a number of buttons to activate special functions. Some systems have only one button and rely on multiple depressions to select the required function; many units have three buttons since this is considered to be the optimum number in terms of user friendliness.

The mouse is connected to the computer by a lead, and this must be positioned to avoid interference with the hand movement. Future developments are likely to include the tail-less mouse with radio frequency or infrared communication with the host. *See* CATHODE RAY TUBE, DIGITIZING TABLET, ICON, INFRARED, LIGHT-EMITTING DIODE, PHOTODIODE, PIEZOELECTRIC, POINTING DEVICE.

mouth. In communications, the open end of a microwave antenna such as a horn. *See* ANTENNA, HORN, MICROWAVE.

***M* out of *N* code.** In codes, a transmission code with inbuilt error detection facilities. A specified number of bits (M), in a character of N bits, must be 1 bits. Any received character not containing a total of M 1 bits initiates an error procedure. *See* ERROR-DETECTING CODE. *Synonymous with* CONSTANT-RATIO CODE.

movable-head disk. (MHD) In memory systems, a magnetic disk unit in which the heads are mounted on a seek arm which moves radially to position the heads over the appropriate track. *Compare* FIXED-HEAD DISK. *See* HEAD, MAGNETIC DISK, TRACK.

moving-coil microphone. In audio, a microphone with a transducer consisting of a coil in a magnetic field attached to a flexible diaphragm. Incident air pressure waves on the diaphragm generate voltages in the coil. *See* MICROPHONE, TRANSDUCER.

moving-coil pickup. In audio, a transducer for sound reproduction from a disc recording. A stylus is connected to a coil in a magnetic field, thus developing voltages resulting from stylus movement. *See* TRANSDUCER.

MP. *See* METAL POWDER.

MPAA. *See* MOTION PICTURE ASSOCIATION OF AMERICA.

MPIP. In video, multi-picture-in-picture; an enhanced version of PIP, providing for multiple insets. *Compare* PIP.

MPU. *See* MICROPROCESSOR.

MR. *See* MEDIUM REDUCTION.

MRDF. In computing, machine-readable data files. *See* MACHINE-READABLE.

ms. *See* MILLISECOND.

MSB. *See* MOST SIGNIFICANT BIT.

MSD. *See* MOST SIGNIFICANT DIGIT.

MS.DOS. In operating systems, a widely used microcomputer disk operating system. It is similar in all respects to PC.DOS. *See* PC.DOS.

MSI. *See* MEDIUM-SCALE INTEGRATION.

M signal. In audio, the signal represented by the sum of the right- and left-hand signal sources in a stereo sound broadcast. *See* STEREOPHONIC.

MSM. In authentication, message stream modification. *See* MESSAGE AUTHENTICATION.

MSS. *See* MASS STORAGE SYSTEM.

MT. *See* MACHINE TRANSLATION.

MTA. In data communications, message transfer agent in the CCITT X.400 message-handling standard. *Compare* MTS, UA. *See* X.400

MTBF. *See* MEAN TIME BETWEEN FAILURE.

MTC. *See* MAGNETIC TAPE CASSETTE.

MTS. In data communications, message transfer service in the CCITT X.400 message-handling standard. *Compare* MTA, UA. *See* X.400.

MTTR. *See* MEAN TIME TO REPAIR.

MTU. Magnetic tape unit. *See* MAGNETIC TAPE TRANSPORT.

MTX. In communications, mobile radio telephone exchange; a radio telephone exchange in a cellular radio system that services a number of radio base stations and provides connection to public switched telephone network. *See* CELLULAR RADIO.

multi. A prefix meaning many.

multiaccess computing. In computing, a mode of computer usage in which a population of users individually controls the operation interactively from a terminal. The user inputs commands, modifies program statements, etc. and awaits the results before proceeding to the next stage. *Compare* BATCH PROCESSING, TRANSACTION PROCESSING. *See* COMPUTER-AIDED DESIGN, ONLINE.

multiburst signal. In television, a video test signal comprising a series of short-duration bursts of continuous waves, with different frequencies, but constant amplitude.

multidrop circuit. In data communications, a circuit rented to a customer for the transmission of data between a central site, usually a computer, and a number of outstation terminals. Two-way transmission is possible between any terminal and the central site, but not directly between terminals. *Compare* POINT-TO-POINT. *See* CIRCUIT. *Synonymous with* MULTIPOINT CIRCUIT.

multiexposure. *Synonymous with* MULTIPLE EXPOSURE.

multifrequency pushbutton set. *See* MF KEYPAD.

multifrequency signal. (MF signal) In communications, a telephone signal made up of several superimposed audio frequency tones.

multifunction workstation. In computing, a computer-based terminal, usually with a display screen and, sometimes, with a printing device that enables a user to perform a variety of tasks (e.g. a personal computer, which is normally capable of performing functions such as word processing, graphics design, computer program development, financial calculations and remote data enquiries). (Philips). *See* PERSONAL COMPUTER.

multi-image. In audiovisual aids, the simultaneous projection of two or more images on adjacent screens using 35-mm slide projectors and sometimes 16-mm and 8-mm motion picture images and multisourced sound. Synchronization and control is carried out using special programmer units. *See* PROGRAMMER.

multilayer. In electronics, a type of compact, printed circuit board that has several layers of circuit etch or pattern, one over the other, interconnected by electroplated holes. These holes can also receive component leads. *See* PRINTED CIRCUIT BOARD.

multilayer colour film. In photography, colour film with two or more layers each sensitive to a different range of colours.

multilayer microfiche. In micrographics, a technique for increasing the number of images on a microfiche by employing several layers with optical effects (e.g. polarization to separate the images). *Compare* MICROFICHE BOOK. *See* MICROFICHE.

multilevel secure. In computer security, a class of system containing information with different sensitivities that simultaneously permits access by users with different security clearances and need-to-know, but prevents users from obtaining access to information for which they lack authorization. (DOD). *See* NEED-TO-KNOW.

multilink. In data communications, a branch between two nodes consisting of two or more data links. *See* DATA LINK.

multilist organization. In data structures, a method of segmenting long chains with an index for the start address of each chain segment. In large databases pointers may be used to link records with common fields (e.g. in a personnel database chains of all employees in given departments may be formed). Searches through long chains may be excessively time-consuming, and a multilist organization enables the search to commence at an intermediate point in the chain. *See* CHAIN, LIST.

multimedia. In audiovisual aids, any combination of motion pictures, slides, video, sound and live action.

multimedia system. (1) In computing, a system architecture based on the use of different media to carry the data and application programs. In a read-only memory compact disc (CD-ROM) system, for example, the data is carried on a CD-ROM disc, whereas the application program is stored in a magnetic medium such as a floppy disk. (Philips). *Compare* SINGLE-MEDIUM SYSTEM. *See* COMPACT DISC – READ-ONLY MEMORY, FLOPPY DISK. (2) In information presentation, a system using more than one medium (e.g. book/audio tape combinations for language learning, teletext subtitling of television programs). *See* TELETEXT.

multimode fiber. In fiber optics, a fiber having a core large enough to permit optical energy to propagate in a number of different modes. *Compare* MONOMODE FIBER. *See* MODE, MODE DISPERSION.

multipass overlapping. In printing, a technique used in dot matrix printers in which the printing head makes several passes, with slight offsets, so as to improve the quality of the printed character. *See* MATRIX PRINTER.

multipath. (1) In fiber optics, a pulse dispersal resulting from the fact that the light rays passing through a fiber have different velocities and paths. *See* MODE DISPERSION. (2) In communications, the reception of a direct very high- or ultra high-frequency wave and another reflected from a surface. The reflected wave travels a longer path, and the two waves can interfere at the receiver. *See* INTERFERENCE.

multiplane. In video and computer graphics, a video image in which different pictures are overlaid, one on top of the other. (Philips). *See* COMPACT DISC – INTERACTIVE, DIGITAL VIDEO, OVERLAY, PLANE.

multiple access. *See* CODE DIVISION MULTIPLE ACCESS, FREQUENCY DIVISION MULTIPLE ACCESS, MULTIACCESS COMPUTING, TIME DIVISION MULTIPLE ACCESS.

multiple exposure. In filming, an optical effect caused by re-exposing camera film more than once. *Synonymous with* MULTIEXPOSURE.

multiple-instruction stream multiple-data stream. (MIMD) In computing, pertaining to a form of parallel computer with multiple control units, arithmetic logic units and memories which virtually operate as individual computers with facilities for work sharing and interaction. *Compare* MULTIPLE-INSTRUCTION STREAM SINGLE-DATA STREAM, SINGLE-INSTRUCTION STREAM MULTIPLE-DATA STREAM, SINGLE-INSTRUCTION STREAM SINGLE-DATA STREAM. *See* ARITHMETIC LOGIC UNIT, CONTROL UNIT, MEMORY, PARALLEL PROCESSING.

multiple-instruction stream single-data stream. (MISD) In computing, pertaining to a form of parallel computer with multiple control units that control a single arithmetic logic unit operating on a single stream of data. *Compare* MULTIPLE-INSTRUCTION STREAM MULTIPLE-DATA STREAM, SINGLE-INSTRUCTION STREAM MULTIPLE-DATA STREAM, SINGLE-INSTRUCTION STREAM SINGLE-DATA STREAM. *See* ARITHMETIC LOGIC UNIT, CONTROL UNIT, PARALLEL PROCESSING.

multiple key retrieval. In databases, the technique of retrieving records based upon the value of several keys, some or all of which are secondary keys. *See* KEY, RECORD, SECONDARY KEY.

multiple precision. In programming, the use of two or more computer words to represent a number so that its precision may be enhanced. *See* DOUBLE PRECISION ARITHMETIC, PRECISION.

multiple routing. In data communications, a method of sending a message where more than one destination is specified in the header of the message. *See* MESSAGE HEADING, ROUTING.

multiplexed analog components. *See* MAC.

multiplexer. (MUX) In data communications, equipment that takes a number of channels and combines the signals into one common channel for transmission. At the remote end, a demultiplexer extracts each of the original signals. *Compare* DEMULTIPLEX-ING, LINE CONCENTRATOR. *See* MULTIPLEXING.

multiplexing. (1) In communications, the process of combining a number of signals so that they can share a common transmission facility, thereby making more efficient use of the shared resource. *See* FREQUENCY DIVISION MULTIPLEXING, TIME DIVISION MULTIPLEXING. (2) In computing, a method of using the same set of signal lines, emanating from a limited set of pins on a chip, to send different sets of signals. *See* TIME DIVISION MULTIPLEXING.

multiplex mode. In data communications, a means of transferring data to or from low-speed input/output devices on a multiplexer channel by interleaving bytes of data. *See* BYTE, INPUT/OUTPUT UNIT, MULTIPLEXER. *Synonymous with* BYTE MODE.

multipoint circuit. *Synonymous with* MULTIDROP CIRCUIT.

multipoint connection. In data communications, a communication link that joins three or more data stations, with the link going from one station to the next in sequence rather than using a star arrangement. *See* STAR.

multiprocessing. In computing, a technique in which two or more processors share a common memory, but operate on different instruction streams. One processor normally has overall control and directs the other through messages placed in the common area of memory. When the slave processor receives an appropriate command it executes its own stored program. Slave processors commonly supervise input/output operations. Processing units are now relatively inexpensive, but backing store remain expensive, and a multiprocessor environment represents an economic way of achieving a high throughput. *Compare* COPROCESSOR. *See* MACHINE CODE INSTRUCTION, PARALLEL PROCESSING, PROCESSOR.

multiprocessor. *See* MULTIPROCESSING.

multiprogramming. In operating systems, a system that allows several programs to be active simultaneously. The system may have a single or multiple processors; if a single

processor is employed the central processing unit services programs, one at a time, according to their priorities and requirements (e.g. a low-priority background program will be serviced during the periods that a high-priority program is suspended, awaiting data from a peripheral). *See* BACKGROUND, CENTRAL PROCESSING UNIT, CONCURRENT PROGRAMMING, DISK DRIVE, MULTIPROCESSING, MULTITASKING, MULTIUSER.

multisatellite link. In communications, a radio link between two ground stations via two or more communications satellites. The link consists of one uplink, two or more satellite-to-satellite paths and one downlink. *See* COMMUNICATIONS SATELLITE SYSTEM, DOWNLINK, GROUND STATION, UPLINK.

Multistream. In data communications, a packet-switching service operated by British Telecom allowing widespread access over dial-up or direct lines. *See* PACKET SWITCHING.

multisystem networking. In distributed processing, the distribution of the data-processing function between two or more host processors in one or several locations using communications facilities. *Compare* PROCESSOR INTERCONNECTION. *See* SYSTEM NETWORK ARCHITECTURE.

multitasking. In programming, the execution of a number of tasks simultaneously. If a task is equivalent to a program, multitasking is synonymous with multiprogramming, but a task may often be a part of a program. *See* MULTIPROGRAMMING, TASK.

multiunit call. In communications, a telephone call for which more than one basic charge unit is levied for an initial minimum interval.

multiuser. In computing, pertaining to an operating system that can service the requests of more than one user or program at once. If a only a single processor is available the users are not handled simultaneously; each is serviced within a short time slice, at high speed, giving the impression to the user of simultaneous operation. *See* MULTIPROCESSING, MULTIPROGRAMMING.

multiwire element. In communications, an antenna consisting of a number of wires connected in parallel. *See* ANTENNA.

Munsell colour system. In computer graphics, a method of colour assessment in which a colour is defined according to its hue, chroma and value. *See* CHROMA, HUE.

mush area. In broadcasting, a region where signals from two or more synchronized transmitters are comparable in strength, producing fading and distortion of received signals.

music flag. In optical media, a flag on the P channel of a compact disc indicating the presence or absence of music. (Philips). *See* COMPACT DISC, FLAG, P CHANNEL.

music synthesizer. In man–machine interfaces, a device that produces musical effects which are a function of digital output of a microcomputer. The synthesizer consists of two channels which cover slightly different pitch ranges, corresponding roughly to those covered by the right and left hands on a piano. The components of a music synthesizer are the data-controlled oscillator (DCO), harmonic generator, voicing circuit, articulator and tempo generator.

The DCO produces a frequency according to a binary number produced from the microcomputer. The harmonic generator adds harmonics to the fundamental frequency produced by the DCO, to give the quality of sound produced by a particular musical instrument. The articulator simulates the effect of the decay of sound which varies from instrument to instrument, and the tempo generator determines the rate at which the composition is stepped from one note to the next. *Compare* SPEECH SYNTHESIZER. *See* ARTICULATOR, DATA-CONTROLLED OSCILLATOR, FOURIER SERIES, HARMONIC, HARMONIC GENERATOR, TEMPO GENERATOR.

mutt. In printing, a typesetting term for the em space. (Desktop). *See* EM.

mutual isolation. In cable television, the attenuation between two system outlets on the network. A minimum figure is normally specified to prevent a spurious signal from one receiver on the network from interfering with another. *See* ATTENUATION, INTERFACE.

mutually prime. *Synonymous with* CO-PRIME.

mutually suspicious. In computer security, pertaining to the state that exists between interactive processes (subsystems or programs), each of which contains sensitive data and is assumed to be designed so as to extract data from the other and to protect its own data. (FIPS).

MUX. *See* MULTIPLEXER.

Mylar. In memory systems, a trade name for a polyester film used as the base for magnetically coated information media. *See* MAGNETIC DISK, MAGNETIC TAPE.

myopia. A visual disorder caused by excessive refractive power of the eyes with the result that only objects close to the eyes appear to be in focus.

N

NAB. *See* NATIONAL ASSOCIATION OF BROADCASTERS.

NAK. *See* NEGATIVE ACKNOWLEDGEMENT.

NAND. A logical operation, A NAND B has the result true if the result of the logical operation A AND B is false. The corresponding truth table is

A	B	A NAND B
0	0	1
1	0	1
0	1	1
1	1	0

Compare AND. *See* TRUTH TABLE.

nano. A prefix indicating 10^{-9}.

nanocode. In computing, a level of programming deeper than microcode. Each individual level of microcode is executed by a separate nanocode program. *Compare* MICROCODE.

nanosecond. One-thousandth of a microsecond. *See* MICROSECOND, NANO.

NAPLPS. In computer graphics, North Atlantic Presentation Level Protocol Syntax, pronounced nap-lips; a graphics standard originally developed to unify videotex systems. NAPLPS is an open-ended syntax facilitating additions and modifications. The standard encompasses the ASCII character set, picture description instructions, mosaic characters, dynamically redefinable character sets, supplementary character sets, macros and colour mappings. The only dynamic control provided is blinking, permitting an image to flash on and off or change colour.

Picture description instructions allow the geometric coding of graphics information independent of the display device resolution. Commands, followed by parameters, cause the display of lines, points, arcs, rectangles and polygons. The coordinates specified in the parameters may be absolute or relative, and are referenced to a standard virtual display that is mapped by the NAPLPS decoder onto the monitor. The picture description instructions also include commands to control display functions such as colour and blinking. Supplementary colour sets complement the basic ASCII set defining special diacritical signs (e.g. umlauts, circumflexes and accents). Macros are sequences of NAPLPS code transmitted by the host computer to the terminal and stored. The macro can be subsequently invoked by the host computer with the transmission of a short command sequence. Color mapping allows a large variety of colours to be defined and animation effects created by making images change their colour at predefined intervals.

The significance of NAPLPS extends beyond computer graphics because it provides for the communication of sophisticated images, just as ASCII code is the de facto standard for the communication of text. *See* ALPHAMOSAIC, AMERICAN STANDARD CODE FOR INFORMATION INTERCHANGE, CIRCUMFLEX, DIACRITIC, DYNAMICALLY REDEFINABLE CHARACTER SET, MONITOR, PICTURE DESCRIPTION INSTRUCTION, UMLAUT, VIDEOTEX.

narrowband. (1) In data communications, pertaining to a channel with a bandwidth less than that of a voice-grade channel. It is normally used for communication speeds of less than 300 bits per second. *See* BANDWIDTH, VOICE-GRADE CHANNEL. (2) In data communications, a range of frequencies contained within a broadband. *See* BROADBAND.

narrowcasting. In cable television, pertaining to a program designed to meet the interests of a minority group.

***n*-ary.** In mathematics, pertaining to a selection, choice or condition that has *n* possible different values or states.

NASA. (1) In communications. *See* NATIONAL AERONAUTICS AND SPACE ADMINISTRATION. (2) In online information retrieval, a database supplied by National Aeronautics and Space Administration (NASA) and American Institute of Aeronautics and Astronautics (AIAA) and dealing with aeronautics and astronautics, science and technology.

National Academy of Television Arts and Sciences. A US organization of television professionals, actors, directors, producers, writers, etc.

National Aeronautics and Space Administration. (NASA) A US government agency that is responsible for administration of the communications satellite program. *See* COMMUNICATIONS SATELLITE SYSTEM.

National Association of Broadcasters. (NAB) A US organization of broadcasters that provides guidelines for programming and advertising practices.

National Bureau of Standards. (NBS) An agency of the US Department of Commerce with the responsibility for setting Federal standards for the effective and efficient use of computer systems. The Bureau was responsible for the original definition and standardization of the encryption system referred to as data encryption standard. *See* DATA ENCRYPTION, FIPS.

National Cable Television Association. (NATA) A US organization representing television cable operators.

National Computer Security Center. A centre of the National Security Agency formed as a result of NSDD-145. The primary goal of the Center is to encourage the widespread availability of trusted computer systems in the USA. It was formerly known as the Department of Defense Computer Security Center. *See* NSDD-145.

National Library of Medicine. (MLM) In online information retrieval, a major producer and vendor of medical databases; Medline is the best known of its many databases. *See* DATABASE PRODUCER, DATABASE VENDOR, MEDLARS, MEDLINE.

National Microfilm Association. (NMA) A US association promoting the use of microfilm. *See* MICROFILM.

National Micrographics Association. (NMA) A US trade association representing the producers of microforms. *See* MICROFORM.

National Oceanographic and Atmospheric Agency. (NOAA) A US government agency that operates weather satellites.

National Security Agency/Central Security Service. The US National Security Agency was established in 1952 as a separately organized agency within the Department of Defense for the signals intelligence and communications security activities of the US government. It was charged with the additional mission of computer security in 1984.

The Central Security Service was established in 1972 to provide a more unified cryptological organization within the Department of Defense. The three primary missions of the National Security Agency/ Central Security Service are communications security, computer security and foreign intelligence information.

native mode. *Synonymous with* ELECTRONIC CODEBOOK.

natural images. *Synonymous with* NATURAL PICTURES.

natural language. (NL) A language in which the rules reflect current usage without being specifically prescribed. The language employed by users in normal communication as compared with restricted language used for communication with computers, indexing documents, etc.

natural pictures. In video, pictures of real-life subjects. (Philips). *Synonymous with* NATURAL IMAGES.

navigation. In databases, the process of moving through a database, following an explicit path from one data item to the next, until the required item is attained.

NBS. *See* NATIONAL BUREAU OF STANDARDS.

NCC. UK National Computing Centre.

n-channel MOS. In microelectronics, a metal oxide semiconductor (MOS) device in which all conduction is through n-type silicon. *Compare* P-CHANNEL MOS. *See* FIELD EFFECT TRANSISTOR, METAL OXIDE SEMICONDUCTOR, N-TYPE MATERIAL.

NCSC. *See* NATIONAL COMPUTER SECURITY CENTER.

NCTA. *See* NATIONAL CABLE TELEVISION ASSOCIATION.

NDC. *See* NORMALIZED DEVICE COORDINATES.

NDR. *See* NON-DESTRUCTIVE READOUT.

near letter quality. (NLQ) In printing, the quality of a printer, normally of the dot matrix type, which may have two or more printing modes. When operating in the near-letter-quality mode the printer runs at a relatively slow rate, producing print of quality suitable for final copies of documents. (Philips). *Compare* BUSINESS QUALITY, DRAFT QUALITY, LETTER QUALITY. *See* DOT MATRIX.

necessary bandwidth. In communications, the bandwidth that is just sufficient to ensure that the transmission of information is at the speed and of the quality required. *See* BANDWIDTH.

needle printer. *Synonymous with* MATRIX PRINTER.

need-to-know. In data security, a policy that restricts access to classified information to personnel whose duties necessitate such access.

negate. In mathematics, to reverse the sign of a numerical quantity.

negative. (1) In photography, a black and white image which is complementary (i.e. black corresponding to white) to an original image. (2) In photography, a colour film image whose colours are complementary to those of the original image.

negative acknowledgement. (NAK) In data communications, a signal sent from receiver to transmitter to indicate that a message with detectable errors has been received. The transmitter then repeats the message. *Compare* AFFIRMATIVE ACKNOWLEDGEMENT.

negative disclosure. In database security, a form of personal disclosure in which it is possible to deduce that an individual does not have a particular attribute (e.g. does not suffer from a particular disease). *See* PERSONAL DISCLOSURE.

negative feedback. A feedback arrangement in which the output signal is effectively subtracted from the input signal and the resulting signal is fed into the system. *Compare* POSITIVE FEEDBACK. *See* FEEDBACK.

negative resist. In microelectronics, pertaining to an imaging process in which the unexposed region of the photoresist is removed in the development process. *Compare* POSITIVE RESIST. *See* CHIP.

negative safeguard. In computer security, a safeguard that is assumed to be functioning when, in fact, it is not.

neighbourhood effect. In computer graphics, an apparent variation in the brightness of a pixel arising from variations in the brightness of neighbouring pixels. *See* PIXEL.

nest. In programming, to embed a subroutine in a larger routine or to embed a loop instruction inside another loop instruction. *See* LOOP, SUBROUTINE.

nesting. In online information retrieval, the use of parentheses in a search statement to specify priority of execution. *See* SEARCH STATEMENT.

network. (1) A series of interconnected points. (2) In communications, a system of interconnected communication facilities. (3) A data structure. *See* NETWORK STRUCTURE.

network architecture. In data communications, the layers, interfaces and protocols of a network. *See* OPEN SYSTEMS INTERCONNECTION, PROTOCOL.

network control program. In computing, a part of the operating system of a host computer that establishes and breaks logical connections with the network. It communicates with the user processes in the host computer on one hand and the network on the other. *See* OPERATING SYSTEM.

network control station. In communications, a station that coordinates the use of a communications network.

network database. In databases, an organization of data relationships such that any record, except the root, may have more than one parent record, and there may be several access paths to a given record. *Compare* HIERARCHICAL DATABASE, RELATIONAL DATABASE. *See* RECORD, ROOT. *Synonymous with* PLEX DATABASE.

network delay. In data communications, the transit time for a packet, in a packet-switched network, defined as the interval between the time that the last bit, of the packet, leaves the entry node and the time at which the first bit enters the destination node. *See* COMPUTER NETWORK, PACKET SWITCHING.

network diagram. A diagram indicating the nodes, and their interconnections, in a network. *See* NODE.

network encryption. In communications security, the provision of secure communications in a network is complicated by the presence of intermediate nodes which receive the messages and redirect them to appropriate output links. There are three methods of dealing with encryption within networks (i.e. link encryption, node encryption and end-to-end encryption).

Link encryption requires cryptographic devices at each end of the communication link. The messages are thus decrypted before they enter the node. They are re-encrypted, under a different key, after leaving the node and before entering the next communication link. Node encryption provides for the message decryption, and re-encryption under a different key for transmission to the next node, within secure modules in the node. End-to-end encryption involves no intermediate decryption and re-encryption. Two users at each end of a communication path must therefore share a common key. *See* CRYPTOGRAPHIC KEY, DATALINK ENCRYPTION, END-TO-END ENCRYPTION, NODE ENCRYPTION.

network layer. In data communications, a layer in the ISO Open Systems Interconnection model. This layer is primarily concerned with the provision of services to establish a path, with a predictable quality of service, between open systems. *Compare* APPLICATION LAYER, DATA LINK LAYER, PHYSICAL LAYER, PRESENTATION LAYER, SESSION LAYER, TRANSPORT LAYER. *See* OPEN SYSTEMS INTERCONNECTION, ROUTING.

network management. In data communications, the systematic procedures necessary to plan, organize and control an evolving communication network with optimum costs and performance.

network management system. In data communications, a system that enables the network supervisor to monitor the status of every communication line, modem and terminal in the network and to locate failures. Usually a controlling unit monitors the network via a low-speed secondary channel independent of the main data channel. *See* CHANNEL, MODEM.

network operating centre. In data communications, an installation that facilitates reliable network operation by the monitoring of network status, supervision and coordination of network maintenance, collecting usage and accounting data, etc.

network operators. In communications, operators of communication networks, normally computer-controlled. (Philips).

Link encryption

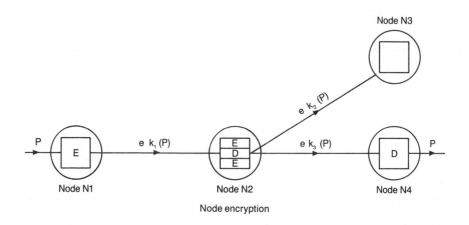

Node encryption

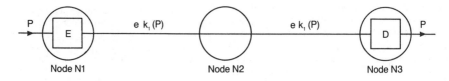

End-to-end encryption

network encryption

network redundancy. In data communications, a property of networks that have more links than are strictly necessary to connect the nodes, thus enabling the network to continue to function if certain links fail.

network structure. In data structures, a structure in which any node can be connected to any other node. *Compare* TREE STRUCTURE. *Synonymous with* PLEX STRUCTURE.

network television station. In communications, a communications satellite earth station that can receive and transmit signals of television network quality. *See* COMMUNICATIONS SATELLITE SYSTEM, GROUND STATION.

network termination unit. In data communications, the part of the network equipment that connects directly with the data terminal equipment. It operates between the local transmission lines and the subscribers' interface. *See* DATA TERMINAL EQUIPMENT.

network timing. In data communications, timing signals transferred from data circuit terminating equipment to data terminal equipment to control the transmission of digits across the transmitted and received data circuits. *See* DATA CIRCUIT TERMINATING EQUIPMENT, DATA TERMINAL EQUIPMENT.

network topology. In communications, the geometric arrangement of nodes and links in a network.

network user identifier. (NUI) In data communications, the identification code used by customers on a public dial port to identify themselves for accounting purposes. *See* PACKET SWITCHING, PUBLIC DIAL PORT.

network weaving. In communications security, a technique using different communication networks to gain access to an organization's system (e.g. a attacker makes a call through AT&T, jumps over to Sprint, then to MCI, and then to Tymnet). The purpose is to avoid detection and trace backs to the source of the call. *See* HACKER.

neural network. In artificial intelligence, a proposed form of parallel processor. It is based upon a large network of individual units each of which operates in a similar manner to a nerve cell (i.e. each unit has a number of input lines and fires whenever the number of input signals exceeds a threshold value). *See* PARALLEL PROCESSING.

neutral density filter. In photography, a grey filter used to reduce exposure and contrast without affecting the colours.

neutral transmission. *Synonymous with* UNIPOLAR TRANSMISSION.

New Century Schoolbook. In printing, a typeface designed for ease of reading. *Compare* AVANTE-GARDE, BOOKMAN, COURIER, HELVETICA, HELVETICA NARROW, PALATINO, SYMBOL, TIMES ROMAN, ZAPF CHANCERY, ZAPF DINGBATS. *See* TYPEFACE.

new-line character. In printing, a control character that instructs a printer to commence a new line.

new media. In information presentation, media now becoming available for mass information presentation (e.g. read-only memory compact disc for use with personal computers, interactive compact discs and optical videodiscs which use dedicated drives). Principal advantages of such media lie in the fast access which makes interactive applications possible and very high storage capacities. (Philips). *See* COMPACT DISC – INTERACTIVE, COMPACT DISC – READ-ONLY MEMORY, OPTICAL DIGITAL DISC, VIDEODISC.

news database. In online information retrieval, a full-text database comprising daily and weekly newspaper editions. It is provided by a newspaper company or wire service. *See* FULL-TEXT DATABASE, WIRE SERVICE.

newsflash page. In videotex, a teletext page in which the information for display is boxed and may be automatically inset or added to a television picture. *See* TELETEXT.

newspaper lines per minute. In printing, a setting speed used for newspaper typesetters. The newspaper line is usually one of 8-point type to an 11-pica line. *See* PICA, POINT, TYPESETTING.

newsprint. In printing, unsized, low-quality, absorbent paper used for printing newspapers. (Desktop). *See* SIZE.

news release. *Synonymous with* PRESS RELEASE.

New York Times Information Bank. In online information retrieval, a database, supplied by the New York Times Company and dealing with world news.

Nexis. In online information retrieval, a database supplied by Mead Data Central and others and dealing with business and industry, economics and news.

Next. In computing, an advanced microcomputer developed for the education market.

nexus. A connection or interconnection.

nib. In peripherals, an electrical conductor used to pass an electrical charge on an electrostatic plotter. *See* ELECTROSTATIC PLOTTER.

nibble. In data structures, a word comprising four bits. *Compare* BYTE. *See* BIT, WORD.

Nicam 728. In television, a standard for the broadcasting of stereo sound for television. It consists of a serial 728 kilobits per second continuous data stream containing 14-bit compounded sound samples along with some control and synchronization information. The data is modulated onto a subcarrier of frequency 6.662 MHz above the vision carrier using quadrature phase shift keying. See CARRIER, PHASE SHIFT KEYING.

Nicem. In online information retrieval, a directory database of educational media. See DIRECTORY DATABASE.

niche markets. Markets demanding specific or specialized products and thus more suited to specialist manufacturers than to large-scale general producers. Wholesale management and industrial management, for example, demand specialized software and equipment of a kind not required in general office management. (Philips).

NIFTP. In data communications, network-independent file transfer protocol. See FILE TRANSFER.

NIIT. National, International and Intercontinental Telecommunication network.

nine's complement. In mathematics, the ten's complement minus one (e.g. the nine's complement of 69 is $99 - 69 = 30$). Compare TEN'S COMPLEMENT.

n,k code. In codes, a coding arrangement in which in a block of n bits, $n - k$ of those bits are used for parity checking. See PARITY CHECKING.

N-key rollover. In peripherals, a keyboard action that produces coded signals in the correct sequence when N keys are depressed virtually simultaneously (e.g. 2-key rollover). Compare LOCKOUT. See KEYBOARD, ROLLOVER.

NL. See NATURAL LANGUAGE.

NLM. See NATIONAL LIBRARY OF MEDICINE.

NLP. In machine translation, natural language processing. See NATURAL LANGUAGE.

NLQ. See NEAR LETTER QUALITY.

NMA. See NATIONAL MICROFILM ASSOCIATION, NATIONAL MICROGRAPHICS ASSOCIATION.

NMOS. See N-CHANNEL MOS.

NMR. In reliability, a form of modular redundancy similar to triple modular redundancy except that N units, N being an odd number, are employed. Compare DUAL REDUNDANCY, TRIPLE MODULAR REDUNDANCY. See MODULAR REDUNDANCY.

NMT. In communications, Nordic Mobile Telephone; a cellular radio system. Compare AMPS, TACS. See CELLULAR RADIO.

NOAA. See NATIONAL OCEANOGRAPHIC AND ATMOSPHERIC AGENCY.

no-circuit signal. In communications, a low tone, periodically interrupted, indicating that no telephone circuit is available.

node. (1) In data communications, a place that has significance for data routing; a point of interconnection to a network. (2) In data structures, an entity on two or more access paths.

node computer. In computer networks, a computer used to interconnect the host computers. The host computers are connected to the communications network via a node computer.

node encryption. In communications security, a method of encryption of network data in which the data is decrypted within an intermediate node, and re-encrypted, under a different key, for onward transmission. The decryption and re-encryption is performed in secure modules, and thus plaintext is not transmitted through the node. Compare DATALINK ENCRYPTION, END-TO-END ENCRYPTION. See NETWORK ENCRYPTION, PLAINTEXT.

no flash. In printing, a command code in phototypesetters that positions the matrix and film, but does not expose the character. The film is thus moved on by a required amount without the formation of an image. See MATRIX, PHOTOTYPESETTING.

noise. (1) In electronics, any signal disturbance that tends to interfere with the normal operation of a device or system. (2) In communications, a random undesired signal. *See* GALACTIC NOISE, HELIOS NOISE, THERMAL NOISE. (3) In information retrieval. *Synonymous with* FALSE DROP.

noise bar. In video recording, a momentary distortion of the picture during playback of a helical scan device. It occurs most commonly during still framing. *See* FREEZE FRAME, STILL FRAME.

noise-cancelling. In microphones, pertaining to devices designed to reduce the effect of ambient noise. The housing is arranged so that ambient noise strikes both sides of the diaphragm, thus cancelling itself out. Sound from a close speaking voice strikes only one side of the diaphragm. *See* DIAPHRAGM.

noise factor. In library science, the proportion of non-relevant items produced by a search. *See* NOISE.

noise temperature. In electronics, the temperature of a thermal noise source producing the same output noise power, in the same bandwidth, as the device under consideration. *See* THERMAL NOISE.

nomenclature. A consistent method for assigning names to elements of a system.

non-aligned. In printing, pertaining to a line of characters in which the baselines vary. *See* BASELINE.

non-ballistic technique. In printing, a method used in the printing head of a matrix printer. The needle is forced forward by a clapper and does not lose contact with it during its flight. *Compare* BALLISTIC TECHNIQUE. *See* MATRIX PRINTER.

non-compatibility. In operations, pertaining to a situation in which one system is unable to retrieve information stored in another or to run programs developed on another. *Compare* COMPATIBILITY.

non-deflected printer. *Synonymous with* DROP ON DEMAND.

non-dense index. In databases, an index that provides information on the location of a group of records. Once the location is

accessed the records must be scanned sequentially until the one corresponding to the appropriate key is found. *Compare* DENSE INDEX. *See* INDEX, KEY, RECORD.

non-destructive cursor. In peripherals, a cursor of a visual display that can be moved about the screen without destroying or changing the information displayed. *Compare* DESTRUCTIVE CURSOR. *See* VISUAL DISPLAY UNIT.

non-destructive readout. (NDR) In memory systems, a reading action that does not change the data held. *Compare* DESTRUCTIVE READOUT.

non-directional microphone. *Synonymous with* OMNIDIRECTIONAL MICROPHONE.

non-impact printer. In printing, a class of printer that aims to provide higher speed and less noise than conventional impact printers. The transfer of images does not depend upon striking a ribbon onto the paper. Methods include ion deposition, ink jet, laser, thermal and electroerosion. *Compare* IMPACT PRINTER. *See* ELECTROEROSION PRINTER, INK JET PRINTER, ION DEPOSITION, LASER PRINTER, PRINTER, THERMAL PRINTER.

non-invertibility. In data security, a property of a cryptographic algorithm. The algorithm is said to be non-invertible if it is computationally infeasible to determine the cryptographic key given the plaintext and corresponding ciphertext. *See* CIPHERTEXT, COMPUTATIONALLY INFEASIBLE, CRYPTOGRAPHIC ALGORITHM, CRYPTOGRAPHIC KEY, PLAINTEXT.

non-linear. In electronics, pertaining to devices in which a change in the input signal does not necessarily produce a proportional change in the output signal. *Compare* LINEAR. *See* AMPLIFIER.

non-linear book. In publishing, a book that is normally read in a random manner rather than from cover to cover. Examples include reference books, catalogues, encyclopaedias and dictionaries. (Philips). *See* VIEWBOOK.

non-linear optics. Pertaining to devices in which light flows are controlled by light signals. *Compare* OPTOELECTRONICS.

non-linear quantization. In communications, quantization using steps of different sizes to distribute the steps more efficiently over the dynamic range. It takes advantage of the fact that quantization errors are less perceptible when signal changes are large. (Philips). *See* PULSE CODE MODULATION, QUANTIZE.

non-lining figures. *Synonymous with* OLD-STYLE FIGURES.

non-polarized return to zero recording. In memory systems, a storage technique in which binary zeros are represented by the absence of magnetization. *Compare* POLARIZED RETURN TO ZERO RECORDING.

non-prime attribute. In databases, an attribute that is not a prime attribute (i.e. it is not a member of a candidate key). *Compare* PRIME ATTRIBUTE. *See* CANDIDATE KEY, RELATIONAL DATABASE.

non-procedural language. In programming, a language in which the user specifies the nature of the desired end result rather than the processes required to attain it (e.g. having specified a family tree and defined a grandson as the son of a grandparent's son or daughter then the user may input a request for the grandsons of a specified person). *Compare* PROCEDURAL LANGUAGE. *See* PROLOG. *Synonymous with* DECLARATIVE LANGUAGE, IMPERATIVE LANGUAGE.

non-reflective ink. In optical character recognition, ink that absorbs light and hence is used to write machine-readable characters.

non-return to zero. (NRZ) (1) In data communications, a method of data transmission in which a voltage of one polarity represents a 1 bit, and the other polarity represents a 0 bit. The circuit carries data whenever it is enabled. It is a common method of data transfer between a computer and its peripherals. (2) In memory systems, a method of recording data on a magnetizable surface so that magnetization in one direction represents a 1 bit, and vice versa. *Compare* NON-RETURN TO ZERO INVERTED, RETURN TO ZERO.

non-return to zero inverted. (NRZI) In memory systems, a method of recording data on a magnetizable surface in which the current in the read/write head is reversed to write a 1 bit and is left unchanged for a 0 bit. *Compare* NON-RETURN TO ZERO.

non-secret design. The principle that aspects of the design of a secure system need not be kept secret because the security lies in secret keys, parameters, etc. (e.g. the data encryption algorithm is public knowledge and the secrecy of the cipher depends upon the secret keys). This principle allows the system to be investigated by a wide variety of specialists searching for potential security design faults. On the other hand it can be argued that the openness increases the risk of discovering a design flaw, or trapdoor, in a system that has become widely used with, potentially, very serious consequences. *See* DATA ENCRYPTION ALGORITHM, TRAPDOOR.

non-standard sector. In software protection, a floppy disk that has been formatted in a non-standard way and so cannot be copied using operating system utilities. *See* EXECUTE PROTECTION, FLOPPY DISK, FORMATTING, OPERATING SYSTEM.

non-switched line. *Synonymous with* LEASED CIRCUIT.

non-transparent mode. In data communications, transmission of characters in a defined format (e.g. ASCII) in which all defined control sequences and characters are recognized and treated. *Compare* TRANSPARENT DATA COMMUNICATION CODE. *See* AMERMCAN STANDARD CODE FOR INFORMATION INTERCHANGE.

non-volatile memory. *Synonymous with* NON-VOLATILE STORAGE.

non-volatile storage. In memory systems, storage media that retains information when the power supply is removed (e.g. bubble memory, magnetic disks). *Compare* VOLATILE STORAGE. *See* BUBBLE MEMORY, MAGNETIC DISK. *Synonymous with* NON-VOLATILE MEMORY, PERMANENT MEMORY.

NOR. A logical operation, A NOR B has the result true if the result of the logical operation A OR B is false. The corresponding truth table is

A	B	A NOR B
0	0	1
1	0	0
0	1	0
1	1	0

Compare OR. *See* TRUTH TABLE.

normal forms.   In databases, a class of relations, in relational databases, with defined properties of interrelationship between the attributes. The use of normal forms in a database reduces problems in the manipulation and storage of data which can arise from inherent interrelationships between attributes. *See* ATTRIBUTE, FIRST NORMAL FORM, RELATION, RELATIONAL DATABASE, SECOND NORMAL FORM, THIRD NORMAL FORM.

normalized device coordinates.   (NDC) In computer graphics, one of the stages in the transformation of images. It is used in the graphical kernel system. Images expressed in world coordinates can be transformed into a single image in normalized device coordinates. A further workstation transformation allows any portion of the image in normalized device coordinates to be displayed at a graphic workstation. Several different workstation transformations can be applied to the same normalized device coordinate image giving different views of it on various devices. *See* GRAPHICAL KERNEL SYSTEM, WORLD COORDINATES.

normal resolution.   (1) In television, the degree of visual definition (400 x 300 pixels) presented by domestic television receiver screens. *See* PIXEL. (2) In optical media, an interactive compact disc display resolution mode of 384 pixels (horizontal) by 280 pixels (vertical). (Philips). *Compare* HIGH RESOLUTION, LOW RESOLUTION. *See* PIXEL.

normal vector.   In computer graphics, a mathematical tool employed to define the orientation of a flat surface. It is a line which is at right angles to every line on the surface. *See* VECTOR.

NOT.   A logical operation, NOT A has the result true if the logical variable A is false. The corresponding truth table is

A	NOT A
0	1
1	0

See BOOLEAN ALGEBRA, TRUTH TABLE.

notarization.   *See* KEY NOTARIZATION.

notepad.   In computer graphics, a program that reserves a portion of main memory as an aide memoire for the user in a windowing environment. *See* WINDOW.

notice of enquiry.   In communications, a public notice issued by the Federal Communications Commission and inviting information, and opinions, to be used in formulating policies, modifying rules or making new rules.

notice of proposed rulemaking.   In communications, a public notice issued by the Federal Communications Commission and inviting comment on a new rule or the modification of an existing rule.

n–p–n transistor.   In electronics, a bipolar transistor with the emitter and collector connected to n-type semiconductor material and

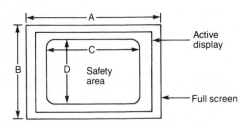

Disc format	Resolution			
	Full screen		Safety area	
	A	B	C	D
525	360	240	320	210
625	384	280	320	250
525/625 compatible	384	280	320	210

normal resolution

the base connected to p-type material. *Compare* P–N–P TRANSISTOR. *See* TRANSISTOR.

NRCd. UK National Reprographic Centre for Documentation.

NRZ. *See* NON-RETURN TO ZERO.

NRZI. *See* NON-RETURN TO ZERO INVERTED.

NSA. US National Security Agency. *See* NATIONAL SECURITY AGENCY/CENTRAL SECURITY SERVICE

NSA COMSEC module. In cryptography, under the Commercial COMSEC Endorsement Program the National Security Agency is endorsing two types of cryptographic products Type I and Type II. A Type-I product is intended for use in protecting classified US government information and is used by the US government and its contractors; it is not available outside government control. A Type-II product is also used by the US government and its contractors, but is also available for the commercial private sector. Type-I and Type-II products cannot be exported. *Compare* DATA ENCRYPTION STANDARD. *See* COMSEC, ORIGINAL EQUIPMENT MANUFACTURE, REVERSE ENGINEERING.

NSDD. US National Security Decision Directive.

NSDD-145. National Security Directive 145; a directive in which the US President recognized the security problem and the susceptibility of private sector communications. As a result of this directive the National Security Agency adapted its Commercial COMSEC Endorsement Program to permit the private sector access to CCEP equipment. *See* DATA ENCRYPTION STANDARD, NSA COMSEC MODULE.

NSI. US National Security Information.

NT1. In communications, an integrated services digital network Network Termination type 1 (NT1) unit. It is located on the user's premises to provide line termination functions for the user-network transmission system. *Compare* NT2. *See* INTEGRATED SERVICES DIGITAL NETWORK.

NT2. In communications, an integrated services digital network Network Termination type 2 (NT2) unit, which provides the private automatic branch exchange facilities (i.e. local switching functions between the terminal equipment and the network, and between the terminals themselves). *Compare* NT1. *See* INTEGRATED SERVICES DIGITAL NETWORK.

NTIS. In online information retrieval, National Technical Information Service; a database supplied by National Technical Information Service and dealing with science and technology.

NTISS. US National Telecommunications and Information System Security.

NTISSC. US National Telecommunications and Information System Security Committee.

NTISSD. US National Telecommunications and Information System Security Directive.

NTSC. *See* VIDEO STANDARDS.

NTSC decoder. In television, the receiver circuitry between the signal detector and the screen that decodes the broadcast signals. *See* VIDEO STANDARDS.

***n*-tuple.** In mathematics, a collection of n elements, normally ordered. *See* TUPLE.

n-type material. In electronics, a semiconductor material doped with an impurity that provides nuclei with loosely bound electrons. These electrons provide negative charge carriers. *Compare* P-TYPE MATERIAL. *See* SEMICONDUCTOR DEVICES.

NUI. *See* NETWORK USER IDENTIFIER.

NUL. *See* NULL CHARACTER.

null character. (NUL) In data communications, a control character that is used as a fill character for transmission, or storage. It may be removed from a sequence of characters without affecting its meaning. The null character may, however, have some significance in the control of equipment or formatting. *See* CONTROL CHARACTER.

null modem. In data communications, a device employed to connect two systems that normally communicate with modems (e.g. if two computers communicate directly using RS-232C interfaces both would transmit data on pin 2 and would expect to receive data on pin 3). In this case a null modem would simply comprise a plug–socket system to connect pin 2 on one computer and to pin 3 on the other, and vice versa. *See* MODEM, RS-232C.

null string. In data structures, a string that contains no characters. *See* STRING.

null suppression. In codes, the bypassing of null characters to be stored or transmitted to save transmission time or storage space. *See* DATA COMPRESSION.

number. A mathematical entity indicating a quantity or amount of units.

number 7 signalling. In communications, a powerful out of band signalling system which supports the whole range of integrated services digital network services. It is a specialized packet-switched network in its own right based on 64 kilobits per second channels in standard pulse code-modulated systems, but it can operate down to 4.8 kilobits per second within an analog transmission network. *See* INTEGRATED SERVICES DIGITAL NETWORK, SIGNALLING.

number crunching. In applications, processing activities that involve a high proportion of mathematical operations on the data, usually arising in scientific applications. Such applications make heavy use of the central processing unit and involve compara-

tively few input/output operations. *Compare* INPUT/OUTPUT-BOUND.

number plan area. *Synonymous with* AREA CODE.

number processing. *See* ARITHMETIC CAPABILITY.

numeral. In mathematics, a discrete representation of a number (e.g. twenty, 20, XX, 14, 10100 all represent the number 20, with the last two examples using the hexadecimal and binary system). *See* HEXADECIMAL.

numerical analysis. In mathematics, the study of methods relating to the development of quantitative solutions to mathematical problems, including the study of errors and the efficiency of the methods in terms of the total computational effort.

numeric database. In online information retrieval, a database of statistical and numeric data rather than text or bibliographic information. *Compare* BIBLIOGRAPHIC DATABASE, DIRECTORY DATABASE, FULL-TEXT DATABASE, REFERRAL DATABASE.

nut. *Synonymous with* EN QUAD.

Nyquist sampling theorem. In control and instrumentation, a theorem that specifies the minimum sampling rate necessary to ensure that the original analog signal can be reconstituted from the sampled values. The theorem states that the sampling rate must be twice as high as the highest frequency present in the sampled signal. *See* ALIASING, COMPUTERIZED INSTRUMENTATION, SAMPLING.

O

OA. Office Automation.

obelisk. *Synonymous with* DAGGER.

obey. In computing, the process whereby the computer performs the set of instructions specified in a program.

object. (1) In computer security, a passive entity that contains or receives information. Access to an object potentially implies access to the information it contains. Examples of objects are: records, blocks, pages, segments, files, directories, directory trees and programs, as well as bits, bytes, words, fields, processors, video displays, keyboards, clocks, printers, network nodes, etc. (DOD). *Compare* SUBJECT. (2) In data structures, an entity in computer memory that contains and protects a set of related data. Objects perform assigned tasks by communicating with each other. For example, a processor object stores vital data for the processor, if another processor is added to the system it is merely necessary to add a corresponding object in memory. (3) In programming, a quantity in an expert system that may be assigned a numerical value and allows the system to reason about real physical quantities. *Compare* ASSERTION.

object code. In programming, the code of a user's program after it has been translated. *Compare* SOURCE CODE. *See* TRANSLATOR.

object graphic. In computer graphics, a form of graphics in which elements such as boxes, circles and patterns can be defined by commands. *See* GRAPHIC PRIMITIVE.

objective. In optics, the image-forming component of the system.

object language. In programming, the output language of a translation process. *Compare* SOURCE LANGUAGE. *See* OBJECT CODE, TRANSLATOR. *Synonymous with* TARGET LANGUAGE.

object program. In programming, a program in object code form. *See* OBJECT CODE. *Synonymous* WITH TARGET PROGRAM.

oblique projection. In computer graphics, a parallel projection in which one face of the object is parallel to the picture plane and the visual rays are inclined to it. *Compare* ISOMETRIC PROJECTION, ORTHOGRAPHIC PROJECTION, PERSPECTIVE PROJECTION. *See* PARALLEL PROJECTION, PICTURE PLANE.

Occam. In programming, a concurrent, control-structured language developed for the transputer to exploit the power of multiprocessing systems. *See* MULTIPROCESSING, PARALLEL PROCESSING, TRANSPUTER.

Oceanic Abstracts. In online information retrieval, a database supplied by Cambridge Scientific Abstracts and dealing with aquatic sciences.

OCI. US Office of Computer Information; an office of the Department of Commerce.

OCLC. In online information retrieval, Online Computer Library Center; a non-profit-making bibliographic utility. It was known as the Ohio College Library Center until 1981, but changed its name when it attracted members outside of Ohio and even from Europe. *See* BIBLIOGRAPHIC UTILITY.

OCR. *See* OPTICAL CHARACTER RECOGNITION.

OCR-A. In optical character recognition, a special typeface intended for optical character recognition (OCR). *Compare* OCR-B.

OCR-B. In optical character recognition, a special typeface for optical character recognition (OCR) considered to be more pleasing to the eye than OCR-A. *Compare* OCR-A.

OCR font. In printing, a set of characters designed to be read by optical character recognition (OCR). *See* OCR-A, OCR-B, OPTICAL CHARACTER RECOGNITION.

octal. In mathematics, pertaining to the number eight. Octal notation uses a base of eight and is a convenient form of representing binary numbers (e.g. hexadecimal 42 = decimal 66 = octal 102 = binary 1 000 010). *Compare* HEXADECIMAL. *See* BINARY.

octet. In data structures, a group of eight binary digits treated as an entity. *Compare* SEPTET, SEXTET. *See* OCTAL.

ODA. In data communications, office document architecture; a set of standards for electronic document interchange. *See* ELECTRONIC DOCUMENT INTERCHANGE.

odd/even check. *Synonymous with* PARITY CHECKING.

odd parity. *See* PARITY.

ODETTE. *See* ORGANIZATION FOR DATA EXCHANGE AND TELETRANSMISSION IN EUROPE.

OEM. *See* ORIGINAL EQUIPMENT MANUFACTURER.

oersted. In electronics, a unit of measure of the magnetizing force necessary to produce a desired magnetic flux across a surface. *See* MAGNETIC FLUX.

OFB. *See* OUTPUT FEEDBACK.

off air. In communications, a broadcast program received either on radio or television.

offcut. In printing, paper left over when the sheet is trimmed to size.

off hook. In communications, a condition in which a unit indicates a busy condition to incoming telephone calls. *Compare* ON HOOK.

office automation. In office systems, the use of any form of machine or system that either replaces or simplifies human activities and operations in office environments. Typically, machines include word processors, facsimile machines, multipurpose photocopying devices and computer terminals. (Philips). *See* ELECTRONIC FILING, ELECTRONIC MAIL, FACSIMILE, OFFICE OF THE FUTURE. WORD PROCESSING.

office of the future. In applications, an office in which all recorded information is held in computer-readable form and there exists a highly integrated database, communication, word- and transaction-processing system. *See* DATABASE, OFFICE AUTOMATION, TRANSACTION PROCESSING, WORD PROCESSING. *Synonymous with* ELECTRONIC OFFICE, PAPERLESS OFFICE.

offline. In operations, pertaining to processing equipment that is not connected to a computer or network, or the operations performed on such equipment. *Compare* ONLINE.

offline printing. In printing, activities that take place without the continual supervision of a computer. *Synonymous with* BACKGROUND PRINTING.

offline shopping. In applications, a development in teleshopping in which the database is distributed to clients, usually in the form of an optical disc, which can be searched at the client's convenience, and without the expense and probable delay of an online search. Goods can then be ordered during a short online connection. (Philips). *See* OPTICAL DISC, TELESHOPPING.

off microphone. In filming, pertaining to the area outside a microphone's pickup pattern. *Synonymous with* OFF MIKE.

off mike. *Synonymous with* OFF MICROPHONE.

offprint. In printing, a feature or other portion of publication made available separately from whole work.

off screen. In filming, pertaining to unseen action that is presumably not far from the perceived action.

offset lithography. *Synonymous with* PHOTOLITHOGRAPHY.

offset printing. In printing, a lithographic method of printing in which the ink is first transferred from the printing surface to a rubber offset blanket and then to the paper or other printing material. *See* LITHOGRAPHY.

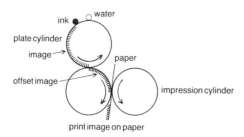

offset printing

OFTEL. UK Office of Telecommunications.

ohm. In electronics, a unit of electrical resistance. One ampere flowing through a one ohm resistance produces a voltage drop of one volt. *See* RESISTANCE.

OIRT. *See* INTERNATIONAL RADIO AND TELEVISION ORGANIZATION.

OIS. Office information system.

O.K. In printing, a mark to indicate that a proof is error-free. *See* PROOF.

Oldstyle. In printing, a US typeface with triangular serifs and stressed strokes. *Compare* AVANTE-GARDE, BOOKMAN, CONDENSED, COURIER, EGYPTIAN, EXPANDED TYPE, HELVETICA, HELVETICA NARROW, NEW CENTURY SCHOOLBOOK, PALATINO, SYMBOL, TIMES ROMAN, ZAPF CHANCERY, ZAPF DINGBATS. *See* SERIF, TYPEFACE.

old-style figures. In printing, a set of type numerals that vary in size, some having ascenders and other descenders. *Compare* LINING FIGURES. *See* ASCENDER, DESCENDER. *Synonymous with* NON-LINING FIGURES.

omega wrap. In video recording, a method of winding videotape around the drum of a helical scan device. The tape is wrapped almost 360° around the drum to form a Greek letter omega. The tracks are diagonal on the tape, there are no video tracks at the top and bottom edges of the tape and the signal is not recorded on tape as the recording head crosses the gap between tracks. *Compare* ALPHA WRAP. *See* HELICAL SCAN.

omission factor. In library science, the number of documents that are relevant to a query, but are not retrieved in a search.

omnidirectional microphone. A microphone that is equally sensitive in all directions. *Compare* UNIDIRECTIONAL MICROPHONE. *Synonymous with* NON-DIRECTIONAL MICROPHONE.

omni player. In optical media, a combined compact disc and LaserVision player that can also play interactive compact discs. (Philips). *See* COMPACT DISC, COMPACT DISC – INTERACTIVE, LASERVISION.

OMR. *See* OPTICAL MARK RECOGNITION.

on board. In microelectronics, additional or supporting functions incorporated into a printed circuit board or within the housing of equipment. (Philips). *See* PRINTED CIRCUIT BOARD.

on chip. In microelectronics, pertaining to a circuit that is on the same chip as other elements. *See* CHIP.

one and one-half spacing. In word processing, an instruction to place one and one-half spaces between lines of text during playback printing.

one-key cryptosystem. *Synonymous with* SYMMETRIC CRYPTOSYSTEM.

one-line initial. In printing, an initial letter larger than the text and lined up with the bottom of the text.

one's complement. In mathematics, a method of representing a negative binary number. In this convention, a binary number is negated by complementing the binary digits. The most significant digit is a sign bit (i.e. one indicates a negative number). Unlike the two's complement, a zero is represented both by all ones or all zeros. *Compare* TWO'S COMPLEMENT. *See* COMPLEMENT.

one shot. In microelectronics, a circuit that receives a pulse as input and generates an output pulse of a specified width that is independent of the width of the input pulse. *See* MONOSTABLE.

one-time pad. In data security, a cipher that uses a non-repeating random key stream. One-time pads are the only ciphers that achieve perfect secrecy, but the length of the key is equal to the length of the message. They are mainly used for diplomatic communications. *See* PERFECT SECRECY, STREAM CIPHER.

one-time passwords. In computer security, passwords that are changed after each use and are useful when the password is not adequately protected from compromise during logon (e.g. the communication line is suspected of being tapped). (FIPS). *See* DYNAMIC PASSWORD, EXPIRED PASSWORD, LOGON, PASSWORD.

one-way cipher. In data security, a cipher that is an irreversible function from plaintext to ciphertext (i.e. it is not computationally feasible to decipher the ciphertext). This technique can be used to store encrypted passwords in a computer system. The passwords are checked by encrypting them, when they are entered, and comparing the result with the stored encrypted passwords. With this technique an attacker cannot determine the cleartext version of the passwords even if illegal access is gained to the computer memory. *See* COMPUTATIONALLY INFEASIBLE, ONE-WAY FUNCTION. *Synonymous with* IRREVERSIBLE ENCRYPTION.

one-way function. (OWF) In data security, a function $f(x)$ such that it is easy to compute $f(x)$ given x, for any x in its domain, but that the inverse is computationally infeasible. In public key cryptography it is possible to multiply two large prime numbers, but computationally infeasible to compute the factors of the product. *See* COMPUTATIONALLY INFEASIBLE, DOMAIN, PASSWORD.

on hook. In communications, a condition in which the telephone is not in use. *Compare* OFF HOOK.

onion skin. In printing, a translucent, lightweight paper used for airmail stationery. (Desktop).

onion skin architecture. In computing and data communications, a layered structure that facilitates communication between processes at the same level, employing lower-level processes in a manner that is largely transparent to the user process. In communication systems this approach facilitates the design and use of complex networks and systems. Processes receive messages from the layer above and pass them to corresponding processes at the same level by initially transmitting them to the layer below. These processes need only be concerned with the passage of messages through two-layer interfaces, although the total system may have many layers. *See* OPEN SYSTEMS INTERCONNECTION, TRANSPARENT.

online. In operations, pertaining to data processing and communication equipment that is connected to a computer or communication channel. *Compare* OFFLINE.

online information. In computing, computer-stored information that may be accessed, displayed, used and interactively modified without recourse to hard copy. *See* HARD COPY.

online information retrieval. In applications, a system that enables a searcher at a remote terminal to interrogate interactively databases, containing bibliographical information or source data, held on a host computer.

Since the end of the World War II there has been a dramatic growth in the amount of scientific and technical information published, particularly in the form of journals and conference proceedings, and this has resulted in a significant increase in the number of abstracting and indexing journals. Online information retrieval originated in the 1960s when computers were introduced for phototypesetting abstracting and indexing journals. Information centres obtained the machine-readable tapes and developed software to enable them to be interrogated, although initially only in batch mode. During the late 1960s the Lockheed Missiles and Space Co. and the System Development Corp. (SDC) were instrumental in developing interactive online systems, and by the mid-1970s such systems were being offered by a number of organizations on a world-wide basis.

The producers of the databases are normally professional institutions, government bodies, commercial companies, etc., and the databases are leased or sold to the suppliers offering the online services. There are now databases covering all subjects and disciplines and although originally they were bibliographical in nature, many now contain factual information and even the full texts of original articles and papers.

To interrogate a database the searcher uses a terminal, with printer attached, connected by a modem or acoustic coupler, to a telephone. The searcher can access the supplier's computer — the 'host' computer — either by dialing directly, if nearby, or by dialing the local node of a data telecommunications network. Having entered the password the user specifies which database is required for the search.

On accessing a relevant database the searcher specifies search terms of keywords that best describe the topic. These are matched with the index to the records on the database and the system responds with the number of matches, or 'postings' found. By combining the search terms using boolean operators (AND, OR, NOT) the search can be narrowed or widened. In bibliographical databases, it is usually possible to narrow a search by specifying the language of the original articles or the publication cut-off date, by searching for matches in titles only, or matches with the terms used by the abstractor to index the publications, by retrieving references to works by a particular author and/or by specifying the formats of original articles (e.g. journal articles, conference papers). The retrieved references or abstracts can be output on the searcher's printer or, if large numbers are involved, may more economically be printed offline by the supplier and posted to the searcher. Various formats may be specified (e.g. bibliographical citation, full record including

abstract and indexing terms, etc.). On some systems it is possible to order reprints of original articles and papers directly at the terminal. Also useful are the selective dissemination of information (SDI) services available on many systems. A search profile (i.e. a combination of search terms) is entered, and details of new relevant references are regularly sent to the searcher as the database is updated.

The initial cost of using an online information retrieval system is incurred in purchasing or leasing the necessary equipment or hardware (i.e. the terminal, printer, modem, telephone, etc.). It is sometimes necessary to pay a subscription to access a particular information system, and manuals, and thesauri of indexing terms will have to be purchased. The direct costs of a search are the telecommunications charges (i.e. telephone call and use of a data communications network). The database connect time charges vary from database to database and from one supplier to another, and the charges made for offline printed references vary. Frequently a charge is also made for any references printed online during a search. On many systems an estimated cost of the search (excluding any telephone charges) is printed when a searcher logs off from the system. Before undertaking online searches it is necessary to have some training in searching techniques and be familiar with some of the retrieval languages used on the various systems. Searches are therefore usually undertaken for enquirers by trained intermediaries, mid-users, information scientists or librarians. *See* ACOUSTIC COUPLER, AND, BOOLEAN ALGEBRA, KEYWORD, MODEM, OR.

online shopping. *Synonymous with* TELESHOPPING.

online storage. In backing storage, devices, and the media they contain, under the direct control of the computer system. *See* ONLINE.

online system. In operations, an information-processing system in which the data or instructions are inserted directly from the point of origin, and the output data is transmitted directly to the appropriate recipient. *Compare* BATCH PROCESSING. *See* ONLINE.

ON-TAP. In online information retrieval, online training and practice; a special training file available from Dialog that contains subjects of various databases. It is available at low cost to persons learning online searching skills. *See* DIALOG.

on the fly printer. In peripherals, an impact printer in which the typing slugs do not stop moving during the time of impression. *Synonymous with* HIT ON THE FLY PRINTER.

on the nose. In photography, pertaining to the use of exposure as indicated by the light meter.

OPAC. Online public access catalogue.

opacity. (1) In printing, pertaining to the degree to which paper will show print through. (Desktop). (2) In optics, the reciprocal of transmittance. *Compare* TRANSMITTANCE. *See* DENSITY.

opaque projector. In audiovisual aids, a device using the principle of reflection to project an image held on a non-transparent medium (e.g. coins, photographs, diagrams) in black and white or colour. *Compare* OVERHEAD PROJECTOR.

op code. *Synonymous with* OPERATION CODE.

open. In programming, an instruction to open a file associates it with the calling program. *Compare* CLOSE. *See* FILE.

open loop. A system in which the input information or signal is not influenced by the output of the system. *Compare* CLOSED LOOP, FEEDBACK.

open reel. In filming and recording, film, video or audio tape on a reel and not enclosed in a cassette or cartridge. *See* CARTRIDGE, CASSETTE.

open shop. In computing, a facility in which the end users can design, develop, test and run their own programs. *Compare* CLOSED SHOP.

open-skies policy. *Synonymous with* DOMSAT DECISION.

open system. In data communications, a system with specified standards and that therefore can be readily connected to other systems that comply with the same standards. *See* STANDARD.

Open Systems Interconnection. (OSI) In data communications, an ISO reference model intended to coordinate the development of standards at all levels of communication. The model has seven layers — physical, data link, network, transport, session, presentation and application. These layers are illustrated in the figure.

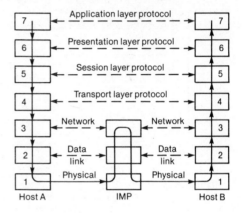

open system interconnection

The concept of the layers provides for a considerable degree of independence between the multifarious and complicated operations involved in data communications. At each level the process believes that it is communicating with its corresponding layer in the receiving host, and it does this by accepting messages from the layer vertically above it, adding control information to it and passing it on to the layer immediately below it. At the receiving end the process is reversed, messages are received from the layer below it, control information is stripped off, and the message is passed up to the next level. The concept can be illustrated by businesses communicating in different countries. Businessman A in Turin is only concerned to pass a business analysis to businessman B in Tokyo. He passes on the analysis to a translator who only speaks Italian and English. The translator produces an English version of the business analysis and hands the result to a

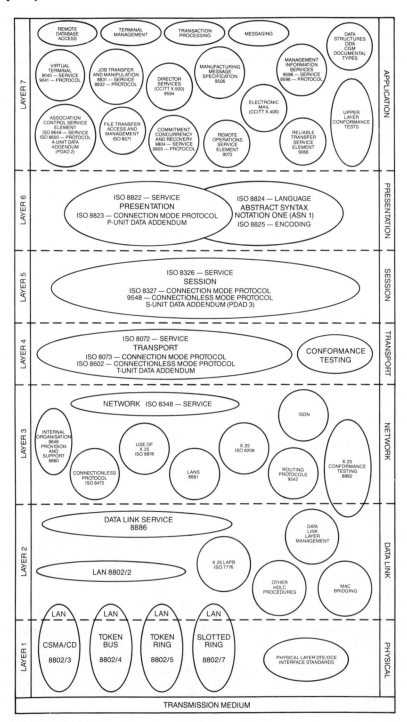

open system interconnection
Fig. 2. Protocol standards and the ISO Reference Model courtesy CAP Industry Ltd.
© Sema Group UK Ltd, 1987/8

post office for transmission. The post office forwards the message by letter to Tokyo where it is handed to a local translator who converts the text from English to Japanese and hands it up to businessman B. The degree of independence is obvious, the translators could agree on a different common language and the post office could select a whole variety of message transmissions; the other layers are unaware and unaffected by the changes.

The lowest layer (i.e. the physical layer) is concerned with the transmission of a raw bit stream. The data link layer uses error-detecting codes and host-to-host control messages to convert an unreliable transmission channel into a reliable one. The network layer in a point-to-point network is primarily concerned with routing and congestion. The transport layer provides reliable host-to-host communication and hides the details of the communication network from the session layer. The session layer is responsible for setting up, managing and tearing down process-to-process connections, whereas the presentation layer performs useful transformations in the text (e.g. text compression) and allows for dialogues with incompatible intelligent terminals. The content of the application layer is left to the users, and standard protocols for specific industries (e.g. banks) are expected to develop. The X.400 message-handling standard is located in the application layer. *Compare* SYSTEM NETWORK ARCHITECTURE. *See* APPLICATION LAYER, DATA LINK LAYER, ERROR-DETECTING CODE, HOST, PHYSICAL LAYER, POINT-TO-POINT, PRESENTATION LAYER, ROUTING, SESSION LAYER, TEXT COMPRESSION, TRANSPORT LAYER, X.400.

operand. In mathematics, the quantity that is to be the subject of a mathematical operation. *Compare* OPERATOR.

operating system. (OS) In computing, a program or group of programs that provides the user with a range of general-purpose facilities for normal usage of the computer. The OS frees the programmer from the chore of writing routines for commonly used functions and provides a uniform, consistent means for all applications software to access the same machine resources. The significance of the OS, from the user's viewpoint, probably lies in the range of application

software available since such software will be designed for use with a particular OS. *See* MS.DOS, PC.DOS, UNIX.

operating time. In communications, the total time required for dialing the telephone call, waiting for connection to be established and coordinating the subsequent transaction with the personnel or equipment at the receiving end.

operation code. In programming, the part of a machine code instruction that specifies the operation to be performed. *Compare* OPERAND. *See* MACHINE CODE INSTRUCTION. *Synonymous with* OP CODE.

operations research. In mathematics, the use of mathematical techniques to represent and study business, management problems, etc. *See* DYNAMIC PROGRAMMING, LINEAR PROGRAMMING.

operator. (1) A person charged to enable a piece of equipment to fulfil its function. (2) In mathematics, a character that designates a mathematical or logical operation (e.g. +). *Compare* OPERAND.

OPSEC. Operations security.

optical axis. An imaginary line drawn through an image-forming system such that the image-forming properties of the system are symmetrical in any plane perpendicular to the line.

optical bar reader. In peripherals, a reader that focuses a beam of light on a bar code label and receives the pulses of reflected light of varying strength and duration. *See* BAR CODE, WAND. *Synonymous with* BAR CODE SCANNER.

optical centre. In printing, a point above the true centre of the page that does not appear as low as the geometrical centre does. (Desktop).

optical character recognition. (OCR) In peripherals, a technique in which printed text is illuminated and the reflected light is passed to photocells which produce a set of electrical signals corresponding to the light/dark sections of the text. In its simplest form a hand-held wand is passed over a small strip of text printed in a font specially designed for OCR. Modern optical scanners can input text from printed pages with few restrictions on the font employed. *Compare* BAR CODE, MAGNETIC INK CHARACTER RECOGNITION, OPTICAL MARK RECOGNITION. *See* INTELLIGENT CHARACTER RECOGNITION, OCR FONT, OPTICAL SCANNER, PHOTOCELL.

optical digital disc. (1) In optical media, an optical disc in which information is stored digitally. It may be a read-only disc, replicated from a master (e.g. a compact disc) or a disc written by a user (e.g. digital optical recording). (Philips). *See* COMPACT DISC, COMPACT DISC-READ-ONLY MEMORY, WORM. (2) In memory systems, the use of plastic and metal discs with minute pits, in one physical form or another, embedded in circular or spiral tracks, which represent the stored bits. The disc is read by a laser beam in a similar manner to a conventional video or compact disc.

There are three main categories of optical digital discs: prerecorded, discs that can be written but not erased, and erasable discs.

The optical digital disc is similar to a videodisc or audio compact disc except that it is used to store binary data rather than pictures or sound. The total storage capacity of optical videodisc systems is of the order of gigabytes and that of interactive or read-only memory compact disc systems is of the order of 500 megabytes, and the cost per bit is currently only 10 per cent of that of magnetic disc systems.

The prerecorded discs may be in read-only memory (ROM) or optical read-only memory (OROM) format. The current read-only memory compact discs (CD-ROM) are 4.72 inches in diameter with spiral tracks and have a storage capacity of 552 megabytes; OROM discs are slightly larger, being 5.25 inches in diameter and may have spiral or circular concentric tracks. The major differences are that the circular track systems are operated in constant angular velocity mode and are used in applications where fast access is important; OROM discs may also be doubled-sided. The prerecorded discs are used to hold large volumes of relatively static data, catalogues, databases, medical and statistical data, encyclopaedias, etc. They cannot therefore be used to hold user-generated data.

The write-once optical disc may be used to store relatively static user data (e.g. for archiving). Such discs do not have the facility to erase, and use again, as conventional magnetic discs. However, they offer the advantages of extremely high storage capacity, over 1 gigabyte for some discs, and a guarantee of data integrity since the data cannot be erased by magnetic fields or careless handling. Moreover, the laser-reading device is not susceptible to head crashes which can cause serious loss of data in magnetic hard-disk systems. The write-once read many times (WORM) discs are available in 5.25- and 12-inch diameter sizes, with corresponding capacities of 250 megabytes and 200–1000 megabytes per side. Such discs may be categorized by the error protection techniques (i.e. direct read after write (DRAW) and direct read during write (DRDW)). In the former case the data block is written and then read, to check for errors, before the next block is written. This technique is rather slow since the disc must make a full rotation to read the data before the next block can be written. The DRDW technique reads the data as it is written, if an error is detected the recording head skips to the next good sector. This method is faster than DRAW but it entails more expensive technology.

The tracks on WORM discs may be spiral or circular, and the data is recorded by ablative pit-forming or bubble-forming techniques. In the first case the laser actually burns a pit in the recording surface. Such pits, however, do not have sharp edges and may therefore be a source of reading errors. In the bubble-forming techniques the laser raises the temperature of a spot in the media to about 2000°C. The lower layer of the recording medium vaporizes and forces up the covering layer to a bubble, such bubbles having no ragged edges.

Erasable optical discs compete more directly with conventional magnetic disks; they have the advantages of very high capacity and are less vulnerable to accidental or malicious erasure. The capacity of a 5.25-inch diameter erasable optical discs is in the range of 200–400 megabytes per side, equivalent to several hundred floppy disks.

Erasable optical discs use a technique termed 'optically assisted magnetic recording' and employ the laser beam to change the disc's magnetic field. The disc is initially magnetized horizontally parallel to its surface. The write head in the drive has both a laser and a magnetic coil; a metal plate designed to intensify the coil's magnetic field is often placed beneath the disc. One bit of data is written by turning on both the laser and the coil. The recording technique is based on the principle that a magnet loses its magnetization when heated to a certain temperature. The low magnetic field of the recording coil can only affect the disc's magnetization over a tiny area heated by the laser beam. At this spot the coil changes the direction of the magnetic field and creates a vertical magnetic bulge. The reading action is again performed by a low-power laser beam, and in this case the polarization of the beam is exploited. As a polarized beam passes through a magnetic field the plane of polarization is rotated slightly, and the reading beam is thus affected by the magnetic bulge. The change in the plane of polarization of the reflected beam is detected and recorded.

Although the bits per inch density of optical disc is some 50 per cent greater than that of hard magnetic disks the massive increase in optical disc capacity is derived from the extremely high track per inch density, of the order of 14 500 TPI compared with 1000 TPI for hard discs. This greater track density arises because the magnetized area of floppy and hard disks is greater in width than in length, whereas the optical disc pit is both smaller and circular. Moreover, the mechanical movement of the magnetic disk reading heads necessarily limits the precision with which the head can be located compared with the high resolution of the laser beam. *See* ABLATIVE PIT FORMING, BUBBLE FORMING, COMPACT DISC – INTERACTIVE COMPACT DISC – READ-ONLY MEMORY, CD-ROM PUBLISHING, DIRECT READ AFTER WRITE, DIRECT READ DURING WRITE, ERASABLE OPTICAL DISC, KERR EFFECT, LASER, MAGNETIC DISK, OROM, POLARIZED, READ-ONLY MEMORY, TRACK, VIDEODISC, WORM, WRITE-ONCE MEDIUM.

optical disc. In optical media, a disc in which information is impressed as a series of pits in a flat surface and is read out by optical means (i.e. by a laser). (Philips). *See* COMPACT DISC, LASER, OPTICAL DIGITAL DISC, VIDEODISC.

optical disc storage. *See* OPTICAL DIGITAL DISC.

optical effects. In filming, special effects produced by an optical printer. *See* OPTICAL PRINTER.

optical fiber. *See* FIBER OPTICS.

optical input. In optical media, the light signal before it is converted into an electrical signal. (Philips).

optically assisted magnetic recording. *See* OPTICAL DIGITAL DISC.

optical mark recognition. (OMR) In character recognition, techniques for recording marks on documents. The marks are usually short lines or filled-in squares on formatted documents (e.g. answers to multiple-choice questions on examination papers, customer order documents). The document is positioned and scanned by a light beam and transmitted, or reflected light is collected by photocells. The significance of the data depends upon its coordinate position on the document and the signals from the photocells are input to a computer. *Compare* OPTICAL CHARACTER RECOGNITION. *See* PHOTOCELL.

optical medium. In optical media, medium employing optics for the storage and distribution of information. (Philips). *See* COMPACT DISC, OPTICAL DIGITAL DISC.

optical memory. *See* OPTICAL DIGITAL DISC.

optical negative. In filming, the negative used in printing the final picture.

optical printer. (1) In filming, a printing device that includes a camera and a projector to form a final optical negative. *See* OPTICAL NEGATIVE. (2) In filming, a device for photographing images from one film onto another for special effects. *See* SPECIAL EFFECTS.

optical recording. *See* OPTICAL DIGITAL DISC.

optical scanner. In office systems, a device that scans a page of printed text, and/or graphics, and produces a bit stream representing the text and/or graphics for entry into a computer or communication network. The bit stream of text represents the digital coding (normally ASCII) of the individual characters and can be used for entry into a word-processing package or desk-top publishing system. Optical scanners can therefore massively reduce the effort normally associated with keyboarding pages of text from a printed page into a computer. The scanner may operate line by line on the printed text or read a whole page in one pass.

The printed page is illuminated by a light source, and the reflected light is directed to a matrix of photodiodes. The electrical outputs from the photodiode matrix correspond to the patterns of white paper and printed text, or graphics, on the page. This analog output is digitized, and the corresponding matrix of binary data is stored in a random-access memory.

The binary matrix is then examined, and small areas of the matrix are systematically checked against patterns of alphanumeric characters. When such a pattern is found the ASCII code for that character is associated with that area of the matrix.

The two methods of matching data employed are template matching and pattern recognition. In the template method the patterns of characters, for a given font, are stored in programmable read-only memories (PROMs) usually on a 24 x 32 pixel frame. The stored pattern is looped through the template patterns until a match is found; sometimes digital filtering is employed to clean up the matrix images. The sets of PROMs can be changed according to the typeface employed on the printed page.

Pattern recognition is based upon artificial intelligence techniques and can be classified into font-specific and font-independent methods. In these techniques the topological features of the characters are recognized: font-specific recognizes them within a given font whereas font-independent can recognize a character independent of the font and can scan proportional fonts, recognizing spaces.

The scanning of graphics is more restricted than that of scanning text. The raster representation of graphics enables images to be edited by pixel manipulation, but more sophisticated manipulation of line art involves raster-to-vector conversion and the

recognition of geometric shapes, points, lines, arcs, etc. *See* ALPHANUMERIC, AMERICAN STANDARD CODE FOR INFORMATION INTERCHANGE, ARTIFICIAL INTELLIGENCE, BIT-MAPPED GRAPHICS, DESK-TOP PUBLISHING, FONT, FONT-INDEPENDENT, FONT-SPECIFIC, PATTERN RECOGNITION, PIXEL, PHOTODIODE, PROGRAMMABLE READ-ONLY MEMORY, RANDOM-ACCESS MEMORY, TEMPLATE MATCHING, WORD PROCESSING.

optical sound track. In filming, a photographic sound track. Light passes through the variable-density striations of the track and is then incident upon a photocell. The electric current variations from the cell are amplified and fed to a loudspeaker system. *Compare* MAGNETIC SOUND. *See* AMPLIFIER, PHOTOCELL.

optical storage. In optical media, storage of information in such a way that it can be read using optics. It is characterized by very high storage density. (Philips). *Compare* MAGNETIC DISK. *See* OPTICAL DIGITAL DISC.

optical technology. In optical media, a technology based upon the use of optical effects for the transmission or storage of information. (Philips). *See* OPTICAL DIGITAL DISC, OPTOELECTRONICS.

optical videodisc. *See* OPTICAL DISC, VIDEODISC.

optional. In standards, a feature not required by a particular standard or not required to meet an optional provision of the standard. (ANSI).

optoelectronics. In microelectronics, pertaining to a device that is responsive to, or that emits, coherent or non-coherent electromagnetic radiation in the visible, infrared or ultraviolet regions. *Compare* NON-LINEAR OPTICS. *See* COHERENCE, FIBER OPTICS.

OR. (1) A logical operation, A OR B has the result true if either, or both, of the logical variables A and B are true. The corresponding truth table is

A	B	A OR B
0	0	0
1	0	1
0	1	1
1	1	1

Compare AND. *See* BOOLEAN ALGEBRA, TRUTH TABLE, XOR. (2) *See* OPERATIONS RESEARCH.

ORACLE. In videotex, Optional Reception of Announcements by Coded Line Electronics; the teletext service operated by the UK Independent Broadcasting Authority. *See* TELETEXT.

Orange Book. In computer security, a set of criteria, for security in a single computer system with several users, designed by the US Department of Defense. The criteria are divided into divisions and classes. A division represents a major improvement in the overall confidence that can be placed in the computer to protect sensitive information. The divisions are divided into classes of increasing desirability from a computer security viewpoint.

Division D deals with minimal protection and contains only one class (i.e. those systems that have been evaluated, but fail to comply with the requirements for a higher evaluation class). Division C deals with discretionary protection, and classes in this division provide need-to-know protection and accountability of subjects for the actions they initiate.

Division B is concerned with mandatory protection. This division requires that the trusted computing bases preserve the integrity of sensitivity labels and employ them to enforce a set of mandatory access control rules. This division has three classes related to labelled security protection, structured protection and security domains.

The Division A is concerned with verified protection; it is characterized by the formal security verification of the mandatory and discretionary controls used to protect sensitive information processed and stored by the computer. *See* ACCOUNTABILITY, COVERT CHANNEL, DISCRETIONARY ACCESS CONTROL, DISCRETIONARY PROTECTION, DISCRETIONARY SECURITY, DOMAIN, GRANULARITY, LABEL, MANDATORY ACCESS CONTROL, NEED-TO-KNOW, OBJECT, REFERENCE MONITOR, SECURITY POLICY, SUBJECT, TRUSTED COMPUTING BASE.

Orbit. In online information retrieval, an information retrieval service operated by the System Development Corp. (SDC).

Orbital Test Satellite. (OTS) In communications, a satellite launched in 1978 for a series of telecommunication experiments and to test the viability of Ku band satellites for Europe. *See* EUTELSAT, GEOSTATIONARY SATELLITE, KU BAND.

ordinal. In data structures, an unsigned integer. When stored in eight bits, ordinals can assume values in the range 0–255, with 16 bits the range is 0–65 535. *Compare* INTEGER.

ordinate. In mathematics, the vertical axis of a two-dimensional coordinate graph. *Compare* ABSCISSA. *See* CARTESIAN COORDINATES, COORDINATE GRAPH. *Synonymous with* Y-AXIS.

Organization for Data Exchange and Teletransmission in Europe. (ODETTE) A European body that sets standards for document layout in order that they can be sent over a data network and understood by the recipient. *See* ELECTRONIC DOCUMENT INTERCHANGE.

original. In photography and recording, an initial photographic image or sound recording as compared with one produced by a duplication or reproduction process.

original equipment manufacturer. (OEM) A manufacturer who purchases equipment, adds value to it (e.g. by enhancing its capabilites or making it suitable for a specific application area) and resells it.

originator. In data communications, the person, institution or other entity that is responsible for and authorized to originate a message. (ANSI). *Compare* RECIPIENT. *See* MESSAGE.

OROM. In optical media, optical read-only memory; an optical digital disc, 5.25 inches in diameter with spiral or circular concentric tracks. *Compare* COMPACT DISC - READ-ONLY MEMORY. *See* OPTICAL DIGITAL DISC.

orphan. In printing, a line of type on its own at the top or bottom of a page. (Desktop). *See* WIDOW.

orthochromatic film. In photography, a black and white film insensitive to the colour red. *Synonymous with* ORTHO FILM.

ortho film. *Synonymous with* ORTHOCHROMATIC FILM.

orthographic projection. In computer graphics, a parallel projection in which the visual rays are perpendicular to the picture plane. *Compare* ISOMETRIC PROJECTION, OBLIQUE PROJECTION, PERSPECTIVE PROJECTION. *See* PARALLEL PROJECTION, PICTURE PLANE.

OS. *See* OPERATING SYSTEM.

OS/2. In programming, operating system for the PS/2. *Compare* PC.DOS. *See* OPERATING SYSTEM, PS/2.

OS-9. In programming, an operating system which forms the basis for the interactive compact disc operating system. (Philips). *See* COMPACT DISC – INTERACTIVE, CD REAL-TIME OPERATING SYSTEM, OPERATING SYSTEM.

oscillator. In electronics, a device that produces a sinusoidal signal of a specified frequency. *See* SINUSOIDAL.

oscilloscope. In electronics, a test instrument comprising a cathode ray tube, time base and amplifiers. It is used for displaying voltage waveforms. *See* AMPLIFIER, CATHODE RAY TUBE, TIMEBASE, WAVEFORM.

OSI. *See* OPEN SYSTEMS INTERCONNECTION.

OTP. In communications, Office of Telecommunications Policy, in the Executive office of the US President; an agency that develops and recommends US public policy in the area of telecommunications.

OTS. *See* ORBITAL TEST SATELLITE.

outage. In reliability, a period of system non-function due to a power supply failure.

outgoing access. In data communications, the ability of a network user to communicate with another user on a different network. *See* GATEWAY.

outline letter. In printing, a letter in which each stroke is represented by two lines (i.e.

one in which the inner part has been removed).

outlining capability. In word processing, a function that permits the system to deal with a multi-indented format and automatically generates the number scheme of the outline.

out-of-band signalling. In communications, a system in which control signals are transmitted at a frequency within the passband of the circuit, but outside the band normally used for voice transmission. *Compare* IN-BAND SIGNALLING. *See* PASSBAND, SIGNALLING.

out of phase. In electronics, a condition between two waveforms of the same frequency in which the waveform peaks do not coincide in time. If the maximum value of one sinusoidal waveform coincides with the minimum value of the other, the waveforms are 180° out of phase. *Compare* IN PHASE. *See* SINUSOIDAL.

output. (1) In computing, pertaining to the action, or the result, of transferring data from the internal storage of a computer to an external device or user. (2) Signals delivered from an audio or video device.

output-bound. Pertaining to a system in which the speed of performance is restricted by the speed of the output unit. *Compare* INPUT-BOUND. *See* OUTPUT UNIT.

output device. *Synonymous with* OUTPUT UNIT.

output feedback. (OFB) In data security, a stream cipher data encryption standard mode of operation. *Compare* CIPHER BLOCK CHAINING, CIPHER FEEDBACK, ELECTRONIC CODEBOOK. *See* DATA ENCRYPTION STANDARD, STREAM CIPHER.

output port. In optical media, an interface used for transferring information out of a computer. (Philips). *Compare* INPUT PORT. *See* INPUT/OUTPUT PORT.

output unit. In peripherals, a device that can receive data from a computer system. *Compare* INPUT/OUTPUT UNIT, INPUT UNIT. *Synonymous with* OUTPUT DEVICE.

overflow. (1) In computing, pertaining to a state in which the result of an arithmetic operation is greater than the value that can be stored in the associated storage location. *Compare* UNDERFLOW. (2) In communications, traffic, in excess of the capacity of channels on a particular route, that is offered an alternative route. (3) In word processing, a condition in which the information exceeds the available storage capacity. (4) In databases, a situation in which a record is allocated a storage area, by an addressing algorithm, and that location is already occupied. The system places the record in an appropriate free area and sets pointers to that area.

overhead bit. In codes, a bit that transmits no information, but is included for control or error-checking purposes. *See* PARITY CHECKING.

overhead projector. In audiovisual aids, a device that projects an image held on a flat, transparent acetate sheet up to about 10 x 10 inches square. A lecturer can write on the sheet during projection or successively build up a total projected image. *See* PROGRESSIVE DISCLOSURE.

overlap. (1) In computing, to perform one operation concurrently with another. *See* PARALLEL PROCESSING. (2) In computer graphics, the ability of two or more windows to be overlaid without any loss of data along the sides where the windows meet. *Compare* TILE. *See* WINDOW.

overlay. (1) In video, laying an image from one source on top of an image from another source. (Philips). *Compare* MIX. *See* CD-I DIGITAL VIDEO, OVERLAY CONTROL. (2) In computing, a method of running a large program with a limited allocation of internal storage. Specified sections of the program are held in backing storage until they are required for execution, when they are read into the internal storage, overwriting some other routine not currently required. This technique seriously slows down the execution of programs and the sections designated for overlay must be selected with care. *See* BACKING STORAGE, VIRTUAL STORAGE.

overlay control. In optical media, the mechanism which controls the transparency between planes in an interactive compact disc image. (Philips). *See* CD-I DIGITAL VIDEO, MULTIPLANE, OVERLAY.

overlay keyboard. *See* KEYBOARD OVERLAY.

overlay network. In communications, a network of transmission links and switching centres superimposed upon another network and interconnected with it at specific points.

overload. (1) In electronics, to draw an excessive current from a device. (2) In filming, to record sound at an excessive level.

overmodulation. In communications, an amplitude-modulated signal in which the amplitude of the carrier is reduced to zero for some part of the cycle of the modulating waveform. *Compare* COMPRESSION. *See* AMPLITUDE MODULATION.

overprinting. In printing, pertaining to printing over an area already printed. It is used to emphasize changes or alterations. (Desktop).

override. A parameter or value that replaces an earlier corresponding parameter or value.

overrun. In data communications, a loss of data caused by the inability of the receiving device to accept data at the rate at which it was transmitted. *Compare* UNDERRUN. *See* TRANSMIT FLOW CONTROL.

overs. (1) In printing, additional paper required to compensate for spoilage in printing. (2) In printing, a quantity produced above the number of copies ordered. (Desktop).

overscan. In television, the part of the television raster outside the visible area of the screen. *See* RASTER.

overstrike. In word processing, a method of producing a character not in the typeface by the appropriate superimposition of two other characters (e.g. a dollar sign produced by the superimposition of an S and a l).

overt channel. In communications security, a path within the system which is designed for the authorized transfer of data. *Compare* COVERT CHANNEL.

overtones. Frequencies that are multiples of the fundamental frequency. Any periodic waveform can be decomposed into a series of sinusoidal waveforms at the fundamental frequency and overtones. *See* FOURIER SERIES. *Synonymous with* HARMONIC.

overwriting. In computer security, the obliteration of recorded data by recording different data on the same surface. (FIPS). *Synonymous with* CLEARING.

OWF. *See* ONE-WAY FUNCTION.

ownership. In data security, the right of users to dispense and revoke privileges for objects they own. (e.g. access on programs and files). *See* ACCESS CONTROL, FILE.

P

P1. In data communications, the relay protocol of the CCITT X.400 message-handling standard. *Compare* P2, P3. *See* X.400.

P2. In data communications, a protocol, of the CCITT X.400 message-handling standard that defines the message header and various parts of the message. *Compare* P1, P3. *See* X.400.

P3. In data communications, the submission protocol, of the CCITT X.400 message-handling standard. *Compare* P1, P2. *See* X.400.

P31. In peripherals, a green, short-persistence phosphor used in monochrome displays. *Compare* P39. *See* PHOSPHOR DOTS.

P39. In peripherals, a green, long-persistence phosphor used in monochrome displays. *Compare* P31. *See* PHOSPHOR DOTS.

PABX. *See* PRIVATE AUTOMATIC BRANCH EXCHANGE.

pacing. In data communications, a method by which a receiving station controls the rate of transmission in order to avoid a loss of data.

pacing device. In audiovisual aids, a device to improve reading skills by indicating a word or phrase for a controlled period. *See* CONTROLLED READING DEVICE, TACHISTOSCOPE.

package. (1) In microelectronics, an integrated circuit chip and its housing. *See* INTEGRATED CIRCUIT. (2) In programming. *See* SOFTWARE PACKAGE.

package count. In microelectronics, the number of integrated circuits necessary to perform a specified function. *See* INTEGRATED CIRCUIT.

packaging. In microelectronics, the number of pins that can be connected to a chip. *See* CHIP.

packed decimal. In data structures, a data representation of a decimal number in which each byte, except the rightmost, represents two digits; the rightmost byte represents the sign and one digit. *See* BINARY-CODED DECIMAL, BYTE.

packet. In data communications, a self-contained component of a message, comprising address, control and data signals, that can be transferred as an entity within a data network. *See* PACKET SWITCHING.

packet assembler/disassembler. (PAD) In data communications, a device, used in conjunction with a packet-switching network that converts the character stream suitable for a simple terminal to packets, and vice versa. *See* PACKET, PACKET SWITCHING.

packet interleaving. In data communications, a form of multiplexing, in a packet-switching network, in which packets from various subchannels are interleaved onto a main channel. *See* MULTIPLEXING, PACKET, PACKET SWITCHING.

packet radio. In data communications, a network with radio links so that a packet may be received by more than one station. *See* ALOHA, PACKET SWITCHING.

packet sequencing. In data communications, a method of ensuring that packets arrive at the receiving station in the same sequential order in which they were transmitted. *See* DATAGRAM SERVICE, PACKET, PACKET SWITCHING.

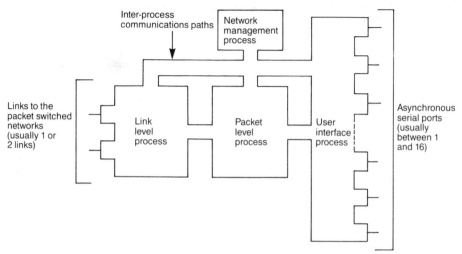

PAD components
Packet assembler/disassembler.

packet switching. In data communications, a method of message transmission in which each complete message is assembled into one or more packets that can be sent through the network, collected and then re-assembled into the original message at the destination. The individual packets need not even be sent by the same route. The communication channels are only occupied during the transmission of a packet as compared with a conventional circuit switching in which a connection is made and maintained for the duration of the complete message transmission. *Compare* CIRCUIT SWITCHING, MESSAGE SWITCHING. *See* DATAGRAM SERVICE, MESSAGE SWITCHING, PACKET, VIRTUAL CIRCUIT.

packet-switching exchange. (PSE) In data communications, the computer system that provides the interface between users and the node-to-node packet-switching network. The functions of the exchange include network protocol, packet sequencing and routing. *See* PACKET, PACKET SEQUENCING, PACKET SWITCHING, PROTOCOL, ROUTING.

packet-switching network. (PSN) In data communications, a network of devices that communicate between each other by transmitting packets addressed to particular destinations. *See* PACKET SWITCHING.

packet terminal. In data communications, a terminal in a packet-switching network capable of forming its own packets and interacting with a network character terminal. *Compare* CHARACTER TERMINAL. *See* PACKET, PACKET SWITCHING.

packing. In memory systems, the process of making the most effective use of storage by placing data elements into contiguous bit positions of words. *See* PACKED DECIMAL.

packing density. (1) In memory systems, the number of bits that may be stored per unit length of recording medium. *Compare* RECORDING DENSITY. *See* BITS PER INCH. (2) In microelectronics, the number of individual logic circuits per unit area on a chip. *See* CHIP.

PACX. In data communications, private automatic computer exchange; a switching and contention system that allows a range of terminals with different speeds to communicate, through a number of output ports, with several other devices such as computers. *See* CONTENTION, PORT.

PAD. *See* PACKET ASSEMBLER/DISASSEMBLER.

padding. In data security, the additional characters added to a plaintext message to ensure that its length is an integral number of blocks for encryption by a block cipher. *See* BLOCK CIPHER.

paddle. In peripherals, a hand-held controller used with microcomputers and video games to control the movement of the cursor or graphic display on the screen. *See* POINTING DEVICE, VIDEO GAME.

page. (1) In word processing, the amount of text designated by the operator to fit onto a sheet of paper. The usually accepted maximum for an A4 sheet is 52 single-spaced lines of 80 characters (i.e. 4160 characters). (2) In memory systems, an area of storage space. *See* PAGING. (3) In videotex, a screenful of information (24 lines x 40 characters) that can be accessed directly. *Compare* FRAME.

page description language. (PDL) In printing and computer graphics, a programming language for arranging text and graphics on an area equivalent to a printed page prior to printing by a raster image device such as a laser printer.

The importance of PDL is related to the development of laser printers and desk-top publishing. Conventional character printers provide for extremely limited control on the appearance of the printed page. Fonts and print sizes are prespecified, and the location of the printed material is fixed by character and line spacing. The only graphics available for conventional printers are those that can be constructed by the placement of printed characters. Laser printers, on the other hand, can produce any image within the constraints of the resolution of the printer, normally of the order of 300 dots per inch. This provides the user with the opportunity to develop attractive printed pages with a variety of typefaces, graphics, etc.

The PDL enables the user to specify the font and print size, and locate the text at any position on the page, or specify a variety of paths for the text (e.g. circular paths). In addition new characters (e.g. special mathematical symbols) may be defined and used. The graphics commands provide for the construction of geometric shapes, specification of line widths, fill areas with designated grey levels and the manipulation of bit graphic images, etc.

The language also contains conventional programming constructs: arithmetic operations, loops, conditional statements, macro routines, arrays, etc. to reduce the effort of specifying complex page layouts. *See* ARRAY, CONDITIONAL JUMP, DESK-TOP PUBLISHING, FONT, LASER PRINTER, LOOP, MACRO.

page end character. *Synonymous with* FORM FEED CHARACTER.

page frame. In memory systems, an area of storage that can store a page. *See* PAGE, PAGING.

page header. In teletext, the top row containing general information (e.g. magazine and page number, day and date, program source and clock time). *See* PAGE.

page make-up. *Synonymous with* MAKE-UP.

page mode. In peripherals, pertaining to terminals that usually have cursor-addressing or some local editing capability. *Compare* FORM MODE, SCROLL MODE.

page numbering. *See* AUTOMATIC PAGINATION.

page printer. In printing, a device that composes a whole page of text before printing. *Compare* LINE PRINTER. *See* PRINTER.

page proof. In printing, the stage following galley proofs in which pages are made up and paginated. (Desktop). *Compare* GALLEY PROOF. *See* PROOF.

page reader. In character recognition, an optical scanning device that examines many lines of text with a scanning pattern determined by program control and/or control symbols intermixed with input data. *See* OPTICAL SCANNER.

page scrolling. In peripherals, scrolling through a whole page of a document displayed on a visual display unit instead of just a line at a time. *See* VERTICAL SCROLLING.

page store. In videotex, a memory unit or audio cassette device that is capable of storing videotex pages for later playback. *See* MEMORY, PAGE.

page view terminal. *Synonymous with* GRAPHIC DISPLAY TERMINAL.

pagination. In printing, the process of splitting the text into pages, and perhaps columns within pages. It may also involve adding illustrations, headers, footers, page numbering, etc. *Compare* COMPOSITION. *See* AUTOMATIC PAGINATION, FOOTER, HEADER.

paging. (1) In memory systems, the transfer of pages of instructions or data between main memory and backing storage. *See* BACKING STORAGE, MAIN MEMORY, PAGE, VIRTUAL STORAGE. (2) In printing, making up into pages or numbering pages. *See* MAKE-UP. (3) In communications, the use of a pocket-sized device to alert the user that he or she is required on the telephone. *See* PAGING RECEIVER.

paging receiver. In communications, a pocket-sized electronic device that emits an audible signal or displays an alphanumeric message when a telephone call is made to the user. *See* RADIO PAGING.

paint. In computer graphics, to fill an area of display (e.g. with a colour, a cross-hatched pattern, etc.).

paint box. In computer graphics, a turnkey system that enables a designer to create colour images electronically. Typically the system comprises five basic elements: a tablet with a pressure-sensitive stylus, computer and software, digital frame store, hard disk and a colour monitor. Menu selection of commands is provided, controlling the selection of colours, brush size, paint mode (water colour, oils, airbrush, gouache), stencils, text, zooming, picture library, etc. The user draws across the tablet, and in some sophisticated systems the colour opacity is controlled by the pressure on the stylus. *See* DIGITIZING TABLET, HARD DISK, TURNKEY SYSTEM, ZOOM.

painter's algorithm. In computer graphics, an algorithm that uses a frame store to hold a three-dimensional image. It is based upon techniques employed by artists. When working with oils the artist first applies the image of distant objects working towards the nearer ones by overlaying paint to form an acceptable representation of true space, where distant objects are masked by closer ones. In the algorithm facets of distant objects are loaded into the frame store first and are then overlaid by near ones thus automatically achieving hidden surface removal. Difficulties arise, however, with concave objects since two objects mask each other at different parts of the picture. *See* FRAME STORE, HIDDEN SURFACE.

pairing. In television, a display fault in interlacing in which alternate scan lines are very close or superimposed. *See* INTERLACE.

PAL. *See* VIDEO STANDARDS.

Palapa. An Indonesian geostationary communications satellite. *See* GEOSTATIONARY SATELLITE.

Palatino. In printing, a Roman typeface with strong inclined serifs. *Compare* AVANTE-GARDE, BOOKMAN, COURIER, HELVETICA, HELVETICA NARROW, NEW CENTURY SCHOOLBOOK, OLDSTYLE, SYMBOL, TIMES ROMAN, ZAPF CHANCERY, ZAPF DINGBATS. *See* ROMAN, SERIF, TYPEFACE.

palette. In video and computer graphics, a range of colours analogous to those in a painter's palette. In interactive compact discs, a palette is used by the user communications manager to support the colour look-up table. The maximum size of the palette at any instant in time is 256 colours, with red, green and blue components each defined to eight-bit accuracy. (Philips). *See* CD-I DIGITAL VIDEO, COLOUR LOOK-UP TABLE, USER COMMUNICATIONS MANAGER.

PAM. *See* PULSE AMPLITUDE MODULATION.

pamphlet. In printing, an unbound treatise on a subject or current topic of interest.

panchromatic film. In photography, black/white film that is sensitive to all colours, thus giving good grey tones. *Synonymous with* PAN FILM.

pan film. *Synonymous with* PANCHROMATIC FILM.

pan scrolling. In peripherals, a form of vertical scrolling with a smoother movement of the text up the screen, similar to the movement of credits following a television program. *See* VERTICAL SCROLLING.

paper bail. In printing, a device on a printer to hold the paper against the platen.

paper jam. In printing devices, a condition in which the paper flow is inhibited causing overprinting of lines, etc.

paperless office. *Synonymous with* OFFICE OF THE FUTURE.

paper throw. In printing devices, paper movement at a rate in excess of the speed for normal line spacing.

parabolic antenna. In communications, a dish antenna in which the cross-section curve is parabolic; the perimeter of such antennae are usually circular. The focal point of parabolic antennae is not affected by the direction of the incident parallel radiation, and the mounting must therefore be adjusted for reception from a single satellite or microwave transmitter. *Compare* SPHERICAL ANTENNA. *See* DISH ANTENNA, FEEDHORN, FOCAL POINT.

paragraph assembly. In word processing, the production of completed documents from portions of text held in computer store. *See* BOILERPLATE.

paragraph mark. *See* REFERENCE MARK.

parallax. In optics, the apparent change of position of an object produced by an actual change of point of observation (e.g. two telegraph poles in a line of sight appear to move relative to one another if the eye is moved to one side).

parallel. (1) In computing, pertaining to processes operating concurrently or systems performing simultaneous actions or in simultaneous active states. *See* PARALLEL PROCESSING, PARALLEL TRANSMISSION. (2) In optics, pertaining to rays or lines that neither converge or diverge.

parallel circuit. In electronics, two or more circuits that share common input and output

nodes or connections. *Compare* SERIES CIRCUIT.

parallel communication. *See* PARALLEL TRANSMISSION.

parallel computer. In computing, a computer with multiple logic or arithmetic units enabling it to perform parallel operations or parallel processing. *Compare* SEQUENTIAL COMPUTER, SERIAL COMPUTER. *See* PARALLEL PROCESSING.

parallel fold. In printing, a folding method in which a sheet is folded and then folded again along a line parallel to the first fold.

parallel interface. In data communications, an interface that permits parallel transmission. *Compare* SERIAL INTERFACE.

parallel mark. *See* REFERENCE MARK.

parallel messages. In data security, stream cipher messages enciphered with the same cryptographic bit stream. *See* CRYPTOGRAPHIC BIT STREAM, STREAM CIPHER.

parallel operation. The performance of simultaneous and usually similar actions, on a related set of inputs. *See* PARALLEL PROCESSING, PARALLEL TRANSMISSION, SERIAL OPERATION.

parallel processing. In computing, pertaining to a system in which more than one process is active at a given instant. The term is sometimes applied to systems that have more than one processor, but where only one is active at any one time.

Conventional von Neumann architectures provide for strictly serial operation and are unsuitable for a wide range of problems involving massive computational tasks (e.g. weather forecasting, three-dimensional simulations, aerodynamics, computer speech and vision, artificial intelligence). The hardware of early computers was very expensive; only one processing unit was provided for all tasks requiring intelligent operation. As the cost of processing power decreased it became more economical to use a variety of processors, many dedicated to particular tasks. For example, many peripherals now have processing power so that input and output data can be locally processed, thus relieving the central computer of routine tasks, such as selecting pens on a plotter or rastering images. In other cases powerful processors are linked to share a total computational load, and this technique is termed multiprocessing.

Supercomputers increase computational speed by including more and more devices onto chips of ever-decreasing size. This development produces densely packed components which must be submerged in liquid coolants to dissipate the heat generated, and leads to extremely expensive units. Current supercomputers such as Cray, link together a small number, four, eight and 16, respectively, of state-of-the-art processors thus producing a combination of serial and parallel processing.

The Inmos transputer very large-scale-integrated chip contains a processor, memory and communications circuitry and was specifically designed for parallel processing. A parallel programming language Occam was designed for this chip, and programs optimized for one chip can be run on a number of transputers sharing a parallel network.

Computer architectures may be classified as SISD, SIMD, MISD and MIMD. Conventional serial computer architectures are single-instruction stream, single-data stream (SISD) (i.e. the instructions are executed sequentially although some degree of pipelining may be present. Vector or array processors have single-instruction stream, multiple-data stream (SIMD) architectures. In this case multiple processing elements are governed by a single control unit, with limited memory to processor communication. The applications areas are those in which identical algorithms are applied to different sets of data in parallel. Multiple instruction streams, single data stream (MISD) systems would operate with several processors performing various operations on the same set of data, whereas multiple instruction stream, multiple data stream (MIMD) involve multiprocessor and tightly coupled parallel-processing computer systems.

Parallel processing may also be considered from the viewpoint of the conceptual architecture. The dataflow concept is one of the most common. Dataflow architectures may be further subdivided into data-driven and demand-driven. In the case of data-driven machines the processes are performed when all the necessary input data for an operation becomes available. Demand-driven devices, on the other hand, only undertake function evaluations as the results are required elsewhere.

Currently parallel processors employing a comparatively large number of simple processors are designed for quite specific tasks, and the development of general-purpose computers will depend upon advances in programming languages and techniques that can exploit the power of the architecture without excessive programming effort. *Compare* SERIAL COMPUTER. *See* ARRAY PROCESSOR, DATA-DRIVEN, DATAFLOW, DEMAND-DRIVEN, MULTIPLE-INSTRUCTION STREAM MULTIPLE-DATA STREAM, MULTIPLE-INSTRUCTION STREAM SINGLE-DATA STREAM, MULTIPROCESSING, PIPELINING, OCCAM, SINGLE-INSTRUCTION STREAM MULTIPLE-DATA STREAM, SINGLE-INSTRUCTION STREAM SINGLE-DATA STREAM, TRANSPUTER, VON NEUMANN. *Synonymous with* SIMULTANEOUS PROCESSING.

parallel projection. In computer graphics, a form of perspective projection in which the observer is assumed to be at infinity so that the lines of projection are parallel. This form of projection simplifies depth calculations and the computation of hidden line algorithms. *Compare* PERSPECTIVE PROJECTION. *See* HIDDEN LINE.

parallel publishing. In communications, a form of publishing in which the information is presented both in printed version and electronically. The printed version may be provided later or, in some cases (e.g. newspaper stories), there is an embargo on the presentation of the electronic form until a specified time after the printed version.

parallel storage. In memory systems, a storage device in which the words or bytes are accessed simultaneously or concurrently. *See* BYTE, WORD.

parallel-to-series converter. In computing, a device that converts a word, or byte, represented in the form of parallel data into an appropriate series of pulses for serial transfer. *Compare* SERIES-TO-PARALLEL CONVERTER. *See* SERIAL TRANSMISSION.

parallel transmission. (1) In data communications, the simultaneous transmission of elements constituting the same code (e.g. each bit of a word is sent simultaneously on an individual wire). It has a higher bit rate than corresponding serial transmission, but requires eight wires to convey individual bytes and is therefore mainly used for transmission over short distances (e.g. for buses within a computer). *Compare* SERIAL TRANSMISSION. *See* BUS. (2) In data communications, a technique for the simultaneous transmission of data using different carrier frequencies. *See* FREQUENCY MODULATION.

parameter. (1) A quantity that individually, or as part of a set, specifies a system or process. (2) A specified variable of a system or process that temporarily assumes the properties of a constant.

parameter passing. In programming, pertaining to the method employed to pass a parameter to a subroutine. *See* PARAMETER, SUBROUTINE.

parent. In data structures, the element, in a hierarchical system, that is immediately superior to the element in question (e.g. in a tree structure the node that points to the particular node in question). *See* TREE STRUCTURE.

parenthesis-free notation. In mathematics, any notation for expressions that does not require the use of parentheses to indicate the order in which individual parts of it are to be evaluated. *See* PREFIX NOTATION, POSTFIX NOTATION.

parity. In codes, pertaining to a condition in which the number of items in a group is odd or even. *See* PARITY CHECKING.

parity bit. In codes, the bit added to a bit grouping, if necessary, in order to produce parity. *See* PARITY, PARITY CHECKING.

parity checking. In codes, a form of redundancy checking. The convention odd or even parity is selected, the number of bits in a grouping is counted, and a parity bit is added, if necessary, to produce parity with the selected convention. Upon receipt of the grouping the number of bits is checked, and an error reported if the selected parity is not found. Parity checking detects the loss, or unwanted inclusion, of an odd number of bits. *See* PARITY, PARITY BIT, REDUNDANCY CHECKING. *Synonymous with* ODD/EVEN CHECK.

parse. In programming, to resolve a string of characters (e.g. representing a program statement) into its elemental parts as defined by (say) the programming language. *See* COMPILER, LEXICAL SCAN.

part. A piece of equipment or a component.

partial dial tone. In communications, a high tone indicating to the telephone caller that dialing has not been completed within a specified time or that not enough digits have been dialed.

partial update. In peripherals, the modification of part of the text, graphics or natural picture displayed on a screen. (Philips). *See* NATURAL PICTURES.

party line. In communications, a line shared by several telephone subscribers, possibly with selective calling. *See* SELECTIVE CALLING. *Synonymous with* SHARED LINE.

Pascal. In programming, a language named after the mathematician Blaise Pascal. It is widely used as a teaching language because its structure and clarity encourage good programming practices. It was originated by Wirth at the Federal Institute of Technology, Zurich in 1970. *See* ADA, BLOCK STRUCTURE, C, STRUCTURED PROGRAMMING.

pasigraphy. A proposed universal system of writing in which the characters represent ideas rather than words.

pass. (1) In programming, a complete cycle (i.e. input, processing, output) of a program execution. (2) In programming, a complete scan of the source code by the compiler or assembler. Compilation and assembly routines make an initial pass to collect details of all names of variables, etc. used in the program. *See* ASSEMBLER, COMPILER.

passband. In communications, the range of signal frequencies that can be satisfactorily transmitted on a given channel (e.g. the passband on voice-grade channels is 300–3000 Hz).

PASSIM. US President's Advisory Staff on Scientific Information Management.

passim. In printing, a term used in footnotes meaning 'here and there'.

passive attack. In data security, an attack in which the intercepted data is recorded and later analyzed. *Compare* ACTIVE ATTACK. *See* PASSIVE WIRETAPPING.

passive bus. In communications, an integrated services digital network point-to-multipoint wiring configuration that allows a number of terminals to be connected in parallel to one interface. It is only available with a basic rate access interface. *See* BASIC RATE ACCESS, INTEGRATED SERVICES DIGITAL NETWORK.

passive device. In electronics, equipment incapable of amplification or power generation. *Compare* ACTIVE DEVICE. *See* AMPLIFIER.

passive mode. In computer graphics, a mode of operation in which the user is unable to modify or interact with the displayed image.

passive threat. In computer security, a potential breach of security, the occurrence of which would not change the state of the system; hardware, software, data, etc. would remain unaltered. Such a threat could arise from unauthorized reading of files or the use of a computer system for an unauthorized application. *Compare* ACCIDENTAL THREAT, ACTIVE THREAT, DELIBERATE THREAT, LOGICAL THREAT, PHYSICAL THREAT. *See* THREAT.

passive wiretapping. In computer security, the monitoring and/or recording of data while the data is being transmitted over a communications link. (FIPS). *Compare* ACTIVE WIRETAPPING. *See* PASSIVE ATTACK.

passphrase. In computer security, a sequence of characters, longer than the acceptable length of a password, that is transformed by a password system into a

virtual password of acceptable length. (FIPS). *See* PASSWORD, VIRTUAL PASSWORD.

password. In computer security, a popular form of knowledge test for access control. A password is a string of alphanumeric data or a phrase that must be entered into a system to gain access to a physical area or a resource. Normally the password is associated with a user identification (user id); the user inputs the user id and then responds to the request for the password. The user id is usually transmitted in clear to the host computer, but the password may be protected in transmission. The use and misuse of passwords are now common. The factors affecting password management are listed below.

(a) Users must be trained and motivated to ensure the effectiveness of the password access control. In particular they must be fully aware of the repercussions of failure to protect their passwords and to ensure that measures are taken to detect a lack of password security (e.g. by auditing accesses).
(b) Passwords should be easy to remember so that users need not make written records of them.
(c) Passwords should be changed regularly.
(d) System records of passwords should be protected (e.g. by encryption).
(e) The system must combat attempts to derive a password by successive logon attempts.
(f) Passwords must not be displayed at a terminal, etc. during logon.

Compare PIN. *See* ACCESS CONTROL, DYNAMIC PASSWORD, EXPIRED PASSWORD, LOGON, ONE-TIME PASSWORDS, PASSPHRASE, TIME-DEPENDENT PASSWORD, USER ID, VIRTUAL PASSWORD. *Synonymous with* KEYWORD.

paste-up. In printing, the various elements of a layout mounted in position to form camera-ready artwork. (Desktop). *See* ARTWORK, CAMERA-READY COPY.

PA system. *Synonymous with* PUBLIC ADDRESS SYSTEM.

patch. (1) In programming, to replace a small set of instructions with a corrected or modified set. (2) In programming, to modify a program by changing its object code rather than its source code. *See* OBJECT CODE, SOURCE CODE. (3) In electronics, to make an electrical connection.

path. In programming, a method of specifying a file in a tree-structured directory. The full specification of a file involves the names of all the subdirectories in the path from the root to the leaf containing the file. *See* DIRECTORY, FILE, ROOT DIRECTORY, TREE-STRUCTURED DIRECTORY.

pattern recognition. In artificial intelligence, the automatic recognition of shapes, patterns and curves. The human optical system and brain are far superior to the most advanced computer system in matching images to those stored in memory. This area is subject to intensive research effort because of its importance in the fields of robotics, and its potential areas of application (e.g. reading handwritten script). *See* MACHINE VISION, ROBOTICS.

pattern-sensitive fault. In reliability, a fault whenever a particular pattern of data arises.

pause. (1) In recording. a temporary interruption of an audio recording or playback. (2) In computing, an interruption in program execution. (Philips).

pause control. In recording, a feature of some tape recorders that permits the tape movement to be stopped without switching from the play or record settings.

pause retry. In data communications, a network control program option enabling a user to specify the number of times that a message should be transmitted in the event of transmission errors and the time interval between each attempt.

PAX. *See* PRIVATE AUTOMATIC EXCHANGE.

pay cable. In cable television, a wired subscription service with a surcharge for optional programs. *See* PAY PER VIEW, PREMIUM TELEVISION.

pay per view. In cable television, pertaining to motion pictures released to subscription television networks and for which subscribers pay an extra fee for viewing. *See* PAY CABLE, PREMIUM TELEVISION, SUBSCRIPTION TELEVISION.

pay television. *Synonymous with* SUBSCRIPTION TELEVISION.

P box. In data security, permutation box; a component of an encryption algorithm that applies a transposition cipher on the input signal. *Compare* S BOX. *See* DATA ENCRYPTION STANDARD, TRANSPOSITION CIPHER.

PBX. *See* PRIVATE BRANCH EXCHANGE.

PC. *See* PERSONAL COMPUTER.

PC board. *See* PRINTED CIRCUIT BOARD.

PC.DOS. In computing, a disk operating system virtually identical with MS.DOS and adopted by IBM for its range of personal computers. *See* MS.DOS.

P channel. In optical media, one of the eight (P–W) compact disc subcode channels. The P channel carries the music flag, indicating the presence or absence of a music track. (Philips). *See* COMPACT DISC, MUSIC FLAG, SUBCODE CHANNEL.

p-channel MOS. In microelectronics, a metal oxide semiconductor (MOS) device in which all conduction is through p-type silicon. *Compare* N-CHANNEL MOS. *See* FIELD EFFECT TRANSISTOR, METAL OXIDE SEMICONDUCTOR, P-TYPE MATERIAL.

PCK. *See* PROCESSOR-CONTROLLED KEYING.

PCM. *See* PLUG-COMPATIBLE MANUFACTURER, PULSE CODE MODULATION.

PCM audio. (1) In audio, a pulse code-modulated (PCM) audio signal. *See* PULSE CODE MODULATION. (2) In optical media, a digital audio compact disc (CD-DA) audio signal after the first stage of encoding (i.e. a multiplexed signal with six 32-bit stereo samples in each audio frame. (Philips). *See* COMPACT DISC – DIGITAL AUDIO, MULTIPLEXING.

PCU. *See* PERIPHERAL CONTROL UNIT.

PDC. Permanent data call. *Synonymous with* PERMANENT VIRTUAL CIRCUIT.

PDI. *See* PICTURE DESCRIPTION INSTRUCTION.

PDL. *See* PAGE DESCRIPTION LANGUAGE.

PDM. *See* PULSE DURATION MODULATION.

PDN. *See* PUBLIC DATA NETWORK.

PE. (1) In word processing, page end character. *Synonymous with* FORM FEED CHARACTER. (2) In printing. *See* PRINTER'S ERRORS.

peak. (1) In character recognition, an unwanted mark extending outwards beyond the stroke edge of a character. *See* STROKE EDGE. (2) In electronics, the maximum positive or negative signal excursion of a signal.

peak envelope power. In communications, the average power supplied to the antenna transmission line by the transmitter during one radio frequency cycle, at the crest of the modulation envelope, under normal operating conditions. *See* MODULATION.

peculiar. *Synonymous with* SPECIAL SORT.

peer entity authentication. In communications security, the action of communicating parties seeking to verify each others identities. *See* AUTHENTICATION, MASQUERADING.

pegging. In recording, a sharp swing in the needle of VUmeter caused by a sudden noise. *See* VUMETER.

pel. *See* PICTURE ELEMENT.

penetration. In data security, an attack on the security of a computer system, undertaken to test the effectiveness of the security and to highlight any areas of weakness. *See* PENETRATION TESTING.

penetration testing. In computer security, the use of special programmer/analyst teams to attempt to penetrate a system for the purpose of identifying any security weaknesses. (FIPS). *See* PENETRATION.

per cent denial. In communications, the average percentage of attempted calls, in the busy hour, that are blocked due to network loading. It is a measure of the grade of service in a dial access circuit group. *See* DIAL ACCESS.

perfect binding. In printing, a common method of binding paperback books. After the printed sections have been collated, the splines are ground off and the cover is glued on. (Desktop). *See* SPLINE.

perfecting. In printing, a method of printing in which both sides of the paper are printed and the paper is ready for folding.

perfector. In printing, a rotary press that prints first one side, then the other, of a sheet, in one pass through the machine. *See* PERFECTING.

perfect secrecy. In information theory, a condition defined by the situation in which the conditional probability that the plaintext message P was sent, if ciphertext message C was received, is equal to the probability that plaintext message P was transmitted. Thus receipt of the ciphertext message provides no additional information to an attacker on the nature of the plaintext message.

perforations. A series of small linearly spaced holes or cuts on a form to facilitate tearing along a desired line.

performance standard. General design criteria defining the desired result without specifying the method of achieving that result. (ANSI). *Compare* DESIGN STANDARD.

perigee. In communications, the point at which a satellite is at a minimum distance from earth in its orbit. *Compare* APOGEE. *See* COMMUNICATIONS SATELLITE SYSTEM.

period. In mathematics, the time interval between two corresponding points on successive cycles of a periodic system. *Compare* FREQUENCY.

periodic. In mathematics, pertaining to any phenomenon that consistently repeats the same cycle of events.

periodic audit. In data processing, a verification of a file or of a phase of processing intended to check for problems and encourage future compliance with control procedures.

peripheral. In computing, a device, under the control of the central processing unit, that performs an auxiliary action in the system (e.g. input/output, backing storage). *See* BACKING STORAGE, CENTRAL PROCESSING UNIT, INPUT/OUTPUT.

peripheral control unit. (PCU) In computing, a unit that provides the necessary interfacing between a peripheral device and the computer input/output system. It provides the decoding of the computer commands relating specifically to a particular device. It also develops the necessary control voltage levels and the timing for the operation of the peripheral device. *See* PERIPHERAL, PERIPHERAL INTERFACE ADAPTOR. *Synonymous with* DEVICE CONTROLLER.

peripheral interface adaptor. (PIA) In computing, a device that provides interface functions between the computer bus and its peripherals. Typical functions include bit serial-to-bit parallel conversion, buffering, addressing, monitoring status and generating interrupts. *See* BUS, INTERRUPT, MICROCOMPUTER, PARALLEL TRANSMISSION, PERIPHERAL, SERIAL TRANSMISSION.

peripheral software drivers. In programming, programs that enable a user to control and communicate with a peripheral. *See* PERIPHERAL.

permanent data call. *Synonymous with* PERMANENT VIRTUAL CIRCUIT.

permanent file. In programming, a file that is stored for later use after the session in which it was created has been terminated. *See* WORKING DATA FILE. *Compare* SCRATCH FILE,

permanent memory. *Synonymous with* NON-VOLATILE STORAGE.

permanent virtual circuit. (PVC) In data communications, a special type of virtual call service in which the logical links between specific terminals are permanently set up so that call set up and release procedures are

eliminated. *See* VIRTUAL CIRCUIT. *Synonymous with* PERMANENT DATA CALL.

permeability. In electronics, the ratio of magnetic flux density in a material to the magnetic field acting on it.

permutation. In mathematics, any one of the total possible number of positional arrangements in a group. *Compare* COMBINATION.

permutation index. In library science, a technique used in machine indexing; each entry in the index is a cyclic permutation of all the words in the original document title. *See* KEYWORD IN CONTEXT.

persistence. In peripherals, the continuation of light emission from phosphor on a cathode ray tube screen after excitation by the electron beam. *See* CATHODE RAY TUBE, FLICKER, PHOSPHORESCENCE. *Synonymous with* AFTERGLOW.

persistence of vision. A physiological effect in which the eye's response to a visual stimulation remains for a short period after the removal of the stimulus. At the average cinematic screen illumination, the average eye detects no flicker for frequencies of intermission above approximately 16 per second. *See* ANIMATION, FLICKER, SILENT SPEED.

persistent conductivity imaging. In printing, an electrophotographic imaging process using photoconductive materials, which retain their increased conductivity for relatively long periods after the light source has been removed. *See* ELECTROPHOTOGRAPHIC PROCESS, PHOTOCONDUCTIVITY.

persistent object. In computer security, a technique in which a resource is given a secret name known only to the programs which can use it, and reference to that resource is then made an inaccessible component of the executable objects which use the resource. For example, a file is given a name and that name is included in the source code of application programs that are allowed to access it. The application programs exist only in a compiled form on the computer, and the name of the file is then removed. The resource is thus hidden from all programs except those which 'know' its secret name. *See* APPLICATION PROGRAM, SOURCE CODE.

personal computer. (PC) In computing, a term generally applied to more powerful microcomputers intended for business applications. *See* MICROCOMPUTER.

personal computer security. The protection of data stored and processed on a personal computer against unauthorized disclosure or modification, and the protection of the hardware and storage media against loss, modification or damage. *See* ACCESS CONTROL, AUDIT TRAIL, BACKUP/RESTORE, RESIDUES PROBLEMS, SOFTWARE PROTECTION, VAN ECK PHENOMENON.

personal computing. In applications, computing performed by an end user on a personal computer, including machine operation and often involving word processing, spreadsheet and database applications. Personal computing is characterized by the informal approach, simplified procedures and on-demand availability, in contrast to conventional electronic data processing. *Compare* ELECTRONIC DATA PROCESSING. *See* DATABASE, END-USER COMPUTING, ELECTRONIC DATA PROCESSING, SPREADSHEET, WHAT IF, WORD PROCESSING.

personal data. In legislation, as defined by the UK Data Protection Act, 1984, data consisting of information that relates to a living individual who can be identified from that information (or from that and other information in the possession of the data user), including any expression of opinion about the individual, but not any indication of the intentions of the data user in respect of that individual. *See* DATA, DATA PROTECTION.

personal disclosure. In database security, a situation in which a user can deduce a previously unknown sensitive statistic concerning an individual. Such disclosure can be approximate, positive or negative. *See* COMPROMISE, INFERENCE CONTROL, NEGATIVE DISCLOSURE,

personal identification number. *See* PIN.

personalization. In microelectronics, the committing a mask- or field-programmable

device to a specific customer requirement. *See* FIELD-PROGRAMMABLE, MASK-PROGRAMMABLE, SEMI-CUSTOM DESIGN.

personal productivity. The degree of efficiency achieved by an individual in the performance of a task. (Philips).

personal productivity software. *Synonymous with* PERSONAL PRODUCTIVITY TOOL.

personal productivity tool. In programming, a software package, such as word processing or a spreadsheet aimed that is improving personal productivity. (Philips). *See* PERSONAL PRODUCTIVITY. *Synonymous with* PERSONAL PRODUCTIVITY SOFTWARE.

personnel security. In computer security, the procedures established to insure that all personnel who have access to any sensitive information have the required authorities, as well as all appropriate clearances. (FIPS).

perspective. In computer graphics, a depth cue in which distant objects are rendered smaller than corresponding objects closer to the observer. *See* DEPTH CUE, THREE-DIMENSIONAL GRAPHICS.

perspective grid. In computer graphics, a grid comprising a perspective view of parallel lines in three orthogonal planes as seen with a specified cone of vision. *See* CONE OF VISION, PERSPECTIVE PROJECTION.

perspective projection. In computer graphics, a projection of a solid object onto a picture plane produced by drawing lines from each significant point of the object through the picture plane to the eye of the observer. *Compare* ISOMETRIC PROJECTION, OBLIQUE PROJECTION, ORTHOGRAPHIC PROJECTION, PARALLEL PROJECTION. *See* PICTURE PLANE.

PERT. In mathematics, program evaluation and review technique; a method used to facilitate the supervision and control of complex projects. *See* CRITICAL PATH METHOD.

pertinent. A quality implying a close logical relationship with, and importance to, the matter under consideration.

petal printer. *Synonymous with* DAISY WHEEL.

Petri net. In mathematics, a method of modelling concurrent systems. The net comprises a set of places, a set of transfer bars and a set of directed edges. A single directed edge connects an input, or output, place to a transition bar, but a place may be linked to a number of different transition bars. The state of a concurrent system is represented by the presence of tokens in places; a transition bar can fire only if there is at least one token in each of its input places. When a bar fires it removes one token from each of its input places and deposits one token in each of its output places. No two bars can fire simultaneously. This technique facilitates the detection of potential deadlocks, looping, etc. in concurrent systems. *See* CONCURRENT PROGRAMMING, DEADLOCK.

pf. *See* PICOFARAD.

phase. In mathematics, an aspect when brought into relation with another aspect. *See* IN PHASE, OUT OF PHASE, PHASE DELAY.

phase angle. In mathematics, a measure of the phase relationship between two sinusoidal waveforms. 'In phase' corresponds to a phase angle of 0°, 360°, 720°,.... *See* IN PHASE, OUT OF PHASE, PHASE, SINUSOIDAL.

phase delay. In communications, the time delay represented by a change in the phase of a sinusoidal wave in passing through two points on a transmission path.

phase equalizer. *Synonymous with* DELAY EQUALIZER.

phase modulation. In communications, a method of modulation in which the phase of the sinusoidal carrier is varied in accordance with the modulating signal. *Compare* AMPLITUDE MODULATION, FREQUENCY MODULATION, PULSE MODULATION. *See* CARRIER, MODULATION, PHASE, SINUSOIDAL.

phase shift keying. (PSK) In data communications, a method of changing the phase of a sinusoidal signal to represent binary data. If only two discrete phases are employed,then each phase corresponds to a binary 1 or 0. If four phase shifts are used then each one may correspond to a dibit. *See* BINARY PHASE SHIFT KEYING, DIBIT, PHASE MODULATION, QUADRATURE AMPLITUDE MODULATION, SINUSOIDAL.

phasing. In communications, an adjustment in a facsimile transmission achieved by a phasing signal to ensure that the reproduced picture corresponds with the original. *See* FACSIMILE.

phon. In acoustics, a measure of sound intensity equivalent to one decibel at 1000 Hz. *See* DECIBEL.

phoneme. In man–machine interfaces, the smallest element of spoken language which distinguishes one utterance from another (e.g. the word bit comprises three phonemes: 'b', 'i' and 't'). *See* ALLOPHONE, SPEECH SYNTHESIZER.

phonetic coding. In audio, a method of encoding speech, or speech-related sound, on the basis of defining the phonemes or phoneme combinations used. (Philips). *See* PHONEME, PHONETIC SYNTHESIS, SPEECH SYNTHESIZER.

phonetic speech. *See* SYNTHESIZED SPEECH QUALITY.

phonetic synthesis. In man–machine interfaces, a speech synthesis technique in which phonemes are linked together and processed to produce the speech output. *Compare* VOCAL TRACT SYNTHESIZER, WAVEFORM ENCODER. *See* PHONEME, PHONETIC CODING, SPEECH SYNTHESIZER.

phonetic transcription. A means of suggesting the pronunciation to the reader using a transformation of the text into another alphabet.

phosphor dots. In electronics, the matrix of dots on a cathode ray tube screen or television set that emits light when bombarded by an electron beam. In colour displays three different types of dots, emitting the colours red, green or blue (RGB), are tightly clustered. *See* CATHODE RAY TUBE, RGB.

phosphor efficiency. In electronics, the ratio of the quantity of light energy emitted by a phosphor dot to the quantity of energy

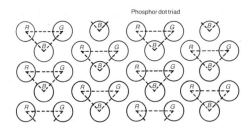

Phosphor dot triad

phosphor dots
Arrangement of phosphor dot triads in a shadow mask tube (R=red; Gr=green; B=blue).

received from the excitation beam. *See* CATHODE RAY TUBE, PHOSPHORESCENCE.

phosphorescence. In electronics, the phenomenon in which certain materials emit light following irradiation by an appropriate form of energy. *See* PHOSPHOR DOTS.

photo. (1) A prefix meaning light. (2) An abbreviation for photograph.

photocell. In optoelectronics, a device employing a photoelectric effect. *See* PHOTO-ELECTRIC. *Synonymous with* PHOTOELECTRIC CELL.

photochromism. In optics, a reversible change of colour produced by exposure to light.

photocomposition. *Synonymous with* PHOTOTYPESETTING.

photoconductivity. In optoelectronics, a phenomenon in which the resistance of a piece of semiconductor material decreases if it receives light energy. *See* SEMICONDUCTOR.

photoconductor. In optoelectronics, a photocell that employs the phenomenon of photoconductivity. *See* PHOTOCELL, PHOTO-CONDUCTIVITY.

photocopy. A photographic copy from an original. *See* PHOTOSTAT.

photodielectric process. In printing, an electrophotographic imaging process in which a photoconductive layer is charged and exposed to a light pattern, and an image is produced on a non-photosensitive dielec-

tric surface. *See* DIELECTRIC, ELECTROPHO-TOGRAPHIC PROCESS, PHOTOCONDUCTIVITY.

photodigital memory. In memory systems, a storage cell produced by writing data onto a film with a laser beam or focused light. Binary data is written by exposing the film for a 1 bit, and vice versa. When the film is developed it forms a read-only memory; it is scanned by a light beam and the transmitted light is collected by a photodiode. *See* BIT, LASER, PHOTODIODE. *Synonymous with* PHOTO-OPTICAL MEMORY.

photodiode. In optoelectronics, a light-sensitive semiconductor diode. The conductivity varies with the intensity of received light. *See* PHOTOCONDUCTIVITY.

photodirect lithography. In printing, a process in which lithographic plates are made direct from the original without an intermediate negative stage. *See* PHOTOLITHOGRA-PHY.

photoelectric. In optoelectronics, pertaining to phenomena in which incident light energy produces an electrical effect. *See* PHOTOCELL, PHOTOCONDUCTIVITY, PHOTO-EMISSION, PHOTOVOLTAIC.

photoelectric cell. *Synonymous with* PHOTOCELL.

photoemission. In optoelectronics, a phenomenon in which light falling onto a material causes the emission of electrons from the surface. *Compare* PHOTOCONDUCTI-VITY, PHOTORESISTIVE, PHOTOVOLTAIC.

photoengraving. In printing, the making of metal relief plates by acid etching on a photographically produced image on metal. *See* RELIEF PRINTING.

photography. The formation of a permanent record of an optical image by exposing a sensitized surface to light or other form of radiant energy.

photogravure. In printing, a photomechanical process in which the printing is performed from a recessed surface and the paper comes into direct contact with the plate. *Compare* OFFSET PRINTING. *See* PHOTO-MECHANICAL.

photoheadliner. In printing, a machine that produces display type by photographic methods. In some versions the machines have special lenses for producing condensed, expanded, slanted or other distorted letter forms.

photolettering. *See* PHOTOHEADLINER.

photolithography. In printing, a method of selectively etching a surface according to a pattern on a mask. The surface is coated with a photoresist material, and the mask is placed in contact with it. The masked surface is exposed to light, the mask is removed, and the photoresist material is developed chemically. The photoresist material is then selectively wasted away according to whether it has or has not been exposed to light. The surface, unprotected by developed photoresist, is then etched away and finally the remaining photoresist is removed. *See* CHIP, ETCHING, LITHOGRAPHY, PHOTORESIST. *Synonymous with* PHOTOLITHO-GRAPHY.

photomechanical. In printing, a complete assembly of type, line art and halftone art, in the form of film positives onto a transparent base from which autopositive diazo proofs can be obtained for checking, and from which a control film negative can be made for the production of printing plates. *See* HALFTONE.

photomechanical plates. In printing, plates produced by exposing positive or negative film on a photosensitive coated plate and then applying chemicals to produce a distinction between printing and non-printing parts. *See* PHOTOENGRAVING, PHOTOLITHOGRAPHY, PHOTOMECHANICAL.

photometry. The science of light measurement.

photomicrography. In photography, a photograph of a magnified image, usually made through a microscope, of a small object. *Compare* CINEMICROGRAPHY, MICRO-PHOTOGRAPHY.

photomontage. In photography, the production of a composite image by the super-imposition and juxtaposition of images from various sources.

photon. A packet of electromagnetic energy. According to Planck's quantum theory, energy is not transmitted in continuous amounts, but in discrete quanta, or photons, and the quantity of energy in a photon is directly proportional to the frequency of radiation.

photonics. Technology employing optical–electronic effects.

photo-optic memory. *Synonymous with* PHOTODIGITAL MEMORY.

photoplastic. An image-recording technique that employs heat or light to deform the surface of a special plastic film.

photopolymer. In printing, a plastic printing plate material which is rendered insoluble in certain solutions by the action of light.

photoresist. Pertaining to photosensitive materials that react to light by hardening. *Compare* PHOTORESISTIVE. *See* CHIP, NEGATIVE RESIST, POSITIVE RESIST.

photoresistive. In optoelectronics, pertaining to a phenomenon in which light falling on a semiconductor releases electrons from parent atoms, causing a reduction in resistance (i.e. an increase in conductivity). *Compare* PHOTOEMISSION, PHOTORESIST, PHOTOVOLTAIC. *See* PHOTOCONDUCTIVITY.

photosensor. In optoelectronics, a device that converts light into an electrical signal. (Philips). *See* PHOTOELECTRIC.

photostat. In printing, a thin photocopy used as part of a paste-up layout.

phototelegram service. In communications, a facsimile service operated by British Telecom. The documents are received by central offices and forwarded to ultimate recipients by express post.

phototext. In printing, text matter set by means of phototypesetting. *See* PHOTO-TYPESETTING.

phototransistor. In optoelectronics, a device that combines the ability to detect light and to provide gain. *Compare* PHOTODIODE. *See* GAIN.

phototypesetting. In printing, the production of textual typesetting by photographic means. *See* TYPESETTING. *Synonymous with* FILMSETTER, PHOTOCOMPOSITION.

phototypography. In printing, the process of producing matter from graphic reproductions via the use of all photomechanical means — cameras, photoenlargers, photocomposing machines and photosensitive substrates. *See* PHOTOMECHANICAL.

photounit. In printing, the unit of a phototypesetter housing the optics, light and energy source and photographic material, on which the typographic image is produced. *See* PHOTOTYPESETTING.

photovoltaic. In optoelectronics, pertaining to a phenomenon in which light falling on the device produces a voltage across it. *Compare* PHOTOCONDUCTIVITY, PHOTOEMISSION, PHOTORESISTIVE.

phracker. In computer security, a person who combines phone 'PHReaking' with computer 'hACKing.' *See* HACKER, PHREAK.

phreak. In communications security, a 'PHone fREAK'; a person fascinated by the telephone system. Commonly, an individual who uses personal knowledge of the telephone system to make calls at the expense of another. *Compare* HACKER. *See* PHRACKER, TELEPHONE INTRUSION.

physical database. In databases, the form that the database is held in for storage, including any pointers that it may contain. A number of different logical databases may be based upon the same physical database. *Compare* LOGICAL DATABASE.

physical data independence. In databases, pertaining to the composition of databases which enable the physical storage structure to be changed without affecting the logical structure. *Compare* LOGICAL DATA INDEPENDENCE. *See* DATA INDEPENDENCE.

physical layer. In data communications, the bottom layer in the ISO Open Systems Interconnection model. This layer is concerned with the transmission of the raw bit stream. *Compare* APPLICATION LAYER, DATA LINK LAYER, NETWORK LAYER, PRESENTATION LAYER, SESSION LAYER, TRANSPORT LAYER. *See* BIT STREAM, OPEN SYSTEMS INTERCONNECTION.

physical record. (1) In data structures, a record associated with a specific area of physical storage. (2) In data structures, the largest unit of data that can be transmitted in a single read or write operation. *Compare* LOGICAL RECORD.

physical threat. In computer security, a threat potentially affecting the actual existence and physical condition of the computer facilities (e.g. theft of equipment, fire, terrorist attack). *Compare* ACCIDENTAL THREAT, ACTIVE THREAT, DELIBERATE THREAT, LOGICAL THREAT, PASSIVE THREAT. *See* THREAT.

PIA. *See* PERIPHERAL INTERFACE ADAPTOR.

pica. (1) In printing, a point system of measurement equivalent to 12 points or 4.217 millimetres. (2) In printing, a typewriter spacing of 10 characters to the inch. *Compare* ELITE. *See* TYPEWRITER FACES. *Synonymous with* TEN PITCH.

pi character. In printing, a type character not included in the font. *See* FONT. *Synonymous with* SPECIAL SORT.

Pick. In computing, a virtual memory, multiuser operating system designed to facilitate information processing and the development of business application programs. It is named after its designer Richard Pick. *See* MULTIUSER, VIRTUAL STORAGE.

picking. In printing, the effect of ink being too tacky and lifting fibers out of the paper. It shows up as small white dots on areas of solid colour. (Desktop).

pickup. In recording, the stylus, cartridge and supporting arm of a disc player.

pickup tube. In television, the tube in a television camera that accepts a visual image and provides an electrical signal corresponding to that image. The image is focused upon a surface coated with a photoconductive material. This surface is scanned by an electron beam, which produces an electrical signal corresponding to the conductivity, and hence illumination, at the corresponding point on the surface. *See* PHOTOCONDUCTIVITY.

pico. A prefix for one-million-millionth (i.e. 10^{-12}).

picofarad. (pf) In electronics, a capacitance of one-million-millionth of a farad. *See* FARAD, CAPACITANCE.

picosecond. (psec) One-millionth of a microsecond. *See* PICO, MICROSECOND.

pictograph. A pictorial sign resembling the thing that the sign represents. *See* GLYPH, ICON.

picture. In programming, a character string used to describe the length and type of data that may be stored in a field of a record, etc. *See* FIELD, RECORD.

picture description instruction. (PDI) In computer graphics, a collection of operation codes that specify the shape and placement of graphic primitives on the screen. The operation codes are followed by a variable number of operands which specify the actual or relative coordinates of the shape (e.g. the end coordinates of a rectangle's diagonals). Some PDIs specify environmental conditions for the image (e.g. set colour). *See* ALPHAGEOMETRIC, GRAPHIC PRIMITIVE, NAPLPS.

picture differencing. In computer graphics, a technique of image processing in which the static picture backgrounds of a sequence of frames are blanked, and the system displays only moving objects, etc. *See* FRAME, IMAGE PROCESSING.

picture element. *Synonymous with* PIXEL.

picture-in-picture. *See* PIP.

picture plane. In computer graphics, the plane in which the image is formed in perspective projections. Lines are drawn from representative points of the object, under view to the eye of the observer. A plane superimposed between the object and the observer is designated the picture plane, and the two-dimensional image is formed by joining the points of intersection of the program lines with this plane. *See* PERSPECTIVE PROJECTION.

Picture Prestel. In videotex, an experimental system which was developed to test the display of a small television-quality picture on a viewdata page. A complete television frame would require about an hour to transmit by viewdata codes over telephone lines. In Picture Prestel only a small area of the screen is used to display a picture (e.g. a signature in a bank retrieval system), and data compression techniques are employed to minimize the transmission time and terminal storage requirements. *See* ALPHAPHOTOGRAPHIC, VIEWDATA.

picture processing. *Synonymous with* IMAGE PROCESSING.

picture stop. In optical media, an instruction encoded in the vertical blanking interval on a videodisc to stop the player on a predetermined frame. *See* FRAME, VIDEODISC.

picture transmission. In communications, a facsimile system with special regard to tone reproduction in which the photographic process is used at the receiving end. *See* FACSIMILE.

picture writing. The use of pictures to represent literally or figuratively things or actions in the recording of events. *See* PICTOGRAPH.

piece fractions. In printing, a fraction that is contained within one symbol and to which one character width is allocated.

pie graph. In computer graphics, a diagram representing proportions as various sized slices of a circular pie (e.g. to represent the manner in which a corporation's budget is spent under the various expenditure headings). *Synonymous with* SECTOR CHART, WHEEL CHART.

piezoelectric. In electronics, the property of certain crystals which change their electrical characteristics (i.e. resistance or voltage) when physical pressure is applied, or change their physical dimensions when an electric voltage is applied. *See* RESISTANCE.

piggyback.   *See* BETWEEN-THE-LINES ENTRY, PIGGYBACK ENTRY, PIGGYBACKING.

piggyback entry.   In data security, the illegitimate access to a computer system via another's legitimate connection (e.g. via an unattended terminal logged onto a remote system). *See* LOGON.

piggyback form.   In word processing, a continuous form carrying stationery, which is usually pasted on. It is often used for printing continuous letters and envelopes.

piggybacking.   In data communications, a method of sending acknowledgements with outgoing messages (e.g. in high-level data link control messages from A to B contain information on the frames received by A from B). *See* ACKNOWLEDGEMENT, FRAME, HIGH-LEVEL DATA LINK CONTROL.

PILOT.   In programming, a textually based computer language developed for computer-assisted learning applications. *See* COMPUTER-ASSISTED LEARNING, COMPUTER-BASED TRAINING.

PIN.   (1) In computer security, personal identification number; a unique, personal number that must be entered by a user before a remote terminal or point-of-sale terminal can be used to transfer information or complete a transaction. *Compare* PASSWORD. *See* POINT-OF-SALE TERMINAL. (2) In banking, the four- to 12-position alphanumeric code or password the customer possesses for authentication. (ANSI). *See* PIN MANAGEMENT AND SECURITY.

pinch plotter.   In peripherals, a hybrid of flatbed and drum plotter. A motor drives the bed along the X-axis and a pen mount moves the paper along the Y-axis. *Compare* DRUM PLOTTER, FLATBED PLOTTER. *See* PLOTTER.

pinch roller.   In recording, a roller on a tape recorder that holds the tape against the capstan during play and record. *See* CAPSTAN.

pincushion distortion.   In optics, an image distortion in which square objects appear

with the corners stretched out. It is caused by lens aberration. *Compare* BARREL DISTORTION. *See* ABERRATION.

pin-feed platen.   In printing, a cylindrical platen that moves the paper by sprocket feed. *See* SPROCKET FEED.

PIN management and security.   In banking and data security, the set of processes involved in the generation, assignment, delivery, issuance, storage, entry, verification, transmission, deactivation and destruction of personal identification numbers (PINs).
   PINs may be employed in two types of environment: (a) an organization where selected employees or members use PINs to gain access to the organization's facilities (e.g. computer systems, databases); (b) an electron funds transfer or electron funds transfer point-of-sale network serving one or more financial institutions and an extremely large, diffuse customer base. *See* ELECTRON FUNDS TRANSFER, ELECTRON FUNDS TRANSFER POINT OF SALE, PIN.

pin photodiode.   In electronics, a p-intrinsic n-photodiode; a comparatively large segment of intrinsic silicon is sandwiched between p- and n-type silicon layers. The diode is biased so that no current flows in the absence of light radiation. When visible light or infrared radiation strikes the diode, hole-electron pairs are formed, and the carriers are swept to the appropriate electrode causing a current flow in the external circuit. *Compare* AVALANCHE PHOTODIODE. *See* ELECTRON, HOLE, PHOTODIODE.

PIP.   In video, picture-in-picture; a facility whereby a reduced picture corresponding to a second video image is inset into the main image of a television or video display. *Compare* MPIP. *See* DIGITAL VIDEO.

pipelining.   In computing, a method of speeding up computer operations by simultaneous operations on instructions. In a strictly sequential processor all operations on one instruction are completed before processing of the next begins. In a pipelining system the third (say) instruction may be fetched from store at the same time as the second one is being decoded and the operations required by the first one are in execution. *See* PARALLEL OPERATION.

pipes. In computing, a Unix facility that passes data from one program to another. The output from the first program is placed in a temporary file, the second program is then run with the temporary file as a source of input data, etc. *See* UNIX.

PIRA. UK Paper, Printing and Packaging Industries Research Association.

Pira. In online information retrieval, a database supplied by the Research Association for the Paper and Board, Printing and Packaging Industries and dealing with pulp, paper and packaging.

piracy. In programming, the illicit copying and distribution of software, usually for financial gain. *Compare* SOFTWARE CREEP. *See* SOFTWARE PROTECTION.

pitch. (1) In typing, the horizontal spacing of characters. *See* TYPEWRITER FACES. (2) In filming, the distance between leading edges of film sprocket holes. (3) In acoustics, the frequency of a sound wave. (4) In communications, a rotation of a satellite about a horizontal axis perpendicular to the direction of flight. *Compare* ROLL, YAW. *See* COMMUNICATIONS SATELLITE SYSTEM.

Pittler classification. A system of classifying technical components using a digital code. *See* CLASSIFICATION.

pixel. In computer graphics, the smallest element of a display space that can be addressed. A picture element will have one or more attributes of colour, intensity and flashing. *Synonymous with* PICTURE ELEMENT. (2) In optical character recognition, an area on a document that coincides with the scanning spot at a given moment. (3) In micrographics, the area of the finest detail that can be effectively reproduced.

pixel multiplication. In optical media, a technique used in decoding pictorial information in an interactive compact disc system to make high-resolution pixel information compatible with a lower-resolution system. (Philips). *See* CD-I DIGI-

TAL VIDEO, HIGH RESOLUTION, LOW RESOLUTION.

pix lock. In video recording, a state in which the playback system is in synchronism with the external synchronizing pulses. *See* SYNCHRONIZATION. *Synonymous with* AUTOMATIC LOCK.

PKC. *See* PUBLIC KEY CRYPTOGRAPHY.

PL/1. In programming, a high-level language designed to encompass both commercial and scientific applications. It contains many of the features of ALGOL, COBOL and FORTRAN plus some facilities not available in previous languages. *See* ALGOL, COBOL, FORTRAN, HIGH-LEVEL LANGUAGE.

PLA. *See* PROGRAMMABLE LOGIC ARRAY.

plaintext. In data security, intelligible text or signals that have meaning and that can be read or acted upon without the application of any decryption. (FIPS). *Compare* CIPHERTEXT. *See* DECRYPT. *Synonymous with* CLEAR DATA, CLEARTEXT.

PLAK. In videotex, public service look-alike system.

plan. A scale drawing with a view vertically above the object or area.

plane. In computer graphics, one layer of a bit-mapped display. (Philips). *See* BIT-MAPPED DISPLAY, MULTIPLANE.

planetary camera. In micrographics, a type of microfilm camera in which the document being photographed and the film remain in a stationary position during exposure and the document is on a plane surface at the time of filming. *Compare* ROTARY CAMERA, STEP-AND-REPEAT CAMERA. *See* MICROFILM. *Synonymous with* FLATBED CAMERA.

planographic. In printing, pertaining to processes in which the printing surface is neither raised nor incised. *Compare* INTAGLIO, LETTERPRESS. *See* LITHOGRAPHY.

planted record. In database security, a type of attack in which plaintext records are added to a encrypted database, and the subsequent changes in database contents provide details of plaintext/ciphertext pairs. *See* CIPHERTEXT, PLAINTEXT, RECORD.

plasma display. *Synonymous with* THIN-WINDOW DISPLAY.

plasma panel. In peripherals, a form of flat-screen display. The device consists essentially of two optically flat glass plates separated by a few hundredths of a millimetre, sealed and filled with neon/argon gas. Vertical parallel conductors are etched on the inside of the front plate, and horizontal parallel conductors are similarly etched on the inside of the rear plate. Each junction, individually addressable, forms a pixel and when activated with a voltage produces a light point of ionized gas. The device has the advantage of simplicity, ruggedness and shape over a conventional cathode ray tube (CRT). It requires no refresh circuitry, has no flicker and is much flatter than a CRT. It can, however, only be used for monochrome displays. *See* CATHODE RAY TUBE, FLAT-SCREEN DISPLAY, PIXEL, VISUAL DISPLAY UNIT.

plate. (1) In printing, a relief, intaglio or planographic printing surface. *See* PLANO-GRAPHIC, INTAGLIO, RELIEF PRINTING. (2) In printing, an illustration of a book printed separately from the text and usually on different paper.

platen. (1) A rubber-covered cylinder in a typewriter or printer around which the paper is guided. (2) In photography, a mechanical device that holds the film in the focal plane during exposure.

plausible reasoning. *Synonymous with* INEXACT REASONING.

playback. In recording, the retrieval of recorded signals, data or information in a form suitable for a human operator.

playback print rate. In computing and word processing, the automatic printing speed of a printer.

plex database. *Synonymous with* NETWORK DATABASE.

plex structure. *Synonymous with* NETWORK STRUCTURE.

Plexus. In library science, a prototype microcomputer-based expert system, developed by the Central Information Service of the University of London to be used in guiding clients with problems to sources of potential assistance. *See* EXPERT SYSTEMS.

plotter. In computing, an output unit used to produce graphs or diagrams. *See* DIGITAL PLOTTER, DRUM PLOTTER, ELECTROSTATIC PLOT-TER, FLATBED PLOTTER, INCREMENTAL PLOTTER, X–Y PLOTTER.

plotting mode. In word processing, a form of printer operation in which dots, or some other suitable characters, are printed at appropriate points to produce a graph or diagram.

PLP. In videotex, AT&T's presentation level protocol; an alphageometric standard. *See* ALPHAGEOMETRIC, NAPLPS.

plug-compatible manufacturer. (PCM) A manufacturer who produces equipment that can be operated in conjunction with another manufacturer's equipment when connected by plug and cable; a term commonly employed in connection with IBM equipment.

plug-in module. *Synonymous with* INSERT MODULE.

plug-in unit. In electronics, an assembly of permanently interconnected components that can be easily plugged into an item of equipment.

PMBX. In communications, private manual branch exchange. *See* PRIVATE BRANCH EXCHANGE.

PMOS. *See* P-CHANNEL MOS.

PMR. In communications, private mobile radio. *See* CELLULAR RADIO.

p–n–p transistor. In electronics, a bipolar transistor with the emitter and collector connected to p-type semiconductor material and the base connected to n-type semiconductor material. *Compare* N–P–N TRANSISTOR. *See* TRANSISTOR.

PN sequence. A sequence of apparently random bits that repeats itself eventually. *See* PSEUDORANDOM NUMBERS.

POB. Point of banking. *Compare* POS.

pocket banking. *See* SUPERSMART CARD.

pocket computer. In computing, a pocket-sized microcomputer with limited processing power, usually restricted to pocket calculator, electronic diary and address book functions, etc. *Compare* BRIEFCASE-PORTABLE. *See* MICROCOMPUTER.

POCSAG. In communications, UK Post Office Code Standardization Advisory Group.

point. In printing, an Anglo-American unit of type measure; one point is equal to 0.3515 millimetres. The measurement in points is taken from the top of a capital letter to the bottom of the descender. *Compare* DIDOT POINT, EM. *See* DESCENDER, PICA.

pointer. (1) In peripherals. *Synonymous with* TRACKING SYMBOL. (2) In data structures, a variable that holds the address of an item of data. In a simple chained list a pointer will hold the address of the next item in the list.

pointing device. In peripherals, a device that enables the user to select a facility by pointing at it or create an image by effectively moving the screen cursor. *See* DIGITIZING TABLET, JOYSTICK, LIGHT PEN, MOUSE, PUCK, TOUCHSCREEN, TRACKER BALL.

point of sale. (POS) A position where a customer pays for goods or services. *See* POINT-OF-SALE TERMINAL.

point-of-sale terminal. In peripherals, a terminal used at a location where customer transactions are performed and designed for particular input functions. In many cases they will be operated by unskilled staff and have facilities for direct reading of data (e.g. automatic reading of coded tags or bar codes). More sophisticated terminals may be linked to the customer's bank for automatic account debiting. *See* BAR CODE, ELECTRONIC FUNDS TRANSFER POINT OF SALE.

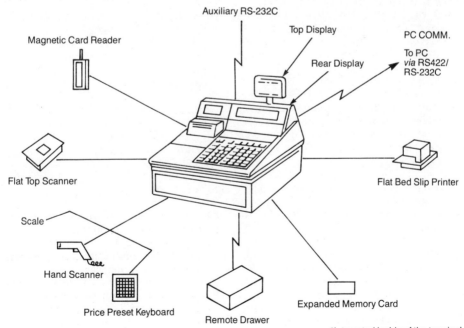

point of sale terminal
PoS terminal with interfaces.

point-to-point. In data communications, pertaining to connection between two, and only two, terminal installations. The connection may include switching facilities. *Compare* MULTIDROP CIRCUIT.

Poisson distribution. In mathematics, a probability distribution pertinent to traffic flows in computing and communication systems. It is used to estimate the size, and waiting times, of queues for service systems in which the arrival and service rates have certain specified statistical properties. *Compare* GAUSSIAN DISTRIBUTION, UNIFORM DISTRIBUTION.

polar coordinates. In mathematics, a method of specifying the location of a point in space. A line is drawn from the origin to the point, and the location is specified in terms of the length of the line and the angle, or angles, between the line and specified axes. *Compare* CARTESIAN COORDINATES.

polar diagram. In recording, a diagram of the pick-up pattern of a microphone.

polarity reversal. In television, an effect in which the polarity of an electronic signal is reversed. The grey scale and colours of the corresponding picture are also reversed. *See* GREY SCALE.

polarization frequency reuse. In communications, a technique of increasing the capacity of a communications satellite in which the same frequency band is used for orthogonally polarized signals. *Compare* SPATIAL FREQUENCY REUSE. *See* FREQUENCY REUSE, POLARIZED.

polarized. Pertaining to electromagnetic radiation in which the electromagnetic vectors are not uniformly distributed in the transverse plane.

polarized return to zero. In communications, a method of signalling with three states, positive and negative signals represent one each of the binary states and the line condition returns to zero voltage between the signals. *Synonymous with* POLAR TRANSMISSION.

polarized return to zero recording. In computing, a storage technique in which binary zeros are represented by magnetization in one direction and binary ones by magnetization in the opposite sense. *Compare* NON-POLARIZED RETURN TO ZERO RECORDING.

polar mount. In communications, a form of adjustable mounting for a dish antenna that enables the reflector to be moved, in elevation, to follow a satellite or to change for reception from one geostationary satellite to another. *Compare* AZ/EL MOUNT. *See* DISH ANTENNA, GEOSTATIONARY SATELLITE.

Polaroid camera. In photography, trade name for a camera that produces a self-developing photograph.

polaroid filter. In photography, a filter that attenuates the intensity of transmitted light according to the plane of polarization. *See* POLARIZED.

polar orbit. In communications, the trajectory of a communications satellite whose orbital plane includes the axis of the earth. *Compare* EQUATORIAL ORBIT, INCLINED ORBIT. *See* COMMUNICATIONS SATELLITE SYSTEM.

polar signalling. In communications, signalling as used in telegraphy where a direct current of one polarity represents a 1 bit and the opposite polarity represents a 0 bit. *Compare* POLARIZED RETURN TO ZERO. *See* NON-RETURN TO ZERO.

polar transmission. *Synonymous with* POLARIZED RETURN TO ZERO.

pole tips. In recording, the part of the magnetic head that protrudes radially beyond the head wheel of a video recorder. *See* HEAD WHEEL.

POLIS. In online information retrieval, Parliamentary Online Information System; a database supplied by Scicon Ltd for the House of Commons Library (UK) and dealing with UK government.

Polish notation. *See* PREFIX NOTATION.

polling. In data communications, a method of controlling terminals on a multidrop or clustered data network where each terminal is interrogated in turn by the computer to determine whether it is ready to receive or

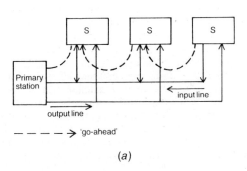

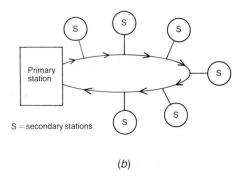

S = secondary stations

- - - - → 'go-ahead'

(a)

(b)

polling
(a) hub polling; (b) loop polling.

transmit data. Data transmission is only initiated by the computer. *See* CLUSTER, HUB POLLING, MULTIDROP CIRCUIT.

polyalphabetic cipher. In data security, a substitution cipher employing a cluster of monoalphabetic ciphers. A cryptographic key is repeatedly written above the plain-text, and the key letter indicates which particular monoalphabetic cipher is to be employed to encrypt the corresponding plaintext letter. *Compare* MONOALPHABETIC CIPHER. *See* CIPHER, CRYPTOGRAPHY, SUBSTITUTION CIPHER.

polynomial code. In codes, an error-detecting code in which a mathematical operation is performed on the data to be sent and is repeated at the receiving end. A check is then performed to detect any data corruption in transmission or transfer. Typically the total obtained from the summation of the binary numbers, corresponding to the bit patterns of the transmitted characters, is divided by an constant specified for the code. The remainder is transmitted as the cyclic check character at the end of the message. At the receiving location the total is then performed as above with the cyclic check character added. If division by the same arbitrarily selected constant is performed and the remainder is zero, the message is accepted as uncorrupted. *See* CYCLIC REDUNDANCY CHECK, ERROR-DETECTING CODE.

POP-2. In programming, an artificial intelligence language derived from LISP. *See* ARTIFICIAL INTELLIGENCE, LISP.

pop filter. In recording, an acoustic filter for use on microphones to reduce overload

effects arising from the sound of hard p's and breath blasts, etc.

pop off. In filming, the instantaneous removal of a pictorial information (e.g. a title from a frame). *Compare* POP ON.

pop on. In filming, the instantaneous appearance of a new image on an existing scene. *Compare* POP OFF.

port. In computing, a functional unit of a node through which data can leave or enter a data network or a computer. *See* NODE, PORT PROTECTION DEVICE.

portability. In programming, pertaining to programs in a form that enables them to be run on more than one computer system.

porta pak. In television, a self-contained, portable, battery-operated video recorder, often with a monitor that can be employed as a viewfinder or for playback. *See* MONITOR, VIDEO RECORDER.

port control. In peripherals, the control of input and output ports on a computer. An example is the control of the printer output port such that the text stored in the computer is transferred to a printer for printing to paper. (Philips). *See* PORT.

port protection device. (PPD) In computer security, a device connected to the communications port of a host computer that has the function of authorizing user access to the port. *Compare* SECURITY MODEM. *See* CALL BACK, TELEPHONE INTRUSION.

portrait. In printing, an upright image or page where the height is greater than the width. (Desktop). *Compare* LANDSCAPE.

POS. Point of sale. *Compare* POB. *See* POINT-OF-SALE TERMINAL.

positional operator. In online retrieval, a system-specific operator that defines the degree of adjacency or proximity of terms to be retrieved. *Synonymous with* CONTEXTUAL OPERATOR.

position-independent code. In programming, a code that can be loaded into, and executed from, any area of store without modification or relinking.

positive. In printing, a true photographic image of the original made on paper or film. (Desktop).

positive feedback. A feedback arrangement in which the output signal is effectively added to the input signal and the resulting signal is fed into the system. In some cases this can result in a self-sustained oscillation. *Compare* NEGATIVE FEEDBACK. *See* FEEDBACK.

positive interlace. In television, a camera system producing exactly spaced sequential scanning of picture tube field lines. *Compare* RANDOM INTERLACE. *See* FIELD, INTERLACE.

positive resist. In microelectronics, pertaining to an imaging process in which the exposed region of the photoresist is removed in the development process. *Compare* NEGATIVE RESIST. *See* CHIP.

positive response. In data communications, a response indicating that the message was received successfully. *See* ACKNOWLEDGEMENT.

post. In computing, to enter data into a record. *See* RECORD.

postcondition. In programming, an assertion, expressed in terms of values of program variables, or relationships between them, that characterizes the state of a program immediately after the execution of a given set of statements. A program is said to be totally correct if it commences in a state corresponding to the precondition and terminates in a state corresponding to the postcondition. *Compare* PRECONDITION. *See* PROOF OF PROGRAM CORRECTNESS.

postcoordinate indexing. In library science, a method of indexing in which the indexing terms are assigned individually and the searcher uses his own combination of terms. *Compare* PRECOORDINATE INDEXING.

post-editing. In machine translation, the editing of material produced by the machine translator to improve the style and make it more acceptable to the end user. *Compare* PRE-EDITING.

poster session. A form of conference in which presenters put their papers in poster form on display boards. Delegates are free to wander around and enter into discussion with presenters, according to their individual interests.

postfix notation. In computing, a logical notation for the representation of arithmetic operations that removes the necessity for brackets to indicate the order in which they are to be performed. The operators follow their associated operands e.g. $(a + b) * c$ would be represented as $ab + c *$. This form considerably facilitates the production of machine code instructions corresponding to high-level language statements. *Compare* INFIX NOTATION, PREFIX NOTATION. *See* HIGH-LEVEL LANGUAGE, MACHINE CODE, OPERAND, OPERATOR. *Synonymous with* REVERSE POLISH NOTATION, SUFFIX NOTATION.

posting. In online information retrieval, the number of records retrieved by a search. *See* HIT.

post mortem. In computing, pertaining to the analysis of an operation after its execution. *See* POST MORTEM DUMP.

post mortem dump. In computing, a dump undertaken after execution to facilitate post mortem analysis. *See* DUMP, POST MORTEM, RESCUE DUMP, SELECTIVE DUMP.

post-production premastering. In optical media, the process of editing, assembly, evaluation, revision and coding of intermediate materials for a videodisc. *Compare*

PREPRODUCTION. *See* INTERMEDIATE MATER-IALS, VIDEODISC.

PostScript. In programming, a page description language produced by Adobe Systems. *See* PAGE DESCRIPTION LANGUAGE.

Post Telephone and Telegraph. (PTT) A government-operated common carrier outside the USA (e.g. British Telecom). *See* COMMON CARRIER.

potentiometer. In electronics, a resistor with a movable contact that may be used as an adjustable resistor or voltage attenuator. *See* ATTENUATION, RESISTOR.

POTS. In communications, 'plain old telephone service'; one used for a conventional telephone service as compared with data communications.

power. (1) In mathematics, the number of times that a quantity is multiplied by itself. (2) In electronics, the product of the instantaneous voltage and the corresponding instantaneous current. In AC circuits, the power consumed in a circuit is zero if the voltages and currents are exactly 90° out of phase with each other. *See* OUT OF PHASE.

powerhouse. In communications, a Federal Communications Commission-licensed radio station permitted to operate at 50 kilowatts power on a frequency assigned to no other full-time licensee.

power keyboard. *See* MAGNETIC KEYBOARD.

power-limited. In communications, pertaining to a situation in which the full bandwidth of a channel cannot be used because the power of the signal is too low to achieve a required signal-to-noise ratio. Some early communications satellite systems were power-limited. *See* BANDWIDTH, COMMUNICATIONS SATELLITE SYSTEM, SIGNAL-TO-NOISE RATIO.

power pack. In electronics, a unit to supply power voltages for equipment.

power restart. In reliability, a facility that detects a fall off in the supply voltage and initiates an interrupt routine enabling the computer to prepare itself for the power loss. The program can be resumed without error when power is restored.

PPD. *See* PORT PROTECTION DEVICE.

PPM. (1) *See* PULSE POSITION MODULATION. (2) In printing, pages per minute.

PRA. *See* PRIMARY RATE ACCESS.

pragmatics. The relationship between signs and those who use them. *See* SEMIOTICS.

pre-amplifier. In electronics, a unit that is used to boost very weak input signals (e.g. the unit that accepts the antenna signals in a television set). *See* AMPLIFIER.

precedence. In programming, rules that govern the order in which operators are applied to operands (e.g. consider $a + b \times c$, the expression is ambiguous unless it is understood that multiplication has precedence over addition). *See* POSTFIX NOTATION.

precedence prosign. In communications, a group of characters indicating the manner in which the message is to be handled.

PRECIS. (1) In library science, Preserved Context Index System; a subject indexing system developed for the British National Bibliography. (2) In library science, precoordinate indexing system. *See* PRECOORDINATE INDEXING.

precision. In mathematics, the degree of discrimination with which a quantity is quoted (e.g. a two-digit number can be selected from a 100 possibilities). *Compare* ACCURACY.

precision ratio. *Synonymous with* RELEVANCE RATIO.

precondition. In programming, an assertion, expressed in terms of values of program variables, or relationships between them, that characterizes the state of a program immediately before the execution of a given set of statements. A program is said to be totally correct if it commences in a state corresponding to the precondition and terminates in a state corresponding to the postcondition. *Compare* POSTCONDITION. *See* PROOF OF PROGRAM CORRECTNESS.

precoordinate indexing.   In library science, an indexing method in which the terms are combined at the time of indexing a document, the combination of terms being shown in the entries. Thus the document can be found listed under the combination of terms. *Compare* POSTCOORDINATE INDEXING. *See* ENTRY, INDEX, TERM.

Predicasts.   In online information retrieval, business and industrial databases that provide both statistics and information. *Synonymous with* PTS.

predicate.   (1) In mathematics, a logical statement made about some state (i.e. it can only assume the value true or false). (2) In databases, a term of a relational calculus expression that specifies the condition to be satisfied by the terms in the retrieved set. *See* RELATIONAL CALCULUS, RELATIONAL DATABASE.

predicate transformer.   In programming, a set of statements that transform a precondition into a postcondition. *See* POSTCONDITION, PRECONDITION, PROOF OF PROGRAM CORRECTNESS.

prediction filters.   In audio, the filters used in adaptive delta pulse code modulation encoding to achieve effective response to audio frequency distribution fluctuations. (Philips). *See* ADAPTIVE DELTA PULSE CODE MODULATION, LINEAR PREDICTIVE CODING.

pre-editing.   In applications, the editing of source material for a machine translation system to make it compatible with the syntax expected by the translator, to remove ambiguities, etc. *Compare* POST-EDITING. *See* LIMITED SYNTAX, MACHINE TRANSLATION.

pre-emphasis.   (1) In recording, the amplification of the high-frequency components of a video-recorded signal prior to the modulation process. *Compare* DE-EMPHASIS. *See* FREQUENCY MODULATION. (2) In recording and communications, an increase in the level of certain signal frequencies relative to the other frequencies, prior to recording or broadcasting, in order to preserve overall frequency definition. Subsequent de-emphasis during reproduction reduces the pre-emphasized frequencies to their proper level. It is used to improve signal-to-noise ratio. (Philips). *Compare* DE-EMPHASIS. *See* SIGNAL-TO-NOISE RATIO.

preferred term.   In definitions, a term recommended as a standard.

prefix.   In communications, a code at the beginning of a message.

prefix notation.   In programming, a method for the representation of one-dimensional expressions, without the need for brackets, by preceding an operand string with a string of operators. The operand string may itself contain operators. *Compare* INFIX NOTATION, POSTFIX NOTATION.

pre-mastering.   (1) In recording, the process in which basic program material is processed to produce a master tape. (2) In optical media, the stage between authoring and mastering in an interactive compact disc and interactive videodisc. (Philips). *See* AUTHORING PROCESS, COMPACT DISC – INTERACTIVE, INTERACTIVE VIDEODISC SYSTEMS.

premium television.   In television, any system that exacts a charge for program viewing. *See* PAY CABLE, SUBSCRIPTION TELEVISION.

premix.   In recording, to combine sound tracks onto one track, which will later be combined with other tracks. *See* SOUND TRACK.

preprint.   In printing, an advanced issue of an article to be published in book or journal form.

preprinted data.   In word processing, data printed on forms to reduce typing effort (e.g. the year in a date field). *Compare* VARIABLE TEXT.

preproduction.   In optical media, the set of design tasks (e.g. flowcharting, storyboarding, scriptwriting, software design, etc.) prior to videodisc production. *Compare* POST-PRODUCTION PRE-MASTERING. *See* STORY BOARD, VIDEODISC.

prerecording.   (1) In word processing, the action of storing text on magnetic media for subsequent playout as part of a repetitive letter or a letter created from boilerplate. *See* BOILERPLATE. (2) In filming, the action of recording sound that will later be played back and used in shooting.

presentation. In information presentation, the method used to show or present information (e.g. a text or graphic display on a visual display unit or television screen). (Philips).

presentation layer. In data communications, a layer in the ISO Open Systems Interconnection model. This layer performs generally useful transformations on the data to be sent (e.g. text compression) and performs the conversions required to allow an interactive program to converse with any one of a set of incompatible intelligent terminals. *Compare* APPLICATION LAYER, DATA LINK LAYER, PHYSICAL LAYER, SESSION LAYER, TRANSPORT LAYER. *See* INTELLIGENT TERMINAL, OPEN SYSTEMS INTERCONNECTION, TEXT COMPRESSION.

press proof. In printing, the last proof to be checked before approval for printing. *See* PROOF.

press release. A statement circulated to newspaper and periodical editors for publication on the specified release date. *Synonymous with* NEWS RELEASE.

pressure pad. In recording, a pad that holds the magnetic tape against the record/playback heads.

Prestel. The UK public viewdata service. *See* VIEWDATA.

prestore. In memory systems, to store data before it is operated on by a computer program or subroutine. *See* SUBROUTINE.

preventive maintenance. In reliability, a regular routine of checking equipment and replacing substandard parts to minimize the possibility of equipment failure. *Compare* CORRECTIVE MAINTENANCE.

primary colours. The minimum set of colours from which all other colours may be obtained. *Compare* SECONDARY COLOUR. *See* ADDITIVE PRIMARY COLOURS.

primary distribution. In publishing, the initial distribution of a document from its publisher to more than one destination.

primary group. In communications, an initial grouping of channels in a multiplexed system. The multiplexing of a large number of channels is often performed in stages. The basic signals are first multiplexed into a primary groups, and these primary groups are then multiplexed, and so on. *See* MULTIPLEXING.

primary key. (1) In databases, a key that uniquely identifies an entity. *Compare* SECONDARY KEY. *See* CANDIDATE KEY, ENTITY. (2) In data security, a cryptographic key employed in the encipherment/decipherment of data. *Compare* SECONDARY KEY. *See* CRYPTOGRAPHIC KEY. *Synonymous with* DATA-ENCRYPTING KEY.

primary letters. In printing, lower-case characters that have neither ascenders or descenders (i.e. a, c, e, etc.). *See* ASCENDER, DESCENDER.

primary rate access. (PRA) In communications, a user network interface in an integrated services digital network system that is normally connected to a digital private branch exchange or computer mainframe. It comprises either 32 x 64 kilobits per second (Australia and Europe) or 24 x 64 kilobits per second (North America and Japan) information transfer full-duplex channels. The Australian and European PRA comprises 30 B channels for user information, one D channel for signalling and one channel for system synchronization and alarms giving a total capacity of 2.048 megabits per second. The Japanese and North American PRA comprises 23 B channels and one D channel, giving an information capacity of 1.536 megabits per second, but with framing and housekeeping overheads the aggregate transmission rate is 1.544 megabits per second. *Compare* BASIC RATE ACCESS. *See* B CHANNEL, D CHANNEL, FRAME, FULL-DUPLEX, INTEGRATED SERVICES DIGITAL NETWORK.

primary station. In data communications, a station on a data link with the right to select a secondary station and transmit a message. There should only be one primary station on a data link at any one time. Primary status is temporary, allocated to a station so that it may transmit a message.

prime attribute. In databases, an attribute of a relational database that is a member of at least one candidate key. *Compare* NON-PRIME ATTRIBUTE. *See* ATTRIBUTE, CANDIDATE KEY, RELATIONAL DATABASE.

prime focus. In communications, a type of dish antenna in which the feedhorn is mounted at the focal point. *Compare* CASSEGRAIN. *See* DISH ANTENNA, FEEDHORN, FOCAL POINT.

prime number. In mathematics, a number that cannot be produced by multiplying integers (other than the number itself and one). The study of prime numbers is extremely important in some aspects of public key cryptography. *Compare* COMPOSITE. *See* PUBLIC KEY CRYPTOGRAPHY.

primitive. A basic or fundamental unit. *See* GRAPHIC PRIMITIVE.

principle of closed environment. *See* CLOSED ENVIRONMENT.

principle of complete mediation. *See* PRINCIPLES OF SECURE SYSTEMS.

principle of least common mechanism. *See* PRINCIPLES OF SECURE SYSTEMS.

principle of least privilege. *See* PRINCIPLES OF SECURE SYSTEMS.

principles of secure systems. In computer security, Saltzer and Schroeder enunciated the following principles of secure systems:

(a) SIMPLICITY. The accuracy of security measures, incorporated in hardware and software, can be more readily checked if those measures are simple and small.

(b) FAIL SAFE. Accesses should require explicit authorization (i.e. the default situation is no access).

(c) COMPLETE MEDIATION. Checking of access against access control informa-

tion must be performed under all circumstances, including normal operation, maintenance, recovery, etc.

(d) SEPARATION OF PRIVILEGE. A two-key philosophy, with each key located in a separate compartment, ensures that a single failure does not result in a security break.

(e) LEAST PRIVILEGE. Every process should operate with the minimum level of privilege necessary to perform the requisite task.

(f) LEAST COMMON MECHANISM. The use of shared mechanisms among users should be minimized for their mutual security.

(g) USER ACCEPTABILITY. Security measures should not interfere unduly with the work of users while, of course, fulfilling all necessary security constraints.

(h) PUBLIC SCRUTINY. Security measures should be available for review by experts (e.g. encryption algorithms can be widely publicized, with their security depending only on the secrecy of the cryptographic key).

See CRYPTOGRAPHIC KEY, NON-SECRET DESIGN.

print. (1) In graphics, an inked impression of an engraved or lithographic plate. (2) In printing, an impression from type of the actual printed matter. (3) In photography, a positive image produced from a negative.

print contrast ratio. In optical character recognition, the quantity obtained from the formula $(M-I)/M$ where I is the reflectance at an inspection area and M is the maximum reflectance found within a specified distance from the inspection area.

print contrast signal. In optical character recognition, the signal generated by the contrast of the zone under examination and its background. *See* PRINT CONTRAST RATIO.

print control character. A control character used in print operations to perform a non-printing action (e.g. carriage return). *See* CARRIAGE CONTROL.

print drum. In printing, a rotating drum holding print characters.

printed circuit board. (PC board) In electronics and computing, a plastic board upon which electronic components such as resistors, capacitors and integrated circuits are mounted and interconnected by plated or etched foil conducting paths. Printed circuit boards are used as plug-in modules in microcomputers. *See* CAPACITOR, EXPANSION CARD, INTEGRATED CIRCUIT, RESISTOR. *Synonymous with* CIRCUIT BOARD.

printer. In peripherals, a device for producing hard-copy text and data output from a computer. Printers can produce both text and graphics, in monochrome or colour, and so the distinction between plotters and printers is not clear cut. Printers are, however, used predominantly for the production of textual outputs and may thus be defined as output devices designed to produce hard-copy two-dimensional images on flexible material, and optimized for the production of characters.

One classification of printers relates to the method of production of the individual characters: fully formed character, dot matrix and stroke. Fully formed character devices are derived from the electric typewriter technology and were used with some early computers. This category now also includes the daisy wheel and thimble printers. These printers contain the complete image of the character and produce high-quality smooth connected character images. Dot matrix printers, on the other hand, build up characters as a matrix of dots. Increasing the number of dots in the matrix and the use of various print head movement strategies to overlap the printed dots can produce character images close to those of fully formed character printers. However, dot matrix technology is commonly used in applications where a functional, legible output will suffice (e.g. program listings). Stroke character devices draw images by the controlled movement of a plotting pen and may therefore be regarded as a special form of plotter. The available fonts on fully formed character systems are contained in the printing wheels, whereas those of dot matrix, and stroke character devices are contained in read-only memories which hold details of the matrix, or strokes, for a given character code.

A second method of classification accords with the quality of the printed output. The categories are letter quality, near letter quality, business quality and draft quality. Letter quality is the top of the range; it is normally associated with fully formed character devices, and accords with that of business correspondence obtained from good office typewriters. Near letter quality can be obtained from dot matrix printers with more than a hundred dots in the matrix and is adequate, for example, for business reports. Business quality can be obtained from most dot matrix printers used with personal computers and, although below that of near letter quality, it is considered to be adequate for internal memoranda. Draft quality is produced by dot matrix printers for program listings, draft reports, etc. where only reasonable legibility is necessary.

The method of image production provides a third means of classification, and in recent years there have been a number of developments to improve the performance of printers in terms of cost, noise, speed of printing, quality of image, range of images, etc. The two broadest categories are impact and non-impact methods. Impact methods are derived from the typewriter convention and are proven, but tend to be slow, noisy and incapable of high graphic resolution. Electric typewriters, daisy wheel, thimble and dot matrix printers, which drive print needles onto print ribbons, are included in this category. Non-impact methods include ink jet, ion deposition, laser, light-emitting diode (LED), thermal and electroerosion printers.

Printers also differ in the manner in which a page of text is produced. Serial printers produce one character after another and are therefore relatively slow; it can take more than one hour to print out the contents of a large floppy disk file. Serial printers can increase their speed by bidirectional printing and logic devices, which decide the optimum print head movements. Line printers form a whole line at a time. Although they provide high-speed output their cost is high and the output does not conform to letter quality. They are, therefore, more commonly associated with minicomputers or mainframes, producing bulk output of data for organizations. Laser printers form a whole page in their print cycle.

The interconnection between a printer and a microcomputer can take the form of a serial RS-232C, current loop or a parallel

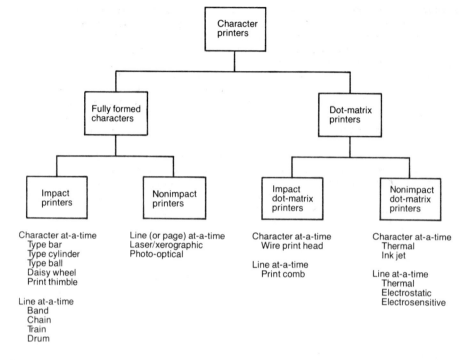

Character at-a-time	Line (or page) at-a-time	Character at-a-time	Character at-a-time
Type bar	Laser/xerographic	Wire print head	Thermal
Type cylinder	Photo-optical		Ink jet
Type ball		Line at-a-time	
Daisy wheel		Print comb	Line at-a-time
Print thimble			Thermal
			Electrostatic
Line at-a-time			Electrosensitive
Band			
Chain			
Train			
Drum			

printer

Centronics interface. Print buffers enable spooling (i.e. the computer loads a buffer with data and can then undertake other tasks until the printer has dealt with the current buffer contents).

Printers are required to operate while unattended, and the methods of paper feed must therefore be automatic, reliable and conform with the requirements of the printed output. Sheet-feed and roll-feed methods rely upon friction as in conventional typewriters. Sheet feed deals with one sheet at a time; these sheets can be fed in manually or automatically from a sheet feeder. Roll feed uses one continual roll of paper, but it can be difficult to ensure proper alignment for long print runs. Pin- or tractor-feed mechanisms ensure that the paper is moved in a regular manner through the printer, but the stationery must have perforated edges for these devices. In some cases the letters or envelopes are affixed to backing paper which has the requisite perforations. Sheet paper bins, similar to those employed for office copiers, are available for the latest laser printers. *See* BUFFER, BUFFER SIZE, CENTRONICS INTERFACE, CURRENT LOOP INTERFACE, DAISY WHEEL, DOT MATRIX, FULLY FORMED CHARACTER, IMPACT PRINTER, INK JET PRINTER, ION DEPOSITION, LASER PRINTER, LED PRINTER, LETTER QUALITY, LINE PRINTER, NON-IMPACT PRINTER, PAGE PRINTER, PIN-FEED PLATEN, PLOTTER, RS-232C, SPOOLING, SPROCKET FEED, THIMBLE, TRACTOR FEED.

printer plotter. In peripherals, a character printer that can also produce some form of graphics output. *See* PLOTTER, PRINTER.

printer's errors. (PE) In printing, a mistake made by the typesetter. *Compare* AUTHOR'S ALTERATIONS.

printing. (1) The production of an image by applying an ink-bearing surface to paper. *See* PRINTER. (2) In photography, the production of a picture by the transmission of light through a negative to light-sensitive paper. (3) In filming, the duplication of a film. It can include the addition of colour and exposure corrections, optical and other effects, and a sound track.

printout. *See* HARD COPY.

printout microfilm. In micrographics, each frame of the microfilm contains data that would otherwise occupy one page of continuous stationery.

print run. (1) In printing, the action of producing a prescribed quantity of copies. (2) In printing, the number of copies produced.

print suppress. In computer security, to eliminate the printing of characters in order to preserve their secrecy (e.g. the characters of a password as it is keyed by a user at an input terminal). (FIPS). *See* PASSWORD.

print to paper. In printing, an instruction to a printer to use all the available supply of paper rather than produce a prescribed number of copies.

printwheel. *Synonymous with* DAISY WHEEL.

priority. In computing, a rank assigned to a task that determines its precedence in receiving system resources.

priority interrupt. In computing, an interrupt that is given precedence over other system interrupts (e.g. an alarm interrupt in a real-time control system). *See* INTERRUPT.

priority processing. In computing, a method of operating a computer system so that the sequence in which programs are processed is fully determined by a system of priorities.

priority scheduler. In computing, a system that uses input and output queues in its job scheduling to improve overall performance. *See* QUEUE.

privacy. In data security, the right of an individual to exercise some form of control both over the information that is stored about him or her and the personnel who are allowed to access such information. A cause of severe concern among many communities particularly when the developments of information technology facilitate the collection, correlation and distribution of sensitive personal information. The legislation governing such activities varies considerably from country to country. *See* DATA PROTECTION, PRIVACY PROTECTION.

privacy protection. In computer security, the establishment of appropriate administrative, technical and physical safeguards to ensure the security and confidentiality of data records and to protect both security and confidentiality against any anticipated threats or hazards that could result in substantial harm, embarrassment, inconvenience or unfairness to any individual about whom such information is maintained. (FIPS). *See* CONFIDENTIALITY, DATA PROTECTION, SECURITY.

private address space. In computing, a range of computer addresses assigned to a particular user. *See* ADDRESS.

private automatic branch exchange. (PABX) In communications, a small automatic branch exchange. In recent years the function of PABXs has moved beyond the interconnection of internal and external telephone users to a role of the central controller of a star-based local area network. In a conventional PABX system each telephone handset is directly connected by a twisted pair cable to a central switch. A connection is made by numerical signalling at relatively low speed and, if the connection cannot be completed, an engaged signal advises the sender to try again. In the great majority of systems this is a limiting factor because it places responsibility for pursuing the connection on the human user. In more advanced PABX systems the problem is eliminated because the switch takes over responsibility for persisting until the connection is made. The same advanced switch can store and forward messages, and can carry data as well as voice at speeds of up to 64 kilobits per second. *See* STORE AND FORWARD.

private automatic computer exchange. *See* PACX.

private automatic exchange. (PAX) In communications, a dial telephone system provided to an organization that does not permit calls to be made over the external telephone network. *See* PRIVATE AUTOMATIC BRANCH EXCHANGE.

private branch exchange. (PBX) In communications, a service provided to an organization comprising switching office trunks, a local switchboard and extension telephones. The extension telephone sets may be connected to each other or to the external trunks. PBXs may be manual or automatic, depending upon the methods used by extensions to place local and outgoing calls. *See* PRIVATE AUTOMATIC BRANCH EXCHANGE.

private cryptography. In communications security, the provision of cryptography that is not transparent to the user. Link and node encryption is transparent to a user; end-to-end encryption may be transparent if it is automatically provided as system service. *See* END-TO-END ENCRYPTION, LINK ENCRYPTION, NETWORK ENCRYPTION, NODE ENCRYPTION, TRANSPARENT.

private dial port. In data communications, a dial-in port of a packet-switching network providing an access port for one customer, with an unlisted telephone number. *Compare* PUBLIC DIAL PORT. *See* PACKET SWITCHING.

private key. In data security, the cryptographic key used to decipher messages in a public key cryptosystem. This key is kept private by the intended recipient of the ciphertext. *Compare* PUBLIC KEY. *See* CIPHERTEXT, CRYPTOGRAPHIC KEY, PUBLIC KEY CRYPTOGRAPHY.

private line. *See* LEASED CIRCUIT.

privilege. In computing, pertaining to a program or user and characterizing the type of operation that can be performed. Privileged users or programs can perform operations normally considered to be the domain of the operating system and which can affect the system performance. *See* OPERATING SYSTEM.

probabilistic model. *Synonymous with* STOCHASTIC MODEL.

probability distribution. In mathematics, a function giving the probability that a random quantity will lie within a given interval. The shape of the probability distribution curve depends upon the mechanisms governing the random event. The three most common in science and technology are the gaussian, Poisson and uniform distributions. *See* GAUSSIAN DISTRIBUTION, POISSON DISTRIBUTION, UNIFORM DISTRIBUTION.

probability theory. In mathematics, a branch dealing with the study of chance events. It is used to predict quantities that characterize the behaviour of a population of such events.

problem-oriented language. In programming, a high-level language developed for the convenient expression of a specified set of problems. *See* PROCEDURE-ORIENTED LANGUAGE, REPORT PROGRAM GENERATOR.

procedural language. In programming, a conventional high-level language (e.g. Pascal) in which the programmer specifies the actions necessary to attain the desired result. *Compare* NON-PROCEDURAL LANGUAGE. *See* PASCAL.

procedural security. *Synonymous with* ADMINISTRATIVE SECURITY.

procedure. In programming, the course taken for the solution of a problem. *See* SUBROUTINE.

procedure-oriented language. In programming, a high-level language oriented towards a given class of procedures. *See* COBOL, FORTRAN, PL/1.

process. (1) In computing, a program in execution. It is completely characterized by a single current execution point (represented by a machine state) and address space. (2) A course of events occurring in accordance with an intended purpose or effect. (3) In computing, a program is a static piece of code, and a process is the execution of that code. When a program is loaded into memory a process is created. (4) In programming, an independent computation, with its own program and data, that can communicate with other concurrent processes.

process camera. (1) In printing, a camera specially designed for process work (e.g. halftone making, colour separation). (2) In filming, a camera designed for special effects. *See* HALFTONE.

process engraving. In printing, the production of a letterpress printing plate by printing down a photographic image onto a plate and etching it to form a relief printing surface. *See* LETTERPRESS, RELIEF PRINTING.

processing. In legislation, as defined by the UK Data Protection Act, 1984, pertaining to the amending, augmenting, deleting or rearranging the data or extracting the information constituting the data and, in the case of personal data, processing means performing any of the abovementioned operations by reference to the data subject. *See* DATA, DATA PROTECTION, DATA SUBJECT, PERSONAL DATA.

process inks. In printing, inks used in three-colour and four-colour printing processes. *See* FOUR-COLOUR PROCESS, THREE-COLOUR PROCESS.

processor. In computing, a device or system capable of performing operations upon data. A central processing unit is a hardware processor. A compiler is a language processor. *See* CENTRAL PROCESSING UNIT, COMPILER, HARDWARE.

processor-controlled keying. (PCK) In peripherals, a technique in which a data entry operator is assisted by a computer which provides prompts, data formatting and validation checks.

processor interconnection. In distributed processing, the distribution of data-processing functions between two or more host processors, in a single location, without the use of communication facilities. *Compare* DISTRIBUTED DATA PROCESSING, MULTI-SYSTEM NETWORKING.

processor utilization. In computing, the proportion of processor time spent in performing useful and necessary tasks in relation to the total available time.

product. In mathematics, the result of multiplying two quantities.

product cipher. In cryptography, a cipher produced by a composition of a number of substitution and transposition ciphers. *See* DATA ENCRYPTION STANDARD, SUBSTITUTION CIPHER, TRANSPOSITION CIPHER.

production cycle. In printing, the cycle towards final production includes markup, original keyboarding, correction keyboarding, typesetting, proof-reading, corrections, page make-up and authors corrections. *See* MARKUP, PROOF-READING, TYPESETTING.

production run. In computing, a routine execution of a commonly used program (e.g. calculation of pay cheques).

production system. *Synonymous with* RULE-BASED SYSTEM.

profile. (1) In library science, the range of interests of a user in an selective dissemination of information system. *See* SELECTIVE DISSEMINATION OF INFORMATION. (2) In programming, a specific set of preferred parameter values for use in a given application. (Philips).

program. In computing, a complete series of definitions and instructions, conforming to the syntax of a given computer language, that when executed on a computer will perform a required task. *See* OBJECT PROGRAM, PROGRAMMING, SOURCE PROGRAM, SYNTAX.

program carrier. The material or a device used to carry or store a program. (Philips). *See* CARRIER.

program check. (1) In programming, a condition arising when programming errors are detected by an input/output channel. *See* CHANNEL. (2) In programming, an interrupt caused by a user program error. *See* INTERRUPT. (3) In programming, a procedure conducted to test the correctness of a program (e.g. by execution with trial data).

program crash. In programming, a failure in a program that produces a computer instruction which cannot be performed and hence prevents further processing. *Compare* BUG.

program development. In programming, the process of writing, inputting, translating and debugging a source program. *See* DEBUG, SOURCE PROGRAM, TRANSLATOR.

program execution time. In computing, the interval during which the instructions of an object program are executed. *See* OBJECT PROGRAM.

program function key. In peripherals, a key on a computer terminal that invokes a utility (e.g. to perform scrolling) or can be programmed by the user (e.g. to insert a repetitive line of data). *Compare* FUNCTION KEY.

program library. In computing, a collection of available general-purpose computer programs held offline or on backing store. *See* BACKING STORAGE, OFFLINE.

program listing. In programming, a printout produced by a translation process displaying the source program, error messages and relevant information on the object program. *See* OBJECT PROGRAM, SOURCE PROGRAM.

programmable. In computing, pertaining to a device that can store a sequence of user-defined instructions. *See* PROGRAMMABLE LOGIC ARRAY, PROGRAMMABLE READ-ONLY MEMORY, PROGRAMMABLE SOUND GENERATOR.

programmable logic array. (PLA) In memory systems, a read-only memory programmed to perform logic operations. *Compare* UNCOMMITTED LOGIC ARRAY. *See* LOGICAL OPERATOR, READ-ONLY MEMORY.

programmable read-only memory. (PROM) In memory systems, a form of read-only memory (ROM) that can be programmed by a user. Blank memory chips are purchased and the required data is input to the chip in a special device (PROM programmer). *See* ELECTRICALLY PROGRAMMABLE READ-ONLY MEMORY, PROM PROGRAMMER, READ-ONLY MEMORY.

programmable sound generator. In audio, an audio signal generator with an integrated microprocessor to control the output signal according to a program set up by the user. (Philips). *See* SOUND SYNTHESIZER.

program maintenance. *Synonymous with* SOFTWARE MAINTENANCE.

programmer. In programming, the role of a professional programmer may range from a leader of a team concerned with the development of a total suite of programs, according to a system specification, to an individual responsible for user advice on and the maintenance of a well-documented program package. Programmers may be roughly divided into four groups: application programmers who are responsible for the development of in-house application programs (e.g. payroll); maintenance programmers who are responsible for updating and correcting an organization's suite of application software; system programmers who develop operating systems, compilers, etc. for computer manufacturers or large software houses; low-level language programmers who produce extremely efficient programs for video games, microprocessor-based devices, etc. *Compare* CODER. *See* APPLICATION PROGRAM, CHIEF PROGRAMMER TEAM, COMPILER, LOW-LEVEL LANGUAGE, OPERATING SYSTEM, SOFTWARE MAINTENANCE, SYSTEM PROGRAM. (2) In audiovisual aids, a multifunction, multichannel controller. A programmer operates in conjunction with a tape recorder or computer with stored instructions, or it may contain its own internal storage. Upon receipt of a signal from an external, or possibly internal, synchronizer the programmer selects the next control function from storage and performs the corresponding action (e.g. turning on lights, selecting a new slide for projection, etc.). *See* PROGRAM, SYNCHRONIZER.

programming. The process by which a computer is made to perform a specialized task. It involves the creation of a formalized sequence of instructions which can be recognized and implemented by the machine. These instructions (the program) are a static entity, but when executed they result in a useful information-handling process. All programs are concerned, either directly or indirectly, with the flow of information. Data, whether stated explicitly or made an intrinsic component of the program is used as an input, which is then processed or computed to generate an output. All of the functions performed by a computer depend, at some stage, upon a program.

The instructions are encoded into a specific programming language. Different languages vary both structurally and syntactically, thus programs are specific to one language, the choice of which depends on both the application and computer for which it is intended. Programming languages may be divided into two main classes: procedural and non-procedural. The majority of the world's programs are written in procedural languages (i.e. the programmer specifies the actions to be taken rather than the nature of the desired result). *See* FOURTH-GENERATION LANGUAGE, HIGH-LEVEL LANGUAGE, INSTRUCTION, LOW-LEVEL LANGUAGE, MACHINE CODE, NON-PROCEDURAL LANGUAGE, PROCEDURAL LANGUAGE.

programming aids. In programming, computer programs provided to aid the user (e.g. compilers, debugging packages, linkage editors, mathematical subroutines, etc.). *See* COMPILER, DEBUG, LINKING.

programming language. In programming, a set of rules to define the manner in which data structures are formulated and the processing instructions are written and organized. *See* HIGH-LEVEL LANGUAGE, LOW-LEVEL LANGUAGE, PROGRAMMING.

programming standards. In programming, a set of rules produced by an organization to impose a discipline on the production of programs. The rules may range from those dealing with the decomposition of large programs into individual modules to the use of individual program constructs (e.g. loops). *See* LOOP, MODULE.

program monitor. In an electronic learning laboratory, a system that enables the instructor to monitor the content and volume level of an audio stimulus before, or during transmission to students.

program patch. In computer security, a section of code added to object code and thus not affecting the source code. Such patches may therefore bypass normal control procedures and could be used for illegal program modification. *See* OBJECT CODE, SOURCE CODE.

program-related data. In optical media, the data concerning the application in an interactive compact disc (CD-I) system. It includes the data modules containing the executable object code for the CD-I pro-cessor, as well as all application data other than audio and video data (e.g. data representing system text or phonetically encoded speech). (Philips). *See* COMPACT DISC – INTERACTIVE.

program specification. In programming, a document providing complete details of a program, giving its function, files accessed, input/output requirements, etc. *See* STRUCTURED SYSTEMS ANALYSIS.

program statement. In programming, an expression or a generalized instruction in a source language. *See* SOURCE LANGUAGE.

program stop. In programming, an instruction that causes the execution to stop (e.g. upon completion of the process).

program switch. In programming, a branch point in a program such that the subsequent path depends upon a condition elsewhere in the program or by some physical state in the system. *See* BRANCH.

progressive disclosure. In audiovisual aids, the process of building up a composite image (e.g. by removing masks on an overhead transparency or adding a new element, or a new slide, while retaining images already exposed). *See* OVERHEAD PROJECTOR.

progressives. In printing, a set of proofs showing each plate of a colour set printed in its appropriate colour and in registered combination. *See* REGISTER.

projection. In databases, an operation in relational algebra. A projection on a given relation, specifying attributes of that relation, produces a second relation containing only a set of tuples with the specified attributes and with all duplicates removed. *Compare* DIVISION, JOIN, SELECTION. *See* RELATIONAL ALGEBRA, RELATIONAL DATABASE.

projection/sound programmer. In audiovisual aids, a device that controls a combined system of sound recorders and projection equipment.

projection television. In television, a television receiver or monitor in which the picture is projected from one or more small cathode ray tubes on to a large screen. (Philips). *See* CATHODE RAY TUBE, LASER KINESCOPE.

projector. (1) In filming, a device that throws motion picture images onto a screen and, with some devices, to reproduce sound from the film sound track. (2) In audiovisual aids, a device that throws slide images onto a screen.

projector dissolve control. In audiovisual aids, a device that controls two or more images so that one can dissolve into or over another. *See* DISSOLVE.

PROLOG. In programming, PRO-gramming in LOGic language; a programming language developed within the artificial intelligence community and designed for symbolic computation. Its greatest usage lies within the area of artificial intelligence, and it has been adopted as the chief language of the Japanese fifth-generation computer project. It also has applications in mathematical logic, relational databases, biochemistry and schools computing. It is a relatively new language, and its range of applications is widening. *See* ARTIFICIAL INTELLIGENCE, LISP, NON-PROCEDURAL LANGUAGE.

PROM. *See* PROGRAMMABLE READ-ONLY MEMORY.

PROM burner. *See* PROM PROGRAMMER.

promiscuous mode. In data communications, a mode of operation of Ethernet local area networks in which a node, with a suitable hardware setting, receives all packets on the bus, rather than those that were only addressed to it. This mode of operation is necessary for network-monitoring purposes, but it may pose communications security problems. *See* ETHERNET, LOCAL AREA NETWORK. *Synonymous with* EAVES-DROPPING MODE.

PROM programmer. In memory systems, a device to input data into a programmable read-only memory (PROM) chip. *See* MICRO-COMPUTER, PROGRAMMABLE READ-ONLY MEMORY.

prompting. In peripherals, a method of requesting specific types of data input from a

terminal user by visual messages and, sometimes, audible signals.

Pronto keyboard. In peripherals, a trade name for a five-fingered keyboard. It has eight keys: five finger keys and three shift keys. *Compare* AZERTY KEYBOARD, DVORAK KEYBOARD, MALTRON KEYBOARD, QWERTY KEYBOARD.

proof. In printing, a sample of a printed output taken for proof reading. *See* PROOF READING.

proof correction marks. In printing, a standard set of signs and symbols used in copy preparation and to indicate corrections on proofs. Marks are placed both in the text and in the margin. (Desktop).

proofing press. In printing, a press used for producing proofs rather than an extensive number of copies. *See* PROOF.

proof of program correctness. In programming, a formal mathematical demonstration that the semantics of the program are consistent with the specification for that program. The traditional method of checking out programs by test data is unreliable, inefficient and provides no guidance on the development of error-free programs.

The results of test runs are unreliable because there is no rigorous method of selecting test data that will ensure that all possible paths through the program are checked. The method is inefficient both because large sets of test data are required, and if the program fails, for any one set of data, then the program must be modified and the complete test run restarted from the beginning to ensure that no additional bugs were inserted with the modification. The most serious shortcoming of this technique, however, is that it provides no disciplined approach to program development. In fact the successive modifications of the program to correct faults, indicated by the test data, can result in final programs that are extremely difficult to maintain or update.

Methods of formal proof of correctness depend, in the first instance, upon a mathematical statement, or assertion, which declares precisely and unambiguously the desired result of the program in terms of the input data and states. This would be a formidable task for substantial programs, but it is interesting to note that this is the form of programming for non-procedural languages. The assertion on the program output data or states is termed the postcondition. The precondition is an assertion on the input data or states prior to the execution of the program. A program is deemed to be correct if its execution, commencing with states corresponding to the precondition, produces a set of states that satisfy the postcondition. The proof of total program correctness requires both that the postcondition is true if the program terminates (known as the proof of partial correctness) and proof that the program does indeed terminate.

Proving that a given program will guarantee to terminate in the specified postcondition is a formidable task for large programs and an uneconomic activity for most commercial or scientific environments. The significance of these formal techniques, however, lies not in the post hoc proof of correctness, but in the disciplined approach that they provide for the production of error-free programs.

Each module within a large program can be developed in an error-free manner by the successive use of pre- and postconditions; in a sequential program the postcondition of one segment becomes the precondition for the succeeding one. This approach can highlight typical potential bugs (e.g. division by zero, string operations on empty strings). Conditional jump statements within a program involve a number of possible paths, and the preconditions must cover both the precondition states for each route and the condition required for that route to be selected. Programs containing loops are the potential source of many bugs, typically endless loops arise in certain conditions or the loop does not terminate with the required set of output states. The formal techniques provide a disciplined approach, to the design of loops, which require the programmer to ensure that the loop commences with the necessary initial condition, that the loop will terminate and when it does the necessary postcondition is met. An important concept is that of a loop invariant which is a state which is true before and after the each execution of the statements in the loop. The selection of the loop invariant provides a new insight into the behaviour of program loops. The formal approach ensures that the loop terminates after a finite number of iterations and that the postcondition is satisfied upon termination.

This topic is now of considerable interest outside the academic world because large organizations and governments are seeking assurances that computer software performs exactly according to specifications, in particular in regard to data security aspects of information-processing systems. *Compare* SPAGHETTI CODE. *See* LOOP INVARIANT, ORANGE BOOK, POSTCONDITION, PRECONDITION, PREDICATE TRANSFORMER.

proof reading. In printing, a detailed examination of a proof for punctuation, spelling and typographical errors. *See* PROOF.

propagated error. In computing, an error in one operation that affects data used in subsequent operations so that the error spreads through much of the processed data.

propagation delay. In communications, the transit time for a signal from one point in the circuit to another.

proportional spacing. In printing, a method of spacing whereby each character is spaced to accommodate the varying widths of letters or figures, so increasing readability. Books and magazines are set proportionally spaced, whereas typewritten documents are generally monospaced. (Desktop). *Compare* MONOSPACE.

proprietary. A system or device produced by a private organization that does not adhere to international standards.

proprietary data. In data security, data that is created, used or marketed by individuals having exclusive legal rights. *See* SOFTWARE PROTECTION.

Pro-Search. In online information retrieval, gateway software that accesses Dialog and BRS databases. It allows BRS commands to be used to search Dialog databases, and vice versa. It can also be used a communications software alone. *See* BRS, DIALOG, GATEWAY SOFTWARE.

prosodic. The stress and intonation of a spoken language.

Prospector. In artificial intelligence, an expert system designed to emulate the reasoning process of an experimental geologist in assessing a given prospective site or region for its likelihood of containing ore deposits of the type represented by the model. *See* EXPERT SYSTEMS.

protected field. In peripherals, data on a visual display screen that may not be modified by an operator. *Compare* INPUT FIELD, UNPROTECTED FIELD. *Synonymous with* FIXED DATA.

protected location. In memory systems, an area of storage whose contents are protected against accidental or improper alteration, or unauthorized access.

protected space. In word processing, an empty space and associated words treated as an entity. If a text is reformatted the space and the words will be contained in a single line and not split. *Synonymous with* REQUIRED SPACE.

protected storage. *See* PROTECTED LOCATION.

protected wireline distribution system. In data security, a telecommunications system that has been approved by a legally designated authority and to which electromagnetic and physical safeguards have been applied to permit safe electrical transmission of unencrypted sensitive information. (FIPS). *Synonymous with* APPROVED CIRCUIT.

protection. *See* DATA-DEPENDENT PROTECTION, DATA PROTECTION, FETCH PROTECTION, PRIVACY PROTECTION.

protection master. (1) In filming and recording, an intermediate duplicate of a film from which prints are made to protect the original. (2) In filming and recording, a spare, reserve copy of a sound recording.

protection ratio. In communications, the minimum value of the required-to-unrequired signal ratio at the receiver input under specified conditions, such that the specified reception quality of the required signal is achieved at the receiver output.

protective ground. In hardware, an electrical connection between two pieces of equipment. It interconnects the chassis of both pieces of equipment for safety reasons. *Compare* SIGNAL GROUND. *See* GROUND.

protective redundancy. In reliability, the use or replicated modules in hardware or software, or the use of error-correcting codes to render a system fault tolerant. *See* ERROR-CORRECTING CODE, FAULT TOLERANCE, REDUNDANCY. *Synonymous with* SPATIAL REDUNDANCY.

protocol. In data communications, a formally specified set of conventions governing the format and control of inputs and outputs between two communicating systems.

protocol converter. In data communications, a device that interfaces two communicating systems working to different protocols (e.g. a protocol converter can interface to a microcomputer, via the asynchronous RS-232C serial port, and to an IBM system network architecture/synchronous data link control synchronous network). All EBCDIC/ASCII code conversions are carried out, as well as cursor positioning, screen buffering and error handling. *Compare* SOFTWARE PROTOCOL CONVERTER. *See* AMERICAN STANDARD CODE FOR INFORMATION INTERCHANGE, ASYNCHRONOUS TRANSMISSION, CODE CONVERSION, EBCDIC CODE, PROTOCOL, RS-232C, SYNCHRONOUS DATA LINK CONTROL, SYSTEM NETWORK ARCHITECTURE.

protocol standards. In data communications, defined protocols which facilitate communication among a wide body of users. Early protocols merely provided for the interconnection of similar devices and the Arpanet was an exception which permitted the interconnection of any two devices. Some early protocols (e.g. BISYNC) became ad hoc standards since they were adopted by many other manufacturers. There are two international bodies concerned with protocol standards—CCITT and ISO. CCITT is responsible for standards in the field of public telecommunication services. It is a permanent committee of the ITU and its best known recommendations are the V-, X- and I-series for analog, digital data transmission and integrated services digital networks. ISO has a large number of member bodies, one for each participating country (BSI in the UK, ANSI in USA,

AFNOR in France). Other bodies such as CCITT and ECMA are also represented. The European Conference of Post and Tele-communications Administrations under-takes standardization in the field of telephony extending into other facilities pro-vided by PTTs (e.g. digital data networks). National organizations such as IEEE pro-mulgate standards (e.g. RS-232C, equiv-alent to CCITT V.24 and a local area network standard IEEE-802). *See* BISYNC, IEEE-802, INTEGRATED SERVICES DIGITAL NETWORK, I-SERIES RECOMMENDATIONS OF CCITT, LOCAL AREA NETWORK, PTT, RS-232C, V-SERIES RECOMMENDATIONS OF CCITT, X-SERIES RECOMMENDATIONS OF CCITT.

protocol transfer. In distributed process-ing, a data transfer in which error checking is employed to ensure that the data is correctly received. Usually the system does not dis-play the data being transferred between the mainframe and the personal computer, but instead gives information on the status of the transfer.

proton. An electrically positive charged particle in the nucleus of an atom. *Compare* ELECTRON.

prototyping. In systems analysis, the pro-cess of building and refining a working model of the final operational system during the development phase. The main purpose of prototyping is to refine inputs, outputs and functions during the design phase rather than having to await the final development of the system.
  Prototyping can take one of three forms. At the simplest level the prototype merely comprises a mockup of system outputs, sample reports, screen layouts, etc. pro-duced in hard copy and reviewed with the user. A more elaborate form is a simula-tion of the final system where users can sit at a terminal and experience the system as it would be after development. This method is useful for demonstrating the system and giving user feedback. The third form of prototyping is the evolutionary system made possible by the development of fourth-generation languages. In this case the proto-type system can evolve into the final system. *See* FOURTH-GENERATION LANGUAGE.

proximity. In online information retrieval, the means by which the relations between two or more terms are specified in order to retrieve relevant items.

PRR. *See* PULSE REPETITION RATE.

PS/2. In computing, a powerful IBM microcomputer.

PSE. *See* PACKET-SWITCHING EXCHANGE.

psec. *See* PICOSECOND.

pseudocode. In systems analysis. *See* STRUCTURED ENGLISH.

pseudo colouring. In computer graphics, a technique of image processing in which colours are assigned to grey levels to enhance, for example, the visual effects of thermal images. *See* GREY SCALE, IMAGE PRO-CESSING.

pseudo-flaw. In computer security, an apparent loophole deliberately implanted in an operating system program as a trap for intruders. (FIPS). *See* ENTRAPMENT, LOOP-HOLE.

pseudorandom numbers. In applications, a sequence of numbers produced by an algorithm and used to approximate to a sequence of random numbers. *See* RANDOM NUMBERS.

PSK. *See* PHASE SHIFT KEYING.

PSN. *See* PACKET-SWITCHING NETWORK, PUBLIC SWITCHED NETWORK.

PSS. (1) In data communications, packet switch service. *See* PACKET SWITCHING. (2) In data communications, Packet Switch Stream; a national, public switched data service provided by British Telecom. It pro-vides full-duplex working up to 48 kilobits per second. *See* KILOSTREAM, MEGASTREAM, SATSTREAM.

PSTN. In communications, public switched telephone network.

PTO. In communications, public telecom-munications operator; an organization that operates a publicly available communications service and supplies associated equipment.

PTS. In online information retrieval, Predicasts Terminal System. *See* PREDICASTS.

PTT. *See* POST TELEPHONE AND TELEGRAPH.

p-type material. In electronics, a semiconductor material doped with an impurity that has electron-accepting nuclei. These impurities effectively produce holes that move through the medium providing positive-charge carriers. *Compare* N-TYPE MATERIAL. *See* HOLE, SEMICONDUCTOR DEVICES.

public access programming. In television, a cable television facility in which which individuals and private organizations are given the opportunity to broadcast their own programs for a nominal fee (e.g. community affairs reports).

public address system. An audio system with a microphone and loudspeaker to enable a speaker to pass information to a large or remote audience. *Synonymous with* PA SYSTEM.

public database. In databases, a database or file of information available to the general public (e.g. Prestel). (Philips). *See* PRESTEL.

public data network. (PDN) In data communications, a network to supply a data transmission service to the public, provided by a public authority, usually a PTT, or recognized private operating agency. *See* PTT.

public dial port. In data communications, a dial-in port providing access to a packet-switched network from a terminal connected to the public telephone network. *Compare* PRIVATE DIAL PORT.

public domain. In copyright, material that has not been copyrighted or for which the copyright has expired. *See* COPYRIGHT.

public key. In data security, the cryptographic key used to encipher messages in public key cryptography. This key is made generally available by the senders of the ciphertext. *Compare* PRIVATE KEY. *See* CIPHERTEXT, CRYPTOGRAPHIC KEY, PUBLIC KEY CRYPTOGRAPHY.

public key cryptography. (PKC) In cryptography, an asymmetric cryptosystem (i.e. one in which the enciphering and deciphering keys are different and it is computationally infeasible to calculate one from the other, given the enciphering algorithm). In public key cryptography the enciphering key is made public, but the deciphering key is kept secret. It has advantages over symmetric ciphers, such as data encryption standard in the areas: (a) security of messages, from a variety of sources, directed to an individual organization; (b) key management; and (c) digital signatures.

If a number of individuals wish to send secure information to a central organization then symmetric ciphers require that initial arrangements be made for the individual, and the organization, to share a unique secret key. Public key cryptography on the other hand enables the organization to publish a single enciphering key, possibly in

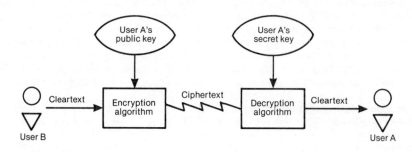

public key cryptosystem

a public directory, and potential senders of the messages need only access this directory, encipher their message using the public key· and agreed algorithm, and transmit it to the organization. Such senders are unable to decipher messages, sent by other individuals using the same key, because the deciphering key is secret and held only by the organization in question. The secrecy of the public key is not required, but it is essential that the integrity of the key in the public directory be guaranteed. If an attacker could replace an organization's public key with an enciphering key produced by the attacker himself who would also hold the corresponding deciphering key, then secret information destined for the organization would be available to the attacker. It is also important that users do not use highly formatted messages because an attacker has a completely free choice in chosen plaintext attacks. Thus an attacker could take an intelligent guess at the meaning of certain repeated blocks in ciphertext messages, encrypted with a given public key, and then check out those guesses by enciphering them with the public key and comparing the results with the ciphertext blocks. *See* DIGITAL SIGNATURE, KNAPSACK CIPHER, MENTAL POKER, RSA, SYMMETRIC CRYPTOSYSTEM.

public key distribution. In public key cryptography, a method of exchanging secret keys between communicating parties that does not require a secure channel.

public switched network. (PSN) In communications, a switching system that provides switching transmission facilities to customers.

puck. In peripherals, a pointing device like a sliding key, or an island, that can be moved around in bounded pool on top of the keyboard housing. *See* POINTING DEVICE.

pulldown. In micrographics, the length of film advanced after each exposure.

pull-down menu. In peripherals, a menu that can be displayed when required. The menu is usually invoked by moving the cursor to an appropriate point on the screen and depressing a specified key. The menu emerges downwards from the cursor position. *See* HELP, MENU, WIMPS.

pulp. In printing, fibrous material of vegetable origin that provides the raw material for paper making.

pulse. In electronics, a change in a voltage or current level for a short duration. *Synonymous with* IMPULSE.

pulse amplitude modulation. (PAM) In communications, a method of pulse modulation in which the amplitude of a train of pulses is adjusted in accordance with the input signal. *See* PULSE MODULATION.

pulse code modulation. (PCM) (1) In communications, a technique for transmitting analog information in digital form. The analog signal is sampled, and the sampled value represented by a fixed-length binary number. This number is then transmitted as a corresponding set of pulses. In telephony, the sampling rate is 8000 per second. *Compare* DELTA MODULATION. *See* ANALOG SIGNAL, PULSE, PULSE MODULATION, SAMPLING. (2) In optical media, the sampling rate for digital audio compact disc is 44 100 samples per second, and the samples are represented by 16-bit binary numbers. A stereo sample therefore comprises 32 bits; it is structured into four eight-bit symbols, with left and right channel symbols interleaved. Six stereo samples (24 symbols) form one stereo frame. (Philips). *See* COMPACT DISC − DIGITAL AUDIO, FRAME, SYMBOL.

pulse duration modulation. (PDM) In communications, a pulse modulation technique in which the width of the pulse, in a pulse train, is adjusted in accordance with the input signal. *See* PULSE MODULATION. *Synonymous with* PULSE WIDTH MODULATION.

pulse generator. In electronics, a device that generates a specified type of pulse or pulse train. *See* PULSE, PULSE TRAIN.

pulse modulation. In communications, a signal transmission system in which the information content is impressed upon a pulse train by adjusting either the pulse amplitude (PAM), pulse duration (PDM), pulse position (PPM) or by binary codes based upon the presence and absence of pulses (PCM). *See* PULSE AMPLITUDE MODULATION, PULSE CODE MODULATION,

PULSE DURATION MODULATION PULSE POSITION MODULATION

pulse period. In electronics, the time interval between the leading edges of two successive periodic pulses. *See* PERIOD, PULSE.

pulse position modulation. (PPM) In communications, a pulse modulation method in which the timing of the individual pulses, in a pulse train, depends upon the modulating signal. *See* PULSE MODULATION.

pulse regenerator. In electronics, a device that accepts a distorted pulse and produces a well-shaped one. *See* PULSE.

pulse repetition rate. (PRR) In electronics, the number of pulses per unit time. *See* PULSE.

pulse stuffing. In data communications, a technique used in some multiplexed systems when an input channel has a low transmission rate. A dummy word is transmitted if the buffer does not contain a full data word at the time that it is read by the multiplexer. *Compare* BIT STUFFING. *See* MULTIPLEXING.

pulse train. In electronics, a series of pulses having similar characteristics; a method of conveying binary information in which the presence, or absence, of a pulse represents a binary 1 or 0, respectively. *See* BINARY CODE, PULSE.

pulse width modulation. *Synonymous with* PULSE DURATION MODULATION.

Pure Aloha. In packet switching, a technique employed in the Aloha system when packet collision occurs. Retransmission is initiated when the terminal does not receive an acknowledgement within a time-out interval, but to avoid repeated overlap the interval before packet retransmission is randomized in each terminal. *See* ALOHA, SLOTTED ALOHA.

pure code. In programming, a code that is never modified in execution. *See* RE-ENTRANT ROUTINE.

pure notation. A notation that is exclusively alphabetical or exclusively numeric.

pure tone. In acoustics, a single-frequency sound without overtones. *See* OVERTONES.

purging. (1) In computing, the orderly review of storage and removal of inactive or obsolete data files. (FIPS). (2) In computer security, the removal of obsolete data by erasure, by overwriting of storage or by resetting registers. (FIPS). *See* OVERWRITING, PERSONAL COMPUTER SECURITY.

purity. In television, pertaining to the degree with which colour signals produce the desired colour on the screen of a receiver or monitor. A slight misalignment of the cathode ray tube deflection system can cause the red beam (say) to strike phosphor dots for green or blue screen colour. *See* CATHODE RAY TUBE, PHOSPHOR DOTS.

pushbutton dialing. In communications, the use of pushbuttons or keys instead of a rotary dial to generate the sequence of dialing digits for the establishment of a call. The signal is normally in the form of multiple tones. *See* MF KEYPAD, TOUCHSTONE. *Synonymous with* TONE DIALING.

pushdown stack. *See* STACK.

push off. In filming, an optical effect in which one image appears to be pushed off the screen by another.

push-up storage. In memory systems, a storage device that handles data such that the next item to be retrieved is the earliest stored item still in the storage device. *See* FIRST IN FIRST OUT, QUEUE.

put down. In printing, an instruction to printer to change to lower-case characters. *Compare* PUT UP. *See* LOWER CASE.

put to bed. In printing, pertaining to the state when a printing apparatus is prepared for the printing action.

put up. In printing, an instruction to a printer to change to capitals. *Compare* PUT DOWN.

PVC. *See* PERMANENT VIRTUAL CIRCUIT.

Q

QAM. *See* QUADRATURE AMPLITUDE MODULATION, QUEUED ACCESS METHOD.

Q channel. In optical media, one of the eight compact disc subcode channels (P–W). The Q channel carries the main control and display information. It identifies track, indexes and running times, and the absolute playing time of the disc. It also indicates whether the recorded information is audio or data, whether pre-emphasis is applied and whether digital copying is permitted. It can also indicate two- or four-channel audio, should four-channel audio be introduced. Optionally, it can include a disc catalogue number and international standard recording code information. Finally, it includes its own cyclic redundancy check. (Philips). *See* COMPACT DISC, CYCLIC REDUNDANCY CHECK, INTERNATIONAL STANDARD RECORDING CODE, PRE-EMPHASIS, QUADRUPHONIC, SUBCODE CHANNEL.

QIC. In memory systems, quarter-inch cartridge; pertaining to a set of standards developed for 1/4-inch tape cartridge systems. *See* MAGNETIC TAPE.

QPSX. In data communications, queued package synchronous exchange; a telephone exchange that can handle both data communications and voice.

quad. *See* EM QUAD, EN QUAD.

quadding. In printing, the action of putting abnormal spacing between words in order to fill out a line. *See* QUAD.

quadrature amplitude modulation. (QAM) In data communications, a method of converting digital signals into analog signals for transmission over a telephone network. It combines both amplitude and phase modulation techniques. A 16-point signal structure, giving 16 carrier states, can be achieved by combining 12 phase angles and four phases with amplitude modulation. The four phases that have modulated amplitudes have two possible amplitude levels. *Compare* AMPLITUDE MODULATION, FREQUENCY SHIFT KEYING, PHASE MODULATION. *See* ANALOG SIGNAL, CARRIER, DIGITAL SIGNAL.

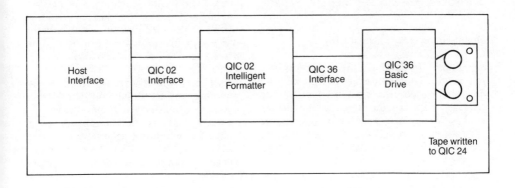

QIC
An example of a system using QIC standards.

417

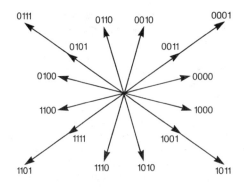

quadrature amplitude modulation

quadruphonic. A frequency modulation broadcast or audio recording system using four speakers, two in front of and two behind the listener. *Compare* MONOPHONIC, STEREOPHONIC.

quadruplex. In video recording, a system using four recording or replay heads on a wheel. *Compare* HELICAL SCAN. *See* TRANS-VERSE SCAN.

quadruture error. In video recording, a playback error condition that arises if the recording, or reading, heads do not arrive at the edge of the tape at the same relative time. *See* QUADRUPLEX. *Synonymous with* SWITCHING ERROR.

quadtree. In computer graphics, a form of run length encoding that exploits area, rather than scan line, coherence. *Compare* RUN LENGTH CODING.

quaint characters. *See* LIGATURES.

quantifier. In databases, a term used in a relational calculus expression. There are two quantifiers used: the existential quantifier read as 'there is'; the universal quantifier read as 'for all'. *See* EXISTENTIAL QUANTIFIER, RELATIONAL CALCULUS, RELATIONAL DATABASE, UNIVERSAL QUANTIFIER.

quantize. In communications, to assign one of a fixed set of values to an analog signal as part of an analog-to-digital conversion process (e.g. in pulse code modulation,

an analog signal is sampled, quantized and a corresponding set of binary pulses is produced). *See* PULSE CODE MODULATION.

quantizing noise. In communications, noise arising from the process of analog-to-digital and subsequent digital-to-analog conversion. The quantization process produces discrepancies in the input and output analog signals. *See* COMPANDOR, QUANTIZE.

Qube. A US videotex and cable television service. *See* CABLE TELEVISION, VIDEOTEX.

query language. In databases, a part of the database management system that provides facilities for the interrogation of data. The complexity of the query facilities vary from language to language. Query languages usually also provide some facilities for database modification and updating. *See* DATABASE MANAGEMENT SYSTEM, RELATIONAL DATABASE.

query modification. In database security, a technique in which user queries are modified to conform to the user access rights. For example if a user were only permitted to access personnel records for a specific department, and the input query were for all females in the organization, then the query would be modified so that the information returned would only relate to females in the aforementioned department.

Questel. In online information retrieval, an information retrieval service operated by Télésystémes Questel (France).

queue. (1) In data structures, a list in which items are added at one end and removed from the other. (2) Processes or items awaiting service on a first in first out principle. *Compare* STACK. *See* FIRST IN FIRST OUT, LIST.

queued access method. (QAM) In programming, any access method that synchronizes the transfer of data between a computer and its peripherals so as to minimize input/output delays.

queued package synchronous exchange. *See* QPSX.

queuing theory. In mathematics, a branch of probability theory used in the study of queues. Given the statistical properties of the servicing and arrival process, it attempts to predict the statistical properties of the queues (i.e. average length, waiting time, etc.). *See* POISSON DISTRIBUTION.

queuing time.   In communications, the time spent in waiting to send or receive a message due to contention on the line. *See* CONTENTION.

quick disc.   In optical media, a one-off optical disc produced on very short delivery (normally during one working day) to a special requirement or for program vali-

dation prior to disc replication. (Philips). *See* COMPACT DISC, OPTICAL DISC.

quire.   In printing, one-twentieth of a ream (i.e 25 sheets). *Compare* REAM.

quonking.   In audio, extraneous noise picked up by a microphone.

qwerty keyboard.   In peripherals, a conventional typewriter keyboard with the keys q,w e,r, t and y on the upper left-hand side. *Compare* AZERTY KEYBOARD, DVORAK KEYBOARD, MALTRON KEYBOARD, PRONTO KEYBOARD. *See* KEYBOARD.

R

race. In electronics, an undesirable state, produced by poor design of digital circuits, in which the output can vary with minor changes in the relative time of arrival of input pulses. *Compare* HAZARD.

RACF. In computer security, Resource Access Control Facility; an IBM software security product that assists in the control of user access to application data sets, volumes, transactions and terminals. *See* ACCESS CONTROL.

rack. (1) In electronics, a metal frame or chassis for the mounting of items of equipment. (2) In photography, to focus a lens.

radial transfer. In memory systems, the transmission of data between a peripheral unit and another device that is closer to the centre than the peripheral unit.

radian. In mathematics, a measure of angle, 3.1416 radians is equivalent to 180°. *Compare* STERADIAN.

radiating element. In communications, a basic unit of an antenna designed to produce electromagnetic radiation. *See* ANTENNA.

radio. In communications, a service for the transmission of speech and music by electromagnetic radiation. *See* ELECTROMAGNETIC RADIATION, RADIOCOMMUNICATION, RADIO WAVES.

radiocommunication. Telecommunication by means of electromagnetic waves at radio frequencies. *See* RADIO WAVES.

radio frequency. (RF) In communications, any frequency that can be used for communication by means of electromagnetic radiation. The range is considered to extend from a few hertz to 300 GHz, but radio frequency communication now extends into the infrared and visible light frequency ranges. *See* FIBER OPTICS, INFRARED, RADIO WAVES.

radio frequency emissions. *Synonymous with* COMPROMISING EMANATIONS.

radio frequency interference. *See* JAMMING. *Synonymous with* ELECTROMAGNETIC INTERFERENCE.

radio microphone. A microphone combined with a low-range radio transmitter, thus requiring no connecting wires to an amplifier that is used for studio or location work. *See* AMPLIFIER, TRANSMITTER.

radio paging. In communications, a method of contacting a user by means of a small portable radio receiver. The caller dials a number on an ordinary telephone, and the called party receives a bleep from the pager. Current systems can emit four tones to convey varying information. Other devices can display a numerical or alphanumerical message.

radio waves. Electromagnetic waves with frequencies in the range 10 kHz to 3000 GHz. *See* ELECTROMAGNETIC RADIATION, RADIO FREQUENCY.

radix. In mathematics, in a radix numeration system the total value of a numeral represented by a string of characters is the sum of each character multiplied by its weight. The ratio of the weight of one digit to the preceding one is the radix for the number system used and is always a positive integer. Thus in a hexadecimal system the radix is 16, and the number 123 has the decimal value of $291 = ((1 \times 16 \times 16) + (2 \times 16) + 3)$. *See* BASE, HEXADECIMAL.

radix point. In mathematics, the character, or implied character, that separates the integral part of the numeral from the fractional part (e.g. the decimal point). *See* RADIX.

Raduga. In communications, a series of Russian C band geostationary satellites; raduga is Russian for rainbow. *See* C BAND, GEOSTATIONARY SATELLITE, GORIZONT, INTER-SPUTNIK, MOLNIYA, STATSIONAR.

ragged centre. In printing, a ragged setting in which any necessary additional spaces are added equally to the left and right of the text. If the total number of necessary additional spaces is not an equal number then the remaining space is added to the left of the text. *See* RAGGED SETTING.

ragged left. In printing, a ragged setting with the text set flush with the right-hand margin and any necessary additional spaces added to the left of the text. *See* RAGGED SETTING.

ragged right. In printing, a ragged setting with the text set flush to the left-hand margin and any necessary additional spaces added to the right of the text. *See* RAGGED SETTING.

ragged setting. In printing, the method used to adjust the length of a line to its desired measure when one interword space value is used. Additional spaces are added to the right or left of text, as necessary, giving a ragged appearance on at least one side. *Compare* JUSTIFY. *See* MEASURE, RAGGED LEFT, RAGGED RIGHT, RAGGED CENTRE.

rag paper. In printing, high-quality paper made from cotton rags. (Desktop).

RAM. *See* RANDOM-ACCESS MEMORY.

RAM disk. *Synonymous with* VIRTUAL DISK.

RAM refresh operation. In memory systems, an operation necessary because dynamic random-access memory (RAM) devices require a periodic rewrite operation to ensure that their contents are retained. *See* DYNAMIC MEMORY, REFRESH.

random. A character set that has equal probability of being selected from the total population of possibilities, hence unpredictable. (ANSI).

random access. In memory systems, access to data such that the next location from which a word or byte is to be retrieved is independent of the location of a previously accessed word or byte. *Compare* SEQUENTIAL ACCESS. *See* DIRECT ACCESS.

random-access memory. (RAM) (1) In memory systems, a memory chip used with microprocessors. Information can be both read from, and written into, the memory, but the contents are lost when the power supply is removed. (2) In memory systems, any form of storage in which the access time for any item of data is independent of the location of the data most recently obtained (e.g. immediate access store has a random-access capability, but magnetic disk does not). *See* IMMEDIATE-ACCESS STORE, MAGNETIC DISK. *Synonymous with* RANDOM-ACCESS STORAGE.

random-access projector. In audiovisual devices, a projector that permits the selection of any sequence of slides independent of their order in the slide tray.

random-access storage. *Synonymous with* RANDOM-ACCESS MEMORY.

random-area update. In computer graphics, an area of any shape, updated as a succession of horizontal whole or partial line updates. (Philips). *See* LINE UPDATE.

random cipher. In data security, a cipher in which, for a given ciphertext message and a given key, the decipherment process is as likely to produce one plaintext message as any other. The result of the decipherment process for a given key and a given ciphertext message is uniformly distributed over the complete range of meaningful and meaningless messages, of the given length, in the language. *See* CRYPTOGRAPHIC KEY, INFORMATION THEORY.

random error. In computing, a spontaneous bit error, usually not reproducible and independent of the data. This type of error can be caused by device operation up to physical boundaries. (Philips).

random interlace. In television, a camera system in which the positioning of horizontal lines of each succeeding vertical field is not fixed, and the line spacing may vary in a random manner. *Compare* POSITIVE INTERLACE. *See* FIELD, INTERLACE.

random numbers. In applications, numbers generated by a random process which have the properties that each number is independent of its predecessors, and the probability distribution of the numbers conforms to a specified distribution (e.g. gaussian, Poisson, uniform). Such numbers are employed in educational software, computer games, simulations, etc.

The application for random numbers arises when an input is required to be unpredictable (i.e. independent of previous inputs). For example, in a teaching package it is often required to present a series of examples drawn at random, computer games similarly require that the player is unaware of the forthcoming event. Simulations are often employed to study complex systems subject to random disturbances (e.g. various strategies for providing service in a supermarket can be tested by the use of random numbers to provide a representation of the arrival of customers).

True random numbers can only be produced by a genuine random process (e.g. the number of electrons emitted by a heated cathode in a small interval of time). An approximation to random number sequences, known as pseudorandom numbers, can, however, be generated by mathematical techniques; pseudorandom number generators can be supplied as software routines or incorporated into the facilities of high-level languages. These pseudorandom numbers are generated by a deterministic procedure and do not therefore conform to the strict definition of a random number, but within their limitations they are suitable for a variety of applications. *See* GAUSSIAN DISTRIBUTION, HIGH-LEVEL LANGUAGE, POISSON DISTRIBUTION, UNIFORM DISTRIBUTION.

random process. A process in which the output cannot be fully predetermined from a knowledge of the system variables. One in which the outcome depends upon one or more random events. *See* RANDOM NUMBERS.

range. In mathematics, the difference between the highest and lowest value that a function or quantity may assume.

ranging figures. *Synonymous with* LINING FIGURES.

rank. (1) To arrange in ascending or descending order according to some criterion. (2) A measure of the relative position in an array, group, series or classification. *See* ARRAY.

Rank-Cintel Flying Spot Scanner. In video, a proprietary device used to produce prerecorded video cassettes from motion picture film. *See* FLYING SPOT SCANNER.

RA paper sizes. *Synonymous with* A, B AND C SERIES OF PAPER SIZES.

rapid-access processing. In photography, a method of processing exposed photographic film or paper using high-temperature chemistry and shallow bath processing to produce dry products in under two minutes.

rapid post-editing. (RPE) In machine translation, a form of post-editing in which only gross errors of machine translation are remedied, but no attempt is made to improve the style of the translation. It is used when the ultimate user needs only to be able to gain an outline of the document's contents. *See* POST-EDITING.

RARC. *See* REGIONAL ADMINISTRATIVE RADIO CONFERENCE.

raster. In peripherals, a predetermined pattern of lines that provides uniform coverage of display space on a visual display unit. *See* VISUAL DISPLAY UNIT.

raster count. In computer graphics, the number of lines in one dimension within a display space. *See* DISPLAY SPACE, RASTER.

raster display. In peripherals, a technique for displaying computer-generated images. For a black/white picture the image is conceptually divided up into a matrix of dots. A frame store holds 0s or 1s in the memory locations corresponding to the locations of the dots. The display controller scans the frame store a line at a time, and switches the electron beam of a cathode ray tube on and off, during the scan, according to the value of the bits in the frame store. Grey levels can be provide for the image by the use of a number of bits for each pixel.

Raster displays may be interlaced or non-interlaced. In the former case the picture is divided into two fields corresponding to the odd and even lines of the scan. Each field is then displayed in succession (i.e. all even lines are displayed, then all odd lines, etc.). This technique is employed in television to reduce flicker, but television images have considerable visual redundancy whereas in computer graphics a horizontal line, which will only be refreshed in every other scan, will flicker for low refresh rates. If high-persistence phosphors are employed to reduce flicker the image will become blurred as items are moved around the screen or deleted. Non-interlaced displays refresh each line during a scan. With a refresh rate of 50–60 Hz there is no perceptible flicker, and long-persistence phosphors can be used.

Raster displays can provide and manipulate solid areas of display, whereas vector displays are effectively restricted to wire frame images. On the other hand low-resolution raster displays are less pleasing to the eye; diagonal lines have a distinct staircase pattern. Early raster displays were limited in resolutions, because of the cost of random-access memory, to resolutions of the order of 256 x 256, but modern devices can provide resolutions as high as 2048 x 1568.

Raster displays can also provide colour images. In this case a number is associated with each dot, or pixel, giving colour attributes. This number is used as an index to a look-up table, which then specifies the red, green and blue mix for the pixel. The additional number of bits required to store colour attributes naturally increases the size of memory required for the frame store. *Compare* DIRECT-VIEW STORAGE TUBE, VECTOR REFRESH, WIRE FRAME. *See* BIT MAP, CATHODE RAY TUBE, COLOUR LOOK-UP TABLE, FIELD, FRAME STORE, GREY SCALE, PIXEL.

raster image processor. (RIP) In printing, a unit in a laser printer. The raster image processor is a hardware-dependent device used to build up an image of a complete page on the photosensitive drum of a laser engine. The RIP interprets the page description language instructions, which include page layout details, font, point size, tint and other details. *See* DESK-TOP PUBLISHING, LASER ENGINE, PAGE DESCRIPTION LANGUAGE.

raster imaging. In computer graphics, the capture, storage, processing and display of an image represented by an array of pixels. An image may be captured in this format by an optical scanner, television camera or self-scanning camera. The stored image may occupy several megabytes of memory; binary thresholding and data compression techniques (e.g. run length coding) may be employed to reduce the storage requirements.

This technique may be employed to store complex images (e.g. engineering or architectural drawings), which can be automatically captured as described above. The raster image can be processed (e.g. to enhance contrast), but this form of storage does not permit the type of computations and manipulations associated with vector generation techniques. However, it is possible to perform processing such as overlaying where, for example, a complex diagram of pipeline distribution is stored separately from a plant layout, and the two images are then combined as required. *Compare* VECTOR IMAGING. *See* BINARY THRESHOLDING, PIXEL, RUN LENGTH CODING, SELF-SCANNING CAMERA.

rasterization. In computer graphics, the process of converting the coordinates representing line end points into the appropriate pattern of bits in a raster display bit map. *See* BIT MAP, RASTER DISPLAY.

raster scan. In peripherals, a technique for recording or displaying an image using a line-by-line sweep across the entire display area. *See* RASTER DISPLAY.

raster unit. In computer graphics, the distance between adjacent pixels. *See* PIXEL.

rate. In information theory, a measure of the average number of bits of information in each character of a message. Consider the set of messages of length N, for a given language, if the entropy of the messages is H then the rate for all sequences of the language of length N is given by H/N. *See* ABSOLUTE RATE, ENTROPY.

rate centre. In communications, a reference point, corresponding to a given geographical location, which is employed by telephone companies in the determination of mileage measurements required for the calculation of interexchange rates.

rate making. In communications, the process of determining the appropriate level of charges to be set by a common carrier for its services. *See* COMMON CARRIER.

rational number. In mathematics, any number that can be expressed by the ratio of two integers where the divider is non-zero.

raw data. In programming, unprocessed and non-reduced data.

raw tape. In recording, blank magnetic tape not previously used for recording. *Compare* VIRGIN.

Rayleigh fading. In communications, the variations in strength of received radio signals due to the different paths travelled; signals may be reflected from moving and stationary objects, various layers in the atmosphere, etc. *See* IONOSPHERE.

ray tracing. In computer graphics, a sophisticated method to produce a high-quality graphic display allowing for object transparency and image reflections off reflective objects. The viewer's space is considered as a window to the object. The ray tracer is considered to send out a ray from each pixel in turn. If the ray does not strike any part of the object or light source it is computed as black or background. If the ray hits part of the object the ray tracer checks for reflectivity, transparency and index of refraction. The path of the reflected and refracted rays is computed according to the orientation of the object surface; the relative magnitudes of light intensity of the rays are also computed. Each ray is then traced further with more subdividing each time an object is intercepted. The subdividing continues until the ray attains a light source or background, or the total number of rays reaches some predetermined limit. When a ray reaches a light source the ray's component for the brightness of the pixel is computed from the intensity of the light source and the relative intensity of the ray. The brightness for the pixel is thus computed by summing the contribution from each ray. This technique produces high-quality displays, but it makes extremely heavy demands on processing power. *See* PIXEL.

RBOC. In communications, Regional Bell Operating Company; a company divested from AT&T which originally offered local telephone services and is now offering other communication services. *See* AT&T.

RBS. In communications, radio base station; the controlling station at the centre of a cell in a cellular radio system. *See* CELLULAR RADIO.

R channel. In optical media, one of the eight compact disc subcode channels (P–W). At present it is only allocated to compact disc graphics. (Philips). *See* COMPACT DISC, SUBCODE CHANNEL.

R-DAT. In recording, one of the proposed formats for digital audio tape recording. In this format a helical scan similar to video tape recorders is implemented to provide the required 20 megabits per second data transfer rate. *Compare* S-DAT. *See* DIGITAL AUDIO TAPE, HELICAL SCAN.

RDC. *See* REMOTE DIAGNOSTIC CENTRE.

R&D. Research and development.

read. In memory systems and peripherals, to acquire or interpret data from an input device, store or some other medium. *Compare* WRITE.

read access. In computer security, permission to read information. (DOD). *Compare* WRITE ACCESS. *See* READ.

reader. (1) In computing, a device that converts data from one form of storage into another. (2) In printing, one who reads text for a specific purpose. *See* COPY READER. (3) In micrographics. *See* MICROFORM READER.

read error. In peripherals, an error in the reading of data from a storage medium. (Philips).

read head. In memory systems, a magnetic head used to read data or signals from a magnetic recording medium. *Compare* WRITING HEAD. *See* MAGNETIC HEAD, READ/WRITE HEAD.

read-mostly memory. (RMM) In memory systems, programmable memory that holds relatively static data. The term may also be applied to programmable read-only memory or to random-access memory that has special safeguards to prevent overwriting. *See* PROGRAMMABLE READ-ONLY MEMORY, RANDOM-ACCESS MEMORY.

read-only memory. (ROM) In memory systems, a storage device whose contents can only be changed by a particular user, by particular operating conditions or by a particular external process. Read-only storage can include storage media where the writing action is inhibited by the operating system or by some mechanical device (e.g. a tag on a diskette). The term read-only memory implies a storage device not designed to be modified by conventional write procedures and which is used to store permanent information in computers and microcomputers. *See* ELECTRICALLY PROGRAMMABLE READ-ONLY MEMORY, FLOPPY DISC, INTERPRETER, OPERATING SYSTEM, PROGRAMMABLE READ-ONLY MEMORY.

read-only memory compact disc. *See* COMPACT DISC – READ-ONLY MEMORY.

read-only storage. *See* READ-ONLY MEMORY.

read out. The retrieval of stored data. *See* READ.

read/write head. In memory systems, a magnetic head capable of both reading and writing actions. *See* MAGNETIC HEAD.

read/write medium. In peripherals and recording, a medium that can be both written (record) and read (playback). Magnetic media can generally be written, read, erased and re-written repeatedly. Optical carriers are at present read-only, or write once, read many times (WORM). Erasable optical discs are the subject of intensive research. (Philips). *See* COMPACT DISC, COMPACT DISC - READ-ONLY MEMORY, DOR, ERASABLE OPTICAL DISC, MAGNETIC DISK, MAGNETIC TAPE, OPTICAL DIGITAL DISC, WORM.

read/write slot. *Synonymous with* HEAD SLOT.

ready state. In data communications, a condition at the data terminal equipment/data circuit terminating equipment (DTE/DCE) interface that indicates the DTE is prepared to accept an incoming call and the DCE is ready to accept a call request. *See* CALL REQUEST, DATA CIRCUIT TERMINATING EQUIPMENT, DATA TERMINAL EQUIPMENT.

real estate. In microelectronics, the area of a chip. *See* CHIP.

real number. In mathematics, a number that may be represented by a finite or infinite number of digits in fixed radix numeration system. *Compare* IMAGINARY NUMBER. *See* RADIX.

real-time. In computing, pertaining to actions that are performed in conjunction with some external process or user and which are required to meet the time constraints imposed by that process or user (e.g. control of an aircraft guidance system, an online information service).

real-time clock. In computing, a unit that produces a timing pulse train. The pulses are used to operate interrupts and thus synchronize computer operations with external events. *See* INTERRUPT, PULSE TRAIN.

real-time data. In optical media, data taken directly from a interactive compact disc, whose flow cannot be interrupted or stopped within the bounds of a real-time data record. (Philips). *See* COMPACT DISC – INTERACTIVE, REAL-TIME DATA RECORD.

real-time data record. In optical media, the smallest amount of real-time data on an interactive compact disc that can be randomly accessed. (Philips). *See* COMPACT DISC – INTERACTIVE, REAL-TIME DATA.

real-time input. In computing, input data received into the system within a time scale, or at instants of time, determined by some other system. *Compare* REAL-TIME OUTPUT.

real-time interactive system. An interactive system that responds to events directly as they occur (i.e. in real time). The interactive compact disc is an example of such a system. (Philips). *See* INTERACTIVE SYSTEM.

real-time operating system. (RTOS) In computing, an operating system that functions within the constraints of real time (e.g. CD RTOS). Such an operating system is essential for full interactivity. (Philips). *See* CD REAL-TIME OPERATING SYSTEM.

real-time operation. *See* REAL-TIME.

real-time output. In computing, output data that must be delivered within a time scale, or at instants of time, determined by some other system. *Compare* REAL-TIME INPUT.

real-time reaction. In computer security, a response to a penetration attempt that is detected and diagnosed in time to prevent the actual penetration. (FIPS). *See* PENETRATION.

real-time sector. In optical media, a interactive compact disc (CD-I) sector with the real-time bit set. The data in this sector must be processed without interrupting the real-time behaviour of the CD-I system. (Philips). *See* COMPACT DISC – INTERACTIVE, REAL-TIME DATA, SECTOR, SYNCHRONIZATION.

ream. In printing, 500 sheets of paper. *Compare* QUIRE.

rear projection. *Synonymous with* BACKGROUND PROJECTION.

rear screen. In filming and audiovisual aids, a screen located between the projector and audience. It is manufactured from translucent glass or plastic with a special coating. The slide or film must be reversed, or a mirror or prism used, to provide the correct image for the viewer.

reasonableness check. In programming, a test for the existence of a gross error (e.g. by checking that a data value lies within a prespecified range).

recall ratio. In library science, the number of documents, retrieved from an index in response to a question on a given theme, divided by the number of documents on the theme known to be indexed. *Compare* RELEVANCE RATIO.

received line signal detector. In data communications, a signal from a modem to a computer to inform it that some device is trying to make contact. It may be used to trigger the computer to generate a logon invitation. *See* LOGON, MODEM, RS-232C. *Synonymous with* CARRIER DETECT.

receive-only. (RO) In data communications, pertaining to terminals or other equipment capable of receiving data or messages, but lacking a keyboard or other input device.

receiver. (RX) (1) In data security, the person, institution or other entity responsible for the receipt of a message. (ANSI). (2) In communications and broadcasting, a device used for detecting and decoding information transmitted down a line, or optical fiber, or as a radiated electromagnetic wave.

recipient. In data communications, the person, institution or other entity that is responsible for an authorized user to receive a message. (ANSI). *Compare* ORIGINATOR. *See* MESSAGE.

reciprocity law. In photography, the density of the developed negative image is proportional to the exposure time. *See* DENSITY.

recognition memory. (REM) In character recognition, a read-only memory in the optical character reader holding the bit patterns of characters in the font. This data is pattern-matched with the corresponding information from the input character. *See* FONT, PATTERN, READ-ONLY MEMORY.

reconfiguration. In computing, to add or remove components of a system or to change their interconnections.

record. (1) In data structures, a collection of related data treated as a unit (e.g. details of name, address, age, occupation and department of an employee in a personnel file). *Compare* FIELD. *See* LOGICAL RECORD, PHYSICAL RECORD. (2) In memory systems, to store signals on a recording medium for later use.

record button. In recording, a plastic button on video cassettes that can be removed to prevent re-recording.

record current optimizer. In recording, a device that facilitates the setting of the optimum current to the magnetic heads. The current to the recording head is adjusted in small steps, and the audio playback voltage is monitored until it just reaches saturation. *See* MAGNETIC HEAD, SATURATION.

recorder. A device used to make a permanent or temporary record of signals, emanating from an audio or audiovisual source. It will normally have playback as well as record facilities. *See* AUDIO CASSETTE RECORDER, AUDIO TAPE RECORDER, VIDEO RECORDER, VIDEO TAPE RECORDING.

record gap. *See* INTERBLOCK GAP.

recording density. Synonymous with packing density.

record layout. In data structures, the manner in which the data is organized in the record (i.e. description and size of fields). *See* FIELD.

record length. In data structures, the number of words or characters in a record. *See* RECORD, WORD.

record lock. In computing, a facility to deny access to a record in a file. It is used in multiuser systems to prevent two users from simultaneously updating the same record. *Compare* FILE LOCK. *See* FILE, MULTIUSER, RECORD.

record separator character. In data structures, the indicator specifying the logical boundary between records. *See* RECORD.

recoverable ABEND. In computing, an ABEND that causes control to be passed to an error-handling routine. The routine enables program execution to continue. *Compare* UNRECOVERABLE ABEND. *See* ABEND.

recoverable error. In computing, a condition that enables the program to continue execution following an error, after any necessary correcting action has been taken. *Compare* UNRECOVERABLE ERROR.

recovery. In reliability, the activity of placing a system back into an error-free state from which normal operation can resume.

recovery procedures. (1) In computer security, the actions necessary to restore a system's computational capability and data files after a system failure or penetration. (FIPS). *See* PENETRATION. (2) In data communications, processes whereby specified stations attempt to resolve erroneous or conflicting conditions arising from some malfunction or external situation in the transfer of data.

rectangular update. In computer graphics, update of a rectangular area, comprising the whole or part of the screen. (Philips). *Compare* LINE UPDATE.

rectangular waveguide. In communications, waveguides of rectangular cross-section used for the transmission of signals over relatively short distances (e.g. from a transmitter to an antenna). *Compare* CIRCULAR WAVEGUIDE. *See* WAVEGUIDE.

recto. In printing, any right-handed, odd-numbered page of a book. *Compare* VERSO.

recursive routine. In programming, a routine that may be used as a routine of itself, calling itself directly or being called by another routine, one that it itself has called. For example in the computation of n x $(n-1)$ x $(n-2)$x ... x 1, the routine is passed the parameter n, if $n = 1$ or 0 it returns the value of 1, otherwise it calls itself with the value $(n-1)$, multiplies the result of the call by n and returns the product. The routine continues to call itself until the parameter passed is 1 when the value of the routine (i.e. 1) is then returned and the successive calls then receive the routine's results. *Compare* ITERATION.

Red Book. In optical media, the informal name for the digital audio compact disc specification. (Philips). *Compare* GREEN BOOK, YELLOW BOOK. *See* COMPACT DISC – DIGITAL AUDIO,

red disc. In optical media, a digital audio compact disc. (Philips). *Compare* GREEN DISC, YELLOW DISC. *See* COMPACT DISC – DIGITAL AUDIO,

red-tape operation. In computing, an operation on data that is necessary for internal purposes, but does not contribute to the final answer.

reduced instruction set computer. (RISC) In computing, a computer designed with a simple instruction set aimed at optimizing the total performance by providing simple and fast decoding for the machine code instructions most commonly employed in computer operation. The concept contrasts with the development of microprocessors with very sophisticated and powerful instruction sets.
  The argument for simpler instruction sets is that a high proportion of all instructions used in execution are comparatively simple. The provision of the less commonly executed complex instructions increases the complexity of chip design and reduces the speed of operation. This is due to the increased number of gates causing longer wire delays, less power available per gate and the interposing of more circuit elements in the information flow (e.g. multiplexers). *See* GATE, INSTRUCTION SET, MACHINE CODE INSTRUCTION, MULTIPLEXER.

reduction. In micrographics, a measure of the linear relationship between the original and final image. A reduction of 16:1 is indicated as 16x. *See* HIGH REDUCTION, LOW REDUCTION, MEDIUM REDUCTION, ULTRA HIGH REDUCTION, VERY HIGH REDUCTION.

redundancy. (1) In information theory, the difference between the absolute rate and the rate of a language. *See* ABSOLUTE RATE, RATE. (2) In reliability, the use of additional system components to mitigate the effects of component malfunction. *See* HARDWARE REDUNDANCY, INFORMATION REDUNDANCY, SOFTWARE REDUNDANCY TIME REDUNDANCY. (3) In communications, the fraction of the gross information content of a message that can be eliminated without losing any essential information. In computing and data communications, redundant characters (e.g. parity bits) are added to data to provide a method of detecting errors in transmission or pro-

cessing. *See* PARITY CHECKING, REDUNDANCY CHECKING.

redundancy checking. In codes, the performance of a calculation on received data and comparison of results with redundant codes to check for certain processing or transmission errors. *See* ERROR-CORRECTING CODE, ERROR-DETECTING CODE, REDUNDANT CODE.

redundant code. In codes, additional bits added to characters for error-checking purposes (e.g. parity bits and Hamming codes). *See* HAMMING CODE, PARITY CHECKING, REDUNDANCY CHECKING.

redundant processing. In data processing, a repetition of processing and an accompanying comparison of individual results for equality.

reel-fed. *Synonymous with* WEB-FED.

reel-to-reel. Pertaining to the copying of signals, or data, from one reel of tape to another (i.e. reel-to-reel recorder). *See* REEL-TO-REEL RECORDER.

reel-to-reel recorder. A tape recorder using magnetic tape threaded on two reels. *Compare* CASSETTE RECORDER. *See* REEL-TO-REEL.

re-entrant routine. In programming, a routine that may be repeatedly entered and may be entered before executions of the same routine have been completed. The calling programs must not, however, change any of the routine's instructions or external parameters. Such routines may be used simultaneously by a number of programs. *See* PURE CODE.

reference mark. In printing, symbols that direct the reader to a footnote or to a given reference. Common reference marks are symbols termed asterisk, dagger, double dagger, section, parallel and paragraph.

reference monitor. In computer security, a security control concept in which an abstract machine mediates accesses to objects by subjects. In principle, a reference monitor should be complete (in that it mediated every access), isolated from modification by system entities and verifiable. A security kernel is an implementation of a reference monitor for a given hardware base. (MTR). *See* OBJECT, SECURITY KERNEL, SUBJECT.

reference volume. In recording, the magnitude of an electrical signal, usually corresponding to speech or music waveforms, that gives a zero reading on a standard volume indicator. It corresponds to 1 milliwatt of power delivered to an electrical load of 600 ohms at 1000 hertz. *See* HERTZ, VOICE UNIT, VUmeter.

referral centre. In distributed processing, an independent body outside the data-processing department that is set up to help coordinate and implement micro–mainframe links. *Compare* INFORMATION CENTRE. *See* COOPERATIVE PROCESSING.

referral database. In online information retrieval, a database that refers users to other, or more additional, sources of information. *Compare* BIBLIOGRAPHIC DATABASE, DIRECTORY DATABASE, FULL-TEXT DATABASE, NUMERIC DATABASE.

reflectance. (1) In optics, the ratio between the quantity of light that is reflected from a given surface and the quantity of light incident on that surface. *Compare* ABSORPTANCE, TRANSMITTANCE. (2) In character recognition, a value assigned to a character or colour of ink relative to its background. *See* REFLECTANCE INK.

reflectance ink. In character recognition, an ink with a reflectance approximating to the acceptable paper reflectance level for the reader used. *See* REFLECTANCE.

reflection. In computer graphics, light incident upon a surface will be partly absorbed, partly transmitted and partly reflected, according to the optical properties of the material and the surface. If the surface is smooth then the rays of a narrow beam of incident light will strike the surface at the same angle, giving a reflected beam with an angle of reflection equal to the angle of incidence. An irregular, rough or matt reflecting surface, however, produces diffuse light with the reflected rays having an almost infinite variety of directions. *Compare* REFRACTION. *See* RAY TRACING.

reflective disc. In optical media, an optical videodisc in which the laser beam is reflected off the shiny disc surface. *Compare* TRANSMISSIVE DISC. *See* OPTICAL DISC.

reflex. In photography, an optical mirror system that permits the viewing of the action field through the camera lens. *See* ACTION FIELD.

reflex camera. *See* REFLEX.

refraction. In computer graphics, when light is transmitted through a number of different materials the direction of the rays change at each interface according to the optical properties of the two materials at the interface. *Compare* REFLECTION. *See* RAY TRACING, REFRACTIVE INDEX.

refractive index. In computer graphics, a measure of the angle through which light is bent when it passes through the interface of two transparent media. The ratio of the sine of the angle of incidence to the sine of the angle of refraction is equal to the ratio of the refractive index of the second medium to that of the first. *See* RAY TRACING, REFRACTION, SINE.

refresh. (1) In memory systems, a signal sent to dynamic random-access memory to enable it to maintain its storage contents. *See* RAM REFRESH OPERATION. (2) In peripherals, the technique of continuously energizing the phosphor coating of a cathode ray tube screen to keep the display visible. *See* REFRESHED CATHODE RAY TUBE.

refreshable program. In programming, a program that may be replaced at any time without affecting either the results or the sequence of processing.

refreshed cathode ray tube. In computer displays, a cathode ray tube screen that must be continually refreshed to keep the display visible. *Compare* DIRECT-VIEW STORAGE TUBE. *See* CATHODE RAY TUBE, REFRESH.

refresh RAM. *See* RAM REFRESH OPERATION.

refresh rate. In peripherals, the number of times per second that a display is drawn on the screen of a refreshed cathode ray tube. *See* REFRESH, REFRESHED CATHODE RAY TUBE.

regeneration. (1) In peripherals, the process of repeatedly producing a display image on a screen of a cathode ray tube so that it remains visible. *See* REFRESH, REFRESHED CATHODE RAY TUBE. (2) In communications, the process of producing a duplicate of a message or data from an unambiguously recognizable, but distorted signal (e.g. a set of on/off pulses attenuated in transmission). *See* PULSE REGENERATOR.

Regional Administrative Radio Conference. (RARC) In communications, an organization that sets frequency allocations for a region of the world. *Compare* WORLD ADMINISTRATIVE RADIO CONFERENCE.

region generation. In video, an overlay technique defining the overlay area separate from the image contents. (Philips). *See* OVERLAY.

region growing. *Synonymous* BLOB GROWING.

register. (1) In printing, the correct positioning of an image especially when printing one colour on another. (Desktop). (2) In computing, a memory device, usually highspeed, and of limited specified length (e.g. one byte, one word); used for special purposes (e.g. arithmetic operations).

registered design. Features of shape, configuration, pattern or ornament applied to an article by any industrial process or means, that have been registered with the appropriate authority.

register insertion. In data communications, pertaining to a technique in which a message to be transmitted, in a local area network, is first loaded into a shift register. The network loop is broken and the shift register inserted either when it is idle or at a point between two adjacent messages. The message to be sent is then shifted out to the network. Any message arriving during this period is shifted into the register behind the transmitted message. *Compare* CONTROL TOKEN, DAISY CHAIN, MESSAGE SLOT. *See* LOCAL AREA NETWORK.

register marks. In printing, marks outside the job area of a trimmed printed sheet used to ensure an accurate register. *See* REGISTER.

regular 8. In filming, 8-mm film with 40 frames per foot. The perforations are the same size as 16-mm film, and there is one perforation per frame line.

regulatory agency. In data communications, an agency controlling the specialized and common carrier tariffs. *See* COMMON CARRIER, SPECIALIZED COMMON CARRIER, TARIFF.

relation. In databases, a flat file. In a relational database the data is stored as entities, and attributes, of those entities in two-dimensional arrays (e.g. a relation) might comprise employee name, employee number, department and salary. *See* FLAT FILE, RELATIONAL DATABASE.

relational algebra. In databases, a language that provides a set of operators for manipulating relations in a relational database (e.g. if there were two relations R1 (employee number, employee department) and R2 (employee number, project) and a user required to know which departments were involved with a given project then a set of operations would be specified and the resulting relation would comprise a table of departments associated with the project). *Compare* RELATIONAL CALCULUS. *See* JOIN, PROJECTION, RELATIONAL DATABASE.

relational calculus. In databases, a language in which a user specifies the set of results required from the manipulation of the data in a relational database. Relational calculus provides a concise unambiguous mathematical notation for statements, such as take the two relations (employee number, project) and (employee number, department) and produce the relation (department) for project = DYNAMO. The result would be a list of departments whose employees were working on the DYNAMO project. The distinction between relational algebra and relational calculus is that the former specifies the actions to be performed and the latter specifies the nature of the desired result. *Compare* RELATIONAL ALGEBRA. *See* RELATIONAL DATABASE.

relational database. In databases, a database in which the individual files, termed relations, hold data in the form of flat files or tables. The restriction upon the form of these tables is given below.

(a) Within the relational system the table must contain only one type of record. Each record has a fixed number of fields, all of which are explicitly named.
(b) The fields within a table are distinct and repeating groups are not allowed.
(c) There are no duplicate records.
(d) There is no predetermined sequence of records.

The processing of data involves operations on whole tables, or relations, rather than upon individual records within a table. The result of such processing is new tables. The table is rectangular, thus all entries must contain data and there are no repeating groups. If a record were to contain an employee's history and the variable number of training courses attended were to be recorded then a separate table would be constructed. This table would contain, for example, four fields: employee's number, name of course, date commenced and result. The variable number of courses attended would thus be accommodated by a variable number of entries in the 'training course' relation.

All the values in a given column refer to the same class of attribute of the entries. These values must be drawn from some domain of possible values (e.g. a date). The fundamental operations on a relational database are selection, projection, join and division; the last is, however, not so commonly employed. Selection produces a new table containing the same number of columns as the original relation, but the rows will contain those of the original relation that satisfy some specified criteria. For example if the table provided details of sales and salesmen then the selection might be on the basis of sales greater than 2000.

The projection operation on a table specifies columns to be selected. The resulting table thus contains only a subset of the columns of the original table. Moreover, it may only contain a subset of the original rows. This is because no duplicate records are permitted in relational databases, and if two rows only differ in the columns deleted by the projection then only one record will be carried forward to the new relation.

The join operation combines information from two or more tables. A common field in two tables is used as the basis of the combination and records with equal values in the common field are concatenated in the resulting relation.

It is necessary to give careful consideration to the contents of relations and to the inherent relationships between attributes of a record, the inclusion of redundant information in a record can lead to problems, and a process of normalization is essential in the construction of a relational database. *See* ATTRIBUTE, DIVISION, DOMAIN, FIELD, FLAT FILE, JOIN, NORMAL FORMS, PROJECTION, RECORD, RELATION, RELATIONAL ALGEBRA, RELATIONAL CALCULUS, REPEATING GROUP, SELECTION.

relational operator. In mathematics, a symbol used to compare two values (e.g. $>$ meaning greater than).

relationship. In databases, a statement linking two entities (e.g. if a personnel database has entities — employee and department — then 'works in' would be a relationship linking these entities). *Compare* ATTRIBUTE, ENTITY. *See* RELATIONAL DATABASE.

relative address. In programming, an address specified in terms of its relationship to a given base address. *Compare* ABSOLUTE ADDRESS. *See* ADDRESS, ADDRESSING MODE. *Synonymous with* DISPLACEMENT.

relative data. In computer graphics, values specifying displacements from the actual coordinates in a display space.

relative error. In mathematics, the ratio of the absolute error of a quantity to its true, theoretically correct or specified value.

relative motion. The motion of one object as observed from another. The motion of object A as seen from object B is the reciprocal of B's motion as observed by A. This effect can be exploited in filming by substituting a camera movement for that of the subject.

relay. In communications, a point-to-point reception and retransmission system.

relay centre. *Synonymous with* MESSAGE-SWITCHING CENTRE.

release graphics. In videotex, the complementary state to 'hold graphics' in which control characters are displayed as spaces. *Compare* HOLD GRAPHICS.

relevance ratio. In library science, the number of retrieved documents actually required divided by the total number of documents retrieved in response to a question on a given theme. *Compare* RECALL RATIO. *Synonymous with* PRECISION RATIO.

reliability. The ability of a system to perform its function under specified conditions for a stated period of time. The overall reliability of a system is measured in terms of the mean time between failure, the mean time to repair and the mean time to recover. *See* MEAN TIME BETWEEN FAILURE, MEAN TIME TO RECOVER, MEAN TIME TO REPAIR, REDUNDANCY.

relief printing. *Compare* INTAGLIO, PLANOGRAPHIC. *Synonymous with* LETTERPRESS.

relocate. In computing, to move a program from one area of main memory to another and to adjust its address values so that it can be executed in its new location.

REM. *See* RECOGNITION MEMORY.

remanence. In computer security, the residual magnetism that remains on magnetic storage media after degaussing. (FIPS). *See* DEGAUSS.

remote. (1) Pertaining to a system connected to a host system by a communication link. (2) In data communications, pertaining to a cluster control unit that is connected to a mainframe via a modem, as compared to a local controller that is directly wired. *See* CLUSTER CONTROL UNIT.

remote diagnostic centre. (RDC) In computing, a centre operated by an equipment supplier to reduce the number of on-site visits by maintenance engineers.

remote eject. In memory systems, a facility of some floppy disk drives in which the disk is automatically ejected before the computer is switched off to ensure that transient voltages do not corrupt disk contents.

remote job entry. (RJE) In computing, the submission of a job to a peripheral that is connected to the processor via a communication link.

remote printing. In printing, the production of hard-copy output from a printer situated at a remote location with respect to the processor which provides the necessary output data. *See* PRINTER.

remote station. (1) In data communications, a station that can call, or be called by, a central station in a point-to-point switched network. (2) In a multipoint network, a tributary station. *See* POINT-TO-POINT, TRIBUTARY STATION.

remote terminal. (1) In computing and communications, a terminal connected via a data link to a system. (2) In peripherals, a visual display unit with its own refresh memory, editing facilities and modem interface. *See* EDIT, MODEM, REFRESH, VISUAL DISPLAY UNIT.

removable cartridge disk. In memory systems, a hard-disk system in which disks, in a cartridge, may be removed and replaced. This system combines the high storage capacity and high data rate of a Winchester drive with the versatility of floppy disk systems. *See* FLOPPY DISK, WINCHESTER DISK DRIVE.

rendezvous. In programming, an interprocess communication mechanism. If two processes pass information to one another through this mechanism then one process attains a transmit state and calls the rendezvous. This process must now suspend itself until the receiving process attains the necessary state to receive the data, at which point communication occurs. Note that this differs from other interprocess communication mechanisms where the transmitting process may deposit a message and continue its operation.

repaginate. In word processing, an editing facility that permits the operator to change the number of lines in each page after final editing. *See* EDIT.

repaint. In computer graphics, to update or redraw a display image.

repeat action key. *Synonymous with* TYPAMATIC KEY.

repeater. In communications, a bidirectional device used to amplify or regenerate signals in channels. Repeaters are spaced along long communication channels subject to excessive attenuation or interference. *See* ATTENUATION, INTERFERENCE.

repeating group. In data structures, a group in a record that can occur any number of times (e.g. the names of dependents in an employee's file). It is not possible to predetermine the number of fields to be allocated to such a group, and records with repeating groups cannot fit into flat files. *See* FIELD, FLAT FILE, RECORD.

repertoire. (1) In programming, a complete set of machine code instructions for a computer or family of computers. (2) In programming, a set of types of instruction for a high-level language. *See* HIGH-LEVEL LANGUAGE, MACHINE LANGUAGE..

repetitive letter. *Synonymous with* FORM LETTER.

replay. In data security, a form of attack in which the message sequence is changed or a stored data item is replaced with a previously stored value. This form of attack can succeed even if the message or stored data item is authenticated or encrypted.

In its simplest form, an attacker can simply record a message, including its authenticator and re-insert it into the communication link. Such a message could, for example, cause a financial transaction to be performed twice. Alternatively an item in a database may be updated by a legitimate user and then restored to its original value by an attacker. *See* MESSAGE AUTHENTICATION.

replication. In recording, the production of copies from a master, usually for commercial distribution. (Philips). *See* MASTERING, STAMPER.

report program generator. In programming, a program that can generate other object programs, which in turn produce user-specified reports from a set of data. *See* OBJECT PROGRAM.

reprint. In printing, the production of subsequent copies of a publication.

reproduce. To copy information so that both the original and duplicate are held on similar storage media.

reprogramming. In programming, changing a program written for one computer so that it will run on another. *See* PROGRAM.

reprographic printing. In printing, a generic term encompassing spirit duplicating, ink duplicating, xerography and small offset printing. *See* OFFSET PRINTING, XEROGRAPHY.

repro proof. In printing, a proof produced with great care, on best quality paper for use in photomechanical reproduction. *See* PHOTOMECHANICAL.

reprotyping. In printing, typing intended for photomechanical reproduction. *See* PHOTOMECHANICAL.

repudiation. In data security, denial by one of the entities involved in a communication of having participated in all or part of the communication. *See* DIGITAL SIGNATURE.

request/response. In communications security, a technique to warn users that a delay/denial of service attack is in operation. If such attacks are initiated during a quiescent traffic state then intended receivers of messages will be unaware that messages are being blocked. Request/response messages may be periodically sent between communicating parties to ensure that open communication paths exist. *See* DELAY/DENIAL OF SERVICE, HOT MODE, TRAFFIC ANALYSIS.

request to send. In data communications, a signal used in conjunction with another — clear to send — as a handshaking protocol in half-duplex operation. The computer generates the request to send signal to the modem and awaits a clear to send signal before transmitting data. *Compare* CLEAR TO SEND. *See* HALF-DUPLEX, HANDSHAKING, MODEM, RS-232C.

required hyphen. In word processing, a hyphen that is not deleted during repagination. *Compare* DISCRETIONARY HYPHEN. *See* REPAGINATE.

required page break. In word processing, a special break instruction that is not deleted during repagination. *See* REPAGINATE.

required space. *Synonymous with* PROTECTED SPACE.

requirements analysis. In systems analysis, a systematic study of user requirements aimed at the production of a definition of the required system.

rerun point. In programming, an intermediate stage of the program from which the execution may be recommenced in the event of an execution error. A program may have more than one rerun point.

rescue dump. In computing, a complete dump of computer storage and states onto a peripheral device so that in the event of a major system failure (e.g. loss of power supply) the program can be recommenced at the state of the last rescue dump. *Compare* POST MORTEM DUMP, SELECTIVE DUMP. *See* DUMP.

reserved word. In programming, one of a set of words that have specific meaning in a programming language and cannot, therefore, be used for names of variables, procedures, etc. *See* PROCEDURE, VARIABLE.

resident software. In computing, any program held permanently in memory to provide a service to other programs (e.g. a resident compiler). *See* COMPILER, SOFTWARE.

residual error rate. In data communications, the ratio of the total number of bits, bytes or blocks incorrectly received, but uncorrected or undetected by the error control device, to the total number of corresponding units transmitted.

residual intelligibility. In communications security, the proportion of a voice-scrambled message that can be understood directly. *See* VOICE SCRAMBLING.

residual magnetism. In electronics, the magnetic effect that remains in a material when the external magnetic field is removed. *See* REMANENCE.

residual risk. In computer security, the portion of risk that remains after security measures have been applied. *See* RISK MANAGEMENT.

residue. In computer security, data left in storage after processing operations and before degaussing or rewriting has taken place. (FIPS). *See* DEGAUSS, RESIDUES PROBLEMS.

residues problems. In computer security, a class of security problems that can arise from information left in storage after processing. Such information may be unavailable to legitimate users, but can be revealed by ingenious programmers (e.g. an erased file may remain on a disk and an erase flag prevents normal access via the operating system, however, the file can be resurrected by requisite programming). *See* PERSONAL COMPUTER SECURITY, RESIDUE.

resin-covered paper. In photography, a photographic high-contrast paper used on phototypesetters. *See* CONTRAST, PHOTOTYPESETTING.

resistance. In electronics, an electrical property of a component relating the voltage drop across its terminals to the current flowing through it. *See* CURRENT, OHM, VOLTAGE.

resistor. In electronics, a device connected into a circuit to provide a specified electrical resistance. *See* RESISTANCE.

resolution. The ability to distinguish fine detail. *See* RESOLVING POWER.

resolver. In recording, a unit controlling the speed of an audio playback device for tape or magnetic film. The speed is determined by synchronous pulses recorded with the original audio track. *See* MAGNETIC FILM, SYNCHRONIZATION.

resolving power. In optics, the maximum number of equal-width black and white lines per millimetre discernible in the image of an optical system (e.g. a lens). *See* RESOLUTION.

resonance. A situation in which a system has a response to a particular excitation frequency that is much greater than its response to neighbouring frequencies.

resource sharing. (1) In computer operations, in an automatic data-processing system, the concurrent use of a resource by more than one user, job or program. (FIPS). *See* AUTOMATIC DATA-PROCESSING SYSTEM. (2) In computer networks, the joint use of resources available on a system or network by users or peripherals (e.g. microcomputer users in a local area network can share a hard disk drive or printer). *See* HARD DISK, LOCAL AREA NETWORK, SERVER.

responder. In communications, a device that automatically transmits a predetermined signal when activated by a received signal. *Compare* TRANSPONDER.

response frame. In videotex, a viewdata frame that enables a user to send information to an information provider (e.g. for booking a hotel room). *See* FRAME, INFORMATION PROVIDER.

response position. In optical mark reading, the area designated for marking information on the form.

response time. (1) The time taken by a system to attain a specified state or to produce a specified output after receiving an input. (2) In peripherals, the time between the generation of the last character at the terminal and receipt of the first character of the reply.

restore. In memory systems, to write data back into memory immediately after a destructive readout. *See* DESTRUCTIVE READOUT.

retention period. In data security, the length of time for which a file is to be kept before it is overwritten. The retention period and the date on which the file was written are used to calculate the earliest date on which the file expires. The date the file was written and the retention period or the expiry date will be written as part of the file label and will be used as a security precau-

tion against the accidental destruction of a file.

reticle lines. In filming, fine guide lines in a camera viewfinder designating various points and areas (e.g. centre of frame, television safe action area). *See* TELEVISION SAFE ACTION AREA.

retouching. In printing and photography, the skilled alteration of halftone images or photographs for improvement or correction.

retree. In printing, a substandard batch of paper.

retrieval. In computing, the process of searching for, locating and reading out data.

retrieval centre. In videotex, a computer centre that hosts the viewdata base for a given set of users, or area, and receives updates from the update centre. *See* UPDATE CENTRE.

retrofit. In computing, to modify a system.

retrospective search. In library science, a search request in the form of a call for all items published on a specific topic since a specified date.

return. (1) In programming, a return jump. *See* RETURN JUMP. (2) In peripherals, a key used to terminate the inputting of information from a keyboard. *See* CARRIAGE RETURN.

return jump. In programming, an instruction that terminates a subroutine and causes a branch to the instruction immediately following the most recent subroutine call. *See* BRANCH, SUBROUTINE CALL.

return to zero. In memory systems, a method of recording in which the reference condition is the absence of magnetization. *Compare* NON-RETURN TO ZERO.

Reuters. An international news-gathering and dissemination organization. It now provides an extremely comprehensive computer-based financial information service.

reveal. (1) In videotex, the facility to produce information on the screen, previously concealed by invocation of conceal mode, with the depression of the reveal key on the user's keypad. It is used for games or quizzes. (2) In videotex, the mode complementary to the conceal mode. *Compare* CONCEAL.

reverberation time. A measure of the acoustic properties of a room or space; the time taken for sound to become attenuated to one-millionth of its initial intensity.

reversal film. In photography, a film normally processed so as to produce a positive image after exposure.

reversal intermediate. In filming, a second-generation duplicate, used for printing to protect the original, reversed so as to make it the same type, positive or negative as the original.

reverse B to W. In printing, an instruction to reverse the image from black to white.

reverse channel. In communications, a channel provided from receiver to transmitter for low-speed control signals.

reverse engineering. A process by which the design of a product is determined by a detailed study of the product itself (e.g. the software on a read-only memory can be determined by a microscopic study of the read-only memory chip). *See* READ-ONLY MEMORY.

reverse indexing. In word processing, the feature that causes the typing position or display pointer to be moved to the corresponding character position of the preceding typing line.

reverse interrupt. In data communications, a control character sequence sent by the receiving station, in a binary synchronous communications system, to request a premature termination of the transmission in progress. *See* BINARY SYNCHRONOUS COMMUNICATIONS.

reverse L to R. In printing, an instruction to reverse the image laterally.

reverse out. In printing, to reproduce as a white image out of a solid background. (Desktop). *See* SOLID.

reverse P. *See* REFERENCE MARK. *Synonymous with* PARAGRAPH MARK.

reverse Polish notation. *Synonymous with* POSTFIX NOTATION.

reverse-reading. In printing, pertaining to text that is read from right to left as on a letterpress printing surface. *See* LETTERPRESS. *Synonymous with* WRONG READING.

reverse video. In peripherals, a visual display unit facility that enables all, or part, of the data to be displayed as a black image on a white background. It is often used to highlight a portion of text. *See* VISUAL DISPLAY UNIT. *Synonymous with* INVERSE VIDEO.

reversible encryption. In data security, a data encryption standard transformation of cleartext in such a way that the encrypted text can be decrypted back to the original cleartext. *Compare* ONE-WAY CIPHER. *See* DATA ENCRYPTION STANDARD.

revise. In printing, an additional proof showing that corrections from an earlier proof have been implemented. *See* PROOF.

RF. Radio frequency.

RFE. Radio frequency emissions. *Synonymous with* COMPROMISING EMANATIONS.

RFI. Radio frequency interference. *See* JAMMING. *Synonymous with* ELECTROMAGNETIC INTERFERENCE.

RF modulation method. In peripherals, a method of connecting a microcomputer output to a domestic television set. The output must be modulated to conform to normal television signal form and is connected directly to the antenna socket of the television set. This is the simplest form of connection for domestic television sets, but the display is affected by noise picked up by the interconnecting lead. *Compare* DIRECT VIDEO INPUT. *See* MODULATION, NOISE.

RGB. (1) In peripherals, the amplifiers that drive the red, green and blue (RGB) electron guns in a colour cathode ray tube. (2) In peripherals, the phosphor dots on a cathode ray tube screen that produce the red, green and blue primary colours. *See*

AMPLIFIER, CATHODE RAY TUBE, GUN, PHOS-
PHOR DOTS, PRIMARY COLOURS.

RGB (5:5:5). In optical media and video, a video encoding technique used for graphics in interactive compact discs. For each pixel the primary colours are each quantized and represented by five bits of information, giving 32 levels of intensity. (Philips). *Compare* DELTA YUV. *See* PIXEL.

RGB encoding. In video, a video encoding technique which transforms the red, blue and green (RGB) components of a video signal into a pulse code-modulated signal. (Philips). *Compare* RGB (5:5:5). *See* PULSE CODE MODULATION RGB.

RGB input. *Synonymous with* DIRECT VIDEO INPUT.

RI. *See* RING INDICATOR.

ribbon cable. In electronics, a flat, plastic-sheathed cable in which the conductors lie parallel to each other.

right-angle fold. In printing, folding a sheet of paper in half twice, with the second fold at right angles to the first. It is a standard fold used for book sections.

right-justified. (1) In printing, pertaining to text that has been moved so that the right margin is straight. (2) In computing, the shifting of a number to the right-hand end of a register. *Compare* LEFT-JUSTIFIED. *See* JUSTIFY, REGISTER.

right-reading. Pertaining to a print, or film, image in the correct lateral orientation with text reading from left to right. *Compare* WRONG-READING.

ring. (1) In data structures, a structure in which the last pointer of a chain list references the first element in the same list. *See* CHAIN LIST. (2) In data communications, a network topology in the form of a ring so that each node is connected only with two neighbours on each side. *Compare* BUS, MESH, STAR. *See* LOCAL AREA NETWORK.

ring back. In data communications, a procedure that allows a telephone to be used both for computer connections and normal voice calls. Computer connections require two calls: the first, which is usually only one ring, alerts the modem which will not answer unless the ringing stops for some period, typically 30 seconds. *Compare* CALL BACK.

ring counter. In electronics, an electronic counter in which the overflow from the last unit is fed back to the input. *See* COUNTER.

Ringdoc. In online information retrieval, pharmaceutical literature documentation; a database supplied by Derwent Publications Ltd and dealing with pharmaceuticals and the pharmaceutical industry.

ring indicator. (RI) In data communications, a signal that indicates that a modem has received a new call. The ring indicator signal goes up and down as the telephone bell rings so that the computer can answer after a specified number of rings. *See* MODEM, RS-232C.

R interface. In communications, an integrated services digital network terminal interface for TE2 equipment. *Compare* S INTERFACE, T INTERFACE. *See* INTEGRATED SERVICES DIGITAL NETWORK, TE2.

RIP. (1) In printing. *See* RASTER IMAGE PROCESSOR. (2) In printing, rest in proportion; an instruction indicating that all elements are to be reduced or enlarged in the same proportion.

RISC. *See* REDUCED INSTRUCTION SET COMPUTER.

rise time. In electronics, the time taken for a voltage pulse to rise from 10 to 90 per cent of its final value. *See* PULSE.

risk. In computer security, the probability or likelihood that a threat agent will successfully mount a specific attack against a particular system vulnerability. *Compare* SAFEGUARD. *See* THREAT, VULNERABILITY.

risk analysis. In risk management, a structured approach to the determination of the optimum security measures and routines for an organization. The objective of a risk analysis project is to enable management to balance the cost of proposed security countermeasures against a realistic estimate of the risk impact.

The methodology of risk analysis comprises the basic steps: asset identification; risk calculation; countermeasure evaluation. The analysis should not be considered to be a once and for all activity. Preferably it is performed at the design phase of a system, or subsystem, because security measures integrated within a system are more effective than those superposed at a later stage. Thereafter the risk analysis should be undertaken periodically to ensure that security measures keep abreast of an organization's development and its changing risk environment. *See* RISK ASSESSMENT.

risk assessment. In risk management, the quantification of probability of an unfavourable outcome in the absence of any deliberate intervention. *See* RISK ANALYSIS.

risk index. In data security, the disparity between the minimum clearance or authorization of system users and the maximum sensitivity (e.g. classification and categories) of data processed by a system. (DOD). *See* SENSITIVITY.

risk management. A disciplined approach adopted to identify, measure and control uncertain events in order to minimize loss and optimize the return on the money invested for security purposes. The objective of risk management is to attain the most effective precautions against: (a) destruction of assets; (b) unauthorized modification or manipulation of company data; (c) unauthorized disclosure of company data; and (d) denial of company assets and data-processing services to unauthorized personnel. In the field of computer security, risk management encompasses risk analysis, management decision making and implementation of security measures and reviews. *See* RISK ANALYSIS, RISK ASSESSMENT.

river. In printing, an undesirable white streak, produced by vertically interconnecting word spaces, that straggles down the text.

RJE. *See* REMOTE JOB ENTRY.

RLIN. Research Libraries Information Network.

RLL. *See* RUN LENGTH-LIMITED.

RMM. *See* READ-MOSTLY MEMORY.

RMS. *See* ROOT MEAN SQUARE.

RO. *See* RECEIVE-ONLY.

roaming. In communications, a capability for travellers to take their telephones on the road. *See* CELLULAR RADIO.

robotics. In control and instrumentation, a discipline that combines aspects of artificial intelligence, and mechanical and electronic engineering. It is concerned with the development of versatile robots which have both sensory units and a degree of intelligence. *See* ARTIFICIAL INTELLIGENCE, INTELLIGENCE.

rogue fiber. In communications, an active wiretap on a fiber optic cable made by fusing a fiber onto the cable by the application of heat. *See* ACTIVE WIRETAPPING, FIBER OPTICS.

role indicator. In library science, a symbol that is assigned to an index term which designates the role of the term in its context (e.g. part of speech).

roll. (1) In filming, a roll of film. (2) In filming, rotation of camera around its axis. (3) In filming, a command to commence filming and recording. (4) In communications, a rotation of a satellite about the central axis. *Compare* PITCH, YAW. *See* COMMUNICATIONS SATELLITE SYSTEM.

rollback. (1) In reliability, a technique of recovery from system failure. Recovery points are inserted at intervals in the program and when such a point is attained, in program operation, the total state of the system is stored in a protected standby memory. When a fault is detected a control unit switches over to standby memory, the status of the machine is restored and the program is re-executed from the recovery point, the original memory now being used as standby. *See* TIME REDUNDANCY. (2) In databases, a technique employed to protect the database against incorrect user actions. The state of the database is preserved and subsequent transactions are stored. If the user decides to implement the total set of transactions a commit command is issued, if the rollback command is employed the transactions are aborted and do not affect the database. *Compare* COMMIT.

rollback recorder. A magnetic tape recorder with a facility to erase on tape motion reversal, to facilitate a rerun of a mix. *See* MIXING.

rolling ball. *Synonymous with* TRACKER BALL.

rolling headers. In teletext, the display of all page headers, of a selected magazine, as they are received, providing the viewer with an indication of the transmitted page sequence. *See* MAGAZINE, PAGE HEADER.

roll in, roll out. In memory systems, a technique employed when a computer simultaneously handles a number of processes. When the process is active then all the relevant data and program code are held in main memory. If a hiatus occurs (e.g. because the program is awaiting input from the user) then the code and data are rolled out to backing storage, and only a buffer is used to accept the input data. Upon completion of data input the code and data are rolled in from backing storage so that processing can continue. *See* BACKING STORAGE, MAIN MEMORY, MULTIPROGRAMMING, SWAPPING.

rollover. In peripherals, a feature of a keyboard that can continue to send the correct codes when more than one key is depressed at any one time. *Compare* LOCKOUT. *See* TWO-KEY ROLLOVER.

roll scroll. *See* VERTICAL SCROLLING.

ROM. *See* READ-ONLY MEMORY.

Roman. In printing, a typeface with vertical stems as compared with italics or oblique which are set at angles. (Desktop). *See* ITALIC, STEM, TIMES ROMAN, TYPEFACE.

ROM cartridge. In memory systems, a read-only memory (ROM) unit, often containing an educational or game program, that mounted in a convenient cartridge and plugged into a microcomputer or video game unit. *See* READ-ONLY MEMORY, VIDEO GAME.

ROM cassette. In memory systems, a plug-in read-only memory (ROM) unit containing data or machine code. (Philips). *See* PLUG-IN MODULE, READ-ONLY MEMORY.

root. (1) In mathematics, a fractional power of a number or quantity. *See* POWER. (2) In data structures, the node that represents the starting point for all paths in a tree structure. *Compare* LEAF. *See* TREE STRUCTURE.

root directory. In computing, the uppermost parent directory in a tree-structured directory (i.e. the one at the root of the tree). *See* DIRECTORY, TREE-STRUCTURED DIRECTORY.

root mean square. (RMS) In electronics, a measure of the amplitude of a waveform. It is equal to the square root of the mean value of the square of the waveform. For sinusoidal voltages it is equal to the amplitude multiplied by 0.7071. *See* SINUSOIDAL.

ROS. In communications security, a Swedish abbreviation for electromagnetic signals. *See* VAN ECK PHENOMENON.

rotary camera. In micrographics, a type of microfilm camera that photographs documents while they are being moved by a transport mechanism. The document transport mechanism is connected to a film transport mechanism, and the film moves during exposure so that there is no relative movement between the film and document image. *Compare* PLANETARY CAMERA, STEP-AND-REPEAT CAMERA. *See* MICROFILM.

rotary press. A sheet- or web-fed printing machine in which the printing surface is cylindrical. *See* SHEET-FED, WEB-FED.

rotate. (1) In video, filming and computer graphics, the rotation of a picture or portion of a picture with respect to its original position. (Philips). *See* TUMBLING. (2) In programming, to shift the contents of a register to the left, or to the right, and directing any overflow bits to the input at the other end. *Compare* SHIFT. *See* INSTRUCTION SET, REGISTER.

rotational latency. In memory systems, the average delay time, caused by the disk rotation needed to gain access, between a request for read or write action and the commencement of that action. (Philips). *Compare* SEEK LATENCY. *See* LATENCY, MAGNETIC DISK.

rotogravure. In printing, the photogravure technique using a web-fed rotary press. *See* PHOTOGRAVURE, ROTARY PRESS, WEB-FED.

round-off errors. In programming, the errors resulting from the rounding-off process. This process is employed when a number is to be stored with a limited number of digits, the least significant remaining digit is adjusted according to the round-off method employed.

round robin. In computing, a method of scheduling resources in a multiuser system. Each user has use of the central processing unit for a specified time interval, at the end of that period control is passed to the next user. *See* MULTIUSER, SCHEDULER.

routine. In programming, a set of instructions to perform a self-contained task. *See* SUBROUTINE.

routing. In data communications, the assignment of a path for a message or packet to attain its ultimate destination. *See* ADAPTIVE ROUTING, DATA COMMUNICATIONS, DIRECTORY ROUTING, HOT-POTATO ROUTING.

routing indicator. In data communications, the address of final circuit or terminal to which a message must be delivered. It is contained in the message header. *See* HEADER.

routing page. *Synonymous with* INDEX PAGE.

routing table. In data communications, a table, at a node of a message-switching network, that indicates the preferred, and sometimes second preference, outgoing line for each destination. *See* DIRECTORY ROUTING.

row. In videotex, one of the 24 information lines, each of which can contain up to 40 characters.

row-adaptive transmission. In teletext, a system in which rows containing no information are omitted from the transmission sequence to improve page access time. *See* ROW.

royal. In printing, a size of printing paper 20 x 25 inches (508 x 635 centimetres).

royalty fee. In online information retrieval, a fee charged by some database producers when their databases are accessed through a database vendor. *See* DATABASE PRODUCER, DATABASE VENDOR.

RPE. *See* RAPID POST-EDITING.

RS. In data communications, a prefix used by the Electronic Industries Association (EIA) for widely used standards in North America. *Compare* V-SERIES RECOMMENDATIONS OF CCITT, X-SERIES RECOMMENDATIONS OF CCITT. *See* ELECTRONIC INDUSTRIES ASSOCIATION, RS-170, RS-232C, RS-366, RS-423A, RS-449.

RS-170. In television, an Electronic Industries Association standard for monochrome television studio facilities. *See* ELECTRONIC INDUSTRIES ASSOCIATION.

RS-232. *See* RS-232C.

RS-232C. In data communications, an extremely popular standard employed in serial connections for computers. The official title is Interface between Data Terminal Equipment and Data Circuit Termination Equipment employing serial binary interface. The C in the suffix indicates that it has been revised.
   The standard has four parts: electrical signal characteristics, interface mechanical characteristics, functional description of the signals and a list of standard interface types. *Compare* CENTRONICS INTERFACE, CURRENT LOOP INTERFACE. *See* DATA CIRCUIT TERMINATING EQUIPMENT, V.24.

RS-366. In data communications, an Electronic Industries Association standard that defines how the computer presents digits, to be dialed, to the autodialer, how the computer signals the end of the number and the actions taken when the autodialer cannot

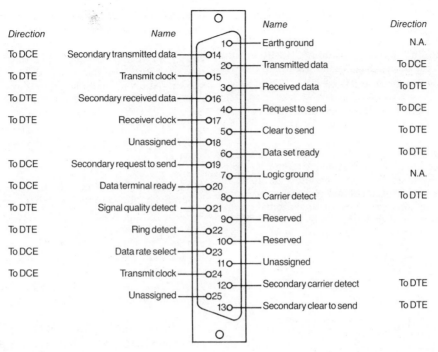

RS-232C
RS-232C pin assignments and signal names of a D-type connector.

complete the call. *See* AUTODIALER, ELECTRONIC INDUSTRIES ASSOCIATION, RS-232C, V.25.

RS-422A. In data communications, an Electronic Industries Association interface standard for high data rates (i.e. 10 megabits per second over 40 feet or 10 000 bits per second over 4000 feet). It uses two wires for each signal. Unlike the RS-232C standard it only comprises the electrical specifications. *Compare* RS-423A. *See* DATA RATE, ELECTRONIC INDUSTRIES ASSOCIATION, RS-232C, V.11, X.27.

RS-423A. In data communications, an Electronic Industries Association interface standard using unbalanced transmissions for lower transmission rates than the RS-422A standard (i.e. 100 000 bits per second over 40 feet and 1000 bits per second over 4000 feet). Like the RS-422A standard it only comprises electrical specifications. *Compare* RS-422A. *See* DATA RATE, ELECTRONIC INDUSTRIES ASSOCIATION, RS-232C.

RS-449. In data communications, a new standard designed to replace RS-232. *See* RS-232C.

RSA. In data security, Rivest-Shamir-Adleman; an algorithm named after its designers that is of extreme importance in public key cryptography. It uses a trapdoor one-way function based upon the computational difficulty of factoring the product of large prime numbers (i.e. integers with several hundred decimal digits). Thus the computation involved in multiplying two large prime numbers p and q is minimal, but it is computationally infeasible to derive the factors p and q from a product n consisting of several hundred decimal digits. A large computer would take about a billion years for a 200-digit number. *Compare* KNAPSACK CIPHER. *See* DATA ENCRYPTION STANDARD, PRIME NUMBER, PUBLIC KEY, TRAPDOOR ONE-WAY FUNCTION.

RSI. Repetitive strain injury; an injury to the nerves and muscles of hand, wrist and arm which, it is believed, is caused by excessive keyboarding operations.

RTECS. In online information retrieval, Registry of Toxic Effects of Chemical Substances; a database supplied by US Public Health Service, National Institute for Occupational Safety and Health (NIOSH) and dealing with toxicology.

RTOS. Real-time operating system. *See* CD REAL-TIME OPERATING SYSTEM,

rubber-banding. In computer graphics, pertaining to the flexible movement of interconnecting lines in computer graphics. In some systems a cut and paste of a section of the graphic provides for the automatic relocation of connecting lines. If this facility is not present the lines must be erased and redrawn in their new location.

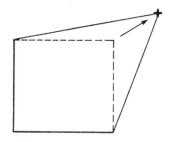

rubber banding

rubric. In printing, heading of book chapter or section, printed in red to contrast with text in black.

rule. In artificial intelligence, a statement in an expert system that enables the likelihood of an assertion, or the value of an object, to be established. A rule combines lower-level assertions or objects to produce a value for a higher-level assertion or object. *See* ASSERTION, EXPERT SYSTEMS, OBJECT, RULE-BASED SYSTEM.

rule-based system. In artificial intelligence, an expert system that consists of a set of antecedent/consequent rules, a database and an executive. The rules are conditional statements that describe how to modify the database when certain patterns are recognized in the data. The executive looks after pattern matching, monitoring database changes, deciding which rule should be executed next and performance of the execu-

tion. *See* DATABASE, EXPERT SYSTEMS. *Synonymous with* PRODUCTION SYSTEM.

ruler. In word processing, a line across the top or bottom of the visual display unit showing the tab and margin settings currently in force. *See* VISUAL DISPLAY UNIT.

run. (1) In computing, the execution of a program. (2) In printing. *Synonymous with* PRINT RUN.

run around. In printing, the fitting of text around an illustration or other display matter.

run in. In printing, the proof correction 'do not start a new line or paragraph'.

run length. In codes, the number of bits between transitions. (Philips). *See* BIT STREAM.

run length coding. (1) In codes, an encoding technique used in digital video. It compresses the data required to store a given image by recording the values of distances between transitions, or changes from one colour or intensity to the next, as well as the values of the colours or intensities between transitions. (Philips). *See* CD-I DIGITAL VIDEO. (2) In computer graphics, a technique to reduce the total storage required for pixel-based images. In the uncoded form pixel attributes are stored for each individual pixel. With run length coding each scan line is examined for successive sets of pixels with identical attributes. The information for this sequence is then stored in three numbers: starting pixel address, finishing pixel address and an index of a look-up table. The appropriate entry in the look-up table holds information on the pixel attributes, colour, etc. This form of coding can produce dramatic reductions in the storage required particularly for regular images such as histograms. *Compare* IMAGE FOLLOWING, QUADTREE, VECTOR GENERATION. *See* FRAME STORE, HISTOGRAM, LOOK-UP TABLE, PIXEL.

run length-limited. (RLL) In codes, pertaining to a system of encoding data for magnetic disk systems in which the number of flux reversals is less than the number of

data bits stored. *See* DATA BIT, FLUX, MAGNE-
TIC DISK.

running head. In printing, type lines above
the main text giving book and/or chapter
titles.

running key. *Synonymous with* CRYPTOGRA-
PHIC BIT STREAM.

running time. In optical media, the time
that an audio track of a digital audio compact disc has been running. It is included in
the subcode and thus available for display
during playback. (Philips). *See* COMPACT
DISC – DIGITAL AUDIO, SUBCODE CHANNEL,
TRACK.

run on. In printing, a term used in price
quotations referring to the cost of increasing
the print quantity.

run time. In computing, the time required
to complete the execution of a single, continuous object program. *See* OBJECT PROGRAM.

run-to-run totals. In data processing, the
utilization of output control totals resulting
from one process as input control totals over
subsequent processing. The control totals
are used as links in a chain to tie one process
to another in a sequence of processes or one
cycle to another over a period of time.

R/W. Read/write. *See* READ/WRITE HEAD.

RX. *See* RECEIVER.

S

S. In electronics, a siemen; an SI unit of conductance (i.e. the reciprocal of resistance). *See* RESISTANCE.

S100 bus. In microcomputers, a bus originally designed for the ALTAIR system and now standardized as the IEEE-696 bus. *See* BUS, MICROPROCESSOR.

sabotage. In legislation, the premeditated destruction of personnel, property or physical plant in an effort to disrupt or terminate manufacturing or other operations by a government or by a private enterprise.

saccadic movements. Brief, rapid eye movements from one fixed point to another (e.g. during reading).

safe area. *Synonymous with* SAFETY AREA.

safeguard. In computer security, a protective measure to mitigate against the effect of system vulnerability. *Compare* RISK. *See* VULNERABILITY.

safety area. In television and computer graphics, the area on a display's surface over which visibility of text or graphics information is guaranteed. The safety area takes account of all allowable tolerances for display monitors and television sets and is less than the total available screen area. (Philips). *Compare* LETTERING SAFETY, TELEVISION SAFE ACTION AREA. *Synonymous with* SAFE AREA.

SAG. *See* SCREEN ACTORS GUILD.

SAGITTAIRE. In banking, Systéme Automatique de Gestion Intégré par Télétransmission de Transaction avec Imputation de Réglements Etrangers; an electronic interbank payment service operated by the Banque de France within France for SWIFT members and submembers located in France and which handles French franc payments only. (ANSI). *See* BANKING NETWORKS, SWIFT.

Sakura. In communications, a Japanese geostationary satellite. *See* GEOSTATIONARY SATELLITE, TELESAT.

salami technique. In data security, a fraud spread over a large number of individual transactions (e.g. a program that does not round off figures, but diverts the leftovers to a personal account).

sales transaction. In applications, the action of entering all the relevant information, including the method used by the customer to pay for the goods or services, into a point-of-sale terminal to complete the sale. *See* POINT-OF-SALE TERMINAL.

same size. In printing, pertaining to a copy from a document-copying machine that is on the same scale as the original.

sample-and-hold circuit. In control and instrumentation, a circuit that samples an analog signal and then holds its output at that value until it takes the next sample. This represents the first stage in an analog-to-digital conversion process. *See* ANALOG-TO-DIGITAL CONVERTER, SAMPLING.

sampling. The process of obtaining a group of representative measurements in relation to some function in order to develop information on that function. The measurements may relate to consecutive values of a continuous variable, or to a set of values from some static group of elements. In sampling a continuous signal the sampling rate must be sufficiently high to ensure that the signal can be accurately reconstructed. The theoretical minimum-required sampling rate is equal to twice the highest frequency contained in the signal. *See* NYQUIST SAMPLING THEOREM, PULSE CODE MODULATION.

sampling interval. The time interval between consecutive samples. *See* SAMPLING.

sandwich tape. In computer security and banking, a material used for magnetic stripes that is designed to increase the difficulty of manufacturing counterfeit cards. The stripe material comprises a low-coercivity material bonded above a high-coercivity material. A high-intensity field is used to encode the stripe such that both materials are magnetized. In the reader the stripe is first subject to a low-intensity erase field which demagnetizes the low-coercivity material. If a counterfeiter uses conventional magnetic material then the forged data will be removed by the erasing field. On the other hand, a counterfeiter using the sandwich material must have access to expensive magnetic encoders capable of developing the high magnetic fields necessary to magnetize the high-coercivity layer. *Compare* WATERMARK TAPE. *See* COERCIVITY, MAGNETIC STRIPE CARD.

sanitization. In data security, the elimination of classified information from magnetic media to permit the re-use of the media at a lower classification level or to permit the release to uncleared personnel or personnel without the proper information access authorizations. (DOE).

sans serif. In printing, a typeface that has no serifs (e.g. Helvetica). *Compare* SERIF. *See* HELVETICA, TYPEFACE. *Synonymous with* GROTESQUE.

Satcom. In communications, a US series of geostationary communications satellites. *See* GEOSTATIONARY SATELLITE.

satellite. (1) In communications, an earth-orbiting radio relay station. A complete satellite communication system comprises the satellite and ground stations which communicate with one another via the satellite. Conventional earth transmitter/receivers that are not in direct line of sight with each other due to the curvature of the earth have to rely upon reflection of radio waves from certain layers outside the atmosphere. Satellites are used to receive and retransmit communication signals for telephone, television and data channels. *See* COMMUNICATIONS SATELLITE SYSTEM, GEOSTATIONARY SATELLITE, GROUND STATION, TELEVISION RECEIVE-ONLY. (2) A system operating as a subsidiary of a central system.

satellite broadcasting. *See* DIRECT BROADCAST SATELLITE.

satellite computer. In computing, a computer performing subsidiary functions under the control of another computer.

Satstream. In data communications, a fully digital British Telecom service offering satellite communication links, initially over Western Europe. Customers will require a small satellite dish antenna. *Compare* KILOSTREAM, MEGASTREAM, SWTICHSTREAM. *See* X-STREAM.

saturation. (1) In optics, the amounts of grey in a hue (i.e. high saturation implies that the hue contains less grey and more colour than is the case with low saturation). *Compare* HUE. (2) In electronics, pertaining to the state of magnetic materials subjected to a magnetic field. With a sufficiently large field the material saturates, and further increases in magnetic field produce no further changes in magnetic flux. *See* FLUX, HYSTERESIS.

saturation testing. In data communications, a technique of checking the performance of a communications network by means of a large bulk of messages. It is undertaken to check for system faults that only arise in exceptional circumstances (e.g. the simultaneous arrival of two messages). *Compare* FLOOD TESTING.

save. In computing, to store a computer program on an auxiliary storage device (e.g. a disk). *Compare* LOAD.

S band. In communications, the frequency range 2–4 GHz. *Compare* C BAND, KU BAND, L BAND.

SBC. *See* SINGLE-BOARD COMPUTER.

S box. In data security, substitution box; a component of an encryption algorithm that performs a substitution cipher on the input signal. *Compare* P BOX. *See* CRYPTOGRAPHY, DATA ENCRYPTION STANDARD, SUBSTITUTION CIPHER.

SBS. In communications, Satellite Business Systems; a private US company that competes in the US domestic communications market. *Compare* COMSAT, INTELSAT.

scalar. In mathematics, a quantity that takes a single numerical value (e.g. height). *Compare* VECTOR.

scalar variable. In programming, a variable that may only assume one of a finite set of values. For example, in Pascal-like languages a variable DAY may be specified and that variable can then be allowed to assume only one of the values — MONDAY, TUESDAY, WEDNESDAY, THURSDAY, FRIDAY, SATURDAY, SUNDAY. *See* PASCAL, VARIABLE.

scaling. (1) A method of readjusting variable values to fit within a specified range. (2) In printing, the process of calculating the degree of enlargement, or reduction of an original image for reproduction.

scallop. In television, a distortion in the form of a wavy picture.

scamp. In printing, a sketch or design showing the basic concept. (Desktop).

scan. (1) In television, the horizontal sweep of an electron beam across a television screen. (2) In data structures, a procedure to investigate every node in the structure. *See* NODE. (3) In office systems. *See* OPTICAL SCANNER.

scan area. In character reading, the area scanned by the optical reader. *See* SCANNER.

scan convertor. In television, a device used in presenting a non-interlaced picture on a normal television screen containing the same number of lines as the original interlaced picture. (Philips). *See* INTERLACE.

scanner. (1) In communications security, a device used to intercept radio commu-nications usually in the citizen band, cellular radio, police, fire and ambulance transmissions areas. (2) A device that examines an object, image or three-dimensional space in a regular manner and produces analog, or digital, signals corresponding to a physical state at each part of the search area. (3) An instrument that automatically samples or interrogates the states of a system and initiates action in accordance with the information so obtained. (4) In office systems. *See* OPTICAL SCANNER.

Scannet. In online information retrieval, a Swedish network and host system.

scanning. In computer security, searching for telephone numbers and passwords by successively trying various combinations of numbers and letters. *See* EXHAUSTIVE ATTACK, HACKER. *Synonymous with* HACK HACK.

scanning device. In micrographics, a device on a microfilm reader that permits shifting of the film, or the entire optical system, so that different portions of the microfilm, frame or reel may be viewed. *See* MICROFILM.

scanning line. In television, a single horizontal line traced across the face of a television screen by an electron beam.

scanning spot. (1) In television, a small area of the target in the camera tube that is covered by the scanning electron beam. (2) In television, the area of the phosphor screen covered by the electron beam in a display tube. (3) In facsimile, the elemental area of the recording medium examined at a given moment by the reading head during transmission, (4) In recording, the elemental area of recording medium acted upon at a given instant by the recording head.

scanning spot beam. In communications, an experimental satellite communications system that broadcasts 600 megabits per second over multiple areas of 10 000 square miles. *See* SATELLITE, SPOT BEAM.

s caps. Small caps. *See* SMALL CAPS.

scatter graph. In mathematics, a representation of the relationship between two quantities as points on a two-dimensional graph when the scatter of the points does not permit a sensible line, or curve, to interconnect the points.

scatter proofs. In printing, proofs of illustrations, in photomechanical processing, arranged in a random manner unrelated to layout. *See* PHOTOMECHANICAL, PROOF.

scavenging. In computer security, searching through residue for the purpose of unauthorized data acquisition. (FIPS). *Compare* BROWSING. *See* RESIDUE.

S channel. In optical media, one of the eight compact disc subcode channels (P–W). At present it is only allocated to compact disc graphics. (Philips). *See* COMPACT DISC, SUBCODE CHANNEL.

scheduled circuits. In data communications, leased circuits provided by British Telecom specially conditioned for data use. *See* CONDITIONING.

scheduler. In computing, a part of an operating system, providing concurrency, that initiates and terminates processes and allocates resources according to priorities assigned to the processes and the availability of resources. *See* CONCURRENT PROGRAMMING, PRIORITY. *Synonymous with* DISPATCHING ALGORITHM.

schema. (1) In databases, a map of the overall logical structure of a database. (2) In databases, in CODASYL it consists of the data description language entries; a complete description of all the area, set occurrences, record occurrences and associated data items and data aggregates as they exist in the database. *See* AREA, CODASYL, DATA DESCRIPTION LANGUAGE, RECORD, SET.

schematic. A diagram of a system's components and their interconnections or interrelationships.

Sci-Mate. In online information retrieval, gateway software produced by the Institute for Scientific Information. It is menu-driven and offers access to the Institute of Scientific Information databases through various vendors. It includes a database management program for use with downloaded data. *See* GATEWAY SOFTWARE, INSTITUTE FOR SCIENTIFIC INFORMATION, MENU.

scintillation. In communications, rapid fluctuations in signal strength.

Scisearch. In online information retrieval, a database supplied by the Institute for Scientific Information and dealing with science and technology.

scissoring. In computer graphics, a form of clipping used in vector display systems. The hardware detects when the cathode ray tube electron beam is to be deflected beyond the normal screen limits and switches it off. The beam is reactivated when the next position within the screen limits is detected. *See* CATHODE RAY TUBE, CLIPPING, VECTOR DISPLAY.

SCPC. *See* SINGLE CARRIER PER CHANNEL.

scrambler. (1) In communications, a coding device applied to communication links for security purposes or to avoid harmful repetitive patterns of digital data. Such repetitive patterns may arise in phase-modulated systems and produce a zero phase shift over a comparatively long period, with a resultant loss in synchronization between the transmitter and receiver decoders. *See* PHASE MODULATION. (2) In communications security. *See* VOICE SCRAMBLING.

scratch. (1) In memory systems, to free an area of storage so that it can be used for another application. (2) In filming, an unintentional abrasive mark on a film.

scratch file. In programming, a file used as a memory workspace. *See* MEMORY WORKSPACE.

scratch pad memory. In memory systems, a small, high-speed memory used as a temporary storage for working data.

screen. *Synonymous with* VIDEO DISPLAY.

Screen Actors Guild. (SAG) A US trade union for motion picture performers.

screen attribute byte. In peripherals, a character position on a screen display that determines the characteristics of the adjacent character to be displayed (e.g. displayable, non-displayable, protected, nonprotected). *See* BYTE.

screen buffer. In peripherals, a buffer used to store the data that is displayed on the screen of a visual display unit. The display unit accesses this buffer in each display scan. *See* REFRESHED CATHODE RAY TUBE, VISUAL DISPLAY UNIT.

screen coordinates. In computer graphics, the coordinate system of the display device. In transforming an image into screen coordinates the characteristics of the display device are taken into account, ensuring that the device is correctly addressed and the image is displayed undistorted. *Compare* EYE COORDINATES, WORLD COORDINATES.

screen editor. In computing, a text editor that displays a screenful of text. A cursor can be moved to any character position and the corresponding section of text modified. *Compare* LINE EDITOR. *See* TEXT EDITOR.

screen format. In computing, the layout or structure of the visual display.

screenful. In videotex, the information contents of a full page. *See* PAGE.

screen overscan. In peripherals, the amount by which the electron beam deflects past the end of a screen in the raster scan of a visual display unit or television set. The horizontal screen line effectively exceeds the width of the screen. *Compare* DISPLAY LINE. *See* RASTER SCAN, VISUAL DISPLAY UNIT.

script. In distributed processing, a prepared set of commands on a microcomputer that automatically initiates logon and password input to a host. *See* LOGON, PASSWORD. (2) In typesetting, a typeface based upon handwritten letterforms. (3) In filming, a set of written specifications for the production of a film.

scroll. In peripherals and video, the continuous horizontal or vertical movement of the video information displayed such that as old data disappears at one edge new data

appears at the opposite edge. (Philips). *See* PAGE SCROLLING, VERTICAL SCROLLING.

scroll mode. In peripherals, pertaining to a terminal with no intelligence. When a key is struck a character is sent over a line, and when it is received it is displayed. *Compare* FORM MODE, INTELLIGENT TERMINAL, PAGE MODE.

SCSI. In peripherals, Small Computer System Interface; an IEEE standard for interfacing a computer to multiple, disparate high-speed peripherals such as floppy or hard disk drives or read-only memory compact disc drives, singly or in combination. (Philips). *See* COMPACT DISC – READ-ONLY MEMORY, HARD DISK, IEEE.

scumming. In printing, a fault in lithography in which the water-accepting layer is worn away from non-image-bearing areas. *See* LITHOGRAPHY.

S-DAT. In recording, one of the proposed formats for digital audio tape recording. In this format a 3.81-mm tape is used but, unlike conventional compact cassette formats, 22 tracks are recorded across the width of the tape. The tracks are recorded longitudinally and read by a multitrack stationary read/write head system. *Compare* R-DAT, *See* COMPACT CASSETTE, DIGITAL AUDIO TAPE.

SDI. *See* SELECTIVE DISSEMINATION OF INFORMATION.

SDIF. In data communications, standard document interchange format.

SDLC. *See* SYNCHRONOUS DATA LINK CONTROL.

SDM. *See* SELECTIVE DISSEMINATION OF MICROFICHE.

SEAQ. In applications, Stock Exchange Automated Quotes; the UK Stock Exchange trading information system. *See* BIG BANG, TOPIC.

search and replace. In word processing, a facility in which every occurrence of a specified string of characters in stored text can be automatically replaced by a second specified string (e.g. in correcting a common spelling error).

Search Helper. In online information retrieval, gateway software produced by Information Access Company (IAC) for use with IAC databases in Dialog. *See* DIALOG, GATEWAY SOFTWARE.

search key. In databases, the data to be compared with a specific part of each item in a search. *See* KEY.

search memory. *Synonymous with* ASSOCIATIVE STORAGE.

search program. In databases, a program that searches a data file or database to find a keyword or key phrase supplied by an operator or another program. (Philips). *See* RETRIEVAL.

search statement. In online information retrieval, a query framed using specific search terms intended to retrieve a set of items. *See* ANSWER SET, SEARCH STRATEGY.

search strategy. In online information retrieval, the search statements used to satisfy the user's requirements in an online search. *See* SEARCH STATEMENT.

SECAM. *See* VIDEO STANDARDS.

SECDED. In codes, single-error correction double-error detection; an error correction and detection code that can detect and correct one-bit errors and detect but not correct two-bit errors. Simple parity checks can only detect but not correct one-bit errors whereas two-bit errors cannot even be detected. *See* BIT, ERROR-CORRECTING CODE, ERROR-DETECTING CODE, HAMMING CODE, PARITY CHECKING, REAL NUMBER.

secondary channel. In data communications, a data channel derived from the same physical path as the main data channel, but completely independent from it. It carries auxiliary information, at a low data rate, dealing with device control, diagnostics, etc. *See* CHANNEL.

secondary colour. A colour produced by the combination of two primary colours. *See* PRIMARY COLOURS.

secondary destination. In data communications, any of the destinations specified in a message except the first.

secondary index. In data structures, an index that holds the keys or locations of all records which have a particular value for a specified field. *See* FIELD, INVERTED FILE, RECORD.

secondary key. (1) In data security. *Synonymous with* KEY-ENCRYPTING KEY. (2) In databases, a key that does not uniquely define a record; a key that contains the value of an attribute other than the unique identifier. *Compare* PRIMARY KEY. *See* ATTRIBUTE.

secondary storage. *Synonymous with* AUXILIARY STORAGE.

second-generation computer. The generation of computers in which solid-state components replaced vacuum tubes. They originated in the late 1950s. *Compare* FIFTH-GENERATION COMPUTER, FIRST-GENERATION COMPUTER, FOURTH-GENERATION COMPUTER, THIRD-GENERATION COMPUTER. *See* SOLID-STATE DEVICE.

second-generation language. In programming, the first generation of high-level languages (e.g. FORTRAN). *Compare* FIRST-GENERATION LANGUAGE, FOURTH-GENERATION LANGUAGE, SECOND-GENERATION COMPUTER, THIRD-GENERATION LANGUAGE. *See* FORTRAN, HIGH-LEVEL LANGUAGE.

second normal form. (SNF) In databases, a property of a relation in a relational database. A relation is in second normal form if it is in first normal form and every non-prime attribute of the relation is fully functionally dependent upon each candidate key of the relation. An example of a relation not in second normal form is EMPLOYEE-NUMBER, PROJECT-NUMBER, PROJECT-NAME, PROJECT-COMPLETION-DATE. The pair EMPLOYEE-NUMBER, PROJECT-NAME is a candidate key for the relation, but PROJECT-COMPLETION-DATE is functionally dependent upon a subset of this key (i.e. PROJECT-NUMBER) and is thus not fully functionally dependent upon the candidate key. The disadvantage of this relation arises if only one employee is assigned to a project and that employee resigns. In this case, all records pertaining to the employee are deleted, and details of the PROJECT-COMPLETION-DATE are lost even though the project may be live. *Compare* FIRST NORMAL FORM, THIRD NORMAL FORM. *See* CANDIDATE KEY, FULLY FUNCTIONAL DEPENDENT, NON-PRIME ATTRIBUTE, NORMAL FORMS, RELATIONAL DATABASE.

second sourcing.   (1) The licensing of rights for manufacturing electronic components, typically a microprocessor. (2) The securing of component supplies from two or more separate sources.

secrecy classification.   In data security, an attribute of data or objects that expresses the relative potential damage arising if the data or object is compromised to an adversary. *See* COMPROMISE.

section.   In printing, a printed sheet folded to make a multiple of pages. (Desktop).

section 214.   In communications, a Federal Communications Commission regulation governing the acquisition, leasing or construction of new telecommunication facilities. *See* FEDERAL COMMUNICATIONS COMMISSION.

section 326.   The section of the Federal Communications Commission Act, 1934, which prohibits censorship. *See* FEDERAL COMMUNICATIONS COMMISSION.

sectioning.   In micrographics, microfilming of an oversize document in two or more parts. *See* MICROFILM.

section mark.   (1) In printing, a character used at the beginning of a new section. (2) A footnote symbol. (Desktop).

sector.   (1) In optical media, the smallest unit of absolutely addressable information on a read-only memory or interactive compact disc. A sector is 2352 bytes long, containing a synchronization pattern, header field and digital data. It may also contain a subheader and EDC/ECC error protection. (Philips). *See* COMPACT DISC - INTERACTIVE, COMPACT DISC - READ-ONLY MEMORY, EIGHT-TO-FOURTEEN MODULATION, ERROR-CORRECTING CODE, ERRROR-DETECTING CODE, HEADER FIELD, SECTOR STRUCTURE, SUB-HEADER. (2) In memory systems, a portion of a rotational magnetic storage device that can be accessed by the magnetic heads in the course of a particular rotation. Magnetic disks are divided into circular tracks, and each track is then subdivided into sectors holding a block of data. A sector is the smallest element of disk store that can be addressed by the computer. *See* BIT COPIER, MAGNETIC DISK, TRACK.

sector address.   In optical media, the physical address of a sector, on an interactive or read-only memory compact disc, expressed in minutes and seconds and sector number. It is contained in the address part of the sector header. (Philips). *See* COMPACT DISC – INTERACTIVE, COMPACT DISC – READ-ONLY MEMORY, HEADER, SECTOR.

sector allocation.   In memory systems, pertaining to the allocation of free magnetic disk sectors to a file that is to be written to disk. *See* FILE, MAGNETIC DISK, SECTOR.

sector chart.   *Synonymous with* PIE GRAPH.

sector id.   In memory systems, the identification (id) header, on a disk sector, preceding the sector data. *See* SECTOR.

sector structure.   In optical media, pertaining to the manner in which the 2352 bytes of

| | CD-ROM | | CD-1 | |
	mode 1	mode 2	form 1	form 2
Synchronization	12 B	12 B	12 B	12 B
Header	4 B	4B	4 B	4 B
Subheader	—	—	8 B	8 B
User Data	2048 B	2336 B	2048 B	2324 B
EDC/ECC	288 B	—	280 B	—

sector structure
CD-ROM and CD-I sector structure.

an interactive or read-only memory compact disc sector are divided. There are four ways in which the data may be divided depending upon the system and the required degree of data integrity. (Philips). *See* COMPACT DISC – INTERACTIVE, COMPACT DISC – READ-ONLY MEMORY, FORM 1, FORM 2, MODE 1, MODE 2, SECTOR.

secure module. *Synonymous with* TAMPER-RESISTANT MODULE.

secure operating system. In computer security, an operating system that effectively controls hardware and software functions in order to provide the level of protection appropriate to the value of the data and resources managed by the operating system. (FIPS). *See* OPERATING SYSTEM.

secure telephone system. In computer security, a telephone system in which the security of the communications is enforced by voice scrambling and/or online supervision circuitry. *See* VOICE SCRAMBLING.

security. The quality or state of being cost effectively protected from undue losses (e.g. loss of goodwill, monetary loss, loss of ability to continue operations, etc.). *See* ADMINISTRATIVE SECURITY, COMMUNICATIONS SECURITY, COMPUTER SECURITY, DATA SECURITY, EMANATION SECURITY, PERSONNEL SECURITY, PROCEDURAL SECURITY, TRAFFIC FLOW SECURITY.

security breach. A violation of security controls producing the danger of loss of system components or compromise of information.

security filter. In computer security, a set of software routines and techniques employed in automatic data-processing systems to prevent automatic forwarding of specified data over unprotected links or to unauthorized persons. (FIPS). *See* SECURITY KERNEL.

security kernel. In computer security, the central part of a computer system (software and hardware) that implements the fundamental security procedures for controlling access to system resources. (FIPS). *See* ACCESS CONTROL, FILTER.

security label. In data security, a sensitivity indicator that is permanently associated with protected data, processes and/or other resources and which may be used in enforcing security policy.

security level. In computer security, the combination of hierarchical classification and a set of non-hierarchical categories that represent the sensitivity of information. (DOD). *See* SENSITIVITY.

security life. In data security, the time span over which cryptographically protected data has value. (ANSI).

security model. In computer security, a model that defines the system-enforced security rules. It specifies the access controls on the use of information and how information will be allowed to flow through the system. It also provides the mechanism for specifying how to change access controls and interfaces dynamically without compromising system security.

security modem. In computer security, a modem installed in a user terminal with integrated security functions. Such modems incorporate outbound call-screening security to control host access from the user end. The user enters a password for a given host computer, the security modem checks the password against host computer telephone numbers, and if a match is found the modem dials up the computer and initiates logon procedures. *Compare* PORT PROTECTION DEVICE. *See* MODEM, TELEPHONE INTRUSION.

security module. *Synonymous with* TAMPER-RESISTANT MODULE.

security paper. In printing, paper incorporating special features (e.g. dyes, watermarks, etc.) for use on cheques. (Desktop).

security policy. In computer security, the statement of the rules for the provision of security services for one or more instances of communication. A security policy is based upon those security services required and enforced by the appropriate system administration and also other security services requested by an entity wishing to communicate with the system. *See* DISCRETIONARY SECURITY, MANDATORY SECURITY.

security testing. In computer security, a process used to determine that the security features of a system are implemented as designed and that they are adequate for a proposed application's environment. This process includes hands-on functional testing, penetration testing and verification. (DOD). *See* PENETRATION TESTING, TIGER TEAM, VERIFICATION.

security threats. In computer and network security, the sources of security threats are: (a) errors and omissions caused by honest employees; (b) dishonest employees who take advantage of some missing control or misuse their authority and who seek to conceal their actions; (c) fire and natural disasters; (d) disgruntled employees or ex-employees who want to cause harm to the management, unlike dishonest employees they do not seek to conceal the results of their actions; (e) water damage; (f) external threats (e.g. terrorism, hackers, riots). *See* HACKER, THREAT.

security violation. In computer security, an incident in which a person defeats or bypasses security controls in order to gain unauthorized access to information, to make unauthorized use of system resources or to remove illegally system components.

seed. In applications, a number supplied to a random-number generator to commence the sequence. *See* RANDOM NUMBERS.

seek error. In memory systems, an error in reading data from a floppy disk when the read/write head does not attain the correct track. *See* FLOPPY DISC, READ/WRITE HEAD, TRACK.

seek latency. In peripherals and recording, the delay between a request for search action and arrival at the location sought. (Philips). *Compare* ROTATIONAL LATENCY.

seek time. In memory systems, the time taken to reposition the heads of a magnetic disk unit in order to read or write data on a different track. It is usually expressed as the average time taken to move over half the

tracks on the disk. *See* MAGNETIC DISK, READ/WRITE HEAD, TRACK.

seepage. In computer security, the accidental flow to unauthorized individuals of data or information access which is presumed to be controlled by computer security safeguards. (FIPS). *Compare* CONFINEMENT. *Synonymous with* DATA LEAKAGE.

see through. In printing, the degree to which an image on an underlying sheet can be seen through a sheet of paper. *Compare* SHOW THROUGH.

segment. (1) In programming, a self-contained portion of a computer program that can be executed without the entire program necessarily resident in the internal store at any one time. (2) In communications, a section of a message that can be held in a buffer. *See* BUFFER.

seize. In data communications, to gain control of a channel in order to transmit a message.

selecting. In communications, inviting another station or node to receive messages.

selection. In databases, an operation on a relational database in which a new relation is formed by selecting records, from the original relation, according to specified criteria on fields. *Compare* DIVISION, JOIN, PROJECTION. *See* FIELD, RECORD, RELATIONAL DATABASE.

selective calling. (1) In data communications, a system in which remote stations are called in for transmissions of messages when required, excluding all other stations on the circuit. (2) In data communications, the facility of a transmitter to select the stations on the same line that are to receive the message.

selective dissemination of information. (SDI) In library science, a service that provides users with abstracts which lie within the user's area of interest. A profile defining each area of interest is compiled for the user and stored on magnetic media for computer processing. Keywords representing documents are automatically matched with the user's profile, and abstracts are sent to the user for each match. *Compare* SELECTIVE DISSEMINATION OF MICROFICHE. *See* ABSTRACT, KEYWORD.

selective dissemination of microfiche. (SDM) In library science, a system that regularly provides large-scale microfiche users with microfiche copies of documents corresponding to their areas of interest. *Compare* SELECTIVE DISSEMINATION OF INFORMATION. *See* MICROFICHE.

selective dump. In computing, a dump of one or more selected areas of storage. *Compare* CHANGE DUMP, DISASTER DUMP, POST MORTEM DUMP, RESCUE DUMP. *See* DUMP.

selectivity. In broadcasting, the ability of a radio receiver to discriminate between two adjacent broadcast carrier signals. *See* CARRIER.

selector. In electronics, a device that looks for the presence of a control pulse, in a pulse train, and consequently directs the pulse train to the appropriate one of the two lines. *See* PULSE TRAIN.

selector channel. In data communications, a channel designed to operate with only one input/output device at any one time. After selection of the input/output device the whole message is transmitted byte by byte. *See* BYTE, CHANNEL.

selenium. In electronics, a chemical element used in photoelectric devices. *See* PHOTOELECTRIC.

self-adaptive system. A system that is able to adjust its performance characteristics according to its environment and to perceived relationships between input and output signals.

self-banking. In applications, the use of automatic tellers, cash dispensers and communication terminals by individual clients to perform banking transactions. The equipment may be located in a bank, place of work, home, etc. *Compare* HOME BANKING. *See* AUTOMATIC TELLER MACHINE.

self-checking circuit. In reliability, a form of hardware and information redundancy in which circuits are able to detect failures in

themselves and fail in a predicted safe manner. *See* HARDWARE REDUNDANCY, INFORMATION REDUNDANCY.

self-checking codes. *Synonymous with* ERROR-DETECTING CODE.

self-correcting code. *Synonymous with* ERROR-CORRECTING CODE.

self-relocating program. In programming, a program that can be loaded into any area of main storage. At initialization the program adjusts its address values so that it can be executed at that location. *See* RELOCATE.

self-scanning camera. In peripherals, a camera used for capture of a static image. It comprises a single-line array of charge-coupled transistors, or photodiodes, which is driven across the back of the lens system by a precision screw drive. Up to 4096 elements may be in the array, and the camera is capable of producing a 4000 x 5000 pixel image with eight- or 12-bit grey scale. Full-colour images can be produced by use of a colour wheel filter and three passes of the image. *See* CHARGE-COUPLED DEVICE, GREY SCALE, PIXEL.

self-synchronizing. In data security, a property of a cipher which provides for an automatic recovery after an error has occurred.

self-test. *Synonymous with* BUILT-IN TEST.

semantics. The study or science of the relationship between symbols and their meaning.

semaphore. In program execution, a method to ensure the synchronization of cooperating processes. It is used to prevent the undesirable interference arising when two processes simultaneously seek to utilize a resource. *See* DEADLOCK.

semiconductor. In electronics, a material with a conductivity midway between that of an insulator and a good conductor. The conductivity is sensitive to temperature, radiation and the presence of impurities. Such materials are used in the manufacture of transistors, diodes, photoelectric devices

and solar cells. *See* DIODE, PHOTOCELL, SEMI-
CONDUCTOR DEVICES, TRANSISTOR.

semiconductor devices. In electronics,
devices manufactured using semiconductor
materials. For some purposes impurities are
deliberately added to the semiconductor to
induce certain conductivity characteristics.
The impurities produce additional positive
or negative electrical carriers in the material,
and the result is a p- or n-type semiconductor, respectively. Semiconductor devices
form the basis of modern electronics because
they are rugged, reliable, cheap to produce,
small and have a very low power consumption. *See* CHIP, SEMICONDUCTOR, TRANSISTOR.

semiconductor laser. In optoelectronics, a
small, rugged, efficient laser well suited for
fiber optics. The laser consists of a semiconductor with p- and n-materials, rather like a
semiconductor diode. A third layer of semiconductor material is inserted at the p–n
junction. This intervening layer has highly
polished surfaces effectively producing mirrors at each end. A forward voltage drives
holes and electrons from the p- and n-
materials, respectively, into the aforementioned layer where they combine and form
photons. The emitted light is reflected to
and fro across the layer, and the layer width
is chosen to provide resonance for the light
wavelength, thus producing a high-intensity
beam of light which is emitted from the
crystal. *See* FIBER OPTICS, LASER, N-TYPE
MATERIAL, PHOTON, P-TYPE MATERIAL, SEMI-
CONDUCTOR.

semiconductor memory. In memory
systems, a memory device, such as used in a
computer, employing semiconductor components or chips. (Philips). *See* MEMORY,
RANDOM-ACCESS MEMORY.

semi-custom design. In microelectronics,
the custom design to meet a specific customer's requirements using less-design-
intensive techniques than full-custom design
(e.g. cell library or masterchip methods).
Compare FULL-CUSTOM DESIGN. *See* CELL
LIBRARY, CUSTOM DESIGN, MASTERCHIP.

semi-micro xerography. (SMX) In micrographics, a copier that accepts input in
micrographic form, via a special reader, and
produces human-readable hard copy. *See*
XEROGRAPHY.

semiology. *Synonymous with* SEMIOTICS.

semiotics. The study of the nature and use
of signs which may be spoken, gesticulated,
written, printed or constructed. *Synonymous with* SEMIOLOGY.

sense. To examine in relationship to some
specified criterion.

sensitive data. In data security, data that,
as determined by a competent authority,
must be protected because its unauthorized
disclosure, alteration, loss or destruction will
cause perceivable damage to someone or
something. (AFR).

sensitive software. In computer security,
any data-processing software that can
bypass, penetrate or damage data-
processing security controls. (AR).

sensitive statistic. In database security, a
statistic from a statistical database that can
be used to reveal information about an
individual. *See* INFERENCE CONTROL, STATIS-
TICAL DATABASE.

sensitive systems. In computer security, a
system that processes sensitive data or performs a sensitive function. The categories of
sensitive systems, in increasing order of sensitivity, are:

(a) Applications providing general process-
    ing support (e.g. engineering calcula-
    tions used in aircraft design).
(b) Funds disbursement, accounting, asset
    management systems (e.g. payroll).
(c) General-purpose information systems
    (e.g. generalized data management
    systems).
(d) Automated decision-making systems
    (e.g. fully automated funds disbur-
    sement and accounting systems).
(e) Real-time control systems (e.g. air traf-
    fic control).
(f) Systems affecting national security or
    wellbeing (e.g. integrated electronic
    funds transfer).

sensitivity. In computer security, the characteristic of a resource that which implies its

value or importance, as well as its vulnerability to accidental or deliberate threats. *See* ACCIDENTAL THREAT, DELIBERATE THREAT, SENSITIVE SYSTEMS.

sensitometer. In photography, a device designed to expose film with an accurately given series of exposures having a systematic progressive relationship.

sensitometric strip. In photography, a strip of film exposed in a sensitometer to determine photographic response and/or processing conditions. *See* SENSITOMETER.

sensor. In electronics, a transducer or similar device that produces an output for monitoring by a system according to the state of some physical phenomenon. *See* TRANSDUCER.

sensor-based system. In computing, a system whose primary source of input is data from sensors. The input data is processed by a computer, and the output may be used to control a physical process, provide monitoring and warning signals to operators, etc.

sentence key. In word processing, a key employed to control text processing one sentence at a time. *See* TEXT PROCESSING.

sentinel. In programming, a marker indicating the beginning or the end of a section of information accessed by a program.

separate and mediate. In computer security, a principle for structuring secure systems in which entities of different security classifications are kept separate except when performing operating operations that require access to entities from more than one level. Such accesses must be performed by trusted reference monitors which ensure compliance with some externally imposed security policy. *See* REFERENCE MONITOR.

separate-channel signalling. In communications, signalling that utilizes the whole or part of a channel frequency band or time slots in a multichannel system in order to provide supervisory and control signals for all the traffic channels in the multichannel system. The time slots or frequency bands that are used for signalling are not used for the message traffic. *Compare* COMMON-CHANNEL SIGNALLING. *See* FREQUENCY DIVISION MULTIPLEXING, SIGNALLING, TIME DIVISION MULTIPLEXING.

separated graphics. In videotex, a display option in which the display of an individual mosaic does not fill the whole of its character space. *Compare* CONTIGUOUS GRAPHICS. *See* MOSAIC.

separation of privilege. In computer security, one of the principles of secure systems. *See* PRINCIPLES OF SECURE SYSTEMS.

separator. *Synonymous with* DELIMITER.

septet. In data structures, a group of seven binary digits (i.e. bits) treated as an entity. *Compare* OCTET, SEXTET.

sequence. An list of items arranged according to a specified set of rules (e.g. arranged alphabetically, numerically or chronologically).

sequential access. In programming, an access mode in which records are obtained from, or placed into, a file in such a way that each successive access to the file refers to the following record in the file. *Compare* DIRECT ACCESS, RANDOM ACCESS. *Synonymous with* SERIAL ACCESS.

sequential computer. In computing, a computer in which events occur one after the other with little or no provision for simultaneousness or overlap. *Compare* PARALLEL COMPUTER.

sequential data set. In memory systems, a data set that is organized on the basis of the successive physical location of records on a storage medium (e.g. magnetic tape). *See* DATA SET, RECORD.

sequential logic. In electronics, a logic circuit in which the output depends upon the previous states of the inputs. *Compare* COMBINATIONAL LOGIC.

SER. *See* SYMBOL ERROR RATE.

serial access. *Synonymous with* SEQUENTIAL ACCESS.

serial communication. *See* SERIAL TRANSMISSION.

serial computer. In computing, a computer with a single arithmetic logic unit. *Compare* PARALLEL COMPUTER. *See* ARITHMETIC LOGIC UNIT.

serial interface. In data communications, an interface (e.g. between data terminal equipment and a modem) that can only pass data in serial transmission form. *Compare* PARALLEL INTERFACE. *See* DATA TERMINAL EQUIPMENT, MODEM, RS-232C, SERIAL TRANSMISSION.

serializer. In computing, a device that converts a space distribution of simultaneous states representing data into a corresponding time sequence of states.

serial operation. The sequential or consecutive execution of two or more operations in a single device (e.g. an arithmetic logic unit). *Compare* PARALLEL OPERATION.

serial printer. In printing, an output device that prints one character at a time. *Compare* LINE PRINTER. *See* PRINTER. *Synonymous with* CHARACTER PRINTER.

serial transmission. In data communications, a method of information transfer in which each bit of a character is sent in sequence. *Compare* PARALLEL TRANSMISSION. *Synonymous with* SERIAL COMMUNICATION.

series circuit. In electronics, a circuit in which the components are connected end to end so that the same current flows through each one. *Compare* PARALLEL CIRCUIT.

series-to-parallel converter. In hardware, a device that accepts the serial input of a word, or byte, on one line and produces a parallel version of that input on *n* lines (*n* being the number of bits in the word or byte). *Compare* PARALLEL-TO-SERIES CONVERTER.

serif. In printing, the short strokes projecting from the principal lines of printed characters. *Compare* SANS SERIF.

server. In computer networks, a unit at a node of a network that provides a specific service for network users (e.g. a printer server provides printing facilities, a file server stores user files). *See* COMMUNICATION SERVER, DISK SERVER, FILE SERVER.

service bureau. In computing, an organization that provides computing or data-processing services for other individuals or organizations.

service centre. In videotex, the computer centre hosting the system for a particular group of users. *See* UPDATE CENTRE.

service message. In data communications, a message, passing between two terminal points, containing or seeking information concerning other messages.

service reference model. (SRM) In computer graphics, the minimum hardware requirements for a NAPLPS decoder. It requires the display of at least 16 simultaneous colours with 256 x 200 pixel resolution. *See* NAPLPS, PIXEL.

service software. In programming, software designed specifically for service and repair work. (Philips). *Synonymous with* DIAGNOSTICS.

servo. *Synonymous with* SERVO MECHANISM.

servo mechanism. In control and instrumentation, a control system that measures the difference between the actual and desired value of a variable and takes action to reduce that difference. *See* FEEDBACK. *Synonymous with* SERVO.

session. (1) In computing, an activity for a period of time; the activity is access to a computer/network resource by a user. A period of time is bounded by session initiation (a form of logon) and session termination (a form of logoff). (DCID). (2) In distributed processing, the period of time during which a user of a terminal can communicate with an interactive system; usually the elapsed time between logon and logoff. *See* LOGOFF, LOGON.

session hold. *Synonymous with* HOT KEY.

session key. In data security, a cryptographic key used only for a limited period (e.g.

a user session at a terminal) and then discarded.

session layer. In data communications, a layer in the ISO Open Systems Interconnection model. This layer provides for connections between processes in different hosts. *Compare* APPLICATION LAYER, DATA LINK LAYER, NETWORK LAYER, PHYSICAL LAYER, PRESENTATION LAYER, TRANSPORT LAYER. *See* OPEN SYSTEMS INTERCONNECTION.

set. (1) In mathematics, an operation on a bit, in binary arithmetic, to adjust its value to 1. *Compare* CLEAR. (2) In mathematics, a collection of elements with a common property. *See* SET THEORY. (3) In databases, a CODASYL term for a named collection of record types. *See* CODASYL, RECORD. (4) In filming, the physical surroundings and background for a studio scene. (5) In printing, a measure of typeface width. *See* SET SIZE. (6) A radio or television receiver.

set off. In printing, a situation in which wet ink on one sheet of paper, which has just been printed, marks the underside of the following sheet on the stack.

set size. In printing, the horizontal dimension of a typeface expressed in sets. One set is equal to one point, the standard dimension of a point is 0.3515 millimetres. The set size indicates the horizontal width allocated to a character, not the size of the printed image. *See* POINT, TYPE SIZE.

set solid. In printing, type set without leading (line spacing) between the lines. Type is often set with extra space (e.g. 9 point set on 10 point). (Desktop). *See* LEADING, POINT, SOLID.

set theory. In mathematics, the study of the properties of sets. *See* SET.

set-top converter. In cable television, a device that interfaces the consumer's television receiver to the network. It will usually contain a frequency changer to enable the receiver to accept any of the wide range of cable signals. It may also contain a decoder to enable authorized subscribers to receive scrambled channels available on premium services. *See* PREMIUM TELEVISION.

set width. In printing, the width of the individual character including the normal amount of space on either side to prevent the characters touching. *See* PHOTOTYPESETTING, SET SIZE.

sextet. In data structures, a group of six binary digits (i.e. bits) treated as an entity. *Compare* OCTET, SEPTET.

sexto. In printing, folded or cut sheet that is one-sixth the area of basic sheet size.

sf signalling. *See* SINGLE-FREQUENCY SIGNALLING.

SGML. *See* STANDARD GENERALIZED MARKUP LANGUAGE.

shade. (1) In printing, the result of adding and mixing small amounts of black with basic hue. (2) In printing, the degree of black mixed into pure hue.

shaded letter. In printing, an outline letter shaded along one side to give a three-dimensional effect of letter and associated shadow. *See* OUTLINE LETTER.

shading. In computer graphics, a realistic representation of a three-dimensional model requires a method of shading the object surfaces. Flat-shading and Gouraud-shading algorithms provide means of representing variations in the illumination over surfaces, but do not support the specular highlights produced by reflection, and they reveal the facetted nature of the image. Ray-tracing techniques provide extremely realistic images, but make excessive demands on computer power. *See* FLAT SHADING, GOURAUD SHADING, RAY TRACING.

shadowmask. In television, a perforated mask located immediately behind a television tube screen and used to separate the electron beams producing red, green and blue. *Compare* BEAM PENETRATION. *See* TELEVISION TUBE.

shallow dish. *See* DISH ANTENNA.

shannon. *See* INFORMATION CONTENT.

Shannon's five criteria. In data security, suggestions for the criteria of secure systems proposed by Shannon in the 1940s: (a) the amount of secrecy offered; (b) the size of the key; (c) the simplicity of enciphering and deciphering operations; (d) the propagation of errors; and (e) extension of the message. *See* INFORMATION THEORY.

Shannon's law.   In communications, a law that provides a measure for the capacity of a communication line in terms of its bandwidth and signal-to-noise ratio. According to this law the maximum transmission in bits per second is given by $W \log (1 + SN)$ where, W = bandwidth, log = logarithm to base 2 and SN = signal-to-noise ratio. *See* BANDWIDTH, SIGNAL-TO-NOISE RATIO.

shared file.   In computing, a file that may be accessed by two systems. It can provide a means of communication between two computer systems.

shared line.   *Synonymous with* PARTY LINE.

shared logic.   In computing, a computer system in which units (e.g. word-processing workstations) operate under a central control sharing the processing power of the central unit. *See* DISTRIBUTED LOGIC.

shareware.   In software, programs that are copyrighted and issued with the request that a modest donation be made to the supplier if they prove to be of value to the user. *See* BULLETIN BOARD. *Synonymous with* FREE-WARE.

sheet-fed.   In printing, pertaining to presses in which paper is fed in a sheet at a time. *Compare* WEB-FED.

sheetwise.   A method of printing a section. One-half of the pages from a section is imposed and printed. The remaining half of the pages is then printed on the other side of the sheet. (Desktop). *See* IMPOSITION, SECTION.

shelf life.   The period of time before deterioration or the effect of external market forces that renders a material or product unusable. *Compare* LOAD LIFE.

shell.   (1) In programming, a program providing an interface between a user and an operating system. *See* SHELL SCRIPT. (2) In

artificial intelligence, an expert system package that can be used in conjunction with a knowledge base produced by a user. *See* EXPERT SYSTEMS, KNOWLEDGE BASE.

shell script.   In computing, a facility in Unix that may be employed to create customized user environments. A shell script contains a sequence of commands which are read by the shell. *See* BATCH FILE, SHELL, UNIX.

SHF.   *See* SUPER HIGH-FREQUENCY.

shielded cable.   In communications, an inner conductor surrounded by an outer grounded metallic braid to protect signals from interference. *See* COAXIAL CABLE, INTERFERENCE.

shielding effectiveness.   In electronics, the measure in decibels of the absorbing property of a conductive shield. In the USA computing devices must comply with Federal Communications Commission emission regulations and special electrically conductive plastics are used for this purpose. *Compare* TEMPEST PROOFING. *See* CONDUCTIVE SHIELDING, DECIBEL.

shift.   (1) In data security, the difference in alphabetic position between a plaintext character, in a translation cipher, and the corresponding ciphertext character. *See* TRANSLATION CIPHER. (2) In computing, a movement of bits in storage to the left or right.

shift codes.   In codes, a method of increasing the number of characters that can be associated with a given number of bits. If a six-bit code is used then 64 characters may be allocated. However, if two of these characters are designated as 'shift' and 'unshift' then they may produce the effect of a shift to and from an alternative character set giving a total of 124 available characters. *See* ESCAPE CODE.

shift key.   In peripherals, a control on a keyboard to enable an alternative character set to be keyed in.

shift register.   In hardware, a register designed for the shifting of data to the left or right. *See* REGISTER.

Ship Movement Service. In communications, a safety service for ships and coastal stations restricted to messages relating to the movement of ships.

SHL. *See* STUDIO TO HEAD END LINK.

short circuit. In electronics, a very low-resistance connection between two electrical points. A short circuit usually results from an accidental connection.

short-wave. Pertaining to radio waves with wavelengths of up to 60 metres. *See* RADIO WAVES.

shotgun microphone. A highly directional microphone. *See* UNIDIRECTIONAL MICROPHONE.

shoulder. In printing, the flat non-printing area surrounding the face of type. *See* TYPE.

shouldering. *Synonymous with* SHOULDER SURFING.

shoulder surfing. In computer security, a method of obtaining knowledge of user passwords, logon procedures, etc. by looking over the shoulder of a terminal user. *Synonymous with* SHOULDERING.

shoulder tap. In computing, a technique enabling one processor to communicate with another.

show through. In printing, the degree to which an image on a reverse side can be seen through a sheet of paper. *Compare* SEE THROUGH.

shrink. In filming and video, a visual effect in which one image becomes gradually smaller until it is replaced completely by another. (Philips). *See* TRANSITION.

shrink-wrapped licence. In software protection, a contract supplied by a software house that is visible through the transparent wrapping around the box of floppy disks and documentation. The contract stipulates conditions under which the software may be used, and it is deemed to come into effect once the wrapping has been torn. The validity of this technique is very questionable in most countries. *See* SOFTWARE HOUSE. *Synonymous with* HAT BOX, TEAR-ME-OPEN.

SI. Systéme Internationale; a metric system of measurement units based upon the metre (length), kilogram (weight), second (time) and amperes (electrical current).

sibilance. In recording, an excessive amount of voice hiss when a consonant such as 's' is spoken.

sideband. In communications, a band of frequencies of a transmitted signal, above and below the carrier frequency, produced by the modulation process. *See* CARRIER, MODULATION.

sidebars. *See* BOX.

side bearings. In printing, the space allocated to either side of a character image to prevent it overlapping with characters on either side. *Compare* KERNING.

side effect. In programming, any external effect produced in the execution of a procedure other than that of giving the required result value.

side heading. In printing, a subheading set flush into the text at the left edge. (Desktop).

side lobe. In communications, one of the lobes between the main and back lobes of an antenna pattern. *Compare* BACK LOBE, MAIN LOBE. *See* ANTENNA PATTERN.

SIGGRAPH. In computer graphics, Special Interest Group on Graphics in the Association for Computer Machinery. *See* ASSOCIATION FOR COMPUTER MACHINERY, CORE.

SIGLE. System for Information on Grey Literature in Europe; an EEC project. *See* GREY LITERATURE.

signal. (1) An intentional time-varying physical phenomenon conveying information. (2) The physical embodiment of a message. (3) A short message, as in a control signal.

signal converter. In cable television, a device located at the head end to convert the received ultra high-frequency signals to frequencies in the very high-frequency range for transmission along the cable system. *See* HEAD END, ULTRA HIGH-FREQUENCY, VERY HIGH-FREQUENCY.

signal element. In data communications, the basic unit by which data is communicated along a channel. Each unit is a state or condition of the channel, representing one or more bits of digital information. A unit may be a DC pulse, or an AC signal of certain amplitude, phase or frequency which is recognized and translated by the receiving equipment.

signal generator. In electronics, a device for producing waveforms of various shapes, frequencies and amplitudes. It is often used for test equipment. *See* WAVEFORM.

signal ground. In electronics, a connection that establishes a common ground reference voltage for all data signals. *Compare* PROTECTIVE GROUND. *See* GROUND.

signalling. In communications, the exchange of information (other than by speech) specifically concerned with the establishment and control of connections and management in a communication network.

signalling distance. In codes, a measure of the degree of difference in two equal-length symbol strings. It is equal to the number of symbol positions that are different in the two strings. *Synonymous with* HAMMING DIFFERENCE.

signal quality detector. In data communications, a signal provided by synchronous modems that indicates whether or not there is a high probability of an error in the received data. *See* RS-232C, SYNCHRONOUS MODEM.

signal-to-noise ratio. (s/n ratio) In communications, the ratio of the power of the required signal to that of the unwanted noise. *See* NOISE.

signature. (1) In printing, a letter or figure printed on the first page of each section of a book and used as a guide when collating and binding. (Desktop). *See* SECTION. (2) In programming. *Synonymous with* FINGERPRINT. (3) In data security. *See* DIGITAL SIGNATURE.

signature analysis. In computer security and data security, written signatures may be employed as a means of identification for access control or authority to initiate a transaction. The automatic verification of signatures is based not only upon the shape of the completed signature but also upon the dynamics of signature production (e.g. pressure deviation, acceleration, time to complete segments). The signature is normally input with an electronic pen, and measurements derived from the input are compared with prestored values appertaining to the purported signature owner.

sign bit. In programming, the bit designated to indicate the numerical sign of the binary number with which it is associated. *See* BIT, FLOATING POINT, ONE'S COMPLEMENT, TWO'S COMPLEMENT.

sign in. *Synonymous with* LOGON.

sign off. *Synonymous with* LOGOFF.

sign on. *Synonymous with* LOGON.

silent speed. In filming, the exposure rate of film consistent with the requirements of persistence of vision. Currently it is set at eighteen frames per second. *See* FRAME, PERSISTENCE OF VISION.

silicon. In electronics, a chemical element having semiconductor properties and used in the manufacture of transistors, solar cells, diodes, etc. *See* CHIP, SEMICONDUCTOR, TRANSISTOR.

silicon-based operating system. In computing, a 32-bit microprocessor operating system in which the operating system primitives are part of the hardware instruction set. *See* INSTRUCTION SET, OPERATING SYSTEM.

silicon foundry. In microelectronics, an organization that enables users to acquire custom-built chips by the provision of both design and manufacturing facilities. The user may employ the organization's computer-assisted design facilities to develop the chip design, and then the organization manufactures batches of the chip. *See* CHIP, MICRO-COMPUTER.

silicon gate. In microelectronics, a form of metal oxide semiconductor technology in which a heavily doped amorphous silicon replaces the usual aluminium gate metallization. *See* CHIP, GATE, METAL OXIDE SEMI-CONDUCTOR.

silicon on sapphire. (SOS) In microelectronics, a fabrication technique in which metal oxide semiconductor devices are built upon a synthetic sapphire substrate. Such devices provide higher speed switching than conventional ones. *See* CHIP, METAL OXIDE SEMICON-DUCTOR.

Silicon Valley. Santa Clara, California; an area famed for its microelectronic manufacturing plants. *See* MICROELECTRONICS.

silk. In photography, a sheet of white fabric stretched on a frame to reduce the harshness of lighting on a subject.

SIMD. *See* SINGLE-INSTRUCTION STREAM MULTIPLE-DATA STREAM.

simplex. (SPX) (1) In communications, pertaining to communication in one direction only. *Compare* DUPLEX, HALF-DUPLEX. (2) In printing, single-sided copying. *Compare* FULL-DUPLEX.

simulation. In computing, a technique by which a system is represented as a mathematical model. The model is then programmed on a computer so that the behaviour of the original system may be studied. *See* COMPUTER, MATHEMATICAL MODEL.

simultaneous processing. In computing, the performance of two or more computing tasks at the same instant of time. *Synonymous with* PARALLEL PROCESSING.

simultaneous transmission. In data communications, a technique in which the transmission of messages in one direction is accompanied with the transmission of control characters or data in the other. *See* FULL-DUPLEX.

sin. An abbreviation for sine. *See* SINE.

sine. In mathematics, the sine of an angle of a right-angled triangle is equal to the ratio of the side opposite the angle to the hypotenuse.

sine wave. In mathematics, a wave that can be expressed as the sine of a linear function of time or distance. Any periodic function can be decomposed into a series of sine waves. This technique can be used to study the passage of a complex waveform through a circuit or transmission system. *See* CIRCUIT, FOURIER SERIES, PERIODIC, SINE.

single-address instruction. In programming, a machine language instruction that contains only an operator and one address. *See* ADDRESS, MACHINE CODE INSTRUCTION.

single-address message. In communications, a message to be delivered to only one destination.

single-board computer. (SBC) In computing, a microcomputer or minicomputer using a single printed circuit board for all logic, timing, internal memory and external interfaces. *See* PRINTED CIRCUIT BOARD.

single carrier per channel. (SPC) In communications, a method of transmitting the audio signal in television transmission in which the audio is contained in a very narrow independent carrier frequency above or below the video signal. *Compare* SUBCARRIER. *See* CARRIER.

single-colour imaging. In office systems, the production of copies with a single colour image. *See* COPIER.

single-error correction, double-error detection. *See* SECDED.

single-frame video recording. In computer graphics, a method of generating animation films from computer displays. The computer program writes an image into frame store, and a video recorder is triggered to store the image corresponding to this frame. The program then clears the frame store and paints the next image. At the end of this process the video recorder is played at normal speed to display the animation sequence. *See* COMPUTER ANIMATION, FRAME STORE.

single-frequency signalling. (sf signalling) In communications, the use of tones to give information for control and supervisory purposes on a channel (e.g. to indicate answer or disconnect states on a direct distance dialing system). *See* DIRECT DISTANCE DIALING.

single-instruction stream multiple-data stream. (SIMD) In computing, pertaining to a form of parallel computer with a single control unit and multiple arithmetic logic units, each arithmetic logic unit having its own memory. The single control unit allocates execution commands to the arithmetic logic units. *Compare* MULTIPLE-INSTRUCTION STREAM MULTIPLE-DATA STREAM, MULTIPLE-INSTRUCTION STREAM SINGLE-DATA STREAM, SINGLE-INSTRUCTION STREAM MULTIPLE-DATA STREAM, SINGLE-INSTRUCTION STREAM SINGLE-DATA STREAM. *See* ARITHMETIC LOGIC UNIT, ARRAY PROCESSOR, CONTROL UNIT, INSTRUCTION, MEMORY, PARALLEL PROCESSING.

single-instruction stream single-data stream. (SISD) In computing, pertaining to a conventional computer system with a single control unit and a single arithmetic logic unit, which operates upon a single stream of data from memory according to a single stream of instructions. *Compare* MULTIPLE-INSTRUCTION STREAM MULTIPLE-DATA STREAM, MULTIPLE-INSTRUCTION STREAM SINGLE-DATA STREAM, SINGLE-INSTRUCTION STREAM MULTIPLE-DATA STREAM. *See* ARITHMETIC LOGIC UNIT, CONTROL UNIT, INSTRUCTION, MEMORY, PARALLEL PROCESSING.

single-medium system. In computing, a system architecture based on the use of a single medium which carries all the software needed for a given application. In interactive compact discs (CD-I), for example, all the program data (video, sound, text and computer) application and driver software are held on the CD-I disc itself. Only the basic operating system kernel is stored in read-only memory in the base case CD-I player, external to the disc. This is in contrast to cases where read-only memory compact disc (CD-ROM) is used as a computer peripheral, and only the program (text or computer) data is held on the CD-ROM, all the applications, driver and operating system software being stored on separate magnetic media. (Philips). *Compare* MULTIMEDIA

SYSTEM. *See* BASE CASE SYSTEM, COMPACT DISC – INTERACTIVE, COMPACT DISC – READ-ONLY MEMORY, DRIVER, KERNEL, OPERATING SYSTEM.

single operation. *Synonymous with* HALF-DUPLEX.

single-scan non-segmented. In video recording, a video tape format that records one television field during each head pass thus permitting freeze framing. *See* FIELD, FREEZE FRAME.

single-sideband transmission. In communications, a method of signal transmission in which one sideband of the modulation signal is suppressed. The upper and lower sidebands are mirror images about the carrier frequency, and thus the suppression of one sideband reduces the power that has to be transmitted without removing any of the information content. *Compare* SUPPRESSED CARRIER TRANSMISSION. *See* MODULATION, SIDEBAND.

single-sided drive. In memory systems, a floppy disk drive that can only read one side of a floppy disk. *Compare* DOUBLE-SIDED. *See* FLIPPY FLOPPY.

single-wire line. In communications, a communication link that uses ground as one side of the circuit. *Compare* FOUR-WIRE CIRCUIT, TWO-WIRE CIRCUIT. *See* GROUND.

sink. *See* DATA SINK.

sink tree. In data communications, the set of all paths to a destination in a communication network, when fixed routing tables are used. *See* ROUTING TABLE.

S interface. In communications, an integrated services digital network terminal interface for TE1 equipment. *Compare* R INTERFACE, T INTERFACE. *See* INTEGRATED SERVICES DIGITAL NETWORK, TE1.

sinusoidal. Pertaining to sine waves. *See* SINE WAVE.

siphoning. In cable television, the transmission of a program originally available by direct broadcast.

SISD. *See* SINGLE-INSTRUCTION STREAM SINGLE-DATA STREAM.

SITA high-level network. In data communications, Société Internationale de Télécommunications Aéronautique; a network serving airlines with a combination of packet- and message-switching facilities. *See* MESSAGE SWITCHING, PACKET SWITCHING.

site polling. In data communications, a technique in which all the terminals at a given location are polled as a group, with the local controller acting as the supervisor for this purpose. *See* POLLING.

sixteen mo. In printing, folded or cut sheet that is one-sixteenth of basic size.

sixteen sheet. In printing, a poster size measuring 120 x 80 inches (305 x 203 centimetres). (Desktop). *Compare* EIGHT SHEET, THIRTY-TWO SHEET.

six-two-five line. In television, the standard number of horizontal sweeps per frame used in Western Europe, Australia and parts of Africa and the Middle East. *Compare* FIVE-TWO-FIVE LINE. *See* FRAME, VIDEO STANDARDS.

size. In printing, a solution based on starch or casein which is added to the paper to reduce ink absorbency. (Desktop).

Sketchphone. In communications, a basic telewriting terminal. The terminal comprises a telephone, digitizing tablet and visual display terminal. The terminal can operate in three modes: speech plus telewriting, speech-only and telewriting-only. *See* DIGITIZING TABLET, TELEWRITING.

skew. (1) In facsimile transmission, a deviation from the rectangular frame due to a lack of synchronism between transmitting and receiving scanner. (2) In character recognition, a condition in which an optically scanned line is not perpendicular to the reference edge or not parallel to preceding and succeeding lines. (3) In printing, the ability to indent text by a varying amount over a specified number of lines. (4) In television, a zig-zag distortion.

skip. (1) In word processing, a facility allowing recorded text to be bypassed. (2) In programming, to ignore one or more instructions in a sequence of instructions.

skip capability. (1) In word processing, during editing, the ability to jump over segments of a document, leaving the corresponding stored sections unchanged. (2) In word processing, the ability to insert instructions between skip codes. Such instructions are displayed on the screen and on draft copies, but not on the final printout.

skip effect. In communications, the long-distance reflection of radio waves from the ionosphere. *See* IONOSPHERE.

sky noise. In communications, electromagnetic radiation from galactic sources and thermal agitation of atmospheric gases and particles. *See* GALACTIC NOISE, NOISE.

sky wave. In communications, a secondary portion of a broadcast signal radiating skywards, part of which is reflected by the ionosphere. *See* IONOSPHERE, SKIP EFFECT.

SL. *See* SOURCE LANGUAGE.

slab serif. In printing, typeface with square-end serifs which may, or may not, be bracketed. *See* BRACKETED, SERIF. *Synonymous with* SQUARE SERIF.

slash. *Synonymous with* SOLIDUS.

slave. (1) Any device that operates under the control of another. (2) In data communications, a remote system or terminal whose functions are controlled by a central master system.

slew. *Synonymous with* HIGH-SPEED SKIP.

slice architecture. In computing, a form of chip architecture that enables the cascading of units to increase the word size. *See* CHIP ARCHITECTURE.

slice network. In data communications, a self-contained modular unit, capable of being located in as many places as necessary or convenient, which in the event of being cut off from the rest of the system will continue to operate independently. Such units can carry out processing functions normally handled by centralized operating centres.

slide/audiotape. In audiovisual devices, a set of slides accompanied with an audiotape recording. Sometimes a signal is available to project the next slide.

slide projector. In audiovisual aids, a device containing a light source and a lens system to project the image of a slide onto a screen. Some devices have a built-in rear viewing screen. The slides may be housed in trays, cartridges and drums. The slide access may be sequential or random.

slide/sync recorder. In audiovisual aids, an audio tape recorder capable of advancing one or more slide projectors on cue. *See* AUDIO TAPE RECORDER.

sliding window protocol. In data communications, a modified form of a stop-and-wait protocol. The sending host is allowed to have multiple unacknowledged frames outstanding simultaneously. Successive frames are given sequence numbers in a given range with numbers being re-used to prevent them growing without bound. The sending host maintains a record of unacknowledged frames and retransmits them after a specified time-out interval, or receipt of negative acknowledgement frames from the receiver, a limit on the maximum permitted number of unacknowledged frames ensures flow control. *Compare* STOP-AND-WAIT PROTOCOL. *See* FRAME, NEGATIVE ACKNOWLEDGEMENT.

slip page. In printing, a galley proof made up on slip, but separated out as a page. *See* GALLEY PROOF.

slit pitch. In peripherals, a measure corresponding to dot pitch on tubes in which rectangular or slit-shaped phosphor triad elements are employed. *Compare* DOT PITCH.

slot. (1) In computing, a single board position on a back plane. *See* BACKPLANE. (2) In filming, a groove in the body of a camera to allow for the insertion of filters or mattes. *See* FILTER, MATTE.

Slotted Aloha. In communications, a packet broadcast system in which packets are timed to arrive at the receiving station in regular time slots, synchronized for all stations. *See* ALOHA.

slotted ring network. In data communications, a ring network with unidirectional

data transmission in which data is transferred in predefined slots in the transmission stream. *See* RING.

slow motion. In optical media, the controlled movement of the laser beam in a videodisc player from frame to frame at a variable rate less than that of normal play. *See* VIDEODISC.

slow-scan television device. (SSTV) In television, a device that compresses the bandwidth of a video signal so that it may be transmitted over a telephone line. The slow speed of transmission mitigates against the communication of moving images. *See* BANDWIDTH, VIDEO COMPRESSOR, VIDEO SIGNAL.

SLSI. *See* SUPER LARGE-SCALE INTEGRATION.

slug. In filming, a strip of film, either blank or image-bearing, used as a leader. *See* LEADER.

slur. In printing, a fault caused by a lateral movement during impression.

small capitals. (small caps) In printing, a design of capital characters with a height equal to the vertical dimension of lower-case characters. *See* LOWER CASE.

small caps. *See* SMALL CAPITALS.

small face. In printing, the smaller of two sizes available on the same body of typeface.

small-scale integration. (SSI) In microelectronics, pertaining to a fabrication technology that produces less than 100 transistors per chip. *Compare* LARGE-SCALE INTEGRATION, MEDIUM-SCALE INTEGRATION, SUPER LARGE-SCALE INTEGRATION, ULTRA LARGE-SCALE INTEGRATION, VERY LARGE-SCALE INTEGRATION. *See* CHIP, GATE.

Smalltalk. In programming, an artificial intelligence programming language.

SMART. In library science, System for the Mechanical Analysis and Retrieval of Text or, more irreverently, Salton's Magical Automatic Retrieval of Text; a computer-based information retrieval system, devised by Professor Salton, that relies entirely, or

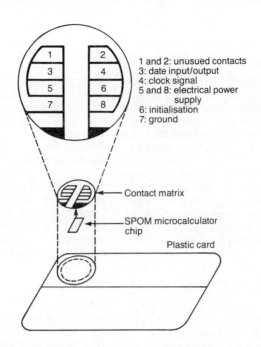

1 and 2: unusued contacts
3: date input/output
4: clock signal
5 and 8: electrical power
         supply
6: initialisation
7: ground

Contact matrix

SPOM microcalculator chip

Plastic card

smart card
The CP8 smart card works as an identity card as well as a form of electronic payment.

almost entirely, on machine processing of text, both of document text and natural language questions. The system is interactive with the user provided with a ranked output from the database which may be evaluated by the user and the results of the evaluation fed back for a modified search. In addition to its use as a retrieval system it is able to compare the effectiveness of one retrieval method against another.

smart. A term used synonymously with intelligent (e.g. a smart terminal). *Compare* DUMB DEVICE. *See* INTELLIGENCE, INTELLIGENT TERMINAL.

smart card. In banking, a plastic card similar in appearance to a normal credit card that has an integrated circuit embedded in the plastic. The circuit has two broad functions: intelligence and memory. The card is activated by insertion into a terminal, and it receives signals from the terminal, performs functions according to those signals, and a program stored in the card's internal memory, sends out response signals and updates its internal memory. Smart cards

may have two forms: one for a set of banking operations and the other, termed an intelligent token, can provide access control, perform encryption and authentication operations, etc.

A multipurpose smart card for banking and financial transactions might perform one or more of the operations: (a) electronic cheque book; (b) electronic wallet; (c) electronic purse; (d) electronic token; (e) telepayment; (f) internal transfer; (g) access; (h) remote banking; and (i) portable file.

An electronic cheque book allows the user to make payments at a point of purchase terminal, in addition to cash withdrawals at a terminal or cash dispenser. The users key in their card personal identification number (PIN) and their bank accounts are only debited when the transactions arrive at the account-holding institution.

The electronic wallet provides for payments of large sums, such as traveller's cheques. The card memory contains details of a prepaid amount which is decreased when the user performs a transaction at a terminal, inputting the PIN and transaction details on a keyboard. Details of the transactions are collected and cleared as for the electronic cheque book. The card may be replenished at a terminal or deactivated when the pre-paid amount has been spent.

The electronic purse is similar to the electronic wallet except that the amounts involved are comparatively small and no customer identification is required. When the prepaid amount is expended the card may be replenished at a special terminal or simply discarded.

The electronic token is a form of electronic purse in which the amount refers to units of consumption (e.g. telephone calls, car parking hours) rather than currency. Again no customer identification is required.

The telepayment service is similar to that of the electronic cheque book except that a guaranteed payment is made to a remote recipient via a terminal connected to a public communication network. The facility includes guaranteed payment for services or goods ordered, and the clearing of the payment has to be initialized by the payee.

The internal transfer facility enables the card holder to transfer funds from one application to another within the same smart card. Access allows the user to gain access to logical or physical facilities such as an account enquiry service, details of transactions stored on the card, safe deposit, etc.

Remote banking relates to the use of smart card terminals, connected to a public communication network, for customer banking transactions. The portable file facility provides functions similar to notebook recording (e.g. transaction details).

The memory of a card may be partitioned for secret data, protected data and a working space. The secret data includes cryptographic keys, PINs, etc. entered onto the card by the card issuer. This data cannot be read from the card and is used only for internal card computations. The protected data can only be accessed via a cryptographic key, and this data may be subdivided such that each sub-area is accessed with a different key. The sub-areas may contain customer name and address, available balance, transaction history, discount facilities for various suppliers, etc. The presence of secret data offers the possibility of checking the PIN keyed in by the card holder with offline terminals; such checks are security against the misuse of lost or stolen cards. *Compare* INTELLIGENT TOKEN, MAGNETICALLY ENCODED

CARD, SUPERSMART CARD, *See* CRYPTOGRAPHIC KEY, PIN. *Synonymous with* CHIP CARD, MICROCIRCUIT CARD.

smart plotters. In peripherals, plotters with built-in intelligence. Such devices can, for example, generate straight lines, circles, several fonts, character and string rotation, line textures, fill patterns, scaling and windowing. *See* AREA INFILL, FONT, PLOTTER, SCALING, WINDOW.

smart terminal. In peripherals, a terminal that provides additional features to those of a dumb terminal. In general such a terminal will have some memory and processing power and can provide formatted displays, graphic displays, upload and download facilities, etc. *Compare* DUMB TERMINAL. *See* DOWNLOAD, UPLOAD.

SMD. In memory systems, storage media module; an industry standard interface for Winchester disk drives. *See* DISK INTERFACE, WINCHESTER DISK DRIVE.

SMPTE. Society of Motion Picture and Television Engineers.

SMX. *See* SEMI-MICRO XEROGRAPHY.

SNA. *See* SYSTEM NETWORK ARCHITECTURE.

snake. *Synonymous with* LOGIC BOMB.

snapshots. In memory systems, the complete state of a computer, memory contents, registers, flags, etc. at a selected instant of time. *See* FLAG, REGISTER.

SNF. *See* SECOND NORMAL FORM.

SNOBOL. In programming, string-oriented symbolic language; a programming language designed for advanced string manipulation. It is used in artificial intelligence, compiler construction applications, etc. *See* ARTIFICIAL INTELLIGENCE, COMPILER, STRING.

snow. In television, a momentary picture distortion caused by a weak video signal. *See* VIDEO SIGNAL.

s/n ratio. *See* SIGNAL-TO-NOISE RATIO.

soak. In programming, a method of detecting program errors and problems by running the program under normal operating conditions while closely supervised by the programmer.

Social Scisearch. In online information retrieval, a database supplied by the Institute for Scientific Information and dealing with social sciences and humanities.

societal vulnerability. In computer security, the possibility of loss, injury or the denial of equal rights to a significant segment of the population, as well as the potential weakening of social stability, or risk to national sovereignty as a result of dependence on computer-based technology. (AFIPS).

Sociological Abstracts. In online information retrieval, a database supplied by Sociological Abstracts Inc. and dealing with sociology.

soft. In electronics, pertaining to magnetic materials that become strong magnets when placed in a magnetic field, but lose their magnetism when the field is removed. The reading and writing heads of magnetic recorders must be manufactured from soft magnetic material. *Compare* HARD.

softback. In printing, a book bound with a paperback cover. (Desktop). *Compare* HARDBACK.

soft copy. In peripherals, information displayed on screen or in audio format. *Compare* HARD COPY.

soft error. (1) In data communications, an intermittent error in a network that requires a retransmission of the message. *Compare* HARD ERROR. (2) In memory systems, an error in reading data from a magnetic disk that can be corrected by re-reading the sector or by moving the read/write head back and forth. *Compare* HARD ERROR. *See* MAGNETIC DISK.

soft hyphen. *Synonymous with* DISCRETIONARY HYPHEN.

softlifting. In computer security, the illegal copying of licensed software for personal use. *See* SOFTWARE PROTECTION.

software. (1) The programs, procedures, routines and possibly documents associated with the operation of a data-processing system. (2) All the non-hardware components of certain information systems (e.g. the tapes and documents associated with complex self-teaching systems). *Compare* FIRMWARE, HARDWARE.

software creep. In software protection, the ad hoc, unauthorized copying of a program for another user, but without a profit motive. *Compare* PIRACY.

software-dependent. In computing, pertaining to a system that is dependent for its operation on specifically defined software. (Philips). *Compare* HARDWARE-DEPENDENT.

software development process. In programming, the steps of a software development cycle are: (a) problem statement; (b) design of abstract algorithms and data structures; (c) statement of flow control and data layouts; (d) coding of program in chosen language; (e) preparation of source code in machine-readable form; (f) translation to object code; (g) loading of machine code program; (h) run time check and debugging; (i) documentation. *See* ALGORITHM, DATA STRUCTURE, DEBUG, OBJECT CODE, SOURCE CODE.

software distribution medium. In memory systems, a device or material used for distributing prerecorded software (e.g. floppy disk, compact cassette, compact disc, optical digital disc). (Philips). *See* COMPACT CASSETTE, COMPACT DISC, FLOPPY DISK, OPTICAL DIGITAL DISC.

software documentation. In programming, a complete description of a software system including program listings, data and file layouts, operating procedures, error messages, etc. *See* FILE, PROGRAM LISTING, SOFTWARE.

software emulation. In programming, a software system, often in microprograms, that enables one computer to execute a program in the machine code of another computer. It is often used to minimize reprogramming when one computer system replaces another. *See* EMULATOR, MICROPROGRAM.

software engineering. In programming, a broadly defined discipline that integrates the various aspects of programming, from writing code to ensure that budgets are met, in order to produce efficient and cost-effective software. *See* SOFTWARE.

software house. In programming, an organization offering software support services to users. *See* SOFTWARE.

software interrupt. In program execution, an interrupt caused by a high-priority program requiring the services of the central processing unit. *Compare* HARDWARE INTERRUPT. *See* INTERRUPT.

software licence. In software protection, an agreement between a user and a vendor of software describing the user's rights to the software. *See* SHRINK-WRAPPED LICENCE, SOFTWARE.

software life cycle. In programming, the phases in the specification, design, development, testing, implementation and maintenance of a software package. They include system requirements, software requirements, overall design, detailed design, component production, component testing, integration and system testing, release, operation and maintenance. In practice the life cycle comprises a number of iterations around the constituent stages of the life cycle. *See* SOFTWARE MAINTENANCE, SYSTEMS ANALYSIS.

software maintenance. In programming, the improvements and changes required to keep programs up to date and ensure effective operation. *See* SOFTWARE. *Synonymous with* PROGRAM MAINTENANCE.

software package. In programming, a set of programs for a specific purpose, usually written by a software house with many users in mind (e.g. Microsoft's Wordstar). *Compare* APPLICATION PROGRAM.

software piracy. *See* PIRACY.

software protection. The adoption of both legal and technical methods to prevent the unauthorized use or exploitation of software. Technical methods usually employ some means of preventing a copied program from being executed. Software may be protected by the intellectual property laws in some countries, but this is usually uncertain and limited. As a result it has become traditional for software suppliers to supplement and enhance that protection by appropriate contractual provisions contained in the software licence.

(a) The legal basis for contractual protection. From a purely legal point of view suppliers have three basic intentions which they aim to achieve by means of a contract with a purchaser, so far as protection is concerned.

(i)   To define the extent to which the purchaser can use the software, on the basis that anything else would constitute an infringement of copyright. Thus the purchaser is granted a limited licence under the copyright, and any use outside the terms of that licence should, in theory, be actionable provided that such use constitutes a restricted act, such as reproduction, translation or adaption within the meaning of the appropriate copyright legislation.

(ii) To maintain the confidentiality of any secret information contained in the software by the imposition of suitable terms. Most countries have some sort of protection of confidential information, but this depends upon the extent to which the information is not in the public domain. The imposition and enforcement of suitable terms can enable confidentiality to be maintained in software, particularly software that has a limited distribution.

(iii) To have a contractual remedy against the recipient of the software. The software supplier may well want to have a contractual remedy against a purchaser, in the event that it has no remedy as a result of the law of copyright or confidentiality, and also where any exclusive rights do not extend to the problem with which the supplier is concerned.

(b) The interests to be protected. Suppliers want to sell the maximum number of their software packages. To achieve this a supplier will want:

(i)   every user to buy their own software package;

(ii) in the case of customer who has many computers, such as a large corporate user, to sell a software package for each computer owned by the customer;

(iii) to limit the use of each software package to the personal use of the particular purchaser, especially where the purchaser is one of a group of a large number of companies.

In addition, software suppliers want to stop the software from being misused or from being used for purposes for which the suppliers could expect to make sales themselves. This means that a supplier wants to prevent:

(i) unauthorized copying, whether for use within the customer's organization, or as a straightforward software piracy for profit;

(ii) unauthorized use on a local area network or remote access entry system;

(iii) the use of the software for the development of competing products.

(c) Traditional software licence agreement. As a practical matter the way in which contractual protection can be applied depends very much on the type of software. Traditionally computer software has always been supplied under licence. The supplier would generally have a standard form of licence agreement, which the end user customer was required to sign before being allowed possession of the software. This type of contract is still widely used, but it can only be used in circumstances where a customer and the supplier, or the supplier's agent, can both sign the agreement. This is still the case where an end user purchases sophisticated software, often tailored to the user's requirements, or is buying an integrated software/hardware system.

On the other hand, such arrangements are no longer appropriate for mass market software for use with microcomputers, and in particular for the home computer market. Nowadays such software is generally sold to an end user by a computer store, or high street dealer, who may be at the end of a distribution chain well removed from the original software supplier. In this situation, particularly with software costing about the same as a hi-fi disc, it is unrealistic or commercially unacceptable for the end user to be expected to sign an agreement.

To overcome this problem software suppliers have tried to develop new techniques to impose contractual conditions upon end users. In particular, throughout the world, distributors of software have followed the technique originally developed in the USA of 'shrink-wrapped licence agreements' whereby the customer is deemed to have accepted restrictions on use by tearing open a sealed package containing the diskette. Unfortunately the validity of this technique is very questionable in most countries.

(d) Shrink-wrapped licence agreement. The object is to impose terms of use, similar to those contained in traditional licence agreements, when the customer purchases software packages from high-street dealers. The shrink-wrapped or tear-me-open, licence agreements were devised to try to meet the need for the customer to purchase software as simply as possible. The manufacturer packs the software in such a way that the user has, in order to obtain access to the diskettes, to open a wrapper or envelope on which the terms of the so-called licence agreement are printed. The envelope is sealed so as to direct the end user to the terms of the licence agreement, together with a statement that opening the diskette package will indicate the purchaser's acceptance of the limitations. The position is reinforced by the inclusion of suitable wording on the pack making it clear to the end user that by buying the pack he or she is accepting the terms of the contract which it contains.

The legal theory behind this method is that the end user has bought outright the diskettes, manuals and other physical manifestations of the package, but only obtains a limited licence to use the programs. In practice it would prove difficult in many jurisdictions, such as the UK, for the manufacturer to enforce any limitations directly against an end user because of the problems of the privity of the contract, bearing in mind that it is the dealer who is the other party to the actual contract of sale.

(e) The terms of the shrink-wrapped agreement. A shrink-wrapped licence agreement usually contains the provisions listed below.

(i) Conditions of purchase. The licence will first make a general statement along the lines that the product is sold subject to limitations on permitted use customary in the sale of microcomputer software for personal use. It will also be expressly brought to the user's notice that the terms of the agreement are set out on the product and that opening the diskette package indicates acceptance of the limitations. It is also common for there to be a statement that if the end user does not accept the limitations, the product should be returned to the dealer and the purchase price refunded.

(ii) Permitted uses. The licence agreement will usually include provisions whereby the licence granted is for personal use only; the software is only to be used on any item of compatible hardware owned or used by the purchaser; and sometimes the software is to be used only on one microcomputer at any one time.

(iii) Uses not permitted. The licence then sets out uses which are not permitted under the licence. These include use of the software on a multiple processor or multiple site arrangement, the use of the software in a computer service business or for remote access entry, the making of copies of the diskettes and associated documentation, except possibly for security purposes, the making of alterations to the software, the right to grant sublicences, disassembly or decompilation, the making of translations of, or modifications to, the software for use with noncompatible hardware.

Quite apart from the validity of these terms as a matter of contract or copyright law, in some jurisdictions there might also be antitrust considerations, particularly in the USA. *See* COPY PROTECTION, COPYRIGHT, DISASSEMBLER, EXECUTE PROTECTION, FLOPPY DISK, LOCAL AREA NETWORK, SHRINK-WRAPPED LICENCE, SOFTWARE LICENCE.

software protocol converter. In distributed processing, the software emulation of a protocol converter. A personal computer linked asynchronously to a host can behave as a synchronous terminal because the appropriate protocol conversions are carried out by software in the host and the personal computer. *Compare* PROTOCOL CONVERTER. *See* ASYNCHRONOUS TRANSMISSION, PROTOCOL, SYNCHRONOUS TRANSMISSION.

software prototyping. *See* PROTOTYPING.

software redundancy. In reliability, that part of a program which would not be necessary if the system were guaranteed to be fault-free. It includes backup copies of key programs, error logging and built-in test programs. *See* BACKUP, BUILT-IN TEST.

software security. In computer security, pertaining to general-purpose software (e.g. operating system, utility, software development tool, and applications programs and routines) which protect data or information handled by a data-processing system and its resources.

software support system. In programming, a system to test the software developed for special-purpose microprocessor systems. The support system executes the object code in the same manner as the microprocessor enabling a programmer to check and debug it. *See* DEBUG, MICROPROCESSOR, OBJECT CODE.

software tool. In programming, a program that is used to facilitate the development of other programs. Most operating systems provide editors to produce and modify source program files, translators to convert from high- or low-level languages to machine language, linking loaders to assemble separately compiled modules into the form suitable for execution and debuggers for the study of programs containing errors. The current trend is to the development of extremely powerful software tools, such as syntax-directed editors, which embody the syntax of a particular language. *See* DEBUGGER, HIGH-LEVEL LANGUAGE, LOW-LEVEL LANGUAGE, MACHINE LANGUAGE. *Synonymous with* DEVELOPMENT TOOL.

software vending machine. In programming, a novel method of purchasing software. The purchaser inserts banknotes or a credit card into a payment slot, chooses the required software by menu selection and keyboard action, inserts a floppy disk, or cassette tape, into the machine and the program is then written to the tape or disk.

solar cell. In electronics, a semiconductor device for collecting the sun's radiation and converting the received energy to electrical power. It is used for remote communication systems lacking access to conventional power supplies (e.g. satellites). *See* COMMU-NICATIONS SATELLITE SYSTEM, SEMICONDUCTOR DEVICES.

solid. In printing, type set with no line spacing between the lines.

solid-state camera. In television, a television camera in which the optical image is projected onto a large-scale integrated circuit device, typically a charge-coupled device, which detects the light image and develops the television signal. *See* CHARGE-COUPLED DEVICE.

solid-state device. In electronics, a device whose operation depends upon the behaviour of electrical or magnetic signals in solids (e.g. transistors, integrated circuits). *See* CHIP, SEMICONDUCTOR, TRANSISTOR.

solidus. In printing, a diagonal typographic sign. *Synonymous with* SLASH.

soliton. In optoelectronics, a pulse of coherent light that either does not change shape or has a shape that varies periodically, with propagation along an optical fiber, returning to its original shape. *See* FIBER OPTICS.

SOM. *See* START OF MESSAGE.

son file. *See* FATHER FILE.

sonic. Pertaining to the audible frequency range (20–20 000 Hz).

sort key. In databases, a field of a data record that is used to determine the order of that record in a set of sorted data (e.g. an employee's name when sorting personnel records in alphabetical order of employees' names). *See* FIELD, RECORD.

SOS. *See* SILICON ON SAPPHIRE.

sound. (1) A train of compression waves transversing air, or other gaseous, liquid or solid material at a frequency, or combination of frequencies in the range 20–20 000 Hz. (2) In filming, a term for all or any of the aural elements in film production.

sound advance. In filming, the physical distance, in frames or inches, between a point

on the sound track and the corresponding visual frame. It is necessary because the sound-reading head cannot occupy the same space as the camera aperture. *See* ADVANCE.

sound attribute. In optical media, a particular property assigned to all or part of the sound information of an interactive compact disc (e.g. language) bandwidth. (Philips). *See* BANDWIDTH, COMPACT DISC – INTERACTIVE.

sound chip. *Synonymous with* AUDIO CHIP.

sound effects. In filming and broadcasting, sounds produced from electronics, recording or other devices to give the impression of realistic effects.

sound effects library. A collection of catalogued sound effects stored on a recording medium. *See* SOUND EFFECTS.

sound film strip projector. In audiovisual aids, a film strip projector with an associated or built-in sound-reproducing unit. *See* FILM STRIP.

sound group. In optical media, part of the user data field in an adaptive delta pulse code modulation (ADPCM) audio sector on an interactive compact disc. Each ADPCM audio sector has 18 sound groups. (Philips). *See* ADAPTIVE DELTA PULSE CODE MODULATION, COMPACT DISC – INTERACTIVE.

sound head. In recording, the device that detects the audio signal from a recording medium. *See* MAGNETIC HEAD.

sound macro. In audio, a predefined sound or sound sequence stored in computer form (e.g. a standard set of words such as the numbers from 1 to 100, or a set of commonly occurring words such as 'yes', 'no'). (Philips). *See* SPEECH SYNTHESIZER.

sound sheets. In recording, a flat magnetic vinyl dictation-recording medium.

sound slide projector. In audiovisual devices, a slide projector with an associated or built-in sound-reproducing unit. The sound unit may control the slide advance automatically. *See* SLIDE/SYNC RECORDER.

sound synthesizer. *See* MUSIC SYNTHESIZER, SPEECH SYNTHESIZER.

sound track. In recording, the audio track of a film or magnetic tape.

source. (1) In data communications, a point of message entry into the system. *Compare* SINK. (2) In electronics, a terminal on an field effect transistor. *See* DRAIN, FIELD EFFECT TRANSISTOR, GATE.

source code. In programming, the original code of a user's program prior to being translated (e.g. compiled, assembled, interpreted). *Compare* OBJECT CODE. *See* ASSEMBLER, COMPILER, INTERPRETER, TRANSLATOR.

source document. (1) In data processing, an invoice, form, voucher or other form of written evidence of a transaction from which the basic data is extracted for processing. (2) In word processing, material from which a secretary prepares final copy.

source language. (SL) (1) In programming, a language in which the user's program is written. *Compare* OBJECT LANGUAGE. *See* ASSEMBLY LANGUAGE, HIGH-LEVEL LANGUAGE, TARGET LANGUAGE. (2) In machine translation, the language from which translation is to be made. *Compare* TARGET LANGUAGE.

source program. In programming, a program written in a source language. *See* SOURCE LANGUAGE.

source suppression. In communications security, the careful design of circuitry and layout so that no compromising signals are emitted. *See* TEMPEST PROOFING.

space. (1) In printing, a blank column or character. *Compare* MARK. (2) In communications, an impulse, or absence of an impulse to signify a binary zero condition. *Compare* MARK. (3) In videotex, a character position filled entirely by background colour.

space craft. A man-made vehicle designed to go beyond the major portion of the earth's atmosphere. *See* COMMUNICATIONS SATELLITE SYSTEM.

space division multiplexing. In communications, the grouping of more than one physical transmission path. In landline communications, many wire pairs may be combined in one cable. In satellite communications, an antenna can focus a number of spot beams to different geographical locations. *Compare* TIME DIVISION MULTIPLEXING. *See* COMMUNICATIONS SATELLITE SYSTEM, MULTIPLEXING.

space division switching. In communications, a method for switching circuits in which each connection through the switch takes a different physical path. *Compare* TIME DIVISION SWITCHING.

space shuttle. A manned space vehicle, capable of launching satellites, that can return to earth and be used for another launch.

space station. In communications, a station located on an object that is, or is to be, located beyond a major portion of the earth's atmosphere. *See* STATION.

space telecommand. In communications, the use of radiocommunication for the transmission of control signals to initiate, modify or terminate functions performed by equipment on a space station or another space object. *See* SPACE STATION.

space telemetry. In communications, the transmission of measurements taken by a space craft, including those relating to the functioning of the craft. *See* SPACE CRAFT, TELEMETRY.

spaghetti code. In programming, a program developed with a lack of structure. The liberal and undisciplined use of 'go to' statements and conditional jumps produces extremely complex lines of program control and renders the programs difficult to test, debug or maintain. *Compare* PROOF OF PROGRAM CORRECTNESS, STRUCTURED PROGRAMMING. *See* CONDITIONAL JUMP, DEBUG, PROGRAM MAINTENANCE.

Spanish n. In printing, the letter n with a tilde, giving a sound as if it were followed by the letter y. *See* ACCENT, TILDE.

sparklies. In television, white flashes or dots that appear intermittently on the screen of a television set employing frequency modulation. It is caused by noise in the frequency-modulated demodulator. *See* FRE-QUENCY MODULATION.

sparse array. In data structures, an array in which most of the entries have a zero value; uneconomic in storage unless special data structures are used. *See* ARRAY.

spatial frequency re-use. In communications, a technique of increasing the capacity of a communications satellite in which the same frequency band is used in several directional beams. *Compare* POLARIZATION FREQUENCY RE-USE. *See* FREQUENCY RE-USE.

spatial redundancy. *Synonymous with* PROTECTIVE REDUNDANCY.

speaker. *Synonymous with* LOUDSPEAKER.

speaker identification. In man–machine interfaces, pertaining to systems that either verify or reject a human speaker's voice. *See* SPEECH RECOGNIZER.

special effects. (1) In filming, any effects unobtainable by straightforward cinematography shooting methods (e.g. explosions). (2) In filming and television, electronic generation of certain graphics effects (e.g. wipes, dissolves). *See* DISSOLVE, WIPE.

specialized common carrier. In communications, a US organization, not a telephone company, authorized by a 1971 Federal Communications Commission decision to provide a domestic point-to-point communication service on a common carrier basis. *See* COMMON CARRIER, POINT-TO-POINT.

special-purpose. Pertaining to systems and devices designed for use in a limited set of applications. *Compare* GENERAL-PURPOSE.

special sort. In printing, a type character not usually included in the font. *See* FONT. *Synonymous with* PECULIAR, PI CHARACTER.

specifications. (specs) The detailed information necessary to describe a task.

specific code. *Synonymous with* ABSOLUTE CODE.

specificity. (1) In library science, the extent to which the system permits precision in specifying the subject of a document to be processed (e.g. the specification of a digital computer has a higher specificity than that of a computer). (2) In library science, a measure expressing the ratio of non-relevant documents not retrieved to the total number of non-relevant documents on file. *Compare* EXHAUSTIVITY.

specs. *See* SPECIFICATIONS.

spectral envelope. The envelope function of a frequency spectrum representing energy distribution as a function of frequency. (Philips). *See* ENVELOPE, FREQUENCY.

spectrum. A range of frequencies. Electromagnetic radiation manifests itself according to its frequency, ranging through low-frequency radio waves, microwaves, infrared heat, visible light, ultraviolet radiation, X-rays to gamma-rays and cosmic rays.

spectrum roll-off. In communications, the attenuation characteristics at the edge of the frequency band of a transmission line or filter. *See* FILTER, FREQUENCY RESPONSE.

speech quality. In optical media, the fourth audio quality level in an interactive compact disc system. A bandwidth of 8.5 kHz is obtained using four-bit adaptive delta pulse code modulation at a sampling rate of 18.9 kHz. It is comparable with amplitude-modulated broadcast sound quality. (Philips). *Compare* CD-DA QUALITY, HI-FI QUALITY, MID-FI QUALITY, SYNTHESIZED SPEECH QUALITY. *See* ADAPTIVE DELTA PULSE CODE MODULATION, AUDIO QUALITY LEVEL, COMPACT DISC – INTERACTIVE, FREQUENCY MODULATION, SAMPLING.

speech recognizer. In man–machine interfaces, a system that receives spoken word inputs and identifies the message. The system output can then be used to initiate appropriate actions or responses. There are currently four main approaches to the problem of speech recognition: acoustic signal analysis, speech production, sensory reception and speech perception. The acoustic signal approach treats speech as a signal waveform and uses mathematical techniques to characterize the waveform and hence identify it. The speech production approach looks to capture the essential ways that speech is produced, rate of vibration of vocal chords, etc. The sensory perception approach suggests duplicating the human auditory process by identifying the parameters and classifying patterns as is performed in the ear. The speech perception approach suggests the extraction of features that are experimentally established as important to human perception of speech (e.g. voice onset times). *Compare* SPEECH SYNTHESIZER.

speech scrambling. *Synonymous with* VOICE SCRAMBLING.

speech synthesizer. In man–machine interfaces, a system that produces a sound, corresponding to spoken words, according to stored text or commands. The current methods fall into three categories: stored digitized sound waveforms; vocal tract synthesis; and phonetic synthesis.

A sound waveform can be represented by binary digits corresponding to the sampled values of the sound wave intensity, as in pulse code modulation. Sampling of speech signals requires some 64 kilobits per second for a reasonable quality output. The storage requirements for this form of speech synthesis are high, but they can be reduced to 16–32 kilobits per second of speech by efficient coding techniques, such as differential pulse code modulation and delta modulation. Further reductions in the storage requirements can be obtained with adaptive delta pulse code modulation techniques which adapt the coding to trends in the speech pattern. The speech output from these stored codes is produced by waveform encoders, which reverse the coding algorithms to reproduce the original waveforms.

Vocal tract synthesis uses a form of speech representation based upon a simulation of the speech production mechanism. In this case the speech waveform for a particular utterance is analyzed in the frequency domain, as compared to the time domain discussed above. The frequency and intensity of various resonant frequencies — term formants — produced by the speech articulators (jaw, tongue, velum and lips) determine the nature of the sound. The variation in the formants of a speech pattern is com-

paratively slow, and thus speech patterns coded in this form can be represented by 2–8 kilobits per second of speech.

The process of reproducing the speech from the coded formants is performed by a series of digital filters corresponding to the formant frequencies. Human speech can be characterized as voiced or unvoiced. When the vocal chords vibrate, and the passage of air is not constricted, a vowel-like sound is produced (i.e. voiced). Voiced sounds like 'l', 'm' or 'ee' have a pitch determined by the rate of vocal chord vibration. Unvoiced sounds such as 's', 'f' and 'sh' have no definite pitch and are produced through constrictions formed by the teeth, tongue or lips. The excitation signal to the filter is either a periodic waveform at a frequency corresponding to a voiced sound or random noise for the unvoiced case.

There are two types of vocal tract synthesizer: linear predictive coder and the formant synthesizer. They differ in the manner in which they compute the coefficients of the digital filter. Linear predictive coders determine the filter coefficients which minimize the difference between the filter output and the required sound waveform. These devices produce acceptable artificial speech for medium data rates. Better quality speech can be obtained from the formant synthesizers which determine the coefficients from the frequency transform of the original speech signal. High-quality speech can be obtained from data rates as low as 900 bytes per second.

Both the stored digitized waveform and formant synthesizer require that the required speech output be uttered by a human, and then recorded for later output. This system does not lend itself to phrases that are generated on demand; attempts to link up prerecorded words, or subphrases, can be somewhat disconcerting to the listener. Phonetic synthesis is a speech analysis technique that can overcome this problem.

Speech data related to unique sounds, termed phonemes, is stored. The set of phonemes required for a word or phrase is generated and output in the required sequence. In practice there is a degree of dependence between phonemes used in a word or phrase, and thus the manner in which a phoneme is spoken will depend upon those adjacent to it.

The coding for phonemes is very efficient, typically less than 50 bytes per second of speech is required. Current phonetic synthesizers have extensive control on timing and intonation. This facility not only provides natural speech output, but also allows for the production of phrases with varying degrees of urgency, male and female voices, and foreign accents.

The application area of speech synthesizers is extremely wide: computer output for telephone users, automatic warning systems, speech training for the handicapped, etc. *Compare* MUSIC SYNTHESIZER, SOUND SYNTHESIZER. *See* ADAPTIVE DELTA PULSE CODE MODULATION, ALLOPHONE, ANALOG, BYTE, DELTA MODULATION, DIFFERENTIAL PCM, DIGITAL FILTER, FORMANT, FORMANT SYNTHESIZER, LINEAR PREDICTIVE CODING, LPC CODER, NOISE, PULSE CODE MODULATION, PHONEME, VELUM, VOCAL TRACT SYNTHESIZER, WAVEFORM ENCODER.

speed. (1) In photography, the light sensitivity of film emulsion. (2) In recording, the rate of movement of the recording material past the reading or writing head. The frequency response of recording devices is a function of the relative speed with which the recording medium moves past the head. In audio recording high fidelity can be attained by increasing the tape speed. In video recording the required frequency response is such that it is not possible to achieve it with a simple linear movement of the tape past the head. Special arrangements, with the heads spinning at an angle to the direction of tape movement, are therefore employed. *See* FREQUENCY RESPONSE, HELICAL SCAN, QUADRUPLEX, TRANSVERSE SCAN, VIDEO TAPE RECORDING.

spelling check. *See* SPELLING CHECK PROGRAM.

spelling check program. In word processing, a program to assist a word processor operator to detect spelling mistakes, typing errors, etc. It checks each word of text against a stored dictionary and signals to the operator when it cannot find a match, indicating the nearest match found to suggest altrnative spellings. *Compare* GRAMMAR-CHECKING PROGRAM.

spherical aberration. In optics, a fault in a lens causing straight lines to be rounded in the reproduced image. *See* ABERRATION.

spherical antenna. In communications, an antenna with a dish shape corresponding to a section of a sphere; the perimeter of such antennae is usually square or rectangular. The focal point of such antennae varies with the direction of the incident parallel rays. Thus, with a fixed mounting, it is possible to adjust for reception from a number of satellites, or microwave transmitters, by appropriate positioning of the feedhorn. *Compare* PARABOLIC ANTENNA. *See* DISH ANTENNA, FEEDHORN, FOCAL POINT.

Spidel. In online information retrieval, a French database vendor linked to Euronet DIANE. *See* DATABASE VENDOR, DIANE.

spike. In electronics, a sharp-peaked, short-duration voltage.

spine. In printing, the binding edge at the back of a book. (Desktop).

splice. In photography and recording, to join two pieces of film or magnetic tape with a special splicing tape.

splicing block. A device to hold the ends of film or tape while a piece of splicing tape is applied.

spline. In computer graphics, a polynomial function used to approximate to a given curve with a high degree of smoothness. *See* B SPLINE.

split keyboarding. In word processing, a system in which keyboarding and editing are performed on one system and playback on another. *See* EDIT, KEYBOARDING.

split knowledge. In data security, a technique in which two or more parties hold data that must be combined in order to reveal a security parameter or to undertake a sensitive operation. *See* DUAL CONTROL.

split screen. In peripherals, a facility that juxtaposes two or more displays on the screen of a visual display unit. *See* VISUAL DISPLAY UNIT, WINDOW.

spoofing. (1) In computer security, the deliberate inducement of a user or a resource to take an incorrect action. (FIPS). *Compare* MASQUERADING. (2) In data communications, a technique to enable a multiplicity of computers to deal with a variety of terminals. Software emulators running on microprocessors in the channel interfaces make the network appear to the terminal as its own type of computer, and the terminals appear to the computer as its own type of terminal. *See* CHANNEL, EMULATOR, SOFTWARE.

spooling. (1) In peripherals, simultaneous peripheral operation online; the use of auxiliary storage as a buffer when transferring data from the processor to its peripherals. This allows programs using slow peripherals (e.g. line printers) to run to completion quickly, thus making room for other programs in the main store. (2) In recording, movement of tape from one reel to another without being in the record or playback mode.

spot. In peripherals, the small area on the screen surface of a cathode ray tube which is bombarded by the electron beam. *See* CATHODE RAY TUBE.

spot beam. In communications, a narrow beam transmitted from a communications satellite. *Compare* GLOBAL BEAM, HEMISPHERIC BEAM, ZONE BEAM. *See* COMMUNICATIONS SATELLITE SYSTEM, FOOTPRINT.

spreadsheet. In programming, a general-purpose package for arithmetic operations favoured by accountants, financial planners, etc. The user is effectively supplied with a large electronic worksheet presented as a grid with cells of adjustable width. Text, numbers or algebraic formulae can be placed in the individual cells. Algebraic formulae relating the quantities in individual cells may be assigned to formula cells; these formulae are not displayed in the cells, but the corresponding result appears when data is placed in the cells referenced by the formulae. When data in a cell is entered or modified, the worksheet is updated and the values

appearing in corresponding formulae cells are automatically updated.

Spreadsheets provide an extremely user friendly alternative to conventional programming, and their mode of operation is closely aligned to the manual method of preparing accounts, financial plans, etc. *See* INTEGRATED SOFTWARE.

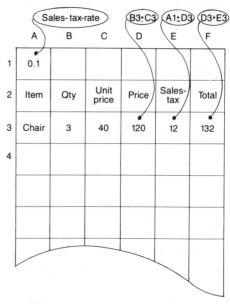

spreadsheet

sprites. In computer graphics, small images on a screen, moving under program control and normally ranging from character sets or cursor shapes to specific patterns as in computer games. (Philips). *Compare* ICON.

sprocket feed. In printing, a method of feeding paper through a device. Toothed, gearlike wheels rotate, and the pins (or sprockets) on these wheels engage in holes along the edge of the film or paper, ensuring a positive drive and accurate positioning. *See* TRACTOR FEED.

SPSS. In programming, Statistical Package for Social Sciences; a software package for statistical analysis.

spur. In communications, a junction on a cable distribution system that connects system outlets to the network.

SPX. *See* SIMPLEX.

square serif. *Synonymous with* SLAB SERIF.

squash. In filming and video, a visual effect in which one image appears to be pushed out from both top and bottom by another. (Philips). *Compare* SQUEEZE. *See* TRANSITION.

squawk box. A low-quality loudspeaker used for an intercom or public address system. *See* INTERCOM, PUBLIC ADDRESS SYSTEM.

squeeze. In filming and video. a visual effect in which one image appears to be pushed out from both sides by another. (Philips). *Compare* SQUASH. *See* TRANSITION.

SRAM. *See* STATIC RANDOM-ACCESS MEMORY.

SRA paper sizes. *Synonymous with* A, B AND C SERIES OF PAPER SIZES.

SRM. *See* SERVICE REFERENCE MODEL.

s/s. In printing, same size; an instruction to reproduce material to the same size as the original.

SSI. *See* SMALL-SCALE INTEGRATION.

SSTV. *See* SLOW-SCAN TELEVISION DEVICE.

stabilization process. In photography, a photographic rapid-access process utilizing special paper in which a developing agent is incorporated in the emulsion layer, thus allowing fast development. In this process a stabilization bath is substituted for the conventional fixing bath. In phototypesetting it is commonly used for paste-up, but is not suitable for long-term storage. *See* FIXATION, PHOTOTYPESETTING, RAPID-ACCESS PROCESSING.

stable state. The state assumed by a system when the transient effects of all signals and disturbances have died away. *See* TRANSIENT.

stack. In data structures, a structure in which items are added at the end of a sequential list and can only be retrieved from the same end. Thus a last in first out.

strategy is employed. *Compare* HEAP, QUEUE. *See* LAST IN FIRST OUT.

stack pointer. In programming, a storage location holding the address of the most recently stored item in a stack. *See* STACK.

STAIRS. In online information retrieval, Storage and Information Retrieval Systems; information retrieval software developed by IBM.

stamper. In recording, a recording mould used to press gramophone records or optical discs. (Philips). *See* METAL FATHER, REPLICATION.

standalone system. A self-contained system independent of another device, system or program.

standalone terminal. In data communications, a terminal that can be directly connected via a modem and is not, therefore, a member of a cluster. *See* MODEM.

standalone word-processing system. A system comprising a single word-processing station that does not share the power of a central computer.

standard. A technical specification that is: (a) available to the public; (b) drawn up with the cooperation and consensus or general approval of all interested parties affected by it; (c) based upon the consolidated results of science and technology experience; (d) aimed at the promotion of optimum community benefits; and (e) approved by a body recognized on the national, regional or international level. *See* PROTOCOL STANDARDS, STANDARDIZATION.

standard deviation. In mathematics, a measure of the spread of values about the arithmetic mean value. *See* ARITHMETIC MEAN.

standard document. In word processing, the primary document that is used in automatic letter writing and is merged with variable information to produce the final letter. *See* AUTOMATIC LETTER WRITING, BOILERPLATE, VARIABLE TEXT.

standard generalized markup language. (SGML) In printing, a method for describing the logical structure of a document. The method is based upon generic coding principles where sections, paragraphs, highlighted words, etc. are tagged as such. *See* GENERIC CODING.

standard input. In computing, a Unix term for the input source provided by the operating system to enable a program to read data. The standard input may be specified at run time. *Compare* STANDARD OUTPUT. *See* FILTER, PIPES, UNIX.

standard interface. In computing, a point of interconnection between two systems (e.g. a central processing unit and a peripheral) at which all aspects of the interconnection — logical, electrical and mechanical — are specified and used in other instances. The existence of standard interfaces is essential when microcomputer users purchase their peripherals from a variety of manufacturers and demand the assurance that the peripheral will function correctly with their particular configuration. Standards may be specific to one manufacturer, and de facto industry standards can be used to interconnect equipment from different vendors (e.g. Centronics parallel interface for printers). Standards are also developed by trade and international associations (e.g. EIA RS-232C and CCITT V.24). *See* CENTRONICS INTERFACE, CENTRAL PROCESSING UNIT, ELECTRONIC INDUSTRIES ASSOCIATION, PERIPHERAL, RS-232C, STANDARDIZATION, V.24.

standardization. In standards, agreement on technical specifications for use by different manufacturers (e.g. standardization of connectors, television signals and formats, international telephone networks, computers and peripherals, digital audio compact disc format and encoding techniques). (Philips). *See* COMPACT DISC – DIGITAL AUDIO, STANDARD INTERFACE.

standard output. In computing, a Unix term for the output provided by the operating system to allow a program to write data to a destination which may be specified at run time. A filter writes it as output to a standard output. *Compare* STANDARD OUTPUT. *See* FILTER, PIPES, UNIX.

standard paragraphs. *Synonymous with* BOILERPLATE.

standards converter. In television, a device that converts television signal characteristics, number of lines, number of fields and colour coding from one national standard to another. *See* VIDEO STANDARDS.

standby. In reliability, a condition in which a complete resumption of stable operation is possible within a short time. *See* COLD STANDBY, HOT STANDBY, WARM STANDBY.

standby equipment. In reliability, a duplicate system to be used if the primary unit becomes unusable as a result of malfunction. *See* STANDBY.

star. In data communications, a network topology in which each node is connected only to one central controller. This network is commonly employed when a number of terminals are connected to a single host computer and the majority of traffic is concerned with host–terminal rather than terminal–terminal communications. However, this topology suffers from the following disadvantages: (a) a breakdown at the host disrupts all traffic; (b) throughput is limited by the host capacity; (c) the cost of cabling may be very high; (d) there is no alternate path in case of failure in the line between a host and a terminal. *Compare* LOOP NETWORK, MESH, RING. *See* LOCAL AREA NETWORK.

start bit. In codes, a bit used in asynchronous transmission preceding a serial character and signalling the start of that character. *Compare* STOP BIT. *See* ASYNCHRONOUS TRANSMISSION. *Synonymous with* START ELEMENT.

start element. *Synonymous with* START BIT.

start of header. In data communications, a control character used at the beginning of a sequence of characters that constitute the address or routing information for the message. *See* HEADER.

start of message. (SOM) In data communications, a character in a poll response that precedes the address, or addresses, of any data stations other than the master station that are to receive the message. *See* POLLING.

start of text. (STX) In data communications, a transmission control character that terminates a message heading and indicates that successive characters relate to the text of the message. *Compare* END OF TEXT.

start/stop envelope. In data communications, a packet in asynchronous transmission comprising start bit, binary data and stop bit. *See* ASYNCHRONOUS TRANSMISSION, START BIT, STOP BIT.

statement. In programming, a meaningful expression used to specify an operation and is usually complete in the context of the language used.

state of the art. That which can be achieved with currently proven technology and practice (i.e. without further research or development).

static. (1) In audio recording, a popping or crackling noise. (2) In radio transmission, interference produced by abnormal atmospheric effects. (3) A non-dynamic system or condition.

static dump. In computing, a dump performed at a particular point in time relative to a machine run (e.g. at the end of the run). *See* DUMP.

static evaluation. In computer security, an examination and analysis of the system documentation and code in order to detect deliberate traps or other unauthorized modifications.

static random-access memory. (SRAM) In memory systems, a form of random-access memory (RAM) that stores each bit in a flip flop. It requires no refresh operation and retains the data as long as power is applied. It is, however, more expensive than dynamic RAM and has a higher power consumption. *Compare* DYNAMIC MEMORY. *See* FLIP FLOP.

station. In data communications, an input or output location of a communication system. It contains the sources and sinks for the messages and those elements that control the message flow on the link.

statistical database. In database security, a database containing aggregate information concerning large subsets of entities (e.g. census data). Such data can be misused to reveal information concerning individuals unless some form of inference control is employed. *See* INFERENCE CONTROL.

statistical time division multiplexing. (stat-mux) In data communications, a version of time division multiplexing in which time slots are only allocated to active terminals. This technique increases the number of terminals that may be connected to a given capacity channel. A buffer memory assembles data and is usually sufficient to store channel characters if traffic temporarily exceeds the multiplexer data link rate. *See* MULTIPLEXER, TIME DIVISION MULTIPLEXING.

statmux. *See* STATISTICAL TIME DIVISION MULTIPLEXING.

Statsionar. In communications, the Russian global communications satellite system; statsionar is Russian for stationary. *See* COMMUNICATIONS SATELLITE SYSTEM, GORIZONT, INTERSPUTNIK, MOLNIYA, RADUGA.

Status. In online information retrieval, information retrieval software that works on free-text principles. It was developed by the UK Atomic Energy Authority. *See* FREE-TEXT SEARCHING.

status line. In word processing, a message on a word-processing display giving details of layout, line currently being typed, etc. to the operator.

status poll. In peripherals, a request, initiated by a computer, for information on the current status of a terminal. *See* POLLING.

STD. Subscriber trunk dialing. *Synonymous with* DIRECT DISTANCE DIALING.

STDM. Synchronous time division multiplexing. *Synonymous with* TIME DIVISION MULTIPLEXING.

steganography. In data security, the concealment of the existence of messages; literally covered writing. In data security this can take the form of filling in intermessage gaps with padding characters, thus although the existence of the communication link is not concealed an attacker is denied information on when messages are being transmitted. *Compare* CRYPTOGRAPHY.

stem. In printing, the main vertical stroke making up a type character. (Desktop).

step. (1) In programming, an individual program operation during execution. (2) In optical media, to advance by one frame either forward or reverse during the playing of a videodisc. *See* FRAME, VIDEODISC.

step-and-repeat camera. In micrographics, a type of microfilm camera that can expose a series of separate images on an area of film according to a predetermined format, usually in orderly columns and rows. *See* MICROFILM.

step-by-step switch. In communications, a switch that is moved to successive positions by line pulses. *See* SELECTOR.

stepped index monomode. *See* FIBER OPTICS.

stepped index multimode. *See* FIBER OPTICS.

stepper motor. In computing, a motor that rotates its shaft by a precise angular amount each time that it is activated.

steradian. In mathematics, a unit solid angle which having its vertex at the centre of a sphere cuts off an area of the surface of the sphere equal to that of a square with sides of length equal to the radius of the sphere. *Compare* RADIAN.

stereo. (1) In filming, a positive transparency used for projection of a rear-screen background. (2) In printing, a duplicate letterpress plate cast from a mould. (3) In audio. *Compare* AMBISONICS. *See* STEREOPHONIC.

stereophonic. (stereo) An effect of three-dimensional sound produced by recording via two separated microphones. The signals from the microphones are recorded or broadcast as separate signals, and these signals are played back through two separately spaced loudspeakers. *Compare* MONOPHONIC, QUADRUPHONIC.

stet. In printing, a proofreader's mark indicating that the copy marked for correc-

tion should remain as it was prior to the correction. *See* PROOF READING.

STI. Scientific and technical information.

still frame. *Synonymous with* FREEZE FRAME.

still-frame audio. *Synonymous with* COMPRESSED AUDIO.

STN. *See* SUPER-TWISTED NEMATIC.

stochastic model. In mathematics, a model of a system that incorporates the effects of random events. *Synonymous with* PROBABILISTIC MODEL.

stop-and-wait protocol. In data communications, a flow control algorithm in which the sending host awaits acknowledgement, from the receiving host, that error-free frames have been received before transmitting further frames. *Compare* FREE WHEELING, SLIDING WINDOW PROTOCOL. *See* FRAME, HOST.

stop bit. In codes, a bit, used in asynchronous transmission, which indicates the end of the character. *Compare* START BIT. *See* ASYNCHRONOUS TRANSMISSION. *Synonymous with* CABOOSE, STOP ELEMENT.

stop code. In word processing, a control code in the body of text that stops playback, or printout, usually to enable the insertion of variable information. *See* VARIABLE TEXT.

stop element. *Synonymous with* STOP BIT.

stop list. In library science, a list of words or terms, or roots of words, that are considered not to be significant for the purpose of information retrieval and that are excluded from indexing. In automatic indexing systems the computer is instructed to ignore common terms such as 'and', 'but', etc. included in the stop list. *See* AUTOMATIC INDEXING.

stop motion cinematography. In filming, a technique to give the trick effect of an instantaneous change (e.g. performers stop their action and an object is placed or removed from the scene). The camera may be stopped during this interval, or the appropriate section of the film removed. On playback the object appears to disappear or to materialize.

stop-watch function. In programming, the function of a stop-watch built into a given computer program. (Philips).

stopwords. *See* STOP LIST.

storage capacity. In memory systems, the amount of data that a particular store can accommodate, generally specified in bytes. Storage can also be quantified in terms of the type of information stored. The over 660-megabyte storage capacity of a compact disc, for example, can hold the data needed to reproduce over 160 000 pages of typed text, 72 minutes of the finest-quality sound or some 5000 video-quality natural pictures. (Philips). *See* BYTE, COMPACT DISC.

storage device. In memory systems, a unit into which data can be entered, retained and later retrieved. *See* MAGNETIC DISK, MAGNETIC TAPE, OPTICAL DIGITAL DISC.

storage dump. Memory dump. *Synonymous with* DUMP.

storage media module. *See* SMD.

storage protection. *See* MEMORY PROTECTION.

storage tube. *See* DIRECT-VIEW STORAGE TUBE.

store and forward. In data communications, a system that stores message packets at intermediate points prior to further transmission. *See* COMPUTER NETWORK, MESSAGE SWITCHING, PACKET.

stored program signalling. In communications, a technique that enables the sequence of controlling, setting up and clearing down calls by an exchange to be stored as a program within a computer memory. *See* SYSTEM X.

story board. (1) In applications, a documentary outline of a computer-assisted learning courseware package when extensive computer graphics, interactive video and/or acoustic magnetic tape sequences are to be employed. The outline contains sketches of graphics annotated with dialogue, screen textual information, etc. *See* COMPUTER-ASSISTED LEARNING, INTERACTIVE VIDEODISC SYSTEMS. (2) In filming, a documentary outline of proposed film sequence with sketches, photographs, details of dialogue, music, sound effects, etc.

straight PCM mode. In audio, the pulse code modulation (PCM) mode, in adaptive delta pulse code modulation, used as predictor for signals having high-frequency characteristics. (Philips). *See* ADAPTIVE DELTA PULSE CODE MODULATION, PULSE CODE MODULATION.

strap. In printing, a subheading used above the main headline in a newspaper article. (Desktop).

strawboard. In printing, a thick board made from straw pulp that is used in bookwork and in the making of envelopes and cartons. It is not suitable for printing. (Desktop).

streaking. Horizontal distortion of a television picture.

stream cipher. In data security, a method of encryption with the capability of providing perfect secrecy. The plaintext is encoded into numbers, usually binary, and a key stream of random numbers is combined with the plaintext to form the ciphertext. The receiving end is supplied with an identical key stream of random numbers, and the mathematical inverse combination of ciphertext and key stream reveals the plaintext. This technique does not require that the plaintext be formed into blocks, with a blocksize determined by the cryptographic algorithm designer, the plaintext may be enciphered in segments of any desired length even down to bit-by-bit encipherment. It is therefore valuable in transmission systems where the messages may need to be encrypted character by character or even bit by bit. *Compare* BLOCK CIPHER, *See* CIPHER FEEDBACK, CRYPTOGRAPHIC BIT STREAM, PERFECT SECRECY.

stream cipher chaining. In data security, a stream cipher in which feedback is employed to generate the cryptographic bit stream.

Compare BLOCK CIPHER CHAINING, OUTPUT FEEDBACK. *See* CIPHER FEEDBACK, CRYPTOGRAPHIC BIT STREAM, STREAM CIPHER.

streamer tape.   In memory systems, a magnetic tape used for archival purposes to record an exact image of all the data stored in a hard disk. It cannot be used to back up or restore individual disk files. (Philips). *See* BACKUP/RESTORE, HARD DISK, TAPE STREAMER.

stress table.   In audio, a table of data defining the way that individual words or syllables are to be stressed when they are regenerated from phonetically coded speech. (Philips). *See* PHONETIC CODING, PHONETIC SYNTHESIS, SPEECH SYNTHESIZER.

strike on.   In printing, a process of setting type by direct impression (e.g. output of a typewriter composing device). *Compare* COLD TYPE, ETCH TYPE.

strike through.   In printing, the effect of ink soaking through the printed sheet. (Desktop).

string.   In data structures, a sequence of characters that can correspond to textual message. *Compare* CHARACTER.

string handling.   In programming, the operations that may be performed on strings are creation, concatenation, extraction of substrings, comparison, determination of string lengths, determination of the position of substrings in strings, replacing substrings within strings, storage and input/output. *See* CONCATENATE, STRING.

string variables.   In programming, variables that can assume values of strings, usually alphanumeric. *See* STRING.

stripe reader.   In peripherals, a device that reads the data encoded on the magnetic stripe of credit cards, etc. and inputs the information into a computer. *See* MAGNETIC STRIPE.

stripping.   In data communications, the process of extracting the essential information elements of a message by removing the header and tail parts of the message envelope. *See* HEADER, TAIL.

strobe.   In electronics, a selection signal.

strobing.   In television, an effect due to a transverse or rotary movement of an object at a speed counteracting the effect of persistance of vision. *See* PERSISTENCE OF VISION.

stroboscopic effect.   A false impression of the speed of revolution of rotating spokes when viewed in a regularly flashing light. It can be used to measure a speed of rotation. *See* WAGON WHEEL EFFECT.

stroke.   (1) In character recognition, an arc or straight line used as a segment of a character. (2) In computer graphics, an arc or straight line used as a segment of a display element. (3) An abbreviation for keystroke. *See* KEYSTROKE.

stroke edge.   In character recognition, the line between a side of a stroke and its background as obtained by averaging out the irregularities along the length of the stroke.

stroke generator.   In computer graphics, a character generator that produces characters composed of strokes. *See* STROKE.

strongly typed.   In programming, pertaining to languages in which the type of each variable is explicitly declared and the compiler can check the type of each variable wherever it appears in the program. This facility enables compilers to detect program errors which might otherwise not become apparent until execution. For example, the compiler can report if an instruction attempts to assign a value to a variable that does not conform to the variable type, such as a floating point value assigned to a string variable. *See* COMPILER, TYPE.

structural redundancy.   In reliability, a form of hardware redundancy applied at a gate level where multiple parallel paths are established between input and output. It has applications in very large-scale integration design, but small-, medium- and large-scale integration systems favour modular redundancy. *Compare* MODULAR REDUNDANCY. *See* GATE, HARDWARE REDUNDANCY, LARGE-SCALE INTEGRATION, MEDIUM-SCALE INTEGRATION, SMALL-SCALE INTEGRATION, VERY LARGE-SCALE INTEGRATION.

structure chart.   In systems analysis, a diagram that indicates the interrelationships of the modules of the system and the data, as well as control, communication necessary for the functioning of those modules. In conjunction with a well-designed data dictionary it provides an essential document for the design evaluation of a system. *Compare* DATA FLOW DIAGRAM. *See* STRUCTURED SYSTEMS ANALYSIS.

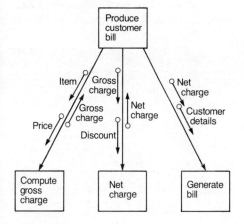

structure chart

structure clash.   *See* JACKSON STRUCTURED PROGRAMMING.

structured English.   In systems analysis, an adaptation of English to express logical program requirements in an unambiguous concise manner. The guidelines for statements in this language are: (a) the statements should be concise, avoiding connectors such as but, except, etc.; (b) the verb should unambiguously describe the required action (e.g. edit rather than handle, process, etc.); (c) the object should be stated explicitly; (d) all nouns should be included in the data dictionary; and (e) adjectives and adverbs should be avoided. *See* DATA DICTIONARY, STRUCTURED SYSTEMS ANALYSIS.

structured   programming.   In programming, a method of designing a program, and associated data structures, that improves clarity, reduces complexity and renders it more amenable to modification and debugging. *Compare* SPAGHETTI CODE. *See* DATA STRUCTURE, DEBUG, JACKSON STRUCTURED PROGRAMMING.

structured   systems   analysis.   In systems analysis, a disciplined approach to the structuring of a system analyst's work. It is concerned not only with the various phases of a system's development, in the form of a structured methodology, but also with the essential communication between, and coordination of, design phases.

The main tools of structured analysis are data flow diagrams or structure charts, a data dictionary, data store structuring and process logic representation. *See* DATA DICTIONARY, DATA FLOW DIAGRAM, DECISION TABLE, STRUCTURE CHART, STRUCTURED ENGLISH.

studio to head end link.   (SHL) In cable television, a fixed microwave link station that transmits signals from the studio to the head end. *See* HEAD END, MICROWAVE TRANSMISSION.

STV.   *See* SUBSCRIPTION TELEVISION.

STX.   *See* START OF TEXT.

style sheets.   In word processing, a file, used in conjunction with some word-processing packages that stores all the formatting information for headings, paragraphs or even whole documents. Once the style sheets have been set up the operator can invoke them using a single command to activate all the formatting codes. *See* WORD PROCESSING.

stylus.   In computer graphics, a hand-held pointer for establishing a coordinate position on a display surface. It may be used to draw figures or move elements of the display. *See* DIGITIZING TABLET, LIGHT PEN, POINTING DEVICE, TRANSDUCER.

subaudio   frequency.   *Synonymous   with* INFRASONIC FREQUENCY.

subcarrier.   In communications, a frequency within a passband of a range of signal frequencies that is modulated with another signal or signal frequency. In satellite communications subcarriers are used to carry audio signals in television channels and may also be used for auxiliary services such as broadcast   radio   signals,   data   communications, etc. *Compare* SINGLE CARRIER PER CHANNEL.

subcode channel. In optical media, one of eight compact disc subchannels, referred to as P to W, that exist in parallel to the main channel. They are used for control and display information. (Philips). *See* COMPACT DISC – DIGITAL AUDIO.

subheader. In optical media, a field in an interactive compact disc sector indicating the nature of the data in the sector, thus allowing real-time interactive operation. (Philips). *See* SECTOR STRUCTURE, SYNCHRONIZATION.

sub-information provider. *See* UMBRELLA INFORMATION PROVIDER.

subject. In computer security, an active entity, generally in the form of a person, process or device, that causes information to flow between objects or changes the system state. (DOD). *Compare* OBJECT.

subliminal. Pertaining to images and sounds below the perception threshold that can influence a subject's behavior.

subprogram. (1) In programming, a program that is invoked by another program. (2) In programming, a part of a larger program that can be compiled independently. *See* COMPILER, SUBROUTINE.

subroutine. In programming, a sequence of instructions to perform an action that is frequently required in a program, or set of programs (e.g. to sort a set of strings into alphabetical order). *Compare* COROUTINE. *See* SUBPROGRAM.

subroutine call. In programming, an instruction that passes control to a subroutine. *See* SUBROUTINE.

subsatellite point. In communications, the point at which a line, drawn from the centre of the earth to the satellite, passes through the earth's surface. *See* LOOK ANGLES.

subschema. In databases, the application programmer's or end user's view of the data.

See SCHEMA. *Synonymous with* EXTERNAL SCHEMA.

subscriber trunk dialing. *Synonymous with* DIRECT DISTANCE DIALING.

subscript. (1) In printing, a letter or number that appears below the baseline in a line of printed text. *Compare* SUPERSCRIPT. *Synonymous with* INFERIOR FIGURE. (2) In programming, a symbol associated with a name of a set to identify a particular element or subset.

subscription television. (STV) In television, a pay broadcast television service. The broadcast signals are scrambled and can only be received by subscribers with special decoders, termed descramblers, attached to their television sets and for which they pay a rental fee. *Compare* CABLE TELEVISION. *See* DESCRAMBLER, PREMIUM TELEVISION. *Synonymous with* PAY TELEVISION.

subset. A set of elements, each one of which is a member of another given set. *See* SET.

substitute character. In codes, a control character put in place of a character that is recognized to be in error or cannot be represented on a given device (e.g. in videotex received characters with parity errors are displayed as white squares). *See* PARITY, VIDEOTEX.

substitution box. *See* S BOX.

substitution cipher. In data security, a cipher in which each character or fixed group of characters is substituted by another character or group of characters. *Compare* TRANSPOSITION CIPHER. *See* CIPHER, CRYPTOGRAPHY, MONOALPHABETIC CIPHER, POLYALPHABETIC CIPHER.

substrate. In microelectronics, the physical material on which a circuit is fabricated. *See* CHIP.

subtitle. *Synonymous with* CAPTION.

subtractive colour mixing. (1) In printing, a means of reproducing colours by mixing or superimposing inks, paints or dyes. (2) In photography, a method of analyzing and resynthesizing colours. A scene is filmed with three light filters, representing the primary colours, and black and white negatives of a subject are produced. A dye positive image is produced for each negative with the dye colour complementary to that of the corresponding filter. These dye images are then superimposed to yield a combined transparent positive image. *Compare* ADDITIVE COLOUR MIXING.

subtractive primary colours. In optics, the colours cyan, magenta and yellow. *Compare* ADDITIVE PRIMARY COLOURS. *See* SUBTRACTIVE COLOUR MIXING.

subtrahend. The number or quantity subtracted from the minuend in the subtraction process. *Compare* MINUEND.

subvoice-grade channel. In communications, a channel with a bandwidth of 240–300 Hz suitable for telegraphy or low-speed (up to some 150 bits per second) data transmission, but not for voice messages. Such channels may be leased from a common carrier or derived as subsets of a voice-grade channel. *Compare* VOICE-GRADE CHANNEL. *See* BIT, COMMON CARRIER.

suffix notation. *Synonymous with* POSTFIX NOTATION.

suitcase-portable. In computing, pertaining to a microcomputer that is considerably larger than a briefcase-portable computer. Such machines evolved from desk-top microcomputers and have a similar range of facilities. The normal weight of these machines ranges from 8 to 16 kilograms. *Compare* BRIEFCASE-PORTABLE, LAP-TOP COMPUTER. *Synonymous with* LUGGABLE, TRANSPORTABLE.

suite. In programming, a collection of programs that is designed to perform a task or a set of closely related task (e.g. the accounting functions of a firm).

summation check. In codes, a check based upon the comparison of the sum of digits of a numeral with a previously computed value to indicate any accidental change in the value of a digit during transmission or transcriptions. *See* CHECKSUM, REDUNDANCY CHECKING.

sun outage. In communications, a period in which a communications satellite system does not function fully due to the relative position of the satellite and the sun. The outage may be caused by the earth's, or the moon's, shadow crossing the solar cells or by the satellite passing in front of the sun. *See* HELIOS NOISE.

sunshine notice. In communications, a notice issued by the Federal Communications Commission stating that members of the public may attend its regulatory proceedings. *See* FEDERAL COMMUNICATIONS COMMISSION.

supercalendered paper. In printing, a glossy, but not coated, paper that is produced by being passed through supercalender rolls under high pressure.

supercomputer. In computing, an extremely powerful mainframe computer used for complex mathematical calculations demanding high speed and storage (e.g. weather forecasting). *Compare* FIFTH-GENERATION COMPUTER. *See* MAINFRAME, PARALLEL PROCESSING.

superconductivity. In electronics, a phenomenon that is produced by extremely low temperatures (i.e. close to the absolute zero of $-273°C$. At these temperatures the resistance of metals becomes extremely low.
The phenomenon of superconductivity is extremely important in the computing and communication fields. It opens up the possibility of small, powerful magnets, very high-speed switching devices, minimal power losses in conduction, etc. The main area of research is directed towards the search for materials that display superconductivity at temperatures sufficiently far above the absolute zero to enable them to be employed in practical devices. *See* JOSEPHSON JUNCTION, RESISTANCE.

superencipherment. (1) In data security, multiple encryption. (2) In data security, a technique in which a plaintext message is first encoded (i.e. each word or phrase is changed to a preselected code) and the resulting encoded message is then enciphered. *See* CIPHER, CODE, CRYPTOGRAPHY.

supergroup. In communications, a collection of five channel groups occupying adjacent bands in the spectrum for the purpose of simultaneous modulation and demodulation. A supergroup comprises 60 voice channels. *See* CHANNEL GROUP, DEMODULATION, MASTER GROUP, MODULATION.

super high-frequency. (SHF) In communications, frequency range of 3–30 Ghz.

superimpose. In computer graphics and video, to place a computer-generated image over an image from another source. *See* OVERLAY.

superimposed circuit. *Synonymous with* SUPERPOSED CIRCUIT.

super large-scale integration. (SSLI) In microelectronics, pertaining to a fabrication technology that produces well in excess of 100 000 transistors per chip. *Compare* LARGE-SCALE INTEGRATION, MEDIUM-SCALE INTEGRATION, SMALL-SCALE INTEGRATION, ULTRA LARGE-SCALE INTEGRATION, VERY LARGE-SCALE INTEGRATION. *See* CHIP, TRANSISTOR.

superlattice. In microelectronics, a chip comprising several layers of semiconductor material. *See* CHIP, SEMICONDUCTOR.

Supermap. In optical media, Australian census database on read-only memory compact disc (CD-ROM) produced by Space Time Research Pty Ltd. *See* CD-ROM PUBLISHING.

super-master group. In communications, CCITT terminology for an assembly of 900 voice channels. *See* CCITT, CHANNEL GROUP, MASTER GROUP, SUPERGROUP.

superposed circuit. In communications, an additional channel obtained from one or more circuits, usually provided for other channels, in such a way that all the channels can be used simultaneously and without mutual interference. *Synonymous with* SUPERIMPOSED CIRCUIT.

superscript. In printing, a small character set, above the normal level of characters, in printed or displayed text. *Compare* SUBSCRIPT.

supersmart card. In banking, a proposed new form of smart card with a microprocessor and 64 kilobytes of memory, a calculator with touch keys, a display window, a synthesized magnetic stripe and battery. Such a card allows offline verification, identification and authorization. It is also possible to use these card with conventional automatic teller machines and terminals; the user will be able to simulate the magnetic stripe of conventional cards by keying instructions with the keyboard. In addition to the functions of conventional smart cards the super card will provide the user with offline display of customer information, transactions, account balances, credit limits, etc. *Compare* MAGNETICALLY ENCODED CARD, SMART CARD. *See* INTELLIGENT TOKEN. *Synonymous with* ULTICARD.

super table of contents. (super TOC) In optical media, the information that is required to start up an interactive compact disc player. The information which is stored in the first track on the disc concerns the disc type and format, the status of the disc as a single entity or part of an album, the data size and the position of the file directory and bootstrap. (Philips). *Compare* TABLE OF CONTENTS. *See* BOOTSTRAP, COMPACT DISC – INTERACTIVE, FILE, TRACK.

super TOC. *See* SUPER TABLE OF CONTENTS.

super-twisted nematic. (STN) In peripherals, a form of liquid crystal display that provides a higher contrast and improved viewing angle as compared with twisted nematic displays. *Compare* TWISTED NEMATIC. *See* LIQUID CRYSTAL DISPLAY.

super videotex. A private videotex system with three sets of attributes: (a) integration with other company information and communication services; (b) integration with word-processing and electronic office facilities; (c) integration with computing facilities (e.g. transaction processing and real-time updating). *See* OFFICE OF THE FUTURE, TRANSACTION PROCESSING, VIDEOTEX, WORD PROCESSING.

supervisor. In computing, the section of a control program that coordinates the use of resources and maintains the flow of the processor unit operations. *Synonymous with* SUPERVISORY PROGRAM.

supervisory program. *Synonymous with* SUPERVISOR.

supervisory sequence. In data communications, a sequence of control characters that performs a defined control function.

supervisory signal. (1) In communications, a signal that indicates whether or not a circuit is in use. (2) In communications, a signal used to indicate the various operating states of circuit combinations.

superzapping. (1) In data security, pertaining to operations that misuse the computer universal access program in order to bypass normal security arrangements and then make illegal modifications to programs or data. (2) In programming, the process of making a direct change to object or machine code. *See* PATCH.

suppressed carrier transmission. In communications, the transmission of a modulated wave in which the carrier signal is to some degree suppressed. The carrier conveys no information, and its suppression reduces the total power of the transmitted signal. *Compare* SINGLE-SIDEBAND TRANSMISSION. *See* CARRIER, MODULATION.

surround sound. *Synonymous with* AMBISONICS.

suspense account. In data processing, a control total for items awaiting further processing. *See* SUSPENSE FILE.

suspense file. In data processing, a file containing unprocessed or partially processed items awaiting further action.

SVC. *See* SWITCHED VIRTUAL CALL.

SVR. In video, super video recorder; a video cassette format developed by Grundig. *Compare* BETA, U-MATIC, VHS.

swapping. In memory systems, the automatic exchange of information between

memory and a mass storage device. *Compare* THRASHING. *See* MASS STORAGE, PAGING.

swash letters. In printing, italic characters with extra flourishes used at the beginning of chapters. (Desktop).

sweep. In television, the repetitive movement of the cathode beam over the phosphor screen. The are two sweeps; one traces horizontal lines, whereas the other moves vertically at a slower rate tracing the assembly of lines into a field. *See* FIELD, FIELD BLANKING, LINE BLANKING INTERVAL, RASTER SCAN.

sweeping. *See* ELECTRONIC COUNTERMEASURES SWEEPING.

SWIFT. In banking, Society for Worldwide Interbank Financial Telecommunications; a private international telecommunication service for banks. (ANSI). *See* BANKING NETWORKS.

swim. In computer graphics, a fault in a display system in which display elements move around the normal position.

switch. In programming, a part of a program that allows control to be passed to one of a number of choices.

switched network. In communications, any network in which connections are made by a switching action (e.g. dialing). *See* SWITCHING.

switched network backup. In communications, an optional facility enabling a user to specify an alternative path if the primary path is, for some reason, not available.

switched star. In cable television, a modern method of cable distribution in which the main cable serves a series of junctions and lines connect the individual subscribers to these junctions. The system has the advantage that the subscriber lines do not have to be of high bandwidth because each subscriber siphons off the signals he requires. Moreover, the system facilitates the development of information services which require the user to send signals back up the line. *Compare* TREE AND BRANCH.

switched virtual call. (SVC) In data communications, a connection between two terminals that is created only when it is required, following a call set-up procedure. *See* PACKET SWITCHING, VIRTUAL CALL SERVICE.

switcher. *Synonymous with* VISION MIXER.

switching. In communications, the provision of point-to-point connections between dynamically changing sources and sinks. *See* CIRCUIT SWITCHING, MESSAGE SWITCHING, PACKET SWITCHING, POINT-TO-POINT, SINK, SOURCE.

switching centre. In communications, a place at which communication lines terminate and where messages can be switched between lines, or interconnections made between circuits. *Synonymous with* SWITCHING OFFICE.

switching error. *Synonymous with* QUADRUTURE ERROR.

switching office. *Synonymous with* SWITCHING CENTRE.

switching overlay. In video and computer graphics, a technique in which every pixel in the displayed image is selected from one or other of the corresponding source images. (Philips). *See* IMAGE, OVERLAY.

switch lock. *See* VERTICAL LOCK.

switch over. In computing and communications, a switching action performed manually or automatically to remove a faulty unit and to connect in an alternative serviceable one.

Switchstream. *Compare* KILOSTREAM, MEGASTREAM, SATSTREAM. *See* X-STREAM.

syllogism. In mathematics, a logical statement that involves three propositions: the major premise, the minor premise and the conclusion. The conclusion is necessarily true if the premises are true (e.g. John likes fishing or singing, John does not like fishing, John likes singing).

Symbol. In printing, a typeface with a collection of useful symbols (e.g. daggers, bullets). *Compare* AVANTE-GARDE, BOOKMAN, COURIER, HELVETICA, HELVETICA NARROW, NEW CENTURY SCHOOLBOOK, OLDSTYLE, PALATINO, TIMES ROMAN, ZAPF CHANCERY, ZAPF DINGBATS. *See* BULLETS, DAGGER, TYPEFACE.

symbol. (1) In communications, one of the unique states of the carrier in digital modulation. *See* CARRIER, MODULATION. (2) In optical media, the basic unit of compact disc digitized data, parity and subcode data. Initially eight bits long, it is expanded to 17 bits by eight-to-fourteen modulation. (Philips). *See* BYTE, COMPACT DISC, EIGHT-TO-FOURTEEN MODULATION, SUBCODE CHANNEL.

symbol error rate. (SER) In data communications, the ratio of incorrect to total number of symbols in a message. *Compare* BIT ERROR RATE. *See* SYMBOL.

symbolic address. In programming, a name or label representing a memory location. *See* LABEL.

symbolic language. In programming, a language for the expression of operation codes and addresses that is more meaningful to a user than machine code representation. *See* ASSEMBLY LANGUAGE, HIGH-LEVEL LANGUAGE, MACHINE LANGUAGE.

symbol table. In programming, a table produced by a compiler or assembler to associate a symbolic name to an actual address or value. *See* ASSEMBLER, COMPILER, SYMBOLIC ADDRESS.

symmetric cryptosystem. In data security, a system in which the enciphering and deciphering keys are equal, or can easily be deduced from one another. *Compare* PUBLIC KEY CRYPTOGRAPHY. *Synonymous with* ONE-KEY CRYPTOSYSTEM.

sync. *See* SYNCHRONOUS.

sync bit. In data communications, a bit used for synchronization. *See* BIT, SYNCHRONIZATION.

synchronization. (1) The process of maintaining common timing and coordination between two or more operations, events or processes.

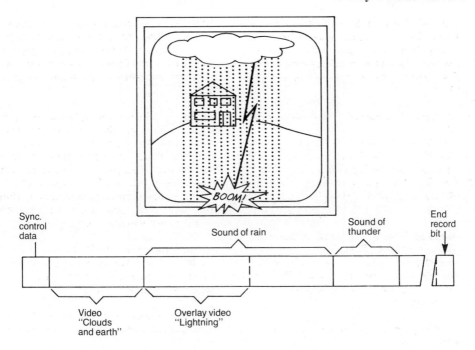

synchronization
Fig. 1. Synchronization of various video and sound elements. Courtesy *Philips*.

(2) In optical media, the process of maintaining a common timing of the various elements (pictorial, sound and text information) which form the total presentation of an interactive compact disc (CD-I). This is the task of the application program under the control of the operating system.

The data stream from the disc, which carries the information to be interpreted by the CD-I player for presentation on the video screen, and reproduction by the hi-fi system, consists of a series of sectors. A subheader at the beginning of each sector, directly following the data stream synchronization and header fields, indicates to the CD-I controlling microprocessor the nature of the information in the user data block which directly follows the subheader information. This user data information can be part of the application program (or the boot or start-up information for the application); it can be data for interpretation by the video processor as pictorial information, or by the audio processor as audio information. It can also be text or other program data to be interpreted by the main microprocessor.

Based on the indication contained in the subheader, the microprocessor switches the user data block to the appropriate circuit. It is then the task of the application program to instruct the microprocessor on how to handle the information once it has passed through the relevant decoding process. In some cases, such as for digital audio compact disc music tracks, the output data will be switched directly to the audio output channels.

In the case of applications program or computing data, the information may well be stored in the main memory, while video data will pass to the video memory to build up a picture for later display.

The synchronization function of the application then relates the various outputs from these data buffers to data coming directly from the appropriate decoding circuitry, to ensure that they are all presented in correct synchronization.

In Fig. 1 the synchronization data control triggers the video memory to indicate when the picture transfer from the disc is complete, and then to pass the background

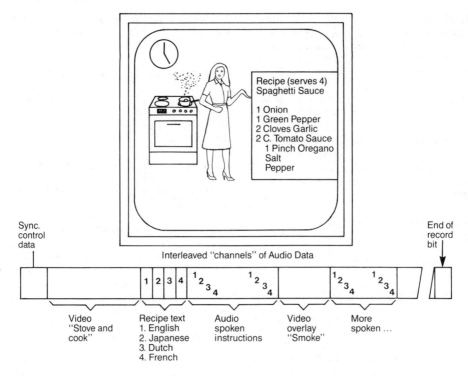

Sync.
control
data

Interleaved "channels" of Audio Data

End of
record
bit

Video
"Stove and
cook"

Recipe text
1. English
2. Japanese
3. Dutch
4. French

Audio
spoken
instructions

Video
overlay
"Smoke"

More
spoken ...

synchronization
Fig. 2. Synchronization of video elements, with multi-lingual commentaries. Courtesy *Philips*.

picture of the clouds, house and earth to the screen. At the same time, the sound representing rain is passed to audio channels. At the appropriate moment, the overlay of the lightning flash is triggered to the video output, and a short time later, the related sound of thunder is passed to the sound channels.

Fig. 2 shows a cooking program, with the additional complexity of multilanguage text in synchronization with multilingual speech. The other elements that make up the presentation, background, clock, smoke and moving head and body are all synchronized in a similar manner to the first example. (Philips). *See* APPLICATION PROGRAM, CD REAL-TIME OPERATING SYSTEM, COMPACT DISC – DIGITAL AUDIO, COMPACT DISC – INTERACTIVE, MAIN MEMORY, OVERLAY, SECTOR, SUBHEADER, TRACK.

synchronization field. In optical media, the first 12 bytes of an interactive or read-only memory compact disc sector containing synchronization data. (Philips). *See* COMPACT

DISC - INTERACTIVE, COMPACT DISC - READ-ONLY MEMORY, SECTOR, SYNCHRONIZATION.

synchronization   pattern. In   communications, a distinctive pattern in a transmitted waveform that is used to establish synchronization. (Philips).

synchronization   pulses. In   electronics, pulses sent to receiving equipment, by transmitting units to keep the two units in step. *Synonymous with* SYNC PULSES.

synchronization signals. In optical media, real-time software interrupts in an interactive compact disc system. They are often generated by a device driver during hardware interrupt processing when a defined condition has been met. (Philips). *See* COMPACT DISC – INTERACTIVE, DRIVER, HARDWARE INTERRUPT, SOFTWARE INTERRUPT, SYNCHRONIZATION.

synchronizer. In audiovisual aids, a single-function control device. It may receive a signal from another device (e.g. a tape recorder) and perform a single control action (e.g. select a new slide). If used in conjunction with a programmer, more complex control functions may be performed with the synchronizer informing the programmer when the next control action is to be undertaken. *See* PROGRAMMER.

synchronous.   Pertaining to two or more processes that require common physical occurrences (e.g. timing pulses for their operation). *Compare* ASYNCHRONOUS. *Synonymous with* SYNC.

synchronous computer.   A computer in which each event is constrained to wait upon the arrival of a timing signal. *Compare* ASYNCHRONOUS COMPUTER.

synchronous data link control.   (SDLC) In data communications, IBM's data link control protocol for System Network Architecture. It is a discipline for managing synchronous, code-transparent, serial-by-bit information transfer over a link. SDLC conforms to subsets of the advanced data link control procedures of ANSI and the high-level data link control of the ISO. *Compare* BINARY SYNCHRONOUS COMMUNICATIONS. *See* ADVANCED DATA COMMUNICATIONS CONTROL PROCEDURE, ANSI, HIGH-LEVEL DATA LINK CONTROL, PROTOCOL, SERIAL TRANSMISSION, SYNCHRONOUS TRANSMISSION, TRANSPARENT.

synchronous data network.   In data communications, a network in which the timing of all network components is controlled by a single timing source.

synchronous idle character.   In data communications, a transmission control character used by data terminal equipment for synchronism or synchronous correction, particularly when no other character is being transmitted. *See* DATA TERMINAL EQUIPMENT, SYNCHRONOUS DATA NETWORK.

synchronous modem.   In data communications, a modem with an internal clock, which produces a continuous stream of data at a fixed transmission rate. Synchronization is required at the bit, byte and message level. *See* MODEM, SYNCHRONOUS TRANSMISSION.

synchronous sound.   In filming, audio signals that are synchronized with the visual image.

synchronous stream cipher.   In data security, a stream cipher in which the next state of the cryptographic bit stream depends only upon the previous state and not upon the input. *See* CRYPTOGRAPHIC BIT STREAM, OUTPUT FEEDBACK, STREAM CIPHER.

synchronous time division multiplexing.   *Compare* STATISTICAL TIME DIVISION MULTIPLEXING. *Synonymous with* TIME DIVISION MULTIPLEXING.

synchronous transmission.   In data communications, a transmission method in which each bit is transmitted according to a given time sequence. It can provide a higher bit rate than asynchronous transmission, but requires that the receiver and transmitter maintain exact synchronization over an extended period. *Compare* ASYNCHRONOUS TRANSMISSION. *See* BIT RATE.

sync pulses.   *Synonymous with* SYNCHRONIZATION PULSES.

sync tip frequency.   In video recording, the frequency of the recorded frequency-modulated signal corresponding to the television synchronization pulse. During synchronization pulses the voltage level of the video signal is at a minimum and thus the synchronization tip frequency is the lowest frequency of the recorded frequency-modulated signal. *See* BLACK LEVEL, FREQUENCY MODULATION, SYNCHRONIZATION PULSES, WHITE LEVEL.

syndetic.   (1) In library science, having entries connected by cross-references. (2) In library science, coordination of two or more related documents.

synonym.   A word denoting the same thing as another but suitable in a different context. *Compare* HOMOGRAPH.

synoptic.   In library science, a concise publication in a journal which presents the key ideas and results of a full-length article.

syntactic error.   In programming, a programming error in which the statement does not conform to the syntax of the language. Such errors are detected and reported in the translation process. *See* SYNTAX, TRANSLATOR.

syntax. (1) The interrelationship of characters or groups of characters independent of their meaning, interpretation or use. (2) In programming, the grammatical rules governing the use of a language.

syntax-directed editor. In programming, a text editor used for the development of programs in a given language. The editor checks the syntax of the program as it is entered, as would a compiler, and gives an early feedback of syntax errors (e.g. the use of a variable name that has not been previously declared). Some syntax editors provide interactive assistance in the development of the program. For example, the user may be provided with a template of program statements which both decreases typing effort and guides the user to forming the statements in the correct syntax. *See* COMPILER, SOFTWARE TOOL, SYNTAX.

synthesis. The building up of separate elements.

synthesis parameters. In audio, the parameters used to regenerate audio information from data stored in a compressed or encoded format (e.g. interactive compact disc). (Philips). *See* CD-I DIGITAL AUDIO.

synthesized-speech quality. In optical media, the fifth and lowest sound quality in interactive compact disc systems; artificially generated speech using phonetic coding. (Philips). *Compare* CD-DA QUALITY, COMPACT DISC – DIGITAL AUDIO, HI-FI QUALITY, MID-FI QUALITY, SPEECH QUALITY. *See* AUDIO QUALITY LEVEL, PHONETIC CODING. *Synonymous with* PHONETIC SPEECH.

SYSGEN. *See* SYSTEM GENERATION.

SYSOP. In applications, systems operator: the operator of a bulletin board who is responsible for the nature of the information provided. *See* BULLETIN BOARD.

system authentication. In data security, the verification of the validity of the system to which access was gained and to which

classified information is to be transferred. *See* MASQUERADING.

system feedback. *See* FEEDBACK.

system generation. (SYSGEN) In computing, a procedure that allows the user to customize the characteristics of an operating system to match the hardware available, and the potential software application programs, that will run under the operating system. *See* APPLICATION PROGRAM.

system integrity. In computer security, the state that exists when there is complete assurance that under all conditions an automatic data-processing system is based on the logical correctness and reliability of the operating system, the logical completeness of the hardware and software that implement the protection mechanisms and data integrity. (FIPS). *See* AUTOMATIC DATA-PROCESSING SYSTEM, DATA INTEGRITY.

system library. In computing, the collection of files and data sets in which the various sections of the operating system are held. *See* DATA SET, OPERATING SYSTEM.

System Network Architecture. (SNA) In data communications, IBM's network architecture for distributed data processing. It allows any distributed system to access any host processor in the network through multisystem networking facilities. It also provides the architecture for distribution between multiple processors, as well as between one or more processors and remote intelligent communication systems. *Compare* OPEN SYSTEM INTERCONNECTION, PROCESSOR INTERCONNECTION. *See* DISTRIBUTED DATA PROCESSING, MULTISYSTEM NETWORKING.

system penetration. In computer security, a violation or circumvention of operating system safeguards. *See* OPERATING SYSTEM, PENETRATION.

system program. In programming, a program that provides a service to another program (e.g. a compiler, operating system). *Compare* APPLICATION PROGRAM. *See* COMPILER, OPERATING SYSTEM, PROGRAMMER.

system saboteur. In computer security, a person who deliberately causes an error in the operating system so as to render it at least unreliable. *See* OPERATING SYSTEM.

systems analysis. The analysis of an activity or system, often in a commercial context, to determine if and how the system may be improved using computer systems. *See* FEASIBILITY STUDY, STRUCTURED SYSTEMS ANALYSIS.

system software. In programming, programs that form part of a computer operating system or its support utilities (e.g. text editors, compilers, interpreters, assemblers, linkage editors and file management programs). (Philips). *See* ASSEMBLER, COMPILER, EDITOR, INTERPRETER, LINKAGE EDITOR, SOFTWARE TOOL.

system text. In optical media, an interactive or read-only memory compact disc message processed by the operating system without the need to load and process any special text-processing application program. (Philips). *See* COMPACT DISC – INTERACTIVE, COMPACT DISC – READ-ONLY MEMORY, OPERATING SYSTEM.

System X. In data communications, a family of digital switching systems developed by British Telecom to provide the next generation of telephone services, handling voice and data over a single line. *See* INTEGRATED SERVICES DIGITAL NETWORK.

SYSTRAN. In machine translation, translation system; a widely used fully automatic machine translation system providing translation between pairs of languages — English, French, Russian and Spanish. *Compare* EUROTRA.

T

T. *See* TERA.

T1. *See* T CARRIER.

T2. *See* T CARRIER.

T4. *See* T CARRIER.

TA. *See* TERMINAL ADAPTOR.

tab. (1) In printing, a preset point on a line at which printing stops. (2) In peripherals, a preset point on a line to which a cursor or printing unit is automatically moved. *See* TABULATION.

table. In data structures, a data array organized so that each element can be located by one or two arguments. *See* ARRAY, LOOK-UP TABLE, SYMBOL TABLE.

table look-up. *See* LOOK-UP TABLE.

table of contents. (TOC) In optical media, information on a compact disc defining the sequential number, start, length and end times of track, together with their type (i.e. digital audio or data). The TOC is contained in the Q subcode channel of the lead-in area of all compact discs. (Philips). *Compare* SUPER TABLE OF CONTENTS. *See* COMPACT DISC, Q CHANNEL, SUBCODE CHANNEL, TRACK.

tablet. *See* DIGITIZING TABLET.

tabloid. In printing, a page half the size of broadsheet. (Desktop). *Compare* BROADSHEET.

tab memory. In word processing, a facility that stores and recalls details of tab stops. *See* TAB, TABULATION.

tabular setting. In printing, text set in columns such as timetables. (Desktop).

tabulation. (1) In printing, the action of automatically moving a printing head to a specified position on a line. (2) To produce a table.

tabulation markers. In peripherals, symbols used to designate protected fields of a visual display or to perform tabulation setting functions. *See* PROTECTED FIELD, TABULATION.

tachistoscope. In visual aids, a device for displaying images or text for brief intervals of time, usually a fraction of a second.

tachometer lock. In recording, a condition in which the tach pulses from a controlled motor arrive in a required relationship with a set of reference pulses. This condition ensures that the reading head follows the same the track, at the same rate, as the original recording head. *See* TACH PULSE.

tach pulse. In recording, a pulse derived from the rotation of a motor shaft. The pulse is produced optically, magnetically or mechanically whenever a given point on the shaft rotates past a fixed point. *See* TACHOMETER LOCK.

TACS. In communications, Total Access Communications System; the standard adopted by the UK government for the cellular radio system. *See* CELLULAR RADIO.

tactile feedback. The use of sense of touch to receive information. *See* BRAILLE MARKS.

tag. (1) In programming, a portion of an instruction. (2) In programming, one or more characters attached to a group of data providing information about the group.

tail. (1) In data structures, a specified data item that indicates the end of a list. *See* LIST.

(2) In data communications, a series of codes used to denote the end of a message. (3) In filming, the end of a film. (4) In printing, the bottom of a book.

take. (1) In printing, a unit of text. It may be one portion of copy taken from a longer piece of matter to be set that is shared among several typesetters. *See* COPY, MATTER, PHOTOTYPESETTING. (2) In filming, a shot or the number of times that a shot has been taken.

take back. In printing, a proof instruction to a printer to take back a part of a line, a whole line or number of lines of type to a previous page or column. *Compare* TAKE IN, TAKE OVER. *See* PROOF.

take in. In printing, an instruction to a printer, on a proof or manuscript, to take in added copy. *Compare* TAKE BACK, TAKE OVER. *See* COPY, PROOF.

take over. In printing, a proof instruction to a printer to take a line or number of lines of type over to the next page or column. *Compare* TAKE BACK, TAKE IN. *See* PROOF.

talkback. In television, a speaker system providing communication between a control room and a television studio.

tamper-resistant module. (TRM) In data security, a device in which sensitive information such as a cryptographic key is stored and sensitive processing is performed. The device has one or more sensors to detect physical attacks, by an adversary trying to gain access to the stored information, in which case the data is immediately destroyed. *See* KEY. *Synonymous with* SECURE MODULE, SECURITY MODULE.

tandem exchange. In communications, a telephone switching office that handles traffic between local exchanges. *Compare* TOLL CENTRE. *See* LOCAL EXCHANGE.

tandem switching. In communications, the use of an intermediate switch or switches to interconnect circuits from the switch of one serving central office to the switch of a second serving central office in the same exchange area. *See* CENTRAL OFFICE, TANDEM EXCHANGE.

tank recorder. In recording, a continuous loop recording system.

tape cartridge. *See* MAGNETIC TAPE CARTRIDGE.

tape counter. In recording, a device that indicates the length of tape that has passed over the magnetic heads. *See* HEAD.

tape deck. (1) *Synonymous with* MAGNETIC TAPE TRANSPORT. (2) In recording, a tape transport mechanism, read/write heads and preamplifier electronics. It is designed to act as a tape recorder with an external sound system. *See* TAPE TRANSPORT.

tape drive. *Synonymous with* MAGNETIC TAPE TRANSPORT.

tape guides. In recording, rollers or posts that position the tape correctly along its path to the tape drive. *See* TAPE DRIVE.

tape library. In computing, a secure room with controlled environmental conditions. It is used to store computer magnetic tapes. *See* MAGNETIC TAPE.

tape memory. In memory systems, secondary storage in the form of magnetic tape. (Philips). *See* AUXILIARY STORAGE, MAGNETIC TAPE.

tape recorder. In recording, an electronic mechanical device to record information on magnetic tape for instant playback. *See* MAGNETIC TAPE. *Synonymous with* MAGNETIC TAPE RECORDER.

tape slide. In audiovisual aids, a 35-mm projector that can be synchronized to a magnetic tape commentary.

tape streamer. In memory systems, a magnetic tape transport designed primarily for reading or writing continuous streams of data, as in backup operations. It is mechanically simpler and hence is cheaper than start/stop units. *See* MAGNETIC TAPE TRANSPORT.

tape timer. In recording, a device that measures the length of tape transported between two reels, usually calibrated in playing time. *See* MAGNETIC TAPE.

tape transport. *Synonymous with* MAGNETIC TAPE TRANSPORT.

target. (1) In micrographics, information photographed on a microfilm preceding or following the associated document. Such information is used for technical or bibliographic control. (2) In television, the light receptive area of the camera tube.

target language. (TL) (1) In programming. *Synonymous with* OBJECT LANGUAGE. (2) In machine translation, the language to which the translation is to be made. *Compare* SOURCE LANGUAGE.

target program. *Synonymous with* OBJECT PROGRAM.

tariff. In communications, the published set of rates, rules and regulations relevant to the equipment and services provided by a telecommunications common carrier. *See* COMMON CARRIER.

TASI. *See* TIME ASSIGNMENT SPEECH INTERPOLATION.

task. In programming, essentially an application program, but it need not be a fully fledged program. It may be a subroutine or subprogram called by an application program for its own use. *See* APPLICATION PROGRAM, SUBPROGRAM, SUBROUTINE.

TBDF. *See* TRANSBORDER DATA FLOW.

T carrier. In communications, a hierarchy of Bell Telephone digital communication systems designated T1, T2 and T4.

TCB. *See* TRUSTED COMPUTING BASE.

T channel. In optical media, one of the eight compact disc subcode channels (P–W). At present it is only allocated to compact disc graphics. (Philips). *See* COMPACT DISC, SUBCODE CHANNEL.

TCSEC. Trusted computer system evaluation criteria. *See* ORANGE BOOK.

TDF. *See* TRANSBORDER DATA FLOW.

TDM. *See* TIME DIVISION MULTIPLEXING.

TDMA. *See* TIME DIVISION MULTIPLE ACCESS.

TDS. *See* TRANSACTION DRIVEN SYSTEM.

TE. In communications, an integrated services digital network terminal that may be a digital telephone, multifunctional workstation, analog telephone, facsimile unit, teletex workstation, etc. *See* DIGITAL TELEPHONE, FACSIMILE, INTEGRATED SERVICES DIGITAL NETWORK, TE1, TE2, TELETEX.

TE2. In communications, an item of equipment that can perform a terminal function in an integrated services digital network (ISDN) system (e.g. computer terminal, facsimile unit, etc.) which conforms to the appropriate X- or V-series of recommendations of CCITT, but does not conform to the I-series requirements of ISDN and therefore requires a terminal adaptor for connection to the network. *Compare* TE1. *See* FACSIMILE, INTEGRATED SERVICES DIGITAL NETWORK, I-SERIES RECOMMENDATIONS OF CCITT, TERMINAL ADAPTOR, V-SERIES RECOMMENDATIONS OF CCITT, X-SERIES RECOMMENDATIONS OF CCITT.

team documentation. A procedure for producing complex documentation (e.g. for a new technological product) in which engineers, technical writers and marketing specialists operate in the context of a common database and make complementary contributions to the documentation. *See* HIERARCHICAL DOCUMENT DESIGN.

tearing. In television, a distortion of image produced by a lack of sweep synchronization. *See* SWEEP.

tear-me-open. *Synonymous with* SHRINK-WRAPPED LICENCE.

technical security. In data security, equipment, components, devices and associated documentation or other media that pertain to cryptography, or to the securing of telecommunications and automated information systems. (NSDD-145).

technical vulnerability. In computer security, a hardware, firmware or software weakness or design deficiency that leaves an automated information system open to potential exploitation, either externally or internally, thereby resulting in risk or compromise of information, alteration of information or denial of service. Technical vulnerability information, if made available to unauthorized persons, may allow an automated information system to be exploited, resulting in potentially serious damage to national security. (DOD). *See* AUTOMATED INFORMATION SYSTEM, DENIAL OF SERVICE, VULNERABILITY.

technological attack.   In computer security, an attack that can be perpetrated by circumventing or nullifying hardware and software access control mechanisms, rather than by subverting system personnel or other users. (FIPS). *See* ACCESS CONTROL.

Telco patch.   In television, a cable connection linking a television station to the local telephone company.

telebanking.   In applications, a facility that performs client banking transactions over a communication network (e.g. videotex, interactive cable television). *See* HOME BANKING, INTERACTIVE CABLE TELEVISION, SELF-BANKING, VIDEOTEX.

telebooking.   In videotex, the use of viewdata response frames to book theatre tickets, reserve hotel accommodation, make travel arrangements, etc. *Compare* TELE-SHOPPING. *See* RESPONSE FRAME.

telecast.   In television, a television broadcast.

telecine.   In television, the apparatus used to transmit motion picture films on television.

Telecom Australia.   The Australian telecommunications agency.

Telecom Gold.   In data communications, the British Telecom version of the US Dialcom system which provides a nationwide electronic mail service. Communication is via a packet switch service or the telephone network. Information may also be undertaken with the US Dialcom service. *See* DIALCOM, ELECTRONIC MAIL.

telecommunications.   Essentially communications over a distance. The technology of the transmission may take one of three forms: electrical signals along a conductor; electromagnetic radiation; or light signals passing along an optical fiber. The signal may, in some cases, have the same shape as the originating signal, but in many cases the information to be transmitted modulates a carrier wave. *See* FIBER OPTICS, MODULATION.

telecommuting.   In applications, pertaining to the use of computers and data communications to avoid the necessity of travelling to one's place of work, by working at home.

teleconferencing.   In applications, the use of computer networks and communication systems to enable participation in conferences or joint projects involving close cooperation by workers separated geographically. At one level the participants are supplied with computer terminals, and they intercommunicate, not necessarily simultaneously, over data communication networks. The operation of the system is controlled by a manager, or management system, responsible for the distribution of information to relevant participants.

More sophisticated systems provide video links, voting systems, recording of conference activities, etc. *See* AUDIO TELECONFERENCING.

telecontrol.   In communications, the remote control of devices using a telecommunication link.

Teledata.   In videotex, Norwegian viewdata system. *See* VIEWDATA.

telefax.   In communications, a system that links photocopying machines for the transmission of images. *See* FACSIMILE, OPTICAL SCANNER.

Teleglobe Canada.   In communications, the Crown corporation that handles Canada's overseas telecommunications.

telegraphy.   In communications, a system in which a direct current is interrupted or its polarity is reversed in order to transmit a signal code,

telegroup. In communications, a group of people linked by a teleconferencing system. *See* TELECONFERENCING.

teleinformatic services. In communications, a CCITT term encompassing all record-type non-voice or non-speech telecommunication services (e.g. telex, videotex, facsimile). *See* COMMON CARRIER, FACSIMILE, VIDEOTEX.

telematics. *See* TÉLÉMATIQUE.

télématique. In communications, a French term coined to describe the combination of computers and telecommunication networks.

telemetering. In data communications, the remote metering of domestic utility consumption. *See* TELEMETRY, TELEMONITORING.

telemetry. In data communications, the transmission of signals derived from measuring devices over long distances.

telemetry, tracking and command. (TT&C) In communications, a system providing two-way communication between a satellite and earth station for the monitoring of spacecraft systems and the transmission of instructions for changes to the system.

telemonitoring. In data communications, the remote monitoring of, usually domestic, measuring devices using a telecommunication link (e.g. reading electricity meters). *See* TELEMETERING.

Telenet. In data communications, Telenet Communication Corp.; a US packet-switching transmission service. *See* PACKET SWITCHING.

teleordering. In publishing, an automated method for bookseller purchasing. Booksellers enter orders for books, using international standard book number (ISBN) identification, into an intelligent terminal during the day. At the end of the working day a central minicomputer automatically dials up these terminals, over the telephone network, collects the details of orders and stores the orders in backing storage. This information is then transferred to a mainframe computer, where they are processed into a format suitable for the publishers. The minicomputer returns a confirmation or otherwise, for each order to the bookseller terminal, where it is stored and printed out the following day. *Compare* TELESHOPPING.

Telepak. In communications, a US leased channel offered by Western Union and telephone companies providing broadband, voice- and subvoice-grade channels. *See* BROADBAND, SUBVOICE-GRADE CHANNEL, VOICE-GRADE CHANNEL.

telephone exchange. *Synonymous with* CENTRAL OFFICE.

telephone frequency. *Synonymous with* VOICE BAND.

telephone intrusion. In computer security, the intrusion into a computer system by dial-up access; a common form of attack by hackers. Such attacks have increased in recent years due to (a) facilities of dial-up networks, (b) availability of penetration equipment, (c) intruder expertise and (d) bulletin boards.

Increases in telephone network facilities in recent years have allowed intruders to dial directly into computer systems from many parts of the world permitting, for example, intruders in the Middle East and Europe to dial up computers in the USA. The decreasing cost and increasing power of personal computers and modems allow even teenagers to acquire sophisticated intrusion equipment. Hackers sometimes display an extremely high level of technical expertise, and pirate bulletin boards allow such hackers to disseminate their knowledge, acquired passwords, intrusion software, etc. *See* BULLETIN BOARD, CALL BACK, PORT PROTECTION DEVICE, SECURITY MODEM.

telephone repeater. A combination of amplifiers and associated equipment to compensate for the attenuation of voice signals along a telephone line. *See* REPEATER.

telephone scrambler. *See* VOICE SCRAMBLING.

telephone set. In communications, a set of equipment comprising telephone transmitter, telephone receiver, switch hook, dialing unit and associated components.

telephone tap. In communications security, an electronic listening device. *See* ELECTRONIC LISTENING DEVICE.

telephony. In communications, a system for the transmission of speech or other signals coded onto audio frequency signals.

telephotography. In communications, a US term for the transmission of news photographs by facsimile. *See* FACSIMILE.

telephoto lens. In photography, a long-focal-length, narrow-angle view lens used for shots of distant objects.

telepoint. In communications, an advanced concept for the extension of public call box facilities. A telepoint would act effectively as a base unit for portable telephones carried by members of the public. It would be installed in streets, public buildings, airports, etc., allowing anyone carrying a portable telephone to make an outgoing call. *See* CORDLESS TELEPHONE, UPT.

teleport. In communications, a high-technology centre serviced with state-of-the-art communication facilities. *See* STATE OF THE ART.

teleprocessing. (1) In data communications, an information transmission system that combines telecommunications, automatic data-processing systems and man–machine interface equipment for the purpose of interacting and functioning as an integrated whole. (FIPS). *See* AUTOMATIC DATA-PROCESSING SYSTEM, TELECOMMUNICATIONS. (2) In data communications, data processing combined with telecommunications (e.g. the use of a telephone network to connect a remote terminal to a computer or to interconnect two computers).

telepublishing. *Synonymous with* ELECTRONIC PUBLISHING.

telerecording. (TVR) In television, a method of recording a television broadcast by directly filming the image on the cathode ray tube screen.

Telesat. In communications, the Canadian communications satellite organization. It was responsible for the world's first domestic telecommunications satellite. *See* ANIK, COMMUNICATIONS SATELLITE SYSTEM.

teleservice. In communications, an integrated service digital network service that provides more facilities than bearer services (e.g. videotex, teletex, facsimile, stereo program sound). *Compare* BEARER SERVICE. *See* FACSIMILE, TELETEX, VIDEOTEX.

teleshopping. In applications, the use of a domestic terminal (e.g. viewdata) to order goods from a supplier. *Compare* TELEBOOKING, TELEORDERING. *See* VIEWDATA. *Synonymous with* ONLINE SHOPPING.

telesoftware. (TSW) In videotex, the transmission of software to an intelligent viewdata or teletext terminal, or to a microcomputer programmed to emulate a videotex terminal. *See* SOFTWARE, TELETEXT, VIEWDATA.

Telestar. In communications, a US series of geostationary communications satellites. *See* GEOSTATIONARY SATELLITE.

Télésystémes–Questel. *See* QUESTEL.

Télétel. The French public videotex service.

teletex. In data communications, an international business correspondence service defined by CCITT and offered by common carriers. The terminals used are primarily sophisticated electronic typewriters and word processors. *See* CCITT, COMMON CARRIER.

teletext. In videotex, a method of transmitting information stored on a computer to domestic television sets suitably adapted. In broadcast services the data signals are transmitted in conjunction with normal television programs. *Synonymous with* BROADCAST VIDEOTEX.

teletext decoder. In videotex, a unit for retrieval and display of teletext pages from a broadcast signal. (Philips). *Compare* TELE-TEXT ENCODER. *See* TELETEXT.

teletext encoder. In videotex, a unit for superimposing teletext information on a television signal before broadcasting. (Philips). *Compare* TELETEXT DECODER. *See* TELE-TEXT.

teletypewriter. In communications, a typewriter device capable of transmitting and receiving alphanumeric information over communication lines. *See* ALPHANUMERIC.

television. In communications, the electronic transmission of pictures and accompanying sound.

television camera. An optical and electronic apparatus for translating an optical image into electrical signals suitable for transmission. *See* COMPOSITE COLOUR VIDEO SIGNAL, PICKUP TUBE, TELEVISION RECEIVER.

television cut-off. In filming, the limitation in the area of a film frame when televised. *See* TELEVISION SAFE ACTION AREA.

television game. *Synonymous with* VIDEO GAME.

television mask. In filming, a mask used on a viewfinder, or on material to be filmed, that indicates the television safe action area. *See* TELEVISION SAFE ACTION AREA.

television monitor. A device that displays television pictures received from a recorder, camera or closed circuit system. It has neither a sound system nor the facilities to receive broadcast signals. *Compare* TELEVISION RECEIVER.

television projector. *See* PROJECTION TELEVISION.

television receive-only. (TVRO) In communications, a ground station used for the reception of satellite television programs. Satellite communications now provide direct-broadcast satellite facilities for the domestic viewer giving access to television programs in areas that have hitherto had either poor terrestrial reception, or none at all, and providing viewers with a massive choice of programs on a free or subscription basis.

The essential components of a TVRO system are a dish antenna, low-noise amplifier, downconverter, satellite receiver, channel selector, radio frequency (RF) modulator and television receiver. The size of the antenna depends upon the frequency band employed by the satellite transponder; C band frequencies require dish antennae 8–12 feet in diameter as compared with the 2–6 foot diameter antenna used with the higher-frequency Ku band systems. The dish antenna serves two purposes: (a) it collects the extremely weak satellite signal incident upon its surface area and focuses it at the feedhorn position; (b) it shields the feedhorn from extraneous noise signals generated by the earth. The feedhorn is located at the focal point of the antenna, it collects the concentrated, but still weak, satellite signal

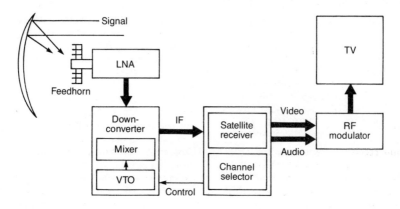

television receive only

and passes it to the low noise amplifier (LNA) which amplifiers the input signal, which is less than 1 microvolt, by a factor of the order of 100 000. An important characteristic of this amplifier is that it minimizes the introduction of noise signals into the early stages of amplification, hence its name.

The output of the LNA is then fed to the downconverter where the signal is converted to a lower intermediate frequency (IF) by mixing it with a signal generated by a voltage-tuned oscillator (VTO), and by filtering out other frequencies produced by the mixing process. The intermediate frequency is constant for all received satellite signals. The particular satellite frequency required by the user is entered into the channel selector, which then adjusts the VTO frequency so that the result of the mixing process is at the intermediate frequency. The use of a constant intermediate frequency, irrespective of the received satellite signal, simplifies the design of the succeeding amplifier stages. The VTO frequency is adjusted by a DC voltage fed from the channel selector.

The IF signal, centred around 70 MHz, is then fed to the satellite receiver, where it is further amplified and filtered before being input to the discriminator. The video and audio signals are extracted from the IF signal in the discriminator, and these two signals pass into the RF modulator.

The function of the RF modulator is to convert the composite video and audio signals into the same form as terrestrially transmitted television signals, so that they may fed into the television set antenna socket. It is also possible to use the video and audio output signals from the satellite receiver to drive separate video monitor and stereo amplifier systems giving enhanced image and sound. *See* C BAND, COMMUNICATIONS SATELLITE SYSTEM, DISH ANTENNA, DISCRIMINATOR, DOWNCONVERTER, FEEDHORN, FOCAL POINT, GROUND STATION, INTERMEDIATE FREQUENCY, KU BAND, LOW-NOISE AMPLIFIER, TRANSPONDER, VOLTAGE-TUNED OSCILLATOR.

television receiver. A device for receiving and reproducing both pictures and sound from broadcast television or modulated cable system signals. *Compare* TELEVISION MONITOR.

television receiver/monitor. A device that can be used to display both broadcast and closed circuit television signals. *See* TELEVISION MONITOR, TELEVISION RECEIVER.

television safe action area. The area of a frame of film which will not be cropped during transmission by television. *See* SAFETY AREA.

television scan. A regular series of horizontal scanning lines on a television screen. The total scan is normally performed in two stages, with the second set of scan lines interlacing the first. *See* INTERLACE, RASTER SCAN, SCANNING LINE, SWEEP, VIDEO STANDARDS.

television tube. A television tube accepts an electrical signal and produces a corresponding visual image. The tube is effectively a cathode ray tube with scanning circuits that cause the spot to trace out a series of horizontal lines across the tube. The signal corresponding to the brightness of the image is fed to the electron gun, thus varying the intensity of the beam striking the phosphor screen. In colour tubes there are three guns corresponding to the red, green and blue signals. Each gun strikes a corresponding phosphor dot on the screen to produce the appropriate colour. *Compare* PICKUP TUBE. *See* CATHODE RAY TUBE, GUN, PHOSPHOR DOTS, SHADOWMASK, TELEVISION SCAN.

telewriting. In communications, a technique that enables the simultaneous transmission of voice and handwritten information over the telephone network. *See* ELECTRONIC BLACKBOARD, SKETCHPHONE.

telex. (TX) In communications, teletypewriter exchange service; an automatic dial-up teletypewriter switching service provided by common carriers. *See* COMMON CARRIER, TELETYPEWRITER.

Telidon. Canadian videotex service that uses alphageometric coding. *See* ALPHAGEOMETRIC, VIDEOTEX.

tempest proofing. In communications security, the prevention of undesirable radiation emission from a computer system which might otherwise enable an eavesdropper to record confidential information. Electromagnetic emission can escape by a variety of routes, and to eliminate this risk source suppression and encapsulation are used, together with shielding of all cables. Fiber optic cables do not radiate electromagnetic radiation. *Compare* SHIELDING EFFECTIVENESS. *See* CONDUCTIVE SHIELDING, FIBER OPTICS, VAN ECK PHENOMENON.

template matching. (1) In computer graphics, an image-processing technique that compares the parts of the image held in computer memory with patterns of candidate objects. *Compare* FEATURE ANALYSIS. *See* IMAGE PROCESSING, MACHINE VISION. (2) In office systems, a technique used in optical scanners in which the binary pattern of an image of an alphanumeric character is matched against font patterns held in programmable read-only memories. *Compare* FONT-INDEPENDENT, FONT-SPECIFIC. *See* ALPHANUMERIC, FONT, OPTICAL SCANNER, PROGRAMMABLE READ-ONLY MEMORY.

tempo generator. In man–machine interfaces, a component of a music synthesizer that determines the rate at which a composition is stepped from one note to the next. It comprises an oscillator with a frequency adjustable from 0.25 to 15 Hz. The oscillator triggers a monostable multivibrator, and the output pulse signals the microprocessor that the next note is to be played. *Compare* ADSR. *See* MONOSTABLE, MUSIC SYNTHESIZER.

temporal separation. *See* ISOLATION ENFORCEMENT.

ten pitch. *Synonymous with* PICA.

ten's complement. In mathematics, the decimal number resulting from the subtraction of a number from the next highest integral power of 10 (e.g. the ten's complement of 69 is $100 - 69 = 31$). *Compare* NINE'S COMPLEMENT, ONE'S COMPLEMENT, TWO'S COMPLEMENT.

tera. (1) One-million-million, eg. 10 to the power 12. (2) In backing storage, eg. 2 to the power 40 (i.e. 1 009 511 627 776).

terahertz. In communications, a frequency of one-million megahertz.

term. (1) The smallest part of an expression to which a value may be assigned. (2) In library science, a label applied to a group of items in a record enabling the items to be retrieved by that label. *See* DESCRIPTOR, HEADING, INDEX. (3) A word or expression that has a precise meaning, in some uses, or is peculiar to a science, art, profession or subject.

term bank. In databases, a database of terms for specialized vocabularies, stored on a computer, that can provide an online service and from which mono-, bi- and multilingual dictionaries can be produced, as well as a range of glossaries and word lists. A facility that can be employed in machine-aided translation, but monolingual term banks also have applications areas (e.g. by standards organizations). *See* MACHINE TRANSLATION. *Synonymous with* TERMINOLOGICAL DATA BANK.

terminal. (1) In peripherals, an input/output device for transmitting and receiving data on a communication line. (2) In communications, a point in the system where information can be transmitted or received. (3) In electronics, a point for the connection to an electrical unit.

terminal adaptor. (TA) In communications, an device that converts a data circuit terminating equipment/data terminal equipment interface to the integrated services digital network (ISDN) S interface. The adaptors are required when users interconnect equipment not conforming to ISDN interfaces to an ISDN system. *See* DATA CIRCUITING TERMINATING EQUIPMENT, DATA TERMINAL EQUIPMENT, INTEGRATED SERVICES DIGITAL NETWORK, S INTERFACE, TE2.

terminal authentication device. In computer security, a two-end device designed to authenticate a specific user terminal. Matching pairs of devices are inserted in the communication channel. For example, one is installed between the terminal and modem, and the other is attached to the host computer port. The host end device generates challenges to the unit connected to the terminal. *See* CHALLENGE/RESPONSE, TELEPHONE INTRUSION, TWO-END DEVICE.

terminal controller. *Synonymous with* CLUSTER CONTROL UNIT.

terminal emulation. In distributed processing, the addition of dedicated software and hardware to a personal computer so that it imitates the essential characteristics of a mainframe terminal. It may be realized by using a special add-in board connected to the microcomputer bus or by an externally connected protocol converter. *Compare* SOFTWARE PROTOCOL CONVERTER. *See* BUS, PROTOCOL CONVERTER, TERMINAL.

terminal handler. In data communications, a part of a data network that services simple character stream terminals.

terminal identification. In computer security, the means used to establish the unique identification of a terminal by an automatic data-processing system. (FIPS). *See* AUTOMATIC DATA-PROCESSING SYSTEM.

terminal identity. In videotex, codes transmitted by a viewdata terminal to the host computer to establish the identity, and hence authorization, of the user. *See* VIEWDATA.

terminal interface. In peripherals, the codes and hardware used to control an input/output device or terminal.

terminal port. In data communications, the functional unit of a node which provides the means by which data enters and leaves the network.

terminal thief. *Synonymous with* HACKER.

terminological data bank. *Synonymous with* TERM BANK.

ternary. A system with three possible states. *Compare* BINARY.

tertiary colour. In printing, a colour produced by the combination of two secondary colours. *See* SECONDARY COLOUR.

test. In banking, a code in a message between sender and receiver used to validate the source of a message that may also validate certain elements of the message such as amount, date and sequence. The code is the result of a bilaterally agreed upon method of calculation. (ANSI). *See* MESSAGE AUTHENTICATION.

test data. (1) In optical media, interactive compact disc data related to the presentation of text as opposed to audio, video or computer data. (Philips). *See* COMPACT DISC – INTERACTIVE. (2) In computer security, data prepared solely to test the accuracy of the programming and logic of a system. Test data is used to prove each branch and combination of branches of a program and should, therefore, be as comprehensive as possible. Deliberate errors should be introduced into the test data, such as inserting alphabetic characters in numeric fields to ensure that these errors are detected by the program. At the end of the test run the output is checked against expected results of processing the data to see if they are compatible. *See* PROOF OF PROGRAM CORRECTNESS.

test pattern. In television, a pattern transmitted by television stations during non-program transmission periods. The pattern may contain information on the time of the next program and can also be used by technicians to check and adjust receiving equipment.

test program. In programming, a program designed to test a unit or system performance. (Philips). *See* DIAGNOSTICS.

text. (1) In word processing, a set of alphanumeric characters that convey information. (2) In communications, the information content of a message.

text animation. In artificial intelligence, a simple form of expert system in which a reference manual is encoded into a knowledge base so that the user can obtain information on a particular topic, or answer a simple query, by a natural language dialogue or menu interaction. *See* EXPERT SYSTEMS.

text compression. In data communications, the elimination of redundant data (e.g. leading zeros, trailing blanks) from a message. *See* DATA COMPRESSION, HUFFMAN CODE.

text editing. In word processing, the insertion, deletion, movement, correction and copying of stored text. *See* TEXT EDITOR.

text editor. In operating systems, a program that enables a user to modify and copy programs and text files in a versatile manner. Characters and strings can be inserted, modified, deleted and moved throughout the text. In many cases it is possible to locate automatically a specific string and to replace every instance of one string by another. *See* LINE EDITOR, SCREEN EDITOR, SEARCH AND REPLACE.

text fonts. In peripherals, system modules that contain the bit map images of a set of alphanumeric characters. (Philips). *See* ALPHANUMERIC, BIT-MAPPED GRAPHICS, FONT.

text move. In word processing, the ability to select a portion of text from a stored document and move it to a new position in that or another stored document. *See* CUT AND PASTE, TEXT EDITOR. *Synonymous with* BLOCK MOVE.

text processing. *See* WORD PROCESSING.

text reader processor. In communications, a device that is able to accept machine-readable data, usually by optical character recognition, and also with limited processing power. The device may be used to write the processed data for a particular application or to transmit it to another location.

text retrieval. In online information retrieval, a computer-based system in which the user is provided with a printout, or display, of whole, or part of the relevant document, instead of merely references to them. Legal literature was the first field to be covered in this way. *See* FULL-TEXT DATABASE.

text size. *See* COMPOSITION SIZE.

text-to-speech synthesis. In man–machine interfaces, a system that receives stored text and produces the corresponding spoken output. Design of a comprehensive system involves algorithms to cope with the vagaries of English spelling and pronunciation plus the design of sound synthesizers which can successfully mimic the human voice. *See* SPEECH SYNTHESIZER.

text type. *See* COMPOSITION SIZE.

TE1. In communications, an integrated services digital network (ISDN) class of terminal which incorporates all the functions standardized by the CCITT for direct connection to ISDN systems. *Compare* TE2. *See* INTEGRATED SERVICES DIGITAL NETWORK, I-SERIES RECOMMENDATIONS OF CCITT.

The Computer Database. In online information retrieval, a database supplied by Management Contents and dealing with computers and the computer industry.

theoretically secure. In data security, a cryptographic system that is secure even when the cryptanalyst has unlimited time, facilities and funds.

thermal imaging. In television, a camera system that responds to the subject's radiated heat rather than light.

thermal noise. In electronics, random signals produced in electronic components with a power proportional to the component's temperature. *See* NOISE.

thermal printer. In printing, a non-impact printer in which a wax-based ink is melted from a ribbon onto the paper in the form of minute dots. *See* NON-IMPACT PRINTER, PRINTER.

thermography. In printing, a print-finishing process that produces a raised image imitating die stamping. The process takes a previously printed image which, before the ink is dry, is dusted with a resinous powder. The application of heat causes the ink and powder to fuse, and a raised image is formed. (Desktop).

thesaurus. In online information retrieval, a list of standard subject terms, or descriptors, in a particular field of knowledge, that can be used to index documents for retrieval in online searching. A thesaurus usually provides synonym control and demonstrates the relationships between terms. *See* DESCRIPTOR, SYNONYM.

thick film. In electronics, a method of integrated circuit fabrication in which the components are mounted and interconnected on a ceramic substrate. *Compare* THIN FILM. *See* CHIP, INTEGRATED CIRCUIT.

thimble. In printing, an element similar to a daisy wheel, but bent into a cup shape. *Compare* DAISY WHEEL.

thin film. In electronics, a method of integrated circuit fabrication in which thin layers of material are deposited on an insulating base in a vacuum. *Compare* THICK FILM, THIN-FILM MEMORY. *See* CHIP, INTEGRATED CIRCUIT.

thin-film memory. In memory systems, a high-speed random-access memory device. Magnetic dots are deposited in a thin film of insulating material. A grid of read/write heads change, and read, the magnetic state of the dots. *Compare* THICK FILM. *See* RANDOM-ACCESS MEMORY.

thin space. In printing, the thinnest space normally used to separate words or numbers. (Desktop).

thin-window display. In word processing, a single line display of 15–32 characters to prompt an operator or display a section of text. *Synonymous with* PLASMA DISPLAY.

third-generation computer. The generation of computers in which integrated circuits replaced individually wired transistors. They originated in about 1964. *Compare* FIFTH-GENERATION COMPUTER, FIRST-GENERATION COMPUTER, FOURTH-GENERATION COMPUTER, SECOND-GENERATION COMPUTER.

third-generation language. In programming, a advanced high-level language providing facilities such as data abstraction and control of asynchronous processes. Modula 2 and Ada are typical third-generation languages. *Compare* FIRST-GENERATION LANGUAGE, FOURTH-GENERATION LANGUAGE, SECOND-GENERATION LANGUAGE, THIRD-GENERATION COMPUTER. *See* ABSTRACT DATA TYPE, ADA, MODULA 2.

third normal form. (TNF) In databases, a property of a relation in a relational database. A relation is in third normal form if it is in second normal form and every non-prime attribute of the relation is non-transitively dependent upon each candidate key of the relation. In effect this requirement states that each field should only depend upon the primary key and not upon any other fields within the relation. An example of a relation not in third normal form is DEPT-NUMBER, PROJECT-NUMBER, PROJECT-NAME, PROJECT-COMPLETION-DATE with DEPT-NUMBER the key. PROJECT-COMPLETION-DATE is functionally dependent upon PROJECT-NUMBER and, if there is only one project per department, PROJECT-NUMBER is functionally dependent upon the key DEPT-NUMBER. Since a number of projects can have the same completion date there is a transitive dependence between PROJECT-COMPLETION-DATE and the key. A relation that is not in third normal form presents problems in the running of the database (e.g. it would not be possible to store a completion date for a project until the project is assigned to a department). *Compare* FIRST NORMAL FORM, SECOND NORMAL FORM. *See* CANDIDATE KEY, FUNCTIONAL DEPENDENCE, NON-PRIME ATTRIBUTE, NORMAL FORMS, RELATIONAL DATABASE, TRANSITIVE DEPENDENCE.

third-party database. In videotex, a database maintained by an information provider on a separate computer, from the videotex service, but accessible by a gateway link between the two computers. *See* DATABASE, GATEWAY, INFORMATION PROVIDER.

thirty-two sheet. In printing, a poster size measuring 120 x 160 inches (304.8 x 406.4 centimetres). (Desktop). *Compare* EIGHT SHEET, SIXTEEN SHEET.

thrashing. In memory systems, a condition in a virtual storage system where an excessive proportion of central processing unit time is spent in moving data between the main and backing storage. This condition arises if the total amount of memory working space required by the individual active processes is very high in relation to the amount of main memory available. *Compare* SWAPPING. *See* CENTRAL PROCESSING UNIT, PAGING, VIRTUAL STORAGE.

threaded code. In programming, a program produced by a code generator in which the code comprises a series of entry points of routines.

threaded tree. In data structures, a tree in which additional pointers assist in the scan of the tree. *See* POINTER, SCAN, TREE.

threat. In computer security, an aspect of the system environment that, if given an opportunity, could cause a harmful event to occur. *Compare* SAFEGUARD, VULNERABILITY. *See* HARMFUL EVENT.

threat analysis. In data security, the process of subjecting cryptographic operations to a series of hypothetical attacks. *See* CRYPT-ANALYSIS.

three-colour process. In printing and photography, a process that uses all three primary colours. *Compare* FOUR-COLOUR PROCESS. *See* PRIMARY COLOURS. *Synonymous with* TRICHROMATIC SYSTEM.

three-dimensional graphics. In computer graphics, the representation of a three-dimensional image on a cathode ray tube (CRT) screen in a form which gives an impression of three-dimensional imagery. Two-dimensional representation of a three-dimensional image can take either wire frame or solid object form. Wire frame images can provide an illusion of depth by intensity depth cuing, perspective and hidden line removal. Solid objects can be viewed realistically on CRT screens with hidden surface removal, transparency, multiple light sources, texturing and shadowing.
   True three-dimensional effects can be produced with a vibrating varifocal mirror or stereoscopic spectacles. The vibrating varifocal mirror reflects a synchronized CRT screen display, and the mirror can produce a three-dimensional image. Such systems, however, suffer from the usual performance limitations of moving mechanical parts.
   A typical stereoscopic system displays two images alternately at about 30 times a second. One of the images is intended for left eye, giving a appropriate perspective view of the image, and the other is for the right eye. Shutters in the form of glasses worn by the user are synchronized to the display presenting each image to the appropriate eye. *See* CATHODE RAY TUBE, HIDDEN LINE, HIDDEN SURFACE, INTENSITY DEPTH CUE, PERSPECTIVE, SHADING.

three two pulldown. In recording, a means of transferring film shot at 24 frames per second into videodisc format at 30 frames per second (NTSC). The first film frame is exposed on three video fields, and the next film frame is exposed on two fields. *See* ANIMATION, FIELD, FRAME, VIDEODISC, VIDEO STANDARDS.

thresholding. *See* BINARY THRESHOLDING.

throughput. A measure of the amount of useful work performed by a system in a given period of time.

tickler file. In data processing, a control file, usually manual, consisting of items sequenced by age for follow-up purposes. *See* AGING.

Tick-Tack. In machine translation, a software package that runs on microcomputer and provides a building block approach to the machine translation of documents with commonly recurring sentences (e.g. business letters). *See* MACHINE-AIDED TRANSLATION.

tie breaker. In computing, a device that resolves a conflict when two central processing units try simultaneously to access the same peripheral. *See* CENTRAL PROCESSING UNIT, PERIPHERAL.

tied letters. *Synonymous with* LIGATURES.

tie line. *Synonymous with* TIE TRUNK.

TIES. Translators and Interpreters Educational Society.

tie trunk. In communications, a point-to-point communication channel linking private branch exchange systems or switchboards. *See* POINT-TO-POINT, PRIVATE BRANCH EXCHANGE.

tiger team. In computer security, a group of people authorized to test the overall security of a system by 'illicit' entry or other means.

tightly coupled. In computing, pertaining to multiprocessing systems in which the constituent computers are linked together so that they may share one or more resources. *Compare* LOOSELY COUPLED. *See* MULTI-PROCESSING.

tilde. In printing, an accent in the form of a small wavy line, usually over the letter n. *See* ACCENT, SPANISH N.

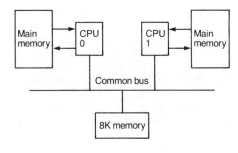

tightly coupled

tile. In computer graphics, a blanked out, or tiled, frame around a window that can hide data on adjoining windows. Overlapped windows do not suffer from this defect, but they may not respond as quickly to user commands. *Compare* OVERLAP. *See* WINDOW.

time address code. In video recording, a digital timing signal recorded on a longitudinal track that provides a display of real time in hours, minutes, seconds and frames. It is used for editing purposes. *See* EDIT.

time assignment speech interpolation. (TASI) In communications, a technique that reassigns a voice channel for the period that a user pauses in speech. *Compare* DIGITAL SPEECH INTERPOLATION.

time base. In electronics, a signal generated to provide an indication of relative timing. In an oscilloscope the time base signal is a waveform that increases linearly to a maximum and then returns rapidly to its reference level, before commencing the next sweep. This signal draws the spot horizontally across the face of the tube for the display of waveforms. In raster scans, the spot is similarly traced across the face of the tube, but in successive horizontal scans the spot is moved vertically down the screen. *See* RASTER SCAN, SWEEP.

time base corrector. In recording, a device that corrects the distortion due to a lack of synchronism between the time base of the recorded signal and that of the playback device. The timing differences are adjusted with the aid of a short-term signal store (e.g. an adjustable delay line). *See* DELAY LINE.

time bomb. In computer security, a variant of the Trojan horse in which malicious code is inserted to be triggered later. *See* TROJAN HORSE.

time-coded page. In teletext, a page in which additional information is added to its normal magazine and page number, thus permitting a number of pages bearing the same magazine and page numbers to be transmitted in sequence. The additional identification is in the form of a four-digit number that may correspond to the time of page transmission. *See* MAGAZINE.

time-dependent password. In computer security, a password that is valid only at a certain time of the day or during a specified interval of time. (FIPS). *See* PASSWORD.

time-derived channel. In data communications, a channel derived by time division multiplexing. *See* TIME DIVISION MULTIPLEXING.

time display. In teletext, the last eight digits of a teletext page header are reserved for clock time, and a receiver may display this information giving a rolling display of current time. *See* PAGE HEADER.

time division multiple access. (TDMA) In communications, a technique whereby groups of users (e.g. several earth stations in a satellite communication system) are allocated time slots to use a common channel employing time division multiplexing techniques. The allocation of frequencies may be made on a fixed or on-demand basis. *Compare* CODE DIVISION MULTIPLE ACCESS, FREQUENCY DIVISION MULTIPLE ACCESS. *See* COMMUNICATIONS SATELLITE SYSTEM, TIME DIVISION MULTIPLEXING.

time division multiplexing. (TDM) In communications, a method of allocating a high-capacity channel to a number of sender recipient pairs. The information from each sender is allocated time intervals in the main channel, and the sections of messages are interleaved, with those from other users at the channel input. The message segments are separated, and the complete messages are reconstructed at the receiving end. The decreasing cost of digital circuitry has rendered time division multiplexing cheaper than frequency division multiplexing, which requires expensive analog filter circuits. However it can only be used for digital signals. Analog signals such as voice must be converted into digital form by pulse code modulation before they can employ this technique. *Compare* FREQUENCY DIVISION MULTIPLEXING, SPACE DIVISION MULTIPLEXING. *See* ANALOG SIGNAL, DIGITAL SIGNAL, PACKET SWITCHING, PULSE CODE MODULATION. *Synonymous with* TIME DIVISION MULTIPLEXING.

time division switching. In data communications, a switching method for time division-multiplexed channels. Data enters a switching stage in one time slot and emerges in another. For switching of pulse code-modulated channels, each time slot contains one coded sample (e.g. eight bits). *Compare* SPACE DIVISION SWITCHING. *See* PULSE CODE MODULATION, TIME DIVISION MULTIPLEXING.

time domain. In electronics, pertaining to the analysis of the effect of a linear circuit on a waveform in terms of time rather than frequency. *Compare* FREQUENCY DOMAIN. *See* WAVEFORM.

time lapse cinematography. In filming, a method of filming processes with invisibly slow movements (e.g. growth of a plant). A greater than normal time interval elapses between the exposure of successive frames. Projection at normal speed then provides an apparent speed up of events.

time lapse recorder. In recording, a video recorder that is operated intermittently to sample video information. It is used for security and surveillance.

time out. (1) In computing, a time interval allotted for certain operations to occur. (2) In computing, a terminal feature that logs off a user if an entry is not made before the end of a specified time interval. *See* LOGOFF.

time redundancy. In reliability, a technique in which a part of a program is used to double check critical computations; either the same subprogram is repeated or a different algorithm is employed. *Compare* PROTECTIVE REDUNDANCY.

time sharing. In computing, a technique that enables a computer to handle simul-

taneous users and peripherals. Each computer operation is performed in sequence, but the high speed of operation, together with the time slice technique, gives the appearance of a simultaneous multiuser service. *See* MULTIPROGRAMMING, TIME SLICE.

time shift viewing. In video recording, the use of a video cassette recorder to replay a television program at a time that is more convenient than the original television broadcast.

time slice. In computing, a non-preemptible interval of processor time allocated to a specific task in a time-shared system. All the tasks receive time slices in rotation until they are completed, thus no one task can monopolize the processor. *See* TIME SHARING.

Times Roman. In printing, a classic typeface designed for the London Times in 1932, noted for its formality and authority. *Compare* AVANTE-GARDE, BOOKMAN, COURIER, HELVETICA, HELVETICA NARROW, NEW CENTURY SCHOOLBOOK, OLDSTYLE, PALATINO, ROMAN, SYMBOL, ZAPF CHANCERY, ZAPF DINGBATS. *See* TYPEFACE.

time study. In office systems, a method for the determination of the optimum method of performing various tasks by a detailed study and analysis of the work content of individual component operations.

timing loop. In programming, a short computer subroutine that produces a precise time delay, usually of the order of milliseconds. *See* SUBROUTINE.

tinny. In recording, an audio output lacking low-frequency components.

tint. In printing, the effect of adding white to a solid colour or of screening a solid area. (Desktop).

T interface. In communications, an integrated services digital network interface between NT1 and NT2 equipment. *Compare* R INTERFACE, S INTERFACE. *See* INTEGRATED SERVICES DIGITAL NETWORK, NT1, NT2.

TIR. *See* TOTAL INTERNAL REFLECTION.

Titan. In videotex, a French viewdata system.

T junction. In electronics, a junction formed to make connection with a cable carrying power or signals.

TL. *See* TARGET LANGUAGE.

TMR. *See* TRIPLE MODULAR REDUNDANCY.

TN. *See* TWISTED NEMATIC.

T network. In electronics, a network comprising three elements interconnected in the shape of a letter T.

TNF. *See* THIRD NORMAL FORM.

TOC. *See* TABLE OF CONTENTS.

TOCTTOU problems. In computer security, time of check to time of use; a class of security problems that can arise from illegal changes, after a check has been performed (e.g. a request to an operating system is checked and found to be valid, but a parameter of the request is then changed before it is performed). *See* ASYNCHRONOUS ATTACKS.

toggle. (1) In distributed processing, to move freely between sessions on a personal computer by depressing a hot key. *See* HOT KEY. (2) In electronics, any device having two stable states. *See* BISTABLE.

token. *See* CONTROL TOKEN.

token bus. In data communications, a bus network in which each node awaits the arrival of a control token before transmitting a message to a downstream node; only one token is on the bus at any one time. *Compare* CARRIER SENSE MULTIPLE ACCESS — COLLISION DETECTION, TOKEN RING. *See* CONTROL TOKEN.

token ring. In data communications, a ring network architecture in which each node awaits the arrival of a control token, from the upstream node, before sending a message towards the next downstream node. Only one token is on the ring at any one time; when a node with a message to send receives a token it transmits its message

followed by the token, which is passed from node to node until it arrives at one with a message for transmission. *Compare* TOKEN BUS. *See* CONTROL TOKEN, LOCAL AREA NETWORK.

toll call. In communications, a telephone call to a connection beyond an exchange boundary.

toll centre. In communications, a switching centre where intercity circuits terminate. Usually one local office in a city is designated the toll centre and is also used for mileage rate measurement. *Compare* TANDEM EXCHANGE. *See* SWITCHING CENTRE. *Synonymous with* TOLL OFFICE, TOLL SWITCHING OFFICE.

toll charge. In communications, a charge for a call outside the local service area of the calling station.

toll office. *Synonymous with* TOLL CENTRE.

toll switching office. *Synonymous with* TOLL CENTRE.

toll switching trunk. In communications, a communication line connecting a local exchange to a toll centre. *See* TOLL CENTRE.

tone. A continuous signal, or sound, of one particular frequency.

tone dialing. *Synonymous with* PUSHBUTTON DIALING.

tone line process. In printing, the process of producing line art from a continuous tone original. (Desktop).

toner. In printing, the material employed to develop a latent image. *See* LASER PRINTER, LATENT IMAGE, XEROGRAPHY.

TOP. In office systems, technical and office protocols; an initiative of a group to computer manufacturers, aimed at the early provision of office systems that can internetwork effectively. The protocol is based upon international standards. *Compare* MAP. *See* OPEN SYSTEMS INTERCONNECTION.

top-down method. A method of designing a system, or computer program, commencing with a simple overall structure, and then successively refining the description of each subcomponent in a similar manner until a detailed structure is obtained. *Compare* BOTTOM-UP METHOD. *See* PROGRAMMING.

TOPIC. In videotex, Teletext Output of Price Information by Computer; the UK Stock Exchange information service. Inputs are received from EPIC, the Stock Exchange information providers, member firm information providers and external information providers, and outputs are available to a nationwide network of viewdata terminals. *See* BIG BANG, EPIC, INFORMATION PROVIDER, SEAQ, VIEWDATA.

top of form. In word processing, a facility on a character printer that automatically advances the paper by one page.

topology. In communications, the form of interconnection of nodes in a network. *See* BUS, NODE, RING, STAR.

total internal reflection. (TIR) In optics, a phenomenon that can occur when light travelling in a medium with relatively high refractive index meets an interface with a medium with a lower refractive index. If the angle of incidence is greater than a given critical angle then the light is not refracted, but is reflected back into the denser

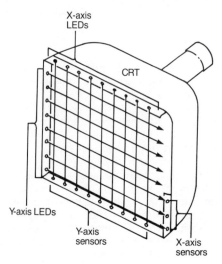

touch screen
Fig. 1. An LCD touch screen.

medium. This phenomenon traps light signals in fiber optic devices and results in their transmission along the fiber. *See* FIBER OPTICS, REFRACTIVE INDEX.

touch pad. *Synonymous with* DIGITIZING TABLET.

touchpanel switch. A switch that operates by capacitance, resistance or physical contact effects and requires no mechanical movement. *See* CAPACITY-ACTIVATED TRANSDUCER.

touchscreen. In peripherals, a pointing device that enables the user to make a selection by touching the screen of a cathode ray tube (CRT). There are three forms of touchscreen: pressure-sensitive, capacitive surface and light beam.

Pressure-sensitive devices comprise two sheets of clear material, separated by a thin air gap, affixed over the CRT screen. The outside sheet is flexible and deforms when pressed with a finger or stylus. Each of the two sheets has either discrete lines or a continuous coating of transparent, thin film conductor deposited onto a non-conductive substrate. When the outer screen is touched the two sheets come into contact, and a conductive path is formed.

When the conducting material is in the form of discrete lines the lines are arranged horizontally on one sheet and vertically on another. Thus the contact affectively closes a unique switch in a grid matrix; the associated touchscreen electronics compute the X,Y-coordinates of the point of contact which are then converted in ASCII code and transmitted to the computer.

The systems using continuous coating of conductive material employ additional circuitry to measure the resistance through the horizontal and vertical paths thus identifying the coordinates of the point of contact. This technique does not require formatted conductor screening and wiring to the discrete conductive lines, but on the other hand the associated electronic circuitry is more complex. The resolution of the pressure-sensitive screen ranges from 256 x 256 to 1024 x 1024.

Pressure-sensitive membranes are subject to fatigue and can be punctured by a sharp stylus. Moreover, penetration of moisture into the air gap can produce fogging.

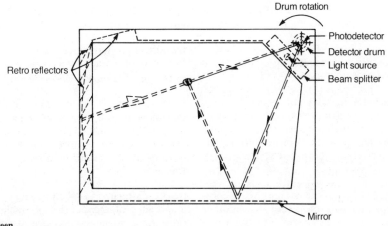

Drum rotation

Photodetector
Detector drum
Light source
Beam splitter

Retro reflectors

Mirror

touch screen
Fig. 2. A single sensor touch screen system.

Capacitive surface systems do not suffer from these diadvantages. In the case of the capacitive surface systems a glass panel is coated with a conductive surface through which phased signals are passed in the horizontal and vertical directions. When the surface is touched with a finger or metal stylus the change in impedance can be measured in a similar manner to that used for the continuous pressure-sensitive screen. However, the variations in the capacitive effects of the stylus or finger inherently limit the resolution to one part in a hundred.

Both the pressure-sensitive and capacitive surface devices involve transparent screens placed over the screen and hence reduce the amount of light transmitted from the device. The light beam systems conventionally use a grid of light beams across the screen. Infrared light-emitting diodes (LED) across the top and one side of the screen send light beams to optical sensors on the opposite sides. The horizontal and vertical beams are interrupted by the user's finger. The optical sensors, which can detect a change in the incident light intensity, provide information on the X,Y-coordinates of the point selected by the user. The light beam optical sensors require compensation for ambient light conditions, and base level readings are taken at regular intervals. The light beam electronics automatically stores these readings and subtracts them from the sensor readings each time the matrix is scanned to detect a break in the beam. The resolution is fixed by the number of light sensors, and a typical system has 40 LED/sensor pairs horizontally and 24 vertically.

A single sensor system has been developed that is less expensive than the grid system. In this case the output from an incandescent screen is optically spread over the screen's surface. The sensor is located in the top right-hand corner and is surrounded by a rotating cylinder with a vertical slit. The screen is surrounded with a frame, and the inside of the bottom part of the frame is coated with a mirror. The inside of the top and left-hand sections of the frame are coated with a material that reflects light back along the same path as the incident beam. As the cylinder around the sensor rotates light is reflected into it either by direct reflection or indirect reflection along a path — bottom mirror (conventional reflection) and top reflecting surface. A finger on the screen thus produces two interruptions to the beam, which are detected by the sensor in one rotation, and the timing of these interruptions provides the necessary information for the calculation of the finger's X,Y-coordinates. *See* AMERICAN STANDARD CODE FOR INFORMATION INTERCHANGE, CAPACITANCE, CATHODE RAY TUBE, IMPEDANCE, LIGHT-EMITTING DIODE, PHOTOSENSOR, POINTING DEVICE, RESISTANCE.

touchtone. In communications, an AT&T term for pushbutton dialing. *See* PUSHBUTTON DIALING.

Toxline. In online information retrieval, a database supplied by National Library of Medicine, Toxicology Information Program, and dealing with biomedicine and toxicology.

TP. *See* TRANSACTION PROCESSING.

TPI. *See* TRACKS PER INCH.

TPS. Transaction-processing system. *See* TRANSACTION PROCESSING.

trace packet. In data communications, a packet that causes a report on each stage of its progress through the network to be transmitted to the network control station. *See* NETWORK CONTROL STATION, PACKET SWITCHING.

trace program. In programming, a program that monitors the actions of another program, or software system. The trace program provides information on the series of actions performed, typically for debugging purposes. The amount of trace information produced may normally be specified by the user (e.g. statement by statement, statements changing the flow of control, changes in the values of specified variables, etc.). *See* DEBUG.

track. (1) In memory systems, a path along which data is recorded, on a continuous or rotational medium (e.g. magnetic tape, magnetic disk). In magnetic disks the data is recorded on a series of circular tracks. *Compare* SECTOR. (2) In optical media, a sequence of contiguous data on a compact disc. The beginning, length, mode and end of the data are defined in the table of contents, which is held in the Q subcode channel of the lead-in area of the disc. The two types of track currently defined are the digital audio compact disc (CD-DA) track according to the CD-DA specification and the data track according to the read-only memory compact disc specification, which is also used in interactive compact discs. In CD-DA the length of a track is related to the playing times (i.e. between 4 seconds and 72 minutes). (Philips). *Compare* SECTOR. *See* COMPACT DISC – DIGITAL AUDIO, COMPACT DISC – INTERACTIVE, COMPACT DISC – READ-ONLY MEMORY, LEAD-IN TRACK, Q CHANNEL, SUBCODE CHANNEL, TABLE OF CONTENTS.

tracker ball. In peripherals, a pointing device that comprises a ball mounted in a box with position sensors. A screen cursor moves at a rate proportional to the speed of ball rotation and in the same direction. *See* POINTING DEVICE. *Synonymous with* ROLLING BALL.

tracking. In peripherals and recording, the following of a track by a readout or pickup device. (Philips). *See* TRACK.

tracking symbol. In computer graphics, a symbol displayed on a screen that indicates the location selected by a corresponding pointing device. *Compare* AIMING SYMBOL. *See* POINTING DEVICE. *Synonymous with* POINTER.

tracks per inch. (TPI) In memory systems, a measure of the density of tracks on an optical or magnetic disk. *See* FLOPPY DISK, HARD DISK, MAGNETIC DISK, OPTICAL DISC, TRACK.

tractor feed. In printing, a feed mechanism for printers comprising a short, continuous belt or chain with teeth that engage in the sprocket holes of continuous stationery. *See* SPROCKET FEED.

traffic. In communications, the signals or messages handled by a communications system.

traffic analysis. (1) In communications security, a form of passive attack in which the intruder observes the source and destination address, frequency and length of messages. *See* TRAFFIC FLOW SECURITY, TRAFFIC PADDING. (2) In communications, a detailed study of a communication system's traffic. It includes a statistical analysis of message headings, receipts and acknowledgements, routings, etc., plus a study of the time variations in the volume of traffic and the type of traffic.

traffic flow security. In communications security, the protection that results from those features in some cryptographic equipment that conceal the presence of valid messages on a communications circuit, usually by causing the circuit to appear busy at all times, or by encrypting the source and destination addresses of valid messages. (FIPS). *See* ENCRYPT, TRAFFIC ANALYSIS, TRAFFIC PADDING.

traffic matrix. In communications, a matrix that records the volume of traffic in a network. The quantity at element (p, q) is a measure of the traffic volume from node p to node q. *See* NODE, TRAFFIC.

traffic padding. In communications security, a technique used to disguise traffic flows. It includes padding messages out to standard lengths with the generation of spurious messages and spurious connections. *See* TRAFFIC ANALYSIS, TRAFFIC FLOW SECURITY.

trailer. (1) In data structures, a label at the end of a magnetic tape giving summary statistics of data recorded. (2) In data structures, a record at the end of a file containing summary information on the constituent data records. *See* FILE, MAGNETIC TAPE, RECORD.

trailer microfiche. In micrographics, a microfiche holding the remaining images of multipage document when the total number of pages exceeds the image area capacity of a single microfiche. *See* MICROFICHE.

trail printer. In word processing, a printer that is shared between work stations.

transaction. In databases, a discrete unit of work. It may involve updating a number of fields in the database, and it must be executed in its entirety to avoid inconsistencies in the data. *See* FIELD.

transaction code. In data processing, a field within a transaction record that designates the nature of the transaction. *See* FIELD, RECORD.

transaction-driven system. (TDS) In computing, a mode of operation in which the arrival of a transaction causes an interrupt of batch-processing activities as resources are diverted to deal with the transaction. *See* BATCH PROCESSING, TRANSACTION PROCESSING.

transaction processing. (TP) In computing, a mode of computer usage in which the user enters data and commands from a remote terminal, often over a communication link. The results of the actions are displayed on the terminal. It has a similar mode of action to multiaccess computing and is often employed when the user is operating with a specific application package. *Compare*

BATCH PROCESSING, MULTIACCESS COMPUTING. *See* ONLINE, TRANSACTION-DRIVEN SYSTEM.

transborder data flow. (TDF) In data communications, the flow of data between countries, or states, and therefore passed from one jurisdiction to another. This represents an area of considerable complexity in the light of differing legislation on data protection, copyright, etc. in the various parts of the world. *See* COPYRIGHT DATA PROTECTION, SOFTWARE PROTECTION, TRANSBORDER RESTRICTIONS.

transborder restrictions. In data communications, regulations concerning the flow of encrypted data across a country's borders. Outside the USA this matter is usually the responsibility of a central government agency, often the PTT. The restrictions may be either: (a) prohibition on the transborder flow of encrypted data; (b) transborder flow of encrypted data is permitted if the cryptographic key is registered with the data protection agency; or (c) no restrictions. The OECD has adopted a minimum set of protection standards that a member country must satisfy described in its publication *Guidelines Governing the Protection of Privacy of Transborder Data Flows of Personal Data*. *See* DATA PROTECTION, TRANSBORDER DATA FLOW.

transceiver. In hardware, a bus driver that can pass data in both directions, hence combining a transmitter and receiver action. *Compare* RECEIVER TRANSMITTER. *See* BUS DRIVER. *Synonymous with* TRANSRECEIVER.

transcoder. In television, a device to convert colour standards, typically from PAL to SECAM, and vice versa. *See* VIDEO STANDARDS.

transcriber. In peripherals, the device that is used to convert the information from a given form of an information-recording system to the data of the computer, and vice versa.

transcription. In office systems, to copy information from one medium to another, or to produce typed copy from a recorded dictation.

Transdoc. An experimental document delivery system supported by the European

Community. It grew out of the Artemis Report and the Adonis project. *See* ADONIS, ARTEMIS.

transducer. In electronics, a device that receives a signal in one physical form and produces an output in another, usually electrical (e.g. a thermocouple produces a voltage proportional to the temperature of the thermocouple junction).

transfer. (1) In programming, to copy a block of information and write it into another part of memory. (2) In programming, to change control. *See* JUMP.

transfer orbit. In communications, an intermediate orbit used in the process of launching a geostationary satellite. *See* GEOSTATIONARY ORBIT.

transformational coding. In codes, the application of a strict set of rules in the transformation of data into a coded form.

transformer. In electronics, a device to change the voltage or current of an AC signal or power supply. *See* AC.

transient. A condition that exists for a limited period following a change in equilibrium states.

transistor. In electronics, a device manufactured from semiconductor material that can be used to control a current flow in a circuit. There are two basic forms: bipolar and unipolar. The bipolar comprises a sandwich of n–p–n or p–n–p semiconductor materials with three terminals: emitter, base and collector. The current flow comprises both positive and negative carriers. In unipolar transistors the terminals are source, gate and drain, and the current flow is by majority carrier only. *See* FIELD EFFECT TRANSISTOR, SEMICONDUCTOR DEVICES.

transistor–transistor logic. *See* TTL.

transition. (1) In filming and video, a change from one image to another. (Philips). *See* FADE, GLOBAL DISSOLVE, LOCAL DISSOLVE, MATCH DISSOLVE, SHRINK, SQUASH, SQUEEZE, WIPE. (2) In facsimile, the change from black to white, and vice versa, at the edge of letters. (3) In data communications, a change of state in a bit stream. *See* BIT STREAM.

transition copier. *Synonymous with* BIT COPIER.

transitive dependence. In relational databases, an indirect dependence between attributes. Suppose A, B and C are three attributes or distinct collections of attributes of a relation R. If C is functionally dependent on B and B is functionally dependent on A, then C is functionally dependent on A; if A is not functionally dependent upon B or B is not functionally dependent on C, then C is transitively dependent upon A. *See* FUNCTIONAL DEPENDENCE.

translate. In programming, the process of transforming a representation of a program in one language into a representation in another language, or some other representation suitable for execution. *See* ASSEMBLER, COMPILER, HIGH-LEVEL LANGUAGE, INTERPRETER, LOW-LEVEL LANGUAGE, TRANSLATOR.

translation. *See* MACHINE TRANSLATION, TRANSLATOR.

translation cipher. In data security, a very simple form of substitution cipher in which each enciphered character is a fixed distance, in the alphabet, from the corresponding plaintext character (e.g. with a shift of five, F replaces A, G replaces B, etc.). *Synonymous with* ADDITIVE CIPHER.

translator. (1) In programming, a program that translates a program from one computer language to another. *See* ASSEMBLER, COMPILER, INTERPRETER. (2) In communications, a device that converts information from one system of representation into another (e.g. converting dialed digits into call-routing information). *See* DIAL-UP.

transliteration. A representation of the characters of one alphabet to those in another, usually on a phonetic basis.

transmission. In communications, the action of sending information from one location to another, leaving the source information unchanged.

transmission loss. In communications, an attenuation of a signal during transmission. *See* ATTENUATION.

transmission medium. In communications, the physical medium that conveys signals between stations (e.g. fiber optics cable). *See* FIBER OPTICS.

transmission window. In fiber optics, the wavelength at which an optical cable is most transparent.

transmissive disc. In optical media, an optical videodisc in which the laser beam is transmitted through the transparent disc. *Compare* REFLECTIVE DISC. *See* OPTICAL DISC.

transmit flow control. In data communications, a procedure designed to ensure that data is only transmitted from one point at a rate at which it can be received at another. *See* FLOW CONTROL, OVERRUN.

transmittance. In optics, the ratio of the amount of light transmitted through a surface to the amount of incident light on that surface. *Compare* ABSORPTANCE, REFLECTANCE.

transmitter. ((TX) 1) In communications, a device that generates a carrier waveform, modulates it with an input signal and radiates the consequent modulated waveform into space. (2) In communications, a device that converts sound waves into electrical signals for transmission along a telephone line. (3) In computing, electronics and communications, the unit that sends signals along a bus or other transmission medium. *See* BUS.

transparency. In photography, a positive image, mounted on acetate or glass that is used for projection.

transparency bit. In optical media, a dedicated bit that controls the overlay transparency in the cursor plane and RGB (5:5:5) plane of an interactive compact disc image. (Philips). *See* CD-I DIGITAL VIDEO, CURSOR PLANE, OVERLAY, RGB (5:5:5).

transparent. (1) In data communications, pertaining to data that is not recognized by the receiving device or software as transmission control characters. (2) Pertaining to a process or procedure invoked by a user without the latter being aware of its existence. *Compare* VIRTUAL. (3) In communications, pertaining to a network or facility that allows a signal to pass through it without a change.

transparent data communication code. In data communications, a mode using a code-independent protocol. Correct functioning is independent of the code or character set. *Compare* NON-TRANSPARENT MODE. *See* TRANSPARENT.

transparent mode. In distributed processing, a mode of operation of a personal computer linked to a mainframe in which all characters, including control characters, are displayed exactly as they are received, but no further action is taken (e.g. to clear the screen). This mode is used for testing purposes or when control characters are intended for another terminal and would otherwise cause unwanted actions.

transphasor. In optoelectronics, an optical transistor. It employs a crystal with a refractive index that varies with the intensity of incident light. Interference effects produce a sudden switch in the intensity of the transmitted beam according to comparatively small changes in the intensity of the input beam. It is capable of very high switching speeds. *See* INTERFERENCE, REFRACTIVE INDEX, TRANSISTOR.

transponder. In communications, a device that receives and retransmits signals. In satellite communications the received signals are amplified and retransmitted at a different frequency. *Compare* RESPONDER. *See* COMMUNICATIONS SATELLITE SYSTEM.

transportable. *Synonymous with* SUITCASE-PORTABLE.

transport layer. In data communications, one of the layers of the Open Systems Interconnection reference mode which provides services for flow control and recovery between open systems with a predictable quality of service. *Compare* APPLICATION LAYER, DATA LINK LAYER, NETWORK LAYER, PHYSICAL LAYER, PRESENTATION LAYER, SES-

SION LAYER *See* BIT STREAM, OPEN SYSTEMS INTERCONNECTION.

transpose. *See* TRS.

transposition cipher. In data security, a cipher in which the characters are reordered, but are not individually disguised. *Compare* SUBSTITUTION CIPHER. *See* CIPHER, CRYPTOGRAPHY.

transposition error. The error arising from the keyboarding of two characters in reverse order.

transputer. In hardware, an Inmos 32-bit microprocessor that is capable of providing a processing power of several million instructions per second with 4 kilobytes of memory and concurrent communication capabilities. The device is designed so that it can implement a set of concurrent processes. The processes are time-shared by the transputer, and instructions are provided to support the process model of communication. Moreover, it is possible to program systems containing multiple interconnected transputers in which each transputer implements a set of processes. A special programming language, Occam, has been developed with facilities for the exploitation of concurrency on the transputer system. *See* BYTE, CONCURRENT PROGRAMMING, OCCAM, PROCESS, TIME SHARING.

transreceiver. *Synonymous with* TRANSCEIVER.

transverse scan. In video recording, a method of scanning a videotape in which the one or more heads rotate in a plane at 90° to the direction of motion of the tape and the tape itself is bent into an arc across its width. *Compare* HELICAL SCAN. *See* QUADRUPLEX.

trap. (1) In programming, a hardware-activated jump to a specified storage location; the address from which the jump was made is recorded. *See* ADDRESS, JUMP. (2) In computing, a state arising from an attempt by a program to perform an illegal action (e.g. to access a resource not allocated to it). The situation is detected by hardware which then transfers control, usually to the operat-

ing system, so that appropriate action may be taken. *See* HARDWARE, OPERATING SYSTEM.

trapdoor. In computer security, a hidden software or hardware mechanism that permits system protection mechanisms to be circumvented. It is activated in some non-apparent manner. *See* TIME BOMB, TROJAN HORSE.

trapdoor one-way function. In mathematics, a function that can be easily computed, but the computation of the inverse function is infeasible unless certain specific information, employed in the design of the function, is available. Thus two large prime numbers may be multiplied together to form a product, but it may be computationally infeasible to derive the factors given only the value of the product. Knowledge of one factor in this case would constitute the trapdoor information. *See* PUBLIC KEY CRYPTOGRAPHY.

trapping routine. In programming, a routine used to identify and trap a specified event (e.g. identifying and verifying input from a keyboard) and trapping inputs that fall outside predetermined limits (e.g. dates) including months beyond the 12th month. (Philips).

treble roll-off. In recording, pertaining to a gradual attenuation of high frequencies.

tree. *See* TREE STRUCTURE.

tree and branch. In cable television, a conventional method of cable distribution in which an area is served by a main cable, and branches from this cable serve a group of subscribers. The disadvantage of this method is that each subscriber cable must have sufficient bandwidth to carry all available channels. This system is also less suitable for interactive information services. *Compare* SWITCHED STAR.

tree database. *Synonymous with* HIERARCHICAL DATABASE.

tree structure. In data structures, a series of connected nodes without cycles. One node is termed the root and is the starting point of all paths, another one or more nodes, termed leaves, terminate the paths.

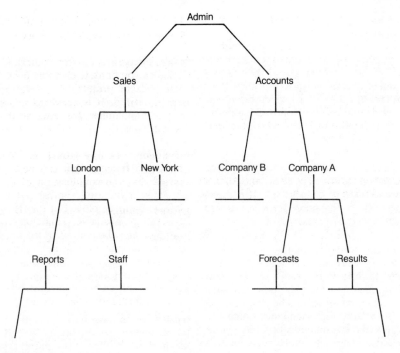

tree-structured directory

A path from any node towards a leaf never passes through any individual node more than once. It can be used to represent hierarchical structures (e.g. a family tree). *Compare* NETWORK STRUCTURE. *See* LEAF, NODE, ROOT.

tree-structured directory. In programming, a facility that permits subdirectories. *See* DIRECTORY. *Synonymous with* HIERARCHICAL DIRECTORY.

trellis coding. In data communications, a protocol that employs forward error correction used in some high-speed modems. *See* FORWARD ERROR CORRECTION, MODEM.

triad. In television, the triangular grouping of red, green and blue phosphors dots on the screen of a shadowmask tube. *See* RGB, SHADOWMASK.

tribit. In data communications, three consecutive bits. In phase-modulated systems a tribit is represented by a phase change of 0, 45, 90, 135, ..., 315°. *Compare* DIBIT. *See* PHASE MODULATION.

tributary station. In data communications, any station, other than the control station on a multipoint circuit. It can communicate with the control station only when polled or selected by it. *See* MULTIPOINT CIRCUIT, POLLING.

trichromatic system. *Synonymous with* THREE-COLOUR PROCESS.

trigram. A three-letter combination (e.g. 'are'). *Compare* DIGRAM.

trim marks. In printing, marks on a printed sheet that show how it is to be trimmed.

triple modular redundancy. (TMR) In reliability, a form of modular redundancy using three active units in parallel. The outputs of all three units are compared and the system output is obtained by taking a majority vote of the three unit outputs. *Compare* DUAL REDUNDANCY, HYBRID REDUNDANCY, NMR. *See* MODULAR REDUNDANCY.

TRM. *See* TAMPER-RESISTANT MODULE.

Trojan horse. In computer security, a program inserted by an attacker in a computer system. It performs functions not described in the program specifications, taking advantage of rights belonging to the calling environment to copy, misuse or destroy data (e.g. a Trojan horse in a text editor might copy confidential information in a file being edited to a file accessible to the attacker). *Compare* MOCKINGBIRD. *See* LEAKAGE.

troposphere. In communications, a layer that extends up to six miles above the earth's surface and scatters radio waves. It is more stable than the ionosphere. *See* IONOSPHERE, TROPOSPHERIC SCATTER CIRCUIT.

tropospheric scatter circuit. In communications, a channel that uses the troposphere to scatter the radio waves, thus providing communication between stations that are not in line of sight. The channels use signals in the ultra high-frequency range and are employed for communication links of up to 600 miles. They are more reliable than high-frequency channels using ionospheric scattering. *See* HIGH-FREQUENCY, IONO-SPHERE, TROPOSPHERE, ULTRA HIGH-FREQUENCY.

troubleshoot. (1) To seek, locate and repair equipment malfunctions. (2) In programming, to debug. *See* DEBUG.

trs. In printing, an instruction on a manuscript or proof to transpose a character or text.

true descender. In printing, pertaining to a displayed, or printed, lower-case character in which the descender appears below the baseline of other characters. *See* DESCENDER.

truncate. (1) In programming, to drop the lower-order digits of a number, usually to fit it into a limited storage space. (2) In programming, an instruction to convert a floating point number to an integer. *See* FLOATING POINT. (3) In online information retrieval, a method used to retrieve all words having a common word stem.

trunk. In communications, a circuit or channel that connects two exchanges or switching units, capable of being switched at both ends and provided with the necessary signalling and terminating equipment.

trunk exchange. In communications, an exchange for trunk lines only.

trusted. In data security, pertaining to software and hardware systems that have been designed, and verified, to avoid compromising, corrupting or denying sensitive information. *See* COMPROMISE, CORRUPT DATA, DELAY/DENIAL OF SERVICE, TRUSTED COMPUTER SYSTEM, TRUSTED COMPUTING BASE.

trusted computer system. In computer security, a system that employs sufficient hardware and software integrity measures to allow its use for processing simultaneously a range of sensitive or classified information. (DOD). *See* TRUSTED, TRUSTED COMPUTING BASE.

trusted computing base. (TCB) In computer security, the totality of protection mechanisms within a computer system — including hardware, firmware and software — the combination of which is responsible for enforcing a security policy. It creates a basic protection environment and provides additional user services required for a trusted computer system. The ability of a TCB to enforce correctly a security policy depends solely on the mechanisms within the TCB and on the correct input by system administrative personnel of parameters (e.g. a user's clearance) related to the security policy. (DOD). *See* SECURITY POLICY, TRUSTED, TRUSTED COMPUTER SYSTEM.

truth table. In logic operations, a means of describing the functions of a logical operation, or a circuit containing logic units. The table lists all the possible input states, together with the corresponding outputs. *See* AND, KARNAUGH MAP.

TSW. *See* TELESOFTWARE.

TT&C. *See* TELEMETRY, TRACKING AND COMMAND.

TTL. In electronics, transistor–transistor logic; logic devices using direct bipolar transistor to transistor coupling (i.e. directly from collector to base). It is characterized by high speed and low power dissipation. *See* LOGIC CIRCUIT, TRANSISTOR.

tty. In peripherals, an abbreviation for teletype. *See* TELETYPEWRITER.

tube shield. A screen or tube around a cathode ray tube display to reduce the effect of reflections. *See* CATHODE RAY TUBE.

tumbling. In computer graphics, turning all or part of a display object about an axis that is continually changing its position. *See* ROTATE.

tunable laser. In optoelectronics, a laser that can be made to vary the frequency of its emitted light. *See* LASER.

tuning. To optimize the performance of a system by fine adjustment.

tuple. (1) In databases, an entry in a relational database. (2) In mathematics, a related set of values. *See* N-TUPLE.

Turing machine. A mathematical model of a device that reads data from a tape, moves the tape zero or one position forward or backward, writes to tape and changes one of its internal states. It was invented by Alan Turing, preceding the first electronic computer, and it provides a useful model for theoretical studies in computation. *See* MATHEMATICAL MODEL.

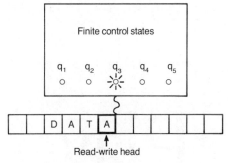

Turing machine
Architecture of a Turing machine.

turnaround documents. In data processing, a computer-produced document that is intended for resubmission into the system.

turnaround time. (1) In office systems, the elapsed time between the despatch and sub-sequent receipt of material. (2) In communications, the time taken in reversing data flow in a half-duplex channel. *See* HALF-DUPLEX.

turnkey system. In computing, a complete system designed for a specific user. With large, complex systems the user needs only to switch on the system, the prime contractor accepting full responsibility for system design, installation, supply of hardware, software and documentation. With software packages the user need not be aware of the operating system; upon loading the disk all operating instructions will be displayed to the user. *See* OPERATING SYSTEM.

turtlegraphics. In computer graphics, a method of creating images by sending instructions to a 'turtle', represented by the screen cursor, to change direction, move specified distances or move through specified points. It is used for educational computer graphics languages. *See* LOGO.

TVR. *See* TELERECORDING.

TVRO. In communications. *See* TELEVISION RECEIVE-ONLY.

TV-SAT/TDF. In television, a German and French satellite project for the broadcasting of television programs in western Europe. *See* DIRECT-BROADCAST SATELLITE.

tweeter. A small loudspeaker used to reproduce high frequencies. *Compare* WOOFER.

twelve mo. In printing, cut or folded sheet that is one-twelfth of basic size.

twelve pitch. *Synonymous with* ELITE.

twin-wire. In printing, pertaining to a paper that has an identical smooth finish on both sides. (Desktop).

twisted nematic. (TN) In peripherals, a form of liquid crystal display. *Compare* SUPER-TWISTED NEMATIC. *See* LIQUID CRYSTAL DISPLAY.

twisted pair. In communications, pertaining to a cable produced by twisting together two individually insulated thin conductors.

This arrangement reduces the capacitance between the wires. *See* CAPACITANCE.

two and a half-dimensional. In computer graphics, pertaining to two-dimensional graphics with special effects. *See* SHADING.

two-dimensional coding. In codes, a data compression technique used in facsimile. Successive scan lines in facsimile transmission are often identical or at least similar. Two-dimensional coding exploits this redundancy by comparing each scan line with a reference line and coding the difference. New reference lines are determined at programmable interval. *Compare* RUN LENGTH CODING. *See* DATA COMPRESSION, FACSIMILE.

two-end device. In computer security, a device installed at both the host computer and legitimate user end of the telephone connection to provide protection against telephone intrusion. *See* TELEPHONE INTRUSION.

two-key lockout. A system used to inhibit further keyboard action when two keys are simultaneously depressed. *Compare* TWO-KEY ROLLOVER. *See* LOCKOUT.

two-key rollover. A system that enables two keystrokes to be correctly interpreted when two keys are simultaneously depressed. *Compare* TWO-KEY LOCKOUT. *See* ROLLOVER.

two's complement. In mathematics, a method of representing a negative binary number. In this convention a binary number is negated by complementing the digits and then adding one to the result. The most significant bit is a sign bit (i.e. a one represents a negative number). *Compare* ONE'S COMPLEMENT. *See* COMPLEMENT.

two-wire circuit. In communications, a circuit that comprises a pair of wires which can be used for simplex, half-duplex or full-duplex transmission depending upon the system design. *Compare* FOUR-WIRE CIRCUIT, SINGLE-WIRE LINE.

TWT. In communications, travelling wave tube.

TWTA. In communications, travelling wave tube amplifier.

TWX. In communications, Teletypewriter Exchange Service; a public switched teletypewriter service offered by AT&T in USA and Canada. *See* TELETYPEWRITER.

TX. *See* TELEX, TRANSMITTER.

Tymnet. In data communications, a US public packet-switching network. *See* PACKET SWITCHING.

typamatic key. In peripherals, a keyboard key that automatically repeats the appropriate character or control action when it remains depressed for more than a given short interval of time. *Synonymous with* AUTOMATIC REPEAT KEY, REPEAT ACTION KEY.

type. (1) In programming, the range of values and valid operations associated with a variable. Types are declared either implicitly or explicitly by the programmer. *See* VARIABLE. (2) In printing, a piece of metal of

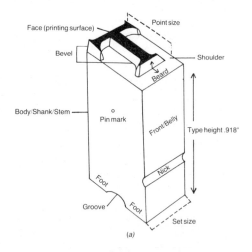

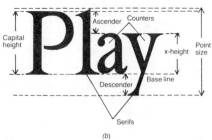

type
(a) parts of a foundry type; (b) elements of typeface.

Times Roman:
The classic typeface designed by Stanley Morrison for the London Times in 1932. The standard for formality and authority.

ABCDEFGHIJKLMNOPQRSTUVWXYZ
abcdefghijklmnopqrstuvwxyz
1234567890

Helvetica:
A traditional 'grotesque' type designed by Max Miedinger in 1957. Often used for children's books on account of its clarity and readability.

ABCDEFGHIJKLMNOPQRSTUVWXYZ
abcdefghijklmnopqrstuvwxyz
1234567890

Helvetica Narrow:
A condensed version of Helvetica, actually treated as a completely separate typeface with its own characteristics.

ABCDEFGHIJKLMNOPQRSTUVWXYZ
abcdefghijklmnopqrstuvwxyz
1234567890

Courier:
An elegant business typewriter typeface.

ABCDEFGHIJKLMNOPQRSTUVWXYZ
abcdefghijklmnopqrstuvwxyz
1234567890

Avant-Garde:
Another grotesque or gothic face. Rounder and lighter weight than Helvetica.

ABCDEFGHIJKLMNOPQRSTUVWXYZ
abcdefghijklmnopqrstuvwxyz
1234567890

Bookman:
A 'primer' typeface designed for ease of reading.

ABCDEFGHIJKLMNOPQRSTUVWXYZ
abcdefghijklmnopqrstuvwxyz
1234567890

New Century Schoolbook:
Another primer typeface. Century Schoolbook was designed in 1894 by L B Benton and T L De Vinne for the Century Magazine.

ABCDEFGHIJKLMNOPQRSTUVWXYZ
abcdefghijklmnopqrstuvwxyz
1234567890

Palatino:
A Roman face with strong, inclined serifs. Designed by Hermann Zapf in 1950 and named after a 16th Century Italian writing-master.

ABCDEFGHIJKLMNOPQRSTUVWXYZ
abcdefghijklmnopqrstuvwxyz
1234567890

Zapf Chancery:
Designed by Hermann Zapf as a cursive face with a handwritten look.

ABCDEFGHIJKLMNOPQRSTUVWXYZ
abcdefghijklmnopqrstuvwxyz
1234567890

Symbol:
A collection of useful symbols and typographic marks such as bullets, daggers and section markers.

"" double quotes ' ' single quotes • bullet — em dash – en dash © ® ¶ §
Ç ü é â ä à å ç ê ë ï î ì Ä Å É æ Æ ô ö ò û ù ÿ Ö Ü ¢ £ ¥ í ó
ú í Ñ ª º ¿ ¡ « »

Zapf Dingbats:
A second collection of rather more illustrative symbols including prettified numbers, printers hands and all sorts of other objects.

✿✛·✢✤✦✧★✡☉☆★★✪✪☆✱✲✳✴✵✹✺✽
❁❂✼✽✾✿❀✽❂✽❂✽●○■□□□□▲▼◆❖▷▐▌▍
☜☞✓✔✗✘✗✘✠✍✌✂✄✁✃✎✐✒✑✇☎✈✉✠✢☇✙☡❡☧

typeface
Typeface guide. Courtesy of *Desktop Publisher*.

standard height with a raised image of a character, or characters, on its upper face. (3) In printing, images produced by composition systems that do not use metal type.

Type I. In cryptography. *See* NSA COMSEC MODULE.

Type II. In cryptography. *See* NSA COMSEC MODULE.

Type B. In video, a form of videotape that records each frame in 51 short tracks. *Compare* TYPE C.

type bar. In printing, a conventional typewriter mechanism with a row of bars that are mechanically driven to form a type impression on the page.

Type C. In video, a form of videotape that records one complete field during each helical scan recording. It can be used for freeze frame display. *Compare* TYPE B. *See* FREEZE FRAME, HELICAL SCAN.

typecasting. In printing, setting type by casting it in molten metal.

typeface. (1) In word processing and printing, the face design of a particular type. (2) In printing, the design of a particular set of type. *See* AVANTE-GARDE, BOOKMAN, CONDENSED, COURIER, EGYPTIAN, EXPANDED TYPE, HELVETICA, HELVETICA NARROW, NEW CENTURY SCHOOLBOOK, OLDSTYLE, PALATINO, SYMBOL, TIMES ROMAN, ZAPF CHANCERY, ZAPF DINGBATS.

type height. In printing, the standard height of type from the bed of a printing press. It is 0.918 inches in the USA and UK. *See* TYPE.

type markup. In printing, to mark the type specifications on layout and copy for the typesetter.

type matter. In printing, type set up in a form ready for printing. *See* FORM.

type-safe language. In programming, a language whose compiler can protect modules and their data from interaction with other modules. *See* COMPILER.

typesetting. The putting of text into typeset form on to a medium, usually photographic film or paper, suitable for making printing plates. *See* DIGITAL TYPOGRAPHY, PHOTO-TYPESETTING.

type size. In printing, the area allocated to a character given in terms of height, width and space. The height is measured in points, the width in sets and the space in ems. The base unit of measurement is 1 point (i.e. 0.3515 millimetres). The em is expressed in terms of height and width except for a square typeface (e.g. an 8 point em represents an 8 point x 8 set typeface). The space refers to that allocated for the typeface, not the area of the printed image. *See* EM, POINT, SET.

typewriter faces. In printing and office systems, the spacing of print characters on typewriters is provided in two standard sizes (i.e. elite, 12 characters to the inch; pica, 10 characters to the inch). *See* ELITE, PICA.

typo. In printing, a typographical error, either in typewriting or typesetting. *See* TYPESETTING.

typographer. *See* COMPOSITOR.

typography. In printing, the art and technique of working with type. *See* TYPE.

U

UA. In data communications, user agent in the CCITT X.400 message-handling standard. *Compare* MTA, MTS. *See* X.400

UART. In computing, universal asynchronous receiver transmitter; a chip that converts parallel byte streams to serial bit streams, and vice versa, for asynchronous devices (e.g. a line printer). *Compare* USART. *See* PARALLEL TRANSMISSION, SERIAL TRANSMISSION.

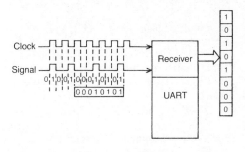

UART

UCA. Uncommitted component array. *See* UNCOMMITTED LOGIC ARRAY.

U channel. In optical media, one of the eight compact disc subcode channels (P–W). At present it is only allocated to compact disc graphics. (Philips). *See* COMPACT DISC, SUBCODE CHANNEL.

UCM. *See* USER COMMUNICATIONS MANAGER.

UCS. *See* UNIVERSAL CHARACTER SET.

UGA. *See* UNCOMMITTED GATE ARRAY.

UHF. *See* ULTRA-HIGH FREQUENCY.

UHR. *See* ULTRA-HIGH REDUCTION.

UKMARC. In online information retrieval, United Kingdom Machine-Readable Cataloguing; a database of bibliographic records of UK publications that is compiled by the Bibliographic Services Division of the British Library. *See* BIBLIOGRAPHIC DATABASE, MACHINE-READABLE.

ULA. *See* UNCOMMITTED LOGIC ARRAY.

u&lc. In printing, an abbreviation for upper and lower case. (Desktop). *See* LOWER CASE, UPPER CASE.

ULSI. *See* ULTRA-LARGE-SCALE INTEGRATION.

ulticard. *Synonymous with* SUPERSMART CARD.

ultrafiche. In micrographics, microfiche images reduced by more than 90x. *Compare* MICROFICHE. *Synonymous with* UMF, UMI.

ultra-high frequency. (UHF) (1) In communications, frequency range of 300–3000 MHz. (2) In television, the frequency range 470–884 MHz. *Compare* VERY HIGH FREQUENCY.

ultra-high reduction. (UHR) In micrographics, a reduction greater than 90x. *Compare* HIGH REDUCTION, LOW REDUCTION, MEDIUM REDUCTION, VERY HIGH REDUCTION. *See* REDUCTION.

ultra-large-scale integration. In microelectronics, a fabrication technology that produces well in excess of 100 000 transistors per chip. *Compare* LARGE-SCALE INTEGRATION, MEDIUM-SCALE INTEGRATION, SMALL-SCALE INTEGRATION, SUPER-LARGE-SCALE INTEGRATION, VERY LARGE-SCALE INTEGRATION. *See* CHIP, TRANSISTOR.

ultrasonic. Air pressure waves at frequencies above audio band.

ultraviolet. (UV) Electromagnetic radiation in a frequency band just above the visible spectrum with wavelengths from some 200 to 4000 angstrom units. *See* ANGSTROM.

ultraviolet-erasable PROM. In memory systems, a programmable read-only memory (PROM) that may be erased by exposure to ultraviolet light, causing stored electrical charges to leak away. *See* PROGRAMMABLE READ-ONLY MEMORY.

U-matic. In recording, a video cassette format for three-quarter-inch tapes developed by Sony. *Compare* BETA, VHS.

umbrella information provider. In videotex, an information provider who rents a large number of pages on a public videotex service and then leases them to a number of other organizations, known as sub-information providers. *See* INFORMATION PROVIDER.

UMF. In micrographics, ultramicrofiche. *Synonymous with* ULTRAFICHE.

UMI. In micrographics, ultramicrofiche. *Synonymous with* ULTRAFICHE.

umlaut. In printing, an accented sign used in German language text, indicated by two dots over an a, o or u. *See* ACCENT.

unary operation. In mathematics, an operation on only one operand (e.g. negation, which reverses the sign of a term). *Compare* DYADIC. *See* OPERAND.

unbalanced transmission. In data communications, a technique employing one wire for each signal and a common return path for all signals. *Compare* BALANCED TRANSMISSION.

unbundling. In programming, the operation of selling software, services and training by a computer manufacturer independent of the sale of computer hardware. *Compare* BUNDLED SOFTWARE. *See* HARDWARE, SOFTWARE.

unclocked. In electronics, a flip flop that changes state at the time of a change of input. Clocked logic units can only change state at the instant that a clock pulse is applied. *See* CLOCK PULSE, FLIP FLOP.

uncommitted component array. *Synonymous with* UNCOMMITTED LOGIC ARRAY.

uncommitted gate array. (UGA) In microelectronics, an uncommitted masterchip array in which the cells are at the functional gate level rather than the component level. *Compare* UNCOMMITTED LOGIC ARRAY. *See* GATE, MASTERCHIP.

uncommitted logic array. (ULA) In microelectronics, an uncommitted masterchip array in which the cells are at a component rather than a functional level. *Compare* PROGRAMMABLE LOGIC ARRAY, UNCOMMITTED GATE ARRAY. *See* MASTERCHIP. *Synonymous with* UNCOMMITTED COMPONENT ARRAY.

unconditional jump. In programming, an instruction to jump to another specified instruction. *Compare* CONDITIONAL JUMP. *See* BRANCH.

underdevelopment. In photography, the result of using a development time shorter than that required to bring up the image fully. *See* DEVELOPING.

underexposure. In photography, any action that results in an insufficient amount of light reaching the film in the camera or printer.

underflow. In mathematics, a condition that arises if the result of an arithmetic operation lies between zero and the smallest number that can be represented by the limited number of digits assigned to the fractional binary number. *Compare* OVER-FLOW.

underline. In word processing, a facility to draw a line automatically under the text. *Synonymous with* UNDERSCORE.

underrun. In data communications, a loss of data caused by the inability of the transmitting device, or channel, to supply data to the communications control logic at the rate required by the attached data link or loop. *Compare* OVERRUN.

underscore. *Synonymous with* UNDERLINE.

unidirectional microphone. In recording, a microphone that has its greatest sensitivity in a given direction. *Compare* OMNIDIRECTIONAL MICROPHONE. *See* MICROPHONE.

uniform distribution. In mathematics, a probability distribution that has a constant value over a specified range and is zero elsewhere. *Compare* GAUSSIAN DISTRIBUTION, POISSON DISTRIBUTION. *See* RANDOM NUMBERS.

uniformly spaced font. *Synonymous with* FIXED-SPACED FONT.

Uniform System of Accounts. In communications, a US classification of accounts for common carriers. *See* COMMON CARRIER.

uninterruptible power supply. (UPS) In computing, a device inserted between a power source and a system to ensure that the system is guaranteed a precise, uninterrupted power supply, irrespective of variations in the power source voltage.

unipolar. (1) In data communications, pertaining to a signal that has excursions from zero to either a positive or negative value, but not both (e.g. it consists of a stream of positive pulses only). *Compare* BIPOLAR. (2) In electronics, a transistor formed from a single type of semiconductor material (i.e. n- or p-type). *Compare* BIPOLAR. *See* FIELD EFFECT TRANSISTOR, TRANSISTOR.

unipolar transmission. In telegraphy, a method in which a mark is represented by current on the line and a space by the absence of current. *See* CURRENT, MARK, SPACE, UNIPOLAR. *Synonymous with* NEUTRAL TRANSMISSION.

unique identification. *Synonymous with* FINGERPRINT.

UNISIST. In online information retrieval, United Nations Information System in Science and Technology; a UNESCO programme intended to foster the development of an international science information network.

unit buffer terminal. In communications, a terminal that does not have a communication buffer.

United States Independent Telephone Association. (USITA) An organization, with members from independent telephone companies in many countries that deals with technical standards and regulatory matters.

unit load. In electronics, the electrical load placed on a driver output by a receiver unit. *See* LOAD.

unit system. In printing, a unit obtained by dividing the square of the type size (i.e. em) into vertical segments. Thus a 36-point em is a square of dimension 36 points; an 18 units to the em system divides the square into 18 vertical segments (i.e. each unit would be 2 points width in this example). Units are thus always relative to the typesize. *See* EM QUAD, POINT.

universal asynchronous receiver transmitter. *See* UART.

universal character set. (UCS) In printing, a facility permitting any standard typeface to be deployed during printing.

Universal Copyright Convention. In printing, a convention that gives protection to authors or originators of text, photographs or illustrations, etc. to prevent use without permission or acknowledgement. The publication should carry the copyright mark, the name of the originator and the year of publication. (Desktop).

Universal Copyright Convention, 1952. In printing, an agreement between signatory countries on copyright. *See* COPYRIGHT.

universal portable telephone. *See* UPT.

Universal Postal Union. (UPU) A United Nations agency that is charged with the responsibility for enhancing international cooperation between national postal services.

universal product code. (UPC) In codes, an agreed bar coding for product labels giving country of origin, manufacturer, etc. It is used for supermarket checkouts, stock control, etc. *Compare* EAN. *See* BAR CODE.

universal quantifier. In mathematics, a symbol employed in predicate calculus and relational calculus that is read as 'for all'. *Compare* EXISTENTIAL QUANTIFIER. *See* PREDICATE, RELATIONAL CALCULUS.

universal set. In mathematics, the total set of elements that have a specified property (e.g. 0, 1, 2, ..., 9) is the universal set of non-negative, single-digit integers. *See* SET.

universal synchronous asynchronous receiver transmitter. *See* USART.

universal synchronous receiver transmitter. *See* USRT.

Unix. In computing, a general-purpose multiuser operating system suitable for use in a wide range of mini- and microcomputers. It originated in the Bell Laboratories in 1969 for the PDP-7 minicomputer, and it became extremely popular among computer scientists. Unix encompasses a range of programming tools that provide a rich, productive environment for the development of software by a team of programmers. *See* PIPES, SHELL, SHELL SCRIPT, SOFTWARE TOOL, STANDARD INPUT, STANDARD OUTPUT.

unjustified. In printing, lines of type that line up vertically on one side, but are ragged on the other. *See* RAGGED SETTING.

unpack. In programming, to recover original data from its packed format. *See* PACKING.

unprotected field. In peripherals, a part of the display on a visual display unit that a user can modify. *Compare* PROTECTED FIELD. *Synonymous with* VARIABLE DATA.

unrecoverable ABEND. In computing, an ABEND that results in abnormal termination of a program execution. *Compare* RECOVERABLE ABEND. *See* ABEND.

unrecoverable error. In computing, an error that results in a premature termination of a program. *Compare* RECOVERABLE ERROR.

unrestricted information transfer. In communications, an integrated services digital network bearer service that makes absolutely no changes to the transmitted bit stream. *Compare* BEARER SERVICE. *See* INTEGRATED SERVICES DIGITAL NETWORK.

up. In computing, pertaining to a device that is functioning correctly. *Compare* DOWN. *See* UPTIME.

up and down propagation time. In communications, the time taken for a signal to travel the distance from a ground station to a satellite and back to a ground station. For geostationary satellites the up and down propagation time is approximately 540 milliseconds. *See* GEOSTATIONARY SATELLITE, GROUND STATION.

UPC. *See* UNIVERSAL PRODUCT CODE.

updatable microfiche. In micrographics, a specially coated microfiche to which images may be added by a combination of microimaging processes and photocopying. *See* MICROFICHE, MICROIMAGE.

update. (1) In programming, to modify stored information with data from recent transactions according to a specified procedure. (2) In word processing, to replace text stored on a file with a revised version.

update centre. In videotex, a computer centre that accepts database updates and transmits them to retrieval centres. *See* RETRIEVAL CENTRE.

update inconsistency. In databases, a phenomenon that can arise in a multiuser database. The sequence of events is: (a) user A retrieves a record; (b) user B retrieves the same record; (c) user A updates a field of the record and writes it back to the database; (d) user B updates a different field of the same record and writes it back to the database overwriting user A's update. Lockout is employed to avoid this situation. *See* FIELD, LOCKOUT, RECORD.

up/down counter. In electronics, a binary counter that accepts two inputs, one to increase the count and the other to decrease it. *See* BINARY COUNTER.

upgradability. A facility allowing easy extension of the performance of a basic unit by adding extra hardware or software, often in the form of add-on modules. (Philips). *See* ADD-ON MODULE.

uplink. In communications, pertaining to transmission from a ground station to a communications satellite. *See* COMMUNICATIONS SATELLITE SYSTEM, GROUND STATION.

upload. In computing, the transfer of programs or data between computers, usually from a microcomputer to a mainframe. *Compare* DOWNLOAD. *See* MAINFRAME.

upper case. In printing, capital or large size characters. *Compare* LOWER CASE.

UPS. *See* UNINTERRUPTABLE POWER SUPPLY.

upstream. In communications, the direction opposite to that of the message flow (i.e. towards the transmitter of the message). *Compare* DOWNSTREAM.

UPT. In communications, universal portable telephone; an advanced concept combining the services of a cordless and mobile radio telephone. Such a device could be used in the home, as a car telephone linking into a cellular radio network, and as a portable telephone in an office building and in public places where suitable telepoints were installed. *See* CELLULAR RADIO, CORDLESS TELEPHONE, TELEPOINT.

uptime. In computing, the time that a computer is available for normal operation. *Synonymous with* AVAILABLE TIME.

UPU. *See* UNIVERSAL POSTAL UNION.

upward compatibility. In computing, the capability of one computer to execute programs written for another, but not vice versa.

Urica. In library science, an automated library system developed by McDonnell Douglas Information Systems.

usage-sensitive pricing. In communications, charges for service based upon usage.

USART. In computing, universal synchronous asynchronous receiver transmitter; a chip that can be programmed under central processing unit (CPU) control for synchronous or asynchronous serial transfer of data between the CPU and an input/output device. *See* ASYNCHRONOUS TRANSMISSION, CENTRAL PROCESSING UNIT, SYNCHRONOUS TRANSMISSION.

USASCII. In codes, USA Standard Code for Information Interchange. *Synonymous with* AMERICAN STANDARD CODE FOR INFORMATION INTERCHANGE.

USASI. United States of America Standards Institute.

user action frame. *See* RESPONSE FRAME.

user application. In programming, a program or related set of programs designed for the user of a system rather than for programmers or service technicians. (Philips). *Compare* SYSTEM SOFTWARE, TEST PROGRAM. *See* APPLICATION SOFTWARE.

user area. In memory systems, the portion of main memory allocated to user programs; the remainder is dedicated to the operating system, buffers, etc. *See* OPERATING SYSTEM.

user communications manager. (UCM) In optical media, a compact disc (CD) real-time operating system module used by an application to manipulate the audio and video output devices of interactive compact disc players. (Philips). *See* CD REAL-TIME OPERATING SYSTEM, COMPACT DISC – INTERACTIVE.

user data. In optical media, data supplied by an information provider for an interactive or read-only memory compact disc application. As such, it includes retrieval software, but not information that the information provider may be required to supply to facilitate authoring. (Philips). *See* AUTHORING, COMPACT DISC – INTERACTIVE, COMPACT DISC – READ-ONLY MEMORY, INFORMATION PROVIDER.

user data field. In optical media, a 2048-byte portion of the data field, in an interactive or read-only memory compact disc addressable sector, that is dedicated to user data. (Philips). *See* COMPACT DISC – INTERACTIVE, COMPACT DISC – READ-ONLY MEMORY, SECTOR.

user feedback. *See* FEEDBACK.

user friendly. Pertaining to any system designed to be used without extensive operator training and that seeks to assist the user to gain maximum benefit from the system. *See* HELP, MENU SELECTION.

user id. In computing, a user identification code which enables a computer to recognize and allocate charges to a user.

user interface. In man–machine interfaces, the interface through which the user and a system or computer communicate. It includes input and output devices, such as a keyboard, a hand control, a digitizing tablet, a touch screen, a printer and a display, and also the software-controlled means by which the users are prompted to supply data needed by the application, and by which they are notified of their errors and how to correct them. (Philips). *See* DIGITIZING TABLET, DISPLAY, HAND CONTROL, KEYBOARD, POINTING DEVICE, TOUCHSCREEN.

user number. In computer security, a code or password by means of which an authorized user can gain access to a computer or to stored information. (Philips). *See* PIN.

user-operated language. *See* PROBLEM-ORIENTED LANGUAGE, PROCEDURE-ORIENTED LANGUAGE.

user profile. (1) A description of the essential parameters of a user with respect to a given system. (2) In computing, a definition of the user type of interaction with a computer network, supplied by the user as a set of parameters, or options, at registration.

user programs. In programming, a group of programs written by the user as compared with manufacturer-supplied software. *See* APPLICATION PROGRAM.

users group. A group of users who share programs, exchange information, etc. on a class of computer systems. *Compare* CLOSED USER GROUP.

user shell. In computing, a program between the operating system and application program on the one hand and the user on the other to enhance the manner of information presentation and command. (Philips). *See* SHELL.

user terminal. *See* TERMINAL.

USITA. *See* UNITED STATES INDEPENDENT TELEPHONE ASSOCIATION.

USPO. United States Post Office.

USRT. In computing, universal synchronous receiver transmitter; an integrated circuit device that can perform timing of synchronous bit serial data and series-to-parallel conversion. *Compare* UART, USART.

utility programs. In programming, a program supplied for common routine tasks (e.g. copying files). *See* FILE.

UTLAS. In library science, University of Toronto Library Automation System; a cooperative Canadian library network.

UV. *See* ULTRAVIOLET.

V

V. (1) In electronics, volt. *See* VOLTAGE. (2) In communications. *See* V-SERIES RECOMMENDATIONS OF CCITT.

V.1. In data communications, equivalence between binary notation symbols and the significant conditions of two condition code.

V.2. In data communications, power levels for data transmission over telephone lines.

V.3. In data communications, international Alphabet Number 5 for transmission of data and messages. *See* INTERNATIONAL ALPHABET NUMBER 5.

V.4. In data communications, general structure of signals of International Alphabet Number 5 for data transmission over public telephone networks. *See* INTERNATIONAL ALPHABET NUMBER 5.

V.5. In data communications, standardization of data-signalling rates for synchronous data transmission in the general switched telephone network.

V.6. In data communications, standardization of data-signalling rates for synchronous data transmission on leased telephone-type circuits.

V.7. In data communications, definitions of terms concerning data communications over the telephone network.

V.10. In data communications, electrical characteristics for unbalanced double-current interchange circuits for general use with integrated circuit equipment in the field of data communications. *See* X.26.

V.11. In data communications, electrical characteristics for balanced double-current interchange circuits for general use with integrated circuit equipment in the field of data communications. *See* X.27

V.13. In data communications, answer back unit simulators.

V.15. In data communications, use of acoustic coupling for data transmission. *See* ACOUSTIC COUPLER.

V.16. In data communications, medical analog data transmission modems. *See* MODEM.

V.19. In data communications, modems for parallel data transmission using telephone signalling frequencies. *See* MODEM.

V.20. In data communications, parallel data transmission modems standardized for universal use in the general switched telephone network. *See* MODEM.

V.21. In data communications, 300 bits per second modem standardized for use in the general switched telephone network. *See* MODEM.

V.22. In data communications, 1200 bits per second duplex modem standardized for use on general switched telephone network and on leased circuits. *See* BITS PER SECOND, MODEM.

V.23. In data communications, 600/1200 baud modem standardized for use in the general switched telephone network. *See* MODEM.

V.24. In data communications, list of definitions for interchange circuits between data terminal equipment and data circuit terminating equipment. *See* RS-232C.

V.25. In data communications, automatic calling and/or answering equipment on the general switched telephone network including disabling of echo suppressors on manually established calls. *See* ECHO SUPPRESSOR, RS-366.

V.26. In data communications, 2400 bits per second modem standardized for use on four-wire leased circuits. *See* FOUR-WIRE CIRCUIT, MODEM.

V.26 bis. In data communications, 2400/1200 bits per second modem standardized for use in the general switched telephone network. *See* MODEM.

V.27. In data communications, 4800 bits per second modem with manual equalizer telephone-type circuits standardized for use on leased circuits. *See* MODEM.

V.27 bis. In data communications, 4800/2400 bits per second modem with automatic equalizer standardized for use on leased telephone-type circuits. *See* MODEM.

V.27 ter. In data communications, 4800/2400 bits per second modem standardized for use in the general switched telephone network. *See* MODEM.

V.28. In data communications, electrical characteristics for unbalanced double-current interchange circuits.

V.29. In data communications, 9600 bits per second modem standardized for use on point-to-point four-wire leased telephone-type circuits. *See* FOUR-WIRE CIRCUIT, MODEM, POINT-TO-POINT.

V.31. In data communications, electrical characteristics for single-current interchange circuits controlled by contact closure. *See* MODEM.

V.35. In data communications, data transmission at 48 kilobits per second using 60–108 kHz group band circuits.

V.36. In data communications, modems for synchronous data transmission using 60–108 kHz group band circuits. *See* MODEM.

V.37. In data communications, synchronous data transmission at a data-signalling rate higher than 72 kilobits per second using 60–108 kHz group band circuits.

V.40. In data communications, error indication with electromechanical equipment.

V.41. In data communications, code-independent error control system.

V.50. In data communications, standard limits for transmission quality of data transmission.

V.51. In data communications, organization of the maintenance of international telephone-type circuits used for data transmission.

V.52. In data communications, characteristics of distortion and error rate measuring apparatus for data transmission.

V.53. In data communications, limits for the maintenance of telephone-type circuits used for data transmission.

V.54. In data communications, loop test device for modems.

V.55. In data communications, specification for an impulsive noise-measuring instrument for telephone-type circuits.

V.56. In data communications, comparative tests of modems for use over telephone-type circuits.

V.57. In data communications, comprehensive data test set for high data-signalling rates.

VAB. *See* VOICE ANSWER BACK.

vacuum fluorescent display. (VFD) In peripherals, a form of flat-screen display with very high brightness and wide viewing angle compared with liquid crystal displays. The blue–green output can, by the use of wavelength filters, produce red, orange, blue, green or yellow displays and may be viewed in daylight, even in bright sunlight. *See* FLAT-SCREEN DISPLAY.

vacuum forming. A means of producing a shape on a thin sheet of plastic by placing it on a relief plate and inducing a vacuum between the sheet and the plate.

vacuum guide. In video, a part of the magnetic head assembly that is used to hold the tape in the correct position by a vacuum action. It is used in transverse scans when the tape must be curved across its width. *See* TRANSVERSE SCAN.

VAD. Value-added distributor.

VADS. *See* VALUE-ADDED DATA SERVICES.

validation. (1) In computer security, the performance of tests and evaluations in order to determine compliance with security specifications and requirements. (FIPS). (2) In programming, a check on input data for correctness against set criteria (e.g. format, ranges, etc.). It may be performed manually or automatically. *See* VALIDITY CHECKING.

validity checking. (1) In programming, a procedure to check that a code group is actually a character of the particular code in use. (2) In programming, a data-screening procedure wherein data input records are checked for range, valid representation, etc. *See* REASONABLENESS CHECK.

value. (1) In printing, the value of a colour is the degree of lightness or darkness relative to a neutral grey scale. (2) In databases, a specific occurrence of an attribute. *See* ATTRIBUTE.

value-added data services. (VADS) In data communications, a term that is replacing value-added network service. Value-added data services are public data networks with added services (e.g. electronic document interchange, viewdata, managed network services). *See* ELECTRONIC DOCUMENT INTERCHANGE, PUBLIC SWITCHED NETWORK, VALUE-ADDED NETWORK SERVICE, VIEWDATA.

value-added network service. (VANS) In communications, a communication service using the communications networks of a common carrier for transmission and providing added data services with separate additional equipment. Added services may include electronic document interchange, viewdata, store-and-forward message switching, terminal and host interfacing. The users include some who do not belong to the organization providing the service. This term is now being replaced by value-added data services. *Compare* COMMON CARRIER, MANAGED DATA NETWORK. *See* STORE AND FORWARD, VALUE-ADDED DATA SERVICES, VALUE-ADDED SERVICE PROVIDER.

value-added service provider. (VASP) In communications, a service, such as a database enquiry facility, offered over a value-added network, but marketed and supported by a separate organization from the value-added network service company. *Compare* CLOSED USER GROUP. *See* VALUE-ADDED DATA SERVICES, VALUE-ADDED NETWORK SERVICE.

value of service pricing. In communications, a pricing system in which the charges are related to the value of the service, to the user, rather than the costs of the supplier.

VANDA. In video, video and audio.

van Eck phenomenon. In computer security, pertaining to radiation from a visual display unit (VDU) or microcomputer. van Eck reported that electromagnetic radiation from a VDU is unique to the particular type of device, and is in the ultra-high-frequency range. Under optimum conditions this radiation can be received as far as 0.66–1.25 miles away and can be translated to readable display.

The radiation can, moreover, be detected and the data displayed with relatively standard electronic components. The van Eck phenomenon is therefore of some concern in computer security fields. *See* COMPROMISING EMANATIONS, TEMPEST PROOFING.

vanilla. In computing, the original version of a system or piece of software; one without later enhancements or modifications. *See* SOFTWARE.

VANS. *See* VALUE-ADDED NETWORK SERVICE.

vapourware. A product that is advertised, but is not commercially available.

variable. In programming, a quantity that is named in the program and can assume any value, within a valid range for its type, and may be operated upon by any valid operator for that type. The name given to a variable is a string of characters which is used to denote the particular memory location in which the current value of the variable is held. The translator of a source program assigns the memory location to the named variable. *See* OPERATOR, TRANSLATOR, TYPE.

variable-area sound track. In filming, a optical sound track that is divided longitud-inally into two components: one essentially opaque and the other essentially trans-parent. *Compare* VARIABLE-DENSITY SOUND TRACK, VARIABLE-HUE SOUND RECORDING. *See* OPTICAL SOUNDTRACK.

variable data. *Synonymous with* UNPRO-TECTED FIELD.

variable-density sound track. In filming, an optical sound track recorded in the form of variable density striations at right angles to the film edge. *Compare* VARIABLE-AREA SOUND TRACK, VARIABLE-HUE SOUND RECORD-ING.

variable-hue sound recording. In filming, a method of sound recording onto a photo-graphic sound track using variations in colour instead of variations in monochrome density or area. *Compare* VARIABLE-AREA SOUND TRACK, VARIABLE-DENSITY SOUND TRACK.

variable-length record. In data structures, a record that can have a length independent of the length of other records with which it is associated. Such a record could contain repeating groups. *Compare* FIXED-LENGTH RECORD. *See* FILE, RECORD, REPEATING GROUP.

variable space. In printing, the length of a line may need to be altered so that the text is justified, and this effect is achieved by varying the space between words. At the time of initial insertion of text this space length is not known so a variable space code is inserted, the actual space length is com-puted at the appropriate time. *See* JUSTIFY, WORD SPACE.

variable text. In word processing, text of a changing nature that is added to recorded text so as to produce the final document.

Compare BOILERPLATE, FIXED DATA, PREPRIN-TED DATA.

VASP. *See* VALUE-ADDED SERVICE PRO-VIDER.

V.bb. In data communications, a speci-fication for 4800 bits per second data trans-mission over voice-grade, telephone line-compatible modems. *See* MODEM, VOICE-GRADE CHANNEL, V-SERIES RECOMMENDA-TIONS OF CCITT.

VBI. *See* VERTICAL BLANKING INTERVAL.

V channel. In optical media, one of the eight compact disc subcode channels (P–W). At present it is only allocated to compact disc graphics. *See* COMPACT DISC, SUBCODE CHANNEL.

VCR. *See* VIDEO CASSETTE RECORDER.

VCS. *See* VIDEO COMPUTER SYSTEM.

VDE. *See* VOICE DATA ENTRY.

VDI. In computer graphics, virtual device interface; an ANSI graphics standard that defines an interface between device-dependent and device-independent code in a graphics environment. VDI makes all device drivers appear identical to the application program. *See* APPLICATION PROGRAM, DEVICE DRIVER, GRAPHIC KERNEL SYSTEM.

VDM. *See* VIRTUAL DEVICE METAFILE.

VDT. *See* VISUAL DISPLAY TERMINAL.

VDU. *See* VISUAL DISPLAY UNIT.

vector. (1) In mathematics, a variable that has magnitude and direction. *See* SCALAR. (2) In data structures, a quantity represented by an ordered set of numbers (e.g. a one-dimensional array). (3) In computer graphics, a line coupled with its direction.

vector display. *See* VECTOR REFRESH.

vector generation. In computer graphics, a data compression technique for images in which the first and last coordinates of straight-line segments are stored. *Compare* IMAGE FOLLOWING, RUN LENGTH CODING.

vector graphics. *See* VECTOR REFRESH.

vector imaging. In computer graphics, the storage and processing of diagrams using representations of the line diagrams, vectors, circles, arcs, etc. *Compare* RASTER IMAGING.

vectoring. In programming, the process of instructing the program to seek additional instructions from a given storage location. *See* INSTRUCTION.

vector processor. *Synonymous with* ARRAY PROCESSOR.

vector refresh. In computer graphics, pertaining to a technique of displaying computer-generated images in which a list of coordinates, representing end points of straight lines, is held in a display file. The display controller repeatedly scans this display file and causes the electron beam of a cathode ray tube to be deflected in straight lines across the screen according to the stored coordinates. The screen phosphor continues to glow for up to 100 milliseconds for each displayed line thus retaining the image on the screen between successive scans. This technique has the advantage that images may be transformed efficiently by display hardware, but if the display file becomes too large the period between successive scans may exceed the phosphor afterglow time and the image begins to flicker. *Compare* DIRECT-VIEW STORAGE TUBE, RASTER DISPLAY. *See* CATHODE RAY TUBE.

Veitch diagrams. In mathematics, a diagram in which a boolean function is represented by a set of squares with each square representing one of the possible states of the function. *Compare* VENN DIAGRAM. *See* BOOLEAN ALGEBRA, KARNAUGH MAP.

vellum. In printing, the treated skin of a calf used as a writing material. The name is also used to describe a thick, creamy book paper. (Desktop).

velum. In man–machine interfaces, the soft palate of the mouth which acts as one of the speech articulators. *See* SPEECH SYNTHESIZER.

Venn diagram. In mathematics, a diagram in which states are represented by regions drawn on a surface (e.g. if state A represents all men with red hair and state B represents all bachelors, the overlapping area then represents all red-haired bachelors). *Compare* VEITCH DIAGRAM.

verification. (1) In computer security, the documentation of penetration or attempts to penetrate an actual online system in support or in contradiction of assumptions developed during system review and analysis. (AR). (2) In computing. *See* KEYSTROKE VERIFICATION.

version number. In computing, an indication of the enhancements contained in a particular offering of an operating system.

verso. In printing, any left-handed, even-numbered page of a book. *Compare* RECTO.

vertical blanking interval. (VBI) (1) In television, the period of time in which the scanning spot is transferred from the end of one raster scan to the beginning of the next. This time period may be employed for teletext signal transmission. *See* RASTER SCAN, TELETEXT. (2) In optical media, blanked lines in each field of a videodisc wherein frame numbers, picture stops, chapter stops, white flags, etc. are encoded. *See* CHAPTER STOP, FIELD, PICTURE STOP, VIDEODISC, WHITE FLAG.

vertical formatting. In word processing, the process of automatically positioning lines of text, in relation to other lines of text, according to prespecified rules.

vertical justification. In printing, the process of redistributing white space, at the bottom of a column, between lines of constituent text so that all columns appear to be of the same length. *Compare* HORIZONTAL JUSTIFICATION. *See* JUSTIFICATION.

vertical lock. In recording, a video recording playback condition in which the playback head rotation is in synchronism with the pulses on the control track. *See* CONTROL TRACK, HELICAL SCAN.

vertical recording. In memory systems, a method of magnetizing a magnetic disk which can provide a higher density than the conventional longitudinal recording technique. *Compare* ISOTROPIC RECORDING, LONGITUDINAL RECORDING. *See* MAGNETIC DISK.

vertical redundancy check. *See* LONGITUDINAL REDUNDANCY CHECK.

vertical resolution. In television, the number of horizontal lines in a television image. *Compare* HORIZONTAL RESOLUTION.

vertical retrace period. In television, the time during which the vertical field scan on a television screen returns to the beginning of the next field. (Philips). *Compare* HORIZONTAL RETRACE PERIOD. *See* FIELD.

vertical scan frequency. *Synonymous with* FRAME FREQUENCY.

vertical scrolling. In peripherals, an action that permits the user to move the screen displayed text up or down, a line at a time, to reveal other parts of the stored text.

vertical tab. *Synonymous with* HIGH-SPEED SKIP.

vertical wraparound. In word processing, the continuation of the cursor movement from the bottom character position in a vertical column to the top character position in the next column. *Compare* HORIZONTAL WRAPAROUND.

very high frequency. (VHF) (1) In communications, the range of frequencies from 30 to 300 MHz. (2) In television, the frequency range 54–16 MHz. *Compare* ULTRA-HIGH FREQUENCY.

very high reduction. (VHR) In micrographics, a reduction in the range 61x to 90x. *Compare* HIGH REDUCTION, LOW REDUCTION, MEDIUM REDUCTION, ULTRA-HIGH REDUCTION. *See* REDUCTION.

very large-scale integration. (VSLI) In microelectronics, pertaining to the fabrication technology that produces of the order of 100 000 transistors per chip. *Compare* LARGE-SCALE INTEGRATION, MEDIUM-SCALE INTEGRATION, SMALL-SCALE INTEGRATION, SUPER-LARGE-SCALE INTEGRATION, ULTRA-LARGE-SCALE INTEGRATION. *See* CHIP, TRANSISTOR.

very low frequency. (VLF) In communications, the range of frequencies from 3 to 30 kHz.

very small-aperture terminal. *See* VSAT.

vesicular film. In photography, film that has the light-sensitive element suspended in a plastic layer. Upon exposure it creates strains within the layer in the form of a latent image. These strains are released, and the latent image is made visual by heating the plastic layer. The image becomes permanent when the layer cools.

vestigial sideband. In communications, a transmission technique of a modulated wave in which one sideband, the carrier and a small part of the opposite sideband are transmitted on a channel. *Compare* SINGLE-SIDEBAND TRANSMISSION, SUPPRESSED-CARRIER TRANSMISSION. *See* CARRIER, MODULATION, SIDEBAND.

VET. *See* VISUAL EDITING TERMINAL.

vf band. In communications, voice-frequency band. *See* VOICE FREQUENCY.

VFD. *See* VACUUM FLUORESCENT DISPLAY.

VHF. *See* VERY HIGH FREQUENCY.

VHR. *See* VERY HIGH REDUCTION.

VHS. In recording, a video cassette format for half-inch tapes developed by JVC. *Compare* BETA, U-MATIC.

Viatel. In videotex, a national viewdata system operated by Telecom Australia. *See* VIEWDATA.

vide. In printing, used in footnotes to direct reader to a given reference.

video. Pertaining to visual images produced or transmitted by a television system.

video bandwidth. In peripherals, the maximum rate at which phosphor dots may be illuminated on display screen. *See* CATHODE RAY TUBE.

video black detector. In television, a device in a television receiver that can recognize the onset of a television commercial by detecting the fade to black image that precedes it.

video camera. In television, a camera for use with a video system. It connects directly to a video recorder or a television receiver and may incorporate a compact video cassette recorder. (Philips). *See* CAMCORDER.

video cassette. In recording, a cartridge holding a loop of video tape. *See* VIDEO TAPE.

video cassette journal. In applications, a journal comprising a video cassette and accompanying booklet. Subscribers receive the journal regularly and return previous editions of cassettes for re-recording. *Compare* ELECTRONIC JOURNAL.

video cassette recorder. (VCR) In television, a cassette recorder for record and playback of video tapes. Various VCR systems are in use, including VHS, VHS-C, Betamax and 8-mm. (Philips). *See* BETA, VHS.

video chip. In video, a dedicated integrated circuit, either in analog or digital integrated circuit technology, designed to fulfil specific video functions. (Philips). *Compare* AUDIO CHIP. *See* INTEGRATED CIRCUIT.

video compressor. In television, a device that converts standard television signals to narrow bandwidth for transmission over voice-grade channels. It may be used in conjunction with a video expander at the receiving end. *See* SLOW-SCAN TELEVISION DEVICE, VIDEO EXPANDER.

video computer system. (VCS) In computing, a microprocessor system with a primary function of providing a video display (e.g. for video games). *See* VIDEO GAME.

video conferencing. In communications, a form of teleconferencing in which participants can view each other with the use of television cameras. *Compare* AUDIO TELECONFERENCING. *See* TELECONFERENCING.

video confidence head. In recording, a device for checking that the video recorder is actually recording. *See* VIDEO RECORDER.

video data. In optical media, interactive compact disc data related to one or more units of video information encoded in delta YUV, RGB, colour look-up table or run length encoding techniques. (Philips). *See* CD-I DIGITAL VIDEO, COLOUR LOOK-UP TABLE, DELTA YUV, RGB, RUN LENGTH CODING.

videodisc. In video recording, a disc that contains recorded television pictures and sound. Videodiscs share the advantage of audio hi-fi discs in that they can be mass produced using low-cost raw materials, whereas prerecorded video cassettes require lengthy recording procedures on expensive magnetic tape. However, such discs do not provide the user with the record facilities of video tape and therefore cannot be used for time-shift television viewing. Certain classes of videodisc have freeze frame, fast/slow motion and random-access search, and the disc player can be controlled from a local microprocessor or linked to a microcomputer. These interactive videodisc systems

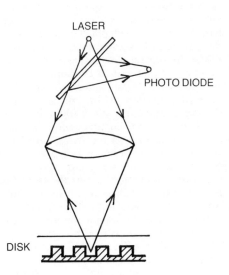

videodisc
Fig. 1. Philips VLP optical pickup, laser and photo diode.

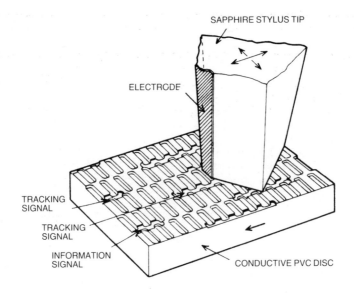

SAPPHIRE STYLUS TIP

ELECTRODE

TRACKING
SIGNAL

TRACKING
SIGNAL

INFORMATION
SIGNAL

CONDUCTIVE PVC DISC

videodisc
Fig. 2. JVC capacitance videodisc with sapphire stylus.

provide excellent facilities for education, training, sales promotion, etc. Videodiscs can also be used as mass storage devices with very high information-packing density and fast random access.

The video signals are frequency-modulated, and the resulting sine wave is clipped. This signal is regarded as a series of pulses of constant amplitude and varying duration. When a videodisc is encoded with these signals the reading system needs only detect the presence or absence of a pulse. The two major forms of consumer disc are capacitive and optical. In the capacitive disc the reading head, or stylus, acts as one plate of a capacitor and the disc as the other. The disc is produced from conducting material, and either the disc, or the stylus, is covered with insulating material to prevent a short circuit between the capacitor plates. The recorded information is in the form of minute pits, as small as half a micrometre, which produces the variation in capacitance.

The optical disc does not employ a stylus, and the information is read by a laser beam which is either reflected or transmitted by the minute encoded pits. The optical discs suffer no stylus wear, and it is possible to display continuously an individual television frame with high quality and no disc damage. The playback quality is relatively insensitive

to fingermarks, etc. on the disc surface and, unlike the capacitive disc, they do not require protective plastic caddys. Since there is no mechanical contact with a reading head the optical disc can rotate at high speed (1800 rpm, NTSC standard) giving one television frame per rotation and therefore very good freeze frame picture quality.

Optical disc players have two modes of operation; CAV (constant angular velocity); CLV (constant linear velocity). In CAV mode the disc is rotated at a constant speed and one frame is recorded on each circular track.

In the freeze frame action the beam jumps back to the start of the frame. Fast and slow motion and forward and reverse play effects are produced by programming the laser beam to jump to appropriate tracks at the start of each frame. In this CAV mode 54 000 individual frames can be accessed, but the total playing time per side is only 30 minutes. A CLV disc has a longer playing time — one hour per side — but it is only suitable for continuous play; fast/slow motion, freeze frame and random access to individual frames are not available with these discs. The additional playing time is achieved by recording more frames per circular track, and the speed of rotation varies from 1800 rpm when the beam reads tracks on the inner circumference to 600 rpm at the outer circumference. The use of videodiscs for education, sales promotion, etc. is described elsewhere (*see* INTERACTIVE VIDEODISC SYSTEMS).

The high-quality freeze frame display of optical discs renders them attractive as storage devices for documents. A single frame on a disc occupies a total surface area of 1 square millimetre, compared with 5 square millimetres on a 3000-frame ultrafiche, and can be accessed in approximately 5 seconds. This use of consumer optical discs for document storage is, however, relatively inefficient in terms of storage capacity, and the data is not suitable for computer or word processor input. With domestic television sets the limited resolution of 525-line (NTSC) or 625-line (PAL) systems only provides comfortable viewing of some 960 characters (videotex standard) compared with 4000 characters on a typed page. This not only limits the total capacity of the disc, but also presents some inconvenience to the user. The latter problem may, however, be overcome by using special high-resolution monitors with 2000 scan lines.

The comparatively low power of the lasers in consumer playback devices does not permit them to be employed as recording devices. Players with record facilities have been demonstrated. They employ nonerasable discs so that each new document can only be recorded on a virgin track. *Compare* COMPACT DISC. *See* CAPACITANCE, FRAME, FREEZE FRAME, FREQUENCY MODULATION, INTERACTIVE VIDEODISC SYSTEMS, OPTICAL DIGITAL DISC, SINE WAVE, VIDEO STANDARDS.

video display. In peripherals, a device that is used to display visual information, text or graphics; usually a cathode ray tube, but may also include light-emitting diodes or plasma panels. *See* CATHODE RAY TUBE, LIGHT-EMITTING DIODE, PLASMA PANEL. *Synonymous with* SCREEN.

video drive. In peripherals, the amplifier and electronic circuits to provide the cathode ray tube signals for a videotex display. *See* VIDEOTEX.

video editing. In video, the editing of video tapes to produce a sequence or program. (Philips). *See* VIDEO TAPE.

video editor. In printing, a photocomposition editing device incorporating a cathode ray tube. *See* CATHODE RAY TUBE, PHOTOTYPESETTING.

video error concealment. In codes, a technique that is used to reduce the visual effect of disturbances arising from erroneous video data. (Philips). *See* CONCEALMENT.

video expander. In recording, a memory device capable of storing one frame of video information. Data may be fed in at a slow rate and used to build up a continuously refreshed image on a television monitor. *See* SLOW-SCAN TELEVISION DEVICE, VIDEO COMPRESSOR.

video game. In applications, a special-purpose microcomputer producing a graphic display and, usually, receiving inputs from a hand controller, thus enabling the player, or players, to participate in games requiring skills and coordination. In some cases the games may be changed by inserting new ROM cartridges. *See* ROM CARTRIDGE. *Synonymous with* TELEVISION GAME.

video generator. In peripherals, a device that generates the signals for a television display according to received commands and signals. *See* SCREEN BUFFER.

videogram. (1) In recording, a prerecorded video tape or cassette. (2) In recording, a generic term for video recording systems encompassing videodisc and video cassette recorders. *See* VIDEO CASSETTE, VIDEODISC.

videographics. In television, the technique of electronic manipulation of pictures.

video input/output. In video, the facility for video input as well as output from a computer. With frame grabbing, for example, video signals can be input to the computer for additional processing and then output to the display. (Philips). *See* FRAME GRABBER.

video layout system. In typesetting, a cathode ray tube system used for layout planning prior to photocomposition. *See* CATHODE RAY TUBE, PHOTOTYPESETTING.

videomatics. The convergence of information technology and video techniques (e.g.

interactive videodisc systems). *Compare* INFORMATICS. *See* INTERACTIVE VIDEODISC SYSTEMS.

videomicrographic system. In micrographics, an information retrieval system in which microforms are retrieved and their images are scanned and transmitted to the user's terminal.

video monitor. In recording, a device for viewing a video recording at the time of recording, or afterwards.

Video Patsearch. In online information retrieval, a patents search service offered by Pergamon in which the indexes to, and the text of, US patents are located in a database and the graphics are held on videodiscs. *See* VIDEODISC.

videophone. In communications, a telephone system that transmits images, usually of the two people making the call.

video player. In recording, a device that can playback a video recording, but cannot itself make video recordings. *See* VIDEODISC.

Video Printing System. (VPS) In communications, a Japanese system in which colour images are transmitted as video signals and are transformed into colour prints or transparencies.

video quality level. In optical media, the reproduction quality of a video signal. Interactive compact discs, for example, provide for four video quality levels (i.e. natural pictures, RGB (5:5:5) graphics, colour look-up table graphics and run length-coded animation). (Philips). *Compare* AUDIO QUALITY LEVEL. *See* CD-I DIGITAL VIDEO, COLOUR LOOK-UP TABLE, NATURAL PICTURES, RGB (5:5:5), RUN LENGTH CODING.

video recorder. In recording, a system that can record television film and sound.

video signal. In television, the signal voltage variations due to picture information and synchronizing pulses. *See* COMPOSITE COLOUR VIDEO SIGNAL.

video standards. In television, there are three common international standards:

(a) NTSC (National Television Standard Committee), commonly used in the USA and Japan, 525 horizontal lines and 60 frames per second;
(b) PAL (phase alternating line), used in western Europe, Australia, parts of Africa and Middle East, 625 horizontal scan lines and 50 frames per second;
(c) SECAM (sequential couleur à mémoire), used in France, Saudi Arabia and USSR, similar to PAL but differs in method of producing colour signals.

A new standard, MAC, is proposed for direct-broadcast satellite systems. *See* DIRECT-BROADCAST SATELLITE, MAC.

video tape. In recording, a flexible tape coated with magnetic material upon which video signals can be recorded. *See* VIDEO TAPE RECORDING.

video tape recording. A tape recorder for television pictures and sound must deal with signals in the frequency range 0–5 Mhz as compared with a 15 kHz bandwidth for audiotape systems. Such high frequencies imply head-to-tape speeds in excess of 12.7 metres per second; the longitudinal recording track schemes of audio tape recorders cannot therefore be employed because they would involve excessive tape velocities, and a one-hour recording would require nearly 46 kilometres of magnetic tape. The necessary head-to-tape speed for video recording is produced by rotating the magnetic heads at a high speed across the width of the tape, as it moves longitudinally at a relatively low speed (12.7–3.81 centimetres per second). The signals are thus recorded as a series of diagonal lines across the width of the tape giving a high effective length of recorded track for a reasonable length of tape.

A second potential problem of video recording is the number of octaves in the signal range of just above DC to 5 MHz; this octave range is reduced by using signal modulation techniques. Given a carrier of 8 MHz the modulated signal ranges from 3 to 13 MHz giving a span of just over two octaves. Frequency modulation is nearly always used because of its tolerance to amplitude variations, which occur in tape recording.

The major components of a video tape recorder are tape deck, head servo, capstan

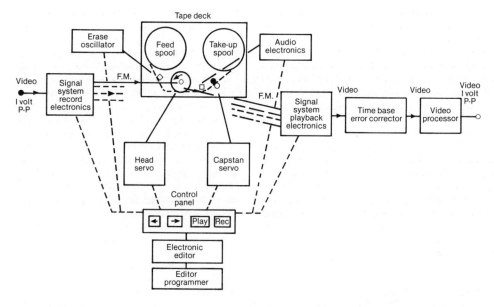

video tape recording

servo, signal system record electronics, signal system playback electronics, time base error correction, video processor, audio electronics and control panel.

The tape deck contains a feed spool and a take-up spool to contain the tape. A capstan, usually with a pinch roller to provide traction, controls the longitudinal speed of the tape. A rotating head wheel, or drum scanner, with a separate motor drive provides the head speed. This assembly has a form of signal coupling so that the radio frequency signal can be fed to the rotating heads. The audio heads are stationary and the audio tracks are recorded longitudinally with the audio erase head preceding the audio playback/record head. A stationary video erase head is located upstream of the video heads.

The rotational speed and phase of the video heads are controlled electronically by a servo mechanism on the head motor. The tape speed and phase are controlled by the capstan servo in more expensive devices. This servo mechanism ensures accurate alignment of the video heads to recorded track during playback.

The signal system record electronics receives the input signal during recording and produces the modulated radio frequency signal at a level high enough to saturate the tape. The signal system playback electronics amplifies the low-voltage signal produced by the magnetic heads during playback, switches between heads in multi-head systems (e.g. quadruplex) equalizes for playback losses and demodulates the frequency modulation signal back to video.

Time base error correction is required to compensate for timing instability arising from the mechanics of the head-scanning process. This electronic system introduces variable delays to ensure the necessary playback signal synchronization. The video processor adds fresh synchronizing pulses and colour bursts to the output video in more expensive units.

The audio electronics unit is similar to that of the audio tape recorders, but the audio quality of video tape recorders is adversely affected by the proximity of stray fields, poor tape contact and low width. The control panel provides the normal control functions — fast spooling, forward or reverse, playback and record. *See* ALPHA WRAP, CAPSTAN, COLOUR BURST, FREQUENCY MODULATION, HELICAL SCAN, MAGNETIC HEAD, OMEGA WRAP, PINCH ROLLER, QUADRUPLEX, SERVO MECHANISM, TRANSVERSE SCAN.

video teleconferencing. In communications, a system providing full audio and visual conferencing facilities. *See* TELECON-FERENCING.

videotex. A term that is used generically to cover teletext, a broadcast videotex service, and viewdata, a wired videotex service. With viewdata a communication link, providing simple two-way communication, is established between the user and host computer through a telephone network. With teletext the information flow is simplex, broadcast over television wavebands in conjunction with normal television programs.

(a) A user's view of videotex. A casual observer would notice very little difference between a viewdata and a teletext display. The general format is of multicoloured sets of alphanumeric characters or simple patterns displayed on a television screen. Across the world there are various videotex standards which affect the form of display, but they fall into two broad categories: alphamosaic and alphageometric. The European systems are based upon the alphamosaic display, and in this case the screen is divided into 24 (row) x 40 (column) spaces. A space is of one colour, and it may contain an alphanumeric character (lower or upper case) or a simple mosaic of six rectangles.

staircase appearance. On the other hand, the NAPLPS system is based upon an alphageometric standard, and the transmitted codes can produce simple line drawings, thus such terminals can be more readily used for educational purposes, for example. The access methods of videotex have been designed on a user friendly basis to ensure that no training is required to retrieve information from the database. There are no complicated logon procedures, and the user is guided to the required information by a series of menu choices provided by the display. A simple hand-held numeric keypad is used to select the next page to be displayed. Videotex organizes its database using a tree structure, although cross-references from one section of the database to another are possible.

A user can also access a page directly by keying in the appropriate page number. Each page can be the start of a small 'pamphlet' to 25 additional frames associated with it. The first page is, say, 121a and successive frames are 121b, 121c, etc. Successive depressions of a control key on the keypad will produce frames b, c, d, etc. The simple tree structure and menu selection allow videotex to be employed by a casual user, but this system does not supply the more sophisticated keyword searches which are possible with other database systems.

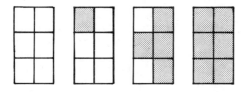

videotex
Fig. 1. Coarse 2×3 graphic dot matrix.

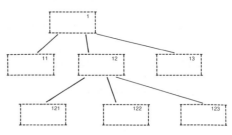

videotex
Fig. 2. Videotex tree structure.

The ASCII codes transmitted to the user either provide details of the pattern, or character, to be displayed in the character space or set certain attributes for the remainder of the line (e.g. switch to graphics, change colour, etc.). The alphamosaic system has the advantage of a simple user decoder system, but in normal operation (i.e. with conventional viewdata terminals) it cannot produce elegant pictures. Even a simple diagonal line has a

(b) Viewdata. In Prestel, the UK national viewdata service, a user dials up the viewdata computer, or uses an autodialer, and the computer responds with an opening page giving instructions on how to proceed.

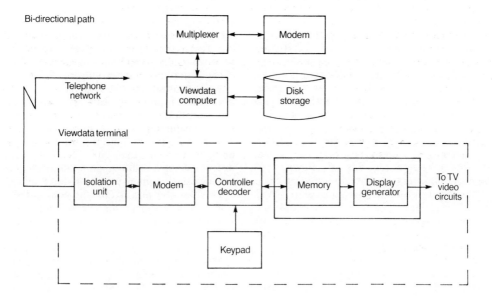

videotex
Fig. 3. Elements of a viewdata system.

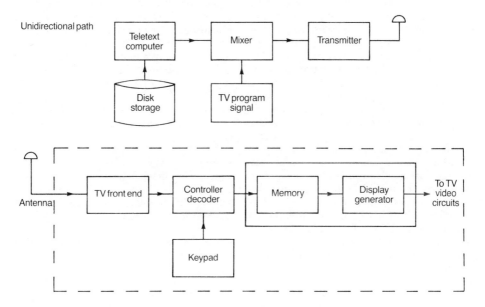

videotex
Fig. 4. Elements of a teletext system.

Each user keypad depression is converted into signals of audio frequency and transmitted to the computer at 75 baud. The computer sets aside a small section of memory for every online user, receives the user requests, selects the appropriate page from the disk store and transmits the information as ASCII codes at user terminal. Details of the user connect time, page accesses, etc. are recorded by the computer for customer billing. The codes transmitted to the user are stored in the decoder random-acess memory (i.e. the screen buffer). The decoder display unit scans this memory, interprets the codes and produces the display on the television screen.

In viewdata, the user forwards requests to the host computer, and it is possible for other information to be similarly transmitted. Thus a response frame can be used as a blank form in which the user inputs appropriate details. For example, a hotel booking service can be provided using viewdata. Information pages provide details of the hotels, prices, location, facilities, etc., and a response frame enables the user to input requirements. The user response information is held in computer store until it is accessed by the hotel reservation unit.

(c) Teletext. To a casual observer the only substantial difference between teletext and viewdata is the delay between a keypad depression and the appearance of the page. Teletext, however, is based on a one-way communication over television broadcast (or cable television) channels.

In radio broadcasts the signal is continuous, but with television the picture information is transmitted in synchronism with the raster scan of the television camera. The picture on the television screen is produced by varying signals to the cathode ray tube gun as the electron beam scans across the face of the tube. The beam commences in the upper left-hand corner of the screen and moves across in a horizontal line. It then jumps back to the left-hand side and paints the next line slightly below the previous one until the whole screen has been covered, at which point the beam flies back from the bottom right-hand to the top left-hand corner. Thus there are short intervals of time, measured in microseconds, when the spot is relocating itself on the screen, and no picture information is transmitted in these flyback periods. A television broadcast signal therefore has periodic gaps in its picture transmission, and it is possible to add a binary pulse train to the normal broadcast signal in these gaps. Teletext, therefore, uses spare capacity on an existing broadcast network and is an efficient and relatively cheap communication technique.

Unlike viewdata, the teletext computer does not respond to user requests, but simply produces each page of the database in rotation. The user requests the desired page by menu selection and inserts the page number on the key pad. The teletext decoder compares the page number of the broadcasted incoming page with that requested by the user and 'grabs' the appropriate frame, storing it in a random-access memory screen buffer, as in viewdata. *See* ALPHAGEOMETRIC, ALPHAMOSAIC, ALPHANUMERIC, ELECTRONIC MAIL, FLY BACK, FRAME, GATEWAY, HALF-DUPLEX, INFORMATION PROVIDER, MODEM, NAPLPS, PRESTEL, RESPONSE FRAME, SIMPLEX, TELEBANKING, TELEBOOKING, TELESHOPPING, TELETEXT, TREE STRUCTURE, VIEWDATA.

videotext. (1) The display of textual material on a cathode ray tube screen or television set. (2) The German term for teletext. *See* TELETEXT.

Videovoice. In television, a device that transmits freeze frame of slow-scan television images over standard telephone connections. *See* FREEZE FRAME, SLOW-SCAN TELEVISION DEVICE.

Vidicon. In television, image pickup tube used in television cameras. *See* MACHINE VISION.

Viditel. In videotex, a Dutch viewdata system. *See* VIEWDATA.

Vidon. In videotex, a Canadian viewdata system. *See* VIEWDATA.

view. In databases, the subset of a database that is made available to a particular user. *See* ACCESS CONTROL.

viewbook. In publishing, a book supplied in the form of floppy disks and read on a microcomputer screen. This form of publishing is applicable to textbooks or reference works where the reader may wish to study sections and have ready access to other sections dealing with allied topics. Automatic searching for specified text strings, facilities for adding and collating reader's margin notes, etc. may also be supplied. *Compare* CD-ROM PUBLISHING, DISK MAGAZINE. *See* ELECTRONIC PUBLISHING.

Viewdata. In videotex, Hongkong viewdata system. *See* VIEWDATA.

viewdata. In videotex, an interactive information service using a telephone link between the user and a host computer. The user employs a special terminal or an adaptor linked to a domestic television set. *Synonymous with* INTERACTIVE VIDEOTEX.

viewing pyramid. In computer graphics, a volume of space containing the coordinate information viewed by an observer. It is constructed in the eye coordinate system with a pyramid formed from an apex at the eye and lines from the apex to the four corners of the picture plane. Two further planes are drawn parallel to the base at distances that represent the nearest and furthest point that can be viewed. The truncated pyramid between these two planes is the pyramid of view. *See* CONE OF VISION, EYE COORDINATES, PICTURE PLANE.

Viewtel. In videotex, a US viewdata system; also called Channel 2000. *See* VIEWDATA.

Viewtel 202. In videotex, a UK viewdata system. *See* VIEWDATA.

vignette. In printing, a small illustration in a book not enclosed in a definite border. (Desktop).

virgin. In video, pertaining to videotape with no recorded signal. *Compare* RAW TAPE.

virtual. In computing and data communications, pertaining to a facility that is offered to a user, or system, as if it were a physical reality. *Compare* TRANSPARENT. *See* VIRTUAL STORAGE.

virtual address. In memory systems, the apparent address of a location in virtual storage. *See* VIRTUAL STORAGE.

virtual call service. In data communications, a packet-switching service in which a logical link is set up prior to transfer. Packets are transferred over the logical link, some of them contain no data, but are used for supervisory purposes. During the data transfer phase, packet sequence and flow control operations are performed. *Compare* DATAGRAM SERVICE. *See* FLOW CONTROL, PACKET SWITCHING, VIRTUAL CIRCUIT.

virtual circuit. In data communications, a circuit that comprises a path established from source to destination in the network. For the duration of the call all packets that are not individually addressed are transmitted through this virtual circuit and arrive in the same order as delivered. *Compare* CIRCUIT SWITCHING, DATAGRAM, PACKET SWITCHING.

virtual device interface. *See* VDI.

virtual device metafile. (VDM) In computer graphics, the definition of a mechanism for storing or transmitting graphical images. In addition to being device-independent the graphical information can be reprocessed and modified in a metafile without regenerating the entire stored picture. *See* GRAPHICAL KERNEL SYSTEM.

virtual disk. In memory systems, an area of main storage in which the data is structured as if it were stored on a floppy disk. It can speed up the operation of microcomputer software that is designed to extract its data from a floppy disk. *See* FLOPPY DISK, MAIN MEMORY. *Synonymous with* RAM DISK.

virtual machine. In computing, a simulation of a computer and its associated devices by another computer system.

virtual memory. (1) In memory systems, a technique that allows the processor to employ its full address space although it exceeds the physical main memory available. The virtual memory space exists on disk, when the processor addresses a portion of its address space, outside the main memory, special hardware locates the required page on disk and transfers it to a section of the main memory. *See* ADDRESS SPACE, PAGE. *Synonymous with* VIRTUAL STORAGE. (2) In computer security, a technique that provides a mechanism to enforce access control. The physical memory is shared among users, but pages of virtual memory can be assigned to individual users or processes. A page entry table can specify the access type (read, write or none) that is allowed from each access node. *See* ACCESS CONTROL.

virtual password. In computer security, a password computed from a passphrase that meets the requirements of password storage (e.g. 64 bits for data encryption standard). (FIPS). *See* PASSPHRASE, PASSWORD.

virtual private network. In communications, a private communications network implemented on a public telephone system. Users contract for a specified traffic capacity at each location and are billed accordingly, with an additional charge for each user call.

virtual push button. In peripherals, a display element that can be selected by a pointing device and programmed to operate as a function key. *See* FUNCTION KEY, POINTING DEVICE. *Synonymous with* LIGHT BUTTON.

virtual service interface. In distributed processing, the mapping of files and services on a mainframe onto a microcomputer to give the impression to users that they are available locally and are running under the microcomputer's operating system. *See* COOPERATIVE PROCESSING.

virtual storage. *Synonymous with* VIRTUAL MEMORY.

virtual telecommunications access method. In data communications, software used to control the flow of information between a host computer and remote terminals.

virtual terminal. In peripherals, an ideal terminal that is defined as a standard for the purpose of uniform handling of a variety of actual terminals. A terminal processor thereafter converts the signals of the real terminal to conform to the standards of the virtual terminal. *See* TERMINAL.

virus. In computer security, a section of code introduced into a disk operating system for malicious purposes. At some stage the inserted code will trigger a process that will eliminate all files from the disk. The effects of the virus can extend to many users. A disk containing the virus is loaded into a computer, and it resides in computer memory. The virus detects when a new disk is loaded into the system and then writes itself onto that disk. *Compare* MOCKINGBIRD.

visible light-emitting diode. (VLED) In microelectronics, a light-emitting diode (LED) with an output in the visible range. Some LEDs produce infrared radiation. *See* LIGHT-EMITTING DIODE.

Visicom. In data communications, an electronic mail service designed for the deaf. *See* ELECTRONIC MAIL.

vision mixer. In television, a device that selects one of a number of image sources (e.g. cameras, video tape recorders) to provide the broadcast picture. It is also used for fades, mixes, etc. *See* MIXER. *Synonymous with* SWITCHER.

visual acuity. The ability of the eye to resolve or discriminate fine detail.

visual display terminal. (VDT) In peripherals, an input/output device comprising a display unit, keyboard and associated circuitry. Cathode ray tube displays are the dominant current technology, and control circuitry is responsible for two basic tasks: timing and character image generation. The alphanumeric displays use dot matrix patterns, typically a 7 x 9 matrix, usually with true descenders. The dot matrix characters are drawn line by line on the screen, and the screen display normally comprises 24 lines of 80 or 132 characters. This screen display is refreshed at 60 Hz (USA), or 50 Hz (UK), to avoid perceptible flicker.

The control circuitry produces an alphanumeric character display by reading the character code in memory, determining the appropriate dot matrix pattern and the next horizontal line of that pattern to be displayed, and developing the on/off signals to drive the cathode ray tube gun as the electron beam scans across the screen. The dot matrix patterns for each character code are stored in a character generator read-only memory.

The three major cathode ray tube terminal types are dumb terminals, smart or editing terminals and intelligent or processing terminals. Dumb terminals have a limited capability and communicate with the computer, one character at a time, under exclusive control of the computer. Editing terminals have an internal buffer memory allowing the operator to check, insert or delete characters or whole lines of text. The data can be entered into the computer in block format, but within the limits of buffer memory terminal data can be manipulated without interaction with the computer. Intelligent terminals have internal microprocessors for limited processing of data; the distinction between an intelligent terminal and a microcomputer linked to a host computer lies in the extent to which the device is operated offline from the host computer.

Display attributes of terminals include character formation, video characteristics and cursor type. The dot matrix patterns can vary from 5 x 7 and 7 x 9 to higher-resolution matrices. The video characteristics include half-intensity, blink, underline, blank and normal/reverse. Similarly, cursors may be steady/blink, block/underline or invisible. The screen intensity can be adjusted by a brilliance control knob or depression of control keys. A screen saver facility removes screen illumination after a certain period of inactivity, and the screen display is made to reappear by depression of any keyboard key. Editing and processing terminals provide editing capabilities, including cursor movement, tab movements, deletion and movement of blocks of data.

Terminals connected to host computers via a communication network require the appropriate interfaces and software to conform to the selected protocols, asynchronous, X.25, synchronous data link control, etc. Graphics display terminals, which demand high-resolution colour displays, make heavy demands upon the performance of the control circuitry and the design of the cathode ray tube. The resolution of colour displays is lower than that of a corresponding monochrome system. The ultimate restriction of the colour display resolution is the grouping of the phosphor dot trios producing the three primary colours of the display. Monochrome displays are brighter than corresponding colour systems both because the colour cathode ray tube has smaller guns and because the shadowmask absorbs a portion of the illumination.

Current graphics display technology uses raster displays, as compared with the earlier vector refresh systems. 1000-line monochrome raster displays can produce images of comparable quality, to vector refresh systems, without the flicker arising when the display file of the vector system becomes large. *Compare* FLAT-SCREEN DISPLAY, VISUAL DISPLAY UNIT. *See* ALPHANUMERIC, ASYNCHRONOUS TRANSMISSION, BUFFER, BUFFER SIZE, CATHODE RAY TUBE, DISPLAY FILE, DOT MATRIX, DUMB DEVICE, EDITING TERMINAL, FLICKER, GUN, INPUT/OUTPUT UNIT, INTELLIGENT TERMINAL, KEYBOARD, MICROPROCESSOR, PHOSPHOR DOTS, RASTER DISPLAY, READ-ONLY MEMORY SHADOWMASK, SYNCHRONOUS DATA LINK CONTROL, TRUE DESCENDER, VECTOR REFRESH.

visual display unit. (VDU) In peripherals, a device for the display of computer output in soft-copy form. The display technologies include cathode ray tube, liquid crystal display, light-emitting diode and plasma panel, but the cathode ray tube displays are likely to remain dominant for some years except where the cost, weight and power requirements are important factors (e.g. in portable microcomputers). A VDU combined with a keyboard, and associated circuitry, comprises a visual display terminal capable of acting as an input/output device for a local or remote computer. *Compare* VISUAL DISPLAY TERMINAL. *See* CATHODE RAY TUBE, FLAT-SCREEN DISPLAY, KEYBOARD, LIQUID CRYSTAL DISPLAY, LIGHT-EMITTING DIODE, PLASMA PANEL, RF MODULATION METHOD, RGB, SOFT COPY. *Synonymous with* DISPLAY DEVICE.

visual editing terminal. (VET) In printing, a visual display terminal used specifically for editing.

visual effects function. In optical media, one of the set of interactive compact disc functions, such as signal mixing and colour palette control, that are used to achieve visual effects. (Philips). *See* COMPACT DISC – INTERACTIVE, PALETTE.

visual literacy. Skills developed in interpreting, judging, responding to and using visual representations of reality.

visual programming. In programming, a method of instructing the computer by showing it what to do rather than keying what to do. For example, instead of writing a lengthy and exacting set of format statements, describing the manner that information is displayed, the user draws a corresponding visual representation by (say) manipulating a cursor on a visual display unit screen. *See* FOURTH-GENERATION LANGUAGE, VISUAL DISPLAY UNIT.

visual search microfilm. *See* VSMF.

viz. In printing, term used in footnotes meaning 'namely'.

VLED. *See* VISIBLE LIGHT-EMITTING DIODE.

VLF. *See* VERY LOW FREQUENCY.

VLSI. *See* VERY LARGE-SCALE INTEGRATION.

vocal tract synthesizer. In man–machine interfaces, a speech synthesizer that accepts the speech, coded on the basis of formants, and produces the original sound waveform. *Compare* PHONETIC SYNTHESIS, WAVEFORM ENCODER. *See* FORMANT, SPEECH SYNTHESIZER.

vocoder. In communications, a device that transmits sufficient information for a voice message to be synthesized, but that does not convey the exact reproduction of the original voice. This means that the synthesizer will produce the same message, but the output will not sound like the original voice. *See* SPEECH SYNTHESIZER.

VOGAD. In communications, voice-operated gain-adjusting device; a unit used in radiocommunications that removes fluctuations in input speech signals and outputs them at a constant level. *Compare* COMPANDOR.

voice activation. Pertaining to any device that is designed to respond to voice signals. *See* SPEECH RECOGNIZER.

voice answer back. (VAB) In man–machine interfaces, an audio response unit that can link a computer system to a telephone network to provide voice responses to enquiries. *See* AUDIO RESPONSE UNIT, SPEECH SYNTHESIZER, VOICE OUPUT.

voice band. In communications, the band of frequencies permitting intelligible transmission of human voice, usually 300–3000 Hz. *See* AUDIO FREQUENCY. *Synonymous with* TELEPHONE FREQUENCY, VOICE FREQUENCY.

voice bank. In communications, a recording system that can store spoken material for ready access.

voice data entry. In man–machine interfaces, a system that accepts the spoken word as input data or commands. The user speaks into a microphone and a digitized version of the audio signal is compared with that of digitized words held in computer memory. When a reasonable match is found the encoded characters (e.g. ASCII) are often displayed on a visual display unit for user confirmation prior to input to the computer. Usually a 'training session' is held to provide the computer with examples of the spoken word. Applications include comments from quality control inspectors on production lines, receipt of telephone orders from salesmen, stock checking, etc. *See* SPEECH RECOGNIZER, VISUAL DISPLAY UNIT.

voice frequency. *See* VOICE BAND.

voice-grade channel. In communications, a channel suitable for the transmission of speech, facsimile, analog or digital data with a frequency range in the voice band, generally about 300–3000 Hz. *Compare* SUBVOICE-GRADE CHANNEL. *See* VOICE BAND.

voice-grade information. In audio, audio information of a quality sufficient for reproducing the human voice, normally having a bandwidth of 4–8 kHz. (Philips). *See* SPEECH QUALITY.

voice guard. In recording, a dictating machine device that emits a loud, steady tone if the recording medium is not moving.

voice input. In man–machine interfaces, human voice input to a given device, such as a computer, where it is normally used for control or information entry purposes. (Philips). *See* SPEECH RECOGNIZER, VOICE DATA ENTRY.

voice mail. In communications, a system in which spoken information is digitized and stored either in a network memory or in the appropriate apparatus at the destination for the message. The spoken message is later retrieved by the called party. *See* VOICE STORE AND FORWARD.

voice message system. *See* VOICE MAIL.

voice notes. In communications, a technique for storing a voice message on a computer. The user views a data message at a visual display unit and inputs the requisite voice message through a microphone. *Compare* VOICE MAIL. *See* VISUAL DISPLAY UNIT.

voice-operated device. In communications, a device used on a circuit to permit the presence of telephone currents to effect desired control. Echo suppressors often use such devices. *See* ECHO SUPPRESSOR.

voice output. In man–machine interfaces, a device that enables a computer to produce output as a spoken word. *See* SPEECH SYNTHESIZER.

voice over. In filming or television, an off-screen voice.

voice print. In computer security, a recorded signal that identifies the voice characteristics of an individual and is used for identification purposes.

voice recognition. *See* SPEECH RECOGNIZER.

voice scrambling. In communications security, the enciphering of voice communications. Voice-scrambling techniques may be categorized as frequency, time division multiplexing and digital techniques. Frequency techniques involve transformations of the constituent frequencies of the voice signal, time division multiplexing permutes short segments of the signal within fixed-length frames, and digital techniques convert the signal into a sequence of binary numbers and then subject those numbers to a mathematical encryption algorithm. *Synonymous with* SPEECH SCRAMBLING.

voice store and forward. In communications, a system that transmits and stores voice messages for playback or demand. *See* STORE AND FORWARD, VOICE MAIL.

voice synthesis. *See* SPEECH SYNTHESIZER.

voice unit. (VU) In communications, a unit measurement of signal level on a telephone line. A VU corresponds to a 1 millivolt sine wave signal into a 600-ohm resistive load. *See* REFERENCE VOLUME, RESISTANCE, SINE WAVE.

volatile storage. In memory systems, storage media in which the stored data is lost when the power supply is removed. *Compare* NON-VOLATILE STORAGE. *See* RANDOM-ACCESS MEMORY.

volatility. In programming, the percentage of records on a file that are added or deleted during a run. *See* ACTIVITY, FILE, RECORD.

voltage. In electronics, the electrical pressure across a circuit causing or capable of causing a current flow. *Compare* CURRENT.

voltage-tuned oscillator. (VTO) In electronics, an oscillator in which the output frequency is a function of an input direct current voltage. *See* OSCILLATOR, TELEVISION RECEIVE-ONLY.

volume. In memory systems, a storage medium holding data that can be mounted or demounted as a unit (e.g. a disk pack). *See* DISK PACK.

volume descriptor. In optical media, the part of an interactive compact disc label that identifies a given disc. (Philips). *See* COMPACT DISC – INTERACTIVE, DISC LABEL.

volume flag. In optical media, the field in an interactive compact disc file structure descriptor containing the logical name of the interactive disc. (Philips). *See* COMPACT DISC – INTERACTIVE.

von Neumann. In architecture, pertaining to the architecture of a conventional computer. It is characterized by: (a) a single computing element, incorporating processor, communications and memory; (b) linear organization of fixed-size memory

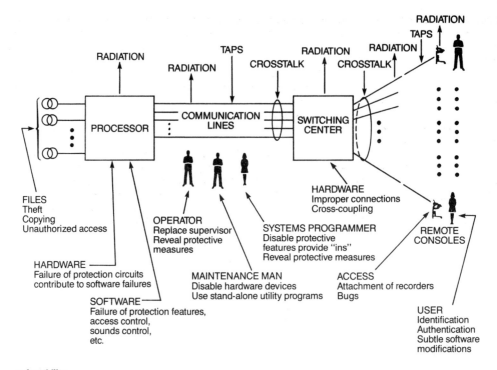

vulnerability
Some of the many possible threats to the security of a computer system. Because security threats arise from such a wide variety of sources, the mechanisms and procedures necessary to provide a secure environment must cover many areas of an enterprise. Source: *Journal of Computers & Security.*

cells; (c) one-level address space of cells; (d) low-level machine language; (e) sequential, centralized control of computation; and (f) primitive input/output capability. *Compare* DATA-DRIVEN, DEMAND-DRIVEN, PARALLEL PROCESSING. *See* ARCHITECTURE, CELL, MACHINE LANGUAGE, MEMORY.

voxel. In computer graphics, a three-dimensional pixel. *See* PIXEL.

VPS. *See* VIDEO PRINTING SYSTEM.

VRC. Vertical redundancy check. *See* LONGITUDINAL REDUNDANCY CHECK.

VSAT. In communications, very small aperture terminals. A VSAT network comprises a central, or hub, dish antenna of 5–8 metres, a geostationary communications satellite and a number of small, remote earth stations with dish antennae of 1.2–2.4 metres in diameter. *See* COMMUNICATIONS SATELLITE SYSTEM, DISH ANTENNA.

V-series recommendations of CCITT. In data communications, a series of recommendations relating to data communications over analog channels. *Compare* I-SERIES RECOMMENDATIONS OF CCITT, X-SERIES RECOMMENDATIONS OF CCITT. *See* PROTOCOL STANDARDS.

VSMF. In micrographics, visual search microfilm file; a 16-mm microfilm catalogue of products approved and listed by the US Department of Defense and their suppliers. *See* MICROFILM.

VTO. *See* VOLTAGE-TUNED OSCILLATOR.

VTR. Video tape recorder. *See* VIDEO TAPE RECORDING.

VU. *See* VOICE UNIT.

vulnerability. In computer security, any weakness or flaw existing in a system; the susceptibility of a system to a specific threat, attack or harmful event, or the opportunity available to a threat agent to mount that attack. *Compare* SAFEGUARD, THREAT. *See* HARMFUL EVENT.

VUmeter. In recording, a meter on sound recorders and playback devices which indicates variations in sound amplitude.

W

WACK. In data communications, Wait before transmitting positive ACKnowledgement; a signal sent by a receiving station to indicate that it is temporarily not ready to receive. *See* ACK, NAK.

WADS. *See* WIDE AREA DATA SERVICE.

wafer. In microelectronics, a very thin slice of cylindrically shaped monocrystalline solid rod of silicon, either before or after integrated circuits have been fabricated on it. After fabrication the wafer is cut into square dice, each of which is an integrated circuit. *See* CHIP, INTEGRATED CIRCUIT, WAFER SILICON INTEGRATION.

wafer silicon integration. In microelectronics, a chip as large as a wafer developed for high-speed computers. In conventional chip technology chips is manufactured on wafers and then cut into individual chips. In subsequent computer manufacture the individual chips are brought together on a circuit and interconnected electrically. This method of computer manufacture results in comparatively long chip interconnections, and the speed of the computer is limited by the time taken for pulses to traverse these interconnections. If the complete set of chips and interconnections is manufactured as a single unit on a wafer then the length of interconnections is considerably reduced. The major disadvantage of this technique lies in the problems of guaranteeing fault-free chips and interconnections in the wafer-manufacturing phase. With conventional chip technology a faulty chip on a wafer can be discarded, with wafer-scale integration techniques, however, it is necessary to employ a high degree of redundancy to ensure that a few isolated faults do not cause the whole wafer to be rejected. *See* CHIP, REDUNDANCY, WAFER.

wagon wheel effect. In filming, a phenomenon in which a spoked wheel appears to move in reverse because a spoke moves almost to the position of its nearest neighbour in the interval between shutter openings. *See* STROBOSCOPIC EFFECT.

wait condition. In computing, a state in which the processor has suspended program execution waiting for an external signal (e.g. data from a peripheral or backing storage). *See* BACKING STORAGE, PERIPHERAL.

wait loop. In programming, a subroutine in a computer program that loops continually until a condition external to the program occurs. *See* INTERRUPT, LOOP, SUBROUTINE.

walkie talkie. In communications, a small portable radio transmitter with limited range.

walk through. In programming, a process of reviewing a computer program, under development, by a structured discussion among a small team. Each member of the team has a well-defined function. The programmer outlines the operation of the program, and a discussion is held to detect any potential problem areas and identify possible improvements.

WAN. *See* WIDE AREA NETWORK.

wand. In peripherals, a hand-held bar code reader. A typical wand comprises an aluminium tube. Illumination from an light-emitting diode, near the reading end of the tube, is focused by a sapphire sphere onto the reflecting bar code label. Reflected light from the label is focused by the sphere onto a phototransistor higher up the tube interior. *See* BAR CODE, LIGHT-EMITTING DIODE, PHOTOTRANSISTOR.

WARC. *See* WORLD ADMINISTRATIVE RADIO CONFERENCE.

warm boot. In computing, the steps necessary to place a computer in fully operational status; typically loading the operating system, when the computer has been switched on and all initial set-up operations have been completed.

warm standby. In reliability, a backup system that can be switched into operation within a few seconds of an active system malfunction. *Compare* COLD STANDBY, HOT STANDBY.

watermark. In printing, a faint mark imparted to certain uncoated papers during manufacture to identify the paper mill.

watermark tape. In computer security and banking, a material used for magnetic stripes that is designed to increase the difficulty of manufacturing counterfeit cards. A permanent magnetic watermark is induced into the material by exposing it to an appropriate varying magnetic field while the magnetic particles are held in a resinous lacquer. The material is then dried thus fixing the orientation of the magnetic particles. One track of the card is used to check the watermark, and the track is subjected to a constant magnetic field before reading. Thus any attempt to counterfeit the watermark pattern by magnetizing a conventional magnetic stripe is thwarted by the erasing effect of the constant magnetic field. *Compare* SANDWICH TAPE. *See* MAGNETIC STRIPE CARD.

WATS. *See* WIDE AREA TELEPHONE SERVICE.

watt. In electronics, a unit of electrical power produced when one amp flows between a potential difference of one volt. *See* AMPERE, VOLTAGE.

wave. A physical activity that increases and decreases, or advances and retreats, periodically as it travels through the medium.

waveband. A range of wavelengths.

waveform. The graphic representation of the amplitude variations of a wave with time. *See* WAVE.

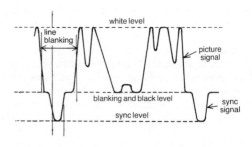

waveform
A typical line in a PAL video transmission showing synchronizing signals.

waveform encoder. In man–machine interfaces, a device that accepts a coded form of digitized speech and produces the original sound waveform. *Compare* PHONETIC SYNTHESIS, VOCAL TRACT SYNTHESIZER. *See* SPEECH SYNTHESIZER.

waveguide. In communications, metal tubes used for the transmission of microwave signals. An optical fiber may be considered to be a waveguide for light waves. *See* CIRCULAR WAVEGUIDE, FIBER OPTICS, RECTANGULAR WAVEGUIDE.

wavelength. The distance between corresponding points on successive waves. The wavelength multiplied by the frequency is equal to the speed of the wave. *See* FREQUENCY.

wavelength division multiplexing. (WDM) In communications, a technique that is identical to frequency division multiplexing. The term is applied to the use of different wavelengths for the light signals along an optical fiber. *See* FIBER OPTICS, FREQUENCY DIVISION MULTIPLEXING.

wayleave. In communications, the right of way granted for the laying of cables.

W channel. In optical media, one of the eight compact disc subcode channels (P–W). At present it is only allocated to compact disc graphics. (Philips). *See* COMPACT DISC, SUBCODE CHANNEL.

WDC. World data centre; a number of such centres were established for the international exchange of scientific information.

WDM. *See* WAVELENGTH DIVISION MULTI-PLEXING.

weak bits. In software protection, a technique in which bits with intermediate polarization values between those of a binary 1 and a binary 0 are prerecorded onto a master floppy disk, along with the software to be protected. When a weak bit is read, the disk controller on a microcomputer sometimes interprets it as a 1 and sometimes as a 0. A special test program checks for this statistical variation by reading the sector concerned several times, and hence determines if a master disk is being used.

If a weak bit is read and then copied across to another disk, along with the protected program, it will be written as a true binary digit and the test program will not detect any variation, in consecutive reads, and therefore conclude that a copy is being used; it will then prevent the program from being executed. *See* EXECUTE PROTECTION, FINGERPRINT. *Synonymous with* FUZZY-SECTOR TECHNIQUE.

weasel word. A word with a meaning changed to manipulate opinion. *Compare* BUZZ WORD.

web. In printing, ribbon or reel of paper as formed on a paper-making machine.

weber. In electronics, a unit of magnetic flux. *See* MAGNETIC FLUX.

web-fed. In printing, pertaining to a machine in which paper is fed from web or reel rather than from flat sheets. *Compare* SHEET-FED. *Synonymous with* REEL-FED.

wedge serif. In printing, a typeface with triangular serifs. *See* SERIF.

weed. In programming, to remove undesired items from a file.

weight. (1) In mathematics, a number assigned to a particular entity when the total effect of dissimilar entities, each of which may have a different number of members, is to established. The weight of each entity is multiplied by the number of members of that entity and summed. (2) In printing, a description of the blackness of a typeface (i.e. light, medium, bold, extra bold and ultra bold). (3) In printing, the weight of 500 sheets of paper of standard size.

weighting. In online information retrieval, a technique used in information retrieval that assigns different weights to search terms, or descriptors, in order to retrieve those documents which are most relevant. *See* DESCRIPTOR.

Westar. In communications, an American series of geostationary communications satellites. *See* GEOSTATIONARY SATELLITE.

Western Library Network. (WLN) In library science, a US library cooperative network that developed software now in wide use, particularly in the Australian and New Zealand bibliographic networks. The WLN was previously known as the Washington Library Network because of its state of origin.

Westlaw. In online information retrieval, a database supplied by West Publishing Co. and others and dealing with business and industry, communications, energy industry, US federal government, insurance and insurance industry, labour and employment, law, US federal law, US state law, patents and US securities.

wet on wet. In printing, a technique in which one colour is printed on another while the first is still wet.

wf. *See* WRONG FONT.

what if. In applications, an interactive decision-making technique in which one or more independent variables in a model are given specific values and the output is computed. *See* PERSONAL COMPUTING, SPREAD-SHEET.

what you see is what you get. (WYSIWYG) In applications, software that exactly reproduces a high-resolution screen image onto the printed output of a laser printer. The document originator can therefore undertake the roles of designer, graphic artist, paste-up and typesetter, with control over the whole process and consequential savings in time and cost. *See* DESK-TOP PUBLISHING.

wheel graph. *Synonymous with* PIE GRAPH.

wheel printer. In printing, a printer with a printing mechanism containing the characters on metal wheels. *See* DAISY WHEEL, PRINTER.

whetstone. In computing, a single program benchmark used to measure the floating point performance of a processor. *See* BENCHMARK TEST, FLOATING POINT.

white-card fraud. (1) In banking, a form of credit card fraud using a counterfeit credit card. A blank white plastic card with a magnetic stripe is manufactured and the stripe is encoded with the details contained in a genuine client's credit card; the information is obtained illegally from the appropriate financial institution. The cards are then used to obtain money from automatic teller machines. The perpetrator may also emboss the account number or other information on the card. *See* AUTOMATIC TELLER MACHINE. (2) In banking, a form of fraud in which a stolen credit card is heated (e.g. by boiling in water) and the old embossed digits are pressed out with new numbers being added.

white flag. In recording, a code that identifies a new film frame on a videodisc. *See* FRAME, VIDEODISC.

white level. In television, the maximum value of video signal voltage (i.e. corresponding to the brightest spot on the television display). *Compare* BLACK LEVEL. *See* VIDEO SIGNAL.

white-level frequency. In video recording, the frequency of the recorded frequency-modulated signal corresponding to the white level. This is the maximum frequency of the signal. *See* FREQUENCY MODULATION, SYNC TIP FREQUENCY, WHITE LEVEL.

white line. In printing, a space between lines of type equal to that left if one line of type is omitted.

white noise. In communications, an unwanted random signal with equal power over all frequencies. *See* NOISE.

white out. *Synonymous with* WHITE-SPACE SKID.

white-space reduction. *See* KERNING.

white-space skid. In communications, a facsimile facility that enables the scanner to skip blank spaces on the document. *See* FACSIMILE. *Synonymous with* WHITE OUT.

wide area data service. (WADS) In data communications, a wide area data transmission service operating on similar principles to a wide area telephone service. *See* WIDE AREA TELEPHONE SERVICE.

wide area network. (WAN) In data communications, a comprehensive multimode network connecting large numbers of terminals and computers spread over a wide area. *Compare* LOCAL AREA NETWORK.

wide area telephone service. (WATS) A flat rate, or measured bulk rate, long-distance telephone service provided on an outgoing or incoming call basis. *Synonymous with* LONG-HAUL NETWORK.

wideband. *Synonymous with* BROADBAND.

wideband channel. In data communications, channels that operate to 50 kilobits per second. The speed can be increased up to 168 kilobits per second with special modems. *See* BIT, MODEM.

widow. In printing, a short line at the top of a page or column. *See* AUTOMATIC WIDOW ADJUST.

width value. In printing, a list or group of widths allocated to a character set. *See* CHARACTER SET.

wild card. In computing, a symbol that may be used to express a set of files (e.g. *.BAS indicates all files with the extension BAS). *See* EXTENSION, FILE.

WIMPS. In man–machine interfaces, windows, icons, mouse and pulldown menus. *See* DESK-TOP PUBLISHING, ICON, MENU, MOUSE, WINDOW.

Winchester. *Synonymous with* WINCHESTER DISK DRIVE.

Winchester disk drive. In backing storage, a rigid magnetic disk system in which the read/write head lands on, and takes off from, a lubricated disk surface and remains in contact with the disk surface, at a safe landing zone, when it is stationary. The read/write heads and disk assembly are located in a sealed module with a closed loop recirculating air system. *Compare* FLOPPY DISK. *See* HARD DISK. *Synonymous with* WINCHESTER.

window. (1) In computer graphics, a software technique for dividing a bit-mapped graphics display into a number of independent, rectangular displays or windows. Each window provides all the necessary functions for a user to interact with an application running in that window. A window may also be used to display the output of a host session when a microcomputer is linked to a mainframe. *See* BIT-MAPPED GRAPHICS. (2) In programming, pertaining to a software technique that facilitates the movement of data between packages. The concept is intended to provide extremely user friendly systems for executives who can view the contents of different packages in 'windows' on the visual display unit screen and cut and paste information from one into another. *See* CUT AND PASTE. (3) In data communications. *See* SLIDING WINDOW PROTOCOL.

wipe. In filming and video, the change from one image to another by wiping out the first image according to a certain pattern to reveal the second image. (Philips). *See* TRANSITION.

wipe-through card reader. In computer security and banking, a card reader in which the card is wiped through an open slot in the read head device.

wire. In printing, the wire mesh used at the wet end of the paper-making process. The wire determines the texture of the paper.

wire frame. In computer graphics, a style of three-dimensional images produced by vector display systems and giving the appearance of objects constructed from wire. *Compare* RASTER REFRESH. *See* VECTOR DISPLAY.

wire printer. In printing, a dot matrix printer that uses wires to produce the pattern of dots. *See* DOT MATRIX.

wire service. In data communications, any telecommunication service over which messages or transmissions can be sent to subscribers (e.g. telex, TWX, SWIFT, BankWire, Fedwire). (ANSI) *See* BANKING NETWORKS, SWIFT.

wiretapping. In communications security, the unauthorized interception of messages. The purpose of passive wiretapping is to disclose message contents without detection, whereas active wiretapping involves the deliberate modification of messages, sometimes for the purpose of injecting false messages, injecting replays of previous messages (e.g. to repeat a credit transaction) or deleting messages. Authentication protects against message modification and injection of false messages by making it infeasible for an opponent to modify or create messages that meet the authentication criteria. *Compare* BETWEEN-THE-LINES ENTRY, EAVESDROPPING, PIGGYBACK ENTRY. *See* ACTIVE WIRETAPPING, BROWSING, PASSIVE WIRETAPPING.

WISE. World Information Systems Exchange; an international cooperative program between hundreds of institutions to foster the exchange of data about information technology.

WLN. *See* WESTERN LIBRARY NETWORK.

woofer. A component of a loudspeaker assembly producing low-frequency sound waves. *Compare* TWEETER.

word. In data structures, a group of bits, bytes or characters, considered as an entity, and capable of storage in one memory location.

word break. In word processing, the use of a hyphen to split a word at the end of a line so as to avoid obvious gaps. *See* EXCEPTION DICTIONARY.

word frame counter. In data communications, a unit to count the number of words in a frame as they are received. It may also count the number of frames. *See* FRAME, WORD.

word length. In data structures, the number of bits, bytes or characters in a word. *See* WORD.

word processing. (WP) In office systems, a office automation facility designed for the generation, manipulation, storage and re-use of bodies of text which are subsequently printed as office correspondence, reports, etc. on character printers, laser printers, etc.

The basic components of the word-processing system are the processor, display screen, printer and software. The processor is commonly a microcomputer, and the rapid expansion of microcomputers in the commercial world was probably due to the demand for cheap word processors.

The word-processing package contains the usual range of text manipulation facilities commonly found in screen editors: ease of insertion, deletion and modification of individual characters, margin and tab settings, automatic word wraparound, search and replace, merging sections from other files, etc. However, business correspondence and reports demand additional formatting facilities (e.g. footnotes, decimal tabs, horizontal scrolling, automatic numbering, paragraph and character formatting).

The footnote facility may simply provide for a one-line page footer, or it could include facilities to move automatically the footnote with the reference and long footnotes (i.e. a continuation of the footnote onto the next page). Decimal tabs provide for the automatic alignment of decimal points in columns of numbers, and horizontal scrolling permits the viewing of wide documents. Automatic numbering may be applied to the numbering of subsections, pages and chapters. This facility can be linked to the automatic production of a table of contents. Paragraph formatting allows for the alignment of paragraphs (flush left, centred, flush right, justified) and for the amount and type of first-line indentation. Character formatting controls such features as bold facing, italics, underlining, subscripting, superscripting, overstriking, print fonts and font sizes. Some systems provide for style sheets to predefine the format specifications for headings, paragraphs or even entire documents.

An important advantage of word processing lies in boilerplating (i.e. the inclusion of standard paragraphs in legal documents, contracts, etc.) or in simply merging sections from various files. Complications with boilerplating can arise from the problems of assigning meaningful file names, within the restrictions imposed by various operating systems, to a multiplicity of small files each containing a stock paragraph. This problem is eased with some packages which allow the creation and easy reference to a library of paragraphs. File merging can also be made more user friendly with windows and split-screen facilities.

Commercial applications often require mail merge facilities with form letters so that a large number of clients receive apparently personalized letters. The minimum requirements of mail merge are the insertion of name and address in the appropriate parts of the letter. However, sophisticated systems provide for the conditional insertion of paragraphs and even the selection of appropriate pronouns for male and female.

Authors may require automatic indexing facilities which allocate page numbers to marked keywords and then sort the index entries alphabetically.

Some word-processing packages are supplied with calculation facilities, but this development has been considerably extended with integrated speadsheet, database and graphics packages. Technical reports comprising tables of data, corresponding histograms or pie charts can be merged easily into the body of reports using such packages. Integrated database systems provide for more sophisticated mail merge systems: records can be selected by specified criteria, sorted, merged into form letters and the corresponding addressed envelopes produced.

Spelling checking is a useful facility to guard against consistent misspelling and typing transcriptions, grammar-checking programs also provide a guard against simple input mistakes or consequential errors when modifications are made to the text. Finally help facilities can range from simple menus invoked by a function key to sophisticated context-sensitive aids.

The major limitation of early word-processing systems lay in the restrictions on the appearance of the printed document imposed by conventional character printers. The advent of desk-top publishing has, however, revolutionized the final product of the word processor. *Compare* DATA PROCESSING. *See* AUTOMATIC DECIMAL TAB, AUTOMATIC FILE SELECT, AUTOMATIC HEADERS/FOOTERS, AUTOMATIC LINE/PARAGRAPH NUMBERING, AUTOMATIC MARGIN ADJUST, AUTOMATIC PAGINATION,

AUTOMATIC TAB MEMORY, AUTOMATIC WIDOW ADJUST, BOILERPLATE, CHARACTER PRINTER, DATABASE, DESK-TOP PUBLISHING, FONT, FORM LETTER, FUNCTION KEY, GRAMMAR-CHECKING PROGRAM, HELP, INTEGRATED SOFTWARE, LOWER CASE, MAIL MERGE, OVERSTRIKE, RECORD, SCREEN EDITOR, SEARCH AND REPLACE, SPELLING CHECK PROGRAM, SPLIT SCREEN, SPREADSHEET, STYLE SHEETS, UPPER CASE, WRAPAROUND.

word processing/office systems. In office systems, the total information-handling system of an organization, including word processing, administrative systems, data processing, micrographics, communications, etc. See OFFICE AUTOMATION.

word serial. In data communications, a parallel data transmission mode in which the words are sent along the bus system one after another. See BUS, PARALLEL TRANSMISSION, WORD.

word space. In electronic typesetting, a code, spaced between words, that can activate the typesetting and produce a non-printing character or space. See VARIABLE SPACE.

words per minute. (wpm) In communications, the rated speed of teletypewriter equipment. See TELETYPEWRITER.

word spotting. In man–machine interfaces, pertaining to systems that can determine whether some subject was mentioned or some word uttered in human spoken phrases.

work and tumble. In printing, a method of printing where pages are imposed together. The sheet is then printed on one side with the sheet being turned or tumbled from front to rear to print on the opposite side. (Desk-top). Compare WORK AND TURN. See IMPOSITION.

work and turn. In printing, a method of printing where pages are imposed in one form or assembled on one film. One side is then printed, and the sheet is then turned over and printed from the other edge using the same forme. The finished sheet is then cut to produce two complete copies. (Desk-

top). Compare WORK AND TUMBLE. See FORME.

work area. Synonymous with MEMORY WORKSPACE.

work factor. In computer security, an estimate of the effort or time that can be expected to be expended to overcome a protective measure by a would be penetrator with specified expertise and resources. (FIPS).

working data file. In programming, a file that is either erased at the end of an editing session or converted to a permanent file. See PERMANENT FILE.

working memory. In word processing, the section of memory holding text during the keyboarding, editing or playback processes. See EDIT, MEMORY.

workspace. Synonymous with MEMORY WORKSPACE.

workstation. (1) An intelligent terminal with facilities designed for specific tasks (e.g. word processing, computer-aided design). See COMPUTER-AIDED DESIGN, INTELLIGENT TERMINAL. (2) In distributed processing, a personal computer either linked to a local area network or attached to a mainframe terminal network upon which the user can call for a number of office automation services (e.g. word processing, electronic mail, computation, remote file access, remote printing). See ELECTRONIC MAIL, LOCAL AREA NETWORK, WORD PROCESSING.

World Administrative Radio Conference. (WARC) In communications, an organization that sets frequency allocation for the whole world. Compare REGIONAL ADMINISTRATIVE RADIO CONFERENCE.

World Aluminum Abstracts. In online information retrieval, a database supplied by American Society for Metals and dealing with metallurgy.

world coordinates. In computer graphics, a coordinate system that is independent of the observer and the characteristics of the display device. Images are usually stored in the world coordinates system and then are transformed to provide views appropriate to a particular observer. They are transformed once again to the device coordinates of the display device for viewing. *Compare* EYE COORDINATES, NORMALIZED DEVICE COORDINATES, SCREEN COORDINATES. *See* CARTESIAN COORDINATES, POLAR COORDINATES.

world disc. In optical media, a interactive compact disc (CD-I) on which the video data is encoded in such a way that it can be played and displayed on any CD-I player, irrespective of 525- or 625-line television standard. (Philips). *See* CD-I DIGITAL VIDEO, VIDEO STANDARDS.

World Reporter. In online information retrieval, a full-text international news database operated by Datasolve Ltd. *See* FULL-TEXT DATABASE.

World Textiles. In online information retrieval, a database supplied by the Shirley Institute and dealing with textiles.

WORM. In optical media, write once read many times; a type of optical digital disc in which the data may be written but not erased and overwritten. *See* DRAW, DRDW, OPTICAL DIGITAL DISC, WRITE-ONCE MEDIUM.

worm. In software protection, a program written by a software publisher that will invoke a penalty if unauthorized use of a program is detected. At best the worm will halt the protected program, at worst it will cause a small amount of corruption each time it is run, eventually leading to a disk crash. Worms are dangerous because they can be activated accidentally and, not surprisingly, packages so protected do not sell well. *Compare* VIRUS. *See* DISK CRASH.

worst-case condition. In data security, the worst-case conditions, from the cryptographer's viewpoint, are when the cryptanalyst: (a) has a complete knowledge of the cipher system; (b) has accumulated a considerable volume of ciphertext; and (c) knows the plaintext equivalent of a certain amount of the ciphertext.

wow. In recording, a low-frequency noise, in audio recording, usually produced by regular variations in the speed of a system's mechanical component. *See* FLUTTER.

WP. *See* WORD PROCESSING.

WPI. In online information retrieval, World Patents Index; an international patents database offered by Pergammon-Infoline.

wpm. *See* WORDS PER MINUTE.

wraparound. (1) In peripherals, the continuation of an operation from the maximum address of working location to the starting address. (2) In word processing, a facility that enables a word to be moved to a succeeding or preceding line, or page, to accommodate insertions and deletions. *See* VERTICAL WRAPAROUND, HORIZONTAL WRAPAROUND.

write. (1) In computer security, a fundamental operation that results only in the flow of information from a subject to an object. (DOD). *Compare* READ. *See* OBJECT, SUBJECT. (2) In computing, to record data in a storage device or data medium. *See* STORAGE DEVICE.

write access. In computer security, permission to write an object. (DOD). *Compare* READ ACCESS. *See* OBJECT, WRITE.

write after read. In memory systems, a technique that restores the data after the read action in those storage devices in which the action of reading erases the data from the device. *See* DESTRUCTIVE READOUT.

write enable. In memory systems, a mechanism that enables data or signals to be recorded on a tape or disk. In the absence of this mechanism the tape or disk is protected against any unwanted or accidental overwriting.

write-once medium. Medium on which data, once written, cannot be erased to permit re-writing. (Philips). *See* DOR.

write/read medium. *See* READ/WRITE MEDIUM.

writer's work bench. In computing, a Unix facility that comprises a package of programs for writers and includes an editor, formatter, proof reader, spelling checker, etc. *See* UNIX, WORD PROCESSING.

writing head. In memory systems, the magnetic head that writes signals onto the storage medium. *Compare* READ HEAD.

writing line. In printing, the maximum line length that can be written by a machine, usually expressed in characters or inches.

wrong font. (wf) In typesetting, a typographic error in which letters of different fonts become mixed. *See* FONT.

wrong-reading. In filming and printing, pertaining to text or graphics that is reversed from left to right. *Compare* RIGHT-READING. *Synonymous with* REVERSE-READING.

WYSIWYG. *See* WHAT YOU SEE IS WHAT YOU GET.

X

X. (1) A prefix for standards used by CCITT and ANSI. *See* ANSI, X-SERIES RECOMMENDATIONS OF CCITT. (2) In micrographics, pertaining to the degree of reduction. *See* REDUCTION.

X.1. In data communications, international user classes of service in public data networks.

X.2. In data communications, international user services and facilities in public data networks.

X.3. In data communications, packet assembly/disassembly facility (packer assembler/disassembler) in a public data network. *See* PACKER ASSEMBLER/DISASSEMBLER.

X.4. In data communications, general structure of signals of International Alphabet Number 5 code for data transmission over public data networks. *See* INTERNATIONAL ALPHABET NUMBER 5.

X.15. In data communications, definitions of terms concerning public data networks.

X.20. In data communications, interface between data terminal equipment and data circuit terminating equipment for start/stop transmission services on public data networks. *See* DATA CIRCUIT TERMINATING EQUIPMENT, DATA TERMINAL EQUIPMENT.

X.20 bis. In data communications, use on public data networks of data terminal equipment that is designed for interfacing to asynchronous duplex V-series modems. *See* DATA TERMINAL EQUIPMENT, MODEM.

X.21. In data communications, interface between data terminal equipment and data circuit terminating equipment for synchronous operation on public data networks. *See* DATA CIRCUITING TERMINATING EQUIPMENT, DATA TERMINAL EQUIPMENT.

X.21 bis. In data communications, use on public data networks of data terminal equipment that is designed for interfacing to synchronous V-series modems. *See* MODEM.

X.22. In data communications, multiplex data terminal equipment/data circuit terminating equipment interface for user classes 3–6. *See* DATA CIRCUIT TERMINATING EQUIPMENT, DATA TERMINAL EQUIPMENT.

X.24. In data communications, list of definitions for interchange circuits between data terminal equipment and data circuit terminating equipment on public data networks. *See* DATA CIRCUIT TERMINATING EQUIPMENT, DATA TERMINAL EQUIPMENT.

X.25. In data communications, interface between data terminal equipment and data circuit terminating equipment for terminals operating in the packet mode on public data networks. *See* DCE, DATA CIRCUIT TERMINATING EQUIPMENT, DATA TERMINAL EQUIPMENT.

X.26. In data communications, electrical characteristics for unbalanced double-current interchange circuits for general use with integrated circuit equipment in the field of data communications. *Compare* X.27. *See* V.10.

X.27. In data communications, electrical characteristics for balanced double-current interchange circuits for general use with integrated circuit equipment in the field of data communications. *Compare* X.26. *See* V.11, RS-423A.

X.28. In data communications, data terminal equipment/data circuit terminating equipment interface for a start/stop mode data terminal equipment accessing the packet assembly/disassembly facility (PAD) on a public data network situated in the same country. *See* DATA CIRCUIT TERMINATING EQUIPMENT, DATA TERMINAL EQUIPMENT, PACKET ASSEMBLER/DISASSEMBLER.

X.29. In data communications, procedures for the exchange of control information and user data between a packet assembly/disassembly facility (PAD) and a packet-mode data terminal equipment or another PAD. *See* DATA TERMINAL EQUIPMENT, PACKET ASSEMBLER/DISASSEMBLER.

X.40. In data communications, standardization of frequency-shift and modulated transmission systems for the provision of telegraph and data channels by frequency division of a group.

X.50. In data communications, fundamental parameters of a multiplexing scheme for the international interface between synchronous data networks. *See* MULTIPLEXING, SYNCHRONOUS DATA NETWORK.

X.50 bis. In data communications, fundamental parameters of a 48 kilobits per second user data-signalling rate transmission scheme for the international interface between synchronous data networks.

X.51. In data communications, fundamental parameters of a multiplexing scheme for the international interface between synchronous data networks. *See* SYNCHRONOUS DATA NETWORK.

X.51 bis. In data communications, fundamental parameters of a 48 kilobits per second user data-signalling rate transmission scheme for the international interface between synchronous data networks using a 10-bit envelope structure.

X.52. In data communications, method of encoding anisochronous signals into a synchronous user bearer. *See* ANISOCHRONOUS TRANSMISSION.

X.53. In data communications, numbering of channels on international multiplex links at 64 kilobits per second. *See* MULTIPLEXING.

X.54. In data communications, allocation of channels on international multiplex links at 64 kilobits per second. *See* MULTIPLEXING.

X.60. In data communications, common-channel signalling for circuit-switched data applications. *See* SYSTEM X.

X.61. In data communications, signalling system No 7 — data user part.

X.71. In data communications, decentralized terminal and transit control signalling system on international circuits between synchronous data networks. *See* SYNCHRONOUS DATA NETWORK.

X.75. In data communications, terminal and transit call control procedures and data transfer system on international circuits between packet-switched data networks.

X.80. In data communications, interworking of interchange signalling system switched data services.

X.87. In data communications, principles and procedures for realization of international user facilities and network utilities in public data networks.

X.92. In data communications, hypothetical reference connections for public synchronous data networks. *See* SYNCHRONOUS DATA NETWORK.

X.96. In data communications, call progress signals in public data networks.

X.110. In data communications, routing principles for international public data services through switched public data networks of the same type. *See* ROUTING.

X.121. In data communications, international numbering plan for public data networks.

X.130. In data communications, provisional objectives for call set-up and clear-down times in public synchronous data networks (circuit switching). *See* CIRCUIT SWITCHING, SYNCHRONOUS DATA NETWORK.

X.132. In data communications, provisional objectives for grade of service in international data communications over circuit-switched public data networks.

X.150. In data communications, data terminal equipment and data circuit terminating equipment test loops for public data networks. *See* DATA CIRCUIT TERMINATING EQUIPMENT, DATA TERMINAL EQUIPMENT, X.21, X.21 bis.

X.180. In data communications, administrative arrangements for international closed user groups. *See* CLOSED USER GROUP.

X.200. In data communications, Open Systems Interconnection reference model for CCITT applications. *See* OPEN SYSTEMS INTERCONNECTION.

X.210. In data communications, Open System Interconnection layer service definition convention. *See* OPEN SYSTEMS INTERCONNECTION.

X.400. In data communications, a standard for message-handling systems that includes specifications for the network architecture,

protocol structure, implementation detail, message transfer elements and content protocols. X.400 is a fully developed application layer of the Open Systems Interconnection model, and it introduces the concept of sublayers termed user agents (UA) and message transfer agents (MTA).

The user agent is analogous to the user of a postal system who addresses and posts a letter. The MTAs are effectively the sorting offices that provide for the distribution and final delivery of the message (Fig. 1). The MTAs as a group are termed the message transfer system.

The three major protocols within X.400 are the relay protocol P1, the message header and body protocol P2, and the submission protocol P3. The user interface is not defined, thus allowing considerable flexibility in the manner in which the message is written, displayed, stored and retrieved.

A typical message has an envelope and a message content that comprises the message header and body. The P2 protocol refers to the message header, including elements such as: originator, recipient, subject, copy

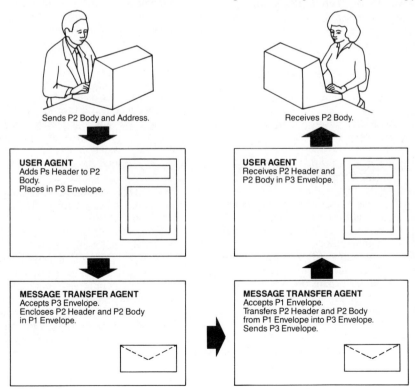

Sends P2 Body and Address.　　　　　Receives P2 Body.

USER AGENT
Adds Ps Header to P2 Body.
Places in P3 Envelope.

USER AGENT
Receives P2 Header and P2 Body in P3 Envelope.

MESSAGE TRANSFER AGENT
Accepts P3 Envelope.
Encloses P2 Header and P2 Body in P1 Envelope.

MESSAGE TRANSFER AGENT
Accepts P1 Envelope.
Transfers P2 Header and P2 Body from P1 Envelope into P3 Envelope.
Sends P3 Envelope.

X. 400

recipients, reply-to indication, reply-by indication, priority, sensitivity, expiry date, blind copy, specification of delivery time, delivery notification address, cross-references to other messages, obsolete message references and reply-to message reference. P2 also defines the various body parts of the message including telex, voice, fax, teletex, videotex.

The P3 protocol covers the envelope standard for the transmissions between the user agent and the message transfer agent. Thus the user sends the message body and address to the user agent who adds the P2 header, to the P2 body and places it in a P3 envelope (Fig. 1).

The P1 protocol refers to the envelope standard when the message is being routed from one message transfer agent to another. The MTA accepts the message in the P3 envelope from the UA, and encloses the P2 header and body in a P1 envelope for transfer to the next MTA. At the receiving end the MTA accepts the P1 envelope, and transfers the P2 header and body into a P3 envelope for submission to the receiving UA. The latter accepts the P3 envelope and passes the P2 body to the receiver.

It is anticipated that the main application area of X.400 will be in office systems using connections between personal computers and networks.

The specific advantages of X.400 to original equipment manufacturers (OEMs), and their customers are listed below.

(a) Reduced development costs resulting from the use of clearly defined specifications.
(b) Purchase of off-the-shelf software reducing development times.
(c) OEM development staff need less specialist knowledge of proprietary communications systems.
(d) Users will not be locked into individual manufacturers.
(e) Elimination of wasteful conversion between different services.
(f) Modular expansion.
(g) Reduction in telephone usage.
(h) Reduction in paper usage.

See APPLICATION LAYER, BLIND COPY, ELECTRONIC MAIL, OPEN SYSTEMS INTERCONNECTION, ORIGINAL EQUIPMENT MANUFACTURER, PROTOCOL, P1, P2, P3.

X-axis. In mathematics, a horizontal axis in a set of three-dimensional cartesian coordinates. *Compare* Y-AXIS, Z-AXIS. *See* CARTESIAN COORDINATES. *Synonymous with* ABSCISSA.

xenon flash. In printing, a high-intensity, short-exposure light source often used in phototypesetting machines.

xerography. In printing, a process that first places an electrostatic charge on a plate. An image is then projected onto the plate, causing the charge to dissipate in the illuminated areas, thus allowing an applied coating of resinous powder to adhere only to the uncharged (dark) areas. The powder is then transferred to paper and is fixed by heat. *See* ELECTROPHOTOGRAPHIC PROCESS, LASER PRINTER, LASER XEROGRAPHY.

x height. In printing, the height of the body of the lower-case letters, exclusive of ascenders and descenders. *Synonymous with* Z HEIGHT.

X-modem. In programming, an asynchronous file transfer protocol that works with almost any microcomputer and host. The protocol is in the public domain and is widely used on bulletin board systems. Data to be transmitted is assembled into 128-byte blocks, the last block being padded with blanks if necessary. Longitudinal redundancy check is used for block checking, and each frame has a sequence number so the receiver will acknowledge and then ignore duplicate frames. *See* BULLETIN BOARD, FRAME, LONGITUDINAL REDUNDANCY CHECK.

XON/XOFF protocol. In data communications, a standard protocol employed when information is transferred from one computer to another, or to a peripheral. The protocol usually requires a full-duplex data link. When the receiving computer, or peripheral, can no longer receive data (e.g. when a computer is required to service another higher-priority task) it sends an XOFF ASCII control character which instructs the transmitting computer to await the reception of a XON character. *See* AMERICAN STANDARD CODE FOR INFORMATION INTERCHANGE, FULL-DUPLEX, PRIORITY, PROTOCOL.

XOR. *See* EXCLUSIVE OR.

X-series recommendations of CCITT. In data communications, a series of recommendations for data transmission over public data networks. *Compare* I-SERIES RECOMMENDATIONS OF CCITT, V-SERIES RECOMMENDATIONS OF CCITT. *See* PROTOCOL STANDARDS.

X-Stream. In data communications, a generic name of four fully digital services, provided by British Telecom — Megastream, Switchstream, Satstream, Kilostream. *See* KILOSTREAM, MEGASTREAM, SATSTREAM, SWITCHSTREAM.

X–Y device. In peripherals, an input device for entering X- and Y-coordinates, mainly used for accurate cursor positioning. (Philips).

X–Y plotter. In peripherals, a plotting device that receives X- and Y-coordinates from a computer and plots a coordinate graph. *See* COORDINATE GRAPH.

Y

yaw. In communications, a rotation of a satellite about an axis that joins the satellite to the centre of the earth. *See* PITCH, ROLL.

Y-axis. In mathematics, a horizontal axis in a set of three-dimensional cartesian coordinates. *Compare* X-AXIS, Z-AXIS. *See* CARTESIAN COORDINATES.

Yellow Book. In standards, informal name for read-only memory compact disc specification. (Philips). *Compare* GREEN BOOK, RED BOOK. *See* COMPACT DISC – READ-ONLY MEMORY.

yellow disc. In optical media, a read-only memory compact disc. (Philips). *Compare* GREEN DISC, RED DISC. *See* COMPACT DISC – READ-ONLY MEMORY.

yoke. In memory systems, a group of read/write heads. *See* READ/WRITE HEAD.

Younger Committee. A UK committee that considered the problems of data protection and privacy. It reported in 1972. *See* DATA PROTECTION, PRIVACY.

YUV. In video, a symbol denoting the luminance signal (Y) and two chrominance signals (U and V). (Philips). *See* CHROMINANCE SIGNAL, DELTA YUV, LUMINANCE SIGNAL, YUV ENCODING.

YUV encoding. In video, a video encoding scheme that takes advantage of the humans eye's reduced sensitivity to colour variations, as opposed to intensity variations. In each picture line, the luminance (Y) information is encoded at full bandwidth, while on alternative lines the chrominance (U and V) signals are encoded at half bandwidth. (Philips). *See* CHROMINANCE SIGNAL, LUMINANCE SIGNAL, YUV.

Z

Z. In electronics, the symbol for impedance. *See* IMPEDANCE.

zap. (1) In programming, a small patch to a program with immediate effect. *See* PATCH. (2) In programming, to delete a large area of a file during an editing session. *See* EDITOR.

Zapf Chancery. In printing, a cursive typeface with a handwritten appearance. *Compare* AVANTE-GARDE, BOOKMAN, COURIER, HELVETICA, HELVETICA NARROW, NEW CENTURY SCHOOLBOOK, OLDSTYLE, PALATINO, SYMBOL, TIMES ROMAN, ZAPF DINGBATS. *See* CURSIVE, TYPEFACE.

Zapf Dingbats. In printing, a typeface providing a collection of symbols including prettified numbers, printers hands and other miscellaneous objects. *Compare* AVANTE-GARDE, BOOKMAN, COURIER, HELVETICA, HELVETICA NARROW, NEW CENTURY SCHOOLBOOK, OLDSTYLE, PALATINO, SYMBOL, TIMES ROMAN, ZAPF CHANCERY, *See* TYPEFACE.

Z-axis. In mathematics, a vertical axis in a set of three-dimensional cartesian coordinates. *Compare* X-AXIS, Y-AXIS. *See* CARTESIAN COORDINATES.

Z-axis intercept. In communications, the intersection of a satellite's Z-axis and the earth's surface. It defines an antenna's pointing direction. *See* COMMUNICATIONS SATELLITE SYSTEM, Z-AXIS.

zero a device. In computing, to erase all the data stored in memory. *See* MEMORY.

zero-bit insertion. *Synonymous with* BIT STUFFING.

zero fill. In computing, to fill an area of memory with zeros. *See* MEMORY.

zeroization. In computer security, a method of degaussing, erasing or overwriting electronically stored data. *See* DEGAUSS, OVERWRITING.

zero knowledge proof. In data security, a technique by which two parties can authenticate each other, but an eavesdropper would be unable to impersonate as one of the parties, irrespective of the number of authentication dialogues known to the eavesdropper. The two parties must share some secret information.

A simple example would be two people who wish to hold a public conversation and establish that one of them had taken a certain action (e.g. paid a bill at a restaurant). However they do not wish to reveal to any third party which one had taken the action. The two parties toss a coin and observe the result, while hiding the coin from others. They then call heads or tails. The person who paid the bill will call the true result of the coin toss, the person who did not pay will call the opposite result of the coin toss. If the two calls are different then each will know that the bill had been paid, but an onlooker would be unable to detect the payee. *See* FIAT SHAMIR ALGORITHM.

zero suppression. In computing, the elimination of zeros to the left of the most significant digits of a number, especially before printing.

z height. *Synonymous with* X HEIGHT.

zigzag folding. *See* ACCORDION FOLD.

zone beam. In communications, a satellite beam pattern with a footprint that can cover less than 10 per cent of the earth's surface. *Compare* GLOBAL BEAM, HEMISPHERIC BEAM, SPOT BEAM. *See* COMMUNICATIONS SATELLITE SYSTEM, FOOTPRINT.

zoom. In photography, to reduce or enlarge the size of the action field by operation of a varifocal lens. *See* ACTION FIELD, in an image. (Philips). *Compare* ZOOM OUT.

zoom in. In video and photography, the facility to enlarge the area of interest

zoom out. In video and photography, the facility to diminish the area of interest in an image. (Philips). *Compare* ZOOM IN.